THE OFFICIAL PRICE GUIDE TO BOTTLES OLD & NEW

BY
THE HOUSE OF COLLECTIBLES, INC.

We have compiled the information contained herein through a *patented computerized process* which relies primarily on a nationwide sampling of information provided by noteworthy collectible experts, auction houses and specialized dealers. This sophisticated retrieval system enables us to provide the reader with the most current and accurate information available.

EDITOR
THOMAS E. HUDGEONS III

SIXTH EDITION
THE HOUSE OF COLLECTIBLES, INC., ORLANDO, FLORIDA 32809

Published by: The House of Collectibles, Inc.
Orlando Central Park
1900 Premier Row
Orlando, FL 32809
Phone: (305) 857-9095

Printed in the United States of America

Library of Congress Catalog Card Number: 78-72029

ISBN: 0-87637-350-3 / Paperback

TABLE OF CONTENTS

ACKNOWLEDGEMENTS

Ezra Brooks Ceramic Co., Gerald F. Marco, Rosemont, IL 60018; Jim Beam Distilling Co., Lucy Freeland, Chicago, IL 60611; McCormick Distilling Co., Weston, MO 64098; Schenley Affliated Brands Corp., New York, NY 10106.

PHOTOGRAPHIC RECOGNITION

Cover and Color Section Photographs: Photographer — Bernie Markell, Orlando, FL 32806; Location — Courtesy Mr. and Mrs. J. Carl Sturm, Orlando, FL 32750.

Color Separations: World Color, Ormond Beach, FL 32074.

INTRODUCTION

Among the various types of collectibles, bottles differ in that they are one of the few types where the collector can actually dig the objects up from the ground. Like an archaeologist, the bottle collector can determine through research and study where to possibly find specimens, locate such spots, and make arrangements to dig there. Quite often, hobbyist first become intrigued with bottles at an antique shop or a flea market. And some are content to buy or swap exclusively from these kinds of sources. But a large number of bottle collectors enjoy the adventure of traipsing around the country using their own ingenuity to find and dig up treasures of bottles. Having to contend with only the cost of digging tools and transportation, the hobbyist can often uncover at least enough extra bottles with sufficient market values so that they have gained more than they have spent. Of course, the beginners usually don't have such luck. It's really not luck, but experience and accumulated knowledge that leads many collectors to find a horde of bottles that are worth quite a bit.

Usually, a collector gets started collecting by selecting any bottles that appeal to him at the time. This kind of collection can include a wide selection of types — cures, food, ink, flask, or modern figurals. But recently, more and more collectors have turned away from general collections to more specialized collecting which has been the trend in most of the antique and collectible fields. Many collectors are not just bottle collectors, but medicine bottle collectors, perfume bottle collectors, or some other particular type of bottle collectors.

Regardless of the type of approach collectors use to acquire their bottles — and many use a variety of methods — the beauty and the history of bottles offer the collector many ways to enjoy them. Many hobbyist delve into the techniques of production and decoration or into the histories of the manufacturers. Since the types of bottles are so extensive, collectors who study their background, find that they can only handle a specialized area. So as bottle collectors become more inquisitive and probing, they have, from necessity, narrowed the types of bottles they collect.

Collecting bottles according to their function is one way to narrow a collection, but not the only way. Some collectors only search for bottles produced by a particular manufacturer; or they collect bottles produced by a particular method, such as the pontil bottles; or they collect bottles with a particular feature, such as the Hutchinson bottles; or some collectors narrow their specialized area even further by collecting only a particular color of a particular type of bottle.

Bottle collecting has recently soared in popularity to become one of America's favorite hobbies. In addition to the usual bottle activity at antique shops and flea markets, bottle clubs have been organized all across the country. More and more bottle buffs spend their weekends digging through the remains of old dumps, or foraging in abandoned mine shafts for relics of the bottlemaker's art.

It has also become big business, as a glance at some of the prices in this book will show. Less than a generation ago, a bottle needed to carry extremely impressive credentials to command a retail value as high as $25. It had to be very old or represent a prime example of a celebrated manufacturer's handiwork. Today nearly every bottle of obsolete design or use, even if not terribly old or good-looking, qualifies as a collectors' item.

There are specialists who are not only interested in any kind of bottle but are willing to risk life, limb and bank account to possess valued specimens. The traditional superstars of this hobby, such as midwest bitters bottles of the Iron Horse era and decorative flasks in cloudy amber that have survived four or five generations, constantly attract more and more buyers. Their prices continually soar to new records. Now they have been joined in the ranks of "collectibles" by legions of others. Any bottle in which merchandise or beverage was sold during the 19th and 20th centuries is an attraction for collectors and often has an established cash value. Although not necessarily great works of art, many bottles of fairly recent origin are valued because of their scarcity.

Demand for bottles has been sufficient enough to boost their prices to seemingly astronomical levels. A beer bottle from the 1930's sells for $22. An ink bottle made around 1900 cannot be purchased for less than $40. As unbelievable as it may seem, collectible bottles are still slightly underpriced in relation to the availability. On the whole, their survival rate has not been lower than that of articles made from most other substances. If they were not thrown away they were accidentally broken. What remains today is but a tiny fraction of the total manufactured.

The general approach to bottle collecting has changed over the years. Yesteryear's hobbyist collected bottles mainly for display, seeking out the most delicate shapes and the warmest colors. He arranged them stylishly on shelves facing a window, so they would sparkle in the sunlight. The present-day collector usually looks far beyond mere beauty into the origin and history of his bottles. Every bottle has a story to tell. It was designed and manufactured for a specific purpose, and has undoubtedly passed through many hands before reaching the collector. By searching through old town directories and old newspaper ads, the collector can discover the names, places, and dates that make the bottle interesting; thus, the bottle becomes not just another flea market "find," but a social document of undeniable historical importance.

Obviously, the history of bottles is closely linked to the history and development of retail merchandising in this country. In spite of the extent to which this subject has been studied, much remains to be learned.

American business firms were the leaders in bottle packaging in the 19th and 20th centuries. Many kinds of merchandise, foodstuffs, medicines, etc., that were sold by other means in foreign countries, came in bottles in the U.S. Pills, for example, were still being dispensed in cartons and tins in most parts of Europe long after bottled pills had become commonplace in the United States. American manufacturers and retailers depended more on bottles, for packaging merchandise suitably, than on any other kind of container. Subsequently, the extent and variety of American bottles available to the collector is enormous. As early as 1870, many items purchased in the average general store in any U.S. town were supplied pre-packaged in bottles. Commercially packaged foodstuffs in bottles were not available in many areas of the world until after World War II.

What came *before* bottles? Obviously, the grocer of Ben Franklin's day did not sell his milk in paper bags. "Portion selling" was the sole method of merchandising in early America. The customer was expected to bring his own container when purchasing liquids or other hard-to-package items. If he wanted milk, he brought his own jar to the store. The grocer would fill it with a ladle from his milk can or barrel. Easily handled items were weighed out, or sold by the piece, and wrapped in paper. Packaging was only meant to get the item home safely, not to serve as a long-range storage container. If there was a bottlemaker nearby, successful merchants had bottles specially made for specific products. Ready-packaged merchandise added slightly to the merchant's cost; but, it saved a lot of time and work. It also increased the shelf life of perishables. Even the most old-fashioned of shopkeepers gradually came to bless the bottle.

As bottles became commonplace, distribtion extended to every corner of the continent. Bottles from the East were carried overland by early settlers. Most were discarded or lost at many points along the way. This is why old bottles turn up just about anywhere — sometimes in the most unlikely locations.

A good indication as to the extent of merchandise sold pre-packaged in bottles can be gleaned from Sears Roebuck catalogues of the 1890's and early 1900's. This was without question the golden age of bottle packaging. These catalogs contain *thousands* of items sold in bottles. Reprint editions are available and invaluable to the collector.

The sales of soft drinks in bottles ushered in another important era in the history of commercial bottle making. Collecting early soft drink bottles from all different retailers has become one of the major specialties of the hobbyist. Prices on many of the more historic soft drink bottles have risen to extraordinary heights, due to the combination of scarcity and high demand. Millions were made, but probably only one in a thousand were saved. No more thought was given to saving them than to the soft drink bottles of today. One reason soft drink bottles are so popular among collectors is the long history of the manufacturing companies. This makes it possible to form a collection exhibiting changes in bottle design. There is no other kind of bottle that lends itself so well to a "developmental" collection.

Definition of a Bottle. For purposes of collecting, a bottle is defined as a container with a cap, lid, or other means of closure. Generally, the device used to cap the bottle is no longer present; but its absence is not detrimental to its value.

There are different categories of bottles. "Store bottles," in which merchandise was sold in stores, comprise the majority of bottles favored by collectors. "Non-store bottles" were made for home use in preserving foodstuffs.

Origin of Bottles. Blown glass bottles were made by the Romans beginning in the late first century B.C. They did a brisk trade in the small pharmacy vials used by the chemists to dispense their pills and potions. These were generally three to four inches in length, narrow, cylendrical, and of pastel color. They did not seal their bottles with cork, since it was unknown in Rome, but rather with a small stone rolled in tar. The glass contained many impurities, such as sand particles and bubbles, and the color was often unevently distributed. Roman glass was more "leathery" and resilient than that of modern times, which accounts for its survival in a fairly good state of preservation for 2,000 years. The Romans also take credit for originating the "store bottle."

Approaches to Bottle Collecting. An individual's approach to bottle collecting is apt to be determined, or at least influenced by, personal finances, available spare time, space in the home or whatever bottles are to be stored and/or displayed, and in what directions the hobbyist's personal taste happens to run. There are attractive advantages to this hobby, one being the absence of "rules" of any kind. The collector can choose to concentrate on bitters bottles, soft drink bottles, milk bottles, or one of the other popular specialties covered in this book. By purchasing according to place of origin, time period, or because the bottle is intriguing, the hobbyist will have a combination of many different types of bottles within his collection, which is perfectly acceptable.

Most collectors, however, choose to specialize because of its distinct advantages. Approximately 70% of active bottle enthusiasts are specialists. A comprehensive representation of every kind of bottle would result in a huge collection. Specialization narrows the field and gives a collection a sense of continuity. Since all the specimens relate to one another, the study and research of their origin can be better organized. The collector can quickly become an authority on bottles in a chosen specialty. Knowledge gained about one maker can be very helpful in researching another. When examining bottles in a shop or at a convention, the collector will very often be in a position of having more knowledge than the seller. A general collector, on the other hand, constantly encounters bottles which he is inclined to buy, but about which he knows next to nothing. The specialist can spot "sleepers" and underpriced items better by having expert knowledge of one or two groups of bottles.

Another benefit in being a specialist is that swapping becomes possible. It is easy to find another collector with the same interest who has duplicates or other unwanted bottles. By specializing in the same type, both parties will know the value of the items to be traded. Bottle collecting has a way of bringing people together, and many collectors become good friends.

There are also a few problems in being a specialist. When the specialized collector comes across a bottle he finds overwhelmingly appealing, for one reason or another, he must make a decision whether to remain 100% faithful to his specialty or to cheat a little. Quite a few specialists occasionally buy outside their field. The result is a little sideline collection which is apt to be very miscellaneous, but very pleasing to the collector. There is always the possibility that by venturing outside his field to make an odd purchase, the specialized collector could abandon his specialty and become a general collector.

If specialization is a primary goal, the pages of this book will show some of the different groups of old and new bottles in which a hobbyist can specialize. Some groups contain a higher proportion of expensive items than others; however, there are specimens of fairly low cost, plus many other which are not listed due to the lack of space. Visits to antique shops and shows will demonstrate the vast selections of bottles available.

A good collection in just about any line can be started without spending a great deal per bottle. Even with a ceiling price of $10 per purchase, it is possible to make impressive inroads into nearly all of the popular groups, especially since many bottles are selling at less than their fair retail values. It would not be worthwhile to venture into a field where most of the better items are very expensive. Coke bottles and 19th century flasks are not for the lean wallet. A collector must be able to compete on an equal financial footing with other buyers. It is best for him to begin on the "ground floor" in specialties that have not yet attracted great hordes of buyers, such as ink bottles and many varieties of food bottles. The prices on these are likely to rise in the future, just as Coke and flask prices skyrocketed from the 1950's to the present time. Every antique dealer knows that old Coke bottles are potentially very valuable. A dealer will not price such an item without checking the value. But many dealers are unaware of the potential value of the less publicized bottles, and may just mark them up at a percentage over the cost price. It is possible to find bottles worth $20 selling for $2 and similar buys, if the collector's field of specialty is a little off the beaten path.

In choosing a type of bottle in which to specialize, the hobbyist must consider what features or aspects of bottles intrigue him the most. Is it the color, shape, printed label, artistic value, historic significance, or impending research that peaks his curiosity? There are collectible bottles to suit every taste and personality. Collecting a certain kind of bottle just because someone else does, or because the local antique shop happens to have a good stock, is fairly unrewarding. Whatever speciality is chosen, the sources of supply for bottles are endless.

Available display space must be a consideration to the serious collector. Where is the collection going to be kept? Approximately how many bottles will the space hold? Is there room for expansion? Space limitations can influence the choice of a specialty. A collector may wish to invest in a moderately expensive class of bottles, and make purchases only occasionally to keep his collection relatively small. Certain kinds of bottles are larger than others and require more space. A hundred ink bottles can be kept in a space that would be used up by half as many soft drink bottles.

Old vs. New. Old bottles are obviously not the only kinds suitable to collect. The Avons, Jim Beams and other figurals of recent and current vintage are not only collectible, but made to be collected. In terms of artistry and as decorative objects, they clearly outshine 1880's bitters bottles and old milk bottles. There are many hobbyists who object to "instant" collectors' items, and prefer bottles which have acquired interest by being preserved over long periods of time. The older bottles have history on their side, and a collection of "oldies" will be much more original than one of limited editions. These two groups are so different in every respect that it should be no problem for any potential collector to decide where his emotions lie.

Technically, there is no clear-cut definition of what separates an "old" from a "new" bottle. Some of the Avons are quite old. By the same token, recent Coke bottles are collected as evolutionary links in the history of Coke bottle manufacturing. The term "antique," though frequently applied to bottles even in this book, really has little practical use in this hobby. By accepted definition, an antique is any article more than one hundred years old. Quite a few of the bottles listed in this book are over one hundred years old, and could deservedly be called antiques; but other bottles, which are just as collectible and sometimes worth even more, are not antiques. There may be a certain magic attached to other collectors' items that rank as antiques, but it makes no difference with bottles. Perhaps this is because bottle making has been going on for 2,000 years, and even a one hundred-year-old specimen is fairly modern. The background, history, use, design, and scarcity of a bottle count with collectors far more than whether it falls in front of or behind the one hundred year mark.

What makes a bottle valuable? No simple answer can be given. Prices are set by supply and demand: the availability of any given bottle on the market versus the number of buyers who want it. Certain bottles are more scarce than others, either from being properly preserved. Demand occurs for some bottles more because of collectors' tastes. Many scarce bottles sell for modest prices simply because they are labeled "slow movers." Dealers have no choice but to mark it low, because there are few customers for that particular kind of bottle. These are the "sleepers," whose values can, and probably will in time, adjust in line with their scarcity. If all buyers had the same tastes and goals in collecting, it would be very easy to say what makes a bottle valuable; but such certainty would also create a very dull hobby.

Will the current merchandise bottles of today ever become valuable? Since a bottle need not gain "antique" status to be collectible, the next generation of sought after bottles could be on supermarket shelves right now. The future potential of the 1970's and the 1980's merchandise bottles has become the only subject of debate among bottle collectors.

Old Bottles for the Collector. The variety of old bottles available to the collector is considerably greater than that of new or recent specimens. This is because old bottles need not be fancy or decorative to have collector appeal; the can simply be *old*. Nevertheless, many old bottles have unusual shapes and command premium prices. An odd or artistically shaped bottle from the 1800's was not made for sale to collectors, but rather to stimulate sale of the product. This is one of the reasons why "old fancies" are, in the opinion of the devotees, more collectible than "modern fancies." In many instances, these "old fancies" were manufactured in greater quantities than modern Jim Beams or Avons, as they were not limited editions; however, the number in existence have a rather low survival rate. With "store bottles," the rate is particularly low because most fell into the hands of people who had absolutely no interest in them, so they were discarded when empty. Only about one out of then "fancies" made before 1900 survives today. With "non-fancies" the survival rate is less than one in twenty or thirty, since they were the ones most frequently discarded.

Following is a list of additional factors that will increase the value of a specimen.

UNUSUAL SHAPE. Shape is the contour or physical outline of the bottle itself. Shapely bottles were produced for expensive products and gift giving. They are collected by topic, such as fish and animals, etc.

UNUSUAL SIZE. Size is important if very large or very small.

ARTISTIC DESIGN. Design is not the same as shape. A bottle may be of standard shape and still be artistic, usually as a result of carrying a design raised on the surface (bas-relief). These ancient bottles were blown in a mold. They were used frequently for store goods in 19th century America, since they had a tendency to promote sales and the cost was no more than that required to make plain bottles. One the mold was made, the bottles could be produced as inexpensively as non-decorative specimens. Labor costs in the 19th century were so low that the price of special molds could be easily absorbed. Spirits flasks are the most familiar 19th century bottles with artistic designs. Numerous motifs can be found. Political subjects are common, including portraits of Presidents. Railroad trains and animals are also frequently encountered. Like bottles of unusual shape, artistically designed bottles lend themselves to topical collecting.

PRESENCE OF BACKGROUND INFORMATION. An old bottle that carries the name and place of business, or other details relating to the manufacturer, will have greater appeal for hobbyists and carry a higher price than if such information were absent. A dated bottle will increase in value, as there are collectors who specialize in certain dates and will buy them regardless of the product or bottle shape, etc. Dates prior to 1900 are especially desirable. The mere presence of this information will not turn a fairly common item into an expensive collectible. Other factors must also be considered. The value will depend on the total characteristics of the specimen.

PRESENCE OF PRINTED LABEL. There are many collectors specializing in bottles with printed paper labels. Such bottles were manufactured in great quantities; but certain kinds, such as *very* old ones or those with highly decorative labels, are not plentiful. The artwork on early labels, especially on tonic bottles, is very original and appealing. The label should not be torn or stained. Fading is expected as an inevitable result of age.

PRESENCE OF ORIGINAL CONTENTS. An old bottle containing a portion of its original contents has a certain attraction for some collectors. It is questionable, however, whether any great premium should be given for such specimens; it is often impossible to know, with any degree of assurance, if the contents *are* original. By the same token, it is possible that evaporation may occur in time. The feature for which a premium was paid will, quite literally, go up in thin air.

Current and Recent Bottles for the Collector. Figurals, manufactured to package spirits and cosmetics, comprise the majority of current and recent bottles of collector interest. The great surge of interest in bottle collecting has prompted many retailers to use decorative bottles for their products and to charge five or six times the price of the contents. While some are bought for gifts or decorative purposes, most are purchased by bottle collectors who have no use for the contents. Advances in glassmaking techniques have enabled figurals to be designed in very intricate and unusual shapes. Competition is keen among manufacturers to create the most original, eye-appealing, and noteworthy designs. The Christmas season is traditionally the peak sale period; but with the present level of collector activity, there is no slow selling period for figurals.

Figurals are collected by manufacturer, such as Jim Beam, Avon, etc. The goal of most collectors is to complete a set of the figurals produced by his favorite manufacturer. The degree of difficulty depends on how many specimens the maker produced, and how scarce they have become on the collector market. A full set of Avons would be a lofty accomplishment; some other sets of figurals can be completed without too much time or expense. If the firm is still in business, a set is never entirely complete for newly issued specimens must constantly be added.

The best time to buy figurals is when first issued on the retail market. When the edition has been sold out, specimens can only be obtained from the collector market with the price always higher, even though the bottle is generally empty by then. The difference between the original retail price and the collector price can be considerable.

SOURCES OF COLLECTIBLE BOTTLES

Collectible bottles are all around and they are just about endless. Bottles the interest collectors turn up in antique shops, flea markets, antique shows and conventions, swap meets, secondhand and salvage stores, pawn shops, Salvation Army thrift shops, in attics and under old front porches.

The beginning collector should realize that the source of a bottle does not contribute to, or detract from, its desirability and value. Once the bottle has left the place where it was found, it matters very little whether it was bought from a posh antique shop, or was dug from a gravel heap. Many specimens in antique shops were unearthed by bottle diggers.

The bottle itself is the important thing, not the source, nor the price. The retail selling prices for all the bottles listed in this book are the average sums for which they sell at the top of the market. There are numerous opportunities, however, to buy for much lower prices, as well as to obtain scarce and desirable bottles absolutely free, if the collector knows what to look for and where to find it. To most bottle collectors, the hunt and chase is as thrilling as the capture. The emotional stimulation and reward of buying a specimen off the counter, in a transaction as routine and uninspiring as buying groceries, does not equal that of making a "find." In this hobby, unlike many others, the collector *can* make "finds," and conceivably build a whole collection. Some bottle buffs own very impressive collections, and have never paid the full retail value for a single specimen.

Listed are some of the possible sources for bottles and the potential they hold.

Retail Dealers. This category includes all dealers who sell collectible bottles at or near the full market prices. Some of them specialize in bottles exclusively, while others carry glassware with bottles comprising the majority of their stock. A number of dealers operate storefronts; others trade only by mail, through pricelists or advertisements in the various collectors' publications.

When buying from such a dealer, the collector will pay a price similar to that listed in this book. Dealers are well informed on the values of all kinds of collectible bottles and rarely make a significant mistake. If they come into possession of a bottle of whose value they are not sure, they put it aside rather than offering it for sale, until they can research the value. They will use this book, as well as the lists from other dealers, to arrive at a price. Even if they bought the bottle for $1, they will price it for $75, if this seems to be the fair retail value. They have a large clientele for bottles and have no trouble making sales at the full retail price.

These specialist dealers serve an important purpose. The offer a huge selection of bottles in an orderly manner. Often their price lists contain helpful background information and details. In buying from a specialist, the collector can be fairly confident that the specimen has been thoroughly examined, is authentic, and that the price has been set in accordance with any flaws or imperfections it may bear. These individuals are expert at noticing damage of all kinds, and they will not try to sell an inferior bottle for the price of a mint one. If a certain bottle is needed to fill out a collection, and time is of the essence, the collector should seek a specialist dealer.

To build an entire collection with purchases from specialists is not only expensive, but also boring. Lists can be obtained from such dealers that detail merchandise being offered in the bottle market. A stamped self addressed envelope is all that need be sent in most cases. A charge of $1 is sometimes imposed, to defray preparation costs, but is usually refundable on the first purchase.

Specialist dealers purchase their bottles from the public, from auction sales, and often from other dealers. Like the more active private collectors, they keep their eyes and ears open for favorable opportunities. They visit the non-specialist antique dealers in the area to check on new arrivals. Bottles are also brought to them by diggers and collectors who have duplicates of which they wish to dispose, or who want to sell their entire collection. These dealers make some very favorable purchases, by knowing exactly what the material is worth and having ready cash when opportunity knocks. Also among their sources of supply are the local auction sales. If the dealer handles rare and costly material in the $200-and-over category, he will undoubtedly be a subscriber to the catalogues of major auction houses, such as Sotheby/Parke-Bernet and Christie in New York, and will place bids on whatever appears to be suitable for his business. When a dealer bids in an auction, he is careful not to go as high as a private collector; he must take his operating expenses and margin of profit into account. Even when a dealer knows for certain that he can sell a bottle at the full retail price, he will not pay more than 60% of the value. A dealer will sometimes bid for a collecotr, as an agent, in an auction sale. The collector will pay the bill from the auction house, plus expenses and the dealer's service charge of approximately 10%.

Non-Specialist Dealers. All general antique shops, which do not specialize in bottles, fall into this category. Many very fine bottles, as good as those handled by the specialists, pass through these shops. The difference is that their selections are not as comprehensive.

Because these dealers are not as knowledgeable as the specialists, they might incorrectly identify a bottle, or overlook damage. This can work to the collector's disadvantage, if he paid for a mint specimen and discovered it was flawed, or advantage, if he finds bottles selling well below the full retail level. The pricing policies of non-specialist dealers vary. If the shop is large, prestigious, and the location is good, the dealer will ask the full retail price. On the other hand, the item may be offered at a discount, if his clientele is not composed solely of bottle collectors. He must offer a bit of inducement to make a sale. If the full retail price is charged, odds are quite good that the bottle will sit for months, tying up capital, and end up being discounted anyway. Some dealers will place the full retail price on newly arrived merchandise, but bring it down quickly if there are no takers. The collector can decide whether he wants to buy at the first price, or gamble that the item will be available in the future at a discount. He should become familiar with the dealer's pricing policies and other methods of doing business.

Often the non-specialist dealers do not have a great deal of reference material on hand. They will have one or two general price guides on antiques which they use in an effort to price everything. If the specific item does not appear in the book, they will try to estimate a price by adding a percentage on to the cost. If they buy a certain bottle for $5 and are not aware of the retail value, they may ask $10 for it. A specialist may be selling the same bottle for $7.50 or as much as $50. If the collector is knowledgeable of market values, he will be able to avoid the overpriced items offered by non-specialist dealers, and take advantage of the opportunities to pick up underpriced merchandise.

Auction Sales. Bottles come up for sale in almost every auction of antiques and general estate contents. Some collectors do a great deal of buying at auction. This is especially suitable if several good auction houses are within driving distance. Making absentee purchases of bottles by auction is a bit risky, because the collector does not have the opportunity to examine the material that the auctioneer describes briefly, without taking note of the item's physical condition or other details of collector interest.

This list is prepared for the bidders who attend the sale as a means of keeping track of the various lots. Frequently the auctioneer is not a bottle authority and cannot even identify the specimens being sold; he merely lists them as "Lot 121 -6 flasks." It may be possible to obtain additional information by calling or writing the auctioneer.

When bidding at a major sale, whether in person or as an absentee, the collector is in competition with hundreds of other collectors, dealers, museums, etc. It is rarely possible to get an item for a bargain price. At a small sale, such as a country auction, there are not bottle people in attendance, he can just about name his price on whatever he choses to purchase. It is certainly worth attending any sales in the area, especially if the announcement does not mention bottles. Chances are dealers who specialize in bottles are not likely to be in attendance.

A collector should not be afraid to bid against dealers. Dealers may have plenty of cash, but they will not bid up to the full retail price or anywhere near it. They are looking to buy only those items for which they can get a favorable price and make a reasonable profit.

By attending the presale exhibition, a collector can critically examine the bottles for sale, checking for flaws, signs of repair, or missing components. Observations should be noted on the auction list, not committed to memory. It is wise to job down the highest bid for each desired bottle to insure a wise purchase.

Secondhand Shops, Salvage Stores, Flea Markets, Thrift Stores, etc. These secondary sources are where old, used and other miscellaneous merchandise of all kinds can be found. Wherever miscellaneous household items are found, so are bottles. The vast majority of what they will have is not in the collectible category; but when they do turn up at these sources, prices are much less than those at an antique shop or auction. These shops must be visited frequently as different antique merchandise is arriving daily. The manager should know which days have the heaviest arrival of material. The specific items a collector wishes to buy should never be mentioned to the manager, as this may lead to a higher price. A collector must rely on his own knowledge of items and their value and not take any written materials along when he shops.

Other Collectors. There are other collectors and bottle clubs that hold swap meets from which bottles can be obtained. Many collectors, especially those who go digging have duplicate or unwanted bottles that they are willing to sell or trade. When buying from another collector, the chances are vry good that he knows the exact retail value of the bottles he has. He may give a substantial break compared to the price charged by a dealer in a shop. A fair price, when buying from a private collector, is 80% of the full retail value.

Getting Bargains. The way to get bargains is to know more about the value of bottle than the person selling it. As we pointed out, you will often be in a position of buying a bottle from a dealer (at a flea market, garage sale, junkshop, etc.) who knows absolutely nothing about the bottle or its value. To his it's just an old bottle and he wants to sell it for as much as he can get. You can end up paying more than you need to in these situations. Never let on that you're a collector. Wear old clothes. Learn to act dumb. The seller may try to get an opinion from you on the bottle's value, directly or indirectly. He may say for example, "That sure is an old one, isn't it?," or "You don't see many like them," or "You must be a collector, to have picked that one out." All of these queries can be effectively dodged. You should have some useful lines up your own sleeve, such as "Hope this one is cheap," "This ought to make a good present for my mother-in-law — I don't want to spend much on her," and "My friend paid $2.50 for one like this — hope you aren't charging that much." Never admit to *liking* the bottle you're about to buy. Never admit to knowing anything about it — or even caring. If the seller should mention something about its age or beauty or anything that would contribute to the price, just brush aside such comments with a casual, "Well, I wouldn't know, and since I'm only going to use it for varnish it doesn't make much difference. Varnish keeps a lot better in glass, you know . . ." In other words, you meet every thrust with a parry. This may be a little damaging to the ego, when you know the complete history of that bottle and could enrapture the seller with half an hour's worth of conversation about it. But it's very healthy on the wallet.

DIGGING FOR BOTTLES

Prospecting for bottles has become one of the favorite pastimes for collectors. Old and collectible bottles are buried in all parts of the country. There is no possible way to imagine the wealth of bottles that is waiting for the enthusiastic prospector.

Bottles are buried along with the discards of past generations. What was junk at one time has become today's treasure. This is true of many old bottles which have often been preserved much better underground than can be imagined. Many bottles were thrown away because they were broken, but some went into the ground whole and stayed that way. The soft earth and sand acted as a cushioning agent to protect them against breakage.

Bringing the science of archaeology to the hobby of bottle collecting represents a big advance. Through the efforts of diggers, many important bottles, historically and artistically, are coming to light, and valuable information is being learned about the history of bottlemaking in this country.

Although these amateur digs have been going on in ernest for more than a decade, the surface has only been scratched. More bottles have yet to be found, and the odds are quite good that the quest will never end. Since bottles are still being discarded, future generations will probably be digging the ones thrown away today. There is a better chance of finding interesting bottles now than for the propector of 100 years ago. Trash disposal methods are not sophisticated in the 19th and early 20th centuries. Many bottles, that would be destroyed today, lay for decades in city dumps.

How *did* so many old bottles succeed in being preserved beneath the earth? Ancient artifacts from the Greek, Roman, Egyptian and other ancient civilizations are being found in the Old World today. They were preserved as the result of cities being abandoned and new cities growing up atop the old ones. With the passage of centuries, layers of soil and sand covered them with the help of the wind, rain, and other actions of nature. Man covered the further with cobblestones and then cement.

The same process has occurred in the United States, but on a smaller scale. Instead of 2,000 years, the time span has been no more than a hundred years. A bottle may be thrown in a ditch and, in time, the ditch becomes partially filled with sand and covers the bottle. Bottles left on beaches are buried as each incoming tide deposits sand and silt. Bottles buried in this manner come under the heading of "accidental burials."

Street paving is an example of an "intentional burial." When a dirt road is being paved, no effort is made to remove any articles mixed in the soil. As bottles are often discarded along roadways, any dirt road is sure to have many of them. In paving the road, bottles and other possible collectors' items are sealed up as if in a tomb. Opportunities to explore sites of this kind occur when the old pavement, which may be forty or fifty years old, is being broken up to lay pipelines or for other maintenance work. Many bottles may be uncovered and are free for the taking; therefore, a chance to check out a site of this type should never be missed.

Sometimes, town dumps have been covered over to become parks or playgrounds. These present golden opportunities. A bit more work on a site of this nature may be necessary, but the results are usually well worth the effort. If the town is old, quite likely the dump has been there for many years. The practice of having town or city dumps goes all the way back to colonial times before the Revolution. Nearly all the junk thrown in them would be collectors' items today. The only problem is that a lot of old dumps were leveled — the contents were taken away and dumped in the ocean or used elsewhere for landfill — before converting the site to its present use. Those that were not leveled were paved with concrete, putting a rather formidable obstacle before the collector. Thorough investigation, however, will help to locate an old dump suitable for digging.

Finding Sites. It is not profitable to attempt random digging. To go into a field and dig, on the chance that bottles may be lying beneath the surface, is an extremely hit and miss affair. Sites must be investigated thoroughly before any actual spadework is done. The best sites are not necessarily those that have already been dug. The success or failure of a "dig" will depend mostly on the decision of where to dig.

A bottle collector who has conducted a successful dig is reluctant to reveal the exact location of his finds. He will not supply specific information on finding the site, because each digger considers his sites personal property. He wishes to rework the site without competition from others. This is understandable since a fertile site may not be located until weeks or months of probing have been completed.

The following suggestions may prove to be helpful in finding a fruitful digging site. First of all, the collector must learn as much as possible about the area in which he lives. Libraries have books on the history of each town, county, or surrounding counties. Old town directories will point out where the business districts used to be. Maps of what the area looked like in the past are available and may help to locate the sites of abandoned dumps. People who have lived in the town for half a century or more should certainly have some recollections that will be helpful. If the town is a big city like New York or Chicago, most of the streets have been paved over for as far back as anyone can remember; but there may be outlying areas of the town, such as the Bronx in New York, which still have vacant lots and dumps.

Some sites may be located by walking or driving through a town. Fairgrounds or reunion grounds are likely to be worthwhile places to investigate further. The areas around ballparks and sandlots are also particularly good, especially if the town is old and these sites have been in use for a long time. Generations of people brought bottles to these places, or purchased them on the spot, and discarded them nearby. Beaches are particularly fertile sites for bottle digging. People have been bringing beverage bottles to beaches for well over 100 years. Odd to say, but the litterbug of yesteryear performed a great service for the collector of today. If all garbage down through the ages had been properly disposed of, not much would remain today in the way of collectors' items.

Ghost towns are high on the list of localities with good potential. The only difficulty is that most of them have been heavily worked over by collectors within recent years and nearly everything worthwhile has been taken. Quite possibly, however, the collectors visiting that site took away only surface material, and did not bother to dig. One of the best places to poke around in a ghost town, is the saloon area, where bottles will most likely be found.

Frequently old bottles are found beside houses, either a few feet under the lawn's surface or beneath porches. It was a common habit in the Midwest, during the late 19th and early 20th centuries, for people to dispose of bottles by placing them beneath the front porch. Valuable bottles, often by the dozens, have been discovered underneath porches in Illinois, Wisconsin, Minnesota and other states of that region.

Prospecting Equipment. A metal detector is a valuable tool for the bottle prospector. Although it will not react to the bottles themselves, it will locate areas where metal objects are buried. Wherever metal objects have been discarded or lost, bottles can often be found. Although a metal detector may cost any where from $200 to $300, none of the other equipment needed in bottle digging is very expensive. Following is a list of the essentials plus some extras that are very useful to have along. Some bottle diggers use nothing but a shovel, while others have extensive equipment. How thoroughly a prospective wishes to outfit himself is a matter of personal choice.

Shovel
Potato Rake (3 or 4 prong)
Small short-handled rake (3 prongs)
Thin steel probing rod
Hunting knife
Hedge shears for cutting roots that get in the way of digging
Bow saw for cutting thicker roots
Tablespoon
Newspaper for wrapping specimens
Hard bristle brush
Canvas sack or wicker basket for carrying specimens
Pad and pencil for making notes and drawing maps
Depending on the terrain, it may be necessary to take along insect repellent, a snakebite kit, and a general first-aid kit.

Here are a few tips on personal safety: Heavy-duty canvas type gloves must be worn at all times. They may take getting used to when picking things up, but the protection is well worth the inconvenience. Even with gloves, it is not a good idea to reach under rocks or into holes in the ground, where there may be broken glass, wasps, or other animals who do not appreciate the intrusion. Instead, use one of the tools to probe in an area that cannot be seen. Sturdy shoes are also essential. If the area might be inhabited by snakes, tall boots are in order, not to mention rugged clothing.

The prospector must never overestimate his ability to climb, leap, swim, or survive in the wilds. The experienced collector never takes any unnecessary chances. Whenever possible, he should form a digging party rather than going out alone, especially when going into woods, deserts, or other unpopulated areas. If he must go alone, he should leave word with someone as to his whereabouts and what time he should be home. When arriving at the digging site, he should take note of the location of the nearest phone.

When digging begins, the prospector starts by clearing away several shovelfuls of earth at a given spot. If no bottles appear, but other man-made relics turn up, further digging should be carried out at that spot; not only deeper into the ground, but in a wider area. Where there are man-made relics of fairly substantial age, there are usually bottles. If nothing turns up within one-and-a-half feet, it is time to move to another spot. The perimeter of the area should be covered first and then work toward the center. It may be necessary to make many test diggings at a site before anything is found, or until it is concluded that the site if bottleless. Some sites that should contain bottles do not. It is also possible that the sites may have been well researched and pinpointed accurately; but digging may be just thirty or forty yards from where the bottles are located. An enthusiast never becomes discouraged. Even professional archaeologists come up empty-handed.

When a bottle is found, **digging must stop!** The bottle must be lifted out gently by hand. If the bottle is imbedded in the soil, the surrounding dirt must be removed bit by bit, using the hands or a small tool, such as a spoon, until the bottle is loosened. In dry soil, a brush sometimes does the trick. The bottle must be handled gingerly since it will be fragile when first exposed to air and sunlight after its many years of burial. It should be wrapped in paper and placed aside. Cleaning of the specimen should never be attempted in the field. It is unusual for a single old bottle to turn up at a site, so when one has been found, there are probably more. Unless absolutely certain that a bottle is worthless, all specimens should be taken home.

HOW TO CLEAN, STORE AND DISPLAY BOTTLES

Compared to many other kinds of collectors' items, bottles require very little care and upkeep. Once the hobbyist has learned to clean his bottles properly and safely, he will have few maintenance problems. Storage and display problems are minimal because bottles are not damaged by sunlight, moisture, or insects.

How to Display Bottles. The chief consideration in display is to prevent breakage while allowing the specimens to be viewed and handled. The collector may wish to keep his bottles in a cabinet, on wall shelving, or distributed at random about the house to provide decorative touches. While certainly appealing, the last approach tends to be riskier. When a collection is not grouped together in one place or one part of the house, it becomes more difficult to guard against accident. This is especially true if pets or small children are around. When a collection is within a cabinet or on shelves, it is out of harm's way.

Almost any kind of cabinet is suitable for a bottle collection. Choice will depend on personal taste, room decor, size of the collection, and the cost of the unit. An ordinary bookcase with glass doors or grillwork will do, *if* it has adjustable shelves and is not too small. A case with wooden sides will not provide as must visibility or light penetration to the inside. With very little expense and trouble, however, a lighting fixture can be installed inside. Cabinets with glass sides are ideal for displaying bottles, and can often be picked up at antique shops or from used furniture dealers.

The usual practice in stocking a display cabinet is according to size — the largest bottles on the bottom shelf, the smallest ones on top. This not only gives a better sense of proportion, but also places the smallest specimens at eye level where their details can be closely examined. Very large specimens can be placed atop the cabinet to provide aesthetic balance. If the collection consists of different kinds of bottles, one shelf can be used for flasks, another for milk bottles, and so forth.

It is important not to overcrowd the shelves by not standing bottles in front of one another. Visibility is reduced and accidents may occur when removing or replacing a specimen. A unit should be large enought to accommodate a growing collection. Any remaining space can always be used for books or curios.

How to Store Bottles. Occasionally bottles may have to be stored rather than displayed. This happens when a collection exceeds the available display space, or when a collector is moving to a new residence. There is no real danger of breakage if reasonable care is exercised. Each bottle should be wrapped in layers of newspaper, and each package taped securely. Extra protection must be given to bottles of unusual shape or with small, delicate components. Placing plenty of crumpled newspaper on the bottom of a sturdy carton and between each bottle will prevent them from knocking against each other. The largest or heaviest bottles must be on the bottom and the lighter ones on top.

This approach, however, is *not suitable* for mailing. Extra protection must be provided when bottles are to be mailed or sent by some other kind of carrier. Each package intended for shipment should contain no more than one bottle. A double carton (one inside the other) should be cushioned with packing material. The bottle should be wrapped and packed securely in the inner carton. The outer carton must be well sealed and tied with strong twine. The address is written directly on the carton, because a label could become detached.

How to Clean Bottles. There is a difference of opinion among collectors as to which is the best technique for cleaning bottles. While some will use abrasives to get their bottles as clean and shiny as when some new, others object to harsh cleaning procedures and would rather let some signs of age remain. It should be noted, however, that the general consensus of opinion is that patina (acquired layers of grime) does *not* contribute to desirability. If the collector does not like the looks of it, he need not be concerned about reducing a specimen's value by removing it.

Bottles bought from an antique dealer will usually have already been cleaned in order to enhance their sales potential. Dealers may do a rather slapdash job, however, and the specimen may need to be recleaned before it can be placed in a collection. In the case of freshly dug bottles, the cleaning task can be challenging.

Cleaning approaches must be varied in some cases. If a bottle is enameled, or surface-painted, extreme care must be taken not to remove any of the enamel. The same is true of bottles with paper labels. Any damage to the label will reduce the bottle's value. Leaving a little dirt is preferable to damaging the label. If immersed in water, the label will dry out; but solvents ought to be avoided, as well as any rubbing or scrubbing across the label.

Some collectors prefer to merely wipe such specimens with rubbing alcohol on a soft cloth, taking care not to touch the label. Wringing out the cloth will prevent any dripping or splashing. This procedure should be repeated several times, allowing the bottle to dry thoroughly between treatments.

Fortunately, most collectible bottles are not enameled and have no label. More rigorous cleaning techniques can be used, but some restraint must still be exercised. Overly enthusiastic cleaning efforts can result in broken bottles.

When a freshly dug bottle has been brought in from the field, the surface condition is likely to be so miserable that it offers very little encouragement of ever being successfully cleaned. Most bottles will clean up well with a bit of patience and hard work. The first step is to remove loose surface particles (sand, small stones, etc.) with a brush. An artist's brush is good for this kind of job. The bottle should soak in lukewarm water for awhile to remove surface dirt.

To soften and break down the tough impacted grime, the bottle must soak in something stronger than plain water. A solution of two tablespoons of bleach in a gallon of lukewarm water can be used. It must be stirred thoroughly before introducing the bottle; otherwise, damage could result. Straight ammonia is also a possibility if there is good ventilation in the room. Kerosene is recommended by some collectors. Bottles should never be put into hot or boiling liquid as they could crack. The length of soaking time will depend on how dirty the specimen is, and how good a job the solvent is doing. A badly caked specimen may need to soak for a week or longer. It will be much more difficult to clean the inside of a bottle. The outside may be spotless, but the bottle may still need to soak for several days. Periodic checks must be made and the solution changed from time to time.

Bottles can, of course, be cleaned with steel wool or a stiff brush. The bottle should be soaked in one of the solutions mentioned above for a couple of hours before scrubbing. It may be necessary to soak it again afterwards and repeat this procedure several times before satisfactory results are achieved.

When the bottle has gotten as clean as can reasonably be expected, it should be soaked again in lukewarm water for a few hours to remove any traces of the cleaning agent. All that remains then is to dry the bottle, which can be done with a rag or by allowing it to air-dry. The bottle can be buffed up with oil to give the glass a shinier appearance. This will be successful only if the bottle came very clean.

If minor traces of dirt or grime remain after cleaning, the collector need not worry. It is better to live with a little dirt than to destroy the bottle in an effort to clean it.

Keeping a Collection Record. A hobbyist should begin to keep a record of his collection as soon as possible. Delay can only mean that the necessary information will be forgotten. A collection record can be kept on index cards, using one card for each specimen. The card identifies the specimen and gives details as to how and when it was obtained. It should include the dealer's name and the purchase price, or the location and date if the specimen was found while digging. Each bottle can also be assigned a number for cataloguing. Such a record is vital for insurance purposes, and will prove enormously useful and informative.

INVESTING

Collectible bottles definitely have investment potential. In the past two years, the retail values of some bottles have increased twofold or more. Even those investors who paid full retail value, at the peak of the bottle market in 1979, would profit by selling their bottles today. When compared to the number of investors in stamps, coins and some other collectibles, there is little doubt that the number of investors and speculators will grow as the general public becomes more aware of the increased prices of certain collectible bottles.

Bottle collecting is obviously not a fad. This hobby has established definite patterns of activity and is growing steadily. The number of bottle collectors, dealers, and auction sales increases each year. While some specimens are found by digging, the majority of them purchased from dealers or through auction sales. As the demand increases for desirable bottles, prices are forced upward. Many bottles that might have been considered expensive at $10 in 1970 are eagerly purchased today for $100 or more. This situation shows every indication of continuing in the future. The prices of today will seem just as expensive in 1991 as those of 1970 seem now.

Anyone interested in buying bottles for investment has to study the market. An investor must learn to interpret trends and do a bit of forecasting. Not all bottles advance in value at the same rate. Those showing the best gains in the past will not necessarily score well in the future. A smart investor will buy the underpublicized, underpriced bottles in any given group, rather than put his money into those which have already attained high price levels. As the star items in each category become to expensive for the average hobbyists, more and more investors will be turning their attention to bottles that are not heavily collected at the moment.

It would be rash to assume that a certain bottle whose price advanced 200% in the past five years will gain another 200% in the next five. It rarely works that way, for various reasons. Coke bottles "shot up" in the 1960's because they were undercollected and underpriced before then. They were selling for much less than their projected value. Then when the wave of Coke collecting came around 1962, prices jumped. By the early 1970's collectors demand was as strong as it had been in the early sixties. As collectors who had "bought cheap" cashed in their holdings, more and more Coke bottles began to flood the market. This increase in supply, as well as demand, helped to keep prices from soaring any higher. Today, Coke bottle prices are just as high as ever, but they are not likely to skyrocket again. There are not enough new Coke collectors to create another rush on the market; only enough to push prices up approximately 10% a year. Anyone investing in Coke bottles today can not hope to do as well as if they had been buying the same bottles in 1960 or earlier.

Beer bottles appear to be underpriced at the moment. Many old specimens can be picked ujp for under $5. This is because "beer collectors" prefer cans to bottles, since the value of cans has surpassed that of bottles. Other soft drink bottles have already been affected by the Coke boom and it is probably that their values will increase further in the years to come.

As far as other types of bottles are concerned, early non-commemorative figurals are a good bet for price increases. Not too many of them are around, and they seldom turn up at "digs." The most collectible milk bottles are those of the small manufacturers — not those of the large companies such as Borden or Sheffield. They should be pre-1940 and in mint condition. Ink bottles have a good steady market, but are not an attractive investment item at the moment. Early bitters bottles are "blue chips" since they hold their value as well as any collectors' item; however, whether any profit can be made by investing in them, now that prices are high, is questionable. Some speculation might be worthwhile in the inexpensive ($10-20) machine-made bitters bottles. Once shunned by collectors, these bottles have acquired a following now that the rarer bitters bottles are costly and beyond the budgets of most buyers.

The more popular groups of non-antique bottles, such as Avon, Luxardo and the rest, have been collected at the top market for many years. Somewhat undercollected have been Kikukawa and Kamotsuru (Japanese) bottles, Garnie, Bardi, and Bralatta, just to name a few.

WHERE AND HOW TO SELL BOTTLES

Undoubtedly every collector will have the occasion to sell all or part of his bottle collection. The need to sell often arises when a collector changes direction and decides to specialize in a group of bottles different than those he had been buying. All collectible bottles are saleable. A profit can be made on most, depending on how they were acquired and the length of time they have been owned.

A collector must think before he sells. If space is not a problem or cash is not needed immediately, he might be better off to hold on to his bottles for awhile longer. If they were purchased recently at full retail value, either from a specialist dealer or at a highly competitive auction sale, the odds are against recouping the full amount of the investment. By checking future editions of this book, as well as price lists and catalogues from dealers, the collector can evaluate the market and sell when the values have advanced far enough for him to break even. There is absolutely no reason for the seller to take a loss. Bottles are collectors' items of established growth and their potential value *will* eventually rise.

There are many different methods of selling. The inexperienced or uninformed seller may take his bottles to a local antique shop and accept whatever is offered. In addition to neighborhood antique shops, there are specialist dealers, auctions, and other collectors.

Selling to a Dealer. A specialist dealer will generally give a higher price than a general antique dealer. Since he deals with customers looking specifically for bottles, he can afford to invest more money in his purchases. He knows just how much he can get for a particular bottle and roughly how long it will take to sell. Usually he will not object to taking some duplicate specimens of scarce bottles, but will not accept an unlimited number of the same item.

Except in rare cases, a specialist dealer sells his bottles at 100% of the retail value. Naturally he tries to obtain his merchandise at the lowest possible prices, since he must pay shop rent, utilities, employee salaries, etc., in addition to turning a reasonable profit. The best prices are received when the seller exhibits his knowledge of the material. The dealer will often ask him to name a price so he must know the current market value of the item.

Bargaining should begin at 80% of the retail value. An offer of 60% is considered quite fair and is generally the best that can be expected. Sometimes the offer may be lower if the dealer does not have the clientele interested in that particular item.

Specialists have fairly high standards in the matter of condition. They are not likely to buy any damaged or repaired bottles, and in the case of inexpensive bottles, they may not want any in less than mint condition. Dealers are constantly bombarded with bottle offers and they have to be selective in what they buy; otherwise, their shops would become junkpiles.

Non-specialist dealers might be more flexible on condition, but will probably pay much less for what they buy. They pay on the basis of what they can safely afford to invest. A non-specialist may have very few customers for bottles. Even if an item is desirable, he may hesitate to buy, because he does not know how long it will take to sell. Most often he will not pay more than 40% of the retail value.

If there are no specialist dealers in a certain area, the seller can check the classified phone directories of other surround communities. A list of names and addresses of bottle dealers, such as the one in the back of this book, can be found in the hobby magazines and newspapers. Even with the task of packing and the expense of postage, the seller may still be farther ahead by not selling to a local non-specialist.

Selling by Auction. Auction selling is unpredictable. Unless the sale is being conducted with reserves (minimum selling prices), there is no way to guard against disappointing, or sometimes disastrous, prices. The risks can be minimized somewhat if the collection is consigned to an auctioneer who handles glassware regularly, and has an established reputation for selling collectible bottles. The results of his past sales will indicate to the seller how his own bottles will fare.

Auctioneers who handle only estate sales are not suitable for selling bottles. One must be found who holds sales of antiques. The odds are quite good that his sales are composed of material put up by many different consignors. He will undoubtedly agree to include, in one of his future auctions, any collection consisting of bottles in the moderate to high price range. It may be difficult to locate an auctioneer willing to sell items that are in the low price category. Auctioneers are paid on commission according to the prices realized by each lot. They do not want to handle inexpensive material because it means little or no profit for them.

Of course, a valuable collection should be consigned to one of the major fine-art auctioneers, such as Sotheby/Parke-Bernet which has offices in New York and Los Angeles. This type of firm allows the collector to place reserves on his consigned items — price, of course, must be agreeable to both parties. They produce lavishly illustrated catalogues that afford the material the best possible chance of selling at a high price.

Selling to Another Collector. Although the best prices are obtained by selling to another collector, the seller should not expect to receive full retail value. If a collector wants to pay top dollar, he will buy from a specialist dealer. Selling to a collector at 80% of the value is far more lucrative than selling to a dealer who has to make a profit. Sometimes collectors can be contacted by taking out ads in the bottle publications, in the general hobby press, or even in the classified section of the local newspaper. The seller will then be contacted by only those collectors interested in his types of bottles.

OLD BOTTLES

OLD BOTTLE INTRODUCTION

As a group, old bottles — especially flasks and bitters bottles — are rising in price at a faster rate than the modern Limited Editions listed in the second part of this book. This is not because of a greater number of collectors specializing in old bottles, but because of their scarcity factor. While modern Limited Editions are readily obtainable from specialist dealers, and from other sources as well, many *old bottles occur* for sale infrequently. They require some searching and hunting to track down. The fortunate hobbyist may succeed in getting a prized specimen by digging, or prospecting, but mostly they will have to be acquired from the trade, in competition with others who want the very same bottle. Demand for the rarer kinds of old bottles is extremely strong. Lists put out by dealers become obsolete quickly. If a list offers 200 cr 300 old bottles, there may be only 20 or 30 remaining in the dealer's stock after the list has been in circulation (through the mail, and given out at shows, etc.) as briefly as two weeks. Yes, the dealer can replenish his stock — by buying from the public or trading with fellow professionals. But each time a specimen of a certain bottle is put back into stock, the dealer is usually forced to pay more for it than for the previous one. Thus, he has no choice but to pass the increase along to his customers — and this is one reason why the retail prices of collectible bottles go up and up.

We have grouped the old bottles listed in this book into categories by *type* or by the contents they originally contained, such as Ale & Beer, Medicine, Spirits, Food, etc. Within each of these classifications, *trade names* will be found in alphabetical order whenever they occur. However, the case of some early bottles (such as flasks), trade names do not appear on the bottle. These have been listed by *subject,* according to the subject embossed or otherwise portrayed.

In using this book, it is important to *read the printed descriptions carefully.* Obviously, it is impossible for any one book to list every existing bottle. The prices given are for the specific bottles listed. If you have a bottle which agrees with a portion of the description (such as subject matter of an embossed flask), but not with all of it, you have a different bottle and most likely *the value is different* than the stated figure. It could be worth more or less. Do not automatically assume that it's worth less than the specimen listed. We have not attempted to list only the rarest items, but a cross-section of bottles in various price ranges in all the various categories.

BOTTLE GRADING

Old bottles, decanters and flasks listed in this book are priced in **Mint Condition.** To be considered mint, an old bottle should be intact, with no chips, cracks, or major flaws. Whittle marks, pontil marks, mold marks and seams should be clearly defined if they are a part of the bottle. Handles and stoppers should be complete (particularly on decanters) and original. Color should be clear and clean.

Labels on old bottles should be intact, clean and bright, no rips, tears or repairs. Label may show wear, and slight discolorations, or yellowing, and still be considered Mint.

BEWARE: *Reproductions are made of many of the most valuable OLD BOTTLES, FLASKS AND BITTERS. The best protection is to buy only from reputable dealers.*

BOTTLE NOMENCLATURE

APPLIED LIP—On older bottles (pre-1880), after removal from the blowpipe, the neck was applied, therefore the seams ended below the top of the lip. This helps distinguish Old Bottles from New—if the seam ends below the top of the lip it is usually a hand-blown applied top. If it runs to the very top of the lip, the bottle was probably machine-made.

AMETHYST COLORED GLASS: clear glass that has been exposed to the sun or a very bright light for a period of time, and has turned a light purple color. NOTE: Only glass containing manganese will turn purple.

BLOB TOP—A large thick blob of glass was placed around the lip of Soda or Mineral Water bottles, the wire that held the stopper was seated below the blob, and anchored the wire when the stopper was closed, to prevent carbonation from escaping.

BLOB SEALS—A popular way of identifying an unembossed bottle was to apply a molten coin-shaped blob of glass to the shoulder of the bottle, into which a seal with the logo, or name of the distiller, date, or product name was impressed.

BLOWPIPE: a long tube used by the blower to pick up the molten glass which is then either blown in mold or Free Blown outside a mold to create unlimited varieties of shapes.

GROUND PONTIL: the pontil scar that has been ground off.

IMPERFECTIONS—Bubbles of all sizes and shapes, bent shapes and necks, imperfect seams, errors in spelling, and embossing, increase rather than decrease the value of Old Bottle, providing these imperfections were formed as a part of the natural production of the bottle. The more imperfections, the greater the value.

KICKUP BOTTOM—An indented bottom of any bottle is known as a "Kick-up." This can vary from deep indentations to a very slight impression. Wine bottles as a group are usually indented.

LADY'S LEG—Called by the manufacturers "long bulbous neck." The shape of the neck earned this type of bottle its nickname.

THREE PIECE MOLD
There are 2 main types:

a.) THREE PIECE DIP MOLD—In which the bottom part of the bottle mold was one piece, and the top, from the shoulder up, was 2 separate pieces. Mold seams appear circling the bottle at the shoulder, and on each side of the neck.

b.) FULL HEIGHT 3 PIECE MOLD—The entire bottle was formed in the mold, and the 2 seams run the height of the bottle to below the lip on both sides.

TURN MOLD BOTTLES—A bottle which was turned in forming, in a mold containing a special solvent. The action of turning, and the solvent, erased all seams and mold marks, and imparted a high luster to the finished bottle. As a group, most old Wine Bottles were made this way.

"WHITTLE MOLD," or "WHITTLE MARKS"—Many molds used in the 1800's, and earlier, were carved of wood. Bottles formed in these molds have genuine "Whittle Marks." The same effect was also caused by forming hot glass in early morning cold molds, this combination caused "goose pimples" on the surface of these bottles. As the mold warmed the later bottles were smooth. "Whittle Mold," and "Whittle Mark" bottles are in demand, and command higher prices.

OPALIZATION—This is the frosty bottle or variated color bottle, that has been buried in the earth, or in mud or silt, and minerals in these substances have interacted with the glass of the bottle to create these effects. Many collectors have a high value on bottles of this type.

PONTIL MARKS—To remove the newly blown bottle from the blowpipe, an iron rod with a small amount of molten glass was applied to the bottom of the bottle after the neck and lip were finished. A sharp tap removed the bottle from the pontil, leaving a jagged glass scar. This "Pontil Scar" can be either round, solid, or ring-shaped. On better bottles, the jagged edges were ground down.

PUMPKIN SEED—A small round flat flask, often found in the western areas. Generally made of clear glass, the shape resembled nothing more than the seed of the grown pumpkin. These bottles are also known as "Mickies," "Saddle Flasks," or "Two-Bit Ponies."

ROUND BOTTOMS—Many soda bottles containing carbonated beverages were made of heavy glass, designed in the shape of a torpedo. This enabled the bottle to lie on its side, keeping the liquid in contact with the cork, and preventing the cork from drying, and popping out of the bottle.

SHEARED LIP—In the early years of bottle making, after the bottle was blown, a pair of scissor-like shears clipped the hot glass from the blowpipe. Frequently no top was applied, and sometimes a slight flange was created. The Sheared Top is a usual feature of Old Patriotic Flasks.

SNAP—A more effective way of detaching the blown bottle from the blowpipe was the "Snap." This device, which made it's appearance in the 1860's, was used to grip the blown bottle in a spring cradle in which a cup held the bottom of the bottle. The bottles, held in a Snap during manufacture, have no pontil scars, or marks, but may have grip marks on the side.

BOTTLE AGE

FREE BLOWN BOTTLES: B.C. to 1860—some are still free blown today.

PONTIL: 1618-1866; also some modern hand blown bottles.

RAISED LETTERS: 1790 to date.

THREE PART MOLD: 1806-1889.

AMETHYST OR SUN COLORED GLASS: 1800 to date.

SHEARED LIP: 1800-1830 (the top has been sheared off).

MACHINE-MADE BOTTLES: 1903 to date (Mold Line runs from base through the top).

BLACK OR DARK OLIVE GREEN GLASS: 1700-1880 approx.

BLOB TOP: thick rounded lip, on most soda and mineral water bottles.

CROWN CAP OR TOP: 1895 to date.

BOTTLE AGE AS DETERMINED BY MOLD LINE

| — 1800 + | — 1880 + | — 1890 + | — 1903 + | 1910 To Date |

BOTTLE SHAPES

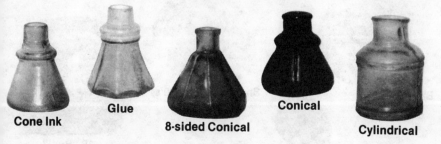

Cone Ink   Glue   8-sided Conical   Conical   Cylindrical

Old Beer

New Beer

Old Soda

New Soda

Shoe Polish

Hutchinson

Tear Drop

Round Bottom

Old Whiskey

New Whiskey

Broken Pontil

Sheared Lip (1800's)

Graphite Pontil

18 "Seal"

2 Part Mold

3 Part Mold

Side Mold

Lady Leg Neck

Medicine or Bitters, label

Old Medicine

New Medicine

Free Blown

Ten Pin

Fire Extinguisher

Squat or Onion

Scroll

Wide Mouth
Case Bottle

FOREIGN TRADEMARKS

A in a circle—Alembic Glass, Industries Bangalore, India
Big A in center of it GM—Australian Glass Mfg. Co. Kilkenny So. Australia.
A.B.C.—Albion Bottle Co. Ltd., Oldbury, Nr. Birmingham, England.
A.G.W.—Alloa Glass Limited, Alloa, Scotland.
A G B Co.—Albion Glass Bottle Co., England, trademark is found under Lea & Perrins, circa 1880 to 1900.
B & Co. L—Bagley & Co. Ltd. Est. 1832 still operating (England).
AVH-A.—Van Hoboken & Co., Rotterdam, The Netherlands, 1800-1898.
Beaver—Beaver Flint Glass Co., Toronto, Ontario, Canada, circa 1897 70 1920.
Bottle in Frame—Veb Glasvoerk Drebkau Drebkau, N.L. Germany.
Crown with 3 dots—Crown Glass, Waterloo, N.S. Wales.
CS & Co.—Cannington, Shaw & Co., St. Helens, England, circa, 1872 to 1916.
Crown with figure of a crown—Excelsior Glass Co., St. Johns, Quebec and later Diamond glass Co., Montreal, Quebec, Canada, circa 1879 to 1913.
D in center of a diamond—Cominion Glass Co., Montreal, Que.
D.B.—in a book frame, Dale Brown & Co., Ltd., Mesborough, Yorks, England.
Fish—Veb Glasvoerk Stralau, Berlin
Excelsior—Excelsior Glass Co., St. John, Quebec, Canada, 1878-1883.
HH—Werk Hermannshutte, Czechoslovakia.
Hamilton—Hamilton Glass Works, Hamilton, Ontario, Canada, 1865-1872.
Hat—Brougba, (Bulgaria).
Hunyadi Janos—Andreas Saxlehner, Buda-Pesth, Austria-Hungary, circa 1863 to 1900.
IYGE—all in a circle, The Irish Glass Bottle, Ltd., Dublin.
KH—Kastrupog Holmeqaads, Copenhagen.

L.—on a bell, Lambert S.A. (Belgium).
LIP—Lea & Perrins, London, England, 1880-1900.
LS—in a circle, Lax & Shaw, Ltd. Leeds, York, England.
M—in a circle, cristales Mexicanos, Monterey, Mexico.
N—in a diamond, Tippon Glass Co., Ltd. Tokyo, Japan.
NAGC—North American Glass Co., Montreal, Quebec, Canada,1883-1890.
PG—Verreries De Puy De Dome, S.A. Paris.
R—Louit Freres & Co., France, circa 1870 to 1890.
S—in a circle, Vetreria Savonese. A. Voglienzone, S.A. Milano, Italy.
S.A.V.A.—all in a circle, Asmara, Ethipia.
S & M—Sykes & Macvey, Castleford, England, 1860-1888.
T—in a circle, Tokyo Seibin Co., Ltd. Tokyo, Japan.
vFo—Vidreria Ind. Figuerras Oliveiras (Brazil).
VT—Ve-Tri S.p.a., Vetrerie Triventa Vicenza, Italy.
VX—Usine de Vauxrot, France.
WECK—in a frame, Weck Glaswerk G. mb.H, ofligen, in Bonn.
Y—in a circle, Etairia Lipasmaton, Athens, Greece.

U.S.TRADEMARKS

The words and letters in bold are only a representation or brief description of the trademark as it appeared on bottle. This is followed by the complete name and location of the company and the approximate period of time in which the trademark was in use.

A—John Agnew & Son, Pittsburgh, PA, 1854-1866.
A in a circle—American Glass Works, Richmond, VA and Paden City, WV, circa 1909 to 1936.
A in a circle—Armstrong Cork Co., Glass Division, Lancaster, PA, 1938-1968.
A & B together (AB)—Adolphus Busch Glass Manufacturing Co., Belleville, IL and St. Louis, MO, circa 1904 to 1907.
A B Co.—American Bottle Co., Chicago, IL, 1905-1930.
A B G M Co.—Adolphus Busch Glass Manufacturing Co, Bellville, IL and St. Louis, MO, circa 1886 to 1928.
A & Co.—John Agnew & Co., Pittsburgh, PA, Indian Queen, Ear of Corn and other flasks, circa 1854 to 1892.
A C M E—Acme Glass Co., Olean, NY, circa 1920 to 1930.
A & D H C—A. & D.H. Chambers, Pittsburgh, PA, Union flasks, circa 1842 to 1886.
AGEE and Agee in script—Hazel Atlas Glass Co., Wheeling, WV, circa 1921 to 1925.
A.G.W. Co.,—American Glass Works Ltd., 1880 to1905.
AGW—American Glass Works, circa 1880.
Anchor figure with H in center—Anchor Hocking Glass Corp., Lancaster, OH, circa 1955.
A.R.S.—A.R. Samuels Glass Co., Philadelphia, PA, circa 1855 to 1872.
A S F W W Va.—A.S. Frank Glass Co., Wellsburg, WV, circa 1859.

ATLAS—Atlas Glass Co., Washington, PA, and later Hazel Atlas Glass Co., 1896-1965.

AVH—A. Van Hoboken & Co., Rotterdam, The Netherlands, 1800-1898.

Ball and Ball in script—Ball Bros. Glass Manufacturing Co., Muncie, IN and later Ball Corp., 1887-1973.

Bernardin in script—W.J. Latchford Glass Co., Los Angeles, CA, circa 1932 to 1938.

The Best—Gillender & Sons, Philadelphia, PA, circa 1867 to 1870.

B F B Co.—Bell Fruit Bottle Co., Fairmount, IN, circa 1910.

B.G. Co.—Belleville Glass Co. IL, circa 1882.

Bishop's—Bishop & Co., San Diego and Los Angeles, CA, 1890 to 1920.

B K—Benedict Kimber, Bridgeport and Brownsville, PA, circa 1822 to 1840.

Boyds in script—Illinois Glass Co., Alton, IL, circa 1900 to 1930.

Brelle (in script) Jar—Brelle Fruit Jar Manufacturing Co., San Jose, CA, circa 1912 to 1916.

Brilliantine—Jefferis Glass Co., Fairton, NJ and Rochester, PA, circa 1900 to 1905.

C in a circle—Chattanooga Bottle & Glass Co. and later Chattanooga Glass Co., since 1927.

C in a square—Crystal Glass Co., Los Angeles, CA, circa 1921 to 1929.

C in a star—Star City Glass Co., Star City, WV, since 1949.

Canton Domestic Fruit Jar—Canton Glass Co., Canton, OH, circa 1890 to 1904.

C & Co. or C Co.—Cunninghams & Co., Pittsburgh, PA, 1880-1907.

CCCo—C. Conrad & Co. (Beer) 1878-1883.

C.V. Co. No. 1 & No. 2,—Milwaukee, Wis. 1880-1881.

C C Co.—Carl Conrad & Co., St. Louis, MO, 1876-1883.

C C G Co.—Cream City Glass Co., Milwaukee, WI, 1888-1893.

C.F.C.A.—California Fruit Canners Association, Sacramento, CA, circa 1899 to 1916.

C G M Co—Campbell Glass Manufacturing Co., West Berkeley, CA, 1885.

C G W—Campbell Glass Works, West Berkeley, CA, 1884-1885.

C & H—Coffin & Hay, Winslow, NJ, circa 1838 to 1842.

C L G Co.—Carr-Lowrey Glass Co., Baltimore, MD, circa 1889 to 1920.

Clyde, N.Y.—Clyde Glass Works, Clyde, N.Y, circa 1870 to 1882.

The Clyde in script—Clyde Glass Works, Clyde, N.Y, circa 1895.

C Milw—Chase Valley Glass Co., Milwaukee, WI, circa 1880.

Cohansey—Cohansey Glass Manufacturing Co., Philadelphia, PA, 1870-1900.

CS & Co.—Cannington, Shaw & Co., St. Helens, England, circa 1872 to 1916.

DB—Du Bois Brewing Co., Pittsburgh, PA, circa 1918.

Dexter—Franklin Flint Glass Works, Philadelphia, PA, circa 1861 to 1880.

Diamond—(plain) Diamond Glass Co. since 1924.

The Dictator—William McCully & Co., Pittsburgh, PA, circa 1855 to 1869.

Dictator—same as above only circa 1869 to 1885.

D & O—Cumberland Glass Mfg. Co., Bridgeton, NJ, circa 1890 to 1900.

D O C—D.O. Cunningham Glass Co., Pittsburgh, PA, circa 1883 to 1937.

D S G Co.—De Steiger Glass Co., LaSalle, IL, circa 1867 to 1896.

Duffield—Duffield, Parke & Co., Detroit, MI, 1866-1875.

Dyottsville—Dyottsville Glass Works, Philadelphia, PA, 1833-1923.

Economy (in script) TRADE MARK—Kerr Glass Manufacturing Co., Portland, OR, 1903-1912.

Electric Trade Mark in script—Gayner Glass Works, Salem, NJ, circa 1910.

Electric Trade Mark—same as above only circa 1900 to 1910.

Erd & Co., E R Durkee—E.R. Durkee & Co., New York, NY, post-1874.

E R Durkee & Co—same as above only circa 1850 to 1860.

Eureka 17—Eurkee Jar Co., Dunbar, WV, circa 1864.

Eureka in script—same as above only 1900-1910.

Everlasting (in script) JAR—Illinois Pacific Glass Co., San Francisco, CA, circa 1904.

Excelsior—Excelsior Glass Co., St. John, Quebec, Canada, 1878-1883.

F inside of a jar outline—C.L. Flaccus Glass Co., Pittsburgh, PA, circa 1900 to 1928.

F & A—Fahnstock & Albree, Pittsburgh, PA, 1860-1862.

FL or FL & Co.—Frederick Lorenz & Co., Pittsburgh, PA, circa 1819 to 1841.

G E M—Hero Glass Works, Philadelphia, PA, circa 1884 to 1909.

G & H—Gray & Hemingray, Cincinnati, OH, circa 1848 to 1864.

Gilberds—Gilberds Butter Tub Co., Jamestown, NY, circa 1883 to 1890.

Greenfield—Greenfield Fruit Jar & Bottle Co., Greenfield, IN, circa 1888 to 1912.

H (with varying numerals)—Holt Glass Works, West Berkeley, CA, circa 1893 to 1906.

Hamilton—Hamilton Glass Works, Hamilton, Ontario, Canada, 1865-1872.

Hazel—Hazel Glass Co., Wellsburg, WV, 1886-1902.

Helme—Geo. W. Helme Co., Jersey City, NJ, circa 1870 to 1895.

Hemingray—Hemingray Brothers & Co. and later Hemingray Glass Co., Covington, KY, since 1864.

H.J. Heinz—H.J. Heinz Co., Pittsburgh, PA, circa 1860 to 1869.

Heinz & Noble—same as above only circa 1869 to 1872.

F. & J. Heinz—same as above only circa 1876 to 1888.

H.J. Heinz Co.—same as above only since 1888.

HS in a circle—Twitchell & Schoolcraft, Keene, NH, 1815-1816.

Hunyadi Janos—Andreas Saxlehner, Buda-Pesth, Austria-Hungary, circa 1863 to 1900.

I G Co.—Ihmsen Glass Co., Pittsburgh, PA, circa 1870 to 1898.

I.G. Co.—Ihmsen Glass Co. circa 1895.

I.G.Co.—monogram, Ill. Glass Co. on fruit jar 1914.

I.P.G.—in diamond, Ill. Pacific Glass Corp. 1925 to 1930.

I G—Illinois Glass F inside of a jar outline, C.L. Flaccus ½ glass ½ co., Pittsburg, PA, circa 1900 to 1928.

Ill. Glass Co.—1916 to 1929.

I G—Illinois Glass Co., Alton, IL, before 1890.

IG Co in a diamond—same as above only circa 1900 to 1916.

Improved G E M—Hero Glass Works, Philadelphia, PA, circa 1868.

I P G—Illinois Pacific Glass Co., San Francisco, CA, 1902-1932.

JAF & Co., Pioneer and Folger—J. A. Folger & Co., San Francisco, CA, since 1850.

J D 26 S—Jogn Duncan & Sons, New York, NY, circa 1880 to 1900.

J R—Stourbridge Flint Glass Works, Pittsburgh, PA, circa 1823 to 1828.

JSB monogram—Joseph Schlitz Brewing Co., Milwaukee, WI, circa 1900.

J T—Mantua Glass Works and later Mantua Glass Co., Mantua, OH, circa 1824.

J T & Co—Brownsville Glass Works, Brownsville, PA, circa 1824 to 1828.

Kensington Glass Works—Kensington Glass Works, Philadelphia, PA, circa 1822 to 1932.

Kerr in script—Kerr Glass Manufacturing Co. and later Alexander H. Kerr Glass Co., Portland, OR; Sand Spring, OK; Chicago, IL; Los Angeles, since 1912.

K H & G—Kearns, Herdman & Gorsuch, Zanesville, OH, 1876-1884.

K & M—Knoz & McKee, Wheeling, WV, 1824-1829.

K Y G W and KYGW Co—Kentucky Glass Works Co., Louisville, KY, 1849-1855.

Lamb—Lamb Glass Co., Mt. Vernon, OH, 1855-1964.

L & W—Lorenz & Wightman, Pa. 1862 to 1871.

L G Co—Louisville Glass Works, Louisville, KY, circa 1880.

Lightning—Henry W. Putnam, Bennington, VT, 1875-1890.

L I P—Lea & Perrins, London, England, 1880-1900.

L K Y G W—Louisville Kentucky Glass Works, Louisville, KY, circa 1873 to 1890.

"Mascot," "Mason" and M F G Co—Mason Fruit Jar Co., Philadelphia, PA, all circa 1885 to 1900.

Mastadon—Thomas A. Evans Mastadon Works, and later Wm. McCully & Co., Pittsburgh, PA, 1855-1887.

MG—slant letters, Maywood Glass, Maywood, Calif. 1930 to 1950 .

M.G. CO.—Missouri Glass Co. 1900.

M.G. Co—Modes Glass Co., Ind. 1895 to 1904.

M. G. W.—Middletown Glass Co. N.Y. C-1889.

Moore Bros.—Moore Bros., Clayton, NJ, 1864-1880.

N B B G Co—North Baltimore Bottle Glass Co., North Baltimore, OH, 1885-1930.

O—Owen Bottle Co.

O-D-1 O & Diamond & I—Owens Ill. Pacific Coast Co., CA, 1932 to 1943. Mark of Owen-Ill. Glass Co. merger in 1930.

P G W—Pacific Glass Works, San Francisco, CA, 1862-1876.

Premium—Premium Glass Co., Coffeyville, KS, circa 1908 to 1914.

Putnam Glass Works in a circle—Putnam Flint Glass Works, Putnam, OH, circa 1852 to 1871.

P & W—Perry & Wood and later Perry & Wheeler, Keene, NH, circa 1822 to 1830.

Queen (in script) Trade Mark all in a shield—Smalley, Kivlan & Onthank, Boston, MA, 1906-1919.

R—Louit Freres & Co., France, circa 1870 to 1890.

Rau's—Fairmount Glass Works, Fairmount, IN, circa1898 to 1908.

R & C Co—Roth & Co., San Francisco, CA, 1879-1888.

Red with a key through it—Safe Glass Co., Upland, IN, circa 1892 to 1898.

R G Co—Renton Glass Co., Renton, WA, 1911.

Root—Root Glass Co., Terre Haute, IN, 1901-1932.

S—in a side of a star-Southern Glass Co. L.A. 1920 to 1929.

S.B. & G. Co.—Streator Bottle & Glass Co., Ill. 1881 to 1905.

S.F. & P.G.W.—John Wieland's extra pale Cac. cal. Bottling Works S.F.

S & C—Stebbins & Chamberlain or Coventry Glass Works, Coventry, CT, circa 1825 to 1830.

S F G W—San Francisco Glass Works, San Francisco, CA, 1869-1876.

S & M—Sykes & Macvey, Castleford, England, 1860-1888.
Squibb—E.R. Squibb, M.D., Brooklyn, NY, 1858-1895.
Standard (in script, Mason)—Standard Coop. Glass Co. and later Standard Glass Co., Marion, IN, circa 1894 to 1932.
Star Glass Co.—Star Glass Co., New Albany, IN, circa 1860 to 1900.
Swayzee—Swayzee Glass Co., Swayzee, IN, 1894-1906.
T C W—T.C. Wheaton co., Millville, NJ, since 1888.
T S—Coventry Glass Works, Coventry, CT, 1820-1824.
W & CO—Thomas Wightman & Co., Pottsburgh, PA, circa 1880 to 1889.
W C G Co—West Coast Glass Co., Los Angeles, CA, 1908-1930.
WF & S MILW—William Franzen & Son, Milwaukee, WI, 1900-1929.
W G W—Woodbury Glass Works, Woodbury, NJ, 1882-1900.
W T & Co—Whitall-Tatum & Co., Millville, NJ, 1857-1935.

ALE & GIN

Not heavily collected until fairly recent years, ale and gin bottles have become one of the more popular divisions of the hobby. Their dark, bold colors and distinctive shapes give them special appeal even though the majority were not made to be collected. These bottles have a definite masculine character and seem to reflect the ruggedness of their original owners. Superb opportunities still prevail to acquire many of these specimens at low prices.

Ale and gin bottles tend to be collected together, which is why we have grouped them in this section. The styles in most instances are similar or identical, and it is not easy to tell, unless information is provided on the bottle itself, whether a given bottle was used for one or the other. These should not be confused with beer bottles, which comprise a separate group and are listed in the appropriate place in this book.

The history of ale and gin is much different than that of wine. Ale has traditionally been a more popular beverage among the common classes than wine. Inexpensive wine has always been available, going all the way back to Roman times, but our ancestors considered it so unpalatable that they preferred almost anything else. Ale was a favorite alternative. The best ale was not expensive, even in 17th century America. Those who did not wish to buy ale ready-made could make it themselves at home with simple ingredients and little fuss. Bottles used by colonial ale-makers were mostly made of pottery and imported from England. Knowing that the ceramics industry was in a primitive state in America, and that demand for bottles and other containers was great, English manufacturers did a brisk trade in the 17th and 18th centuries selling their bottles in the U.S. (One of the first lessons to be learned by diggers is that a bottle is not necessarily of America origin just because it was found on American soil — regardless of the age.)

The oldest of these specimens had a matte or unglazed surface, while the later examples are generally glazed. These cannot be classified as store bottles. They were intended for the home brewer, even though many (with contents) must have been publicly sold.

Though inexpensive, certain hazards were attached to home brewing of ale. When corks were used as stoppers, it was important to keep them moist. Otherwise they contracted slightly, and the ale's carbonation could force them out of the bottle — therby allowing the contents to go flat.

Gin, unlike ale, beer and wine, does not have ancient origins. It was invented — quite by accident — in the 17th century. Francesco de la Bor, a Dutch physician, was experimenting with treatments for kidney disease and prepared gin as a medicinal compound. It was supposed to purify the blood. At first it was sold exclusively by chemists. While its effectiveness in blood purifying was questionable, gin drinking became a fad — even among persons with sound kidneys. Many chemists went into the gin-brewing business fulltime, to meet the demand. Eventually it began to be sold in taverns and its popularity spread from Holland into Germany, England and elsewhere. For reasons still unexplained, it never caught on in some countries, such as France and Italy. But it became popular in America in colonial times and gin consumption increased steadily during the 19th century.

Modern gin bottles still bear much resemblance, in shape at least, to their forerunners of the 1600's. Gin bottles were designed with square bodies to facilitate packing them in a case and prevent shifting around in transit. There were a dozen bottles to a case, which was made of wood (at first by the local cooper, then by packing firms). These were called "case bottles." The first case bottles were octagonal, but the standard four-sided design was introduced not long thereafter. Early case bottles had very short necks. The later trend was toward long necks. It is often impossible to distinguish between early gin bottles of Dutch and American origin. The styles are very similar, as American bottle makers employed a good many Dutch workers.

Most case bottles with tapered collars can safely be dated to the 19th century. Plate molds began to be used in bottle making in the late 1800's. Such molds carried plates with lettering or designs which were transferred to the bottle. Case bottles are found with embossed likenesses of animals, human figures, stars or geometrical motifs. Though retaining the traditional shape, case bottles vary in size from a half pint to multiple gallons. Early specimens are crudely made and bear pontil scars.

You will encounter many unusual and bizarre names among the early ale and gin makers, as reflected in the following list. For example there was "Antediluvian Luyties Brothers" of New York. The word "antediluvian" means "occuring before the Biblical flood" (the great flood for which Noah built his ark). How this relates to an alcoholic beverage is difficult to comprehend. More explainable, but still seemingly confusing just for the sake of being confsing, was "Ameliorated Schiedam Holland Gin." To ameliorate means to improve something. Why didn't they just say "improved Schiedam Holland Gin?" Probably because a long word, that few people understood, might be mistaken for something grand and exotic. Can't you picture someone arriving home a few gererations ago with a prized package beneath his arm, and breathlessly announcing, "Hey, I've got a bottle of real genuine *ameliorated* gin."

ALE & GIN

A

NO.	DESCRIPTION	PRICE RANGE	
☐ 1	**ABMYERSAM**		
	Rock Rose, New Haven, Md., dark green, 9⅛"	7.00	10.00
☐ 2	**A & D.H.C.**		
	Yellow amber, 9½"	14.00	20.00
☐ 3	**A.H.**		
	In seal, roll top, green amber, 11⅜"	38.00	52.00
☐ 4	**A.I.**		
	With an anchor in seal on shoulder, honey amber, 8¾" ..	36.00	49.00
☐ 5	*ALE, label, dark green, turn mold, 9½"*	5.00	8.00
☐ 6	*ALE, label, olive, turn mold, kick-up, 8½"*	5.00	8.00
☐ 7	*ALE, label, green, kick-up, 6"*	5.00	8.00
☐ 8	*ALE, label, c. 1916 A under bottom, olive, 9½"*	3.00	5.00
☐ 9	*ALE, label, aqua, 9½"*	4.00	6.00
☐ 10	*ALE, label, aqua, kick-up, 8"*	3.00	4.00
☐ 11	*ALE, label, aqua, Root under bottom, 11¾"*	4.00	6.00
☐ 12	*ALE, label, dark olive, turn mold, 9½"*	9.00	12.00
☐ 13	*ALE, label, amber, ground pontil, 11¼"*	32.00	41.00

A & D.H.C.

2   5   6   7   8

9   10   11   12   13

14   15   16   17

☐	14	*ALE, label, amber, 8¾"*	**17.00**	**23.00**
☐	15	*ALE, label, light green, small kick-up pontil, 9"*	**18.00**	**26.00**
☐	16	*ALE, label, olive, kick-up, 7½"*	**19.00**	**27.00**
☐	17	*ALE, label, olive, kick-up with broken pontil, 12"*	**18.00**	**26.00**
☐	18	*ALE, label, olive, kick-up pontil, three-part mold, 8¾"*	**22.00**	**30.00**
☐	19	*ALE, label, amber, pontil, 9"*	**31.00**	**42.00**
☐	20	*ALE, label, milk glass, 11"*	**18.00**	**26.00**
☐	21	*ALE, label, five dots under bottom, small kick-up, black, 10"*	**7.00**	**10.00**
☐	22	*ALE, label, light aqua, 9½"*	**4.00**	**6.00**
☐	23	*ALE OR WINE, label, three-part mold, B under bottom, dark olive, 10"*	**7.00**	**10.00**
☐	24	*ALE OR WINE, label, kick-up, dark olive, 9½"*	**3.00**	**5.00**
☐	25	*ALE OR WINE, label, kick-up, dark olive, 10"*	**3.00**	**5.00**
☐	26	*ALE, plain, 7¼", free-blown, 2" diameter, pontil, crude top*	**22.00**	**32.00**
☐	27	*ALE, plain, aqua, free-blown, kick-up, pontil, light-weight bottle, very crude top, 2¾" diameter, 9½"*	**27.00**	**38.00**
☐	28	*ALE, plain, free-blown, aqua, kick-up, pontil, 2¼" diameter, crude top, 8½"*	**22.00**	**32.00**
☐	29	*ALE, plain, quart, 3" neck, very crude applied top, pontil in kick-up, very light blue, 6"*	**22.00**	**32.00**
☐	30	*ALE, plain, eight panels, graphite pontil, green, 7"*	**23.00**	**33.00**
☐	31	*ALE, plain pottery, brown and white, 8½"*	**5.00**	**8.00**
☐	32	*ALE, plain pottery, white, 8½"*	**7.00**	**10.00**
☐	33	*ALE, plain, white, pottery, 11½"*	**7.00**	**10.00**
☐	34	**S. ALVARES** *On seal, clear, kick-up, 11½"*	**11.00**	**15.00**
☐	35	**AMELIORATED SCHIEDAM HOLLAND GIN** *Amber, 9½"*	**19.00**	**27.00**
☐	36	**ANTEDILUVIAN LUYTIES BROTHERS, NEW YORK** *Small kick-up, olive, 12"*	**9.00**	**12.00**
☐	37	**ASCR** *In a seal, olive, kick-up, pontil or plain, 10½"*	**45.00**	**60.00**
☐	38	**ASPARAGUS GIN** *THE ROTHENBERG CO. on front in circle, slug plate, S.F. CALIF., same shape as a Duffy malt, graduated collar, aqua, 10⅛"*	**21.00**	**29.00**
☐	39	**AVAN HOBOKEN & CO.** *On front, seal on shoulder AVH, case bottle, olive, 11¼"* .	**33.00**	**43.00**

B

☐	40	**BAIRD DANIELS CO. DRY GIN** *Taped and ring top, aqua, 9"*	**10.00**	**15.00**
☐	41	*Same as above, except MISTLETOE DRY GIN, 8½", clear or amethyst*	**10.00**	**15.00**
☐	42	*Same as above, except CORONET under bottom, aqua* ..	**12.00**	**18.00**
☐	43	**BART E.L.** *In Old English type on one line, on the other Dry Gin, light green, 8½"*	**7.00**	**10.00**
☐	44	**BASS' PALE ALE** *Label, three-part mold, amber, 9½"*	**5.00**	**8.00**
☐	45	**B.B. EXTRA SUPERIOR** *Whiskey, amber, 10½"*	**15.00**	**21.00**

☐ 46	**B. C. W.**		
	Dark olive, pontil, 9"	55.00	75.00
☐ 47	**BENEDICTINE**		
	Dark green, kick-up, F22 on bottom, 8¾"	14.00	20.00
☐ 48	**BERGOMASTER**		
	Geneva Gin, Cobb Hersey Co., Boston on round label, also ship on bottom of label, case type, 10½", olive	12.00	16.00
☐ 49	**BERRY BROS.**		
	323 E. 38th St. N.Y. in circle on front, aqua, 11¼"	4.00	6.00
☐ 50	**BILL & DUNLOP**		
	Dark olive, 11½"	22.00	35.00
☐ 51	BLACK BOTTLE, beer or ale, three-part mold, kick-up with one dot, 4½" body, 2" neck, crude top, bottom 3", dark olive, 7¾"	15.00	21.00
☐ 52	BLACK BOTTLE, 4¾" body, 2" neck, 3" bottom, three-part old, kick-up, dark olive	15.00	21.00
☐ 53	BLACK BOTTLE, 5½" body, 2½" lady's leg neck, improved pontil, 2¾" bottom, crude top	15.00	21.00
☐ 54	BLACK BOTTLE, beer or ale, three-part mold, 6½" body, 3" neck, 2½" bottom, dark olive	10.00	15.00
☐ 55	BLACK GLASS, plain, three-part mold, kick-up, 7¾"	7.00	10.00
☐ 56	BLACK GLASS, C.W. & Co. under bottom, three-part mold, kick-up	7.00	10.00
☐ 57	**BLAKE BROS PALE ALE, LANGPORT,**		
	Label, P & R B under bottom, three-part mold, olive, 9½" .	12.00	16.00
☐ 58	**BLANKENHEYM & NOLET**		
	On front, ½" letters, case bottle, olive, 9½"	22.00	30.00
☐ 59	**BLANKENHEYM & NOLET**		
	Dark olive, 7½"	19.00	27.00
☐ 60	**BLANKENHEYM & NOLET**		
	Green or amber, 9½"	16.00	23.00
☐ 61	Same as above, except brown or amber, 8½"	16.00	23.00
☐ 62	Same as above, except brown, 7⅞"	18.00	27.00
☐ 63	Same as above, except clear, 9⅜"	12.00	16.00
☐ 64	Same as above, except green, 9½"	22.00	30.00
☐ 65	**BOUVIER'S BUCHU GIN**		
	On front, on back, Louisville, Ky., square fancy shoulder and neck, purple	13.00	19.00
☐ 66	**DR. C. BOUVIER'S BUCHU GIN**		
	Vertical in two lines, fancy quart bottle, 11¾"	15.00	22.00
☐ 67	**BOUVIER'S BUCHU GIN**		
	Clear or amethyst, 11¾"	7.00	10.00
☐ 68	**BOUVIER'S BUCHU GIN**		
	Clear, machine made, 6"	4.00	6.00
☐ 69	**BOWER & TUFT'S**		
	New Albany, Ind. around bottom in ten panels, L & W under bottom, dark amber, 9½"	29.00	38.00
☐ 70	**E.J.F. BRANDS** (ale)		
	In seal, case type, ribbed sides, tapered top, 9½"	32.00	45.00
☐ 71	**B. R. P. CO.**		
	Mold-blown, tapered top, green or amber, 8⅞"	16.00	23.00
☐ 72	**BUNGALOW**		
	Gin label, tapered top, amber, 10½"	12.00	17.00

C

☐ 73 **C.A. & C. DOS VINHOS DO PORTO**
   Vertical, 11¾", whittle mold, olive, amber .... | 13.00 | 17.00
☐ 74 **CARL MAMPE, BERLIN**
   Ale, small kick-up, tapered top .... | 16.00 | 23.00
☐ 75 *CASE BOTTLE with two dots under bottom, crude applied
   top, 9½"* .... | 18.00 | 27.00
☐ 76 *CASE BOTTLE, plain, broken pontil, curved bottom, dark
   olive, short neck, 10"* .... | 50.00 | 65.00
☐ 77 *CASE BOTTLE, plain, curved bottom, dark olive, crude
   applied top, full of bubbles, short neck, 9¼"* .... | 19.00 | 27.00
☐ 78 *CASE BOTTLE, plain, clear, long neck, on front, sunken
   circle, 9"* .... | 13.00 | 17.00
☐ 79 *CASE BOTTLE, plain, five dots under bottom, short neck,
   crude top, olive, 10½"* .... | 16.00 | 23.00
☐ 80 *CASE BOTTLE, plain, short neck, crude top, olive, 10½"* . | 16.00 | 23.00
☐ 81 *CASE BOTTLE, plain, small kick-up, dark olive, 9½"* ..... | 16.00 | 23.00
☐ 82 *CASE BOTTLE, plain, milk glass, roof type shoulder, 2"
   neck and top, 1¼" deep circle under bottom, 9½"* ...... | 45.00 | 60.00
☐ 83 *CASE BOTTLE, plain, curved or plain bottom, dark olive,
   tapered top, short neck, 10"* .... | 16.00 | 23.00
☐ 84 *CASE BOTTLE, plain, curved or plain bottom, dark olive,
   tapered top, short neck, 3⅞"* .... | 16.00 | 23.00
☐ 85 *CASE BOTTLE, plain, curved or plain bottom, brown-olive,
   light olive, tapered top, short neck, 10"* .... | 16.00 | 23.00
☐ 86 *CASE BOTTLE, label, black, 8"* .... | 13.00 | 17.00
☐ 87 *CASE GIN, label, green, cross on bottom, 10"* .... | 19.00 | 27.00
☐ 88 *CASE GIN, label, pontil, black, 10"* .... | 28.00 | 38.00
☐ 89 *CASE GIN, label, dark olive, green, 9"* .... | 22.00 | 32.00
☐ 90 *CROWN SEAL, label, kick-up, aqua, 11"* .... | 7.00 | 10.00
☐ 91 **C.S. & CO.**
   Under bottom, three-part mold, olive, 10" .... | 11.00 | 15.00
☐ 92 **C. W.& CO.**
   *Under bottom, kick-up, dot in center, three-part mold, 5"
   body, 2" bob neck type, 3" bottom, dark olive* .... | 12.00 | 17.00

D

☐ 93 **JOHN DE KUYPER & SON**
   Olive, 10¼" .... | 14.00 | 19.00
☐ 94 **DE KUYPER GIN**
   Label, dark amber, 10½" .... | 10.00 | 15.00
☐ 95 **DE KUYPER, L.G. CO.**
   Square face gin, dark green, 7⅜" .... | 13.00 | 17.00
☐ 96 *DEMIJOHN, sample label, clear or amethyst, 4"* .... | 11.00 | 15.00
☐ 97 *DEMIJOHN, olive, 12"* .... | 12.00 | 16.00
☐ 98 *DEMIJOHN, label, cobalt, 12"* .... | 28.00 | 37.00
☐ 99 *DEMIJOHN, pontil, dark green, 16½" x 6½" x 8"* .... | 40.00 | 55.00
☐ 100 **DE MONDARIZ V.H.P. ACUAR**
   A round shoulder, snap-on top, olive, machine made, 8½" | 7.00 | 10.00

□101 **DOUBLE EAGLE SEAL**
Kick-up on bottom, turn mold, ring top, light green, 9¾" . 16.00 23.00
□102 **DREWS DOPPEL KRONENBIER**
Squat bottle, ale, dark amber, 8" 18.00 27.00
□103 **D^R K**
*In center of a circle with INTRODUCED ON MERIT around
edge of circle, on bottom, Established D^R K 1851 inside a
circle, applied top, quart size, amber* 30.00 42.00
□104 **D-SEARS**
In a seal, ale, tapered collar, olive, 10½" 29.00 38.00
□105 **DUB & G**
In seal, olive, 8¼" and 6½" 45.00 60.00
□106 *DUNMORE OR SQUAT, label, different sizes and heights,
dark olive, green, pontil, free-blown* 130.00 170.00
□107 **J. & R. DUNSTER**
On front panel, tapered top, olive green, 9½" 30.00 42.00
□108 **F. DUSCH, RICHMOND, VA., T.B.I.N.S.**
Reverse side XXX Porter, squat type, aqua, 6¾" 38.00 50.00
□109 **DUTCH ONIONS**
Ale, free-blown, open pontil, olive 125.00 160.00
□110 **DYOTTVILLE GLASS WORKS, PHILA.**
Under bottom, three-part mold, olive, graphite pontil, 11" . 22.00 32.00
□111 **DYOTTVILLE GLASS WORKS, PHILA. 5**
Under bottom, three-part mold, amber, 11" 15.00 22.00

E

□112 **W. EAGLE, CANAL ST, NY.**
*(Missing period after N); Philadelphia Porter 1860 on back,
ice blue, 7"* 23.00 31.00
□113 **EMON COLL**
In seal, kick-up, olive, 11½" 20.00 27.00
□114 **D.H. EVANS, ST. LOUIS**
*Ale, three-piece mold, tapered top and ring, quart, black
glass* 29.00 38.00

F

□115 *F under bottom, label, amber, 6"* 5.00 8.00
□116 **FABRICADE GIJON**
Under bottom, dark olive, 11" 7.00 10.00
□117 **F.C.G. CO., LOU., KY.**
Under bottom, amber, 12" 10.00 15.00
□118 **F E S & CO. GIN**
Aqua, 9¾" 12.00 17.00
□119 **FINEST OLD WINDMILL GIN**
Tapered top, clear, 10½" 23.00 32.00
□120 **FLORA TEMPLE HARNESS TROT 219**
Horse on front, amber, 8½" 90.00 120.00

G

☐ 121 **GARNET DRY GIN**
Clear, 8¾" 9.00 12.00

☐ 122 **GINEBRA DE LA CAMPANA**
In center a bell in seal, dog bottle, a Star of David on base,
TRADE MARCA REGISTRADA, tapered case gin, green,
9⅛" 45.00 60.00

☐ 123 *GIN, label, free-blown, open pontil, wide collar, green, 11"* 19.00 25.00

☐ 124 *GIN, label, free-blown, flared lip, open pontil, amber*
green, 13" 19.00 25.00

☐ 125 *GIN, label, free-blown, roll lip, pontil, green or amber,*
15½" 55.00 75.00

☐ 126 *GIN, label, free-blown, improved pontil, dark green, 8½"* . 25.00 34.00

☐ 127 *GIN, label, clear or amethyst, 9½"* 5.00 8.00

☐ 128 *GIN, label, green, 10½"* 7.00 10.00

☐ 129 *GIN, plain, clear, 3¼"* 4.00 6.00

☐ 130 **GOLDEN SPRAY**
Clear or amethyst, 9½" 7.00 10.00

☐ 131 **GORDON'S DRY GIN**
On front, on one side England, the other London, under
bottom in sunken circle a wild boar, green or clear, seam
to top, 8½" or 8⅝" 6.00 9.00

☐ 132 *Same except seam to top ring, the boar is a little different,*
amber 8.00 11.00

☐ 133 **GRAVES GIN**
Label, clear, 6" 5.00 8.00

H

☐ 134 **H D B & C**
Roll lip, green or amber, 6¼" 16.00 22.00

☐ 135 **P. F. HEERING**
Amber, 11" 29.00 41.00

☐ 136 **P. F. HEERING**
On a seal, amber, 10¼" 29.00 41.00

☐ 137 **P.F. HEERING**
On ribbon shield, kick-up, double ring top, dark green,
8¾" 47.00 62.00

☐ 138 **J.H. HENKES, DELFSHAVEN**
Tapered top, green, 8½" 16.00 23.00

☐ 139 **J.H. HENKES**
Tapered top, green, 10⅜" 21.00 28.00

☐ 140 **HIGHEST MEDAL, VIENNA 1873**
In circle, head in circle, green, 8¼" 45.00 60.00

☐ 141 **I.C. HOFFMAN**
In seal, kick-up, dark olive, 9" 38.00 52.00

☐ 142 **P. HOPPE, SCHIEDAM**
In seal, flared top, improved pontil, dark green, 9⅜" 32.00 42.00

☐ 143 *Same as above, green, 9½"* 32.00 42.00

☐ 144 **A. HOUTMAN & CO., SCHIEDAM**
Same on reverse side, roll lip, amber green, 11" ... 32.00 42.00

☐ 145 **H.T. & CO. LONDON & N.Y.**
*Under bottom, Capacity 24½ oz on shoulder, sheared top,
aqua* 7.00   10.00
☐ 146 **HERMAN JANSEN, SCHIEDAM HOLLAND**
In seal, dark green, 9⅜" 23.00   32.00

J

☐ 147 **C.A. JOURDE BORDEAUX**
Dots under bottom, olive, 10½" 11.00   15.00
☐ 148 **JUNIPER BERRY GIN, BOTTLED BY QUININE WHISKEY CO.,
LOUISVILLE KY.** *Wide ring top, aqua, 10½"* 22.00   30.00
☐ 149 **JUNIPER LEAF GIN**
Case type, amber, 10½" 16.00   23.00

K

☐ 150 **KAISERBRAUEREI, BREMEN**
Vertically in ¾" letters, olive, inside screw top, 9¼" 16.00   23.00
☐ 151 **KEY SEAL**
Dark olive, 9½" 40.00   52.00
☐ 152 **E. KIDERLEN**
Dark olive, 5¾" 22.00   31.00
☐ 153 **H.B. KIRK & CO. N.Y.**
*"Bottle Remains The Property Of" in back, right
face, amber, 11"* 14.00   19.00
☐ 154 *Same as above, except left face* 14.00   19.00
☐ 155 **A.B. KNOLL REGISTERED ERIE, PA.**
Amber, 9½" 13.00   18.00
☐ 156 **KOPPITZ MELCHERS, DETROIT, MICH.**
A B & Co under bottom, aqua, 9½" 13.00   18.00

L

☐ 157 **L.M.G. CO.**
In seal, flared top, improved pontil, brown, green, 9½" . . .   45.00   60.00
☐ 158 **LONDON JOCKEY**
*N's in London backward, Club House Gin on one side,
man riding a horse on back, dark olive, 9¾"* 115.00   140.00
☐ 159 *Same except N is correct* 60.00   80.00
☐ 160 **LONG NECK PORTER**
Free-blown, open pontil, olive 45.00   60.00
☐ 161 **P. LOOPUYT & CO. DISTILLERS, SCHIEDAM**
Dark olive, 9½" 33.00   42.00
☐ 162 **LOTHARINGEN**
Pontil, dark olive, 10" x 18" 120.00   150.00
☐ 163 **L & T GIN**
Anchor on front, olive, 9" 40.00   53.00

M

☐ 164 **MADISON ORIGINAL ALE**
*John Fennell Louisville, Ky. on front, tapered ring top, star
under bottom, amber, 7⅛"* .... | 15.00 | 20.00
☐ 165 **THE MALTINE M'F'G CO., NEW YORK**
Amber, 6" .... | 13.00 | 18.00
☐ 166 **V. MARKER & CO.**
Semi-script, tapered top, green or amber, 9⅜" .... | 23.00 | 32.00
☐ 167 **J. MEBUS**
In seal, olive 9¾" .... | 42.00 | 60.00
☐ 168 **MEDER & ZOON**
*Swan with W.P. in center, all in a seal, amber or green,
9¼"* .... | 32.00 | 44.00
☐ 169 **J. MEEUS**
*Anchor with J.M. over it, improved pontil, clear or amber,
9¾"* .... | 43.00 | 55.00
☐ 170 **L. MEEUS, ANTWERP**
Key in center, green, brown, 10¼" .... | 43.00 | 55.00
☐ 171 **V. MEIER, INDIANAPOLIS, IND.**
Dark amber, 8¾" .... | 28.00 | 37.00
☐ 172 **MELCHER GIN**
Label, dark olive, 10¾" .... | 13.00 | 18.00
☐ 173 **J.J. MELCHERSWZ COSMOPOLIET**
*On top, J.J. Melcherswz under, in center, a man holding a
bottle, on base Schiedam, case type, short neck, tapered
top, dot under bottom, dark olive, 10"* .... | 50.00 | 65.00
☐ 174 *MONK Label, amber, 10"* .... | 60.00 | 80.00

N

☐ 175 **NATHAN BROS,** *(c. 1863)* **PHILA.**
Amber, 9½" .... | 100.00 | 130.00
☐ 176 **A.C.A. NOLET, SCHIEDAM**
Greenish brown, 8⅞" .... | 31.00 | 39.00
☐ 177 **I.A.I. NOLET, SCHIEDAM**
Dark green, amber, 8¼" .... | 33.00 | 42.00
☐ 178 **NOLETS MISTLETOE BRAND**
Dark green, amber .... | 55.00 | 70.00

P

☐ 179 **PALMBOOM**
*With palm tree, in a seal, Ilyes & Co., Schiedam, improved
pontil, green, 11"* .... | 65.00 | 85.00
☐ 180 **P & C**
Tapered top, green, 11¾" .... | 17.00 | 24.00
☐ 181 **J.J. PETERS**
*On one side, Hamburg other side, sunken panel under bot-
tom, green, 8½" x 3¼" x 3¾"* .... | 40.00 | 55.00

☐ 182 **J.J.W. PETERS**
Tapered top, figure of dog on one side, green, 7¾" x 2½"
x 2½" 60.00   80.00

☐ 183 **J.J.W. PETERS, HAMBURG**
On bottom, dog figure, tapered lip, two-piece mold, oval,
amber, 7¾" 75.00   100.00

☐ 184 *Same as above, except dark amber, 8¼"* 75.00   100.00

☐ 185 **J.J.W. PETERS**
In vertical line, tapered lip, case type, dog figure, green,
10½" x 3¼" x 3" 75.00   100.00

☐ 186 **P.G. & OLD BRISTOL**
Seal, pontil, dark olive, 9" 100.00   135.00

☐ 187 **PHILANTROP**
only imported by Lrucipsoila Demerara Mein, crown over
head, amber, green, 10¾" 55.00   75.00

☐ 188 **G.W., PORTER, XX PORTER & ALE**
Hollow P on reverse side, tapered top with ring, light
green, 7¼" 70.00   90.00

☐ 189 **POSEN, WRONKERSTR. NO 6, HARTWIG KANTOROWIC**
Eagle under bottom, amber, 10" 35.00   50.00

☐ 190 **P.S.**
In seal, ale, double ring top, pontil, olive, 10" 31.00   42.00

R

☐ 191 **JAMES RAY, SAVANNAH, GA.**
In front, in back, XX Ale, 4" body, 2¾" neck, blob top,
aqua 45.00   60.00

☐ 192 **T.M. REEVE** *(c. 1732)*
In a seal on shoulder, square, refined pontil, olive, 10" ... 65.00   85.00

☐ 193 **RELYEA, CARTER & CO's**
On one side Royal, other side Schiedam Schnapps, olive,
9½" 45.00   60.00

☐ 194 *ROMAN BOTTLE, teardrop catcher, free-blown, aqua, 4"* . 45.00   65.00

☐ 195 *ROMAN BOTTLE, teardrop catcher, pontil, aqua, 4½"* ... 45.00   65.00

☐ 196 **ROSS'S IRISH GIN**
Label, three-part mold, quart, aqua 7.00   10.00

☐ 197 **ROYAL CHAMPI**
Dark olive, 8¾" 30.00   40.00

☐ 198 **RUCKER DRY GIN**
1 under bottom, aqua, 9" 12.00   17.00

☐ 199 **R.W.**
In a seal on shoulder, squat body, ale, long neck, olive,
6¼" 55.00   75.00

☐ 200 **JOHN RYAN, SAVANNAH, GA.**
Two dots under a, in front, XX Philadelphia Porter on back,
cobalt, improved pontil, 6½" 70.00   90.00

☐ 201 **JOHN RYAN**
In 1" letters around bottle, ½" letters under John Ryan,
XX Porter & Ale, Philada, blue, ground pontil, 7¾" 75.00   100.00

☐202 **JOHN RYAN** *(c. 1886)*
In 1" hollow letters around bottle, ½" under J.R., XX
Porter & Ale, Philada, blue, 4¾" 65.00 85.00

☐203 **JOHN RYAN** *(c. 1866)* **SAVANNAH, GA.**
In front, Philadelphia XXX Star on each side of Ale on
back, squat body, blue, 7¼" 65.00 85.00

☐204 **JOHN RYAN** *(c. 1866)* **SAVANNAH, GA**
In front, Philadelphia XXX Star on each side of Porter on
back, squat body, blue, 7¼" 60.00 80.00

☐205 **JOHN RYAN PORTER & ALE, PHILADA, XX** *(c. 1859)*
Graphite pontil, cobalt, 7" 65.00 85.00

☐206 SAMPLE, label, square, free-blown, black glass, 6" 22.00 32.00

S

☐207 **SARGENT** *(c. 1830)*
(Reverse 3 on front), dark amber, 8½" 90.00 120.00

☐208 **SEAHORSE HOLLANDS GIN**
Tapered top, three dots under bottom, green, 9⅝" 30.00 45.00

☐209 **ST. ANGELINE**
#1136 under bottom, dark amber, 11" 50.00 65.00

☐210 **ST. DOMINIC**
Indentation in back for label, dark olive, 9¼" 30.00 45.00

T

☐211 **T.C.C.R.**
In a seal at the base, three-piece mold, dark green, 11" ... 32.00 48.00

☐212 **A. THELLER**
Label, Theller Arnold under bottom, dark olive, 8¾" 13.00 18.00

V

☐213 **VANDENBURGH & CO**
Bell in a seal on shoulder of bottle, case gin, avocado or
olive, crude top, 11" 80.00 100.00

☐214 Same except 9" 80.00 100.00

☐215 **VANDENBURGH & CO.**
Bell with ribbon in center, flared top, dark amber, 8⅞" 45.00 60.00

☐216 **VANDENBURGH & CO.**
Bell with ribbon in center, improved pontil, green or
amber, 9" 80.00 100.00

☐217 **J. VANDERVALK & CO., ROTTERDAM**
Green, 9½" 37.00 48.00

☐218 **VANDERVEER'S MEDICATED GIN OR REAL SCHIEDAM
SCHNAPPS**
Flared top, amber, 8½" 17.00 24.00

☐219 **VAN DUNCK'S GENEVER, TRADE MARK**
Ware & Schmitz in back, amber, 9" 135.00 175.00

☐220 **S. VAN DYKE, AMSTERDAM**
Cross in center, dark green, 10¼" 25.00 35.00

☐221 **H. VAN EMDEN POSTHOORN GIN**
M in a ring under bottom, clear or amethyst, 10⅝" 19.00 26.00

☐222 **J.H. VANGENT, SCHIEDAM**
Tapered top, three dots under bottom, brown, 9⅜" 22.00 29.00

☐223 **A. VANPRAAG & CO'S. SURINAM GIN**
Dark green, 9¾" 30.00 40.00

☐224 *Same except dark amber* 30.00 40.00

☐225 **V.G.& C.**
Flared top, pontil, green or amber, 10" 32.00 43.00

☐226 **VH & C**
Under bottom, dark olive, 9½" 23.00 31.00

☐227 **VHOYTEMAEC**
*Vertical, case bottle, 2¼" x 2¼", short neck, tapered top,
dark olive, 9"* 36.00 48.00

☐228 **V.H.P.**
*Aquas De Mondariz around shoulder, three-part mold,
olive, 6½"* 22.00 30.00

☐229 **VIII**
Pontil, dark olive, 9" 65.00 85.00

☐230 **DANIEL VISSER & ZONEN, SCHIEDAM**
Tapered top, amber, 9" 27.00 36.00

W

☐231 **WARNERS IMPORTED**
B Gin in back, sky blue, 9" 26.00 35.00

☐232 **WATSON BILTONPARK**
Olive, 9" 110.00 140.00

☐233 **WEISS BIER**
On front, KARL HUTTER, N.Y. on bottom, blob top, 7¼" . 10.00 15.00

☐234 **R. WHITE & SONS LD, LONDON**
*Around a W on bottle top, on bottom J in a shield, whittle
mark, dark olive, 10¼"* 23.00 31.00

☐235 **WOODMAN'S**
Pontil, three-part mold, black glass, 8" 130.00 160.00

BEER

Beer bottles were among the least popular of the bottle for many years. The similarity of design of beer bottles detracted from their collector appeal, as well as the fact that old beer bottles were considered to be so common that they could never achieve any real value. This, of course, has now changed. As you will note in our listings, a number of specimens command double-digit prices, and beer bottle devotees claim that these sums will appear ridiculously low in the not-too-distant future. Their commonness may be misjudged. Certainly enormous quantities were manufactured, but the percentage that were saved cannot be too great. Oddly enough, beer bottle collecting was mainly stimulated (in the early 1970's) by interest in beer *can* collecting — a rare instance of a newer version of a product exciting interest before its predecessor.

Beer is of ancient origins. It was made by nearly every civilization of the ancient world, including the Egyptians and Romans. At that time its consumption was restricted exclusively to the upper classes. Poor people drank a beverage called *mulsum* — made from the leavings of grapes and other fruits, after the juice had been extracted for wine.

Beer was brewed in the medieval monasteries, and was (supposedly) taken on the Mayflower with the pilgrims in 1620. George Washington and Thomas Jefferson both did their own home brewing. So did many other prominent early Americans, and made no effort to hide the fact. Since beer contained so much less alcohol than hard liquor, anyone who preferred it was considered a model citizen. Beer was not even among the targets of early temperance agitators.

You will search in vain for American beer bottles dating before the mid 19th century. Despite the large amounts of beer consumed in this country up to 1850, beer bottles did not exist. All the beer at that time was either made in the home or drank at taverns, where it was dispensed from wood barrels. Old-timers who spanned the era from barrel beer to the bottled variety swore that the latter did not compare in flavor to the former, apparently, the beer acquired special mellowing from the wood.

Taverns, naturally, tried to discourage the sale of beer in bottles, as this hurt their trade. But, try as they might, they were unable to stand in the way of progress. By 1870, beer was obtainable in bottles in most parts of the country. To meet this very unwelcome competition, tavernkeepers offered special inducements to their patrons, such as free lunch with the purchase of beer. They also tried to get into the business of selling take-out beer, but the laws of most states prohibited this.

The first bottle used for beer in the U.S. were made of pottery. Glass became dominant following the Civil War. The average beer bottle of 1870 was made of glass, contained a quart of beer and was cork stoppered. Breweries did not emboss their names and emblems on bottles until early 1870.

Commercial sale of bottled beer naturally led to advertising wars between manufacturers, as with other products. Makers concentrated very much on extolling the medicinal virtues and purity of their beers. David Nicholson of St. Louis called his beer "liquid bread." The only common ingredient was yeast. Hoff's Malt Extract (beer was not always called beer, for fear the word might offend the genteel) was advertised as "a remedy recommended by European Physicians for complaints of the chest, dyspepsia, obstinate cough, hoarseness, and especially consumption."

C. Conrad and Company, a wholesaler for Adolphus Busch in St. Louis, sold the original Budweiser from 1877 to 1890. The Budweiser name was a trademark of C. Conrad but in 1891 the company sold it to the Anheuser-Busch Brewing Association. By that time Adolphus Busch, founder of the company, had already established two companies to make beer bottles. In addition to furnishing bottles for Budweiser, they supplied other breweries from about 1880 to 1910.

Corks were replaced as stoppers on beer bottles with the invention by William Painter in 1891 of the "crown cork closure," containing a thin slice of cork within a tight-fitting metal cap. This continues to be used today.

Until the 1930's beer was customarily retailed in green glass bottles. There were some exceptions, such as the aforementioned David Nicholson, who used cobalt blue glass. When production of beer was resumed following Prohibition, green glass was abandoned in favor of brown. It was believed that brown glass would repel sun rays better and thereby prolong freshness.

BEER BOTTLES

A

NO.	DESCRIPTION	PRICE RANGE	
☐ 1	**ABC Co.**		
	Aqua, 9½"	3.00	5.00
☐ 2	**A.B.G.M. CO.**		
	E27 on bottom in circle, aqua, 11½"	5.00	8.00
☐ 3	**A.B.G.M.CO.**		
	C13 under bottom, aqua, 9½"	3.00	5.00
☐ 4	**A.B.G.M. CO.**		
	S4 under bottom, aqua, 10"	4.00	6.00
☐ 5	**A.B.G.M. CO.**		
	In a circle under bottom, in center E27, aqua, 11¼"	5.00	7.00
☐ 6	**A.B.G.M. CO.**		
	Under bottom, aqua, 9¾"	4.00	7.00
☐ 7	**ABERDEEN BREWING CO., ABERDEEN, WASH.**		
	Blob top, amber, clear, 9¼"	7.00	11.00
☐ 8	**AB6G**		
	4 under bottom, aqua, 9½"	3.00	5.00
☐ 9	**A.661**		
	2 under bottom, aqua, 9½"	3.00	5.00
☐ 10	**ACME BREWING COMPANY**		
	Aqua, 9½"	9.00	13.00
☐ 11	**ALABAMA BREWING CO., BIRMINGHAM, ALA.**		
	Aqua, 9½"	7.00	11.00

☐	12	**AMERICAN BREWING & C. I. CO., BAKER CITY, ORE.**		
		Crown top, amber, 11¼ "	7.00	11.00
☐	13	**ANHEUSER BUSCH INC.**		
		Amber, machine made, 9½ "	1.50	2.25
☐	14	**ARNAS**		
		Under bottom, amber, round, 8"	3.00	4.00
☐	15	**AROMA**		
		F under bottom, amber	4.00	7.00
☐	16	**AUGUSTA BREWING CO., AUGUSTA, GA.**		
		Around outside of circle, in center of circle, a large A with bottle shape embossed over A, crown top, aqua, 9¼ "	7.00	11.00
☐	17	Same except Hutchinson Bottle, 7"	17.00	23.00

B

☐	18	**THE BAKER CO., DAYTON, OHIO**		
		On front in oval slug plate, blob top, quart, amber, 11¼ "	7.00	11.00
☐	19	**BEADLESTON & WOERZ**		
		Excelsior Empire Brewery in a cirle, in center of it two ladies, eagle, monogram, New York. This Bottle Not To Be Sold, round, aqua, 9"	9.00	12.00
☐	20	**BECHER & CO. BOTTLE BEER, LANCASTER, O.**		
		Blob top, aqua, 10½ "	7.00	11.00
☐	21	**THE GEORGE BECHTEL BREWING CO.**		
		This Bottle Not To Be Sold on back, aqua, 9"	7.00	11.00
☐	22	BEER, amber, A.B.G.M. Co. in center, K 17 all under bottom of bottle, opalescent, 9½ "	4.00	7.00
☐	23	BEER, brown, 11½ "	3.00	4.00
☐	24	BEER, green, 11¼ "	3.00	4.00
☐	25	BEER, label, plain, amber, 8½ "	3.00	5.00
☐	26	BEER, label, plain, light amber, 8¾ "	3.00	5.00
☐	27	BEER, label, M.G.Co. under bottom, amber, 9¼ "	3.00	5.00
☐	28	BEER, label, star under bottom, amber, 7¾ "	7.00	11.00
☐	29	BEER, label, dark green, 9"	7.00	11.00
☐	30	BEER, label, cobalt, 9¼ "	22.00	31.00
☐	31	BEER, label, on bottom, I inside ring, clear or amethyst, 9½ "	3.00	5.00
☐	32	BEER, label, Root 8 on bottom, amber, 9½ "	3.00	5.00
☐	33	BEER, label, crown top, amber, 11½ "	3.00	5.00
☐	34	BEER, label, lady's leg neck, amber, 12"	6.00	9.00
☐	35	BEER, label, blob top, 9½ "	7.00	11.00
☐	36	BEER, label, pontil, aqua, 10½ "	17.00	26.00
☐	37	BEER, milk glass, wine type, crown top, ABM, 10¼ "	11.00	16.00
☐	38	BEER, plain, amber, 8¾ "	3.00	5.00
☐	39	BEER, plain, amber, 11½ "	3.00	5.00
☐	40	BEER, plain, blue, light green, 11¼ "	3.00	5.00
☐	41	BEER, plain, blue, 11¾ "	6.00	9.00
☐	42	**BERGHOFF**		
		On shoulder, FT. WAYNE, IND. at base, crown top, ABM, aqua	3.00	4.00
☐	43	**BERGHOFF, FORT WAYNE, IND.**		
		Blob top, amber 9"	9.00	12.00

☐ 44 **B. 42**
On bottom, dark green, turn mold, 9½" 5.00 8.00

☐ 45 **BIERBAUER BREWING CO., CANA—JOHARIE, NY**
On front in slug plate, blob top, aqua, 9⅜" 6.00 9.00

☐ 46 **BLATZ, MILWAUKEE**
On shoulder, olive, 9¼" 3.00 5.00

☐ 47 **BLATZ, OLD HEIDELBERG**
Stubby bottle, amber 9" 9.00 12.00

☐ 48 **BLATZ, PILSNER**
Amber, 10½" 4.00 6.00

☐ 49 **BLATZ, VAL BREWING CO., MILWAUKEE,**
On shoulder in a star VB, under bottom V.B. & Co., Milw.,
blob top, amber, 12" 7.00 11.00

☐ 50 **BOHEMIAN LAGER BEER, BODIE BOTTLING WORK,**
BODIE, CAL., Crown top, aqua 9.00 12.00

☐ 51 **BORN & CO., COLUMBUS, OHIO**
In a diamond shape, blob top, quart, amber 6.00 9.00

☐ 52 **BOSCH LAKE, LINDEN, MICH.**
On front, T.B.N.T.B.S. on bottom, blob top, amber, 12" ... 6.00 9.00

☐ 53 **BOSCH LAKE, LINDEN, MICH., T.B.N.T.B.S.**
On bottom, blob top, amber, 12" 7.00 11.00

☐ 54 **BOSCH LAKE, LINDEN, MICH.**
Blob top, quart, amber 4.00 6.00

☐ 55 **R. BOVEE**
Large block outline of a B, Troy, N.Y., reverse T.B.N.T.B.S.,
N.B.B. & Co., aqua, 12" 7.00 10.00

☐ 56 **BUFFALO BREWING CO., SACRAMENTO, CAL.**
In form of circle, horseshoe with buffalo jumping through,
blob top, quart, amber, 12" 10.00 15.00

☐ 57 **BUFFALO BREWING CO., S.F. AGENCY, BB Co.**
Monogram, crown top, amber, 9⅛" 10.00 15.00

☐ 58 **E & J BURKE**
E & B on bottom (cat), ABM, amber, 8" 3.00 5.00

☐ 59 **C.W. BURR, RICHMOND, VA.**
In a circle, reverse T.B.N.T.B.S., blob top, aqua, 9¼" 7.00 11.00

C

☐ 60 **CAIRO BREWING CO.**
On shoulder, amber, round, wire-porcelain stopper, clear,
9" 4.00 6.00

☐ 61 Same as above except aqua 5.00 8.00

☐ 62 **CAMDEN CITY BREWERY**
Amber, various numbers on bottom, 9" 5.00 9.00

☐ 63 **CANTON, OHIO**
Star under bottom, aqua, 9¾" 10.00 15.00

☐ 64 **CAS-CAR-RIA BOTTLE**
With 45 in a circle, amber, 9¼" 10.00 15.00

☐ 65 **CB CO.**
Monogram in circle, under it, Chattanooga, Tenn., light
amber, 11½" 9.00 13.00

☐ 66	**CB CO.**		
	Monogram near shoulder, under it, Chattanooga, Tenn., amber, 11¼ "	4.00	7.00
☐ 67	**THE CENTRAL BRAND EXTRA LAGER BEER**		
	Label, aqua, 9¼ "	3.00	5.00
☐ 68	**CHAS JOLY**		
	Phila on back, amber, 9¼ "	7.00	10.00
☐ 69	**CHATTAHOOCHEE BREWING CO.**		
	This Bottle Not To Be Sold, Phoenix City, Ala. on back, aqua, 9½ "	7.00	10.00
☐ 70	**CHATTAHOOCHEE BREWING CO., COLUMBUS, GA.**		
	Aqua, 9½ "	7.00	10.00
☐ 71	**CHATTAHOOCHEE BREWING CO., BROWNSVILLE, ALA.**		
	Aqua, 9½ "	7.00	10.00
☐ 72	**CHATTANOOGA BREWING CO.**		
	Aqua, 9½ ", C on bottom	5.00	8.00
☐ 73	**CLAUSSEN BREWING ASS'N., SEATTLE, WASH.**		
	Crown top, 9½ ", clear amber	9.00	12.00
☐ 74	**CLAUSSEN SWEENEY BREWING CO.**		
	Blob top, 10½ ", aqua	6.00	9.00
☐ 75	**THE CLEVELAND & SANDUSKY BREWING CO.**		
	Under bottom M, in center of bottle C.S.B.C. monogram, blob top, aqua, 9"	9.00	12.00
☐ 76	**COBALT BLUE BEER**		
	Label, graduated and flared band collar, 9¾ "	17.00	23.00
☐ 77	**THE CONNECTICUT BREWERIES CO.**		
	The Connecticut, Bridgeport, Conn. in a circle, in center Breweries Co., blue green, 9½ "	3.00	4.00
☐ 78	Same except Registered on shoulder	8.00	11.00
☐ 79	**C. CONRAD & CO.**		
	Original" Budweise," U.S. Patent no. 6376, under bottom CCCO, short tapered top with ring, aqua, 9¼ "	11.00	15.00
☐ 80	**CONSUMERS ICE CO.**		
	Hygeia Water, Memphis, Tenn., around lower bottom, round, tapers, to small neck, 10" tall, base 4¼ ", porcelain-spring stopper	6.00	9.00
☐ 81	**THE COOK & BERNHEIMER CO.**		
	On one side, other side Refilling Of This Bottle Prohibited, on the bottom, C&B.Co. Bottling, 2¼ " x 4", amber, 6¾ "	9.00	12.00
☐ 82	**THE COOK & BERNHEIMER COMPANY**		
	Refilling Of This Bottle Prohibited other side, amber	10.00	15.00
☐ 83	**COOK BOCK BEER**		
	Label, amber, 9¼ "	3.00	5.00
☐ 84	**COOKS 500 ALE**		
	Label, amber, 9½ "	5.00	8.00
☐ 85	**CROWN**		
	On shoulder, Label, applied lip, twisted neck, deep grooves, three-piece mold, iron pontil, dark olive, 8½ "	17.00	23.00
☐ 86	**CRYSTAL BREWAGE, BALTIMORE, MD. U.S.A.**		
	Amber, 10½ "	8.00	11.00
☐ 87	**C 6 CO.**		
	I on bottom, aqua, 9¼ "	3.00	5.00

D

☐	88	**DALLAS BREWERY**		
		Machine made, amber, 7½"	3.00	5.00
☐	89	**DALLAS BREWERY**		
		Clear or amethyst, 9"	6.00	9.00
☐	90	**DAYTON BREWERIES**		
		Amber, 9½"	7.00	10.00
☐	91	**DIAMOND JIMS BEER**		
		Label, aqua, 9¼"	5.00	8.00
☐	92	**DIXIE BREWERY, PHENIX [sic] CITY, ALA,**		
		Aqua, 9½"	8.00	11.00
☐	93	**DU BOIS**		
		Blob top, 8", amber	6.00	9.00
☐	94	**DUBUQUE BRG. & MALTING CO.**		
		Dubuque, 1A under bottom, amber, 8¾"	8.00	11.00
☐	95	**DUKEHART & CO.**		
		Maryland Brewery, Baltimore on front, three lines, squat body, long neck, amber, round, 8"	13.00	18.00

E

☐	96	**EAGLE SPRING DISTILLERY CO.**		
		On front, rectangular, amethyst, 7"	4.00	6.00
☐	97	**E.B. CO., ESCANABA, MICH.**		
		Amber, 8½"	8.00	9.00
☐	98	**E.B. & CO. LD 11614**		
		On bottom, aqua, 12"	5.00	8.00
☐	99	**THE EBLING BREWING CO., NEW YORK, USA** *on front*		
		Crown top, aqua, 9¼"	6.00	9.00
☐	100	*Same as above except blob top*	9.00	13.00
☐	101	**THE JOHN EICHLER BREWING CO., NEW YORK, REGISTERED,**		
		(written fancy) on front, blob top, aqua, 9"	7.00	10.00
☐	102	**EL DORADO BREWING CO.**		
		E.B.D. Co. monogram, STOCKTON, CAL., crown top, four-piece mold, quart, amber, 12"	17.00	23.00
☐	103	**EL PASO BREWERY**		
		Amber, 8"	7.00	10.00
☐	104	*Same as above except aqua*	7.00	11.00
☐	105	**ENGEL & WOLF'S NO. 26 & 28, DILLWYN ST., PHILA.**		
		Applied lip, graphite pontil, blue green, 7¼"	23.00	32.00
☐	106	**ENTERPRISE BREWING CO., S.F., CAL.**		
		Vertical on front, four-piece mold, quart, blob top, light amber, 11¾"	12.00	17.00
☐	107	**C.H. EVANS & SONS ALE**		
		On shoulder, crown top, amber, 9"	4.00	6.00
☐	108	**EXCELSIOR**		
		M under bottom, 9¼", aqua	10.00	15.00
☐	109	**EXCELSIOR LAGER BIER FROM VALENTINE BLATZ BOTTLING DEPT., CHICAGO**		
		In a circle, blob top, T.B.I.N.S. on reverse side, aqua, 9" ..	10.00	15.00

F

☐110 **FALSTAFF LEMP, ST. LOUIS**
Inside of shield, crown top, aqua, 9" 5.00 8.00

☐111 **FEE BROS., ROCHESTER, N.Y., BEL ISLE**
8 fl. oz., 6" 6.00 9.00

☐112 **JOHN E. FELDMAN, RICHFIELD SPRINGS, N.Y.**
In oval slug plate, blob top, 9¼", clear 7.00 10.00

☐113 **F.H.G.W.**
4 under bottom, amber, 10" 3.00 4.00

☐114 **F.H.G.W.S.**
Tapered top with ring, blob neck, 12" 7.00 10.00

☐115 **FINLEY BREWING CO., TOLEDO, O.**
Under bottom, trade mark, an F in a diamond on shoulder,
blob top, quart, aqua 7.00 10.00

☐116 **FINLEY BREWING CO., TOLEDO, O.**
Trade Mark on top of diamond shape in center of which is
an F, all on bottom, aqua, 10¾", ... 7.00 10.00

☐117 **THE FLORIDA BREWING CO., TAMPA, FLA.**
In sunken panel, aqua, under bottom F.B.Co., 6¾" 5.00 8.00

☐118 **THE FOSS-SCHNEIDER BREWING CO.**
Aqua, 7½" 6.00 9.00

☐119 **THE FOSS-SCHNEIDER CO.**
In a horseshoe shape, under it BREWING CO., CINCIN-
NATI, O., crown top, aqua, 11" 7.00 10.00

G

☐120 **J. GAHM & SON TRADE MARK**
(Mug with J.G. monogram) BOSTON, MASS. on front; blob
top, amethyst, 9" 7.00 10.00

☐121 *Same as above, except old crown top* 6.00 9.00

☐122 *Same as above, except amber, ABM* 5.00 8.00

☐123 **GALLITZIN BOTTLING CO.**
326 under bottom, clear, 10" 6.00 9.00

☐124 **GALLITZIN BOTTLING CO.**
Aqua, 9½" 4.00 6.00

☐125 **GALVESTON BREWING CO.**
Guaranteed Pure, Galveston, Tex., aqua, round, 7¾" 5.00 8.00

☐126 **GALVESTON BREWING, GALVESTON, TEX.**
Reverse T.B.N.T.B.S., aqua, 9½" 7.00 10.00

☐127 **G-B-S** *(with arrow)*
Baltimore, Md., Trade Mark on the shoulder, clear, round,
porcelain wire top, 9¼" 7.00 10.00

☐128 **GEO. CH. GEMUNDEN, SAVANNAH, GEO.**
In a circle in center, Lager Beer on back, This Bottle Is
Loaned Only in three lines, blob top, 8" 16.00 20.00

☐129 **GEORGIA BREWING ASSOCIATION**
Aqua, 9¾" 7.00 10.00

☐130 **THE GERMANIA BREWING CO.**
Aqua, 7½" 8.00 11.00

☐ 131 **A. GETTLEMAN BREWING CO.**
Pure Malt & Hops, Milwaukee, round, hand holding hops,
amber, 9¼" 10.00 15.00

☐ 132 **GREAT SEAL STYRON, BEGGS & CO., NEWARK, OHIO**
Round, clear, 9" 6.00 9.00

☐ 133 **CHARLES S. GROVE CO.**
78 & 80 Merimac Street Boston, Sparkling Lager Beer,
with CSG Co. monogram all inside of diamond-shaped
panel on front, blob top, clear, 9" 9.00 12.00

☐ 134 **GUTSCH BREW CO.**
13 under bottom, red or amber, 8½" 11.00 15.00

H

☐ 135 **A. HAAS BREWING CO, HOUGHTON, MICH.**
In circle on front, blob top, large size, REGISTERED at
base, amber, 12" 5.00 8.00

☐ 136 **A. HAAS BREWING CO.**
Written fancy at slant, blob top, amber, 9½" 6.00 9.00

☐ 137 **HACK & SIMON**
Aqua, 9½" 5.00 8.00

☐ 138 **THE JOHN HAUCK BREWING CO.**
Cincinnati, O., on the bottom A.B. Co., round, clear or
amber, 11⅜", ... 9.00 12.00

☐ 139 **HENNINGER**
Machine made, amber, 11½" 5.00 8.00

☐ 140 **HEUSTIS' E.M.**
Main St., Charleston, Mass., This Bottle Not To Be Sold,
Registered, aqua, round, 9" 5.00 8.00

☐ 141 **H.G. CO.** *on base*
Tapered top, blob top, amber, 9½" 7.00 10.00

☐ 142 **HOME BREWING CO., RICHMOND, VA.**
On shoulder, number under bottom, aqua, 9½" 8.00 11.00

☐ 143 **HOME BREWING CO., INDIANAPOLIS**
Blob top, clear 7.00 10.00

☐ 144 **HOSTER CO, O**
665 and mark under bottom, amber, 11¾" 7.00 10.00

☐ 145 **HOSTER'S** *in script,* **COLUMBUS, O., WEINER BEER**
Blob top, quart, amber 7.00 10.00

☐ 146 *Same as above, except dark amber, 7½"* 7.00 10.00

☐ 147 **HOUSTON ICE & BREWING CO.**
Crown top, ABM, aqua, 7¾" 7.00 10.00

☐ 148 **HUDSON, N.Y., EVANS ALE**
On shoulder, crown top, ABM, amber, 10" 3.00 4.00

☐ 149 **A. HUPFEL'S SON'S**
161-St. & 3rd Ave. New York, blob top, amber, 9⅜" 5.00 7.00

☐ 150 *Same as above except crown top, 9"* 4.00 6.00

I

☐ 151 **INDEPENDENT BR'G ASS'N**
On bottom in circle form with big E and building on top
and small B at bottom of E, amber, 11¼" 9.00 12.00

☐ 152	**INDEPENDENT BREWING CO. OF PITTSBURGH**		
	On front, crown top, light amber, 9"	4.00	6.00
☐ 153	*Same as above, except PITTSBURGH misspelled PITTS-*		
	BRUGH	13.00	18.00
☐ 154	**IND. BR'G. ASSN., MARION**		
	in a circle	6.00	9.00
☐ 155	**INDIANAPOLIS BREWING CO.**		
	R.C. Co. under bottom, amber, 7¼"	6.00	9.00
☐ 156	**INDIANAPOLIS BREWING CO., INDIANAPOLIS, IND.**		
	Angel holding a glass of beer, sitting on a wheel on world,		
	USA, all on front, aqua, 9½"	13.00	18.00
☐ 157	**IROQUOIS BRG. CO., BUFFALO**		
	Inside of circle, INDIAN HEAD in center, crown top, ABM,		
	amber	7.00	10.00

J

☐ 158	**JACKSON & CO.**		
	Hop leaves with B in center, YONKERS, N.Y. on front, 1904		
	on bottom, blob top, clear, 9½"	7.00	10.00
☐ 159	**JACOB JACKSON, 803 & 805 DICKINSON ST., PHILADA.**		
	Blob top, reverse T.B.N.T.B.S., aqua, 9½"	7.00	10.00

K

☐ 160	**THE KANSAS CITY BREWERIES CO.**		
	On front, Crown top, amber, 9"	7.00	10.00
☐ 161	**KAUFMAN BEV. CO., CINCINNATI, O. USA.**		
	Clear, 7"	7.00	10.00
☐ 162	**A.W. KEMISON CO.**		
	In horseshoe shape, blob top, blob neck, amber, 7¾"	7.00	10.00
☐ 163	**KESSLER MALT EXTRACT**		
	Squat body, crown top, amber	7.00	10.00
☐ 164	**KOPPITZ-MELCHERS BREWING CO.**		
	Trademark star in center, Reg. Detroit Mich. in a circle		
	slug plate, blob top, aqua, 11¼"	9.00	12.00
☐ 165	**M. KRESS, REDWOOD CITY, T.B.N.T.B.S.**	9.00	12.00
☐ 166	**THE KRESS WEISS BEER CO.**		
	Amber, 7¼"	6.00	9.00
☐ 167	**C.A. KRUEGER**		
	D.O.C. 36 under bottom, amber, 9¾"	8.00	11.00
☐ 168	**K.S.**		
	Monogram, KUEBELER STRONG, SANDUSKY, OHIO,		
	blob top, aqua, 7½"	6.00	9.00
☐ 169	*Same as above, except 11"*	8.00	11.00
☐ 170	**K.S.** *monogram on front*		
	Crown top, ABM, aqua, 9"	3.00	4.00
☐ 171	**THE JOHN KUHLMAN BREWING CO., ELLENVILLE, N.Y.**		
	Aqua, 7"	6.00	9.00
☐ 172	**JOHN KUHLMAN BREWING CO., ELLENVILLE, N.Y.**		
	On front in oval slug plate, crown top, aqua, 9¼"	5.00	8.00

L

☐ 173 **LAKE ERIE BOTTLING WORKS, TOLEDx, OHIO**
In a cirle, aqua, 10½" 8.00 11.00

☐ 174 *LARGE AQUA BOTTLE, round blob-top, THIS BOTTLE LOANED NOT SOLD, SIX PINTS, near base, place for large label, 13¼"* 7.00 10.00

☐ 175 **LEECHEN BEER, GERMANY**
Label, amber, 9¼" 5.00 8.00

☐ 176 **LEISY**
Peoria, Ill on back, amber, 9½" 6.00 9.00

☐ 177 **LEMP**
AB Co. under bottom, aqua, 9½" 3.00 4.00

☐ 178 **LEXINGTON BREWING CO., LEXINGTON, KY.**
Blob top, S.B. & CO. under bottom, amber, 12" 9.00 12.00

☐ 179 **LIMP, ST. LOUIS**
In a shield, blob top, amber, 8¾" 7.00 10.00

☐ 180 **D. LUTZ & SON BREWING CO., ALLEGHENY, PA.**
On front in oval slug plate, blob top, 9¾", aqua, 9¾" 9.00 12.00

M

☐ 181 **MALZBIER BEER GERMAN**
Amber, 8½" 5.00 8.00

☐ 182 **THE MARYLAND BREWING COMPANY**
Amber, 9" 10.00 15.00

☐ 183 **MASSACHUSETTS BREWERIES CO., BOSTON**
Crown top, amber, 9½" 3.00 5.00

☐ 184 **M. MAYER**
This Bottle Not To Be Sold in back, 4 under bottom, aqua, 9" 7.00 10.00

☐ 185 **McAVOY BREWING CO., LAGER BEER, CHICAGO**
Blob top, aqua, 9½" 7.00 10.00

☐ 186 **D.W. McCARTHY**
D.W. McC. monogram, STOCKTON, CAL. on front, blob top, four-piece mold, quart, amber, 12" 10.00 15.00

☐ 187 *Same as above, except 9½"* 10.00 15.00

☐ 188 **McLYMAN & BRADY, TOLEDO, OHIO**
Blob top, aqua, 11½" 7.00 10.00

☐ 189 **GEORGE MEYER BEER**
Aqua, 7½" 7.00 10.00

☐ 190 **GEORGE MEYER, SAVANNAH, GA.**
Aqua, 9½" 17.00 23.00

☐ 191 **C. & J. MICHEL BREWING CO., LACROSSE, WIS.**
Reverse side B.N.T.B.S., blob top, amber, 7½" 10.00 15.00

☐ 192 **MILLER BECKER CO.**
On back Send Me Home When I Am Empty, on base This Bottle Not To Be Sold, machine made, aqua, 11½" 7.00 10.00

☐ 193 **MINERAL SPRING BEER**
Label, aqua, 9" 3.00 5.00

☐ 194 **MOBILE BREWERY, MOBILE, ALA.**
Aqua, 10" 9.00 12.00
☐ 195 **THE CHRISTIAN MOERLEIN BREWING CO., CINCINNATI, O.**
In a circle, in center of circle monogram M, aqua, 9½" ... 5.00 8.00
☐ 196 **THE CHRISTIAN MOERLEIN BREWING CO., CINTI., O.**
In four lines, amber, fifth, blob top, blob neck 9.00 12.00
☐ 197 **MOFFATS-ALE BREWERY-INC.**
On both sides, large M on bottom, ABM, crown top, grass
green, 9⅜" 4.00 6.00
☐ 198 **MUNCHNER BAVARIAN TYPE BEER**
Aqua, 9¼" 7.00 10.00

N

☐ 199 **NATIONAL LAGER BEER, H. ROLTRBACHER AGT.,**
STOCKTON, CAL., H.R.
Monogram all on front, four-piece mold, blob top, amber,
11½" 9.00 12.00
☐ 200 *Same as above, except pint size* 10.00 15.00
☐ 201 *Same as above, except 8"* 10.00 15.00
☐ 202 **NEBRASKA BREWING CO., OMAHA, NEB.**
In a circle, amber, 9" 8.00 11.00
☐ 203 *Same except clear* 5.00 8.00
☐ 204 *Same except red or amber* 13.00 18.00
☐ 205 **T.L. NEFF'S SONS**
Case bottle trade mark on back, aqua, 11" 10.00 15.00
☐ 206 **DYSON NELSON**
Trade Mark, round, aqua, inside screw, 6¾" 10.00 15.00

O

☐ 207 **OAKLAND BOTTLING CO., OAKLAND, CAL.**
Around shoulder, blob top, amber, 9" 10.00 15.00
☐ 208 **O.B. CO.**
Under bottom, label, amber, 9¾" 5.00 8.00
☐ 209 **OCONTO BREWING CO.**
Blob top, amber 7.00 10.00
☐ 210 **THE PROPERTY OF OHLSSON'S CAPE BREWERY**
Inside screw cap 13.00 18.00
☐ 211 **W. OLMSTED & CO.**
On one side, reverse NEW YORK, roof type shoulders, on
roof in front CONSTITUTION, pontil, 10½" 60.00 80.00

P

☐ 212 **PABST BREWING CO. OF MILWAUKEE**
Amber, 12" 7.00 10.00
☐ 213 **PABST**
Milwaukee, Trade Mark, crown top, amber, 9¼" 6.00 9.00

94

97 E.B.C. ESCANABA MICH.

98

103 EL PASO BREWERY

108 EXCELSIOR LAGER BEER

134 ...SCH BREW. CO ...HEBOYGAN WIS.

137 ...ACKE...AND... EAGLE BREWERY VINCENNES IND.

144 HOSTER COL. O.

155 ...POLIS BREWING CO ...IAPOLIS IND. U.S.A.

156 ...POLIS BREWING CO ...IAPOLIS IND. U.S.A.

177 LEMP STD. & SUMM...

192 ...LER-BECKER CO CLEVELAND, O. ...ARTS PER... ...8 OZ...

205 Schlitz BREWING CO ...TON, S...

208

224 ROBERT PORTNER BREWING CO TIVOLI ALEXANDRIA VA

☐214 **PABST, MILWAUKEE**
In circle in center, leaves and in circle big P, Trade Mark under it, on bottom Registered, This Bottle Not To Be Sold, amber, 9¼" 7.00   10.00

☐215 **THE PALMEDO BREWING CO, CHARLESTON, S.C.**
In a circle in center, large monogram P, aqua, 7¾" 7.00   10.00

☐216 *Same except no P, crown top, aqua, 9½"* 4.00   6.00

☐217 **C. PFEIFFER BREWING CO., C.P.B. CO., DETROIT, MICH.**
In circle on shoulder, blob top, amber, 9¼" 6.00   9.00

☐218 **PHOENIX BREWING CO.**
An eagle with trade mark under it, VICTORIA, B.C., tapered top, amber, 8¼" 13.00   18.00

☐219 **PIEL BROS**
This Bottle Not To Be Sold on back, clear, 9" 6.00   9.00

☐220 **PIEL BROS**
P.B. and arrow in shield, EAST NEW YORK BREWERY, all on front, crown top, amber, 9¼" 6.00   9.00

☐221 *Same as above, except dark aqua* 6.00   9.00

☐222 **PIEL BROS**
Above P.B. inside of circle, under the East New York Brewery, aqua, 9" 7.00   10.00

☐223 **PITTSBURGH BREWING CO.**
Crown top, amber, 12¼" 7.00   10.00

☐224 **ROBERT PORTNER BREWING CO.**
Amber, 7¼" 13.00   18.00

☐225 **PROSPECT BREWERY, CHAS WOLTER'S PHILA**
Reverse T.B.N.T.B.S., blob top, amber, 8" 13.00   10.00

☐226 *Same as above, except 7¼"* 10.00   15.00

☐227 **W.O. PUTNAM**
Clear, 9½" 6.00   9.00

R

☐228 **RAHR'S BEER**
Label, amber, 9¼" 4.00   6.00

☐229 **JOHN RAPP & SON, S.F., CAL.**
On front, blob top, quart, light amber, 11½" 10.00   15.00

☐230 *Same as above, except 9½"* 11.00   16.00

☐231 *Same as above, except 8¼"* 7.00   10.00

☐232 **R.C. & A.**
Reverse NEW YORK, tapered top, cobalt blue, 9" 19.00   27.00

☐233 **RENO BREWING CO., RENO, NEV.**
Tapered top, amber, 10¾" 7.00   11.00

☐234 **ROSE NECK BREWING CO., RICHMOND, VA.**
Embossed star, round, crown top, aqua, 9¾" 7.00   10.00

☐235 **ROSESSLE BREWERY, BOSTON**
T.B.T.B.R. on front, Premium Lager on back, crown top, aqua, 9" 5.00   8.00

☐236 **ROTH & CO.**
In center monogram, letters RCO, SAN FRANCISCO in a circle, tapered top, amber, 10¼" 11.00   16.00

☐ 237	**ROYAL RED**		
	Not To Be Refilled, No Deposit No Return, on base, ABM, red, 9½"	16.00	23.00
☐ 238	**RUBSAM & HORRMANN BREWG. CO.**		
	In horseshoe shape in center, Staten Island, N.Y., Registered, in four lines on back near bottom This Bottle Not To Be Sold, blob top, under bottom KH, 1906, aqua, 9"	7.00	10.00
☐ 239	**JACOB RUPPERT BREWER, NEW YORK**		
	On shoulder in circle, crown top, yellowish green or amber, 9¼"	5.00	8.00
☐ 240	**JOHN RYAN**		
	ALE XXX Star 1866, blob top, cobalt, 8¼"	50.00	65.00

S

☐ 241	**SAKURA BEER** *on base*		
	Foreign writing on back, dark amber, 11¼"	6.00	9.00
☐ 242	**SANTA CLARA COUNTY BOTTLING CO., SAN JOSE**		
	Four-piece mold, ½ pint, light amber, 7¾"	7.00	10.00
☐ 243	**F. & M. SCHAEFER MFR'G CO., NEW YORK**		
	Around base on front, crown top, aqua, 9"	3.00	5.00
☐ 244	**THE SCHAEFER-MEYER BRO. CO., TRADE MARK LOUISVILLE, KY.**		
	In a shield, amber, 11"	10.00	15.00
☐ 245	**SCHLITZ BREWING CO.**		
	124 on bottom, amber, 9½"	9.00	12.00
☐ 246	**C. SCNEER & CO.**		
	In horseshoe letters, under it SACRAMENTO, CAL., blob top, blob neck, amber, 7½"	7.00	10.00
☐ 247	**CHAS SEILER, MILWAUKEE, BEER**		
	In two lines on front, on back Empty Bottle to Be Returned, blob top, aqua, 8"	7.00	10.00
☐ 248	**G.B. SELMER, CALIFORNIA POP BEER**		
	Reverse Pat. Oct. 29, 1872, tapered top, amber, 10½"	23.00	32.00
☐ 249	**SMITH BROS. BREWERS, NEW BEDFORD, MASS.**		
	Inside of slug plate, TO BE WASHED AND RETURNED on front also, blob top, clear	6.00	9.00
☐ 250	**SOUTHERN BREWING CO.**		
	Machine made, green, 9½"	3.00	4.00
☐ 251	**L. SPEIDEL & CO., BOSTON, MASS.**		
	Hop Leaf and B on center front, Registered LS Co. monogram on back, blob top, clear, 9"	10.00	15.00
☐ 252	**SPRINGFIELD BREWERIES CO., BOSTON BRANCH, BOSTON, MASS., TRADE MARK**		
	S.B. Co. monogram, blob top, clear, 9"	6.00	9.00
☐ 253	**STETTNER & THOMAS, WEISS BEER BREWERS, ST. LOUIS, MO.**		
	Blob top, amber, 9½"	10.00	15.00
☐ 254	**ST. MARY'S BOTTLING WORKS, ST. MARY'S, OHIO**		
	In a circle, quart, blob top, aqua	9.00	13.00
☐ 255	**JOHN STROHM, JACKSON, CAL.**		
	J.S. monogram on front, four-piece mold, light amber, 7¾"	10.00	15.00
☐ 256	**PETER STUMPF**		
	This Bottle Not For Sale on back, amber, 8½"	10.00	15.00

T

☐ 257 **TEIKOKU BEER**
Japanese writing on back, graduated collar and ring, Amber, 11¾" **6.00** **9.00**

☐ 258 **TERRE HAUTE BREWING CO.**
2½" diameter, R.G. CO. on bottom, aqua, 9½" **6.00** **9.00**

☐ 259 **GEO. A. TICOULET SAC.** *on front*
Four-piece mold, amber, 7¾" **7.00** **10.00**

☐ 260 **TOLEDO BREWING & MALTING CO.**
Amber, 9½" **5.00** **8.00**

☐ 261 **JOHN TONS**
JT monogram, STOCKTON, CAL, on front, four-piece mold, blob top, quart, amber, 11½" **9.00** **13.00**

☐ 262 **S.A. TORINO**
Gray snake around bottle, RED EYE, RED TONG, clear, 12¼" **13.00** **18.00**

☐ 263 *Same as above, except aqua* **11.00** **15.00**

☐ 264 **TROMMER'S EVERGREEN BR'Y**
Aqua, 9¼" **8.00** **11.00**

U

☐ 265 **UNION BREWING CO., LTD., BEER, TARRS, PA.**
On bottom Union Made C & CO., brown, 8" **7.00** **10.00**

☐ 266 **UNITED STATES BREWING CO., CHICAGO, ILL.**
Aqua, 9" **7.00** **10.00**

V

☐ 267 **VA. BREWING CO.**
Aqua, 9¾" **6.00** **9.00**

☐ 268 **A.G. VAN NOSTRAND, CHARLESTOWN, MASS.**
Inside of ribbon, BUNKER HILL LAGER, BUNKER HILL BREWERIES, EST. 1821 REG., amber, 9¾" **17.00** **24.00**

☐ 269 **C.J. VATH & CO., SAN JOSE**
On front in slug plate, blob top, amber, 12" **11.00** **16.00**

☐ 270 **VICTORIA BREWING CO.**
On base Not To Be Sold, Victoria, B.C., amber, 9" **8.00** **12.00**

☐ 271 *Same except red amber* **9.00** **12.00**

W

☐ 272 **THE WACKER & BIRK BREWING CO., CHICAGO**
Reverse T.B.N.T.B.S., aqua, 9½" **7.00** **10.00**

☐ 273 **SIDNEY O. WAGNER**
On shoulder, crown top, 11¼", ... **3.00** **5.00**

☐ 274 **THE J. WALKER BREWING CO., CINCINNATI, OHIO**
In a circle, amber, 11¼" **5.00** **8.00**

☐ 275 **HENRY K. WAMPOLE & CO., PHILADA.**
Around should, graduated collar and ring, light amber, 8½" **8.00** **12.00**

☐276 **WASHINGTON BREWING CO.**
Trade Mark with picture of eagle, REG. WASH. D.C., aqua,
9¼" 13.00 18.00

☐277 **WEST END**
Written fancy, BRG. CO. UTICA, N.Y., crown top, ABM,
amber, 9½" 8.00 11.00

☐278 **W.F. & G.P MIL**
Under bottom, clear, 9¼" 5.00 8.00

☐279 **W.F. & S.**
On bottom, crown top, aqua, 9½" 3.00 4.00

☐280 **W.F. & S MIL**
Under bottom, aqua, 9" 3.00 5.00

☐281 *Same except #39 and amber* 3.00 5.00

☐282 **WIEDEMANN**
0179 under bottom, amber, 9½" 8.00 11.00

☐283 **WISCONSIN SELECT BEER**
Aqua, 9¼" 5.00 8.00

☐284 **THE P.H. WOLTERS BREWING CO.**
This Bottle Never Sold in back, aqua, 9½" 6.00 9.00

☐285 **WUNDER BOTTLING CO.**
W.B. Co. monogram, SAN FRANCISCO, CAL., on front,
amber, 7⅝" 7.00 10.00

☐286 *Same as above, except OAKLAND* 7.00 10.00

Y

☐287 **Y** *under bottom*
Label, amber, 9¾" 7.00 10.00

☐288 **YOERG BREWING CO., ST. PAUL, MINN.**
Aqua, 9½" 6.00 9.00

☐289 **GEO. YOUNG CALIFORNIA POP BEER**
Reverse Pat. 29th 1872, amber, 10½" 23.00 31.00

☐290 **THEO. YOUNG**
With large stars, hop leaves, buds, in a monogram, T.Y.
Union Ave., 165th & 166th St. N.Y., all on front, crown top,
amber, 9" 7.00 10.00

BITTERS

Bitters bottles have long ranked as favorites in the bottle hobby. In fact, they were being saved and admired ("collected" might not be the right word) before most other kinds of old bottles. Some people — certainly not the majority but some here and there — who bought bitters in the 19th century used the bottles for display in their homes after their contents had been consumed. This was not the case with most bottles of that time. Hence, bitters bottles have survived in somewhat greater numbers than most other old bottles, but demand for them is so great that prices are strong nevertheless.

Bitters was a liquor of varying alcoholic content, popular first in England and then in America. It was advertised primarily as a tonic and could be bought from supply houses and stores that did not sell other kinds of liquor — as well as from liquor dealers. The motive for such advertising was twofold: first, to promote sales among people who were not customarily liquor drinkers; second, and probably of greater importance, to provide an excuse for customers for having it in the home. One could freely consume bitters — to ward off a chill, because the weather was damp, or for numerous reasons — without stirring up gossip.

Indeed, some bitters did have very low alcoholic content — only 15%. But brands were available ranging up to 120 proof, higher than the hardest of most hard liquor.

The decorative shapes of some bitters were likewise intended to promote sales, thus providing yet another excuse for their purchase. The more creative ones featured likenesses of pigs, fish, cannons, drums, ears of corn and the like. Generally, the bitters collector will either specialize in these "figurals," or in the bottles a particular manufacturer, such as Hostetter.

Bitters originated in England during the reign of George II (1727-1760.) In an effort to curb drunkenness, stiff taxes were imposed on "spirituous liquors." To avoid this tax, aimed mainly at gin, ginmakers added herbs to their product and sold it as medicine. Bitters became popular in America because the colonists could import it from England — which they did in huge quantities — without having to pay the liquor tax. Many physicians reached the point of becoming convinced that bitters *did* possess medicinal value. This not only aided sales but made the beverage more socially acceptable. No less an authority than Dr. Benjamin Rush, the most noted physician of his time, put his stamp of approval on bitters in 1785. This line of thought prevailed as late as 1862, when the Revenue Act imposed a smaller tax on bitters than on liquor.

Jacob Hostetter of Lancaster County, Pennsylvania, was a physician who made his own bitters and used it for his patients. Upon his retirement in 1853, he gave his son, David, permission to manufacture it commercially. Thus began the most successful bitters firm in the nation. Hostetter's was known for its colorful and dramatic, if somewhat overblown, advertising. The company not only displayed its ad messages on billboards and in magazines, but published its own yearly almanac crammed with ads for the product. Ads cautioned that Hostetter's Bitters was not a panacea. It wouldn't cure *everything,* but the list of ailments supposedly overcome by its regular use was lengthy: "dyspepsia (indigestion), diarrhea, dysentery, general debility, chills and fever, liver complaint, bilious remittent fevers (fevers thought to be caused by bile impurities), and the pains and weaknesses that come with old age." "Weaknesses that come with old age" was a gentle way of saying impotence.

The following is a sample of the Hostetter ad prose:

"It lives, and continues to thrive and increase in popularity, with marvelous rapidity, simply because the world wants it, will have it, cannot do without it . . . Furnished with this preventative, the pioneer of California may fearlessly prosecute his search for gold and silver . . . He may sleep wrapped in his blanket or buffalo robe on the damp ground by night, and brave the hot beams of the sun by day without incurring the usual penalties . . . provided he reinforces his constitution, his appetite and his strength by moderate and regular use of the Hostetter's Bitters."

As fate would have it, David Hostetter died from an ailment that his product was supposed to cure — kidney failure — in 1888.

Over 1,000 types of bitters bottles are known, most of them produced from 1860 to 1905. In addition to the figurals already mentioned, shapes included round, square, rectangle, barrel-shaped, gin bottle shaped, twelve-sided, and flask-shaped, as well as others. Figurals are the scarest and in general the most desirable to collectors.

Bitters bottles were usually embossed with a design and the manufacturer's name. Many carried paper labels. The embossed variety are generally older, scarcer, and more valuable. By the 1880's, it had become a common practice to sell the bottles in cardboard boxes, which carried illustrations and lengthy maker-to-buyers messages. The boxes are collectible, too, but very few were preserved. Pictures in early Sears Roebuck catalogues give an idea of what they looked like.

The most common color for bitters bottles was amber in various shades, ranging from pale golden yellow to dark amber-brown. Next was aqua (light blue.) Green and clear glass bottles were sometimes used. The rarest colors are dark blue, amethyst, milk glass, and puce.

Since many collectors of bitters bottles specialize by manufacturer, certain specimens have become more valuable than they might be expected to on grounds of design or scarcity. Generally speaking, the American-made bitters bottles will command higher prices than those of foreign origin when sold in this country if design and color are similar.

NOTE: The great popularity of bitters bottles as a collectors' item has encouraged the making of reproductions. Some are of quite good quality and can fool an inexperienced buyer. Take care, and do not buy unless you can be certain of the specimen's authenticity.

BITTERS BOTTLES

A

NO.	DESCRIPTION	PRICE RANGE	
☐ 1	**ABBOTT'S BITTERS (C.W. ABBOTT & CO. BALTIMORE)**		
	Round bottle, amber, machine made	10.00	14.00
☐ 2	**ABBOTT'S BITTERS**		
	On base, C. W. Abbott & Co., Baltimore on shoulder, machine made, amber, 8"	6.00	8.00
☐ 3	**ABBOTT'S BITTERS**		
	6½", machine made	6.00	8.00
☐ 4	**DR. ABELL'S SPICE BITTERS**		
	Label, pontil, aqua, 7½"	50.00	70.00
☐ 5	**ACORN BITTERS**		
	Amber, tapered lip, 9"	65.00	85.00
☐ 6	**AFRICAN STOMACH BITTERS**		
	In three lines near shoulder, amber, 9½"	38.00	55.00
☐ 7	**AFRICAN STOMACH BITTERS**		
	In three lines near shoulder, amber, round, under Bitters small letters Spruance Stanley & Co., 9½"	55.00	75.00
☐ 8	**AIMAR'S SARRACENIA BITTERS**		
	On back Charleston S. C., aqua, 7½"	45.00	60.00
☐ 9	**AIMAR'S SARRACENIA FLY TRAP BITTERS**		
	Label, on back embossed A. S. B. Charleston S. C., aqua, 7¼"	115.00	135.00
☐ 10	**ALEX VON HUMBOLDT'S**		
	On back Stomach Bitters, tapered neck, ring top, amber, 9¾"	75.00	95.00
☐ 11	**ALPINE HERB BITTERS**		
	In two lines in front, in back in a shield TT&CO, amber 9¾"	55.00	75.00
☐ 12	**WILLIAM ALLEN'S CONGRESS BITTERS**		
	Rectangular bottle, deep green, clear, light amber, 10" ...	110.00	135.00
☐ 13	*Same except pontil, amethyst, 7¾"*	110.00	135.00
☐ 14	**DR. ALTHER'S BITTERS**		
	Lady's leg shape, clear, 5"	38.00	50.00
☐ 15	**AMAZON BITTERS**		
	Reverse side Peter McQuade N.Y., amber, 9¼"	90.00	110.00
☐ 16	**AMERICAN CELEBRATED STOMACH BITTERS**		
	Amber, 9¼"	38.00	50.00
☐ 17	**AMERICAN LIFE BITTERS**		
	Back same, P. Eiler Mfg. Tiffin, Ohio, log effect, cabin type bottle, tapered lip, light amber to amber	160.00	190.00
☐ 18	**AMERICAN LIFE BITTERS**		
	Same as above, except Omaha, Neb.	160.00	190.00
☐ 19	**AMERICAN STOMACH BITTERS**		
	Amber, 8½"	70.00	90.00
☐ 20	**DR. ANDREW MUNSO BITTERS**		
	Lady's leg shape, amber, 11¼"	85.00	110.00
☐ 21	**DAVID ANDREW'S VEG. JAUNDICE BITTERS**		
	Open pontil, aqua	85.00	110.00

☐ 22	**ANGOSTURA**		
	Bitters on back, Rheinstorom Bros, N.Y. & Cin. on bottom, amber	40.00	55.00
☐ 23	**ANGOSTURA BARK BITTERS**		
	Clear or aqua, 9½"	38.00	52.00
☐ 24	**ANGOSTURA BARK BITTERS**		
	Figural bottle, "EAGLE LIQUOR DISTILLERIES", amber, 7"	50.00	65.00
☐ 25	**ANGOSTURA BITTERS**		
	On base, green, 7¾"	30.00	38.00
☐ 26	**APPETINE BITTERS, GEO. BENZ & SONS, ST. PAUL, MINN. MFG.**		
	Label, amber, 7¼"	18.00	23.00
☐ 27	**ARABIAN BITTERS**		
	In back, Lawrence & Weicesslbaum, Savannah, Ga., square, tapered top, amber, 9½"	85.00	105.00
☐ 28	**ARGYLE BITTERS, E. B. WHEELOCK, NO.**		
	Tapered lip, amber, 9¾"	115.00	140.00
☐ 29	**AROMATIC ORANGE STOMACH BITTERS**		
	Square bottle, amber	45.00	62.00
☐ 30	**ARPS STOMACH BITTERS**		
	Ernest L. Arp & Kiel, label, round, aqua, 11¼"	30.00	38.00
☐ 31	**ASPARAGIN BITTERS CO.**		
	Clear to aqua, 11"	45.00	60.00
☐ 32	**ATHERTON'S DEW DROP BOTTLES**		
	On base 1866 Lowell Mass., ringed shoulder, short tapered top, amber, 10"	50.00	65.00
☐ 33	**ATWELL'S WILD CHERRY BITTERS**		
	Label, oval bottle, aqua, 8"	15.00	20.00
☐ 34	**ATWOOD'S GENUINE BITTERS**		
	Round bottle, aqua, 6½"	8.00	11.00
☐ 35	**ATWOODS QUININE TONIC BOTTLES**		
	Rectangular bottle, aqua, 8½"	37.00	49.00
☐ 36	**ATWOOD'S BITTERS—VEGETABLE JAUNDICE**		
	Round bottle, aqua, Moses F. Atwood	10.00	14.00
☐ 37	**ATWOOD GENUINE PHYS. JAUNDICE BITTERS, GEORGTOWN, MASS.**		
	12-sided, aqua, 6½"	18.00	23.00
☐ 38	**ATWOOD JAUNDICE BITTERS**		
	by Moses Atwood on panels, clear or aqua, 6"	9.00	12.00
☐ 39	Same as above, except pontil	22.00	30.00
☐ 40	**ATWOOD JAUNDICE BITTERS**		
	Formerly made by Moses Atwood, clear or aqua, 6"	7.00	10.00
☐ 41	**ATWOOD JAUNDICE BITTERS**		
	Machine made, clear or aqua, 6"	3.00	4.50
☐ 42	**ATWOOD'S / GENUINE / BITTERS**		
	Marked on base, N. WOOD SOLE PROPRIETOR on domed shoulder, aqua, round, 6"	22.00	27.00
☐ 43	**ATWOOD'S / JAUNDICE BITTERS / M.C. ARTER & SON / GEORGETOWN / MASS**		
	Aqua, 12-sided, ring top, 6"	18.00	23.00

☐ 44 **ATWOOD JAUNDICE BITTER**
*Formerly made by Moses Atwood, clear or aqua, screw
top, 6"* 1.75 2.50

☐ 45 **ATWOOD'S QUININE TONIC BITTERS**
Aqua, 8½" 50.00 65.00

☐ 46 **ATWOOD'S QUININE TONIC BITTERS, GILMAN BROS.
BOSTON**
Label, aqua, 9" 55.00 70.00

☐ 47 **ATWOOD'S VEG. DYSPEPTIC BITTERS**
Pontil, short tapered top, aqua, 6½" 55.00 70.00

☐ 48 **AUGAUER BITTERS**
Green, 8¼" 65.00 85.00

☐ 49 **AUNT CHARITY'S BITTERS**
*Label, Geo. A. Jameson Druggist, Bridgeport, Conn., clear
and amber, 8½"* 18.00 23.00

☐ 50 **DR. AURENT IXL STOMACH BITTERS, BARKERS,
MOORE & MEIN**
Mfg. Wholesale Merch. Phila., clear, 8½" 27.00 35.00

☐ 51 **AYALA MEXICAN BITTERS**
*On back M. Rothenberg & Co. San Francisco, Cal., long
collar with ring, amber, 9½"* 60.00 80.00

☐ 52 **DR. M. C. AYERS RESTORATIVE BITTERS**
Aqua, 8½" 65.00 85.00

B

☐ 53 **E. L. BAILEY'S KIDNEY AND LIVER BITTERS**
On back Best Blood Purifier, amber, 7¾" 60.00 80.00

☐ 54 **BAKER'S HIGH LIFE BITTERS**
*The Great Nerve Tonic embossed on back, tapered top,
machine made, pint* 20.00 25.00

☐ 55 **BAKERS ORANGE GROVE**
On back Bitters, roped corners, tapered top, amber, 9½" . 95.00 110.00

☐ 56 *Same as above, except yellow* 175.00 225.00

☐ 57 **BAKERS STOMACH BITTERS**
Label, lady's leg shape, amber, 11¼" 55.00 70.00

☐ 58 **E. BAKERS PREMIUM BITTERS**
Richmond, Va., aqua, 6¾" 50.00 65.00

☐ 59 **DR. BALLS VEG. STOM. BITTERS**
Pontil, aqua, 7" 75.00 95.00

☐ 60 **BALSDONS GOLDEN BITTERS**
1856 N.Y. other side, amber, 10½" 100.00 125.00

☐ 61 **BARBER'S INDIAN VEG. JAUNDICE BITTERS**
12-sided, aqua, 6¼" 70.00 90.00

☐ 62 **BARTLETT'S EXCELSIOR BITTERS**
*On bottom BARTLETT BROS. N. Y., 8-sided, aqua and
amber, 7¾"* 175.00 225.00

☐ 63 **BARTO'S GREAT GUN BITTERS**
*In circle in center Reading, Pa., cannon shop bottles,
amber, olive amber, 11" x 3¼"* 800.00 1100.00

☐ 64 **BAVARIAN BITTERS**
Hoffheimer Brothers other side, amber, 9½" 100.00 135.00

☐ 65	**BAXTERS MANDRAKE BITTERS**		
	Lord Bros. Prop. Burlington, Vt. on vertical panels, amethyst, 6½"	22.00	27.00
☐ 66	**BEECHAM BITTERS**		
	Woodward Drug Co. Portland, Org., label, amber, 8¼"	14.00	18.00
☐ 67	**BEGG'S DANDELION BITTERS**		
	Rectangular bottle, clear, 8"	80.00	100.00
☐ 68	**BEGG'S DANDELION BITTERS**		
	Square bottle, amber, 9¼"	65.00	85.00
☐ 69	**BEGG'S DANDELION BITTERS**		
	Chicago, Ill other side, amber, 9"	60.00	80.00
☐ 70	**BEGG'S DANDELION BITTERS** in 3 lines		
	Tapered top, base to neck a plain band, amber, 7¾"	21.00	26.00
☐ 71	**BELLE OF ANDERSON BITTERS**		
	Amber, 7"	55.00	75.00
☐ 72	**DR. BELLS BLOOD PURIFYING BITTERS**		
	Amber, 9¼"	50.00	70.00
☐ 73	**BELLS COCKTAIL BITTERS**		
	Lady's leg shape, amber, 10¾"	90.00	115.00
☐ 74	**BELMONTS TONIC HERB BITTERS**		
	Amber, 9½"	85.00	105.00
☐ 75	**BEN-HUB CELEBRATED STOMACH BITTERS**		
	New Orleans in 3 lines, same in back, tapered top, 9"	90.00	110.00
☐ 76	**BENDERS BITTERS**		
	Aqua, 10½"	60.00	80.00
☐ 77	**BENGAL BITTERS**		
	Amber, 8½"	70.00	90.00
☐ 78	**BENNETTS CELEBRATED STOMACH BITTERS**		
	Amber, 9¼"	60.00	80.00
☐ 79	**BENNETTS WILD CHERRY STOMACH BITTERS**		
	Amber, 9¼"	90.00	115.00
☐ 80	**BERKSHIRE•BITTERS, AMANN & CO., CINCINNATI, O.**		
	Ground top, dark amber, 10½"	800.00	1100.00
☐ 81	**BERLINER MAGEN BITTERS**		
	S. B. Rothenberg sole agents S. F., label, green, 9½"	90.00	115.00
☐ 82	**BERLINER MAGEN BITTERS**		
	Amber, 9½"	60.00	80.00
☐ 83	**DR. L. Y. BERTRAMS LONG LIFE AROMATIC STOMACH BITTERS**		
	Aqua, 9"	55.00	75.00
☐ 84	**BERRY'S VEGETABLE BITTERS**		
	Labeled only, square bottle, amber, iron pontil, 9½"	30.00	40.00
☐ 85	**THE BEST BITTERS OF AMERICA**		
	Cabin shape, amber, 9¾"	100.00	135.00
☐ 86	**BIG BILL BEST BITTERS**		
	Amber, 12"	90.00	115.00
☐ 87	**BILLING'S MANDRAKE TONIC BITTERS**		
	Labeled only, rectangular bottle, aqua, 8"	18.00	23.00
☐ 88	**BIRD BITTERS**		
	Philadelphia Proprietor, clear, 4¾"	60.00	80.00

☐ 89	**DR. BIRMINGHAM ANTI BILIOUS BLOOD PURIFYING BITTERS**		
	Round, green, 9¼"	50.00	70.00
☐ 90	**DR. BISHOPS WAHOO BITTERS**		
	Amber, 10¼"	100.00	130.00
☐ 91	**BISMARCK BITTERS**		
	½ pint, amber	30.00	40.00
☐ 92	**BOTANIC STOMACH BITTERS**		
	Same on reverse, paper label, amber, 9"	70.00	90.00
☐ 93	*Same as above, except back reads BACH MEESE & CO. S.F., amber, 9"*	60.00	80.00
☐ 94	**BOURBON WHISKEY BITTERS**		
	Barrel, bright puce, 9"	175.00	225.00
☐ 95	**BOURBON WHISKEY BITTERS**		
	Barrel, yellow olive, 9"	175.00	225.00
☐ 96	**BOWES CASCARA BITTERS**		
	Has No Equal, P. F. BOWES, Waterbury, Conn. U.S.A., clear, 9¼"	60.00	80.00
☐ 97	**DR. BOYCE'S TONIC BITTERS**		
	Francis Fenn Prop. Rutland, Vt. on panels, bottle has twelve panels, aqua blue, 7¼"	45.00	60.00
☐ 98	**DR. BOYCE'S TONIC BITTERS**		
	Label, sample size, twelve panels, aqua, 4½"	13.00	17.00
☐ 99	**BOYER'S STOMACH BITTERS**		
	Bottle in shape of an arch, fancy bottle, round, clear, 11" .	75.00	95.00
☐ 100	**BOYER'S STOMACH BITTERS CINCINNATI**		
	Whiskey shape bottle, fluted shoulder and round base, clear	115.00	140.00
☐ 101	**BITTER DE**		
	2 Lions Bordeaux in a seal on shoulder, tapered top, ring, piece mold, Dr. Olive, 12¼"	60.00	80.00
☐ 102	**BITTER**		
	Secrestat in a seal, turn mold, Dr. Oiva, 12"	60.00	80.00
☐ 103	**THE BITTERS PHARMACY**		
	Label, clear, 4½"	4.00	6.00
☐ 104	**DR. BLAKE'S AROMATIC BITTERS N.Y.**		
	Aqua, pontil, 7¼"	70.00	90.00
☐ 105	**BLAKE'S TONIC & DUERETIC BITTERS**		
	Round, aqua, 10¼"	30.00	40.00
☐ 106	**DR. BOERHAVES STOMACH BITTERS**		
	Olive amber, 9¼"	65.00	85.00
☐ 107	**BOERHAVES HOLLAND BITTERS**		
	One side B. Page Jr., other side Pittsburg, Pa., aqua, 8" ..	60.00	80.00
☐ 108	**BOSTON MALT BITTERS**		
	Round, green, 9½"	35.00	50.00
☐ 109	**BRADY'S FAMILY BITTER**		
	On three sunken panels, amber, 9½"	70.00	90.00
☐ 110	**BROPHYS BITTERS**		
	Aqua, 7"	60.00	80.00
☐ 111	**BROWN, N.K.**		
	On other side Burlington, Vt., on front Iron & Quinine Bitters, ring top, aqua, 7¼"	55.00	75.00

☐ 112 **BROWN'S CELEBRATED INDIAN HERB BITTERS**
*In a shield shaped panel at base on left side, on base
Patented-Feb. 11-1867, Indian Maiden, amber, golden
amber, other shades of amber which are common for this
bottle* 210.00 265.00

☐ 113 **Rare in green,** *clear, aqua* 300.00 450.00

☐ 114 **BROWN'S AROMATIC BITTERS**
Oval bottle, aqua, 8½" 60.00 80.00

☐ 115 **BROWN & LYONS BLOOD BITTERS**
Amber, 8" 100.00 130.00

☐ 116 **BROWN CHEMICAL CO.**
Brown Iron Bitters on other side, amber, 8" 18.00 23.00

☐ 117 **F. BROWN BOSTON SARSAPARILLA STOMACH
BITTERS**
Pontil, aqua, 9¼" 80.00 100.00

☐ 118 **DR. BROWN'S BERRY BITTERS**
Aqua or clear, 8¼" 40.00 55.00

☐ 119 **BROWN'S CASTILIA BITTERS**
Round, tapered, amber, 10" 70.00 90.00

☐ 120 **BROWN'S CELEBRATED INDIAN HERB BITTERS**
Amber, 12½" 335.00 425.00

☐ 121 **BROWN'S CELEBRATED INDIAN HERB BITTERS**
Indian maiden figural, black, 12½" 345.00 440.00

☐ 122 **BROWN'S INDIAN QUEEN BITTERS**
Reddish amber, 12½" 250.00 335.00

☐ 123 **BRYANT'S**
*Stomach Bitters on three panels, green, small kick-up
with dot* 175.00 225.00

☐ 124 **BRYANTS STOMACH BITTERS**
On two panels, 8-sided, pontil, olive, 11¾" 135.00 170.00

☐ 125 **GEO.J.BYRNE:**
*Professor-New York, on 1 panel in back, The Great-Univer-
sal-Compound-Stomach-Bitters-Patented-1890, all in
FANCY panels, very fancy decor bottle, amber, 10"* 700.00 1000.00

☐ 126 *Same as above, clear or amethyst* 350.00 425.00

☐ 127 **H. E. BUCKLEN & CO.**
Electric Brand Bitter on each side, amber, 9" 18.00 23.00

☐ 128 *Same except no Electric* 18.00 23.00

☐ 129 **BURDOCK BLOOD BITTERS**
Canadian type, early ABM, clear, 8½" 14.00 18.00

☐ 130 **BURDOCK BLOOD BITTERS**
*T. Milburn & Co., Toronto, Ont. on back, tapered neck,
aqua blue, 8½"* 30.00 40.00

☐ 131 **BURDOCK BLOOD BITTERS**
*Foster Milburn Co. on one side, other side Buffalo, N.Y.,
clear, 8"* 22.00 27.00

☐ 132 *BITTERS, label, McC on bottom, gold, 9½"* 6.00 8.00

☐ 133 *BITTERS, label, amber, lady's leg neck, 12"* 50.00 65.00

☐ 134 *BITTERS, label under glass in circle, bar bottle, clear,
12¼"* 22.00 27.00

☐ 135 *BITTERS, label, crock, light olive, brown trim, 10¼"* 30.00 40.00

☐ 136 *BITTERS, label, different colors and sizes, reproductions* 8.00 11.00

☐ 137 *BITTERS or WHISKEY, label, green* 60.00 80.00

C

☐ 138 **CALDWELL'S HERB BITTERS**
Multi-sided bottle, "GREAT CONIC" amber, pontil, 12⅝" .   175.00   225.00

☐ 139 **DR. CALLENDER & SONS LIVER BITTERS**
Square bottle "CELEBRATED LIVER BITTERS", light amber, 9⅝" 75.00   95.00

☐ 140 **CALIFORNIA FIG BITTERS**
Square bottle, "CALIFORNIA EXTRACT OF FIG CO.", amber, 9⅝" 70.00   90.00

☐ 141 *Same as above, except Fig & Herb Bitters, black* 180.00   230.00

☐ 142 **CALIFORNIA HERB & FIG BITTERS**
Amber, 9¾" 80.00   100.00

☐ 143 **CALIFORNIA WINE BITTERS**
M. KELLER, L.A. in shield on shoulder, M. K. around bottle, olive green, 12¼" 105.00   125.00

☐ 144 **CAPITAL BITTERS** *one side*
Dr. M. M. Fenner's Fredonia, N.Y. on reverse side, aqua, 10½" 35.00   47.00

☐ 145 **CARACAS BITTERS**
Amber to emerald green, 8¼" 32.00   42.00

☐ 146 *Same as above, in dark green* 45.00   60.00

☐ 147 **CARMELITE BITTERS**
For the Kidney and Liver Complaints on one side, on back, Carmelite, Frank R. Leonori & Co. Proprietors, New York, square, amber, olive, 10½" 60.00   80.00

☐ 148 **CARMELITER KIDNEY & LIVER BITTERS**
Square bottle, "CARMELITER STOMACH BITTERS CO.-NEW YORK", amber, 10⅝" 45.00   60.00

☐ 149 **CARONI BITTERS**
Pint, amber 19.00   26.00

☐ 150 **CARONI BITTERS**
½ pint, green 25.00   33.00

☐ 151 **CARPATHIAN HERB BITTERS**
Hollander Drug Co. Braddock P. on other side, amber, 8½" 40.00   55.00

☐ 152 **CARPENTER & BURROWS, CINCINNATI, O.**
In 2 lines, cabin type bottle, tapered top, amber, label stated bitters-S is reverse in Burrows, 9½" 225.00   300.00

☐ 153 **CARTER'S LIVER BITTERS**
Oval bottle, w/label, amber, 8⅝" 70.00   90.00

☐ 154 **CASSINS GRAPE BRANDY BITTERS**
Triple ringed top, dark olive green, 10" 115.00   140.00

☐ 155 **CASTILIAN BITTERS**
In vertical letters, round shape and tapered from bottom to neck, narrow square top and ring in center of neck, narrow square top and ring in center of neck. Light amber, 10" 75.00   95.00

☐ 156 **CATAWBA WINE BITTERS**
Cluster of grapes in front and back, green, 9" 70.00   90.00

☐ 157 **CELEBRATED BERLIN STOMACH BITTERS**
Square bottle, light green, 9½" 95.00   115.00

2

15

22

64

109

112

116

126

127

131

133

135

136

137

151

171

☐158 **CELEBRATED PARKERS BITTERS—STOMACH**
In 3 lines, side mold, amber, tapered top, 8¼" 90.00 115.00

☐159 **CELEBRATED CROWw BITTERS**
F. Chevalier & Co. Sole Agents, amber, 9¼" 80.00 100.00

☐160 **CELEBRATED HEALTH RESTORING BITTERS**
Dr. Stephen Jewetts, pontil, aqua, 9½" 50.00 65.00

☐161 **CELERY & CHAMOMILE BITTERS**
Label, square, amber, 10" 18.00 23.00

☐162 **CHALMER'S**
On shoulder on base Proprietors in center, Catawka Wine Bitters. ¼ moon letters under it Trade Mark, center of it circle with mill tree, under it it in ¼ moon letters Sutters Old Mill. Spurance Stanley & Co., round, ring tapered top. aqua, 11½" 85.00 105.00

☐163 **CHANDER'S, DR., JAMAICA GINGER ROOT BITTERS**
All in 4 lines, barrel type bottle, on shoulder in 2 lines Chas. Nichols Jr. & Co. Props. Lowell Mass., amber, double ring top, 10" 225.00 275.00

☐164 **CHRISTIAN XANDER'S STOMACH BITTERS**
Label, Washington, D.C., amber, 12" 35.00 48.00

☐165 **DR. E. CHYDER STOMACH BITTERS, N.O.**
Amber, 9" 18.00 23.00

☐166 **CINTORIA BITTER WINE** *on shoulder*
On shoulder, amber, 11" 18.00 23.00

☐167 **CLARKE'S COMPOUND MANDRAKE BITTERS**
In 3 lines, aqua, ring top, 7⅝" 40.00 53.00

☐168 **CLARK'S GIANT BITTERS**
Rectangular bottle, ring top, "PHILADA, PA.", aqua, 6¾" 40.00 53.00

☐169 **E. R. CLARKE'S SARSPARILLA BITTERS**
Sharon, Mass., Rectangular bottle, aqua, pontil, 7⅞" 90.00 115.00

☐170 **CLAYTON & RUSSELL'S BITTERS**
Labeled only, square bottle, "CELEBRATED STOMACH BITTERS", Label, amber, 8⅞" 20.00 25.00

☐171 **CLARKES SHERRY WINE BITTERS**
Clear, blue green pontil, 8" 35.00 47.00

☐172 **CLARKE'S SHERRY WINE BITTERS**
Only 25¢, pontil, blue green, 8" 90.00 115.00

☐173 **CLARKS VEG. BITTERS**
Only 75¢, pontil, aqua, 8" 100.00 130.00

☐174 **CLAW BITTERS**
Label, light amber, 4¾" 30.00 40.00

☐175 **CLIMAX BITTERS**
On back S. F. Cal., golden amber, 9½" 60.00 80.00

☐176 **CLOTWORTHY'S**
Oriental Tonic Bitter on back, amber, 10" 85.00 105.00

☐177 **COCA BITTERS ANDES MTS.**
Trademark, picture of Indian carrying man across stream, also THE BEST TONIC 100.00 130.00

☐178 **COCAMOKE BITTERS**
Hartford, Con., square bottle, amber, tapered top, 9" 60.00 80.00

☐179 **COCKTAIL BITTERS**
Cribbs Davidson & Co other side, 9¼" 125.00 145.00

☐ 180 **DR. A. W. COLEMAN'S ANTIDYSPEPTIC TONIC BITTERS**
Pontil, ground pontil, green **90.00** **115.00**

☐ 181 **COLLETON BITTERS**
Pontil, aqua, 6½" **60.00** **80.00**

☐ 182 *Same as above, without pontil*...................... **18.00** **23.00**

☐ 183 **COLUMBO PEPTIC BITTERS**
*On back L. E. Junc, New Orleans, La., square bottle, under
bottom SB&CO, amber, 8¾"* **35.00** **45.00**

☐ 184 **COMPOUND HEPATICA BITTERS**
*H.F.S. monogram, oval bottle, "H.F. SHAW M.D.", aqua,
ring top, Mt. Vernon, Me., 8⅜"* **65.00** **85.00**

☐ 185 **COMPOUND CALISAYA BITTERS** *in 2 lines*
Tapered top, square, amber, 9½" **14.00** **18.00**

☐ 186 **COMUS STOMACH BITTERS** *in 2 lines*
*Back Clerc Bros & Co. Limited sole proprietors, New
Orleans, La. in 3 lines, tapered top, amber, 9"* **70.00** **90.00**

☐ 187 **CONGRESS**
On other side, Bitters, amber or clear, tapered top, 9" **60.00** **80.00**

☐ 188 **CONSTITUTION BITTERS**
*Rectangular bottle, "SEWARD & BENTLEY", Buffalo,
N.Y., green, round. Below shoulder A.M.S. 2 at base 1864,
9½"* **90.00** **115.00**

☐ 189 **CONSTITUTION BITTERS 1880**
Bodeker Bros Prop. Rich. Va., amber, 7" **115.00** **145.00**

☐ 190 **CORN JUICE BITTERS**
Flask-shaped bottle, quart, aqua, pint also **70.00** **90.00**

☐ 191 **CORWITZ STOMACH BITTERS**
Amber, 7½" **45.00** **60.00**

☐ 192 **CRIMEAN BITTERS**
*Under it on base, Patent 1863, on other side Romaines Cri-
mean Bitters, amber, 10¼"* **175.00** **225.00**

☐ 193 **H.M. CROOKESS**
*Stomach bitters, letters separated from the mould seam,
round big blob neck, long tapered top, small kick up olive
green, 10½"* **325.00** **400.00**

☐ 194 **CUNDERANGO BITTERS**
Same on back side, greenish amber, 7¾" **60.00** **80.00**

☐ 195 **CURTIS CORDIAL CALISAYA, THE GREAT STOMACH
BITTERS**
Tapered neck, amber, 11½"........................ **140.00** **190.00**

D

☐ 196 **DAMIANA BITTERS**
*Baja, Calif. on back, 8-pointed star under bottom, Lewis
Hess Manufr. on shoulder, aqua, 11½"* **70.00** **90.00**

☐ 197 **DAMIANA**
*Same as above, except no Lewis Hess Manufr. on
shoulder* **35.00** **48.00**

☐ 198 **DANDELION BITTERS**
Rectangular bottle, clear, amber, tapered top, 8" **35.00** **48.00**

☐ 199 **DANDELION XXX BITTERS**
Aqua or clear, 7" **60.00** **80.00**

☐200 **DEMUTH'S STOMACH BITTERS**
Philada., square bottle, amber, 9⅝" 45.00   60.00

☐201 **DEVIL-CERT STOMACH BITTERS**
Round bottle, clear, ABM, 8" 15.00   20.00

☐202 **DEXTER LOVERIDGE WAHOO BITTERS, DWD**
1863 XXX on roof tapered top, Eagle faces down to left
with arrow. dark amber, 10" 90.00   115.00

☐203 Same as above, except Eagle faces up to right, light
yellow 95.00   120.00

☐204 **DIGESTINE BITTERS**
P.J.Bowlin Liquor Co. sole proprietors-St. Paul, Minn. in
lines, tapered top, amber, 8½" 140.00   185.00

☐205 **DIMMITT'S 50CTS BITTERS**
Flask bottle, "ST. LOUIS", amber, tapered top, 6½" 70.00   90.00

☐206 **DeWITTS STOMACH BITTERS**
Chicago, amber, 8" 55.00   75.00

☐207 **DeWITTS STOMACH BITTERS**
Chicago, amber, 9¾" 55.00   75.00

☐208 **DOC DUNNING OLD HOME BITTERS**
Greensboro, N. Carolina, dark red, amber, 13" 75.00   95.00

☐209 **DOYLE'S HOP BITTERS**
Cabin shape, 1872 on roof, several shades of amber and
many variants of colors 60.00   80.00

☐210 **S.T.DRAKES**
On top of roof panel, 1860 plantation on next panel, Bitters on next, reverse center panel Patented 1862 with six
logs, front plain for label, other covered with logs, some
have five logs and the earliest have four logs, amber the
most common, others: citron, pale yellow, green, scarce
in olive green, 10" 120.00   160.00

E

☐211 **EAGLE AROMATIC BITTERS**
Round bottle, "EAGLE LIQUOR DISTILLERIES", yellow
amber, 6¾" 18.00   23.00

☐212 **EAST INDIA ROOT BITTERS**
Geo. P. Clapp, sole Prop., gin shaped bottle, "BOSTON
MASS", amber, 9⅝" 110.00   140.00

☐213 **EMERSON EXCELSIOR BOTANIC BITTERS**
Rectangular bottle, "E.H. Burns-Augusta-Maine", amber,
9" 14.00   18.00

☐214 **DR. E.P. EASTMAN'S YELLOW DOCK**
Pontil, rectangular bottle, "LYNN, MASS.", aqua, tapered
top, 7¾" 70.00   90.00

☐215 **ELECTRIC BITTERS**
Square bottle, "H.E. BUCKLEN & CO., CHICAGO, ILL.",
amber, 9" 35.00   48.00

☐216 **EGON BRAUN HAMBURS**
Embossed on shoulder, Universal Mercantile Co. San
Francisco", Original Amargo Bitters, etc., all on label,
double ring top, green, 5" 40.00   55.00

☐217 **ENGLISH FEMALE BITTERS**
On reverse Dromgoole, Louisville, Ky., clear or amber,
8½" 70.00   90.00

☐ 218 **EXCELCIOR**
On back Bitters, tapered top, amber, 9" 60.00   80.00

☐ 219 **EXCELSIOR HERB BITTERS**
J.V. MATTISON, WASHINGTON, N.J., rectangular, roofed shoulder, amber, 10" 115.00   145.00

F

☐ 220 **FAVORITE BITTERS**
Powell & Stutenroth, barrel shape with swirl ribbing, amber, 9¼" 90.00   115.00

☐ 221 **FEINSTER STUTTGARIES MAGEN BITTERS**
Brand Bros. Co., label, 3-sided bottle, long neck and ring top, amber, 10" 60.00   80.00

☐ 222 **DR. M.M. FENNER'S CAPITOL BITTERS**
Aqua, 10½" 30.00   40.00

☐ 223 *Same as above, green* 40.00   55.00

☐ 224 **FER-KINA GALENO**
(Bitters) on shoulder, beer type bottle, brown, machine made, 10⅛" 14.00   18.00

☐ 225 **FERNET GIGLIANI BITTERS**
San Francisco, label, wine type bottle, kick-up bottom, green 25.00   32.00

☐ 226 **FERRO QUINA STOMACH BITTERS BLOOD MAKER**
Dogliani Italia, D.P. Rossi, 1400 Dupont St. S.E. sole agents, U.S.A. & Canada, lady's leg type neck, amber, 9¼" 70.00   90.00

☐ 227 **THE FISHBITTERS** *(on side of eye)*
On reverse W.H. Ware Patented 1866, on base W.H. Ware Patented 1866, plain rolled top, amber, 11½", 3½" x 2½", 210.00   260.00

☐ 228 *Same as above, except clear* 400.00   575.00

☐ 229 **FITZPATRICK & CO.**
Shape of stubby ear of corn, amber, 10" 220.00   275.00

☐ 230 **A.H. FLANDERS M.D. RUSH'S BITTERS**
Clear, amethyst, amber, 9" 40.00   55.00

☐ 231 **DR. FLINTS** *on other side PROVIDENCE, R.I.*
On front Quaker Bitters, aqua, ring top, 9½" 50.00   70.00

☐ 232 *Same except Dr. Flint's, on back Quaker* 60.00   80.00

☐ 233 **FISCHER'S-N.E., COUGH BITTERS**
Atlanta, Ga. all in 3 lines, tapered top, aqua, 6" 45.00   60.00

☐ 234 **DR. FORMANECK'S BITTER WINE**
Amber, round, 10½" 10.00   15.00

☐ 235 **FOWLER'S STOMACH BITTERS**
Fancy bottle, square, light amber, "STOMACH BITTERS", 10" 110.00   140.00

☐ 236 **FRANK'S LAXITIVE TONIC BITTERS**
Flask type, on bottom 502, amber, tapered top, 6¼" 90.00   115.00

☐ 237 **FRANCKS PANACEA BITTERS**
(Frank Hayman & Rhine Sole Proprietors), round, light house, amber, 10" 95.00   120.00

☐ 238 **FRENCH AROMATIQE**
The finest stomach bitters in 4 lines on shoulder, ring top, aqua, 7⅜" 30.00   40.00

G

☐ 239 **GARRY, OWEN STRENGTHENING BITTERS**
On one side Sole Proprietor's, on other side Ball & Lyon's,
New Orleans, La., front plain, under bottom W.McC & Co.
Pitts., amber, 9" 70.00   90.00

☐ 240 **GERMAN BALSAM BITTERS, W. M. WATSON & CO.**
Sole agents for U.S., milk glass, 9" 85.00   105.00

☐ 241 **GERMAN HOP BITTERS**
Square, amber, "READING, MICH.", 9½" 55.00   75.00

☐ 242 **GERMAN TONIC BITTERS**
Pontil, square, aqua, "BOGGS, COTMAN & CO.", 9¾" ... 60.00   80.00

☐ 243 **DR. GILMORES LAXATIVE—KIDNEY & LIVER BITTERS**
Oval bottle, amber, 10⅜" 90.00   115.00

☐ 244 **THE GLOBE TONIC BITTERS**
Tapered top, square bottle, amber, 10" 60.00   80.00

☐ 245 **GLOBE BITTERS**
Manufactured only by Byrne Bros. & Co. New York, fluted
tapered neck, amber, 11" 135.00   170.00

☐ 246 **GLOBE BITTERS**
Manufactured only by John W. Perkins & Co., Sole Proprietors, Portland, Me., amber, 10" 165.00   210.00

☐ 247 **DR. GODDIN'S BITTERS**
Square, aqua, "GENTIAN BITTERS", 10" 185.00   230.00

☐ 248 **GOLDEN SEAL BITTERS**
Square bottle, amber, 9" 100.00   130.00

☐ 249 **GODFREYS CELEBRATED CORDIAL BITTERS**
Iron pontil, aqua, 10" 45.00   60.00

☐ 250 **GEO. C. GODWINS**
Reverse Indian Vegetable Sarsaparilla, each side reads
Bitters, all lettering reads vertically, pontil, aqua, 8¼" ... 160.00   200.00

☐ 251 **GOFF'S BITTERS**
Label, Camden, N.H., aqua 15.00   20.00

☐ 252 **GOFF'S BITTERS**
H on bottom, machine made, clear and amber, 5¾" 30.00   40.00

☐ 253 **GOLD LION BITTERS**
Round bottle, labeled, clear, 6" 18.00   23.00

☐ 254 **DR. GOODHUE'S ROOT & HERB BITTERS**
Rectangular bottle, "J.H. RUSSELL & CO.", aqua, 10⅜" .. 65.00   85.00

☐ 255 **ST. GOTTHARD HERB BITTERS**
Mette & Kanne Bros. St. Louis, Mo. in vertical line on
front, tapered top, 8¾" 50.00   65.00

☐ 256 **GRANGER BITTERS**
Clear, flask bottle, labeled, amber, anchor on front, 7⅞" .. 18.00   23.00

☐ 257 **W.H.GREEG LORIMER'S JUNIPER TAR BITTERS**
Elmira, N.Y., blue green, 9½" 70.00   90.00

☐ 258 **GREELEY'S BOURBON BITTERS**
Amber, puce, 9½" 140.00   170.00

☐ 259 **GREER'S ECLIPSE BITTERS**
Louisville, Ky. on side, amber, 9" 100.00   130.00

☐ 260 Same as above, except puce 140.00   170.00

☐261 **GRIEL'S HERB BITTERS**
Lancastle, Pa., round bottle, "GRIEL & YOUNG", aqua,
9½" 60.00 80.00

☐262 **J. GROSSMAN**
Old Hickory Celebrated Stomach Bitters on back, amber,
4½" 35.00 48.00

☐263 **J. GROSSMAN**
Old Celebrated Stomach Bitters on other side, amber,
8¼" 65.00 85.00

☐264 **DR. GRUESSIE ALTHER'S KRAUTER BITTERS**
Label, B under bottom, amber, 10½" 80.00 100.00

☐265 **GUNCKELS EAGLE BITTERS**
Square bottle, labeled only, amber, 9⅜" 20.00 30.00

H

☐266 **HAGANS BITTERS**
Amber, 9½" 55.00 75.00

☐267 **E. E. HALL, NEW HAVEN**
Established 1842 on base, amber 10¼" 70.00 90.00

☐268 **HALL'S BITTERS**
E.E. Hall, New Haven, Established 1842 on back, barrel
shape, amber, 9¼" 170.00 220.00

☐269 **DR. T. HALL'S, CALIF. PEPSIN WINE BITTERS**
In three lines, amber, tapered top, 9¼" 85.00 105.00

☐270 **DR. THOS. HALL'S / CALIFORNIA / PEPSIN WINE
BITTERS**
Vertically on three lines on front, light amber, 9" tall, 2½"
base 60.00 80.00

☐271 **HANSARD'S HOP BITTERS**
Crock, tan and green, 8" 60.00 80.00

☐272 **DR. MANLEY HARDY'S GENUINE JAUNDICE BITTERS,
BOSTON, MASS.**
Long tapered neck, aqua, 7½" 90.00 115.00

☐273 Same as above, except BANGOR, MAINE 90.00 115.00

☐274 Same as above, except 6½" 80.00 105.00

☐275 Same as above, except no pontil 25.00 32.00

☐276 **DR. HARTER'S WILD CHERRY BITTERS**
St. Louis or Dayton, O., rectangular, amber, 7¾" 28.00 37.00

☐277 Same except miniature 28.00 37.00

☐278 **DR. HARTER'S WILD CHERRY BITTERS**
Dayton, O., four sunken panels, rectangular, 4¾" 35.00 47.00

☐279 **DR. HARTER'S WILD CHERRY BITTERS**
St. Louis all in four lines, embossed cherries on both side
panels, 2 under bottom, amber, 7¼" 160.00 210.00

☐280 **HART'S STAR BITTERS**
Philadelphia, Pa., aqua, 9¼" 90.00 115.00

☐281 **HARTWIG'S CELEBRATED ALPINE BITTERS**
Base Wm. Mc. & Co., Pittsburgh, Pa., square bottle, "ST.
JOSEPH, MO.", golden amber, 9⅜" 85.00 110.00

☐282 **HARTWIG KANTOROWICZ**
Posen, Germany, case type bottle, milk glass, 4" 80.00 105.00

☐283 Same as above, except 9½" 75.00 95.00

☐284 **HARZER KRANTER BITTERS**
Reverse Herman C. Asendorf, Brooklyn, N.Y., amber, 9½" 45.00 60.00

179

196

217

245

258

259

263

266

267

356

379

291

400

300

410

417

☐ 285 **HAVIS IRON BITTERS**
*In base the WILLIAMSBURG DRUG CO., square bottle,
"WILLIAMSBURG, KY.", amber, 8"* 85.00 110.00

☐ 286 **H.H. HAY CO.**
*Selling Agents Portland Me. on back, on bottom L.F.
Atwood, in center L.F., 6¾"* 45.00 60.00

☐ 287 **HENDERSON'S CAROLINA BITTERS**
Trademark H.C.B., square bottle, amber, 9⅝" 85.00 110.00

☐ 288 **DR. HENLEY'S CALIFORNIA IXL** *(in oval)* **BITTERS**
W.Frank & Sons, Pitt. reverse side, sky blue 60.00 80.00

☐ 289 **DR. HENLEY'S SPICED WINE**
*OK in a circle, Bitters label, reverse OK Bitters, round bot-
tle, ring top, bluish aqua, 12"* 45.00 60.00

☐ 290 **DR. HENLEY'S WILD GRAPE ROOT**
*Reverse IXL in an oval, Bitters under it, tapered and ring
top, square bottle, under bottom W. F. G. Sons, amber,
12"* 60.00 80.00

☐ 291 **HENTZ'S CURATIVE BITTERS**
Phila., label, embossed, clear, 9½" 55.00 75.00

☐ 292 **H. P. HERB WILD CHERRY BITTERS**
*Reading, Pa., in back wild cherry and tree, Bitters on all
four sides of the roof, amber, 10"* 90.00 115.00

☐ 293 *Same as above, except green* 130.00 165.00

☐ 294 **DR. I. HESTER'S STOMACH BITTERS**
Amber, 8¾" 80.00 100.00

☐ 295 **HERKULES BITTER**
*Monogram, G.A. inside of circle, figural-ball shape bottle,
"1 QUART", labeled, also 1 pint, deep green, 7¾"* 85.00 105.00

☐ 296 **DR. R.F. HIBBARD'S WILD CHERRY BITTERS**
*Proprietor, N.Y., round bottle, "C.N.CRITTENTON", aqua,
8"* 95.00 120.00

☐ 297 **HIERAPICRA BITTERS**
*Reverse side Extract of Fig, Botanical Society, other side
California, aqua, 6½"* 70.00 90.00

☐ 298 **HIGHLAND BITTERS & SCOTCH TONIC**
Barrel-shaped bottle, ring top, amber, 9½" 160.00 200.00

☐ 299 *Same as above, except olive* 185.00 230.00

☐ 300 **HI HI BITTER CO.**
Triangular shape, amber, 9½" 80.00 100.00

☐ 301 **HILL'S HOREHOUND BITTERS**
Round bottle, labeled only, "IRISH MOSS", 6½" 11.00 15.00

☐ 302 **HILL'S MOUNTAIN BITTERS**
*Rectangular bottle, "EMBOSSED INDIANA DRUG SPE-
CIALTY COMPANY", amber, tapered top, 7¾"* 30.00 40.00

☐ 303 **HOBOKEN AVAN BITTERS**
Olive, 9¼" 35.00 47.00

☐ 304 **HOFFHEIMER BROS.**
Reverse BAVARIAN BITTERS, amber, 9½" 42.00 56.00

☐ 305 **DR. HOFFMAN'S GOLDEN BITTERS**
Label, ACW under bottom, amber, 9" 15.00 20.00

☐ 306 **HOLTZERMANN'S PATENT STOMACH BITTERS**
*On the roof of cabin-shaped bottle, shingle roof, tapered
top, amber, 9¾"* 150.00 190.00

☐307	**HOLTZERMANN'S PATENT STOMACH BITTERS**		
	Label, amber, 4¼"	140.00	170.00
☐308	*Same as above, except 9¾"*	140.00	170.00
☐309	**HOME BITTERS,**		
	On the side, Saint Louis, Mo., square, beveled corners, long tapered top, 9", amber	70.00	90.00
☐310	**DR. HOOFLAND'S GERMAN BITTERS**		
	Rectangular bottle, aqua, pint, pontil, in back C.M. Jackson, Phila., 4"	40.00	55.00
☐311	**HOP & IRON BITTERS**		
	Square bottle, in back "UTICA, N.Y.", amber, tapered top, 8⅝"	65.00	85.00
☐312	**DR. VON HOPFS CURACO BITTERS**		
	In back Chamberlain & Co. Des Moines Iowa, tapered top, amber, 9¼"	95.00	120.00
☐313	*Same as above, in a flask type bottle*	70.00	90.00
☐314	**HOPS & MALT BITTERS**		
	Roofed shoulder, Trademark (Sheafil Grain), square bottle, yellow amber, amber, tapered top, 9⅝", ...	80.00	100.00
☐315	**DR. A.S. HOPPINS**		
	Union stomach bitters, in three lines, tapered top, off shade of amber, beveled corners, 9¾"	45.00	60.00
☐316	**HORSE SHOE BITTERS**		
	Horse Shoe Med. Co., Base Pat. App. for, Horseshoe shape, amber, COLLINSVILLE, ILL."	130.00	160.00
☐317	**DR. J. HOSTETTER'S STOMACH BITTERS**		
	Square, light amber, amber, 9"	11.00	15.00
☐318	*Same except yellow green*	22.00	29.00
☐319	*Same except machine made*	6.00	8.00
☐320	**DR. J. HOSTETTER'S** *[sic]*		
	Amber, 8¾"	25.00	32.00
☐321	**DR. J. HOSTETTER'S**		
	Amber, 8¾	16.00	21.00
☐322	**DR. HOSTETTER'S STOMACH BITTERS**		
	On base I.G.L., square, amber, 9"	11.00	15.00
☐323	*Same as above, except on back 18 Fluid oz., 8¾"*	11.00	15.00
☐324	*Same as above, machine made*	5.00	7.00
☐325	**DR. J. HOSTETTER'S STOMACH BITTERS**		
	(J is backwards), amber, 8½"	60.00	80.00
☐326	**DR. J. HOSTETTER'S STOMACH BITTERS**		
	L & W 10 on base, yellow amber, 9½"	18.00	23.00
☐327	*Same as above, except dark amber*	18.00	23.00
☐328	*Same as above, except S. McKEE & CO., 2 on base*	18.00	23.00
☐329	*Same as above, except #2 on base*	18.00	23.00
☐330	**HUA**		
	On base, small lady's leg, amber, 7½"	21.00	27.00
☐331	**H. U. A.**		
	Monogram on bottom, Bitters label, lady's leg shape, amber, 10½"	32.00	43.00
☐332	**GEO. C. HUBBEL & CO.**		
	On each side, blank front and back, tapered top, aqua, golden bitters, 10½"	160.00	210.00

☐333 **HUTCHINS** on side, **DYSPEPSIA BITTERS**
On front, New York on other side, tapered top, aqua, pontil, 8½"... 115.00 140.00

☐334 **J.W. HUTCHINSON'S**
Reverse Tonic Bitters, Mobile Ala., aqua, 8¾".......... 120.00 145.00

☐335 **HYGEIA BITTERS**
Square bottle, "FOX & CO.", amber, tapered top, base L & W, 9"... 60.00 80.00

I

☐336 **IMPERIAL RUSSIAN TONIC BITTERS**
Rope design on sides, clear or aqua, 9¼"............... 90.00 115.00

☐337 **I.N.C. BITTERS**
(Reedy, Pa.), round, long neck, barrel-shape, amber, 10½" 90.00 115.00

☐338 **IMPERIAL BITTERS**
One side, Victor Rivaud, other side, Louisville, Ky., amber, 10½"... 85.00 105.00

☐339 **INDIAN VEGETABLE SARSAPARILLA**
Reverse Bitters, Boston, all vertical lettering, pontil, aqua, 8¼"... 90.00 115.00

☐340 **IRON BITTERS**
Square bottle, "BROWN CHEMICAL Co.", 8⅝".......... 17.00 23.00

☐341 **ISAACSON SEIXAS & CO. BITTERS**
CO, with eye in center, monogram, square, light amber, "66 & 68 COMMON ST.", push up with five star pontil, etc. 160.00 210.00

☐341 **ISHAM'S STOMACH BITTERS**
Square bottle, amber, 9⅜"........................... 80.00 100.00

J

☐343 **JACOB'S CABIN TONIC BITTERS**
Cabin shape bottle, "LABORATORY-PHILADELPHIA", clear glass, pontil, 7⅜"............................... 175.00 225.00

☐344 **DR. JACOB'S BITTERS**
S. A. Spencer, rectangular bottle, "NEW HAVEN", aqua, 10"... 100.00 130.00

☐345 **JENKINS STOMACH BITTERS**
In two lines, under bottom, W.McC & Co., tapered top, amber... 70.00 90.00

☐346 **JEWEL BITTERS**
Reverse John S. Bowman & Co., amber, 9"............. 50.00 65.00

☐347 **JEWEL BITTERS**
On side, John S. Bowman & Co., California on back, tapered top, quart, amber........................... 45.00 60.00

☐348 **JOCKEY CLUB HOUSE BITTERS**
J. H. Dudley & Co., green, 9½"...................... 90.00 115.00

☐349 **A. H. JOHNSON & CO.**
On the side Collingwood, Ont., on front Johnson's Tonic Bitters, clear or amethyst, double ring top, 8¾"........ 45.00 60.00

☐350 **JOHNSON'S INDIAN DYSPEPTIC BITTERS**
Each on four sides, rectangular, aqua, tapered top, pontil, ring top, 6¼"....................................... 70.00 90.00

□351 **A.H. JOHNSON & CO.**
Other side Collingwood, Ont., on front Johnson's Tonic
Bitters, clear or amethyst, double top, 8¾".............   21.00   27.00

□352 **JONES INDIAN SPECIFIC HERB BITTERS**
SW. Jones - Prop. Phila; square, amber, "PATENT", 1868,
tapered top, 9"...............   65.00   85.00

□353 **DR. HERBERT JOHN'S INDIAN BITTERS**
Great Indian Discoveries; amber, 8½"................   70.00   90.00

□354 **JOHNSON'S CALISAYA BITTERS**
Reverse Burlington Vt.; tapered top, amber, 10"........   35.00   48.00

K

□355 **KAISER WILHELM BITTERS CO.**
Sandusky O.; bulged neck, ringed top, round bottle,
amber, clear, 10"....................   175.00   225.00

□356 **KELLY'S OLD CABIN BITTERS**
Patd March 1863 on one side; green, 10"..............   275.00   350.00

□357 **KELLY'S OLD CABIN BITTERS**
Patented 1868 or 1870 on each side of roof, amber, 9¼"..   275.00   350.00

□358 **KENNEDY'S EAST INDIA BITTERS**
Clear, Omaha Neb., 6½".........................   55.00   70.00

□359 **KEYSTONE BITTERS**
Barrel-shaped bottle, ringed top, amber, 10"...........   65.00   85.00

□360 **KIMBALL'S (has backward S) JAUNDICE BITTERS**
Troy N.H. on side; tapered top, pontil, dark amber, 6¾"..   175.00   225.00

□361 **KIMBALL'S JAUNDICE**
On other side Troy, N.H.; beveled corners, rectangular,
olive green, tapered top, pontil, 7¼" x 2¾" x 2"........   115.00   140.00

□362 **KING SOLOMON BITTERS**
Seattle, Wash.; rectangular bottle, amber, 8½"........   95.00   115.00

□363 **KING SOLOMON'S BITTERS**
Other side Seattle, Washington; rectangular, amber, 10
oz......................................   45.00   60.00

□364 **KLAS'S OREGON PEACH BITTERS**
In large letters on shoulder; round, aqua, 11½"........   50.00   65.00

□365 **KOEHLER & HENRICH RED STAR STOMACH BITTERS**
St. Paul Minn. in a circle; label in red, black and white cir-
cle; 1908, 11½"....................   175.00   225.00

□366 **KOEHLERS STOMACH BITTERS CO.**
Amber, 12½"......................   30.00   40.00

L

□367 **LANDSBERG'S CENTURY BITTERS**
In three lines; over it a bird or eagle; in back The Ader
Company, St. Louis also in three lines; 13 stars around
shoulder, also 1776 & 1876; corner diamond effect, very
decorative bottle, tapered top and ring, 11½"..........   315.00   385.00

□368 **LACOUR'S BITTERS**
Sarsoparipher, round fancy bottle, amber, yellow-green,
9⅛"......................................   90.00   115.00

☐369 **DR. LANGLEY'S ROOT & HERB BITTERS**
76 Union St. Boston on front; round, ringed top, light green, 6¾" 35.00   48.00

☐370 **DR. LANGLEY'S ROOT & HERB BITTERS**
99 Union St. Boston on front; ringed top, amber, 8½" 45.00   60.00

☐371 *Same as above, but embossing in indented panel* 45.00   60.00

☐372 **LASH'S BITTERS CO.**
N.Y., Chicago, San Francisco; round, clear, dark amber, amethyst, 10¾" and 11" x 3" 27.00   36.00

☐373 *Also with label Cordol Bitter* 6.00   9.00

☐374 **LASH'S / BITTERS CO. / NEW YORK, CHICAGO / SAN FRANCISCO**
Amber, round, ABM only 10.00   14.00

☐375 **LASH'S BITTERS CO. N.Y., CHICAGO, SAN FRANCISCO**
Round, fluted neck and shoulder, tapered top and ring, amber, 10½" 30.00   40.00

☐376 **LASH'S KIDNEY & LIVER BITTERS AND BLOOD PURIFIER**
In back; square, tapered top and ring, amber, beveled corners, 9½" 45.00   60.00

☐377 **LASH'S BITTERS**
With circle between words KIDNEY and LIVER, on back in two lines, The Best Cathartic and Blood Purifier, 2¾" x 2¾", amber, 9" 15.00   20.00

☐378 *Same except 1" x 1" x 3"* 10.00   14.00

☐379 **LASH'S LIVER BITTERS**
Nature's Tonic Laxative on back, machine made, amber, 7½" 9.00   12.00

☐380 *Same as above, except screw top* 15.00   20.00

☐381 **LEAK KIDNEY & LIVER BITTERS**
Reverse side The Best Blood Purifier and Cathartec, amber, 9" 60.00   80.00

☐382 **LEDIARDS**
On side Celebrated Stomach, on back Bitters, tapered top, sea green, 10" 70.00   90.00

☐383 **LEIPZIGER BURGUNDER WEIN BITTERS**
All in a circle in center "A" around it, The Hockstadter Co. all under bottom, ring & tapered top. Round, 3pt. mould, green 35.00   48.00

☐384 **DR. LERIEMONDIE'S SOUTHERN BITTERS**
Dark green, 10" 60.00   80.00

☐385 **LEWIS RED JACKET BITTERS**
Around bottom, three-piece mold, amber, 11" 55.00   75.00

☐386 **LIFE EVERLASTING BITTERS, ATLANTA, GA.**
Amber, 10" 75.00   95.00

☐387 **LIPPMAN'S GREAT GERMAN BITTERS**
Other side N.Y. & Savannah, Geo., amber, 9¾" 120.00   150.00

☐388 **LITTHAUER STOMACH BITTERS**
In center Invented 1884 by Josef Lowenthal, Berlin in vertical lines, tapered top, milk glass, 9¾" 100.00   130.00

☐389 *Same as above, except Berlin omitted* 70.00   90.00

☐390 *Same as above, except clear and "J" is backward, Invented, 7"* 130.00   170.00

☐391	**LINCOLN BITTERS**	
	Rectangular bottle, labeled only, clear glass, 9⅜"	22.00	29.00
☐392	**LOHENGRIN BITTERS**	
	Adolph Marcus, Van Buton German, square-gin shape,	
	milk glass, 9½"	200.00	250.00
☐393	**LOWELL'S INVIGORATING BITTERS**	
	Square bottle, "BOSTON, MASS.", aqua, 8¼"	50.00	70.00
☐394	**DR. LOEW'S CELEBRATED STOMACH BITTERS &**	
	NERVE TONIC	
	Amber, 3½"	50.00	65.00
☐395	**DR. LOEW'S CELEBRATED STOMACH BITTERS &**	
	NERVE TONIC	
	Reverse The Loew & Son Co., tapered top and swirled	
	ribbedneck, fancy bottle, apple green, 9½"	170.00	220.00
☐396	**LORD BROS., DR. MANDRAKE BAXTO'S BITTERS**	
	Amber, 12"	25.00	33.00
☐397	*Same as above, except clear or amber*	12.00	17.00
☐398	**LORENTZ MED CO. TRADEMARK**	
	Around shoulder, bitters label, amber, 9¾"	17.00	23.00
☐399	**LORENTZ MED CO.**	
	On bitters label, Trade To-Ni-Ta Mark around shoulder,	
	amber, 10"	15.00	20.00
☐400	**LORIMER'S JUNIPER BITTERS**	
	Blue green, square, 9½", 2¼"	70.00	90.00
☐401	**DR. XX LOVEGOODS FAMILY BITTERS**	
	On roof of cabin-shaped bottle, tapered neck, amber,	
	10½"	90.00	115.00
☐402	**DR. LOVEGOODS FAMILY BITTERS**	
	(E left out of BITTERS), amber, 9½"	225.00	315.00
☐403	**E. DEXTER LOVERIDGE WAHOO BITTERS DWD**	
	1863 XXX on roof, tapered top, eagle faces down and left	
	with one arrow, dark amber, 10"	90.00	115.00
☐404	*Same except eagle faces up to right, light yellow*	90.00	115.00
☐405	**LOWELL'S INVIGORATING BITTERS**	
	Square bottle, "BOSTON-MASS.", aqua, 8¼"	55.00	75.00
☐406	**LUTZ**	
	Isaac D, Reading, Pa., red amber, double ring top, label	
	stated bitters, 7¼"	55.00	75.00
☐407	**DR. LYFORD'S BITTERS**	
	C.D. Herrick, Tilton, N.H., on bottom W.T. & Co. C, ringed	
	top, aqua, 8"	50.00	70.00
☐408	**E. G. LYONS & CO., MFG. SAN. F. CA.**	
	(n in SAN is backward), tapered top, amber, 9"	70.00	90.00

M

☐409	**MACK'S SARSAPARILLA BITTERS**	
	In back Mack & Co. Prop's S. F., amber, 8½"	50.00	70.00
☐410	**MAGADOR BITTERS**	
	(E. J. Rose's) in back, superior tonic, cathartic and blood	
	purifier, amber, 9"	90.00	115.00
☐411	**MAGIC BITTERS**	
	Prepared by Minetree & Jackson, Petersburg, Va., two	
	panels and rounded sides, tapered top, olive, 14½"	75.00	95.00

☐412	**MALARION BITTERS** Snyder Gue & Condell, St. Louis, Mo., amber, 8½"	**65.00**	**85.00**
☐413	**MALT BITTERS CO.** Boston U.S.A. under bottom, round, emerald green, 8½" .	**45.00**	**60.00**
☐414	**MAMPE BITTERS** Label, back embossed same with Carl Mampe, Berlin, dark green, 6"	**75.00**	**95.00**
☐415	**PROFESSOR B.E. MANNS ORIENTAL STOMACH BITTERS** Amber, 10¼"	**55.00**	**75.00**
☐416	**MARIANI COCO BITTERS** Green, 7½"	**15.00**	**20.00**
☐417	**MARSHALL'S BITTERS** The Best Laxative and Blood Purifier on back, amber, 8¾"	**35.00**	**47.00**
☐418	**McNEIL'S INDIAN VEGETABLE BITTERS** Oval bottle, labeled only, aqua, 6¾".	**18.00**	**24.00**
☐419	**McKEEVER'S ARMY BITTERS** On shoulder, drum-shaped bottom, cannonballs stacked on top, tapered top, amber, 10¼"	**600.00**	**775.00**
☐420	**MILLS BITTERS** A. M. Gilman, sole prop., lady's leg shape, ringed top, 6 ounce, amber.	**55.00**	**75.00**
☐421	Same except sample size, 2 ounce	**55.00**	**75.00**
☐422	**MISHLER'S HERB BITTERS** S. B. Hartman & Co. in back, under bottom Stoeckels Grad Pat. Feb. 6, 66, tapered top, amber, 8¾"	**55.00**	**75.00**
☐423	Same as above, except back reads Wm. McC & Co.	**55.00**	**75.00**
☐424	**MOHICA BITTERS** On back Roth & Co. S. F., ringed top, amber, 9".	**55.00**	**75.00**
☐425	**MORNING STAR BITTERS** (with Iron Pontil), fancy triangular, amber, "INCEPTUM 5869", Patented (curve) 5869, 13"	**175.00**	**225.00**
☐426	Same without pontil	**90.00**	**115.00**
☐427	**G. N. MORRISON'S** Invigorating - other side, G.N. Morrison, New Orleans, amber, tapered top, 9¼"	**190.00**	**235.00**
☐428	**MOULTONS OLOROSO BITTERS** Trade (Pineapple) Mark, round, aqua, ribbed bottle, 11½" .	**80.00**	**100.00**
☐429	**MURRAY'S PURIFYING BITTERS** Rectangular bottle, labeled only, aqua, 8"	**18.00**	**24.00**

N

☐430	**NATIONAL BITTERS , EAR OF CORN** Patent 1867 under bottom, amber, corn, 12¼"	**200.00**	**250.00**
☐431	**NEW YORK HOP BITTERS CO.** Tapered top, aqua, 9"	**115.00**	**140.00**
☐432	**DR. NISKIAN'S STOMACH BITTERS** On one side, Morrin-Powers, Merc.-sole agents-Kansas City, Mo. on other side, other two plain, tapered top, clear, 8¼"	**150.00**	**190.00**
☐433	**NIGHTCAP BITTERS, SCHMIDLOPP & CO.** Distillers, Cincinnati, O., a good Beverage, multi-sided bottle, tapered top with ring, clear, 9"	**100.00**	**125.00**

☐434 **NORMAN BITTERS**
In back Dr. Bohlins, clear, 8¾" 40.00 50.00
☐435 **NORTHCRAFTS BOTANIC BITTERS**
Square bottle, labeled only, machine made, amber, 9¼" . 10.00 14.00

O

☐436 **WM. G. OESTING, GERMANIA BITTERS**
Amber, 9¼" 55.00 75.00
☐437 **O.K. PLANTATION**
Triangular shape, amber, 11"........................ 275.00 350.00
☐438 **OLD ABE'S AQUE & STOMACH BITTERS**
*In three lines, ring top, under bottom in a clove lief-H B &
C, 0-12 oz., aqua, 7¼"* 25.00 34.00
☐439 **OLD CABIN BITTERS**
*Schnudlapp & Co., Cincinnati, O., etx., cabin-shape bottle,
"PATENTED 1863", amber, 9"* 150.00 190.00
☐440 **OLD DR. SOLOMON'S INDIAN WINE BITTERS**
Rectangular bottle, aqua, 8½" 65.00 85.00
☐441 **OLD HICKORY CELEBRATED STOMACH BITTERS**
On other side J. Grossman, N.O.LA, amber, 4½" 45.00 60.00
☐442 **OLD HOMESTEAD WILD CHERRY BITTERS**
*Cabin shape, golden amber, clapboards not logs and
shingled roof, 10"* 170.00 220.00
☐443 **OLD HOMESTEAD CABIN BITTERS**
Amber, 9½".. 125.00 150.00
☐444 **OLD HOMESTEAD WILD CHERRY BITTERS**
Cabin shape, amber, 10" 140.00 170.00
☐445 *Same except PATENT on roof, clapboards not logs and
shingled roof, amber, 10"* 90.00 115.00
☐446 *Same except cobalt blue* 500.00 675.00
☐447 *Same except inside thread, marked on top PAT. 1861* 175.00 225.00
☐448 **OLD SACHEM BITTERS & WIGHAM TONIC**
*Barrel type bottle, ringed top, puce, amber, yellow amber,
9¾"* 140.00 170.00
☐449 *Same except green* 140.00 170.00
☐450 *Same except with label MERRICK & MOORS OLD
SACHEM BITTERS & WIGWAM TONIC, NEW HAVEN,
CONN.* 120.00 150.00
☐451 **O'LEARY'S 20th CENTURY BITTERS**
In vertical line, tapered top, light amber, 8½" 85.00 105.00
☐452 **OREGON GRAPE ROOT BITTERS**
Round, clear, 9¾"................................. 50.00 65.00
☐453 **ORIGINAL POCAHONTAS BITTERS**
*In center above it 10 hoops and 10 below, barrel shape,
short neck, ring top, aqua, 9½"* 1000.00 1300.00
☐454 **ORIZABA BITTERS**
*On back J. Maristany Jr., round bottle, tapered top, amber,
9½"* 65.00 85.00
☐455 **ORANGE BITTERS**
*Round bottle, labeled only, machine made, pale green,
six-pointed star with 3 dots on base, 11¾"* 10.00 14.00
☐456 **ORRUSO BITTERS**
Around shoulder, round, ABM, dark green, 11¼" 25.00 34.00

☐457 **OSWEGO BITTERS**
 Amber, 7¼" 45.00 60.00
☐458 **OXYGENATED BITTERS**
 Pontil, aqua, 6¾" 80.00 100.00

P

☐459 **DR. PALMERS TONIC BITTERS**
 Square bottle, labeled only, aqua, 8¾" 10.00 14.00
☐460 **PAINE'S CELERY COMPOUND BITTERS**
 Rectangular bottle, amber, 8" 9.00 12.00
☐461 *Same as above, clear glass* 7.00 10.00
☐462 **PARKER.R.MASON-CHICAGO**
 *In two lines, other side Aromatic-Golden Bitters, amber,
 tapered top, 9¼"* 110.00 135.00
☐463 **PATENTED BITTERS**
 *(T. Pirters & Co., 31 & 33 Mich. Ave., Chicago), square bot-
 tle, "CHICAGO", amber, 9¼"* 75.00 95.00
☐464 **PAWNEE BITTERS**
 Indian Medicine Co. S.F., amber, 11¼" 70.00 90.00
☐465 **DR. PELZOLDS GENUINE GERMAN BITTERS**
 Cabin type bottle, amber 120.00 150.00
☐466 **PETER VIERLING'S BLOOD PURIFYING BITTERS**
 (Evansville, Ind.), square bottle, amber, 10" 70.00 90.00
☐467 **PENNS BITTERS FOR THE LIVER**
 On front panel, square, beveled edge, amber, 6½" 55.00 75.00
☐468 **DR. PETZOLD'S CABIN BITTERS**
 Except 1862, amber, 11" 115.00 140.00
☐469 **PEYCHAUD'S AMERICAN AROMATIC BITTERS CORDIAL**
 *L.E. JUNG, SOLE PROP. N.O., round tapered top, amber,
 10½"* 40.00 55.00
☐470 **PERUVIAN BITTERS**
 *On shoulder, in black in shield P.B. CO., square bottle,
 amber, 9¼"* 35.00 48.00
☐471 **PEPSIN BITTERS**
 *On one side, with R.W. Davis Drug Co., Chicago, U.S.A. in
 two lines on other side, shoulder and neck are raised, but
 not on ends, sunken panels on front and back, yellow
 green, 8¼" tall, 4¼" x 2⅛"* 80.00 100.00
☐472 **PEPSIN CALISAYA BITTERS**
 *In two lines, opposite side Dr. Russell Med. Co., rec-
 tangular, green, olive green, beveled corners with three
 vertical ribs, 7½" tall, 4¼" x 2¼"* 25.00 34.00
☐473 **PERRINS APPLE GINGER, PHILA.**
 Embossed apple on front, cabin type bottle, amber, 10¼" 90.00 115.00
☐474 **DR. D.S. PERRY & CO.**
 *On other side New York Excelsior Aromatic Bitters, roofed
 shoulder, tapered top, amber, 10½"* 110.00 140.00
☐475 **JOHN A PERRY'S, DR. WARREN'S BILIOUS BITTERS**
 Boston Mass., aqua, 10" 70.00 90.00
☐476 **PHILADELPHIA HOP BITTERS**
 *In three lines, top of it a man holding a bottle, roof
 shoulder, tapered top, aqua, 10¼"* 175.00 225.00

☐477	**PHOENIX BITTERS**		
	On back J.N° Moffat, on one side Price $1.00, other side		
	N.Y., pontil, dark olive, 5"	60.00	75.00
☐478	**DR. GEO. PIERCES INDIAN RESTORATIVE BITTERS**		
	On side Lowell, Mass., tapered top, aqua, pontil, 7½" ...	60.00	75.00
☐479	**PINEAPPLE BOTTLE**		
	Bitters label, light amber, 9¼"	120.00	150.00
☐480	*Same except yellow green*	350.00	425.00
☐481	**PIPER BITTERS**		
	In a seal on shoulder, tapered top and ring, Dr. Olive, 3 Pt.		
	mold, 12¼"	60.00	75.00
☐482	**DR. PLANETTS BITTERS**		
	Iron pontil, aqua, 9¾"	70.00	90.00
☐483	**PLOW'S SHERRY BITTERS**		
	A large leaf on back of label, amber, 7¾"	350.00	425.00
☐484	**POMLO BITTERS CO.**		
	N.Y. on back, tapered top and ring, light green, 11½"	65.00	85.00
☐485	**POND'S BITTERS CO. CHICAGO**		
	Label, Ponds Genuine Ginger Brandy on back, clear,		
	11½"	22.00	29.00
☐486	**POND'S BITTERS**		
	Reverse side Unexcelled Laxative, on base 76, amber,		
	9¾"	42.00	47.00
☐487	*Same except machine made, clear*	18.00	24.00
☐488	**POOR MAN'S FAMILY BITTERS**		
	Ringed top, aqua, 6½"	30.00	40.00
☐489	*Same except label reads POOR MAN'S BITTERS CO.,*		
	OSWEGO N.Y., Entered according to Act of Congress in		
	1870	45.00	60.00
☐490	**DR. POTER'S STOMACH BITTERS**		
	(Dr. Poter New York), rectangular bottle, labeled, clear		
	glass, embossed, round boud top, 5½"	15.00	20.00
☐491	**R.W. POWERS & CO. AROMATIC PERUVIAN BITTERS**		
	Rich. Va. 1881, amber, 10½"	75.00	95.00
☐492	**PRICKLEY ASH BITTER CO.**		
	In two line in sunken panel, other sides are flat for labels,		
	beveled corners, 2¾" x 2¾", 10"	25.00	32.00
☐493	**PRUSSIAN BITTERS**		
	Tapered top, amber, 9½"	55.00	75.00
☐494	**PRUNE STOMACH & LIVER BITTERS**		
	(The best cathartic & blood purifier), square, amber, on		
	base 2280, tapered top, 9"	85.00	105.00

Q

☐495	**THE QUININE BITTER CO.**		
	184-196 Congress St. Chicago, Ill. U.S.A., diamond shape,		
	concave sides, clear, 8½"	60.00	80.00

R

☐496	**RAMSEY'S TRINIDAD BITTER** *on shoulder*		
	(Bitters misspelled on bottom), dark olive, 8¼"	80.00	100.00

☐ 497 **RAMSEY'S TRINIDAD BITTERS**
Round, dark olive, body 5", 3¼" neck on a shoulder, under bottom, Ramsey Trinidad Bitter (no date) 50.00 70.00

☐ 498 **DR. MILLER'S RATAFIA,** *(Sphinx)*
Under it, Damiana Silbe Bros. Jr. Plagemann, S.F. sole agents, Pacific Coast, round bottle, tapered and ringed top, amber, 12" 55.00 75.00

☐ 499 **RED CLOUD BITTERS**
Square bottle, "TAYLOR & WRIGHT Chicago", green, also amber, 9½" 100.00 120.00

☐ 500 **RED JACKET BITTERS**
Square bottle, "BENNET & PIETERS", amber, 9½" 65.00 85.00

☐ 501 **RED JACKET BITTERS**
Rectangular bottle, "MON-HEIMER & CO.", amber, 8½" . 50.00 65.00

☐ 502 **REED'S BITTERS**
(In back curved letters Reed's Bitters), round, lady's leg neck, on ring, 12½" 200.00 250.00

☐ 503 **DR. RENZ'S HERB BITTERS**
Tapered and ring top, light green, 9" 60.00 80.00

☐ 504 **REX BITTERS CO., CHICAGO**
Whiskey shape, amber, clear, 10¼" 35.00 48.00

☐ 505 **REX KIDNEY & LIVER BITTERS**
Square bottle, in back "LAXATIVE & BLOOD PURIFIER", red amber, 10" 55.00 75.00

☐ 506 **RICHARDS, C.A. & Co.**
18 & 20 Kilby St., Boston, Mass., amber, label stated wine bitters, 9½", with label 55.00 75.00

☐ 507 *Same as above, without label* 30.00 40.00

☐ 508 **S.O. RICHARDSON** *vertically on front*
Bitters So. Reading on side, other side Mass., flared top, pontil, light green, 6½" 60.00 80.00

☐ 509 **R.C. RIDGWAY & PHILA.**
Big 3 under bottom, amber, 11" 80.00 105.00

☐ 510 **RIVAUD'S** *(reverse apostrophe)* **IMPERIAL BITTERS**
Victor Rivaud on side, Louisville Ky on other side, amber, 10½" 85.0 110.00

☐ 511 **DR. C.W. ROBACKS**
Cincinnati, O, in small circle in center, Stomach Bitters, dark brown, barrel shape, ten ribs on top, ten ribs on base, 9¾" 160.00 215.00

☐ 512 **ROCK CITY BITTERS**
50¢ size in two lines, side mold, amber, 7½" 70.00 90.00

☐ 513 **ROHRER'S**
On one side Lancaster Pa., on the other side Expectoral-Wild Cherry Tonic, 10½" 90.00 115.00

☐ 514 **ROMAINES CRIMEAN BITTERS**
Fancy square, amber, "PATEND 1863", on base, 10" 160.00 210.00

☐ 515 **E.J. ROSE'S**
Superior Tonic, Cathartic and Blood Purifier on back, amber, 9" 55.00 75.00

☐ 516 **ROSSWINKLE'S CROWN BITTERS**
Square bottle, amber, tapered top, 8¾" 60.00 80.00

☐517 **S.B. ROTHENBERG**
*In a semicircle inside of which is SOLE / AGENT / U.S. /,
the reverse has an applied blob seal stamped PAT.
APPLIED FOR, bottle is in the shape of asquare face gin,
milk glass color, top, 8½" tall, 2" at base, 3" at shoulder* . 70.00 90.00

☐518 **ROYAL ITALIAN BITTERS**
Round, tall, red amber, wine type bottle, 13½" 85.00 105.00

☐519 **ROYAL PEPSIN STOMACH BITTERS**
Amber, 8½" 75.00 95.00

☐520 *Same as above, except no embossing* 15.00 20.00

☐521 **W.L. RUCHARDSON'S BITTERS**
Pontil, rectangular bottle, "MASS.", aqua, 7" 80.00 100.00

☐522 *Same except no pontil* 35.00 48.00

☐523 **RUSH'S BITTERS**
*Square bottle, "A.H. FLANDERS, M.D. N.Y."' aqua, pint
size* 10.00 14.00

☐524 *Same as above, amber, 9"* 30.00 40.00

☐525 **RUSS'S ST. DOMINGO BITTERS**
Square bottle, NEW YORK, amber, also olive green, 10" .. 50.00 65.00

☐526 **DR. RUSSELL'S ANGOSTURA BITTERS**
Round tapered top, amber, medium green, clear, 7¾" 90.00 115.00

☐527 *Same except olive green (rare)* 85.00 110.00

S

☐528 **SAIDSCHITSER-FURSTLICH-LOBKOWITZ BITTER
WASSER**
In circle, tan crock, four panels, round bottom, 9½" 90.00 115.00

☐529 **SAINSEVINS WINE BITTERS**
Label, ringed top, aqua, 12" 18.00 24.00

☐530 **SALMON'S PERFECT STOMACH BITTERS**
Tapered top, square beveled corners, amber, 9½" 80.00 100.00

☐531 **SANBORN'S KIDNEY & LIVER VEGETABLE LAXATIVE
BITTERS**
*On bottom B, tapered bottle to paneled shoulder with
fluted neck, amber, 10"* 90.00 115.00

☐532 **SAN JOAQUIN WINE BITTERS**
*On back at bottom B. F. C. Co., deep kick-up in base,
amber, 9¾"* 40.00 55.00

☐533 **SARSAPARILLA BITTERS**
*On side E. M. Rusha, back side Dr. De Andrews, amber,
10"* 55.00 75.00

☐534 **SAZERAC AROMATIC BITTERS**
*In a circle on shoulder in monogram DPH & Co., milk
glass, also in blue, green, 12½"* 250.00 325.00

☐535 **SAZERAC AROMATIC BITTERS**
D.P.H. in seal, lady's leg shape, light amber, 10¼" 175.00 235.00

☐536 **DR. S.B. & CO.**
ML under bottom, clear or amethyst, 7¼" 6.00 8.00

☐537 **SCHROEDER'S BITTERS**
*Louisville, Ky-in three lines, base in one line, Ky.G.W.Co.,
lady's leg, ring top, amber, 11½"* 200.00 250.00

☐538 *Same except tapered top and ring, 5½"* 215.00 270.00

☐539 **SEGRESTAT BITTERS** *in seal*
Kick-up bottom, dark olive, 11¾" 70.00 90.00

☐540 **SEGUR'S GOLDEN SEAL BITTERS, SPRINGFIELD, MASS.**
Pontil, aqua, 8" 85.00 110.00

☐541 **W. F. SEVERA**
On back Stomach Bitters, tapered top, red amber, 10".... 35.00 48.00

☐542 **SHERMAN BITTERS**
Myer Bros. Drug. Co., St. Louis, label, amber, 7¾" 10.00 14.00

☐543 **DR. B.F. SHERMAN'S PRICKLY ASH BITTERS**
Machine made, amber, 10" 8.00 10.00

☐544 **SIMONS AROMATIC STOMACH BITTERS**
Clear or amber, 7¼" 70.00 90.00

☐545 **SIMONS CENTENNIAL BITTERS TRADE MARK**
Bust shape bottle, double ring top, amber, clear or aqua,
10¼" 285.00 340.00

☐546 **DR. SIMS ANTI-CONSTIPATION BITTERS**
Amber, 6½" 65.00 85.00

☐547 **DR. SKINNER'S CELEBRATED 25 CENT BITTERS**
So. Reading, Mass., pontil, aqua, 9½" 80.00 100.00

☐548 **DR. SKINNER'S SHERRY WINE BITTERS**
Rectangular bottle, "SO. READING MASS.", aqua, pontil,
8½" 85.00 110.00

☐549 **S.C. SMITH'S DRUID BITTERS**
Barrel shape bottle, brown, 9½" 165.00 200.00

☐550 **DR. SMITHS COLUMBO BITTERS**
Label and embossed, amber, 9¾" 30.00 40.00

☐551 **SNYDER BITTERS**
Jonesboro, Ark., tapered top, amber, 9½" 60.00 75.00

☐552 **SOMER'S STOMACH BITTERS**
Square shape bottle, amber, 9½" 65.00 80.00

☐553 **SOLOMON'S STRENGTHENING & INVIGORATING BITTER**
On one sunken panel, on the other "Savannah Ga.", on
other side, sunken panels, back flat, roofed shoulders,
beveled corner, cobalt, 9½" 250.00 325.00

☐554 **DR. SPERRY'S FEMALE STENGTHENING BITTERS**
Waterbury, Conn., label and embossed, 10" 90.00 115.00

☐555 **STAAKE'S ORIGINAL VITAL-TONE BITTERS**
Around shoulder, ringed top, clear, 8¼" 50.00 65.00

☐556 **STANDARD AMERICAN AROMATIC BITTERS CORDIAL**
Yochim Bros in seven lines, New Orleans, round bottle,
tapered top and ring, quart, amber, 10½" 18.00 24.00

☐557 **S. STANLEY & CO. AFRICAN STOMACH BITTERS**
Amber, 9½" 55.00 75.00

☐558 **STAR KIDNEY & LIVER BITTERS**
Tapered top, amber, 9½" 32.00 43.00

☐559 *Same as above with label* 37.00 48.00

☐560 **STEINFIELD'S BITTERS**
Light amber, tapered top, in back on shoulder First Prize-
Paris, 10" 100.00 125.00

☐561 **STEKETEES BLOOD PURIFYING BITTERS**
Amber, 9½" 60.00 75.00

☐562 **DR. STEWARTS TONIC BITTERS**
Columbus Ohio under bottom, amber, 8" 50.00   65.00

☐563 **ST. GOTTHARDS BITTERS**
Amber, 8½" 75.00   95.00

☐564 **ST. GOTTHARDS HERB BITTERS**
Amber, 8½" 55.00   70.00

☐565 **STONGHTON BITTERS**
Clear, 7" 18.00   24.00

☐566 **DR. STOEVER'S BITTERS**
Established 1837, square, "KRYER & CO.", amber, 9" 75.00   95.00

☐567 **SUFFOLK BITTERS**
Other side Philbrook & Tucker, Boston, shape of a pig, ground lip, light amber, 9½" x 3½" 400.00   550.00

☐568 **SUMTER BITTERS**
On front and back Charleston S.C., on back Dowie Moise & Davis Wholesale Druggist, amber, 9½" 90.00   115.00

☐569 **SUN KIDNEY & LIVER BITTERS**
Square bottle, "VEGETABLE LAXATIVE", amber, machine made, 9½" 50.00   65.00

☐570 **SWAN'S, C.H.**
on back Bourbon Bitters, square, tapered top, beveled corners, amber, 9" 70.00   90.00

☐571 **DR. SWEET STRENGTHENING BITTERS**
Long tapered top, aqua, 8¼" 55.00   70.00

T

☐572 **THORN'S HOP & BURDOCK TONIC BITTERS**
Square bottle, "BRATTLEBORO, VT.", amber, label states this is a bitters, 8" 15.00   20.00

☐573 **TIP-TOP BITTERS**
Multi-sided bottle, labeled only, amber, 8½" 15.00   20.00

☐574 **TIPPECANOE**
Amber, clear, aqua, 9" 75.00   95.00

☐575 **TIPPECANOE**
Misspelled Rochester under bottom, amber, 9" 80.00   105.00

☐576 **TODD'S BITTERS**
Machine made, clear, 8¼" 10.00   14.00

☐577 **TONOLA BITTERS**
Trade mark Eagle, square, aqua, "PHILADELPHIA", 8" .. 60.00   75.00

☐578 **TONECO STOMACH BITTERS**
Square bottle, tapered top, "APPETIZER & TONIC", clear glass, ABM 30.00   40.00

☐579 **TONECO BITTERS**
Clear, under bottom a diamond shape with number 35.00   45.00

☐580 **OLD DR. TOWNSEND CELEBRATED STOMACH BITTERS**
In six lines, handled jug, amber, plain band, pontil, 8¾" .. 160.00   210.00

☐581 **TRAVELLERS BITTERS**
A man with a cane standing up, oval, amber, 1834-1870, 10½" 270.00   340.00

☐582 **TUFTS ANGOSTURA BITTERS**
Label, green, 9¾" 15.00   20.00

☐583 **TUFTS TONIC BITTERS**
Rectangular bottle, labeled only, aqua, 9" 10.00 14.00
☐584 **TURNER BROTHERS N.Y.**
Buffalo N.Y., San Francisco Calif., tapered top, pontil,
amber, 9½" 160.00 210.00
☐585 **TYLER'S STANDARD AMERICAN BITTERS**
Square bottle, amber, 9" 85.00 110.00
☐586 **TURNER'S BITTERS**
Rectangular, clear glass, 8" 60.00 75.00

U

☐587 **THE ULLMAN**
Einstein Co., Cleveland, O., Germania Mager Bitters —
back and front labels, complete label information, under
bottom a diamond in center of it, #337, golden amber, ring
top, round should, 3 blob in neck 115.00 140.00
☐588 **ULMER MT. ASH BITTERS**
Aqua, 7" 85.00 110.00
☐589 **UNCLE TOM'S BITTERS**
Square bottle, "THOMAS FOULD & SON", Trevorton, Pa.,
pale amber, tapered top, 10" 95.00 125.00
☐590 **UNDERBERG-ALBRECHT**
On base H.U.A., round bottle, labeled, red-amber, lady's
leg neck, also ABM, 12" 18.00 24.00
☐591 **UNIVERSAL BITTERS**
Pontil, aqua 100.00 125.00
☐592 **UNIVERSAL BITTERS**
Mfg. by Aug. Horstmann Sole Agent F.J. Schaefer, 231
Market St. Louisville, Ky, lady's leg shape, emerald green,
12" 300.00 380.00
☐593 **UNKA**
Within a ball on front, picture of an eagle on top of the
ball, Army & Navy around all this, Unka Bitters 1895 under
all this, label, tapered and ringed top, amber, 8½" 25.00 34.00
☐594 **USAACSON SEIXAS & CO.**
Other side reads 66 & 68 Common St., C.O. Witheye, bit-
ters monogram under it, bulged neck, tapered and ring
top, kick-up 75.00 95.00
☐595 **U.S. OF COLOMBIA**
Colon on bottom, Bitters Colombian around shoulder,
tapered top and ring, 3-piece mold, black, beer type bottle,
8½" 65.00 85.00
☐596 **U.S. GOLD BITTERS**
(In center $20 Gold Piece, Marked on roof), square, aqua,
U.S. 1877, (Reg. in U.S. Patent Office), 10" 175.00 225.00
☐597 **USQEBAUGH BITTERS**
High domed, square tapered bottle, aqua, 10½" 70.00 90.00

V

☐598 **VAN OPSAL & CO. MORNING DEW BITTERS, N.Y.**
Amber, 10½" 100.00 125.00

☐ 599 **VEGETABLE STOMACH BITTERS**
Reverse side Dr. Ball's, Northboro, Mass., aqua, 7¼" 80.00 105.00

☐ 600 **VERMO STOMACH BITTERS**
Reverse side Tonic & Appetizer, tapered top, machine made, 9½" 35.00 47.00

☐ 601 **VICTORIA TONIC BITTERS**
(William & Ross, L & W), square bottle, "MEMPHIS, TENN.", pale amber, 9½" 90.00 115.00

☐ 602 **PETER VIERLING'S BLOOD PURIFYING BITTERS**
Square bottle, amber, 10" 85.00 110.00

☐ 603 **DR. VON HOPF'S CURACO BITTERS**
Chamberlain & Co. Des Moines, Iowa on back, amber, 9¼" 45.00 60.00

☐ 604 **VON HUMBOLDT,**
German bitters in 2 lines, on one side liver complaint other dyspepsia & Co. domed panels on all sides, Double rings top, pontil, 6¼", aqua 120.00 165.00

☐ 605 **ALEX VON HUMBOLDT**
on back stomach bitters square beveled corners, base a dot, ring & tapered top, lt. amber, 10¼" 75.00 95.00

☐ 606 **ALEX VON HUMBOLDT'S STOMACH BITTERS**
Square bottle, pale amber, 10" 80.00 105.00

W

☐ 607 **WAHOO & CALISAYA BITTERS**
Near shoulder on two sides, Jaocob Pinkerton, on roofed shoulder Y!! - Y!!, 1,M - ok, amber, tapered top, 10" 115.00 140.00

☐ 608 **WAITS KIDNEY & LIVER BITTERS**
In back, three lines, Calif. own, true laxative and blood purifier on bottom P.C.G.W., amber, tapered top and ring, 9" 45.00 60.00

☐ 609 **J. WALKER VINEGAR BITTERS**
Aqua, 8½" 10.00 14.00

☐ 610 **WALLACE'S TONIC STOMACH BITTERS**
(George Powell & Co., Chicago, Ill.), square bottle, amber, base L & G, 9" 70.00 90.00

☐ 611 **WAMPOO BITTERS**
On other side, Siegel & Bro., N.Y., amber, tapered top and ring, 10" 50.00 65.00

☐ 612 **C.H. WARD'S EXCELSIOR BITTERS**
Rectangular bottle, "C.H. WARD & CO.", clear glass, 8" .. 45.00 60.00

☐ 613 **WARNERS SAFE BITTERS**
Figure of a safe in center, on base Rochester N.Y., oval shape, round collar, amber, 9¾" 90.00 115.00

☐ 614 **DR. WARNER'S OLD QUAKER BITTERS**
Old Dr. Warner's on one side, Quaker Bitters on other, aqua, rectangular, 9½" 65.00 85.00

☐ 615 **WARNER SAFE TONIC BITTERS**
Pint, various shades of amber 175.00 225.00
☐ 616 *Same as above, except ½ pint* 150.00 200.00
☐ 617 *Same as above, except square ring top* 90.00 115.00

☐618 **WARNER'S SAFE TONIC BITTERS**
(On a base A & DHC), oval bottle, labeled, "ROCHESTER,
N.Y.", amber, embossed, 9¼" 80.00   105.00

☐619 **WARNERS SAFE BITTERS**
Ring top under bottom A.U.D.H.C., amber, 7¾" 135.00   165.00

☐620 *Same as above, except plain smooth bottom, 7½"* 175.00   225.00

☐621 *Same as above, except square ring top* 90.00   115.00

☐622 **WEIS MEDICINE CO.**
The Dr. H.F. Guard on the Rhine-Stomach Bitters-Dayton,
Ohio in four lines running vertically; ring top, amber, 9¼" 80.00   105.00

☐623 **WEST INDIA STOMACH BITTERS**
(W.I.M.C.); square, amber, "ST. LOUIS, MO.", base 10" ... 65.00   85.00

☐624 **WHEELER'S BERLIN BITTERS**
Hexagonal, olive green, "BALTIMORE", iron pontil, 9½" . 300.00   375.00

☐625 **DR. WHEELER'S TONIC SHERRY WINE BITTERS**
Round, pontil, plain or aqua, 8¼" 90.00   115.00

☐626 **WHITE'S STOMACH BITTERS**
Square bottle, amber, 9⅜" 65.00   85.00

☐627 **WHITEWELL'S TEMPERENCE BITTERS**
Boston; pontil, aqua, 7" 140.00   170.00

☐628 **WILD CHERRY & BLOOD ROOT JAUNDICE BITTERS**
Round bottle, labeled only, aqua, 9½" 18.00   24.00

☐629 **WILD CHERRY BITTERS**
Mfg. by C.C. Richards & Co. Yarmouth N. S. L. & Co.; aqua,
6¼" 60.00   80.00

☐630 **EDW. WILDER & CO.**
Edw. Wilder Stomach Bitters on back; Patented 5 on one
roof; very light green, 10½" 170.00   220.00

☐631 **WILDERS STOMACH BITTERS**
(Edw. Wilder Co.); square cabin shape bottle, "WHOLE-
SALE DRUGGISTS", Louisville, Ky., clear glass, 10½" ... 140.00   170.00

☐632 **DR. WILSON'S HERBINE BITTERS**
(Bragley Sons & Co., Montreal); oval, aqua, 8½" 70.00   90.00

☐633 *(Edw. Wilder Co.), also 6"* 70.00   90.00

☐634 **J. T. WIGGINS GENTION BITTERS**
Ribbed sides, amber, 11" 60.00   75.00

☐635 **WILMERDING & CO.**
Sole agents for Peruvian Bitters, 214 & 216 Front St. S.F.
in a circle; flask shape bottle, amber, 6" 350.00   425.00

☐636 **L.Q.C. WISHART'S**
Pine tree trademark on one side; Pine Tree Tar Cordial
Phila on other side; different sizes and colors 90.00   115.00

☐637 **DR. WISTERS OXYGENATED BITTERS FOR DYSPEPSIA &**
GENERAL DEBILITY
Pontil, aqua, 6" 130.00   170.00

☐638 **DR. WONSER'S U.S. INDIAN ROOT BITTERS**
Fancy round type bottle, tapered top, amber, 10½" 390.00   485.00

☐639 *Same as above, except aqua* 500.00   625.00

☐640 **N. WOOD'S BILOUS BITTERS**
Rectangular bottle, labeled only, aqua, Portland, Maine,
6" 12.00   16.00

☐641 **WOODCOCK PEPSIN BITTERS**
(JOHN SCHROEDER), rectangular, smoky amber 95.00   120.00

☐642 **WOODBURY'S BITTERS**
Steinhardt Bros. & Co., N.Y., round bottle, tapered top,
amber, 8" 40.00 52.00
☐643 **WOOD'S TONIC**
Wine Bitter on side, Cincinnati, Ohio other side, aqua 60.00 75.00
☐644 **WRYGHTE'S BITTERS**
Appears on all four sides, London also appears on four
sides, ringed top, pontil, dark olive, 5¾" 90.00 115.00

Y

☐645 **YAZOO VALLEY BITTERS**
(Fulton M. McRae), amber, 8¾" 70.00 90.00
☐646 **YOCHIM BROS. CELEBRATED STOMACH BITTERS**
Amber, 8¾" 70.00 85.00
☐647 **YERBA BUENA BITTERS***
Flask bottle, "S.F. CAL.", amber, 8⅜" 80.00 100.00
☐648 **DR. YOUNGS WILD CHERRY BITTERS-BROOKLYN, N.Y.**
Amber, 8½" 85.00 105.00

Z

☐649 **ZOELLER'S STOMACH BITTERS**
Rectangular bottle, amber, 9½" 80.00 100.00
☐650 **ZINGARI BITTERS**
Round bottle, lady's leg neck, amber, 11¾" 190.00 240.00
*Other "Yerba Buena" Bottles 190.00 240.00
Dark amber, pint bottle 125.00 150.00

COSMETIC

The category cosmetic includes all bottles that contained products to improve or beautify personal appearance, as well as perfume bottles. Because of the nature of their contents, and the class of people who purchased them, these bottles were frequently designed to be eye-appealing. Not only would an attractive bottle promote impulse sales, it stood to be selected over others for its decorative contributions to milady's dressing table. Thus, competition was keen among manufacturers not only to have the best products, but also (and sometimes more so) to sell them in the most appealing containers. Unfortunately for the glass bottle buff, the substance used for making bottles was often ceramic.

Cosmetic bottles include a number of well-executed figurals — including the Avons of today. In the main, however, they are *not* figurals but are decorative in other ways, such as the use of imaginative variations on standard traditional shapes, attractive color, and artistic embossing. Most of the brand names are a thing of the past, but some familar ones will be encountered, such as Colgate.

The European cosmetic industry had a long head start on America's, and the U.S. manufacturers mostly styled their products, as well as the containers for them, after foreign prototypes. It is sometimes claimed that cosmetics, in the form of perfume, were the earliest products to be stored or distributed in bottles. This may or may not be so; certainly, wine was kept in bottles in the distant past. In any event, glass bottles known to have contained perfumes and sweet oils used in embalming can be traced to the 18th dynasty of Egypt (3,000 B.C., or 5,000 years ago).

Cosmetics were used extensively in the ancient world. Prepared perfumes and colored grease used in the fashion of modern lipstick and rouge could be bought from dealers, as well as all sorts of other preparations. To judge from historical accounts, the Roman empresses and all the leading ladies (as well as, in fact, many of the leading men) of ancient times made themselves up heavily. The cosmetics industry waned in the Middle Ages, but revived grandly in the Renaissance and has flourished uninterrupted since.

Cosmetics have not always served the same purpose as today. Traditionally, the use of perfumes and aromatic lotions was to hide body odors. Our ancestors bathed infrequently, the usual excuse being given as the lack of running water or other facilities. One contemporary observer of those days wrote that the combination of perfumes plus body odor was worse than if no perfume had been used.

As bathing gradually caught on during the 19th century, fragrances in perfumes were toned down and made more delicate.

The most celebrated American maker of perfume bottles in the 18th century was Casper Wistar, whose factory was founded in New Jersey in 1739. Martha Washington's perfume bottle, which she carried at all times, is said to have been made by Wistar. Another well-known domestic manufacturer of perfume bottles in the 18th century was Henry William Stiegel. He entered the trade in 1763. While Wistar's bottles were mainly plain and functional, those of Stiegel include many decorative specimens that appeal greatly to collectors.

In the 1840's Solon Palmer of Cincinnati began to manufacture and sell perfumes. A few had rather unusual names, Jockey Club and Baby Ruth among them. Though Jockey Club definitely carried sporting overtones, Baby Ruth had no connection with the Yankee baseball star. It was introduced well before his time and referred to Ruth Cleveland, baby daughter of President Cleveland. In 1871, Solon Palmer moved to New York and by 1879 his products were being retailed in drugstores throughout the country. Palmer bottles are appealing to collectors, because of their brilliant emerald green color.

So-called "Charley Ross Bottles," containing perfume, appeared around 1880. These are of great interest to collectors for their historical overtones. Young Charley Ross was kidnapped in Pennsylvania in 1874 and never heard from again. The case became one of the major news stories. Charley Ross perfume bottles were sponsored by the child's father, who saw this as a means of reminding the public of his son's name and thereby perhaps finding clues or leads. The bottles carry a likeness of a youth's face, but it was to no avail.

Perfumes for men became popular in the second half of the 19th century. Left to themselves, American males might not have adopted the use of colognes and other fragrances this early, but they were very popular in Europe, and whatever was current or fashionable in Europe was sure to be copied in the U.S. Just as manufacturers of bitters and other preparations often overstated their virtues, makers of perfumes and colognes were guilty of this as well. A trade card for Florida Water, an after-shave lotion, claimed it to be "the richest, most lasting, yet most delicate of all perfumes for use on the handkerchief, at the toilette and in the bath, delightful and healthful in the sickroom. Relieves weakness, fatigue, prostration, nervousness, and headache." Whatever benefits derived from its use were probably attributable to the alcoholic content which ran to 75%.

Avon had its beginnings in the 1880's. David H. McConnell, a door-to-door book salesman, began luring prospective customers by giving away sample vials of perfume. His book sales increased, but he soon discovered that customers showed more interest in the perfume than in the books. In 1886, he established the California Perfume Co. in New York which in 1939 changed its name to Avon.

COSMETIC

A

NO.	DESCRIPTION	PRICE RANGE	
☐ 1	**AUBRY SISTERS**		
	Pat Aug 22, 1911 under bottom, milk glass, 1"	1.25	.25

B

☐ 2	**C. R. BAILEY**		
	Aqua, 3½"	5.00	7.00
☐ 3	**BAKER'S PERFUME**		
	Ring top, clear, 3"	4.50	6.50
☐ 4	**BALDWINS QUEEN BESS PERFUME**		
	Reverse side Sample Baldwins Perfume, label, ring top, 5½"	7.00	10.00

☐ 5 *BARBER BOTTLE, milk glass, ring top, 4¾" x 2½", sunken panel on front of bottle for label, round, 9"* **15.00** **20.00**

☐ 6 *BARBER BOTTLE, label, clear or amethyst, 7¼"* **8.00** **11.00**

☐ 7 *BARBER BOTTLE, label, milk glass, 12"* **20.00** **25.00**

☐ 8 *BARBER BOTTLE, label, clear or amethyst, 10½"* **11.00** **15.00**

☐ 9 *BARBER BOTTLE, label, aqua, 8"* **6.00** **9.00**

☐ 10 *BARBER BOTTLE, label, blue green, 8½"* **16.00** **21.00**

☐ 11 *BARBER BOTTLE, label, aqua, 8½"* **10.00** **14.00**

☐ 12 *BARBER BOTTLE, plain, red, 3½"* **15.00** **20.00**

☐ 13 **BAY RUM**
On one panel, Barber bottle, six 1¾" panels, root type shoulder, lady's leg neck, neck 3¼", ring top, milk glass, body, neck and shoulder 4½" **22.00** **30.00**

☐ 14 *BELL, plain, perfume, clear, 2" round, 3"* **6.00** **9.00**

☐ 15 *BOOT, perfume label, clear or amethyst, 3½"* **13.00** **18.00**

☐ 16 **BRUNO COURT PERFUMEUR**
Green with gold neck, 5½" **10.00** **14.00**

C

☐ 17 **CALIF. PERFUME CO.**
Fruit flavors on the front of panel, rectangular, amethyst, 5½" **15.00** **20.00**

☐ 18 **CARD COLOGNE** *or* **OPIUM SQUARE**
Decorated, frosted, tapered **4.50** **7.00**

☐ 19 **C CO.**
Perfume, fancy shape, screw top, clear, 3¼" **4.50** **7.00**

☐ 20 **CHAPOTEAUT**
Reverse side Paris, BL4063 on bottom, clear or amethyst, 2¾" **3.00** **4.00**

☐ 21 **CHAPOTEAUT**
On back Paris, clear **3.00** **4.00**

☐ 22 **CHRISTIAN DIOR**
Clear, 4" **8.00** **11.00**

☐ 23 **CHRISTIANI DE PARIS**
Perfume, fancy shape, thin flared lip, open pontil, aqua, 3⅜" **30.00** **38.00**

☐ 24 **CLARKE & CO.**
Woodard under bottom, cosmetic, square, cobalt, 4¼" .. **6.00** **9.00**

☐ 25 **C. L. Q. CO.**
Under bottom, inside screw, clear or amethyst, 4¼" **7.00** **10.00**

☐ 26 **C.M.**
Label, clear, 1¾" **3.00** **4.00**

☐ 27 **COLGATE & CO.**
Clear or amethyst, 6¼" **6.00** **8.00**

☐ 28 **COLGATE & CO., NEW YORK**
In a circle, through center of circle PERFUMERS, clear or amethyst, 3⅝" **3.00** **4.00**

☐ 29 **COLGATE & CO.**
New York on back, clear, 4¾" **4.00** **6.00**

☐ 30 **COLGATE & CO. NEW YORK**
On bottom, fancy shape, five concave panels on side, step on shoulder, ring collar, amethyst, 5¼" **6.00** **8.00**

☐	31	**COLGATE & CO. N.Y. COLEO SHAMPOO** *X on sides, flask, AMB, amethyst*	3.50	6.00
☐	32	**COLGATE & CO. PERFUMER 4 N.Y.** *On bottom, machine made, clear, 4¼"*	3.00	4.00
☐	33	**COLGATE & CO. PERFUMERS, NEW YORK** *Rectangular, long neck, amethyst, 3⅝"*	4.00	5.75
☐	34	**COLGATE AND CO. PERFUMERS, N.Y.** *On one panel, rectangular, amethyst or clear, 3¾"*	6.00	8.00
☐	35	*COLOGNE, decorated trunk and shoulder, applied lip, six panels, amethyst or clear, 5¼"*	4.00	6.00
☐	36	*COLOGNE, cathedral type, ring top, 1¼" square at bottom, improved pontil, cobalt, 5¾"*	75.00	95.00
☐	37	*COLOGNE, label, fancy shape, panels, milk glass, 7¼"* ..	22.00	28.00
☐	38	*COLOGNE, label, fancy shape, open pontil, flared lip, aqua, 4¾"*	25.00	33.00
☐	39	*COLOGNE, label, 603 on bottom, clear or amethyst, 3"* ...	3.00	4.00
☐	40	*COLOGNE or PEPPERSAUCE, label, five stars on three panels, light green, 7½"*	11.00	15.00
☐	41	*COLOGNE, label, pontil, cobalt, 8¾"*	15.00	20.00
☐	42	*COLOGNE, plain, round, clear or opalescent, 2¾"*	1.35	2.25
☐	43	*COSMETIC JAR, round, cream, 1¾" base 2¼"*	4.00	5.75
☐	44	*COSMETIC, plain, square, metal screw top, cobalt, 6"* ...	1.30	2.20
☐	45	*CREAM, label, milk glass, 2¼"*	1.30	2.20
☐	46	*CREAM, label, milk glass, 2"*	1.30	2.20
☐	47	*CREAM, label, tan, 2"*	2.50	3.50
☐	48	*CREAM, label, milk glass, 2"*	2.50	3.50
☐	49	*CREAM, label, milk glass, 2½"*	2.50	3.50
☐	50	*CREAM, label, tan, 2¾"*	2.50	3.50
☐	51	*CREAM, label, milk glass, 2½"*	2.50	3.50
☐	52	*CREAM, label, milk glass, 2¾"*	2.50	3.50
☐	53	*CREAM, label, milk glass, 1¾"*	2.50	3.50
☐	54	*CREAM, label, tan, 3¼"*	2.50	3.50
☐	55	*CREAM, label, milk glass, 2¾"*	2.50	3.50
☐	56	**CREME SIMON** *J.S. 80 under bottom, milk glass, sheared top, 2½"*	4.00	6.00
☐	57	**THE CROWN PERFUMERY CO.** *Amber, 2½"*	4.00	6.00
☐	58	**CRUSELLASH** *Wood marks, aqua, 11½"*	11.00	15.00
☐	59	**CUTEX** *Rectangular, frosted, 1½" x 1¾" x 2½"*	2.35	3.25

D

☐	60	**DAGGETT & RAMSDELL** *Perfect Cold Cream, Trade Mark Made in U.S.A. on base, round, screw top, clear, 2¾"*	1.25	2.15
☐	61	**DAYBROOKS DETROIT PERFUMERS** *On top in a round design, 3 on bottom, clear or amethyst, 6"*	4.00	6.00
☐	62	**DEPAS PERFUME** *Clear, 4"*	7.00	10.00

☐ 63	**DERWILLO** *On the front panel, For The Complexion on the back,* *tapered to shoulders, square, clear, 3¾"*	7.00	10.00
☐ 64	**DE VRY'S DANDERO-OFF HAIR TONIC** *Label, clear, 6½"*	5.00	7.00
☐ 65	**DOLL** *Figural, perfume, clear, 2½"*	11.00	15.00
☐ 66	**DRYDEN & PALMER** *D&P under bottom, clear, 7½"*	5.00	7.00

E

☐ 67	**EAGLE BRAND NOVA** *Milk glass, 1½"*	3.00	4.00
☐ 68	**MARIE EARLE, PARIS** *Under bottom, clear, 2¾"*	7.00	10.00
☐ 69	**EAU DENTIFRICE DU DOCTEUR, JEAU-PARIS** *In four lines, clear or amethyst, 3"*	3.00	4.00
☐ 70	**ELCAYA** *Milk glass*	2.35	3.20
☐ 71	**EMPRESS JOSEPHINE TOILET CO.** *Milk glass, 6¼"*	9.00	12.00

F

☐ 72	*FACE CREAM, label, cream and black, 1½"*	2.35	3.20
☐ 73	**FLORIDA WATER** *Label, clear, 568 on bottom, 7¼"*	4.00	6.00
☐ 74	**FLORIDA WATER** *Label, pontil, aqua, 8"*	7.00	10.00
☐ 75	**FRANCO AMERICAN HYGIENIC CO, CHICAGO** *On front panel, Toilet Requisites on left side, Franco-* *American on the right side, rectangular, amethyst, 6"* ...	6.00	8.00
☐ 76	**FRANCO AMERICAN HYGIENIC CO.** *Other side Franco American Toilet Requisites, clear, 1½"* *x 1½" base, 7"*	6.00	8.00
☐ 77	**FROSTILLA** *On front panel, Elmira N.Y., U.S.A. on side, Fragrant* *Lotion on other side, clear, 4½"*	5.00	7.00

G

☐ 78	*GERMAN ENAMELLED BOTTLE, on front, painted on* *panels: a girl drinking from a glass, in back: five lines in* *German script, on each side on a panel: flowers, seven* *panels in all, pontil, small crude neck, OF BOSTON, On* *bottom, cold cream, eight panels, screw top, amethyst,* *2½"*	3.00	40.00
☐ 79	*GERMAN ENAMELLED BOTTLE, hand painted, pontil,* *around 1650, blue green, 5½"*	150.00	190.00
☐ 80	**GOURAUD'S ORIENTAL CREAM** *New York on side, London other side, machine made 4¼"*	3.00	4.00

55

56 CREME SIMON

57 THE CROWN PERFUMERY COMPANY LONDON

58 CRUSELLAS PERFUMES HABANA

67 EAGLE BRAND NO.

70 ELCAYA

72

73

76 FRANCO-AMERICAN HYGIENIC CO. CHICAGO

78

87

95

121 S.W. LAIRD PERFUMER NEW YORK

122 Larkin Co. BUFFALO

123

139 FLORIDA WATER MURRAY & LANMAN

117 KERKOFF PARIS

146 THEO NOEL

151 PARIS

158 Palmer

160 Palmer

□	81	**L.L.E. GRAND**		
		P.L. on bottom, clear 3½"	6.00	8.00
□	82	**GRIMAULT & C^{IE}PARIS**		
		Reverse side PHARMACIE, DY, pontil, clear, 4"	19.00	26.00
□	83	**GUERLAIN PARIS**		
		Depose in back, clear, 6¾"	5.00	7.00
□	84	**GURRLAIN**		
		Eau Lustrale LUS other side, broken pontil, raspberry, 6¼"	18.00	25.00

H

□	85	**HAGANS MAGNOLIA BALM**		
		In three line on front, beveled corners, ring top, milk glass, 5"	11.00	15.00
□	86	*Same as above, except turned-under top, 4½"*	10.00	14.00
□	87	**HAIR OIL**		
		Label on back, amber, 10¼"	40.00	52.00
□	88	**HARMONY OF BOSTON**		
		On bottom, cold cream, eight panels, screw top, amethyst, 2½"	3.00	4.00
□	89	**HARRISON'S COLUMBIAN PERFUMERY**		
		Clear, 2¾"	6.00	8.00
□	90	**J. HAUEL**		
		Reverse Philadelphia, on side Perfumer, square, flared lip, open pontil, aua, 3"	23.00	32.00
□	91	**H.B. & H. N.Y.**		
		On shoulder, clear, 3½"	6.00	8.00
□	92	**C. HEEMSTREET & CO., TROY N.Y.**		
		Eight panels, ring top, pontil, blue, 7"	38.00	47.00
□	93	**HESSIG-ELLIS CHEMIST, MEMPHIS TENN**		
		Q Ban For The Hair on back, clear, 6½"	7.00	10.00
□	94	**HILBERT'S DELUXE PERFUMERY**		
		Flattened heart shape with long neck, clear, 3¼"	6.00	8.00
□	95	**H.J.**		
		Perfume label, 2¼"	3.50	4.50
□	96	**HOGG & CO.**		
		Three-cornered bottle, 8"	7.00	10.00
□	·97	**HOLT'S NICKEL COLOGNE**		
		In a sunken front panel, round, amethyst or clear, 2⅞" ...	4.00	6.00
□	98	**HOMATROPIN**		
		Perfume dropper, blue, 2"	11.00	15.00
□	99	**F HOYT & CO. PERFUMERS, PHILA.**		
		In sunken panel, round, amethyst, 3"	5.00	7.00
□	100	**HOYT'S**		
		Clear, 3¼"	3.50	4.50
□	101	**HUBBARD, HARRIET, AYER N.Y.**		
		In a square with monogram, 3¾" ounces on the trunk, square, screw top, clear, 4¾"	2.35	3.20
□	102	**HUBBARD, HARRIET, AYER N.Y.**		
		Cosmetic jar, milk glass, square, screw top, 1½" or 2½"	5.00	7.00

☐103 **RICHARD HUDNUT, N.Y.**
Monogram, 4 fl. Ozs. Net, rectangular, clear, 5¾" 2.35 3.20
☐104 **RICHARD HUDNUT, N.Y. U.S.A.**
With eagle and monogram, tapered neck, round, clear,
5¼" 5.00 7.00
☐105 **RICHARD HUDNUT PERFUMER N.Y.**
Square, amethyst, 3" or 3½" 3.00 4.50
☐106 **RICHARD HUDNUT**
Clear or amethyst, 3" 4.00 6.00
☐107 **RICHARD HUDNUT**
Machine made, clear, 4" 2.35 3.20
☐108 **C. W. HUTCHINS PERFUMER, NEW YORK**
Clear, 3¼" 3.00 4.00
☐109 **HYACINTHIA TOILET HAIR DRESSING**
Crude applied lip, open pontil, rectangular, aqua, 6" 24.00 33.00

I

☐110 **IMPERIAL CROWN PERFUMERY & CO.**
Clear, 5" 6.00 8.00
☐111 **INGRAMS MILKWEED CREAM**
On shoulder, screw top, milk glass jar, white, 2¼" 1.30 2.15
☐112 **INGRAMS SHAVING CREAM**
On shoulder, screw top, round, cobalt, 2¼" 5.00 7.00

J

☐113 **JEAN MARIE FARINA COLOGNE**
Six-sided, pontil, clear, 4⅝" 22.00 30.00
☐114 **JEWELETTE LABORATORIES, PERFUMERS, CHICAGO**
Clear, 8" 8.00 11.00
☐115 **JUILLET 1827, 28, 29, 30,**
Perfume, shaped like a harp with a rooster at base,
improved pontil, double coated with a turquoise milk
glass effect on the outside and a brilliant ultramarine
effect on the inside, 5¼" 130.00 160.00

K

☐116 **D. KERKOFF, PARIS**
Tapered, footed, rectangular, amethyst, 3¼" 1.30 2.15
☐117 **KERKOFF**
Clear or amethyst, 5¼" 4.00 6.00
☐118 **KIKEN ST. LOUIS**
Under bottom, label, clear or amethyst, 8¼" 7.00 10.00
☐119 **DR. KOCH'S TOILET ARTICLES, WINONA, MINN.**
Ring top, clear or amethyst, 5¼" 5.00 7.00
☐120 **KRANKS COLD CREAM**
Jar, milk glass, round, screw top, 2¾" 3.00 4.00

L

☐ 121 **G. W. LAIRD**
Milk glass, 4¾" 9.00 12.00

☐ 122 **LARKIN CO.**
Dark green, 1½" x 1¼" base, 3" 7.00 10.00

☐ 123 **LARKIN CO.**
Under bottom, milk glass, 2" 3.00 4.00

☐ 124 **L B**
Under bottom, clear or amethyst, 4" 6.00 8.00

☐ 125 **DR. H. HOWARD LEVY**
Milk glass, 1" 3.00 4.00

☐ 126 **L. H.**
On bottom, shape of a slipper, perfume, improved pontil,
flared lip, clear, 3½" long 30.00 40.00

☐ 127 **LIGHTNER'S HELIOTROPE PERFUMES**
Lightning on back, in center, hollow letters L.E.N. & Co.
Detroit, Mich., milk glass, 6½" 15.00 20.00

☐ 128 **LIGHTNER'S JOCKEY CLUB PERFUMES**
Lightning on back, in center, hollow letters L.E.N. & Co.
Detroit Mich., milk glass, 6½" 15.00 20.00

☐ 129 **LIGHTNER'S MAID OF THE MIST**
Lightning on back, in center, hollow letters L.E.N. & Co.
Detroit Mich., milk glass, 6½" 15.00 20.00

☐ 130 **LIGHTNER'S WHITE ROSE PERFUMES**
Lightning on back, in center, hollow letters L.E.N. & Co.,
Detroit Mich., milk glass, 6½" 15.00 20.00

☐ 131 **LIT. PIVER PARIS**
Under bottom, clear or amethyst, 3" 3.00 4.00

☐ 132 **LUBIN**
Clear, 1½" diameter, 3" 3.00 4.00

☐ 133 **LUBIN PARFUMERS PARIS**
Pontil, clear, 3½" 15.00 20.00

M

☐ 134 **MACK'S FLORIDA WATER**
Tapered top, aqua, 8½" 6.00 8.00

☐ 135 **MELBA**
Label, machine made, clear, 4¾" 4.00 6.00

☐ 136 **MINERALAVA FACE FINISH N.Y.**
Scotts Face Finish on back, clear, 5¼" 6.00 8.00

☐ 137 **MONELL'S TEETHING CORDIAL, N.Y.**
On three of eight panels, aqua, 1⅛" round 5" 5.00 7.00

☐ 138 **MORTON, CARPENTER CO., COLONITE BOSTON, MASS.**
Square, amethyst or clear, 4" 4.00 6.00

☐ 139 **MURRAY & LANMAN**
Machine made, aqua 3.00 4.50

☐ 140 **MURRAY & LANMAN, AGUA DE FLORIDA, NEW YORK**
6" or 9" 5.00 6.50

☐ 141 **MURRAY & LANMAN, AGUA DE FLORIDA, NO. 69 WATER ST., N.Y.**
Pontil, aqua, 9" 18.00 25.00

☐ 142 **MURRAY & LANMAN DRUGGISTS, FLORIDA WATER, NEW YORK**
In four vertical lines, aqua, 5½" body, 3¾" neck 5.00 7.00

☐ 143 *Same as above, except smaller bottle* 5.00 7.00

N

☐ 144 **NEWTON, LONDON**
Shape of a schoolhouse, flared lip, milk glass, 2⅝" 40.00 55.00

☐ 145 **THEO NOEL**
Aqua, 4½" 4.00 6.00

☐ 146 **NUIT DE MONE**
Around top, black glass, 3¾" 15.00 20.00

O

☐ 147 **OBOL**
Under bottom in sunken panel, Front and back 1¼" panels, plain, on each side three panels, three-part mold with short round neck facing out, ½" open on one side, milk glass, 2⅛" x ¾", 4¼" 12.00 18.00

☐ 148 *Same as above, except no writing, flat bottom, 2"* 10.00 13.00

☐ 149 **ORIENTAL CREAM**
On side, Gourands, New York, square bottle with short neck, clear or amethyst, 5¼" 5.00 7.00

☐ 150 **ORIZA-OIL L. LEGRAND PARIS**
Modele Exclush Depose on back, clear, 5¼" 3.50 4.75

P

☐ 151 **PALANGIE**
BL 2874 under bottom, clear, 5¾" 3.50 4.75

☐ 152 **PALMER**
In script, vertically on flat sides, some round bottles, emerald green, 4½" 11.00 15.00

☐ 153 **PALMER**
Metal crown, with Salon Palmer Perfumer and two stars, fancy shape, ribbed shoulders, emerald green, 5¾" 14.00 19.00

☐ 154 *Same as above, except with rings instead of ribs, glass stopper, Salon Palmer Perfumer on shoulder, 4½"* 13.00 18.00

☐ 155 **PALMER**
In script in center of bottle, ring top, 2" round, 4½" body, 2" neck 11.00 15.00

☐ 156 *Same as above, except oval, 7¼"* 11.00 15.00

☐ 157 **PALMER**
Clear or amethyst, 3¼" 4.00 6.00

☐ 158 **PALMER**
Clear, 2½" 4.00 6.00

☐ 159	**PALMER** Flat front, round back, blue green, 4¾"	12.00	16.00
☐ 160	**PALMER** C2 under bottom, oval shape, blue green, 5"	11.00	15.00
☐ 161	**PARIS PERFUME CO., JERSEY CITY, N.J.** **GUARANTEED FULL 2 OZ.** Ring top, clear or amethyst, 6"	5.00	7.00
☐ 162	**L. PAUTAUBERGE PHARMACIEU, PARIS** In three lines, on bottom R 6, 5862, beveled corners, cobalt, 2¼" square base, 6" body, 2" neck	16.00	21.00
☐ 163	**P.D.** On base, aqua, 4¾"	11.00	15.00
☐ 164	PERFUME, fancy shape, four sides, round ribs on three sides, one plain ring, ring top, ring vase type body, 3¼" tall, 2" neck	11.00	15.00
☐ 165	PERFUME, fancy shape, clear, 3"	9.00	12.00
☐ 166	PERFUME, label, aqua, 6½"	13.00	18.00
☐ 167	PERFUME, label, clear or amethyst, 6¼"	3.50	4.25
☐ 168	PERFUME, label, blue, 2¾"	4.00	6.00
☐ 169	PERFUME, label, fancy shape, clear, 3¼"	4.00	6.00
☐ 170	PERFUME, label, clear, 6½"	6.00	8.00
☐ 171	PERFUME, label, clear, 5½"	3.50	4.25
☐ 172	PERFUME, label, clear or amethyst, 3"	3.50	4.25
☐ 173	PERFUME, label, clear, 2¾"	4.00	6.00
☐ 174	PERFUME, label, various colored stripes around bottle, 2"	8.00	11.00
☐ 175	PERFUME, label, clear or amethyst, 3"	2.35	3.15
☐ 176	PERFUME, label, aqua, 6"	4.00	6.00
☐ 177	PERFUME, label, clear, sheared top, 2½"	8.00	11.00
☐ 178	PERFUME, label, pontil, clear or amethyst, 4"	14.00	19.00
☐ 179	PERFUME, label, aqua, 7½"	6.00	9.00
☐ 180	PERFUME, label, clear or amethyst, 4¾"	4.00	6.00
☐ 181	PERFUME, label, eight panels, clear or amethyst, 1¾" . .	3.50	4.25
☐ 182	PERFUME, label, pontil, aqua, 3¾"	16.00	21.00
☐ 183	PERFUME, label, clear, 5¼"	4.00	6.00
☐ 184	PERFUME, label, clear or amethyst, 5½"	16.00	21.00
☐ 185	PERFUME, label, pinch bottle, pontil, green, 6"	16.00	21.00
☐ 186	PERFUME, label, gold frame around bottle with marble on each corner, aqua, 4"	16.00	21.00
☐ 187	PERFUME, label, flat front, round back, clear, 6½"	6.00	8.00
☐ 188	PERFUME, label, pontil, clear, 12¼"	16.00	21.00
☐ 189	PERFUME, label, clear, 6½"	13.00	18.00
☐ 190	PERFUME, label, cut glass flower satin glass, sheared top, 5"	6.00	9.00
☐ 191	PERFUME, label, clear, 4"	3.50	4.25
☐ 192	PERFUME, label, clear, 6½"	12.00	16.00
☐ 193	PERFUME, label, pontil, cobalt, 5"	40.00	50.00
☐ 194	PERFUME, label, snail design, machine made, satin, clear, 7½"	6.00	8.00
☐ 195	PERFUME, label, flowers around bottle, square, milk glass, pontil, 5"	16.00	21.00
☐ 196	PERFUME, label, cobalt, 5½"	10.00	14.00
☐ 197	PERFUME, label, fancy shape, clear or amethyst, 3¼" . . .	3.50	5.00
☐ 198	PERFUME, label, fancy shape, clear or amethyst, 3¼" . . .	5.00	7.00
☐ 199	PERFUME, label, clear or amethyst, 3¾"	8.00	11.00

☐200	*PERFUME, ½ bell shaped, clear or amethyst, 3"*	8.00	11.00
☐201	*PERFUME, eight vertical panels, ring collar, glass stopper, improved pontil, clear, 3⅛"*	14.00	19.00
☐202	*PERFUME, fancy hand-painted gold-lead design, open pontil, deep purple appears black, 6½"*	30.00	40.00
☐203	*PERFUME, very ornate, fancy scroll work around gothic letter M, reverse side has blank oval area for label, flared lip, open pontil, clear, 4"*	40.00	50.00
☐204	*PERFUME, shaped like a clam shell, still has partial paper label with round mirror glue to label, very crude, open pontil, clear, 3½"*	45.00	60.00
☐205	*PERFUME, shaped like a woven basket with handles, small oval circle on front for paper label, open pontil, aqua, 2⅞"*	30.00	40.00
☐206	*PERFUME, figure of an Indian maiden sowing seeds on front, each side has a potted plant, fancy shape, fluted neck, clear, 4⅞"*	22.00	28.00
☐207	*PERFUME, violin or corset shaped, flared lip, open pontil, clear, 5⅜"*	45.00	58.00
☐208	*PERFUME, picture of an Indian holding a spear between gothic arches, open pontil, turquoise, 4"*	35.00	45.00
☐209	**PERFUMERIE** *Clear, 3½"*	3.00	5.00
☐210	**J. PICARD** *Clear, 3¼"*	2.35	3.15
☐211	**ED PINAUD** *Clear or amethyst, 7"*	5.00	7.00
☐212	**ED PINAUD** *Aqua, 6"*	4.00	6.00
☐213	**ED PINAUD** *Clear, 3¾"*	2.35	3.15
☐214	*PINCH BOTTLE SHAPED, plain, light amber, 3½" body, 4½" neck*	12.00	16.00
☐215	*Same as above, except smaller*	8.00	10.00
☐216	**POMPEIAN MASSAGE CREAM** *Clear or amethyst, 2¾"*	4.00	6.00
☐217	**POMPEIAN MFG. CO.** *Machine made, clear or amethyst, 3¼"*	3.00	4.00
☐218	**POND'S** *Milk glass, 1¾"*	2.00	3.00
☐219	**POND'S EXTRACT** *1846 on bottom, machine made, clear, 5½"*	4.00	6.00
☐220	**PREPARED BY N. SMITH PRENTISS, ESPRIT DE _____, NEW YORK** *Perfume, fancy shape, picture of young girl with an armful of flowers on front, on reverse an embossed vase and plant, open pontil, flared lip, aqua, 5½"*	50.00	65.00
☐221	**BY N. PRENTISS** *Reverse 28 John St. N. York, one side Bearsoil, other side Perfumes, square, flared lip, open pontil, clear, 2¾"*	38.00	52.00
☐222	*PUMPKIN SEED, perfume, plain, clear or amethyst, 3¼"* .	3.00	4.00
☐223	*PUMPKIN SEED, label, side strap, clear or amethyst, 3½"*	6.00	8.00

Q

□ 224	**QUENTIN**		
	Clear, 3"	3.50	4.25
□ 225	**Q. T.**		
	On base, perfume, monument shaped with round ball supported by eagles, flared lip, open pontil, clear, 5"	40.00	50.00

R

□ 226	**RICKSECKER'S**		
	Clear, 3½"	4.00	6.00
□ 227	**RIEGER'S CALIFORNIA PERFUMES**		
	Crooked neck, clear, 3¼"	7.00	10.00
□ 228	**R & M**		
	Shoe shaped, clear, 3½"	11.00	15.00
□ 229	**ROGER & GALLET**		
	Clear or amethyst, 4¾"	4.00	6.00
□ 230	**ROGER & GALLET PARIS**		
	On back, 8897 H.P. under bottom, clear or amethyst, 5½"	5.00	7.00
□ 231	**ROGER & GALLET**		
	Clear or amethyst, 4¼"	4.00	6.00
□ 232	**J. ROIG**		
	Clear, 3¼"	3.50	4.25
□ 233	**CHARLEY ROSS**		
	Picture of a boy, four sizes	40.00	50.00

S

□ 234	**C.H. SELICK, PERFUMER N.Y.**		
	Ring top, clear, 2⅝"	5.00	7.00
□ 235	**STIEGEL**		
	Teardrop shaped, sixteen swirls to the left, improved pontil, clear, 3⅛"	40.00	50.00

T

□ 236	**T**		
	Oz. on shoulder, square, cobalt, 2¾"	5.00	7.00
□ 237	**TOILET WATER**		
	On one panel of a six-paneled bottle, roof type shoulder, lady's leg neck, barber bottle, milk glass, 3¼" body, neck and shoulder 4½"	22.00	30.00
□ 238	*TOILET WATER, label, amber, 7¼"*	3.00	4.00
□ 239	**T.P.S. & CO., NY**		
	On base, man's head figural, three-part mold, metal cap, 7"	40.00	50.00
□ 240	**TREVILLE PARIS**		
	Green, 8¼"	7.00	10.00

V

☐ 241	**VAIL BROS**		
	Green, 3″	8.00	11.00
☐ 242	**VALENTINES**		
	Green, 2¾″	4.00	6.00
☐ 243	**VAN BUSKIRB'S**		
	Aqua, 5″	2.50	3.35
☐ 244	**VELVETINA**		
	Velvetina Skin Beautifier Goodrich Drug Co Omaha on back, milk glass, 5¼″	15.00	20.00
☐ 245	**VIN DE CHAPOTEAUT PARIS**		
	Clear or amethyst, 10½″	3.25	4.50
☐ 246	**VIOLET DULCE VANISHING CREAM**		
	Eight panels, 2½″	4.00	6.00
☐ 247	**VOGN**		
	In script, in two lines Perfumery Co. New York, case type body, seam end at collar, clear, 7¾″	7.00	10.00

W

☐ 248	**W.B. & CO.**		
	Under bottom, aqua, 3½″	5.00	7.00
☐ 249	**W & H. WALKER**		
	Clear, 8¾″	6.00	8.00
☐ 250	**WHITE ROSE**		
	Label, second label picture of a bird holding a note which reads Faith and Love, cucumber shaped, turquoise green, 4⅜″ long	25.00	35.00
☐ 251	**WITCH HAZEL**		
	Milk glass, 9¼″	15.00	20.00
☐ 252	**ALFRED WRIGHT, PERFUMER, ROCHESTER, N.Y.**		
	Cobalt or amber, 7½″	14.00	20.00
☐ 253	**W.T. & CO.**		
	Beveled corners, ring top, milk glass, 5″	8.00	11.00

CROCKS

Crocks are not made of glass, but pottery. Because many collectors of glass bottles are likewise collectors of crocks, we have included a brief selection of them. Many more styles, types and manufacturers exist than we have space to list.

Crocks are appealing for their variety of shapes, painted or stenciled decorations and lustrous finishes. Of ancient origin — older than glass — they were used extensively in the sale of store products in America during the 19th century and into the 20th. Alcoholic beverages were only one of many products kept in crocks; nevertheless, the association became so well planted that the term "old crock" came to refer to perpetual imbibers.

Pottery containers were made in the U.S. as early as 1641 in Massachusetts, just 21 years after the Mayflower. They might have taken the place of glass for widespread commercial use but for several drawbacks. One of these was that the product could not be seen through the bottle, as it could with glass. This not only hurt sales, but made it difficult for consumers to know when the bottle was getting empty. There was also some problem in convincing the public about the cleanliness of pottery bottles, since the interior was not visible. One big plus in their favor was that they could be manufactured more cheaply than glass. Pottery bottles also kept beverages cooler and presumably extended shelf life as they prevented entry of light.

Pottery bottles and jars continue to be used for store products today, but not as widely. Imported jams and jellies are often sold in them. The British manufacturers use pottery containers to a greater extent today than do their American counterparts. (Very possibly the well-decorated crock jars now at your supermarket, containing Scottish marmalade and the like, could be collectors' items of tomorrow.)

The pottery industry in early America usually followed the movement of immigrants from one territory to another. The pioneer settlers in Pennsylvania and Ohio were famous for their pottery: bottles, jugs and mugs of fired clay made for holding beverages, medicines, condiments and inks. Many early jugs were imaginatively hand painted and rank as prime examples of folk or primitive art.

A very differently styled group of crocks, in all sizes and designed for all purposes, was brought to the U.S. by the first major wave of Chinese immigrants. They arrived in California and set up communities there, then spread out to establish additional communities elsewhere (notably in Vancouver, British Columbia). Nearly all of their household goods, foodstuffs, and medicines were carried about in pottery crocks, bearing delicately enameled or shaped designs. Of course, the art of pottery making was very old in China by then, and had reached levels of achievement that Americans could not hope to duplicate. While American designers derived some inspiration from these Chinese specimens, they were well aware that they could not successfully imitate them and rarely tried to. Chinese crocks are eminently collectible, but because of their foreign origin they fall outside the scope of this book and are not included in the listings.

Upon discovery of the role of microbes in disease-causing bacteria in the late 1800's, patent-medicine makers were given a golden opportunity to fleece the public. Here was something else to be added to the long list of things for which their tonics and potions offered protection or remedy (some of which continue to baffle medical science to the present day). One of the more infamous of these cures was marketed in pottery containers by William Radam, a Prussian immigrant living in Texas. He was granted a patent for his "Microbe Killer" in 1886. The Pure Food and Drug Act put an end to his profitable business in 1907. It was discovered that his "cure" was simply a combination of wine and water. Since the wine was only a fraction of 1% of the total contents, he was making a profit of over 20,000% on each sale.

Most household pottery jars were made in the 19th century. Jugs glazed on the inside date to after 1900. The advent of the automatic glassblowing machine in 1903 made glass bottles cheaper and easier to produce and the use of pottery declined.

CROCKS

A

NO.	DESCRIPTION	PRICE RANGE	
☐ 1	**ALASKAN YUKON 1909 PACIFIC EXPO. OF SEATTLE**		
	Flower on shoulder, jug, 2¾"	23.00	35.00
☐ 2	**P. H. ALDERS, COMPLIMENTS OF THE EAGLE SALOON, ST. JOSEPH, MO.**		
	Cream and brown, 3"	27.00	39.00
☐ 3	*ALE, Label, tan, 8½"*	12.00	17.00
☐ 4	*ALE, Label, brown, 6"*	5.00	8.00
☐ 5	**THE ALTMAYOR & FLATAU LIQUOR CO., FINE LIQUORS, MACON, GA.**		
	Round, tan, 6½"	32.00	45.00
☐ 6	**ALLEN & HANBURY'S LTD. BYNOL MALT & OIL**		
	Black on prints, enormous amount of writing	12.00	17.00
☐ 7	**AMERICAN STONE WARE**		
	In 2 lines, blue letters also near top a large 6, 14 X 13, gray, 13½"	25.00	34.00
☐ 8	**F. A. AMES & CO.**		
	Owensboro Ky in back, flat, tan and brown, 3½"	32.00	45.00
☐ 9	**ANDERSON'S WEISS BEERS**		
	7¼"	7.00	10.00
☐ 10	**ARMOUR & COMPANY, CHICAGO**		
	Jug, pouring spout, white, 7¼"	20.0	25.00
☐ 11	**B. & J. ARNOLD, LONDON ENGLAND**		
	Master Ink, dark brown, 9"	12.00	17.00

B

NO.	DESCRIPTION	PRICE RANGE	
☐ 12	**B & H**		
	Cream, 3"	26.00	37.00
☐ 13	**BASS & CO. N.Y.**		
	Cream, 9½"	15.00	20.00
☐ 14	*BEAN POT, label, light blue, 4¼"*	4.00	6.00
☐ 15	**L. BEARD**		
	On shoulder, cream & blue, blob top, 8½	16.00	22.00
☐ 16	**BELLARMINE JUG**		
	Superb mask, two horseshoe decorations below mask, 13"	23.00	32.00

☐ 17 **BISCUIT SLIP GLAZE STONE PORTER**
Blob top with small impressed ring for string. Firmly impressed towards base J, Heginbotham, Kings Arms, Stayley Bridge. Reserve has other letters impressed below shoulder which cannot be clearly deciphered: UBL?T ??? ?EA TODY. Towards base are a further possible 14 characters which cannot be deciphered. MINT STATE & EARLY 1800's, 9½ " 45.00 65.00

☐ 18 **COMPLIMENTS OF BENISS & THOMPSON, SHELBYVILLE, KY**
Tan and brown, 3¾ " 25.00 38.00

☐ 19 **JAS. BENJAMIN, STONEWARE DEPOT, CINCINNATI, O.**
Blue stencil lettering, mottled tan, 9" 30.00 45.00

☐ 20 *Same as above, except tan, 13½ "* 30.00 42.00

☐ 21 **BLACK'S FAMILY LIQUOR STORE, H.P. BLACK,**
2042-43 Fresno in blue glaze letters, 1 Gal. Jug, ivory and dark brown 25.00 38.00

☐ 22 *BITTER, label, olive, brown trim, 10¼ "* 30.00 45.00

☐ 23 **B. B. BITTER MINERAL WATER, BOWLING GREEN, MO.**
White, five gallon, 15" 30.00 45.00

☐ 24 **BLACK FAMILY LIQUOR STORE**
Stamped in blue glaze, brown and tan, gallon 17.00 24.00

☐ 25 **BLANCHFLOWER & SONS, HOMEMADE,**
4 Prize Medals, GT, Yarmouth, Norfolk, cream with black, 6 sided lid 16.00 22.00

☐ 26 **BLUE PICTURE PRINT GINGER JAR,**
Picture extends entire circumference of jar, building and junk in sail, 3½ " 22.00 33.00

☐ 27 **BLUE PRINT OINMENT POT BEACH & BARNICOTT,**
Successors to Dr. Roberts Bridport, Poor Man's Friend, crisp print 11.00 15.00

☐ 28 **BLUE TOP & PRINT CREAM POT,**
Golden Pastures, Thick Rich Cream, Chard, picture of maid milking cow 12.00 17.00

☐ 29 **BROWNINGS PALE ALE, LEWES,**
Sparkled biscuit glazed finish, string rim at neck. Cork closure, impressed: 8¾ " 15.00 20.00

☐ 30 **BROWNINGS PALE ALE, LEWES,**
Potters Mark: STEPHEN GREEN'S LAMBETH 15.00 20.00

☐ 31 **BOSTON BAKED BEANS**
HHH on back, brick color, 1½ " 5.00 8.00

☐ 32 **BOSTON BAKED BEANS**
OK on back, brick color, 1½ " 5.00 8.00

☐ 33 **BOWERS THREE THISTLES SNUFF**
Cream color with blue lettering, two to three gallon 35.00 50.00

☐ 34 **BURGESS, JOHN & SON, ANCHOVY PASTE, WAREHOUSE 107 STAND,**
Black print on White, 3½ ", curved shoulder type, print 2 X 2¾ " 25.00 38.00

☐ 35 **BRYANT & WOODRUFF, PITTSFIELD, ME.**
Handled jug, blue gray, 7" 23.00 34.00

☐ 36 **BYNOL MALT & OIL, ALLEN & HANBURY'S**
Black on white, print 2¾ " X 3¾ ", height, lots of writing on this pot, 4⅕" 18.00 24.00

☐	37	*BUTTER CROCK, no label, handle, blue-gray decoration,* *4"*	23.00	34.00
☐	38	*BUTTER CROCK, no label, blue-gray decoration, 5¼"*	17.00	24.00

C

☐	39	**CALIFORNIA POP** *Pat. Dec. 29, 1872, blob top, tan, 10½"*	55.00	75.00
☐	40	**CALIFORNIA COUGH BALM** *Dose teaspoon full, children ½, 10– brown, crock jug with handle, 3¼"*	90.00	120.00
☐	41	**CAMBRIDGE SPRINGS MINERAL WATER** *In 2 lines, 2½", brown & tan*	18.00	27.00
☐	42	*CANNING CROCK, inscribed Hold Fast That Which is Good, dark brown, 6½"*	23.00	34.00
☐	43	*CANNING CROCK, wax sealer, 6"*	19.00	28.00
☐	44	*CANNING CROCK, wax sealer, reddish brown, 8"*	19.00	28.00
☐	45	*CANNING CROCK, blue with a gray decorative design, 8½"*	19.00	28.00
☐	46	*CANNING CROCK, mustard color, 7"*	16.00	22.00
☐	47	*CANNING CROCK, maple leaf design in lid, caramel color, 6"*	10.00	15.00
☐	48	*CANNING CROCK, brown, 5"*	14.00	20.00
☐	49	*CANNING CROCK, wax channel, brown, 8½"*	15.00	21.00
☐	50	*CANNING CROCK, reddish brown, green on the inside, 6¾"*	16.00	22.00
☐	51	*CANNING CROCK, crude, brown, 4"*	10.00	15.00
☐	52	*CANNING CROCK, was sealer, dark brown, 5½"*	14.00	20.00
☐	53	*CANNING CROCK, wax sealer, tan, 5½"*	14.00	20.00
☐	54	*CANNING CROCK, wax sealer, dark brown, 5½"*	10.00	15.00
☐	55	*CANNING CROCK, wax sealer, dark brown, 6½"*	9.00	13.00
☐	56	*CANNING CROCK, wax sealer, mottled gray, 5"*	8.00	12.00
☐	57	*CANNING CROCK, wax sealer, brown, 5½"*	11.00	16.00
☐	58	*CANNING CROCK, barrel, dark brown, 5½"*	11.00	16.00
☐	59	*CANNING CROCK, lid, star design, dark brown, 8¾"*	16.00	22.00
☐	60	*CANNING CROCK, dark brown, 7½"*	14.00	20.00
☐	61	*CANNING CROCK, tan, 9"*	16.00	22.00
☐	62	*CANNING CROCK, wax channel, brown, 7½"*	16.00	22.00
☐	63	**CASPER CO., FROM THE, WINSTON-SALEM, LOWEST PRICE WHISKEY HOUSE,** *Write for confidential list, tan crockery, blue letters, with wire handle, 9¼"*	60.00	80.00
☐	64	**18th CENTURY BELLARMINE,** *Superb large decorative mark approx. 2½" x 2½", large star decoration beneath contained in oval with decorative border, 9¼"*	225.00	300.00
☐	65	**GEO. M. CHERNAUCKAS BUFFET, TELEPHONE CANAL 1756,** *1900 S. Union St., Corner 19th St., Chicago, large hall, etc., in a square under it ½ gal. liquid measure, gal. brown & white, black lettering, 8½"*	40.00	55.00
☐	66	**CHINESE CROCK JUG** *Vase, wide, flared mouth, black or dark brown, 6"*	10.00	15.00
☐	67	*Same as above, except Federal Law Forbids*	3.00	5.00

☐ 68 **CHRIS MORLEY'S**
Under it in a scroll, Ginger Beer, under it Victorias B. C.,
brown & cream, inside screw, 7¾" **16.00** **21.00**

☐ 69 **CLARK BROS.**
Pat. May 17, 1899, Zanesville, Ohio, brown, 7½" **18.00** **25.00**

☐ 70 **CLARK BROS. GROCERS, BIRMINGHAM, ALA.**
Handle, jug, white and brown, 10½" **20.00** **28.00**

☐ 71 **JOHN CLIPP & CO.,**
Lambeth in a circle on base, lt. brown (crock), 5¾" **18.00** **25.00**

☐ 72 **COMMEMORATIVE WHISKEY / SPIRIT JUG**
By Copeland Spode & bearing their marks on base.
Underglazed transfer in band around neck reads: CORONA-
TION OF KING GEORGE 5TH & QUEEN MARY, June 22, 1911.
Distillers, Edinburgh, 8½". Main body in Royal Blue with 2
inch band at neck in grey, ¾" bottom ornamental white
embossed relief Royal Crown with 2 flags, the left bearing
portrait of King George V on background of Union Jack &
the right bearing Portrait of Queen Mary on background of
Royal Standard. Whole measures Approx. 3¾" X 3¾",
reverse of jug: Crowned Royal Coat of Arms surrounded by
Garter. Thistle to left top. Rose to right top. Shamrock
either side of base. Rose thistle & shamrock relief in white
around top of neck **80.00** **100.00**

☐ 73 **COMPLIMENTS OF M. A. CLAUTON, 26 FARM ST.**
Brown and tan, 3" **22.00** **32.00**

☐ 74 **COMPLIMENTS OF MARTIN COLLINS, CARTERSVILLE, GA.**
Brown and tan, 3" **25.00** **37.00**

☐ 75 **COMPLIMENTS OF COLUMBIA LIQUOR COMPANY**
AUGUSTA, GA.
Handle, tan and brown, 3" **24.00** **35.00**

☐ 76 **CONNER'S BLOOD REMEDY**
Cream, 6⅜" **11.00** **15.00**

☐ 77 **COMPLIMENTS OF J.R. COPELAND, 781 24TH ST.**
Miniature jug, brown and white, blue lettering, 5¼" **17.00** **24.00**

☐ 78 **COOK FAIRBANK & CO., AKRON, OHIO**
On shoulder, 11 X 6½" with handle. gray **13.00** **19.00**

☐ 79 **COOPER'S FRANK SEVILLE MARMALADE,**
Black on white, 3¾", large print with lots of writing **5.00** **8.00**

☐ 80 **CORNISH MEAD CO., LTD.,**
Penzance, Cornwall. ONE PINT TWO TONE STONE JAR
WITH HANDLE, Underglaze Mary-print on side: The
Honey-moon Drink, Ye Olde Mead. 25% Proof, black top . **18.00** **25.00**

☐ 81 **COWDEN & CO., HARRISBURG, PA.**
Dark brown, 6½" **18.00** **25.00**

☐ 82 **CRAMER'S KIDNEY CURE, ALBANY N.Y.**
N's are backward, aqua, 4½" **18.00** **25.00**

☐ 83 *CROCK BOTTLE, gray, 10"* **9.00** **12.00**

☐ 84 *CROCK, label, cathedral type, brown and tan, 8½"* **30.00** **40.00**

☐ 85 *CROCK FLASK, red and brown glaze, 7½"* **45.00** **60.00**

☐ 86 *CROCK, label, brown, green and tan, 7"* **11.00** **16.00**

☐ 87 *CROCK, label, light gray, 6½"* **12.00** **17.00**

☐ 88 *CROCK, label, brown, 7"* **11.00** **16.00**

☐ 89 *CROCK with seal, Amsterdam, tan, 12"* **14.00** **20.00**

☐ 90 *CROCK, label, tan and cream, 6¾"* **9.00** **12.00**

☐ 91 *CROCK, label, tan and cream, 5½"* **9.00** **12.00**

☐	92	*CROCK, plain, ring top, two tone, tan and cream, 8½"* ...	5.00	8.00
☐	93	*CROCK, plain, Kinney on base, ring top, two tone, tan and cream, 8½"*	9.00	12.00
☐	94	*CROCK, plain, bottle type, tapered crown, cream and tan, 7½"*	6.00	9.00
☐	95	*CROCK, plain, roof type shoulder, cream and tan, 8"*	5.00	7.00
☐	96	**DR. CRONK'S SARSAPARILLA BAR**		
		Blob top, sand color, 9½"	18.00	24.00
☐	97	**CROWOUS, J.W. DRUG CO., 1 LB. MERCURY,**		
		Dallas, Tex. in 4 lines, tan crock, ring top, 2¾"	35.00	48.00
☐	98	**CROWN GINGR BEER CO., CLEVELAND, OHIO**		
		In a circle in center, brown, 6¾"	11.00	15.00
☐	99	**CRUISKEEN LAWN**		
		Cream and brown, 8"	17.00	24.00
☐	100	**PRESENTED BY, P. J. CURRIN, A MERRY CHRISTMAS AND HAPPY NEW YEAR**		
		Pint jug, brown and tan with blue stencil lettering, 6½" ..	23.00	32.00

D

☐	101	**DAWSON SALTS & WATER CO. DISTRIBUTORS HAMBY SALTS, IRON AND LITHIA WATER, DAWSON SPRINGS, KY.**		
		Large 5 above, jug, brown and white, blue lettering, 18" ..	27.00	38.00
☐	102	**D.C.**		
		Gray, 11"	9.00	12.00
☐	103	*Same as above, except tan, 10½"*	9.00	12.00
☐	104	**THE D.C.L. SCOTCH WHISKEY DISTILLERS LIMITED, LONDON, EDINBURGH, GLASGOW, GOLD MEDALS, EDINBURGH 1886**		
		Under bottom Bengimark, Doulton, Shicon, England	50.00	65.00
☐	105	**DEACON BROWN VINEGAR**		
		in 3 lines, tan & brown, 3¼"	25.00	37.00
☐	106	**GEO. A. DICKEL & CO., CASCASE DISTILLERY HAND MADE SOUR MASH TENNESSEE WHISKEY**		
		White with black lettering, blue bands, 9½"	22.00	33.00
☐	107	**D. J. AND CO., NO. 2A LUMBER STREET, N. YORK, 1795**		
		Preserves crock, seal top, salt glaze, 5"	90.00	120.00
☐	108	**A. P. DONAGHHO, PARKERSBURG, W. V.**		
		Canning crock, tan, blue stencil, 8"	22.00	23.00
☐	109	**A. P. DONAGHHO, PARKERSBURG, W. V.**		
		Written at a slant, blue-gray stencil, 8"	22.00	33.00
☐	110	**DOSTER-NORTHINGTON DRUG CO., BIRMINGHAM, ALA.**		
		Jug with handle, white and brown, 11"	18.00	25.00
☐	111	**DOSTER-NORTHINGTON DRUG CO., BIRMINGHAM, ALA.**		
		Brown and cream, ½ gallon	18.00	25.00
☐	112	**DOTRICK DISTILLING CO.,**		
		Dayton, O. MOTTO JUG, "EAT, DRINK AND BE MERRY", in 3 lines, crock brown & cream with hand, 5½"	38.00	50.00
☐	113	**COMPLIMENTS OF A. J. DRESEL, SECOND & MAGNOLIA AVE., LOUISVILLE, KY.**		
		Brown and tan, 2¼"	25.00	37.00

☐114 **DRINKOMETER**
In back, tan, 5″ 9.00   12.00

E

☐115 **EAGLE LIQUEUR DIS., CINCINNATI, O.**
Ring top, eagle and shield in center, green, 2¼″ 25.00   38.00
☐116 **EELAARKI, ADRSV., SCHIEDARN**
Crock with handle, ring around bottom, tan, 4″ 17.00   25.00
☐117 *Same as above, except 12″* 9.00   12.00
☐118 **ENGLAND NATOINE**
*In two lines on base, four rings near shoulder, spout, brick
brown, 10″* 9.00   12.00
☐119 *Same as above, except in all colors and sizes, some with
panels, some with plain tops* 9.00   12.00
☐120 **ETRUIA STONE CHIN**
2518 under bottom, syrup label, tan, 6″ 18.00   25.00

F

☐121 **J. W. M. FIELD & SONS WHOLESALE LIQUORS,
OWENSBORO, KY.**
Cream, 3¼″ 25.00   38.00
☐122 **FOCKIN, WYNAND, AMSTERDAM**
Beer jug with handle, tan, 12″ 14.00   20.00
☐123 **FOWLKES & MYATT CO. CIDER VINEGAR**
Miniature jug, brown and white, blue lettering, 3″ 27.00   38.00
☐124 **FRANC, L. & CO.,**
*Toledo, Ohio, M.C. Kingon Hand Made Sour Mash
Whiskey in a frame, blue letters, tapered top & ring, 10½″* 18.00   25.00
☐125 **FREIBERG & KAHN DISTILLERIES, METROPOLITAN
CLUE,**
In a form in 4 lines, tan & cream, 3½″ 14.00   20.00
☐126 **J FRIEDER**
Hand-painted picture, ring around bottom, tan, 12″ 22.00   29.00
☐127 **FROG,**
Sheared top, coming out of mouth, green, 6½″ 13.00   19.00
☐128 *Same as above, except B. FRANKFER* 22.00   29.00
☐129 **G. W. FULPER & BROS., FLEMINGTON, N.J.**
Tan and blue decorations, 11¼″ 26.00   35.00

G

☐130 **GALLAGHER & O'GARA, DEALERS IN FINE
WHISKEY, BESSEMER, ALA.**
Tan 18.00   28.00
☐131 **GALLOWAY'S EVERLASTING JAR**
*Pat'd Feb. 8th Pat. Applied for 1870, canning crock with
wax sealer, gray, 7¾″* 16.00   25.00
☐132 *GINGER POT, fancy decoration, no lettering, turquoise,
3½″* 9.00   12.00
☐133 *GOLD TESTER, crock, 4″* 6.00   8.00

109

114

129

Happy Patty,
348 Mangum St.,
Durham N.C.

142

153

VINEGAR

158

167

168

169

184

☐ 134 **CHARLES S. GOVE COMPANY, WHOLESALE LIQUOR DEALERS, BOSTON, MASS.**
Jug with handle, brown top and cream base, 9" 18.00 25.00

☐ 135 **COMPLIMENTS OF H. GRAFF & CO., FRESNO, CAL.**
In three lines, jug with handle, letters stamped in blue glaze, ivory and dark brown, 3½" 23.00 34.00

☐ 136 **H. GRAFF & CO., COMPLIMENT OF FRESNO, CAL.**
In 3 lines, blue glaze letters, cream brown, 3¼", with handle 17.00 24.00

☐ 137 **GRASSELLI ARSENATE OF LEAD**
Poison crock, cream, 6½" 17.00 24.00

☐ 138 **THE O. L. GREGORY VINEGAR CO.**
Tan and brown, 3½" 17.00 24.00

H

☐ 139 **HAILWOODS MANCHESTER, BROWN TOP CREAM POT,**
Outline picture of cow at center, height 4" 22.00 33.00

☐ 140 **HAMMERSLEY'S CREAMERY, BLUE PRINT CREAM POT,**
Broughton, three hammers pictured at center, 4" 17.00 24.00

☐ 141 *Same but height 3"* 26.00 38.00

☐ 142 **HAPPY PATTY**
With handle, brown and tan, 8½" 17.00 24.00

☐ 143 **I. W. HARPER, NELSON CO., KY**
Cream, 3¼" 38.00 52.00

☐ 144 **HARPER, I. W. NELSON CO., KENTUCKY**
Wluses & many doz. a ribbing etc. on front of jug with handle, tan neck, etc. ring top, cream, 7½" 75.00 100.00

☐ 145 **I. W. HARPER, GOLD MEDAL WHISKEY**
Square base, long twisted neck, cobalt, 8¾" 35.00 50.00

☐ 146 **W. P. HARTLEY, LIVERPOOL & LONDON**
London Tower in center, under it Trademark Reg., eleven panels, tan, 4" 9.00 12.00

☐ 147 **VINCENT HATHAWAY & CO.**
Blob top, tan, 9½" 10.00 14.00

☐ 148 **HAYNER LOCK, BOX 290, DAYTON, OHIO**
White, 8" 20.00 30.00

☐ 149 **HELMENT RYE**
Blue lettering, cream, 3" 17.00 24.00

☐ 150 **HESSIG-ELLIS DRUG CO., MEMPHIS, TENN**
1 lb. Mercury, Cream, ring top 13.00 19.00

☐ 151 **DISTILLED BY JAMES R. HOGO, JIM WHISKEY, POPULAR BLUFF, MO.**
White and brown, blue lettering, 9¾" 40.00 60.00

☐ 152 **COMPLIMENTS OF HOLBERG, MOBILE AND CINCINNATI**
Brown and white, 3¼" 25.00 38.00

☐ 153 **E. J. HOLLIDGE**
Label, cream, 6" 9.00 12.00

☐ 154 **HOLLOWAY'S FAMILY OINTMENT FOR THE CURE OF CTC.,**
8 lines (London), 1 x 1½ round crock, in back 7 lines, ring top 17.00 24.00

☐ 155 **HOLLOWAY'S OINTMENT, GOUT & RHEUMATISM,**
Height 1½" 9.00 12.00
☐ 156 **J. W. HOOPER & BRO., GROCERIES AND LIQUORS,**
NASHVILLE, TENN.
Jug, tan with brown top and blue lettering, 8¼" 26.00 38.00
☐ 157 **HORTON CATO MFG. CO., DETROIT, MICHIGAN,**
ROYAL SALAD DRESSING
Wide mouth jug, white and brown with black lettering,
10¼" 21.00 29.00
☐ 158 **R. M. HUGHES & CO'S**
Monogram, VINEGAR, blue label, white, 9¼" 28.00 39.00
☐ 159 **HUMPHREY & MARTIN**
Tan and brown crock, 8¾" 28.00 39.00

I

☐ 122 *INK CROCK, conical, light gray, 2¾"* 9.00 12.00
☐ 160 *INK CROCK, round pouring lip, cream, 10¾"* 9.00 12.00
☐ 161 *INK CROCK, round pouring lip, brown, 7¾"* 9.00 12.00
☐ 162 *INK CROCK, plain, roof type shoulder, pouring lip, 6"* 13.00 18.00
☐ 163 *INK CROCK, plain, tan, 2¾"* 9.00 12.00
☐ 164 *INK CROCK, plain, no neck, round collar, brown, 1¾"*
round, 1¾" tall 10.00 14.00
☐ 165 *INK CROCK, label, light gray, 5¾"* 11.00 15.00
☐ 166 *INK CROCK, label, tan, 2½"* 9.00 12.00
☐ 167 *INK CROCK, label, tan, 2½"* 10.00 14.00
☐ 168 *INK CROCK, label, tan, 2¾"* 10.00 14.00
☐ 169 *INK CROCK, label, tan, 7"* 9.00 12.00
☐ 170 *INK CROCK, label, cream, 5"* 7.00 12.00
☐ 171 *INK POTTERY, light blue, short neck* 9.00 12.00
☐ 172 *INK POTTERY, some have embossing, brick brown, 10"* .. 9.00 12.00
☐ 173 *INK POTTERY, plain, conical, light gray, 2¾" around bot-*
tom, 2⅛" 8.00 11.00
☐ 174 *Same as above, except brown* 8.00 11.00
☐ 175 *INK POTTERY, plain, ring top, light brown, 1¾" round, ¼"*
neck 9.00 12.00

J

☐ 176 **JONES BROS. & CO.**
Brown and tan, 3½" 25.00 37.00
☐ 177 **JONES BROS., COMPLIMENTS OF J. CARR MFG.'S OF**
HIGH GRADE CIDER & VING., LOUISVILLE, KY.
Tan and cream, 3½" 25.00 37.00
☐ 178 **JORDAN & STANLEY, WINE & SPIRIT MERCHANTS,**
NEWPORT, I.W., SPIRIT JUG, CORK CLOSURE,
Brown top, light fawn bottom, incised across top front,
handle at neck, round section jug with waist towards bot-
tom third, 8" 18.00 26.00
☐ 179 *JUG, very crude bell shape, red and tan, 7"* 9.00 12.00

K

☐ 180 **KABBENBEER LTD., LONDON, PATENTED ONE LITRE LIDDED BEER JUG.**
White glaze, handle at side, impressed below neck, IL. base impressed "W", black underglaze printed lid reads THIS JUG IS THE PROPERTY OF KABBENBEER, LTD., LONDON, PATENTED. Handle at side, brass thumb plate for opening lid, over center brass clip to keep lid closed, 9¼", hairline crack extends 3½" down from neck on one side only. Unusual Brewery item. No other damage except defect mentioned 35.00 48.00

☐ 181 **KAEHLER BROS., FRESNO, CAL.**
In a circle with a medicine trademark, ivory and brown, gallon 18.00 25.00

☐ 182 **KAN 2**
in seal on shoulder, ring neck, ring top, handle, tan, 12", round 26.00 37.00

☐ 183 **JAMES KEILLER & SONS, DUNDEE MARMALADE, LONDON,** *(c. 1862),* **GREAT BRITIAN**
Gray, 4" 7.00 10.00

☐ 184 **KENNEDY**
Tan and beige, 8½" 11.00 16.00

☐ 185 **THE KINTORE**
Cream and brown, 8¼" 18.00 25.00

☐ 186 **C.B. KIRBY, LATE R. CROOK & CO., HERVEY STREET, IPSWICH**
Tan and cream, two gallon 23.00 34.00

☐ 187 **J.W. KOLB & SON, 4471 ST. LOUIS AVE., ST. LOUIS, MO.**
Jug, stamped letters, dark brown and cream, 3¼" 25.00 37.00

☐ 188 **RETURN TO KUTNER & GOLDSTEIN & CO., WHOLESALE GROCERS, FRESNO, CALIF.**
Wire handle, cream, gallon 23.00 34.00

☐ 189 **KUTNER GOLDSTEIN & CO., RETURN TO,**
Wholesale Grocers Fresno, Calif. in 4 lines in blue glaze letters, bucket type handle, 1 gal., cream 24.00 36.00

L

☐ 190 **LAMBRECHT** *in script,* **BUTTER**
White and blue lettering, 2⅞" 7.00 10.00

☐ 191 **LITTLE BROWN JUG**
Engraved, brown pottery, 2¾" 25.00 36.00

☐ 192 **LITTLE BROWN JUG 1876**
Dark brown, 3" 25.00 36.00

☐ 193 **LIVERPOOL**
On base, brown and white, tapered top, 7¼" 11.00 16.00

☐ 194 **LYMANS CLARE & CO., 384 & 386 ST. PAUL STREET, MONTREAL**
Tan, blue incising, 6" 18.00 25.00

M

□ 195 **MANCHESTER, HAILWOODS PURE RICH CREAM,**
Cream Pot, Stone Color, creamery, Broughton, 4" 13.00 18.00
□ 196 *Same but height 3¼"* 22.00 33.00
□ 197 **COMPLIMENTS OF J.C. MAYFIELD MFG. CO.**
BIRMINGHAM, ALA.
Tan, 3¼" 40.00 60.00
□ 198 **MAYFIELD VINEGAR & CIDER CO., MAYFIELD, KY,**
THE FAMILY & PICKLING VINEGAR
Cream, 3¼" 37.00 53.00
□ 199 **McCOMB POTTERY**
Pottery Pat. Pend. on bottom, canning crock, tan and
brown, 6" 20.00 30.00
□ 200 **McCOMB POTTERY & CO.**
Pat. Jan. 24, 1899, canning crock, white, 7" 16.00 23.00
□ 201 **COMPLIMENTS OF, McDONNEL, JOHN A.**
269 Conception St. in 4 lines, crock with handle, cream, 3" 40.00 60.00
□ 202 **THE MEDENHALL HOTEL BATHS, CLAREMORE, OKLA.,**
Radium Water from, Cures rheumatism, stomach trouble,
eczema and other ailments, letters in blue, 1 gal. jug, ivory
and brown with handle 22.00 34.00
□ 204 **MELCHERS, J. J. WZ — SCHIEDORM —**
Honey Suckle, Old Gin in 4 lines on base, tan, 12½" x 2¾"
with handle, ring top 14.00 20.00
□ 204 **M.H. MELICK, ROSEVILLE, OHIO**
Canning crock, gray, 8¼" 13.00 18.00
□ 205 **MERCURY**
Tan and white crock, 5" 7.00 10.00
□ 206 **MERCURY SPURLOCK NEAL CO.,**
NASHVILLE, TENN.
Jug, white and blue lettering, 3¼" 40.00 60.00
□ 207 **MEREDITH'S DIAMOND CLUB PURE RYE WHISKEY**
White, 8" 45.00 65.00
□ 208 **METROPOLITAN CLUB, FREBERG & KAHN DISTILLERS**
Miniature jug, brown and white, blue lettering, 3¼" 25.00 37.00
□ 209 **MILLER, C. J.,**
Fine Whiskies, Vicksburg, Miss. in 3 lines, crock jug with
handle, brown, tan, 7½", qt. 20.00 30.00
□ 210 **MINN. STONEWARE CO., RED WING, MINN.**
On bottom, wide mouth, reddish brown, 7" 20.00 30.00
□ 211 **MINN. STONEWARE CO. SAFETY VALVE PAT.**
Canning crock, white and blue markings, 8½" 19.00 27.00
□ 212 **CHRISTIAN MOERLEIN BREWING CO., CIN. O.**
In a circle on shoulder, TRADEMARK on top of it in center,
MOERLEINS OLD JUG LAGER RUN BEER with fancy
design around it, dark brown, 8" 2.00 37.00
□ 213 **COMPLIMENTS OF D. MONROE, SR.**
303-305 South 18th St., brown and tan, 3½" 40.00 60.00

□214 **MOTTO JUG "AS I GO UP THE HILL OF PROSPERITY, MAY I NEVER MEET A FRIEND,"**
Dotrick Distillery Co., Dayton, O., brown and cream crock with handle, 4½" 40.00 60.00

□215 **MOUTH WASH,**
Letters running bottom left to top right with 3 leaf clover, applied top, elephant stopper, pale blue, 5" 11.00 15.00

□216 **MOUTARDE DESSAUZ FILS ORLEANS FRANCE**
On back, cream, 4" 11.00 16.00

□217 **WM. J. MOXLEY'S SPECIAL OLEOMARGARINE**
The Taste is the Test, Pat. 6-2-14, white and black lettering blue bands, 7½" 18.00 25.00

□218 **GRAPE JUICE PREPARED BY MYERS, BENTON & CO., CLEVELAND**
Tan, 5½" 30.00 40.00

N

□219 **N. K. A.**
In a circle near shoulder, tan with handle, short neck, double ring top, tan, 11¼" 14.00 20.00

□220 **D. NEWMAN**
Tan and white crock, 7" 6.00 8.00

□221 **NORDJAUSEN KORNSCHNAPPS**
Tan and cream, 7½" 18.00 25.00

□222 **NORTON & CO., J. BENNINGTON, VT.,**
With #2 and flower Dis. (blue) Sand color, 2 gal., flat ring top 70.00 90.00

□223 **COMPLIMENTS OF NORTON & NORTON, SAVANNAH, GA.**
Brown and tan, 3¼" 25.00 36.00

□224 **E. & L. P. NORTON, BENNINGTON, VA.**
Gray with blue decorative design, 8" 45.00 65.00

□225 **E.B. NORTON & CO., WORCESTER, MASS.**
Handle, gray with blue decorative design, 14" 45.00 65.00

O

□226 **JOHN H. OELKERS 730 S. RAMPART ST., N.O. L.A.**
Tan and brown, 4½" 25.00 37.00

□227 **OLD**
In center a picture of a Jug on it, Rye, Jug, tan, 3½" 28.00 39.00

□228 **OLD CONTINENTAL WHISKEY**
Miniature size, brown and tan, 3¼" 25.00 37.00

□229 *Same as above, except cream* 25.00 37.00

□230 **OLD CONTINENTAL WHISKEY**
Brown and cream, 3" 25.00 37.00

□231 **OLD CUTTER RYE, A.E. CAMPBELL CATERING CO., BIRMINGHAM, ALA.**
Tan, 3¼" 25.00 37.00

☐232 **OLD DEXTER DIS. CO., BUTLER, KENTUCKY**
Dis. in a circle a flower in center in back Pat. Aug. 11, 1919,
The Old Dexter Jug Whiskey, rib side, round jug with han-
dle and vase bottom, 8" 55.00   75.00

☐233 **OLD JUG, BOURBON, G. HANNEMAN, PORTLAND, ORE.**
In 4 lines, handle, silver-plated, pouring spout, 10½" 100.00   130.00

☐234 **OLD JUG LAGER**
The Fashionable Beverage of the Day, Brilliant in Color,
Absolutely Pure, Stimulating, Rejuvenating, Truly Cul-
tured, Veritable Luxury, Nashville, Tenn. all in ornate let-
tering, cream, 8¾" 18.00   25.00

☐235 **OLD NECTAR RYE**
R.P. Blalack, Mobile, Ala., cream, 3" 25.00   37.00

☐236 **OLD PRIVATE STOCK PURE RYE**
In 2 lines, brown and gray crock with handle, double ring
top, 3¼ 28.00   40.00

☐237 **OLD TAYLOR**
On side, Reverse S.H. TAYLOR & SONS DIST., FRANK-
FORT, KY., tan, quart 22.00   33.00

☐238 **OREGON IMPORT COMPANY, PORTLAND, OREGON,**
With handle, brown and cream crock, ½ gal. 28.00   40.00

☐239 **D.L. ORMSBY, 1850**
With star in a circle, reverse at base in shield Patent
Pressed W. Smith N.Y., twelve-sided, very crude, tan, ½
pint 18.00   25.00

☐240 **OTTMAN BROS. & CO, FORT EDWARD, N.Y.**
Blue bird, gray with cobalt decoration, 11" 70.00   95.00

P

☐241 **J. W. PALMER**
Tan, 3" 25.00   37.00

☐242 **PAIN & BAYLOR**
Tan and white, 7" 9.00   12.00

☐243 **RICHARD PEARCE**
Tan, 7" 9.00   12.00

☐244 **PEWTRESS, S. L.**
Conn, #2, Blue Flower Dis., tapered ring top, same color . 90.00   120.00

☐245 **G.W. PIPER**
Cream, 7¼" 9.00   12.00

☐246 **PRICE & BRISTOL**
On base, brown and white, tapered top, 7¼" 11.00   16.00

Q

☐247 **M. QUINN, WHOLESALE GROCER, KANSAS CITY, MO.**
Wire handle with wooden grip, white with blue lettering,
10" 22.00   35.00

R

☐248 **WM. RADAM'S MICROBE KILLER NO. 1**
Handle on jug, white with blue lettering, 10¾" 37.00   52.00

☐249 **RANDOLPH & CO.**
Brown and tan, 3" 25.00 37.00

☐250 **THEO RECTANUS CO.**
Pure Old Hand Made Sour Mash Louisville, brown and
cream, 3¼" 25.00 37.00

☐251 **RELIABLE MIDDLE QUALITY FRUIT PRESERVES**
Gray with black lettering, 6" 18.00 26.00

☐252 **JACOB RICHTER CO., FRESNO, CAL.**
Best Wines & Liquors $5 per gal. in four lines, brown and
ivory, gallon 35.00 48.00

☐253 **H.E.N. ROSS**
In a circle, In a circle under it a cross and Cross Flag,
under it in one line Phein Preussen, Pottery or Crock on
shoulder, handle, tan, 12" tall, 3¼" round 14.00 19.00

☐254 **ROYAL DOULTON DEWARS WHISKEY**
With Scottish figure, crock jug, qt. 40.00 58.00

☐255 **RUSSELL, M. C. & SON,**
Corner 3rd & Market Sts. Maryville, Ky. in a frame, brown
and sand with handle, 6" 28.00 37.00

S

☐256 **SAINSBURY'S BLOATER PASTE,**
Black or white, 3" 5.00 7.00

☐257 **SANFORD'S INKS, THE QUALITY LINE PASTES**
Jug with pouring spout, white with blue lettering, 10½" .. 22.00 33.00

☐258 **SATTERLEE & MORY, FT. EDWARDS, N.Y.**
Gray with blue decorative design, 7½" 35.00 48.00

☐259 **JAMES SCHAM**
Pat. July 13, 1909, embossed Sherwood, canning crock,
glass lid, white, 7½" 17.00 26.00

☐260 **CHRISTIAN SCHMIDT, SHENANDOAH, PA.**
Cream, 7" 12.00 17.00

☐261 **COMP. OF H. SCHRODER, 401 & 403 BROUGHTON**
Brown and tan, 3½" 25.00 37.00

☐262 **SHUSTER, BEN J., COMPLIMENTS OF,**
Selma, Ala. in 3 lines, beige and brown with handle, 3¾" . 22.00 37.00

☐263 **FRED L. SCHWANTZ, UP-TO-DATE GROCER, FINE
LIQUOR,
63 BEALE ST., MEMPHIS, TENN.**
Jug, tan with brown top, 8½" 27.00 38.00

☐264 **SCOTLAND EXPORT CO. LTD. CHIVAS REGAL**
Tan, 12" 27.00 38.00

☐265 **B. J. SIMOND'S**
Blob top, 10" 45.00 65.00

☐266 **SIMPLEX HEKTOGRAPH,**
Composition for Hall's Patent Simplex, large picture of
hatted man blowing trumpet, very large print 3 x 3 inches,
printed at rear with instructions "For Use" 18.00 25.00

☐267 **D. F. SMITH & SNOWS**
Whitefoot, Pat. July 17, 66, blob top, tan, 10" 45.00 60.00

☐268 **J. L. SMITH**
Inside under lip, crude Southern pottery, brown, 11" 18.00 25.00

☐269 **SMOKY MT. 1880**
Vinegar jar, brown, 5" 14.00   19.00

☐270 **COMP. OF SOUTHERN GRO. CO., 114 BERNARD ST.**
Brown and tan, 3½" 25.00   36.00

☐271 **SOY SAUCE**
Pottery jug, short neck, ring top, side spout, brown, 5" ... 10.00   15.00

☐272 **SOYER'S PERFECT SAUCE, MEADVILLE, PA.**
On front in 3 lines, crock with handle, ring top, 7½" 14.00   19.00

☐273 **W. M. SPENCER**
Clarks improved, Pat. May 19th 92, Zanesville, Ohio on bottom, white with blue lettering, 9" 22.00   30.00

☐274 **STONE MASON PAT'D APPLIED FOR**
On shoulder, canning crock, tan and brown 18.00   25.00

☐275 **THE WEIR STONEWALL FRUIT JAR, PAT. 1892**
Tan and brown, 6½" 14.00   19.00

☐276 **STOUT & GINGER BEER,**
Tan and brown, 6", a cross in center 7.00   10.00

☐277 **E. SWASEY & CO., PORTLAND, ME.**
Butter crock, white and brown, 3½" 18.00   25.00

☐278 **DR. SWETT'S ORIGINAL ROOT BEER, REGISTERED, BOSTON, MASS.**
Brown and tan, 7¾" 9.00   12.00

T

☐279 **E. B. TAYLOR, RICHMOND VA.**
At an angle, gray with blue stencil lettering, 8" 22.00   29.00

☐280 **THWAITES DUBLIN,**
Tan tapered top, short neck, 6¾" 8.00   11.00

☐281 **TIGER GLAZED & 17th CENTURY,**
8½", large oval decoration below composed of shield with 5 ears of corn erect above, 2½" in height by 1¾" in width, salt glaze 275.00   335.00

☐282 **TIMOTHY WHITE CO., LTD. EXTRACT OF MALT & COD LIVER OIL,**
Black on white, 5⅗", print size 3½" x 3¼", crisply printed 13.00   18.00

☐283 **TODE BROS.**
T.B. and arrow through a ring on bottom, dark tan 9.00   12.00

U

☐284 **N.M.URI & CO. R.H. PARKER**
Tan, 2¾" 40.00   60.00

☐285 *VASE, label, 3½"* 9.00   12.00

☐286 *VOODOO FACE JUG, 2 under bottom, gray, 6" x 6"* 40.00   60.00

W

☐287 **VITREOUS STONE BOTTLING, J. BOURNE & SON**
Patentees Denby Pottery, near Derby P&J Arnold Sondon, 4¼" x 2½", pouring lip, brown 14.00   10.00

☐288	**WALKDENS COPYING INK**		
	Salt glaze, 7½"	90.00	120.00
☐289	**WATERLOW & SONS, LIMITED**		
	Brown, 7½"	13.00	18.00
☐290	**WESSON OIL**		
	Blue lettering, 5"	18.00	25.00
☐291	**WESTERN STONEWARE CO.**		
	Pat. Jan. 24, 1899 on bottom, brown and tan, 7"	18.00	25.00
☐292	**WEYMAN'S SNUFF**		
	On base, tan, 6¾"	17.00	24.00
☐293	*Same as above, except cream*	17.00	24.00
☐294	*WHISKEY, Label, tan and cream, 4"*	15.00	23.00
☐295	**N. A. WHITE & SONS, UTICA, N.Y.**		
	Blue iris flower on front, tan, 6¾"	32.00	45.00
☐296	**WHITE-HALL, W. H.**		
	Monogram, S. P. & S. Co. Whitehall, Ill., canning crock, 7"	23.00	35.00
☐297	**WIGTOWNSHIRE CREAMERY CO., CREAM JUG**		
	White, black underglaze transfer. 4½", transfer measures 3½" x 2½", picture of lady holding milking stool and milk pail, ribbon above contains: PURE FRESH CREAM. Ribbon below contains: WIGTOWNSHIRE CREAMMERY CO.	18.00	25.00
☐298	**WING LEE WAI, HONG KONG**		
	Under bottom, CHINESE RICE WINE: Federal Law Forbids Sale or Re-Use of This Bottle on back, brown, 6"	11.00	15.00
☐299	**WOAPOLLINARIS-BRANNEN**		
	M with an anchor in center of the seal, under it CEBRY KREUYBER AHR WEILER, RHEIN PRAUSSE, under it #65, handle, tan, 12"	19.00	27.00
☐300	**COMP. OF WORRELL & FOSTER, WEST END, ALA.**		
	Tan and brown, 3¼"	25.00	38.00
☐301	**WRIGHT & GREIG, GLASGOW.**		
	Whiskey Jug, 3½", biscuit color, handle at neck, underglaze transfer: Roderick Dhu, Highland Whiskey, Sole Proprietors: Wright & Greig, Glasgow, bottom incised C & F Glasgow, trasver measures 4¼" x 3½" and is picture of Highland Chief in full dress against background of mountains	35.00	50.00

X

☐302	**X**		
	On shoulder, brown pottery, 6½" tall, 3¾" diameter	9.00	12.00

Y

☐303	**COMPLIMENTS OF MRS. J. M. YOCKERS, 500 WILKINSON ST.**		
	Tan and cream, 3¼"	10.00	30.00

CURE BOTTLE

Cure bottles are among the most intriguing — certainly from a historical viewpoint — of any in the hobby. They serve as documentary evidence of how the public was fooled in the 19th and early 20th centuries when tonics and other preparations were advertised to cure all manner of physical and emotional problems. Strict modern laws enforced by the Food and Drug Administration, and Federal Trade Commission, do not allow the sale of such products any longer — except when the ad claims are vastly toned down.

The great number of cure bottles preserved for collectors bears testimony to public gullibility. It does not speak too well of the morals or motives of early manufacturers, either, who frequently not only failed to help the users of their products, but actually caused them harm. By leading people to believe that ailments and diseases could be cured by taking their preparations, they delayed or prevented many from seeking proper medical aid. All was fair in the "cure game." In 1816, J. Andrus of Hillsborough, New Hampshire, placed a cancer cure on the market. W. Stoy of Lebanon, Pennsylvania, had preceeded him seven years earlier with a hydrophobia (rabies) cure.

One reason for the success of quack patent medicines was general public distrust of doctors. Though the medical profession of the 19th century was not as well informed as today, it did not deserve much of the criticism heaped upon it. When a physician pronounced a case incurable, but a patent medicine maker said he could remedy it with a few swallows of such-and-such, the medicine maker was automatically considered smarter than the physican. This kind of thinking was not totally eradicated until well after 1900. Nor, in fact, might it be today, as many persons still rely on store-bought preparations rather than consulting doctors.

Patent medicine cures became such big business that road shows were organized around them. They worked not only out of wagons, but were booked into vaudeville theatres throughout the country. Various forms of entertainment were offered along with sales pitches for the product. Generally, the cast included several persons who had been "chronic sufferers" but due to repeated use of the cure, were totally healed. They came forward to tell their stories in long dull monologues. The show traditionally closed with cases of the product being carried onstage for the public to come up and purchase by the case or bottle. Patent medicine shows were extremely successful. They often realized better profits than the legitimate theatre, since they collected both from an admission fee and sale of the product (and, sometimes, sales of books, and quack appliances). Theatrical managers were always glad to book medicine shows into their theatres.

Manufacturers made a game of inventing bizarre product names. Some used foreign-sounding names or blatantly claimed that their product was of foreign origin. This was commonplace in retailing in the 19th century, not only for medicinal cures but other products. Coffee was customarily called Brazilian, leather Moroccan, rubber Indian, silk Persian, and tea Chinese, even if domestically produced. To suggest that something was imported not only lent charm, but imply that it was better. So far as medicines were concerned, slapping on foreign names gave the impression that somebody, somewhere in the world, had an inside track on curing ailments that baffled American science. One example of this was Carey's Chinese Cure (a very collectible bottle). Catarrh was the old-fashioned name for headcold. For all the American public knew, it was going along sneezing while 10,000 miles away the Chinese were merely downing this simple remedy whenever a cold struck. Of course, there was no cold cure in China — or anyplace else, but it sounded good, and it sold.

Some cures were supposingly composed of Indian medicine. It was widely known that indians did not visit the white man's physicians, did not take their medicines, but made cures of their own from closely-guarded recipes. Quite likely, if commercially sold "Indian cures" had followed the authentic recipes, some good might have been accomplished. But they merely used the name to sell worthless potions. They included the Ka-Ton-Ka Cure, and Kickapoo Indian Cough Cure. If the latter sounds familiar, Al Capp picked up the name and used it many years later in his comic strip, "Li'l Abner," transforming it into moonshine liquor called Kickapoo Joy Juice.

Try as you might, it would be difficult to name a disease, ailment or complaint for which a "cure" was not sold in the 19th century — usually many of them, by different makers. In fact, the following listings read like a compendium of bodily ills.

Many cure bottles are embossed with an owl and the traditional druggist symbol of mortar and pestle. The Owl Drug Store, established in San Francisco in 1882, became associated with Rexal in 1919. Owl Drugs sold its rights to the patent firm of Rexall, the United Drug Co., in 1933, and then was known as Owl-Rexall Drug Co.

CURES BOTTLES

A

NO.	DESCRIPTION	PRICE RANGE	
☐ 1	**A NO.** *1 self cure* *The specific-(label), aqua, 5"*	4.50	7.00
☐ 2	**ACID CURE SOLUTION, EMPIRE MFG. CO., AKRON, OHIO** *In a circle, crock, white, 4¾"*	9.00	12.00
☐ 3	**ABBOTT-BROS. - RHEUMATIC CURE** *Estd. 1888 all in four lines one side, Abbott Bros. other, amber, 7¾"*	14.00	21.00
☐ 4	**DR. ADAMS, COUGH CURE** *Prepared by E.J. Parker, Cortland, N.Y. all in 4 lines, flat ring top, beveled corner, clear, 5½"*	14.00	21.00

☐	5	**DR. AGNEWS CURE FOR THE HEART**		
		Ring top, clear, 8½"	9.00	12.00
☐	6	**DR. AGNEWS CURE FOR THE HEART**		
		In two lines, clear, ring top, 7½"	12.00	16.00
☐	7	*Same as above, except only two lines on front*	9.00	12.00
☐	8	**ALEXANDER'S SURE CURE FOR MALARIA, AKRON, OHIO**		
		On side Alexanders Liver & Kidney Tonic, ring top, amber, 8"	9.00	12.00
☐	9	**ALEXANDER'S SURE CURE FOR MALARIA**		
		Ring top, amber, 6½"	9.00	12.00
☐	10	**ALEXANDER'S SURE CURE FOR MALARIA, Akron**		
		Other side ALEXANDER'S LIVER & KIDNEY TONIC, Akron, Ohio, ring top and ring in center of neck, amber, 7¾"	20.00	30.00
☐	11	**ALKAVIS SURE CURE FOR MALARIA**		
		Label, ring top, amber, 8¼"	7.00	10.00
☐	12	**ALLCOCK'S**		
		On one side, other DANDRUFF CURE, ring top, clear, 6½"	9.00	12.00
☐	13	**ALMYR SYSTEM OF TREATMENT FOR CATARRH**		
		ALMYR CATARRH CURE in three lines, aqua, ring top, 8¼"	25.00	32.00
☐	14	**ANCHOR WEAKNESS CURE**		
		Amber, 8¼"	8.00	11.00
☐	15	**ANTIMIGRAINE CURE EVERY VARIETY OF HEADACHE**		
		Clear or amethyst, 5¼"	7.00	10.00
☐	16	**ANTIBRULE CHEMICAL CO.**		
		Other side St. Louis, Mo. U.S.A., on front ANTIBULE CURES BURRUS-WOUNDS-SKIN DISEASES-AND ALL INFLAMMATION in three lines, clear, 6¼"	15.00	20.00
☐	17	**ATLAS KIDNEY & LIVER CURE, ATLAS MEDICINE CO., HENDERSON, N.C. U.S.A.**		
		With fancy monogram, AM CO. in sunken panel, honey amber, 9"	11.00	15.00
☐	18	**AMERICAN**		
		On one side, COUGH CURE other, front Howard Bros., aqua, 6½"	12.00	16.00
☐	19	*Same as above, except Prepared by W. B. Jones, M.D.* ...	12.00	16.00
☐	20	**AQUE**		
		Front one side, AQUE CURE other, Lowell, Mass., double ring top, aqua, 7"	8.00	11.00
☐	21	**ARCTIC FROSTBITE CURE**		
		Label, ring top, clear or amber, 2¾"	7.00	10.00
☐	22	**AYER'S**		
		In sunken panel, one side AQUE CURE, other Lowell, Mass., aqua, pontil, 7"	18.00	25.00
☐	23	*Same as above, except no pontil*	8.00	11.00

B

☐	24	**B.H. BACON, ROCHESTER N.Y., OTTO'S CURE**		
		Clear, 2½"	6.00	9.00
☐	25	**BAKER'S BLOOD & LIVER CURE**		
		Large crown with a flag, amber, 9½"	55.00	70.00

☐	26	**BAKER'S SOUTH AMERICAN FEVER AND AGUE CURE**		
		Ring top, amber, 9¾"	38.00	52.00
☐	27	**BAUER'S COUGH CURE**		
		On front, clear, 2⅞"	6.00	9.00
☐	28	**BAUER'S INSTANT COUGH CURE**		
		Aqua, 7"	10.00	13.00
☐	29	**BAUER'S INSTANT COUGH CURE**		
		Mt. Morris, N.Y. in three lines, tapered top, aqua, 7"	16.00	22.00
☐	30	**P. A. BENJAMIN'S LIVER & KIDNEY CURE**		
		Tapered top, aqua, 7½"	6.00	9.00
☐	31	**BENSON'S CURE FOR RHEUMATISM**		
		In three lines, three ring top, pontil, aqua, 6½"	16.00	22.00
☐	32	**DR. BENNETT'S**		
		Other side A. L. Scoville & Co., front, quick cure, aqua, 4½"	15.00	21.00
☐	33	**BIRD'S LUNG CURE**		
		In two lines vertical, ring top, aqua, 2½"	16.00	22.00
☐	34	**BISHOP'S GRANULAR CITRATE OF MAGNESIA, SAN FRANCISCO, COUGH CURE**		
		Blue, 6½"	7.00	11.00
☐	35	**BLISS LIVER & KIDNEY CURE**		
		Aqua or clear, 9¼"	8.00	12.00
☐	36	**BLISS LIVER & KIDNEY CURE**		
		Clear, 7"	10.00	14.00
☐	37	**THE BLISS REMEDY CO., BLISS LIVER & KIDNEY CURE, STOCKTON, CAL.**		
		Aqua, 9¼"	11.00	15.00
☐	38	**BOERIKE & RUNYON , S.F. & PORTLAND**		
		Clear or amethyst, 5½"	7.00	11.00
☐	39	**DR. BOSAKO'S RHEUMATIC CURE**		
		Aqua, 5¾"	6.00	9.00
☐	40	**BREEDENS RHEUMATIC CURE**		
		Label, BREEDEN MEDICINE CO., CHATTANOOGA, TENN. on front, aqua, 6½"	9.00	12.00
☐	41	**BRIGGS TONIC PILLS, NEVER FAIL TO CURE**		
		M.A. Briggs, Valdosta, Ga., clear, 3"	6.00	9.00
☐	42	**BRIGHTSBANE, THE GREAT KIDNEY AND LIVER CURE**		
		Vertical on front, square beveled corners, light amber, 8⅞"	10.00	14.00
☐	43	**BROWN'S BLOOD CURE, PHILDELPHIA**		
		Green, 6½"	15.00	21.00
☐	44	**BROWNS HOUSEHOLD PANACEA AND FAMILY LINIMENT**		
		Vertical on front panels, Curtis & Brown on side, Mfg. Col'd. New York on opposite side, rectangular, square collar, aqua, 5⅛"	8.00	12.00
☐	45	**BUCHAN'S HUNGARIAN**		
		Balsam of Life, London, vertical lines Kidney Cure, round short neck, green, 5¾"	6.00	9.00
☐	46	**DR. L. BURDICK'S KIDNEY CURE**		
		In two lines, amber, ring top, 7¼"	20.00	27.00
☐	47	*Same as above, except with Lodewick*	16.00	22.00
☐	48	**DR. L. BURDICK'S KIDNEY CURE**		
		In two lines, vertical, ring top, amber, 7¼"	23.00	32.00

☐ 49 **SAN JAK BURNHAM'S**
Kidney Cure all in 3 vertical lines, on shoulder Chicago,
ring top, clear, 7" **15.00** **21.00**
☐ 50 **DR. SAN JAK BURNHAM'S**
KIDNEY CURE in three lines vertical, on shoulder,
Chicago, ring top, clear, 7¼" **15.00** **21.00**
☐ 51 **BUXTON'S RHEUMATIC CURE**
Aqua, 8½" **7.00** **10.00**
☐ 52 **THE DR. D. M. BYE OIL CURE CO.**
Reverse side, 316 N. Illinois St., other side Indianapolis,
Ind., ring top, clear, 6½" **7.00** **10.00**

C

☐ 53 **C** *(small letters)* **ubeb, ouch, ure**
All in one word, vertical, double ring top, clear, 5¼" **9.00** **13.00**
☐ 54 **CANADIAN BOASTER HAIR TONIC**
Reverse side Dandruff Cure, clear, 8¼" **7.00** **10.00**
☐ 55 **CAMPBELL & LYON**
On one side, other Detroit, Mich., front UMATILLA-
INDIAN-COUGH CURE in two lines, vertical, tapered top,
aqua, 5½" **21.00** **30.00**
☐ 56 **CAPUDINE HEADACHE CURE**
Oval, aqua, 3⅜" **6.00** **10.00**
☐ 57 **CARSON'S AGUE CURE**
Jamestown, N. Y. in three lines vertical, ring top, aqua,
7¼" **15.00** **21.00**
☐ 58 **CERTAIN CURE FOR RHEUMATISM**
Vertical on front in sunken panel, Chas. Dennin on side,
Brooklyn on opposite side, aqua, 6¾" **11.00** **15.00**
☐ 59 **CHASE'S DYSPEPSIA CURE**
Newburgh, N. Y. in three lines vertical, double ring top,
aqua, 8¾" **15.00** **21.00**
☐ 60 **CHAMBERLAINS CURE FOR CONSUMPTION**
Aqua, 5" **7.00** **10.00**
☐ 61 **CILL'S CATARRH CURE**
Vertical on front, sheared top, round bottom, clear, 3¼" . **11.00** **15.00**
☐ 62 **THE CLINIC KIDNEY & LIVER CURE**
In two lines, on back M'fr'd by Foley & Co., Stubenville, O.
& Chicago, amber, tapered top, 9½" **21.00** **28.00**
☐ 63 **DR. J.W. COBLENTZ CURE, FT. WAYNE, IND.**
Label, cobalt, 7¾" **6.00** **10.00**
☐ 64 **COE'S DYSPEPSIA CURE OR STOMACH BITTERS,**
THE C. G. CLARK CO., NEW HAVEN, CONN. U.S.A.
Clear or aqua, 7½" **11.00** **15.00**
☐ 65 **COKE DANDRUFF CURE**
On bottom, large ring top, clear, 6½" **11.00** **15.00**
☐ 66 **MRS. M.E. CONVERSE'S SURE CURE FOR EPILEPSY**
Ring top, clear, 6¾" **10.00** **15.00**
☐ 67 **C.C.C. (CORN CURE) BY MENDENHELL CO.,**
EVANSVILLE, IND.
Ring top, clear or aqua, 4¼" **13.00** **19.00**

☐ 68 *Also C.C.C. (Certain Cough Cure)* **13.00** **19.00**
☐ 69 **DR. COSTA'S RADICAL CURE FOR DYSPEPSIA**
In sunken panels, double ring top, aqua, 5½" **7.00** **10.00**
☐ 70 **CRAIG'S KIDNEY**
(c. 1887)in ½ moon circle, under it Liver Cure Company, amber, double ring top, bottle same as Warner Safe Cure, 9½" **23.00** **32.00**
☐ 71 **CRAIG'S KIDNEY**
in ¼ moon letters under it in 4 lines & Liver Cure Company, oval, double ring top, amber, 9¼" **21.00** **30.00**
☐ 72 **DR. CRAIG'S COUGH & CONSUMPTION CURE**
In four lines vertical, double ring top, amber, 8" **140.00** **190.00**
☐ 73 **CRAMERS KIDNEY & LIVER, CURE**
In 3 lines, ring top, aqua, 7" **12.00** **17.00**
☐ 74 **CRAMER'S COUGH CURE**
In two lines, ring top, aqua, 6¼" **15.00** **21.00**
☐ 75 **CRAMER'S KIDNEY CURE SAMPLE**
Albany, N.Y. in four lines, ring top, round bottle, aqua, 4½" **15.00** **21.00**
☐ 76 **CRISWELL'S BROMO-PEPSIN CURES HEADACHE**
Vertical, round, ring top, amber, 2½" **10.00** **14.00**
☐ 77 **CRISWELL'S BROMO-PEPSIN CURES HEADACHE AND DIGESTION**
Vertical on front, amber, 4¾" **10.00** **14.00**
☐ 78 **CROSBY-5-MINUTE CURE**
In three lines vertical, ring top, amber, 2¾" **8.00** **12.00**
☐ 79 **CROW'S CHILL CURE**
In two lines vertical, tapered top, aqua, 9½" **12.00** **17.00**
☐ 80 **CURTIS COUGH CURE**
C.C.C. on each side, J. J. Mack & Co. - sole Proprietors, San Francisco, Cal., ring top, aqua, 7" **9.00** **13.00**
☐ 81 **CURTIS COUGH CURE**
In two lines on top Ointment in center C.C.C., also on each side C.C.C., ring top, aqua, 7" **16.00** **21.00**
☐ 82 **J.M. CURTIS CURE FOR THE BALDNESS**
Providence, R.I., flared top, aqua, ½ pint **10.00** **14.00**
☐ 83 **THE CUTICURA SYSTEM OF CURING CONSTIPATIONAL HUMORS**
On front of panel, Potter Drug and Chemical Corp. Boston, Mass, U.S.A. on reverse of panel, rectangular, aqua, 9¼" **10.00** **14.00**

D

☐ 84 **DaCOSTAS RADICAL CURE**
On 3 panels Morris & Heritage on one side other Philadelphia, SSS monogram at top, in back panels, ring top, aqua, 8¼" **16.00** **21.00**
☐ 85 **DR. DANIEL'S COLIC CURE**
Ring top, clear or amethyst, 3¾" **6.00** **9.00**
☐ 86 **DR. DANIEL'S COLIC CURE NO. 1**
On front, square, clear, 3½" **6.00** **9.00**

☐ 87	**DR. DANIEL'S COLIC CURE NO. 2** *Same as above*	6.00	9.00
☐ 88	**DR. DANIEL'S VETERINARY COLIC CURE NO. 1** *On front, square, clear, 3½"*	7.00	10.00
☐ 89	**DR. DANIEL'S VETERINARY COLIC CURE NO. 2** *Same as above*	7.00	10.00
☐ 90	**DATILMA-A RADICAL CURE FOR PAIN** *In three lines vertical, clear, ring top, 4½"*	7.00	10.00
☐ 91	**DEAN'S KIDNEY CURE** *The Langham Med. Co. LeRoy, N.Y. in 3 lines, ring top,* *7¼", aqua*	11.00	15.00
☐ 92	**DEERING & BERRY — GREAT KIDNEY CURE** *Saco, Me. in three lines vertical, ring top and ring on neck,* *clear, 6⅛"*	9.00	12.00
☐ 93	**DeWITTS COLIC & CHOLERA CURE** *Green, 4½"*	6.00	9.00
☐ 94	**DR. DeWITT'S LIVER, BLOOD, & KIDNEY CURE** *Amber, 8½"*	28.00	37.00
☐ 95	**DR. DeWITT'S** *Electric Cure, W.J. Parker & Co. Baltimore Md., tapered* *top, aqua, 6½"*	10.00	15.00
☐ 96	**E. C. DeWITT & CO., CHICAGO U.S.A., ONE MINUTE COUGH CURE** *Tapered top, aqua, 4½"*	7.0	10.00
☐ 97	**E.G. DeWITTS & CO., CHICAGO** *Label, side mold, Dyspepsia Cure on back, clear, 9¼"* ...	10.00	15.00
☐ 98	**W. H. DOLF'S SURE CURE FOR COLIC** *Flat ring top, T.C.W. & Co. under bottom, aqua, 3½"*	10.00	15.00
☐ 99	**DUFFY'S TOWER MINT CURE (TRADEMARK EST 1842)** *Tapered bottle, wide ring top, embossed tower and flag,* *amber, 6½"*	85.00	105.00

E

☐100	**ELECTRICITY IN A BOTTLE** *Around shoulder, on base The West Electric Cure Co., ring* *top, blue or amber, 2½"*	8.00	11.00
☐101	**ELEPIZONE, A CERTAIN CURE FOR FITS AND EPILEPSY, ELEPIZONE, H.G. ROOT M.C.** *183 Pearl St., New York on front, ring top, aqua, 8½"*	30.00	40.00
☐102	**ELLIS'S SPAVIN CURE** *In two lines vertical, ring top, aqua, 8"*	15.00	21.00
☐103	**EMERSON'S RHEUMATIC CURE** *Emerson Pharmaceutical Company, Baltimore, Md. in five* *lines, ring top, amber, 5"*	9.00	12.00

F

☐104	**FALEY'S [sic] KIDNEY & BLADDER CURE** *On front, Foley's & Co. on one side, Chicago, U.S.A. on* *reverse, amber, 9½"*	7.00	10.00

☐105	**DR. M.M. FENNER'S** *Amber, 10¼"*	**14.00**	**20.00**
☐106	**DR. M.M. FENNER'S PEOPLES REMEDIES, N.Y., U.S.A.,** **KIDNEY & BACKACHE CURE 1872-1898** *All on front horizontally, amber, 10½"*	**32.00**	**47.00**
☐107	**FITCH'S DANDRUFF CURE, IDEAL DANDRUFF CURE CO.** *Ring top, 6¼"*	**7.00**	**10.00**
☐108	**FITZGERALD'S MEMBRANE CURE** *Vertical on front in sunken panel, aqua*	**12.00**	**17.00**
☐109	**FOLEY'S KIDNEY & BLADDER CURE** *On front, on one side Foley & Co., reverse Chicago U.S.A.,* *double ring top, amber, 7½"*	**9.00**	**13.00**
☐110	**SAMPLE BOTTLE FOLEY'S KIDNEY CURE, FOLEY & CO.,** **CHICAGO, U.S.A.** *Vertical around bottle, aqua, 4¼"*	**7.00**	**10.00**
☐111	**FOLGER'S OLOSAONIAN** *On front on one side Doct. Bobt. T.B., deeply leveled corner, long neck, tapered top, pontil, aqua, 7½"*	**15.00**	**20.00**
☐112	**FOLEY'S SAFE DIARRHEA & COLIC CURE, CHICAGO** *Panels, aqua, 5½"*	**7.00**	**10.00**
☐113	**FONTAINE'S CURE** *One side, other FOR THROAT & LUNG DISEASES, front in* *three lines FONTAINE'S COLIT, Brooklyn, N.Y., U.S.A, ring* *top, aqua, 5½"*	**8.00**	**12.00**
☐114	**H.D. FOWLE, BOSTON** *In back, label, Fowle's Pile & Humor Cure, ring top, aqua* *5½"*	**9.00**	**13.00**
☐115	**DR. FRANK, TURKEY FEBRIFUGE FOR THE CURE OF** **FEVER AND AGUE** *Pontil, aqua, 6"*	**15.00**	**22.00**
☐116	**FREE SAMPLE CRAMERS KIDNEY CURE** *Albany and N.Y. are reversed, aqua, 4¼"*	**11.00**	**16.00**
☐117	**FRENCHS** *Under it a crown, on each side Trade Mark, under it Kidney* *& Liver & Dropsy Cure Co., on base Price 1.00-all on front,* *round corners double ring top, Trade Mark in reverse,* *9½", amber*	**24.00**	**32.00**
☐118	**FROG POND CHILL & FEVER CURE** *Flat ring top, amber, 7"*	**31.00**	**42.00**

G

☐119	**G.R. & N. CURE &, MAGICAL PAIN, EXTRACTOR** *In 3 lines on front, ring top, aqua, 4¼"*	**12.00**	**18.00**
☐120	**GANTER'S L. F., MAGIC CHICKEN CHOLERA CURE** *L. P. Ganter Medicine Co. - Glasgow, N. Y., U.S.A. in nine* *lines, ring top, amber, 6¾"*	**38.00**	**52.00**
☐121	**GARGET CURE, C.T. WHIPPLE PROP., PORTLAND, ME.** *Ring top, aqua, 5¾"*	**7.00**	**10.00**
☐122	**Dr. A.F. GEOGHEGAN, LOUISVILLE KY., CURE FOR** **SCROFULA** *Graphite pontil, aqua, 9¼"*	**55.00**	**77.00**

☐ 123 **GLOVER'S IMPERIAL DISTEMPER CURE, H. CLAY GLOVER, NEW YORK**
Vertical on front, amber, 5" **7.00** **10.00**

☐ 124 **GLOVERS IMPERIAL MANGE CURE**
H. Clay Glover DU'S one side, New York on other side, amber, 7" **7.00** **10.00**

☐ 125 **GOLD DANDRUFF CURE**
Vertical on center front, ring top, clear, 7½" **10.00** **15.00**

☐ 126 **GOLDEN ROD LOTION, A SAFE AND CERTAIN CURE**
Amber, 6" **12.00** **17.00**

☐ 127 **GRAHAM'S DYSPEPSIA CURE**
S. Grover Graham Co., Newburgh, N.Y., clear, 8½" **7.00** **10.00**

☐ 128 **GRAY'S BAKAM, BEST COUGH CURE**
In 2 lines, one side S.K. Pierson, other LeRoy, N.Y., tapered top, clear, 6½" **15.00** **22.00**

☐ 129 **S. GROVER GRAHAM'S DYSPEPSIA CURE, NEWBURG, N.Y.**
Vertical on front in large letters, amethyst, 8¼" **13.00** **18.00**

☐ 130 **GROVE'S CHRONIC CHILL CURE**
All on front in 2 lines, ring top, clear, 7¼" **12.00** **17.00**

☐ 131 **DR. GRAVES HEART REGULATOR, CURES HEART DISEASE**
Ring top, aqua, 5¾" **7.00** **10.00**

☐ 132 **THE GREAT DR. KILMER SWAMP ROOT KIDNEY LIVER & BLADDER CURE SPECIFIC**
Aqua or clear, 8¼" **9.00** **13.00**

☐ 133 *Same as above, except THE GREAT & SPECIFIC* **9.00** **13.00**

☐ 134 **GREGORY'S INSTANT CURE**
Pontil, aqua, 4" and 6" **11.00** **16.00**

H

☐ 135 **HALL'S CATARRH CURE**
Aqua, 4½" **8.00** **11.00**

☐ 136 **HALL'S CATARRH CURE**
Aqua, 5½" **9.00** **13.00**

☐ 137 **HALL'S CATARRH CURE**
Aqua, 6½" **9.00** **13.00**

☐ 138 **DR. B. W. HAIR'S ASTHMA CURE**
Hamilton, Ohio in three lines, tapered top, 8" **12.00** **17.00**

☐ 139 **HAMILTON'S MEDICINES CURE**
All in side of a 7 pts. star, under it, Auburn, N.Y., rectangular, ring top, aqua, 8½" **16.00** **23.00**

☐ 140 **DR. HANFORD'S CELERY CURE OR NERVE FOOD CURE**
Rheumatism - neuralgia - insomnia & C & C all in nine lines on front, double ring top, aqua, 7½" **9.00** **12.00**

☐ 141 **DR. HARDING'S**
Celebrated, Catarrh Cure, in 3 lines on front, ring top, clear, 3" **12.00** **17.00**

☐ 142 **HARTS HONEY & HAREHOUND**
Cure, coughs, colds, group, 4 lines on front on one side Lincoln, ILL. U.S. Other Harts Med. Co., ring top, clear 7" **12.00** **17.00**

☐143 **HART'S SWEDISH ASTHMA CURE**
Buffalo N.Y. on side, rectangular, beveled corners, light amber, 6⅝" 7.00 10.00

☐144 *Same as above, except by INDIAN MED. CO., CLINTONVILLE, CONN.* 6.00 9.00

☐145 **HEALY & BIGELOWS KICKAPOO INDIAN COUGH CURE**
On panels, ring top, aqua, 6¼" 6.00 9.00

☐146 **HEBBARD'S, Dr. CURE FOR FITS**
New York in three lines, vertical, ring top, clear, 8½" 15.00 22.00

☐147 **DR. J.B. HEMOUS**
Reverse side Sure Cure For Malaria, cobalt, 6¼" 9.00 12.00

☐148 **HEPATICURE FOR BLOOD, LIVER & KIDNEYS**
In 2 lines on front, on one side Marshall Med. Co., other Kansas City, Mo., ring top, clear or amethyst, 9½" 22.00 32.00

☐149 **DR. HERMAN'S**
Vegetable, Catarrh Cure on round type bottle in 3 lines, ring top, clear, 2¾" 12.00 17.00

☐150 **DR. HERNDON'S**
On one side, other Gypsey Gift Bank, plain front, in over lap letter H.G.G. in side of a circle under it in 5 lines. That is medicine which cures, Balt, DMD. rectangular, long neck & ring top, clear, 6½" 15.00 22.00

☐151 **HERRICK'S HOREHOUND SYRUP**
Cures all throat and lung infections all in 3 lines, ring neck & top, aqua, 6" 15.00 22.00

☐152 **HICK'S CAPUDINE CURES ALL HEADACHES, ETC.**
Amber, 5¾" 12.00 17.00

☐153 **HILLEMANS AMERICAN CHICKEN CHOLERA CURE, ARLINGTON, MINN.**
Flared top, cobalt, 6½" 40.00 55.00

☐154 **DR. HILLER'S COUGH CURE**
Tapered top, aqua, 7½" 9.00 12.00

☐155 **HILLS**
With block H letters and arrow, under it DYS-PEP-CU-CURES CHRONIC DYSPEPSIA, INDIAN DRUG SPECIALTY CO., St. Louis, Indianapolis on front, tapered top, amber, 8½" 20.00 30.00

☐156 **HIMALAYA, THE KOLA COMPOUND, NATURES CURE FOR ASTHMA, NEW YORK, CINCINNATI**
Embossed horizontally on indented front panels, square, amber, 7½" 12.00 18.00

☐157 **HIRES**
Cough Cure, Phila. Pa. on sides, aqua, 4½" 9.00 12.00

☐158 **HIRES**
On front on one side Cough Cure, other side Phila., ring top, aqua, 4½" 12.00 17.00

☐159 **HITE'S PAIN CURE**
Staunton, Va. 2 lines on front, ring top, clear, 5½" 12.00 17.00

☐160 **HOLLOWAY'S — CORN CURE**
In two lines running vertically, ring top, clear, 2¼" 6.00 9.00

☐161 **HOLLENSWORTH'S RUPTURE CURE**
In three lines, aqua, ring top, 6¼" 15.00 22.00

105

124

136

157

182

208

215

225

237

268

294

296

319

330

335

☐162	**HOWARD BROS.**		
	On front, one side AMERICAN, other COUGH CURE, aqua, 6½"	12.00	17.00
☐163	**HOWARD BROS.**		
	On front, on one side Cough Cure, other side Pettit's American, tapered top, aqua, 7"	8.00	12.00
☐164	**DR. S.D. HOWE'S ARABIAN MILK CURE FOR CONSUMPTION**		
	Clear, 6"	9.00	12.00
☐165	*Same as above, except 7½"*	17.00	23.00
☐166	**C. H. HOWE**		
	On the other side CURE, ring top, aqua, 7¼"	9.00	12.00
☐167	**C. I. HOOD & CO.**		
	Lowell, Mass. in back, TUS SANO CURES COUGHS in three lines, aqua, double ring top, 2½"	15.00	22.00
☐168	**HOOD'S PILLS CURE LIVER ILLS**		
	All in a circle, ring top, sim. round bottle, 1"	6.00	9.00
☐169	**DR. HOXSIE'S**		
	On the side Buffalo, N.Y. Certain Croup Cure in two lines, clear, ring top, 4¾"	7.00	10.00
☐170	**HUFFMAN'S**		
	In script, GOITRE CURE - NAPANEE, ONT. in three lines vertical, ring top, clear. 4¼"	11.00	15.00
☐171	**HUNNICUTT'S**		
	Reverse side Rheumatic Cure, ring top, aqua, 8"	7.00	10.00

I

☐172	**INDIAN MED. CO., CLINTONVILLE, CONN., KICKAPOO INDIAN COUGH CURE**		
	Aqua, 5¾"	7.00	10.00

J

☐173	**W. M. JOHNSON'S PURE HERB TONIC, SURE CURE FOR ALL MALARIAL DISEASES**		
	Vertical lettering, clear, 6"	10.00	14.00

K

☐174	**K.K.K., KAY'S KENTUCKY KURE OR LINIMENT**		
	Vertical around bottle, aqua, 3¾"	20.00	27.00
☐175	**DR. J. KAUFFMAN'S ANGELINE, INTERNAL RHEUMA-TISM CURE, HAMILTON, OHIO**		
	Vertical in three lines on front, flared top, clear, 7⅞"	15.00	22.00
☐176	**DR. L. E. KEELEY, KEELEY'S CURE FOR DRUNKNESS**		
	Etc., Dwight, Ill., ring top, clear or amethyst, 5½"	9.00	12.00
☐177	**KEESLING CHICKEN CHOLERA CURE C.C.C.**		
	Package 25 cents, B. F. Keeslings, Logansport, Ind.	9.00	12.00
☐178	**KENDALL'S SPAVIN CURE FOR HUMAN FLESH**		
	Vertical on two panels, ten vertical panels, aqua, 5¼"	7.00	10.00

☐179	**KENDALL'S SPAVIN CURE**		
	Around shoulders, Enosburgh Falls, Vt. on bottom, twelve		
	vertical panels, amber, 5½"	7.00	10.00
☐180	**KELLUM'S · SURE CURE FOR INDIGESTION AND DYSPEPSIA**		
	In six lines, ring top, clear, 6¾"	15.00	22.00
☐181	**KICKAPOO COUGH CURE**		
	Vertical on indented panel, round, aqua, 6¼"	9.00	13.00
☐182	**E. J. KIEFFER**		
	Amber, 8"	9.00	13.00
☐183	**E. J. KIEFFER**		
	Amber, 9"	9.00	13.00
☐184	**K. K. CURE'S BRIGHTS DISEASE AND CYSTITIS**		
	All in six lines, one side K. K. Med. Co., other side New		
	Jersey, aqua, tapered top, 7½"	11.00	16.00
☐185	**DR. KILMER'S SURE HEADACHE CURE**		
	25 doses in a box	6.00	9.00
☐186	**DR. KILMER'S INDIAN COUGH CURE CONSUMPTION OIL**		
	Vertical on front, BINGHAMTON, N.Y. on side, rectan-		
	gular, aqua, square collar, ball neck, 7⅛"	12.00	17.00
☐187	**KILMER'S Dr. — SAMPLE BOTTLE SWAMPROOT KIDNEY CURE**		
	London, E.C., aqua, double ring top, 4½"	15.00	22.00
☐188	**DR. KILMER'S SWAMPROOT KIDNEY LIVER AND BLADDER CURE**		
	London, E.C. vertical on front, rectangular, aqua, double		
	band top, 5¾"	15.00	22.00
☐189	*Same as above, only 7¼"*	15.00	22.00
☐190	**SAMPLE BOTTLE DR. KILMER'S SWAMPROOT KIDNEY CURE**		
	London, E.C., aqua, cylindrical, square top, 3¼"	15.00	22.00
☐191	**SAMPLE BOTTLE DR. KILMER'S SWAMPROOT KIDNEY CURE**		
	London, E.C. vertical on front, aqua, cylindrical, square		
	collar, 4⅛"	22.00	32.00
☐192	**SAMPLE BOTTLE DR. KILMER'S SWAMPROOT KIDNEY CURE**		
	Binghamton, N.Y. vertical on front, cylindrical, aqua,		
	square collar, 4⅜", 3⅛", 4⅛", 4¼"	12.00	17.00
☐193	**DR. T. J. KILMER'S COUGH CURE**		
	Schoharie, N.Y. vertical on front, rectangular, aqua,		
	square band collar, 5⅝"	12.00	17.00
☐194	**THE GREAT / DR. KILMER'S SWAMPROOT KIDNEY LIVER AND BLADDER CURE**		
	In embossed kidney shape panel / SPECIFIC, on front,		
	BINGHAMTON, N.Y. on side, aqua, double band collar,		
	rectangle, 8¼", 8⅛", 8", 8½", 9"	14.00	22.00
☐195	**DR. KILMER'S SWAMPROOT KIDNEY LIVER AND BLADDER CURE**		
	BINGHAMTON, N.Y., USA embossed on front, rectan-		
	gular, aqua, double band collar, 7"	7.00	10.00
☐196	*Same as above, only square band collaring neck7¼"*	7.00	10.00
☐197	*Same as above, only square band collar, 4¾"*	7.00	10.00

☐ 198 **DR. KILMER'S INDIAN COUGH CURE CONSUMPTION OIL**
Vertical on front, BINGHAMTON, N.Y. on side, rectangular, aqua, double band collar, 5⅝" **18.00 23.00**

☐ 199 **DR. KILMER'S COUGH CURE CONSUMPTION OIL**
(In embossed lung shape panel) CATARRH SPECIFIC all on front, BINGHAMTON, N.Y. on side, rectangular, aqua, double band collar, 8¾" **60.00 80.00**

☐ 200 **DR. KILMER'S SWAMP ROOT KIDNEY CURE, BINGHAMTON, N.Y.**
Aqua, 1½" **7.00 11.00**

☐ 201 **THE GREAT KILMERS**
Swamp-Root Kidney Liver and Bladder Cure Specific on front, Binghamton, N.Y. on left, Dr. Kilmer & Co. on right, aqua, rectangular, 8¼" **9.00 12.00**

☐ 202 **DR. KING'S NEW CURE FOR CONSUMPTION**
Clear or aqua, 6" **7.00 10.00**

☐ 203 **KODOL DYSPEPSIA CURE**
On side, E. C. DeWitt & Co., Chicago on opposite side, rectangular, aqua, 6⅞" **8.00 11.00**

L

☐ 204 **LANGERBACH'S DYSENTARY CURE**
Vertical on front, San Francisco, Cal., round bottle, blob type, amber, 6" **20.00 27.00**

☐ 205 **LASH'S KIDNEY & LIVER CURE**
Amber, 9" **25.00 34.00**

☐ 206 **JARABE DE LEONARDI**
Para La Tos Creostodado, Leonardi Cough Cure Creosoted, New York and Tampa, Fla. in four lines in sunken panel, plain back, plain sunken side panels, aqua, under bottom W. T. Co 4, U.S.A., 5¼" **6.00 9.00**

☐ 207 **LEONARDI'S COUGH CURE, CREOSOTED**
N.Y. & Tampa, aqua, 5½" **7.00 10.00**

☐ 208 **LEONARDI'S TASTELESS**
Clear or amethyst, 6¼" **6.00 9.00**

☐ 209 **LIEBIG'S FIT CURE — AN ENGLISH REMEDY**
Dr. A. B. Meserole, 96 John St., N. Y. in five lines, ring top, aqua, 5½" **10.00 14.00**

☐ 210 **LIGHTNING KIDNEY AND LIVER CURE**
No Relief, No Pay, in 2 lines on front, on one side Herb Med. Co. other Weston, W. Va., double ring top, aqua, 9½" **23.00 32.00**

☐ 211 **LIGHTNING KIDNEY & LIVER CURE, NO RELIEF, NO PAY, HERB MED. CO.**
Weston, West Va., aqua, 9½" **35.00 45.00**

☐ 212 **LIGHTNING OIL**
On one side, other Oil, front sure cure, back plain, rectangular, ring top, aqua, 5½" **12.00 17.00**

☐ 213 **LITTLE GIANT CATARRH CURE**
In two lines back, Warsaw, N. Y., one side only Mfd. by A. F. Mann, ring top, amber, 3½" **16.00 22.00**

☐214 **LONG'S STANDARD MALARIA CURE CO.,**
ROCHESTER, N. Y., *in six lines*
Amber, double ring top, 7½" 10.00 14.00
☐215 **LOOKOUT MOUNTAIN MEDICINE CO.**
Amber, 10½" 16.00 22.00
☐216 **LUCAS, D. D. CO. — VINELAND, N. J. —**
BOHEMIAN CATARRH CURE
Ring top, clear, 3¼" 6.00 9.00

M

☐217 **J.J. MACK & CO., S.F. CAL., CURTIS COUGH**
CURE, C.C.C.
On both sides, 7" 11.00 16.00
☐218 *MAGIC MOSQUITO BITE CURE & INSECT*
EXTERMINATOR, SALLADE & CO. N.Y.
On front, oval, tapered collar, aqua, 7⅞" 10.00 15.00
☐219 **MALOY OIL H.F.M.**
In leaf, Instant Relief Cure Rheumatism, clear, 4¾" 7.00 10.00
☐220 **DR. J. B. MARCHICI**
On other side Utica, N.Y., ring top, aqua, 6¼" 9.00 12.00
☐221 **MARNE'S FAMOUS ANISEED CURE**
In two lines, clear, ring top, 5" 15.00 22.00
☐222 **MARVINIS CHERRY COUGH CURE**
Label, tapered top, amber, 9½" 15.00 22.00
☐223 **MAYER'S MAGNETIC CATARRH CURE**
In two lines vertical, ring top, clear, 3½" 9.00 13.00
☐224 **MERTOL DANDRUFF CURE**
Clear, 5½" 7.00 10.00
☐225 **DR. MILES NEW HEART CURE**
Vertical on front in sunken panel, double band collar,
aqua, 8½" 11.00 15.00
☐226 *Same as above, free sample size, 4¼"* 12.00 16.00
☐227 **MINER'S DAMIANA NERVE DISEASE CURE**
Embossed woman, amber, 8¼" 65.00 85.00
☐228 **PETER P. MINIOTTIS — RHEUMATISM CURE**
In center, in a circle man with a bear around it - Great
West Indian Discovery, etc. - 10 Wyckoff St., Brooklyn,
N.Y. Registered, under bottom "21", tapered top, aqua,
Label only, 10" 12.00 16.00
☐229 *Embossed* 20.00 27.00
☐230 **MORRIS & HERITAGE**
On one side, other Philadelphia, SSS monogram in back,
on front DACOSTO'S RADICAL CURE in three lines, ring
top, aqua, 8¼" 30.00 42.00
☐231 **MORRIS-MORTON DRUG CO.**
On one side, other, Ft. Smith, Ark. on front, SWAMP-CHILL
AND FEVER CURE in four lines, tapered top, clear or
amethyst, 6½" 23.00 32.00
☐232 **MOXIE CATARRH CURE**
Around flat watch type bottle, clear, 1½" 23.00 32.00

☐ 233	**MUNYON'S INHALER, CURES COLDS, CATARRH AND ALL THROAT & LUNG DISEASES**		
	On front, Patented, Fill to the Line on back, round, olive green, 4⅛"	15.00	20.00
☐ 234	**MYSTIC CURE**		
	Other side MYSTIC CURE, on front for Rheumatism and Neuralgia, ring top, clear or Aut., 6¼"	9.00	12.00
☐ 235	**MYSTERIOUS PAIN CURE — A SCOTCH REMEDY**		
	In three lines, vertical, ring top, clear, 5½"	9.00	12.00

N

☐ 236	**NAU'S DYSPEPSIA CURE**		
	Amber, 5"	8.00	10.00
☐ 237	**NO. 1 LABOREE'S COLIC CURE**		
	Clear, 3½"	8.00	10.00

O

☐ 238	**ONE MINUTE COUGH CURE**		
	Vertical on front in sunken panel, E.C. DeWitt & Co. on one side, Chicago, U.S.A. on opposite side, rectangular, aqua, 5½"	9.00	13.00
☐ 239	*Same as above, except 5"*	7.00	10.00
☐ 240	**ONE MINUTE COUGH CURE**		
	Vertical on front, E.C. DeWitt & Co. Chicago, U.S.A. vertical on back, rectangular, aqua, 4¼"	7.00	10.00
☐ 241	**THE ORIGINAL COPPER CURE**		
	Two lines in script, ring top, amber, 7¾"	70.00	100.00
☐ 242	**THE ORIGINAL, COPPER CURE**		
	In 2 script lines, oval shape bottle, ring top, amber, 7¾"	45.00	60.00
☐ 243	**THE ORIGINAL · DR. CRAIG'S · KIDNEY CURE,** *(c. 1889)*		
	In three lines, on base Rochester, N.Y., double ring top, amber, Bottle same as Warner Safe Cure, 9½"	25.00	35.00
☐ 244	**OTTO'S CURE FOR THE THROAT & LUNGS**		
	On front indented panel, B.H. Bacon on right panel, Rochester, N.Y. on reverse side, aqua, 6"	7.00	10.00
☐ 245	**OTTO'S CURE FOR THE THROAT & LUNGS**		
	Vertical on front indented panel, oval, aqua, 2¾"	6.00	9.00

P

☐ 246	**PARIS MED. CO., ST. LOUIS, GROVE'S CHRONIC CHILL CURE**		
	Aqua, 2¾"	7.00	10.00
☐ 247	**PARK'S SURE CURE (KIDNEY CURE)**		
	Aqua, 6½"	9.00	12.00
☐ 248	**PARK'S LIVER & KIDNEY CURE**		
	In three lines, in back Free Samples, aqua, tapered top, 3"	22.00	30.00
☐ 249	*Same as 248 except aqua, 5"*	35.00	45.00

☐ 250	**DR. PARK'S COUGH SYRUP**		
	Geo. H. Wells, other side Le Roy, N.Y., tapered top, label		
	reads The Throat & Lungs - A Positive Guarantee of Cure		
	of Any Throat or Lung Disease, etc., aqua, 6¼"	11.00	15.00
☐ 251	**DR. PARKER'S & SONS CO. — BATAVIA, N.Y.**		
	"RED CHERRY COUGH CURE FOR CONSUMPTION" all		
	in four lines, running vertically, ring top, aqua, 5½"	11.00	15.00
☐ 252	**DR. PARKER'S COUGH CURE**		
	Ring top, aqua, 6"	7.00	10.00
☐ 253	**DR. LEE'S LINIMENT, PACKED BY THE PERSIAN BALM**		
	CO., N.S. PKG. PR.		
	On front DR. LEE'S LINIMENT; on other side A Sure Cure		
	For Quinsy Store Throat and Croup; back 75 Years Before		
	the Public a Sure Test; ring top, ring neck, clear, 2½"	9.00	12.00
☐ 254	**PERUVIANA-NATURE'S KIDNEY CURE —**		
	Peruviana Herbal Remedy Co. - Cincinnati, Ohio in four		
	lines vertical, tapered top, amber	45.00	60.00
☐ 255	**S. K. PIERSON, GRAY'S BALSAM**		
	"Best Cough Cure" in two lines, vertical, tapered top,		
	clear, 5½"	9.00	12.00
☐ 256	**PISO'S CURE**		
	On side, FOR CONSUMPTION on front, other side HAZEL-		
	TONE & CO., emerald green, 5"	7.00	10.00
☐ 257	Same as above, except clear	6.00	9.00
☐ 258	**POLAR STAR COUGH CURE**		
	With embossed star in center, vertical on front in sunken		
	panels, rectangular, aqua, 5¾"	6.00	9.00
☐ 259	Same as above, except 4"	6.00	9.00
☐ 260	**PORTER'S CURE OF PAIN, CLEVELAND, OHIO**		
	Clear, 6½"	7.00	10.00
☐ 261	**PRATT FOOD CO.**		
	Phila. U.S.A. in two lines vertical, PRATT'S BLOAT CURE		
	in two lines vertical, double ring top and ring in neck,		
	aqua, 6½"	22.00	30.00
☐ 262	**PRATT'S DISTEMPER & PINK EYE CURE**		
	Amber, 7"	7.00	10.00
☐ 263	**PRATTS DISTEMPER CURE, PRATT FOOD CO.**		
	Phila, U.S.A., ring top, amber, 7"	11.00	15.00
☐ 264	**DR. CHARLES T. PRICE**		
	THE CURE FOR FIT - 67 William St.-New York in 5 lines,		
	ring top, clear, 8½"	30.00	40.00
☐ 265	**PRIMLEY'S IRON & WAHOO TONIC**		
	All in 4 lines, tapered top & ring, back Jones & Primley Co.,		
	Elkhart, Ind., amber, 9½"	15.00	20.00
☐ 266	**PRIMLEY'S SPEEDY CURE**		
	For Cough and Colds, all on front, rectangular, ring top,		
	aqua, 6½"	15.00	20.00

Q

☐ 267	**QUICK HEADACHE CURE, B.F. KEESLING,**		
	LOGANSPORT, IND.	9.00	13.00

R

☐ 268	**WM. RADAMIS**		
	Amber, 10½"	**25.00**	**35.00**
☐ 269	**RAY'S GERMICIDE CURES MANY DISEASES**		
	On front in gold paint, hand painted flowers on top half, top half is white, lower half is brown pottery somewhat glazed, sheared type, handle, jug shape, 8½"	**15.00**	**20.00**
☐ 270	**RED STAR COUGH CURE**		
	On one side, other side THE CHARLES A. VOGELER CO., Baltimore, U.S.A on base, tapered top, aqua, 7½"	**9.00**	**12.00**
☐ 271	**REDDISH & CO., FRANK O.**		
	On one side, other LeRoy, N.Y., on front PARKER LIVER & KIDNEY CURE in three lines vertical, amber, tapered top, 9½"	**45.00**	**60.00**
☐ 272	**REEVE'S COMP. TEREBENE COUGH CURE**		
	Clear, 4"	**7.00**	**10.00**
☐ 273	*Same as above, except 6"*	**7.00**	**10.00**
☐ 274	**3913 — RHEUMATISM CURE**		
	In two lines, ring top, clear or aqua, 5¾"	**11.00**	**15.00**
☐ 275	**RHODES FEVER & AGUE CURE**		
	Aqua, 8½"	**7.00**	**10.00**
☐ 276	**RHODE'S,** *other side* **FEVER & AGUE CURE**		
	Front, Antidote to Malaria in three lines, aqua, tapered top, 8½"	**35.00**	**47.00**
☐ 277	**RIVER SWAMP CHILL AND FEVER CURE**		
	Embossed alligator, ring top, amber or clear, 10¼"	**18.00**	**25.00**
☐ 279	**RIVER SWAMP, THE**		
	Under it chill and alligator, fever cure under it Augusta, Ga. flat ring top, amber, 7"	**70.00**	**100.00**
☐ 280	**ROCK'S COUGH & COLD CURE, CHAS. A. DARBY, N.Y.**		
	Vertical on front in sunken panel, rectangular, aqua, 5⅝" .	**9.00**	**13.00**
☐ 281	**ROLL'S SYRUP WILD CHERRY WHITE PINE AND TAR, CURES COUGHS AND COLDS**		
	Flared top, clear	**15.00**	**20.00**
☐ 282	**DR. ROPER'S,** *other side* **CURE**		
	Front, INDIAN FEVER, clear, tapered top, aqua, 7"	**9.00**	**13.00**
☐ 283	**H. G. ROOT M.C., 183 PEARL ST. N.Y., ELEPIZONE, A CERTAIN CURE FOR FITS AND EPILEPSY**		
	Ring top, amber, 8½"	**18.00**	**26.00**
☐ 284	**ROSEWOOD DANDRUFF CURE, PREPARED BY J.R. REEVES CO., ANDERSON, IND.**		
	Vertical on front, rectangular, paneling on collar, amethyst, 6½"	**11.00**	**15.00**

S

☐ 285	**SAWYER, DR. A. P.**		
	One side, other CHICAGO, front FAMILY CURE, double ring top, aqua, 7½"	**22.00**	**30.00**

☐ 286 **SAYMAN'S VEGETABLE LINIMENT**
*In two lines on one side Cures Catarrh & Colds, other side
Relieves All Pain, tapered top, ring on neck, aqua, 6½"* .. **11.00** **15.00**

☐ 287 **SAMPLE SHILOH'S CURE**
Vertical on front, rectangular, aqua, 4¼" **7.00** **10.00**

☐ 288 **SANFORD'S** *on one side,* **RADICAL CURE**
On opposite side, rectangular, cobalt blue, 7¾" **18.00** **25.00**

☐ 289 **SAVE-THE-HORSE, REGISTERED TRADE MARK, SPAVIN
CURE, TROY CHEMICAL CO., BINGHAMTON, N.Y.**
On front, ring top, aqua, 6½" **7.00** **10.00**

☐ 290 *Same as above, except TROY N.J.* **12.00** **16.00**

☐ 291 **SAMPLE SHILOH'S CURE**
In two lines, aqua, ring top, 4½" **11.00** **15.00**

☐ 292 **SHILOH'S CONSUMPTION CURE**
*In three lines, S. C. Wells & Co. other side - Leroy, N.Y.,
aqua, was made in three sizes, tapered top, 8"* **7.00** **10.00**

☐ 293 *Same as above, except S.C. Wells, 6½"* **9.00** **13.00**

☐ 294 **DR. SHOOP'S COUGH CURE**
Clear, 6½" **5.00** **7.00**

☐ 295 **SIMONDS** *other side* **PAIN CURE**
Ring top, aqua, 4¾" **12.00** **17.00**

☐ 296 **SLOANS SURE COLIC CURE**
Ring top, clear or amethyst, 4¾" **7.00** **10.00**

☐ 297 **H. K. SMITH CURE**
All in two lines, ring top, aqua, 5" **8.00** **12.00**

☐ 298 **SPARKS KIDNEY & LIVER CURE**
Ring top, amber, 9¾" **60.00** **80.00**

☐ 299 **THE SPECIFIC A NO. 1, A SELF CURE, TRADE MARK**
On front and bottom, aqua, 5½" **7.00** **10.00**

☐ 300 **SPEEDY CURE FOR COUGHS AND COLDS**
*On one side Jones & Primley Co., other side Elkhart, Ind.,
ring top, clear, 8"* **9.00** **12.00**

☐ 301 **SPOHN'S DISTEMPER CURE, SPOHN MEDICAL
COMPANY, GOSHEN, INDIANA U.S.A.**
Vertical on front in sunken panel, aqua, 5" **7.00** **10.00**

☐ 302 **STEWART D. HOWE'S — ARABIAN MILK CURE**
*In three lines, vertical, one side For Consumption, other
New York, aqua, ring top, 7½"* **22.00** **30.00**

☐ 303 **DR. STRUBLES KIDNEY CURE**
In a circle, under it Himrode, N. Y., ring top, cobalt, 6½" .. **100.00** **140.00**

☐ 304 **DR. SYKES SURE CURE FOR CATARRH**
In four lines, aqua, 6½" **5.00** **7.00**

☐ 305 **DR. SYKES SURE CURE FOR CATARRH**
In front, four-part mold, aqua, round, short neck, 6¾" ... **8.00** **11.00**

☐ 306 **SYLVAN REMEDY CO.**
*Peoria, Ill. in back, REIDS-GERMAN COUGH & KIDNEY
CURE, one side No Danger from Overdose, other Contains
no Poison, aqua, 5½"* **9.00** **12.00**

T

☐307 **TA-HA COUGH CURE**
In two lines vertical, ring top and ring on neck, aqua, 6" .. **15.00 20.00**

☐308 **TAMALON SAFE ANIMAL CURE**
Amber, 11¼" **28.00 40.00**

☐309 **E. E. TAYLOR'S CATARRH CURE**
All in a circle, in center a star, ring top, clear, 2¾" **9.00 13.00**

☐310 **TAYLOR'S HOSPITAL CURE FOR CATARRH**
N.Y. WT Co. U.S.A. under bottom, clear or amethyst, 6¼" **15.00 20.00**

☐311 **THREE-NINE-ONE-THREE**
In numbers, under it Rheumatism cure, rectangular, clear,
ring top, 5½" **12.00 17.00**

☐312 **TIGER OIL — CURE PAIN**
In 2 lines vertical, ring top and neck, aqua, 4½" **9.00 12.00**

☐313 **DR. W. TOWNS EPILEPSY CURE, FOND DUL LAC,**
WISCONSIN, U.S.A.
Amber, 7½" **9.00 13.00**

U

☐314 **UPHAM'S FRESH MEAT CURE**
Pat. Feb. 12, 1867 Phila., flared top, aqua, 6¾" **11.00 15.00**

W

☐315 **WADSWORTH LINIMENT**
Rheumatism on one side, Cure on other side, side mold,
aqua, 5½" **25.00 33.00**

☐316 **WAKEFIELD'S** *other side* **BLOOMINGTON**
Front MAGIC PAIN CURE, all running vertically, ring top,
aqua **22.00 30.00**

☐317 **WARNER'S SAFE ANIMAL CURE**
Amber, 11¼" **32.00 45.00**

☐318 **WARNER'S SAFE CURE**
Embossed, sample, amber **30.00 42.00**

☐319 **WARNERS SAFE CURE**
London England on side, Toronto Canada other side,
amber, 9½" **38.00 50.00**

☐320 **WARNER'S SAFE KIDNEY & LIVER CURE**
In center a safe, under it, Rochester N.Y., various numbers
under bottom, oval, amber, 9½" **8.00 11.00**

☐321 *Same as above, except RHEUMATIC CURE, amber* **10.00 14.00**

☐322 *Same as above, except amber, 6½"* **8.00 11.00**

☐323 *Same as above, except NERVINE, clear, 6½"* **4.00 6.00**

☐324 **WARNER'S WHITE WINE OF TAR SYRUP CONSUMPTION**
CURE, C.D. WARNER M.D.
Coldwater Mich., aqua, 4½" and 6¼" **9.00 13.00**

☐325 **"WARNER'S WHITE WINE OF TAR SYRUP —
CONSUMPTION CURE"**
*Cures a cold in 24 hours on label, Mfg. by C. D. Warner
M.D., Cold Water, Mich., aqua, 7¼"* 14.00 20.00

☐326 **DR. WEAVER'S — CANKER CURE**
In two lines vertical, aqua, pontil, ring top, 5¼" 38.00 50.00

☐327 **THE WEST ELECTRIC CURE CO., ELECTRICITY
IN A BOTTLE**
Ring top, cobalt 16.00 22.00

☐328 **C.T. WHIPPLE PROP., PORTLAND ME.
GARGET CURE**
Aqua, 6" 5.00 7.00

☐329 **A.J. WHITE CURATIVE SYRUP**
On sides in sunken panel, rectangular, aqua, 5⅛" 9.00 12.00

☐330 **WHITE'S QUICK HEALING CURE**
Amber, 6¼" 9.00 12.00

☐331 **FAITH WHITCOMB'S BALSAM**
*In two lines on front, one side CURES COUGHS & COLDS,
other CURES CONSUMPTION, double ring top, 9½"* 15.00 20.00

☐332 **WINANS BROS., INDIAN CURE FOR BLOOD**
Price $1, aqua, 9¼" 20.00 30.00

☐333 **DR. J. L. WOODS TASTELESS CHILL CURE**
*Wood Drug Co., Bristol, Tenn. in four lines, vertical, ring
top and neck, aqua, 7"* 15.00 20.00

☐334 **WOOD'S GREAT PEPPERMINT CURE FOR COUGHS
& COLDS**
Clear, 6½" 7.00 10.00

☐335 **WOOLDRIDGE WONDERFUL CURE CO.**
Columbus Ga., amber, 8½" 10.00 15.00

☐336 **WYKOOP'S FEVER & AGUE CURE**
Tapered top, pontil, cobalt, 6½" 55.00 75.00

Y

☐337 **DR. YARNALL'S, GOLD CURE FOR ALCOHOLISM**
*Prepared Only By The Yarnall Gold Cure Co., ring top,
clear, 5½"* 70.00 100.00

Z

☐338 **ZEMO CURES ECZEMEE**
*E.W. Rose Med. Co. St. Louis on one side, reverse side,
Zemo Cures Pimples and all Diseases of the Skin and
Scalp, fancy bottle, ring top, clear, 6½"* 9.00 12.00

FLASKS

Flask bottles have become one of the most popular varieties of bottles in the hobby. Their myriad designs and shapes, and their mottos reflecting sentiments of the time render them important artistic, as well as historical objects. Prices (as you will note in the following listings) have attained very high levels for the most desirable examples. This is not mostly due to rarity, but the fact that flask bottles have long been collected and demand has been building up for many years. Some of the original owners of these 19th century flasks undoubtedly put them up for display when empty. While flasks were not likely to be used as objects d'art in well-to-do homes, the middle classes of that time seized upon anything ornamental to decorate their homes — including advertising bills taken from fences.

Todays we think of a flask as a small, rather flat spirits bottle that can be carried in the pocket. Many of those on the collector market fit the description, but others are of figural shape and various sizes. All were made to contain whiskey. It would be easy to assume that they were created as collectors' items, but this was not the case. Their attractive designs and the presence of slogans or sayings was merely intended to catch the eye and hopefully promote sales. In some instances, they were used as propaganda when manufacturers installed the name and/or likeness of their favorite Presidential candidate on flasks, or publicized some cause. Political flasks enjoy a strong following among collectors. It should not be presumed, though, that every political flask had propaganda intent. Many pictured George Washington long after his death. These should be correctly classified as patriotic.

Mottos were numerous. They included such popular patriotic sayings as "Don't tread on me," coined by the revolutionists of '76 and deeply ingrained into our language by the 19th century. Curiously, there were also "warnings slogans" of the over-indulgence in spirits, probably inspired by the early temperance movement. One of these was, "Use me, don't abuse me." It was really to manufacturers' advantage if whiskey was not abused. Over-use might have led to its being outlawed, or very heavily taxed, as gin was in England.

It is important to note — if you wonder about the time and effort put into flask manufacture — that they were not intended as throw-aways. Flasks were designed to be reused. When empty, they were taken to the spirits dealer, who filled them up again. You did not need to buy a new flask each time you purchased its contents.

The earliest American flasks were probably those of the Pitkin Glasshouse, set up in 1783 near Hartford, Connecticut. At first, they were freeblown, or made without aid of a mold. By 1850, some 400 design variations had been used. These flasks have black graphite pontil marks. The pontil was coated with powdered iron to enable the flask's bottom to be broken away without damaging the glass. The several hundred additional types made between 1850 and 1870 carry no such markings, thanks to invention of the snapcase. This was a spring device to cradle the flask in the finishing process.

Competition to devise the most original designs and slogans in the flask trade was intense. Plagiarism of mold designs by rival companies occurred frequently.

Thomas W. Dyott, an English immigrant who had worked as a bootblack, became proprietor of the Philadelphia and Kensington Glass Works, one of the major flask manufacturers. Among his portrait flasks was one picturing himself, along with a likeness of Benjamin Franklin (patriarch of Philadelphia) on the reverse. Another of Dyott's flasks honors the French general, Lafayette, an important figure in the American Revolutionary War. When Lafayette returned in old age to tour America in 1824, Dyott presented him with a specimen of the Lafayette Flask — thereby achieving immense publicity for himself.

Masonic flasks were plentiful. Many bore the order's emblems on one side and the symbolic American eagle on the other. Public sentiment turned against the Masons when William Morgan of Batavia, New York, mysteriously disappeared after threatening to reveal Masonic secrets. Gradually, the incident was forgotten and Masonic flasks continued to flourish. These now constitute a major specialty for collectors.

George Washington was a perennially popular subject for flasks, just as he was for engravings (engravers and lithographers were still profitably selling his likeness as late as 1850 — to persons who had not been born during his lifetime). At first, he appeared on flasks as a soldier in uniform. Some people objected to this kind of commercializing of Washington's memory, especially when used to promote sale of liquor. But collectors have no regrets of it being done!

Many celebrated persons, including some who were still living at the time, were portrayed on flasks. Singer Jenny Lind, the Swedish operatic soprano, was among them. It is quite possible she was the only female to be pictured on a flask in her lifetime.

The Presidential elections of 1824 and 1828 produced a number of special flasks promoting Andrew Jackson and his rival John Quincy Adams.

Events of the time were likewise memorialized on flasks. Those reading "For Pike's Peak," and "Pike's Peak or Bust," appeared in 1859. Pike's Peak was a goldrush to the Colorado mountains that fizzled into nothingness, after thousands of hopeful prospectors descended upon the region.

FLASKS

A

NO.	DESCRIPTION	PRICE RANGE	
☐ 1	**JOHN Q. ADAMS**		
	In a circle, Eagle facing to right, on base J.T. & CO., beaded edge, sheared top, pontil, green, pint	750.00	1000.00
☐ 2	**A.G.W.L.**		
	Under bottom, saddle flask, amber, ½ pint	8.00	11.00

☐ 3 **ALL SEEING EYE;**
Star and large eye in center, under it A.D., in back, six-pointed star with arms, Masonic emblem, under it G.R.J.A., pontil, sheared top, amber, pint 200.00 265.00

☐ 4 *ANCHOR FLASK, double ring, amber or clear, ½ pint, quart* 25.00 35.00

☐ 5 *AQUAMARINE, pint* 32.00 45.00

B

☐ 6 **BALTIMORE GLASS WORKS**
Aqua, very thin glass, pontil, on back a stack of wheat ... 140.00 190.00

☐ 7 **BALTIMORE MONUMENT**
And under it Balto. door with step railing, in back sloop with pennant flying, sailing to right above it Fells below point, ½ pt. 3 ribbed on side, plain top, pontil, aqua, qt. (c. 1840) 115.00 145.00

☐ 8 *Same as above, except plain bottom,* 95.00 120.00

☐ 9 **B.P. & B.**
Yellow green, ½ pint 40.00 55.00

☐ 10 **BRIDGETON, NEW JERSEY**
Around a man facing to left, in back a man facing to the left with Washington around it, ribbed sides, sheared top, pontil, aqua, pint 75.00 95.00

☐ 11 **BRYON & SCOTT**
One picture of each, Byron on front and Scott in back, ribbed sides, sheared top, pontil, 5½" amber 165.00 200.00

C

☐ 12 **CALABASH**
Hunter and fisherman, aqua, quart 40.00 55.00

☐ 13 **CANNON FLASK**
Cannon and balls lengthwise of flask, cannon balls at left of wheel in foreground, rammer and swab beneath, A rammer leans against cannon in front of right wheel. In horseshoe circle around cannon — GEN. TAYLOR NEVER SURRENDERS — Vine and grapes for a frame in center of it — A LITTLE MORE GRAPE CAPT BRAGG, vertically ribbed with heavy medial rib, plain top, pontil, puce, ½ pint, aqua 350.00 425.00

☐ 14 **CHAPMAN P., BALT., MD**
Soldier with a gun on front, a girl dancing on a bar in back, sheared top, aqua, pint 140.00 180.00

☐ 15 **CLASPED HANDS · Eagle Flask** *(c. 1860-75)*
Union 13 stars, clasped hands, eagle above banner mark, "E", Wormer & Co., Pittsburg, aqua, quart 90.00 120.00

☐ 16 **CLASPED HANDS — Eagle Flask** *(c. 1860-75)*
Deep golden amber, ½ pint ....(90.00).......... 100.00 140.00

☐ 17 **CLASPED HANDS — Flask** *(c. 1860-75)*
One with eagle and banner, above oval marked Pittsburgh, Pa., other cannon to left, flag and cannonballs, aqua, pint 75.00 95.00

☐ 18 **COLUMBIA — Eagle Flask** *(c. 1820-50)*
*Columbia with Liberty Cap facing left, 13 stars - ½ moon
circle around bust, in back eagle facing right under eagle
"B & W", plain top, pontil, yellow, pint* 250.00 325.00
☐ 19 *Same as above, except aqua (c.1830)* 245.00 310.00
☐ 20 **CORN FOR THE WORLD**
*In ½ moon around ear of corn, in back design on large
oval panels, Baltimore Monument and under it "BALTI-
MORE", the step railing of the entrance door facing left,
pontil, round top, golden yellow, quart (c. 1835)* 275.00 350.00
☐ 21 *Same as above, except the door is facing right, ½ pt.
smooth edge, sheared top, pontil, aqua. (c. 1840)* 115.00 145.00
☐ 22 **CORNUCOPIA**
*Designs on oval panels, beading on edges and at top,
inverted cornucopia coiled to left and filled with produce,
in back large circular, in center of it large geometric star
-around it 8 petalled rosette - under it palm (6), plain top,
pontil, light blue green, ½ pint* 1300.00 1700.00
☐ 23 **CORNUCOPIA — Flask**
*Cornucopia coiled to the left and filled with produce, Urn
in back with 6 bars and filled with produce, pontil, plain
top, light amber, ½ pint* 60.00 80.00
☐ 24 *Same as above, except aqua* 60.00 80.00
☐ 25 *Same as above, except olive amber, pint* 60.00 80.00
☐ 26 **CORN FOR THE WORLD**
Amber, 8¼" 150.00 190.00
☐ 27 *CORNUCOPIA, emerald green, pint* 45.00 60.00
☐ 28 *CORNUCOPIA and EAGLE, aqua, ½ pint* 235.00 305.00
☐ 29 *Same as above, except inverted cornucopia* 235.00 305.00
☐ 30 *CORNUCOPIA and URN, olive, pint* 50.00 65.00
☐ 31 *CORNUCOPIA and URN, amber, ½ pint* 50.00 65.00
☐ 32 *CORNUCOPIA and URN with twig, open pontil, olive or
amber, ½ pint* 60.00 80.00
☐ 33 **CUNNINGHAM, PITTSBURGH, PA.**
Indian, hunter and eagle 95.00 120.00

D

☐ 34 *Delicate powder blue, ½ pint* 35.00 47.00
☐ 35 *18 diamond quilted flask, green, 6¼"* 95.00 120.00
☐ 36 *DOG in center, in back man in uniform on a horse, pontil,
sheared top, aqua, quart* 110.00 135.00
☐ 37 *DOUBLE EAGLE (eagles lengthwise), open pontil, olive
green* 100.00 125.00
☐ 38 *DOUBLE EAGLE, aqua, pint* 125.00 160.00
☐ 39 *DOUBLE EAGLE, light green, pint* 100.00 125.00
☐ 40 *DOUBLE EAGLE, beneath unembossed oval, sheared top,
pontil, amber, 6¼"* 30.00 40.00
☐ 41 *DOUBLE EAGLE, STODDARD, N.H., olive or amber, pint* . 100.00 125.00
☐ 42 *DUCK FLASK, picture of a duck in water, under duck
SWIM, above duck WILL YOU HAVE A DRINK, aqua, pint* . 120.00 150.00

E

☐ 43 AMERICAN EAGLE, facing left, shield with bars on breast, above eagle 13 stars, 3 arrows in right talons, branch in left, back big bunch of grapes and smaller one at right, above it two large leaves, qt., aqua — fine vertical ribbing, pontil, plain top, (c. 1835) 80.00 100.00

☐ 44 EAGLE FLASK, circle below eagle, aqua, 6" 60.00 80.00

☐ 45 EAGLE facing left, shield with eight vertical bars on breast, 4 arrows in left. Claw large branch in right, 23 sun rays around head. Eagle stand on oval frame in side frame 20 small pearls, a bar connects the claw, back same, pt. aqua, 3 side ribbed, pontil, plain top. (c. 1840) 80.00 100.00

☐ 46 EAGLE facing to right resting on a shield and rock pile, aqua, pint 60.00 80.00

☐ 47 EAGLE facing left, ribbon held in back with 5 star extending to the right, below eagle large stellar Motif — same in back, all in Designs on oval panels, qt. corrugated horz. with vertical rib., aqua, plain top, pontil (c. 1845) 120.00 150.00

☐ 48 EAGLE and MASONIC FLASK
Large eagle with rays over head and OHIO in a circle under eagle, under that J. SHEPARD & CO., on shoulder ZANESVILLE, reverse Masonic arch, ornaments under arch, pontil, green, amber or olive, pint 200.00 260.00

☐ 49 EAGLE resting on arrows and olive branch with ribbon in beak, an oval panel under eagle, CUNNINGHAM & CO., PITTSBURGH, PA., ring neck, olive green, quart 125.00 150.00

☐ 50 EAGLE and Clasped Hands, aqua, pint 45.00 60.00

☐ 51 EAGLE and Cornucopia, clear, pontil, aqua, ½ pint 165.00 200.00

☐ 52 EAGLE and DYOTTVILLE G.W., aqua, pint 100.00 125.00

☐ 53 **EAGLE TREE — Flask**
Eagle head turned to left, shield with 8 vertical bars on breast, large olive branch in right, etc., in back large tree in foliage, plain top, pontil, aqua, Kensington Glass Works, common flask, pint 115.00 145.00

☐ 54 EAGLE and Flag, aqua, pint, pontil, (c. 1830) 120.00 150.00

☐ 55 EAGLE and Girl on bicycle, A & DHA, aqua, pint 70.00 90.00

☐ 56 EAGLE, head to the left, wing partly up, large shield with 6 bars on breast, above eagle liberty, eagle stands on wreath branches, in back 4 lines Willington Glass co. West Willington, Conn., qt. tapered top, plain base, dark olive green (c. 1860) 90.00 115.00

☐ 57 EAGLE, MASONIC, blue green, pint 160.00 200.00

☐ 58 EAGLE on oval panels, 25 sun rays in ¼ circle around eagle head, 8 vertical bars on shield. End of olive branch & arrows under claws in oval frame with 23 small pearls around. T.W.D., in back full sailing to right. U.S. flag at reas., waves beneath frigate and in semi-circle beneath Franklin pt. 3 vertically ribbed on side, sheared top, pontil, aqua, (c. 1830) 115.00 145.00

☐ 59 EAGLE and Stag, aqua, ½ pint 160.00 205.00

☐ 60 EAGLE and Tree, aqua, pint 80.00 100.00

20

64

65

66

67

82

84

89

106

152

F

☐	61	*FLASK, plain, amber, ½ pint*	7.00	10.00
☐	62	*FLASK, plain, bulbous neck, ½ pint, 6¾"*	5.00	7.00
☐	63	*FLASK, plain, bulbous neck, ½ pint, 7"*	6.00	9.00
☐	64	*FLASK, Label, pontil, very pale olive, 6"*	40.00	55.00
☐	65	*FLASK, Label, dark olive, 5½"*	12.00	17.00
☐	66	*FLASK, Label, ribbed base, clear, 6¾"*	11.00	15.00
☐	67	*FLASK, Label, amber, 7½"*	10.00	14.00
☐	68	*FLASK, Round Label, amber, 6½"*	11.00	15.00
☐	69	*FLASK, Label, pontil, clear, 6¾"*	18.00	24.00
☐	70	*FLASK, plain, sheared top, pontil, green, pint*	140.00	190.00
☐	71	*Same as above, except clear*	140.00	190.00
☐	72	**FLORA TEMPLE**		
		Aqua, pint	190.00	240.00
☐	73	**FLORA TEMPLE**		
		Handle, puce or amber, pint	190.00	240.00
☐	74	**FLORIDA UNIVERSAL STORE BOTTLE**		
		Clear, pint	4.00	7.00
☐	75	**H. FRANK, PAT'D. AUG. 6th 1879**		
		Under bottom, two circles in center, reverse plain, ring top, ribs on sides	35.00	47.00
☐	76	**H. FRANK, PAT. AUG. 6, 1872**		
		All on bottom, circular shaped flask, two circles in center on front, reverse side plain, wide rib on sides, ring neck, aqua, pint	40.00	55.00
☐	77	**FRANKLIN & FRANKLIN**		
		Aqua, quart	120.00	160.00

G

☐	78	**Gen. MacArthur and GOD BLESS AMERICA**		
		Purple or green, ½ pint	10.00	15.00
☐	79	**G.H.A.**		
		Concord, N.Y. 1865, aqua, ½ pint	16.00	22.00
☐	80	**GIRL FOR JOE**		
		Girl on bicycle, aqua, pint	65.00	85.00
☐	81	**GRANITE GLASS CO.**		
		In three lines, reverse Stoddard, N.H., sheared top, olive, pint	140.00	190.00
☐	82	**GUARANTEED FLASK**		
		Clear or amethyst, 6¼"	4.00	7.00
☐	83	**GUARANTEED FULL**		
		Clear, 6½"	7.00	10.00

H

☐	84	*HISTORY FLASK, Label, aqua, side panels, 7¼"*	12.00	16.00
☐	85	*HUNTER and Dog, puce, pint*	275.00	340.00

I

☐ 86 IRON *Pontil, double collared, pint* 35.00   47.00
☐ 87 **ISABELLA G.W.**
    Sheaf of wheat, pint 70.00   90.00

J

☐ 88 **GENERAL JACKSON** — Eagle Flask
    Jackson, three-quarter view facing left in semi-circle above bust, in back -eagle head turned to right, laurel branch in eagle's beak, nine stars above eagle. Eagle stands on oval frame with inner band of 16 large pearls, J.R. in oval frame below eagle, in semi-circle below oval frame -LAIRD. SC.PITT,Edge horizonal beading rib, plain top, pontil, aqua, pint 1000.00   1300.00
☐ 89 **JENNY LIND**
    With wreath, reverse picture of glass works, above is FISLERVILLE GLASS WORKS, wavy line on neck, pontil, tapered top, aqua, quart 100.00   135.00
☐ 90 *Same as above, except S. HUFFSY* 55.00   75.00
☐ 91 **JENNY LIND LYRE**
    Aqua, pint 100.00   140.00

K

☐ 92 **KEEN — P & W — SUNBURST FLASK** *(c. 1814-30)*
    Olive amber, ½ pint 175.00   260.00
☐ 93 **KEENE Masonic**
    Tooled lip, pontil, pint 180.00   230.00
☐ 94 **KEENE Sunburst**
    Green 280.00   340.00

L

☐ 95 *LAFAYETTE, large bust in uniform, face slightly to the right, General-LA-Fayette in ¾ circle around bust. Back, on edges, Republican Gratitude-Kensington Glass Works, Philadelphia, under eagle facing left in oval frame T.W.D. Pontil, aqua, pt., (c. 1830)* 360.00   450.00
☐ 96 *LAFAYETTE and Eagle, amber* 70.00   100.00
☐ 97 *LAFAYETTE and Eagle, KENSINGTON, open pontil, aqua, pint* 120.00   150.00
☐ 99 *LAFAYETTE and Dewitt Clinton, olive, amber, ½ pint* 180.00   240.00
☐ 100 *LAFAYETTE and Liberty Cap, aqua, pint* 110.00   145.00
☐ 101 *LAFAYETTE and Masonic, ½ pint* 180.00   240.00
☐ 102 **L.C. & R. CO.**
    On bottom, Eagle in a circle, reverse plain, clear, ½ pint . 35.00   47.00
☐ 103 **LEGENDARY GRANDFATHER**
    Broken swirl pattern, reddish amber 100.00   135.00

☐ 104	**LIBERTY & UNION**		
	In three lines, in back BALTIMORE Monument, in above semi-circle BALTIMORE, entrance to door is without step railing, edges smooth, plain lip, pontil, yellow olive, pint .	3500.00	4250.00
☐ 105	**LOUISVILLE G.W.**		
	And eagle, aqua, ½ pint	90.00	120.00
☐ 106	**LOUISVILLE, KY. GLASS WORKS**		
	In lower part of flask, rectangular panel, near shoulder, in oval panel, American eagle, facing right, wings raised above and paralleled to body, eagle rests on shield, no bars, in eagle's beak narrow ribbon extending upward above eagle and below, through shield, in back no design or inscription all covered with decidedly angular vertical ribbing, eagles vertical, ribbing plain with laid on ring, base plain, yellow green, pint	95.00	130.00
☐ 107	**LOWELL R.R.**		
	Olive, amber, ½ pint	120.00	150.00
☐ 108	**LYNDEBORO, L.G. CO.,**		
	PATENT on shoulder, aqua, pint	18.00	25.00
☐ 109	**LYNDEBORO, L.G. CO.**		
	Golden amber, quart	32.00	43.00

M

☐ 110	*MAN with a gun and bag, reverse side running dogs, double ring top, aqua, pint*	120.00	150.00
☐ 111	*MAN with a gun and bag and a feather in hat, reverse side grape vine, with bunches of grapes and leaves, ribbed sides, sheared top, pontil*	90.00	120.00
☐ 112	*MARKED Double Eagle, olive or amber, pint*	70.00	90.00
☐ 113	**MASONIC ARCH**		
	Pillars & pavement, no stars etc., pt. 2 rings at shoulders, fine horizontal corrugations around flask etc. sheared top, pontil O., amber, in back eagle head turning left. shield with bars and tiny dots on breast, 3 arrows in its left claw. Olive branch in right, plain ribbon above head, plain oval frame below eagle, (c. 1825)	975.00	1250.00
☐ 114	**MASONIC ARCH**		
	Pillars & pavement, 6 stars surrounding quarter moon & without comet at right of pillars, Eagle facing left. No shield on breast., etc. under it in plain oval frame KCCNC. pt. O. amber, one single vertical rib. Sheared top, pontil, (c. 1825)	115.00	145.00
☐ 115	**MASONIC — Eagle Flask** *(c. 1814-50)*		
	Pillars and pavement, except 6 stars surrounding quarter moon and without comet to right of pillars, in back, eagle facing to left KCCNC in oval frame, mold work error should read KEENE, olive amber, pint	215.00	290.00
☐ 116	*MASONIC and Eagle, pint, pontil, green*	500.00	675.00
☐ 117	*MASONIC and Eagle, olive or amber, pint*	120.00	150.00
☐ 118	*MASONIC and Eagle, pontil, pint, blue green*	135.00	170.00

☐119	*MONUMENT and corn in a circle under this, BALTIMORE, reverse side a large ear of corn, aqua, quart*	**120.00**	**150.00**
☐120	*Same as above, except amber*	**140.00**	**175.00**
☐121	*MOUNTED Soldier and dog, citron, quart*	**225.00**	**285.00**

N

☐122	**NEW GRANITE GLASS WORKS**		
	In horse shoe letters, in center of it Stoddard, N.H. in back on a pole a flag with 13 stars and 9 stripes flying to the right, rib sides, sheared top, pontil, amber, 5¾"	**85.00**	**110.00**
☐123	**"NEW LONDON GLASSWORK"** — *Anchor Eagle Flask*		
	Golden amber, pint, (c. 1860-66)	**375.00**	**500.00**

P

☐124	**PIKES PEAK**		
	Man with pack and cane walking to left, reverse eagle with ribbon in beak in oval panel, aqua, pint	**85.00**	**110.00**
☐125	*Same as above, except several colors*	**70.00**	**90.00**
☐126	**FOR PIKE'S PEAK**		
	Reverse side, man shooting a gun at a deer, aqua, 9½" ..	**30.00**	**42.00**
☐127	**FOR PIKE'S PEAK**		
	Old rye, aqua, pint	**40.00**	**55.00**
☐128	**PIKES PEAK**		
	Traveler and hunter, olive, amber, pint	**190.00**	**240.00**
☐129	**PIKE'S PEAK HISTORICAL FLASK** — **Penn.** — *(c. 1859-70)*		
	Ring top, Eagle - Prospector to right, under it "For Pike's Peak", yellow amber, pint	**525.00**	**650.00**
☐130	**PITTSBURGH**		
	Double eagle, citron, pint	**190.00**	**240.00**
☐131	**PITTSBURGH**		
	Double eagle, aqua, pint	**28.00**	**37.00**
☐132	**PITTSBURGH, PA.**		
	In raised oval circle at base, with an eagle on front, back same except plain for label, aqua, applied ring at top, pint, 7½"	**38.00**	**47.00**
☐133	*PITKIN type, light green, pint*	**50.00**	**70.00**
☐134	*POTTERY FLASK, figure of a man and horse, same on reverse side, pint*	**250.00**	**325.00**

Q

☐135	*QUILTED Pattern Flask, sheared top, pontil, reddish brown, amber, green, olive amber, ½ pint*	**475.00**	**600.00**
☐136	*Same as above, except amethyst*	**600.00**	**775.00**
☐137	*Same as above, except white bluish cast*	**165.00**	**200.00**

R

☐ 138 **RAILROAD — Eagle Flask** *(c. 1830-48)*
Amber, pint **140.00 175.00**

☐ 139 **RAILROAD FLASK**
On oval panels, horse drawing long cart on rail to right. Cart filled with barrels and boxes, under it Lowell and above it Railroad in back eagle facing left. Shield with 7 vertical & 2 horizontal bars on breast, 3 arrows in eagles left claw, olive branch in right, 13 large stars surround edge, ½ pt. 3 ver. ribbed on side, sheared top, pontil, O. amber, (c. 1860) **100.00 140.00**

☐ 140 **RAILROAD FLASK**
Designs on oval panels, crude locomotive to left on rail, embossed success to the Railroad, reading around locomotive-back but the line connecting the tender with rear wheel shows a slight break and E in success carries a conbex dot attached to the upper bar pt. 3 vertically ribbed on side, sheared top O. amber, (c. 1830) **110.00 150.00**

☐ 141 **RAVENNA GLASS WORKS — Star Flask** *(c. 1857-60)*
Ohio, aqua, pint **140.00 180.00**

☐ 142 **RAVENNA GLASS WORKS**
In three lines, ring top, yellow green, pint **120.00 155.00**

☐ 143 **RAVENNA**
In center, anchor with rope, under it GLASS COMPANY, ring top, aqua, pint **130.00 165.00**

☐ 144 **RAVENNA TRAVELERS COMPANION**
Pontil, amber, quart **220.00 310.00**

☐ 145 **REHM BROS**
Bush & Buchanan Sts & O'Farrel & Mason Sts, in a sunken circle, ribbed bottom, two rings near shoulder, coffin type, metal and cork cap, clear or amethyst, ½ pint **90.00 125.00**

☐ 146 *RIBBED FLASK, fluted base to shoulder, sheared top, pontil, aqua, ½ pint* **150.00 190.00**

☐ 147 *Same as above, except yellow or amber* **180.00 235.00**

S

☐ 148 *SAILING VESSEL and COLUMBIAN JUBILEE, amber, pint* **80.00 105.00**

☐ 149 *SAILOR BOTTLE, dancing sailor on back, amber, 7½"* ... **60.00 80.00**

☐ 150 *SCROLL, one star, smooth base, aqua, 7"* **8.00 11.00**

☐ 151 *Same as above, except two stars* **28.00 37.00**

☐ 152 *SCROLL, one star, clear, aqua or amber, pontil, ½ pint to quart* **38.00 50.00**

☐ 153 *Same as above, except two stars CIX-17, (c. 1855)* **100.00 125.00**

☐ 154 *SCROLL, aqua, 9"* **270.00 340.00**

☐ 155 *SCROLL, open pontil, aqua, pint* **50.00 70.00**

☐ 156 *SCROLL FLASK, Penn. (c. 1845-60), aqua, 2½ quart* **270.00 340.00**

☐ 157 *Same as above, except deep sapphire blue, quart* **2100.00 2500.00**

☐ 158 *SCROLL FLASK (c. 1845-50), Deep golden amber, pint* ... **330.00 410.00**

☐ 159	*SCROLL FLASK, scroll decoration framing acanthus leaves. Diamond motif at center, four petalled flower motif at top and leaf motif at base, same in back, pt. vertical medial rib., pontil D, aqua, sheared top., (c. 1850)*	750.00	925.00
☐ 160	*SCROLL, large heart shaped frame with elaborate scrolls, one eight-pointed star on shoulder, in center 6 pointed star. Same in back pt., pontil, plain top, blue aqua, (c. 1850)*	65.00	85.00
☐ 161	*SCROLL, M.C. on side in script, blue or aqua, pint*	45.00	65.00
☐ 162	*SCROLL, D.C. MOTT, ½ pint*	28.00	37.00
☐ 163	*SCROLL, green, pint*	55.00	75.00
☐ 164	*SCROLL, banded neck, aqua*	40.00	55.00
☐ 165	*SCROLL, aqua, quart*	85.00	110.00
☐ 166	*SCROLL, iridescent blue, pint*	120.00	150.00
☐ 167	*SCROLL, aqua, 2½ quart*	130.00	165.00
☐ 168	*SCROLL FLASK (c. 1845-60), blue green, pint*	360.00	450.00
☐ 169	*Same as above, except yellow green*	335.00	425.00
☐ 170	*SCROLL FLASK (c. 1845-60), sapphire blue, pint*	850.00	1100.00
☐ 171	**S.G. CO.**		
	And anchor on bottom, aqua, 6¼"	12.00	16.00
☐ 172	*Same as above, except amber*	9.00	13.00
☐ 173	*SHEAF OF WHEAT-Westford Glass Co. Conn. pt., read amber, double top collared, plain base, (c. 1860)*	65.00	85.00
☐ 174	*SHEAF OF WHEAT-Westford Glass Co. Pictorial Flask GX111-36, double-ring top, plain base, amber, pint, GX111-36. Conn., (c. 1865)*	85.00	110.00
☐ 175	*SHEAF OF WHEAT and GRAPES, open pontil, aqua, ½ quart*	110.00	140.00
☐ 176	**SOLDIER-DANCER FLASK, Md.** *(c. 1830-52)*		
	Chapman, below dancer, Balt. Md. under soldier, yellow green, pint	320.00	400.00
☐ 177	**SOUTH CAROLINA DISPENSARY**		
	With palm tree, aqua, pint	55.00	75.00
☐ 178	*Same as above, except amber, ½ pint*	75.00	100.00
☐ 179	*SPIRAL FLASK, spiral to the left, pontil, sheared top, amber, ½ pint*	250.00	325.00
☐ 180	*Same as above, except spiral to the right, green, pint*	160.00	210.00
☐ 181	**SPRINGFIELD G.W. and CABIN**		
	Aqua, ½ pint	60.00	80.00
☐ 182	**SPRING GARDEN**		
	In center, anchor, under it GLASS WORKS, reverse side, log cabin with a tree to the right, ring top, aqua, ½ pint ..	120.00	155.00
☐ 183	**SPRING GARDEN GLASSWORK FLASK, Md.**		
	Yellow olive, pint	320.00	400.00
☐ 184	*STAG and Tree, aqua, pint*	60.00	80.00
☐ 185	**STAR — Cornucopia Flask**		
	Designs oval panels banded at top, sides by same on edge, inverted cornucopia, coiled to left and filled with produce, in back large circular in center, star-shaped design with six ribbed points and in center circle with small eight-petalled rosette, Under it medallion modified symmetrical palm motif rising from pointed oval with hatching, plain top, pontil, horizontal beading edges, light blue green, ½ pint	2500.00	3500.00

171

172

197

218

220

223

224

250

251

☐186 STAR with a circle around it on shoulder, light amber, saddle flask, ½ pint 10.00 15.00

☐187 **STODDARD** double eagle, **GRANITE GLASS CO., STODDARD, N.H.**
Pontil, golden amber, pint 90.00 120.00

☐188 **STODDARD, N.H.**
In panel under eagle facing left, reverse same except blank panel, sheared top, pontil, amber, pint 115.00 140.00

☐189 **STODDARD, N.H.**
In 2 lines, in back 3 lines Granite Glass Co. tapered top, light amber, plain bottom 85.00 110.00

☐190 Same as above, except tapered top, olive green 110.00 135.00

☐191 STRONGMAN and two gentlemen, clear, ½ pint 105.00 130.00

☐192 **S.T.R.A.**
In a five point star, reverse plain, ring collared top, amber, ½ pint 95.00 125.00

☐193 Same as above, except double ring top 90.00 120.00

☐194 **SUNBURST FLASK, Conn.** (c. 1813-30)
Olive amber, pontil, ½ pint 90.00 120.00

☐195 Same as above, except olive green 300.00 400.00

☐196 **SUCCESS TO THE RAILROAD**
With a horse and a cart on rail around it, same on reverse side, sheared top, pontil, olive or aqua, pint 200.00 265.00

☐197 **SUCCESS TO THE RAILROAD**
Around it a horse and cart on a rail, in back an eagle with wings spread, also an arrow and a branch, 17 stars around this, sheared lip and pontil, amber, ½ pint 200.00 280.00

☐198 **SUCCESS TO R.R.**
Eagle, olive, pint, pontil, (c. 1850) 115.00 140.00

☐199 Same as above, except aqua, pint 125.00 155.00

☐200 Same as above, except olive green or amber, pint 100.00 130.00

☐201 **SUCCESS TO RAILROAD — Flask, N.H.** (c. 1830-50)
Keene Glassworks, olive, amber, pint 140.00 180.00

☐202 SUMMER and WINTER FLASK, aqua, ½ pint 80.00 105.00

☐203 Same as above, except quart 80.00 105.00

☐204 **SUNBURST**
Large elliptical sunburst 26 triangulas, sectioned rays, flatted at ends forming closed ellipse, in center, back same, edges horizontally corrugated, corrugations extend around flask at juncture of neck and body, tapered top, 3 rings around neck at shoulder, pontil, olive amber, ½ pint 1500.00 2100.00

☐205 SUNBURST FLASK, large Elliptical sunburst (4¹⁄₆ X 2½") 24 rounded rays rounding downward to surface of flask and forming ellispe, back same... pt. Horizontal corrugation extends around side at base & around upper part between neck & squared and concave shoulder (3 rings), sheared top, pontil, o. green, (c. 1820) 475.00 575.00

☐206 SUNBURST FLASK, aqua, pint 80.00 105.00

☐207 SUNBURST, KEENE, olive or amber, pint 135.00 170.00

☐208 SUNBURST, KEENE P & W, olive or amber, pint 175.00 170.00

☐209 SUNBURST, KEENE, amber, ½ pint 175.00 170.00

☐210 *SWIRLED PITKIN, amber* 125.00 155.00
☐211 *SWIRLED PITKIN, blue green, pint* 70.00 90.00

T

☐212 **TAYLOR — CORNSTALK — Flask, Md.** *(c. 1800-52)*
Clear or amethyst, large mouth, pint 900.00 1175.00
☐213 **TAYLOR, GENL**
Facing right in ¼ moon circle, bust in uniform, back,
"Fells point" in semi circle above monument under it
Balto. pt. ver. 3 ribbed, with heavy medial rib., aqua, pontil,
plain top, Maryland (c. 1850) 75.00 100.00
☐214 **TAYLOR & RINGGOLD**
Pontil, plaintop, aqua, pint (c. 1845) 110.00 140.00
☐215 **TRAVELERS**
In center a sunflower, under it COMPANION, in back
Ravenna, in center sunflower, under it Glass Co., sheared
top, amber, pint 110.00 145.00
☐216 **TRAVELERS COMPANION**
And sheaf, amber, quart 100.00 135.00
☐217 **TRAVELERS COMPANION**
And star, aqua, ½ pint 60.00 80.00

U

☐218 **UNION**
Side mold, ball and cannon on back, aqua, 7½" 80.00 105.00
☐219 **UNION**
Clasped hands in shield, eagle with banner on reverse
side, pint 55.00 75.00
☐220 **U 2266**
On bottom, clear or amethyst, 5" 3.00 4.50

V

☐221 *VIOLIN FLASK, curled ornaments in a heart shape, with a*
panel with two stars and a C, reverse same except no C,
collared neck, green, pint 150.00 190.00
☐222 **VERTICALLY RIBBED SUNBURST FLASK** *(c. 1810-50)*
Light blue green, ½ pint 180.00 230.00

W

☐223 **WARRANTED FLASK**
Clear or amethyst, 7½" 9.00 12.00
☐224 *G. WASHINGTON, prune color, pontil, 10½"* 100.00 130.00
☐225 *WASHINGTON and ALBANY, aqua, ½ pint* 120.00 150.00
☐226 *G. WASHINGTON and A. Jackson, olive green, pint* 125.00 155.00
☐227 *G. WASHINGTON and T. Jefferson, dark amber, pint* 140.00 180.00

☐228 WASHINGTON G. in ½ moon circle above bust, in back
eagle facing right, pontil, plain top, beading edge, pt.,
aqua (G1-10) 65.00   85.00

☐229 WASHINGTON GENERAL, in ¾" moon circle above bust
facing left in back eagle facing right, e. Pluribus Unum
above sun rays, T.W.D. in oval frame near base, vertically
ribbed and inscription July 4, A.D. 1776, Kensington Glass
Works, Phila., three star afoe 1776, pt., aqua, pontil, plain
top 165.00   200.00

☐230 G. WASHINGTON and sheaf of wheat, aqua, pint 120.00   155.00

☐231 **WASHINGON** (c. 1810-52)
Bust facing left, Fells above bust below point, back,
Baltimore Monument, under it, BALTO., plain top, pontil,
(c. 1835,) aqua, pint, qt. 225.00   325.00

☐232 **WASHINGTON — TAYLOR** (c. 1820-40)
No inscription around Washington bust, facing right, in
back "Baltimore X Glass Woks," (r omitted), in center
Taylor facing right, heavy vertical medial rib with narrow
rib each side and two narrow ribs forming out edge of
each panel, plain top, pontil, deep puce, quart 1300.00   1675.00

☐233 **WASHINGTON — TAYLOR FLASK**
Washington bust facing left without queue, in back Taylor
facing left in uniform, smooth edge, deep yellow green,
tapered top and ring, quart 350.00   450.00

☐234 **WASHINGTON — TAYLOR FLASK** (c. 1860-75)
Dyottville Glass Work, Washington facing left, Taylor fac-
ing left, in uniform, four buttons on coat, light blue, quart   300.00   375.00

☐235 **WASHINGTON**
In ½ moon circle above bust in back eagle facing left, B.K.
in oval frame near base, P.T., edge, vertical ribbing, pontil,
plain top, yellow green, (G1-13) 55.00   75.00

☐236 **WASHINGTON**
Above bust in ¾ circle, The Father of His country in back I
have endeavour, D. Do my duty above bust in ¾ circle, qt.
plain edge, plain top, aqua 70.00   100.00

☐237 **WASHINGTON BUST**
In back tree, Calabash flask, qt., aqua sloping collared
with ring, vertical fluting, pontil, (c. 1850) 70.00   95.00

☐238 **WASHINGTON FLASK** (c. 1840-60)
Father of His Country around bust, back plain, N.Y., plain
top, light green, pint 90.00   120.00

☐239 **WASHINGTON — TAYLOR** (c. 1833-60)
Washington facing left, back, Taylor facing left, deep blue
green, quart 350.00   450.00

☐240 **WASHINGTON**
Bust, Washington in ½ moon circle, above bust, back
Gen. Z Taylor in ½ moon circle above bust, qt. smooth
edge, aqua, plain top, (c. 1850) 70.00   90.00

☐241 **WASHINGTON**
Facing left in ½ moon circle above bust, in back
Baltimore Glass Works in ¾" around monument, side 3
ribbed, pontil, plain top, pale blue green, (c. 1840) 170.00   215.00

☐242 **WASHINGTON — TAYLOR**
*Washington facing left, in back Taylor facing left, deep
sapphire blue, pint* 260.00 310.00
☐243 *Same as above, except yellow green, plain back, double
ring top* 120.00 155.00
☐244 **WASHINGTON**
*Facing right, in ¾" moon circle Bridgetown, New Jersey,
above bust unknown bust facing right, in ¾" moon circle,
above bust Bridgetown, New Jersey, side 3 ribbed with
heavy medial rib, deep wine, pontil, plain top, quart
(c. 1830)* 1150.00 1375.00
☐245 **WASHINGTON**
*Facing right in ½ moon circle, bust, back Jackson facing
left-½ moon circle, bust ½ pint, pontil, plain top, conven-
try Glass Work, Conn., olive amber, (c. 1840)* 105.00 135.00
☐246 **WASHINGTON**
*Facing right, fells, above bust below point, buck Balto,
below Monument, pontil, plain top, aqua, quart, (c. 1840)* . 140.00 180.00
☐247 **WESTFORD — Eagle Flask**
*Eagle head turned to left, shield on breast, eagle stands
on large laurel wreath, above eagle LIBERTY, in back
Westford Glass Co. Westford, Conn., double ring top, pontil, olive amber, ½ pint* 85.00 110.00
☐248 **WESTFORD GLASS CO.**
*In ½ circle, under it WESTFORD, CONN., reverse side a
stack of wheat, green, pint* 70.00 100.00
☐249 **WHEELING, VA.**
*A bust facing to the right, in a horseshoe shape WHEAT
PRICE & CO., WHEELING, VA., reverse a building, around
it FAIRVIEW WORKS, sheared top, pontil, green* 400.00 475.00
☐250 *WHISKBROOM, clear, 7½"* 12.00 17.00
☐251 *WHISKEY FLASK, quilt design, clear or amethyst, 8"* 10.00 15.00
☐252 **WILLINGTON — Eagle Flask** *(c. 1860-72)*
Bright green, pint 90.00 120.00
☐253 *Same as above, except olive amber, ½ pint* 85.00 115.00
☐254 **WILLINGTON GLASS CO., WEST WILLINGTON, CONN.**
*On four lines, reverse eagle and shield, under it a wreath,
on shoulder LIBERTY, amber, pint* 85.00 115.00
☐255 **WILL YOU TAKE A DRINK? WILL A DUCK SWIM?**
Aqua, pint 125.00 155.00
☐256 *WINTER and SUMMER FLASK, tree with leaves and a bird
on right side, above it SUMMER, reverse side tree without
leaves and bird, above it WINTER, tapered top, aqua,
quart and pint* 100.00 140.00
☐257 *Same as above, but with Summer on front and Winter on
back* 85.00 110.00

Z

☐258 **ZANESVILLE CITY GLASS WORKS**
In oval panel, reverse plain, ring top, amber 75.00 11.00
☐259 *Same as above, except aqua* 55.00 75.00

FOOD

Food bottles are defined as those made for commercial sale of all consumable food items, *as well as cooking aids such as oil,* but excluding beverages of most kinds. The line of demarcation is somewhat thin. Milk bottles are classified as food bottles; soda bottles aren't.

This is one of the largest fields in bottle collecting, as well as one of the most diversified. It is, therefore, ideal for beginners. Since food bottles on the whole have not been heavily collected until recently, many are still underpriced in relation to scarcity and interest. Additionally, you will find that antique dealers — except for specialists — sometimes fail to realize the value of certain food bottles and price them very low. Anyone with some knowledge in this field (our listings will provide a good working introduction) will have no problem getting bargains.

The amatuer historian, paricularly, will enjoy food bottle collecting. The pages of 19th and early 20th century magazines, as well as newspapers, are filled with pictorial ads for the products sold in these bottles. Some food bottle collectors keep scrapbooks of these ads. They serve as an excellent means of placing approximate dates on specimens.

Introduction of bottled foodstuffs revolutionized the food industry much more dramatically than might be imagined (canning helped, too, of course). Prior to bottling, food could not be transported long distances or kept for more than a short length of time in stores because of spoilage. Everything that a community used, in the way of perishable food, had to be locally produced. Farmers and dairymen could, of course, produce their own, but most people had to depend on the grocer. Everything in the colonial grocery store, and up to the second quarter of the 19th century, was arrayed loosely. You picked out what you wanted, and the proprietor sold it to you by the pound, or slice, or quart, or however it was being sold. When you wanted milk, you took your own quart container to the store; the grocer filled it from his can or barrel with a ladle. (Nobody was overly concerned about the milk not being pasteurized, or laying in an unchilled, uncovered container hour after hour.) Non-messy foodstuffs were generally wrapped in paper. Nothing came in any kind of container; the grocer had to package it for you. Even crackers, which could easily have been retailed in paper boxes or cartons, were normally sold by the pound from barrels.

Glass bottles ushered in the age of "portion packaging." They not only saved labor for the grocer, they enabled him to sell products from distant localities. Very shortly thereafter, firms were established for the purpose of wholesaling foodstuffs to grocers. A new chapter began in American business.

It was not considered wise to go to any great expense in making food bottles, since most customers were only interested in the contents and the lowest-priced brand was likely to be the best seller. Nevertheless, many very interesting and collectible specimens were created, mostly from the motive of each manufacturer trying to make his bottles recognizable from those of the competition. Certain shapes came to signify certain products. In time, these bottles began to carry slogans and/or advertising messages, either through embossing or (later) paper labels.

Peppersauce bottles were fashioned in the shape of a Gothic cathedral with arches and windows on each side. Most were made between 1860 and 1890, the earlier ones being pontil scarred. Apparently, the use of this motif relates to the popularity of peppersauce (hot sauce) in central Europe where Gothic architecture is prevalent. These bottles are in shades of green. Tomato sauce bottles were made of clear glass.

Mustard jars came in various shapes. Differences include varying numbers of rings around the jar and sizes of jar mouths. Colors were green or clear. Older mustard jars have pontil scars. Some are embossed, as are some chili sauce bottles. One chili sauce bottle bears a Maltese cross.

Cooking oil was not commonly sold in bottles until 1890. The early specimens are tall and slim. A few are embossed, though embossing was largely discontinued at the turn of the century; paper labels were not only more inexpensive, they could carry lengthy messages that would be impossible to emboss.

Though round bottles traveled better in shipments because they could withstand more pressure, manufacturers sometimes departed from the standard round shape. Pickle or chutney bottles were large and square. Spice bottles, too, were a risk in transit due to their concave front and back panels. Both early pickle and spice bottles have pontil scars.

Worcestershire sauce, originally made in Worcester, England, was as much in demand in the 19th century as today. C.W. Dyson Perrins, director of the Lea and Perrins sauce company, parlayed Worcestershire sauce into a great fortune — much of which he used to indulge his interest in art, antiques, and rare books. These bottles are quite common. Most are in shades of green.

Henry J. Heinz began manufacturing "Good Things for the Table" in 1869. This Pittsburgh, Pennsylvania company started on a small scale. Its goal was to instill public confidence in pre-packaged foodstuffs. One innovation was to use clear glass — some people were skeptical of colored glass containers, thinking they were used to hide impurities in the food. (Actually their purpose, aside from being distinctive and eye-catching, was to screen out light and preserve product shelf life.) Heinz's first bottled product was horseradish. It was a success and the company began bottling catsup in 1889. These items are still largely sold in glass bottles, though the plastic squeeze-bottle for catsup is likely to spell the doom of glass.

A Brooklyn milkman is reported to have been delivering milk in bottles to homes as early as 1878. This could not have been factory-packaged milk, however. Apparently the bottles were bought empty from a supplier and filled by the retailer. The ancestor of the 20th century milk bottle was invented in 1884 by Dr. Harvey D. Thatcher, a druggist of Potsdam, New York. Thatcher's first milk bottle was embossed with a picture of a Quaker farmer milking his cow while seated on a three-legged barn stool. The words "Absolutely Pure Milk" were stamped into the glass on the bottle's shoulder. Waxed containers began replacing milk bottles in the early 1950's.

FOOD BOTTLES

A

NO.	DESCRIPTION		PRICE RANGE	
☐ 1	**THE ABNER ROYCE CO.**			
	The Abner Royce Co. Pure Fruit Flavor, Cleveland, Ohio in			
	back, clear, 5¼ "		4.00	6.00

☐	2	**THE ABNER ROYCE CO.** *Aqua, 5½"*	5.00	7.00
☐	3	**A.E.B.B., PURE OLIVE, DEPOSE FRANCE** *Aqua, 10"*	3.00	4.50
☐	4	**A.G. 5 & CO.** *4-Patented April 5, 1898, clear, quart*	12.00	16.00
☐	5	**ALART & McGUIRE TRADEMARK "OK" PICKLES** *Amber, 7"*	5.00	7.00
☐	6	**ALART & McGUIRE N.Y.** *Under bottom, aqua, 5"*	3.00	4.50
☐	7	**ALEXIS GODILLOT JEUNE** *Bordeaux on back panel, eight panels, green, 6¼"*	10.00	14.00
☐	8	**AMERICAN GROCERY CO. PAT APP. FOR N.Y.** *Under bottom, clear, 10"*	3.00	4.50
☐	9	**ANCHOR** *Screw top, clear or amethyst, quart, 9"*	9.00	12.00
☐	10	**THE A-1 SAUCE** *Aqua, 7¾"*	4.00	6.00
☐	11	**THE A-1 SAUCE** *Aqua, 11"*	4.00	6.00
☐	12	**ARMOUR AND COMPANY, CHICAGO** *In four lines on cathedral type panels, round corner, lady's leg neck, milk glass, 5¼"*	11.00	15.00
☐	13	**ARMOUR & CO. PACKERS, CHICAGO** *Under bottom, milk glass, 2¼"*	2.50	3.50
☐	14	**ARMOUR & CO.** *Aqua, 4"*	3.00	4.50
☐	15	**ARMOUR & CO.** *Milk glass, 5¼"*	11.00	15.00
☐	16	**ARMOUR'S TOP NOTCH BRAND, CHICAGO** *Under bottom, clear or amethyst, 5¾"*	2.50	3.50
☐	17	**A-10** *under bottom* *Clear or amethyst, 8"*	3.00	4.50

B

☐	18	**BABBLIN BROOK** *Milk bottle, clear, pint*	2.50	4.00
☐	19	**BABY TOP** *Two-face milk bottle, Brookfield on other side, 1 qt. liquid 2 Reg. Sealed 157 on base, clear*	20.00	30.00
☐	20	**BAKER'S** *Aqua, 4¾"*	4.00	6.00
☐	21	**BAKER'S FLAVORING EXTRACTS, BAKER EXTRACTS CO.** *On one side Strength & Purity, on the other side Full Measure, machine made, clear*	2.50	4.00
☐	22	**BANQUET BRAND CHARLES GULDEN, N.Y.** *On slug plate, flare lip, amethyst, 5⅛"*	3.50	4.75
☐	23	*BARREL MUSTARD, plain, two rings on top, three on bottom, amethyst or clear, 4½"*	3.00	4.25
☐	24	*BARREL MUSTARD, plain, three rings on top and bottom, clear or amethyst, 4½"*	3.00	4.25
☐	25	**B.B.G. CO. 326** *Under bottom, clear or amethyst, 8"*	1.35	2.15

8

12

13

15

16

21

25

26

27

38

40

42

58

57

64

66

☐	26	**B.B.G. CO. 78**		
		On bottom, clear or amethyst, 7½ "	2.40	3.25
☐	27	**B & CO. LD. B**		
		13 under bottom, aqua, 8½ "	2.40	3.25
☐	28	**B C CO.**		
		Clear or amethyst, 4½ "	4.00	6.00
☐	29	**BECKER'S PURE HORSE-RADISH, BUFFALO**		
		Aqua, 4¼ "	6.00	8.00
☐	30	**B.F.B. CO. 109**		
		2845 on bottom, aqua, 8"	2.35	3.15
☐	31	**B & FB CO.**		
		2445 under bottom, aqua, 8"	2.35	3.15
☐	32	**BIRELEY'S TRADEMARK REG. HOLLYWOOD, CAL.**		
		Milk bottle, clear, 5¼ "	4.00	6.00
☐	33	**BISHOP & COMPANY**		
		Under bottom, clear or amethyst, 5½ "	5.00	7.00
☐	34	**BISHOP & COMPANY**		
		On bottom, fourteen vertical panels, ring at base, catsup, amethyst, 9¾ "	3.00	4.50
☐	35	Same as above, except 7⅝"	3.00	4.50
☐	36	**A. BOOTH & CO. BALT.,**		
		Label, Oyster Cocktail Catsup Salad Dressing under bottom, clear or amethyst, 7½ "	3.00	4.50
☐	37	Same as above, except 6"	1.25	2.10
☐	38	**BORDENS CONDENSED MILK CO.**		
		Milk glass, clear or amethyst, 4¼ "	6.00	8.00
☐	39	BREAST PUMP, sheared top, clear, 4"	4.00	6.00
☐	40	**H. B. BROOKS**		
		Amber, 10¼ "	15.00	20.00
☐	41	Same as above, except clear	6.00	10.00
☐	42	**B-33**		
		On bottom, aqua, 5"	1.25	2.15
☐	43	**BURNETT'S STANDARD FLAVORING EXTRACTS**		
		In sunken panel, aqua, 5¼ "	2.50	3.25
☐	44	**BURNETT'S STANDARD FLAVORING EXTRACTS**		
		Long neck, medicine bottle type, clear or amethyst, 4½ " .	1.25	2.15
☐	45	Same as above, except 5⅝"	1.25	2.15
☐	46	**BWCA**		
		In monogram, eight panels, clear or amethyst, 10"	3.00	4.25

C

☐	47	**JOSEPH CAMPBELL PRESERVE CO.**		
		Clear or amethyst, 8"	4.00	6.00
☐	48	**CANDY BROS MFG. CO. CONFECTIONERS**		
		Label, aqua, 12"	6.00	8.00
☐	49	CANNON BOTTLE, amber or olive, 9½ "	24.00	32.00
☐	50	CAPER, plain, green, 6½ "	7.00	11.00
☐	51	Same as above, except machine made	2.50	3.25
☐	52	CAPER BOTTLES, several different sizes and colors, some embossed, some not	9.00	12.00

☐ 53	CAPERS, eight indented panels in neck, two-ring top, three sizes	12.00	18.00
☐ 54	**DON CARLOS CYLINDER** Pat. June 19, 1894 N.Y. under bottom, clear, 5¼"	6.00	8.00
☐ 55	**CARNATION'S FRESH MILK** Chicago Sealed 1 qt., milk bottle, amber	5.00	7.50
☐ 56	CATHEDRAL PEPPERSAUCE, double collared mouth, pontil, 9¼", blue green	50.00	65.00
☐ 57	CATHEDRAL PICKLE, label, light blue, 9½"	22.00	30.00
☐ 58	CATHEDRAL, ground pontil, blue green, 8½"	70.00	100.00
☐ 59	CATSUP, plain, clear or amethyst, 7½"	1.50	2.25
☐ 60	CATSUP, ten panels, amethyst or clear, 8" or 9¾"	3.00	4.50
☐ 61	CATSUP, ten panels, top and bottom panels alternate, clear or amethyst, 10"	3.00	4.50
☐ 62	CATSUP, two mid-sections, ten panels, clear or amethyst, 8"	4.00	6.00
☐ 63	CATSUP, plain, tapered body, ring at shoulder, tapered neck, ring top, clear or amethyst, 7½"	4.50	6.50
☐ 64	CATSUP, plain, clear or amethyst, 10" tall, 2½" diameter	5.00	7.00
☐ 65	CATSUP, label, 1600 on bottom, clear or amethyst, 10"	1.50	2.25
☐ 66	CATSUP, label, clear or amethyst, 9¾"	3.00	4.50
☐ 67	CATSUP, plain, clear or amethyst, 9"	5.00	7.00
☐ 68	CATSUP, plain, clear or amethyst, 8½"	5.00	7.50
☐ 69	CATSUP, label, 403 on bottom, clear or amethyst, 7½"	2.00	3.50
☐ 70	CATSUP, label, aqua, panels, 8"	7.00	10.00
☐ 71	CATSUP, plain, clear or amethyst, 8½"	5.00	7.00
☐ 72	CATSUP, label, clear or amethyst, 10½"	5.00	7.50
☐ 73	CATSUP, label, swirl design, clear or amethyst, 8"	5.00	7.50
☐ 74	CATSUP, label, 10F under bottom, clear or amethyst	5.00	7.50
☐ 75	CATSUP, label, clear, 9½"	4.00	6.00
☐ 76	CATSUP and PRESERVE BOTTLES, embossed	3.00	4.50
☐ 77	**C B B** Under bottom, aqua, 8"	4.00	6.00
☐ 78	**C.B.K. and 1233 on bottom** Aqua, 7¼"	2.50	3.50
☐ 79	**C B W** Under bottom, clear or amethyst, 10¼"	4.00	6.00
☐ 80	**C & D** Under bottom, aqua, 7¾"	9.00	12.00
☐ 81	**CENTRAL MFG. COMPANY** Clear or amethyst, 5"	4.00	6.00
☐ 82	CHAMPAGNE CATSUP, round, screw top, amethyst or clear, 7½"	3.00	4.50
☐ 83	CHAMPAGNE CATSUP, applied top, one ring, amethyst, 9¾"	3.50	5.00
☐ 84	**CHAMPION VERMONT MAPLE SYRUP** Label, clear or amethyst, 8½"	6.00	8.00
☐ 85	**CHAMPION'S VINEGAR** Aqua, 14½"	22.00	30.00
☐ 86	**CHAMPION'S VINEGAR** Aqua, 15½"	19.00	25.00
☐ 87	**R.C. CHANCE'S SONS, TABLE TALK KETCHUP, PHILA** Label, clear or amethyst, 9¼"	5.00	7.00

☐ 88	*CHERRY, label, B under bottom, clear, 4½"*	1.50	2.25
☐ 89	*CHERRY, plain, 33 and a star on bottom, clear or*		
	amethyst, 6¼"	1.50	2.25
☐ 90	*CHERRY PICKLE, plain, clear or amethyst, 6"*	1.50	2.25
☐ 91	**THE C.I. CO. LTD.**		
	This Trademark Registered, Maple Sap & Boiled Cider		
	Vinegar, on front, East Ridge, NH, three rings near base,		
	flint shoulder, tapered neck and ring top, cobalt, 11½" ..	30.00	40.00
☐ 92	**THE J.M. CLARK PICKLE CO., LOUISVILLE, KY.**		
	Round, clear, 5"	5.00	7.00
☐ 93	**COLEMAN DIARY**		
	Belvidere, Ill., all in a circle in center Quality milk, on		
	shoulder one qt. liquid, blob top, clear, B.T.M.A.L.	12.00	17.00
☐ 94	**COLEMAN, L.E.**		
	Belvidridere, Ill. all in a circle (milk bottle) B.I.M.L.A., pt.,		
	clear	15.00	20.00
☐ 95	**N.L. CLARK & CO., PERUVIAN SYRUP**		
	Aqua, 8½"	6.00	8.00
☐ 96	**CONDIMENT**		
	Plain milk bottle type, clear or amethyst, 6½"	4.00	6.00
☐ 97	*Same as above, except vase type bottle, 4"*	3.00	5.00
☐ 98	**THE COOPERATIVE**		
	Ideal Feeder in three lines, in center of an one side ounces		
	table other table spoon, oblong — bottle and turn up top,		
	6¼ long (English)	19.00	25.00
☐ 99	**COTTAGE CHEESE**		
	Ten panels, clear or amethyst, 4½"	5.00	7.00
☐100	**COURTENAY & CO.**		
	A & P under bottom, clear or amethyst, 7"	6.00	8.00
☐101	**COURTENAY & CO.**		
	Clear or amber, 7"	4.00	6.00
☐102	**C.R.B.**		
	Under bottom, label, aqua, 8"	3.00	5.00
☐103	**CROWN**		
	Under bottom, pickle label, 14"	9.00	12.00
☐104	**CRUIKSHANK BROS & CO.**		
	Allegheny Pa. under bottom, clear or amethyst, 8"	2.50	3.50
☐105	**C.S. & CO. LD5302**		
	On bottom, eight panels, aqua, 6½"	2.50	3.50
☐106	**CURTICE BROTHERS CO.**		
	1613 under bottom; 2¼" round, clear or amethyst, 8"	5.00	8.00
☐107	**CURTICE BROS.**		
	Machine made, clear or amethyst, 10"	3.00	5.00
☐108	**CURTICE BROS. CO.**		
	Preserves on the shoulders, ridges all around, amethyst		
	or clear, 7¼"	3.00	5.00
☐109	**CURTICE BROTHERS CO. PRESERVES ROCHESTER, NY**		
	In circle on tapered neck, 8", 10½" or 12¼"	6.00	8.00
☐110	**CURTIS BROS. PRESERVES**		
	Clear, 10½" or 12½"	6.00	8.00
☐111	**GEORGE M. CURTIS, PURE OLIVE OIL**		
	Clear, 17"	3.00	5.00

☐ 112 **GEO M. CURTIS, PURE OLIVE OIL**
Slim, round 1.50   2.25
☐ 113 **CURTIS & MOORE**
Clear or amethyst, 2¼ " x 2¼ ", 10" 8.00   11.00

D

☐ 114 **DAVIS OK BAKING POWDER**
Round, aqua, 4½ " 3.00   5.00
☐ 115 **DAWSON'S PICKLES**
Ten panels, clear or amethyst, 7½ " 4.00   6.00
☐ 116 **D. & C.**
Pontil, clear or amethyst, 11½ " 11.00   15.00
☐ 117 **D. & CO**
Mustard, clear or amethyst, 4½ " 2.50   3.50
☐ 118 **DIXIE** *under bottom*
Clear, 7¾ " 3.00   5.00
☐ 119 **DODSON & HILS MFG CO.**
Aqua, 8" 4.00   6.00
☐ 120 **DUNDEE**
Gray 8.00   11.00
☐ 121 **J. DUPIT BORDEAUX ELIXIR DE SOULAC LES BAINS**
Amber, 3" 7.00   10.00
☐ 122 **A. DURANT & FILS BORDEAUX**
Round, aqua and blue, 7⅛ " 4.00   6.00
☐ 123 *Same as above, except no embossing, fancy* 3.00   5.00
☐ 124 **E. R. DURKEE & CO., N.Y.**
Pontil, aqua, 4½ " 15.00   20.00
☐ 125 **E. R. DURKEE & CO. CHALLENGE SAUCE**
Sample, amethyst, 4" 6.00   8.00
☐ 126 **E.R. DURKEE & CO. SALAD DRESSING, N.Y.**
Vertically, Bottle Patented April 17, 1877 on bottom,
round, amethyst, 6½ " 4.00   6.00
☐ 127 **E.R. DURKEE & CO., N.Y.**
Round, screw top, amethyst, 3½ " 1.50   2.25
☐ 128 **E.R. DURKEE & CO., SALAD DRESSING, N.Y.**
Round shoulder, Patented April 17, 1877 on the bottom,
round, clear, 4½ " or 7¾ " 1.50   2.25
☐ 129 **E.R. DURKEE & CO., NEW YORK**
In vertical lines, clear or amethyst, 5", 6¾ " or 8¼ " 2.50   3.50
☐ 130 **E. R. DURKEE AND CO.**
Sheared top, eight panels, clear or amethyst, 4" 3.00   5.00
☐ 131 **E. R. DURKEE & CO.**
Clear or amethyst, 6" 6.00   8.00
☐ 132 **E.R. DURKEE & CO.**
Clear or amethyst, 7" 4.00   6.00
☐ 133 **E. R. DURKEE & CO.**
Clear or amethyst, 1½ " diameter, 4" 6.00   8.00
☐ 134 **E.E. DYER & CO. EXTRACT OF COFFEE, BOSTON, MASS**
Graphite pontil, green, 6" 30.00   40.00

E

☐ 135 **E.H.V.B.**
Graphite pontil, six panels, light blue, 9½" 38.00 50.00

☐ 136 **EIFFEL TOWER LEMONADE**
G. Foster Clark & Co. Manufacturer on opposite side,
clear, 2¾" 3.00 5.00

☐ 137 **CHARLES ELLIS SON & CO. PHILA.**
Aqua, 6" 4.00 6.00

☐ 138 **ENO'S FRUIT SALT**
W on bottom, 7" tall, 1½" x 2½" 5.00 7.00

☐ 139 **ESKAY'S**
pat. J11-93 Albumenized 163 Food on bottom, sheared
top, amber, 7½" 3.00 5.00

☐ 140 **ESKAY'S**
pat July 93 Albumenized 179 Food on bottom, machine
made, amber, 7½" 3.00 5.00

☐ 141 **EVANGELINE PEPPERSAUCE**
Made in St. Martinville, La., U.S.A. on one side panel,
twelve panels, tiny screw top, 5¼" 2.50 3.50

☐ 142 **EXTRACT TABASCO**
Under bottom, clear, 4¾" 2.50 3.50

F

☐ 143 **F**
In center of bottle, Refined pontil, clear, 5" 7.00 10.00

☐ 144 **FANCY OLIVE OIL**
Small base with five rings, six rings at shoulder, long
bulbous neck, aqua, 7" 6.00 8.00

☐ 145 **F.G.W.**
Under bottom, clear, 7¾" 3.00 5.00

☐ 146 **J.A. FOLGER & CO.**
Golden Gate High Grade Flavoring Extracts, 2 oz Full
Measure on front panel, rectangular, amethyst, 5½" 2.50 3.50

☐ 147 **FOLGERS GOLDEN GATE FLAVORING**
On panel, rectangular, amethyst, 5¼" 1.50 2.25

☐ 148 **FORBES DELICIOUS FLAVORING EXTRACTS**
Made by Forbes Bros. & Co, St. Louis on front panel,
rectangular, clear, 4¾" 1.50 2.25

☐ 149 **4N**
Under bottom, clear or amethyst, 9¾" 3.00 5.00

☐ 150 **THE FRANK TEA & SPICE CO.**
Machine made, clear, 5½" 3.00 5.00

☐ 151 **FRANK TEA & SPICE CO, CINCINNATI O**
Jumbo Peanut Butter, Made from No. 1 Spanish and No. 1
Va. Peanuts, Salt Added, 5 oz, embossed head of
elephant, round ridges on bottle, clear 3.00 5.00

☐ 152 **LOUIT FRERES & CO. BORDEAUX**
Mustard barrel, three rings at base and shoulder, crude
ring collar, open pontil, amethyst, 4¾" 5.00 8.00

☐ 153 Same as above, except graphite pontil 14.00 20.00

G

☐ 154	**G.A.J.**		
	Under bottom, sheared top, 7"	3.00	5.00
☐ 155	**GARRETTS FOOD PRODUCTS**		
	Garrett & Co. Inc. Monticello, N.Y., St. Louis Est. U.S. Pat. Off., round, green, 10½" and 12⅛"	5.00	8.00
☐ 156	**GEBHARDT EAGLE**		
	On the side panel, Chile powder on the opposite panel, Eagle embossed on the front with Trademark, screw top, rectangular, clear or amethyst, 3½" or 5½"	4.00	6.00
☐ 157	**THE M.A. GEDREY PICKLING CO.**		
	Aqua, 9¼"	5.00	7.00
☐ 158	**GIBBS**		
	B on bottom, clear or amethyst, 8¼"	3.00	4.50
☐ 159	**GOLDBERG-BOWEN & CO.**		
	Sierra Madre Olive Oil San Francisco, Cal, shaped like a gin bottle, flared collar, bulbous type neck, amethyst, quart, 11¼"	4.00	6.00
☐ 160	**GOLDEN TREE PURE SYRUP**		
	Crown top, aqua, 11¼"	3.00	4.50
☐ 161	**THE GRADUATED NURSING BOTTLE**		
	Clear, 6¾"	11.00	15.00
☐ 162	*GRAPE JUICE, plain, aqua, 6"*	3.00	4.50
☐ 163	**GRAPETTE PRODUCTS CO. CAMDEN ARK.**		
	Under bottom, ABM, clear, 7¼"	6.00	8.00
☐ 164	**GRARY & CO**		
	Stag head on shoulder, Worcestershire Sauce on side, a stag on neck, clear or amethyst	5.00	7.00
☐ 165	**CHARLES GULDEN**		
	Clear or amethyst, 4¾"	3.00	4.50
☐ 166	**CHAS. GULDEN, NEW YORK**		
	On bottom, pickle jar, four large bulbous rings, flared collar, clear, 5½"	4.00	6.00
☐ 167	**CHAS. GULDEN**		
	16 under bottom, aqua or clear, 8½"	5.00	7.00
☐ 168	**CHAS. GULDEN, NEW YORK**		
	Four rings on base, three on shoulder, mustard barrel, amethyst, 4⅝"	4.50	6.50
☐ 169	**CHAS. GULDEN, N.Y.**		
	Under bottom, clear, 4¼"	5.00	8.00
☐ 170	**CHAS. GULDEN, N.Y.**		
	Under bottom, clear or amethyst, 4¼"	3.00	4.50

H

☐ 171	**H**		
	Under bottom, clear, 4½"	2.50	3.50
☐ 172	**HALFORD LEIGESTERSHINE**		
	Aqua, 7⅛"	2.50	3.50
☐ 173	**HANANC**		
	Aqua, 6"	4.00	6.00

☐174 **THOMAS L. HARDIN CO.**
Clear or amethyst, 7" 5.00 8.00

☐175 **GEO HARM**
This Bottle To Be Washed and Returned, Not To Be
Bought Or Sold on back, clear, quart 11.00 15.00

☐176 **H.J. HEINZ CO. NO. 37 GOTHIC HORSERADISH**
Aqua, 6" 3.00 4.50

☐177 **H.J. HEINZ CO.**
On bottom, also large notch on bottom, 18 panels, round,
clear, 8¾" 4.00 6.00

☐178 **H.J. HEINZ CO.**
Patent on the bottom, eight panels, amethyst, 9¼" 4.00 6.00

☐179 **H.J. HEINZ CO. 69 PATD.**
Under bottom, clear, 6" 5.00 8.00

☐180 **H.J. HEINZ CO.**
122 Patd under bottom, ten panels, clear or amethyst,
4¾" 3.00 4.50

☐181 **H.J. HEINZ CO.**
7 Patented and an X on bottom, clear or amethyst, 8¼" .. 3.00 4.50

☐182 **HEINZ**
Clear or amethyst, 6" 4.00 6.00

☐183 **HEINZ**
No. 28 under bottom, aqua, 7¼" 2.50 3.50

☐184 **HEISEY RELISH**
Label, eight panels, lead glass, clear or amethyst, 4" 5.00 7.00

☐185 **HERB JUICE**
On panel, rectangular, clear, 8⅜" 3.00 4.50

☐186 **HILL'S**
Label, machine made, L.B. CO monogram on back, aqua,
11" 6.00 8.00

☐187 **HIRES IMPROVED ROOT BEER**
Panel, Mfg. by The Charles Hires Co., panel, Philadelphia
Pa, U.S.A., panel, Make Five Gallons of a Delicious Drink,
aqua, 4¾" 4.00 6.00

☐188 **HOLBROOK & CO.**
P.B. on bottom, aqua, 7½" 3.75 5.00

☐189 **HOLBROOK & CO.**
Aqua, 4½" 5.00 8.00

☐190 **HOLBROOK & CO.**
R.B.B. under bottom, aqua, 8¾" 9.00 12.00

☐191 **HONEY**
Clear or amethyst, 8" 7.00 10.00

☐192 **HONEYWELL**
Sauce type bottle, rolled lip, concave panels, front and
back, three concave on sides, open pontil, aqua, 6¾" ... 14.00 20.00

☐193 **HORLICK'S TRADEMARK, RACINE, WIS., MALTED MILK**
M.M. U.S.A. 1 GAL.
Round, clear, 10¾" 2.00 3.00

☐194 **HORLICK'S**
Twice on shoulders, round, screw top, clear, 2¾" 1.40 2.10

☐195 **HORLICK'S**
Clear or amethyst, 5" 3.00 4.25

☐196 **HORLICK'S**
Aqua, different sizes 3.00 4.25

☐ 197 **HORTON-CATO MFG CO, DETROIT, MICH**
In three lines, three round panels, on bottom T.P., clear, 5½" 5.00 8.00

☐ 198 **HORTON-CATO CO.**
Clear, 7" 3.00 4.50

☐ 199 **HORTON-CATO & CO., DETROIT**
Reverse side Crown Celery Salt, gold, 8" 19.00 25.00

☐ 200 **HORTON-CATO MFG. CO., DETROIT, MICH**
Under bottom, clear, 6" 3.50 5.00

☐ 201 **J.W. HUNNEWELL & CO.**
On side, Boston on opposite side, three concave panels, aqua, 1½" 3.00 4.50

☐ 202 *Same as above, except aqua green* 5.00 7.00

☐ 203 **H.W.P. 394**
Under bottom, sheared top, clear, 6" 4.00 6.00

☐ 204 **HYMAN PICKLE CO., LOUISVILLE, KY.**
Under bottom, yellow, 8" 5.00 7.00

I

☐ 205 *INDIA PACKING CO., PORTLAND, ORG.*
Moon in center, aqua, 6" 7.00 10.00

J

☐ 206 *JELLY, label, Patented June 9-03 June 23 03 under bottom, clear, 3½"* 2.50 3.50

☐ 207 *JELLY, label, 2 under bottom, clear or amethyst, 4¾"* .... .50 3.50

☐ 208 *JELLY, label, sheared top, 2¼"* 2.50 3.50

☐ 209 *JELLY, label, Patented June 9-03 June 23 03 under bottom, clear or amethyst, 2½"* 2.50 3.50

☐ 210 **JOSLYN'S MAPLE SYRUP**
Eight sides, ground lip, aqua, 8" 5.00 8.00

☐ 211 **J.P.S.**
Under bottom, clear or amethyst, 7¼" 2.50 3.50

☐ 212 **J.P.S.**
Under bottom, pickles, green, 6" 5.00 8.00

☐ 213 **J.P.S.**
Under bottom, green, 6" 5.00 8.00

☐ 214 **J.P.S.**
Under bottom, clear or amethyst, 5" 3.00 4.50

☐ 215 **J. Wm JUNKINS CATSUP, BALTIMORE MD.**
Clear or amethyst, 8" 9.00 12.00

K

☐ 216 **KELLOGGS**
On base, oval, clear, 4¼", 6" or 7" 1.50 2.25

☐ 217 **KEPLER**
On four sides on shoulder, tapered bottle, ring top, under bottom Snowhill RW&CO, London, green, 1¾" x 2¼", 1¼" neck, 5¼" 7.00 10.00

☐218	*Same as above, except no Kepler on shoulder, 7½" tall, 2¼" x 3¼"*	9.00	12.00
☐219	**KARL KIEFER PAT** *In glass lid to fit pickle bottle, round, amethyst or clear, 6"*	4.00	6.00
☐220	**KITCHEN BOUQUET** *On bottom, round, ABM, aqua, 5¾"*	2.50	3.50
☐221	**KLEASNER P.C.** *Belvidere, Ill. in center Pure Milk all in a circle, on shoulder B.I.M.A.L., clear, base K*	11.00	15.00

L

☐222	**LAM A & F** *Under bottom, green, 9¼"*	12.00	17.00
☐223	*LAMP CANDY BOTTLE, aqua, 3"*	5.00	8.00
☐224	**LEA & PERRINS** *J10D,S on bottom, aqua, 11½"*	3.00	4.50
☐225	*Same as above, except 8½"*	3.00	4.50
☐226	*Same as above, except 7¼"*	2.50	3.50
☐227	**LEVER BROS. CO. NEW YORK** *Label, amber, 10"*	7.00	10.00
☐228	**LINCOLN BANK BOTTLE** *On base, Pat 1959 Lincoln Foods Inc. Lawrance Mass 3-17-3 under bottom, clear, 8½"*	8.00	11.00
☐229	**LIPTON** *Number on bottom, aqua, 8½"*	4.00	6.00
☐230	**JOSHUA LONGFIELD** *North of England Sauce around shoulder, aqua, 7"*	5.00	8.00
☐231	**LONG SYRUP REFINING CO., S.F. CAL.** *Wine color, 4¾"*	6.00	8.00
☐232	**LUHMAN** *Belvidere, Ill. in center Dairy all in a circle, B.I.M.A.L., clear*	12.00	16.00
☐233	**LUNDBORG** *Clear or amethyst, 2½"*	3.00	4.50
☐234	**E.G. LYONS & RAAS CO.** *Clear or amethyst, 4"*	5.00	7.00

M

☐235	**M** *Under bottom, amber, 6½"*	5.00	8.00
☐236	**MANDER WEAVER & CO.** *Cream crock, 4"*	9.00	12.00
☐237	**MANSFIELD DAIRY** *Clear, quart*	8.00	11.00
☐238	**SGDG GRAND MARNIER** *On back, snap on, machine made, light amber, 6"*	10.00	14.00
☐239	**MASON** *Belvidere, Ill. in center Dairy all in a circle, ½ pt. base M, Dots on shoulder #24, B.I.M.A.L., clear*	11.00	
☐240	**D. MAURER & SON** *Under bottom, 3"*	2.00	3.00

☐ 241	**F.E. McALLISTER'S**		
	Aqua, 7"	3.50	4.50
☐ 242	**McCORMICK & CO. SPICE GRINDERS, BALTIMORE**		
	Eight panels, sheared top, clear or amethyst, 3¾"	4.00	6.00
☐ 243	**McCORMICK & CO., EXTRACTS, SPICES & ETC., BALTIMORE MD.**		
	Clear, 4½"	4.00	6.00
☐ 244	**McCORMICK & CO., BALTIMORE**		
	Triangular, clear, 3½"	4.50	6.00
☐ 245	**McCORMICK & CO.**		
	Clear or amethyst, 4¾"	4.00	6.00
☐ 246	**McCORMICK & CO.**		
	Clear, 5¼"	3.50	4.75
☐ 247	**McCORMICK & CO.**		
	Round, aqua, 5¼"	3.50	4.75
☐ 248	**McILHENNY CO., AVERY ISLAND LA.**		
	Clear or amethyst, 8"	5.00	7.00
☐ 249	**McILHENNY CO., AVERY ISLAND LA.**		
	Swirl pattern, clear, 8"	9.00	13.00
☐ 250	**MELLINS FOOD, FREE SAMPLE**		
	P on bottom, aqua, 3¾"	3.25	4.50
☐ 251	**MENLEY-JAMES LIMITED**		
	N.Y., London on bottom, milk glass, 1¾"	2.50	3.25
☐ 252	*MILK BOTTLE, HA under bottom, clear*	7.00	10.00
☐ 253	**MILKS' EMULSION**		
	F.C.W. under bottom, machine made, amber, 6¼"	2.50	3.25
☐ 253	**MILKS' EMULSION**		
	#1054 under bottom, machine made, amber, 6¼"	2.50	3.25
☐ 255	**M&M**		
	On one line, T in center, CO on bottom line, pumpkin seed type bottle, clear, 3¾"	3.00	4.50
☐ 256	**MOUTARDE DIAPHANE / LOUIT FRERES & CO.**		
	Mustard barrel, three rings at base and shoulders, crude ring collar, graphite pontil, amethyst, 5"	14.00	20.00
☐ 257	*Same as above, except clear*	9.00	12.00
☐ 258	**MUSKOGEE WHO. GRO. CO.**		
	Clear, 8¼"	4.00	6.00
☐ 259	*MUSTARD, label, clear or amethyst, 4½"*	2.50	3.25
☐ 260	*MUSTARD, label, small kick-up, six-part mold, clear or amethyst, 5½"*	2.50	3.25
☐ 261	*MUSTARD, label, Patented under bottom, twelve panels, clear or amethyst, 4¾"*	2.50	3.25
☐ 262	*MUSTARD BARREL, plain, three rings at top and bottom, sheared top, clear or amethyst, 1¾" round*	4.00	6.00
☐ 263	*Same as above, except no sheared top, 4½"*	3.00	5.00
☐ 264	**MY WIFE'S SALAD DRESSING**		
	Machine made, blue green, 8"	5.00	8.00

N

☐ 265	**BIBO NEWMAN & KENBERG**		
	BNI monogram, San Francisco, Cal., round, ring collar, clear, 5¼"	5.00	8.00

☐ 266 **NUT HOUSE**
Figure of house and other writing, store jar, ball shape,
clear 11.00 15.00

O

☐ 267 **OLD DUFFY'S 1842 5 YEAR OLD APPLE JUICE VINEGAR**
On top shoulder, Duffy's in diamond shape and 1842 in circle on neck, eight panels, amber, 6¾" 12.00 16.00
☐ 268 OLIVE OIL, long neck, ring collar, graphite pontil, light
aqua, 12½" 7.00 10.00
☐ 269 OLIVE OIL, plain, old flared lip, round with tapered neck,
aqua, 11¼" 5.00 8.00
☐ 270 OLIVE OIL, plain, three-part mold, flat ring top, under bottom, sunken circle, cobalt, 4¼" tapered body, 2½" neck . 9.00 13.00
☐ 271 OLIVE OIL, amber, 1½" round, 6¼" tall, 2½ neck 3.50 4.50
☐ 272 OLIVE OIL, slim, bulbous neck, clear or aqua, three sizes,
7¼" to 12½" 5.00 7.00
☐ 273 OLIVE OIL, label, aqua, 7½" 4.00 6.00
☐ 274 OLIVE OIL, aqua, 10¼" 2.75 4.25
☐ 275 OLIVE OIL, free-blown, pontil, small kick-up, aqua, 10" ... 11.00 15.00
☐ 276 OLIVE OIL, label, clear, 6½" 2.50 3.25
☐ 277 OLIVE OIL, label, kick-up, aqua, 12¾" 7.00 10.00
☐ 278 OLIVE OIL, label, clear or amethyst, 8" 3.50 4.50
☐ 279 OLIVE OIL, aqua, 10" 4.00 6.00
☐ 280 OLIVE OIL, label, clear or amethyst, 5½" 2.35 3.15
☐ 281 OLIVE OIL, label, free-blown, pontil, aqua, 13½" 14.00 20.00
☐ 282 OLIVE OIL, label, free-blown, pontil, aqua, 10" 14.00 20.00
☐ 283 OLIVE OIL, label, applied ring top, deep kick-up, aqua,
9½" 5.00 8.00
☐ 284 **J. M. OLIVER & SONS**
On blob seal, Olive oil, aqua, 7" 5.00 8.00
☐ 285 **F.A. OSTEN'S PURE SALAD OIL**
Eight-ring top, long neck, flared bottom, aqua 7.00 10.00

P

☐ 286 **PARKER BROS.**
Vertically, on shoulder, London Club Sauce, crude top,
round, aqua, 7¼" 5.00 8.00
☐ 287 **PASKOLA'S, THE PRE-DIGESTED FOOD CO., TRADEMARK**
Embossed Pineapple, amber, 6" 5.00 8.00
☐ 288 **PEPPERMINT**
Marble in center of neck, aqua, 7¼" 9.00 12.00
☐ 289 PEPPERSAUCE, 20 rings around bottle, round, space for
label, clear or aqua, 6¼" 8.00 12.00
☐ 290 PEPPERSAUCE, 22 rings around bottle, space for label,
oval, clear or aqua, 7" 8.00 12.00
☐ 291 PEPPERSAUCE, cathedral, gothic arch in lower half of six
panels two windows in upper half of each panel, aqua,
8½" 15.00 20.00
☐ 292 PEPPERSAUCE, clear, 8" 7.00 10.00
☐ 293 PEPPERSAUCE, label, 4¾" 2.75 3.50
☐ 294 PEPPERSAUCE, label, X on bottom, aqua, 9" 9.00 12.00

☐ 295	PEPPERSAUCE, clear or amethyst,1½" square, 6½"	7.00	10.00
☐ 296	PEPPERSAUCE, label, clear or amethyst, 6½"	1.50	2.25
☐ 297	PEPPERSAUCE, label, aqua, 7"	4.00	6.00
☐ 298	PEPPERSAUCE, label, aqua, 10½"	9.00	13.00
☐ 299	PEPPERSAUCE, label, 24 rings, clear, 8¼"	8.00	12.00
☐ 300	PEPPERSAUCE, label, NYMM and monogram under bottom, aqua	9.00	13.00
☐ 301	PEPPERSAUCE, label; leaded glass, clear or amethyst, 7¼"	5.00	8.00
☐ 302	PEPPERSAUCE, label, swirl pattern, clear or amethyst, 8½"	5.00	7.00
☐ 303	PEPPERSAUCE, fifteen rings, cathedral type, G.C.O. Pat. Sept 26, 1875 on base, double ring top, aqua, 8½"	14.00	20.00
☐ 304	PEPPERSAUCE, label, C & B on base, clear or amethyst, 7½"	11.00	15.00
☐ 305	PEPPERSAUCE, label, clear, 12½"	5.00	7.00
☐ 306	PEPPERSAUCE, label, amber, 7¾"	7.00	10.00
☐ 307	PEPPERSAUCE, label, D.E. under bottom, aqua, 8"	5.00	8.00
☐ 308	**PEPSINE CHAPOTEAUT** Ten panels, clear or amethyst, 3½"	3.00	4.50
☐ 309	**PEPTOGENIC MILK POWDER** Around shoulder, machine made, tin measure top, amber, 5¾"	4.00	6.00
☐ 310	**PHOENIX BRAND** Machine made, clear, 6"	4.00	6.00
☐ 311	PICKLE BOTTLE, cathetral, square, four gothic panels, applied ring and lip, aqua, 11½"	22.00	30.00
☐ 312	PICKLE, cathedral, cobalt, ½" square, 5½"	30.00	40.00
☐ 313	PICKLE, plain, paneled corner, tapered neck, yellow, 2½" square, 7¼"	11.00	16.00
☐ 314	Same as above, except no panel, under bottom Pat. Apr 4 1882, Heinz 16 in circle, aqua	4.00	6.00
☐ 315	PICKLE, label, clear or amethyst, 3¾" square, 13½"	5.00	8.00
☐ 316	PICKLE, label, machine made, 165 under bottom, clear or amethyst, 7"	2.50	3.25
☐ 317	PICKLE, label, pontil, aqua, 10"	11.00	15.00
☐ 318	PICKLE, label, broken pontil, aqua, 7¼"	65.00	85.00
☐ 319	PICKLE, label, kick-up, pontil, aqua, 8½"	19.00	25.00
☐ 320	PICKLE, label, W.T. & CO. under bottom, aqua, 6¼"	1.50	2.25
☐ 321	PICKLE, label, aqua, 8¼"	4.00	6.00
☐ 322	PICKLE, label, aqua, 6½"	3.25	4.50
☐ 323	PICKLE, label, green, 11"	5.00	7.00
☐ 324	PICKLE, label, clear or amethyst, 6¾"	7.00	10.00
☐ 325	PICKLE, label, small kick-up, aqua, 9"	6.00	9.00
☐ 326	PICKLE, label, clear or amethyst, 7½"	3.00	4.50
☐ 327	PICKLE, label, Patented Aug. 20, 1901 under bottom, clear or amethyst, 7"	1.50	2.25
☐ 328	PICKLE, label, Pat Applied For #16 under bottom, clear, 11¼"	4.00	6.00
☐ 329	PICKLE, label, Pat July 11th 1893 under bottom, sheared top, clear, 7"	3.00	4.50
☐ 330	PICKLE, label, 3 under bottom, aqua, 3½"	5.00	8.00
☐ 331	PICKLE, label, sheared top, clear or amethyst, 5"	4.00	6.00
☐ 332	PICKLE, label, sheared top, aqua, 12¾"	19.00	25.00
☐ 333	PICKLE, label, aqua, 10½"	7.00	10.00

☐ 334	*PICKLE, label, clear or amethyst, 5"*	5.00	7.00
☐ 335	*PICKLE, label, small kick-up, green, 7½"*	10.00	15.00
☐ 336	*PICKLE, label, eight panels, clear or amethyst, 6½"*	3.00	4.50
☐ 337	*PICKLE, label, amber, 6¾"*	11.00	15.00
☐ 338	*PICKLE, label, clear, 7"*	5.00	8.00
☐ 339	*PICKLE, label, clear or amethyst, 11" tall, 2½" x 3¼"* ...	5.00	8.00
☐ 340	*PICKLE, label, green, 5½"*	4.00	6.00
☐ 341	*PICKLE, label, ten panels, clear or amethyst, 10¼"*	3.00	4.50
☐ 342	*PICKLE, AM on bottom, clear*	2.50	3.50
☐ 343	*PICKLE, label, Pat Apr. 20, 1901 on bottom, clear or amethyst, 8¼"*	2.50	3.50
☐ 344	*PICKLE, label, Pat O.P. 1900 on bottom, clear or amethyst, 6"*	3.50	4.75
☐ 345	*PICKLE, label, sunken bottom, aqua, 2½" diameter, 9"* ..	3.00	4.50
☐ 346	*PICKLE, label, aqua, 8½"*	7.00	10.00
☐ 347	*PICKLE, label, pontil, aqua, 9"*	6.00	9.00
☐ 348	*PICKLE, label, clear, 4½"*	3.50	4.50
☐ 349	*PICKLE, label, broken pontil, aqua, 6½"*	14.00	20.00
☐ 350	*PICKLE, label, improved pontil, amber, 10"*	25.00	32.00
☐ 351	*PICKLE, label, cathedral design, blue green, 13½"*	75.00	95.00
☐ 352	*PICKLE, label, sheared top, green, 3¼"*	4.00	6.00
☐ 353	*PICKLE, label, small kick-up, amber, 7½"*	5.00	8.00
☐ 354	*PICKLE, label, four side panels, pontil, aqua, 6¼"*	25.00	32.00
☐ 355	*PICKLE, label, green, 8½"*	5.00	8.00
☐ 356	*PICKLE, label, Pat. App. For under bottom, aqua, 9¼"* ...	7.00	10.00
☐ 357	*PICKLE, label, pontil, aqua, 7½"*	14.00	20.00
☐ 358	*PICKLE, label, three-piece mold, light blue, 12"*	5.00	8.00
☐ 359	*PICKLE, label, aqua, 9"*	3.00	4.50
☐ 360	*PICKLE, label, ten panels halfway down, small kick-up, aqua, 12"*	5.00	8.00
☐ 361	*PICKLE or CHERRY, label, Pat. App. For under bottom, clear or amethyst, 5"*	4.50	7.00
☐ 362	**PICKMAN'S CHOCOLATE** *Machine made, aqua*...............................	3.00	4.50
☐ 363	**E. D. PINAUD** *Aqua, 2¼"*	4.00	6.00
☐ 364	**PIN MONEY** *Clear, 5¼"*	5.00	8.00
☐ 365	**PLANTERS** *Same in back, peanut figures on each corner, glass top with a peanut nob, clear*	75.00	100.00
☐ 366	**PLANTERS** *Same in back, square, glass top with peanut nobs, clear* .	25.00	35.00
☐ 367	**PLANTERS SALTED PEANUTS** *Same in back, glass top with peanut nob, clear*	38.00	50.00
☐ 368	**PLANTERS** *Same in back on base, glass top with peanut nob, clear* ..	18.00	24.00
☐ 369	**PLANTERS** *On shoulder, PENNANT 5c SALTED PEANUTS on front, on each side a Planters Peanut Man figure, glass top with peanut nob, clear*	45.00	60.00
☐ 370	**P/P CO.** *Under bottom, clear, 1¾" diameter, 5"*	2.75	4.25
☐ 371	**DR. PRICE'S** *Clear or amethyst, 5¾"*	2.50	3.75

☐372	**PRICE-BOOKER MFG. CO.**		
	Clear or amethyst, 8"	4.00	6.00
☐373	**PRIDE OF LONG ISLAND**		
	Clear or amethyst, 9¾"	4.00	6.00
☐374	**POMPEIAN BRAND VIRGIN LUCCA OLIVE OIL**		
	In four lines, aqua, 7½"	4.00	6.00
☐375	*Same as above, except other sizes*	4.00	6.00
☐376	**THE POTTER PARLIN CO.**		
	Under bottom, sheared top, clear or amethyst, 4"	5.00	7.00
☐377	**PRIMROSE SALAD OIL WESTERN MEAT CO.**		
	Vertically on one panel, aqua, 9½"	4.00	6.50
☐378	*Same as above, except quart*	5.00	7.00
☐379	**PURE OLIVE OIL S.S.P.**		
	Bulb shaped base, long neck, amethyst, 7¼"	4.00	6.50

Q

☐380	**QUERUS**		
	Pontil, aqua, 5¼"	18.00	25.00

R

☐381	*RADISH, label, eight panels, clear or amethyst*	4.00	6.00
☐382	*RADISH, label, ten panels, clear, 4½"*	2.50	3.50
☐383	*RADISH, label, square on bottom, clear or amethyst, 7"* ..	3.00	4.25
☐384	*RADISH, label, 2 on bottom, sheared top, clear or amethyst, 10¾"*	4.00	6.00
☐385	*RADISH, label, green, 5½"*	3.00	4.25
☐386	*RADISH, label, clear or amethyst, 9½"*	2.50	3.50
☐387	*RADISH, label, clear or amethyst, 5¼"*	2.50	3.50
☐388	*RADISH, label, Pat April 2nd, 1901 under bottom, clear or amethyst, 5½"*	3.00	4.25
☐389	*RADISH, label, ribbed base, clear or amethyst, 7½"*	3.00	4.25
☐390	*RADISH, label, eight panels, clear or amethyst, 6½"*	3.00	4.25
☐391	*RADISH, label, 169 under bottom, clear or amethyst, 8¾"*	2.75	3.75
☐392	*RADISH, label, clear or amethyst, 6"*	3.00	4.25
☐393	*RADISH, label, clear or amethyst, 5¾"*	3.00	4.25
☐394	*RADISH, label, 56S in triangle under bottom, clear, 4½"* .	2.75	3.75
☐395	**RED SNAPPER SAUCE CO., MEMPHIS, TENN.**		
	Six sides, clear, 9½"	7.00	10.00
☐396	**RED SNAPPER**		
	Clear or amethyst, 7½"	3.50	4.50
☐397	**RESTORFF & BETTMANN, N.Y.**		
	Under bottom, light green, 4½"	4.00	6.00
☐398	**RESTORFF & BETTMANN F.F., N.Y.**		
	Under bottom, Mustard, aqua, 4½"	5.00	8.00
☐399	**R.J. RITTER CONSERVE CO.**		
	Under bottom, clear, 8¼" or 10½"	5.00	7.00
☐400	**ROWAT & CO.**		
	Same in back, light green, 10"	5.00	8.00
☐401	**ROYAL LUNCHEON CHEESE**		
	Milk glass, 2½"	2.50	3.50

☐ 402 **ROYAL LUNCHEON CHEESE**
Under bottom, milk glass, 3" 2.50   3.25

S

☐ 403 *SALAD DRESSING, label, clear or amethyst, 6¼"* 4.00   6.00
☐ 404 **M. SALZMAN CO., PURITY ABOVE ALL**
855 under bottom, amber, 10½" 11.00   15.00
☐ 405 *SAUCE, round, tapered neck, sixteen concave vertical panels all around, aqua, 8"* 5.00   8.00
☐ 406 *SAUCE, coffin shape, ring on base and top of neck, clear, 8¼"* 3.50   4.50
☐ 407 *SAUCE, olive oil shape, round, tapered neck, graduated collar, pontil, aqua, 5¾"* 9.00   12.00
☐ 408 *SAUCE, square, tapered neck, sixteen rings, sunken panel on front, aqua, 8⅜"* 4.00   6.00
☐ 409 *SAUCE, tapered neck, 23 rings, oval, sunken panel on front, ABM, aqua, 8"* 3.00   4.50
☐ 410 *SAUCE, triangular, tapered neck, diamond shape down center on all three sides, crude collar, amethyst, 8¾"* ... 5.00   7.00
☐ 411 **SKILTON FOOTE & COS., BUNKER HILL PICKLES**
Light olive, 11½" 22.00   30.00
☐ 412 **SKILTON FOOTE & COS., BUNKER HILL PICKLES**
In outer ring, picture of pickle barrels, trees, fence, tower, all in center, round, aqua, 6⅜" 7.00   10.00
☐ 413 *Same as above, except gold, 7½"* 13.00   17.00
☐ 414 **SNOWHILL B.W. & CO. LONDON**
On bottom, amber, 6½" 3.00   4.50
☐ 415 **SOCIETE HYGIENIQUE, NO. 5 RUE J.J. ROUSSEAU, PARIS**
Vertically around bottle, cylindrical, graphite pontil, clear, 6⅜" 14.00   20.00
☐ 416 **STRONG COBB & CO., CLEVELAND O.**
Pure Concentrated Flavoring Extracts embossed, clear, 6½" 5.00   7.00

T

☐ 417 **TILLMANN'S**
In small panel at top, star with T in center in circular panel, OIL in square panel at base, square, aqua, 8" 5.00   7.00
☐ 418 *TABASCO or DRY FOOD, wide mouth, 2½" opening, pontil, dark green, 7½"* 22.00   30.00
☐ 419 **TOURNADES KITCHEN BOUQUET**
Clear or amethyst, 5¼" 3.00   4.50
☐ 420 **TRAPPEY'S TABASCO PEPPERS**
On center panels, vertical panels on upper and lower half, four large rings divide the panels, crown top, oval, ABM, clear, 6¾" 3.00   4.50

U

☐ 421 **WILLIAM UNDERWOOD & COMPANY**
Around bottom, aqua, 10" 9.00   12.00

☐ 422 **U. S. NAVY**
Pepper, eight panels, aqua 12.00   16.00

V

☐ 423 **VALENTINES**
Amber, 3¼" 5.00   8.00

☐ 424 **VALLEY FARM DIARY**
In center John H. Bowen, Pikesville, Md., in a circle above
it one quart liquid, on back MTC under bottom E in circle &
#28, ring on neck & ring top, clear 5.00   8.00

☐ 425 **V.D. CO.**
Pat April 27, 1875 under bottom, aqua, 7" 5.00   8.00

☐ 426 **VINEGAR**, label, milk glass, 5½" 5.00   8.00

☐ 427 **VIRGINIA FRUIT JUICE CO., NORFOLK, VA.**
In script on front, machine made, tenpin shape, clear or
amethyst, 7½" 3.00   4.50

W

☐ 428 **M.T. WALLACE & CO. PROP. BROOKLYN N.Y.**
Brasst's Purifying Extract 1850, pontil, aqua, 9½" 38.00   50.00

☐ 429 **WM. R. WARNER & CO.**
Clear, 8¼" 7.00   10.00

☐ 430 **WARSAW PICKLE CO.**
Aqua, 8¾" 7.00   10.00

☐ 431 **WATERS BROS. OLIVE OIL AND EXTRACTS, OAKLAND,
CAL.**
Round, light aqua, 11½" 5.00   8.00

☐ 432 **WDS N.Y.**
Graphite pontil, dark green, 8" 38.00   50.00

☐ 433 **C. WEISBECKER, MANHATTAN MARKET, NEW YORK**
Pickle jar, corner panels, square, ring on neck, square collar, aqua, 6¼" 5.00   8.00

☐ 434 **WELLCOME CHEMICAL WORKS**
Under bottom, Kepler around top, machine made, amber,
6½" 3.00   4.50

☐ 435 **THE J. WELLER CO.**
Clear or amethyst, 7½" 5.00   7.00

☐ 436 **WELLS & RICHARDSON CO.**
Cereal Milk on each side, amber, 7¾" 9.00   12.00

☐ 437 **H. WICKERT**
Aqua, 7¼" 5.00   8.00

☐ 438 **THE WILLIAMS BROS CO.**
Pickle label, clear, 7½" 3.00   4.50

☐ 439 **WOOD COOPER PURE OLIVE OIL, SANTA BARBARA, CA.**
Inside of crude blob seal on shoulder, band collar, round,
aqua, 11" 5.00   8.00

FRUIT JAR

Fruit jars, as defined by collectors, are jars originally sold empty, intended for use in home preservation of foodstuffs (not necessarily just fruit). Jars in which pre-packaged fruit was sold by grocers are not included in this category — they come under the heading of Food Bottles (see previous section).

While home production of jellies, preserves vegetables and fruit is still popular in some parts of the country, it's now more in the class of a hobby than a necessity. During the 1800's, when many kinds of foodstuffs were not available pre-packaged, home canning served an important purpose. Many varieties of fruit jars are available to the collector, ranging from the mid 19th century to recent date. They are distinctively different in character than most other kinds of bottles since they carry no product name or advertising (because they were sold empty). However, they cannot be termed "plain," as the bottle maker's name is usually in large lettering, along with (sometimes) the patent date. Ornamental motifs on fruit jars are not common, but will be encountered on some. There are also specimens on which the maker's name appears in artistic lettering. When grouped together as a collection, they can make a handsome display. Prices are still very modest, on the whole, for fruit jars. Excellent buys will be found by anyone touring the flea markets, garage sales and thrift stores. Another plus in their favor is that fruit jars haven't been extensively facsimilized — hence there is little danger of acquiring reproductions.

The origin of fruit jars dates to the 18th century. The problem of preserving perishable foodstuffs seemed for generations to be unsolvable. Food was often put on blocks of ice but the ice was not always available; there were no refrigeration devices in those days to manufacture it. The problem was especially acute when traveling. Military troops in battle ate very poorly, because there was no way of supplying them with a variety of fresh foods. Napoleon Bonaparte, recognizing that a well-nourished army was likely to have an advantage over the enemy, proposed a competition with a prize of 12,000 francs to anyone who could develop a means of effectively preserving food. Some 14 years later, Nicolas Appert claimed the prize. His method was incredibly simple: enclose the food in a glass container, seal it, then boil to destroy bacteria. His findings were published in book form in New York in 1812. The volume created a sensation and the public soon clamored for glass preserving jars.

Thomas W. Dyott, a prestigeous bottle maker, was selling fruit jars by 1829 and possibly earlier. It was his advertising campaign that gave preserving bottles the name "fruit jars."

The most common closure used on fruit jars in the first 50 years of their production was cork sealed with wax. The process was improved upon in 1855 when Robert Arthur invented an inverted saucerlike lid, which was inserted into the jar. This provided greater air tightness.

Philadelphia's Hero Glass Works developed a glass lid in 1856. There was strong competition to arrive at a better fruit jar which presumably would earn a fortune for whoever took out the patent. This was seemingly achieved in 1858, just two years later, when a zinc lid for fruit jars was patented by John Landis Mason. The so-called Mason jars — which many people erroneously believe have Masonic connections — were named for John L. Mason. At first, they were widely hailed and Mason had trouble making them fast enough to meet orders. It was then observed by the medical profession that zinc coming into contact with foodstuffs could be potentially harmful. This problem was resolved by the Hero company's development of a glass lid for Mason's jars in 1868. Mason transferred his patent rights on the jar to the Consolidated Fruit Jar Co., which subsequently let the patent expire. Ball Brothers of Municie, Indiana, then began distributing Mason jars in 1880. They were sold in dime stores, through mail-order catalogues, and in general stores throughout the country. Literally, millions were made.

By then, Mason had invented other objects, including a folding liferaft, a soap dish, a brush holder and a sheet metal cap dye. But none of these proved as popular as the Mason jar. With his rights to that invention gone, he sank into poverty and died penniless in 1902.

Use of a semiautomatic bottle making machine in Buffalo, New York, in 1898 increased output of the Mason jars. A fully automatic machine came along in 1903.

FRUIT JARS

A

NO.	DESCRIPTION	PRICE RANGE	
☐ 1	**ABGA**		
	In script, under it Mason Perfect, under it made in U.S.A., screw band and lid, made in U.S.A., ABGA Trade mark sheared top, qt., aqua or lt. blue	20.00	25.00
☐ 2	**ABGM CO.**		
	Under bottom, Groove ring wax sealer, qt., aqua	32.00	42.00
☐ 3	**ACME**		
	In center in star surrounded by L.G. Co. under it Trade Mark, 1893, in back, Mason's Patent Nov. 30th 1858, sheared top, qt. aqua	120.00	150.00
☐ 4	**AGEE**		
	In large letters under it Lightning Seal, sheared top, old Lightning seal (Australian) qt., aqua	13.00	18.00
☐ 5	**AIR TIGHT FRUIT JAR**		
	In center of barrel shape jar, wax sealer, Iron pontil on bottom, amber, 1 qt., clear	2250.00	2600.00
☐ 6	**ANCHOR MASON'S**		
	Patent in 3 lines, sheared top, Mason seal, qt., clear	9.00	12.00
☐ 7	**ATLAS EZ SEAL**		
	In 3 lines all in a circle, sheared top, lightning seal, qt., aqua, lt. blue	12.00	17.00
☐ 8	**ATLAS E.Z.**		
	Seal all in 3 lines, under bottom Atlas E-Z seal, aqua pt. jar, clear or aqua	7.00	10.00
☐ 9	**ATLAS IMPROVED MASON** (c. 1890's)		
	Glass lid, metal screw band, aqua or green	4.00	6.00
☐ 10	**ATLAS MASON'S PATENT** (c. 1900)		
	Zinc lid, olive green, quart	14.00	20.00
☐ 11	**ATLAS MASON'S PATENT NOV. 30, 1858**		
	Zinc lid, olive green, ½ gallon	19.00	26.00

☐ 12 **ATLAS MASON'S PATENT NOV. 30th, 1858**
Screw top, olive green, quart **19.00** **26.00**

☐ 13 **ATLAS MASON'S PATENT**
Screw top, green, quart **3.00** **4.50**

☐ 14 **ATLAS SPECIAL** *(c. 1910)*
Screw top, clear or blue **6.00** **8.00**

☐ 15 **ATLAS SPECIAL MASON** *(c. 1910)*
Zinc lid, wide mouth, aqua, quart **6.00** **8.00**

☐ 16 **ATLAS STRONG SHOULDER MASON**
Green or clear, 5⅛" or 6⅞" **4.00** **6.00**

☐ 17 **ATLAS STRONG SHOULDER MASON** *(c. 1915)*
Zinc lid, aqua, green, clear or blue, pint, quart **7.00** **10.00**

☐ 18 **ATLAS WHOLEFRUIT JAR**
*Glass lid and wire bail, wide mouth, clear, pint, quart, ½
gallon* **5.00** **8.00**

☐ 19 **ATMORE & SON**
*Glass lid and metal screw band, wide mouth, aqua, green,
quart* **11.00** **15.00**

☐ 20 **THE AUTOMATIC SEALER** *(c. 1895)*
Glass lid with spring wire bail, aqua, green, quart **19.00** **25.00**

B

☐ 21 **B & CO. LD**
*Under bottom, stopper finish (neck) per glass stopper,
cork jacket (English) 2 Sizes lt. green* **14.00** **20.00**

☐ 22 **BAKER BROS.** *(c. 1865)*
Wax sealer, groove ring, green or aqua, pint **35.00** **45.00**

☐ 23 **BALL**
Vaseline glass, screw top, pint, quart **6.00** **8.00**

☐ 24 **BALL** *(c. 1890)*
Screw top, green, three sizes **7.00** **10.00**

☐ 25 **THE BALL** *(c. 1890)*
Screw top, green, quart **7.00** **10.00**

☐ 26 **BALL** *in script,* **IDEAL**
Wire top clamp, clear, 3" or 4¾" **6.00** **8.00**

☐ 27 **BALL** *in script,* **IDEAL**
*In back, Pat. July 14, 1908, wire top clamp, green or clear,
three sizes* **5.00** **7.00**

☐ 28 **BALL IDEAL PATD JULY 14 1988**
(error in date), blue green, pint **18.00** **24.00**

☐ 29 **BALL IDEAL PAT'D JULY 14, 1908**
Wire and glass lid, aqua or blue, quart, 7¼" **6.00** **8.00**

☐ 30 **BALL IDEAL PATD JULY 14, 1908**
Lid and wire, aqua or blue, quart **4.00** **6.00**

☐ 31 **BALL IMPROVED**
Aqua, pint **4.00** **6.00**

☐ 32 **THE BALL JAR, MASON'S PATENT NOV. 30, 1858**
Screw-on lid, aqua, quart **7.00** **10.00**

☐ 33 **BALL** *in script,* **MASON'S PATENT 1858**
Green, three sizes **4.00** **6.00**

☐ 34 **BALL** *in script,* **MASON**
Clear or green, six sizes 5.00 8.00

☐ 35 **BALL MASON**
Aqua, quart 3.00 4.50

☐ 36 **BALL** *in script,* **PERFECT MASON**
Screw top, six sizes 4.00 6.00

☐ 37 **BALL PERFECT MASON**
Clear, quart 3.00 4.50

☐ 38 **BALL** *(printed)* **PERFECT MASON**
Deep aqua, pint 5.00 7.00

☐ 39 **BALL PERFECT MASON**
Aqua, quart 4.00 6.00

☐ 40 **BALL PERFECT MASON**
No line under BALL, zinc lid, aqua, pint, quart 5.00 7.00

☐ 41 **BALL PERFECT MASON** *(c. 1900)*
Zinc lid, vertical lines around sides are cup and pint measurements, amber, olive, blue or clear 25.00 35.00

☐ 42 **BALTIMORE GLASS WORKS** *(c. 1865)*
Aqua, quart 120.00 165.00

☐ 43 **BAMBERGER & CO.**
In center made for, sure seal, all in a circle, sheared top, lightning seal, qt., light blue 22.00 30.00

☐ 44 **BANNER TRADE MARK WARRANTED**
Glass top, aqua, quart 9.00 12.00

☐ 45 **BANNER WIDEMOUTH WARRANTED** *(c. 1910)*
Glass lid, full wire bail, wide mouth, blue, quart 11.00 15.00

☐ 46 **B. B. G. M. CO.** *(c. 1887)*
Glass lid and metal screw band, blue, green or aqua, quart 40.00 55.00

☐ 47 **BEAVER** *(c. 1897)*
Glass lid and screw band, amber, green, clear or amethyst, pint, quart 20.00 27.00

☐ 48 **BEAVER**
4 under bottom, amber, 7¼ " 30.00 40.00

☐ 49 **BEECH NUT TRADE MARK** *with leaf*
Green, quart 5.00 7.00

☐ 50 **BEE HIVE**
Zinc band and glass insert, blue 25.00 32.00

☐ 51 **BENNETT'S** *(c. 1875)*
Green, quart 37.00 49.00

☐ 52 **BERNARDIN MASON**
Zinc lid, clear, quart 8.00 12.00

☐ 53 **BEST**
Zinc screw band and glass insert, wide mouth, green, quart 24.00 36.00

☐ 54 **THE BEST** *(c. 1875)*
Glass stopper that screws into the neck, quart 21.00 32.00

☐ 55 **THE BEST FRUIT KEEPER**
Glass lid and wire clamp, green, quart 2.00 30.00

☐ 56 **BEST WIDE MOUTH**
Zinc band and glass insert, aqua or clear.............. 3.00 4.50

☐ 57 **BLUE RIBBONS GOODS**
Always reliable in 3 lines, screw band glass insert & sheared top, (Canadian pro. Jar.) qt., clear.............. 12.00 17.00

☐ 58 **BOLA ESPECIAL**
Mason seal. Ribs sides on lid Bola., (Japan), qt., clear 5.00   7.00
☐ 59 **BOLDT MASON JAR**
Zinc lid, blue green 14.00   20.00
☐ 60 **BORDEN'S MILK CO.** *(c. 1885)*
Hexagonal, metal band and glass insert, clear, pint 11.00   15.00
☐ 61 **BOSCO DOUBLE SEAL**
Glass lid and full bail, clear, quart 4.00   6.00
☐ 62 **BOYD MASON** *(c. 1910)*
Zinc lid, olive green, pint, quart 5.00   8.00
☐ 63 **BOYD PERFECT MASON**
Zinc lid, green, ½ pint, pint, quart 5.00   7.00
☐ 64 **BOYDS GENIUNE**
Mason under bottom inside of diamond IG Co. sheared
top, Mason seal, qt., aqua 5.00   8.00
☐ 65 **BRAUN SAFETEE MASON**
Zinc lid, aqua 4.00   6.00
☐ 66 **BRAYTON & CO. A.P.**
In ½ moon, under it San Francisco, Cal. Pressed on laid
on ring, Iron closure, William Haller, Patd. Aug. 7, 1860,
aqua, quart 420.00   510.00
☐ 67 **BRELLE JAR**
Glass lid and wire clamp, wide mouth, clear, quart 22.00   30.00
☐ 68 **BRIGHTON** *(c. 1890)*
Glass lid, metal wire clamp, clear, amber or amethyst,
quart 38.00   50.00
☐ 69 **GEO. D. BROWN & CO.** *(c. 1875)*
Glass lid and heavy metal clamp, green, quart 15.00   20.00
☐ 70 **THE BURLINGTON** *(c. 1880)*
Zinc band, clear or aqua, quart 30.00   40.00
☐ 71 **BURNHAM & CO.** *(c. 1865)*
Iron lid, green, quart 45.00   60.00

C

☐ 72 **CANADIAN KING**
Glass lid and full wire bail, clear, quart 5.00   8.00
☐ 73 **CANADIAN SURE SEAL**
Metal lid and wire metal screw band, wide mouth, clear,
quart 4.00   6.00
☐ 74 **CANTON DOMESTIC FRUIT JAR** *(c. 1895)*
Glass lid and wire bail, clear, quart 25.00   35.00
☐ 75 **CASSIDY** *(c. 1885)*
Glass lid and wire bail, clear 30.00   42.00
☐ 76 **C. F. J. CO.** *(c. 1871)*
Glass lid and metal band, green, quart 15.00   21.00
☐ 77 **C. G. CO.** *(c. 1890)*
Screw lid, clear, quart 14.00   20.00
☐ 78 **A. & D. H. CHAMBERS UNION FRUIT JAR, PITTS**
Clear, quart 9.00   12.00
☐ 79 *same as above, except Cornflower blue* 110.00   140.00
☐ 80 **THE CHAMPION, PAT. AUG. 31, 1869**
Glass lid and top, metal screw band, aqua, quart 40.00   55.00

☐	81	**CLARKE FRUIT JAR CO.** *(c. 1886)*		
		Glass lid and wire bail with lever lock clamp, aqua, quart .	**48.00**	**62.00**
☐	82	**CLARKE FRUIT JAR CO., CLEVELAND O.**		
		54 under bottom, aqua, 7¼"	**25.00**	**35.00**
☐	83	**CLARK'S PEERLESS** *(c. 1882)*		
		Wire bail and glass lid, blue, quart	**7.00**	**10.00**
☐	84	**CLIMAX**		
		Full wire bail and glass lid, green, pint	**12.00**	**16.00**
☐	85	**CLYDE LIGHTNING**		
		Screw top, clear or green, quart	**9.00**	**12.00**
☐	86	**CLYDE MASON** *(c. 1880)*		
		Screw top, green, quart	**14.00**	**20.00**
☐	87	**COHANSEY** *(c. 1870)*		
		Glass lid and clamp, barrel shaped, aqua, quart	**19.00**	**26.00**
☐	88	**COHANSEY GLASS MFG. CO.**		
		Pat MCH 20 77 under bottom, barrel shaped, aqua	**14.00**	**20.00**
☐	89	**COLUMBIA**		
		Glass lid with clamp, amber, quart	**14.00**	**20.00**
☐	90	**COMMONWEALTH FRUIT JAR**		
		Glass lid and wire bail, green, quart	**30.00**	**40.00**
☐	91	**CORONA JAR IMPROVED**		
		Beaded neck design, clear, all sizes	**7.00**	**10.00**
☐	92	**CORONET**		
		Top of it a crown, screw band & glass insert with a crown,		
		sheared top, clear, quart	**75.00**	**100.00**
☐	93	**CROWN** *(c. 1890)*		
		Glass lid and zinc screw band, aqua, quart	**13.00**	**19.00**
☐	94	**CROWN** *(c. 1870)*		
		Glass lid and zinc screw band, aqua, all sizes	**8.00**	**12.00**
☐	95	**CROWN**		
		Glass lid and zinc screw band, all sizes	**4.00**	**6.00**
☐	96	**CROWN MASON**		
		Zinc screw band, white opal insert, round with vertical ribs		
		on the sides, all sizes	**4.00**	**6.00**
☐	97	**CRYSTAL JAR**		
		Clear or amethyst, 6½"	**14.00**	**20.00**
☐	98	**CRYSTAL JAR C.G.**		
		Sheared top, clear, quart	**18.00**	**25.00**
☐	99	**CUNNINGHAM & IHMSEN** *(c. 1868)*		
		Wax seal, cobalt blue, quart	**50.00**	**65.00**
☐	100	**CUNNINGHAM'S & CO.** *(c. 1879)*		
		Wax seal, aqua, quart, iron pontil	**60.00**	**85.00**

D

☐	101	**THE DAISY**		
		In a circle, glass lid and wire bail, aqua, quart	**14.00**	**20.00**
☐	102	**THE DAISY JAR** *(c. 1885)*		
		Heavy iron clamp, round, aqua, quart	**32.00**	**45.00**
☐	103	**DALBEY'S FRUIT JAR** *(c. 1866)*		
		Glass lid, round extending wax seal neck, deep aqua,		
		quart	**55.00**	**75.00**

☐ 104 **THE DANDY** *(c. 1885)*
Glass lid and wire clamp, round and slender, light green,
quart 25.00 35.00

☐ 105 **THE DANDY**
Gilberds 9 under bottom, amber, 7½ " 14.00 20.00

☐ 106 **THE DARLING** *(c. 1885)*
Zinc screw band and glass insert, round tapering sides,
aqua, quart 25.00 35.00

☐ 107 **DECKER DEPENDABLE FOOD, JACOB E. DECKER &
SON, MASON CITY, IOWA**
Clear, quart 4.00 6.00

☐ 108 **DECKER'S IOWANA**
Glass lid and wire bail, clear, quart 5.00 8.00

☐ 109 **DEXTER** *(c. 1865)*
Zinc band with glass insert, aqua, quart 30.00 40.00

☐ 110 **DIAMOND FRUIT JAR**
Glass lid and full wire bail, clear, quart 7.00 10.00

☐ 111 **DICTATOR D.D.I. HOLCOMB PATENTED DEC. 14TH, 1869**
Wax seal, blue, quart 20.00 30.00

☐ 112 **DILLON** *(c. 1890)*
Wax seal, round, aqua, quart 25.00 35.00

☐ 113 **DOMINION** *(c. 1886)*
Zinc band and glass insert, round, clear, quart 32.00 43.00

☐ 114 **DOMINION WIDEMOUTH SPECIAL**
Zinc lid, round, clear, quart 5.00 8.00

☐ 115 **DOOLITTLE, THE SELF SEALER**
Glass lid, wide mouth, clear, quart 25.00 35.00

☐ 116 **DOUBLE SAFETY**
Glass lid and full wire bail, clear, quart 3.00 4.50

☐ 117 **DOUBLE SAFETY**
In script, smalley Kiviare Onthank, Boston Mass., in
center #4, clear, 7⅜ " 5.00 8.00

☐ 118 **DOUBLE SEAL**
In script, clear, 7¼ " 3.00 4.50

☐ 119 **DREY EVER SEAL**
Glass lid and full wire bail, clear or amethyst, quart 2.00 3.00

☐ 120 **DREY IMPROVED EVER SEAL**
Glass lid and full wire bail, round, clear, quart 2.50 3.50

☐ 121 **DREY MASON**
Screw top, round, aqua, all sizes 2.50 3.50

☐ 122 **DREY** in script, **PERFECT MASON**
Screw top, clear or green, several sizes 3.00 4.25

☐ 123 **DREY PERFECT MASON**
Zinc lid, green, pint, quart 3.00 4.25

☐ 124 **DREY SQUARE MASON**
Zinc lid, square, clear or amethyst, quart 1.50 2.15

☐ 125 **THE DUNKLEY CELERY CO., KALAMAZOO**
Four-piece mold, ground top, amethyst, quart 18.00 25.00

☐ 126 **THE DUNKLEY PRESERVING CO.** *(c. 1898)*
Glass lid, metal clamp, clear, quart 14.00 19.00

☐ 127 **DU PONT**
Screw top, round, aqua, quart 17.00 24.00

☐ 128 **DURHAM**
Glass lid and wire bail, round, aqua, quart **9.00** 12.00
☐ 129 **DYSON'S PURE FOOD PRODUCTS**
Metal band, round, clear, quart **4.00** 6.00

E

☐ 130 **EAGLE** *(c. 1876)*
Glass lid and iron thumbscrew to tighten, green, quart ... **30.00** 40.00
☐ 131 **EASI-PAK MASON-METRO**
Screw top, clear **5.00** 8.00
☐ 132 **EASY VACUUM JAR** *(c. 1895)*
Glass lid, tall and round, clear, quart **12.00** 17.00
☐ 133 **THE ECLIPSE** *(c. 1868)*
Wax seal, aqua, quart **35.00** 50.00
☐ 134 **THE ECLIPSE** *(c. 1868)*
Wax seal, aqua, quart **35.00** 50.00
☐ 135 **ECLIPSE WAX SEALER** *(c. 1868)*
Wax seal, green, quart **25.00** 37.00
☐ 136 **ECONOMY**
Metal lid and spring wire clamp, amethyst, pint, quart, ½
gallon **4.00** 6.00
☐ 137 **ECONOMY, TRADE MARK**
Clear or amethyst, quart **3.00** 4.50
☐ 138 **ECONOMY, TRADE MARK, PAT. JUNE 9, 1903**
Clear or amethyst, quart **3.00** 4.50
☐ 139 **E.G.CO.** *(monogram)* **IMPERIAL**
Clear, quart **9.00** 12.00
☐ 140 **ELECTRIC**
Glass lid and wire bail, round, aqua, quart **19.00** 26.00
☐ 141 **ELECTRIC FRUIT JAR** *(c. 1900-15)*
Glass lid and metal clamp, round, aqua, quart **30.00** 40.00
☐ 142 **ELECTROGLAS N.W.**
Clear, quart **3.00** 4.50
☐ 143 **EMPIRE**
In maltese cross, clear, quart **7.00** 10.00
☐ 144 **EMPIRE** *(c. 1860)*
Glass stopper, deep blue, quart **55.00** 75.00
☐ 145 **THE EMPIRE** *(c. 1866)*
Glass lid with iron lugs to fasten it, aqua, quart **42.00** 55.00
☐ 146 **ERIE FRUIT JAR** *(c. 1890)*
Screw top, clear, quart **19.00** 27.00
☐ 147 **ERIE LIGHTNING**
Clear, quart **7.00** 10.00
☐ 148 **EUREKA** *(c. 1864)*
Wax dipped cork or other, extending neck, aqua, pint **25.00** 35.00
☐ 149 **EUREKA, PAT. FEB 9TH, 1864, EUREKA JAR CO.,**
DUNBAR, W. VA. *(c. 1870)*
Aqua, quart **14.00** 20.00
☐ 150 **EVERLASTING IMPROVED JAR** *(c. 1904)*
In oval, quart **7.00** 10.00

□ 151 **EVERLASTING JAR** *(c. 1904)*
Glass lid and double wire hook fastener, round, green,
pint, quart, ½ gallon 14.00 19.00
□ 152 **EXCELSIOR** *(c. 1880-90)*
Zinc screw band and glass insert, aqua, quart 24.00 32.00
□ 153 **EXCELSIOR IMPROVED** *(c. 1890)*
Aqua, quart 14.00 20.00
□ 154 **EXWACO**
Clear or green, quart 9.00 12.00

F

□ 155 **F.A. & CO.** *(c. 1860)*
Glass stoper, aqua, quart, iron pontil 60.00 80.00
□ 156 **FAHNSTOCK FORTUNE & CO.**
Green, quart 14.00 20.00
□ 157 **FAMILY FRUIT JAR**
Wire top, clear, quart, base, Patd Oct. 18,1887 .... 120.00 165.00
□ 158 **FARLEY**
Glass lid and full wire bail, square, slender, clear, quart .. 3.00 4.50
□ 159 **F.C.G. CO.** *(c. 1875)*
Metal cap, amber or green, quart 40.00 50.00
□ 160 **FEDERAL FRUIT JAR** *(c. 1895)*
Glass lid and wire bail, olive green, quart 25.00 35.00
□ 161 **FHANESTOCK ALBREE & CO.**
Pontil, sheared top, aqua, 7¼" 70.00 100.00
□ 162 **FINK & NASSE, ST. LOUIS**
Green, quart 14.00 20.00
□ 163 **FLACCUS CO., E.C. TRADE MARK**
Elk and floral design, milk glass 100.00 130.00
□ 164 **W.L.J. FLEET LIVERPOOL**
Glass stopper, aqua, quart 45.00 60.00
□ 165 **FOSTER SEALFAST**
Glass lid and full wire bail, clear or amethyst, quart 5.00 8.00
□ 166 **FRANKLIN DEXTER FRUIT JAR** *(c. 1865)*
Zinc lid, aqua, quart 14.00 20.00
□ 167 **FRANKLIN FRUIT JAR** *(c. 1866)*
Screw-on lid, green, quart 29.00 40.00
□ 168 **FRUIT GROWER'S TRADE CO.**
Wax dipped cork, oval, extending wax seal neck, green,
quart 20.00 30.00
□ 169 *FRUIT JAR, label, graphite pontil, seal top, aqua, 9½"* ... 95.00 120.00
□ 170 *FRUIT JAR, label, sheared top, 4¼"* 5.00 7.00
□ 171 *FRUIT JAR, label, pontil, clear, quart* 130.00 160.00
□ 172 *FRUIT JAR, ground pontil, blue green, 8¼"* 55.00 75.00
□ 173 *FRUIT JAR, label, 4 under bottom, sheared top, black, 7"* . 120.00 150.00
□ 174 *FRUIT JAR, label, graphite pontil, aqua, 10"* 115 140.00
□ 175 **FRUIT KEEPER**
Glass lid and metal clamp, deep green, quart 25.00 35.00

G

☐176 **THE GAYNER**
Glass lid and wire bail, clear, quart 7.00 10.00

☐177 **THE GEM** *(c. 1856)*
Zinc band and glass insert, amber, aqua or green, quart .. 8.00 12.00

☐178 **GEM** *(c. 1868)*
Zinc screw band and glass insert, green, quart 11.00 15.00

☐179 **GEM** *(c. 1869)*
Zinc screw band and glass insert, aqua, quart 12.00 17.00

☐180 **THE GEM, C.F.J.** *(c. 1882)*
Monogram, wide zinc screw band and glass insert, aqua,
green, quart 14.00 20.00

☐181 **GEM** *(c. 1884)*
Zinc screw band and glass insert, green, quart 14.00 20.00

☐182 **GEM**
With maltese cross, aqua, quart 3.00 4.50

☐183 **GEM HGW**
Aqua, quart 4.00 6.00

☐184 **GEM IMPROVED MADE IN CANADA**
Clear, quart 5.00 8.00

☐185 **GEM IMPROVED** *(c. 1860)*
Zinc band and glass insert, round, green, pint 14.00 20.00

☐186 **THE GEM, PAT. NOV. 26, 1867**
Clear, quart 5.00 8.00

☐187 **GENUINE BOYDS MASON** *(c. 1900)*
Zinc lid, green, quart 7.00 10.00

☐188 **GENUINE MASON** *(c. 1900)*
Zinc, olive green, pint, quart 22.00 30.00

☐189 **G.G. CO.**
Screw top, clear 8.00 11.00

☐190 **GILBERDS**
Gilberds Improved Jar Cap Jamestown N.Y. Oct. 13, 1885
Pat July 31, 82 on top, small kick-up, sheared top, aqua,
quart 70.00 90.00

☐191 **GILBERDS IMPROVED JAR** *(c. 1885)*
Glass lid and wire bail, aqua, quart 40.00 55.00

☐192 **GILBERDS JAR** *(c. 1884)*
Glass lid and screw band, aqua, quart 55.00 75.00

☐193 **GILCHRIST** *(c. 1895)*
Zinc lid and dome shaped opal liner, wide mouth, aqua
green, quart 7.00 10.00

☐194 **GILLAND & CO.** *(c. 1890)*
Glass stopper, aqua, quart 14.00 20.00

☐195 **G.J.** *monogram*
Clear, quart 7.00 10.00

☐196 *GLASS SCREW-CAP JAR, Pat. Oct. 24, 1905, six panels,*
Warm Cap Slightly To Seal Or Unseal on top of cap, ame-
thyst, 5" 5.00 8.00

☐197 **GLASSBORO** *(c. 1880-1900)*
Trademark, zinc band and glass insert, light to dark green,
three sizes 12.00 17.00

☐ 198 **GLASSBORO IMPROVED** *(c. 1880)*
Wide zinc screw band and glass insert, aqua or pale
green, quart **12.00** **17.00**

☐ 199 **GLENSHAW G. MASON**
(G in square), clear, quart **3.00** **4.50**

☐ 200 **GLOBE**
*Glass lid, metal neck band, top wire bail and bail clamp,
amber, green or clear, quart* **14.00** **20.00**

☐ 201 **GLOCKER, PAT. 1911 OTHERS PENDING SANITARY**
Aqua, quart **3.00** **4.50**

☐ 202 **GOLDEN STATE,**
*S in a triangle, Pat. Dec. 20, 1910, Pat. Pending under it,
amethyst* **7.00** **10.00**

☐ 203 **GOLDEN STATE**
Metal screw-on lid, wide mouth, four sizes **9.00** **12.00**

☐ 204 **GOLDEN STATE IMPROVED**
Thin metal screw-on lid, clear, two sizes **8.00** **11.00**

☐ 205 **GOOD HOUSE KEEPER'S MASON JAR** *(c. 1935-1946)*
Screw-on metal lid, clear, quart **3.00** **4.50**

☐ 206 **GOOD HOUSE KEEPER'S,** *R in circle,* **WIDE MOUTH MASON**
Screw top, clear, quart **3.00** **4.50**

☐ 207 **GREEN MOUNTAIN G.A. CO.**
Wire clamp, aqua **5.00** **8.00**

☐ 208 **G SQUARE MASON**
Metal screw-on lid, clear, quart **5.00** **8.00**

H

☐ 209 **HAINES** *(c. 1882)*
Glass lid and iron clamp, green, quart **40.00** **55.00**

☐ 210 **HAINES IMPROVED** *(c. 1870)*
Glass lid and top wire bail, aqua green, quart **40.00** **50.00**

☐ 211 **HAMILTON GLASS WORKS**
Green, quart **14.00** **20.00**

☐ 212 **HANSEE'S PLACE HOME JAR**
Pat. Dec. 19 1899 under bottom, aqua, 7" **25.00** **35.00**

☐ 213 **HARRIS** *(c. 1860)*
Metal lid, ground top, deep green, quart **55.00** **75.00**

☐ 214 **HARRIS IMPROVED** *(c. 1875-1880)*
Glass lid and iron clamp, green, quart **45.00** **60.00**

☐ 215 **HASEROT COMPANY** *(c. 1915-1925)*
Zinc lid, green, quart **7.00** **10.00**

☐ 200 **THE HASEROT COMPANY, CLEVELAND MASON PATENT**
Screw top, ground top, green, quart **9.00** **12.00**

☐ 216 **E.C. HAZARD & CO., SHREWSBURY, N.J.**
Wire clamp, aqua, quart **7.00** **10.00**

☐ 217 **HAZEL**
Glass lid and wire bail, aqua, quart **8.00** **10.00**

☐ 218 **HAZEL-ATLAS LIGHTNING SEAL**
Full wire bail and glass lid, green, quart **8.00** **11.00**

☐ 219 **H. & D.** *(c. 1915)*
Glass top, metal band **5.00** **7.00**

28

48

105

161

170

190

220

287

291

320

321

322

327

449

479

484

☐ 220 **HELME'S RAILROAD MILLS**
Amber, 7³/₄" 11.00 15.00
☐ 221 **HELMES RAILROAD MILLS**
Amber, quart 12.00 16.00
☐ 222 **THE IMPROVED HERO**
Glass top, metal band, green, base, Patd Nov. 26, 1867 ... 11.00 15.00
☐ 223 **HERO**
With cross and lightning at top, green, quart 14.00 20.00
☐ 224 **THE HEROINE**
Wide zinc screw band and glass insert, light green, quart . 19.00 26.00
☐ 225 **THE HIGH GRADE**
Zinc screw-on top, clear 15.00 22.00
☐ 226 **HOLZ, CLARK, & TAYLOR** (c. 1878)
Screw-on glass lid, aqua, quart, Salem, N.J. 65.00 85.00
☐ 227 **HOM-PAK**
Metal lid, clear 3.00 4.50
☐ 228 **HOM-PAK MASON**
Two-piece lid, clear, pint, quart 5.00 8.00
☐ 229 **THE HOUSEHOLD**
In center W.T. CO., under it FRUIT JAR, aqua, quart 9.00 12.00
☐ 230 **H & R** (c. 1886)
Round wax sealer, ground top, milk glass insert, blue,
quart 11.00 16.00
☐ 231 **HUDSON BAY**
Picture of a beaver on side coat of arms, rawhide clamp
top, square, clear, quart 13.00 20.00

I

☐ 232 **THE IDEAL** (c. 1890)
Zinc lid, clear, pint, quart 7.00 10.00
☐ 233 **IDEAL WIDE MOUTH JAR**
Flat metal lid, clear, quart 3.00 4.50
☐ 234 **THE IMPERIAL** (c. 1886)
Glass lid and wire clamp, green, quart 20.00 26.00
☐ 235 **IMPERIAL IMPROVED QUART**
Glass lid and wide zinc screw band, aqua or green, quart . 9.00 12.00
☐ 236 **IMPROVED EVERLASTING JAR**
In a watermelon panel, under bottom Illinois Pacific Glass
Co. S.F. Cal., Pat. in center, amethyst, 6½" 7.00 10.00
☐ 237 **INDEPENDENT** (c. 1888)
Screw-on glass lid, clear or amethyst, quart 27.00 36.00
☐ 238 **INDEPENDENT JAR** (c. 1882)
Screw-on glass lid, clear or amethyst, quart, G.T. 25.00 35.00
☐ 239 **IVANHOE**
Glass lid and wire bail, clear, quart 5.00 8.00
☐ 240 **IVANHOE**
4 under bottom, clear, 4¼" 5.00 8.00

J

☐ 241 **J. & B. FRUIT JAR** (c. 1898)
Zinc lid, light green, pint, quart, G.T. 15.00 22.00

☐242 **JEANNETTE,** *a J in a block under it,* **MASON HOME PACKER**
Clear, quart 2.50 3.25

☐243 **JEWEL JAR**
Wide zinc screw band and glass lid, clear or amethyst, quart 3.00 4.50

☐244 *Same as above, except also made in Canada* 3.00 4.50

☐245 **J.G. CO.**
Monogram, zinc lid and domed opal liner, wide mouth, green, quart 19.00 25.00

☐246 **JOHNSON & JOHNSON, NEW BRUNSWICK, N.J. U.S.A.**
(c. 1890), ground top, square, amber, 4¼" or 6½" 5.00 8.00

☐247 **JOHNSON & JOHNSON, NEW BRUNSWICK, N.J. U.S.A.**
Cobalt blue 75.00 100.00

☐248 **JUG**
Glass ears with wire handle, round, amethyst, ABM, gallon 7.00 11.00

K

☐249 **KALAMAZOO, THE JAY B. RHODES** *(c. 1875)*
Wax seal, Kalamazoo, Mich., quart 4.00 6.00

☐250 **K.C. FINEST QUALITY** *in banner,* **MASON**
Square, spacesaver style, zinc lid, clear or amethyst, quart 4.00 6.00

☐251 **KEEFER'S · No. 1 & 2**
In two lines, inside threads, threaded glass stopper, G.M. Keefer Patd Dec 20th 1870, aqua 155.00 185.00

☐252 **KERR ECONOMY TRADE MARK**
Chicago on base, metal lid and narrow clip band, clear or amethyst, pint, quart 4.00 6.00

☐253 **KERR ECONOMY** *in script, under it* **TRADE MARK**
Under bottom Kerr Glass Mfg. Co., Sand Spring, Okla., clear, 3¾" 14.00 20.00

☐254 *Same as above, except Chicago Pat. under bottom* 3.00 4.50

☐255 **KERR GLASS TOP MASON**
Flat metal lid, clear, pint, quart 2.50 3.25

☐256 **KERR SELF SEALING, TRADE MARK REG.** *in banner,* **PAT. MASON**
Clear, quart 2.50 3.25

☐257 *Same as above, except indigo blue* 11.00 15.00

☐258 **KERR SELF SEALING WIDE MOUTH MASON**
Base reads: Kerr Glass Mfg. Co., Sand Springs, Okla., Pat. Aug. 31, 1915, clear 2.50 3.25

☐259 **KERR** *in script,* **SELF SEALING TRADE MARK** *in a ribbon, under it* **MASON**
Clear, 6¾" 1.50 2.15

☐260 *Same as above, except square, clear, 9"* 1.50 2.15

☐261 **KERR SELF SEALING TRADE MARK 65TH ANNIVERSARY**
(c. 1903-1968), Gold 18.00 25.00

☐262 **KERR WIDE MOUTH MASON**
Clear, ½ pint 15.00 22.00

☐263 **KG**
In oval, wire clamp, clear, quart 4.00 6.00

☐ 264 **THE KILNER JAR**
Zinc screw band and glass insert, clear, quart **7.00** **10.00**
☐ 265 **KING**
Full wire bail and glass lid, clear or amethyst, quart **9.00** **12.00**
☐ 266 **KINSELLA TRUE MASON** *(c. 1874)*
Zinc lid, clear, quart **7.00** **10.00**
☐ 267 **KLINE PAT. OCT. 27, 1863**
A on glass stopper, aqua, quart with jar **80.00** **105.00**
☐ 268 **KLINE A.** *(c. 1863)*
Glass fitting lid and clamp, aqua, quart **22.00** **29.00**
☐ 269 **KNIGHT PACKING CO.**
Base 01 within diamond, paneled, screw top, clear, quart . **3.00** **4.50**
☐ 270 **KNOWLTON VACUUM FRUIT JAR**
With star in center, clear or aqua, quart **7.00** **10.00**
☐ 271 **KNOWLTON VACUUM FRUIT JAR**
Zinc lid and glass insert, blue, quart **20.00** **27.00**
☐ 272 **KNOX MASON**
Zinc lid, clear, quart **3.00** **4.50**
☐ 273 **KOHRS**
Glass lid and half wire bail, clear, quart **3.00** **4.50**
☐ 274 **KYGW CO.**
On base, amber, quart **22.00** **30.00**

L

☐ 275 **LAFAYETTE** *(c. 1864)*
Wax dipped cork, with profile, aqua or blue, quart **75.00** **100.00**
☐ 276 **LAMB MASON**
Zinc lid, clear, pint, quart **5.00** **8.00**
☐ 277 **THE LEADER**
One line, glass lid and wire clamp, clear, quart **38.00** **50.00**
☐ 278 **LEE & CO., J. ELWOOD**
Zinc screw, ground top, amber **9.00** **12.00**
☐ 279 **LEGRAND IDEAL CO., L.I.J.**
Monogram, screw top, blue, quart **14.00** **20.00**
☐ 280 **LEOTRIC**
In oval, glass lid, ground top, medium green, quart **9.00** **12.00**
☐ 281 **LIGHTNING TRADE MARK REGISTERED U.S. PATENT OFFICE**
Putnam 4 on bottom, lid with dates, aqua, pint **5.00** **7.00**
☐ 282 **LIGHTNING TRADE MARK**
Putnam 199 on bottom, aqua, ½ gallon **6.00** **8.00**
☐ 283 *Same as above, except wire and lid, pint* **6.00** **8.00**
☐ 284 **LIGHTNING TRADEMARK**
Glass top, round, aqua, 6″ **7.00** **10.00**
☐ 285 *Same as above, except Putnam on base, aqua, quart, ½ gallon* **8.00** **11.00**
☐ 286 *Same as above, except amber, pint, quart, ½ gallon* **15.00** **20.00**
☐ 287 **LIGHTNING**
Putnam 824 under bottom, sheared top, aqua **9.00** **12.00**
☐ 288 **LINDELL GLASS CO.** *(c. 1870)*
Wax sealer, amber, quart **40.00** **55.00**

☐ 289 **LOCKPORT MASON**
Zinc top, aqua, ½ gallon 6.00   9.00
☐ 290 **LOCKPORT MASON, IMPROVED**
Zinc screw band, glass insert, aqua, quart 6.00   9.00
☐ 291 **LORILLARD & CO**
On base, glass top, metal clamp, amber, pint 13.00   17.00
☐ 292 **P. LORILLARD & CO.**
Sheared top, amber, 6¼" 12.00   16.00
☐ 293 **LUSTRE R.E. TONGUE & BROS. CO. INC. PHILA.**
In circle or shield, wire clamp, quart 3.00   4.50
☐ 294 **LUSTRE**
Glass top and wire bail, aqua 5.00   8.00
☐ 295 **L. & W.** *(c. 1860)*
Cleveland, Ohio, wax sealer, green, quart 25.00   35.00
☐ 296 **W.W. LYMAN** *(c. 1862)*
Glass top and wire clamp, ground top, aqua, quart 22.00   30.00
☐ 297 **LYON & BOSSARD'S JAR**
Glass lid and iron clamp, aqua, quart 45.00   60.00
☐ 298 **LYON & BOSSARD'S JAR, EAST STROUDSBURG, PA.**
(c. 1890), iron clamp, ground top, aqua, quart 100.00   130.00

M

☐ 299 **MACOMB POTTER CO. PAT. APPLIED FOR**
On base, screw top, white crock 11.00   16.00
☐ 300 **THE MAGIC FRUIT JAR** *(c. 1890)*
Glass top and iron clamp, amber, quart 60.00   80.00
☐ 301 **THE MAGIC FRUIT JAR**
Star in center, ground top, aqua, quart 45.00   60.00
☐ 302 **MALLINGER**
Zinc top, clear, quart 7.00   10.00
☐ 303 **MANSFIELD IMPROVED MASON**
Clear, quart 5.00   8.00
☐ 304 **THE MARION JAR**
#5 under bottom, sheared top, aqua, quart 14.00   20.00
☐ 305 **THE MARION JAR** *(c. 1858)*
Zinc top, green, quart 10.00   14.00
☐ 306 **THE MASON**
Zinc top, light green, quart 5.00   7.00
☐ 307 **MASON FRUIT JAR**
Zinc lid, clear, quart 6.00   9.00
☐ 308 **MASON FRUIT JAR**
Zinc top, clear, quart 5.00   7.00
☐ 309 *Same as above, except amber* 45.00   58.00
☐ 310 **MASON FRUIT JAR**
Zinc top, aqua, quart 5.00   8.00
☐ 311 **MASON FRUIT JAR PATENT NOV. 30TH, 1858**
Zinc top, aqua, quart 6.00   8.00
☐ 312 **THE MASON JAR OF 1858**
Zinc top, aqua, quart 6.00   8.00
☐ 313 **MASON KEYSTONE**
Clear, quart 4.00   6.00

☐ 314 **MASON PATENT NOV. 30TH, 1880**
Zinc top, clear, pint, quart 7.00 10.00

☐ 315 **MASON PATENT NOV. 30TH, 1858**
With dots on letters, hand painted with hot glass, screw
top, green, quart 6.00 8.00

☐ 316 **MASON PAT. NOV. 30TH, 1858** (c. 1910)
Clear, quart 3.00 4.50

☐ 317 **MASON PORCELAIN**
Tan, quart 11.00 15.00

☐ 318 Same as above, except black 160.00 210.00

☐ 319 **MASON**
Star design jar, zinc top, clear, pint 7.00 11.00

☐ 320 **MASON'S**
Sheared top, pale green, 7¼" 4.00 6.00

☐ 321 **MASON'S**
Pat Nov. 26-67 under bottom, aqua, 5½" 5.00 8.00

☐ 322 **MASON'S**
Sheared top, black, 7¼" 160.00 210.00

☐ 323 **MASON'S**
Swirled milk glass, 7¼" 75.00 90.00

☐ 324 **MASON'S CG, PATENT NOV 30, 1858**
Zinc lid, green, quart 5.00 8.00

☐ 325 **MASON'S-C-PATENT NOV. 30TH 1858**
Green, 7" 3.00 4.50

☐ 326 **MASON'S IMPROVED**
Zinc screw band and glass insert, aqua or green, pint 10.00 14.00

☐ 327 **MASON'S IMPROVED BUTTER JAR**
Sheared top, aqua, ½ gallon 10.00 14.00

☐ 328 **MASON'S IMPROVED**
Hero F J Co. in cross above, zinc band and glass lid covered with many patent dates, earliest Feb. 12, '56, aqua .. 10.00 14.00

☐ 329 **MASON'S KEYSTONE** (c. 1869)
Zinc screw band and glass insert, aqua, quart 15.00 20.00

☐ 330 **MASON'S "M" PATENT NOV. 30TH 1858**
Green, 7" 5.00 8.00

☐ 331 **MASON'S,** under it **"M" PATENT NOV. 30TH 1898**
Screw top, aqua, quart 11.00 15.00

☐ 332 **MASON'S PATENT 1858**
Zinc lid, amber or green, pint 15.00 20.00

☐ 333 **MASON'S PATENT 1858**
Zinc top, aqua, quart 7.00 10.00

☐ 334 **MASON'S PATENT NOV. 30, 1858**
Zinc top, amber or yellow, quart 10.00 15.00

☐ 335 **MASON'S PATENT NOV. 30, 1858**
Zinc top, aqua or green, pint 30.00 45.00

☐ 336 **MASON'S PATENT NOV. 30, 1858**
Zinc top, clear, quart 5.00 8.00

☐ 337 **MASON'S** (cross) **PATENT NOV. 30TH, 1858**
Pat. Nov. 26, 67, 45 in center on bottom, blue or aqua, pint 7.00 10.00

☐ 338 **MASON'S PATENT NOV. 30TH 1858, C.F.J. Co.**
Monogram, aqua, pint 5.00 7.00

☐339 **MASON'S,** *under it an arrow, under that* **PATENT NOV. 30TH 1858**
Sheared top, quart **14.00** **20.00**

☐340 **MASON'S**
With flat type cross, H.F.J. Co. in each corner, Patent Nov. 30th 1858, ½" letters, sheared top, aqua, gallon **11.00** **15.00**

☐341 **MASON'S PATENT**
Zinc lid, aqua, green or clear, quart **3.00** **4.50**

☐342 **MASON'S PATENT, NOV. 30TH 1858**
Three errors on M, P, N, reads ASONS ATENT, OV., aqua, quart **17.00** **24.00**

☐343 **MASON'S PAT. NOV. 30TH 1858**
(Backward S), New Reproduction, sheared top, amber, pint **14.00** **20.00**

☐344 **MATHIA'S & HENDERSON**
Glass lid and heavy wire clamp, clear, quart **7.00** **10.00**

☐345 **M. C. CO.**
On base, screw top, amber, quart **14.00** **20.00**

☐346 **McDONALD NEW PERFECT SEAL**
Wire bail and glass lid, blue, quart **5.00** **8.00**

☐347 **McDONALD NEW PERFECT SEAL, PATENT JULY 14, 1908**
Clear, quart **5.00** **8.00**

☐348 **METRO EASI-PAK MASON**
Threaded neck, clear, quart **3.00** **4.50**

☐349 **M.F.A.**
Metal screw-on top, clear, quart **11.00** **16.00**

☐350 **MICHIGAN MASON**
Zinc top, clear, quart **14.00** **20.00**

☐351 **MID WEST**
(Canadian Made), wide zinc band and glass top, clear or amethyst, quart **5.00** **8.00**

☐352 **MILLER'S FINE FLAVOR**
Around top, three bees in circle in center, aqua, quart **11.00** **15.00**

☐353 **MILLVILLE ATMOSPHERIC FRUIT JAR**
In back Whitall's Patent June 18, 1861, clamp top **35.00** **45.00**

☐354 **MILLVILLE IMPROVED** *(c. 1885)*
Zinc lid and glass insert, aqua, quart **25.00** **35.00**

☐355 **MISSION,** *a bell and trademark on each side, under it,* MASON, JAR, MADE IN CALIF.
On bottom Los Angeles Calif. Mfg by W. J. Latchford Co., screw top, clear or green, three sizes **11.00** **15.00**

☐356 **MODEL MASON** *(c. 1910)*
Zinc top, clear, quart **10.00** **14.00**

☐357 **JOHN M. MOORE** *(c. 1865-1875)*
Glass top and heavy iron clamp, aqua, quart **65.00** **85.00**

☐358 **MOORE'S PATENT, DEC. 3, 1861**
Glass top with cast iron clamp and screw, aqua or green, quart **50.00** **65.00**

N

☐359 **NATIONAL** *(c. 1885)*
On base, metal top, quart **5.00** **7.00**

☐360 **NATIONAL SUPER MASON** *(c. 1870)*
Glass top and iron clamp, clear, quart 9.00 12.00
☐361 **NEWARK**
Zinc top, clear, quart 11.00 15.00
☐362 **NEWARK SPECIAL EXTRA MASON JAR**
Base, Mfg. for M. A. Newark & Co., L.A. 11.00 15.00
☐363 **NEWARK**
Zinc top, clear, quart 7.00 10.00
☐364 **NEW GEM**
Wide zinc top, clear, quart 3.00 4.50
☐365 **NEWMAN'S**
*Patent, Dec. 20th, 1859 in 4 lines, sheared top, metal top
cover with rubber band, aqua, quart* 160.00 210.00
☐366 **N STAR**
Metal top and wax seal, blue, quart 14.00 20.00
☐367 **N.W. ELECTROGLASS WIDE MOUTH MASON**
Screw top, clear or amethyst, quart 3.00 4.50
☐368 **N.W.**
*In large letters, under it monogram Electroglas, under it
Mason, sheared top, zinc lid, square jar, clear, quart* 5.00 8.00
☐369 **N.W. ELECTROGLASS WIDE MOUTH MASON**
Zinc top, aqua, quart 5.00 7.00
☐370 **NORGE**
*Script, under bottom Drammens Glass DG. sheared lip,
glass lid & wire seal (Norway), clear, quart* 12.00 17.00

O

☐371 **OC**
On base, glass top, wire clamp, quart 9.00 12.00
☐372 **OK**
*On shoulder, on top wax seal, Groove, 3 Port Mold, inside
lip ground, aqua, quart* 160.00 210.00
☐373 **OHIO QUALITY MASON**
Clear, quart 5.00 7.00
☐374 **OPLER BROTHERS INC., OB** *monogram,* **COCOA AND
CHOCOLATE, NEW YORK U.S.A.**
Glass top, wire clamp, clear 5.00 7.00
☐375 **OSBURN. N**
*In ½ moon under it Rochester, under it slant N.Y., wax
cork seal, aqua, quart* 200.00 260.00
☐376 **OSOTITE**
In diamond, clear, quart 6.00 9.00
☐377 **OSOTITE**
*Inside of a diamond, metal spring clamp and glass lid on
lid Pat. pending, sheared top, clear, quart* 11.00 15.00

P

☐378 **PACIFIC GLASS WORKS**
Zinc band and glass insert, green, quart 45.00 60.00

☐379	**PACIFIC MASON**		
	Zinc top, clear, quart	**14.00**	**20.00**
☐380	**PACIFIC S.F. GLASS WORKS** *(c. 1880)*		
	Green, quart	**25.00**	**35.00**
☐381	**PARAGON, NEW**		
	Glass top and iron clamp, green, quart	**37.00**	**49.00**
☐382	**PATENT APPLIED FOR**		
	Metal top and wax seal, extending wax seal neck, green,		
	quart	**14.00**	**20.00**
☐383	**P.C.G. CO.**		
	Wax seal, aqua, quart	**19.00**	**25.00**
☐384	**THE PEARL**		
	Zinc screw band and glass insert, ground top, green, quart	**14.00**	**20.00**
☐385	**PEERLESS**		
	Wax dipped cork, green, quart	**55.00**	**75.00**
☐386	**THE PENN**		
	Metal cap and wax seal, green, quart	**28.00**	**37.00**
☐387	**PEORIA POTTERY**		
	Metal top and wax seal, glazed brown stoneware, quart ..	**9.00**	**12.00**
☐388	**PERFECTION**		
	Double wire bail and glass top, clear, quart	**25.00**	**35.00**
☐389	**THE NEW PERFECTION**		
	Clear or amethyst, ½ gallon	**19.00**	**26.00**
☐390	**PERFECT SEAL**		
	Full wire bail and glass top, clear, quart	**4.00**	**6.00**
☐391	**PERFECT SEAL** *in shield,* **MADE IN CANADA**		
	Clear, quart	**3.00**	**4.50**
☐392	**PET**		
	Glass stopper, green, quart	**45.00**	**60.00**
☐393	**PET**		
	Glass stopper and wire bail, aqua, quart	**28.00**	**37.00**
☐394	**H.W. PETTIT, WESVILLE N.H.**		
	Under bottom, ground top, aqua, quart	**7.00**	**10.00**
☐395	**THE GORAGAS PIERIE CO., PHILA., ROYAL PEANUTENE**		
	Sheared top, clear, quart	**9.00**	**12.00**
☐396	**PINE DELUXE JAR**		
	Full wire bail and glass top, clear, quart	**4.00**	**6.00**
☐397	**PINE** *(P in square)* **MASON**		
	Zinc top, clear, quart	**4.00**	**6.00**
☐398	**PORCELAIN LINED**		
	Zinc top, aqua, quart	**15.00**	**20.00**
☐399	*Same as above, except green, 2 gallon*	**12.00**	**17.00**
☐400	**POTTER & BODINE PHILADELPHIA**		
	In script, glass top and clamp, aqua, quart	**40.00**	**55.00**
☐401	**PREMIUM COFFEYVILLE KAS.**		
	Wire ring and glass top, clear or amethyst, quart	**11.00**	**15.00**
☐402	**PREMIUM IMPROVED**		
	Glass top and side wire clips, clear, quart	**7.00**	**10.00**
☐403	**PRESTO**		
	Screw-on top, clear	**2.50**	**3.25**
☐404	**PRESTO FRUIT JAR**		
	Screw-on top, clear	**2.50**	**3.25**

☐405 **PRESTO GLASS TOP**
Half wire bail and glass top, clear or amethyst, quart **2.50** **3.25**
☐406 **PRESTO SUPREME MASON**
Threaded neck, clear, pint **2.50** **3.25**
☐407 **PRESTO WIDEMOUTH GLASS TOP**
Threaded neck, clear, quart **2.50** **3.25**
☐408 **PRINCESS**
Fancy shield, glass top and wire bail, clear, quart **14.00** **20.00**
☐409 **PROTECTOR**
Flat zinc cap and welded wire clamp, aqua, quart **17.00** **24.00**
☐410 **PROTECTOR**
6 under bottom, sheared top, six panels, aqua **14.00** **20.00**
☐411 **THE PURITAN**
Glass top and wire clamp, aqua, pint **27.00** **36.00**
☐412 **PUTNAM GLASS WORKS**
On base, Zanesville, O, wax seal, green, quart **30.00** **40.00**

Q

☐413 **THE QUEEN**
Circled by Pat. Dec 28th Patd. June 16th 1868, wax seal,
green, quart **18.00** **25.00**
☐414 **THE QUEEN**
Patd. Nov. 2 1869, #39 under bottom, clear, quart **14.00** **20.00**
☐415 **THE QUEEN** *(c. 1875)*
Zinc band, aqua or green, quart **11.00** **16.00**
☐416 **QUEEN IMPROVED**
Shield design, glass lid and wire clamps, clear, quart **3.00** **4.50**
☐417 **QUICK SEAL**
In circle, glass lid and wire bail, green, blue or clear, quart **3.00** **4.50**
☐418 **QUONG HOP & CO., 12 OZ. NET**
Glass lid and wire bail, Chinese writing, clear, pint **3.00** **4.50**
☐419 **QUONG YEUN SING & CO.**
Half wire bail and glass lid, clear, pint **5.00** **7.00**

R

☐420 **RAMSEY JAR**
Base, April 1866 6 Nov. 67, glass lid, twelve-sided jar,
aqua, quart **100.00** **130.00**
☐421 **RAU'S IMPROVED GROOVE RING JAR** *(c. 1910)*
Wax sealer, pink, pint, quart **30.00** **40.00**
☐422 **RED KEY MASON**
2 under bottom, Pat. Nov. 30th 1858, clear or amethyst,
6½" **9.00** **12.00**
☐423 **RED MASON'S,** *embossed key,* **PATENT NOV. 30TH, 1858**
Zinc lid, aqua or green, pint **12.00** **17.00**
☐424 **REID MURDOCK & CO. CHICAGO**
Zinc lid, clear, quart **3.00** **4.50**
☐425 **RELIABLE HOME CANNING MASON** *(c. 1940's)*
Zinc screw band and glass insert, clear, quart **2.50** **3.25**

☐426 **RELIANCE BRAND WIDE MOUTH MASON**
Screw-on lid, clear, three sizes 3.00 4.50
☐427 **ROOT** *(c. 1925)*
Clear, quart 4.00 6.00
☐428 **ROOT MASON** *(c. 1910)*
Zinc screw-on lid, aqua, green or blue, quart 5.00 8.00
☐429 **ROOT MASON** *(c. 1925)*
Clear, quart 4.00 6.00
☐430 **THE ROSE** *(c. 1920)*
Screw-on lid, clear, three sizes 7.00 10.00
☐431 **ROYAL OF 1876**
Screw top, ground top, band 2 collared on ears, aqua,
quart 30.00 40.00
☐432 **ROYAL TRADE MARK**
With crown, glass lid and full wire bail, light green or
clear, pint, quart, ½ gallon 6.00 8.00
☐433 **ROYAL TRADE MARK FULL MEASURE** *(c. 1900)*
REGISTERED with crown, green, quart 3.00 4.50

S

☐434 **SAFE SEAL, PATD. JULY 14, 1908**
Clear, quart 3.00 4.50
☐435 **SAFE SEAL** *(c. 1935)*
Glass lid and wire bail, aqua or clear, pint, quart 3.50 4.75
☐436 **SAFETY** *(c. 1900)*
Full wire bail and glass lid, amber, pint, quart, ½ gallon .. 45.00 60.00
☐437 **SAFETY SEAL MADE IN CANADA**
Half wire bail and glass lid, clear, pint, quart 5.00 8.00
☐438 **SAFETY VALVE PATD. MAY 21, 1895**
With emblem in center on bottom, ground top, aqua, pint . 7.00 10.00
☐439 **SAFETY VALVE PATD. MAY 21, 1895**
Midget jar, ground top, clear, 3¾" 30.00 40.00
☐440 **SAFETY WIDE MOUTH MASON, SALEM GLASS WORKS,**
SALEM, N.J.
Zinc lid, aqua or green, quart, ½ gallon 10.00 14.00
☐441 **SAMCO** *in center,* **GENUINE MASON**
Zinc screw band and opal insert, clear, all sizes 5.00 8.00
☐442 **SAMCO SUPER MASON** *(c. 1920)*
Zinc screw band and opal insert, clear, all sizes 1.35 2.10
☐443 **SAMPSON IMPROVED BATTERY** *(c. 1895)*
Screw-on lid, aqua, quart 12.00 17.00
☐444 **SANETY WIDE MOUTH MASON** *(c. 1920)*
Zinc lid, wide mouth, aqua, quart 13.00 18.00
☐445 **SANFORD** *(c. 1900)*
Metal screw band and glass insert, clear, quart 16.00 22.00
☐446 **SANITARY** *(c. 1900)*
Glass lid and wire bail, aqua, quart 7.00 10.00
☐447 **SAN YUEN CO.** *(c. 1925)*
Glass lid and half wire bail, clear, quart 4.00 6.00
☐448 **THE SCHAFFER JAR, ROCHESTER N.Y.**
Monogram S.J.C., aqua, quart 14.00 20.00

☐ 449	**SCHRAM**		
	Schram St. Louis on bottom, clear or amethyst, 4"	7.00	10.00
☐ 450	**SCHRAM AUTOMATIC SEALER**		
	In ribbon, flat metal lid and wire clamp, clear, all sizes ...	9.00	13.00
☐ 451	**THE SCRANTON JAR** (c. 1870-1880)		
	Glass stopper and wire bail, aqua, quart	45.00	60.00
☐ 452	**SEALFAST**		
	Sold by W.H. Vanlew, Dayton, Wash. Bakery & Grocery in an oval, wire clamp top, green, 6¾"	6.00	8.00
☐ 453	**SEALFAST** (c. 1915)		
	Full wire bail and glass lid, clear or amethyst, all sizes ...	3.00	4.50
☐ 454	**SEALTITE TRADE MARK**		
	Green, quart	3.00	4.50
☐ 455	**SEALTITE WIDE MOUTH MASON**		
	Flat metal top and screw band, green, quart	4.00	6.50
☐ 456	**SEASON'S MASON**		
	Metal band and glass insert, three sizes	5.00	8.00
☐ 457	**SECURITY**		
	Glass top and wire bail, clear, quart	5.00	8.00
☐ 458	**SECURITY SEAL**		
	Half wire bail and glass top, green or blue, pint, quart	7.00	10.00
☐ 459	**SELCO SURETY SEAL**		
	Half wire bail and glass top, green or blue, pint, quart	7.00	10.00
☐ 460	**SELCO SURETY SEAL** in circle, **PATD. JULY 14, 1908**		
	Green, quart	3.00	4.50
☐ 461	**SILICON GLASS COMPANY, PITTSBURG, PENN.**		
	Wire bail and glass top, clear or aqua, quart	7.00	10.00
☐ 462	**SIMPLEX**		
	Glass screw top, clear, pint, quart	6.00	10.00
☐ 463	**SIRRA MASON JAR**		
	Made in Calif., zinc top, clear, pint, quart	7.00	10.00
☐ 464	**SMALLEY**		
	Zinc screw band and milk glass insert, amber, quart	7.00	10.00
☐ 465	**SMALLEY**		
	Zinc top, clear, quart	5.00	8.00
☐ 466	**THE SMALLEY FRUIT JAR, SPET. 23, 84**		
	Aqua, quart	14.00	20.00
☐ 467	**SMALLEY FULL MEASURE QUART**		
	Patented Dec. 1889, Apr. 1896, Dec. 1896 under bottom, sheared top, clear or amethyst	5.00	7.00
☐ 468	**SMALLEY SELF-SEALER WIDE MOUTH**		
	Full wire bail and glass top, clear, pint, quart	5.00	7.00
☐ 469	**SMALLEY'S ROYAL, ROYAL TRADE MARK NU-SEAL**		
	Crown, clear, pint	3.00	4.50
☐ 470	**J.P. SMITH SON & CO., PITTSBURGH**		
	Clear, quart	14.00	20.00
☐ 471	**SNYDER ROBERTA**		
	Star Route, Dairy, Oregon, 97625, fruit jar	14.00	20.00
☐ 472	**SPENCER** (c. 1865)		
	Glass top and iron clamp, aqua, quart	35.00	45.00
☐ 473	**SPENCER'S PATENT** (c. 1868)		
	Wax dipped cork, aqua, quart	30.00	40.00

☐ 474	**STANDARD MASON LYNCHBURG**		
	Aqua, quart	**4.00**	**6.00**
☐ 475	**STANDARD** *with ribbon and* **MASON** *inside*		
	Aqua, quart	**5.00**	**8.00**
☐ 476	**STANDARD, W.C. & CO.**		
	Aqua	**5.00**	**8.00**
☐ 477	**STANDARD**		
	Wax sealer, aqua, quart	**12.00**	**17.00**
☐ 478	**STANDARD MASON**		
	Zinc top, light aqua or light green, pint, quart	**5.00**	**8.00**
☐ 479	**STAR**		
	6 under bottom, aqua, 6½"	**35.00**	**45.00**
☐ 480	**STAR** *(c. 1895)*		
	Zinc band and glass insert, clear, quart	**17.00**	**24.00**
☐ 481	**STAR GLASS CO., NEW ALBANY, IND.**		
	Aqua	**14.00**	**20.00**
☐ 482	**STERLING MASON**		
	Zinc top, clear, pint, quart	**3.00**	**4.50**
☐ 483	**STEVEN'S** *(c. 1875)*		
	Wax sealer, green, quart	**45.00**	**60.00**
☐ 484	**A. STONE & CO. PHILA**		
	Aqua	**14.00**	**20.00**
☐ 485	**STONE MASON FRUIT JAR, UNION STONEWARE CO., RED WING MINN.**		
	Sand crock, ½ gallon	**12.00**	**17.00**
☐ 486	**STONE MASON FRUIT JAR**		
	Zinc top, white crock, quart	**9.00**	**12.00**
☐ 487	**SUEY FUNG YUEN CO.**		
	Chinese writing, clear, quart	**5.00**	**8.00**
☐ 488	**SUN**		
	Glass top and metal clamp, light green, quart	**27.00**	**35.00**
☐ 489	**SUPREME MASON**		
	Screw top, clear, quart	**3.00**	**4.50**
☐ 490	**SURE SEAL**		
	Full wire bail and glass top, deep blue, quart	**5.00**	**7.00**
☐ 491	**SWAYZEE'S FRUIT JAR**		
	Zinc top, aqua, pint, quart	**11.00**	**15.00**
☐ 492	**SWAYZEE'S IMPROVED MASON**		
	Blue or aqua, pint	**4.00**	**6.00**
☐ 493	**SWAYZEE'S IMPROVED MASON**		
	Zinc lid, green or aqua, pint	**3.50**	**4.75**

T

☐ 494	**TAYLOR & CO.**		
	Wire bail and glass top, aqua, quart	**4.00**	**6.00**
☐ 495	**TELEPHONE JAR**		
	Full wire bail and glass top, green, quart	**11.00**	**15.00**
☐ 496	**THE TELEPHONE JAR, TRADE MARK, REG. WHITNEY GLASS WORKS**		
	Clear, quart	**2.50**	**3.25**

□497 **THE WIDE MOUTH TELEPHONE JAR, TRADE MARK REG.**
Clear, quart 4.00 6.00
□498 **TEXAS MASON**
Made in Tx by Tx under bottom, clear, 6¾" 3.00 4.50
□499 **TF**
Monogram on base, clear, quart 3.00 4.50
□500 **TIGHT SEAL PAT'D. JULY 14, 1908**
Half wire bail and glass lid, green or blue, all sizes 3.00 4.50
□501 **TROPICAL CANNERS**
Metal top, clear, quart 3.00 4.50
□502 **TRUE FRUIT** *(c. 1900)*
Glass top and metal clamp, clear, quart 9.00 12.00

U

□503 **UNION** *(c. 1865)*
Wax seal and metal lid, extending neck, sheared top, deep
aqua, quart 19.00 27.00
□504 **U.G. CO.**
On base, Groove Wax sealer, pressed laid-on ring, panels
jar, 2 round & 4 flat, aqua, quart 45.00 60.00
□505 **UNDERWOOD & CO. Wm.**
Front back Boston, under bottom, kick up & pontil, rolled
lip, cork closure, flower-leaf, used for ink, cobalt, quart . . 130.00 160.00
□506 **UNION FRUIT JAR** *(c. 1866)*
Wax seal and metal top, sheared top, aqua, quart 14.00 20.00
□507 **UNITED DRUG CO., BOSTON MASS**
Clear, quart 3.00 4.50
□508 **UNIVERSAL**
Screw top, clear, quart 5.00 7.00
□509 **UNIVERSAL L.F. & CO.**
Clear, quart 2.50 3.25

V

□510 **VACU-TOP**
On base, flat metal lid and clamp, light green, quart 23.00 32.00
□511 **THE VACUUM SEAL**
Glass top, slender extending neck, clear, quart 10.00 14.00
□512 **THE VALVE JAR CO. PHILADELPHIA**
Base, Pated Mar 10th 1868, glass or metal lid and wire coil
clamp, sheared top, aqua, 1½ pint 125.00 155.00
□513 **THE VALVE JAR** *(c. 1868)*
Zinc screw-on top, aqua, quart 25.00 35.00
□514 **THE VAN VLIET** *(c. 1881)*
Glass top and iron band with screw, aqua or green, quart . 140.00 175.00
□515 **VETERAN**
Bust of soldier, clear, quart 10.00 14.00
□516 **THE VICTOR** *(c. 1899)*
Flat metal top and clamp, light green, quart 13.00 20.00
□517 **THE VICTOR, PAT. FEB 20, 1900**
M monogram in circle and diamond, clear, quart 14.00 20.00

☐518 **VICTORY** (c. 1875)
Flat glass top and side wire clips, clear, quart 8.00 11.00
☐519 **VICTORY HOM-PAK MASON**
Clear, quart 3.00 4.50

W

☐520 **"W"** (c. 1885)
Wax seal, green, quart 7.00 10.00
☐521 **W & CO.**
On base, green, quart 14.00 20.00
☐522 **GEO. E. WALES**
On base, glass lid and metal clamp, clear, quart 11.00 15.00
☐523 **WALLACEBURG GEM**
Glass insert and zinc screw band, clear or amethyst, quart 7.00 10.00
☐524 **WAN-ETA COCOA, BOSTON**
Zinc top, amber, blue, quart 12.00 17.00
☐525 **WAN-ETA COCOA, BOSTON**
½ pint, 4¾" 10.00 14.00
☐526 **THE WARSAW SALT CO.**
In center, monogram W.S. CO., under it Choice Table Salt
Warsaw, N.Y., screw top, quart 9.00 13.00
☐527 **WEARS JAR**
Glass top and wire clamp, clear, quart 7.00 11.00
☐528 **WEIDEMAN BOY BRAND, CLEV.**
Clear, quart 5.00 8.00
☐529 **THE WEIR, PAT. MAR. 1ST 1892**
Wire bail, crock, quart 8.00 12.00
☐530 **WEIR SEAL**
White stoneware lid and wire bail, white, quart 7.00 11.00
☐531 **WESTERN PRIDE** (c. 1880)
Wax seal, clear, quart 45.00 65.00
☐532 **WHEATON** on base
Clear, quart 3.00 4.50
☐533 **WHEELER** (c. 1889)
Glass top and wire bail, aqua or green 30.00 40.00
☐534 **WHITALL'S**
Glass top and clip with screw tightener, green, quart 22.00 32.00
☐535 **WHITALL'S PATENT, JUNE 18, 1861**
In form of circle, On back, Millville Atmospheric Fruit Jar,
aqua, quart 25.00 35.00
☐536 **WHITE CROWN MASON**
Framed in circle and oblong, aqua, quart 3.00 4.50
☐537 **WHITNEY MASON PATD. 1858**
In a circle, clear, 9" 5.00 8.00
☐538 **WHITNEY MASON** (c. 1858)
Zinc lid, aqua or light green, quart 9.00 12.00
☐539 **WILCOX** (c. 1867)
Flat metal lid and clamp, green, quart 23.00 29.00
☐540 **WILLS & CO.** (c. 1880-1885)
Glass stopper and metal clamp, blue green 40.00 55.00

☐541 **WINSLOW JAR** *(c. 1870-1873)*
Glass lid and wire clamp, green, quart 33.00   45.00
☐542 **WOODBURY** *(c. 1884-1885)*
Glass lid and metal band clamp, aqua, quart 23.00   34.00
☐543 **WOODBURY IMPROVED, WGW**
Monogram, Woodbury Glass Works, Woodbury, N.Y. on
bottom, aqua, quart 9.00   12.00
☐544 **WOODBURY IMPROVED** *(c. 1885)*
Zinc cap, aqua, three sizes 25.00   35.00
☐545 **WOODBURY**
Woodbury Glass Works Woodbury, N.J. 2 under bottom,
aqua, 7" 22.00   31.00
☐546 **WORCESTER**
Clear or amber, quart 35.00   45.00
☐547 **JOSHUA WRIGHT, PHILA.**
Pontil, barrel type 120.00   150.00

X

☐548 **XNOX** *in center, a block with* **K** *in middle,*
MASON *under it,* **XNOX** *is an error, should read* **KNOX**
Clear, quart 18.00   25.00

Y

☐549 **YELONE JAR** *(c. 1895-1900)*
Glass lid and wire bail, clear 12.00   17.00
☐550 **YEOMAN'S FRUIT BOTTLE** *(c. 1855-1870)*
Wax sealer, small mouth, aqua 35.00   45.00

HUTCHINSON

Charles A. Hutchinson of Chicago developed a novel and revolutionary kind of bottle in the late 1870's, the rights for which were sold to a number of manufacturers and resulted in great proliferation of the Hutchinson Bottle. The Hutchinson Bottle had the distinction of originating the phrase "pop bottle," and this is how soda came to be known as "pop." That's exactly what the Hutchinson bottles did — they popped when being opened.

It wasn't really the Hutchinson bottle that was different, but the stopper. Hutchinson patented the stopper on April 8, 1879. It was intended as an improvement on cork stoppers, which could shrink and allow air to seep into the bottle. It consisted of a rubber disc held between two metallic plates, attached to a spring stem. This spring stem was figure 8 in shape, the upper loop being larger than the lower (to prevent the stem from falling into the bottle). The lower loop could pass through the bottle's neck to push down the attached disc and permit filling or pouring from the bottle. After filling, the bottle was sealed by pulling the disc up to the bottle's shoulders, where it made a tight fit. To open, was the spring hit — thereby creating the "POP" sound. Three different lengths and five sizes of gaskets were made to fit bottles of various proportions. Hutchinson bottles ceased to be made when health authorities warned of the dangers of metal poisoning from consuming beverages sold in them. They were last manufactured in 1912, but they had already become obsolete by that time.

As curiosities, the Hutchinson bottles rank high, and they enjoy a strong following among collectors. In the main, they are not decorative, and, of course, figurals were not made (it was tough enough adapting this device to a standard-shape bottle).

Prices on Hutchinson bottles tend to vary more sharply by geographical locale than prices of most other collector bottles. Specimens that are scarce and highly priced in one part of the country are sometimes common and inexpensive in another. We have attempted to provide median or average prices, but you will undoubtedly find examples selling above the highest and below the lowest of our range of figures. Obviously, it makes sense for the Hutchinson collector to contact dealers in distant states and, whenever possible, buy specimens that are common in a certain dealer's area, but scarce in the collector's territory.

ABBREVIATIONS

Hutchinson bottles often carried abbreviations, in the form of a series of initial letters spelling out a message. They include the following:

> tbntbs — this bottle not to be sold
> T.B.M.B.R. — this bottle must be returned
> T.B.I.N.S. — this bottle is not sold

These instructions or warnings to the customer were not without their purpose. Hutchinson bottles were easily reusable, and manufacturing firms wanted to be certain that beverage companies would buy only from them rather than from the public. This problem was later solved by the "deposit bottle," after the Hutchinson era.

A

NO.	DESCRIPTION	PRICE RANGE	
☐ 1	**ABA, FORGO, N.D.**		
	All in a circle, light blue, 7"	27.00	35.00
☐ 2	**A.B.A. GRAND FORKS, N.D.**		
	All in a circle, panels base aqua, 7"	15.00	20.00
☐ 3	**A.B. CO. ALLIANCE, O.**		
	All in a circle, aqua, 6½"	12.00	17.00
☐ 4	**ACME BOTTLING WORKS, J.J. RUTISHAUSER, FERNANDINA, FLA.**		
	All in a circle aqua, 7"	12.00	17.00
☐ 5	**ACME, THE WATER CO, PITTSBURG, REGISTERED**		
	In back W.A.S. Co. in hollow letters. clear or aqua, 6½" ..	12.00	17.00
☐ 6	**AETNA BOTTLING**		
	Concord, N.H., all in a circle, aqua, 6¾"	12.00	17.00
☐ 7	**A.F. LUCAS, WILMINGTON, N.C.**		
	All in a circle, aqua, 6⅞"	12.00	17.00
☐ 8	**ALABAMA BOTTLING CO.**		
	"a" under bottom, a bid in a circle "This Bottle Prop. of A.B. Co. Not To Be Sold", aqua, 7½"	11.00	15.00
☐ 9	**ALAMEDA SODA WATER COMPANY**		
	Show clasped hard, light green, 6½"	17.00	24.00
☐ 10	**ALBUQUERQUE BOTTLING WORKS**		
	All in a circle, aqua, 6¼"	15.00	20.00
☐ 11	**ALLEN, WM. T. & SON, PETERSON, N.J. REG'S**		
	In 5 lines' Live & Let Live, trademark, clear, 6½"	17.00	24.00
☐ 12	**ALHOUN & BRASWELL, STANFORD, FLORIDA**		
	All in a circle, in center trademarks, registered, on base. registered #33 under bottom in back a harp, clear, 7"	15.00	20.00
☐ 13	**AMAN, H. CHEYENNE, WYO.**		
	All in a circle, aqua, 6½"	15.00	20.00
☐ 14	**AMAN, H. CHEYENNE, WYO.**		
	All in a circle, clear, 6½"	12.00	17.00
☐ 15	**AMERICAN BOTTLING WORKS**		
	In horse shape under it Alboirn, and Detroit, Mich. clear, 6½"	12.00	17.00
☐ 16	**AMERICAN BOTTLING CO. 323-325, SARASOTA**		
	All in a circle, on bottom AB Co. aqua, 7"	15.00	20.00
☐ 17	**AMERICAN MINERAL WATER, S.F.**		
	In a circle aqua, 7¼"	27.00	36.00
☐ 18	**AMERICAN**		
	In center a flag under it soda works, S.F. clear, 6½"	12.00	17.00
☐ 19	**AMERICAN SODA FOUNTAIN CO.**		
	All on front, aqua, 6¾"	15.00	20.00
☐ 20	**AMORY L.B. BOTTLER GRAFTON, AL.**		
	On base T.B.N.T.B.S. light blue, 6¾"	12.00	17.00
☐ 21	**ANCHOR STEAM BOTTLING WORKS**		
	In center, an anchor, Shawnee, O.T. all in a circle, on base anchor, aqua, 6¾"	110.00	140.00

☐ 22 **A ANCHOR UNDER IT BOTTLING WORKS**
All in a circle. Shawnee, Okla. aqua, 6¾" **15.00** **20.00**

☐ 23 **ANCHOR, THE BOTTLING WORKS, CINCINNATI O.**
All in a circle in center of it an anchor, in back registered
bottle never sold in 2 lines, on base D, panels base 6¾"
aqua **17.00** **24.00**

☐ 24 **ANCHOR, THE BOTTLING WORKS, CINCINNATI, OHIO**
All in a circle, in center, anchor, aqua, 7" **15.00** **20.00**

☐ 25 **ANCHOR STEAM BOTTLING WORKS, SHAWNEE, OKLA.**
All in a circle, in center an anchor, anchor on base,
6¾" **15.00** **20.00**

☐ 26 **A. ANCHOR STEAM BOTTLING WORKS, SHAWNEE, OKLA.**
Ty all in a circle, aqua, 6¾" **45.00** **65.00**

☐ 27 **ANDRAE, G. PORT HURON, MICH.**
All in a circle, blue, 6¾" **25.00** **35.00**

☐ 28 **ANNESTON, AL.**
Coca-cola in block letters, aqua, 7¾" **100.00** **130.00**

☐ 29 **ARCO, CAPE, SODA WORKS, MARSHFIELD, ORG.**
All in 3 lines, aqua, 7¾" **17.00** **24.00**

☐ 30 **ARDMORE BOTTLING & MFG. CO.**
Ardmore, I.T. under bottom O.F., aqua, 6¾" **140.00** **190.00**

☐ 31 *Same as above, except O under bottom* **140.00** **190.00**

☐ 32 **ARDMORE BOTTLING WORKS**
All on front, aqua, 7" **27.00** **36.00**

☐ 33 **ARDMORE BOTTLING WORKS, ARDMORE, I.T.**
All in a horse shoe (5 lines) letters aqua **140.00** **190.00**

☐ 34 **ARIZONA BOTTLING WORKS, PHOENIX, ARIZONA**
All in a circle, on base 329, aqua, 6⅞" **15.00** **20.00**

☐ 35 **ARIZONA BOTTLING WORKS, PHOENIX, ARIZONA**
All in a circle, aqua, 7" **15.00** **20.00**

☐ 36 **A.R.O.**
Mel around shoulder in side of horse shoe. Eclispe car-
bonating company, on base St. Louis, in center
monogram EC. Co., amber, 6¼" **23.00** **34.00**

☐ 37 **ARTESIAN BOTTLING WORKS, DUBLIN, GA.**
In sunken circle, with panels, C.C. Co. on one panel, aqua
or clear, 7" **13.00** **18.00**

☐ 38 **ARTIC SODA WORKS, HONOLULU**
On vertical panels, clear, 7" **17.00** **24.00**

☐ 39 **ASHLAND BOTTLING WORKS**
All in a circle, amber, 7" **25.00** **35.00**

☐ 40 **ASTLEY, LYMAN CHEYENNE, WYO.**
All in 3 lines, aqua, 7" **30.00** **45.00**

☐ 41 **ASTORG SPRINGS MINERAL WATER, S.F. CAL.**
All in 5 lines, light green, 6½" **15.00** **20.00**

☐ 42 **A.T.G.**
On base, amber, 7" **32.00** **43.00**

☐ 43 **ATLANTA COCA—COLA, ATLANTA, GA.**
All in block letters, clear, 6½" **130.00** **180.00**

☐ 44 **ATLANTA CONSOLIDATED BOTTLING CO.**
All on front, aqua, 7½" **12.00** **17.00**

☐ 45	**AUGUSTA B.C., AUGUSTA, GA.**		
	All in a circle in center large a with bottle in center, aqua,		
	9½"	15.00	20.00
☐ 46	*Same except 7"*	8.00	15.00
☐ 47	**AUSTIN BOTTLE WORKS, MINN.**		
	All in a circle, clear, 6¾"	16.00	23.00
☐ 48	**AUSTIN BOTTLE WORKS, AUSTIN, TX.**		
	All on front, clear, 7"	10.00	20.00
☐ 49	**AUSTIN ICE & BOTTLING, REG.**		
	Must not be sold on back, 71 under bottom, aqua, 7¼" ..	12.00	17.00
☐ 50	**A & W. H. BEAUMONT**		
	In ½ moon letters under it in 2 lines Atlanta, Ga. 5 points star under bottom. Semi round base panels base & shoulder, aqua, 7"	14.00	21.00
☐ 51	**AYLMER, WM. FARGO**		
	In 2 lines, blue, 7"	32.00	45.00
☐ 52	**AYLMER, WM. FARGO**		
	In 3 lines O.T., blue, 6½"	130.00	180.00

B

☐ 53	**BACON'S SODA WORKS**		
	In horse shoe letters, under it Sonora, Cal., lt. blue, 7" ...	15.00	20.00
☐ 54	**J. ED BAKER**		
	Clear, 9½"	6.00	9.00
☐ 55	**BARTH F.E.**		
	In ½ moon under it Green Port, L.I.N.Y. under it Reg., aqua, 7½"	11.00	16.00
☐ 56	**BARTLESVILLE BOTTLING WORKS**		
	Coombs & Martin Prop., aqua, 7"	14.00	21.00
☐ 57	**BARTLESVILLE BOTTLING WORKS**		
	Coombs & Martin Prop, aqua 7"	14.00	22.00
☐ 58	**BARTNER, E.D.**		
	Glenville, Pa. all in a circle, on base D.O.C. 54, aqua, 6¼"	14.00	22.00
☐ 59	**BARTOW**		
	Fla. Coca-Cola in black letters, clear, 7"	125.00	175.00
☐ 60	**BATE'S, DR**		
	Trademark National Tonic Beer, 1876, green 8"	37.00	46.00
☐ 61	**BATT BROTHERS BOTTLING WORKS**		
	Tonawanda, N.Y. all in a circle, light blue, 6⅛"	14.00	22.00
☐ 62	**BAUER, L.J.**		
	Woodsfield, Oh. all in a circle, aqua, 6"	11.00	16.00
☐ 63	**BAUMON F. SANTA MARIA, CAL.**		
	All in a circle, aqua or clear, 7"	14.00	22.00
☐ 64	**BAY CITY BOTTLING WORK**		
	All in a circle, aqua, 6¼"	12.00	21.00
☐ 65	**BAYVIEW BOTTLING WORKS**		
	Seattle, all in a circle, clear, 7"	24.00	36.00
☐ 66	**B & B BOTTLING WORKS**		
	Hawkinsville, Ga. all in a circle, aqua, 6¼"	11.00	16.00

☐ 67 **B.B. & M.F.G. CO.**
*All on front, in back on base T.B.N.T.B.S. under bottom
"S", aqua, 7"* 12.00   17.00

☐ 68 **B.B. & W. BOTTLING WORKS**
Hattiesburg, Miss. all in a circle, 7" 22.00   32.00

☐ 69 **R.M. BECKER'S**
"B" under bottom, aqua, 6½" 12.00   17.00

☐ 70 **R.M. BECKER'S**
"B" on bottom, aqua. 7¼" 11.00   15.00

☐ 71 **BECKER R.M.**
Waterford, Miss. all in a circle, aqua, 7" 9.00   13.00

☐ 72 **BECKER, HENRY**
*In a horse shoe letters, in center of it, Terre Haute, In.,
aqua, 6½"* 14.00   22.00

☐ 73 **BEEBETAFT & CO.**
*Wardner, Idaho Ter. all in a circle on base 33, clear or
aqua, 6¼"* 130.00   170.00

☐ 74 **BEEBETAFT & CO.**
*Colfax, Washington Ter. all in a circle, under bottom 33,
aqua, 6¾"* 115.00   160.00

☐ 75 **BENSON BOTTLING CO.**
Minneapolis all in a circle on back T.B.N.T.B.S., aqua, 8" . 16.00   23.00

☐ 76 **BENNETTVILLE BOTTLING WORKS, BENNETTVILLE, S.C.**
All in a circle, registered on base T.B.N.T.B.S., 6½" 11.00   16.00

☐ 77 **BENSON BOTTLING CO., MINNEAPOLIS**
All in a circle, in back T.B.N.T.B.S., aqua, 8" 14.00   23.00

☐ 78 **BERGER, JOHN M.**
*Bottle Works in center Felk Point, Baltimore all in a circle
aqua, 8"* 12.00   19.00

☐ 79 **BESSEMER COCA—COLA: in script (Ala.)**
All in a circle, aqua, 6½" 190.00   265.00

☐ 80 **BEST A.**
Cincinnati all in a circle, aqua, 6½" 11.00   16.00

☐ 81 **BICKAL JAS. P.**
*Stuebenville, Oh. all in a circle, under bottom J.B.P., aqua,
6½"* 11.00   16.00

☐ 82 **BICKAL JAS. P.**
Steubenville, Oh., all in a circle, aqua, 6½" 11.00   16.00

☐ 83 **BIEDENHARN COUNTY CO.**
All in a circle, "B" under bottom, 7¼" 80.00   105.00

☐ 84 **BIEDENHARN CANDY CO.**
All in a circle B.C.C., under bottom, aqua, 7¼" 45.00   60.00

☐ 85 **BILLINGS E.L.**
Under it Sac City, in back Geyser soda, aqua, 6¾" 12.00   17.00

☐ 86 **BINDER, CHAR**
*C.B. Mongroft C.B., all in a circle in back, under bottom
C.B., aqua, 7"* 12.00   17.00

☐ 87 **BIRMINGHAM BOTTLING WORKS**
*Birmingham, Al. all in a water mellow letters under it
T.B.M.B.R., aqua, 8"* 12.00   17.00

☐ 88 **BIRMINGHAM "COCO—COLA in script"**
Bottling A. all in a circle, aqua, 7" 200.00   275.00

☐ 89 **BISMARKS, REMINGTON, P.C.**
All in a circle, clear, 7" 16.00 22.00

☐ 90 **BIWABIK BOTTLING WORKS Biwabik, Minn.**
All in a circle, under bottom N & L, clear, 7" 12.00 17.00

☐ 91 **BLACK DIAMONDZ**
A T in center Soda Works all in a circle, under bottom
P.C.G.W., aqua, 6¾". 16.00 22.00

☐ 92 **BLACKWELL BOTTLING**
In horse shoe letters in center works W.S., under it
Blackwell O.T. panel base, aqua, 6⅜" 130.00 170.00

☐ 93 **BLACK & ROGERS, BOTTLERS OKLAHOMA**
Ter. all in a circle (Guthrie, O.T.) under bottom B & R panel
base, yellow aqua, 6⅝" 115.00 155.00

☐ 94 **BLACK R.W.**
Oklahoma Ter. in a circle, panel base, aqua, 6¼" 130.00 170.00

☐ 95 **BLISS, CHAS. F.**
In ½ moon under it Racine, Wis. star & 8 under bottom,
light blue, 6¾" 12.00 17.00

☐ 96 **BLUFF CITY BOTTLING**
All in horse shoe letters in center Co., under it Memphis,
Tenn., panels base, light aqua, 7" 14.00 19.00

☐ 97 **BLAIR, J.R.**
Bottler Oklahoma City O.T. all in a circle, light aqua, 6¾" 130.00 170.00

☐ 98 **BOARD T.M.**
Coshocton Oh. all in a circle, clear, 7" 12.00 17.00

☐ 99 **BODE NO. 5**
All in a circle, plain back, clear, 6¾" 12.00 17.00

☐ 100 **BODE, GA., BOTTLERS EXTRACTS, CHICAGO**
In a circle, clear, 6¾" 12.00 17.00

☐ 101 **BOISE**
Idaho on front, paneled base, aqua, 7" 26.00 37.00

☐ 102 **BOISE J.H.**
Idaho all in a circle, aqua, 7" 32.00 45.00

☐ 103 **BOKOSHE BOTTLING WORKS G.W. GILES, PROFS.**
All in a circle (Bokoshe, Okla.), aqua 6⅜" 17.00 24.00

☐ 104 **BONANZA BOTTLING CO.**
In ½ moon letters under it, Dawson N.W.T., greenish, 7¾" 130.00 170.00

☐ 105 **BORTNER E.D., GLENVILLE, PA.**
All in a circle, on base D.O.C.54, clear, 6½" 12.00 17.00

☐ 106 **BOSTELMANN, D.W.**
In ½ moon circle, under it trade anchor mark, Chicago, Ill,
aqua, 6½" 16.00 23.00

☐ 107 **BOTTLE MADE FOR HUTCHINSON'S PATENT,**
SPRING STOPPER
All in a circle, plain back, aqua, 6¾" 15.00 20.00

☐ 108 **BOTTLING: P.S.: CO.**
Spartanburg, S.C. all in a circle in back, TBNTBS, aqua
6½" 21.00 27.00

☐ 109 **BOVEE. T., TROY, N.Y.**
All in a circle, aqua, 7¼" 12.00 17.00

☐110 **BOONVILLE MINERAL SPRINGS, N.Y.**
All in a circle, amber, 6½" 28.00   42.00

☐111 **BOWDEN, BOONTON, N.J.**
In 3 lines panel base, aqua, 7⅛" 12.00   17.00

☐112 **BOWDEN, D., BOONTON, N.J.**
In 3 lines, panels, base clear or light blue, 7½" 15.00   20.00

☐113 **BOWLING GREEN, BOTTLING WORKS**
Bowling Green, Oh. all in a circle, aqua, 7" 15.00   20.00

☐114 **BOYLAN & STURR BOTTLING CO., PATERSON, N.J.**
*Registered 1902, in four lines vertical, slug plate in back,
large letters B & S under it, registered under bottom B & S,
light blue, 6½"* 15.00   20.00

☐115 **BOYLE, DAVID, CO., PATERSON, N.J.**
*In center of it 65 & 87 Washington St. 1904 all in a circle,
on base registered, aqua, 9"* 15.00   20.00

☐116 **BOYLAN & STURR BOTTLING CO.**
*Paterson, N.J. Re . 1902 in 4 lines vertical in slug plate in
back large B & S under it Reg. under bottom B & S, light
blue 7½"* 15.00   20.00

☐117 **BOYNTON**
*In ½ moon letters under it in 4 lines bottler, North Hamp-
ton, Mass. Reg. B under bottom, aqua, 6¾"* 12.00   17.00

☐118 **BRADCOCK J.M.**
Pawnee, Okla. all in a circle, aqua, 6½" 12.00   17.00

☐119 **BRANHAWL & CO.**
*In ½ moon, under it Woodfield, Oh. in block D.O.C., aqua,
6⅜"* 15.00   20.00

☐120 **BRANDON, THOS, TOPEKA, KS.**
All in a circle, clear, 6¾" 27.00   34.00

☐121 **BRAZELL, THOS.**
*201-205 Pleasant St. West Yardner, Mass. all in horse
shoe letters, panels under it Reg., clear, 6¼"* 12.00   17.00

☐122 *Same as above, except words all in a circle and reg. on
shoulder, amethyst, 6½"* 12.00   17.00

☐123 **BRECHEISEN, THE BOTTLING CO.**
Kenton, Oh., aqua, 7" 12.00   17.00

☐124 **BRENNAN & MC GRATH**
*In ½ moon letters under it Naugatuck, Conn., dark aqua,
6½"* 15.00   20.00

☐125 **BRIG & SCHAFFER S.F.**
In 2 lines over it a fish, lt. green, 6¼" 17.00   23.00

☐126 **BROADWAY**
*In ½ moon letters, under it Bottling Works, silver City,
N.M., clear, 6"* 17.00   23.00

☐127 **BROADWAY BOTTLING WORKS**
*Silver City, N.M. all in a circle, star under bottom, aqua,
6⅛"* 17.00   23.00

☐128 **BROE & GORMAN**
*In a horseshoe letters under it in 3 lines, 404-6 East 60th
St., New York, in back B.G. under it registered, clear, 6¾"*   12.00   17.00

☐ 129 **BROE & GORMAN**
In horse shoe letters under it in three lines. 404-6 East
60th St. N.Y. in back B.C. under it reg., clear, 6¾" **12.00** **17.00**

☐ 130 **BROOKS BOTTLING WORKS**
Durant, I.T. all in a circle, aqua, 6⅞" **135.00** **185.00**

☐ 131 **BROUGH, THE CO.**
Contents mfg., by, in 2 ¼ moon letters under it Trade
Mark Egle, under it reg. Cleveland, Oh., aqua, 6¾" **18.00** **27.00**

☐ 132 **BROWN'S VALLEY BOTTLING CO.**
All in a circle, clear, 7" **12.00** **17.00**

☐ 133 **BRUNSWICK**
Coca-Cola Bottling Co. Brunswick, Ga. all in a water
mellow letters, under bottom Reg, aqua, 8" **125.00** **160.00**

☐ 134 **BRUNSWICK COCA—COLA**
Brunswick, Ga. all in block letters, clear **125.00** **160.00**

☐ 135 **BUFFALO**
In center Trade Mark Reg. under it T.B.N.S., aqua, 6½" .. **15.00** **20.00**

☐ 136 **BUFFALO, N.Y.**
Panels shape bottle, aqua, 7" **17.00** **23.00**

☐ 137 **BURNS & ARMSTRONG**
Running vertical, in center of double round ring a arm
holding scale, clear or aqua, 7" **15.00** **20.00**

☐ 138 **BURK. J., MACON BOTTLING WORK**
Macon, Ga. all in a circle. Panel base, light blue, 7½" **15.00** **20.00**

☐ 139 **BURGIE J.L.**
Dyesburg, Tenn., all in 3 lines, aqua, 6¾" **17.00** **23.00**

☐ 140 **BURGOYNE, P.M.**
Memphis, Tenn. all in a circle, 25 under bottom, aqua, 6⅝" **15.00** **20.00**

☐ 141 **BURKHARDT, HENRY**
H.B. under bottom, 6¾" **11.00** **15.00**

☐ 142 **BURN'S T., TUCSON, ARZ.**
In a circle, under bottom T.B.N. 'S, clear, 6½" **17.00** **23.00**

☐ 143 **BURN'S T., TUCSON, ARZ.**
In a circle, T.B.N.S on base, clear, 6¾" **17.00** **23.00**

☐ 144 **BUSCH, HENRY**
Minnemucca, N.Y. all in a circle, should be Winnemucca,
33 under bottom, aqua, 6⅞" **22.00** **31.00**

C

☐ 145 **C.B. CO. CONCORD, N.H.**
All in a circle, aqua, 6¾" **17.00** **23.00**

☐ 146 **C.C.S. & M CO. 270T0274**
Royal New Orleans T.B.N.S. in 4 lines, vertical, ¼ moon
on base, aqua, 7¾" **15.00** **20.00**

☐ 147 **C.M.S. CO., ALLIANCE, OH.**
In center a crown, Reg. all in a circle, aqua, 6⅝" **18.00** **25.00**

☐ 148 **C & O, WELLSTON, OH.**
In 3 lines, aqua, 7" **12.00** **17.00**

☐ 149 **CALESBURY BOTTLING WORKS**
A. Davis Prop's Calesbury, Ill. Panels base, aqua, 6½" ... **12.00** **17.00**

☐ 150 **CALIFORNIA BOTTLING WORKS**
T. Blauth, 407 K St. Sacramento in 5 lines, light green 6¾" **17.00** **23.00**

☐ 151 **CALIFORNIA SODA WORKS**
In a circle Eagle in center, aqua, 7" **24.00** **33.00**

☐ 152 **CALWIN, JAMES**
In center Monogram J.C., Lowel, Mass. all in a circle, Reg.
near shoulder, aqua, 8½" **15.00** **20.00**

☐ 153 *Same as above, no monogram* **12.00** **17.00**

☐ 154 *Same as above, under it center, Lowell, Mass. in a circle,*
Mispelled Calvin **23.00** **33.00**

☐ 155 **CALUMENT BOTTLING WORKS**
M. Cols-West Pullman, Ill. all in a circle. Panels base
under bottom C.B.W., clear, 7¾" **15.00** **20.00**

☐ 156 **CALVERT W.H. BROWNSVILLE, PA.**
All in a circle. Panels base, aqua, 6¾" **12.00** **17.00**

☐ 157 **CALVIN BOTTLING WORKS, CALVIN, I.T.**
All in a circle on base, big H 3 top, 3 bottom in the big H.
Yellowish aqua, 6½" **130.00** **180.00**

☐ 158 **CALVIN BOTTLING WORKS, CALVIN, OKLA.**
All in a circle on base, 3 on top 3 bottom in Big H., aqua,
6½" **15.00** **20.00**

☐ 159 **CALVIN JAMES (CALVIN) LOWELL, MASS.**
All in a circle, aqua, 3½" **16.00** **23.00**

☐ 160 **CAMDEN BOTTLING COMPANY**
All in a circle, aqua, 8½" **12.00** **17.00**

☐ 161 **CAMEL BOTTLING WORK**
Clear, 7" **12.00** **17.00**

☐ 162 **CAMMON BOTTLING WORKS, SCAMMON, KANSAS**
All in a circle under it Artificial Flavor and color, clear,
6½" **16.00** **23.00**

☐ 163 **CAMBELL, C.H., ASHEVILLE, N.C.**
All in a circle, aqua, 7" **12.00** **17.00**

☐ 164 **CAMBELL C.H., ASHEVILLE, N.C.**
All in a circle, under bottom Pat. 85, aqua, 7" **16.00** **23.00**

☐ 165 **CAPE ARCO**
In ½ moon under it in 2 lines, Soda Works MARSHFIELD,
ORE, light green, 7" **15.00** **20.00**

☐ 166 **CAPE ARGO**
Soda Work Marshfield all in 3 lines, aqua, 7" **15.00** **20.00**

☐ 167 **CAPITAL CITY BOTTLING WORK, ATLANTA, GA.**
All in a circle, under bottom a diamond, aqua, 7" **12.00** **17.00**

☐ 168 **CAPITAL, S.W. CO.**
Aqua, 8½" **12.00** **17.00**

☐ 169 **CARDEN BROS., LITTLE FALLS, N.Y.**
All in a circle, clear, 6⅞" **15.00** **20.00**

☐ 170 **CARMEN BOTTLING WORKS**
Carmen O.T., aqua, 6⅜" **125.00** **160.00**

☐ 171 **CARR P., PHILA., PA.**
In 2 lines, light green, 7½" **15.00** **20.00**

☐ 172 **CARRE E. MOBILE, ALA.**
All in a circle, aqua, 7¼" **12.00** **17.00**

☐173 **CARROLL, NEW BURGH, N.Y.**
In 3 lines, C under bottom, light aqua, 6½" **12.00**   **17.00**

☐174 **CASEY & CRONAR'S**
In ½ moon letters, under it in two lines, Eagle Soda
Works, aqua, 7½" **12.00**   **17.00**

☐175 **CASEY & CRONAR'S**
In ½ moon letters, under it Eagle, Soda Works, light green
7¼" **12.00**   **17.00**

☐176 **CASEY, HUGH**
Eagle Soda Works all in 3 lines, aqua, 7" **15.00**   **20.00**

☐177 **CASEY HUGH**
Eagle, Soda Works, 50 K St. Sacramento, Cal. all in 6 lines,
aqua, 7" **16.00**   **23.00**

☐178 **CASEY, HUGH**
Eagle Soda Works in large letters 3 lines, light green 7" . .   **12.00**   **17.00**

☐179 **CAWLEY, W.H., D.B.W. PHILLIPSBURG, N.J.**
All in a water mellow letters under it T.B.N.T.B.S. on
shoulder Reg., aqua, 6¾" **15.00**   **20.00**

☐180 **CAWLEY, W.H., CO D.B.W. DOVER, N.J.**
All in a circle above it Registered on base T.B.N.T.B.S. on
base C, aqua, 6¾" **15.00**   **20.00**

☐181 **CAWLEY, THE W.H. CO S.B.W., SOMERVILLE, N.J.**
All in a circle, top Reg. on base T.B.N.T.B.S., aqua 6¾" . .   **15.00**   **20.00**
☐182 *Same as above, except blue* **20.00**   **30.00**
☐183 **CAWLEY, THE W.H., SOMERVILLE DOVER**
FLEMINGTON, N.J.
T.B.N.T.B.S. in 8 lines under bottom "C", aqua, 6½" **15.00**   **20.00**

☐184 **CEDAR POINT, PLEASURE, RESORT CO.**
All in a circle, aqua, 7¾" **16.00**   **23.00**

☐185 **CENTRAL BOTTLING WORKS, DETROIT, MICH.**
All in a circle, under bottom J.J.G., blue, 7" **30.00**   **40.00**

☐186 **CHICAGO CONSOLIDATED BOTTLING CO.**
14 to 18, Lomax Place Chicago, Ill all in 6 lines in back
Trade Mark in center Mary C.C.B. Co. under it Reg. on
base T.B.I.N.S. & M.E.R.E., B.B.Co. 1900, aqua 6" **16.00**   **23.00**

☐187 **CHICAGO CONSOLIDATED BOTTLING CO.**
14 to 18 Charles Place, Chicago, Ill. in 6 lines, in back
Trade Mark & Reg., aqua, 6½" **15.00**   **20.00**

☐188 **CHACTAW BOTTLING WORKS**
All in front, aqua or clear, 6¾" **15.00**   **20.00**

☐189 **CHAMPION**
In center Soda Works, under it, PLYMOUTH, CAL. aqua 7"   **15.00**   **20.00**

☐190 **CHAMPION BOTTLING WORKS**
All in ½ moon letters under bottom it Ironton, Ohio, aqua,
6½" **12.00**   **17.00**

☐191 **CHAMPION BOTTLING WORKS**
Ironton, Ohio, all on front, aqua, 6¾" **15.00**   **20.00**

☐192 **CHAMPION SODA WORKS, PLYMOUTH, CAL.**
All in a water mellow letters, clear, 6¾" **15.00**   **20.00**

☐ 193 **CHARLESTON BOTTLING WORKS**
Charleston, W. Va. all in a circle, aqua, 6¾" **15.00** **20.00**

☐ 194 **CHEADLE N.F. GUTHRIE, OKLA.**
All in 3 lines on base C, aqua, 6½" **12.00** **17.00**

☐ 195 **CHECOTAH BOTTLING WORKS**
Checotah, I.T. all in a circle, on base C, 6¾" **135.00** **180.00**

☐ 196 **CHICKASAW BOTTLING CO.**
Pauls Valley, Okla. all in a circle, on base S.B., light aqua, 7⅛" **15.00** **20.00**

☐ 197 **CHICKASAW BOTTLING WORKS**
S. Bros. Props. all in a circle S.B. on base (Pauls Valley, Okla.), aqua, 7½" **15.00** **20.00**

☐ 198 **CHICKASHA**
In one line under it in ½ moon letters Bottling Works, under it Chickasha, I.T., aqua, 6⅜" **135.00** **180.00**

☐ 199 **CHICKASHA BOTTLING WORKS**
Chickasha, IT all in a circle, aqua, 6⅜" **135.00** **180.00**

☐ 200 **CHICO SODA WORKS**
In 2 lines, clear, 6¼" **11.00** **15.00**

☐ 201 **CHICO SODA WORKS**
In large letters in 2 lines, clear, 6½" **15.00** **20.00**

☐ 202 **CHILLICOTHE, THE, BOTTLING WORKS**
Chillicothe, Oh. all in a circle, aqua, 6½" **15.00** **20.00**

☐ 203 **CILLEY, H.D. LANCONIA N.H.**
In horse shoe letters on base C, 36, light aqua, 6¾" **15.00** **20.00**

☐ 204 **CINCINNATI, THE, SODA WATER & GINGER ALE CO.**
In a horse shoe letters in center 5 pt. stars through it Trade choice marks, on base T.B.I.N.S., clear, 6⅝" **15.00** **20.00**

☐ 205 **CIRCLEVILLE, MINERAL WATER CO.**
Circleville, Oh. all in a circle, in back K.C.B. Co., clear 6⅝" **15.00** **20.00**

☐ 206 **CITY BOTTLING CO.**
In ½ moon letters in center or it LIMITED, under it in 4 lines 322 to 332 S. LIBERTY ST. New Orleans, La. on base T.B.N.T.B.S., aqua, 7¾" **12.00** **17.00**

☐ 207 **CITY BOTTLING CO. LIMITED**
69 & 71 South Liberty St. New Orleans, L.A. in 5 lines on base A.C.G. Co. T.B.N.T.B.S., on bottom 6 leaves flower, 7⅞", ... **15.00** **20.00**

☐ 208 **CITY BOTTLING WORKS**
In large letters, Horizon in 3 lines on back. M.G.W. in back in 3 lines City Bottling Works Toledo, Oh. under bottom C.B.W., aqua, 6⅞" **15.00** **20.00**

☐ 209 **CITY BOTTLING WORKS, BRADDOCK, PA.**
All in a circle, aqua, 6½" **12.00** **17.00**

☐ 210 **CITY BREWING CO., WAPAKONET, OH.**
In moon letter, aqua, 7" **12.00** **17.00**

☐ 211 **CITY ICE**
In center, & Bottling Works, GEORGETOWN, under it Texas, all in a circle, aqua, 6½" **12.00** **17.00**

☐ 212 **CITY ICE & BOTTLING WORKS, GEORGETOWN, TX.**
All in a circle, aqua, 6½" **15.00** **20.00**

☐213	**CLAREMORE BOTTLING WORKS**		
	Claremore, I.T., all in 5 lines, aqua, 6½"	135.00	180.00
☐214	**CLARKSBURG BOTTLING WORKS**		
	Clarksburg, W. Va., aqua, 6¾"	15.00	20.00
☐215	**CLEBURNE BOTTLING WORKS, CLEBURNE, TEXAS**		
	All in a circle, aqua, 7½"	12.00	17.00
☐216	**CLEVELAND LIQUOR LEAGUE**		
	In horse shoe letters in center a horse head, under it Bottling Work C., aqua, 6¾"	15.00	20.00
☐217	**CLING & LUDWIG, BRUNSWICK, GA.**		
	In horse shoe letters in slug plate, under bottom Dixon in back T.B.T.B.R., clear, 7½"	15.00	20.00
☐218	**COALGATE BOTTLING WORKS**		
	Coalgate, I.T. all in a circle, 6⅝", ...	135.00	180.00
☐219	**COBB, ROB. T., WELMINGTON, N.C.**		
	All in a circle, aqua, 6½"	30.00	40.00
☐220	**COCA—COLA (SLANTED LETTERS) BOTTLING WORKS**		
	Under it in a ½ circle, Richmond, Va., aqua, 7"	150.00	200.00
☐221	**COCA—COLA**		
	(In script around it in black letters) Property of, clear, 7" ..	150.00	200.00
☐222	**COCA—COLA BOTTLING CO., CHATTANOOGA, TENN.**		
	All in a circle, Block letters, light green, 7"	150.00	200.00
☐223	**COCA—COLA BOTTLING CO., TUSKEGEE, AL.**		
	All in a circle, Block letters, clear, 7"	150.00	200.00
☐224	**COLDMAN BROS.**		
	in center (mong. 1 & H.) Trenton, N.J. in a circle, Panels base, under bottom 674, aqua, 8¾"	15.00	20.00
☐225	**COLE'S SODA**		
	By N.J. Cole, So. Action, Mass., clear, 7½"	12.00	17.00
☐226	**COLLINS JNA, GROVETON, TX.**		
	All in a circle, clear or aqua, 6½"	12.00	17.00
☐227	**COLONY BOTTLING WORKS, COLONY, OKLA.**		
	All in a circle, aqua, 6½"	15.00	20.00
☐228	**COMANCHE BOTTLING WORKS**		
	Comanche, I.T. all in a circle, 6¾"	135.00	180.00
☐229	**COMANCHE BOTTLING WORKS**		
	Miller & Co. Comanche, I.T. all in a circle on base M & Co. Panels base, aqua, 7⅛"	170.00	220.00
☐230	**CONCHO BOTTLING WORKS, SAN ANGELO, TEXAS**		
	All in a circle, aqua, 7½"	15.00	20.00
☐231	**CONCORD BOTTLING CO.**		
	In a horse shoe shape letters, under it Concord, N.H., aqua, 6⅝"	16.00	23.00
☐232	Same as above, except a star in center	16.00	23.00
☐233	**CONCORD BOTTLING CO.**		
	In horse shoe letters, under it Concord, N.H., aqua 6½" ..	12.00	17.00
☐234	**CONCORD BOTTLING CO., CONCORD, N.H.**		
	Star in center, aqua, 6¾"	12.00	17.00
☐235	**CONSOLIDATED BOTTLING CO., HURON S. DAK.**		
	All in a circle, Panels base, clear or aqua, 6¾"	15.00	20.00
☐236	Same as above, except AB 126 under bottom	19.00	25.00

☐237 **CONSOLIDATED, THE, BOTTLING CO.**
All in a circle: Lima, Ohio, aqua, 6½″ 12.00 17.00
☐238 **CONSUMERS BOTTLING CO.; KEY WEST, FLA.**
In 4 lines all in a circle, clear, 7″ 11.00 15.00
☐239 **CONSUMERS BOTTLING CO., KEY WEST, FLA.**
All in a circle on base Reg. etc., clear, 6¼″ 12.00 17.00
☐240 **CONSUMERS S & M**
*Waters Mfg. Co. Ltd. New Orleans, La. in 5 lines, on base
Y.B.N.T.B.S., under bottom M, clear, 6¾″* 16.00 23.00
☐241 **CONSUMERS SAND. M. WATER MFG. CO. LIMITED
NEW ORLEANS, LA.**
In 4 lines, vertical, aqua, 6¼″ 16.00 23.00
☐242 **COOK H.E., WHEELING, W. VA.**
All in a circle, clear, 6½″ 15.00 20.00
☐243 **COOS BAY SODA WORKS**
J.A. Golden, Marshfield Org. in 4 lines, aqua, 6⅝″ 15.00 20.00
☐244 **CORBETT, JOHN, DEMING, N.M.**
All in a circle, clear, 6⅜″ 15.00 20.00
☐245 **CORDOVA BOTTLING WORKS**
Aqua, 6¾″ 12.00 17.00
☐246 **CORONETT & CO., WHEELING, W. VA.**
*All in a circle in center of it a 6 pts. star. Trade Mark, clear
6½″* 16.00 23.00
☐247 **CORTES, H. & CO.**
*Prop Tx Bottling Works Galveston, Tx, around base A &
D.H.C., aqua, 8″* 12.00 17.00
☐248 **CRAMER JACKY**
In ½ moon letters, under it Phillipsburg, mon., aqua, 6½″ 12.00 17.00
☐249 **CRAWLEY, W.A., CLARKSDALE, MISS.**
All in a circle, clear, 7¼″ 12.00 17.00
☐250 **CRESSON SPRINGS SOFT DRINKS WORK, CRESSON, PA.**
Aqua, 7¾″ 15.00 20.00
☐251 **CRIPPLE CREEK**
*In center of it Bottling Works, Cripple Creek, Colo. all in a
circle, aqua, 6¾″* 16.00 23.00
☐252 **CRIPPLE CREEK BOTTLING WORKS, CRIPPLE CREEK,
COLO.**
All in a circle, clear, 6¾″ 16.00 23.00
☐253 **CRIPPLE CREEK BOTTLING WORKS, CRIPPLE CREEK,
COLO.**
All in a circle, aqua, 6¾″ 20.00 30.00
☐254 **CRIPPLE CREEK BOTTLING WORKS, CRIPPLE CREEK,
COLO.**
All in a circle, V.P. under bottom, clear, 6½″ 16.00 23.00
☐255 **CROGAN, J.F., LEXINGTON, KY.**
All in a front, blue, 7½″ 16.00 23.00
☐256 **CRONAR, M., 230 K ST. SACRAMENTO**
In 3 lines, aqua, 6½″ 15.00 20.00
☐257 **CROSS J.C.**
Kingfisher O.T. in 3 lines, aqua, 6¼″ 130.00 175.00
☐258 **CROWN BOTTLING CO., BUFFALO, N.Y.**
All in a circle in a crown. Panels base, aqua, 7⅛″ 15.00 20.00

☐ 259 **CROWN BOTTLING CO.**
Coalgate, I.T. Base 15, aqua, 6⅝" 100.00   135.00

☐ 260 **CROWN BOTTLING & MFG. CO.**
All in front aqua, 6½" 12.0   17.00

☐ 261 **CROWN BOTTLING & MFG. CO.**
In center a crown, Ardmore, I.T. all in a circle, big Y under
bottom (120), aqua, 6¾" 135.00   175.00

☐ 262 **CROWN BOTTLING & MFG. CO., ARDMORE, OKLA.**
Crown in center, on base "C", clear, 6¼" 15.00   20.00

☐ 263 **CROWN BOTTLING WORKS**
In horse shoe letters, under it Sandusky, O., aqua, 7" 12.00   17.00

☐ 264 **CROWN BOTTLING WORKS**
In horse shoe letters in center of it, a crown, under it Ard-
more, I.T., G on base, clear, 6½" 135.00   175.00

☐ 265 **CROWN BOTTLING WORKS, DELAWARE, O.**
All in a circle, aqua, 7" 15.00   20.00

☐ 266 **CROWN BOTTLING WORKS**
Hugo I.T. all in a circle B & D, aqua, 7⅛" 135.00   175.00

☐ 267 **CROWN BOTTLING WORKS**
Muskogee, I.T. all in a circle, aqua, 6⅝" 135.00   175.00

☐ 268 **CROZIER**
In center an elk Orangeville, Ont., clear or aqua, 6¾" 15.00   20.00

☐ 269 **CRUSELLASH**
Wood marks, aqua, 11½" 14.00   19.00

☐ 270 **CRYSTAL BOTTLING CO., CHARLESTON, W. VA.**
All in a circle, aqua, 6¾" 15.00   20.00

☐ 271 **CRYSTAL BOTTLING WORKS**
Lehigh I.T. all in a circle S on base, aqua, 6½" 130.00   170.00

☐ 272 **CRYSTAL S.W. CO. S.F.**
In 3 lines, diamond under bottom, Dr. aqua, 6¼" 16.00   23.00

☐ 273 **CRYSTAL SODA WATER CO. S.F.**
In 3 lines, 7¼" 15.00   20.00

☐ 274 **CRYSTAL SODA WORKS, HONOLULU, HI.**
Aqua, 7½" 45.00   60.00

☐ 275 **CRYSTAL SODA WORKS, HONOLULU, HI.**
Trade Mark J.A.P. under bottom aqua, 6½" 22.00   31.00

☐ 276 **CRYSTAL SPRING BOTTLING CO., BARNET, VT.**
All in a circle, clear, 6½" 16.00   23.00

☐ 277 **CRYSTAL SPRING BOTTLING CO., BARNET, VT.**
All in a circle, clear, 7½" 16.00   23.00

☐ 278 **CRYSTAL SPRING BOTTLING WORKS, COLUMBUS, KANS.**
All in a circle, light blue, 7" 16.00   23.00

☐ 279 **CRYSTAL WATER CO., JOHNSTOWN, PA.**
All in a circle Cak. 8 oz. Reg., under bottom L & H., aqua,
6¼" 12.00   17.00

☐ 280 **CUMAER BARKMAN, PORT JERVIS, N.Y.**
In 4 lines, aqua, 6¾" 15.00   20.00

☐ 281 **CUMMINGS, T.D.**
In ½ moon circle under it Phila, in black large "C" under
it, T.B. is Regst., light green, 6½" 15.00   20.00

☐282 **CUNNINGHAM SUPPLY CO.**
Phila. in scripts under it. Regst.#1907 under bottom, in
back (Mong.) large C. S.C., clear, 7½" **15.00** **20.00**

☐283 **CUNNINGHAM SUPPLY CO., 518 LOCUST ST. PHILA., PA.**
All in 5 lines on base T.B.N.T.B.S. under bottom 1895,
aqua, 7¼" **14.00** **19.00**

☐284 **CUNNINGHAM WESLEY, REG. HAMPTON, VA.**
All in a water mellow circle, aqua, 6½" **15.00** **20.00**

☐285 **CUSHING BOTTLING WORK: G.F. KNOWLES CUSHING,**
OKLA.
All in a circle, aqua, 6⅞" **15.00** **20.00**

☐286 **CUSHING CROWN BOTTLING, THE, CO. W. CORLIS**
PROP. CUSHING, OKLA.
All in a circle, aqua, 6⅞" **15.00** **20.00**

☐287 **CURRIERS**
Orange phosphate all in a horse shoe letters, aqua, 6¾" . **15.00** **20.00**

☐288 **CURRIERS VANILLA**
All in a circle, aqua, 7" **12.00** **17.00**

☐289 **CUTTING, THE, MINERAL WATER BOTTLING CO.**
In a horse shoe letters, in center Trade Mark, C.M.W. Co.
(Mong.) Regs. 422 Morres St. Phila., clear, 7¼" **15.00** **20.00**

D

☐290 **DAHLSTROM, JOHN, ISHKEMING, MICH.**
All in a circle, light blue, quart **18.00** **25.00**

☐291 **DAHLSTOM, JOHN, ISHIKEMING, MICH.**
All in a circle, 10 panels base, aqua, 7" **12.00** **17.00**

☐292 **DALINGER J.E.**
Tacoma all in a circle, aqua, 7" **12.00** **17.00**

☐293 **DARLING W.H., & SON**
In a horse shoe letters under it, Newport, Vt., aqua, 7" ... **16.00** **23.00**

☐294 **DAVIS BOTTLING**
In ½ moon letters in center works under it Davis L.T. bot-
tom M. yellowish aqua, 6½" **110.00** **140.00**

☐295 **DAVIS & WORCHESTER, EHE CO.**
All in a circle, on base No. 3, aqua, green, 6½" **15.00** **20.00**

☐296 **DEAMEP**
In a hollow letters, under it Grass Valley, back W.E.J.,
7½" **12.00** **17.00**

☐297 **DEAN, H.E., GREAT BEND, KANS.**
All in a circle, clear or amber **18.00** **25.00**

☐298 **DECKER BOTTLING, DAYTON, OH.**
On 3 panels bottle, aqua, 7" **19.00** **25.00**

☐299 **DEIS & TIBBALS, LIMA, OH.**
All in a circle, aqua, 7" **12.00** **17.00**

☐300 **DELANEY & CO. BOTTLERS, PLATTSBURG, N.Y.**
All in a circle, aqua, 7" **12.00** **17.00**

☐301 **DELANEY & YOUNG, EUREKA, CAL.**
All in a circle, pale blue, 6½" **15.00** **20.00**

□ 302 **DELTA BOTTLING WORKS, YAZOO CITY, MISS.**
In 4 lines, Panel base, aqua, 7¼" **16.00** **23.00**

□ 303 **DELTA MFG. CO., "DELTA"**
In a triangle under bottom, aqua, 7¼" **12.00** **17.00**

□ 304 **DELTA MFG. CO., GREENVILLE, MISS.**
All in a circle, aqua, 6½" **13.00** **17.00**

□ 305 **DENHALTER, H. SALT LAKE CITY, UT.**
In 4 lines, clear, 6½" **15.00** **20.00**

□ 306 **DENHALTER & SON, SALT LAKE CITY, UT.**
All on front, aqua, 6½" **15.00** **20.00**

□ 307 **DENNALTER, THE, BOTTLER, SALT LAKE, UT.**
All in a circle & a shield, clear, 6¾" **12.00** **17.00**

□ 308 **DENNAULTER H.G. SON**
In ½ moon circle under it Salt Lake City, Ut., aqua, 6½" .. **22.00** **30.00**

□ 309 **DEWAR JAMES**
In ½ moon letters under it, Elko, Nev., aqua, 6¾" **16.00** **23.00**

□ 310 **DIAMOND BOTTLING WORKS, COLUMBUS, KANS.**
All in a circle, aqua, 7½" **16.00** **23.00**

□ 311 **DIAMOND BOTTLING WORKS, MIAMI, OKLAHOMA**
All in a circle under bottom M., aqua, 7⅜" **15.00** **20.00**

□ 312 **DIAMOND BOTTLE WORKS, MIAMI, OK. T.**
All in a circle under bottom M., Panels base, aqua, 7¼" .. **80.00** **105.00**

□ 313 **DIAMOND BOTTLING WORKS, MIAMI, OKLAHOMA**
All in a circle. Panels base, M under bottom, aqua, 7" **15.00** **20.00**

□ 314 **DIEHL & DANBURY, D**
In back on shoulder, D under bottom,6½" **12.00** **17.00**

□ 315 **DIEHL & LORD**
*In hollow letters, under it Nashville, Tenn., under bottom a
star, aqua, 7"* **15.00** **20.00**

□ 316 **DIETZ, A.F.**
In ½ moon letters in center Knowersville, N.Y., aqua, 7" .. **12.00** **17.00**

□ 317 **DIETZ, A.F., ALTAMONT, N.Y.**
Reg. all in a circle, clear, 7" **12.00** **17.00**

□ 318 **DISBORO YEO & CO., CHICAGO**
All in a circle, clear, 6¾" **22.00** **30.00**

□ 319 **DISTILLED SODA WATER CO., OF ALASKA**
All in a circle, Panel base, light aqua, 7¼" **22.00** **30.00**

□ 320 **DOBBS, FERRY, MINERAL WATER CO, DOBBS FERRY,
N.Y.**
All in a circle, aqua, 6½" **12.00** **17.00**

□ 321 **DONAT & MOTIS, CHICAGO, ILL.**
*All in a circle in center through it 576, W. 19th St. in back
on base D.O.C. under bottom Big D, aqua or clear, 6½"* .. **12.00** **17.00**

□ 322 **DOOLEY & MULLEN, BELVIDERE, ILL.**
All in a circle, 511 on back, aqua, 6¾" **12.00** **17.00**

□ 323 **DUNCAN BOTTLING WORKS, DUNCAN, OKLA.**
All in a circle, Panels base under bottom S, aqua, 7¼" ... **16.00** **23.00**

THE PROPERTY OF
Mrs J. ED. BAF
NEWBURG NY

REGISTER

54

REGISTERED

BIEDENHARN
CANDY CO.
VICKSBURG
MISS.

83

BURKHARDT

18 TH &
JEFFERSON STS
CHICAGO.

141

CAMDEN BOTTLING
COMPANY
CAMDEN
N.J.

REGISTERED

160

FEHR BOTTLING WORKS
BIRMINGHAM ALA

161

CAPITAL S.W. CO.

COLUMBUS
OHIO

168

WORKS

COMANCHE

228

DELTA MFG. CO.
TRADE MARK
DELTA

GREENVILLE
MISS.

303

WIEHL & DANIE
MEMPHIS
TENN.

314

ELEPHANT
STEAM BOTTLING
WORKS
BIRMINGHAM
ALA.

348

FAYETTE
GA.

362

BOTTLING

TEXAS

397

GUETTE & COMPANY
REGISTERED
DETROIT. MICH.

432

☐324 **DURANT, PROPERTY OF, BOTTLING WORKS, DURANT, I.T.**
All in a circle, aqua, 7" 130.00 160.00

☐325 **DURESEN, JOHN, MINNEAPOLIS, MINN.**
All in a circle, Panels base, clear, 7¼" 15.00 20.00

E

☐326 **E.B. CO. EVARNSVILLE, IND.**
All in a circle, aqua, 7" 12.00 17.00

☐327 **E.B. CO. EVANSVILLE, IND.**
"B" under bottom panels bottle, aqua, 7" 12.00 17.00

☐328 **E.O.H., PARKERSBURG, W. VA.**
All in a circle, aqua, 6¾" 12.00 17.00

☐329 **EAGLE**
Under it an Eagle, Soda Water and Bottling Co. Santa Cruz, California. All in 4 lines, on base T.B.N.S., aqua, 6½" 15.00 20.00

☐330 **EAGLE BOTTLE WORKS, KNOXVILLE, TENN.**
All in a circle, in center of it an Eagle, in back B.N.S., aqua, 7¼" 16.00 23.00

☐331 **EAGLE BOTTLING WORKS**
In center spray wing Eagle on one side J., other L.,Davenport, Ia. all in a circle, under bottom J & L all in a circle. aqua, 6¾" 15.00 20.00

☐332 **EAGLE BOTTLING WORKS**
In center Eagle and flag, etc., Tacoma, Washington in a circle, aqua, 6½" 15.00 20.00

☐333 **EAGLE BOTTLING WORKS, LAWTON O.T.**
All in a circle, yellow aqua, 6¾" 130.00 175.00

☐334 **EAGLE SODA WATER & BOTTLING CO., SANTA CRUZ, CALIF.**
Under Eagle in a spray wing, eagle on base T.B.N.S., aqua, 6½" 12.00 17.00

☐335 **EAST, THE, IND. BOTTLING WORKS**
In a horse shoe letters in center in 3 lines, F.V. Cleveland, Ohio, clear, 6⅞" 12.00 17.00

☐336 **EASTERN**
Chicago in center through it Bottling Works under bottom E.B.W., aqua, 6½" 12.00 17.00

☐337 **EASTON, ALEX, FAIRFIELD, IOWA**
All in a circle, aqua, 6½" 15.00 20.00

☐338 **EASTERN BOTTLE WORKS**
Chicago, all in a circle, back Trade Mark, ship Reg. T.B.N.S. under bottom, E.B.W., aqua, 6½" 15.00 20.00

☐339 **EBNER P.**
In ½ moon letters, under it bottle Wil Del. in back in large hollow letters P.E., under bottom P.E., Panels base, aqua, 7½" 16.00 23.00

☐340 **ECLIPSE CARBONATIONS COMPANY**
In horse shoe in center E.C. Co., under it St. Louis, on shoulder ARO, in back M.E.L., 2 ½ cents deposit Required for Return of this bottle, under bottom E.C. Co. amber, 6⅜" 30.00 40.00

☐341	**EL PROGRESSO DU, LA.**		
	Havana arsenal in four lines (Cuba), light aqua, 6⅞"	**30.00**	**40.00**
☐342	**EL RENO**		
	1 line under it in ½ moon letters Bottling Works, under it in 2 lines El Rind O.T., aqua	**135.00**	**180.00**
☐343	**EL RENO BOTTLING WORKS**		
	All in a circle, El Reno O.T., clear, 6½"	**135.00**	**180.00**
☐344	**ELECTRIC BOTTLING CO.**		
	In ½ moon letters under it T.B.L.M.B.R.W. in 4 lines, on base Valdosta, Ga., aqua, 7"	**12.00**	**17.00**
☐345	**ELECTRIC BOTTLING WORKS, WEST POINT, MISS.**		
	All in a circle, aqua, 6½"	**12.00**	**17.00**
☐346	**ELEPHANT BOTTLING CO.**		
	On base D.O.C., under bottom "D", aqua, 8"	**12.00**	**17.00**
☐347	**ELEPHANT ON SHOULDER BOTTLING WORKS**		
	Chicago, M. Levin, Prop. in 3 lines, in back a ship, over it Trade Mark, under it Reg. T.B.N.S., aqua, 6½"	**15.00**	**20.00**
☐348	**ELEPHANT STEAM BOTTLING WORKS**		
	All on front under bottom "D", aqua, 6½"	**14.00**	**19.00**
☐349	**ELK VALLEY BOTTLING WORKS, LARIMORE, N.D.**		
	All in a circle, aqua, 6½"	**16.00**	**23.00**
☐350	**ELKO BOTTLING WORKS, ELKO, NEV.**		
	All in a circle, aqua, 6½"	**40.00**	**40.00**
☐351	**ELWICK C.L.Z: LINCOLN, NEB.**		
	All in a water mellow circle, on base 8-13-33, aqua, 6¾" ..	**16.00**	**23.00**
☐352	**ELWICK, NEB., LINCOLN, NEB.**		
	All in a circle, aqua, 6¾"	**15.00**	**20.00**
☐353	**EMPIRE SODA WORK, VALLYO, CAL.**		
	All on front, aqua, 6¾"	**12.00**	**17.00**
☐354	**ENGEL, DAVID**		
	Under it a horse shoe, in it Mineral Trade Mark, under it Cincinnati, O.T.B.I.N.S. in 3 lines, aqua, 7"	**15.00**	**20.00**
☐355	**ENGLAND, NEW BOTTLING CO., MINNEAPOLIS**		
	All in a circle, under bottom T.B.N.T.B.S., aqua, 6¾"	**12.00**	**17.00**
☐356	**ENGLE F.E., F.E., LANCASTER, PA.**		
	In 3 lines, 8 fl. ozs. on shoulder, aqua, 6¾"	**12.00**	**17.00**
☐357	**ERIE BOTTLING WORKS, UTICA, N.Y.**		
	All in a circle, on base Reg. clear, 6¾"	**12.00**	**17.00**
☐358	**ERTEL JOHN M.**		
	Under bottom B & E, clear, 6¾"	**12.00**	**17.00**
☐359	**ERTS, J.M., POUGHKEEPSIE, N.Y.**		
	All in a circle, Reg. on base E. under bottom, clear, 7"	**12.00**	**17.00**
☐360	**ESPOSITO G., PHIADE.**		
	All in a circle, aqua, 6¾"	**12.00**	**17.00**
☐361	**ESPOSITO, J.**		
	812 & 814 Washington Ave. Kaca Kola, aqua, 7½"	**12.00**	**17.00**
☐362	**ETTA BOTTLING WORK, LAFAYETTE, LA.**		
	Clear, 6¾"	**12.00**	**17.00**
☐363	**EUREKA BOTTLING WORKS, FT. SMITH, ARK.**		
	The words stolen from are at the top, aqua, 7"	**15.00**	**20.00**

☐364 **EUREKA CALIFORNIA SODA WATER CO., S.F.**
In center of it, a bird, light green, 6¾" 16.00   23.00
☐365 **EVENCHIK, BROS. BOTTLING WORKS, CLEVELAND, OHIO**
In center an Eagle, all in a circle, aqua, 7" 15.00   20.00
☐366 **EWA BOTTLING WORK**
In a horse shoe letters, under it H.T., Panels base, clear, 7½" 75.00   95.00
☐367 *also aqua* 85.00   110.00
☐368 **EXCELSIOR BOTTLING CO., BLOOMINGTON, ILL.**
All in a circle, under bottom E.B. Co., aqua, 7" 14.00   10.00
☐369 **EXCELSIOR BOTTLING CO., CLARKSBURG, W. VA.**
All in a circle, aqua, 6¾" 12.00   17.00
☐370 **EXCELSIOR BOTTLING WORKS, HOUSTON, TEXAS**
All in a circle, aqua, 7¼" 15.00   20.00

F

☐371 **F.A.B.**
In a large horse shoe, in center, Galveston, Tx. near base, aqua, 7½" 12.00   17.00
☐372 **FARGO, THE MINERAL SPRINGS CO.**
In a horse shoe letters, in center of it Pure & Clean, Warren O., clear, 6⅝" 12.00   17.00
☐373 **FELBRATH, H, PEORIA, ILL.**
All in a circle at base S.B. & Co., aqua, 7" 12.00   17.00
☐374 **FIDELITY BOTTLING WORKS**
Reg. Monroe, La. all in a circle, Panels Base, under bottom, Fidelity, aqua, 7" 15.00   20.00
☐375 **5TH WARD BOTTLING WORKS, HOUSTON, TX.**
All in a water mellow letters, in center 5th Ward, aqua, 7¾" 15.00   20.00
☐376 **FINLEY & SON**
In ½ moon letters in center 1893, under it Bottlers, 1806 D St. N.W. Washington, D.C. in back, T.B.N.T.B.S., under bottom F, aqua, 6½" 15.00   20.00
☐377 **FISCHER & CO., SANTA FE, N.M.**
All in a circle, aqua, 6¼" 15.00   20.00
☐378 **F.K. & SON, SOCARRO, N.M.**
All in a circle, aqua, 6½" 30.00   40.00
☐379 **FLADUNG & SONS, REG. READING, OHIO**
All in a circle, aqua, 7½" 15.00   20.00
☐380 **FLA. BREWING CO., FOSTORIA, OHIO**
All in a circle, aqua, 7" 15.00   20.00
☐381 **FLETCHER, H.W., BELLAIR, OH.**
All in a circle, aqua, 6½" 15.00   20.00
☐382 **FLECKENSTEIN'S BOTTLING WORKS, COLUMBIA, PA.**
In an oval on top & Reg. under it Panel base, aqua, 6¾" .. 15.00   20.00
☐383 **THE FLORIDA BREWING CO., TAMPA, FLA.**
All in a circle, on base F.B. Co., aqua, 6½" 15.00   20.00
☐384 **FREIDMAN, WM.**
Champion, Soda Factory, Key West, Fla. all in a circle, on base Reg. Etc., clear, 6¾" 15.00   20.00

☐385 **FOLGER'S BOTTLING WORKS, GRAND RAPIDS, MICH.**
All on front in 5 lines, aqua, 6½" 15.00 20.00

☐386 **FONDA D.C., BOULDER, COLO.**
All in a circle, aqua, 7" 15.00 20.00

☐387 **FORSTER & POLHEMUS, POUGHKEEPSIE, N.Y.**
All in 4 lines, CLEAR, 7" 15.00 20.00

☐388 **FORTHOFEER, JOHN**
In ½ moon letters under it Mt. Vernon, Ind., light aqua, 6½" 15.00 20.00

☐389 **FOSTORIA BOTTLING WORKS, FOSTORIA, OHIO**
All in a circle, aqua, 7" 15.00 20.00

☐390 **FORT TOWSON BOTTLING WORKS, FORT TOWSON, OKLA.**
All in a circle, under bottom B & D, Panel base, aqua, 7½" 15.00 20.00

☐391 **FURA, J., BOTTLING CO.**
All in a circle, aqua, 6½" 15.00 20.00

G

☐392 **G.A.K.**
In large block letters in center of bottle, aqua, 6¾" 15.00 20.00

☐393 **GADSEN BOTTLING WORK, GADSEN, ALA.**
All in a circle, clear, 6½" 15.00 20.00

☐394 **GADSEN COCA—COLA, GADSEN, ALA.**
In block letters, clear, 7" 170.00 225.00

☐395 **GALLAGER & CO.**
in ½ moon circle under it Philade, in back Big "C", in side of it & Co., light blue, 6⅞" 22.00 32.00

☐396 **GALLUP BOTTLING WORKS, GALLUP, N.M.**
All in a circle, light aqua, 6½" 22.00 32.00

☐397 **GAPERA BOTTLING, FT. WORTH, TEXAS**
All in a circle, clear, 6½" 15.00 20.00

☐398 **GARRISON, E.J., PATERSON, N.J.**
All in a circle, aqua or clear, 5¼" 15.00 20.00

☐399 **GEARY BOTTLING WORKS, GEARY O.T.**
All in a circle, yellow aqua, 6⅜" 170.00 225.00

☐400 **GEARY BOTTLING WORKS, GEARY, OKLA.**
All in a circle, aqua, 6⅞" 45.00 65.00

☐401 **GENTSCH, E., BUFFALO, N.Y.**
In three lines under bottom "G", squat type bottle, light amber, 5¾" 15.00 20.00

☐402 **GEORGIA BOTTLING CO., ATLANTA, GA.**
All in a circle, aqua, 7" 15.00 20.00

☐403 **JOS GFROERER & CO.**
In ½ moon letters under it Millbank D.T., quart, aqua 140.00 180.00

☐404 **GIERING J.F., YOUNGSTOWN, O.**
clear, 6⅝" 15.00 20.00

☐405 *Same as above, except aqua* 15.00 20.00

☐406 **GILBERT BOTTLING WORK, MINN.**
All in a circle, clear, 7½" 15.00 20.00

☐407	**GILBERT BOTTLING WORKS, GILBERT, MINN.**		
	All in a circle, bottom R., aqua, 6¾"	**15.00**	**20.00**
☐408	**GILLIGAN, A.C.**		
	In ½ moon letters under it, Cincinnati, O., T.B.I.N.S. in back, Eagle, under it Trade Mark, E.H.E. Co., aqua, 7½" ..	**15.00**	**20.00**
☐409	**GIMLICH & WHITE, PITTSFIELD, MASS**		
	All in a circle, aqua, 7"	**15.00**	**20.00**
☐410	**GLASSER & REASBECK, BELLAIRE, O.**		
	All in a circle, aqua, 6½"	**15.00**	**20.00**
☐411	**GLENN & BARTOY, NEW ULM, TEXAS**		
	All in a circle, aqua, 6¾"	**15.00**	**20.00**
☐412	**GOLDEN WEST SODA WORKS, BRUNS & NASH MOUNTAIN VIEW, CAL.**		
	All in 5 lines, light green, 7"	**15.00**	**20.00**
☐413	**GORDON, A., HALF WAY HOUSE**		
	Tannerville N.Y., in a circle, under it registered, on base in back, Not to be Sold, clear, 6¾"	**12.00**	**20.00**
☐414	**GORNY, A.**		
	In center Trade A.G. Mark, Chicago, Ill. under it, R.T.B. on bottom AG, aqua, 7"	**12.00**	**17.00**
☐415	**GRAFTON BOTTLING WORKS, GRAFTON, N.D.**		
	clear, 6¾"	**1.20**	**17.00**
☐416	**GRAFTON BOTTLING WORKS, GRAFTON, N.D.**		
	Ill. in a circle, clear, 6¾"	**15.00**	**20.00**
☐417	**GRAMERCY, BOTTLING WORKS, GRAMERCY, LA.**		
	clear, 7"	**12.00**	**17.00**
☐418	**GRAMERCY BOTTLING WORKS, GRAMERCY, LA.**		
	aqua, 7"	**15.00**	**20.00**
☐419	**GRANT, C.E., OHIO**		
	In 2 lines, aqua, 6½"	**12.00**	**17.00**
☐420	**GRANT & UPTON**		
	In ½ moon letters under it in 2 lines Columbus, Ohio, aqua, 6½"	**12.00**	**17.00**
☐421	**GREENHOUSE, L., NEWARK, N.J.**		
	In a circle, in back T.B.N.T.B.S., aqua, 7"	**15.00**	**20.00**
☐422	**GREENVILLE BOTTLING & MFG. CO., GREENVILLE, TEXAS**		
	All in a circle, bottom G, aqua, 6¼"	**16.00**	**23.00**
☐423	**GRERA BOTTLING, FT. WORTH, TEXAS**		
	All in a circle, clear	**12.00**	**17.00**
☐424	**GROCERY & CANDY CO.**		
	In horse shoe letters, under it Fairmont, W. Va., clear, 8¼"	**12.00**	**17.00**
☐425	**GRUBEL, GEO.**		
	In ½ moon letters, under it in 2 lines Kansas City, Kans., aqua, 6¾"	**12.00**	**17.00**
☐426	**GRUBEL, GEO., KANSAS CITY, KANSAS**		
	In three lines, aqua, 6½"	**8.00**	**15.00**
☐427	**GRUBEL, GEO, KANSAS CITY, KANSAS**		
	In three lines, clear, 6½"	**128.00**	**17.00**
☐428	**GUAYMAS BOTTLING WORKS, GUAYMAS, MEXICO**		
	In 4 lines, clear, 7¼"	**32.00**	**42.00**

□ 429 **GUILBER, YREKA**
In a circle, aqua, 7¼" **15.00** **20.00**
□ 430 **GUILBER, YREKA**
In a circle, clear, 7" **12.00** **17.00**
□ 431 **GUTEKUNST, O.J.**
Registered all on front, clear, 6¾" **12.00** **17.00**
□ 432 **GUYETTE & COMPANY, DETROIT, MICH.**
Reg. in center, G under bottom, cobalt blue, 6¼" **42.00** **55.00**
□ 433 **GWINN BOTTLING WORK**
Mich. in 3 lines, clear **12.00** **17.00**

I

□ 434 **ICE PLANT BOTTLING WORKS, OKLAHOMA CITY**
All in a circle under bottom B, aqua, 6¾" **16.00** **23.00**
□ 435 **IDABEL MFG. & BOTTLING CO., IDABEL, OKLA.**
All in a circle, aqua, 6¾" **16.00** **23.00**
□ 436 **IMPERIAL BOTTLING WORKS, MONTGOMERY, ALA.**
All in 4 lines, aqua, 7" **12.00** **17.00**
□ 437 **INDEPENDENT BOTTLING WORK**
In center hand shake, S McAlester, Okla. Trade Mark, reg. all in a circle, aqua, 6¾" **16.00** **23.00**
□ 438 **INDEPENDENT BOTTLING WORKS**
In center B.C. Chicago, under bottom C.B., light blue, green, 6¼" **16.00** **23.00**
□ 439 **INGO SODA WORKS**
In a horse shoe letters, under it Bishop, Calif., 6½" **15.00** **20.00**
□ 440 **IRELAND BROS.**
(B.W., inter blocking Mong.) Bottling Works, Malleawan, N.Y. all in a circle, aqua, 9⅜" **15.00** **20.00**
□ 441 **IRON CITY**
"11" on bottom, "96" on base, aqua, 6½" **12.00** **17.00**
□ 442 **ISAAC CRANS & SONS, MISSLWTOWN, N.Y.**
All in slug plate, pale aqua, 6¾" **12.00** **17.00**
□ 443 **ISAAC, MERKEL, PHATTSBURG, N.Y.**
All in a circle, on bottom A.G.W., Panel base, aqua, 7¼" **12.00** **17.00**
□ 444 **ISIAH BUNN**
Reg Riverside Bottling Works Warwick, N.Y. all in a circle, under bottom a star, clear, 6⅝" **18.00** **27.00**
□ 445 **ISIAH BUNN**
(top Reg.) Riverside Bottling Works. Warwick, N.Y. all in a circle, in back T.B.N.T.B.S., quart, clear, 8¾" **22.00** **32.00**
□ 446 **IUKA MINERAL**
Spring all in a circle, aqua, 6¾" **16.00** **23.00**

J

□ 447 **JACKSON BOTTLING WORKS**
W.A. Lake, all on front, aqua, 7" **16.00** **23.00**
□ 448 **JACOBS, J.L., CAIRO, N.Y.**
All in a circle, light aqua, 7" **12.00** **17.00**

☐ 449 **JASPER COCA—COLA CO., JASPER, ALA.**
All in block letters, 6¾" **130.00** **165.00**
☐ 450 **J & F BORDE, TAMPICO, MEXICO**
All in water mellow letters, Panels base, light blue **23.00** **32.00**
☐ 451 **JEFFERSON BOTTLING WORKS, JEFFERSON, TEXAS**
All in a circle, aqua, 7½" **23.00** **32.00**
☐ 452 **JOHN & HUGH, O'REILLY, STATEN ISLAND**
All in a circle, T.B.N.T.B.S., light blue, 6⅞" **16.00** **20.00**
☐ 453 **JOHNSON & BROS., DELTA, PA.**
All in a circle, amber, 6½" **23.00** **34.00**
☐ 454 **JOHNSON & CORBETT**
In ½ moon letters, under it Socorro, N.M., aqua, 6¼" **16.00** **23.00**
☐ 455 **JONES, A.**
In 2 lines, aqua, 6¾" **12.00** **17.00**
☐ 456 **JONES GEO.**
In 2 lines, aqua, 7" **12.00** **17.00**
☐ 457 **JONES, LEWIS F., PHILIPS BURCH, PA.**
All in a circle in back T.B.N.S., aqua, 7" **16.00** **23.00**
☐ 458 **JOYCE, A.L.**
Bottling Work, Traverse City, Mich. all in a circle, aqua,
6½" **12.00** **17.00**
☐ 459 **JOYCE BROS., GREENVILLE, MICH.**
All in a water mellow circle, Panels base, aqua to light
green, 6¼" **12.00** **17.00**
☐ 460 **JUMBO BOTTLING WORK**
In ½ moon letters, in center elephant, under it Trade Mark,
Cincinnati, O., aqua, 7" **16.00** **23.00**
☐ 461 **JUMBO BR'G CO.**
The Mineral Water Dept. Cincinnati, O. all in a circle, on
base J.B. Co., aqua, 7" **16.00** **23.00**

K

☐ 462 **KAMMERER, G.**
"A.G.W.L." on base, aqua, 7" **12.00** **17.00**
☐ 463 **KANTER BROS AND CO.**
All in a circle, aqua, 7" **9.00** **13.00**
☐ 464 **L. KARNAHRENS**
A star-Bottling Jacksonville, Fla. all in 4 lines, aqua **12.00** **17.00**
☐ 465 **KARSCH & SONS, JOHN, EVANSVILLE, IND.**
Aqua, 6½" **12.00** **17.00**
☐ 466 **KEARNEY WM., A., SHAMOKIN, PA.**
Amber, 7¼" **27.00** **38.00**
☐ 467 **KEAVENY BUCKLEY & CO.**
348 & 350 Bienville Street, New Orleans in 4 lines, under
bottom star, aqua, 7⅛" **15.00** **20.00**
☐ 468 **KEE, GEORGE F.**
In center a key Congers, N.Y. all in a circle, under it
T.B.N.T.B.S., clear, 7" **12.00** **17.00**
☐ 469 **KEE, GEORGE F.**
In center a key, CONGERS N.Y. all in a circle, under it
T.B.N.T.B.S., clear, 7" **12.00** **17.00**

☐ 470 **KEENAN MFG. CO., BUTTE MT.**
In a circle, ten panels at base, aqua, 7¼" 18.00 27.00

☐ 471 **KEENAN MFG. CO., BUTTE, MONT.**
All in a circle, aqua, 6¾" 18.00 27.00

☐ 472 **KELLER'S BOTTLING CO.**
In horse shoe letters in center Big K, under it Cleveland,
O., clear, 7¼" 12.00 17.00

☐ 473 **KELLY, T.H. & CO.**
Eagle Bottling Works, Steubenville, O. all in a circle, aqua,
6½" 12.00 17.00

☐ 474 **KELLY T.H. & CO.**
Eagle Bottling Works, Steubenville, O. all in a circle, on
base C & Co. 3, aqua, 6¾" 12.00 15.00

☐ 475 **KELLY, T.H., EAGLE BOTTLING WORKS,**
STEUBENVILLE, O.
All in a circle, aqua, 6" 12.00 17.00

☐ 476 **KENNEDY, C.H., BUTLER, PA.**
In 2 lines in center, clear, 6½" 15.00 20.00

☐ 477 **KENRICK, E.J. & SON**
In ½ moon circle, under it Portsmouth, O., aqua, 6½" . . . 12.00 17.00

☐ 478 **KING, N.Y. ROGERS, ARK.**
All in a circle, aqua, 6" 12.00 17.00

☐ 479 **KING & JOYCE, CHICAGO**
On base T.B.I.N.S. under bottom K & J, aqua, 7½" 12.00 17.00

☐ 480 **KINGFISHER BOTTLING WORKS F.C. BROWN**
KINGFISHER, O.T.
All in a circle, aqua, 6¾" 120.00 155.00

☐ 481 **KINNEY BOTTLING WORKS, MC CURTAIN, I.T.**
All in a circle, aqua, 6½" 65.00 85.00

☐ 482 **KINNEY'S BOTTLING WORKS, MC CURTAIN, OKLA.**
All in a circle, aqua, 6½" 16.00 23.00

☐ 483 **KINGSTON BOTTLING WORK, I.V. WAGNER PROP.,**
KINGSTON, N.C.
In a horse shoe, letters in back T.B.N.T.B.S., clear, 7" 15.00 20.00

☐ 484 **KLUETSCH, CHARLES**
In center (mong. KC) Chicago, Ill. all in a circle, Bolton
CK., aqua, 6½" 16.00 23.00

☐ 485 **KNOWN**
(besides what is listed in this book) Coca-Cola, Tuskgee,
Al, Brunswick, Ga., Atlanta, Ga., Gadsen, al., Chatt, Tenn.,
all in block letters, Jasper, Al. 150.00 350.00

☐ 486 **KOEHLER, HENRY, POMEROY, OHIO**
All in a circle under it registered, aqua, 7" 12.00 17.00

☐ 487 **KREBS UNION**
In ½ moon letters under it in 3 lines Bottling Works,
Krebs, I.T., clear, 6½" 120.00 155.00

☐ 488 **KROGER BROS., BUTTE, MT.**
In a circle, aqua, 8" 30.00 40.00

☐ 489 **KROGER BROS., BUTTE, M.T.**
All in a circle, clear, 6½" 185.00 235.00

☐490 **KRUEGER, H.O., GRAND FORKS, N.D.**
aqua, 6½" 45.00   65.00

☐491 **KRUSLING & HUESMANN**
In a horse shoe, letters in center a flag on 3 strip, Union
Trade Mark, under it Cincinnati, aqua, 7" 15.00   20.00

☐492 **KRUSLING, J.A. & HUESMANN, FLAG, CINCINNATI**
clear, 7" 12.00   17.00

☐493 **KUEHNE, FRANK, SISTERVILLE, W. VA.**
aqua, 7" 12.00   17.00

☐494 **KUHLMAN THE JOHN BREWING CO., ELLENVILLE, N.Y.**
All in a circle bottom A & D, aqua, 7" 16.00   23.00

☐495 **KULY BOTTLING WORKS, DECATUR, ILL.**
All in a circle bottom A & D, aqua, 6½" 12.00   17.00

L

☐496 **LA. PRULVA**
Farrica de Aguss, Gasedsas, Jose Ma. Samchez, Jerez,
Zac all in a circle, under bottom A.R., aqua, 6¾" 16.00   23.00

☐497 **LAKE W.W., JACKSON BOTTLING WORKS,**
JACKSON, MISS.
In 3 lines, under bottom L, aqua, 7" 12.00   17.00

☐498 **LAYER, C., RATON, N.M.**
All in a circle, Panel base, clear, 7¼" 16.00   23.00

☐499 **LAUBE, JAS. X, ACKRON, O.**
All in a circle, blue, 6¾" 23.00   32.00

☐500 **LAUGMONT BOTTLING WORKS**
All in a circle, clear or aqua, 6½" 12.00   17.00

☐501 **LAUTERBACK, JOHN**
In a horse shoe letters, under it Springfield, Ill., on base
N.B.B.G. Co., 46, aqua, 7⅛" 12.00   17.00

☐502 **LAVIN, M.F., ASHLLEY, PA.**
In a horse shoe letters, under it Reg., light blue, 6¾" 12.00   17.00

☐503 **LAWRENCE, LOUIS, MANAIMO, B.C.**
All in a circle, aqua, 7½" 16.00   23.00

☐504 **LEHIGH BOTTLING**
In horse shoe letters, Works under it Lehigh, Ind. Ter.,
aqua, 6½" 130.00   170.00

☐505 **LEHIGH, BOTTLING WORKS, LEHIGH, I.T.**
All in a circle, light aqua, 6⅝" 130.00   170.00

☐506 **LEHIGH BOTTLING WORKS, LEHIGH, OKLA.**
All in a circle, under bottom "S", aqua, 6⅝" 16.00   23.00

☐507 **LEMAIRE**
On front 4 piece mold, aqua, 6½" 12.00   17.00

☐508 **LEMON BEER**
Noona & Irmiger, Manitowac, Wisc., all in 4 lines, amber,
6½" 32.00   43.00

☐509 **LEMON BEER, MOONAN & MANITOWAC, WISC.**
All in a circle, amber, 6¼" 32.00   43.00

☐510 **LETTENMAYER O., KEEN, N.H.**
All in a circle H 2-5 under bottom, aqua, 6½" 12.00   17.00

☐511 **LINDSEY, J.A.**
A harp on back, "33" under bottom, aqua, 7" 12.00 17.00
☐512 *Same except clear ....* 12.00 17.00
☐513 **LION A.**
In front, aqua, 6¼" 11.00 15.00
☐514 **LIQUID THE**
In side of diamond, on bottom, on base M.B. & g. Co. 33, aqua, 6¾" 12.00 17.00
☐515 **LODI SODA WORKS**
All in a circle, large letters, aqua, 6½" 16.00 23.00
☐516 **LOHR, ANDREW**
Ridge on back mold, on bottom C. & Co. LIM, clear or aqua, 6½" 12.00 17.00
☐517 **LOMAX**
Chicago, Etc. on front, in back T.B.M.B.R., cobalt, 7" 55.00 75.00
☐518 **LOMAX J.A.**
Ginger ale all on front, aqua, 6½" 12.00 17.00
☐519 **LOMAX J.A.**
14-16 & 18 Charles Place, Chicago, Trade Mark Reg. in a diamond square in center of it 4 bottle in a diamond in center J.A.L. all on front, base T.B.M.B.R., bottom J.L., 6¾" 60.00 80.00
☐520 **LOMAX, K.A.**
Chicago all in a circle, cobalt, 7" 45.00 60.00
☐521 *Same except in back T.B.M.B.R. ....* 50.00 70.00
☐522 **LONG, F.C., THE BOTTLING CO.**
Chicago in 3 lines, aqua, 6½" 12.00 17.00
☐523 **LOW, JOHN S.**
All in a circle, aqua, 7" 12.00 17.00
☐524 **LUCAS, A.E., WILMINGTON, N.C.**
All in a circle, aqua, 6⅞" 16.00 23.00
☐525 **LUDWIG A., NAPA, CAL.**
In 3 lines, clear or aqua, 6½" 16.00 23.00
☐526 **LUDWIG, L., BRUNSWICK, GA.**
In horse shoe letters, in back T.B.T.B.R., under bottom Dixon, smoke color, 7¼" 12.00 17.00
☐527 **LUTHER & MYERS**
In ½ moon letters, under it Albany, N.Y., Panels base, under bottom, L & M, aqua, 7" 16.00 23.00
☐528 **LYMAN ASTLEY, CHEYENNE, WYO.**
All in a circle, 6¾" 25.00 34.00

M

☐529 **M.B.W. MINOT, N.D.**
All in a circle, aqua, 7¼" 12.00 17.00
☐530 **M & M STAR BOTTLING CO., OSKALOOSA, IA.**
Aqua, 6½" 15.00 23.00
☐531 **MACON BOTTLING WORKS**
E.J. Burk, aqua, 6⅝" 12.00 17.00
☐532 **MADDEN, GEORGE E.**
Aqua, 7" 15.00 20.00

☐ 533 **MAGINNIS, GEO. T. & CO.**
All in a circle, aqua, 7" 12.00 17.00

☐ 534 **MAHASKA BOTTLING WORKS**
All in a circle, clear, 7" 12.00 17.00

☐ 535 **MAHASKA BOTTLING WORKS**
All in a circle, aqua, 6¾" 12.00 17.00

☐ 536 **MANFIELD BOTTLE WORKS, MANFIELD, ARK.**
All in a circle "M" etc. under bottom, light green, 6½" ... 15.00 20.00

☐ 537 **MANHATTAN, THE — BOTTLING CO., CHICAGO, ILL.**
In center of it Trade Mark a horse head Registered under
bottom Trade Mark Registered in center head, aqua, 6¾" 16.00 23.00

☐ 538 **MANHATTAN, THE, BOTTLING CO.**
Trade Mark registered Chicago, Ill. all in a circle, in center
of it a horse head, aqua, 6½" 12.00 17.00

☐ 539 **MARIETTA BOTTLING WORKS, MARIETTA, GA.**
All in a circle, clear, 7" 12.00 17.00

☐ 540 **MARIETTA BOTTLING WORKS, MARIETTA, OKLA.**
All in a circle, panels base, aqua, 7¼" 75.00 100.00

☐ 541 **MARION BOTTLING & ICE CREAM CO.**
Made from, Mo-Cola, original Coca-Cola Formula not an
imitation, Ocala, Fla. all in a circle, aqua, 6¾" 12.00 17.00

☐ 542 **MARION BOTTLING & ICE CREAM CO.**
Made from Mo-Cola original, Coca-Cola Formula, not an
imitation, all in a circle, clear, 6¼" 55.00 75.00

☐ 543 **MARION BOTTLING WORKS, FAIRMONT, W.VA.**
All in a circle, aqua, 6¾" 12.00 17.00

☐ 544 **MARKOWITZ, L., BRUNSWICK, GA.**
In 3 lines in back T.B.T.B.R., aqua, 7⅝" 16.00 23.00

☐ 545 **MARSH, J.I., PORTMOUTH, O.**
All in a circle, aqua, green, 6¼" 12.00 17.00

☐ 546 **MARTINS BOTTLING CO., MINNEAPOLIS**
In 3 lines, aqua, 6½" 12.00 17.00

☐ 547 **MATHIEU, JACOB, BYESVILLE, O.**
All in a circle, aqua, 7" 12.00 17.00

☐ 548 **MAUSER G. & CO., ADAMS, MASS.**
Registered all in a circle, aqua, 7¼" 12.00 17.00

☐ 549 **MAYER & BERNSTEIN, ALBANY, N.Y.**
Registered in 3 lines, clear or aqua, 7" 12.00 17.00

☐ 550 **MAYER, CHAS. H. CO.**
Trade Mark large G D all in a ½ moon letters under it Registered, Hammond, Ind., Registered "M" under bottom,
light green, 7¼" 15.00 20.00

☐ 551 **MAYER, CHAS. H.M. & CO.**
In ½ moon circle, in it Trade G.D., under it in 3 lines
Registered, Hammond, Ind. also extra Registered panel
base in back T.B.I.N.S., under bottom "M", light blue, 7" . 15.00 20.00

☐ 552 **MAYER, JACOB, EVANSVILLE, IND.**
Under bottom, J.M., panels base, aqua, 6¼" 12.00 17.00

☐ 553 **MAYFIELD**
(in script Celery Cola) not script Standard Bottling Co.
Atlanta, Ga. all in a circle, Panels base, aqua, 7" 32.00 42.00

☐554 **MAYFIELD**
*(in script Celery Cola) not script, Rome Bottling Works
Rome, Ga. all in a circle, aqua, 6½"* **32.00** **42.00**

☐555 **MAYFIELD, CELERY—COLA**
J.C. Mayfield Mfg. Co. Birmingham, Ala., aqua, 6½" **12.00** **17.00**

☐556 **McBRIDE EARL & POLLAND**
*In a horse shoe letters, under it Registered, Detroit, Mich.,
aqua, 7"* **12.00** **17.00**

☐557 **McCARTHY, PERRY O.T.**
All in a circle, bottom 77, panel base, aqua, 7¼" **75.00** **100.00**

☐558 **McCARTHY, PONOA CITY, O.T.**
All in a circle, on bottom, 77, aqua, 7¼" **75.00** **100.00**

☐559 **McCREEDY, PROVIDENCE, R.I.**
*All in a circle, on shoulder Registered panels base, clear,
7"* **23.00** **32.00**

☐560 **McCREEDY, S.E., PROVIDENCE, RI.**
in a circle, panels base, aqua, 6¼" **12.00** **17.00**

☐561 **McDONOUGH & COMPANY**
*First and Henderson, J.C. in 4 lines vertical, No. 1 under
bottom, aqua, 6½"* **12.00** **17.00**

☐562 **McGRAW, J.C., HARPER'S FERRY, W. VA.**
All in a circle, clear, 7" **12.00** **17.00**

☐563 **McGUINESS**
*Eagle in center, Utica, N.Y. all in a circle, bottom star, light
aqua, 6⅞",* **135.00** **175.00**

☐564 **McKINNEY, VAN ALSTYNE & PLANO**
Clear, 6¾" **135.00** **175.00**

☐565 **McMAHAN, PAULSVILLEY, I.T.**
Clear, 6¾" **12.00** **17.00**

☐566 **McNEIL B., WHEELING, W. VA.**
In center mong. all in a circle, clear, 6⅝" **12.00** **17.00**

☐567 **McPALIN, DON, PARK CITY, UTAH**
All in a circle, clear 6½" **16.00** **23.00**

☐568 **GEORGE L. McREEVY**
*In ½ moon letters, in center GL & McCm mong letters,
trade Mark Reg. Baltimore, Md. all in a circle, Registered
in back T.B.I.N.S., bottom CL McC, aqua, 7"* **12.00** **17.00**

☐569 **MEEHAN BROS.**
M under bottom, light green, 6½" **12.00** **17.00**

☐570 **MEISIER BROS., PLEASANT CITY, O.**
All in a circle, in back M.B. & G Co., aqua, 7" **16.00** **23.00**

☐571 **MEMPHIS BOTTLING AND MFG. CO., MEMPHIS, TENN.**
All in a circle, aqua, 6½" **16.00** **23.00**

☐572 **MENDOCINO BOTTLING WORKS, A.L. REYNOLDS**
All in 3 lines, light green, 7" **16.00** **23.00**

☐573 **MENTON, M., BELTON, TEXAS**
In a center a rooster, aqua, 6¾" **12.00** **17.00**

☐574 **MERIDAN STEAM BOTTLING CO.**
(Miss) all in a circle, clear, 6¾" **16.00** **23.00**

☐575 **MERRIT MOORE, JR. BOTTLER**
All in a circle, back T.B.N.T.B.S., clear, 7" **12.00** **17.00**

☐576 **MERRIT MOORE JR. BOTTLER**
"This Bottle Not To Be Sold" on back, clear or amethyst,
7" 12.00 17.00

☐577 **MERRITT MOORE JR. BOTTLER, HUDGINS, P.O. VA.**
Aqua, 6⅞" 12.00 17.00

☐578 **MESSALL**
(M.E. Mong.) Mark, Enid, O. T. Registered, all in a circle,
light aqua, 6⅝" 90.00 120.00

☐579 **MESSALL,E.J., CONCORDIA, KANS.**
All in a circle, aqua, 6⅞" 18.00 26.00

☐580 **MESSALL AND MESSALL**
All in a circle (Guthrie, OK), aqua, 6¾" 80.00 105.00

☐581 **METTE BROS., CHICAGO, ILL.**
In 3 lines under bottom, mong. M.B., clear or amethyst,
6½" 12.00 17.00

☐582 **MEW, W.B., & LANGTON CO.**
All in a circle, green, 7" 16.00 23.00

☐583 **MEYER & RADCLIFFE, WHEELING, W. VA.**
In center mong. all in a circle, clear, 6⅝" 12.00 17.00

☐584 **MILES, A.S.**
All on front, aqua, 6½" 12.00 17.00

☐585 **MILLER, A.H.**
aqua, 6½" 12.00 17.00

☐586 **MILLER WM., BOTTLING WORKS, MONTPELIER, V.T.**
All in a circle, bottom E. 3, aqua, 6⅞" 16.00 23.00

☐587 **MILLER, W.J., WOODSFIELD, O.**
In center a star all in a circle, clear, 6½" 12.00 17.00

☐588 **MILWAUKEE BOTTLING CO., N. PLATTE, NEB.**
In a sunken panel, aqua, 7¼" 16.00 23.00

☐589 **MINERAL WATER MFG. CO. THE, DEFIANCE, OHIO**
All in a circle, under it registered in back T.B.I.N.T.B.S.,
aqua, 7" 18.00 26.00

☐590 **MINOT BOTTLING WORKS CO., MINOT, N.D.**
All in a circle, aqua, 7" 16.00 23.00

☐591 **MISSOULA BOTTLING WORKS**
Clear or aqua, 7" 12.00 17.00

☐592 **MOE, J.M., TOMAHAWK, WIS.**
In three lines, clear, 5¼" 14.00 19.00

☐593 **MOE, J.M., TOMAHAWK, WIS.**
In three lines, aqua, 6¾" 12.00 17.00

☐594 **MOKELUMNE HILL SODA WORKS**
All in a circle, aqua, 6½" 12.00 17.00

☐595 **MONROE BOTTLING**
In a horse shoe letters, under it Works, Monroe, La., clear,
7¼" 12.00 17.00

☐596 **MONROE CIDER & VINEGAR, EUREKA, CAL.**
All in 3 lines, aqua 6¾" 12.00 17.00

☐597 **MOORE JOHN R., SWAINSBORO, GA.**
All in a circle under bottom 201, aqua, 6½" 12.00 17.00

☐598 **MORJARITY & CARROLL**
All in a circle, aqua, 6½" 12.00 17.00

☐599 **MORLEY C. VICTORIA, B.C.**
In 3 lines under bottom diff Nos., aqua, 7½" 23.00 32.00

☐600	**MORNINGSTAR D., SALEM, OHIO** *All in a circle under it T.B.N.T.B.S., aqua, 7"*	12.00	17.00
☐601	**MOULTON & SCOTT, NORTON, KANS.** *All in a circle, clear, 6½"*	15.00	20.00
☐602	**MT. CARMEL ICE & BOTTLING CO. MT., CARMEL, ILL.** *All in a circle, aqua, 6¾"*	12.00	17.00
☐603	**MT. HOOD SODA WATER, PORTLAND, ORE.** *Etc. all in a circle, panels base, light green, 7"*	16.00	23.00
☐604	**MOXIE** *In large letters near shoulder, aqua, 6½"*	45.00	60.00
☐605	**MULLEN B.J., ALBANY N.Y.** *In 3 lines under bottom (mong.) B.J.M., clear, 7¼"*	12.00	17.00
☐606	**MULLEN B.J.E.** *In ¼ moon letters in center mong. M.B.J.E., 1886, clear,* *7¼"*	12.00	17.00
☐607	**MULLINS, J.** *In 1" hollow letters under it Buffalo, N.Y. under bottom,* *"M", on base C & Co., aqua, 6½"*	11.00	15.00
☐608	**MUSKOGEE BOTTLING WORKS, MUSKOGEE, I.T.** *Aqua or clear, 6½"*	90.00	125.00
☐609	**MUSKOGEE BOTTLING WORK, MUSKOGEE, I.T.** *All in a circle Bottom E.R.R., aqua, 6⅜"*	100.00	130.00
☐610	*Same except panels base*	120.00	155.00
☐611	**MUSKOGEE BOTTLING WORKS, MUSKOGEE, I.T.** *All in a circle bottom, S, light aqua, 6¼"*	115.00	140.00
☐612	**MUSKOGEE FRUIT CO., MUSKOGEE, I.T.** *All in a circle, clear, 7"*	100.00	130.00
☐613	**MUSKEGON BOTTLING WORKS, MUSKEGON, MICH.** *Panels base, dark aqua, 6½"*	15.00	20.00
☐614	**MUTCHLER & WEISER, CHERRY VALE, KANS.** *All in a circle, clear, 6⅞"*	16.00	23.00

N

☐615	**NATIONAL BOTTLE WORKS** *John J. Ball Prop. York, Pa. all in a circle, under it reg.* *under bottom #4, clear, 6½"*	12.00	17.00
☐616	**NATIONAL, DOPE CO., BIRMINGHAM, AL.** *All in a water mellow letters, under it T.B.I.N.S., aqua, 8"* .	11.00	15.00
☐617	**NATIONAL SODA WATER** *All in a circle, aqua, 6½"*	12.00	17.00
☐618	**HOPE, NEW SELTZ & MINERAL WATER MFG. CO.** *L. M. 350 Bienville's N.O. La. in 7 lines, vertical, under bot-* *tom a anchor, aqua, 8"*	12.00	17.00
☐619	**NEW LIBERIA ICE & BOTTLING CO.** *In 4 lines, clear, 7"*	12.00	17.00
☐620	**NEW LIBERTY SODA CO.** *All in a circle, clear, 6½"*	12.00	17.00
☐621	**NEWMANN & FUNKE, DETROIT, MICH.** *All in a circle, under bottom N & F, aqua, 7"*	12.00	17.00

☐622 **NEWPORT MINERAL WATER CO., NEWPORT, KY.**
All in a circle, under it Reg. on base T.B.I.N.S. D.O.C. 92,
under bottom W., light aqua, 6⅞" **12.00** **17.00**

☐623 **NEW YORK BOTTLING WORKS, FAYETTE CITY**
All in a circle, under it SS, clear, 6½" **18.00** **25.00**

☐624 **NEVADA CITY SODA WATER WORKS**
E.T.R. Powell in 2 lines vertical lines, light green, 6¾" ... **12.00** **17.00**

☐625 **NEVADA CITY SODA WORKS**
In horse shoe letters under it E.T.R. Powell, aqua, 6½" ... **15.00** **20.00**

☐626 **NEVADA CO.**
Col. all in 5 lines, light green, 7" **12.00** **17.00**

☐627 **NEVADA SODA WATER**
Grass Valley all in a circle, aqua, 6½" **12.00** **17.00**

☐628 **NOCK'S BOTTLING WORKS, NILES, OHIO**
All in a circle, clear, 7¼" **12.00** **17.00**

☐629 **NORRIS, G, & CO. CITY BOTTLING WORKS, DETROIT, MICH.**
Cobalt, 6¼" **32.00** **41.00**

☐630 **NORTHROP & STURGIS CO., PORTLAND, OR.**
In 4 lines, light blue, 6¼" **16.00** **23.00**

☐631 **NORTHWESTERN BOTTLING CO., BUTTE, MONT.**
All in a circle, aqua, 6½" **33.00** **42.00**

☐632 **NORTHWESTERN BOTTLING WORKS, WASHINGTON, D.C.**
In center 1601 5th St. N.W.J.H. Schlueter, on back Reg.
N.T.B.S., 6½" **16.00** **23.00**

O

☐633 **O.K. CITY BOTTLING WORKS C.G. FROST**
All in a circle, bottom F., aqua, 6⅜" **16.00** **23.00**

☐634 **O.K. CITY BOTTLING WORKS C.G. FROST**
All in a circle, F, under bottom, amber, 6¾" **45.00** **60.00**

☐635 **OK MULGEE BOTTLING WORKS OK, MULGEE I.T.**
All in a circle, aqua, 6⅝" **170.00** **225.00**

☐636 **O.P.S.W. CO.**
In center, O & a bottle, Trade Mark, under it Oakland, Al.
Reg. on base T.B.T.N.S., aqua, 6½" **16.00** **23.00**

☐637 **OAKLAND STEAM SODA WORKS**
In center, a sun and 1882 - on bottom B.N.S., 6¼" **16.00** **23.00**

☐638 **OCEANVIEW BOTTLING WORKS**
N & B Prop. Mendoceno, Cal. all in a water mellow letters,
aqua, 6½" **13.00** **18.00**

☐639 **OGDEN, BOTTLING SODA WORKS, OGDEN, UTAH**
All in a circle, clear, 6¾" **16.00** **23.00**

☐640 **OHIO BOTTLING CO. THE CLEVELAND, O.**
In a circle in center, Eagle, Trade Mark Reg., aqua, 7¼" .. **16.00** **23.00**

☐641 **OHIO BOTTLING WORKS**
In horse shoe letters in center a (mong.) under it San-
dusky, O., light green, 5¼" **16.00** **23.00**

☐642   *Same except all in a circle, aqua, 5½″* **12.00**   **17.00**

☐643   **OHIO BOTTLING WORK**
In center mong. O.N. Sandusky, O. all in a circle, aqua, 5½″ **12.00**   **17.00**

☐644   **OHIO BOTTLING WORKS**
In ½ moon letters in center mong., under it in 1 line Sandusky, O., aqua, 7⅝″ **12.00**   **17.00**

☐645   **OKLAHOMA CITY BOTTLING WORKS**
Stiller Bros., all in a circle, under bottom S, aqua, 6¼″ ...   **16.00**   **23.00**

☐646   **OLIN & ORENDORFF, SO. PUEBLO, COL.**
All in a circle, aqua, 6¼″ **16.00**   **23.00**

☐647   **OLIN & ORENDORFF, SO. PUEBLO, COL.**
Aqua, 6½″ **16.00**   **23.00**

☐648   **OMAHA BOTTLING CO.**
All in a circle, aqua, 6¼″ **16.00**   **23.00**

☐649   **OMAHA BOTTLING CO.**
In 2 ½ moon lines under it Omaha Nebr. "O" under bottom, light aqua, 6½″ **16.00**   **23.00**

☐650   **OTTENVILLE, E. "MC"**
In 2 lines, under bottom "25", cobalt, 6″ **70.00**   **90.00**

☐651   **OTTENVILLE, NASHVILLE, TENN.**
All in a circle, blue **33.00**   **42.00**

☐652   **OTTENVILLE, E.**
"McC" on base, "25" under bottom, cobalt, 6″ **70.00**   **90.00**

☐653   **OTTENVILLE, NASHVILLE, TENN.**
Blue, 6½″ **70.00**   **90.00**

P

☐654   **PABLO & CO.**
Man in a canoe and dog, T.B.N.S., etc. N.O., aqua, 7″ **33.00**   **42.00**

☐655   **PABLO & CO. J.**
In center, man in canoe with dog, Trade Mark, on base T.B.N.S. Seltzer & Mineral Mfg. Nos.-475-477 & 479 St. Claude, St. N.D. **17.00**   **23.00**

☐656   **PABST & SONS, J.**
In ½ moon, in center a big P, under it Hamilton, aqua, 6½″ **15.00**   **20.00**

☐657   **PACIFIC BOTTLING WORKS**
In a horse shoe letters under it, Tacoma, Wash., light green, 6¾″ **15.00**   **20.00**

☐658   **PACIFIC PUGET SOUND SODA WORKS, SEATTLE, W.T.**
In 5 lines, under bottom a diamond with "A" in side of it, aqua, 6¾″ **100.00**   **140.00**

☐659   **THE PACOLET GRAPE JUICE CO., TRYON, N.C.**
In a circle, cob. top, aqua, 7″ **12.00**   **17.00**

☐660   **D. PALISER**
"Paliser" should be "Palliser" (misspelled), aqua, 6¼″ ..   **22.00**   **32.00**

☐661 **PALISRODE**
Eagle in center, on other side Bottling Co., shield and monogram in center, 6½" 12.00 17.00

☐662 **D. PALLISERS SONS**
Aqua, 7" 12.00 17.00

☐663 **PALMER S.C. WASHING CO.**
All in a circle, amber, 6¾" 60.00 80.00

☐664 **PAPE, THE CHAS BOTTLING WORKS, MARITTA, O.**
All in a circle, under it registered, in back T.B.I.N.S., aqua, 7" 12.00 17.00

☐665 **PARSON, T., SALT LAKE CITY**
In 3 lines, light blue, 6½" 15.00 20.00

☐666 **PASTOL, HENRY J., SACRAMENTO, CAL.**
All in 3 lines, aqua, 7" 12.00 17.00

☐667 **PAWNEE ICE & COLD STORAGE CO. BOTTLING WORKS, PAWNEE, OKLA.**
All in a circle, light aqua, 6¾" 16.00 23.00

☐668 **PEARSON BROS.**
Aqua, 6" 12.00 17.00

☐669 **PEARSON BROS.**
Placerville in 2 lines, aqua, 6½" 12.00 17.00

☐670 **PENNSBORO BOTTLING WORKS, PENNSBORO, W. VA.**
All in a circle, aqua, 6¾" 12.00 17.00

☐671 **PENSACOLA BOTTLING WORKS, PENSACOLA, FLA.**
All in a circle, dark aqua, 6" 15.00 20.00

☐672 **PEPSI-COLA**
In script, PENSACOLA, FLA., clear, 7" 235.00 315.00

☐673 **PERKINS, P.W.**
Star in center, Tannerville, N.Y., under bottom K. Hutter, 10 D.N.Y., aqua or clear, 6½" 12.00 17.00

☐674 **PERKINS STEAM BOTTLING WORKS**
L.O. Martz Proprietor, Perkins, Okla. all in a circle, aqua, 6½" 16.00 23.00

☐675 **PETER WESP & CO., BUFFALO, N.Y.**
All in a circle, under bottom, W.K., light blue, 6½" 12.00 17.00

☐676 **N.C. PETERS, LARAMIE, WYO.**
All in a circle, clear, 6" 15.00 21.00

☐677 **PHOENIX BOTTLING WORKS, MOBILE, ALA.**
All in a circle, under bottom B & H, aqua, 7" 12.00 17.00

☐678 **PIEDMONT STEAM**
In ½ moon letters, under it in 2 lines Bottling Co on base C. & Co LIM, clear, 6¼" 12.00 17.00

☐679 **PINE-APPLE NECTAR**
In front, back Curcia Bros. S.F., clear, 6¾" 12.00 17.00

☐680 **PINE BLUFF BOTTLING CO., PINE BLUFF, ARK.**
All in 4 lines, under bottom "P", aqua, 6" 15.00 20.00

☐681 **PINE BLUFF BOTTLING CO., PINE BLUFF, ARK.**
All in 4 lines, "P" under bottom, aqua, 6" 12.00 17.00

☐682 **PIONIER BOTTLING WORKS, BROOKSIDE, ALA.**
In a circle, aqua, 6½" 12.00 17.00

☐683 **PIONEER SODA WORKS**
Smith & Brian Co. Reno, Nev. all in a circle, aqua, 6¾" ... 16.00 23.00

☐684 **POLICASTRO STEAM CARBONATING CO.,
HELENA, ARK.**
Property of in 5 lines, panels, base, light blue, 6¾" **12.00** **17.00**
☐685 **PAUL POMEROY, LUDINGTON, MICH.**
Aqua, 7" **12.00** **17.00**
☐686 **POND BOTTLING CO., A.J. ENCLERT POND CREEK, O.T.**
All in a circle, on shoulder, R, clear, 6¾" **140.00** **190.00**
☐687 **POP BOTTLE, LABEL**
Aqua, 7" **11.00** **15.00**
☐688 **POPULAR SODA WORKS CO.**
All in a circle, aqua, 6½" **12.00** **17.00**
☐689 **PORT BOTTLING CO.**
All in a circle, sold at sloe 85, aqua, 6¼" **12.00** **17.00**
☐690 **PORTNER, ROBERT, BREW COMP**
*In center a diamond with Trade, Tivoli, Mark, under it Alex-
andria, Va. all in a circle, clear, 7½"* **15.00** **20.00**
☐691 **POTEAU BOTTLING**
*In horse shoe letters in center works, under it, bottom S,
Poteau I.T., aqua, 6½"* **140.00** **190.00**
☐692 **POTEAU BOTTLING WORKS, POTEAU, I.T.**
All in a circle no sundy bottom, aqua, 6⅝" **130.00** **175.00**
☐693 **POTEAU BOTTLING WORKS, POTEAU, I.T.**
All in a circle, under bottom S, aqua, 6¾" **140.00** **190.00**
☐694 **POUND CREEK BOTTLING CO., A.J. ENCLERT POUND
CHECK**
Should be Pound Creek, O.T., clear, 6¾" **135.00** **185.00**
☐695 **PRESCOTT BOTTLING WORKS, PRESCOTT, A.T.**
Clear, 6¾" **150.00** **210.00**
☐696 **PRIDE BOTTLING CO.**
All in a circle, aqua or clear, 6¼" **12.00** **17.00**
☐697 **PROPERTY OF C.C. BOTTLING CO.**
Clear, 6¾" **150.00** **210.00**
☐698 **PURDY BOTTLE CO.**
All in a circle, under bottom P., aqua, 6½" **12.00** **17.00**

Q

☐699 **QUERBES, ANDREW, SHREVEPORT, LA.**
All in a circle, Q under bottom, aqua, 6¾" **15.00** **20.00**

R

☐700 **R & W, LAS VEGAS, N.M.**
All in a circle, aqua, 7⅛" **16.00** **23.00**
☐701 **R & W, LAS VEGAS, N.M.**
In a sunken panel, Ten sided base, aqua, 7½" **16.00** **23.00**
☐702 **RAINIER, SODA CO. BOTTLING WORKS, SEATTLE**
All in a circle, clear, 7" **16.00** **23.00**
☐703 **RALSTON BOTTLING WORKS, RALSTON, O.T.**
Clear, panel base, clear, 7¼" **135.00** **180.00**
☐704 **RALU, H.A., COLON, R.P.**
*All in a water mellow letters, in back T.B.N.T.B.S., Panels
base, clear, 8"* **16.00** **23.00**

☐705 **RANFTS BOTTLING WORKS, JOLIET, ILL.**
Reimers & Voitik-successors, all in a circle, aqua, 6½″ .. **12.00** **17.00**

☐706 **RAVENNA, O.**
In center E.S.H. Bottling works all in a circle, aqua, 6¾″ . **12.00** **17.00**

☐707 **RAVENNA, O.S.**
In center E.S.H. Bottling works, all in a circle on base Reg.
T.B.N.T.B.S., A.B. Co., 0191, under bottom H., clear **23.00** **32.00**

☐708 **RAVIA BOTTLING WORKS, RAVIA, I.T.**
Under bottom 16, light aqua, 6¾″ **130.00** **175.00**

☐709 **RAY, JAS., SAVANNAH, GA.**
All in a circle, aqua, 6½″ **16.00** **23.00**

☐710 **REASBECK, C.J., MARTINS FERRY, O.**
on 2 panels, 10 panels bottle, aqua, 6⅞″ **16.00** **23.00**

☐711 **REASBECK, C.J., MARTINS FERRY, O.**
All in a circle, aqua, 6⅞″ **12.00** **17.00**

☐712 **REASBECK, P.H., BRADDOCK, PA.**
Clear or aqua, 7″ **12.00** **17.00**

☐713 **RED FOX BOTTLING WORKS, STEUBENVILLE, O.**
All in a circle, aqua, 6⅞″ **12.00** **17.00**

☐714 **REED, J.R., FERNANDINA, FLA.**
All in a circle, aqua, 6½″ **12.00** **17.00**

☐715 **REEDER BOTTLING WORKS, REEDER, N.D.**
All in a circle, aqua, 6¾″ **27.00** **36.00**

☐716 **REICHERT, F.A., WASHINGTON C.H. OHIO**
All in a circle, under it Reg., aqua, 7″ **12.00** **17.00**

☐717 **RENFRO MFG. CO., ATLANTA, GA.**
All in a circle, Panels base, under bottom A.C. Co. aqua,
7″ **12.00** **17.00**

☐718 **RICHARD & THALHEIMER**
Under bottom Dixie, clear or amethyst, aqua, 7½″ **12.00** **17.00**

☐719 **RICHARDSON, THE BOTTLING CO., MANSFIELD, O.**
All in a circle, aqua, 6¾″ **12.00** **17.00**

☐720 **RICHTER'S BOTTLING WORKS, FRESNO, CAL.**
In 3 lines, R under bottom, aqua, 6¼″ **12.00** **17.00**

☐721 **RIDER C.W., WATERTOWN, N.Y.**
All in a circle, amber, 7″ **23.00** **32.00**

☐722 **RIGGS & DOLAN**
Clear, 7″ **12.00** **17.00**

☐723 **RILEY, C.F.**
Near should, cobalt blue, 6½″ **32.00** **43.00**

☐724 **RINN EMIL F.**
Bottle Work, all in a circle, dark green, 6½″ **12.00** **17.00**

☐725 **RIVIERA MINERAL WATER, TYLER, TEXAS**
All in a circle, under bottom X Panels base, aqua, 7¼″ ... **15.00** **20.00**

☐726 **ROBERT J., UNION CITY, TENN.**
On 2 panels, 10 panels bottle on base C & Co., aqua, 6¾″ **12.00** **17.00**

☐727 **ROBINSON, A.B., BANGOR, ME.**
All in a circle, aqua, 7½″ **16.00** **23.00**

☐728 **ROCKY, THE, MOUNTAIN BOTTLE WORKS**
All in a circle, clear or aqua, 6½" 12.00 17.00

☐729 **ROESEN, W.F., JEFFERSON CITY, MO.**
In center lady with glass & banner riding, ale bottle on wheels, etc., aqua, 6¼" 16.00 23.00

☐730 **ROGATZ H.**
Chicago in center, mong. H. R. under bottom "28", aqua, 16½" 12.00 17.00

☐731 **ROLFE BOTTLING WORKS, ROLFE, IA.**
All in a circle, aqua, 6½" 12.00 17.00

☐732 **ROLL, HENRY, BLUEISLAND, ILL.**
In 3 lines under bottom H.R., clear, 7¼" 12.00 17.00

☐733 **ROSE BOTTLING WORKS**
Reg. 1909, Cleveland, O. all in a circle, aqua, 7" 12.00 17.00

☐734 **ROSE & CO. W.L., WHEELING, W. VA.**
All in a circle, aqua, 6½" 12.00 17.00

☐735 **RUBIN BROS**
In center R.B. Philade. all in a water mellow letters, under it Reg., aqua, 7¾" 12.00 17.00

☐736 **RUMFF, PETER**
Spokane Fall, all in a circle, clear or aqua, 6¾" 22.00 31.00

☐737 **RUMMEL, HENRY, CHARLESTON, W. VA.**
All in a circle, aqua, 7" 12.00 17.00

☐738 **RUMMEL, HENRY, CHARLESTON, W. VA.**
All in a circle, aqua, 6¾" 12.00 17.00

☐739 **RUONA, K.A. & CO., REG. ISHPEMING, MICH.**
All in a circle, quart, clear, 6¾" 15.00 20.00

☐740 **RUSSELL, GEORGE**
Aromatic, Gingerale, 369 Jay St. New Willonghyde, Brooklyn on 8 panels virtual, aqua, 6¾" 15.00 20.00

☐741 **RYAN BOTTLING WORKS, CHICAGO, ILL.**
All in a circle, aqua, 6⅜" 12.00 17.00

☐742 **RYAN BOTTLING WORKS**
Trade, R.B.W., Mark, Chicago, aqua, 6¾" 15.00 20.00

S

☐743 **S.C.O.N.M.W. ASS.**
In ½ moon in center Trade Mark, under it registered Sacramento, Cal., aqua, 6½" 12.00 17.00

☐744 **ST. HELENA SODA WORKS**
In 2 lines, aqua or clear, 6¼" 16.00 23.00

☐745 **ST. MARY'S BOTTLING WORKS, ST. MARY, O.**
All in a circle, aqua, 7" 15.00 20.00

☐746 **SALLISAW BOTTLING WORKS, SALLISAW, OKLA.**
All in a circle, 33 on base, aqua, 6¾" 15.00 20.00

☐747 **SALT LAKE, UTAH**
In a circle in center of it in a shield, The Danhalter Bottle Co., under bottom in a shield 3 cross, Denhalter, on base 40, clear, 6¾" 15.00 20.00

☐748 **SAN FRANCISCO SODA WORKS**
In 2 lines, aqua, 7" 12.00 17.00

☐749 **SAN JOSE SODA WORKS**
John Balzhouse, Prop. San Jose, Cal. all in a water mellow circle, aqua, 7" **15.00** **20.00**

☐750 **SANDER, JOHN, L.**
On back T.B.N.T.B.S., aqua, 7" **12.00** **17.00**

☐751 **SANDBERG BROW**
In 2 lines, aqua, 6⅜" **12.00** **17.00**

☐752 **SANDERS, JOHN L.**
In Baltimore, Md. in center a shield J.L.S., on base Reg. semi-round bottle, aqua, 7" **15.00** **20.00**

☐753 **SANDUSKY BOTTLING WORKS**
In 3 lines, 12 panels, on base G.H., aqua, 6¾" **16.00** **23.00**

☐754 **SAPULPA BOTTLING WORKS, SAPULPA, I.T.**
All in a circle, A.S., clear, 6½" **200.00** **285.00**

☐755 **SARATOGA BOTTLING WORKS**
In 2 lines, panels base, blue, 7" **45.00** **60.00**

☐756 **SASS & HAFNER**
In ¼ moon letters, in center of it Trade Mark, under it in 2 lines S & H Chicago, frosted blue, 7" **18.00** **25.00**

☐757 **SATINSKEY B.**
In script, 338 So 4th Phila. Reg. all in 4 lines, in back T.B.N.T.B.S., under bottom a star, aqua, 3" **12.00** **17.00**

☐758 **SCAMMON BOTTLING WORKS, SCAMMON, KANS.**
All in a circle, clear, 7" **16.00** **23.00**

☐759 **SCHAUR, FRED B.**
Registered, Utica, N.Y., clear, 6¾" **15.00** **20.00**

☐760 **SCHARR FRED**
In 2 lines, 6½" **12.00** **17.00**

☐761 **SCHEMRICH, L.G.**
In center a big S. Benwood, W. Va., clear, 6½" **12.00** **17.00**

☐762 **SCHERRER, JAS., MOLINE, ILL.**
All in a circle, aqua, 6¾" **12.00** **17.00**

☐763 **SCHILLE, P.**
Center (mong.) S.S. Columbus, O. all in a circle, aqua, 7" . **15.00** **20.00**

☐764 **SCHILLE P..**
Fancy script S.B. Columbus, Ohio, aqua, 7" **12.00** **17.00**

☐765 **SCHINERS, C.**
And Co., Sacramento, Cal. Capital Soda Works all in a circle, aqua, 6½" **12.00** **17.00**

☐766 **SCHLEGED G.W., SCHELEGED, CHANDLER, O.T.**
All in a circle, clear, 6¾" **130.00** **170.00**

☐767 **SCHLEGEL G.W.**
In horse shoe letters, under it Chandler O.T., on base S, light aqua, 6½" **160.00** **215.00**

☐768 **SCHMIDT, F., LEADVILLE, COLO.**
Blush aqua, 6½" **15.00** **20.00**

☐769 **SCHMIDT L., THOMASVILLE, GA.**
All in a circle, aqua, 6½" **14.00** **19.00**

☐770 **SCHMUCK'S GINGER ALE**
In 2 lines, vertical, 12 panels, amber, 8" **28.00** **37.00**

☐771 **SCHNERR, C., SACRAMENTO, CAL.**
In 3 lines, aqua, 7" **15.00** **20.00**

441

445

523

616

662

750

872

890

892

958

989

☐772 **SCHRADER, A.W.**
In ½ moon letters, in center a bottle, under it Scranton, Pa.,Panels base, under bottom S, in back "S", aqua, 6½ "   16.00   23.00

☐773 **SCHRAMM, HENRY**
Anvil in center, Fullersburge, III. all in a circle, aqua, 6¼ "   12.00   17.00

☐774 **SCHWCINHART, PITTSBURG**
In back 10th Ward Bottling Works, under bottom J.J., aqua, 6¾".......................................   12.00   17.00

☐775 **SCOTT, ED**
In center (mong.) Trade Mark Parkenburg, W. Va. all in a circle, aqua, 7".....................................   15.00   20.00

☐776 **SEATTLE SODA WORKS**
In a circle #16 under bottom, aqua, 6¾".............   12.00   17.00

☐777 **SEATTLE SODA WORKS**
In 2 lines, aqua, 6¾".............................   16.00   23.00

☐778 **SEETZ BROS., EASTON, PA.**
All in a circle, panel base, light green, 6½".............   15.00   20.00

☐779 **SELMA PRODUCE CO., SELMA, AL.**
All in a circle, aqua, 6¾".........................   12.00   17.00

☐780 **SERWAZI, P.J., MANAGUNK, PA.**
All in a circle, olive green, 7".....................   80.00   105.00

☐781 **SESSETON BOTTLING WORKS**
in 2 lines, aqua, 6¾".............................   12.00   17.00

☐782 **SEWELL BOTTLING WORKS, SEWELL, W. VA.**
All in a circle, aqua, 6½".........................   15.00   20.00

☐783 **SHAWEE BOTTLING WORKS F. SCHNEITER & CO. SHAWEE, OKLA.**
All in a circle, aqua, 6⅞".........................   14.00   19.00

☐784 **SHAWEE BOTTLING WORKS, SHAWEE, O.T.**
All in a circle back, this bottle not to be sold, under bottom F.S., yellow aqua, 6⅝".........................   160.00   215.00

☐785 **SHEEP**
In center of Trade Mark Reg. under it T.B.N.S., aqua, 6½"   15.00   20.00

☐786 **SHERIDAN BOTTLE WORK, SHERIDAN, ARK.**
Aqua, 6".......................................   12.00   17.00

☐787 **SHEYNNE BOTTLING WORKS, VALLEY CITY, N.D.**
Stevens & Co. Prop. all in a circle panels base, aqua, 6¾"   15.00   20.00

☐788 **SHIPLEY S.J., WHEELING, W. VA.**
All in a circle, aqua, 6⅞".........................   12.00   17.00

☐789 **SHONE, T.**
In one line, aqua, 6½".............................   12.00   17.00

☐790 **SHOULDER BOTTLING WORKS, THE, AKRON, O.**
All in a circle, aqua,.6¾".........................   12.00   17.00

☐791 **SING SING SODA WORKS**
In 3 lines in cathedral slug plate, aqua, 6½"............   16.00   23.00

☐792 **SISTECK, FRANK**
In horse shoe letters, under it Bottling Works, Irwin, Pa., panels base, on base C & Co. LIM No. 6, aqua, 7"........   15.00   20.00

☐793 **SMITH BERT, BROWNSVILLE, TENN.**
All in a circle, aqua, 7" 32.00   41.00

☐794 **SMITH & BRIAN CO.**
Pioneer Soda Works Reno, Nev. all in 3 lines, 4 Part Mold,
Light blue green 80.00 105.00

☐795 **SMITH DAVID, JOHNSTOWN, N.Y.**
In a circle, panels base, under bottom C26, aqua, 6¾" ... 12.00   17.00

☐796 **SMITH, DAVID, JOHNSTOWN, N.Y.**
In a circle letters, panels base, under bottom C-26, aqua,
6¾" 15.00   20.00

☐797 **SMITH, H.D., TENNILLE, GA.**
In a water mellow letters, on base T.B.N.T.B.S., clear, 6½"
.... 12.00   17.00

☐798 **SMITH, H.D., TENNILLE, GA.**
All in a circle, under it reg. T.B.N.T.B.S., clear, 6½" 12.00   17.00

☐799 **SMITH, H.D., TENNILLE, GA.**
All in a circle, no. 4 under bottom, clear, 7" 12.00   17.00

☐800 **SMITH WATER, ROCKWOOD, TENN.**
All in a circle, aqua, 6¾" 16.00   23.00

☐801 **SOMERSET ICE CO.**
Under it Steam Bottling Works, Somerset, Ky., all in a
horse shape letters panels, aqua, 7" 15.00   20.00

☐802 **SOUTH BEND SODA BOTTLING WORKS**
In a circle, in center of it South Bend, Wash., aqua, 7" ... 12.00   17.00

☐803 **SOUTH McALISTER**
In ½ moon letters, under it in 4 lines Bottling Works South
McAlister, Ind. Ter., aqua, 6½" 190.00 250.00

☐804 **SOUTH RANGE BOTTLING WORKS, SOUTH RANGE,**
MICH.
All in a circle, aqua, 6¾" 12.00   17.00

☐805 **SOUTHERN BOTTLING WORKS**
All in horse shoe letters, under it F.J. Hyatt, Prop.
Houston, Tx. in 4 lines, aqua, 7¼" 16.00   23.00

☐806 **SOUTHERN SODA WATER CO., NASHVILLE, TENN.**
All in a circle, on base D.O.C., 8 panels base, aqua, 7¼" . 15.00   20.00

☐807 **SOUTHWESTERN, THE BOTTLING CO., TULSA, I.T.**
Panels base, under bottom S, aqua, 7⅛" 190.00 250.00

☐808 **SPANCENBERGER, J. & W.**
In ½ moon letters, under it Springfield, O., aqua, 6¼" ... 15.00   20.00

☐809 **SPARKS & CHARLES E., DELEWARE**
In center of it, 210 E 4th St., Wilmington all in a circle on
base reg., aqua, 7¼" 12.00   17.00

☐810 **SPARKS & GRIFFITH, LEHIGH, I.T.**
All in a circle fluted base, aqua, 7¼" 115.00 140.00

☐811 **SPEIDEL BROS. (BOSTON)**
Aqua, 6" 12.00   17.00

☐812 **SPEIDEL, BROS, WHEELING W. VA.**
All in a circle, aqua, 7" 12.00   17.00

☐813 **SPENCER & BUTTLER, DES MOINES, IOWA**
State capital all on front, aqua, 7¼" 18.00   25.00

☐814 **SPRENGER J.J.**
In a horse shoe shape letters, under it Atlanta, Ga., aqua,
7" 12.00   17.00

☐815 **SPRING ST. BOTTLING WORKS**
J.A. Smith, Warwick, N.Y. all in a horse shoe letters, on
top Reg., aqua, 6¼" 12.00   17.00

☐816 **STAMP ICE & FULL CO., STAMP, ARK.**
All in a circle, under bottom S, aqua, 6¾" 15.00   20.00

☐817 **STANDARD BOTTLING CO., ATLANTA**
In back, T.B.T.B.R., aqua, 8" 12.00   17.00

☐818 **STANDARD BOTTLING CO., DENVER, COLO.**
In 2 lines (vertical), base S.B. Co., amethyst, 6⅛" 16.00   23.00

☐819 *Same except aqua* 11.00   15.00

☐820 **STANDARD BOTTLING CO., DENVER, COLO.**
All in a circle, clear or amethyst, 6½" 16.00   23.00

☐821 **STANDARD BOTTLING CO., FT. BRAGG**
All in 3 lines, aqua, 7" 15.00   20.00

☐822 **THE STANDARD BOTTLING CO., ODGEN, UTAH**
Clear, 6¾" 16.00   23.00

☐823 **STANDARD BOTTLING CO., SILVERTON, COLO.**
Peter Orello, Prop. all in a circle, aqua, 6¾" 15.00   20.00

☐824 **STANDARD BOTTLING, DENVER, COLO.**
In 3 lines (vertical), clear, 6¼" 22.00   31.00

☐825 **STANDARD, THE, BOTTLING MFG., CRIPPLE CREEK,**
COLO.
All in a circle, on bottom #20, clear, 6½" 18.00   27.00

☐826 **STANDARD BOTTLING WORKS, MINNEAPOLIS, MINN.**
All in a circle, K.R. under bottom, amber, 6¼" 27.00   37.00

☐827 **STANDARD BOTTLING WORKS, MINNEAPOLIS, MINN.**
All in a circle H.R. on base, amber, 6½" 55.00   75.00

☐828 **STANDARD BOTTLING WORKS, MINNEAPOLIS, MINN.**
In 4 lines, amber, 6¾" 30.00   40.00

☐829 **STAR BOTTLING**
In center a star under it Works Co., under it Houston,
Tx.,on shoulder 3 stars, aqua, 6½" 12.00   17.00

☐830 **STAR BOTTLING WORKS**
In ½ moon letters in center a 5 points star in center of
it,(mong.) under it in 2 lines Reg. New Haven, Conn., on
base T.B.N.T.B.S., aqua, 6" 12.00   17.00

☐831 **STAR BOTTLING WORKS**
Under it a star (mong.), in center of it Reg. New Haven,
Conn., on base T.B.N.T.B.S., aqua, 6½" 12.00   17.00

☐832 **STAR BOTTLING WORKS, ANADARO, O.T.**
T & M, 16 on base, clear, 6⅝" 170.00   220.00

☐833 **STAR BOTTLING WORKS, THE, CINCINNATI, O.**
In center a star with KK Trade Mark all in a circle, under it
Reg. T.B.N.T.B.S. in 3 lines, aqua, 7" 15.00   20.00

☐834 **STAR BOTTLING WORKS, GALENA, KANS.**
Panels bottom, star on base, aqua, 7¼" 18.00   27.00

☐835 **STAR BOTTLING WORKS, ST. PAUL, MINN.**
Con. 8 Fl. oz., in back T.B.I.N.S., aqua, 6¾" 15.00   20.00

☐836 **STAR BOTTLING WORKS, SANDUSKY, O.**
All in a circle, aqua, 6¼" 12.00   17.00

☐837 **STAR BOTTLING WORKS, SANDUSKY, O., THE**
Around a star, aqua, 6¾" 12.00 17.00

☐838 **STAR BOTTLING WORKS, STAR, N.C.**
All in a circle, aqua, 6¾" 32.00 42.00

☐839 **STAR BOTTLING WORKS CO.**
*All in a water mellow letters, in center faceted star, under
it in 2 lines, Houston, Tx., clear, 7¼"* 16.00 23.00

☐840 *Same except flat star* 12.00 17.00

☐841 *Same except on shoulder 3 star* 16.00 23.00

☐842 **STEAM BOTTLING WORKS**
*In center, anchor, Trade Mark, in ½ moon letters, under it
Reg. Shawnee, O.T., aqua, 6½"* 170.00 230.00

☐843 **STEAM BOTTLING WORKS, SHAWNEE, OKLA. I.T.**
Clear, 7" 95.00 130.00

☐844 **STENSON, HAS.**
In back Chicago, Ill., aqua, 6¼" 12.00 17.00

☐845 **STETSON, JAS, CHICAGO, ILL.**
In 2 panels, under bottom J.S., light blue, 6¾" 15.00 20.00

☐846 **STEPHEN, P.G.**
Hexagon shape (panels bottle), aqua, 7" 16.00 23.00

☐847 **STEPHENS & JOSE**
In ½ moon letters, under it Virginia City, Nevada, aqua, 7"
.... 18.00 27.00

☐848 **STERLING SPRING MINERAL WATER CO.**
*In (mong.) "PL" Hancock, Mid all in a circle under bottom
PL, aqua, 6¾"* 12.00 17.00

☐849 **STERLING SPRING MINERAL WATER CO., .P.L.**
*(mong.) Hancock, Mich. all in a circle, under bottom P.L.,
aqua, 6¾"* 12.00 17.00

☐850 **STEUBEN B.T. IOWA**
In 3 lines, aqua, 7" 12.00 17.00

☐851 **STEUBENVILLE BOTTLING**
*In a horse shoe letters, in center Works, under it J.W.
Sharp, aqua, 6½"* 15.00 20.00

☐852 **STEUBENVILLE BOTTLE WORKS, J.W.**
Sharp all in a horse shoe letters, aqua, 6½" 12.00 17.00

☐853 **STILLWATER BOTTLING WORKS**
G.F. Knowles, Stillwater, Okla., aqua, 6¾" 16.00 23.00

☐854 **STILLWATER BOTTLING WORKS**
G.F. Knowles, Stillwater, Okla., aqua, 6¾" 12.00 17.00

☐855 **STOCKDER, F., CANNON CITY, COLO.**
All in a circle, aqua, 7" 12.00 17.00

☐856 **STOLEN FROM, EUREKA BOTTLING WORKS, FT. SMITH,
ARK.**
3 on base, aqua, 6¾" 12.00 17.00

☐857 **STROUD BOTTLING WORKS, STROUD, OKLA.**
All in a circle, light aqua, 6½" 12.00 17.00

☐858 **STROUD BOTTLING WORKS STILLER BROS., STROUD,
OKLA.**
All in a circle, under bottom S, light aqua, 6½" 12.00 17.00

☐859 **SUCCESS BOTTLING WORKS**
In 2 lines, clear, 6¼" 12.00 17.00

☐860 **SUMTER BOTTLER BOTTLING WORKS, SUMTER, S.C.**
All in a circle, on base T.B.R., clear, 7" 12.00 17.00
☐861 **SUMTER BOTTLING WORKS, SUMTER, S.C.**
All in a circle, aqua, 6½" 16.00 23.00
☐862 **SUNSET BOTTLING WORKS**
All in a circle, aqua, 7" 12.00 17.00
☐863 **SUPERIOR BOTTLING WORKS, SUPERIOR, WIS.**
Aqua, 7½" 12.00 17.00
☐864 **SUPERIOR BOTTLING WORKS, SUPERIOR, WIS.**
All in a circle, aqua, 6⅜" 12.00 17.00
☐865 **SUTTON BOTTLING WORKS, SUTTON, W. VA.**
In center Juepcene & Walker Props. (mong.) J.W., under it
T.B.N.T.B.S., aqua, 7" 15.00 20.00
☐866 **SWINDLER & BERNSTEIN, CHICAGO**
All in a circle, S.B. under bottom, aqua, 6½" 16.00 23.00

T

☐867 **T.H.**
Monogram, in side of slug plate, aqua, 6½" 12.00 17.00
☐868 **T. & S. PORT TOWNSEND SODA WORKS P.T.W.T.**
In 4 lines vert., greenish aqua, 6⅛" 22.00 32.00
☐869 **TABLE WATER CO.**
Reg. Hallett all near top, in center an Indian head, under it
Nonquit Trade Mark Bridgeport, Conn., on base
T.B.N.T.B.S., clear, 7½" 16.00 23.00
☐870 **TALLODEGA, AL.**
Coca-Cola in block letters, clear, 7" 130.00 190.00
☐871 **TAMPA BOTTLING WORKS, TAMPA, FLA.**
All in a circle, clear, 6½" 12.00 17.00
☐872 **TAMPA CIDER & VINEGAR CO.**
All in a circle, clear, 6" 12.00 17.00
☐873 **TANNER, T.J., PORT TWONSEND, WASH.**
In 4 lines, aqua, 7" 35.00 50.00
☐874 **TAWASENTHA SPRINGS CO.**
In 3 lines, under it Indian maid Trade Mark, under it Cincin-
nati, O., aqua, 6¾" 15.00 20.00
☐875 **TAYLOR E., ERIE, PA.**
Around bottle, large T under bottom, aqua, 6¼" 12.00 17.00
☐876 **TAYLOR, ERIE PA.**
Around bottle, large T under bottom, aqua, 6¼" 12.00 17.00
☐877 **TAYLOR, JAS., F., NEW BERN, N.C.**
All on front, aqua, 6¾" 16.00 23.00
☐878 **TAYLOR SODA WATER MFG. CO., BOISE, IDA.**
All in a circle, panels bottom, light aqua, 6¼" 16.00 23.00
☐879 **TEXAS PRODUCE CO., TEXARKANA, TEX.**
All in a circle, clear, 6¼" 15.00 20.00
☐880 **THIMELIN, THOS., SOUTH BRIDGE, MASS.**
All in a circle, aqua, 6½" 15.00 20.00
☐881 *Same except pale aqua* 12.00 17.00
☐882 **THOMAS, W.Z., NILES, OHIO**
All in a circle, clear, 8" 12.00 17.00

☐883 **THOMAS W.Z., NILES, OHIO**
All in a circle, T.B.N.T.B.S. on base, clear, 8¼" **15.00** **20.00**

☐884 **TIMPSON BOTTLING WORKS, TIMPSON, TEXAS**
All in a circle, panels base, under bottom J & B, aqua, 7" . **16.00** **23.00**

☐885 **TIP TOC BOTTLING WORKS, M & C, GREENWICH, N.Y.**
All in a diamond shape letters, in back T.B.N.T.B.S., aqua,
6½" **16.00** **23.00**

☐886 **TIPTON BOTTLING WORKS, TIPTON, IOWA**
In many diff. town in Iowa, clear or aqua, 7" **12.00** **17.00**

☐887 **TOLLE BOTTLING WORKS, T., LITCHFIELD, ILL.**
All in a circle, clear, 6½" **12.00** **17.00**

☐888 **TONOPAH SODA WORK, NEV.**
In 3 lines, clear, 6¾" **27.00** **36.00**

☐889 *Also greenish aqua* **27.00** **36.00**

☐890 **TOWNE'S**
On front, aqua, 7" **12.00** **17.00**

☐891 **TRINIDAD**
In center BOTTLING WORKS, Trinidad, Colo. all in a circle,
aqua, 7" **23.00** **32.00**

☐892 **TRINIDAD BOTTLING WORKS**
All in a circle, clear or amethyst, 6½" **16.00** **23.00**

☐893 **TULSA BOTTLING WORKS, TULSA, I.T.**
All in a circle, aqua, 6⅛" **135.00** **185.00**

☐894 **TUSKALOOSA BOTTLING WORKS, C.C. SIMPSON**
MGA Tuskaloosa, Ala. all in a circle, back T.B.N.T.B.S.,
aqua, 6½" **12.00** **17.00**

☐895 **TUSKGEE, ALA**
In block letters, clear, 6¼" **16.00** **23.00**

☐896 **TUSKGEE COCA-COLA BOTTLING (ALA.)**
All in a circle, clear, 6½" **120.00** **165.00**

☐897 **TWIN CITY BOTTLING WORKS, DENNISON, O.**
All in a circle, aqua, 6½" **12.00** **17.00**

☐898 **TWIN SPRINGS BOTTLING WORKS, KANSAS CITY, MO.**
All in a circle, under bottom P.S., aqua, 9½" **15.00** **20.00**

☐899 **TYLER UNION BOTTLING WORKS**
All in a circle, aqua, 6¾" **16.00** **23.00**

U

☐900 **U.N. BOTTLING**
In center WORKS, N.Y. Canandaiqua all in a circle under it
Reg. in back, T.B.N.T.B.S., under bottom "33", clear, 6¾" **12.00** **17.00**

☐901 **UNAKA BOTTLING WORKS, ERWIN, TENN.**
All in a circle, on base C.G. Co., aqua, 7" **15.00** **20.00**

☐902 **UNION B. WORKS, HOUSTON, TX.**
Interlocking F.P. & Co. in triangle, Trade Mark, aqua, 7½" **16.00** **23.00**

☐903 **UNION BOTTLING CO., SEATTLE**
All in a circle, aqua, 7" **16.00** **23.00**

☐904 **UNION BOTTLING WORK**
All in a circle, aqua, 6¾" **16.0** **23.00**

☐905 **UNION BOTTLING WORK**
In ½ moon letters, under it in 4 lines F.H. Potthoff & Co.
Props., Houston, Tx., in back Interlocking E.P. & Co. in
triangle, under it Trade Mark, aqua, 7¼" **23.00** **32.00**

☐906 **UNION BOTTLING WORK**
In ½ moon letters, under it Houston, Tex. in triangle, Inter-
locking F.P. & Co., under it Trade Mark, clear or aqua, 7½"
.... **16.00** **23.00**

☐907 **UNION BOTTLING WORKS**
In horse shoe letters, in center of it "U", under it Eveleth,
Minn., aqua, 6¾" **12.00** **17.00**

☐908 **UNION BOTTLING WORKS, MILWAUKEE**
All in a circle, under it T.B.I.N.S., aqua, 6¾" **12.00** **17.00**

☐909 **URMANN, A.**
Under bottom, 649, aqua, 7¼" **12.00** **17.00**

☐910 **UVALDE BOTTLING WORKS, UVALDE, TEXAS**
Aqua, 6¼" **12.00** **17.00**

V

☐911 **VALAER C., BOTTLING WORKS, CHARLOTTE, N.C.**
All in a circle, aqua, 6¾" **23.00** **32.00**

☐912 **VANCOUVER SODA WORKS, VANCOUVER, WASH.**
Star & Trade Mark in a sunken Panel, aqua, 7½" **16.00** **23.00**

☐913 **VARUNA MINERAL WATER**
Wills in a horse shoe letters, in center Richwood, Ohio,
under it 1. Miles Pro. T.B.N.S. M.B.R., clear, 6½" **12.00** **17.00**

☐914 **VERNER J. NO.**
In center a beaver, under it Toronto, aqua, 7" **12.00** **17.00**

☐915 **VERNON & O. BRYAN**
'X' under bottom, 7" **12.00** **17.00**

☐916 **VETH & HAZEK, RACINE, WIS.**
In a circle, V & H under bottom, aqua, 7" **12.00** **17.00**

☐917 **VICKSBURG STEAM BOTTLING WORKS**
"P" under bottom, aqua, 6¼" **12.00** **17.00**

☐918 **VIEREGG, GRAND ISLAND, NEB.**
All in a circle, aqua, 6¾" **16.00** **23.00**

☐919 **VINITA BOTTLING CO., VINITAT. I.T.**
All in a circle, aqua, 6⅝" **150.00** **210.00**

☐920 **VINITA BOTTLING WORKS, VINITA**
All in a circle, I.T. under bottom 33, light aqua, 6¾" **150.00** **210.00**

☐921 **VOCELGESANG, H.**
In ½ moon letters, under it, Elk. Canton, O., aqua, 7½" .. **15.00** **20.00**

☐922 **VOGEL BOTTLING WORKS, HOUSTON, TX.**
All in a circle, on base T.B.N.T.B.S., aqua or clear, 8¼" .. **16.00** **23.00**

☐923 **VOGEL, HENRY M.**
Norwalk Bottling Works Norwalk, O., all in a circle, aqua,
6½" **12.00** **17.00**

W

☐ 924 **W.F.& S.**
*Star in center, Mil's under bottom, a star in center of bot-
tle, aqua, 6¾"* **16.00** **23.00**

☐ 925 **W.H.H.**
*In one inch letters Chicago, Ill., panels base, light blue,
6¾"* **15.00** **20.00**

☐ 926 *Same except in back I.G. Co. blue* **19.00** **25.00**

☐ 927 **WAGNER, B.W., WAGONER, I.T.**
All in a circle, panel base, aqua, 7" **130.00** **170.00**

☐ 928 **WAGNER W.K.**
In ¼ moon letters under it, Youngstown, Ohio, aqua, 6⅝" **15.00** **20.00**

☐ 929 **WAGNER BROS.**
In ½ moon, under it Tiffin, Ohio, aqua, 6¾" **15.00** **20.00**

☐ 930 **WAGONER BOTTLING WORKS, WAGONER, I.T.**
All in a circle, under bottom G, Panels base, aqua, 7⅛" ... **140.00** **190.00**

☐ 931 **WAHRENBERGER J., NEW HAVEN, CONN.**
In 4 lines, aqua, 7" **15.00** **20.00**

☐ 932 **WAIALNA SODA WORKS**
In 2 lines (Hawaii), aqua, 7¾" **23.00** **32.00**

☐ 933 **WALDRON BOTTLING WORKS, WALDRON, ARK.**
All in a circle, clear, 6⅜" **15.00** **20.00**

☐ 934 *Same as above except aqua* **15.00** **20.00**

☐ 935 **WALLER R.**
*In center 176 Spring St. Saratoga, N.Y., in back
T.B.N.T.B.S., aqua, 7½"* **15.00** **20.00**

☐ 936 **WALLIS J.A., BANGOR, ME.**
All in a circle, under bottom W., 6⅝" **16.00** **23.00**

☐ 937 **WARNER P.**
*421 So. 2nd St. Philad., Pa. all in a circle, in back inside of
a star Trade Mark, under it T.B. Reg., panels base, clear,
7¾"* **15.00** **20.00**

☐ 938 **WATERLOO BOTTLING WORKS**
Waterloo in water mellow circle, aqua, 6½" **12.00** **17.00**

☐ 939 **WATERLO BOTTLING WORKS, WATERLO, IOWA**
All in a circle, aqua, 6½" **15.00** **20.00**

☐ 940 **WAXAHACHIE, TEXAS**
In 2 lines, aqua, 7" **15.00** **20.00**

☐ 941 **WEBB & RILEY, JOLIET, ILL.**
Trade Mark all in a circle, aqua, 7" **12.00** **17.00**

☐ 942 **WEIGEL, H.**
Under botttom "W", aqua, 6½" **12.00** **17.00**

☐ 943 **WEIGEL, H., YORK, PA.**
All in a circle, Big W under bottom, green aqua, 7" **15.00** **20.00**

☐ 944 **WEIGEL, R.**
*in center 176 Spring St., Saratoga, N.Y., back TBNTBS,
aqua, 7½"* **16.00** **23.00**

☐ 945 **WEILER, PINE BLUFF, ARK.**
All in a circle, aqua, 6¾" **15.00** **20.00**

☐946 **WEILER, R., SARATOGA, N.Y.**
All in a circle, aqua, 6½" 15.00 20.00

☐947 **WELLS STEAM BOTTLING WORKS, GALVESTON, TX.**
*Caveman carrying a huge club over shoulder, Trade Mark
on back side, 6¾"* 23.00 32.00

☐948 **WENGS & SON, CARLISLE, PA.**
In a horse shoe letters, aqua, 6¾" 12.00 17.00

☐949 **WENGR, G.R. & SONS, CARLISLE, PA.**
In horse shoe shape letters, aqua, 6¾" 15.00 20.00

☐950 **WENTZ, FRANK, LEWISTOWN, PA.**
All in a circle, light blue, 6½" 12.00 17.00

☐951 **WERLE, C.A.**
In ½ moon letters, under it Nok Hill, aqua, 7" 12.00 17.00

☐952 **WERRBACK, MILWAUKEE**
*In 2 lines, on base I.G. Co., under bottom L.W. in back
T.B.N.T.B.S., Pure Ginga beer on shoulder, aqua, 7"* 16.00 23.00

☐953 **WESLEY CUNNINGHAM**
*In ½ moon letters, under it Hampton, Va. Registered
under bottom FTS, panels base, clear, 7½"* 16.00 23.00

☐954 **WEST END BOTTLING WORKS, LITTLE ROCK, ARK.**
All in a circle, under bottom W.E., aqua, 7" 15.00 20.00

☐955 **WESTERHOLM & CO.**
*In a horse shoe letters, in center mong. C.W. Co. Reg., on
base A.G.W.L., under bottom, mong. C.W.C., aqua, 7"* ... 15.00 20.00

☐956 **WHALEN & FARRELL, WILKESBARRE, PA.**
In 2 lines on shoulder, under bottom FW, aqua, 6⅝" 15.00 20.00

☐957 **WHEELER BROS.**
*On shoulder Waukesha, Soda Water Co. Waukesha, Wis.
all in a circle, clear, 6¼"* 12.00 17.00

☐958 **WHELAN, D.J.**
On back "Mineral Water", aqua, 7½" 16.00 23.00

☐959 **WHELAN & FERGUSON**
*In center Trade Mark, monogram circle etc. Reg., Halifax
N.S. Canada in 3 lines, vertical semi-round bottom, aqua,
7½"* 16.00 23.00

☐960 **WHITE JNO., ST. LOUIS**
All in a circle, aqua, 6¾" 15.00 20.00

☐961 **WHITE W.P.**
All in a circle, clear, 7" 12.00 17.00

☐962 **WHITE, W.P., DANIELSON, CONN.**
*All in a circle, on base Registered, semi round bottom,
clear, 6"* 15.00 20.00

☐963 **WHITMER & BARNETT, REG. CANTON, O.**
All in a circle, aqua, 6⅝" 12.00 17.00

☐964 **WIEGAND, CHR., LAS VEGAS, N.M.**
All in a circle, panels base, clear, 7⅛" 27.00 36.00

☐965 **WIEGAND, CHRIS, E. LAS VEGAS, N.M.**
All in a circle, panels base, aqua, 7¼" 16.00 23.00

☐966 **WIESER, ADAM**
Spokane in 2 lines, aqua, 7" 16.00 23.00

☐967 **WIGGS J.J. & CO., LITTLE ROCK, ARK.**
In a circle, aqua, 6¾" 15.00 20.00

☐968 **WIGGS, J.J. & CO., LITTLE ROCK, ARK.**
All in a circle, aqua, 6¾" 12.00 17.00

☐969	**WILBURTON BOTTLING WORKS**		
	All in a circle, (Okl.), aqua, 6¾"	32.00	42.00
☐970	**WILLIAMS BROS.**		
	In ½ moon letters, under it in 2 lines San Jose, Cal., aqua, 7½"	15.00	20.00
☐971	**WILLIAMS, P.H.**		
	In ½ moon letters, under it Gross Valley, light green, 6½"	15.00	20.00
☐972	**WILLIAMS, S.M., MATTEAWAN, N.Y.**		
	On front, SMW mong. on back, panels base, clear, 6½" ..	15.00	20.00
☐973	**WILLINGTON, N.C.**		
	In 2 lines, clear	12.00	17.00
☐974	**WISEOLA BOTTLING CO., BIRMINGHAM**		
	All in a circle, under bottom a star, clear, 7"	12.00	17.00
☐975	**WISEOLA BOTTLING CO.**		
	All in a circle, under bottom a star, clear, 7"	12.00	17.00
☐976	**WOODBURY, H., YORK, PA.**		
	All in a circle, aqua, 7"	15.00	20.00
☐977	**WOOTAN WELLS CO.**		
	By Wootan Wells, Texas in Vertical lines, aqua, 6½"	12.00	17.00
☐978	**WRIGHT FRANK**		
	Registered, Norwalk, O. all in a circle, aqua, 6½"	12.00	17.00
☐979	**WRIGHTSVILLE BOTTLING WORKS, WRIGHTSVILLE, GA.**		
	All in a circle, aqua, 6½"	12.00	17.00
☐980	**WUHBMANN, JOHN, ELLERVILLE, N.Y.**		
	All in a circle, light green, 6½"	12.00	17.00

Y

☐981	**YORK MINERAL WATER CO., E.W.**		
	In center a bull, all in a circle Cincinnati, O., aqua, 7"	16.00	23.00
☐982	**YOUNG, A., BUFFALO, N.Y.**		
	In 2 lines, Double "Y" on bottom, light green, 6⅞"	12.00	17.00
☐983	**YUNCKER BOTTLING CO., TACOMA, WASH.**		
	All on front, aqua, 7"	16.00	23.00

Z

☐984	**ZANG & KAPMEYER, SCRANTON, PA.**		
	In 3 lines panel top, aqua, 6¾"	12.00	17.00
☐985	**ZEMMERMAN, B., NEW BRUNSWICK, N.J.**		
	All in a circle, Numbers under bottom, in back T.B.N.T.B.S., aqua, 7"	12.00	17.00
☐986	**ZIEGERS SODA WATER, TUSCON, ARIZ.**		
	All in a circle, under bottom Z, panels base, aqua, 6½" ..	16.00	23.00
☐987	**ZIMMERMAN, MRS. B., NEW BRUNSWICK, N.J.**		
	All in a circle, under it T.B.N.T.B.S., on bottom O.D., clear or amethyst, 6½"	12.00	17.00
☐988	**ZIMMERMAN, MRS. B., NEW BRUNSWICK, N.J.**		
	In two ½ moon lines, under it N.J., on base T.B.N.T.B.S., clear, 6½"	18.00	26.00
☐989	**ZIPPERER, OTTO J**		
	Aqua, 6½"	12.00	17.00

INK

Ink bottles have a lengthy history and quite likely have been made in a greater variety of designs than any other single class of bottles. Figurals are numerous among ink bottles, some of them of extremely imaginative shapes and high-quality modeling.

You might wonder why a product so cheap as ink would be retailed in decorative bottles. There is no mystery about this. Most other things sold in bottles were quickly used up and the bottle discarded; or the bottle and its contents were kept in a cupboard out of view. Ink bottles not only remained in the home for a while (one bottle might last for months or longer), they were prominently displayed on desks in offices, dens and studies. The manufacturers felt it was advantageous for ink bottles to be styled as ornamental objects and be suitable beside fine writing sets or any objets d'art that might be on the desk. Very likely, many buyers in the late 1800's chose their ink not by brand, but by the bottle's appeal.

Ink has been, of course, manufactured since ancient times for use with various kinds of writing pens. Ink writing in the form of Egyptian hieroglyphics dates to at least 3,000 B.C. and possibly earlier. Prior to ink, writing and drawing was done by etching into stone. The Egyptians used paper made from the dried plinth of the papyrus plant, native to the Nile valley. Neither they nor *any other* people of the ancient world wrote with quill pens, a common misbelief fostered (in part) by Hollywood "Biblical epics" showing scribes writing with quills. There were two common varieties of pens in the ancient world. One was called a stylus and was made of metal. It came to a point at the tip, something like a modern pen, but had no provision for holding the ink and had to be constantly dipped and redipped. After writing a few strokes it was dry. There was also another problem with the ancient stylus: it had a habit of tearing the papyrus which was delicate. In an attempt to solve both dilemmas, reed pens were introduced. These were common field reeds pulled from the ground. The tip was chewed to feather it and make it like a brush. This held more ink and was not as hard on the papyrus. Quill pens, such as were used in George Washington's time, did not make their appearance until about the 6th century A.D., or about 1,500 years ago.

Ink has been made and sold in many different ways. At certain times, such as in the European middle ages, it was in short supply and very expensive, and the difficulty of obtaining ink was responsible in part for the high rate of illiteracy. The Egyptians used various vegetable dyes for their inks. Ancient Romans used the black bile secreted by the cuttlefish as an ingredient in ink. Later, medieval monasteries often depended upon making ink from soot and oils.

It was not possible, in most parts of Europe, to buy ready-made ink until around the year 1500. This era saw the dawn of the stationer's shop which at that time mainly sold books, but also dealt in writing materials. (There were no bookshops at that time: books were available either from a stationer or directly from the printer.)

The ink used around 1500 was not as good as the ink made prior to this time. some of its predecessors. Many experiments were made over the succeeding years, with changes in ingredients to improve quality and reduce price. Ink was so expensive in some places — such as Italy — that students who did a great deal of writing were forced to water down their ink. The "faded" writing often seen in early letters and notebooks has not faded at all — it originally appeared that way.

Prior to the 18th century, ink was generally sold in copper or brass containers, and this is how the common people used it. Well-to-do persons transferred the contents of these jars into their ornate silver inkwells. The nobility of Europe and other wealthy individuals often owned magnificent inkwells on which their family coat of arms was engraved. These are now very desirable and costly collectors' items.

Ink was being sold in glass and pottery bottles in England in the 1700's, but the bottling was done by retailers rather than manufacturers. Hence, these bottles carry no brand names and often cannot be identified as having contained ink. The first patent for the commercial production of ink was granted in England in 1792. In America, the first patent for ink was given to Maynard and Noyes of Boston in 1816. Naturally, patents on as ink only covered the specific recipe used by the maker or developer; patents did not prevent rivals from selling ink made from other formulas. Until 1816, most of the ink used in the U.S. had been imported from Britain and France and was fairly costly.

The first American-made master bottles — bottles containing a pint or quart of ink from which inkwells could be filled in offices and schools — were of poor quality glass containing many bubbles and other imperfections.

The early ink industry in America was hampered by the lack of good writing pens. Quills, which were awkward to use, continued to be used until the mid 19th century. Peregrine Williamson of Baltimore invented a metal pen (really a re-invention of the Egyptian stylus) in 1809, but it failed to win widespread acceptance until 1858. In that year, Richard Esterbrook opened a factory to make metal pens at Camden, New Jersey. These pens were not an immediate success, as they had to be dipped in the ink often having no ink supply of their own. This resulted in messy ink spills. Bottle manufacturers set about to create "untippable" bottles and this gave birth to many unusual shapes and designs. Umbrella-shaped ink bottles were popular, as were the teakettle shapes — complete with pouring spout. Other shapes included turtles, barrels, shoes, buildings, boats, schoolhouses and cathedrals.

A man named Hyde, from Reading, Pennsylvania, invented the fountain pen in 1830. But for one reason or another — lack of financing, or advice of people who thought the idea was silly — it was not commercially manufactured until 1884. As the fountain pen gained in use, ink bottles gradually became plainer. Since the pen now carried its own ink supply, it was not necessary to keep ink on the desk top. Bottles could be stored in drawers where they were out of sight. With nobody seeing them, it was unnecessary to make them fancy. Thus, the majority of decorative American ink bottles belong to the era dating from 1860 to about 1890.

INK BOTTLES

A

NO.	DESCRIPTION	PRICE RANGE	
☐1	**ALLING'S**		
	Sheared top and teapot spout, green, 2¼"	9.00	12.00
☐2	**ALLING'S INK**		
	Triangular, green, 1⅞" x 2¼"	14.00	21.00
☐3	**ALONZO FRENCH**		
	Barrel, Pat. March 1st, 1870, aqua, 2" tall, 2" long	20.00	28.00
☐4	**ANGUS & CO.**		
	Cone, aqua, 3½"	4.00	6.00
☐5	**ANTOINE ET FILS**		
	Straight top with pouring lip, brown pottery, 8⅜"	7.00	10.00
☐6	**P & J ARNOLD**		
	Collar with pouring lip, brown, 9¼"	9.00	12.00
☐7	**ARNOLD'S**		
	Round, clear or amethyst, 2½"	5.00	7.00
☐8	**A3**		
	Pat July 9, 1895 under bottom, aqua, 2¼"	7.00	9.00

B

NO.	DESCRIPTION	PRICE RANGE	
☐9	**B & B**		
	Pottery bottle, tan, 7½"	5.00	8.00
☐10	*BELL, sheared top, clear or amethyst, 3"*	5.00	7.00
☐11	*BELL, label, crock, double ring top, tan*	13.00	20.00
☐12	*BELL TOP, on side and under bottle patd. Apr. 21st 1868, flare top, ring on base and shoulder, aqua, 2½" x 2¹⁄₁₆"* ...	13.00	20.00
☐13	**BERTINGUIOT**		
	Sheared top, amber, 2"	12.00	18.00
☐14	**BILLING & CO.**		
	Banker's Writing Ink, B in center, aqua, 2" x 1½"	7.00	10.00
☐15	**BILLING & CO.**		
	Banker's Writing Ink: B embossed in center on bottom, aqua, 2"	5.00	7.00
☐16	**BILLINGS, J. T. & SON**		
	Sheared top, aqua, 1⅞"	5.00	8.00
☐17	**BILLINGS/MAUVE INK**		
	Near base, dome shaped, sheared top, aqua, 1¾" tall, 2¹¹⁄₁₆" deep base	13.00	20.00
☐18	**S.M. BIXBY & CO.**		
	Aqua, 2½"	13.00	20.00
☐19	**BIXBY**		
	On bottom, aqua, 2½"	3.00	4.00
☐20	**BIXBY**		
	On bottom, clear or amethyst, 2½"	2.50	3.50

☐ 21	**BIXBY**		
	Under bottom, ink or polish, Patented Mch, 83 under		
	shoulder, square base, round corners slanting upward so		
	the bottle gradually becomes round, bulbous shoulder,		
	amber, 2" base, 4"	5.00	8.00
☐ 22	*Same as above except plain, no BIXBY*	4.00	6.00
☐ 23	**BIXLEY MUSHROOM INK**		
	Aqua, 2"	11.00	15.00
☐ 24	**C. BLACKMAN**		
	Green, 2½"	9.00	12.00
☐ 25	**BLACKWOOD & CO.**		
	On one panel, under it on panel London, 10 panels, aqua,		
	snap top, 2¼" x 2"	12.00	16.00
☐ 26	**BLACKSTONE'S, INK, U.S.A.**		
	Cones type bottle, ring shoulder and ring top, clear, 2⅛" x		
	2⅛"	13.00	20.00
☐ 27	*BOAT SHAPED, plain, blue, 1¾"*	5.00	7.00
☐ 28	*Same as above except clear*	5.00	7.00
☐ 29	**BONNEY W.E. BARREL INK**		
	Aqua, 5½"	40.00	55.00
☐ 30	**BONNEY CONE INK**		
	Bonney Premium French Ink, South Hanover, Mass, aqua,		
	5½"	40.00	50.00
☐ 31	**W. E. BONNEY INK, SOUTH HANOVER, MASS**		
	Aqua, 2¼"	9.00	12.00
☐ 32	**W. E. BONNEY**		
	Aqua, 2½" x 3" x 1½"	85.00	105.00
☐ 33	**J. BOURNE & SONS NEAR DERBY**		
	On base, Carter's Ink, tan, 7"	11.00	15.00
☐ 34	**J. BOURNE & SON, PATENTEES, DERBY POTTERY NEAR**		
	DERBY, P. J. ARNOLD, LONDON, ENGLAND		
	Embossed near the base, Pottery, round, pouring spout		
	lip, light brown, 9½" tall, 3¾" diameter	7.00	10.00
☐ 35	**BOURNE DERBY**		
	Crock, brown, 8½"	5.00	7.00
☐ 36	**BRICKETT J. TAYLOR INK**		
	Cylindrical, flared lip, 4½"	70.00	100.00
☐ 37	**D. B. BROOKS & CO. INK**		
	Blue green, 2⅛"	9.00	12.00
☐ 38	**D. B. BROOKS & CO.**		
	Amber, 2" x 2½"	13.00	20.00
☐ 39	*BULLDOG HEAD, milk glass, 4"*	70.00	100.00
☐ 40	**J. J. BUTLER**		
	Aqua, 2"	7.00	10.00

C

☐ 41	**CALUMBINE INK**		
	Between four pointed stars, ring top, aqua, 1¾" x 1½" x		
	1½"	21.00	30.00
☐ 42	**CARDINAL BIRD INK**		
	Turtle, aqua	65.00	80.00

19

20

39

42
47

52

CARTER'S
Rubber
Stamp Ink

PURPLE

CARTER'S
INDELIBLE
INK
53

64

CAW'S INK
NEW YORK
90

CONQUEROR
RED INK
98

DAVIDS'
BLUE
BLACK
Electro Chemical
WRITING FLUID

112

115

120

REGISTERED
TRADE MARK
DIAMOND & ONYX
PHILADELPHIA
U.S.A.
123

REGISTERED
TRADE MARK
DIAMOND & ONYX
PHILADELPHIA
U.S.A.
124

119

HALEY
INK Co
163

FOXBORO
RECORDER
INK
150

154

168

198

215

□43	**CARDINELL INK OU TRADE MARK, MONTCLAIR, N.J.** *Cardinell Erado Trade Mark Montclair, N.J. on back, square, collar, ABM, amber, 1" x 2⅛"*	3.00	4.25
□44	**CARTER** *#11 under bottom, aqua, 2½"*	4.00	6.00
□45	**CARTER** *Under bottom, milk glass, 3"*	13.00	20.00
□46	**CARTER INK** *Made in U.S.A. under bottom, tea kettle, clear, 2½" x 4"*	40.00	60.00
□47	**CARTER INK** *Clear or amethyst, 2¼"*	3.00	4.25
□48	**CARTER'S** *On bottom, double V band collar, ring on shoulder and base, round, aqua or amethyst, 2⅝"*	3.50	4.50
□49	*Same as above except CARTER'S 7½ MADE IN USA on bottom, aqua*	5.00	7.00
□50	**CARTER'S** *On bottom, cone, large and small raised ring at base of neck, two round bands on collar, aqua, 2½" x 2⅞"*	5.00	7.00
□51	**CARTER'S** *On lid, screw-on top, 13 embossed on bottom, clear, 1⅛"*	5.00	7.00
□52	**CARTER'S** *Cobalt, 6½"*	7.00	10.00
□53	**CARTER'S** *Eight panels, aqua, 1¾"*	9.00	13.00
□54	**CARTER'S** *On shoulder, three-part mold, ring collar and pouring lip, light green, pint*	13.00	18.00
□55	**CARTER'S** *One ring tapers at neck, round base, amethyst, 2¼"*	3.00	4.50
□56	**CARTER'S** *Three dots close together under bottom, aqua, 2½"*	4.00	6.00
□57	**CARTER'S FULL ½ PINT** *On shoulder, applied ring, round, aqua, 6¼"*	8.00	12.00
□58	**CARTER'S** *On back, Full ½ Pint on bottom, Pat Feb. 14-99, 6" tall, 2½" round*	7.00	10.00
□59	**CARTER'S FULL QUART** *On top shoulder, under that Made in U.S.A., aqua, 9½"*	12.00	16.00
□60	**CARTER'S FULL QUART, MADE IN U.S.A.** *Around shoulder, Pat. Feb. 14, 99 on base, round, applied lip, aqua, 9⅝"*	11.00	15.00
□61	**CARTER'S** *House Ink, turtle, double door with two windows on dome near spout, Ink, and below that, Carter's*	140.00	180.00
□62	**CARTER'S INK** *Plain, three-part mold, round, pouring lip, light green, ½ pint, quart, 10¼" tall, 3" bottom, 2¼" neck*	11.00	15.00
□63	*Same as above except ring collar, two-part mold*	11.00	15.00
□64	**CARTER'S INK MADE IN U.S.A.** *Under bottom, label, aqua, 2¾"*	5.00	7.00

☐65 **CARTER'S INK CO.**
Two porcelain bottles, one in the shape of a man and one in the shape of a woman, woman has red blouse, red and white skirt, black shoes, yellow hair, and rolling pin in her left hand, man has tan trousers, blue jacket and red tie, 3⅝" 32.00 42.00

☐66 **CARTER'S KOAL BLK INK**
Label, machine made, clear, 2" 3.00 4.25

☐67 **CARTER'S MADE IN U.S.A.**
On shoulder, also Full Qt. Bulk Ink, aqua, 9¾" 4.00 6.00

☐68 **CARTER'S**
Under bottom, ring base and ring shoulder, double ring top, honey amber, 2⅛" x 2 .... 13.00 20.00

☐69 **CARTER'S MADE IN U.S.A.**
Under bottom, ring top, four pen ledge, aqua, square, 1¼" x 2¼" 11.00 15.00

☐70 **CARTER'S**
On base Made in U.S.A. 1897, round base, tapers at neck, one ring, green or aqua, 2½" tall, base 2⅜" 5.00 7.00

☐71 *Same as above except brown* 9.00 12.00

☐72 **CARTER'S/NON-COPYING/CARMINE/WRITING/FLUID**
Imprinted on jug, The Carter's Ink Co., seal, powderhorn, etc., brown and tan glaze, gallon 19.00 25.00

☐73 **CARTER'S NO. 1**
On base, round, cobalt blue, 32 fluid ounces, 9½" 13.00 20.00

☐74 **CARTER'S NO. 5 MADE IN U.S.A.**
On bottom, machine made, clear or amethyst 3.00 4.00

☐75 **CARTER'S NO. 5 MADE IN USA**
On bottom, ring collar, large ring forms shoulder, cone, ABM, amethyst, 2½" 3.00 4.00

☐76 **CARTER'S #6 MADE IN USA**
On bottom, round, ring collar, ring on shoulder and base, aqua, 2½" diameter, 3" 4.00 5.50

☐77 **CARTER'S #6½ MADE IN USA**
On bottom, 16 FLUID OZ. on shoulder, sheared type collar and ring on neck, bulbous shoulder, ring at base, round, ABM, amethyst, 3" diameter, 7½" 7.00 10.00

☐78 **CARTER'S #9 MADE IN USA**
On bottom, double ring collar, step on shoulder, amethyst, 2" x 2" x 2" 3.00 4.00

☐79 **CARTER'S #9**
On bottom, ring collar, ABM, square, clear, 2" 2.50 3.25

☐80 **CARTER'S 1897**
On bottom, cone, wide and narrow raised rings, rings at base of neck, narrow, round band collar, aqua, 2½" 5.00 8.00

☐81 **CARTER'S 1897 MADE IN U.S.A.**
Under bottom, cone, aqua 7.00 9.00

☐82 **CARTER'S 1897 MADE IN U.S.A.**
Under bottom, cone, emerald 7.00 9.00

☐83 **CARTER'S PENCRAFT COMBINED OFFICE & FOUNTAIN PEN FLUID**
Clear, 7½" 5.00 8.00

☐84	**CARTER'S PRO WRITING FLUID** *Label, machine made, G11 Sk No. 1 under bottom, on shoulder 32 Fl. Oz., cobalt, 9½"*	12.00	17.00
☐85	**CARTER'S RYTO PERMANENT** *Blue-black ink for fountain pen and general use, The Carter's Ink Co., Carter embossed near base, The Cathe- dral, label, 9¾"*	35.00	43.00
☐86	**CARTER'S 2 C-101** *Under bottom, Cathedral type, in bottom of each window Ca, machine made, cobalt blue, 10", set of 4*	37.00	48.00
☐87	*Same as above except 8"*	37.00	48.00
☐88	**CAW'S BLACK FLUID INK** *Light blue, 7¾"*	17.00	24.00
☐89	**CAW'S INK** *New York on one side, circle on top of shoulder with raised square on top of circle, clear, aqua or light blue, 2¼" x 1¾"*	5.00	8.00
☐90	**CAW'S INK** *Aqua, 3½" x 2" x 2"*	5.00	8.00
☐91	**CHALLENGE** *Green, 2¾"*	6.00	10.00
☐92	**CHASE BROS.** *Excelsior Office Ink, Haverhill, Mass., label, under bottom Feb. 15, 1886, cobalt, 9"*	13.00	20.00
☐93	**CLAR-O-TYPE CLEANER** *Label, Clar-O-Type embossed on each side, 3 under bot- tom, cobalt, 2½"*	4.00	6.00
☐94	**CLIMAX** *On shoulder, machine made, square, curved bottom, clear, 3¾"*	5.00	7.00
☐95	**THE CLUB INK CARTER HEXAGONAL** *Four-leaf clover, cobalt, 4 ounces*	22.00	30.00
☐96	**COMP. S.I. HOUSE INK BOTTLE** *On roof S.I. Comp., doors and windows around square bottle, flat round top, fancy bottle, 2⅝" x 1¾" x 1½"*	130.00	160.00
☐97	*CONFEDERATE HAT INK WELL, copper and tin, 3¾" x 1½"*	40.00	50.00
☐98	**CONQUEROR** *Label, blue or aqua, 2¼"*	9.00	12.00
☐99	**CONTINENTAL JET BLACK INK MFG. CO., PHILADELPHIA** *Label, two dots under bottom, clear*	4.00	6.00
☐100	**CONTINENTAL INK** *Long tapered collar and pouring lip, aqua, 7¾"*	9.00	12.00
☐101	**COVENTRY GEOMETRIC INK** *Open pontil, amber, 1⅝"*	65.00	80.00
☐102	**CROLIUS, C.** *Manufacturer, Manhattan, Wells, N.Y., round crock with holder for pen, ring top, tapered shoulder, gray and blue glaze, 2⅜" x 3¼"*	1300.00	1700.00
☐103	**CROSS PEN CO.** *Aqua, 2¾"*	13.00	20.00
☐104	**CROSS PEN CO. INK** *CPC trademark, aqua, 2¾"*	11.00	15.00

☐ 105	**APPLE GREEN CROSS PEN CO.**		
	Embossed monogram, 2½"	9.00	13.00
☐ 106	**CURRIER & HALL, CONCORD, N.H. POT INK**		
	Brown, quart	30.00	40.00
☐ 107	**CURRIER & HALL POTTERY MASTER INK**		
	Two-tone label	9.00	12.00
☐ 108	**CURRIER & HALL'S INK, CONCORD, N.H.**		
	1840, label, twelve-sided, open pontil, aqua, 2½"	50.00	65.00

D

☐ 109	**DANSK DESIGNS, LTD. FRANCE IHQ,**		
	Under bottom, wide ring top and base, (A.B.M.) 2⅛" x 2" wide, flare top	12.00	17.00
☐ 110	**DAVID'S**		
	On base, Turtle Ink, sheared top, aqua, 2" x 2¼"	25.00	35.00
☐ 111	**DAVID CO., N.Y. THAD**		
	Square label, Davids Red Ink, 1⅞" x 1⅛", ring top	14.00	19.00
☐ 112	**DAVID'S ELECTRO CHEMICAL WRITING FLUID**		
	Label, M 3 under bottom, machine made, cobalt blue, 9" .	12.00	17.00
☐ 113	**DAVID'S TURTLE INK**		
	Green	30.00	40.00
☐ 114	**T. DAVID'S & CO.**		
	Aqua, 1¾"	7.00	10.00
☐ 115	**THAD DAVID'S CO. N.Y.**		
	On bottom, amber, 2¾"	5.00	7.00
☐ 116	**THAD DAVID'S INK**		
	Beveled edges, slope shoulder, green, 1¾" square	6.00	9.00
☐ 117	**THADDEUS DAVID'S CO.**		
	Pinched pouring lip, clear, 6⅜"	12.00	16.00
☐ 118	**THADDEUS DAVID'S & CO.**		
	Label, Writing Fluid, New York, cream crock, 5¾"	30.00	38.00
☐ 119	**DAVIES**		
	Sheared top, Patd Sept 4-80 under bottom, clear or amethyst, 2½"	31.00	42.00
☐ 120	**W.A. DAVIS CO.**		
	In back, U.S. TREASURY on front shoulder, clear or amethyst	14.00	21.00
☐ 121	**W.A. DAVIS**		
	Clear, 2¼"	4.00	5.50
☐ 122	**W.A. DAVIS CO/BOSTON, MASS/U.S.A.**		
	Embossed on shoulder, decorated cylinder with sixteen curved panels at top of body, and sixteen near base of body, base pedestal flared, double rings at base of neck, mold lines end at base of neck, flared ring on lip, greenish aqua, 8"	11.00	15.00
☐ 123	**DIAMOND & ONYX**		
	Aqua, 9"	9.00	12.00
☐ 124	**DIAMOND & ONYX**		
	Aqua, 9¼"	4.00	6.00
☐ 125	**DIAMOND & ONYX**		
	Aqua, 3" and 5½"	7.00	10.00

☐126 **DIAMOND INK CO., MILWAUKEE**
In a circle under bottom, pinch type bottle, in each pinch a
diamond, round ring on shoulder, ring at base, clear, ½"
neck 9.00 13.00

☐127 **DIAMOND INK CO., MILWAUKEE**
On base, Patented Dec 1st, 03, No. 622, square, amethyst,
1⅝" 4.00 5.50

☐128 **DIAMOND INK CO.**
Clear, 1½" 4.00 5.50

☐129 **DIAMOND INK CO.**
Wash pen point, one large and small connected jar 11.00 15.00

☐130 **DOULTON, LAMBETH**
Pouring lip, brown pottery, 4½" 7.00 10.00

☐131 **DOVELL'S**
In ¼ moon, under it Patent, cones type bottle, ring on
shoulder, ring top, aqua, 2¼" x 2¼" 13.00 20.00

☐132 **DOVELL'S PATENT**
Cone, blue, 2½" 7.00 10.00

☐133 **S.O. DUNBAR**
Stopper or cork, aqua, 2½" 7.00 10.00

☐134 **S.O. DUNBAR, TAUNTON**
Cone, eight-sided, open pontil, aqua 100.00 140.00

☐135 **S.O. DUNBAR, TAUNTON**
Cone, eight-sided, open pontil, aqua 22.00 30.00

☐136 **DUNBAR, S.O., TAUNTON**
On one panel in 2 lines, cones type bottle, ring top, pontil,
aqua 32.00 40.00

☐137 **S.O. DUNBAR, TAUNTON, MASS.**
Round, graduated collar, aqua, 5¾" x 2¾" 9.00 12.00

E

☐138 **EARLES INK CO.**
Pouring lip, crock, beige, 6⅛" 7.00 10.00

☐139 **E. B.**
Inside threads, cone, clear or amethyst, 2⅛" 5.00 7.00

☐140 **EDISON FOUNTAIN PEN INK, PETERSBURG VA.**
Under bottom A.C.W. 232, ring tip and neck, square, clear 8.00 10.00

☐141 **ESBINS INDELIBLE INK**
Aqua, small bottle 5.00 7.00

☐142 **ESTES, N.Y. INK**
Pontil, aqua, 6¾", ... 18.00 25.00

F

☐143 **FARLEY'S INK**
Open pontil, olive or amber, 2" x 2" 185.00 230.00

☐144 **FARLEY'S INK**
Eight-sided, open pontil, aqua, 2" x 2" 65.00 85.00

☐145 **L.P. FARLEY CO**
Sheared top, dark green, 2" 17.00 22.00

☐146 **FINE BLACK WRITING INK**
Label, pontil, aqua, 5" 13.00 20.00

□ 147	**H.B. FORSTER**		
	Aqua, 7¾"	7.00	10.00
□ 148	**PATENT FORTSCHMITT, CANADA**		
	Long metal cap with P, clear, 6"	13.00	20.00
□ 149	**FOUNTAIN INK CO., N.Y., USA**		
	Clear, 3½"	11.00	15.00
□ 150	**FOXBORO**		
	Clear, 2½	5.00	7.00
□ 151	**FRANKLIN INK**		
	Aqua, 4" long, 2" at tallest part	35.00	47.00
□ 152	**FRENCH INK CO., HANOVER, MASS.**	22.00	30.00
□ 153	**FULLER'S BANNER INK, DECATUR, ILL.**		
	Aqua, 8"	13.00	20.00

G

□ 154	**GATES**		
	Round, clear, 6"	1.35	2.15
□ 155	**GEOMETRIC INK WELL**		
	Coventry Black Glass, round open pontil, dark olive amber		
	or olive green, 1½" x 1½"	90.00	125.00
□ 156	**GLENN & CO.**		
	Round, clear, 1⅝"	5.00	8.00
□ 157	*GLUE or INK, label*		
	Clear, 2¾"	3.00	4.00
□ 158	*GLUE or INK, label*		
	Eight panels, aqua	7.00	10.00
□ 159	**G.M.W.C.A.A.S.**		
	Turtle, ink pen rest slot, oval, aqua	9.00	12.00
□ 160	**GREENWOOD'S**		
	Sheared top, under bottom Patd March 22, 92, tapered,		
	clear or aqua green, 1½"	7.00	10.00

H

□ 161	**HALEY, MADE IN U.S.A., INK CO.**		
	In 3 lines, ring shoulder and base, ring top, aqua, 1¼" x		
	1¼"	15.00	24.00
□ 162	**HALEY INK CO.**		
	Aqua, 2¾"	7.00	10.00
□ 163	*Same as above except clear*	5.00	7.00
□ 164	**HALEY INK CO., MADE IN USA**		
	Two rings on shoulder, four rings on base, clear or		
	amethyst, 6¾"	9.00	12.00
□ 165	*Same as above except brass spout, aqua*	12.00	16.00
□ 166	**HARRIS INK**		
	Label, pontil, black glass, 10½"	22.00	29.00
□ 167	**HARRISON'S COLA INK 2**		
	Open pontil, aqua	50.00	65.00
□ 168	**HARRISON'S COLUMBIAN INK**		
	Eight panels, pontil, aqua, 2"	30.00	42.00
□ 169	**HARRISON'S COLUMBIAN INK**		
	In 3 lines, round, ring top, pontil, cobalt, 4½" x 1¼"	85.00	115.00

☐170 **HARRISON'S/COLUMBIAN/INK**
Eight-sided squat, open pontil, aqua, 1¾" tall, 1¾" base   45.00   60.00

☐171 **HARRISON'S COLUMBIAN INK**
Open pontil, cobalt, 1½" x 1½" 110.00   135.00

☐172 **HARRISON'S/COLUMBIAN/INK**
*Embossed vertically on three of twelve panels, Patent
embossed on shoulder, iron pontil, aqua 3⅛", x 1½"* 35.00   50.00

☐173 **HARRISON'S/COLUMBIAN/INK**
Open pontil, Pat. on Shoulder, aqua, 3⅛", x 1½" 32.00   47.00

☐174 **CHAS. M. HIGGINS & CO.**
Aqua, 7½" 5.00   8.00

☐175 **HIGGINS DRAWING INK**
Under bottom, machine made, clear, 3" 3.00   4.00

☐176 **HIGGINS INKS, BROOKLYN, N.Y.**
On bottom, round, squat, clear, 3¾" 5.00   7.00

☐177 *Same as above except ABM* 2.50   3.25

☐178 **HIGGINS INKS, BROOKLYN, N.Y.**
Round, amethyst or clear, 2" 4.00   6.00

☐179 **H.J.H. WRITING INK**
B.B. on panels, sheared top, clear or aqua, 2½" 12.00   16.00

☐180 **HOGAN & THOMPSON**
Phila, cone, open pontil, aqua, 2" x ⅜" 100.00   150.00

☐181 **JOHN HOLLAND, CINCINNATI**
*Square bottle with rounded corners, ring top and neck,
aqua, 2¼"* 5.00   7.00

☐182 **HOOKER'S**
Sheared top, round, aqua, 2" 9.00   12.00

☐183 **HOUSE INK**
Light blue, 2⅞" 5.00   7.00

☐184 **HOVER, PHILA**
On two panels, eight panels, umbrella shape, aqua, 2" ...   38.00   49.00

☐185 **HOVER PHILA**
*In 2 lines on one panel, umbrella type bottle, ring top, pon-
til, ring top, blue-green, 2¼" x 2⅛"* 27.00   38.00

☐186 **HUNT MFG. CO., SPEEDBALL, U.S.A., STATESVILLE, N.C.**
Embossed on bottom, cone, clear, 2¾" 2.50   3.25

☐187 **HUNT PEN CO. SPEEDBALL, U.S.A., CAMDEN, N.J.**
Embossed on bottom, round, clear, 2¾" 2.50   3.25

I

☐188 **IGLOO INK**
*Dome shaped, plain with neck on side, sheared top, 1¾"
or 1¼" tall, 2" round, sapph. blue* 170.00   225.00

☐189 *Same as above except cobalt* 225.00   290.00

☐190 **IMPROVED PROCESS BLUE CO.**
Aqua, 2⅜" 2.75   4.25

☐191 *INK, ring around base, base of shoulder and neck, amber,
2⅜" x 1⅞"* 4.00   6.00

☐192 *Same as above except aqua or clear* 2.75   4.25

☐193 *INK; cone, ring collar, bulbous ring forms shoulder, ring
on base of neck, amber, 2½" x 2½"* 5.00   7.00

☐ 194	INK; square, ABM, cobalt blue, 2" x 2¼"	3.50	5.00
☐ 195	INK; round, cobalt blue, 2½" x 3"	5.00	7.00
☐ 196	INK; round, ABM, cobalt blue, 1⅞" x 2¾"	5.00	7.00
☐ 197	INK; cone type, yet not a true cone, base is cone shape with two large graduated flared bands on shoulder and neck, sheared collar, aqua, 3⅜"	7.00	10.00
☐ 198	INK; cone, honey amber, 2½"	4.50	6.00
☐ 199	INK; cone, tan, crock, 2½"	8.00	11.00
☐ 200	INK; cone, cobalt blue, 2½"	11.00	15.00
☐ 201	INK; cone, amber, 2⅝"	11.00	15.00
☐ 202	INK; cone, light blue, 2¾"	7.00	10.00
☐ 203	INK; cone, plain, clear or amethyst, 2½"	2.50	3.75
☐ 204	Same as above except blue or amber	11.00	15.00
☐ 205	INK; cone, amethyst, 3"	5.00	7.00
☐ 206	INK; design Patd. Feb 16th, 1886 under bottom in sunken circle, five different size rings on top or shoulder, one 1¼" ring on base, clear 12¼"	7.00	10.00
☐ 207	Same as above except one ring near shoulder, green	7.00	10.00
☐ 208	INK; no emboss, 8 panels, umbrella type bottle, pontil, plain top, brilliant blue, aqua, 2¼" x 2¼"	13.00	20.00
☐ 209	INK; three-piece mold, crude graduated collar, ice blue, pint, 7⅜"	7.00	10.00
☐ 210	INK; ice cube shaped, solid glass, heavy, small well, metal collar, desk type, clear, 2" x 2" x 2"	3.50	4.75
☐ 211	INK; label, three-part mold, aqua, 2¾"	7.00	10.00
☐ 212	INK; label, black, 7½"	22.00	30.00
☐ 213	INK; label, cone, ring shoulder, 2½"	6.00	8.00
☐ 214	INK; label, crock, tapered neck, brick red, 4"	5.00	7.00
☐ 215	INK; label, aqua, 2¾"	4.00	6.00
☐ 216	INK; label, crock, green and white, 2½" x 2½"	11.00	15.00
☐ 217	INK; label, clear, 2½"	3.00	4.00
☐ 218	INK; label, light blue, 2¾"	4.00	6.00
☐ 219	INK; label, tin box, 1½"	22.00	30.00
☐ 220	INK; label, dark aqua, 2¾"	4.00	6.00
☐ 221	INK; label, clear, 6½"	5.00	8.00
☐ 222	INK; label, clear, 2½" at base tapering to 2" at top	12.00	16.00
☐ 223	INK; label, wood, brick red, 3"	11.00	15.00
☐ 224	INK; plain, checked bottom, clear, 3" tall, 1¾" x 1¾" base .	18.00	25.00
☐ 225	INK; label, aqua, 5¾"	5.00	7.00
☐ 226	INK; label, three-part mold, green, 9¼"	13.00	20.00
☐ 227	INK; label, sheared top, pontil, clear, 2"	13.00	20.00
☐ 228	INK; label, desk bottle, sheared top, clear or amethyst, 1¾"	9.00	12.00
☐ 229	INK; label, Pat Oct. 17, 1865 around bottom, clear or amethyst, 2¾"	22.00	30.00
☐ 230	INK; label, desk bottle, sheared top, clear or amethyst, 1½"	9.00	12.00
☐ 231	INK; label, clear, 1½"	6.00	8.00
☐ 232	INK; label, sheared top, panels on shoulder, clear or amethyst, 1¼" x 1½" x 1½"	9.00	12.00
☐ 233	INK; label, green, 2½"	60.00	80.00
☐ 234	INK; label, broken pontil, green, 7½"	25.00	34.00
☐ 235	INK; label, sheared top, aqua, ½" tall, 5½" long	38.00	50.00
☐ 236	INK; label, long square body, neck on end, clear, 3¾" x ¾"	12.00	16.00
☐ 237	INK; label, round, dark green, 2¼"	10.00	14.00
☐ 238	INK; pen rest on both sides at shoulder, sheared collar, amethyst, 2⅝" x 2⅜" x 2⅜"	6.00	8.00

216

217

218

219

220

221

222

224

270

231

223

232

233

234

277

278

235

☐ 239	*Same as above except aqua, 2" x 2¼" x 2¾"*	**6.00**	**8.00**
☐ 240	*INK or GLUE; plain, heavy ring forms shoulder, slightly raised ring above at base of neck, conical, aqua, 2¼" tall, 2½" base*	**3.00**	**4.00**
☐ 241	*Same as above except brown or amber*	**4.00**	**6.00**
☐ 242	*Same as above except green or blue*	**6.00**	**8.00**
☐ 243	*Same as above except cobalt*	**7.00**	**10.00**
☐ 244	*INK; plain, has two deep rounded troughs on shoulder on either side of neck for pen rest, plain top, sunken bottom, clear or amethyst, 2¼" x 2½", neck ¾"*	**9.00**	**12.00**
☐ 245	*INK; plain, ring encircling base, another forming shoulder, small ring on base of neck, round, clear, 2¼" x 2"*	**3.00**	**4.00**
☐ 246	*Same as above except different colors*	**7.00**	**10.00**
☐ 247	*INK; plain, no emboss, flare lips, ring shoulder and base, round, clear, 2⅛" x 2"*	**11.00**	**15.00**
☐ 248	*INK; plain, 2¾" round bottom, trench from shoulder to shoulder ¾" wide for clamp of some kind, flat ring, ring at bottom of neck, 1½" ring top, ½" neck, machine made, clear*	**5.00**	**7.00**
☐ 249	*INK; plain, round, inside of flower stand, two prongs on left top to hold pen, all metal is gold color, clear, 2½" tall, 3½" round*	**22.00**	**30.00**
☐ 250	*INK; plain, round, green, clear or amethyst, 2⅝"*	**3.00**	**4.00**
☐ 251	*INK; plain, round bottom, green, 9"*	**7.00**	**10.00**
☐ 252	*INK; plain, square top, on top and bottom fancy gold colored metal stand, round base, clear, 2"*	**13.00**	**20.00**
☐ 253	*INK; plain, square, green or clear, 2"*	**3.00**	**4.50**
☐ 254	*INK; square, squat, cobalt blue, 2⅜"*	**5.00**	**8.00**
☐ 255	*INK; square, amethyst or aqua, 2½"*	**3.00**	**4.00**
☐ 256	*INK; 2 oz. on short neck, square, rounded corners, machine made, cobalt, clear or blue, 2" x 2"*	**3.00**	**4.00**
☐ 257	*INK WELL; sunken desk type, flat, round, ABM, clear, 3" x 1½"*	**3.00**	**4.00**
☐ 258	**IRVING** *Square, aqua, 2½"*	**22.00**	**32.00**

J

☐ 259	**J & IEM** *Imprinted in each panel, Turtle with six panels, on base Patd Oct 31, 1865, under bottom J, aqua*	**28.00**	**37.00**
☐ 260	*Same as above except no patent date, amber*	**90.00**	**120.00**
☐ 261	*Same as above except cobalt*	**300.00**	**400.00**
☐ 262	**JASMINE INK CORP., NORFOLK, VIRGINIA** *Square, labeled Perfumed Jasmine Ink, ABM, clear*	**3.00**	**4.00**
☐ 263	**J. M & S IGLOO INK** *Early*	**18.00**	**24.00**
☐ 264	**JOHNSON INK CO., WILLINGTON, CONN.** *Fancy label, Stoddard, tapered and sheared top, dark green, 5⅞"*	**24.00**	**30.00**
☐ 265	**JOSIAH JONSON'S** *Japan, Writing Fluid, London, one word on each panel, teakettle type crock, 2½" x 2¼", gray and brown glazes* .	**160.00**	**210.00**

K

☐ 266	**KEENE GEOMETRIC INK**			
	Open pontil, amber	85.00	105.00
☐ 267	**KEENE UMBRELLA INK**			
	Eight-sided pontil, green	40.00	55.00
☐ 268	**KELLER**			
	Double ring top, clear or amethyst, 2½"	6.00	8.00
☐ 269	**KELLER INK, DETROIT**			
	Square, screw top, machine made, clear or amethyst	3.00	4.00
☐ 270	**THE ROBERT KELLER INK CO.**			
	Clear, 9¼"	9.00	12.00
☐ 271	**KELLERS INK**			
	Under bottom, clear, 1¼" x 1½", ½" neck	12.00	16.00
☐ 272	**F. KIDDER IMPROVED, INDELIBLE INK**			
	Around bottle, square, aqua, 2½" x 1½" x 1½"	27.00	36.00
☐ 273	*Same as above except 5", clear*	23.00	31.00
☐ 274	**KIRKLAND WRITING FLUID**			
	Ring on shoulder and base, aqua, 2¼" x 1½"	6.00	8.00

L

☐ 275	**L & B**			
	Monogram in center, cone, aqua, 2½"	10.00	14.00
☐ 276	**LAKE'S**			
	Cone, aqua, 2½"	17.00	24.00
☐ 277	**LEVISON'S**			
	Machine made, clear, 7¼"	7.00	10.00
☐ 278	**LEVISON'S INKS**			
	Amber, 2½"	100.00	135.00
☐ 279	**LOCHMAN'S LOCOMOTIVE INK**			
	Train shaped, trademark, Patd, Oct, 1874, plain collar, aqua, 2³⁄₁₆" x 2"	38.00	50.00
☐ 280	**LOMBARD'S LILAC INK**			
	Diamond shape label, house type, clear, 2⅜"	5.00	7.00
☐ 281	**LYNDEBORO**			
	Rectangular, slots for two pens, aqua, 2¼"	11.00	15.00
☐ 282	**LYNDEBORO**			
	Rectangular, slots for two pens, green, 2¼" x 2⅜"	9.00	12.00

M

☐ 283	**MAGNUS**			
	Tan pottery, 4⅝"	7.00	10.00
☐ 284	**CARL MAMPE BERLIN**			
	Amber, 2"	13.00	20.00
☐ 285	**MANCHESTER NOVELTY CO.**			
	Aqua, 2⅝"	12.00	16.00
☐ 286	**MANN'S**			
	Label, Design Patd Feb 16, 1886 under bottom, amber, 9¼" .	13.00	20.00

☐287 **MASSACHUSETTS STANDARD RECORD INK**
On shoulder, clear, $7\frac{3}{4}$" ... 12.00 16.00

☐288 **MAURIN A. DEPOSE, PARIS,**
In 3 lines, square bottle, ring top, clear, $2\frac{1}{2}$" x $1\frac{1}{4}$" ... 22.00 35.00.00

☐289 **MAYNARD & NOYES'**
Label only, flare top, pontil, olive green, $4\frac{1}{4}$" x $1\frac{1}{6}$" ... 20.00 30.00

☐290 **MAYNARD'S WRITING INK**
Sheared top, amber case, eight panels, umbrella type, dark green, 2" ... 29.00 40.00

☐291 **JULES MIETTE, PARIS**
Sheared top, blue green, $2\frac{3}{4}$" ... 14.00 20.00

☐292 **MON-GRAM INK**
Round, clear or amethyst, $2\frac{1}{2}$" ... 5.00 7.00

☐293 **MOORE**
Square or cylindrical, aqua, 2" ... 6.00 8.00

☐294 **MOORE & SON**
Sheared top, aqua or clear, $1\frac{5}{8}$" ... 7.00 10.00

☐295 **MOORE J & IEM**
Igloo, round, $2\frac{1}{2}$" to $6\frac{1}{2}$", several other types and sizes . 18.00 32.00

☐296 **M.S. CO.**
Sanford's #216 on bottom, clear ... 4.00 6.00

☐297 **MT. WASHINGTON GLASS CO.**
New Bedford, Mass, Bubble Ball Inkwell, clear, 2" ... 30.00 40.00

☐298 **MY LADY INK**
On base, Carbonine Ink Co., N.Y., aqua, $1\frac{3}{8}$" ... 7.00 10.00

N

☐299 **NA**
On one panel, 10 base panels concave, ring top, aqua, clear, $2\frac{1}{4}$" x $2\frac{1}{2}$" ... 30.00 40.00

☐300 **NATIONAL INK N.W.W. & CO.**
Label, clear, 2" ... 3.00 4.00

☐301 **NATIONAL SURETY INK**
Round, two rings on shoulder and base, 32 oz. on shoulder, ABM, clear, 9" ... 7.00 10.00

☐302 **NAYMARD & MOYES** *[sic]* **BOSTON**
Label, pontil, clear ... 43.00 52.00

☐303 **P. NEWMAN & CO., GILSUM, N.H.**
Label, umbrella type, eight panels, olive green, $1\frac{1}{2}$" ... 18.00 27.00

☐304 **NEWTON'S INK**
In 2 lines, ring shoulder and top, and ring base of neck, sheared top, aqua, $2\frac{7}{8}$" x $2\frac{1}{4}$" ... 11.00 16.00

☐305 **NICHOLS & HALL**
Label, house type, clear, $2\frac{7}{8}$" ... 7.00 10.00

O

☐306 **OCTAGON INK**
Mushroom shaped, pontil, aqua ... 24.00 31.00

☐307 **THE OLIVER TYPEWRITER**
Round, clear, 2" **5.00** **8.00**

☐308 **1 X L**
Fancy ink, ring top, clear, 2½" **13.00** **20.00**

☐309 **OPDYKE**
Barrel shaped bottle with four rings around it, opening in center, clear, 2" **13.00** **20.00**

☐310 *Same as above except panels around bottom, ring top, Opdyke under bottom, clear, 2¼"* **22.00** **30.00**

☐311 **OPDYKE BROS. INK**
Barrel with opening in center, ring top, aqua, 2½" x 2⅜". **20.00** **30.00**

☐312 **OPDYKE BROS. INK**
Barrel, Patd March 11, 1870, opening in center, aqua, 2½" x 2⅜" **22.00** **30.00**

P

☐313 **PALMER**
Round, sheared top, golden amber, 4¼" **30.00** **45.00**

☐314 **PARKER**
Panels on shoulder, ring top, ABM, clear, 2½" **9.00** **12.00**

☐315 *Same as above except Parker's "Quink" under bottom, Made in U.S.A. #1, ABM, 1½"* **6.00** **8.00**

☐316 **PAUL'S INKS**
N.Y., Chicago on back, cobalt, 9½" **15.00** **20.00**

☐317 **PAUL'S SAFETY BOTTLE & INK CO. N.Y.**
On shoulder, squat, ring top, clear, 1⅜" **13.00** **20.00**

☐318 **PAUL'S WRITING FLUID**
N.Y., Chicago, flared neck, ring top, three-part mold, 5½" **13.00** **20.00**

☐319 **P.B.CO. INK**
Round, aqua, 2½" **9.00** **12.00**

☐320 **PEERLESS**
On two panels, eight panels, umbrella type, bulbous shoulder, sheared top, clear or amethyst **13.00** **20.00**

☐321 **J.W. PENNELL**
Embossed on eight panels on base, round top, ring top, aqua, 2" **13.00** **20.00**

☐322 **PENN. MFG. WORK, PHILA.**
Eight flat sides, white, 2½" **37.00** **50.00**

☐323 **PERRY & CO., LONDON, PATENT**
In two lines, on top ½" hole for ink and funnel hole for pen, flared ring bottom 3" to 2¼" top, sunken bottom, cream pottery, 3" round, 1¾" tall **21.00** **30.00**

☐324 **PITKIN INK KEENE**
Open pontil, dark aqua, 1¾" **125.00** **155.00**

☐325 **PITKIN INKWELL**
36-rib mold, swirls to left, flared lip, lime green, 1¾" x 2½" x 2¼" **250.00** **325.00**

☐326 **POMEROY INK, NEWARK, N.Y.**
Label, two rings on base and shoulder, ring top, aqua, 2¾" **7.00** **10.00**

☐327 **G.A. POTTER**
Pottery, tan, 9⅞" **12.00** **17.00**

R

☐328 **RAVEN'S**
Label, design Patd Feb 16th 1886 under bottom, 7¾" **13.00 20.00**

☐329 **READING INK CO., READING, MICH., SUPERIOR BLUE INK**
Label, round, wide collar, flared top, aqua, 6³⁄₁₆" x 1⁹⁄₁₆" ... **9.00 13.00**

☐330 **READING INK CO., READING, MICH.**
Diamond shaped label, on base Pat. April 18, 1875, round, crude pouring lip, aqua, 6⅛" **11.00 15.00**

☐331 **READING INK CO.**
Violet Ink, label, crude cone with pronounced mold lines, 2¾" x 2⅝" **11.00 15.00**

☐332 **READS INKSTAND AND INK**
Pat. Nov. 25, 1872, ring top, aqua blue, 2" **21.00 28.00**

S

☐333 **SI**
Under bottom pontil, umbrella type bottle, 8 panels, plain top, pontil, aqua, 2¼" x 2½" **29.00 40.00**

☐334 **SSS**
Under bottom, 8 panels, umbrella type, bottle plain top, aqua, 2¼" x 2¼" **13.00 20.00**

☐335 **SAFETY BOTTLE & INK CO., N.Y.**
Paul's pat. on shoulder, diagonal swirls, sunburst pattern on base, clear, 2⅛" x 2¾" **13.00 20.00**

☐336 **SANFORD HORSE-SHOE INK**
Sanford 217 Pat. apl. for, aqua **9.00 13.00**

☐337 **SANFORD/INKS/ONE QUART/AND LIBRARY PASTE**
Vertically, raised ¾" ring around base and shoulder, round, square collar and ring, ABM, amber, 3¾" diameter, 9⅜" tall **6.00 8.00**

☐338 *Same as above except embossing on pouring cap, Pat. Feb. 27, 06, 10½* **10.00 15.00**

☐339 **SANFORD MFG. CO.**
Pat. May 23, 1899 on bottom, clear or amethyst, 3" **3.50 4.25**

☐340 **SANFORD'S BELLWOOD, ILL**
Made in U.S.A. 44CC. embossed on bottom, metal screw-on top, red plastic, 1½" **5.00 7.00**

☐341 **SANFORD'S MFG. CO.**
Vertically in sunken panel, 1 oz. on next panel, S.I. Co. monogram on next panel, square collar, ABM, amethyst, 1½" x 2½" **3.25 4.25**

☐342 **SANFORD'S FREE SAMPLE NEVER SOLD**
Sheared top, 3½" **6.00 8.00**

☐343 **SANFORDS #6**
On bottom, 1½ oz. on one panel, large step on shoulder, double band collar, clear, 1¾" x 2¼" **2.75 3.75**

☐344 **SANFORD'S #8**
Under bottom, light green, 2½" **4.00 6.00**

☐345 **SANFORD'S 9**
Under bottom, machine made, clear or amethyst, 2½" ... **3.25 4.50**

☐346	**SANFORD'S 25-8**		
	On bottom, aqua, 2½"	4.00	6.00
☐347	**SANFORD'S #27**		
	On bottom, machine made, clear, 2½"	2.50	3.25
☐348	**SANDFORD'S #29 PAT APP'D FOR**		
	On bottom, boat shaped, clear, 2" x 2¾" x 2¼"	9.00	12.00
☐349	**SANFORD'S 30 PATENT APPLIED FOR**		
	On bottom, boat shaped, aqua, 2" tall, 2¼" x1¾" base	11.00	15.00
☐350	**SANFORD'S #39**		
	On bottom, large ring with deep groove at base and shoulder, step on shoulder, small and large ring collar, round, aqua or amethyst, 2" x 2⅜"	3.50	4.25
☐351	**SANFORD'S #39 3N**		
	On bottom, aqua, 2½"	4.00	6.00
☐352	**SANFORD'S #88**		
	Bell shaped, sheared collar, amethyst, 2½" diameter, 3⅜" tall	7.00	10.00
☐353	**SANFORD'S #89**		
	Somewhat conical, sheared collar, amethyst, 2¼" diameter, 2½" tall	3.00	4.25
☐354	**SANFORD'S #98 CHICAGO, NEW YORK 1½ OZ.**		
	On bottom, large ring on base and shoulder, two rings on collar, round, ABM, clear, 1¾" x 2½"	2.50	3.25
☐355	**SANFORD'S CHICAGO, #187** *under bottom*		
	Under bottom, round, flared top, clear, 1½" x 1½"	12.00	16.00
☐356	**SANFORD'S #219**		
	On bottom, large ring on base and shoulder, large ring and small ring collar, round, ABM, clear, 1⅞" x 2¼"	2.50	3.25
☐357	**SANFORD'S #276**		
	On bottom, S.I. Co. monogram in sunken bull's-eye panel, rings at base of neck, ABM: three other plain bull's-eyes, clear, 1⅞" x 2⅝"	2.50	3.25
☐358	**SANFORD'S PREMIUM WRITING FLUID**		
	Label, ABM, amber, 9"	6.00	8.00
☐359	**SCHLESINGER'S HYDRAULIC INK**		
	Whitm and black crock, copper top, 6"	35.00	50.00
☐360	**SHEAFFER'S/SKRIP/THE SUCCESSOR TO INK**		
	Embossed on metal plate in top of wooden cylinder, container for an ink bottle, wooden threaded screw-on top, 3⅝" tall, 2 7/16" diameter	7.00	10.00
☐361	*SHOE, label, clear, 6" long*	9.00	12.00
☐362	*SHOE with buckle, clear, 3⅞" long*	7.00	10.00
☐363	**SIGNET INK**		
	Threaded for screw top, cobalt blue, 7¾"	12.00	16.00
☐364	**S. SILL-** *(cannot decipher balance)*		
	Chester, Conn., blue label under bottom, 3¼" round ring at bottom and top, vase shaped, four different side holes to hold quill pens, in center top a bottle for ink, all wood, brown, 1¾"	21.00	30.00
☐365	**SISSON & CO.**		
	Sheared top, round, pale aqua green, 1⅝"	7.00	10.00
☐366	**SKRIP**		
	Tighten cap, tip bottle to fill the well on metal top, Pat'd 1759866 on bottom, ink well, screw-on top, clear, 2¾"	12.00	16.00

☐367	**S.M. CO 6**		
	Under bottom, aqua, 2¼"	1.00	10.00
☐368	**SONNEBORN & ROBBINS**		
	Flared lip, cork stopper topped with brass, tan pottery, 5½"	7.00	10.00
☐369	**SO. STAMP & STATIONERY CO., MFG. STATIONERS, RICHMOND, VIRGINIA**		
	Amber, 9½"	24.00	31.00
☐370	**STAFFORD'S COMMERCIAL INK**		
	Round, Pat. Jan 13-85, S.M. CO, clear, 2"	9.00	12.00
☐371	**STAFFORD'S INK**		
	In two lines running vertically, two rings on shoulder and bottom, amber, 4¼" body, 2" neck	9.00	12.00
☐372	**STAFFORD'S INK**		
	Green, 8"	12.00	16.00
☐373	**STAFFORD'S INK**		
	Round, aqua, 3"	5.00	7.00
☐374	**STAFFORD'S INK**		
	Near base, round bottle, aqua, 2⅛" x 2¼"	12.00	16.00
☐375	**S.S. STAFFORD INK, MADE IN U.S.A.**		
	In two lines, in a sunken panel, under it This Bottle Contains One Full Quart, two rings on bottom, two on shoulder, short neck, aqua, 2"	11.00	16.00
☐376	Same as above except 7"	11.00	16.00
☐377	Same as above except 6"	12.00	18.00
☐378	Same as above except 4¾"	12.00	18.00
☐379	**STAFFORD'S INKS, MADE IN U.S.A.**		
	Pouring spout, cobalt blue, 6"	13.00	20.00
☐380	**STAFFORD'S INK SS, MADE IN U.S.A.**		
	In sunken panel, under it, This Bottle Contains One Full Qt., aqua or light blue, 9½"	6.00	8.00
☐381	**STAFFORD'S NO. 5, PAT NOV. 17, 1896, NOV. 22, 1892**		
	On base, shoe shaped, aqua, 2½" neck, 3¼"	13.00	18.00
☐382	**STAFFORD'S VERMILION INK**		
	Two pen slots, aqua with blue label	9.00	12.00
☐383	**STANFORD**		
	Square roof and 1½" chimney, ½" base, Stanford's Fountain Pen Inks, machine made, 2" x 2"	2.75	4.25
☐384	**STANFORD'S BLUE INK**		
	Label around body, ring on base, neck and shoulder, 2⅜" neck, 2" tall, 2" round	4.50	6.50
☐385	**HENRY C. STEPHENS, LTD.**		
	Pouring spout, dark brown, 9"	7.00	10.00
☐386	**STODDARD MASTER INK**		
	Olive amber around pontil, 9⅜"	28.00	36.00
☐387	**STODDARD UMBRELLA INK**		
	Eight-sided, open pontil, amber	50.00	60.00
☐388	**SUPERIOR INK**		
	Tan and brown, 2"	7.00	10.00
☐389	**SWIFT & PEARSON**		
	Top and neck drawn out and shaped by hand, bulbous neck, dark green, 7⅝"	34.00	41.00
☐390	**SYR-RHEL INK**		
	Pontil, cobalt, 8"	45.00	60.00

T

☐391	**BRICKETT J. TAYLOR INK**		
	Cylindrical, flared lip, Keene, open pontil, 4½"	130.00	165.00
☐392	*TEA KETTLE, stars on eight panels, metal top, cobalt, 2½"*	140.00	180.00
☐393	*Same as above except no stars and long neck, clear, 6"* ..	90.00	120.00
☐394	*Same as above except no stars and short neck with eight panels, metal top, blue*	135.00	170.00
☐395	*TEA KETTLE, place for two pens on top, Pat. App. For and cloverleaf under bottom, aqua, 2"*	35.00	50.00
☐396	**AM (TEA KETTLE TYPE)**		
	Snap top, clear, 1½" x 2¼"	75.00	100.00
☐397	**TEA KETTLE INK**		
	Label, eight panels, 2½" sheared top, cobalt, 2" x 4"	175.00	240.00
☐398	*Same as above except clear*	60.00	80.00
☐399	*Same as above except neck is close to the eight panels, metal top, aqua*	60.00	80.00
☐400	**THOMAS**		
	On bottom, cone, bulbous shoulder, double collar, amethyst	6.00	8.00
☐401	**L.H. THOMAS & CO.**		
	Clear or aqua, 2¼" x 3⅛"	3.25	5.00
☐402	**L.H. THOMAS CHICAGO CO. #57**		
	On bottom, double band collar, large and small ring on shoulder, large ring on base, round, aqua, 2½"	7.00	10.00
☐403	**L.H. THOMAS INK**		
	Aqua, 5¼"	12.00	16.00
☐404	**L.H. THOMAS INK**		
	Bell shaped, aqua, 2¾"	19.00	26.00
☐405	**L.H. THOMAS INK**		
	Pat. April 13, 1875 under bottom, aqua, 8"	12.00	16.00
☐406	**W.B. TODD**		
	Ring top, round, green, 2⅞"	8.00	11.00
☐407	**TRAVEL INK**		
	Label, with fitted hard leather case, six panels, aqua, 2" .	9.00	12.00
☐408	*TURTLE, plain rim around bottle at bottom, spout extends 1⅟₁₆" on side, sheared top, aqua, 1½" wide, 2⅛" tall*	21.00	28.00
☐409	*TURTLE, aqua, 2" x 4"*	45.00	60.00
☐410	*TURTLE, twelve lines lower half, granite, sheared top, aqua, 1½" x 2"*	33.00	42.00

U

☐411	*UMBRELLA INK, eight-sided, tapers into small round neck, open pontil, olive amber, 2½" tall, 2½" base*	65.00	80.00
☐412	*Same as above except brown*	26.00	37.00
☐413	*Same as above except blue*	26.00	37.00
☐414	*Same as above except no pontil*	18.00	27.00
☐415	*Same as above except no pontil, brown or blue*	11.00	15.00
☐416	*UMBRELLA INK, six panels, pontil, aqua or blue, 2½"* ...	60.00	80.00

☐417 *Same as above except no pontil* **35.00** **50.00**
☐418 *Same as above except smaller type* **25.00** **35.00**
☐419 *UMBRELLA INK, rolled lip, eight vertical panels, aqua, 2⅝"* **11.00** **15.00**
☐420 *UMBRELLA INK, rolled lip, open pontil, light amber, 2½" diameter, 2⅜" tall* ....OCT............... **41.00** **52.00**
☐421 *UMBRELLA INK, eight vertical panels, rolled lip, whittled effect, open pontil, emerald green, 2⅜"* **45.00** **56.00**
☐422 *UMBRELLA INK, label, twelve panels, open pontil, aqua* . **22.00** **29.00**
☐423 **UNDERWOOD**
Aqua, 3" **9.00** **12.00**
☐424 **UNDERWOOD INKS**
Cobalt blue, 6½" **40.00** **55.00**
☐425 **UNDERWOOD INKS**
Embossed, cylindrical, two pen rests on shoulder, flared lip, cloudy, mold line ends at base of neck, aqua, 1⅞" tall, 2⅛" base **15.00** **23.00**
☐426 **UNDERWOOD INKS**
Under bottom, circle or ring, tapered bottle, space for label, aqua, 3¼" x 2¼" **45.0** **57.00**
☐427 **JOHN UNDERWOOD & CO.**
Cobalt blue, 9½" **30.00** **38.00**
☐428 **UNION INK CO.**
Ring top, aqua, 2¼" **9.00** **12.00**
☐429 **UNION INK CO./SPRINGFIELD, MASS.**
On sloping front, dome shaped, sheared top, aqua, 1½" . **21.00** **28.00**
☐430 **UNION INK CO./SPRINGFIELD MASS.**
Aqua, 2" **12.00** **17.00**

V

☐431 **VOLGERS INK**
Label, house type, T.C.V. under bottom, ring top, clear, 2" **12.00** **17.00**

W

☐432 **WWW**
Enter lock large letters, under it trademark, flare ring top, round, blue-green, 2⅞" x 2⅛" **18.00** **25.00**
☐433 **SAMUEL WARD & CO.**
Sheared top, clear, 3" **9.00** **12.00**
☐434 **WARD'S INK**
Pouring spout, round, olive green, 4¾" **9.00** **12.00**
☐435 **WATERLOW & SONS, LIMITED, COPYING INK**
Label, Crock, brown, 7½" **9.00** **12.00**
☐436 **L.E. WATERMAN CO.**
Squat band, ABM, aqua **3.00** **4.00**
☐437 **WATERMAN'S WELLTOP**
2 oz., A.B.M., clear, square, screw top and well top, clear, 3⅛" x 1⅞" **11.00** **15.00**

☐438 **E. WATERS**
Vertically words, Troy, N.Y., round, amber, 6½" 350.00   475.00

☐439 **WATERS INK, TROY, N.Y.**
*On panels, six panels, pontil, ring on shoulder and ring
top, tapered, aqua, 2½" x 2"* 120.00   160.00

☐440 **J.M. WHITALL**
Round, green, 1¾" 7.00   10.00

☐441 **WHITTEMORE BROS & CO.**
Dark green, 9½" 9.00   12.00

☐442 **WILBORS INK**
*On shoulder, ring top and base, ring top, round, aqua,
2½" x 2"* 12.00   16.00

☐443 **WILLIAMS & CARLETON, HARTFORD, CONN.**
Round, aqua 18.00   23.00

☐444 **GEORGE W. WILLIAMS & CO.**
Hartford, Conn., cone, aqua, 2½" 19.00   26.00

☐445 **WOODS, PORTLAND, MAINE BLACK INK**
Tapered, ring top, aqua, 2½" 19.00   26.00

☐446 **WORDEN & WYATT'S**
*In 3 lines, in back 1 XL Fancy Inks, square, ring top, clear,
2½" x 1¼"* 24.00   36.00

☐447 **WRIGHT-CLARKSON, MERC. CO. DULUTH, MINN.**
On base, clear, 6½" 5.00   7.00

☐448 **WRITEWELL & CO/INK/CHEMICALLY PURE**
Label, cobalt blue, 7¼" x 2¹⁵⁄₁₆" 12.00   17.00

Y

☐449 **YALE**
Dickinson & Co., Rutherford, N.J., amber, 1¾" 6.00   8.00

MEDICINE

This category includes all patent medicines specially sold as medicine. It excludes bitters, a liquor generally advertised as medicinal tonic, since bitters collecting is a major specialty in itself (see the section on Bitters Bottles). Likewise excluded are all bottles carrying the word "Cure," which also are collected as a specialty in themselves (see the section on Cure Bottles).

Many of the comments made in the introduction to Cure Bottles listings apply to medicine bottles. Like Cures, they were generally of questionable value, but gushingly praised in advertising, and successfully sold due to public distrust of the legitimate medical profession.

Patent medicine refers to preparations whose formulas were covered by a patent registered with the U.S. Patent Office. In the 19th century, such patents could be obtained by anyone whether a licensed physician, pharmaceutical company or (as was generally the case) a fast-buck artist who knew nothing about medicine. So long as the ingredients were not deemed poisonous in ordinary dosages, the patent would be granted. They were treated as "products" rather than medicines, After passage of the Pure Food and Drug Act of 1907, most patent medicine companies went out of business. They were required to list ingredients on labels and upon learning the ingredients, few people wanted to buy them. Many consisted of nothing more than liquor diluted with ordinary water, sometimes with the addition of opiates. Others contained small amounts of strychnine or arsenic. Some quack manufacturers considered it good business to load up their preparations with powerful ingredients; they felt that if users experienced *some* kind of reaction, even if just dizziness or faintness, they'd believe in the product's effectiveness.

Not all medicines were patented. The U.S. Patent Office opened in 1790, but it was six years later before a patent was taken out for medicine. Many makers hesitated to take out patents as this required them to reveal the contents.

One of the oldest types of medicine bottles came out of England, the embossed Turlington's "Balsam of Life" bottles made between 1723 and 1900. The earliest American-made medicines came in plain bottles from domestic production. The first embossed U.S. medicine bottles date from around 1810. By 1906, the making of medicine bottles had become an $80,000,000 per year industry. Today's medicine bottles are largely made of plastic.

MEDICINE BOTTLES

A

NO.	DESCRIPTION	PRICE RANGE	
☐1	**THE P.L. ABBEY CO.**		
	Clear, 8¾"	11.00	16.00
☐2	**THE ABBOTT AIKAL CO. CHICAGO**		
	In vertical lines, ring top, clear, 2⅝"	5.00	8.00
☐3	**THE ABBOTT AIKLORD CO., CHICAGO**		
	Clear or aqua, 2⅝"	7.00	12.00
☐4	**ABBOTT BROS., CHICAGO**		
	Reverse side Rheumatic Remedy, amber, 6½"	15.00	24.00

☐5 **THE ABNER ROYCE CO.**
Clear or amethyst, 5½ " 3.00 5.00

☐6 **ABRAMS & CORROLLS ESSENCE OF JAMAICA GINGER, SAN FRANCISCO**
Aqua, 5¼ " 10.00 15.00

☐7 **ABSORBINE**
Springfield, Mass. U.S.A., amber, 7½ " 9.00 13.00

☐8 **A & CO.**
Under bottom, label, amber, 5¼ " 7.00 10.00

☐9 **A.C. CO. COMFORT, JACKSONVILLE, FLA.**
Under bottom, clear, 5½ " 3.00 5.00

☐10 **ACEITE ORIENTAL RESSERT**
In back, cobalt, 3½ " 17.00 24.00

☐11 **ACEITE ORIENTAL RESSERT**
Moon and star on back, amber, 3½ " 8.00 11.00

☐12 **ACID IRON EARTH**
Reverse side Mobile, Ala., amber, 6¾ " 12.00 16.00

☐13 **DR. ACKER'S TU-BER-KU**
Catarrh Of The Head other side, clear, 8" 6.00 9.00

☐14 **ACKER'S ELIXER, THE GREAT HEALTH RESTORER**
Label, amber, 6½ " 5.00 8.00

☐15 **AFFLECKS DRUG STORE, WASHINGTON, D.C.**
Clear or amethyst, 3¼ " 5.00 8.00

☐16 **AFRICANA**
In script, amber, 8" 14.00 19.00

☐17 **AGUA PERUBINAT CONDAL**
Label, round, 10½ " 6.00 9.00

☐18 **AIMARS**
Reverse side Charleston S.C., reverse Sarsaparilla & Queens Delight, amber, 9⅝ " 50.00 65.00

☐19 **ALBANY CO. PHARMACY, LARAMIE, WYO.**
Aqua 6.00 9.00

☐20 **DR. ALEXANDER**
On side, Lung Healer on opposite side, rectangular, square collar, aqua blue, 6½ " 6.00 9.00

☐21 **DR. W. H. ALEXANDERS WONDERFULL HEALING OIL**
Label, aqua 4.00 6.00

☐22 **ALLAIRE WOODWARD & CO., PEORIA, ILL**
Reverse side Elixir & Nutrans, amber, 10" 17.00 23.00

☐23 **ALLAN ANTIFAT BOTANIC MED CO., BUFFALO, N.Y., 1895**
Aqua, 7½ " 8.00 12.00

☐24 **MRS. A. ALLEN'S**
Worlds Hair Restorer one side, New York other side, amber, 7½ " 6.00 9.00

☐25 **MRS. S.A. ALLEN'S**
Worlds Hair Restorer, 355 Produce St. N.Y. on two panels, dark purple, 7" 17.00 23.00

☐26 **ALLEN'S ESSENCE OF JAMAICA GINGER**
Aqua, 5½ " 7.00 10.00

☐27 **ALLEN'S NERVE & BONE LINIMENT**
Vertical around bottle; square collar, round, aqua, 3⅞" 6.00 9.00

☐28 **ALLEN'S SARSAPARILLA**
Vertical on front; oval shape, narrow square, aqua, 8⅛" ... 15.00 23.00

☐ 29	**ALLE-RHUME REMEDY CO.**		
	Machine made, clear, 7¾"	6.00	9.00
☐ 30	**T.C. CAULK ALLOY**		
	On bottom, sunken panel, clear, 2¼"	4.00	6.00
☐ 31	**AMERICAN DRUG STORE N.O.**		
	In center, tapered top, amber, 9¼"	40.00	55.00
☐ 32	*Same except sample size, 4¼"*	45.00	60.00
☐ 33	**AMER'S**		
	In vertical writing, clear or amethyst, 1¾"	4.00	7.00
☐ 34	**SP. AMMON AR**		
	Clear, 9¼"	15.00	20.00
☐ 35	**AMMONIA,** *Flask, all sizes, aqua*	3.00	5.00
☐ 36	**AMMONIA,** *label, aqua, 10½"*	4.00	7.00
☐ 37	**SPIRITUS AMMONIAE**		
	Label, machine made, amber, 6½"	3.00	5.00
☐ 38	**DR. H. ANDRES & CO.**		
	On each side, picture of face of sun, under it Haurieshal		
	Fontevitale, ground top, pontil, aqua, 9"	45.00	60.00
☐ 39	**ANGIERS EMULSION**		
	Aqua, 7"	4.00	7.00
☐ 40	**ANGIERS PETROLEUM EMULSION**		
	Under bottom in three lines, sunken panel in front, back		
	side is rounded, aqua, 7"	5.00	8.00
☐ 41	**ANGIERS PETROLEUM EMULSION**		
	Aqua, 7"	4.00	7.00
☐ 42	**ANODYNE FOR INFANTS**		
	Vertical on front in sunken arch panel, Dr. Groves on side,		
	Philada on opposite side, rectangular, clear, 5¾"	5.00	8.00
☐ 43	**ANTHONY, 501 BROADWAY N.Y.**		
	On front, Flint Varnish for Negatives on label on back,		
	round, clear, 5½"	4.00	6.00
☐ 44	**E. ANTHONY, NEW YORK**		
	Vertical on front, oval, cobalt blue, 6"	7.00	11.00
☐ 45	*APOTHECARY JARS, open pontil, round, ground stopper,*		
	aqua 8½" and 10"	7.00	11.00
☐ 46	*APOTHECARY (drug store), different sizes, clear, 2" and*		
	up	7.00	11.00
☐ 47	*APOTHECARY (drug store), different sizes, green, amber,*		
	light amber, blue, etc., 2" and up	8.00	12.00
☐ 48	*APOTHECARY (drug store), different sizes, pontil, 2" and*		
	up	12.00	19.00
☐ 49	*APOTHECARY, label, 100 under bottom, amber, quart size*		
	....	11.00	16.00
☐ 50	**ARMOUR & CO.**		
	Amber, 4"	4.00	7.00
☐ 51	**ARMOUR AND COMPANY, CHICAGO**		
	In four lines on cathedral type panels, round corner, lady's		
	leg type neck, taller than milk glass, 5¼"	16.00	23.00
☐ 52	**ARMOUR LABORATORIES', CHICAGO**		
	In egg shape circle in center, amber, 7¾"	4.00	7.00
☐ 53	**ARMOUR LABORATORIES, CHICAGO**		
	On fancy oval panel, rectangular, amber, 5"	7.00	11.00
☐ 54	**ARMOUR'S VIGORALS CHICAGO**		
	Squat body, amber	3.00	5.00

☐55	**ARNICA LINIMENT, J.R. BURDSALL'S, NEW YORK**		
	On front and sides, aqua, flask, 5⅝"	6.00	8.00
☐56	**ARNICA & OIL LINIMENT**		
	Vertical on two panels, eight vertical panels, aqua, 6½" .	3.00	5.00
☐57	**DR. SETH ARNOLD'S BALSAM, GILMAN BROS., BOSTON**		
	On front and sides, rectangular, amethyst, 3¾"	6.00	9.00
☐58	**DR. SETH ARNOLD'S BALSAM, GILMAN BROS., BOSTON**		
	Aqua, 7"	11.00	15.00
☐59	**DR. SETH ARNOLD'S**		
	On side Cough Killer, sunken panels, rectangular, banded		
	collar, aqua, 5½"	6.00	9.00
☐60	**AROMATIC SCHNAPPS**		
	(S is backwards), dark olive, 8"	30.00	40.00
☐61	**ASTER**		
	In script running up, The Puritan Drug Co. Columbus O. on		
	base, aqua, 8¾"	7.00	10.00
☐62	**ASTYPTODYAE CHEMICAL CO.**		
	Clear or amethyst, 4½"	3.00	5.00
☐63	**ASTYPTODYAE CHEMICAL CO.**		
	In two lines, 3¾" body, 1" round, 1" neck, clear or		
	amethyst	3.00	5.00
☐64	**ATHIEU'S COUGH SYRUP**	3.00	5.00
☐65	**DR. A. ATKINSON, N.Y.**		
	Pontil, aqua, 8¼"	15.00	20.00
☐66	**THE ATLANTA CHEMICAL CO., ATLANTA, GA. U.S.A.**		
	On side, amber, 8½"	5.00	8.00
☐67	**ATLAS MEDICINE CO.**		
	Henderson, N.C., U.S.A. 1898, amber, 9¼"	10.00	15.00
☐68	**ATRASK OINTMENT**		
	Square bottle, aqua, 2½"	1.50	2.50
☐69	**C. W. ATWELL, PORTLAND, ME.**		
	Vertical on front in large letters, oval, light aqua, 8"	5.00	7.00
☐70	**C. W. ATWELL**		
	Long tapered lip, vertical C. W. Atwell Portland Me, oval		
	shape, open pontil, aqua, 7½"	15.00	22.00
☐71	**ATWOODS JANNAICE LAXATIVE**		
	Machine made, clear, 6"	3.00	5.00
☐72	**AYER'S AGUE CURE, LOWELL MASS**		
	Aqua, 5¾"	6.00	9.00
☐73	**AYER'S CHERRY PECTORAL, LOWELL MASS**		
	Aqua, 7¼"	6.00	9.00
☐74	**AYER'S CONCENTRATED SARSAPARILLA**		
	Pontil, aqua	19.00	31.00
☐75	**AYER'S HAIR VIGOR**		
	Label, aqua, 7½"	11.00	16.00
☐76	*Without label*	4.00	7.00
☐77	**AYER'S**		
	Lowell Mass U.S.A. on back, 8½"	5.00	7.00
☐78	**AYER'S PILLS**		
	Square, clear, 2⅜"	1.50	2.50
☐79	**AYER'S PILLS, LOWELL MASS.**		
	Rectangular, aqua, 2"	5.00	8.00

15

Mrs. S.A. ALLEN'S
25

ALLEN'S
27

36

SPIRITUS
AMMONIAE
AROMATICUS
U.S.P.
37

39

41

ROYAL
CERMETUER
66

ATWOOD'S
Jamaica Laxative
71

76

BABY EASE
84

62

75

109

DR. BELL'S
126

130

BISM.
SUBNITR
134

H C BLAIR
CHEMIST
136

☐80 **AYER'S**
In sunken panel, aqua, 6¼" 1.50   4.00
☐81 **AYER'S SARSAPARILLA**
Lowell, Mass., U.S.A., Compound Ext., aqua, 8½" 2.75   4.25
☐82 **AYER'S**
Reverse side, Lowell, Mass., on side Pectoral, other side
Cherry, aqua, 7¼" 8.00   11.00

B

☐83 **ELIXIR BABEK FOR MALARIA CHILLS FEVERS,**
WASHINGTON, D.C.
Vertical on front in sunken panel, rectangular, clear, 6" .. 6.00   9.00
☐84 **BABY EASE**
Aqua, 5½" 3.00   5.00
☐85 **WM. A. BACON, LUDLOW, VT.**
Pontil, aqua, 5½" 14.00   20.00
☐86 **DR. BAKER'S PAIN PANACEA 1855**
Pontil, aqua, 5" 27.00   38.00
☐87 **DR. IRA BAKER'S HONDURAS SARSAPARILLA**
Aqua or clear, 10½" 16.24   24.00
☐88 **JOHN C. BAKER & CO., COD LIVER OIL**
9½" 7.00   10.00
☐89 **JN. C. BAKER & CO.**
On one side 100 N. 3rd. St., on other side Phild., pontil,
Aqua, 4¾" 17.00   24.00
☐90 **S. F. BAKER & CO., KEOKUK, IOWA**
Aqua, 8½" 6.00   9.00
☐91 **BALLARD SNOW LINIMENT CO.**
Clear or amethyst, 4½" 4.00   9.00
☐92 **BALL BALSAM OF HONEY**
Ringed top, pontil, aqua, 3½" 16.00   22.00
☐93 **BALM-ELIXIR REMEDIES, OSSIPEE, N.H.**
Clear, 5¾" 4.00   6.00
☐94 **BALSAM OF HONEY**
Pontil, aqua, 3¼" 24.00   31.00
☐95 **BALSAM VEGETABLE PULMONARY**
Around bottle, aqua, 5" 6.00   9.00
☐96 **JNO. T. BARBEE & CO.**
Clear or amethyst, 6" 5.00   8.00
☐97 **JNO. T. BARBEE & CO.**
Clear or amethyst, machine made, 6" 3.00   5.00
☐98 **BARBER MEDICINE CO., KANSAS CITY, MO.**
Label, aqua, 7½" 10.00   15.00
☐99 **BARKER MOORE & MEIN MEDICINE CO., PHILADELPHIA**
On front and side, rectangular, aqua, 6⅜" 4.00   6.00
☐100 **BARKER MOORE & MEIN**
Vertical on front, Druggist on side, Philadelphia on op-
posite side, aqua, 5¼" 4.00   6.00
☐101 **WM. JAY BARKER, HIRSUTUS, NEW YORK**
Vertical on front in sunken panel, pewter stopper, square
collar, ABM, clear, 6⅝" 6.00   9.00

☐ 102 Same as above except aqua, 5¼" 6.00 9.00
☐ 103 **DR. BARKMAN'S NEVER FAILING LINIMENT**
On front, light green, 6¼" 5.00 7.00
☐ 104 **BARNES & PARKE, N.Y., BALSAM OF WILD CHERRY &
TAR**
7½" 11.00 15.00
☐ 105 Same as above except 6¼" 11.00 15.00
☐ 106 **BARRY'S TRICOPHEROUS FOR THE SKIN & HAIR, N.Y.**
Pontil, 5¼" 12.00 17.00
☐ 107 Same as above except five other different sizes 12.00 17.00
☐ 108 **T.B. BARTON**
Clear or amethyst, 4½" 3.00 5.00
☐ 109 **BARTOW DRUG CO.**
Clear or amethyst, 3½" 4.00 6.00
☐ 110 **BATCHELOR'S**
Clear or amethyst, 3" 5.00 7.00
☐ 111 **BATEMANS DROPS**
Vertical, cylindrical, amethyst, 5¼" 3.00 5.00
☐ 112 **GEO. H. BATTIER DRUGGIST, 120 BEALE ST.**
5¼" 5.00 7.00
☐ 113 **J. A. BAUER, S. F. CAL.**
Lime green, 8¼" 7.00 10.00
☐ 114 **BAYER ASPIRIN**
In circles, Bayer Aspirin run up and down as cross sign,
screw top, machine made, clear, buttle type bottle, 2½". 3.00 5.00
☐ 115 **X-BAZIN SUCCRTO, E. ROUSSEL**
Philadelphia, six panels, sheared top, clear, 2¾" 6.00 9.00
☐ 116 **B.B.B., ATLANTA, GA.**
Amber, 3¾" x 2¼" 9.00 12.00
☐ 117 **BEASON'S VEGO SYRUP COMPOUND**
Smith Chemical Corp. Johnson City, Tenn., label, clear,
8½" 4.00 6.00
☐ 118 **BEE-DEE MEDICINE CO., CHATTANOOGA TENN.**
On one side Bee Dee Liniment, double ring top, clear, 5½"
.... 6.00 9.00
☐ 119 **BEGGS CHERRY COUGH SYRUP**
Rectangular, aqua, 5¾" 3.00 4.00
☐ 120 **BEGGS DIARRHOEA BALSAM**
Aqua, 5½" 6.00 9.00
☐ 121 **DR. BELDING'S MEDICINE CO.**
On one side of sunken panel, other side Minneapolis,
Minn., side sizes 1¾", 3" wide panel, one side plain for
label, other in script, Dr. Belding's Wild Cherry, Sarsaparilla, body 6", neck 3", aqua 18.00 26.00
☐ 122 **DR. BELDING'S WILD CHERRY SARSAPARILLA**
In sunken panel in front, back plain, Dr. Belding Medicine
Co. on one side in sunken panel, other side Minneapolis,
Minn., aqua, 10" 11.00 15.00
☐ 123 **BELL ANS**
On both sides, round, ABM, amber, 3¾" 3.00 4.00
☐ 124 **BELL & COMPANY INC. MFG. CHEMISTS, NEW YORK**
In three lines, ring top, bottom M.B.W. U.S.A., clear, 7"... 7.00 10.00
☐ 125 **BELL, PA PAY ANS BELL & CO. INC., ORANGEBURG,
NEW YORK, USA**
On opposite sides, rectangular, ABM, amber, 2¾" 3.00 4.00

☐ 126 **DR. BELL'S**
*The E.E. Sutherland Medicine Co. Paducah, Ky., Pine Tar
Honey, aqua, 5½″* 3.00 5.00
☐ 127 **BELT & SON, SALEM, ORE.**
Aqua, 5½″ 5.00 7.00
☐ 128 **J.A. BERNARD DRUGGIST**
*552 Westminister St. Providence, R.I., rectangular, clear,
flared lip, 5½″* 5.00 7.00
☐ 129 **BERRY BROS., 323 E. 38TH ST. N.Y.**
In circle on front, aqua, 11¼″ 4.00 6.00
☐ 130 **THE BETTES PHARMACY**
Label, clear, 4½″ 3.50 5.50
☐ 131 **EL BIEN PUBLICO DRUG STORE, WEST TAMPA, FLA.**
Clear, 3¼″ 3.00 5.00
☐ 132 **BIOKRENE HUTCHINGS & HILLYER, N.Y.**
Aqua, 7½″ 3.00 5.00
☐ 133 **DR. BIRNEY'S CATARRAH ALL POWER**
Clear, 2¼″ 3.00 5.00
☐ 134 **BISM SUBNITR**
Clear, 5¼″ 6.00 9.00
☐ 135 **B-L TONIC, THE B-L-CO. ATLANTA, GA.**
Label, B-L Made in U.S.A. embossed in back, amber, 10″ . 3.00 5.00
☐ 136 **H.C. BLAIR**
*8th & Walnut Philada on side of bottom, clear or
amethyst, 6½″* 5.00 8.00
☐ 137 **E. BLOCH & CO.**
W.B. under bottom, clear, 3½″ 5.00 8.00
☐ 138 **BLOOD BALM CO.**
Label, amber, 9″ 8.00 12.00
☐ 139 **DR. E. BLRICKERS TONIC MIXTURE FOR FEVER AND
CHILLS**
Small tapered top, aqua, 6″ 22.00 30.00
☐ 140 **BLUD-LIFE**
Clear or amethyst, machine made, 8½″ 3.00 4.50
☐ 141 **DR. A. BOCHIE'S GERMAN SYRUP**
In two vertical lines, square, aqua, 6¾″ 3.00 4.50
☐ 142 **BOERICKE & RUNYON COMPANY**
In script on front, clear, 7¾″ 2.50 3.25
☐ 143 **BOERICKE & RUNYON CO.**
*In large letters vertical on one panel, square, beveled cor-
ner, amethyst, 8⅛″* 4.00 6.00
☐ 144 *Same as above except sample size, amber, 2½″* 4.00 6.00
☐ 145 **BOLDWIN CHERRY PEPSIN & DANDELION TONIC**
Amber, 8″ 22.00 30.00
☐ 146 **W. H. BONE CO. C.C. LINIMENT, S.F. CAL. U.S.A.**
Aqua, 6½″ 4.00 6.00
☐ 147 **BON-OPTO FOR THE EYES**
Clear or amethyst, 3¼″ 3.00 5.00
☐ 148 **BOOTH'S HYOMEI**
Buffalo N.Y., Rorterie, Canada, black, 3″ 3.00 5.00
☐ 149 **BORAX**
Clear, 5¼″ 10.00 15.00

☐ 150 **DR. BOSANKO'S PILE REMEDY**
Phila. Pa., aqua, 2½" 3.00 5.00

☐ 151 **DR. BOSANKO'S**
Trial Size on one side, aqua, 4" 3.00 5.00

☐ 152 **DR. A. BOSCHEES GERMAN SYRUP**
In vertical lines, long neck, aqua, 6¾" 3.00 5.00

☐ 153 **BOSTON, MASS**
On front panel, Egyptian Chemical Co., square, clear, screw top, measured, 7½" 2.75 3.50

☐ 154 **DR. C. BOUVIER'S**
Clear, 4½" 6.00 9.00

☐ 155 **BRADFIELD'S, ATLANTA, GA.**
Aqua, 8¾" 5.00 7.00

☐ 156 **BRANDRIFF'S FOR AGUE**
On front, Piqua, Ohio, ring top, aqua or green, 8" 8.00 11.00

☐ 157 **BRANDRIFF'S VEGETABLE ANTIDOTE, PIQUA, O.**
Aqua, 8" 6.00 9.00

☐ 158 **BRANT'S INDIAN PULMONARY BALSAM, MT. WALLACE PROPRIETOR**
Vertical on three panels, 8" wide vertical panels, aqua, 6¾" . 38.00 52.00

☐ 159 **BREIG & SHAFER**
On bottom, on top of it a fish, green 2.75 3.50

☐ 160 **G.O. BRISTO BACKWAR, BUFFALO**
Six panels, pontil, 4¾" 29.00 41.00

☐ 161 **BRISTOL'S**
On one side in sunken panel, other side, New York, front panel plain for label, on back in sunken panel Genuine Sarsaparilla, under bottom in circle panel #18, 2¼" neck, 3¾" wide, 2¼" thick, aqua 6.00 9.00

☐ 162 **BRISTOL'S SARSAPARILLA**
Pontil, green 33.00 47.00

☐ 163 **B & P**
Amber, Lyons Powder on shoulder of opposite side, 4¼" 3.00 5.00

☐ 164 **B.P. CO.**
On front, also BP back to back with circle around it, cobalt, oval, 3" 11.00 15.00

☐ 165 **B.P. CO.**
On front, also BP back to back with circle around it, oval, 1½" 10.00 14.00

☐ 166 **BROMATED PEPSIN, HUMPHREY'S CHEMICAL CO., NEW YORK**
Vertical on front, square, cobalt blue. 3¾" 5.00 7.00

☐ 167 **BROMO CAFFEINE**
Light blue. 3¼" 3.00 5.00

☐ 168 **BROMO LITHIA CHEMICAL CO.**
Amber, 4¼" 2.75 3.50

☐ 169 **BROMO LITHIA CHEMICAL CO.**
Amber, 3¼" 3.00 5.00

☐ 170 **BROMO-SELTZER**
On shoulder, round, machine made, cobalt, under bottomM1 in a circle, 5" 1.50 2.25

☐ 171 **BROMO-SELTZER EMERSON DRUG, BALTIMORE, MD.**
On front, round, cobalt, 5" 1.50 2.25

137

138

140

151

154

168

169

189

190

195

214

215

222

228

245

247

261

267

271

282

☐ 172 **BROMO-SELTZER EMERSON DRUG, BALTIMORE, MD.**
On front, round, cobalt, machine made, 5" 1.50 2.25
☐ 173 **BROMO-SELTZER EMERSON DRUG, BALTIMORE, MD.**
On front, round, cobalt, machine made, 4" 1.50 2.25
☐ 174 **BROMO-SELTZER EMERSON DRUG, BALTIMORE, MD.**
On front, round, cobalt, 5" 7.00 11.00
☐ 175 **BROMO-SELTZER EMERSON DRUG, BALTIMORE, MD.**
On front, round, cobalt, machine made, 6½" 1.50 2.25
☐ 176 **BROMO-SELTZER EMERSON DRUG, BALTIMORE, MD.**
On front, round, cobalt, machine made, 8" 1.50 2.25
☐ 177 **BROMO-SELTZER EMERSON DRUG, BALTIMORE, MD.**
On front, round, cobalt, machine made, 2½" 1.50 2.25
☐ 178 **BROMO-SELTZER EMERSON DRUG, BALTIMORE, MD.**
On front, round, cobalt, machine made, screw top, 4¾".. 1.50 2.25
☐ 179 **BROMO-SELTZER**
Around shoulder, machine made, screw top, cobalt 2.00 3.25
☐ 180 **THE BROOKS DRUG CO., BATTLE CREEK, MICH.**
Label, 887 under bottom, clear, 8" 3.00 5.00
☐ 181 **BROOKS & POTTER DRUGGISTS, SENATOBIA, MISS.**
Clear or amber, 7¼" 3.00 5.00
☐ 182 **THE BROWNE PHARMACY**
1st to 203 Union St., New Bedford, Mass. (B in Wreath),
rectangular, clear, flared lip, 4" 10.00 15.00
☐ 183 **BROWN CO., W.T. & CO.**
Cobalt, 8" 7.00 10.00
☐ 184 **DR. BROWN'S RUTERBA**
Side mold, amber, 8" 8.00 12.00
☐ 185 **DR. C.F. BROWN, YOUNG AMERICAN LINIMENT,
NEW YORK**
Ring top, aqua, 4" 5.00 8.00
☐ 186 **F. BROWNS ESSENCE OF JAMAICA GINGER, PHILADA.**
Tapered top, pontil, aqua, 5½" 15.00 20.00
☐ 187 Same except no pontil 6.00 9.00
☐ 188 Same except no pontil and has ringed top 6.00 9.00
☐ 189 **F. BROWN'S**
Aqua, 5½" 4.00 6.00
☐ 190 **BROWN-FORMAN CO.**
Clear or amethyst, 4½" 3.00 5.00
☐ 191 **BROWN HOUSEHOLD PANACEA AND FAMILY
LINIMENT**
Vertical on front in sunken panel, Curtis & Brown on side,
Mfg. Co. L. D. New York on opposite side, rectangular,
aqua, 5⅛" 4.00 6.00
☐ 192 **J. T. BROWN, 292 WASHINGTON ST., BOSTON,
PREPARATION**
Pontil, aqua, 6" 15.00 20.00
☐ 193 **DR. O. PHELPS BROWN**
Aqua, 3½" 4.00 6.00
☐ 194 **DR. O. PHELPS BROWN**
On side Jersey City, N.J., ring top, aqua, 2½" 3.00 5.00
☐ 195 **BROWN SARSAPARILLA**
Aqua, 3x1¾x9½" 6.00 9.00
☐ 196 **W. E. BROWN DRUGGIST, MANCHESTER, IOWA**
Clear 5.00 8.00

☐197 **W. E. BROWN DRUGGIST, MANCHESTER, IOWA**
Mixing jar and an eagle over it, clear, 5½" **6.00**   **8.00**

☐198 **BROWN'S INSTANT RELIEF FOR PAIN**
Aqua, embossed, 5¼" **3.00**   **5.00**

☐199 **B. S. #30**
Under bottom, drop bottle, clear, 3½" **7.00**   **10.00**

☐200 **BUCHAN'S HUNGARIAN BALSAM OF LIFE, LONDON**
Vertical lines Kidney Cure, round short neck, green, 5¾" .   **18.00**   **25.00**

☐201 **BUCKINGHAM**
On one side, Whisker Dye on other side, brown, 4¾" **4.00**   **6.00**

☐202 **DR. BULL'S HERBS & IRON**
Pat. Oct. 13, 85 on base, 9½" **17.00**   **23.00**

☐203 **DR. J. W. BULL'S VEG. BABY SYRUP**
Trademark, round, aqua, 5¼" **4.00**   **6.00**

☐204 **W.H. BULL MEDICINE CO.**
Amber, 9½" **5.00**   **8.00**

☐205 **W.H. BULL'S MEDICINE BOTTLE**
Pat Oct 1885 under bottom, clear, 5¼" **4.00**   **6.00**

☐206 **DR. BULLOCK'S NEPHRETICURN**
Providence R.I., aqua, 7" **9.00**   **13.00**

☐207 **BUMSTEADS WORM SYRUP**
Philada, aqua, 4½" **9.00**   **13.00**

☐208 **A. L. BURDOCK LIQUID FOOD, BOSTON, 12½ PERCENT SOLUBLE ALBUMEN**
On four consecutive panel, twelve vertical panels on bottle, square collar, amber, 6" **7.00**   **10.00**

☐209 **J.A. BURGON, ALLEGHENY CITY, PA.**
Label on back, Dr. J.A. Burgon standing and holding a bottle and table, clear, 8¼" **13.00**   **18.00**

☐210 **BURKE & JAMES**
W.T. CO. A.A. U.S.A. under bottom, clear or amethyst, 6¼" **7.00**   **10.00**

☐211 **E.A. BURKHOUT'S DUTCH LINIMENT, PREP. AT MECHANICVILLE, SARATOGA CO., N.Y.**
Pontil, aqua, 5¼" **80.00** **105.00**

☐212 **BURLINGTON DRUG CO., BURLINGTON, VT.**
Label, clear, 5½" **8.00**   **11.00**

☐213 **BURNAM'S BEEF WINE E.J.B. & IRON**
On front, thumb print on back, oval, aqua, 9¼" **7.00**   **10.00**

☐214 **BURNETT**
Clear, 6¾" **3.00**   **5.00**

☐215 **BURNETT**
Boston on other side, clear, 4¼" **3.00**   **5.00**

☐216 **BURNETT**
On side, Boston on opposite side, beveled corners, square collar, oval shape, aqua, 6½" **5.00**   **7.00**

☐217 **BURNETTS COCAINE**
Vertical on front, Burnetts on side, Boston on opposite side, large beveled corners, tapered shoulders, aqua, 7⅜"   **6.00**   **9.00**

☐218 **BURNETTS COCAINE, BOSTON**
Ringed top, aqua, 7¼" **5.00**   **8.00**

☐219 **BURNETTS COCAINE, 1864-1900**
Ringed top, clear **11.00**   **15.00**

☐ 220 **BURNHAM'S BEEF WINE & IRON**
Aqua, 9½" 5.00   8.00
☐ 221 **BURNHAM'S CLAM BOUILLON, E.S. BURNHAM CO., NEW YORK**
Five lines, machine made, 4½" 3.00   4.00
☐ 222 **BURNHAM'S**
Aqua, 4¾" 3.50   5.00
☐ 223 **BURRINGTON'S VEGETABLE GROUP SYRUP, PROVIDENCE, R.I.**
Vertical around bottle, ring collar, cylindrical, clear, 5½" . 5.00   7.00
☐ 224 *Same as above except aqua* 5.00   7.00
☐ 225 **BURTON'S MALTHOP TONIQUE**
Label, three-part mold, dark olive, 7½" 5.00   8.00
☐ 226 **BURWELL-DUNN**
R.S.J., 969 under bottom, clear or amethyst, 3¾" 3.00   5.00
☐ 227 **BUTLER'S BALSAM OF LIVERWORT**
Pontil, aqua, 4¼" 55.00   75.00

C

☐ 228 **CABOT'S SULPHO NAPTHOL**
Vertical on front, oval back, beveled corners, square collar, amber, 6½" and 4¾" 5.00   9.00
☐ 229 **CABOT'S SULPHO NAPTHOL**
Written fancy, large beveled corners, oval back, square collar, aqua, 5⅛" 6.00   9.00
☐ 230 **CALDWELLS SYRUP PEPSIN**
Mfd by Pepsin Syrup Co., Monticello, Ill., aqua, rectangular, 3" 3.00   5.00
☐ 231 **CALDWELLS SYRUP PEPSIN**
Mfd by Pepsin Syrup Co. Monticello, Ill., aqua, rectangular, machine made, screw top, all sizes 1.35   2.15
☐ 232 **CALIFORNIA FIG SYRUP CO.**
On front panel, Louisville, Ky. on left side, San Francisco, Calif. on right side, rectangular, amethyst, 7¼" 3.00   5.00
☐ 233 **CALIFORNIA FIG SYRUP CO.**
On front on side Wheeling, W. Va., 6" ABM, clear 5.00   7.00
☐ 234 **CALIFORNIA FIG. SYRUP CO., SAN FRANCISCO, CAL**
Vertical on front, Syrup of Figs on both sides, rectangular, square collar, amethyst, 6½" 5.00   8.00
☐ 235 **CALIFORNIA FIG SYRUP CO.**
Califig, Sterling Products (inc) Successor on front, rectangular, clear, 6¾" 3.00   5.00
☐ 236 **CALIFORNIA FIG SYRUP CO.**
Califig, Sterling Products (inc) Successor on front, rectangular machine made, screw top, all sizes and colors .. 1.35   2.15
☐ 237 **CALIFORNIA FIG. SYRUP CO., S.F., CAL.**
Syrup of Fig, clear or amber, 6¾" 3.00   4.50
☐ 238 **PROF. CALLAN'S WORLD RENOWNED BRAZILIAN GUM**
Vertical on one panel, square collar, aqua, 4⅛" 3.00   4.50
☐ 239 **DR. CALLAN'S WORLD RENOWNED BRAZILIAN GUM**
Clear, 4½" 3.00   4.50

☐240	**EXT. CALUMB. FL.**		
	Cobalt, 9½″	17.00	23.00
☐241	**CALVERT'S**		
	Clear or amethyst, 8″	11.00	15.00
☐242	**THE CAMPBELL DRUG CO., THE GENERAL STORE, FOSTORIA, OHIO**		
	On back Camdrugo, green, 5¼″	7.00	10.00
☐243	**CAMPBELL V. V.**		
	In script, the genuine always bears this signature in the front panel, diamond shaped base, clear, 5⅛″	4.00	6.00
☐244	**CAPLION**		
	Label, clear, TCWCO. U.S.A. on bottom, 5″	4.00	6.00
☐245	**CAPUDINE CHEMICAL CO. RALEIGH, N.C.**		
	In center, G under bottom, label, machine made, amber, 7½″	2.50	3.25
☐246	**CAPUDINE FOR HEADACHE**		
	On front panel, amber, oval, 3¼″	1.35	2.10
☐247	**DR. M. CARABALLO**		
	Vermicida in back, aqua, 4¼″	5.00	7.00
☐248	**CARBONA**		
	On the base, paneler, aqua, 5½″ and 6″	3.00	5.00
☐249	**CARBONA, CARBONA PRODUCTS CO.**		
	Carbona in three lines, hair oil, aqua, 6″	1.40	2.15
☐250	**CARBONA, CARBONA PRODUCTS CO.**		
	Carbona in three lines running vertically, round, aqua, hair dressing, 6″	3.00	4.00
☐251	**CARBONA & CARBONA PRODUCTS CO.**		
	Carbona on three vertical panels, twelve panels, square collar, aqua, 5⅛″	6.00	8.00
☐252	**CARLES HYPO · COD.**		
	Clear, double ring top, one big under it small top, 8″	12.00	16.00
☐253	**CARLO ERBA MAINO, OLEO PICINO**		
	Clear or amber, 3¾″	10.00	15.00
☐254	**CARLSBAD**		
	Clear, 5½″	5.00	8.00
☐255	**CARLSBAD AH**		
	Under bottom, sheared top, clear, 4″	3.00	5.00
☐256	**CARLSBAD RA**		
	Under bottom, sheared top, clear, 4″	5.00	9.00
☐257	**CARPENTER & WOOD, INC.**		
	Est. 1883 Providence, R.I. with eagle and shield on center front, glass stopper, round, clear or amethyst, 2¼″	3.00	5.00
☐258	**CARTER'S SPANISH MIX**		
	Pontil, green, 8″	16.00	23.00
☐259	**CARY GUM TREE COUGH SYRUP**		
	S. Fran. U.S.A., aqua blue, 7½″	10.00	15.00
☐260	Same as above except lime green	13.00	19.00
☐261	**CASSEBEER**		
	Reverse side N.Y., amber, 7½″	7.00	10.00
☐262	**CASTOR OIL, PURE**		
	2 fl. oz., The Frank Tea & Co, cintion front, clear, flask, 5¼″ .	7.00	10.00
☐263	Also machine made and screw top, all sizes and colors ..	1.50	2.20

☐264	**CASTOR OIL**		
	4" body, 3" neck, 1¼" round bottle, cobalt blue	13.00	18.00
☐265	Same, except smaller, some in different sizes	13.00	18.00
☐266	Castor oil label, W.C. 30z under bottom, cobalt, 8¼"	11.00	15.00
☐267	**C.B. 6B**		
	On bottom, green, 7¼"	3.00	5.00
☐268	**C & C**		
	Inside two concentric circles, sides fluted, amethyst rectangular, 4½"	3.00	5.00
☐269	**C.C.C. TONIC, BOERICKE & RUNYON NEW YORK**		
	Vertical on front in large letters, beveled corners, rectangular, large flared square collar, clear, 8"	26.00	34.00
☐270	**C & Co**		
	Clear or amber, 3½"	3.00	5.00
☐271	**CELERY MEDICINE CO**		
	Bitters label, clear or amethyst, 9"	12.00	17.00
☐272	**CELERY-VESCE, CENTURY CHEMICAL CO**		
	Indianapolis, Ind. U.S.A., amber, 4"	6.00	9.00
☐273	**CELRO-KOLA, PHIL BLUMAUER & CO., PORTLAND, OR.**		
	Clear, 10"	6.00	9.00
☐274	**CENTOUR LINIMENT**		
	Ringed top, aqua, 5¼"	3.00	5.00
☐275	**CENTOUR LINIMENT**		
	On shoulder, aqua, 3½"	1.40	2.25
☐276	**CENTOUR LINIMENT**		
	On shoulder, aqua, round, 5"	3.00	5.00
☐277	**CENTOUR LINEMENT**		
	On shoulder, round bottle, machine made, aqua, 5"	1.50	2.35
☐278	**CENTRAL DRUG CO.**		
	Laramie Wyo, clear	6.00	9.00
☐279	**CERTAIN GROUP REMEDY**		
	Vertical on front in sunken panel, Dr. Hoxsie's on side, Buffalo, N.Y. on opposite side, rectangular, clear, 4½" ..	6.00	9.00
☐280	**CHAMBERLAIN'S COLIC CHOLERA AND DIARRHEA REMEDY**		
	Chamberlain Med. Co. Des Moines, Ia USA on front and sides, rectangular, aqua, 4½"	6.00	9.00
☐281	Same as above except 6"	5.00	8.00
☐282	**CHAMBERLAIN'S COUGH REMEDY**		
	On other side Chamberlains Med. Co., aqua, 5½"	5.00	8.00
☐283	**CHAMBERLAIN'S**		
	On side panel, Bottle Made in America on opposite side, rectangular, aqua, 4½"	3.00	5.00
☐284	**CHAMBERLAIN'S COLIC CHOLERA DIARRHEA REMEDY**		
	On front, Des Moines, Iowa U.S.A. on side panel, Chamberlain Med. Co. on opposite, aqua, rectangular, 5¼"	4.00	6.00
☐285	**CHAMBERLAIN'S COUGH REMEDY**		
	On front, Des Moines, Ia. U.S.A. on left side, Chamberlain Med. Co. on right side, rectangular, aqua or clear, 6¾" ..	4.00	6.00
☐286	**CHAMBERLAIN'S PAIN-BALM**		
	On front, Des Moines, Ia. U.S.A. on left side, Chamberlain Med. Co. on right side, aqua, rectangular, 7"	3.00	5.00

281

293

301

307

311

330

336

337

354

357

360

358

359

365

368

372

☐287 **CHAMPLIN'S LIQUID PEARL**
On front, rectangular, square collar, milk glass, 5" 7.00 11.00
☐288 Same as above except 6" 6.00 10.00
☐289 **DR. P. H. CHAPELLE, N.Y.**
Label, flask, clear, 6¾" 6.00 9.00
☐290 **CHELF CHEM. CO.**
Cobalt, machine made, 4" 2.50 3.25
☐291 **CHEMICAL BOTTLE**
Label, crystal glass, clear, 6½" 8.00 11.00
☐292 **CHEMICAL CO. D.D. N.Y. SAMPLE**
On the front panel, amber, square, 5" 1.50 2.15
☐293 **CHESEBROUGH**
Clear or amethyst, 3½" 2.50 3.25
☐294 **CHESEBROUGH MFG. CO.**
In horseshoe letters, under it Vaseline, clear, 2⅞" 1.50 2.15
☐295 **CHESEBROUGH VASELINE**
Clear, 2¾" 3.00 5.00
☐296 Same except 3¾" 4.00 6.00
☐297 Same except ABM, amethyst, thread top, 3¼" and 2½" . 3.00 4.00
☐298 Same as above except ABM, amber 3.00 4.00
☐299 Same as above, ABM, clear 3.00 4.00
☐300 **CHESEBROUGH VASELINE TRADE MARK, NEW YORK**
On front, mold threads, pint size, amethyst 3.50 5.50
☐301 **PROF CHEVALIER**
Clear, 4¼" 3.50 5.50
☐302 CHINESE BOTTLE, clear, 2½" 3.50 5.50
☐303 **CHINIDIN**
Clear, 5¼" 6.00 9.00
☐304 **CHLORATE POTASSIQUE**
Pontil, clear glass painted brown, 6½" 16.00 23.00
☐305 **CHRISTIES MAGNETIC FLUID**
Flared top, aqua, 4¾" 6.00 9.00
☐306 **CHURCH, C.M.**
In script in center on one side of it Druggist, other
Belvidere, Ill. ring top, on bottom A.M.F. & Co., 6½" clear 5.00 8.00
☐307 **T.R. CIMICIFUG**
Clear, 7¾" 3.00 5.00
☐308 **CIRCASSIAN BLOOM**
Clear or amber, 5" 4.00 7.00
☐309 **THE CITIZENS WHOLESALE SUPPLY CO.**
Label, clear, 7½" 3.00 5.00
☐310 **THE CITIZENS WHOLESALE SUPPLY CO.**
Columbus O. Camphorated Oil on label, clear, 7½" 3.00 5.00
☐311 CITRATE MAGNESIA, clear or amethyst, 8" 3.00 5.00
☐312 CITRATE MAGNESIA, clear or amethyst, 8¾" 3.00 5.00
☐313 CITRATE MAGNESIA in script around bottom, Sanitas
bottle, clear or amethyst, 8" 2.50 3.50
☐314 CITRATE MAGNESIA in script on bottom, Sanitas bottle,
clear or amethyst, 8" 1.35 2.15
☐315 CITRATE MAGNESIA, National Magnesia Co. Inc., clear,
round, 7" 3.00 5.00
☐316 CITRATE MAGNESIA, in a sunken circle, in center O Dot,
4T around it, double-ring top, aqua, 7" 3.00 5.00

☐317 *CITRATE MAGNESIA, embossed in indented bands, blob top, green, 8"* **6.00** **9.00**

☐318 **CITY DRUG COMPANY**
103 Main St., Anaconda Mont., clear, 4¼" **3.00** **5.00**

☐319 **CITY DRUG COMPANY**
Meridian, Tex., amethyst, rectangular, 3¼" **1.35** **2.15**

☐320 **OTIS CLAPP & SONS MALT & COD LIVER OIL COMPOUND**
Vertical on front in fancy lettering, large square collar, amber, 7¼" **5.00** **8.00**

☐321 **C. G. CLARK & CO.**
Restorative other side, aqua, 7¾" **4.00** **7.00**

☐322 **THE C. G. CLARK CO.**
Vertical on one panel, New Haven, Ct. on third panel, twelve vertical panels, square collar, aqua, 5½" **3.50** **5.00**

☐323 **CLARK'S CORDIAL**
On front in diamond shape panel, (Note: you can see where the words Clark's Calif. Cherry Cordial were slugged out of the mold), amber, 8¼" **27.00** **36.00**

☐324 **DR. J. S. CLARK'S, THROAT & LUNGS**
Reverse side Balsam For The, aqua, 8½" **11.00** **15.00**

☐325 **CLOUDS CORDIAL**
On each side, tapered type bottle, tapered top, amber, 10¾" x 3 x 2" **24.00** **33.00**

☐326 **W.W. CLARK, 16 N. 5TH ST. PHILA.**
Pontil, aqua, 5⅜" **15.00** **22.00**

☐327 **CLEMENTS & CO.**
Rosadalis other side, aqua, 8½" **5.00** **8.00**

☐328 **CREME DE CAMELIA FOR THE COMPLEXION**
On side, The Boradent Co. Inc., San Francisco on opposite side, beveled corners, rectangular, flared collar, New York in slug plate, cobalt blue, 5⅛" **7.00** **10.00**

☐329 *Same as above except San Francisco & New York embossed* **7.00** **10.00**

☐330 *COD LIVER OIL, aqua, 9¾"* **4.00** **6.00**

☐331 *COD LIVER OIL, with fish in center, screw top, machine made, two sizes, amber, round* **3.00** **5.00**

☐332 *COD LIVER OIL, in front with a fish in sunken panel, square, amber, screw top, machine made, 9"* **3.00** **5.00**

☐333 *COD LIVER OIL, in front with a fish in sunken panel, square, amber, screw top, machine made, 6"* **3.00** **5.00**

☐334 *COD LIVER OIL-FISH, different sizes and many different colors, some made in Italy* **15.00** **20.00**

☐335 **COFFEEN'S PAIN SPECIFIC**
Clear, 7¼" **4.00** **7.00**

☐336 **COLLEGE HILL PHARMACY**
Clear or amethyst, 4½" **3.00** **5.00**

☐337 **N.A. COLLINGS**
WT Co. U.S.A. under bottom, clear, 6¼" **3.00** **5.00**

☐338 **COLY TOOTH WASH**
Backward S in WASH, clear, 4½" **13.00** **19.00**

☐339 **COMPOUND ELIXIR**
Aqua, 8¾" **9.00** **12.00**

☐340 **W. H. COMSTOCK**
On back Moses Indian Root Pills, on side Dose 1 to 3,
amber, 2½" 4.00 6.00
☐341 **CONE ASTHMA CONQUEROR CO.**
Cincinnati, O., clear, 8" 5.00 8.00
☐342 **CONNELL'S BRAHMNICAL MOON PLANT EAST INDIAN**
REMEDIES
On base in back ten stars around a pair of feet, under it
trade mark, amber, 7" 18.00 27.00
☐343 **CONNELL'S BRAHMNICAL EAST INDIAN REMEDIES**
Amber 7.00 11.00
☐344 **COOPE'S NEW DISCOVERY**
Tonic, label, aqua, 8¾" 1.35 2.10
☐345 **CHAS. D. COOPER PHARMACIST**
Walden, N.Y., rectangular, amethyst, 4½" 5.00 7.00
☐346 **COOPER'S NEW DISCOVERY**
Aqua, 9" 6.00 9.00
☐347 **COSTAR'S**
Very light blue, 4" 5.00 7.00
☐348 **COSTAR'S, N.Y.**
On shoulder, amber, 4" 6.00 9.00
☐349 **GEORGE COSTER**
Side mold, aqua, 5½" 4.00 6.00
☐350 **CRARY & CO.**
Aqua, 4¼" 2.50 4.00
☐351 **W. H. CRAWFORD CO.**
Clear, 4¼" 2.50 4.00
☐352 **CREENSFELDER & LAUPHEIMER DRUGGISTS,**
BALTIMORE, MD.
On three panels, twelve panels, on shoulder A.R.B.,
amber, 8½" 9.00 13.00
☐353 **CREOMULSION FOR COUGHS DUE TO COLDS**
Amethyst or clear, rectangular, 8¼" 4.00 6.00
☐354 **CRESOL U.S.P.**
Label, clear, 7¼" 3.00 5.00
☐355 **DR. CROSSMANS SPECIFIC MIXTURE**
Vertical around bottle, square collar, aqua, 3¾" 6.00 9.00
☐356 **CROWN CORDIAL & EXTRACT CO. N.Y.**
Amethyst, round, 10¼" 4.00 6.00
☐357 **THE CRYSTAL PHARMACY**
Clear or amethyst, 7" 3.00 5.00
☐358 **C.S. & CO. LD 6045**
On bottom, aqua, 8¾" 3.00 5.00
☐359 **C.S. & CO. LD 10296**
On bottom, dark green, 9¾" 6.00 9.00
☐360 **DR. CUMMING'S VEGETINE**
Aqua, 9¾" 3.00 5.00
☐361 **CURLINGS CITRATE OF MAGNESIA**
Vertical on front, large beveled corners, crude ring top,
cobalt blue, 6⅛" 4.00 6.00
☐362 **CUSHING MEDICAL SUPPLY CO., N.Y. & BOSTON, FULL**
QT.
Aqua, 10" 6.00 9.00

☐363 **CUTICURA TREATMENT FOR AFFECTATIONS OF THE SKIN**
Aqua, 9⅛" 4.00   7.00

D

☐364 **DAD CHEMICAL CO.**
On the shoulders, amber, round, 6" 1.35   2.15
☐365 **DALBYS**
Carminative on back, 3751 under bottom, clear, 3¾" 2.50   3.25
☐366 **DALBYS CARMINATIVE**
Pontil, clear or aqua, 3½" 16.00   23.00
☐367 **DALTON'S SARSAPARILLA AND NERVE TONIC**
Belfast, Maine USA on opposite sides, rectangular, aqua, 9¼" 12.00   17.00
☐368 **C. DAMSCHINSKY**
Aqua, 3¼" 4.00   7.00
☐369 **DAMSCHINSKY LIQUID HAIR DYE, N.Y.**
Aqua, 3½" 5.00   7.00
☐370 **D. DAMSCHINSKY LIQUID HAIR DYE, NEW YORK**
In sunken panels, aqua, 3½" 5.00   7.00
☐371 *Same as above except 2¾"* 5.00   7.00
☐372 **DANA'S**
Aqua, 9" 5.00   7.00
☐373 **DANA'S SARSAPRILLA**
In two lines in a sunken panel, side and back are plain sunken panels, aqua, 9" 12.00   17.00
☐374 **DANIEL'S**
Front side, other sides Atlanta, Ga., aqua, 4½" 4.00   6.00
☐375 **DR. DANIEL'S CARBO-NECUS**
Disinfectant Deordorizer Purifier & Insecticide, clear, 6½" .. 3.00   5.00
☐376 **DR. DANIEL'S VETERINARY**
Clear, 3½" 4.00   7.00
☐377 **DR. DANIEL'S VETERINARY COLIC DROPS NO. 1**
Square, amethyst, 3½" 7.00   10.00
☐378 **DR. A.G. DANIEL'S LINIMENT, OSTER COCUS OIL, BOSTON, MASS. USA**
Vertical on front, oval back, beveled corners, clear, 6¾" . 6.00   9.00
☐379 **DARBY'S PROPHYLACTIC FLUID**
J.H. Zeilen & Co. Phila., aqua, 7½" 6.00   8.00
☐380 **CHAS. F. DARE MENTHA PEPSIN**
Bridgetown, N.J. 6.00   9.00
☐381 **DR. DAVIS'S COMPOUND SYRUP OF WILD CHERRY & TAR**
On 5 panels, 8 paneled bottle, tapered top, aqua, 7¼" ... 12.00   16.00
☐382 **DAVIS**
In an upper sunken panel, bottom of it flat, back full sunken panel, on one side Geoetable, other side Pain Killer, aqua or light blue, 6" 4.00   6.00
☐383 **DAVIS**
In sunken panel in front, medical, aqua, 6⅝" 4.00   6.00
☐384 **DAVIS**
In sunken panel in front, medical, blue, 6½" 4.00   6.00

☐385 **DAVIS VEGETABLE PAIN KILLER**
On front and sides, rectangular, sunken panels, aqua, 6" .   4.00   6.00

☐386 **D.D. CHEMICAL Co. N.Y. SAMPLE**
On front of panel, amber, square, 5" 3.00   4.50

☐387 **D.D.D.**
On front of panel, amethyst, square, 3½" and 5½" 5.00   7.00

☐388 **DEAD SHOT VERMIFUGE**
Pontil, amber or clear 19.00   26.00

☐389 **PROF. DEAN'S BARBED WIRE REMEDY**
Amber, 5½" 3.00   5.00

☐390 **DELAVAN'S SYRUP WHOOPING COUGH CROUP, PHILADELPHIA**
Vertical on front, rectangular, square collar, aqua, 6¼" .   6.00   9.00

☐391 **DELAVAN'S WHOOPING COUGH REMEDY**
Phila., aqua, 6¼" 4.00   6.00

☐392 **DR. J. DENNIS GEORGIA SARSAPARILLA**
Augusta, Ga., graphite pontil, tapered top, aqua, 10½" ..   90.00   120.00

☐393 **DERMA-ROYALE FOR THE SKIN AND COMPLEXION**
Vertical The Derma Royale Comp'y Cincinnati, O. also on front, inside of circle, flared lip, square, clear, 6⅛" 6.00   9.00

☐394 **PAUL DEVERED & CO., GENUINE C.V.E.**
Geo. Raphael & Co. sole proprietor, pontil, flared top, clear or amber, 3½" 16.00   22.00

☐395 **DEWITT'S SOOTHING SYRUP, CHICAGO**
Amethyst, round, 5" 5.00   7.00

☐396 **DEWITTS**
Aqua, 9" 18.00   26.00

☐397 **E.C. DEWITT & CO.**
Aqua, 9¼" 6.00   9.00

☐398 **DICK'S LIVER AC PILLS**
In three lines, round bottom, ring top, clear, 2⅜" 6.00   9.00

☐399 **DIAMOND OIL**
On two sides of panel, aqua, rectangular, 5½" 3.00   5.00

☐400 **DIAMOND & ONYX**
Phila. U.S.A., aqua, 4¾" 3.00   5.00

☐401 **MAXIMO M. DIAZ**
Aqua, 7" 3.00   5.00

☐402 **DICKEY CHEMIST, S.F.**
In center Pioneer 1850, blue, 5¾" 14.00   19.00

☐403 **JOHN R. DICKEY'S**
Old Reliable Eye Water, Mfg. by Dickey Drug Co., Briston, Va., aqua, round, 3¾" 4.00   6.00

☐404 **DILL'S BALM OF LIFE**
Vertical on front, rectangular, ABM, clear, 6" 4.00   6.00

☐405 **DILL'S COUGH SYRUP**
Vertical on front, Dill Medicine Co. on side, Norristown, Pa. on opposite side, sunken panels, rectangular, clear, 5⅞" ..   5.00   7.00

☐406 **A.M. DINIMOR & CO., BINNINGERS OLD DOMINIAN WHEAT TONIC**
Tapered top, amber, 9½" 16.00   23.00

☐407 **MRS. DINMORE'S COUGH & CROUP BALSAM**
Vertical on front in oval end of sunken panel, rectangular, aqua, 6" 6.00   9.00

☐408 **DIOXOGEN**
Amber, 4" 3.00   5.00

☐409 **DIOXOGEN**
The Oakland Chem C. on back, amber, 7¾" 4.00   7.00

☐410 **DIPPER DANDY**
*On neck, sheared bottom, 10 to 60 cc grad scale, metal
shaker bottom, clear, 6"* 5.00   8.00

☐411 **DR. E. E. DIXON**
Clear or amethyst, 6½" 4.00   7.00

☐412 **DODGE & OLCOTT CO, NEW YORK, OIL ERIGERON**
Label, cobalt, machine made, D & O under bottom, 7" 6.00   9.00

☐413 **DODSON'S**
*On one side of panel, Livertone on other side, aqua or
amethyst, rectangular, 7"* 5.00   8.00

☐414 **DODSON & HILS, ST. LOUIS U.S.A.**
Amethyst, round, 8¼" 4.00   7.00

☐415 **DOLTON'S SARSP. & NERVE TONIC**
Aqua, 9" 6.00   9.00

☐416 **DONALD KENNEDY & CO., ROXBURY MASS**
Label, aqua, 6½" 3.00   5.00

☐417 **DONNELL'S RHEUMATIC LINIMENT**
*Vertical on front, J.T. Donnell & Co., St. Louis, Mo. on
opposite sides, rectangular, aqua blue, 7¼"* 5.00   8.00

☐418 **C. K. DONNELL, M.D./809 SABATTUS ST.,
LEWISTON, ME.**
*Vertical on front in sunken panel, square collar, rectangu-
lar, amethyst, 6¼"* 3.00   5.00

☐419 **DOUGHERTY, W. T.**
*In center a mortar with 3 lines City Drug Store, on base
Marengo, Ill., all on front, tapered top, clear, 6½"* 14.00   19.00

☐420 **GEORGE DOWDEN CHEMIST & DRUGGIST**
No. 175 Broad St. Rich. Va., pontil, aqua, 4½" 32.00   40.00

☐421 **REV. N. H. DOWN'S, VEGETABLE BALSAMIC ELIXER**
*Vertical on four panels, twelve vertical panels in all, aqua,
5½"* 5.00   8.00

☐422 **DR. DOYEN STAPHYLASE DU**
Clear or amethyst, 8" 5.00   7.00

☐423 **D.P.S. Co.**
Amber, 3½" 3.00   4.00

☐424 **DR. DRAKE'S GERMAN CROUP REMEDY**
*Vertical on front in sunken panel, The Glessner Med. Co.
on side, Findlay, Ohio on opposite side, square collar, rectangular, aqua, 6⅜"* 7.00   10.00

☐425 **DREXEL'S**
Clear, 4½" 5.00   7.00

☐426 **DROP BOTTLE**
#45 under bottom, aqua, 4" 9.00   13.00

☐427 **THE DRUGGISTS LINDSEY RUFFIN & CO.**
Senatobia, Miss., clear or amber, 6¼" 5.00   8.00

☐428 **J. DUBOIS**
*On other panels around bottle, Great Pain Specific and
Healing Balm, Kingston, N.Y., aqua, 2¼"* 6.00   9.00

☐429 **DUCH POISON, ZUM K. VERSCHLUSS**
Under bottom, clear or amethyst, 8¼" 9.00   13.00

376 396 397 400 408 411

422 423 425 430 435

436

439 443 446 449 462

☐430 **DR. DUFLOT**
Clear or amethyst, 4¼" 5.00 7.00
☐431 **DRUG STORE MEAS. BOTTLE**
Clear with handle, long neck, body has Oz. Measure, 3⅛" x 7" . 10.00 15.00
☐432 **S. O. DUNBAR, TAUNTON, MASS.**
Aqua, 6" 7.00 10.00
☐433 **T. J. DUNBAR & CO.**
On side Cordial Schnapps, other side Schiedam, green, 10" . 25.00 32.00
☐434 **DUTTON'S VEGETABLE**
Other side Discovery, aqua, 6" 4.00 6.00

E

☐435 **E**
In square, very light green, 4" 5.00 7.00
☐436 **THE EASOM MEDICINE CO.**
On back a house in center of trade mark, aqua, 2¼" 6.00 9.00
☐437 **EASTMAN, ROCHESTER, N.Y.**
Clear or amber, 6½" 3.00 5.00
☐438 **A.W. ECKEL & CO. APOTHECARIES**
Charleston, S.C., clear, 4" 4.00 6.00
☐439 **EDDY & EDDY**
Clear, 1" x 1¾", 5" 3.00 5.00
☐440 **EDDY & EDDY CHEMIST, ST. LOUIS**
Round, amethyst, 5" 4.00 6.00
☐441 Same as above except clear, 6" 5.00 7.00
☐442 **EDDY'S**
Round, green, 5¼" 4.00 6.00
☐443 **W. EDWARDS & SON**
Clear, 5" 3.00 5.00
☐444 **W. EDWARDS & SON, ROCHE EMBROCATION FOR WHOOPING COUGH**
Clear, 5" 6.00 9.00
☐445 **FRANK H. E. EGGLESTON**
Pharm., Laramie, Wy., clear or amber 6.00 9.00
☐446 **THE E.G.L. CO.**
Aqua, sheared top, 5¾" 7.00 10.00
☐447 **E. H. CO. MO COCKTAILS**
Same on reverse side, three-sided bottle, dark olive, 10" . 100.00 130.00
☐448 **EHRLICHER BROS. PHARMACISTS, PEKIN, ILL**
Clear, 4¼" 5.00 8.00
☐449 **E.L. & CO.**
Under bottom, amber, 7¼" 3.00 4.50
☐450 **ELECTRIC BRAND LAXATIVE**
Label, amber, 9¾" 6.00 9.00
☐451 **ELIXIR ALIMENTARE**
On side, Ducro A. Paris on opposite side, beveled corners, large square collar, rectangular, light green, 8¼" 5.00 7.00
☐452 **COMPOUND ELIXIR OF PHOSPHATES & CALISAYA**
Aqua, 8¾" 8.00 11.00
☐453 **ELLEMAN'S ROYAL EMBROCATION FOR HORSE**
Aqua, 7½" 11.00 15.00

☐454 **CHARLES ELLIS, SON & CO., PHILADA.**
Vertical around bottle, round double band, light green, 7"   5.00   7.00

☐455 **ELY'S CREAM BALM**
*Ely Bros. New York, Hay Fever Catarrh on front and sides,
sheared lip, rectangular, amber, 2⅝"* 4.00   6.00

☐456 *Same as above except 3¼"* 5.00   8.00

☐457 **ELYS CREAM BALM**
On front panel, rectangular, amber, 2½" 4.00   6.00

☐458 **C.S. EMERSONS AMERICAN HAIR RESTORATIVE,
CLEVELAND, O.**
Pontil, clear or amber, 6½" 32.00   41.00

☐459 **EMPIRE STATE DRUG CO. LABORATORIES**
Aqua, 6½" 4.00   7.00

☐460 **THE EMPIRE MED CO., ROCHESTER, N.Y.**
Blob top, aqua, 8¼" 6.00   9.00

☐461 **EMPRESS**
Written on front, round, flared lip, amber, 3¾" 3.00   5.00

☐462 **E.R.S. & S. 3**
Under bottom, label, amber, 7½" 2.50   3.25

☐463 **E.R.S. & S.**
Under bottom, amber, 4½" 3.00   5.00

☐464 **ESCHERING**
Clear or amethyst, 5¼" 3.00   5.00

☐465 **ESPEY'S**
Clear, 4½" 3.00   5.00

☐466 **E. ESTANTON**
*Sing Sing, N.Y. other side, Prepared by Block Hunt's,
aqua, pontil, 5"* 32.00   41.00

☐467 **EUREKA HAIR RESTORATIVE**
P. J. Reilly, San Fran., dome-type bottle, aqua, 7" 10.00   15.00

☐468 **EUTIMEN**
Clear or amethyst, 5¼" 3.00   5.00

☐469 **D. EVANS CAMOMILE PILLS**
Pontil, aqua, 3¾" 22.00   32.00

☐470 **THE EVANS CHEMICAL CO.**
Clear or amethyst, round back, 6¼" 3.50   5.00

☐471 **THE EVANS CHEMICAL CO. PROPRIETORS,
CINCINNATI, O. U.S.A.**
On front with big G, oval, clear, 5" 3.00   4.75

☐472 **DR. W. EVANS TEETHING SYRUP**
Flared lip, pontil, aqua, 2½" 19.00   26.00

☐473 **EWBANKS TOPAZ CINCHONA CORDIAL**
Amber, 9½" 10.00   15.00

☐474 *EYE CUP, S under bottom, clear or amethyst, 2"* 4.00   5.75

☐475 **EYE-SE**
*Around shoulder twice, on bottom Gilmer Texas, deco-
rated, round, aqua, 9¼"* 3.00   5.00

F

☐476 **G. FACCELLA**
On bottom, aqua, 6" 4.00   6.00

☐477 **B. A. FAHNESTOCKS**
In back Vermifuge, pontil, aqua, 4" 15.00   20.00

☐478 **DR. FAHRNEY'S**
Uterine other side, clear or amethyst, 8½" 3.00   5.00

☐479 **DR. PETER FAHRNEY**
71 under bottom, clear, 6" 4.00   7.00

☐480 **FARBENFABRIKEN OF ELBERFELD CO., N.Y.C.**
Label, 90 under bottom, amber, 4¼" 3.00   5.00

☐481 **FARR'S GRAY HAIR RESTORER, BOSTON, MASS. 6 OZ.**
All on front at a slant, beveled corners, ABM, amber, 5⅝" . 3.00   5.00

☐482 **H.G. FARRELLS ARABIAN LINIMENT**
Pontil, aqua, 4¼" 15.00   20.00

☐483 **FATHER JOHN'S MEDICINE**
Lowell Mass., ring top, wide mouth, dark amber, 12" 7.00   10.00

☐484 *Same as above except 8¾"* 8.00   11.00

☐485 **FEBRILENE TRADE MARK**
On front, aqua, rectangular, 4½" 1.50   2.25

☐486 **FELLOWS & CO.**
Aqua, 7¾" 3.50   4.75

☐487 **FELLOWS & CO. CHEMISTS ST. JOHN. N.B.**
Vertical on front, flask, 8" 6.00   9.00

☐488 *Same as above except ABM* 3.50   4.75

☐489 **FELLOW'S LAXATIVE TABLETS**
Clear or amber, 2½" 5.00   8.00

☐490 **FELLOW'S SYRUP OF HYPOPHOSPHITS**
Deep indentation on lower trunk on face of bottle, oval,
aqua, 7¾" 5.00   8.00

☐491 **DR. M. M. FENNER, FREDONIA, N.Y., ST. VITUS**
DANCE SPECIFIC
Ringed top, aqua, 4½" 8.00   11.00

☐492 **DR. M. M. FENNERS PEOPLES REMEDIES**
Vertical on front, U.S.A. 1872-1898 on side, Fredonia, N.Y.
on opposite side, graduated collar, rectangular, amethyst,
6" 6.00   8.00

☐493 **FERRO CHINA MELARO TONICO**
Lion embossed on three-sided bottle, tapered top with
ring, green 32.00   41.00

☐494 **FERROL THE IRON OIL FOOD**
One side Iron & Phosphorus, other side Cod Liver Oil,
amber, 9¼" 10.00   15.00

☐495 **B. W. FETTERS DRUGGIST**
Phila. Pat. Aug. 1, 1876, beer bottle shape, blue green, 8¾" . 14.00   19.00

☐496 **FIFIELD & CO., 263 MAIN STREET, BANGOR, ME.**
Rectangular, clear, 4¾" 7.00   11.00

☐497 **B. F. FISH, SAN FRANCISCO, FISH HAIR RESTORATIVE**
Aqua, 7¾" 8.00   12.00

☐498 **DR. S. S. FITCH & CO., 714 BROADWAY, N.Y.**
Pontil, aqua, 3¼" 21.00   29.00

☐499 **DR. S. S. FITCH**
On side, 707 Broadway N.Y. on opposite side, sheared col-
lar, rectangular, beveled corners, pontil, aqua, 3¾" 32.00   41.00

☐500 **DR. S.S. FITCH, 701 BROADWAY N.Y.**
Pontil, aqua, 1¾" 18.00 25.00
☐501 *Same as above except 6½"* 18.00 25.00
☐502 *Same as above except tapered top, oval* 18.00 25.00
☐503 **DR. S.S. FITCH, 714 BROADWAY N.Y.**
Vertical on front, oval, aqua, 6½" 28.00 39.00
☐504 **FIVE DROPS**
*On side, Chicago USA on opposite side, rectangular,
aqua, 5½"* 4.00 6.00
☐505 **FLAGG'S GOOD SAMARITANS IMMEDIATE RELIEF,
CINCINNATI, O.**
Pontil, five panels, aqua, 3¾" 16.00 23.00
☐506 **A.H. FLANDERS M.D., N.Y.**
On back, amber, 9" 50.00 65.00
☐507 **FLETCHERS VEGE-TONIO**
*On front panel, beveled corner, 2½" square, amber, roof
shoulder, under bottom, DOC, 8½"* 13.00 18.00
☐508 **FLIPPINS**
Clear, 6½" 3.00 5.00
☐509 **R.G. FLOWER MEDICAL CO.**
Amber, 9" 8.00 12.00
☐510 **THE FLOWERS MANUFACTURING CO.**
Clear, 6¼" 5.00 7.00
☐511 **FOLEY & CO.**
Clear or amethyst, 5½" 4.00 6.00
☐512 **FOLEY & CO., CHICAGO, FOLEY'S KIDNEY PILLS**
Aqua, 2½" 3.00 5.00
☐513 **FOLEY & CO. CHICAGO, U.S.A.**
Sample bottle, Foley's Kidney Cure, round, aqua, 4½" ... 10.00 15.00
☐514 **FOLEY'S CREAM**
*On one side, Foley & Co., Chicago, U.S.A. on opposite
side, square, clear, 4¼"* 3.00 5.00
☐515 **FOLEY'S HONEY AND TAR, FOLEY & CO., CHICAGO, USA**
Vertical on front, rectangular, sample size, aqua, 4¼" ... 4.00 6.00
☐516 **FOLEY'S HONEY & TAR**
Foley's & Co. Chicago, aqua, 5¼" 6.00 9.00
☐517 **FOLEY'S KIDNEY PILLS, FOLEY & CO. CHICAGO**
On front vertically, round, clear, 2½" 5.00 7.00
☐518 **J. A. FOLGER & CO., ESSENCE OF JAMAICA GINGER,
SAN FRA.**
Tapered top, aqua, 6¼" 10.00 15.00
☐519 **J. A. FOLGER & CO., ESSENCE OF JAMAICA GINGER,
SAN FRANCISCO**
*Vertical on front in oval slug plate, graduated collar, oval,
aqua, 6"* 5.00 8.00
☐520 **DR. ROBT. B. FOLGER'S, OLOSAONIAN N.Y.**
Beveled corners, tapered top, aqua, 7¼" 13.00 18.00
☐521 **THE FORBES DIASTASE CO.**
Cincinnati, O., amber, 7⅞" 8.00 12.00
☐522 *Same as above except clear* 11.00 15.00
☐523 **B. FOSGATES ANODYNE**
Round, flared top, aqua, 4½" 7.00 10.00
☐524 *Same except ringed top, 5"* 5.00 8.00

□525 **H. D. FOWLE, BOSTON**
Aqua blue, 5½" 7.00 10.00

□526 **DR. FRAGAS**
Cuban Vermifuge on two other panels, eight panels, aqua,
3¾" 6.00 9.00

□527 **FRANCO AMERICAN HYGENIC CO.**
Perfumer Chicago other side, clear, 3" 4.00 6.00

□528 **FRASER**
Cobalt, 4½" 7.00 10.00

□529 **FRASER & CO.**
Amber, 5" 3.00 5.00

□530 **FRENCH EAU DE QUININE HAIR TONIC, ATLANTA,**
Label, clear, 10½" 6.00 9.00

□531 **J. H. FRIEDENWALD & CO.**
Balt. Md., Buchen Gin For All Kidney & Liver Troubles,
Friedenwalds Buchen Gin on other side, green, 10" 10.00 15.00

□532 **FROG POND CHILL & FEVER TONIC**
Cobalt, 7" 10.00 15.00

□533 **THE FROSER TABLET CO.**
Label, clear, 5¾" 3.00 5.00

□534 **FRUITOLA**
On side panel, Pinus Med. Co., Monticello, Ill., U.S.A. on
other side, rectangular, aqua, 6½" 3.00 5.00

□535 **F.S. & CO. 299**
2 under bottom, 4" 2.75 3.75

□536 **DR. FURBER'S CORDIAL OF MT. BOLM**
Flat ring top, 7¾" 12.00 16.00

G

□537 **G.F.P. FOR WOMEN**
On side L. Gerstle & Co., other Chattanooga, Ten., amber 6.00 9.00

□538 **GALLED ARMPITS & CO.**
One side For Tender Feet, other side Turkish Foot Bath,
aqua, 7½" 6.00 9.00

□539 **GARGLING OIL, LOCKPORT, N.Y.**
Tapered top, green, 5½" 8.00 12.00

□540 **GARRETT DRUG CO.**
R.W. Garrett Mgr., Will Point, Texas, clear, 4⅛" and 5¾" . 3.00 5.00

□541 **D.H. GEER & CO., BOSTON, MASS., STUMP OF THE**
WORLD TRADEMARK
Aqua, 9½" 15.00 20.00

□542 **A.M. GERRY PHARMACIST, SOUTH PARIS, ME.**
Rectangular, aqua, 6" 4.00 6.00

□543 **GILBERT BROS. & CO.**
Baltimore Md., green, 7¾" 5.00 8.00

□544 **J. A. GILKA**
9 Schutzen str. 9 on back, pour spout, plain bottom,
amber, 9" 70.00 90.00

□545 **J.A. GILKA**
Two men with club and crown on bottom, black, 9" 50.00 65.00

□546 **GIROLAMO PAGLIANO**
On front and back in large vertical letters, rectangular, beveled corners, apple green, 4⅜" 19.00 26.00

□547 **M.H. GLEESON & BROTHER**
Apothecaries, Boston, aqua, oval flask shape, 8½" 10.00 15.00

□548 **GLOVER H. CLAY CO., N.Y.**
On the front panel, rectangular, amber, 5" 1.35 2.15

□549 **GLOVER'S**
412 under bottom, amber, 5" 3.00 5.00

□550 **GLOVER'S IMPERIAL MANGE MEDICINE**
On the front of panel, 6½ fl. oz., H. Clay Glover Co. on the left side, N.Y. on the right side, rectangular, amber 6¾" .. 1.35 2.15

□551 **GLOVER'S IMPERIAL CANKER WASH., H. CLAY GLOVER D.V.S., NEW YORK**
Vertical on front, rectangular, amber, 5¼" 5.00 7.00

□552 **GLOVER'S IMPERIAL MANGE MEDICINE 6½ FL. OZ., NEW YORK, H. CLAY GLOVER**
On front and sides, rectangular, ABM, amber, 7" 4.00 6.00

□553 **GLOVER'S IMPERIAL "MANGE REMEDY," H. CLAY GLOVER D.V.S., NEW YORK**
On front and sides 4.00 6.00

□554 **GLYCEROLE**
On side slot, aqua, applied ring at top, 6¼" 1.35 2.15

□555 **GLYCOTHYMOLINE 1 LB. NET**
Amethyst, oval, 8¼" 4.00 7.00

□556 **GLYCOTHYMOLINE 3 FL. OZ.**
Around shoulder, amethyst, oval, 4" and 4¾" 3.00 5.00

□557 **GLYCO THYMOLINE**
Slanted lower right to top left, square, ABM, clear, 4½" .. 3.00 5.00

□558 **S.B. GOFF'S OIL LINIMENT, CAMDEN, N.J.**
On front and side, rectangular, aqua, 5¾" 5.00 7.00

□559 **S.B. GOFF'S COUGH SYRUP, CAMDEN, N.J.**
On front and opposite side, rectangular, aqua, 5¾" 4.00 6.00

□560 **J.P. GOLDBERG, JACKSON'S ORIGINAL AMERICAN MED.**
Indian with bow and arrow, pontil, 9" 13.00 18.00

□561 **GOLDEN'S LIQUID BEEF TONIC**
Circular around bottle, in center of the circle, in round sunken panel, C. N. Crittenton, Prarr, N.Y., champagne type bottle, green, ring top, 9½" 6.00 9.00

□562 **GOMBAULTS J.E., CAUSTIC BALSAM**
On front panel, The Lawrence Williams Co., Sole Props For The U.S. and Canada on the left and right side of panels, aqua, rectangular, 6½" 7.00 10.00

□563 **GOODE'S SARSAPARILLA, W.S.G. GOODE**
Practical Pharmacist, Williamsville, Va. 16.00 23.00

□564 **V.V. GOOGLER**
Clear, 5" 5.00 7.00

□565 **GOOSE GREASE LINIMENT, MFG. G.G.L. CO. OF GREENSBORO, N.C.**
Ring top, picture of a goose on it, aqua, 7¼" 6.00 9.00

□566 **W.J.M. GORDON PHARMACEUTIST, CINCINNATI, OHIO**
On three lines, blob top, blue green, 7½" 14.00 19.00

☐567 **GOURAUD'S ORIENTAL CREAM**
New York on one side, London on the other, clear, 4¼" .. 3.00   5.00

☐568 **GRA CAR CERTOSA OF PAVIA**
Aqua, 9½" 16.00   23.00

☐569 **GRACE LINEN** *around shoulder*
Around shoulder, monogram on bottom, round, aqua, 2¼" 4.00   6.00

☐570 **GRAHAMS NO. 1 HAIR DYE LIQUID**
3½" 9.00   12.00

☐571 **GRAND UNION E.T.A. CO., GRAND UNION TEA CO.**
On each side, clear or amber, 5¼" 4.00   6.00

☐572 **A.C. GRANT, ALBANY, N.Y., GERMAN MAGNETIC LINIMENT**
Beveled corners, pontil, aqua, 5" 16.00   23.00

☐573 **GRANULAR CITRATE OF MAGNESIA**
Kite with letter inside it, ring top, cobalt, 8" 22.00   31.00

☐574 *Same except 6"* 22.00   31.00

☐575 **GRAY'S CELEBRATED SPARKLING SPRAY & EXQUISITE TONIC**
Blob top, clear 5.00   8.00

☐576 **GRAY'S ELIXIR, GRAY LAB**
Amber, 7¼" 3.00   5.00

☐577 **GRAY'S SYRUP OF RED SPRUCE GUM**
On opposite sides, sunken panels, rectangular, ABM, aqua, 5½" 3.00   5.00

☐578 **DR. T.W. GRAYDON, CINCINNATI, O., DISEASES OF THE LUNGS**
Vertical on front in slug plate, square collar, light amber, 5⅞" 6.00   9.00

☐579 **GREAT ENGLISH SWEENY**
Vertical on front in sunken panel, Specific on side, Carey & Co. on opposite side, rectangular, aqua, 6" 4.00   6.00

☐580 **L. M. GREEN**
Other side Woodbury, N.J., clear or amethyst, 4¼" 3.00   5.00

☐581 **S.L. GREEN, DRUGGIST**
Camden, Ark., 3 iv on shoulder, ring top, under bottom, W.T. & Co., U.S.A., amber, 3" 3.00   5.00

☐582 **DRS. E.E. & J.A. GREENE, N.Y. & BOSTON**
Aqua, 7½" 7.00   10.00

☐583 **DRS. E.E. & J.A. GREENE**
Aqua, 7½" 6.00   9.00

☐584 **DRS. E.E. & J.A. GREEN**
On side, New York & Boston on opposite side, square collar, rectangular, aqua, 7½" 4.00   6.00

☐585 **GREEVER-LOT SPEICH MGF. CO.**
Clear, 6¼" 3.00   4.00

☐586 **DR. GREN'S SARSAPARILLA**
Rectangular, aqua, double ring top, 9¼" 14.00   19.00

☐587 **GRIMAULT & CO.**
Clear, 6½" 3.00   5.00

☐588 **GRODERS BOTANIC DYSPEPSIA SYRUP**
Waterville, Me on one side, U.S.A. other side, aqua, 8¾" . 6.00   9.00

☐589 **DR. GROVE'S**
On other side Philadelphia, on front Anodyne for Infants,
ring top, aqua, 5¼" 9.00 12.00
☐590 **GROVE'S TASTELESS CHILL TONIC**
Prepared By Paris Med. Co. on the front panel, clear or
amethyst, oval, 5¾" and 5⁵⁄₁₆" 3.00 5.00
☐591 **S. GROVER GRAHAM, DYSPEPSIA REMEDY, NEWBURGH**
N.Y. USA
Vertical on front, rectangular, clear, 6⅛" 4.00 6.00
☐592 **GUN OIL**
Vertical in sunken panel, rectangular, clear, 4¾" 4.00 7.00
☐593 **GURRLAIN**
Other side Eau Lustrale, open pontil, raspberry color, 4¾" .. 11.00 15.00

H

☐594 **HAGAN'S MAGNOLIA BALM**
On front of panel, milk glass or clear, rectangular, 5" 7.00 10.00
☐595 **HAGAR'S NERVINA TONIC, THE GREAT BLOOD**
MEDICINE
Label, double band collar, light apple green, 8¾" 5.00 7.00
☐596 **HAIR BALSAM**
Olive green, blob top 5.00 8.00
☐597 **HAIR HEALTH, DR. HAYS**
On opposite sides in sunken panels, rectangular, amber,
6¾" 4.00 6.00
☐598 *Same as above except ABM* 3.00 4.00
☐599 **HAIR RESTORATIVE DEPOTS**
Vertical on front in sunken panel, Professor Woods on
side, St. Louis & New York on opposite side, rectangular,
sunken panels, aqua, 7" 30.00 40.00
☐560 **H.H. HACKENDOHL**
Milwaukee, Wis. in two lines (Scrip), under bottom Pat.
June 17 - 88 - S.B., ring top, clear, 5½" 9.00 12.00
☐601 **LEON HALE**
Clear or amethyst, 6" 3.00 5.00
☐602 **LEON HALE**
Clear or amethyst, 5" 3.00 4.00
☐603 **E. W. HALL**
Aqua, 3½" 3.00 5.00
☐604 **R. HALL & CO., PROP. DR. BARNES, ESSENCE OF**
JAMAICA GINGER
Aqua, 5" 6.00 9.00
☐605 **HALL'S BALSAM FOR THE LUNGS** *vertical on front,*
Vertical on front, fancy arch panels, sunken panel, rectan-
gular, aqua, 7¼" 11.00 15.00
☐606 **HALL'S BALSAM FOR THE LUNGS**
On the front panel, John F. Henry & Co. on side, New York
on opposite, rectangular, aqua, 7¾" and 6⅝" 6.00 9.00
☐607 **HALL'S CATARRAH MEDICINE**
Vertical, round, ABM, clear, 4½" 3.00 4.00
☐608 **HALL'S HAIR RENEWER, NASHUA, N.H.**
Label, S&D 112 under bottom, aqua, 7¼" 6.00 9.00

☐609 **HALL'S** *(on one side)*
Hair Renewer on opposite side of panel, this bottle is pret-
tier than Ayer's Hair Vigor, rectangular, peacock blue,
6½" 16.00   23.00

☐610 **HALL'S SARSAPARILLA**
Vertical on sunken arch panel, J. R. Gates & Co. on side,
Proprietors, S.F. on opposite side, rectangular, aqua, 9¼" 22.00   30.00

☐611 **HALSEY BROS. CO., CHICAGO**
Amber, 6¾" 5.00   8.00

☐612 **HAMILTON'S OLD ENGLISH BLACK OIL**
Vertical on three panels, eight vertical panels, aqua, 6¾" ... 4.00   6.00

☐613 **HAMLIN'S WIZARD OIL, CHICAGO, USA**
Aqua, rectangular, 5¾" 3.00   4.00

☐614 **HAMLIN'S WIZARD OIL, CHICAGO, ILL. USA**
On front and sides, rectangular, sunken panels, aqua, 6¼" . 3.00   4.00

☐615 *Same as above except 8"* 3.00   4.00

☐616 **HAMMOND'S SARSAPARILLA By sear**
Label, aqua, 8½" 9.00   12.00

☐617 **HAMPTON'S**
Amber, 6½" 6.00   9.00

☐618 **HANCE BROTHERS & WHITE**
Phila. U.S.A. in back, amber, 7" 3.00   5.00

☐619 **HANCOCK LIQUID SULPHUR CO.**
Baltimore Md. on side, clear 4.00   6.00

☐620 **HAND MED. CO., PHILADELPHIA**
On front, oval, aqua, 5⅛" 3.00   4.00

☐621 **HANSEE EUROPEAN COUGH SYRUP, R.H. HANSEE
PRO, MONTICELLO, N.Y.**
Vertical on front in sunken panel, rectangular, amethyst,
5¼" 4.00   6.00

☐622 **HARLENE FOR THE HAIR**
In four lines, ring top, on one side sample, same on other,
aqua, 3" 9.00   12.00

☐623 **HARPER HEADACHE REMEDY, WASH., D.C.**
Clear, 5" 3.00   5.00

☐624 **DR. HARRISON'S CHALYBESTE TONIC**
Teal blue, 7¾" 16.00   22.00

☐625 **DR. HARTER'S IRON TONIC**
Label, amber, 9" 12.00   16.00

☐626 **DR. HARTER'S IRON TONIC**
Amber, 9¼" 9.00   12.00

☐627 **DR. HARTER'S LUNG BALM**
On front, clear 5.00   8.00

☐628 **HARTSHORN'S FAMILY MEDICINE**
Tall-canted roof shoulder, long neck, collared lip, with
bulls eye, aqua, 9½" 10.00   15.00

☐629 *Same except ring lip, oval shoulders, rectangular, Royal*
Gall Remedy, large cats eye bubble, red amber, 7¼" 11.00   15.00

☐630 **E. HARTSHORN & SONS, ESTABLISHED 1850, BOSTON**
Vertical lettering on slug plate, rare flask shape, aqua ... 9.00   12.00

☐631 **HARTSHORN & SONS ESTABLISHED 1850, BOSTON**
On center front, rectangular, clear, 6¼" 5.00   8.00

☐632 *Same as above except 4⅞"* 5.00   8.00

☐633	**DR. HASTINGS NAPHTHA SYRUP**		
	On front, London on other side, aqua, pontil, 6½"	14.00	19.00
☐634	**HAVILAND & CO., NEW YORK, CHARLESTON, & AUGUSTA**		
	Pontil, tapered top, aqua, 5¾"	20.00	30.00
☐635	**L. F. H. H. HAY SOLE AGENT**		
	On shoulder, L. F. Atwood on base, aqua, 6½"	3.00	5.00
☐636	**R. HAYDEN'S**		
	H.V.C. on other side, light blue, 4½"	5.00	8.00
☐637	**DR. HAYDEN'S**		
	Viburnum on back, aqua, 7"	3.00	5.00
☐638	**DR. HAYES**		
	Three stars on bottom, clear	3.00	5.00
☐639	**DR. HAYNE'S ARABIAN BALSAM, R. MORGAN & SONS, PROVIDENCE, R.I.**		
	On four consecutive panels, twelve panels, band collar, aqua, 4¼"	4.00	6.00
☐640	**DR. HAY'S**		
	Amber, 6"	4.00	6.00
☐641	**HAY'S**		
	On side, Hair Health on opposite side, label on back, adopted April 1, 1912, ABM, amber, 7½"	4.00	7.00
☐642	**CASWELL HAZARD & CO.**		
	Square, cobalt, 7½", 2¾." x 2¾"	7.00	10.00
☐643	**CASWELL HAZARD & CO.**		
	In three lines near top, in center in a circle Omnia Labor Vincit, under this in four lines Chemists, New York & Newport, square, beveled corner, short neck, cobalt, 3¾", 7½"	11.00	16.00
☐644	**HEALTH NURSER**		
	Clear or amber, 6⅓"	8.00	12.00
☐645	**HEALTH SPECIALIST SPROULE**		
	Clear, 8¼"	5.00	8.00
☐646	**HEALY & BIGELOW'S INDIAN OIL**		
	1¼" round, aqua, 5¼"	5.00	8.00
☐647	**HEALY & BIGELOW**		
	Reverse side Indian Sagwa, aqua, 8¾"	7.00	10.00
☐648	**HECEMAN & CO.**		
	On front of panel, one one side Chemists, other side New York, 3" x 2" body, 6½" neck, aqua, 3¾"	6.00	9.00
☐649	**HECEMAN & CO.**		
	Vertical in large letters on front, Chemists on side, New York on opposite side, rectangular, aqua, 10½"	4.00	6.00
☐650	**G. M. HEIDT & CO.**		
	Aqua, 9½"	5.00	7.00
☐651	**H. T. HELMBOLD**		
	Philadelphia on side, Genuine Fluid Extracts on front, side mold, aqua, 7¼"	6.00	9.00
☐652	**H. T. HELMBOLD'S GENUINE PREPARATION**		
	Pontil, aqua, 6½"	20.00	30.00
☐653	**H. T. HELMBOLD**		
	Philadelphia other side, Genuine Fluid Extracts front side, side mold, aqua, 6½"	9.00	12.00

☐654 **HEMOGLOBINE DESCHIENS**
Cobalt, 7¾" 11.00   15.00
☐655 **HENRY'S CALCINED MAGNESIA, MANCHESTER**
Pontil, 4¼" 16.00   22.00
☐656 **HENRY'S CALCINED MAGNESIA, MANCHESTER**
Vertical on all four sides, rolled lip, clear, 4¼" 7.00   10.00
☐657 **HENRY'S THREE CHLORIDES**
Amber, 7¼" 3.00   5.00
☐658 **THE HERB MED. CO., SPRINGFIELD, O.**
Reverse side Lightning Hot Drops No Relief No Pay, aqua, 5"   6.00   9.00
☐659 **HERB MED CO., WESTON, W. VA.**
Aqua, 9½" 6.00   9.00
☐660 **HERBINE**
St. Louis on the left side, Herbine Co. on the right side,
rectangular, clear, 6¾" 2.00   3.00
☐661 **HERRINGS MEDICINE CO., ATLANTA, GA.**
Label, clear, 7¾" 3.00   5.00
☐662 **H. 82**
Under bottom, green, 7¼" 3.00   5.00
☐663 **H**
On bottom, amber, 4" 1.40   2.30
☐664 **E.H. CO.**
Aqua, 3½" 3.00   5.00
☐665 **H.H.H. MEDICINE**
The Celebrated one side, D.D.T. 1869 other side, aqua ...   7.00   10.00
☐666 **HIAWATHA HAIR RESTORATIVE, HOYT**
Long neck, light green, 6¾" 8.00   12.00
☐667 **HICKS & JOHNSON**
C.L.C. CO-2 under bottom, clear, 6½" 4.00   7.00
☐668 **HICKS' CAPUDINE**
Three different sizes, amber 3.00   5.00
☐669 **HICKS' CAPUDINE**
Amber, 5¾" 4.00   6.00
☐670 **HICKS' CAPUDINE CURES ALL HEADACHES &**
& COLD ETC.
Amber, 5¾" 8.00   12.00
☐671 **DR. H.H. HIGGINS SARSAPARILLA**
Romney Va., pontil, aqua, 10" 29.00   42.00
☐672 **DR. H.R. HIGGINS**
In back Romney Va., on one side Sarsaparilla, other side
Pure Extract, pontil, tapered top, aqua, 10" 40.00   55.00
☐673 **HILL'S**
Vertical on front, Hair Dye No. 1 on back, square, oval
sides, aqua, 3¼" 3.00   4.00
☐674 **HILLSIDE CHEM. CO.**
On bottom, amber, 7½" 3.00   5.00
☐675 **HIMALYA**
Ring top, amber, 7½" 4.00   6.00
☐676 **HIMALYA**
Amber, 7½" 3.00   5.00

□677 **HINDS HONEY AND ALMOND CREAM, A.S. HINDS CO., PORTLAND, MAINE USA, IMPROVED THE COMPLEXION, ALCOHOL 7%**
On front and sides, rectangular, 2⅞", clear 4.00   6.00

□678 **A. S. HINDS**
Portland, Me other side, clear, 5½" 4.00   6.00

□679 **HOBO MED. CO.**
Beaumont, Texas Registered Trademark, H.B. on the front panel in a diamond, rectangular, clear, screw top, 8⅛" . . .   3.00   5.00

□680 **HOFFMAN'S ANODYNE**
Label, rectangular, square collar, clear, 5" 3.00   4.00

□681 **HOFFMAN'S**
In center in large letters, Great Find Trade Make in three lines on front, one ring in neck, ring top, aqua, 6¼" 7.00   10.00

□682 **HOFF'S GERMAN LINIMENT**
Goodrich & Jennings, Anoka, Minn. vertical on three panels, twelve vertical panels, ring collar, aqua, 5¾" 5.00   8.00

□683 **HOFF'S LINIMENT**
Goodrich Drug Co., Anoka, Minn. vertical on three panels, twelve vertical panels, ring collar, ABM, aqua blue, 7" . . .   4.00   6.00

□684 **DR. J.J. HOGAN**
Next to post office, Vallejo, Cal. in circle, W.T. & CO. U.S.A. under bottom, ringed top, cobalt blue, 7¼" 27.00   36.00

□685 **HOLLAND**
Aqua, 3½" 3.00   5.00

□686 **HOLLAND DRUG CO.**
Prescriptions A Specialty, Holland, Tx. on the front, on the bottom USP, rectangular, amethyst, 4¾" 1.35   2.25

□687 **HOLLIS BALM OF AMERICA**
Cylindrical, square collar, aqua, 5" 7.00   11.00

□688 **HOLMAN'S NATURES GRAND RESTORATIVE, J. B. HOLMAN, PROP.**
Boston, Mass., pontil, olive green 225.00   275.00

□689 **HOLTONS ELECTRIC OIL**
On bottle vertically, round, amethyst, 3¼" 3.00   5.00

□690 **HOLTON'S ELECTRIC OIL**
Vertical on bottle, cylindrical, square collar, clear, 3¼" . .   5.00   8.00

□691 **THE HONDURAS CO'S. COMPOUND EXTRACT SARSAPARILLA, 1876**
Aqua, 10½" 25.00   33.00

□692 **HONDURAS MOUNTAIN TONIC CO.**
Fancy writing in sunken panel, double band collar, aqua, 9" .   16.00   23.00

□693 **HONE DEURE**
On one panel, Colours on back panel, six panels, flared top, clear, t.p. pontils, small bottles, 2¾" 11.00   16.00

□694 **HOODS SARSAPARILLA**
Aqua, 8¾" 5.00   8.00

□695 **HOOD'S**
Machine made, clear, 8½" 3.00   5.00

□696 **HOOD'S TOOTH POWDER**
Clear, C.I. Hood & Co., Lowell, Mass, 3½" 5.00   8.00

☐697 **W.H. HOOKER [sic] & CO. PROPRIETORS, NEW YORK, U.S.A.**
Vertical on front in sunken panel, For the Throat and Lungs on side, Acker's English Remedy on opposite side, cobalt, 5¾" 14.00   19.00

☐698 Same as above except N.&S. AMERICARS, 6½" 11.00   15.00

☐699 Same except round and ACKER'S BABY SOOTHER, aqua 7.00   11.00

☐700 **W. H. HOOPER & CO.**
Proprietors New York, U.S.A. in three lines in sunken panel, on one side in sunken panel Acker's English Remedy, on other For The Throat & Lungs, 1½" neck, ring top, cobalt, 5¾" 13.00   20.00

☐701 **G. W. HOUSE CLEMENS INDIAN TONIC**
Ring top, aqua, 5" 60.00   80.00

☐702 **THE HOWARD DRUGS & MEDICINE CO.**
Prepared By, Baltimore, Md., Frixie Hair Oil in sunken panel on front in script, six lines, clear or amethyst 2¼" x 1" x 4" 3.00   5.00

☐703 Same size as above except Rubifoam For the Teeth, Put Up By E.W. HOYTH & CO., Lowell Mass in six lines, not in sunken panel 5.00   8.00

☐704 **HUGHEL'S DANDER-OFF HAIR TONIC DANDRUFF REMEDY**
All on front side, square bottle, clear, 6¼" 6.00   9.00

☐705 **HUMPHREY'S**
Humphrey's Homeophathic on back, clear, 3½" 3.00   5.00

☐706 **HUMPHREY'S MARVEL OF HEALING**
Clear or amethyst, 5½" 3.00   5.00

☐707 **HUMPHREY'S MARVEL WITCHHAZEL**
Machine made, clear, 5½" 3.00   5.00

☐708 **R. H. HURD PROP.**
No. Berwick, Me. U.S.A. Backer's Specific, clear, 4½" ... 6.00   9.00

☐709 **HURLEY**
Clear or amethyst, 5" 3.00   4.00

☐710 **HUSBAND'S CALCINED MAGNESIA, PHILA.,**
Vertical on all four sides, square, sheared collar, aqua, 4¼" . 4.00   6.00

☐711 **HUSBAND'S CALCINED MAGNESIA, PHILA.**
Square, sheared lip, clear or amber, 4½" 5.00   8.00

☐712 **HYATT'S, other side LIFE BALSAM, N.Y.**
On front Pulmonic, olive green, pontil, applied top, 12⅛" . 60.00   80.00

☐713 **HYATT'S**
On front, Pulmonic other side, Life Balsam, N.Y., aqua, applied top, pontil, 11" 45.00   60.00

I

☐714 **I. G. CO.**
Under bottom, aqua, 7" 6.00   9.00

☐715 **IMPERIAL HAIR/TRADE MARK**
Shield with crown in center, Regenerator vertical on front, Imperial Chemical Manufacturing Co. on side, New York on opposite side, rectangular, beveled corners, square collar, 4½", light green, 4½" 6.00   9.00

☐716 **INDIA CHOLAGOGUE**
Vertical on front, Norwich, Conn. U.S.A. on side, Osgood's on opposite side, rectangular, beveled corners, machine made, aqua, 5½" 3.00 5.00

☐717 *Same as above except NEW YORK embossed on side, not machine made, aqua, 5⅜"* 5.00 8.00

☐718 **DR. H.A. INGHAM'S VEGETABLE PAIN EXTRACT**
Aqua, 4½" 5.00 7.00

☐719 *IODINE, machine made, amber, 2¼"* 3.00 5.00

☐720 **I.R.**
Label, fancy bottle, graphite pontil, aqua, 6½" 16.00 23.00

☐721 **ISCHIROGENO O BATTISTA FARMACIA INGLESE DEL CERVO NAPOLI**
Amber, 7" 14.00 19.00

J

☐722 **J & J**
Under bottom, sheared top, cobalt, 2½" 3.00 5.00

☐723 **JACKSON MFG. CO., COLUMBUS, O.**
Ring top, clear, 6¼" 3.00 5.00

☐724 **JACOB'S PHARMACY**
Other side Atlanta, Ga., Compound Extract Pine Splinters, clear, 7½" 3.00 5.00

☐725 **JACOB'S PHARMACY**
W.T.&CO. C. U.S.A. under bottom, amber, 6" 5.00 8.00

☐726 **ST. JACOB'S OEL, THE CHARLES A. VOGELER COMPANY, BALTIMORE, MD. U.S.A.**
Vertical around bottle, cylindrical, aqua, 6⅝" 5.00 8.00

☐727 *Same as above except amethyst* 5.00 8.00

☐728 **JAD SALTS, WHITEHALL PHARMACY CO., N.Y.**
Label, screw top, clear, 5¾" 3.00 4.00

☐729 **JAMAICA GINGER**
Label, clear, 5¾" 3.00 4.00

☐730 **JAMAICA GINGER FRUIT CORDIAL, MANUFACTURED BY C.C. HINES & CO., BOSTON, MASS.**
On two sides, square, clear, 6½" 3.00 5.00

☐731 **JAQUES**
Aqua, 4½" 4.00 6.00

☐732 **DR. D. JAYNES TONIC VERMIFUGE, 242 CHEST ST., PHILA**
On front, aqua, rectangular, 5½" 3.00 4.00

☐733 **DR. D. JAYNES EXPECTORANT**
On front panel, on back Philada on each side, three panels, short neck, aqua, pontil, 6¾" 16.00 23.00

☐734 **DR. D. JAYNES EXPECTORANT**
Vertical on front in sunken panel, Twenty Five Cents on side, Quarter Size on opposite side, rectangular, square collar, aqua, 5¼" 4.00 6.00

☐735 **DR. D. JAYNES**
Half Dollar on one side, Half Size on other side 5.00 8.00

☐736 **DR. D. JAYNES**
Pontil, aqua, 7" 11.00 15.00

☐737 **JAYNES & CO., BOSTON**
Screw top, amber, 9½" 6.00   9.00

☐738 **T.E. JENKINS & CO., CHEMISTS, LOUISVILLE, KY.**
Graphite pontil, aqua, 7" 15.00   20.00

☐739 **JOHNSON'S AMERICAN ANODYNE LINIMENT**
Around bottle, aqua, 4½" or 6½" 3.00   5.00

☐740 **JOHNSON'S AMERICAN ANODYNE LINIMENT**
Vertical, round, aqua, 4¼" 3.00   5.00

☐741 *Same as above except 6½"* 3.00   5.00

☐742 **JOHNSON'S CHILL AND FEVER TONIC**
Clear, 5¾" 3.00   5.00

☐743 **JOHNSON & JOHNSON OIL**
Label, C1637 under bottom, aqua, 5" 3.00   5.00

☐744 **S. C. JOHNSON & SON, RACINE, WIS.**
Under bottom, clear, 3" 3.00   5.00

☐745 **DR. E.S. JOHNSON BLOOD SYRUP, FARMINGTON, ME.**
Vertical on front in oval slug plate, large square collar,
oval, aqua, 9⅝" 9.00   12.00

☐746 **DR. JOHNSON'S HORSE REMEDIES PREPARED BY**
NEW YORK VETERINARY HOSPITAL
Vertical on front in slug plate, oval, flared collar, aqua,
6¾" 7.00   10.00

☐747 **DR. JONES' AUSTRALIAN OIL**
Not To Be Taken on each side, amber, 5" 9.00   12.00

☐748 **DR. JONES' LINIMENT**
Aqua, 6¾" 3.00   5.00

☐749 **J.P.L.**
Under bottom, aqua, 7½" 3.00   5.00

☐750 **DR. JUG'S MEDICINE FOR LUNGS, LIVER & BLOOD**
Brown, neck ¾", jug with handle, 6¼" x 3½" 16.00   22.00

☐751 **L.E. JUNG**
Machine made, amber, 11" 3.00   5.00

☐752 **JUNKET COLORS**
With monogram on one side, Little Falls, N.Y., Chas.
Hansen's Laboratory, square, aqua, 3½" 3.00   5.00

K

☐753 **KALIUM**
Clear, 5½" 6.00   9.00

☐754 **KALO COMPOUND FOR DYSPEPSIA, BROWN MFG. CO.,**
GREENVILLE, TENN.
(N's in TENN. are backwards), all on front in oval end of
sunken panel, rectangular, square collar, amethyst, 9½" .. 16.00   22.00

☐755 **KA:TON:KA, THE GREAT INDIAN REMEDY**
On opposite sides, rectangular, graduated collar, aqua, 8¾" 8.00   12.00

☐756 **KEASBEY & MATTISON CO.**
Aqua or amber, 3¼" 4.00   6.00

☐757 **KEASBEY & MATTISON CO.**
Light blue, 3½" 3.00   5.00

☐758 **KEASBEY & MATTISON CO. CHEMISTS, AMBLER, PA.**
On front, light blue, rectangular, 5" 3.00   4.00

☐759	**KEASBEY & MATTISON CO, AMBLER, PA.**		
	On front, smoky blue, round, 5¾"	3.00	5.00
☐760	**KEASBEY & MATTISON, PHILADELPHIA**		
	Around shoulder, cylindrical, ring collar, cobalt blue, 6" ..	7.00	10.00
☐761	**THE KEELEY REMEDY NEUROTENE**		
	Discovered by Dr. L.E. Keely Dwight, clear, 5⅝"	7.00	10.00
☐762	**DR. KELLINGS PURE HERB MED.**		
	Pontil, green, 6"	18.00	25.00
☐763	**J.W. KELLY & CO.**		
	C in triangle on bottom, clear or amethyst, 6"	3.00	5.00
☐764	**KEMP'S**		
	O.F. Woodward on one side, Leroy, N.Y. on other side, light blue, 5½"	3.00	5.00
☐765	**KEMP'S BALSAM**		
	Vertical on front, sample size, heavy glass, unusual flask shape, band collar, aqua, 2⅞"	4.00	6.00
☐766	**KEMP'S BALSAM FOR THROAT AND LUNGS, LEROY, N.Y., O.F. WOODWARD**		
	Front and sides, rectangular, square band collar, aqua, 5¾"	4.00	6.00
☐767	**KENDALL'S SPAVIN TREATMENT**		
	On shoulder, Enosbury Falls, Vt. on base, amber, twelve panels, 5½"	5.00	8.00
☐768	**DR. KENDALL'S QUICK RELIEF**		
	Vertical on front in sunken panel, rectangular, double band collar, aqua, 5"	3.00	5.00
☐769	**DR. KENNEDY'S**		
	Aqua, side mold, 9"	4.00	6.00
☐770	**DR. KENNEDY'S FAVORITE REMEDY, KINGSTON, N.Y. U.S.A.**		
	Vertical on front in sunken panel, clear, 7"	3.00	5.00
☐771	**DR. D. KENNEDY'S**		
	On side, Favorite Remedy on front, Kingston, N.Y. U.S.A. on opposite side in sunken panels, graduated collar, rectangular, amethyst, 8¾"	4.00	6.00
☐772	*Same as above except aqua*	3.00	5.00
☐773	**DR. KENNEDY'S LINIMENT, RHEUMATIC LINIMENT, ROXBURY, MASS.**		
	Aqua, 6¼"	6.00	9.00
☐774	**DR. KENNEY'S**		
	On other side, aqua, 9"	6.00	9.00
☐775	**KEYSTONE DRUG CO.**		
	So. Boston Va., tapered top, clear or amber, 9"	6.00	9.00
☐776	**MRS. E. KIDDER CORDIAL**		
	Marked vertically Mrs. E. Kidder Dysentery Cordial, Boston, round, open pontil, aqua, 8"	16.00	23.00
☐777	**KIDNEY BOTTLE PILLS**		
	Label, kidney shape, ring top, clear, 5½"	11.00	15.00
☐778	**E.J. KIEFFER & CO.**		
	Round back, clear or amethyst, 6½"	4.00	6.00
☐779	**E. J. KIEFFER'S**		
	Amber, 6½"	5.00	8.00
☐780	**KILLINGER**		
	On front, aqua, square, 7⅞"	4.00	6.00

☐781 **DR. KILMER'S**
Swamp Root Kidney Liver and Bladder Remedy, Binghampton, N.Y., U.S.A. on front, aqua, rectangular, 7" 5.00   8.00

☐782 **DR. KILMER'S**
Aqua, 7" 5.00   8.00

☐783 **DR. KILMER'S**
Swamp-Root, Kidney & Bladder Remedy on front, Binghampton, N.Y. on left, aqua, rectangular, 8" 5.00   9.00

☐784 **DR. KILMER'S**
Swamp-Root, Kidney Remedy, Binghampton, N.Y., sample bottle, aqua, round, 4¼" 8.00   11.00

☐785 **DR. KILMER'S U & O ANOINTMENT, BINGHAMPTON, N.Y.**
On front, round, aqua, 1¾" 3.00   5.00

☐786 **DR. KILMER'S**
Clear, machine made, 7¼" 3.00   5.00

☐787 **KINA**
Laroche on back, aqua, 7¾" 3.00   5.00

☐788 **DR. KING'S NEW DISCOVERY**
On front, Chicago, Ill. on side, H.E. Bucklem & Co. on right side, rectangular, aqua, 4½" 4.00   6.00

☐789 **DR. KING'S NEW DISCOVERY FOR COUGHS AND COLDS**
On front panel, clear, rectangular, 6¾" 5.00   8.00

☐790 **DR. KING'S NEW LIFE PILLS**
On front, clear, square, 2½" 3.00   4.00

☐791 **KINNEY & CO.**
Clear or amethyst, 3" 5.00   8.00

☐792 **S. B. KITCHEL'S LINIMENT**
Aqua, 8¼" 5.00   9.00

☐793 **KLINKER'S HAIR TONIC, CLEVELAND**
Vertical on front in fancy panel, ring collar, ring on neck, three ribs on side, base crown shape, fancy shape, clear, 6" .   6.00   9.00

☐794 **KNAPPS**
Aqua, 4" 3.00   5.00

☐795 **KOBOLE TONIC MED. CO., CHICAGO, ILL.**
Milk glass, 8½" 22.00   32.00

☐796 Same as above except amber or aqua 16.00   22.00

☐797 **DR. KOCH'S REMEDIES, EXTRACTS & SPICES**
On one side Dr. Koch Vegetable Tea Co., other Winona, Minn., clear, 9" 4.00   6.00

☐798 **KODEL NERVE TONIC, FREE SAMPLE**
Under bottom E. C. Dewich & Co., Chicago, wide ring top, aqua, 3¼" 3.00   5.00

☐799 **KOKEN, ST. LOUIS, U.S.A., 10 FL. OZ.**
On front, clear, round, 7" 1.40   2.15

☐800 **KOKO FOR THE HAIR**
Clear, 4¾" 4.00   6.00

☐801 **KOLA-CARDINETTE**
On each side, The Palisade Mfg. Co., Yonkers, N.Y. under bottom, amber, 9" 4.00   7.00

☐802 **KONING TILLY**
In vertical line, sheared top, round, aqua, ¾" 5.00   7.00

☐ 803 **KONJOLA MOSBY MED. CO., CINCINNATI, U.S.A.**
On front, Konjola on left and right panels, clear, rectangular, screw top, 8¼ " 1.40   2.20

☐ 804 **DR. Wm KORONG HAIR COLORING MFG. CHEMIST**
Louisville, Ky. with teaspoon on each side, 3ii on shoulder, Simplex in scrip, clear, double ring top, 4½ " ... 9.00   12.00

☐ 805 **THE KREBS-OLIVER CO.**
Amber, 5¾ " 4.00   6.00

☐ 806 **KUHLMAN'S KNOXVILLE TENN.**
W.&T. Co. U.S.A. under bottom, clear, 4½ " 5.00   8.00

☐ 807 **KUTNOW'S POWDER**
Vertical on front in large letters, rectangular, large square collar, corner panels, aqua, 4¾ " 3.00   5.00

L

☐ 808 **LA AMERICA**
Clear or amethyst 5.00   8.00

☐ 809 **L.B. CO.**
Clear, 11½ " 3.00   5.00

☐ 810 **LACTO-MARROW CO.**
Other side N.Y., U.S.A., clear or amethyst, side mold, 9¼ " .. 4.00   7.00

☐ 811 **LACTOPEPTINE, NEW YORK**
Clear or amethyst, 4" 3.00   5.00

☐ 812 **LACTOPEPTINE FOR THE DIGESTIVE AILMENTS**
Around cross, dark green, sheared top, 3" 5.00   7.00

☐ 813 **LA-CU-PIA**
Under bottom, aqua, four-part mold, 8¼ " 4.00   6.00

☐ 814 **LAINE CHEM CO.**
Amber, 5½ " 3.00   5.00

☐ 815 **LAINE CHEM CO.**
Amber, 4" 4.00   6.00

☐ 816 **LAINE CHEM CO.**
Amber, 341 under bottom, 6½ " 4.00   6.00

☐ 817 **GEO. L. LAIRD & CO.**
In horseshoe shape, OLEO-CHYLE in vertical line, cathedral type bottle, ring top, blue, 6¾ " 21.00   28.00

☐ 818 **LAKE SHORE SEED CO., DUNKIRK, N.Y.**
Vertical on front in large sunken panels, rectangular, ring on neck, aqua, 5½ " 3.00   5.00

☐ 819 **LANGLEY & MICHAELS, SAN FRANCISCO**
Vertical on front in round sunken panels, round graduated collar, aqua, 6¼ " 7.00   10.00

☐ 820 **LANMAN & KEMP** one side,
One side, other side N.Y., aqua, 6" 3.00   5.00

☐ 821 **LANMAN & KEMP**
Aqua, Cod Liver Oil one side, other side N.Y., 10½ " 7.00   11.00

☐ 822 **LANMAN & KEMP**
Aqua, 8½ " 4.00   6.00

☐ 823 **LARKIN CO., BUFFALO**
Clear, 6" 3.00   5.00

☐824 **LARKIN CO.**
Clear or amethyst, 4¼" 3.00 5.00
☐825 **LARKIN SOAP CO., MODJESKA DERMA-BALM,**
MODJEST DERMA-BALM
On three sides, square, flared lip, clear, 4¾" 6.00 9.00
☐826 **LAUGHLIUS & BUSHFIELS WORM POWER,**
WHEELING, VA. 1850
Pontil, aqua, 3¼" 18.00 25.00
☐827 **A.J. LAXOL, WHITE, NEW YORK**
In two indented panels on front, oval back, triangular,
round band collar, cobalt blue, 7" 11.00 15.00
☐828 **LAXOL**
2½" neck, triangular, cobalt blue, 7" 9.00 12.00
☐829 **L-C 1903**
On bottom, blue, sheared top, 4" 5.00 8.00
☐830 **JOHN P. LEE**
Clear, 4½" 3.00 5.00
☐831 **LEGRANDE'S ARABIAN CATARRH REMEDY, N.Y.**
On front, flask type bottle, aqua, 9½" 9.00 12.00
☐832 **LEHN & FINK, NEW YORK**
On bottom, amber, seven-part mold, 7¼" 5.00 8.00
☐833 **DR. H.C. LEMKE'S**
On other side, aqua, 10" 14.00 19.00
☐834 **LEMON ELIXIR** *under bottom,*
Under bottom, Paper label reads DR. H. MOYEY'S LEMON
ELIXIR HERB COMPOUND, ATLANTA, GA., aqua, 7¼" .. 6.00 9.00
☐835 **LEONARDI'S**
On one side, other New York, N.Y., front Golden Eye Lotion,
relieves without pain all in sunken panels, aqua, 4½" 9.00 12.00
☐836 *Same except Tampa, Fla.* 9.00 12.00
☐837 *Same except A.B.M.* 5.00 8.00
☐838 **LEONARDI'S BLOOD ELIXIR**
The Great Blood Purifier, Tampa, Fla. all in 4 lines, bev-
eled corners, ring top, amber, 8¼" 14.00 19.00
☐839 *Same except New York and Tampa, Fla.* 14.00 19.00
☐840 **LEONARDI & CO.,**
Pharmacists, Jackson Black, Tampa, Fla. all in 3 lines,
oval, thin tapered top, clear, 4¾" x 6¾" 9.00 12.00
☐841 **S.B. LEONARDI & CO.**
Amber, 8¼" 6.00 9.00
☐842 **JARABE DE LEONARDI**
5 under bottom, aqua, 5½" 3.00 5.00
☐843 **LEONARDI, JARABE**
De., Para Latos Creasotado, Leonardi's Cough syrup creo-
sated, New Rochelle, N.Y. all in 4 lines, ring top, clear and
aqua, 5¼" 5.00 7.00
☐844 *Same except New York and Tampa, Fla.* 5.00 7.00
☐845 **LEONARDI'S WORM SYRUP,**
The Great Worm Killer, S. B. Leonardi & Co., N.Y. & Tampa,
Fla. in 4 lines, square ring top, aqua, 5¹/₁₆" 5.00 8.00
☐846 *Same except Prepared only by S.B.L. & Co., & New York,*
aqua, 4¼" 5.00 7.00

☐ 847	**W.F. LEVERA**		
	On side, Cedar Rapids, Iowa on opposite side, amber, 5½"	4.00	6.00
☐ 848	**LEWIS & CO.**		
	Amber, 7½"	3.00	5.00
☐ 849	**J.A. LIMCRICK'S GREAT MASTER OF PAIN, RODNEY, MASS.**		
	Pontil, tapered top, aqua, 6¼"	22.00	30.00
☐ 850	**DR. LINDSEY'S BLOOD SEARCHER, DR. J.M. LINDSEY, GREENBURG, PA. 1850**		
	Sold by agent Robert Emory Sellers & Co., Pittsburgh, 1880, clear, 8½"	16.00	22.00
☐ 851	**DR. LINICK'S MALT EXTRACT**		
	Vertical on front, ring collar, square, shaped like pickle jar, clear, 6"	5.00	8.00
☐ 852	**LINIM**		
	Clear, 5¾"	6.00	9.00
☐ 853	**LINIMENT OR OIL OF LIFE 16 OZ.**		
	On side in sunken arch panel, C.C. TAYLOR on side, Fairport, N.Y. on opposite side, rectangular, graduated collar, clear, 10½"	6.00	9.00
☐ 854	Same as above except 5⅞"	6.00	9.00
☐ 855	**LIPPMAN'S LIVER PILLS**		
	Aqua, 2¼"	3.00	5.00
☐ 856	**LIQUID FRANCONIA, LEROY, N.Y.**		
	O.F. Woodward on front and sides, rectangular, amethyst, 4¼"	3.00	5.00
☐ 857	**LIQUID PEPTONOIDS, ARLINGTON CHEMICAL CO., YONKERS, N.Y.**		
	Sunken in arched panel, square, amber, 7⅝"	3.00	5.00
☐ 858	**LIQUID OPDELDOC**		
	Cylindrical, two-piece mold, square band collar, aqua, 4½".	6.00	9.00
☐ 859	**LIQUOZONE**		
	3" diameter, amber, 8"	3.00	5.00
☐ 860	**LIQUID VENEER**		
	Under bottom, clear or amber, 6¼"	4.00	6.00
☐ 861	**LISTERINE**		
	Near shoulder, at bottom Lambert Pharmacal Co. in two lines, three sizes, clear or amethyst	3.00	5.00
☐ 862	Same except machine made	1.40	2.20
☐ 863	**LITTLE GIANT SURE DEATH TO ALL KINDS OF BUGS**		
	Every bottle warranted, Little Giant Co., Newburyport, Mass, aqua, 8½"	9.00	12.00
☐ 864	**LIVE & LET LIVE CUT RATE DRUG CO.**		
	Chattanooga, Tenn., clear, 3½"	3.00	5.00
☐ 865	**L.L.L.**		
	In front, ring top, aqua, 7¾"	5.00	8.00
☐ 866	**LOG CABIN COUGH AND CONSUMPTION REMEDY**		
	Under bottom Pat. Sept. 6th, 1887, amber	14.00	19.00
☐ 867	**LOG CABIN EXTRACT**		
	Label, Rochester, N.Y., Pat'd. Sep. 6 1889, amber, 6¼" ...	60.00	80.00
☐ 868	**LONDON**		
	Pontil, light green, 5½"	9.00	13.00

LOG CABIN EXTRACT. *Medicine, amber, 8"* 100.00   125.00

Left to right:
FIDDLE BOTTLE. *Cobalt, 10"* 15.00   25.00
VERTICAL RIBBED FLASK. *Amber, halfpint, 6"* 50.00   75.00
TIPPECANOE BITTERS. *Amber, 9½"* 70.00   90.00

Left to right:

GILMORE'S AROMATIC WINE. *LeRoy, N.Y., amber, 10" ....* 20.00   25.00
CHICKEN ON BICYCLE. *Labled bitters, amber, 8½"* .. 100.00   150.00
VIEUX COGNAC. *Olive green, 10½"* 18.00   25.00

Left to right:
SUCCESS TO THE RAILROAD GV-1. *O.P., aqua, pint* . **270.00   300.00**
CAMPBELL'S HAIR INVIGORATOR AURORA N.Y.
O.P., 6½" **60.00   80.00**
DR. JAYNES INDIAN EXPECTORANT. *O.P., 5"* **50.00   75.00**
LONDON. *O.P., aqua, 5"* **17.00   24.00**

Left to right:

WARNERS SAFE CURE. *London, green, pint, 9½"* . . . 100.00   125.00
MUNYON'S INHALER CURE. *Green, 4¼"* 15.00   20.00
BROWN'S BLOOD CURE. *Green, 7¼"* 90.00   120.00
HANDYSIDE'S CONSUMPTION CURE. *Green, 6¼"* . . 100.00   125.00

Left to right:
LONDEN'S CURE FOR PILES. *O.P., aqua, 6¾"* 140.00   160.00
AYER'S AGUE CURE. *O.P., aqua, 7"* 125.00   150.00
PORTER'S CURE OF PAIN. *I.P., aqua, 6½"* 125.00   150.00
JAS. NEWTON'S CURE FOR CROUP. *O.P. aqua, 5"* . . 225.00   250.00

Left to right:

SPARKS KIDNEY AND LIVER CURE. *Amber, 9½"* . . . 350.00   375.00

HILLS DYS-PEP-CU CURE. *Amber, 8½"* 40.00   50.00

JAS. MITCHNER'S OCCIDENTAL DIPTHERIA CURE.
Amber, 8½" 40.00   60.00

Left to right:
HOPS BITTERS. *Amber, 9½"* 20.00 30.00
HIGHEST MEDAL VIENNA 1873. *Case gin, olive green, 8½"* 40.00 65.00
J.J.W. PETERS, DOG BOTTLE. *Labled bitters, amber, 8½"* 40.00 60.00

☐869 **L.O.R. CO.**
Around an eye, tapered top, 4¾" 22.00   30.00
☐870 **LORD'S OPDELDOC**
With embossed man breaking and tossing away his
crutches, on front in arched panel, oval, square collar,
aqua, 5" 14.00   19.00
☐871 **LORENTZ MED. CO.**
Amber, 4" 5.00   8.00
☐872 **DON LORENZO**
Same on reverse side, dark olive, 10" 16.00   22.00
☐873 **J.M. LOTRIDGE**
W.T.Co. under bottom, clear, 6¼" 3.00   5.00
☐874 **THE LOUIS DAUDELIN CO.**
Clear, 8¾" 3.00   5.00
☐875 **LOUIT FRERES & CO, BOR DEAUX**
On front, mustard barrel, three rings at base and shoulder,
crude ring collar, amethyst, graphite pontil, 4¾" 11.00   15.00
☐876 **LUFKIN ECZEMA REMEDY**
Label, clear, 7" 5.00   8.00
☐877 **LUNDBORG, N.Y.**
Teal blue, 8⅝" 5.00   7.00
☐878 **LUYTIES**
Amber, 7" 5.00   8.00
☐879 **LYMAN ASTLEY-CHEYENE, WYO.**
In a circular panel, aqua, 7" 9.00   13.00
☐880 **DR. J.B. LYNAR & SON**
Logansport, Ind., J.B.L. in seal on shoulder, clear, 6" 9.00   13.00
☐881 **DR. J.B. LYNAR & SON**
Clear or amethyst, 6" 5.00   8.00
☐882 **LYON'S**
Pontil, aqua, 6¼" 12.00   17.00
☐883 **LYON'S**
Aqua, 6¼" 5.00   8.00
☐884 **LYON'S LAXATIVE SYRUP, LYON MED. CO.**
Reverse Louisville, Ky., clear, 6¼" 3.00   5.00
☐885 **LYON'S FOR THE HAIR, KAT HAIRON, NEW YORK**
On front, back and sides, sunken panels, rectangular,
pontil, aqua, 6⅛" 32.00   40.00
☐886 **LYON MFG' CO.**
Mexican Mustang Liniment on back, aqua, 7¾" 6.00   9.00
☐887 **LYON MFG' CO.**
Same as above except 7½" 5.00   8.00
☐888 **LYRIC 3 — Y**
Under bottom, machine made, clear or amethyst, 4½" . . .   1.45   2.25
☐889 **LYSOL**
Amber, 3½" 1.45   2.25

M

☐890 **J. J. MACK & CO., SAN FRANCISCO, DR. A. E.**
FLINT'S HEART REMEDY
Amber, 7½" 11.00   16.00

☐891 **MACK DRUG CO., PROP'S N.Y., DR. FLINTS REMEDY**
Flat ring top, amber, 7½" 11.00 15.00
☐892 **MACON MEDICINE CO.**
*"Guinns Pioneer Blood Renerver" on other side, amber,
11"* 9.00 13.00
☐893 **MADAME M. YALE FRUITCURA WOMANS TONIC**
Reverse side Chicago & N.Y., aqua, 9" 7.00 10.00
☐894 **MAGGI #2**
Rectangular, tapered neck, 6" 6.00 9.00
☐895 **MAGNESIE CALCINEE**
Clear glass, painted brown, 8" 7.00 11.00
☐896 **J. J. MAHER & CO., PROPRIETORS, AUGUSTA, MAINE**
Amber, 8½" 6.00 9.00
☐897 **P.H. MALLEN CO. CHICAGO**
Under bottom W.T. Co. U.S.A., amber, 9" 6.00 9.00
☐898 **THE MALTINE MFG. CO.**
#3 under bottom, amber, 7½" 6.00 9.00
☐899 **THE MALTINE MFG. CO. CHEMISTS, NEW YORK**
*In five lines on front, various numbers under bottom,
amber or brown, short neck, 6½"* 5.00 8.00
☐900 **MALYDOR MFG. CO., LANCASTER, O. U.S.A.**
*On front, large beveled corners, one corner is sunken,
amethyst, 5"* 5.00 7.00
☐901 **MANSFIELD MEDICINE CO. N.Y. and MEMPHIS**
*On front, Proprietors S. Mansfield on each side, tapered
top, aqua, 5½"* 9.00 13.00
☐902 **S. MANSFIELD & CO.**
Reverse side Memphis, aqua, 5¾" 7.00 10.00
☐903 **CHAS. MARCHAND**
Amber, 4" 3.00 5.00
☐904 **CHAS. MARCHAND**
Clear or amethyst, 8½" 5.00 7.00
☐905 **MARCHAND'S**
Amber, 5½" 3.00 5.00
☐906 **J.B. MARCHISI M.D.**
Aqua, 7½" 5.00 8.00
☐907 **MARINE HOSPITAL SERVICE 1798 U.S.**
*1871 around a crossed anchor and staff, near base 1000
c.c., ringed top, clear, 9¼"* 19.00 26.00
☐908 **MARINE HOSPITAL SERVICE**
Aqua, 5½" and other sizes 17.00 24.00
☐909 **MARSHALL'S**
Aqua, 4¾" 4.00 6.00
☐910 **DR. MARSHALL'S CATARRH SNUFF**
*On oppposite sides in large letters, rectangular, round
band collar, aqua, 3⅜"* 7.00 10.00
☐911 **WM. J. MATHESON & CO. LTD**
Sheared top, clear, 3½" 4.00 6.00
☐912 **MATHIS QUARTER DOLLAR FAMILY LINIMENT**
Aqua, 4¼" 3.00 5.00
☐913 **C. B. MATHIS**
Aqua, 4" 3.00 5.00

☐914 **MATHIS QUARTER DOLLAR FAMILY LINIMENT,**
B. MATHIS, TOMS RIVER, N.J.
In seven lines on front, oval, aqua, 4" 5.00 8.00
☐915 **MAZON PARFUM**
Vertical on front, square, aqua, 4" 3.00 5.00
☐916 **J. O. McCANN**
Clear, 2¾" 3.00 5.00
☐917 **McCANNON & CO., WINONA, MINN.**
Vertical on front in sunken panel, rectangular, double
band collar, aqua, 7⅛" 3.00 5.00
☐918 **McCOMBIE'S COMPOUND RESTORATIVE**
Pontil 23.00 31.00
☐919 **McCORMICK & CO.**
Clear, 3¾" 3.00 5.00
☐920 **DRS. McDONALD & LEVY**
Sacramento City, Calif., aqua, 4¾" 9.00 12.00
☐921 **McELREES WINE OF CARDUI**
On side, Chattanooga Medicine Co. on opposite side,
sunken oval panels, graduated collar, clear, 8½" 5.00 8.00
☐922 **McFADDEN THE DRUGGIST, SENATOBIA, MISS.**
Clear or amber, 5¾" 4.00 6.00
☐923 **McKESSON & ROBBINS**
Amber, 3" 3.00 5.00
☐924 **McKESSON & ROBBINS**
In two lines, amber, 2¼" square, 1⅞" wide 3.00 5.00
☐925 **DR. McLANE'S, AMERICAN WORM SPECIFIC**
Round, pontil, 4" 14.00 20.00
☐926 **DR. McLEAN'S LIVER & KIDNEY BALMS, ST. LOUIS, MO.**
Aqua, 8¾" 9.00 13.00
☐927 **McLEAN'S STRENGTHENING CORDIAL**
Graphite pontil, aqua, 9¼" 22.00 31.00
☐928 **DR. McLEAN'S LIVER & KIDNEY BALM, ST. LOUIS**
Aqua, oval flask, 9" 5.00 8.00
☐929 **DR. J.H. McLEAN'S VOLCANIC OIL LINIMENT**
On the front, square, aqua, 4" 5.00 7.00
☐930 **DR. J.H. McLEAN'S**
Aqua, sheared top, ten panels, 3½" 4.00 6.00
☐931 **McMILLAN & KESTER, ESS. OF JAMAICA GINGER, S. F.**
All on front, flask, graduated collar, aqua, 6¾" 6.00 9.00
☐932 **McMILLAN & KESTER, ESS. OF JAMAICA, GINGER, S. F.**
Aqua, 6" 12.00 17.00
☐933 **DR. McMUNN'S ELIXIR OF OPIUM**
Pontil, round, aqua, 4½" 12.00 17.00
☐934 **DR. McMUNN'S ELIXIR OF OPIUM**
Vertical around bottle, cylindrical, square collar, aqua,
4½" 5.00 8.00
☐935 **FURST McNESS CO., FREEPORT, ILL.**
Vertical on front in sunken panel, rectangular, ring and
band collar, ABM, aqua, 8½" 3.00 4.00
☐936 *Same as above except 6¼"* 3.00 4.00
☐937 **M.C.W. 10½ OZ** *under bottom, Amber, 7½"* 3.00 4.00
☐938 **M.C.W. 43** *under bottom, Round, amber, 3"* 3.00 5.00

☐939 **M.D. U.S.A.** *in center of bottle, Ring top, 9½"* 14.00 19.00
☐940 **MEADE & BAKER**
Clear or amethyst, 3½" 5.00 8.00
☐941 **MEADE & BAKER**
Clear, 4¼" 3.00 5.00
☐942 *MEDICINE, plain, square, aqua, applied top, kick-up, pontil, 9¾"* 12.00 17.00
☐943 *MEDICINE, plain, round, cobalt, 3" round, 7½"* 7.00 10.00
☐944 *MEDICINE, plain, twelve-sided, round, pontil, 1¼" x 2½"* 11.00 16.00
☐945 *MEDICINE label, clear, 4"* 3.00 4.00
☐946 *MEDICINE label, pontil, aqua, 6¾"* 11.00 15.00
☐947 *MEDICINE label, amber, 8"* 3.00 4.00
☐948 *MEDICINE label, cobalt, 4½"* 6.00 9.00
☐949 *MEDICINE label, clear or amethyst, W on bottom, 6"* 3.00 5.00
☐950 *MEDICINE label, clear or amethyst, 5"* 1.45 2.25
☐951 *MEDICINE label, aqua, pontil, 6½"* 11.00 15.00
☐952 *MEDICINE label, amber, 7¼"* 3.00 4.00
☐953 *MEDICINE label, free-blown, pontil, clear, 3⁹⁄₁₆" diameter .* 13.00 18.00
☐954 *MEDICINE label, kick-up, cobalt, 6"* 5.00 8.00
☐955 *MEDICINE label, amber, 7¼"* 3.00 5.00
☐956 *MEDICINE label, cobalt, 5¾"* 6.00 9.00
☐957 *MEDICINE label, pontil, aqua, 1½" diameter, 5¼"* 11.00 15.00
☐958 *MEDICINE label, aqua, pontil, 2¼" round* 11.00 15.00
☐959 *MEDICINE label, clear, pontil, 2¾"* 8.00 12.00
☐960 *MEDICINE label, light blue, small kick-up, 7½"* 4.00 6.00
☐961 *MEDICINE label, W under bottom, clear, 4½"* 2.00 3.00
☐962 *M, plain medicine label, amber, 8½"* 3.00 5.00
☐963 *MEDICINE label, three-cornered bottle, clear, 4"* 3.00 4.00
☐964 *MEDICINE label, three-part mold, aqua, 6¼"* 4.00 6.00
☐965 *MEDICINE label, cobalt, 5½"* 5.00 8.00
☐966 *MEDICINE label, B under bottom, aqua* 3.00 5.00
☐967 *MEDICINE label, aqua, 6¼"* 3.00 4.00
☐968 *MEDICINE label, clear, 4½"* 3.00 4.00
☐969 *MEDICINE label, twelve panels, aqua, 4½"* 3.00 4.00
☐970 *MEDICINE label, 400 under bottom, amber, 6¼"* 3.00 5.00
☐971 *MEDICINE label, 5 on bottom, aqua, 8"* 2.00 3.00
☐972 *MEDICINE label, 17 on bottom, amber, 7¾"* 3.00 5.00
☐973 *MEDICINE label, amber, 9"* 5.00 8.00
☐974 *MEDICINE label, free-blown, pontil, aqua, 9¾"* 14.00 19.00
☐975 *Also Pat. March 1893, St. Louis, Mo. under bottom, clear, 7½"* 4.00 6.00
☐976 *MEDICINE label, aqua, 1¾"* 3.00 5.00
☐977 *MEDICINE label, clear, 2½"* 3.00 5.00
☐978 *MEDICINE label, amber, 2423 under bottom, 8"* 3.00 5.00
☐979 *MEDICINE label, 933 on bottom, amber, 8¾"* 3.00 5.00
☐980 *MEDICINE label, amber, nine-part mold, machine made, 7½"* 4.00 6.00
☐981 *MEDICINE label, clear or amethyst, 5"* 3.00 5.00
☐982 *MEDICINE label, pontil, clear or amethyst, 3½"* 7.00 10.00
☐983 *MEDICINE label, three-part mold, clear, 5¾"* 3.00 5.00
☐984 *MEDICINE label, clear, pontil, 4"* 7.00 10.00
☐985 *MEDICINE label, W.T.Co. U.S.A. under bottom, cobalt blue, 5¾"* 7.00 10.00

☐986	*MEDICINE label, three-part mold, cobalt blue, 9½"*	7.00	10.00
☐987	*MEDICINE label, clear, 4¾"*	1.50	2.25
☐988	*MEDICINE label, 171 under bottom, aqua, 5"*	1.50	2.25
☐989	*MEDICINE label, aqua, 6"*	1.50	2.25
☐990	*MEDICINE label, E.L. & Co. under bottom, amber, 7"*	3.00	5.00
☐991	*MEDICINE label, round back, clear or amethyst, 6¾"*	3.00	5.00
☐992	*MEDICINE label, clear or amethyst, 8½"*	5.00	8.00
☐993	*MEDICINE label, front has sunken panel, other side flat, 14 under bottom, amber, 7¾" x 2½" x 2½"*	3.00	5.00
☐994	*MEDICINE label, amber, 7"*	3.00	5.00
☐995	*MEDICINE label, cobalt, 3"*	4.00	6.00
☐996	*MEDICINE label, numbers under bottom, cobalt, 7½"* ...	6.00	9.00
☐997	*MEDICINE label, ringed top, milk glass, 4½"*	7.00	10.00
☐998	**MEDICAL DEPT. U.S.N.**		
	Reverse side 50c.c., clear or amber, 4"	14.00	19.00
☐999	*Same as above except 8½"*	14.00	19.00
☐1000	**C.W. MERCHANT CHEMIST, LOCKPORT, N.Y.**		
	In vertical lines, tapered top, amber, 5¾"	9.00	13.00
☐1001	**C.W. MERCHANT, LOCKPORT, N.Y., OAK ORCHARD ACID SPRINGS**		
	Tapered top, dark green, 9¼"	30.00	40.00
☐1002	**THE WM. S. MERRELL CO.**		
	Label, amber, machine made, 7¾"	4.00	6.00
☐1003	**THE WM. S. MERRELL CO.**		
	FGN on bottom, machine made, amber, 7¾"	3.00	5.00
☐1004	**THE MERZ CAPSURE CO.**		
	Clear, twelve panels, 3¾"	3.00	4.00
☐1005	**T. METCALF & CO.**		
	Clear, 8"	6.00	9.00
☐1006	**MRS. S. METTLER'S MEDICINE**		
	Aqua, 6½"	5.00	8.00
☐1007	**MEXICAN MUSTANG LINIMENT**		
	In three vertical lines, round, aqua, pontil, 4½"	16.00	23.00
☐1008	*Same except no pontil*	3.00	5.00
☐1009	**MEXICAN MUSTANG LINIMENT**		
	On back, clear, 7½"	7.00	10.00
☐1010	**A.C. MEYER & CO. BALTO., MD. U.S.A., DR. J.W. BULLS COUGH SYRUP**		
	Aqua, 6½"	6.00	9.00
☐1011	**JOHN MEYER CHEMIST, MT. CLEMENS, MICH.**		
	Amber, 9½"	9.00	12.00
☐1012	**MEYERS MFG. CO.**		
	Vertical on side, shaped like a miniature pop bottle, crown top, amethyst, 4"	4.00	6.00
☐1013	**DR. MILE'S NERVINE**		
	On the front panel, aqua, rectangular, 8¼"	3.00	4.00
☐1014	**DR. MILE'S RESTORATIVE NERVINE**		
	On the front panel, rectangular, aqua, old bubbles, 8¼" .	4.00	6.00
☐1015	**DR. MILE'S MEDICAL CO.**		
	On the front panel, aqua, rectangular, 8¼"	3.00	4.00

☐ 1016 **DR. MILES MEDICAL CO.**
Vertical in sunken panel on front, label on reverse side, Dr. Miles Alterative Compound, picture of man with diagram of blood veins, double band collar, rectangular, ABM, aqua, 8¾" 9.00   12.00

☐ 1017 **DR. J.R. MILLERS'**
On side, Balm on opposite side, arch panels, rectangular, square collar, clear, 4¾" 5.00   9.00

☐ 1018 **MINARD'S LINIMENT, BOSTON**
Seven vertical panels on front half, back plain, round, round band collar, amethyst, 5⅛" 4.00   6.00

☐ 1019 **MINARD'S**
Clear or amethyst, 5" 4.00   6.00

☐ 1020 **MINARD'S LINIMENT**
Six panels, round back, clear or amethyst, 6" 5.00   8.00

☐ 1021 **MINUTE OIL MED. CO. LTD, NEW ORLEANS**
Aqua, 10¼" 16.00   22.00

☐ 1022 **MITCHELL'S**
Cobalt, on side Eye Salve 5.00   8.00

☐ 1023 **M.J. & CO.**
Amber, 8" 5.00   8.00

☐ 1024 **MOE HOSPITAL, SIOUX FALLS, SO. DAK.**
Vertical on front, side panels show scales, oval back, fluting on back, amethyst, 8¼" 6.00   9.00

☐ 1025 **MONTECATINI SALTS, ITALY**
Amber, 4" 7.00   10.00

☐ 1026 **GEORGE MOORE**
Clear, 5¾" 4.00   6.00

☐ 1027 **DR. J. MOORE'S ESSENCE OF LIFE**
Vertical around bottle, cylindrical, pontil, aqua, 3¾" 22.00   29.00

☐ 1028 **MOORE'S LIVER-AX**
Aqua, 7" 6.00   9.00

☐ 1029 **MOORE'S REVEALED REMEDY**
Amber, 8¾" 9.00   12.00

☐ 1030 **DR. MORENO**
Aqua, side mold, W.T. & CO. 5 U.S.A. under bottom, 8" ... 7.00   10.00

☐ 1031 **E. MORGAN & SONS, SOLE PROPRIETORS, PROVIDENCE, R.I.**
(E left out of Providence), twelve panels, on shoulder Dr. Haynes Arabian Balsam, aqua, 7½" 9.00   12.00

☐ 1032 **MORLEY BROS**
Label, aqua, 7" 4.00   6.00

☐ 1033 **MORNING CALL-C. LEDIARD, ST. LOUIS**
Olive amber, 10½" 6.00   9.00

☐ 1034 **H.S. MORRELL, N.Y.**
Pontil, tapered top, aqua, 5¾" 22.00   28.00

☐ 1035 **MORSE'S CELEBRATED SYRUP**
Vertically, oval, long tapered neck, graphite pontil, 9½" . 19.00   26.00

☐ 1036 **MORTON & CO.**
Clear or amethyst, 5½" 3.00   5.00

☐ 1037 **MORTON & CO., TAMPA, FLA., W.T. & CO.**
Clear or amber, 4½" 4.00   6.00

☐ 1038 **MOUTARDE DIAPHANE LOUIT FRERES & CO.**

On front, mustard barrel, three rings at base and shoulders, amethyst, crude ring collar, graphito pontil, 5"   11.00   15.00

☐ 1039 **MOXIE NERVE FOOD, TRADE MARK REGISTERED, MOX-IE**

On front and back, round, crown top, aqua, 10¼" 12.00   16.00

☐ 1040 **MOXIE NERVE FOOD, LOWELL, MASS**

Thick embossed line, graduated collar, round, aqua, 10" .   9.00   12.00

☐ 1041 **MOYER'S OIL OF GLADNESS, BLOOMSBURG, PA.**

Vertical on front in sunken panel, graduated collar, aqua, 5⅝" 7.00   10.00

☐ 1042 **MUEGGE BAKER, OREGON**

Muegge's on reverse shoulder, green, 8" 10.00   15.00

☐ 1043 **H.K. MULFORD CO., PHILA.**

Amber, 7¼" 7.00   10.00

☐ 1044 **MUNYON'S**

In one sunken side panel, other Paw-Paw, in front on top a tree, two board lines with Munyon's Paw-Paw, plain back, amber, long tapered top, 10" 13.00   18.00

☐ 1045 **MUNYON'S GERMICIDE SOLUTION**

Side mold, green, 3¼" 5.00   8.00

☐ 1046 **MUNYON'S GERMICIDE SOLUTION**

Green, 3½" 7.00   10.00

☐ 1047 **MURINE EYE REMEDY CO., CHICAGO U.S.A.**

Round, clear, 3½" 4.00   6.00

☐ 1048 **MURPHY BROTHERS, PORTLAND**

On front in oval end panel, rectangular, square collar, aqua, 4⅞" 3.00   5.00

☐ 1049 **SIR. J. MURRAY'S RE-CARBONATED PATENT MAGNESIA**

Vertical on front, crude band and small band collar, oval, light green, 7¼" 5.00   7.00

N

☐ 1050 **NATRIUM**

Clear, 4¾" 7.00   10.00

☐ 1051 **NELSON BAKER & CO.**

Amber, 9" 4.00   6.00

☐ 1052 **NERVE & BONE LINIMENT**

Round bottle, old type mold, aqua, 4¼" 5.00   8.00

☐ 1053 **NERVINE**

Prepared by the Catarrhozone Co., Kinston, Ont. vertical on front in oval sunken panel, rectangular, square collar, amethyst, 5¼" 6.00   9.00

☐ 1054 **NEWBROS HERBICIDE KILL THE DANDRUFF GERM**

Ring top, clear or amber, 5½" 6.00   9.00

☐ 1055 **THE NEW YORK PHARMACAL ASSOCIATION**

In two lines in a sunken panel on one side, on other side Lactopeptine, in front The Best Remedial Agent In All Digestive Orders, round 6" body, 1½" neck, 2¾" square, corners, cobalt 17.00   23.00

☐ 1056 **N.Y. MEDICAL**

Reverse side University City, cobalt, 7½" 17.00   23.00

☐ 1057 **NORTH**
Pontil, 6¼" 18.00   25.00
☐ 1058 **NORTON**
Clear or amethyst, 5" 3.00   5.00
☐ 1059 **NOYES, GRANULAR EFFERVESCENT MAGNESIA SULPHATE**
Vertical on front, rectangular, corner panels, square collar, aqua, 6" 5.00   8.00
☐ 1060 **NUCO-SOLVENT DR. GRIFFIN**
Aqua, 5¼" 6.00   9.00
☐ 1061 **NYAL'S EMULSION of COD LIVER OIL**
Amber, 9" 4.00   6.00
☐ 1062 **NYAL'S LINIMENT**
Amber, ring in neck, " 4.00   6.00
☐ 1063 **N.Y. PHARMACAL ASSOCIATION**
In two vertical lines, cobalt, 8½" 13.00   18.00

O

☐ 1064 **THE OAKLAND CHEMICAL CO.**
Amber, 4¾" 3.00   5.00
☐ 1065 **THE OAKLAND CHEMICAL CO.**
Amber, 5¼" 5.00   8.00
☐ 1066 **OD CHEM. CO., NEW YORK**
In two lines, amber, 6¾" 3.00   4.00
☐ 1067 **ODOJ** *under bottom,*
Under bottom, milk glass, M632 on one panel, 4½" 11.00   15.00
☐ 1068 **O.K. PLANTATION**
Triangular, amber, 11" 200.00   240.00
☐ 1069 **OL. AMYGDAL**
Clear, 5¾" 7.00   10.00
☐ 1070 **OLD DR. TOWNSEND'S SARSAPARILLA**
Pontil, green 40.00   55.00
☐ 1071 **OLDRIDGE BALM OF COLUMBIA FOR RESTORING HAIR**
Aqua, 6¼" 35.00   50.00
☐ 1072 **OLD DRUG STORE APOTHECARY JARS**
Open pontils, round, glass stoppers, 10½" 9.00   12.00
☐ 1073 **OLEUM, DR. PETER'S**
In back, tree in center of it, P-B under it 1783-1880, on base Trade Mark, ring top, clear, 5⅞" 14.00   20.00
☐ 1074 **OLIVE OIL**
Open pontil, no embossing, 10½" 9.00   12.00
☐ 1075 **OMEGA OIL CHEMICAL CO., NEW YORK**
In three lines at bottom, above bottom, a leaf with words Omega Oil It's Green, ring under this with Trade Mark, flared top with ring, under bottom, various numbers in circle, light green, 4½" 10.00   15.00
☐ 1076 **OMEGA OIL IT'S GREEN, TRADE MARK**
All inside of leaf embossed on front, THE OMEGA CHEMICAL CO. NEW YORK at base on front, sheared collar, clear, 6" 6.00   9.00
☐ 1077 *Same as above except 4½"* 6.00   9.00
☐ 1078 *Same as above except ABM, thread top, 6"* 3.00   4.00

☐ 1079 **OMEGA OIL**
Vertical on front, cylindrical, aqua, 3¼" 3.00   4.00
☐ 1080 *OPIUM BOTTLES, in different sizes, 1 drop to ½ ounce,*
most are clear, some amethyst 9.00   13.00
☐ 1081 *OPIUM, aqua, 2½"* 9.00   13.00
☐ 1082 **ORIENTAL CONDENSED COFFEE, TRADE MARK,**
ORIENTAL TEA COMPANY, BOSTON, MASS.
Vertical on front in slug plate, square collar, oval, aqua,
6½" 5.00   8.00
☐ 1083 **ORIENTAL CREAM, GOURAND'S, NEW YORK**
On flat front, front panels and sides, corner panels, flared
lip, rectangular, clear, 5½" 5.00   8.00
☐ 1084 **OTIS CLAPP & SON**
Amber, 7½" 7.00   11.00
☐ 1085 **C. OWENS**
Clear, 2½" 1.50   2.30
☐ 1086 **OWL**
J.B. Co., P.C. CO. in diamond shape on bottom, clear, 3½" . .   7.00   10.00
☐ 1087 **OWL DRUG CO.**
Clear, 5¼" 7.00   10.00
☐ 1088 **THE OWL DRUG CO. SAN FRANCISCO**
On bottom, double wing owl on mortar on front, clear, 8⅜"   11.00   15.00
☐ 1089 *OWL BOTTLE, double wing owl on mortar, thread top, rec-*
tangular, clear, 3⅜" 4.00   6.00
☐ 1090 **THE OWL DRUG CO.**
On back, double wing owl, rectangular, square collar,
ABM, clear, 5¾" 4.00   6.00
☐ 1091 *Same as above except 4"* 7.00   10.00
☐ 1092 **THE OWL DRUG CO.**
On back, single wing owl, hair tonic type bottle, ring col-
lar, tapered neck, round, amethyst, 7" 7.00   10.00
☐ 1093 **OWL DRUG STORE**
Embossed owl in center, diamond and 2 under bottom,
clear, 1½" x 2³⁄₁₆" 7.00   10.00
☐ 1094 **OX**
Pontil, cobalt blue, 8½" 40.00   50.00
☐ 1095 **OXIEN PILLS, THE GIANT OXIEN**
Augusta, Me., clear, 2" 5.00   8.00
☐ 1096 **OXIEN PILLS**
The Giant Oxien Co., Augusta Me., clear, 2" 4.00   6.00
☐ 1097 **OZOMULSION**
Amber, 5½" 3.00   5.00
☐ 1098 **OZON ANTISEPTIC DRESSING: W.H. DUNCAN,**
NATURES PINE REMEDY
Label, rectangular, square collar, ABM, clear, 6" 3.00   5.00
☐ 1099 **THE OZONE CO. OF TORONTO, LIMITED**
Same in back, double ring top, clear, 7" 7.00   10.00
☐ 1100 **THE LIQUID OZONE CO.**
8 under bottom, amber, 8" 7.00   10.00

P

☐ 1101 **PAINES CELERY COMPOUND**
Aqua, 10" 7.00   10.00

☐ 1102 *Same as above except amber* **7.00** **11.00**
☐ 1103 **PALACE DRUG STORE**
    Clear, 4½" **3.00** **5.00**
☐ 1104 **PALACE DRUG STORE**
    Clear or amethyst, 6" **4.00** **6.00**
☐ 1105 **PALATINE MED. CO.**
    Japanese Dropper, MAN'F'D By, tapered type bottle, ring
    top, clear, 5¼" **9.00** **12.00**
☐ 1106 **THE PALISADE MFG. CO.**
    Yonkers, N.Y. on bottom, clear or amethyst, 7¾" **5.00** **8.00**
☐ 1107 **THE PALISADE MFG. CO., YONKERS, N.Y.**
    Under bottom, amber, 7¼" **5.00** **9.00**
☐ 1108 **JAS. PALMER & CO., PHILADA.**
    One side Wholesale, other side Druggists, aqua, 5" **5.00** **9.00**
☐ 1109 **PALMOLIVE SHAMPOO, B.J. JOHNSON, TORONTO,**
    ONT. CANADA
    On front and back, rectangular, ring collar, ABM, clear,
    7¼" **5.00** **8.00**
☐ 1110 *10 Panel, bluish, 4"* **5.00** **9.00**
☐ 1111 **PA-PAY-ANS BELL**
    Ring top, amber **5.00** **8.00**
☐ 1112 **PA-PAY-ANS BELL**
    (Orangburg, N.Y.) **7.00** **11.00**
☐ 1113 **JOHN D. PARK**
    Cincinnati, O., Dr. Cuysotts Yellow Dock & Sarsaparilla in
    five vertical lines on front, 8½" body, 2" neck, tapered
    top, graphite pontil, aqua, 2¼" x 4¼" **32.00** **41.00**
☐ 1114 **JOHN D. PARK, CINCINNATI, O., DR. WISTARS**
    BALSAM OF WILD CHERRY
    Aqua, 7½" **11.00** **15.00**
☐ 1115 **PARKE DAVIS & CO.**
    Label, amber, 5½" **3.00** **5.00**
☐ 1116 **PARKE DAVIS & CO.**
    Label, 343 under bottom, amber **4.00** **6.00**
☐ 1117 **PARKE DAVIS & CO.**
    Label, black glass, 3½" **5.00** **8.00**
☐ 1118 **PARKE DAVIS & CO.**
    Label, P.D. & CO. 274 under bottom, amber, 5¼" **3.00** **5.00**
☐ 1119 **PARKER**
    On one side, New York other side, 17 under bottom,
    amber, 7" **3.00** **5.00**
☐ 1120 **PARKER'S HAIR BALSAM, NEW YORK**
    On front and sides in sunken oval panels, rectangular,
    ABM, amber, 7½" **5.00** **8.00**
☐ 1121 **PARKER'S HAIR BALSAM, NEW YORK**
    On front and sides, rectangular, amber, 6½" **4.00** **7.00**
☐ 1122 **DR. PARK'S INDIAN LINIMENT, WYANOKE**
    Clear, 5⅜" **4.00** **7.00**
☐ 1123 **PAUL WESTPHAL**
    Clear or amethyst, 8" **5.00** **8.00**
☐ 1124 **PAWNEE INDIAN TA-HA**
    Price 25¢, Jos. Herman Agt., aqua, 8½" **14.00** **19.00**

☐1125 **PAWNEE INDIAN, TOO-RE**
Vertical on front in sunken panel, plain sides and back, rectangular, aqua, 7¾" 9.00   12.00

☐1126 **P D & CO.**
Under bottom, amber, 3¼" 3.00   4.00

☐1127 **P D & CO. 119**
Under bottom, amber, 4" 3.00   4.00

☐1128 **P. D. & CO.**
Under bottom, amber, 3¾" 3.00   4.00

☐1129 **P D & CO.21.S**
Under bottom, machine made, amber, 2½" 3.00   4.00

☐1130 **P D & CO. 334**
Under bottom, amber, 4¾" 3.00   5.00

☐1131 **PEARL'S WHITE GLYCERINE**
Cobalt, 6¼" 9.00   13.00

☐1132 **EBENEZER A. PEARL'S TINCTURE OF LIFE**
Vertical on front in sunken panels, rectangular, aqua, 7¾" 6.00   9.00

☐1133 **PEASE'S EYE WATER**
Newman, Ga., aqua, 4¼" 3.00   5.00

☐1134 **PROF. W.H. PEEK'S REMEDY**
N.Y., amber, 8" 7.00   10.00

☐1135 **DR. H.F. PEERY'S**
On back Dead Shot Vermifuce, amber, 4" 4.00   7.00

☐1136 **DR. H.F. PEERY'S**
Clear or amethyst 3.00   5.00

☐1137 **WM. PENDELTON**
Rockland, Me. vertical on three panels, twelve panels, square collar, aqua, 4⅜" 4.00   7.00

☐1138 **PEOPLES CHEMICAL CO., THE SCIENTIFICALLY PREPARED RED CROSS**
With cross embossed in circle, BEEF WINE & IRON PROVIDENCE, R.I. all on front, flask shape, flared collar, clear, 7½" 7.00   10.00

☐1139 **PEPERAZINE EFFERVESCENTE MEDY**
In three vertical lines, amber, 2¾" x 1¼", 6¼" 4.00   6.00

☐1140 **PEPTENZYME**
Cobalt, 2½" 10.00   15.00

☐1141 **PEPTENZYME**
At slant on front in sunken panel, cobalt blue, 3¼" 7.00   10.00

☐1142 **PEPTO-MANGAN GUDE**
Six panels, aqua, 7" 5.00   8.00

☐1143 **PEPTONOIDS, THE ARLINGTON CHEMISTS**
Yonker, N.Y., amber, 6" 4.00   6.00

☐1144 **PERRIN & STEPHENSON NO PERCENTAGE PHARMACY PORTER BUILDING**
San Jose, Cal., rectangular, aqua, square collar, 4½" 4.00   7.00

☐1145 **DR. PETER'S KURIKO**
On one of the panels, Prepared By Dr. Peter Fahrney & Sons, Co., Chicago, Ill., U.S.A. on the other side, amethyst, square, paneled, 9" 4.00   6.00

☐1146 **PETER MOLLER'S PUR COD LIVER OIL**
Label, clear, 5¾" 3.00   5.00

☐1147 **DR. J. PETTIT'S CANKER BALSAM**
Vertical on front, flask shape, clear, 3¼" 6.00   9.00

☐ 1148 **DR. PETTIT'S EYE WATER**
Buffalo, N.Y. on front, amethyst and clear, ring top, scale on back, 3" 9.00 12.00

☐ 1149 **PFEIFFER CHEMICAL CO., PHILA & ST. LOUIS**
On back, aqua, 6" 4.00 6.00

☐ 1150 **PHALON'S CHEMICAL HAIR INVIGORATOR**
Pontil, clear, 5½" 13.00 18.00

☐ 1151 **DR. O. PHELPS BROWN**
Vertical on one panel, ring collar, square, wide mouth, aqua, 2¾" 4.00 6.00

☐ 1152 **JOHN H. PHELPS PHARMACHIST, PHELPS RHEUMATIC ELIXIR**
Scranton Pa., clear, 5½" 4.00 6.00

☐ 1153 **PHILLIPS EMULSION COD LIVER OIL, NEW YORK**
Vertical on front in sunken panel, rectangular, amber, 9¼" 4.00 7.00

☐ 1154 **C.H. PHILLIPS, N.Y.**
Amber, 9½" 7.00 10.00

☐ 1155 **PHILLIPS' EMULSION**
(N backwards), amber, 9½" 27.00 35.00

☐ 1156 **PHILLIPS' EMULSION**
#1 under bottom, sample, 4¾" 6.00 9.00

☐ 1157 **PHILLIPS' EMULSION**
Amber, 7½" 4.00 6.00

☐ 1158 **PHILLIPS' MILK OF MAGNESIA**
Light blue, 7" 4.00 7.00

☐ 1159 **PHOLON'S VITALIA**
Same on reverse side, sunken arched panels, rectangular, flared lip, amethyst, 6⅜" 5.00 8.00

☐ 1160 **PHOSPHOCYCLO-FER**
On back label, depose on bottom, 4½" 3.00 5.00

☐ 1161 **DR. GEO. PIERCE'S**
On front, on back Indian Restorative Bitters, on side Lowell, Mass, aqua, pontil, 7½", 9" and other variants ... 55.00 75.00

☐ 1162 **DR. PIERCE'S GOLDEN MED. DISC.**
On the front panel, Buffalo, N.Y. on the left side, RV Pierce, M.D. on the right side, rectangular, aqua, 8¼" ... 3.00 5.00

☐ 1163 **R.V. PIERCE, M.D.**
On one side of panel, Buffalo, N.Y. on opposite side of panel, aqua, rectangular, 9⅛" 3.00 5.00

☐ 1164 **DR. PIERCE'S ANURIC TABLE FOR KIDNEYS AND BACKACHE**
On the front, aqua, round, 3½" 3.00 5.00

☐ 1165 **DR. PIERCES, ANURIC**
Embossed inside of kidney, TABLETS FOR KIDNEYS AND BACKACHE all on front, cylindrical, clear, 3" 5.00 8.00

☐ 1166 **DR. PIERCE'S FAVORITE PRESCRIPTION**
On the front panel, Buffalo, N.Y. on left side, R.V. Pierce, M.D. on right side, aqua, rectangular, 8½" 6.00 9.00

☐ 1167 **L. PIERRE VALLIGNY**
La-Goutte-A-Goutte, New York, old type screw top, amber, rectangular, 5½" 9.00 12.00

☐1168 *PILL BOTTLE; plain, oval, shear top, screw top, clear, 2½"* 3.00 5.00
☐1169 *PILL BOTTLE; plain, oval, shear top, screw top, clear, 1½"* 3.00 5.00
☐1170 *PILL BOTTLE; plain, aqua, 1¾"* 3.00 5.00
☐1171 *PILL BOTTLE; plain, clear, amber, 3½"* 3.00 5.00
☐1172 **THE PILLOW-INHALE CO. PHILA.**
Aqua, 7½" 3.00 5.00
☐1173 **PINEOLEUM FOR CATARRHAL CONDITIONS**
On both front and back, conical, pewter neck and top, amber, 6⅜" 5.00 8.00
☐1174 **PINE TREE TAR CORDIAL, PHILA.**
On one panel, on another panel a tree and patent 1859, another panel L.Q.G. Wisharts, blob top, green, 8" 45.00 60.00
☐1175 **PINE TREE TAR CORDIAL, PHILA. 1859**
With tree embossed, green, 8" 26.00 37.00
☐1176 **PINEX**
On both sides, rectangular, aqua, 5¾" 3.00 4.00
☐1177 **DR. PINKHAM'S EMMENAGOGUE**
Tapered top, pontil, kick-up in base, light blue, 5" 45.00 60.00
☐1178 **LYDIA E. PINKHAM'S**
Aqua, C8 under bottom, 8¼" 4.00 6.00
☐1179 **PINKSTON & SCRUGGS PHARMACISTS**
W.T. CO., O., U.S.A. under bottom, 4½" 3.00 5.00
☐1180 **PIPERAZINE**
Gold, 5" or 6" 11.00 16.00
☐1181 **THE PISO COMPANY**
In two lines in front sunken panel, on one side in sunken panel Trade-Piso's-Mark, on other side Hazeltine & Co., under bottom different numbers, green, clear, amber, 5¼" 4.00 6.00
☐1182 **DR. S. PITCHER'S**
On the side panel, Castoria on the other side, rectangular, aqua, 5⅞" 3.00 5.00
☐1183 **PITCHER'S CASTORIA**
Aqua, 6¼" 4.00 6.00
☐1184 **DR. W.M. PITT'S CARMINATIVE**
Aqua, 4" 4.00 6.00
☐1185 **DR. W.M. PITT'S CARMINATIVE**
Clear or amethyst, 4" 5.00 7.00
☐1186 *PLAIN MEDICINE BOTTLE, twelve panels, broken pontil, body 3", neck 1", clear* 5.00 7.00
☐1187 *PLAIN LABEL, clear, 4¾"* 6.00 9.00
☐1188 *PLAIN LABEL, clear, 4¾"* 5.00 7.00
☐1189 **DR. PLANETT'S BITTERS**
Iron pontil, amber, 9¾" 48.00 62.00
☐1190 **PLANK'S CHILL TONIC CO.**
Chattanooga, Tenn., clear or amber, 6½" 5.00 8.00
☐1191 **PLANTER'S OLD TIME REMEDIES**
One side Chattanooga Tenn., other side Spencer Med. Co., aqua 5.00 8.00
☐1192 **PLATT'S CHLORIDE**
Clear or amethyst, quart 5.00 8.00

☐ 1193 **PLUMMER & THOMPSON DRUGGIST**
*(P & T MONOGRAM) Lakeport, N.H., rectangular, ame-
thyst, flared lip, 4½"* 7.00 10.00

☐ 1194 **PLUTO WATER**
*Under bottom, a devil and Pluto, round, light green o
clear, 3¼" and other sizes* 3.00 5.00

☐ 1195 **P.M.F.S. & CO.**
On bottom, amber, 2¼" 3.00 4.00

☐ 1196 **POMPEIAN MASSAGE CREAM**
Clear or amber, 2¾" 4.00 6.00

☐ 1197 **POMPEIAN MASSAGE CREAM**
On front, barrel shape, ABM, clear, 2¾" 4.00 6.00

☐ 1198 **POND'S EXTRACT**
Label, 1846 under bottom, 5½" 3.00 5.00

☐ 1199 **POND'S EXTRACT CATARRH REMEDY**
Cobalt, 5¾" 11.00 15.00

☐ 1200 **POND'S MONARCH LINIMENT**
On front in sunken panel at slant, rectangular, aqua, 6" .. 5.00 8.00

☐ 1201 **PORTER'S PAIN KING**
*On opposite sides, sunken panels, rectangular, clear,
6¾"* 4.00 6.00

☐ 1202 **PORTER'S PAIN KING**
Same as above except ABM 3.00 4.00

☐ 1203 **DR. PORTER, NEW YORK**
Vertical on front, rectangular, aqua, 4¼" 5.00 8.00

☐ 1204 **PORTER'S**
*Pain King on other side, G.H.R. under bottom, clear or
amethyst, 7"* 5.00 8.00

☐ 1205 **POSEN**
Wronkerstr. No. 6, amber, 10" 18.00 24.00

☐ 1206 **POTTER & MERWIN**
*On front, plain back, on one side St. Louis, on other
Missouri, beveled corner, roofed shoulder, aqua, tapered-
top, 5½"* 7.00 10.00

☐ 1207 *Same except pontil* 17.00 23.00

☐ 1208 **PP**
(Back to back) label, cobalt, 2½" 5.00 8.00

☐ 1209 **PRESTON & MERRILL, BOSTON 1871**
Clear, 4¼" 3.00 5.00

☐ 1210 **PRESTON OF NEW HAMPSHIRE**
*On front, mold threads, sheared collar, glass stopper with
metal cup cover, emerald green, 3½"* 5.00 8.00

☐ 1211 **PROTONUCELN [sic],**
Amber, 2⅞" 3.00 5.00

☐ 1212 **PROTONUCLEIN,**
Amber, sheared top, 2" 4.00 6.00

☐ 1213 **WM. PRUNDER'S OREGON NO. 7138**
*(Embossed child's head with ribbon wreath) on center,
REGISTERED MARCH 25th 1879, BLOOD PURIFIER, WM.
PRUNDER & CO., PORTLAND, ORE. all on front in slug
plate ring and flared collar, oval, amber, 7½"* 17.00 24.00

☐ 1214 **THE PURDUE FREDERICK CO., NEW YORK**
Clear or amber, 8" 4.00 6.00

☐1215 **PURE COD LIVER OIL BYNE ATWOOD, PROVINCETOWN, MASS.**
Vertical on front, oval, aqua, 7" 5.00 8.00

☐1216 **PURE & GENUINE FOUR FOLD LINIMENT, R. MATCHETTS**
On front and sides, rectangular, clear, 5¼" 3.00 5.00

☐1217 **PYNCHON**
At base on front, Boston on opposite side at base, oval, aqua, 4¾" 5.00 8.00

Q

☐1218 **Q BAN**
Machine made, amber, 6¾" 3.00 4.00

R

☐1219 **DEL DR. RABELL**
Reverse side Emulsion, aqua, 9½" 3.00 5.00

☐1220 **RECINE de GUIMAUVE**
Cut glass, blue, 9¼" 23.00 32.00

☐1221 **R.R.R. RADWAY & CO., NEW YORK, ENTD. ACCORD. TO ACT OF CONGRESS**
On flat front panel and opposite sides in large letters, rectangular, aqua, 6⅜" 6.00 9.00

☐1222 **RADWAY'S** on side, **SARSAPARILLIAN RESOLVENT**
On front, R.R.R. on opposite side, Entd. Accord. to Act of Congress, sunken panels, rectangular, aqua, 7¼" 14.00 19.00

☐1223 **RAMSON'S NERVE & BONE OIL, BROWN MFG. CO. PROPRIETORS**
Vertical on front in sunken panel, Greenville, Tenn. on side, New York, NY, on opposite side, rectangular, aqua 5¾" 7.00 10.00

☐1224 **RAWLEIGH**
In vertical script, under it in ribbon, Trade Mark, clear or amethyst, 7⅝" 4.00 6.00

☐1225 **W.T. RAWLEIGH MED. CO.**
Freeport Ill on other side, clear 8¼" 3.00 5.00

☐1226 *Rectangular; almost square, no embossing, pontil, aqua, 2½"* 6.00 9.00

☐1227 *Same as above, concave corner panels, crude flared lip pontil, aqua, 5¼"* 6.00 9.00

☐1228 **RED CROSS FAMILY LINIMENT**
Label, Cooperative Drug Mfg., Jackson, Tenn., clear, 5½" 3.00 5.00

☐1229 **RED CROSS PHARMACY, W.T. CO. U.S.A.,**
Savanah [sic] Ga., clear, 5½" 9.00 12.00

☐1230 **REDINGTON & CO., ESSENCE OF JAMAICA GINGER, SAN FRANCISCO**
Vertical on front, aqua, 5¼" 5.00 8.00

☐1231 **REED & CARNRICK, JERSEY CITY, N.J.**
In three slanting lines, in back, Peptenzyme, cobalt, ring top, 2¾" x 2½" x 8½" 11.00 15.00

☐1232 *Same, two smaller sides* 9.00 12.00

□ 1233 **REED & CARNRICK**
Same except 4½" 8.00 11.00

□ 1234 **REED AND CARNRICK PHARMACISTS, NEW YORK**
In five lines on front panel, amber, 7½" 6.00 9.00

□ 1235 **REED & CARNRICK, N.Y.**
On bottom, amber, 4¾" 5.00 8.00

□ 1236 **REED & CARNRICK, N.Y.**
Dark blue, 6¼" 21.00 28.00

□ 1237 **REED & CARNRICK, NEW YORK**
Peptenzyme on back, cobalt, 4½" 9.00 12.00

□ 1238 **REESE CHEMICAL CO., BLOOD & SYSTEM TONIC**
Ring top, green, 3¾" 7.00 10.00

□ 1239 **REID'S**
Aqua, 5½" 4.00 6.00

□ 1240 **RENNE'S**
Aqua, 5" 3.00 4.00

□ 1241 **RENO'S NEW HEALTH UTERINE TONIC**
In center a lady head. Prepared only by S.B. Leonardi &
Co., New York, N.Y. all in 8 lines on front, ring top, 7½"
aqua 14.00 19.00

□ 1242 **RENO'S NEW HEALTH**
Or Woman's Salvation, Prepared only by S.B. Leonardi &
Co. Tampa, Fla. all in 7 lines, 7½" aqua 14.00 19.00

□ 1243 **RENWAR**
On each side, ring top, cobalt, 6" 7.00 10.00

□ 1244 **RESINAL BALTO. MD. CHEMICAL CO.**
Under bottom, milk glass, 3¼" 3.00 5.00

□ 1245 **RESTORFF & BETTMAN N.Y.**
Six panels, aqua, 4¼" 5.00 8.00

□ 1246 **REXALL**
3VIII on shoulder, rectangular, flared lip, emerald green,
6½" 7.00 10.00

□ 1247 **C.A. RICHARDS**
Amber, 9½" 18.00 25.00

□ 1248 **RICH-LAX**
Label, aqua,7½" 9.00 12.00

□ 1249 **F.A. RICHTER & CO. MANUFACTURING, CHEMISTS,
NEW YORK**
With embossed anchor, vertical on front, anchor on side,
Pain Expeller on opposite side, rectangular, aqua, 5" 7.00 10.00

□ 1250 **RICKER HEGEMAN OR HEGENAK DRUG STORES**
In center, cobalt, 5½" 14.00 20.00

□ 1251 **RIKER'S COMPOUND SARSAPARILLA**
Vertical in sunken panel on front, beveled corners, rectangular, sunken panels on all sides, aqua blue, 10" 24.00 32.00

□ 1252 **C.B. RINCKERHOFFS, PRICE ONE DOLLAR**
On side, Health Restorative, New York, tapered top, olive,
7¼" 65.00 85.00

□ 1253 **THE RIVER SWAMP CHILL and FEVER CURE**
With alligator in center, Augusta Ga, clear or aqua, 7" ... 32.00 45.00

□ 1254 **JAMES S. ROBINSON, MEMPHIS, TENN.**
Clear, 7" 5.00 8.00

☐ 1255 **ROCHE'S EMBROCATION FOR THE WHOOPING COUGH,**
W. EDWARDS & SON
On consecutive panels, flared lip, clear, 5" **7.00** **10.00**

☐ 1256 **RODERIC'S WILD CHERRY COUGH BALSAM**
Flared collar, ABM, clear, 5½ " **6.00** **9.00**

☐ 1257 *Same as above except amber, 4½ "* **5.00** **8.00**

☐ 1258 **RON-BRE**
Amber, 6½ " **3.00** **5.00**

☐ 1259 **ROOT JUICE MED. CO.**
Aqua, 9" **3.00** **5.00**

☐ 1260 **ROOT JUICE MED. CO.**
Label, clear or amethyst, 6" **3.00** **5.00**

☐ 1261 **DR. ROSE'S**
Philadel on other side, pontil, aqua **10.00** **15.00**

☐ 1262 **ROSHTON & ASPINWALL, NEW YORK**
On back Compound Chlorine Tooth Wash, flared top, pontil, golden olive, 6" **160.00** **210.00**

☐ 1263 *Round, crude ring collar, cylindrical, whittled effect, pontil, aqua blue 5¾"* **7.00** **10.00**

☐ 1264 **V. ROUSSIN, DRUGGIST, MUSKEGON, MICH.**
Clear, 7¼ " **5.00** **8.00**

☐ 1265 **ROWLANDS MACASSAI (OIL)**
Pontil **14.00** **20.00**

☐ 1266 **ROYAL FOOT WASH, EATON DRUG CO.**
Atlanta, Ga. **7.00** **10.00**

☐ 1267 **ROYAL GALL REMEDY**
Machine made, dark amber, 7½ " **7.00** **10.00**

☐ 1268 **ROYAL GERMETUER**
Same on reverse side, one side Kings Royal Germeturer Co., other side Atlanta Ga. U.S.A., amber, 8½ " **16.00** **23.00**

☐ 1269 **RUBIFOAM FOR THE TEETH, PUT UP E.W. HOYT & CO., LOWELL, MASS.**
All on front, oval, clear, 4" **5.00** **8.00**

☐ 1270 **RUSH'S** *on one side,* **REMEDY** *on reverse,*
Other two sides A.H.F. Monthly, double ring top, aqua, 6" **7.00** **10.00**

☐ 1271 **RUSH'S**
Vertical on front in small rectangular panel, Lung on side, Balm on opposite side, A.H. Flanders, MD. on back side, sunken panels, rectangular, aqua, 7" **14.00** **19.00**

☐ 1272 **RUSHTON'S**
F.V. on back, Cod Liver Oil on other side, N.Y. other side, ice blue, 10½ " **10.00** **15.00**

☐ 1273 **RUSS'S AROMATIC**
Side panel Schnapps, other side N.Y., dark olive, 8" **23.00** **32.00**

☐ 1274 **JOHN RYAN CITRATE OF MAGNESIA, SAVANNAH, GA.**
On front in four lines, aqua, short neck, round, 7" **42.00** **55.00**

S

☐ 1275 **SKEYHAN' PHARMACY, ROCKFORD, ILL.**
All in 3 lines on front, on shoulder 3IV, on bottom C.L.M. & Co., 2½ ", clear **7.00** **10.00**

☐ 1276 **DR. SAGE'S**
On one side, on other side Buffalo, Catarrah Remedy on front, on back Dr. Price Propr., all on sunken panels, #1 under bottom, 2¼" 7.00 10.00

☐ 1277 **SALVATION OIL, AC MEYER & CO., BALTIMORE, MD.**
In four lines in a sunken panel in front, round sides, under bottom, letter D, rectangular, 2¼" x 1" 5.00 8.00

☐ 1278 **SALVATION OIL, A.C. MEYER & CO.,TRADE MARK, BALTIMORE, MD. USA**
All on front, arched panel, rectangular, aqua, 6¾" 6.00 9.00

☐ 1279 **SALVATION TRADE MARK OIL, A.C. MEYER & CO., BALT. MD. U.S.A.**
Ring top, aqua, 6¾" 6.00 9.00

☐ 1280 **SAMMY'S MEDICINE**
Reverse side Baltimore Md. U.S.A., under bottom S.R. Scoggins, front side Reaches through the Entire System, sky blue, 7" 7.00 10.00

☐ 1281 **SAND'S SARSAPARILLA, NEW YORK**
Pontil, aqua, 6¼" 23.00 32.00

☐ 1282 **DR. SANFORD, NEW YORK**
On each side, aqua, 7½" 6.00 9.00

☐ 1283 **SANITAL DE MIDY**
Clear, twelve panels, 2¾" 4.00 6.00

☐ 1284 **THE SANITAS CO.**
Label, aqua, 9" 4.00 6.00

☐ 1285 **SANITOL**
For The Teeth on other side, clear, 4½" 5.00 8.00

☐ 1286 **DR. R. SAPPINGTON**
Reverse side Flaxseed Syrup, ring top, aqua, 7½" 5.00 8.00

☐ 1287 **A. SARTORIUS & CO., NEW YORK**
On front, round, clear, 2¾" 3.00 5.00

☐ 1288 **SASSAFRAS**
Under it an eye cup, Eye Lotion, Sassafras Eye Lotion Co., Maugh Chunk Pa., cobalt blue, 6" 13.00 18.00

☐ 1289 **SAVE**
Label, tan, 2¼" 1.45 2.20

☐ 1290 **SAVER**
Three-sided, amber, 3½" 15.00 20.00

☐ 1291 *Same as above except aqua, 4½"* 15.00 20.00

☐ 1292 **E.R. SCHAEFER'S**
Round back, clear, 4" 3.00 5.00

☐ 1293 **SCHEFFLER'S HAIR COLORINE, BEST IN THE WORLD**
On front, rectangular, beveled corners, clear, 4¼" 5.00 8.00

☐ 1294 **SCHENBS PULMONIC SYRUP**
Pontil 13.00 18.00

☐ 1295 **DR. SCHENCK'S PINE TAR FOR THROAT AND LUNGS**
Vertical in oval sunken end panel, rectangular, square collar, aqua, 6⅛" 9.00 12.00

☐ 1296 **SCHENCK'S PULMONIC SYRUP, PHILADA.**
On four panels, eight vertical panals, aqua, 5¾" 7.00 10.00

☐ 1297 **SCHENCK'S SYRUP**
Vertical on front, oval end sunken panel, aqua, 6¼" 5.00 8.00

☐ 1298 **SCHENCK'S SYRUP, PHILADA**
On three panels, eight vertical panels, aqua, 7¼" 7.00 10.00

☐ 1299 **HENDRICK WALTER SCHIEDAM, AROMATIC SCHNAPPS**
Olive, 7" 33.00 42.00
☐ 1300 **SCHLOTTERBECK & FUSS CO., PORTLAND ME.**
*Vertical on front in sunken panel, rectangular, sheared
collar, amber, 5"* 5.00 8.00
☐ 1301 **SCHUTZEN STR. NO. 6**
J. E. Gilke on back panel, 10" 26.00 35.00
☐ 1302 **SCOTT'S EMULSION**
*Cod Liver Oil on one side, With Lime Soda on other side,
aqua, various sizes* 4.00 6.00
☐ 1303 **S. & D. 8**
Under bottom, amber, 6" 3.00 5.00
☐ 1304 **S & D 83 2**
Under bottom, sheared top, amber, 3½" 3.00 5.00
☐ 1305 **S & D 2S**
Under bottom, amber, 4½" 1.50 2.25
☐ 1306 **S & D 100**
Under bottom, sheared top, clear, 2½" 3.00 5.00
☐ 1307 **S & D 73**
Under bottom, amber, 6¼" 3.00 5.00
☐ 1308 **S & D 83**
Under bottom, amber, 3½" 1.50 2.25
☐ 1309 **SEABURY**
Cobalt, sheared top, 3¾" 5.00 8.00
☐ 1310 **SEABURY**
Sheared top, amber, 3¾" 5.00 8.00
☐ 1311 **R. N. SEARLES**
*On side, Athlophoros on opposite side, rectangular, aqua,
6¾"* 5.00 7.00
☐ 1312 **SHAKE**
Label, amber, 6" 3.00 5.00
☐ 1313 **SHAKER FLUID EXTRACT VALERIAN**
On front and back, square, aqua, 3¾" 3.00 5.00
☐ 1314 **DR. S.&H. AND CO.**
P.R. Registered on base, amethyst or aqua, round, 9¼" .. 7.00 10.00
☐ 1315 **SHARP & DOHME**
Baltimore Md. under bottom, amber, 5¾" 3.00 5.00
☐ 1316 **SHARP & DOHME**
Three corners, round back, cobalt, 3½" 5.00 8.00
☐ 1317 **SHECUTS SOUTHERN BALM FOR COUGHS, COLD 1840**
Aqua, 6¾" 17.00 23.00
☐ 1318 **WM. H. SHEPARD, MARBLEHEAD, MASS.**
Label, aqua, 9" 9.00 12.00
☐ 1319 **J.T. SHINN**
Clear, 4¾" 3.00 5.00
☐ 1320 **S.H.K.C. EXT. P.C.**
Clear or amethyst, 4" 3.00 5.00
☐ 1321 **DR. SHOOP'S FAMILY MEDICINES**
Racine Wisc, aqua, ring top, 5½" 5.00 8.00
☐ 1322 **SHORES**
Label, clear, 9½" 3.00 5.00
☐ 1323 **SHORT STOP FOR COUGHS, H.M. O'NEIL, N.Y.**
Vertical on front in sunken panel, square, aqua, 4" 3.00 5.00
☐ 1324 **SHULTZ**
Dr. Shultz on other side, aqua, 6½" 5.00 8.00

☐ 1325 **SHUPTXINE**
In script, Druggist, Savannah, Ga., in two lines on front flap panel, top 31V, panel each side, round blank back, under bottom Pat 18/17 C.L. Co., Freen, 5¼" tall, 2" x 1¼" 11.00 15.00

☐ 1326 *Same as above, 3½" tall, 1½" x ¾"* 7.00 10.00

☐ 1327 *Same as above, 2½" tall, 1⅛" x ¾"* 8.00 11.00

☐ 1328 **THE SILBURT CO., TRADEMARK**
Cleveland, Sixth City, clear, 4¼" long 5.00 8.00

☐ 1329 **SIMMONS**
Aqua, 7" 4.00 7.00

☐ 1330 **SIMMON'S LIVER REGULATOR**
In three sunken panels on front, Philadelphia on side, Macon, Ga. on opposite side, J.H. Eeilin & Co. vertical on back, rectangular, aqua, 9" 6.00 9.00

☐ 1331 **DR. SIMMON'S SQUAW VINE WINE COMPOUND**
Vertical lines, tapered top, aqua, 8½" 5.00 8.00

☐ 1332 **DR. M.A. SIMMON'S LIVER MEDICINE**
St. Louis, aqua, 5¾" 5.00 8.00

☐ 1333 **DR SIMMON RANDALL'S**
Amber, 9" 10.00 15.00

☐ 1334 **DR. T.J. SIMPSON'S**
Aqua, 7¼" 7.00 11.00

☐ 1335 **C. SINES**
One side, Phila. Pa. reverse side, front side Tar Wild Cherry & Hoar Hound, pontil, aqua, 5" 17.00 24.00

☐ 1336 **SIPHON KUMY SGEN BOTTLE FOR PREPARING KUMYSS**
FROM REED & CARREIC, N.Y.
Cobalt, 8¾" 24.00 33.00

☐ 1337 **S.J.S. FOR THE BLOOD**
On one side L.G. Gerstle & Co., other side Chattanooga, Tenn., amber, 9" 9.00 13.00

☐ 1338 **SKABCURA DIP CO.**
Chicago U.S.A., aqua, 5" 5.00 8.00

☐ 1339 **SKODA'S SARSAPARILLA**
On side Skoda's, opposite side Discovery with Belfast, Me, on indented panel, front indented panel marked Concentrated Extract Sasaparilla Compound, back panel has label, amber, 9" 16.00 23.00

☐ 1340 *Same as above except Wolfville on one side, Nova Scotia on other side* 16.00 23.00

☐ 1341 **SKODA'S WOLEFIRLLE DISCOVERY**
Aqua, 9" 16.00 23.00

☐ 1342 **DR. SLEDGE'S HOREHOUND PECTORAL**
HOREHOUND PECTORAL in indented front panel, Memphis, Tenn. one side, Dr. Sledge's other side, graphite pontil, aqua, 7¼" 21.00 28.00

☐ 1343 **SLOAN'S LINIMENT**
Clear or amethyst, 7" 5.00 8.00

☐ 1344 **SLOCUM'S COLTSFOOT EXPECTORANT**
On bottom, flask or oval shape, aqua, 2¼" 3.00 5.00

☐ 1345 **SLOCUM'S EXPECTORANT COLTSFOOT**
Under bottom, aqua, 2¼" 4.00 6.00

☐ 1346 **T.A. SLOCUM CO. MFG., CHEMISTS, N.Y. & LONDON**
With anchor seal, one side reads For Consumption, other
side Lung Troubles, beveled corners, long collar, aqua,
9½" 12.00   17.00

☐ 1347 **T.A. SLOCUM MFG. CO., PSYCHINE CONSUMPTION,**
181 PEARL ST. N.Y.
Aqua, 8½" 5.00   8.00

☐ 1348 **MFG. SLOUGH, ELLIMAN'S ROYAL EMBROCATION FOR**
HORSES
Double ring top, aqua, 7½" 9.00   13.00

☐ 1349 **SMITH'S GREEN MOUNTAIN RENOVATOR**
Tapered top & ring, Green 9.00   13.00

☐ 1350 **S. SMITH, GREEN MOUNTAIN RENOVATOR**
East Georgia, Vt. in 3 lines, tapered top, olive & amber,
pontil 22.00   28.00

☐ 1351 **SMITH'S BILE BEANS**
Clear, 1¾" 3.00   4.00

☐ 1352 **SMITH GREEN MT. RENOVATORE.**
E. Ga. Vt., olive amber, stoddard glass, 6⅛" 165.00   210.00

☐ 1353 **DR. SMITH'S WORM OIL**
Aqua, 4" 3.00   5.00

☐ 1354 **T.B. SMITH KIDNEY TONIC, CYNTHIANA, KY.**
Aqua, 10½" 11.00   15.00

☐ 1355 **SOLOMONS CO**
In script, Branch Drug Stores, Bull St., Savannah, Ga., in
three lines in front, under bottom WTCo, U.S.A. in two
lines, aqua or amethyst, 7" 4.00   6.00

☐ 1356 *Same only different sizes* 4.00   6.00
☐ 1357 *Same only cobalt* 12.00   16.00

☐ 1358 **SOLOMONS & CO., SAVANNAH, GA.**
Aqua, 6" 7.00   10.00

☐ 1359 **A.A. SOLOMONS & CO., DRUGGISTS MARKET SQUAE**
(misspelled Square), aqua, 3¾" 12.00   16.00

☐ 1360 **SOZONDONT**
On each side, clear, 2½" 3.00   5.00

☐ 1361 **SPARKLENE**
Registered on back, amber, 5" 3.00   5.00

☐ 1362 **SPARKS PERFECT HEALTH**
For Kidney & Liver Diseases, three lines in sunken panel
on front, round, aqua, 4" 5.00   8.00

☐ 1363 **SPENCER MED. CO.**
On one side sunken panel, front, Nubian Tea and Trade
Mark, other side panel, Chattanooga Tenn., amber,
square, 4" 4.00   6.00

☐ 1364 **SPENCER MED CO.**
One side panel, Chatt. Tenn., Nubian Tea in sunken panel
on front, golden, 4" 4.00   6.00

☐ 1365 **P.H. SPILLANE, PHARMACIST, COHOES, N.Y.**
W. T. CO. under bottom, clear, 5" 4.00   6.00

☐ 1366 **SPITH SAN FRANCISCO PHARMACY**
11th & Railroad Avenues, flared lip, 5¼" 5.00   7.00

☐ 1367 **SPIRIT OF TURPENTINE, FRANKLIN, OHIO**
Label, Pat April 21, 1896 under bottom, clear, 8¾" 5.00   8.00

☐ 1368 **E.R. SQUIBB 1864**
Round, green, 6″ 7.00 10.00

☐ 1369 **DR. L.R. STAFFORD OLIVE TAR**
*Label, Directions, J.R. Stafford on side, Olive Tar opposite
side, rectangular, double band collar, clear, 6″* 4.00 6.00

☐ 1370 **J.R. STAFFORD'S OLIVE TAR**
On opposite side, rectangular, aqua, 6″ 4.00 6.00

☐ 1371 **STANDARD OIL CO.**
*Vertical on front, Cleveland O. on one side, Favorite on
opposite side, rectangular, amethyst, 6¼″* 3.00 5.00

☐ 1372 **STAPHYLASE DU DR. DOYEN**
Clear, 7½″ 4.00 6.00

☐ 1373 **STEIN & CO., APOTHECARIER, JERSEY CITY**
M-W U.S.A. under bottom, clear or amethyst, 5⅜″ 4.00 6.00

☐ 1374 **STEELMAN & ARCHER, PHILADELPHIA, PA.** *on front,*
Rectangular, clear, 5″ 5.00 8.00

☐ 1375 **R.E. STIERAUX PILLS**
*In front in form of circle about the size of a half dollar,
clear, 1¾″* 3.00 5.00

☐ 1376 **A. STONE & CO.**
Inside screw top, 3 Philada on screw top, aqua, 7½″ 18.00 25.00

☐ 1377 **STRAUSS, SPRINGFIELD AVE., N. HIGH ST. NEWARK,
N.J.**
Clear, 5¼″ 3.00 5.00

☐ 1378 **STRONTIUM**
Aqua, 7½″ 4.00 6.00

☐ 1379 **F.E. SUIRE & CO., CINCINNATI**
Reverse side Waynes Duiretic Elixir, amber, 8″ 9.00 12.00

☐ 1380 **SULPHO LYTHIN**
Amber, 3″ 3.00 4.00

☐ 1381 **SULTAN DRUG CO.**
St. Louis & London on other side, amber, 7¼″ 5.00 8.00

☐ 1382 **THE E.E. SUTHERLAND MEDICINE CO.**
Aqua, 5½″ 3.00 4.00

☐ 1383 **SUTHERLAND SISTERS HAIR GROWER, NEW YORK**
*All seven sisters on front in a sunken panel, Sutherland
Sisters on the side, New York on opposite side, rec-
tangular, ABM, clear, 5¼″* 7.00 10.00

☐ 1384 **SUTHERLAND SISTERS HAIR GROWER**
Aqua, 6″ 7.00 10.00

☐ 1385 **L.B. SUTTON**
Amber, 5½″ 3.00 5.00

☐ 1386 **SWAIM'S**
*Other panels, Panacea, Established 1820 Philada, aqua,
7″* 9.00 12.00

☐ 1387 **SWAIM'S**
Other panels, Panacea, Philada, pontil, olive, 8″ 50.00 75.00

☐ 1388 **SWIFTS**
Cobalt blue, 9″ 17.00 24.00

☐ 1389 **DR. SYKES**
Specific Blood Medicine, Chicago, Ills, clear, 6½″ 4.00 6.00

☐ 1390 **SYR:RHOEAD**
Cobalt blue, pontil, 8½″ 31.00 40.00

☐ 1391 **SYRUP OF THEDFORD'S BLACK DROUGHT**
Vertical on front in sunken panel, rectangular, ABM, clear 3.00 4.00

T

☐ 1392 **DR. TAFT'S ASTHMALENE N.Y.**
On the front panel, rectangular, 3½" 3.00 5.00

☐ 1393 **TANGIN**
Same on reverse side, 9" 9.00 12.00

☐ 1394 **TARRANT & CO.**
Clear, 5¼" 5.00 8.00

☐ 1395 **TAYLOR'S CELEBRATED OIL**
*On front, back plain, one side Leraysville, Other Penn.,
aqua, 6⅛"* 9.00 12.00

☐ 1396 **TAYLOR'S DRUG STORE**
Clear or amethyst, 4" 3.00 5.00

☐ 1397 **TAYLOR'S DRUG STORE**
Clear, 4¾" 5.00 8.00

☐ 1398 **TAYLOR'S ESSENCE OF JAMAICA GINGER**
Clear, 5½" 7.00 10.00

☐ 1399 **TEABERRY FOR THE TEETH & BREATH**
Clear, 3½" 7.00 10.00

☐ 1400 **TEINTURE D'FOTIDA**
Amber, 5½" 9.00 12.00

☐ 1401 **TERISSIER PREVOS A PARIS**
Graphite pontil, blue, 7½" 65.00 85.00

☐ 1402 **A TEXAS WONDER, HALL'S GREAT DISCOVERY**
*For Kidney, Bladder Troubles, E.W. Hall, St. Louis, Mo.,
clear, 3½"* 3.00 5.00

☐ 1403 **DR. THACHER'S**
*Liver and Blood Syrup, Chattanooga, Tenn. on the front
panel, rectangular, amber, 7¼" and 8¼"* 4.00 6.00

☐ 1404 **DR. THACHER'S LIVER AND BLOOD SYRUP**
*On the front, Chattanooga, Tenn. on one side of the
panels, Sample on the opposite panel, amber, rectangular, 3½"* 4.00 6.00

☐ 1405 **DR. H.S. THACHER'S DIARRHEA REMEDY,
CHATTANOOGA**
On one of the panels, amethyst, square, 3⅜" 4.00 6.00

☐ 1406 **DR. THACHER'S VEGETABLE SYRUP, CHATTANOOGA,
TENN.**
On the front, amethyst, rectangular, 7" 4.00 7.00

☐ 1407 **DR. H.S. THACHER'S WORM SYRUP**
*On the side panel, Chattanooga, Tenn. on other panel,
aqua, square, 4¼"* 4.00 7.00

☐ 1408 **DR. THACHER'S**
Olive, 3¼" 4.00 7.00

☐ 1409 **DR. THACHER'S**
Chattanooga Tenn. on side, aqua, 3¼" 3.75 6.00

☐ 1410 **DR. H.S. THACHER'S**
Amber, 2½" 4.00 6.00

☐ 1411 **HENRY THAYER**
Amber, 9½" 21.00 28.00

☐ 1412 **THOMAS ELECTRIC OIL**
Vertical on front in sunken panel, Internal & External on side, Foster Milburn Co. on opposite side, rectangular, clear, 4¼" 3.00 5.00

☐ 1413 **DR. S.N. THOMAS ELECTRIC OIL**
Vertical on front, External on side, Internal on opposite side, Northrum & Lyman, Toronto, Ont. on back, double band collar, rectangular, aqua, 5½" 3.00 5.00

☐ 1414 **THOMPSON'S HERBAL COMPOUND, NEW YORK**
Label, clear or aqua, 6¾" 3.00 5.00

☐ 1415 **DR. THOMPSON'S SARSAPARILLA, GREAT ENGLISH REMEDY**
On front indented panel, Calais, Me. U.S.A. side, St. Stephens, N.B. opposite side, rectangular, aqua, 9" 11.00 15.00

☐ 1416 **THOMPSON'S**
Philada other side, Diarrhea syrup on back, aqua 5.00 8.00

☐ 1417 **DR. THOMPSON'S**
Eye Water, New London, Conn., aqua, round, pontil, 3¾" . 21.00 29.00

☐ 1418 **THURSTON & KINGBURY TAK FLAVORING EXTRACT, BANGOR, MAINE**
Vertical on front in oriental style letters, Finest Quality Full Strength, clear, 5" 5.00 8.00

☐ 1419 **DR. TICHENOR'S**
Aqua, Antiseptic on other side, 3¾" 7.00 10.00

☐ 1420 **DR. TICHENOR'S**
On one side of panel, Antisepetic on the other side, rectangular, aqua, 5⅞" 3.00 5.00

☐ 1421 **DR. G.H. TICHENOR'S ANTISEPTIC REFRIGERANT**
One side Sherrouse Medicine Co., other side Ltd., New Orleans La., aqua, 5¾" 9.00 13.00

☐ 1422 **TIKHELL**
Light blue, 6½" 5.00 8.00

☐ 1423 **TILDEN**
Under bottom, amber, 5" 3.00 5.00

☐ 1424 **TILDEN**
Amber, 7½" 3.00 5.00

☐ 1425 **CLAES TILLY**
Aqua, 3¾" 3.00 5.00

☐ 1426 **G.De KONING TILLY**
Oil, aqua, 1" 3.00 5.00

☐ 1427 **TIPPECANOE**
Amber, clear, aqua, 9" 75.00 95.00

☐ 1428 **TIPPECANOE**
Misspelled Rochester under bottom, amber, 9" 85.00 110.00

☐ 1429 **DR. TOBIAS, NEW YORK**
In large letters vertically on front, Venetian Liniment in large letters on back, large beveled corner panels, aqua, graduated collar, 6¼" 4.00 6.00

☐ 1430 **DR. TOBIAS, NEW YORK**
Vertical on front, same as above except oval, 4¼" 4.00 6.00

☐ 1431 **DR. TOBIAS, NEW YORK**
Aqua, 8" 6.00 9.00

☐1432 **DR. TOBIAS VENETIAN HORSE LINIMENT, NEW YORK**
   On front and back, rectangular, aqua, 8¼" 7.00   10.00
☐1433 **TOKA**
   Reverse Blood Tonic, aqua, 8½" 10.00   15.00
☐1434 **T. TOMLINSON**
   Aqua, 10½" 7.00   10.00
☐1435 **TONICIO ORIENTAL PARA EL CABELLO**
   In three lines on sunken panel on front, on one side New
   York, on other, Lanman Y Kemp, both in sunken panels,
   under bottom #34, aqua, flat collar, ringed neck, 6" 7.00   10.00
☐1436 **TO-NI-TA LORENTS MED. CO. TRADE MARK**
   Around shoulder, bitters label, amber, 9¾" 9.00   13.00
☐1437 **R.E. TOOMBS JR.**
   Clear or amethyst, 5¼" 3.00   5.00
☐1438 **TOOTH POWDER**
   Label, milk glass, 2" 9.00   13.00
☐1439 **DR. TOWNSEND**
   Reverse Sarsaparilla, 1850, 9½" 75.00   95.00
☐1440 **DR. TOWNSEND**
   Sarsaparilla on other sides, pontil, amber, 9½" 95.00   120.00
☐1441 **A. TRASKS**
   Magnetic Ointment on back, aqua, 2½" and 3¼" 5.00   8.00
☐1442 **M. TREGOR SONS, BALTIMORE MD., WASH. D.C.**
   E.R.B., clear, 8" 6.00   9.00
☐1443 **J. TRINER, CHICAGO**
   On one panel, six panels, clear, 5¼" 7.00   10.00
☐1444 **TRUAX RHEUMATIC REMEMDY, BEN O. ALDRICH,**
   KEENE, N.H.
   Label, clear 4.00   6.00
☐1445 **DR. TRUES ELIXIR ESTABLISHED 1851,**
   DR. J.F. TRUE & CO. INC.
   Auburn, Me., Worm Expeller, Family Laxative on front and
   opposite side in sunken panel, rectangular, ABM, clear,
   5½" 3.75   5.50
☐1446 *Same as above except 7¾"* 5.00   8.00
☐1447 **H.A. TUCKER M.D., BROOKLYN N.Y., MO.**
   DIAPHORTIC COMPOUND on front, ring top, aqua, 5½" .   5.00   8.00
☐1448 **J. TUCKER, DRUGGIST**
   Reverse Mobile, pontil, aqua, 7½" 22.00   29.00
☐1449 **NATHAN TUCKER M.D.**
   Star & Shield Specific for Asthma, Hay Fever and All
   Catarrhal Diseases Of The Respiratory Organs all on front,
   round, clear, 4" 5.00   8.00
☐1450 **JOHN S. TUFTS APOTHECARY**
   (J. S. T. Monogram), Plymouth, N.H., oval, clear, 6¾" 4.00   6.00
☐1451 **TURKISH FOOT BATH, GALLED ARMPITS & CO.** 7.00   10.00
☐1452 **TURKISH LINIMENT**
   Aqua, 4¾" 3.00   5.00
☐1453 **ROBT. TURLINGTON** *(TURLINGTON misspelled)*
   One one side June 14, 1775, other side London, back side
   By The Kings Royal Patent Granted on back; aqua, 2¾" . .   17.00   23.00
☐1454 **ROBT. TURLINGTON**
   By The Kings Royal Patent Granted on back, aqua, 2¾" .   26.00   35.00
☐1455 *Same except no pontil* 9.00   13.00

☐ 1456 **TURNER BROTHERS**
New York, Buffalo, N.Y., San Francisco Cal. on front,
graphite pontil, tapered top, amber, 9½" 70.00 90.00
☐ 1457 **TUSSICON**
In one line vertical, Ring top, clear, 5" 7.00 10.00
☐ 1458 **DR. TUTT'S**
New York on other side, Asparagine on front, aqua, 10¼" 9.00 12.00
☐ 1459 **DR. S.A. TUTTLE'S, BOSTON, MASS.**
On vertical panels, twelve vertical panels, aqua, 6¼" 6.00 9.00
☐ 1460 **TUTTLE'S ELIXIR CO., BOSTON, MASS.**
On two vertical panels, twelve panels, amethyst, 6¼" . . . 5.00 8.00

U

☐ 1461 **UDOLPHO WOLFE'S**
On front panel, on back Aromatic Schnapps in two lines,
right side plain, left Schiedam, 2¼" square, beveled cor-
ners, 1½" neck, golden amber 15.00 20.00
☐ 1462 *Same except light amber, 9½"* 13.00 20.00
☐ 1463 *Same except olive* 18.00 25.00
☐ 1464 **UDOLPHO WOLFE'S**
Aromatic Schnapps on back, Schiedam on side, other
side plain, olive, 8" 14.00 19.00
☐ 1465 **UDOLPHO WOLFE'S**
Aromatic Schnapps Schiedam on two sides, green, 7½" . 17.00 23.00
☐ 1466 **UDOLPHO WOLFE'S**
Schiedam Aromatic Schnapps on three panels, yellow, 8" 16.00 22.00
☐ 1467 **DR. ULRICH**
Aqua, 7½" 7.00 10.00
☐ 1468 **UNCLE SAM'S NERVE & BONE LINAMENT**
Aqua 5.00 8.00
☐ 1469 **UNION DRUG CO.**
Union Makes Strength (shield) San Francisco, Cal. in slug
plate, oval, fancy, clear, flared lip, 6¼" 5.00 8.00
☐ 1470 **UNITED STATES MEDICINE CO.**
New York in three lines, flat ring top, clear or amethyst, 5½" 7.00 10.00
☐ 1471 **U.S. MARINE HOSPITAL SERVICE**
Clear, 5" 11.00 16.00
☐ 1472 **U.S.A. HOSPITAL DEPT.**
In a circle, flared top, oval, cornflower blue, 2½" 75.00 95.00

V

☐ 1473 **VAN ANTWERP'S**
Clear, 6½" 3.00 5.00
☐ 1474 **VAN SCOY CHEMICAL CO., SERIAL #879,**
MT. GILEAD, O. U.S.A.
Clear, 6" 4.00 6.00
☐ 1475 **VAN SCOY CHEMICAL CO., SERIAL NO. #8795,**
MT. GILEAD, O. U.S.A.
Clear, 6" 3.00 5.00

☐1476 **VANSTANS**
Aqua, 2″ 3.00 5.00
☐1477 **VAN VLEET & CO.**
W.T. Co. on bottom, amber, 10″ 7.00 11.00
☐1478 **DR. VAN WERTS BALSAM**
Vertical on front in sunken panel, Van Wert Chemical Co.
on side, Watertown, N.Y. opposite side, beveled corners,
aqua, 5¾″ 5.00 8.00
☐1479 **VASELINE**
Chesebrough New York, in three lines, clear or amethyst,
2½″ 3.00 5.00
☐1480 **VASELINE**
Dark amber, machine made, 3″ 3.00 5.00
☐1481 **VASEY' STARE**
Anti-cholera in 2 lines all on front, (med. bottle) Double
ring top, 8¼″ clear 9.00 12.00
☐1482 **VASOGEN**
Amber, 3¼″ 4.00 6.00
☐1483 **VICKS**
On one side, on other Drops, cobalt, screw top, machine
made, 1¼″ wide, ½″ thick,, very small, 1⅞″ 3.00 5.00
☐1484 **VIN-TONE THE FOOD TONIC**
Amber, 8¾″ 7.00 10.00
☐1485 **THE CHARLES A. VOGELER COMPANY**
Aqua, 6¼″ 3.00 5.00
☐1486 **THE CHARLES A. VOGELER CO., ST. JACOBS OIL,**
BALTIMORE, MD. U.S.A.
Round, 6¼″ 5.00 8.00

W

☐1487 **J.C. WADLEIGH, DELIGHTS SPANISH LUSTRAL**
Tapered top, aqua, 6″ 5.00 8.00
☐1488 **DR. R.B. WAITES, LOCAL ANAESTHETIC, SAFE,**
RELIABLE, NON-SECRET
Vertical around bottle, ring collar, round, clear, 3″ 5.00 8.00
☐1489 **DR. R.B. WAITE'S LOCAL ANAESTHETIC**
Safe Reliable Non-Secret, The Anticolor Mfg. Co., Spring-
ville, N.Y. U.S.A., clear, 2¾″ 5.00 8.00
☐1490 **WAIT'S WILD CHERRY TONIC**
The Great Tonic on back, amber, 8½″ 9.00 13.00
☐1491 **WAKEFIELDS BLACK BERRY BALSAM**
Vertical on front, rectangular, blue aqua, 5″ 5.00 8.00
☐1492 **WAKELEE'S CAMELLINE**
Vertical on front, rectangular, beveled corners, cobalt blue,
4¾″ 9.00 12.00
☐1493 *Same as above except amber* 4.00 6.00
☐1494 **WALKER'S TONIC, FREE SAMPLE**
Clear, 3⅜″ 14.00 19.00
☐1495 **HENRY K. WAMPOLE & CO.**
Clear or amethyst 4.00 6.00
☐1496 **HENRY K. WAMPOLE & CO.**
Clear or amethyst, 8¾″ 5.00 8.00

☐ 1497 **HENRY K. WAMPOLE & CO. INC.**
Clear or amethyst, 408 on bottom, 8½" 3.00   5.00
☐ 1498 **HENRY K. WAMPOLE & CO. INC.**
Clear or amber, 8½" 3.00   5.00
☐ 1499 **HENRY K. WAMPOLE & CO. INC., PHILDELPHIA, PA. U.S.A.**
On flat front panel, rectangular, amethyst, 8¼" 7.00   10.00
☐ 1500 *Same as above except ABM* 3.00   4.00
☐ 1501 **DR. WARDS TRADE MARK**
With line through it, The J.R. Watkins Med. Co. on side, Winona, Minn. on opposite side, amber, 8¾" 5.00   8.00
☐ 1502 **W.R. WARNER & CO.**
Clear, 2¼" 3.00   5.00
☐ 1503 **WARNER & CO.**
Round bottom, sheared top, clear, 2¾" 5.00   8.00
☐ 1504 **WM. R. WARNER & CO., PHILADELPHIA**
In a race track circle in center, W&Co on front, 6" body, 1½" neck, 2¼" square, square corners, under bottom #67 cobalt 9.00   12.00
☐ 1505 **WM. R. WARNER & CO.**
Label, amber, 5¼" 3.00   5.00
☐ 1506 **W.R. WARNER & CO.**
Clear, 2½" 4.00   7.00
☐ 1507 **W.R. WARNER & CO.**
Phila on back, aqua, three-part mold, 8" 7.00   10.00
☐ 1508 **WM. WARNER & CO., PHILADA.**
Vertical on front, round, clear, 4" 4.00   6.00
☐ 1509 **WARNER'S SAFE REMEDY**
Machine made, amber, 9" 14.00   19.00
☐ 1510 **WARREN'S MOCKING BIRD FOOD**
Round, sheared top, aqua, 7" 7.00   10.00
☐ 1511 **WASHINGTONIAN SARSAPARILLA**
Label, pontil, aqua 14.00   19.00
☐ 1512 **WATKINS CHILL TONIC**
Label, picture of J.R. Watkins and Watkins Trade Mark embossed on opposite sides, ABM, clear, 8½" 4.00   6.00
☐ 1513 **WATKINS DANDRUFF REMOVER AND SCALP TONIC**
On side, J.R. Watkins Co. Winona, Minn, USA. on opposite side, rectangular, beveled corners, ABM, clear, 6¾" 4.00   6.00
☐ 1514 **WATKINS TRIALMARK**
Aqua, 8½" 4.00   6.00
☐ 1515 **THE J.R. WATKINS CO.**
In a sunken panel, clear, amber, 7¹/₁₆" 3.00   5.00
☐ 1516 *Same except machine made* 1.50   2.20
☐ 1517 **J.R. WATKINS MED. CO.**
Clear or amethyst, 5¼" 3.00   5.00
☐ 1518 **J.R. WATKINS MEDICAL CO.**
Clear or amethyst, 5¼" 3.00   5.00
☐ 1519 **THE J.R. WATKINS MEDICAL CO.**
Winona, Minn. U.S.A. other side, round bottom, clear, machine made, 3¼" 3.00   5.00
☐ 1520 **WATSON'S PHARMACY, HOMER, N.Y.**
W.T. CO. U.S.A. under bottom, clear or amethyst, 4¾" . . . 3.00   5.00

☐ 1521 **WEB'S A NO. 1 CATHARTIC TONIC**
Reverse side, The Best Liver Kidney & Blood Purifier, amber   26.00   35.00

☐ 1522 **WEBSTER LITTLE**
W.T. CO. M U.S.A. under bottom, celar, 4¾" 4.00   6.00

☐ 1523 **WEEDON DRUG CO.**
515 Franklin St. Tampa, Fla. in two lines, regular medical
bottle, clear or amethyst 3.00   5.00

☐ 1524 **DR. T. WEST**
Clear, 5" 3.00   5.00

☐ 1525 **W.D. CO. 6A**
Under bottom, amber, 6" 3.00   5.00

☐ 1526 **J.B. WHEATLEY'S COMPOUND SYRUP, DALLASBURGH, KY.**
Graphite pontil, aqua, 6" 55.00   75.00

☐ 1527 **WHEELER'S TISSUE PHOSPHATES**
In two lines in a sunken panel, 2½" square, three panels
plain, beveled corners, under bottom monogram WBYU or
other letters, aqua, 9" 7.00   10.00

☐ 1528 **WHEELOCK LINLAY & CO., PROPRIETORS, DR. WILHOFT'S ANTIPERIODIC OR FEVER & AGUE TONIC, NEW ORLEANS**
Clear, 5" 3.00   5.00

☐ 1529 **A.J. WHITE**
On other panels, Design Pat 1894 on bottom, green, 7" . . .   7.00   10.00

☐ 1530 **WHITE & CO.**
Proprietors, New York, amber, 9½" 12.00   16.00

☐ 1531 **DR. WHITE'S**
On other side Dandelion Alternative, applied top, aqua,
9⅝" x 3¼" x 2" 7.00   10.00

☐ 1532 **WHITE'S CREAM**
Aqua, 5¼" 3.00   4.00

☐ 1533 **WHITE'S LINIMENT, WHITE & JONES PROPRIETORS, BLAINE, MAINE**
Vertical around bottle, ground top for glass stopper, clear,
5" 4.00   6.00

☐ 1534 **WHITEHURST**
Vertical on center front, flask, shape, aqua, 3½" 3.75   5.75

☐ 1535 *Same as above except ABM* 3.00   4.00

☐ 1536 **WHITE WINE AND TAR SYRUP**
Vertical on front in sunken panel, Warners on side, Cold-
water, Mich., aqua, 7" 4.00   6.00

☐ 1537 **WILLIAMS & CARLTON WHOLESALE DRUGGISTS**
Hartford, Conn., aqua 6" 4.00   6.00

☐ 1538 **WILLIAMS MAGNETIC RELIEF**
On one side A.P. Williams, other side Frenchtown, N.Y.,
aqua, 6½" 5.00   8.00

☐ 1539 **WILSON FAIRBANK & CO.**
10" 9.00   12.00

☐ 1540 **J.H. WILSON**
Reverse side Brooklyn, N.Y., front side Wilsons Carbo-
lated Cod Liver Oil, aqua, 8" 9.00   12.00

☐ 1541 **THE WILSON LABORATORIES**
Machine made, clear 3.00   5.00

☐1542 **WINCHESTER CRYSTAL CLEANER**
Label, clear, 6¾" 3.00 5.00

☐1543 **J. WINCHESTER, N.Y., DR. J.F. CHURCHILL'S SPECIFIC REMEDY FOR CONSUMPTION, HYPOPHOSPHITES OF LIME & SODA**
Tapered top, aqua, 7¼" 5.00 8.00

☐1544 **WINGFIELD**
Clear or amethyst, 5½" 3.00 5.00

☐1545 **MRS. WINSLOW'S SOOTHING SYRUP**
Curtis & Perkins Proprietors, in four vertical lines, short neck, small bottle, aqua, 5¼" 4.00 6.00

☐1546 *Same as above except pontil* 11.00 15.00

☐1547 **MRS. WINSLOW'S SOOTHING SYRUP, CURTIS & PERKINS, PROPRIETORS**
Aqua, 5" 18.00 25.00

☐1548 **MRS. WINSLOW'S SOOTHING SYRUP**
Curtis & Perkins, Prop., aqua, O.P., 5" 17.00 23.00

☐1549 **WINSTEAD'S**
Lax-Fox on other side, amber, 7¼" 3.00 5.00

☐1550 **WINTERSMITH**
Amber, 9¼" 5.00 8.00

☐1551 **WINTERSMITH**
Amber, 8½" 4.00 7.00

☐1552 **L.Q.C. WISHART'S**
Pine tree trademark on one side, Pine Tree Tar Cordial Phila. on other side, different sizes and colors 35.00 47.00

☐1553 **DR. WISTAR'S BALSAM OF WILD CHERRY, CINC. O**
Aqua, 5½" 17.00 24.00

☐1554 **DR. WISTAR'S BALSAM OF WILD CHERRY, 1848-1896**
Six panels, pontil, clear or aqua 25.00 35.00

☐1555 **DR. WISTAR'S BALSAM OF WILD CHERRY PHILADA.**
On five consecutive panels, eight panels in all, aqua, 5" .. 5.00 8.00

☐1556 **DR. WISTAR'S**
Same as above, ⅝" 5.00 8.00

☐1557 **DR. WISTAR'S BALSAM OF WILD CHERRY, SETH W. FOWLER & SONS, BOSTON**
On six consecutive panels, 3⅝", aqua 7.00 10.00

☐1558 **WOLFE'S**
Schnapps on one panel, X under bottom, amber, 8" 18.00 25.00

☐1559 **WOLFSTIRNS RHEUMATIC & GOUT REMEDY, HOBOKEN, N.J.**
Vertical on front, rectangular, aqua, 5" 4.00 6.00

☐1560 **THAT WONDROUS LINIMENT**
On front vertical, A. Schoenhelt on side, San Jose, Cal. on opposite side, rectangular, beveled corner, aqua, 4¼" ... 5.00 8.00

☐1561 **WOOD'S PINE SYRUP COMPOUND**
Aqua, 5¾" 3.00 5.00

☐1562 **N. WOOD & SON**
On one side panel, Portland, Me. other panel, clear or amethyst, 5¾" 7.00 10.00

☐1563 **WOODARD CLARK & CO. CHEMIST, PORTLAND CO.**
Clear or amber, 6¼" 3.00 5.00

☐ 1564 **THE WRIGHT RAPID RELIEF CO.**
Clear, 5¾" 7.00 10.00

☐ 1565 **WRIGHT'S CONDENSED SMOKE**
Label with directions, ABM, amber, 9½" 3.00 4.00

☐ 1566 **W T CO.**
Under bottom, amber, 3¼" 5.00 8.00

☐ 1567 **W.T.CO 4 U.S.A.**
Under bottom, aqua, 7¾" 3.00 4.00

☐ 1568 **W.T. CO. 9**
Under bottom, aqua, 2½" 1.50 2.25

☐ 1569 **W.T. CO. 3**
Under bottom, amber, 4¾" 1.50 2.25

☐ 1570 **W & T 50**
Under bottom, clear, 6½" 1.50 2.25

☐ 1571 **W.T.U.D. CO. 16**
Under bottom, amber, 8" 7.00 10.00

☐ 1572 **WYETH**
Amber, 6¼" 6 .... 3.00 4.00

☐ 1573 **WYETH 119 6**
Under bottom in sunken panel, 1¾" x 1¹³⁄₁₆", clear,
amethyst, 3⅝" 5.00 8.00

☐ 1574 **WYETH**
Under bottom, clear or amethyst, 3½" 3.00 5.00

☐ 1575 **WYETH**
Under bottom, amber, 3¼" 1.50 2.25

☐ 1576 **WYETH & BRO. PHILADA**
In a circle, saddle type flask, under bottom 226A, amber,
1½" neck, 7½" 3.00 5.00

☐ 1577 *Same except cobalt blue* 17.00 24.00

☐ 1578 **WYETH & BRO.**
Saddle type flask, amber, 7½" 5.00 8.00

☐ 1579 **JOHN WYETH**
Clear, 3" 1.50 2.25

☐ 1580 **JOHN WYETH & BRO. BEEF JUICE**
On front, round, amber, 3½" 3.00 5.00

☐ 1581 **JOHN WYETH & BRO.**
Pat May 16th 1899 under bottom, cobalt, 6½" 15.00 20.00

☐ 1582 *Same except 3½"* 9.00 12.00

☐ 1583 **JOHN WYETH & BROTHER**
Philadelphia, Liquid Extract Malt, squat body, amber, 9" . 7.00 10.00

☐ 1584 **JOHN WYETH & BROTHER, PHILA. 1870**
Round, blue, 9" 17.00 24.00

☐ 1585 **JOHN WYETH & BROTHER**
Saddle shape, clear, 7¾" 6.00 9.00

☐ 1586 **JOHN WYETH & BRO. TAKE NEXT DOSE AT**
Around base of neck, Pat. May 16, cap shows hours 1 to
12, square, cobalt blue, 5¾" 13.00 18.00

☐ 1587 *Same as above except ABM* 5.00 8.00

☐ 1588 **DR. WYNKCOP'S KATHATISMIC HONDURAS,**
SARSAPARILLA, N.Y.
10½" 17.00 24.00

X

☐ 1589 **X-LALIA, BOSTON, MASS.**
Clear or amethyst, 7¼" **5.00** **8.00**

Y

☐ 1590 **YAGER'S SARSAPARILLA**
Golden amber, 8½" **13.00** **18.00**
☐ 1591 **MADAME M. YALE CO., N.Y. & CHICAGO U.S.A.**
On each side La Freckla, clear, 6½" **7.00** **10.00**
☐ 1592 **BEN LEE YOUNG**
Clear, 3½" **3.00** **5.00**
☐ 1593 **YUCATAN CHILL-TONIC**
Label, embossed Yucatan Chill-Tonic Improved, Evansville, Ind., clear, 6¼" **7.00** **10.00**

Z

☐ 1594 **ZIPPS**
In fancy letters, Cleveland, O., clear, 5½" **4.00** **6.00**
☐ 1595 *Same except amber* **7.00** **10.00**
☐ 1596 **XOA-PHORA,** *(c. 1900)*
.... **5.00** **8.00**
☐ 1597 **ZOA-PHORA, WOMAN'S FRIEND**
In front, on side Kalamazoo, Mich. USA, ring top, blue green, 7½" **6.00** **9.00**
☐ 1598 **ZOLLICK HOFFERS, ANTI-RHEUMATIC CORDIAL**
Phil., tapered top, pontil, 6½" **17.00** **23.00**

MINERAL WATER

The bottling and selling of mineral water was a major industry in the U.S. in the 19th century. It was consumed by some for supposed health benefits, by others who simply liked the taste, and, to a large extent, by those who wanted to be chic. The mere fact that European royalty plus such American royalty as the Astors and Vanderbilts drank mineral water was enough recommendation for the public.

Mineral water was popular nearly a full century, but the peak period was from about 1860 to 1900. The majority of collectible bottles, such as those listed below, fall into that era. Shapes of mineral water bottles are not extremely creative, but they all feature bold attractive lettering and, sometimes, designs — either with embossing or a paper label. The variety, in terms of manufacturers and places of origin, is enormous — so much so that the hobbyist may want to specialize by geographical locale. Another intriguing point about mineral water bottles is that the *sizes* vary greatly, from about 7 inches in height up to Goliaths of 14 inches that make very impressive displays. Although specimens with paper labels are not highly sought after by some collectors because they're more recent in date than embossed bottles, the labels are often very colorful with entertaining messages.

The motive for drinking mineral water in the 19th century was somewhat different than that for use of spring water today. Ordinary drinking water of that time did not contain the chemical additives to which some persons now object. It was essentially pure water, but mineral water — from mineral springs — had the supposed advantage of a higher mineral content which was thought to be healthful. Mineral water might be classified as a fad but, if so, it was one of long duration. The Greeks were extolling the virtues of mineral water as early as 400 B.C. Hippocrates, the Greek "father of medicine," mentioned it favorably in his writings. During the Italian Renaissance (c.1400-1550 A.D.), when classical ideals came back into vogue, mineral water returned to popularity. For the next several centuries, Europe's well-to-do flocked to mineral springs in their leisure time, to swim in mineral water, bathe in it, relax in it, and drink it. In early times, it was possible to obtain mineral water for drinking only by visiting the springs. Visitors would gleefully fill their jugs, pack them into wagons, and hope that the supply would last until their next trip. Eventually, the popularity of mineral water reached such a point that shopkeepers made efforts to supply it. This was not easy at first since there were no distributors. The shopkeeper had to engage an agent at one of the spas to fill barrels or tubs with the water and ship it to him. Upon its arrival it was placed into bottles which the retailer had to buy empty from a glass manufacturer. This was a costly process, resulting in mineral water selling in such places as London and Paris for very high sums — more than most wine and spirits. The so-called "carriage trade" (customers who arrived in their own carriages) bought it and it became evident that the general public would, too, if prices could somehow be lowered.

Since America also was blessed with mineral springs, spas began opening up in the U.S. — as early as colonial times. In 1767, a Boston spa started bottling its water. It was followed by one in Albany in 1800 and by a Philadelphia spa in 1819.

Competition naturally developed between the spas. Claims of the curative powers of the various bottled waters were often as outlandish as those of bottled medicines. The sparkling waters were believed to cure rheumatism, diabetes, kidney disorder, gout, nervous afflictions, and all sorts of other ailments. Doctors recommended it to their patients.

European immigrants to America were so convinced of the powers of these salted waters that they imported their favorite brands from the "old country." These arrived in crudely made pottery bottles. The first American bottles for mineral water were unadorned but made of glass.

George Washington had a speculative eye on Saratoga Springs in upstate New York and in August 1783, attempted to purchase controlling interest in it. The effort failed and several years later Saratoga Springs was opened to the public. "Saratoga water" was not commercially bottled until 1820. In that year, the Rev. D.O. Griswold, who called himself "Dr. Clarke," began putting it on the market. By 1850, the remarkable total of over 7,000,000 bottles of Saratoga water were being sold annually — nearly one bottle for every adult in the country.

Sellers of mineral water were quick to capitalize on stories about its powers. During the Civil War, it was said that wounded soldiers at Gettysburg made rapid recoveries by drinking the mineral water there. Almost as soon as the report had been circulated, Gettysburg Katalysine Spring Water was available in shops.

When mineral water sales began declining after the Civil War, distributors tried desperately to inject new interest into the product. A major advertising campaign declared that mineral water contained lithium, an alkali metal supposingly with healing abilities. An investigation after passage of the Pure Food and Drug Act of 1907 found only minor traces of lithium in the bottled water. The name "Lithia Water" promptly disappeared from labels.

Bottled spring water began to replace mineral water in the late 19th century. Most collectible mineral water bottles were cork-stoppered.

MINERAL WATER BOTTLES

A

NO.	DESCRIPTION	PRICE RANGE	
☐ 1	**ABILENA NATURAL CATHARTIC WATER**		
	On the bottom, amber or brown, 11½"	7.00	9.00
☐ 2	**ABILENA NATURAL CATHARTIC WATER**		
	On the bottom, blob top, amber, 10⅛"	9.00	12.00
☐ 3	**ADERONDACK SPRING, WESTPORT, NY**		
	Tapered top with Reg., plain bottom, quart, Emerald green, (30.00)	39.00	50.00
☐ 4	**ADERONDACK SPRING, WHITEHALL, N.Y.**		
	Mineral Water tapered top and ring emerald green, pt., (45.00)	44.00	55.00
☐ 5	**AETNA MINERAL WATER**		
	Aqua, 11½"	6.00	9.00
☐ 6	**AETNA SPOUTING SPRING**		
	In horseshoe letters in center, A & E in block letters, Saratoga, N.Y., aqua, pint	70.00	100.00
☐ 7	**AKESION SPRINGS**		
	Owned By Sweet Springs Co., Saline Co., Mo., amber, 8".	15.00	22.00

☐ 8 **ALBERT CROOK**
Saratoga Co. N.Y. in a circle, through center of it Paradise
Spring, tapered top, six rings, green or aqua, pint **75.00**   **95.00**

☐ 9 **ALEX EAGLE**
In center, 1861 MINERAL WATER, tapered top, aqua, 7¼″ .   **13.00**   **20.00**

☐ 10 **ALHAMBRA NAT. MINERAL WATER CO.,**
MARTINEZ, CAL.
Applied top, aqua, 11¼″ **12.00**   **16.00**

☐ 11 **ALLEGHANY SPRING, VA.**
Amber **15.00**   **22.00**

☐ 12 **ALLEN MINERAL WATER**
Horizontal letters placed vertically on bottle, blob top,
golden amber, 11½″ **12.00**   **16.00**

☐ 13 **ALLEN MINERAL WATER**
Big ring top, 7½″ **12.00**   **16.00**

☐ 14 **AMERICAN KISSINGER WATER**
In vertical lines, tapered top and ring, aqua, pint **55.00**   **70.00**

☐ 15 **AMERICAN MINERAL WATER CO., NEW YORK**
M.S. monogram all inside slug plate, THIS BOTTLE NOT
TO BE SOLD at base, blob top, aqua, 9¼″ **14.00**   **20.00**

☐ 16 **ARTESIAN BALLSTON SPA**
Green **24.00**   **32.00**

☐ 17 **ARTESIAN SPRING CO., BALLSTON, N.Y.**
Ballston Spa. Lithia Mineral Water on back, dark aqua, 7¾″   **28.00**   **37.00**

☐ 18 **ARTESIAN WATER**
Pontil or plain, Dupont on back, dark olive, 7¾″ **55.00**   **70.00**

☐ 19 **ARTESIAN SPRING CO.**
In center an "S" super-imposed over an "A". under it
Ballston, N.Y., tapered top and ring pt. emerald green,
(40.00) **36.00**   **48.00**

☐ 20 **ASTORG SPRINGS MINERAL WATER, S.F., CAL.**
Blob top, green, 7″ **11.00**   **15.00**

B

☐ 21 **JOHN S. BAKER**
Mineral Water, this bottle never sold on panels, blob top,
eight panels, pontil, aqua **37.00**   **50.00**

☐ 22 **BARTLETT SPRING MINERAL WATER, CALIFORNIA**
In a slug plate, blob top, 11⅝″ **15.00**   **22.00**

☐ 23 **BATTERMAN H.B.**
In ½ moon circle, in center, 1861, under it in 2 lines
Brooklyn, N.Y., tapered top, ground pontil (C1860), aqua,
7½″ **35.00**   **48.00**

☐ 24 **BAUMAN, N., POTTSVILLE, PA.**
In 4 lines, slug plate, (c. 1860) ground pontil, tapered top
and ring, green, 7½″ **65.00**   **85.00**

☐ 25 **BEAR LITHIA WATER**
Aqua, 10″ **6.00**   **9.00**

☐ 26 **J. & A. BEARBOR, NEW YORK MINERAL WATER**
Eight panels, star on reverse side, graphite pontil, blue, 7¼″   **40.00**   **60.00**

☐ 27 **BEDFORD WATER**
Label in back, aqua, 14″ **5.00**   **9.00**

☐ 28 **BITTERQUELLE SAXLEHNERS JANOS**
On bottom, whittle mark or plain, ring top, avocado green,
10½" 5.00 8.00

☐ 29 **BLOUNT SPRINGS NATURAL SULPHUR**
Cobalt, 8" and 11" 60.00 80.00

☐ 30 **BLUE LICK WATER CO., KY**
Mineral Water bottle, double ring top, pontil, pt. amber .. 110.00 135.00

☐ 31 **J. BOARDMAN & CO. MINERAL WATER**
Eight panels, graphite pontil, cobalt, 7¾" 70.00 100.00

☐ 32 **BOLEY & CO., SAC. CITY, CAL.**
Reverse side Union Glass Work, Phila. slug plate, blob
top, graphite pontil, blue, 7½" 65.00 85.00

☐ 33 **J. BORN MINERAL WATER, CINCINNATI**
Reverse below B, T.B.N.T.B.S., blob top, green, 7¾" 15.00 22.00

☐ 34 **J. BORN MINERAL WATER, CINCINNATI**
In three lines, reverse side large B and T.B.N.T.B.S., blob
top, blue, 7½" 22.00 33.00

☐ 35 **BOWDEN LITHIA WATER**
Under it a house and trees, under that Lithia Spring Ca.,
blob top, aqua 12.00 17.00

☐ 36 **BROWN DR, N.Y.**
In 1 line, vertical big B in back, tapered top, pontil (c.1850),
green, 7½" 65.00 85.00

☐ 37 **BUCKHORN MINERAL WATER**
Label, aqua, 10¼" 5.00 8.00

☐ 38 **BUFFALO LICK SPRINGS**
Clear or amethyst, 10" 6.00 9.00

☐ 39 **BUFFALO LITHIA SPRING WATER**
Aqua, 10½" 11.00 15.00

☐ 40 **BUFFALO LUTHIS' WATER**
Natures Materia Medica, lady sitting with pitcher in hand,
under it, Trade Mark, round, aqua, 11½" 11.00 15.00

☐ 41 **BYTHINIA WATER**
Tapered top, amber, 10¼" 6.00 9.00

C

☐ 42 **CAL. NAT. MINERAL WATER, CASTALIAN**
Around shoulder, amber, 7¼" 8.00 11.00

☐ 43 **CALIFORNIA NATURAL SELTZER WATER**
Reverse side picture of a bear, H.&G., blob top, aqua, 7¼" .. 18.00 26.00

☐ 44 **CAMPBELL MINERAL WATER, C., BRULINGTON, VT.**
(c.1870), plain bottom, tapered top and ring, aqua, quart .. 120.00 170.00

☐ 45 **W. CANFIELD**
Agt. for S.H.G., graphite pontil, squat, blob top, green, 6¼" . 50.00 65.00

☐ 46 **CANTRELL, THOS. J.**
Bellfast, Medicated aerated water, all in 5 vertical lines,
blop top, round bottom, aqua, 9¼", (c.1900) 17.00 23.00

☐ 47 **CARLSBAD L.S.**
Sheared collar, cylindrical, ground top, clear, 4" 6.00 9.00

☐ 48 **CARLSBAD L.S.**
On bottom, short tapered top, quart, green, 10¼" 11.00 15.00

☐ 49 **CARTERS SPANISH MIXTURE**
Pontil, 8½" 45.00 60.00

☐ 50 **C.C. & B., SAN FRANCISCO**
In two lines, reverse side Superior Mineral Water, ten-sided base, blob top, graphite pontil, blue, 7" 140.00 175.00

☐ 51 **CHAMPION SPOUTING SPRING SARATOGANY**
In four lines all on front, in back in 2 lines Champion Water, green, pint 100.00 130.00

☐ 52 **CHAMPLAIN SPRING, HIGHGATE, VT.**
Mineral Water, tapered top & ring, emerald green, qt. 55.00 75.00

☐ 53 **CHASE & CO. MINERAL WATER, SAN FRANCISCO, STOCKTON, MARYSVILLE, CAL.**
In five lines, graphite pontil, blob top, green, 7¼" 65.00 85.00

☐ 54 **CITY BOTTLING WORK**
Under it a girl seated, Mt. Vernon, O., tapered top, clear, 11" . 25.00 35.00

☐ 55 **C. CLARK**
On front, Mineral Water on back, dark olive, ground pontil, 7" 38.00 50.00

☐ 56 **JOHN CLARKE, NEW YORK**
Around shoulder, two-piece mold, pontil, olive, 9¼" 55.00 75.00

☐ 57 **JOHN CLARK, N.Y. SPRING WATER**
Back New York, green, pint, 7" 35.00 47.00

☐ 58 **LYNCH CLARK, N.Y.**
Dark olive, pint 45.00 60.00

☐ 59 **CLARK & WHITE**
In U, under it New York, in center C Mineral Water, olive green, 9¼" 18.00 25.00

☐ 60 **CLARK & WHITE**
In horseshoe, in center big C, in back Mineral Water, olive green, 9½" 13.00 18.00

☐ 61 **CLARKE & CO., N.Y.**
In two lines, tapered top and ring, pontil, blue green, 7¾" 50.00 65.00

☐ 62 **CLARKE & WHITE**
Wide mouth, dark olive, 7" x 3¾" 19.00 27.00

☐ 63 **CLARKE & WHITE**
Olive, 8" 19.00 27.00

☐ 64 **CLARK & WHITE, NEW YORK**
Mineral Water Bottle qt. & pt. olive green, tapered top with ring, ... 55.00 75.00

☐ 65 **C. CLEMINSON SODA & MINERAL WATER, TROY, N.Y.**
Blob top, blue, 7¼" 17.00 25.00

☐ 66 **COLUMBIA MINERAL WATER CO., ST. LOUIS, MO.**
Aqua, 7¼" 9.00 12.00

☐ 67 **COLWOOD, B.C., HYGENIC MINERAL WATER WORKS**
Blob top, crock, white and brown, 8" 17.00 25.00

☐ 68 **CONGRESS & EMPIRE SPRING CO.**
Hotchkiss Sons & Co. New York, Saratoga, N.Y., large hollow letters, CW in center, olive, 7" 50.00 65.00

☐ 69 **CONGRESS & EMPIRE SPRING CO., SAROTOGA, N.Y.**
Reverse side Congress Water, dark olive, 7¾" 33.00   45.00

☐ 70 **CONGRESS & EMPIRE SPRING CO.**
In horseshoe shape, Big C in center, above it Hotchkiss Sons, under the big C, New York, Saratoga, N.Y., pint, under bottom two dots, green, wood mold, 7¾" 26.00   37.00

☐ 71 **CONGRESS & EMPIRE SPRING CO., NEW YORK, SARATOGA**
In a horseshoe shape, in center of it a big C in frame, under it, Saratoga, N.Y., tapered and ring top, emerald green, 7¾" 50.00   70.00

☐ 72 **CONGRESS & EMPIRE SPRING CO.**
On back Empire Water, dark green, under bottom a star, 3" diameter, 7½" 32.00   43.00

☐ 73 **CONGRESS & EMPIRE SPRING CO., NEW YORK, SARATOGA**
Olive green, 7½" 24.00   32.00

☐ 74 **CONGRESS & EMPIRE SPRING CO.**
In U, under it Saratoga, N.Y.: in center of big C, Mineral Water, blue green, 9¼" 24.00   32.00

☐ 75 **CONGRESS SPRING CO., SARATOGA, N.Y.**
Dark green, quart, tapered top and ring 32.00   43.00

☐ 76 **CONGRESS SPRING CO.**
In horseshoe shape, in center large C, under it Saratoga, N.Y., in back Congress Water, quart, dark green, 7¾" . . .   26.00   37.00

☐ 77 **CONGRESS SPRINGS CO. S S, N.Y.**
In a circle, under the bottle in center #4, old beer type, wood mold, blue green, 9½" 12.00   18.00

☐ 78 **CONGRESS SPRINGS CO.**
In horseshoe shape, in center a G, Saratoga, N.Y., emerald green, tapered top and ring, 8" 37.00   50.00

☐ 79 **CONGRESS WATER**
In two lines, tapered and ring top, green, 8" 37.00   50.00

☐ 80 **CONNOR, C.**
In ½ moon letters, in back also Union Glass Works, Phila., tapered top with ring, pontil, green, 7½" (c. 1844) 65.00   85.00

☐ 81 **CONONT'S, F.A.**
In ½ moon letters under it in 4 lines Mineral Water, No. 252, Girod St., N.O., ring top large C in back ground pontil aqua, 7" (c. 1850) 37.00   50.00

☐ 82 **P. CONWAY BOTTLER, PHILA.**
Reverse side No. 8 Hunty, 108 Filbert, Mineral Water, blob top, cobalt, 7¼" 23.00   35.00

☐ 83 **COOPERS WELL WATER**
BCOO on back base, aqua, 9¾" 16.00   23.00

☐ 84 **CORRY BELFAST**
In 2 hollow letters lines, ver. tea drop bottle, blob top, aqua, 9½" (c. 1910) 17.00   25.00

☐ 85 **COULEY'S FOUNTAIN OF HEALTH, No. 38 BALTIMORE'S BALTIMORE**
Symbol of a fountain in the center, tall whiskey bottle shape, pontil, aqua, 10" 24.00   31.00

☐ 86 **COURTLAND STREET 38 N.Y.**
T. Weddle's Celebrated Soda Mineral Water on back, graphite pontil, cobalt, 7½" 75.00   95.00

☐ 87 **COWLEY'S FOUNTAIN OF HEALTH**
Pontil, aqua, 9½" 24.00 35.00
☐ 88 **CROWN**
On shoulder, olive green, beer type bottle, 8½" 7.00 10.00
☐ 89 **CRYSTAL SPRING WATER**
In horseshoe shape, under it, C.R. Brown Saratoga Spring,
N.Y., quart, green, 9½" 90.00 125.00
☐ 90 **CRYSTAL SPRING WATER CO., N.Y.**
Around base, aqua, 9½" 6.00 9.00

D

☐ 91 **DEARBORN, J & A**
In ¼ moon letters under it New York, in back "D" tapered
blob top, pontil, blue, 7½" (c.1857)................... 75.00 95.00
☐ 92 **DEEP SPRING**
Three-part mold, C in a diamond under bottom, amber,
12¾" 16.00 23.00
☐ 93 **DOBBS FERRY MINERAL WATER CO., DOBBS FERRY,
N.Y.**
Aqua, 6½" 6.00 9.00
☐ 94 **DOBBS FERRY MINERAL WATER CO. WHITE PLAIN, N.Y.**
All inside slug plate, CONTENTS 7 OZ. REGISTERED on
front at base, amethyst and clear, 8" 6.00 9.00
☐ 95 **D.P.S. CO.**
Rochester, N.Y. U.S.A., amber, 3½" 4.00 7.00

E

☐ 96 **EAGLE SPRING DISTILLERY CO.**
On front, rectangular, amethyst, 7" 5.00 7.00
☐ 97 **EAGLE'S W.E., SUPERIOR SODA & MINERAL WATER**
All in 4 lines in black large W.E., pontil, blob top, blue,
7½" (c.1856) 80.00 100.00
☐ 98 **G. EBBERWEIN**
Savannah, Geo. in three lines on front, on back between
words Mineral Water, monogram EGB, under bottom monogram E, light blue, blob top, 7½" 26.00 37.00
☐ 99 Same except aqua 17.00 25.00
☐100 Same except amber or dark blue 40.00 55.00
☐101 Same except short neck, vertical in back Ginger Ale, 8" .. 40.00 55.00
☐102 Same except amber 25.00 34.00
☐103 **ELK SPRING WATER CO., BUFFALO, N.Y.**
On front in oval slug plate, blob top, ½ gallon, clear 17.00 25.00
☐104 **C. ELLIS & CO., PHILA.**
Short neck, graphite pontil, green, 7" 45.00 60.00
☐105 **EMPIRE SPRING CO.**
E in center, Sarotoga, N.Y., back, Empire Water, green,
tapered top and ring, 7½" 27.00 36.00
☐106 **EMPIRE WATER**
Pint, star under bottom, green 17.00 25.00
☐107 **A.C. EVANS SUP^R MINERAL WATER, WILMINGTON, N.C.**
Written vertically, graphite pontil, green, 7½" 45.00 60.00

☐ 108 **EXCELSIOR SPRINGS, MO.**
Roselle under bottom, clear or amethyst, 8" 9.00 12.00

☐ 109 **EXCELSIOR, SPRING, SARATOGA, N.Y.**
Plain bottom, tapered top & ring, emerald green, qt.
(c.1870) 47.00 60.00

☐ 110 **THE EXCELSIOR WATER**
Blue, ground pontil, 7" 47.00 60.00

☐ 111 **THE EXCELSIOR WATER**
On eight panels, blob top, graphite pontil, green, 7¼" ... 65.00 85.00

F

☐ 112 **FARREL'S MINERAL WATER, EVANSVILLE, IND.**
Graphite pontil, aqua, 7½" 47.00 60.00

☐ 113 **FRANKLIN SPRING, MINERAL WATER**
Ballston, SPA Saratoga Co. N.Y. Mineral Water bottle,
emerald green, pt. 95.00 125.00

☐ 114 **FRIEDRICHSHALL, C. OPPEL & CO.**
On the bottom, label, blob top, green, 9" 8.00 11.00

G

☐ 115 **J.N. GERDES**
S.F. Mineral Water, blob top, green, eight-sided, 7½" 32.00 43.00

☐ 116 **J.N. GERDES S.F. MINERAL WATER**
Vertical on four panels, eight panels in all, blob top, aqua
blue, 7⅛" 32.00 43.00

☐ 117 **GETTYSBURG KATALYSINE WATER**
X under bottom, green, 10" 23.00 29.00

☐ 118 **GEYSER SPRING, SARATOGA SPRING, STATE OF N.Y.**
Light blue, 7¾" 24.00 35.00

☐ 119 **GEYSER SPRING, SARATOGA SPRINGS**
In horseshoe, in center State of New York, in back vertically The Saratoga Spouting Spring, about a quart, light
blue, 7¾" 32.00 43.00

☐ 120 **GILBEY'S SPEY ROYAL**
Label, three dots and number under bottom, golden
amber, 8" 13.00 18.00

☐ 121 **GLACIER SPOUTING SPRING**
Glacier misspelled, In horseshoe shape, letters under it
Saratoga Spring, N.Y., in back a fountain, green, pint 130.00 165.00

☐ 122 **GLENDALE SPRING CO., THIS BOTTLE NOT TO BE
SOLD,**
Blob top, aqua, 7" 11.00 16.00

☐ 123 **GRANITE STATE SPRING WATER CO., AKINSON DEPOT,
N.Y., TRADEMARK**
Embossed, two Indians taking water from stream and
large granite rock, crown top, aqua, 10" 15.00 22.00

☐ 124 **GREAT BEAR SPRING**
Fulton N.Y., This Bottle Is Loaned And Never Sold on bottom, aqua, 11½" 11.00 16.00

☐ 125 **CHARLES S. GROVE & CO. SPARKLING MINERAL WATER, NO. 30 CANAL ST. BOSTON**
In a diamond shape, reverse side T.B.N.S. Deposit On Same, Refund When Returned, aqua, 7½" 18.00 24.00

☐ 126 **GUILFORD MINERAL SPRING WATER**
Blue green, 9¾" 16.00 23.00

☐ 127 **GUILFORD MINERAL SPRING WATER**
Green 16.00 23.00

☐ 128 **GUILFORD MINERAL, SPRING WATER, GUILFORD, VT.**
Tapered top with ring, yellow green, qt. 75.00 95.00

☐ 129 **GUILFORD & STAR SPRING**
Green or amber 16.00 23.00

☐ 130 **GUILFORD MINERAL SPRING WATER**
Inside of a diamond in center, also G.M.S., under it Guilford, Vt., short neck, dark green, 10" 31.00 40.00

H

☐ 131 **HANBURY SMITH**
Light olive, 8" 7.00 10.00

☐ 132 **HANBURY SMITH'S MINERAL WATERS**
Dark green, 7¾" 23.00 32.00

☐ 133 **HARRIS**
Amber, 9¼" 6.00 9.00

☐ 134 **HARRIS ALBANY MINERAL WATERS**
Graphite pontil, tapered top, aqua, 7¼" 24.00 33.00

☐ 135 **DR. HARTLEY'S MINERAL WATER, PHILA.**
In front, in back Improved Patent, pontil, flared top, light emerald green, 6¾" 50.00 65.00

☐ 136 **HATHORN**
Saratoga, N.Y., Amber, 9¼" 22.00 29.00

☐ 137 **HATHORN SPRING**
In horseshoe shape, under this, Saratoga, N.Y., dark amber, under bottle a "drop" and a letter H, round, 7½". 31.00 42.00

☐ 138 *Same except bottom plain, very dark green* 31.00 42.00

☐ 139 **HATHORN WATER, SARATOGA, N.Y.**
Paper label, amber, 9½" 5.00 8.00

☐ 140 **HEADMAN**
In a dome shape, under it Excelsior Mineral Water, reverse F.W.H. in hollow letters, graphite pontil, green, 7½" 40.00 60.00

☐ 141 **HECKINGS MINERAL WATER**
Green 15.00 22.00

☐ 142 **HIGH ROCK CONGRESS SPRING, SARATOGA, N.Y.**
Mineral Water bottle, tapered top & ring, qt., yellow olive (c.1870) 60.00 80.00

☐ 143 **HIGHROCK CONGRESS SPRING**
Rock, under it C&W, SAT, NY, green 60.00 75.00

☐ 144 *Same except amber* 40.00 60.00

☐ 145 **HOLMES & CO. MINERAL WATER**
Ground pontil, blue, 7½" 40.00 60.00

☐ 146 **HOLMES & CO.**
Ground pontil, Mineral Water in back, light blue, 7¼" 40.00 60.00

136

HATHORN

147

HONESDALE GLASSWORKS

161

JUBILEE SPRING WATER CO. BUFFALO N.Y.

176

LEMON SOUCH

179

MAGEE'S CHLORINATED LITHIA SPRING WATER CLARKSVILLE, MECKLENBURG CO. VA.

220

VICHY WATER PATTERSON & FRAZEAU N.Y.

228

THE PURITAN WATER CO NEW YORK

231

ROCKBRIDGE ALUM WATER R.A.S.Co. ROCKBRIDGE CO. VA.

232

ROUND LAKE MINERAL WATER SARATOGA CO. N.Y.

235

JOHN RYAN EXCELSIOR MINERALWATER SAVANNAH

240

SARATOGA RED SPRING

244

SARATOGA VICHY SPOUT V SARATOGA N.Y.

257

SYRACUSE SPRINGS EXCELSIOR

267

UNION SPRING SARATOGA N.Y.

279

WITTER SPRINGS WATER

291

WHITE SULPHUR WATER GREENBRIER, VA.

295

☐ 147 **HONESDALE GLASS WORKS, AP**
("PA" backwards), Mineral Water in back, aqua, 7½ " 22.00 29.00
☐ 148 **HONESDALE GLASS WORKS, PA.**
In a dome shape, reverse side Mineral Water, graphite
pontil, blob top, green 55.00 75.00
☐ 149 **J. HOPKINS, PHILA.**
Pontil, short neck, dark aqua 24.00 32.00
☐ 150 **HORAN P., 75, WEST 27th ST., N.Y.**
All in 4 lines, pontil, blob top, green, 7½ " (c.1860) 55.00 75.00
☐ 151 **HUBENER, J.**
In ¼ moon letters under it New York, in back Mineral
Water big "H", tapered top, pontil, blue, 8" (c.1850) 70.00 90.00
☐ 152 **HYGEIA WATER**
Cons. Ice Co., Memphis, Tenn. around base, aqua, 9¾ " .. 6.00 9.00
☐ 153 **HYPERION SPOUTING SPRING**
In a horseshoe shape, under it Saratoga, N.Y., in back
American Kissinger Water, tapered and ring top, aqua,
pint 130.00 160.00

I

☐ 154 **IMPROVED MINERAL WATER**
Short tapered top, graphite pontil, cobalt, 7½ " 38.00 52.00
☐ 155 **IMPROVED MINERAL WATER**
Blob top, graphite pontil, blue, 6¼ " 31.00 40.00
☐ 156 **INDIAN SPRING**
In center, Indian head under bottom, aqua, 10½ " 15.00 22.00
☐ 157 **IODINE SPRING, L, SOUTH HERO, VT.**
Qt. golden amber, tapered top, with ring 155.00 190.00

J

☐ 158 **JACKSON NAPA SODA**
On front, in back Natural Mineral Water, Jacksons
T.B.I.N.S., aqua, 7½ " 9.00 12.00
☐ 159 **JACKSON'S NAPA SODA SPRING**
On front, reverse side Natural Mineral Water, blob top,
aqua, 7½ " 8.00 12.00
☐ 160 **JOHNSTON & CO. PHILA.**
In large block letters, on back large fancy 2" J., tapered
top, sea green, 6¾ " 15.00 22.00
☐ 161 **JUBILEE SPRING WATER CO.**
101 under bottom, 5 pt on back, aqua, 11½ " 15.00 22.00

K

☐ 162 **J. KENNEDY, MINERAL WATER, PITTSBURG**
In three lines on back, script letters J.K., graphite pontil,
blob top, green, 7½ " 35.00 43.00
☐ 163 **KISSINGER WATER**
Dark olive, 6¼ " 29.00 37.00

☐ 164 **KISSINGER WATER PATTERSON & BROZEAU**
Tapered top, olive, 7" 17.00 24.00

☐ 165 **D.A. KNOWLTON**
In a dome shape, under it Saratoga, N.Y., tapered top,
olive, 9½" 42.00 55.00

☐ 166 **KNOWLTON, D.A., SARATOGA, N.Y.**
In 3 lines, tapered top & ring, em. green pt. (c.1850) 45.00 60.00

☐ 167 *Same except amber ....* 140.00 190.00

☐ 168 *Same except blue ....* 140.00 190.00

L

☐ 169 **R.T. LACY, NEW KENT CO., VA., PROP. BELMONT LITHIA**
WATER
In a circle in center two men turning a hand drill, under
that DEUS AQUAM CREAVIT BIBAMUS and AD 1877, blue
green. 10" 22.00 33.00

☐ 170 **J. LAMPPIN & CO. MINERAL WATER, MADISON, LA.**
In back Madison Bottling Establishment, graphite pontil,
blob top, blue green, 6½" 60.00 80.00

☐ 171 **LIVITI DISTILLED WATER CO., PASADENA, CAL.**
Around base in small letters, crown top, I.P.G. CO. 841
LIVITI on bottom, round, ABM, tapered neck, aqua, 7¾" . 5.00 8.00

☐ 172 **J.A. LOMAX, 14 & 16 CHARLES PLACE, CHICAGO**
Four-piece mold, amber, 9¾" 15.00 22.00

☐ 173 **LYNCH & CLARK, NEW YORK MINERAL WATER**
Tapered top & ring pontil, olive amber, pt. 100.00 130.00

☐ 174 **LYTTON SPRING**
In center a pelican, SWEET DRINKS under it, in three lines
P.M.H. Co., San Franciso, C.H.B., aqua, 6½" 15.00 22.00

M

☐ 175 **MACNISH & SON, JAMAICA**
In 2 ver. lines, semi round bottom, applied crown top,
aqua, 9½" (c.1910) 13.00 18.00

☐ 176 **MADDEN MINERAL WATER CO.**
Label, aqua, 7" 9.00 12.00

☐ 177 **MADURO, I.L. CANAL ZONE**
All in a water mellow circle, marble bottle, applied top,
aqua, 9¼" (c.1910) 15.00 22.00

☐ 178 *Same except, Jr. add to name ....* 13.00 18.00

☐ 179 **MAGEE'S**
Aqua, 10½" 12.00 17.00

☐ 180 **MAGNETIC SPRING**
Amber 29.00 40.00

☐ 181 **MAGNETIC SPRING, HENNIKER, N.H.**
Tapered top & ring, qt. Go. amber plain bottom (c.1868) .. 80.00 100.00

☐ 182 **J. MANKE & CO, SAVANNAH**
In two lines, in back Mineral Water, blob top, aqua, 7" ... 16.00 24.00

☐ 183 **MASSENA SPRING, WATER, MINERAL WATER**
Tapered top & ring, emerald green, qt. 55.00   75.00

· ☐ 184 **FREDERICK MEINCKE**
In horseshoe shape, in center of horseshoe 1882, under it
in two lines, Savannah, Geo., on back 2" monogram F.M.,
on top of it Mineral Water, under it Water, under bottom is
monogram M, cobalt, 7¾" 40.00   60.00

☐ 185 **MEINCKE & EBBERWEIN**
Savannah, Geo. in horseshoe shape, in center 1882, on
back monogram between words Mineral Water, M&E,
under bottom, monogram ME, cobalt, blob top 45.00   60.00

☐ 186 **MERCHANT, LOCKPORT, N.Y.**
Plain bottom tapered top & ring, emerald green, qt.
(c.1870) 50.00   65.00

☐ 187 **MICUELPIRIS MINERAL WATER, NO. 334 ROYAL ST.,
N.O.**
Ground pontil, aqua, 7½" 40.00   60.00

☐ 188 **MIDDLETOWN HEALING SPRING**
Amber 22.00   30.00

☐ 189 **MIDDLETOWN MINERAL SPRING, NATURE REMEDY
MIDDLETOWN, VT.**
Tapered top with rings, emerald green, qt. 75.00   95.00

☐ 190 **MIDDLETOWN SPRING, VT.**
Amber 18.00   25.00

☐ 191 **J. & D. MILLER, MARIETTA, OHIO**
Reverse side Mineral Water, blob top, aqua, 7½" 16.00   22.00

☐ 192 **MILLS SELTZER SPRING**
Under bottom M, blob top, aqua, 7½" 16.00   22.00

☐ 193 *MINERAL WATER, tapered top, graphite pontil, green,
7¼"* 32.00   43.00

☐ 194 *Same as above except cobalt* 55.00   75.00

☐ 195 *MINERAL WATER, tapered top, six panels, improved pon-
til, dark green, 7"* 28.00   39.00

☐ 196 *MINERAL WATER, label, light green, 10¾"* 6.00   9.00

☐ 197 *MINERAL WATER, ground pontil, green, 7¼"* 31.00   43.00

☐ 198 **MINERAL WATER**
In ¼ moon letters, tapered top, pontil, 7", green (c.1850) .   31.00   43.00

· ☐ 199 **MISSISQUOI. A, SPRING, PAPOOSE MINERAL WATER**
Tapered top & ring, plain base, Y. olive, qt. (c.1868) 130.00   165.00

☐ 200 **MOSES, POLAND WATER**
Figural Mineral Water bottle, tapered top, plain bottom,
aqua, qt. (c.1875) 34.00   48.00

☐ 201 *Same except some have a screw cap, ABM (they were
made for Hiram Ricker Co., c.1885). Just a few of the
originals are left or survived, then came in different sizes,
colors are clear, green and amber* 32.00   46.00

☐ 202 **MURTHA & CO.**
In front running ver. in back Mineral Water in 2 lines runn-
ing ver., tapered top, pontil, green, 7½" (c.1842) 60.00   80.00

N

☐203 **NAPA SODA, PHIL CADUC**
*Reverse Natural Mineral Water, tapered neck, blob top,
blue, 7½"* **27.00** **36.00**

☐204 **NATURAL**
*In center, a man with sleeping cap and handkerchief
around neck, under it MINERAL WATER, blob top, 7½"* .. **15.00** **22.00**

☐205 **NEW ALMADEN**
*In a horseshoe shape, under it MINERAL WATER, blob
top, aqua, 6¾"* **14.00** **20.00**

☐206 **NEW ALMADEN MINERAL WATER, W&W**
*On panels, ten panels, tapered top, blob top, graphite pon-
til, green, 7½"* **40.00** **60.00**

☐207 **N.Y. BOTTLING CO., N.Y.**
*Star on shoulder 10cts. Deposit on back, This Bottle is
Loaned, 10¢ Will Be Paid For Its Return under bottom,
aqua, 12"* **8.00** **11.00**

O

☐208 **OAK ORCHARD ACID SPRING**
*On shoulder H.W. BOSTWICK AGT., NO. 574 BROADWAY,
N.Y., on bottom From F. Hutchins Factory Glass,
Lockport, N.Y., light amber, 9"* **32.00** **45.00**

☐209 **O.K. BOTTLING CO.**
*O.K., in center 526, 528, 530, W. 38th St., N.Y., reverse side
Indian holding a flag, aqua, 10¾"* **16.00** **23.00**

☐210 **O'KEEFE BROS. HIGH GRADE MINERAL WATER,
MATTEWAN, N.Y.**
With monogram, crown top, amethyst, 7¾" **6.00** **9.00**

☐211 **OLYMPIA WATER CO.**
*In a dome shape, under it MINERAL WELLS, TEX., blob
top, several different sizes, aqua* **16.00** **23.00**

☐212 **OLYMPIA WATER CO., MINERAL WELL, TEX.**
Aqua, 9½" **11.00** **16.00**

☐213 **ORIGINAL CALIF. MINERAL WATER CO.**
Sweetwater Springs, San Diego, Calif., aqua, 11" **16.00** **23.00**

☐214 **E.O. OTTENVILLE**
*Large E.O. on front, reverse Ottenville, Nashville, Tenn.,
amber, 9¼"* **25.00** **32.00**

P

☐215 **P**
On base, round bottle, blob top, aqua, 9¾" (c.1900) **8.00** **11.00**

☐216 **PABLO & CO.**
Mineral Water Factory on back, aqua, 7½" **14.00** **19.00**

☐217 **PACIFIC CONGRESS WATER**
On bottom, crown top, four-piece mold, aqua, 8¼" **7.00** **10.00**

☐218 **PACIFIC CONGRESS WATER**
*In horseshoe shape, under it WATER, applied top, light
blue, 7"* **11.00** **16.00**

☐ 219 **PARAISO MINERAL WATER BOTTLED BY P. STEGELMAN, SALINAS, CAL.**
On front, four-piece mold, crown top, aqua, 8¼" 7.00 9.00
☐ 220 **PATTERSON & BRAZEAU, VICHY WATER, N.Y.**
Dark green, 6¾" 7.00 9.00
☐ 221 **PAVILION & UNITED STATE SPRING CO.**
Dark olive, 3" diameter, 7¾" 22.00 31.00
☐ 222 **PARIS, MIGUEL, MINERAL WATER, NO.334, ROYAL ST. N.O.**
All in 5 lines in back Big "P", blob ring top, pontil, aqua, 7½" (c.1850) 40.00 60.00
☐ 223 **P.H. CRYSTAL SPRING WATER COMPANY N.Y.**
Around base, crown top, tenpin shape, aqua, 9¼" 7.00 9.00
☐ 224 **POLAND WATER**
Aqua 27.00 36.00
☐ 225 **PRIEST NATURAL SODA**
Aqua 8.00 11.00
☐ 226 **PRIST NAPA**
A Natural Mineral Water Recarbonated At St. Helena From The Priest, Mineral Spring, Napa Co., Calif., applied crown, aqua, 7¼" 8.00 11.00
☐ 227 **PURE NATURAL WATERS CO., PITTSBURG, PA.**
Inside fancy shield, with house embossed in center, crown top, ABM, aqua, 12¼" 5.00 8.00
☐ 228 **THE PURITAN WATER CO., N.Y.**
Aqua, 12¼" 7.00 9.00

Q

☐ 229 **QUAKER SPRINGS, I.W. MEADER & CO., SARATOGA CO. N.Y.**
All in 3 lines, tapered top & ring, plain bottom, green and teal blue, qt. (c.1880) 90.00 120.00

R

☐ 230 **R.C. & T.**
In hollow letters under it New York, tapered top, pontil, green, 7½", (c.1853) 60.00 85.00
☐ 231 **ROCKBRIDGE ALUM WATER**
Aqua, 9½" 11.00 15.00
☐ 232 **ROUND LAKE MINERAL WATER**
Saratoga, N.Y., amber 7¾" 80.00 100.00
☐ 233 **RUTHERFORDS PREMIUM MINERAL WATER**
Ground pontil, dark olive, 7½" 55.00 75.00
☐ 234 **RUTHERFORD & KA**
On shoulder, three-piece mold, graduated collar, olive amber, 10½" 23.00 34.00
☐ 235 **JOHN RYAN**
Excelsior Mineralwater, Savannah in front, back Union-glass Work, Phila. This Bottle Is Never Sold, cobalt, improved pontil, 7" 40.00 60.00

S

☐236 **ST. REGIS MASSENA WATER**
Green 12.00 17.00

☐237 **SAN FRANCISCO GLASS WORKS**
Tapered neck, blob top, sea green, 6⅞″ 14.00 19.00

☐238 **SAN SOUCI SPOUTING SPRING**
In a horseshoe shape, in center a fountain and Ballston
Spa, N.Y., tapered top and ring, aqua, pint or amber, quart 110.00 140.00

☐239 **SARATOGA SPRING**
Honey amber, 9¾″ 26.00 34.00

☐240 **SARATOGA RED SPRING**
Green, 7½″ 45.00 60.00

☐241 **SARATOGA**
Under it a big A, under it Spring Co., N.Y., tapered top and
ring, olive green, round, pint and quart, 3¼″ x 9″ 75.00 95.00

☐242 **SARATOGA SELTZER SPRING**
Olive green, quart, tapered top and ring, 8″ 30.00 40.00

☐243 Same except pint, 6¼″ 50.00 75.00

☐244 **SARATOGA VICHY SPOUTING SPRING**
In a horseshoe shape, in center a hollow letter V, under it
Saratoga, N.Y., tapered top, aqua, 7½″ 35.00 47.00

☐245 **J. SCHWEPPE & CO.**
"51 Berners Street Oxford Street, Genuine Superior,
Aerated Waters,; around bottle, tear drop type, light
green, 8½″ 26.00 35.00

☐246 **SEVEN SPRINGS MINERAL WATER CO., GOLDSBORO, N.C.**
Aqua, 8″ 7.00 9.00

☐247 **SHASTA WATER CO.**
Mineral Water Co., amber, 10½″ 7.00 9.00

☐248 **E.P. SHAW & CO. LTD. WAKEFIELD**
Paper label, green, 5″ 6.00 9.00

☐249 **SHOCO LITHIA SPRING CO., LINCOLN, NEB.**
Crown top, aqua, 7¾″ 6.00 9.00

☐250 **S. SMITHS, KNICKERBOCKER MINERAL & SODA WATER, N.Y.**
Pontil, green, 7″ 45.00 60.00

☐251 **SPARKLING LONDONBERRY SPRING LETHA WATER, NASHUA, N.H.**
Label, green, 11⅝″ 4.00 6.00

☐252 **STAR SPRING**
Saratoga, N.Y., aqua 21.00 28.00

☐253 **STEINIKE & WEINLIG SCHUTZ MARKE,**
Embossed hand holding some tools, Seltzers in large letters on back, three-piece mold, blob top, emerald green,
9¾″ 13.00 20.00

☐254 **STODDARD MAGNETIC SPRING, HENNICKER, N.H.**
Amber 45.00 60.00

☐255 **SUMMIT MINERAL WATER**
J.H. in three lines, blob top, green, 7½″ 11.00 15.00

☐256 **SUNSET SPRING WATER, CATSKILL MT., HAMES FALLS, N.Y.**
On base This Bottle Loaned Please Return, aqua, 13" 13.00   20.00

☐257 **SYRACUSE SPRiNGS**
Different sizes, amber 38.00   50.00

T

☐258 **TAYLOR**
Never surrenders in 3 lines, slug plate in back Union Glass Works, Phila. in 2 lines, tapered top, pontil, blue, 7¼" (c.1850) 110.00   140.00

☐259 **THOMPSON'S,** *in center* **PREMIUM MINERAL WATERS**
Tenpin shape, reverse side Union Soda Works, San Francisco, blob top, aqua, 7½" 15.00   21.00

☐260 **TOLENAS SODA SPRINGS**
Reverse side Natural Mineral Water, tapered neck, blob top, aqua blue, 7" 15.00   21.00

☐261 **TRITON SPOUTING SPRING**
In horseshoe shape, in center block letter T, under it, Saratoga, N.Y., in back Triton Water, pint, aqua 85.00   110.00

☐262 **TWEDDLES CELEBRATED SODA OR MINERAL WATER**
Reverse side Courtland Street, in center #38, under it New York, tapered top, graphite pontil, cobalt, 7½" 45.00   60.00

U

☐263 **UNDERWOOD SPRING, FALMOUTH FORESIDE, ME.**
On front in oval slug plate, crown top, 8⅞" 6.00   9.00

☐264 **UNGARS OFNER BITTERWASSER**
Green, 9½" 6.00   9.00

☐265 *Same as above with no embossing* 3.00   5.00

☐266 **UNION GLASS WORKS, PHILA.**
Under it SUPERIOR MINERAL WATER, panel base, blob top, graphite pontil, blue, 7" 45.00   60.00

☐267 **UNION SPRING**
Saratoga, N.Y. in a circle, green, 8" 75.00   100.00

☐268 **UTE CHIEF OF MINERAL WATER**
Maniton, Colo., U.T. on base, crown top, clear or purple, 8" 5.00   8.00

V

☐269 **VARUNA MINERAL WATER WELLS**
In a horseshoe shape, Richwood, Ohio, under it I. Miller, Prop. T.B.N.S. and must be returned, clear, 6½" 15.00   22.00

☐270 **VERMONT SPRING SAXE & CO.**
Green 15.00   22.00

☐271 **VERMONT SPRING, SAXE & CO., SHELDON, VT.**
Qt., yellow green, tapered top with rings 65.00   85.00

☐272 *Same except emerald green* 65.00   85.00

□273	**VERONICA MEDICINAL SPRING WATER**		
	Amber, 10½"	**7.00**	**9.00**
□274	**VERONICA MINERAL WATER**		
	Around shoulder, square, amber, clear, 10¼"	**8.00**	**11.00**
□275	*Same as above except ABM*	**6.00**	**9.00**
□276	**VERONICA MINERAL WATER**		
	On square shoulder, square, amber, 10½"	**8.00**	**11.00**
□277	**VICHY ETAT**		
	Label, reverse side embossed Establishment Thermal De		
	Vichy, cobalt, 6¾"	**18.00**	**24.00**
□278	**VICHY WATER CULLUMS SPRING, CHOCTAW CO., ALA.**		
	Dark olive, 7¼"	**32.00**	**41.00**
□279	**VICHY WATER, PATTERSON & BRAZEAU, N.Y.**		
	Vertically on front, pint size, dark green, 6¾"	**13.00**	**20.00**

W

□280	**WASHINGTON, SPRING, SARATOGA, N.Y.**		
	In 4 lines, plain bottom, tapered top & ring, O. green, pt. .	**48.00**	**62.00**
□281	*Same except single ring lip*	**48.00**	**62.00**
□282	*Also in green*	**48.00**	**62.00**
□283	*Also in amber*	**75.00**	**100.00**
□284	**WASHINGTON SPRING**		
	Picture of Washington's head, pint, emerald green, 6¼" .	**50.00**	**75.00**
□285	*Same except quart, 8¼"*	**27.00**	**36.00**
□286	**WELLER BOTTLING WORKS, SARATOGA, N.Y.**		
	Blob top, aqua	**8.00**	**12.00**
□287	**G.W. WESTON & CO.**	**16.00**	**22.00**
□288	**G.W. WESTON & CO., MINERAL WATER,**		
	SARATOGA, N.Y.		
	Amber	**100.00**	**130.00**
□289	**WHELAN TROY**		
	Embossed tulips, Hutchinson, 7½" 11.00	**15.00**	
□290	**D.J. WHELAN**		
	Mineral Water on back, aqua, 7½"	**10.00**	**14.00**
□291	**WHITE SULPHUR WATER**		
	Blue green, 8¾"	**11.00**	**15.00**
□292	**WITTER**		
	Witter Medical Spring under bottom, amber, 9½"	**7.00**	**9.00**
□293	**WITTER SPRING WATER**		
	Witter Medical Springs Co. under bottom, amber, 9½" ...	**7.00**	**9.00**
□294	**WITTER SPRING WATER, W.M.S. CO., SAN FRANCISCO**		
	Around should and bottom, amber, 9¼"	**10.00**	**14.00**
□295	**W.S.S. WATER**		
	Machine made, 9-2-8 O.I. with diamond shape under bot-		
	tom, green, 5½"	**5.00**	**7.00**

X

☐ 297 **XXX (xxx)**
In two lines, blob top, graphite pontil, green, 7" 21.00   32.00

Y

☐ 298 **ADAM W. YOUNG, CANTON, OHIO**
In slug plate, squat shape, graduated collar, aqua, 9¼" . .   7.00   9.00

Z

☐ 299 **ZAREMBO MINERAL SPRING CO., SEATTLE, WASH.**
Blue, tapered top, 7½" 16.00   22.00

POISON

Poison bottles have come in for much greater popularity in the collector market recently. The mere deadliness of their original contents gives poison bottles a special allure. Though obviously it would have been sense-less to promote sales of such products by using decorative bottles, quite a few poison bottles *are* ornamental — not for sales reasons, but to make them readily identifiable on the home shelf. The figural skull and cross-bones or just the skull, is the most familiar. For many years, collectors were prejudice against these bottles to the point where they were almost offended by them. Today, it is quite a different story. They're recognized as the historical and decorative objects they are and no one is offended at the sight of them any longer.

The sale of poison in bottles dates back to very early times. For centuries, chemists dispensed toxic substances in vials stoppered with corks. The poisons of the ancients were chiefly derived from vegetable substances, such as the hemlock Socrates drank to carry out his death sentence. They were used (as were poisons of later times) in very small quantities as ingre-dients in medicine, usually as stimulants or relaxants.

Preparation of poisons became a very advanced art in Europe in the 16th and 17th centuries. There was a great demand for effective poisons, from persons who wished to do away with enemies, rid themselves of unwanted spouses, or collect an inheritance. Murder by poisoning was extremely widespread at this time. Underworld scientists worked to perfect special poisons, sometimes on commission for a certain client, which would be odorless, tasteless, and difficult to detect by autopsy. The favorite poisons for murder were "slow poisons" which could be given daily over a long period of time and cause death by absorption into the system. This kind of poisoning was almost impossible to detect by autopsy. Vials of "slow poi-sons" were sold for their weight in gold — or more. Its use became so extensive that some countries, notably Italy, imposed the death penalty on anyone other than a chemist selling any poisonous substance.

Because of the abuse of poisonous substances, their sale was restricted or prohibited in much of Europe in the 18th and 19th centuries. There was the further danger — in those pre-safety-cap days — of such products fall-ing into the hands of children.

It gradually became apparent, however, that society had a need for these preparations, and that to prevent sale of anything which could be poisonous was unfair to the public. Solvents used in cleaning, for example, were a necessary article in the Industrial Age. Attention was then focused on providing the containers with unmistakable identification, either by shape or a special texture or other means, to prevent accidental consump-tion. As early as 1853, the American Pharmaceutical Association recom-mended national laws to identify poison bottles. The American Medical Association suggested in 1872 that poison containers be uniformly identi-fied by a rough surface on one side and the word "poison" on the other. Despite much discussion and debate on the subject, no laws for uniform poison containers were ever enacted. Each manufacturer remained at lib-erty to identify his product and provide warning in whatever fashion he selected.

The skull and crossbones became the traditional symbol of poisonous substances, at first in the form of figural bottles then gradually being downplayed to the point where it ended up as a tiny symbol on bottle labels of the 20th century. The skull and crossbones were originally a Christian religious symbol, indicating life after death. It came to signify poison after pirates used it on their flags in the 18th century.

Most poison bottles were strong shades of blue or brown. Colorless specimens are very uncommon; there was too much danger of them being mistaken for tonic bottles (remember, literacy was not high in the 19th century — not everybody could read labels on bottles). In addition to the skull and crossbones, another shape sometimes used was the coffin, or sometimes "longbones." Containers were also likely to have quilted or ribbed surfaces to further distinguish them. This was probably intended as an aid to blind persons.

John Howell of Newton, New Jersey, designed the first safety closure in 1886. However, such closures were not considered vital until poison bottles began to be made in less identifiable shapes. This did not occur until well into the 20th century.

Most poison bottles range in size from a half an ounce to 16 ounces capacity with a few being larger.

POISON BOTTLES

A

NO.	DESCRIPTION	PRICE	RANGE
☐ 1	ACID, round, clear or green, 6⅞"	3.00	4.00
☐ 2	Amber, vertical ribs all around, rectangular, ring collar, ABM, 3¼"	5.00	8.00
☐ 3	**SP. AMMON AR.**		
	Label, clear, 9½"	10.00	15.00

B

☐ 4	**BALTIMORE, MD.**		
	Under bottom, amber, 3"	3.00	4.00
☐ 5	**BETUL-OL, W.T. CO. U.S.A.**		
	Under bottom, clear, 4¼"	3.00	5.00
☐ 6	**BOWKERS PLROX**		
	670-2 under bottom, clear or amethyst, 4¼"	3.00	5.00
☐ 7	Same as above except 8"	14.00	19.00
☐ 8	**BOWMANS**		
	In script, Drug Stores on side panels, ribs, hexagonal cobalt, 5¼"	30.00	45.00
☐ 9	**BROWNS RAT KILLER**		
	Under it C. WAKEFIELD CO., applied lip, aqua, 3"	7.00	11.00
☐ 10	**BROWN**		
	Three-sided, ABM, 4½"	3.00	5.00

C

☐	11	*CARBOLIC ACID, 3 oz. on each side, poison crosses all around it, ring top, cobalt, 5"*	**20.00**	**30.00**
☐	12	*Same as above except no carbolic acid, 8½"*	**32.00**	**45.00**
☐	13	**THE CLARKE FLUID CO., CINCINNATI** *Poison on side, 8 to 64 oz. graduated measure on other side, clear or amethyst, quart size*	**20.00**	**30.00**
☐	14	**C.L.C. CO PATENT APPLIED FOR** *Under bottom, cobalt, 2¼"*	**5.00**	**8.00**
☐	15	**C.L.C. & CO. PATENT APPLIED FOR** *Under bottom, hexagonal, emerald green, ½ ounce to 16 ounces*	**22.00**	**30.00**
☐	16	*Same as above except cobalt*	**30.00**	**45.00**
☐	17	*Cobalt blue, seven concave vertical panels on front half, ½ oz. at top on front, square collar, oval, ABM, 2⅞"*	**4.00**	**6.00**
☐	18	**COCAINE HYDROCHLOR POISON** *Label, triangular, vertical ribs, ring top, amber, 5"*	**12.00**	**17.00**
☐	19	*Crossbones & star, snap-on top, amber, 2½"*	**22.00**	**30.00**
☐	20	*CURTICE BROS. PRESERVES, ROCHESTER, N.Y.* *Four-part mold, clear or amethyst, 7"*	**14.00**	**19.00**

D

☐	21	*DAGGER on front, square, pouring lip, aqua, 5"*	**12.00**	**17.00**
☐	22	**D. D. D.** *Clear or amethyst, 3¾" and 5½"*	**5.00**	**8.00**
☐	23	**D. D. CHEMICAL CO., N.Y.** *SAMPLE on front of panel, square, amber, 5"*	**2.00**	**3.00**
☐	24	**DEAD STUCK** *Non-poisonous, won't stain in small letters, For Bugs on same line but small letters, in center a bug, on each side Trade Mark, under it Gottlieb Marshall & Co., Cersal, Germany, Philadelphia, Pa. in three lines, under bottle X, aqua, 7" tall, 3½" x 1½"*	**20.00**	**30.00**
☐	25	**DEPOSE** *On bottom, four-cornered, label reads Riodine Organic Iodine 50 capsules, 4⅛" tall, 1¾" x ½" neck*	**6.00**	**9.00**
☐	26	**FINLAY DICKS & CO DISTRIBUTORS, NEW ORLEANS, LA DICKS ANT DESTROYER** *Sheared top, clear or amethyst, 6½"*	**6.00**	**9.00**
☐	27	**DPS** *Below skull and cross on front, Poison of each side, cross on four sides, ring top, cobalt*	**8.00**	**12.00**
☐	28	**DURFREE EMBALMING FLUID CO.** *8 to 64 oz. graduated measure, clear or amethyst, ½ gallon*	**16.00**	**23.00**
☐	29	**DURFEE EMBALMING FLUID CO.** *Clear or amethyst, 8¾"*	**17.00**	**24.00**

E

☐	30	**ECORC:QUINGUINA PULV:** Pontil, clear, painted brown, 5¾"	15.00	22.00
☐	31	**ELI LILLY & CO.** Poison on each panel, amber, 2", four other different sizes	7.00	10.00
☐	32	**E.R.S.&.S.** Under bottom, vertical ribbing on all sides, space for label, double ring top, square, cobalt, 4½"	15.00	22.00
☐	33	**EVANS MEDICAL LTD., LIVERPOOL** Label, Chloroform B.A., Poison, number and U.Y.B. under bottom, ABM, amber, 6½"	5.00	8.00
☐	34	**EXTRAIT FL: DE QUINQUINA** Amber, 6½"	15.00	22.00
☐	35	**EXTRAIT FL: DE QUINQUINA** Amber, 6½"	15.00	22.00

F

☐	36	**FERRIS & CO. LTD., BRISTOL** Near base, poison in center, vertical ribbing, wide ring top, aqua, 7½"	11.00	15.00
☐	37	**FORTUNE WARD DRUG CO.** Larkspur Lotion Poison, 119 Maderson, Memphis, Tenn. on label, on each side for External Use Only, ring top, amber, 5½"	7.00	11.00
☐	38	**FREDERIA** Vertical, flask type, hobnail clover, clear, ½ pint	50.00	70.00
☐	39	**THE FROSER TABLET CO.** St. Louis-N.Y., Brooklyn, Chicago, Sulphate poison tab- lets, label, ABM, clear, 5¾"	5.00	8.00
☐	40	**F.S. & CO. P.M.** On base, POISON vertically, surrounded by dots, two sides plain, rectangular, ring top, amber, 2¾"	11.00	16.00

G

☐	41	**J.G. GODDING & CO, APOTHECARIES, BOSTON, MASS.** In three lines in center, ribs on each side, ring top, cobalt, 4⅛" hexagon	18.00	25.00
☐	42	**GRASSELLI ARSENATE OF LEAD** POISON on shoulder, different sizes	50.00	65.00

H

☐	43	**HB CO** Under bottom within an indented circle, glass top orna- ments with Poison around half of bottle, nobs and lines, very few lines or nobs in back, cobalt, 6½"	7.00	10.00
☐	44	Same as above except smaller, 3¾"	5.00	8.00
☐	45	Same as above except plain bottom	4.00	6.00

☐ 46 **HOBNAIL POISON**
*Collared neck, made using double gather, attributed to N.
England, clear, 6"* **60.00** **80.00**

I

☐ 47 **IKEY EINSTEIN, POISON**
On each side of it, rectangular, ring top, clear, 3¾" **18.00** **25.00**
☐ 48 **IODINE POISON TINCT.**
Machine made, amber, 2¼" **4.00** **6.00**
☐ 49 **IODINE TINCT**
*No embossing on bottle, but stopper in glass tube is em-
bossed: THE S. H. WESTMORE CO./PAT. AUG. 19, 1919,
square, ring collar, ABM, light amber, 3½"* **4.00** **7.00**

J

☐ 50 **JTM & CO.**
*Under bottom, 1¼" slim letters Poison, label reads Milli-
ken's Tri-Sept., Bernays No. 2 Unofficial Poison on two
panels, tablet container, amber, 3"* **6.00** **9.00**
☐ 51 **J.T.M. & CO.**
*Under bottom, three-cornered, Poison on one side, two
plain sides, ring top, amber, 10"* **100.00** **135.00**

L

☐ 52 **LIN, AMMONIAE**
Label, green, 6¾" **18.00** **25.00**
☐ 53 **LIN BELLAD**
Label, green, 7¾" **26.00** **37.00**
☐ 54 **LIN BELLAD**
Label, cobalt, 7" **55.00** **75.00**
☐ 55 **LIN BELLADON**
Label, under bottom Y.G. CO., green, 7" **18.00** **25.00**
☐ 56 **LIN SAPONIS**
Label, green, 6¾" **18.00** **25.00**
☐ 57 **LIQ. ARSENIC**
Label, green, 5¾" **18.00** **25.00**
☐ 58 **LIQ:HYD: PERCHLOR POISON**
Label, green, 9" **22.00** **33.00**
☐ 59 **LIQ. MORPH. HYDROCHL POISON**
Label, cobalt, 4½" **33.00** **46.00**
☐ 60 **LIQ. STRYCH. HYD.**
Label, green, 6" **18.00** **25.00**
☐ 61 **LRAY POISON**
Label, embossed ribs on edges, amber, 3½" **14.00** **20.00**

M

☐	62	**EDWARD R. MARSHALL CO.**		
		Dead Stuck Insecticide, green, 9"	30.00	45.00
☐	63	**McCORMICK & CO., REGISTERED TRADE MARK., BALTO,**		
		MD. PATENTED		
		Three-sided, cobalt, 4"	7.00	10.00
☐	64	*Same as above except July 8th 1882 ....*	8.00	11.00
☐	65	**McCORMICK & CO., BALTIMORE**		
		Three-sided, clear or amethyst, 3¾"	6.00	9.00
☐	66	**McCORMICK & CO., BALTO.**		
		In a circle, in center a fly or been under it, Patent Applied For, triangular, ring top, cobalt, 1½" tall	6.00	9.00
☐	67	**MELVIN & BADGER, APOTHECARIES, BOSTON, MASS**		
		Ribbing on side, ring top, cobalt, 7½"	100.00	130.00
☐	68	**R.C. MILLINGS BED BUG POISON**		
		Charleston, S.C., shoulder strap on side, clear, 6¼"	12.00	17.00

N

☐	69	**N 16 OZ.**		
		Poison label, cobalt, 6½"	25.00	38.00
☐	70	**N 8 OZ.**		
		Poison label, cobalt, 6"	12.00	17.00
☐	71	**NORWICK**		
		On base, coffin shape, Poison vertical down center of front, also horizontal in back on shoulder, covered with diamond embossing, amber, 7½"	12.00	17.00
☐	72	*Same as above except ABM, cobalt ....*	12.00	17.00
☐	73	*Same as above except BIMAL ....*	27.00	36.00
☐	74	**THE NORWICK PHARMACY CO., NORWICK, N.Y.**		
		Label, M under bottom, ABM, cobalt, 3½"	11.00	16.00
☐	75	**NOT TO BE TAKEN**		
		In center vertically, vertical wide ribbing on sides, rectangular, ring top, cobalt, 6¾"	11.00	16.00
☐	76	**NOT TO BE TAKEN**		
		In center of bottle on each side in three vertical lines, #12 under bottom, cobalt, 7¾"	45.00	65.00
☐	77	*Same as above except in two lines Poison, Not to Be Taken, cobalt ....*	45.00	65.00
☐	78	*Same as above except emeral green, clear ....*	17.00	25.00

O

☐	79	**O1. CAMPHOR FORTE**		
		Label, crystal glass, amber, 5"	25.00	35.00
☐	80	**O1. EUCALYPTI**		
		Label, crystal glass, amber, 6½"	26.00	35.00
☐	81	**O1. SINAP. AETH.**		
		Label, crystal glass, amber, 5"	26.00	35.00

☐ 82 **ORGE MONDE**
Label, cut glass, blue 27.00   35.00
☐ 83 **OWL POISON AMMONIA**
Label, three-cornered, cobalt, 5¼" 30.00   40.00
☐ 84 **THE OWL DRUG CO.**
Poison other side, three-cornered, cobalt, 8" 100.00   130.00

P

☐ 85 **POISON BOTTLE**
On one side, irregular diamond shape, ridges on three corners, amber, four sizes 5.00   8.00
☐ 86 Some have Poison on two sides 7.00   100.00
☐ 87 Same machine made 4.00   6.00
☐ 88 POISON on one panel, nobbed on three sides, 16 on bottom, round back, 3⁹⁄₁₆", also four other sizes 10.00   15.00
☐ 89 POISON on each side panel, no round back, four-cor-
nered, three sides nobbed, other plain, amber, 2¾" 6.00   9.00
☐ 90 POISON on each side panel, round back; three sides
nobbed, machine made, amber, four different sizes 6.00   8.00
☐ 91 POISON, TINCTURE IODINE under a skull and crossbones, ½ on one side of skull, Oz. on the other, oval, 5
panels on front, under bottom At. 1-7-36, amber, 2¼" tall,
¾" x 1" 9.00   13.00
☐ 92 POISON on each side, P.D. & CO. on bottom, amber, 2½" 6.00   9.00
☐ 93 POISON, plain, cobalt, different sizes 13.00   18.00
☐ 94 POISON, label, dark blue, 8" 8.00   12.00
☐ 95 POISON, ribs in front, 90 under bottom, black back, cobalt, 13½" 85.00   115.00
☐ 96 POISON, casket type, hobnail finish, amber, 3½" 35.00   48.00
☐ 97 Same except cobalt, 7½" 46.00   62.00
☐ 98 POISON, Use with Caution on other side, cobalt, 8¾" ... 18.00   25.00
☐ 99 POISON DO NOT TAKE (N in Not backward), DCP under
bottom, 4¼" 20.00   28.00
☐ 100 POISON, label, cobalt, 8" 25.00   35.00
☐ 101 POISON, machine made, ground top, clear, 13½" 17.00   26.00
☐ 102 POISON, 12 under bottom, Not To Be Taken on side,
cobalt, 7¾" 45.00   60.00
☐ 103 POISON, label, three-cornered, 74 under bottom, cobalt,
2½" 4.00   6.00
☐ 104 POISON, label, cobalt, 5" 18.00   25.00
☐ 105 POISON, flask, made rough to avoid a mistake in the dark,
sheared top, aqua, ½ pint 130.00   170.00
☐ 106 Same as above except pontil, green 45.00   60.00
☐ 107 X around POISON in one panel, X around plain side, 1 oz.
use with caution, diamond shape with letter D under bottom, ring top, cobalt, 3¼" 20.00   30.00
☐ 108 POISON, label, dark blue, 8" 12.00   18.00
☐ 109 POISON, label, cobalt or amber, 3½" 7.00   10.00

☐ 110 *POISON, label, cobalt, 3¼"* 9.00 13.00
☐ 111 *POISON, skull, Pat. Applied For on bottom rim, S under bottom, ceramic reproduction, cobalt, 3½"* 35.00 48.00
☐ 112 *POISON, clear, 6½", embossed picture of rat on front, machine made* 7.00 10.00
☐ 113 **PYROX BOWKER INSECTICIDE CO., BOSTON & BALTIMORE**
Cream crock, glass top, 7½" 10.00 15.00

R

☐ 114 **RAT POISON**
Horizontal on round bottle, clear or amethyst, 2½" 18.00 26.00
☐ 115 **RIDDES**
7073 under bottom, 6½", three-cornered with ribs or edges, ring top, aqua 18.00 26.00
☐ 116 **REESE CHEMICAL CO., CLEVELAND, OHIO**
For External Use Only, etc., rectanglar, 5½", sides ribbed, flat and ring top, cobalt, green, clear 16.00 24.00
☐ 117 **RIGO**
Embossed on base, vertical on left panel, Use with Caution, in center Not to be Taken, right usage extreme with stars all around bottle, ring top, cobalt 30.00 40.00
☐ 118 **ROMAN INC.**
Vertical in script in center, ribbed on each side, hexagonal, ring top, emerald green, 5¼ 20.00 28.00

S

☐ 119 **S & D**
173 under bottom, ABM, poison label, cobalt, 2½" 17.00 25.00
☐ 120 **SHARP & DOHME**
On one panel, Phila on other panel, label, X126-1 under bottom, three cornered, cobalt, 2" 9.00 12.00
☐ 121 **SHARP & DOHME/BALTIMORE**
On two panels, six vertical panels, bulbous shoulder ring collar, amber, ABM, 2½" 4.00 6.00
☐ 122 **SHARP & DOHME**
On one panel, Baltimore, Md., three cornered, cobalt, 3½" 6.00 9.00
☐ 123 **SHARP & DOHME**
On one panel, other Phila, label reads Ergotole D & D, three cornered, 2", cobalt, under bottom X-126-1 .... 9.00 12.00
☐ 124 *Skull & Crossbones on each of six vertical panels, also GIFT embossed on each panel, (gift means poison in German), aqua or clear, flared collar, 8⅛"* 13.00 18.00
☐ 126 *Skull, POISON on forehead, crossbones under bottom, 2" round, 3" tall, 1" neck, ring top, cobalt, Pat. Appl'd For on base in back* 120.00 160.00
☐ 127 **SPIRITS**
Silver and milk glass, 9" 25.00 35.00

☐ 128	**SOL. TRYPAFLAVIN**		
	1 + 49, crystal glass, amber, 5"	23.00	32.00
☐ 129	**SYR: HYPOPH: CO.**		
	Green,9"	21.00	29.00
☐ 130	**SYR: FER: PA: CO.**		
	Cobalt, 7"	48.00	62.00
☐ 131	**SYR: FER: IODID**		
	Cobalt, 7"	75.00	100.00

T

☐ 132	**TEINTURE de COCHENILLE, LABEL**		
	Amber, 7½"	14.00	20.00
☐ 133	**F.A. THOMPSON & CO., DETROIT**		
	On front, Poison on sides, ribbed corner, coffin type, ring top, 3½"	35.00	48.00
☐ 134	**TINCT CELLADON, POISON**		
	Round bottle, vertical ribbing, aqua and green	32.00	45.00
☐ 135	**TINCTURE IODINE**		
	In three lines under skull and crossbones, square, flat ring and ring top, amber, ABM	6.00	9.00
☐ 136	Same as above except BIMAL	9.00	13.00
☐ 137	Same as above except 2¾"	6.00	9.00
☐ 138	**TINCT. ACONITI., LABEL**		
	Green, 6"	18.00	26.00
☐ 139	**TINCT. ACONITI., LABEL**		
	Green, 7¾", Y.G. Co. under bottom	25.00	34.00
☐ 140	**TINCT. CAMPH: CO. POISON, LABEL**		
	Green, 9"	22.00	30.00
☐ 141	**TINCT. CHLOROF. et MORPH CO., LABEL**		
	Green, 7¾"	25.00	34.00
☐ 142	**TINCT. CONII, POISON, LABEL**		
	Cobalt, 6"	32.00	43.00
☐ 143	**TINCT. ERGOTAE. AMM**		
	Y.G. Co. under bottom, green, 7¾"	25.00	34.00
☐ 144	**TINCT. IODI MIT., LABEL**		
	Green, 7¾"	25.00	34.00
☐ 145	**TINCT. LOBELLIAE AETH, LABEL**		
	Green, 6"	17.00	24.00
☐ 146	**TINCT. NUX VOM, LABEL**		
	Green, 6"	17.00	24.00
☐ 147	Same except wide mouth and different label	17.00	24.00
☐ 148	**TINCT. OPII, LABEL**		
	Green, 6"	17.00	24.00
☐ 149	**TINCT. OPII.**		
	POISON on base, cobalt, 7"	35.00	46.00
☐ 150	**TINCTURE: SENEGAE, LABEL**		
	Under bottom number 6 U.G.B. ABM, amber, 6"	10.00	15.00
☐ 151	**TRILETS**		
	Vertical, other side poison, triangular, cobalt, 3½", ribbed corner, ABM	7.00	10.00
☐ 152	Same as above except BIMAL	12.00	17.00

☐ 153 **TRILOIDS**
On one panel of triangular bottle, Poison on another, the other plain, corners nobbed, number under bottom, cobalt, 3¼" 6.00   9.00

☐ 154 **TRI-SEPS, MILIKEN POISON**
One ribbed side, two for label, under bottom in sunken panel JTM & Co., ring top, 1½" X 2" tall, ¾" neck, 1¼" letters Poison on side 6.00   8.00

U

☐ 155 **U.D.O.**
On base, Poison vertically on two panels, triangular, 5¼", ring top, cross stitch around Poison, cobalt 18.00   25.00

☐ 156 Same as above except - 8½" 22.00   32.00

V

☐ 157 **VAPO-CRESOLENE CO.**
Vertical on one panel with four rows of nail heads, Patd. U.S. July 1794 Eng. July 23, 94 on next panel with nail heads, square, double band collar, aqua, ABM, 5½" 5.00   8.00

☐ 158 Same as above except clear, 4" 5.00   8.00

☐ 159 Same as above except S is reversed, dated July 23, 94 ... 8.00   12.00

☐ 160 **VICTORY CHEMICAL CO.**
Quick Death Insecticide, 148 Fairmont Ave. Phila, Pa., 8 oz., clear, 7" 11.00   16.00

W

☐ 161 **W.R.W. & CO.**
Under bottom, Poison on each side, ribbed corner, rectangular, 2½", ring top 12.00   17.00

☐ 162 **JOHN WYETH & CO., PHILA**
On front, oval, cobalt, 4", cross around base and side, flat ring collar 6.00   9.00

☐ 163 **JOHN WYETH & BROS., PHILA.**
In two lines on side, square, 2¼" 17.00   23.00

☐ 164 **WYETH POISON**
Vertical in back, round ring base and top, cobalt, 2¼" ... 10.00   15.00

☐ 165 Same as above except amber 6.00   9.00

PONTIL BOTTLES

Pontil Bottles are not a type of bottle, but a characteristic of bottles indicating the method of production and can be helpful in providing old bottles with approximate dates.

"Pontil" is a glassmaker's word, meaning a glass rod used to hold a bottle after the bottle is blown. The pontil is placed on the bottle's bottom to permit removal from the blowpipe and also, if desired, add finishing work to the lip. Pontils were introduced in the ancient world and continued throughout the era of handblown glass. It was felt that nothing else would serve the purpose as well.

When work on the bottle was completed and the pontil no longer needed, it would be broken away — leaving a scar or rough projection. This is known as a PONTIL SCAR. Its presence is evidence of the bottle being handblown. In cases where the pontil scar was large and might interfere with the bottle standing level, an attempt was usually made to grind it off. It then becomes a GRAPHITE PONTIL. The origin of this term is unclear; graphite was not used in the grinding.

The following is a rough timetable of the handblown bottle and its characteristics:

BLOWPIPE. c. 100 B.C.-c. 1965 A.D. There is strong debate on dating the blowpipe's origin. An Egyptian tomb painting is known, of about 4,000 years ago, showing workers holding pipes to their mouth, but it is not established whether they represent glass workers. No identifiable blown glass of Egyptian origin is known. Some modern bottles are still made by hand blowing.

PONTIL SCAR. c. 100 B.C.-c. 1900 A.D. Pontil scarring is uncommon on bottles made after 1900, because of improved glassblowing equipment.

SOLID BLOWN BOTTLES. c. 100 B.C.-c. 1910

REDDISH-BLACK MARK ON BOTTOM. c. 1800 A.D.-1860 A.D.

WHITE MARK ON BOTTOM. c. 1800 A.D.-1860 A.D.

PONTIL BOTTLES

A

NO.	DESCRIPTION	PRICE RANGE	
☐ 1	ADUFOUR & CO.		
	Bordeaux in center of barrel shape fruit jar, 3 ring on top 3, under bottom, sheared top (French), clear, qt.	15.00	21.00
☐ 2	ALLEN MRS. S.A.		
	On side other New York, (Med.) on front World's Hair Balsam, 355 Broone St. in 3 lines, Rect. tapered top, aqua, 6½ "	19.00	27.00
☐ 3	AMERICAN		
	On one side, other Buffalo, N.Y. on front in 2 lines, Rheumatic Balsam, (Med.) rect. Med neck, small tapered top, aqua, 6¼ "	70.00	90.00

☐ 4 **ARTES & WILSON**
Manuf., Boston all in 4 vertical lines, (soda), tapered top,
lt. green, 7" 40.00 55.00

B

☐ 5 **BACH'S**
One side other, Auburn, N.Y., front American Compound
in 2 lines, rectangular, (Med.), flat & round ring top, aqua,
7¼" 35.00 45.00

☐ 6 **BACON WM. A., LUDLOW, VT.**
In 2 lines, oval, (Med.), tapered top, aqua, 5½" 24.00 37.00

☐ 7 **BAKE'S DR.**
On front Pain Panaga, rectangular, (Med.), tapered top,
pale aqua, 5" 24.00 37.00

☐ 8 **BAKER'S E., PREMIUM BITTERS, RICHMOND, VA.**
All in 4 vertical lines, oval, wide flonged inverse top, aqua,
6½" 48.00 62.00

☐ 9 **BALSAM OF HONEY**
In 3 lines vertical round bottle (Med.), ring top, pontil,
aqua, 3½" 19.00 27.00

☐ 10 **BALSAM OF HONEY**
Vertical in 3 lines, (Med.), small round bottle, ring top,
aqua, 3½" 13.00 18.00

☐ 11 **BATTERMAN, H.B.**
In ½ moon letters in center of it 1861, under it Brooklyn,
N.Y., tapered top, (soda), aqua, 7½" 20.00 27.00

☐ 12 **BERRY'S**
On one side, other New York, on front in 3 lines,
Tricopherous for the skin and hair, (Med.), aqua, 6" 20.00 27.00

☐ 13 **BININGER'S REGULATOR**
Clock Whiskey bottle, double ring top, golden amber, pt. . 240.00 310.00

☐ 14 **BIRMINGHAM D. ANTIC BILLIOUS**
Blood Purifying, Bitters on 4 panels in back on one panel,
This Bottle No to be sold, other 7 panels plain, round, wide
flare top, med. green, 9" x 4" 90.00 130.00

☐ 15 **BLUE LICK WATER CO.**
Ky. Mineral Water bottle, double ring top, amber, 6½" ... 80.00 110.00

☐ 16 **BOGLE'S, HYPERION, FLUID**
For the hair in 4 lines, ver. (Med.) oval, wide ring top, aqua,
5½ 35.00 45.00

☐ 17 **BOLEY & CO., SAC. CITY, CALIF.**
All in 2 lines, tapered top, (soda), cobalt blue, 7¼" 40.00 55.00

☐ 18 **BONNEY, W.E.**
Around in center of barrel shape bottle, 3 near shoulder, 2
in center, 3 on base, (ink), short neck with ring top, aqua,
2¾" 110.00 130.00

☐ 19 **BRANT'S INDIAN**
Purifying extract, M.T. Wallace, Proprietor, on 3 panels, 8
panels, (Med.), tapered top, aqua, 6½" 40.00 50.00

☐ 20 **BRINKERHOFF'S C.**
In half moon letters, ver. on front, on one side Health restorative, other New York, rect. (Med.), tapered top, olive green, 7½" .... 130.00　170.00

☐ 21 **BROWN DR., N.Y.**
In 1 line, ver. Big "B" in back, (Mineral Water), green, 7½" 45.00　55.00

☐ 22 **BROWN'S F.**
Boston, Sarsaparilla & Tomato Bitters in 4 lines, ver. (bitters) tapered top & ring, oval, aqua, 9½" .... 90.00　115.00

☐ 23 **BROWN'S, F.**
Ess of Jamaica Ginger, Philad. in 4 lines, ver., (Med.), tapered top, oval, aqua, 5½" .... 10.00　15.00

☐ 24 **BURGIN & SONS**
In one line over it in ½ moon letters Philad. Glass Works, (soda) tapered blob top, med. green, 7¼" .... 52.00　68.00

☐ 25 **BURT, W.H., SAN FRANCISCO**
In 2 lines, (soda), tapered blob top, dark green, 7¼" ..... 40.00　55.00

C

☐ 26 **CANNINGTON SHAW & CO LTD.**
St. Helens on top of L.D., beaded decoration around shoulder, qt., lt. green (British fruit jar) .... 14.00　21.00

☐ 27 **CEPHALICK SNUFF TREE**
By the King Patent, all around ver., words in 4 lines, plain top, round, (Med.), aqua, 3½" .... 55.00　70.00

☐ 28 **CLARKE, JOHN**
New York in 2 lines (Mineral Water), low shoulder & neck, tapered & ring top, qt., dark olive green .... 65.00　85.00

☐ 29 **COLTON**
Back Bitters, rectangular, wide beveled corners, tapered top, long neck, aqua, 6½" x 2¼" x ¼" .... 50.00　70.00

☐ 30 **COLOGNE**
Fancy Round Toilet Water bottle, with stopper, flared top, with bold blue & white spiral stripes, clear, 6" .... 55.00　75.00

☐ 31 **COOKE'S CARMINE INK**
In 2 lines, (ink), bell shaped, ring top, aqua, 1½" .... 15.00　21.00

☐ 32 **CORBETT'S DR.**
On one side, other Shaker Bitters, front renovating, domed indented panels, one flat & plain, rect., beveled corners, double ring top, aqua, 9½" .... 50.00　70.00

D

☐ 33 **D.S. & CO. SAN FRANCISCO**
In 2 lines, tapered blob top, (soda), cobalt blue, 7" .... 40.00　55.00

☐ 34 **DALBY'S CARMINATW**
In 2 lines ver. tapered type bottle, round, light ring top, (Med.), 3¾" .... 20.00　27.00

☐ 35 **DAVID'S & BLACK**
New York on shoulder (ink), round, tapered top, dark green 6¼" .... 65.00　85.00

☐ 36 **DAVIS**
In sunken panel, on each side, Vegetable, Pain Killer, double ring top, (Med.), rect., aqua, 5" **12.00** **18.00**

☐ 37 **De HALSEY**
Back Patents, around bottle, domed, nick in center, crude double ring top, black glass, 3¼" **100.00** **130.00**

☐ 38 **DEMIJOHN**
Freeblown, tapered collared top, (wine) one gallon, olive amber **30.00** **40.00**

☐ 39 **DUNHAM J.S.**
Panels bottle (ink), ring top, aqua, 2½" **25.00** **34.00**

☐ 40 **DURKEE & CO. E.R., NEW YORK**
In 2 ver. lines, (Med.), flare top, round, aqua, 4¾" **12.00** **18.00**

E

☐ 41 **E.K.B.**
On base over it soda water, on shoulder aerated, all in 3 lines, tapered blob top, cobalt, 6¾" **85.00** **100.00**

☐ 42 **EAGLE'S W.**
Superior in 1 lines under it, soda or Mineral water, tapered top, green, 7½" **40.00** **60.00**

F

☐ 43 **FARRELL'S, H.G., ARABIAN, LEMIMENT**
In 3 ver. lines, round, (Med.) light ring top, aqua, 4½" **12.00** **18.00**

G

☐ 44 **GILLET T.W., NEW HAVEN**
Soda bottle, heavy ring top, sapphire blue, 6½" **75.00** **95.00**

☐ 45 **GOODWIN'S, GEO. C.**
Front back Indian Vegetable and Sarsaparilla, on one side Bitters, other Boston, all in vertical lines, tapered top, beveled corners, aqua, 8½" **55.00** **75.00**

☐ 46 **GRASFENBERG CO.**
On one side other New York, on front, Dysentery Syrup, all in vertical lines, (Med.), light ring top, rect., aqua, 4¾" ... **12.00** **18.00**

H

☐ 47 **HARRISON**
In back Tippecanoe, log cabin type bottle, long neck, flare top (ink), clear, 3¾" **1,500.00** **2,250.00**

☐ 48 **HARRISON'S COLUMBIAN INK**
In 3 lines, round, ring top, cobalt, 4½" **30.00** **42.00**

☐ 49 **HARRISON'S, COLUMBIAN INK**
Bottle, applied flared top, octagonal type bottle, aqua, 3¾" **35.00** **48.00**

☐ 50 **HART'S**
On one panel, other side Bitters, front Virginia Aromatic, rectangular, beveled corners are curved, tapered top, emerald green, 7¾" 900.00 1,200.00

☐ 51 **HAUEL J.**
Phila. in 2 lines in sunken panel, (Med.), oval, light ring top, aqua, 3¾" 12.00 18.00

☐ 52 **HEATHS INDELIBLE**
Black Writing Ink, pontil, 8 panels, ring top, green, 4" 22.00 28.00

☐ 53 **HEWETT'S DR. STEPHEN**
On 1 panel in center, celebrated Health, Restoring Bitters in 2 lines, other panel Rindge, N.H., wide bevel corners, ring top, olive amber, 7" 85.00 115.00

☐ 54 **HONESDALE**
In ½ moon circle under it, ½ moon glass work in center of it Pa., blob top, (soda), dark green, 7" 30.00 42.00

☐ 55 **HOVER PHILA.**
On shoulder, flare top, (ink) round, lt. green, 6¼" 25.00 35.00

☐ 56 **HOVER, PHILA.**
Vertical line, 12 panels, umbrella, ink, ring top, light green, 1⅜" 18.00 27.00

☐ 57 **HUMBOLDT VON.**
German Bitter in 2 lines on front, on one side Liver Complaint, other Dyspepsia & c. all have indent domed panels, rect., double ring top, aqua, 6½" 60.00 80.00

I

☐ 58 **I.B.**
Under it 1779 all in a seal in center of bottle, squat type bottle ring top (wine), black glass, 10½" 100.00 135.00

☐ 59 **INDIAN COLOGNE BOTTLE**
Rolled top, aqua, 5" 60.00 85.00

☐ 60 **ITALIAN, SODA WORKS, MANUFACTURING, SAN FRANCISCO**
All in 4 lines, blob top, dark green, 7" 48.00 62.00

J

☐ 61 **JACOB'S, CHOLERA &, DYSENTERY, CORDIA**
In 3 vertical lines, (Med.) ring top, aqua, 7" 55.00 70.00

☐ 62 **JAYNE'S DR. D, EXPECTORANT, PHILA.**
In 3 vertical lines, rectangular (Med.), aqua, 7" 25.00 35.00

K

☐ 63 **KERR M.G., & BERTOLETON**
Front, back compound Asiatic Balsam, right side blank other Norristown, Pa. & Med., flare top, rectangular, aqua 4½" 35.00 50.00

☐ 64 **KIDDER MRS. E.**
Dysentery, Cordial, Boston all in 4 vertical lines, (Med.) round, tapered top, aqua, 5½" 25.00 35.00

L

☐	65	LABEL, vertical ribbing, panel for label, (ink) cones, aqua, flare top, aqua blue green, 2⅛"	22.00	28.00
☐	66	LABEL bottle (ink) ring top, cones, ink, blue green, 2½"	18.00	27.00
☐	67	LABEL bottle, umbrella type, aqua, 2½"	12.00	18.00
☐	68	LABEL bottle, umbrella type bottle, double ring top (ink) 8 panels, blue green, 2½"	12.00	18.00
☐	69	LABEL INK bottle, round, pewter hinged top, no neck, clear, 3" X 1½"	20.00	27.00
☐	70	LABEL INK bottle, round, ring & tapered top with pouring lip, emerald green, 7½"	15.00	21.00
☐	71	LABEL TYPE bottle, flare top, round, (ink), 3½" neck, black glass, 1"	10.00	15.00
☐	72	LABEL TYPE bottle, tapered top with pouring lip (ink) round, olive green, 4½"	10.00	15.00
☐	73	**LANGLEY'S DR., ROOT & HERB** Bitters, 76 Union St. Boston all in 5 vertical lines, wide ring top, round, aqua, 8½"	40.00	50.00
☐	74	**LESTER E.** In ½ moon letters, near base in large letters, St. Louis, blob top, (soda), dark aqua, 7"	40.00	50.00
☐	75	**LOS ANGELES WINE CO., SPOKANE WASH.** Chestnut type bottle with handle, ¾ qt., amber	52.00	68.00
☐	76	**LYNDE & PUTNAM** Mineral Water, San Francisco, Cal. A all in 4 lines, tapered blob top, cobalt, 7¼"	40.00	55.00

M

☐	77	**MILLVILLE GLASS WORK** In ½ moon circle, (soda), dark green, 7"	40.00	55.00
☐	78	**MINERAL WATER** In ½ moon letters, tapered blob top, med. green, 7"	40.00	55.00

N

☐	79	**NEWTON'S, I.** Other side Norwich, VT. on front in 2 lines Jaundice Bitters, rect. beveled corners, thin flare top, aqua, 6½"	52.00	68.00
☐	80	**NURSING FREEBLOWN** Bottle with enameled female figure and other decorations, sheared top with pewter ring, 6"	120.00	155.00

O

☐	81	**OLD SACHEM** Bitter and, Wigwam Tonic, in center of the barrel, 10 hoap on bottom, 10 on top, round, ring top, amber, 9½"	80.00	105.00

☐ 82 **OLDRIGE'S**
On one side, on front Balm of Columbia for the restoring of Hair in 3 lines, rectangular, (Med.) flare top, aqua, 6" ..   65.00   85.00

☐ 83 **OWEN CASE**
Eagle Soda Work in 3 lines back Sac City, tapered top, cobalt, 7½" 42.00   58.00

P

☐ 84 **PATTERSONS T.**
In ½ moon circle in center of it 140 under it in 2 lines Church St. New York, 7" blob top, dark blue, (soda) 38.00   50.00

☐ 85 **PLAIN**
No emboss (label) (ink) cones, ring top, emerald green, 2¼" 32.00   45.00

☐ 86 **PURDY'S, COTTAGE BITTER**
On one side, other wide side indented, end flat, rectangular beveled corners, double ring top, amber, 9" 55.00   70.00

R

☐ 87 **R**
On one panel near base, panels bottel (ink), umbrella type   20.00   27.00

☐ 88 **RICHARDSON'S W.L.**
On front on one side Bitters other Mass., in back South, Reading short neck, flare top, wide bevel corners, aqua, 7" 68.00   88.00

S

☐ 89 **SCOTTS, JAMES P.**
In ½ moon letters in center of it, Onk, square, ring top, aqua, 2½" 30.00   40.00

☐ 90 **SNUFF BOTTLE**
Label, round, sheared top, olive green, 3¾ 25.00   35.00

☐ 91 **SNUFF**
Label Bottle, flare top, short neck, beveled corners, olive amber, 4½" 12.00   18.00

☐ 92 **STONE & CO.**
A. Philad. in 2 lines, (fruit jar) tapered neck, big ring top, wax sealer, qt., aqua 220.00   275.00

T

☐ 93 **TAYLOR**
Facing left in uniform in back Rob^T Ramsey Wine & Liquor March^T 281 8th Avenue, N.Y. all in 5 lines, flask Pt. smooth edges, plain lip, aqua 350.00   450.00

☐ 94 **TAYLOR & CO.**
Valparaiso Chile in 3 lines, blob top, dark green, 7¼" (soda) 45.00   62.00

☐ 95 **TEA KETTLE**
Type Ink bottle, pouring neck from side, pattern molded
under bottom, 24 ribs, big flare top, ring top on spout,
clear, 2¾" 130.00 170.00

☐ 96 **TURNER'S BALSAM**
On 2 panels, vertical (Med.) small 8 panels, round bottle,
ring top, aqua, 4¾" 40.00 50.00

U

☐ 97 **UNION GLASS WORKS**
In ¼ moon circle, in center of it Phila., under it in 3 lines,
This bottle never sold, blob tapered top, (soda), cobalt, 7" 38.00 52.00

W

☐ 98 **WATERS E., TROY, N.Y.**
In 2 lines, fancy shoulder (ink), wide ring top, short neck,
round, aqua, 2½" 70.00 90.00

☐ 99 *Same except, 3¼"* 70.00 90.00

☐ 99 **WOOD'S DR.**
On one side in center Sarsaparilla & Wild Cherry, other
side Bitters, Rect., tapered top, wide bevel corners,
aqua, 9" 70.00 90.00

☐ 100 **WOOD'S BLACK INK**
Portland, Isabella Glass Works, N.J. in 3 lines, bell type
bottle, ring top, aqua, 2½" 22.00 29.00

SODA

Soda bottles probably have as many collectors as any other group of bottles on the hobby market. The only thing that has prevented prices from going higher is the relatively recent dates of most specimens and the rather high preservation rate. Nevertheless, a number of Coke bottles (and others) are already well into double digit prices and the time may well be ahead when soda bottles sell for as much on the average as 19th century flasks. There is certainly tremendous enthusiasm for them which shows no sign of waning.

Figurals are not to be found among soda bottles, but there are some mild "fancies": specimens with concave or convex bodies, or with various kinds of longitudinal fluting. Each manufacturer (and there are many) faced the task of producing his bottles as cheaply as possible, yet rendering them distinctive in some way so they could be readily recognized by customers in retail stores. This was often accomplished by the use of very large, originally styled lettering and/or logos, embossed or printed (rarely supplied by means of paper labels; paper labels were not considered ideal for soda bottles as they could "sweat" off).

One of the intriguing aspects of soda bottle collecting is that the evolution of each maker's bottles can be traced down to the present time. It is possible to assemble complete collections showing every type of bottle in which any popular soft drink was retailed over the years.

Soda is one of the few bottled beverages which does not have ancient origins. It was unknown to the Greeks and Romans, to medieval Europe, and even to George Washington and Abraham Lincoln. Nothing even similar to soda was available until late in the 19th century. The mere thought of a beverage not containing alcohol would have been unappealing. No one would have believed — until they tasted soda — that it stood any chance of selling. Seltzer water was on the market a very long while before anyone got the idea of making a flavored drink from it without including spirits.

Originally, seltzer water was consumed straight without additives in the belief it could aid digestion, cure headaches, or provide other medicinal benefits. The fact that belching occurred after drinking seltzer water seemed to confirm this; the seltzer was credited with breaking up gas in the stomach and expelling it.

After it was discovered that some natural mineral springs contained carbonation, efforts were made to artifically introduce carbonation into water. These repeatedly failed, for more than a century. Finally in 1772 an English scientist, Joseph Priestley, succeeded in carbonating water. He quickly proclaimed the medicinal properties of carbonated water in an effort to popularize it; later, makers simply took Priestley's lead and the claims got more and more overblown.

Nobody would dare suggest that carbonated water should be drunk because it tasted good and was harmless. But gradually, as more and more people tried it, they started to like it, and were not terrible concerned about the validity of advertising claims. For one thing, it was a lot cheaper than liquor.

Small quantities of soda water (unflavored) were sold by Professor Benjamin Silliman of Yale in 1806. By 1810 a New York druggist was selling homemade seltzers, claiming them to be sure cures for overweight — the presumption probably being that if you filled your stomach and enough gas-forming seltzer, you might succeed in killing your appetite. But — remarkably — nobody got the idea of putting flavorings into seltzer until 1881. The telegraph, telephone, electric light and railroad train were all developed before a drop of flavoring went into seltzer water.

The first commercially sold soda was Imperial Inca Cola. Not very many Inca Indians drank soda, but makers were still stressing medicinal benefits and that accounted for the Indian tie-in (the Indians were believed to have secret knowledge on curing ailments without chemical medicines). Imperial Inca Cola did not exactly set the world on its ear, but it encouraged further experimentation. Suddenly, people started flavoring their own seltzer just to see how it tasted. Bottlers did the same. Results were mixed.

Coca-Cola, the first really successful cola drink, was developed in 1886. On a May afternoon in 1886, "Doc" Pemberton of Atlanta diligently stirred a mixture in a three-legged pot in his back yard. When it was finished he sampled it, liked it, and brought a glassful to the local druggist for his opinion. Willis Venable, proprietor of Jacob's Drug Store, added ice and tap water to the syrup, tested it, and *he* liked it, too. Venable agreed to sell the drink as a headache cure. Only one customer bought a Coca-Cola that day, but sales have now reached 95 million daily, including bottles, cans and restaurant consumption. Poor Doc wasn't able to cash in on the international success of his invention. What became one of the major companies of the world yielded him just $50 in its first year.

When carbonated water was added to Coca-Cola, beginning in 1887, sales improved. Pemberton died in 1888, with "Coke" still in its infancy. It did not become a corporation until 1892. At that time, it was still being sold exclusively at druggists' fountains mainly in the South. It occurred to Joseph A. Biedenharn in 1894 that if he bottled Coca-Cola he could sell a great deal more of it. He loaded the bottles on his horse-drawn truck and peddled the beverage throughout the countryside around Vicksburg, Mississippi. Bottled Coke was a hit.

After bottling started, the references to Coke as a headache cure disappeared from advertising. Instead, it was claimed to be refreshing, invigorating and energy-building.

Alex Samuelson is credited with designing the familiar Coke bottle in 1915. A supervisor of the Root Glass Co. of Terre Haute, Indiana, he studied drawings of cola nuts, the brown bitter-tasting seeds from which Coca-Cola syrup was made. The result was the "hobble skirt" or "Mae West" bottle adopted by the Coca-Cola company in 1916. Though it was similar to the cola nut in shape, it was named "hobble skirt" after a ladies' fashion of the time. Except for a minor trimming in the middle, the bottle has remained the same. Prior to 1916, a variety of shapes can be found.

Many people tried cashing in on Coke's rising popularity by mixing their own cola drinks. The most successful of these was Caleb D. Bradham of New Bern, North Carolina, who began producing Brad's Drink in 1890. In 1896, he changed its name to Pep-Kola and two years after to Pipi-Cola. Not until 1906 did it become known as Pepsi-Cola.

Most of the early soda bottlers made their own products and sold them locally. It was not until c. 1900 that these small local plants began going nationwide. Many early bottles can be found with pontil scars.

SODA

A

NO.		DESCRIPTION	PRICE RANGE	
☐	1	**ABILENA**		
		Label, #1 under bottom, amber, 6"	**6.00**	**9.00**
☐	2	**ALABAMA GROCERY CO.**		
		Register on shoulder, clear, 8"	**4.00**	**6.00**
☐	3	**ALA COLA**		
		Aqua, 7¾"	**5.00**	**8.00**
☐	4	**ALEXANDRIA BOTTLING, INDIANA**		
		Aqua, 7½"	**7.00**	**10.00**
☐	5	**ALPHA**		
		B.H.A. in back, light green or aqua, 6"	**4.00**	**6.00**
☐	6	**ALVAN VALLEY BOTTLE WORKS, EVERETT, WASH.**		
		Aqua, 6"	**6.00**	**9.00**
☐	7	**THE A.M. & CO., REG. WACO TEXAS & ST. LOUIS, MO.**		
		Reverse side, We Pay For Evidence Conv. Thieves For Re- *filling Our Bottles, aqua, 8½"*	**8.00**	**11.00**
☐	8	**AMERICAN SODA WORKS, TRADE MARK, PORTLAND, OR.**		
		Green, 7¾	**6.00**	**9.00**
☐	9	**AQUA DIST & BOT CO.**		
		Aqua, 8½"	**6.00**	**9.00**
☐	10	**ARIZONA BOTTLING WORKS**		
		A under bottom, This Bottle Must Be Returned on vase, *aqua, 7"*	**7.00**	**10.00**
☐	11	**ARTER & WILSON, MANUF.**		
		Boston in 4 vertical lines, tapered top, graphite pontil, *light green, 7"*	**60.00**	**80.00**
☐	12	**AUGUSTIN VITALE, PROVIDENCE, R.I., A.V.**		
		Monogram all in slug plate on front, blob top, clear, 9¼" .	**6.00**	**9.00**

B

☐	13	**B**		
		Large letter, tapered top, (Belding, Cal.), aqua or clear, *7½"*	**17.00**	**23.00**
☐	14	**B**		
		On front, gravitating stopper made by John Matthews, *N.Y. Pat. Oct. 11, 1864 on bottom, blue aqua, 7¼"*	**6.00**	**9.00**
☐	15	**B & G**		
		Large letters under it San Francisco in 2 lines, blob top, *7½" base panels, iron pontil, cobalt blue*	**70.00**	**90.00**
☐	16	**BABB & CO., SAN FRANCISCO, CAL.**		
		In three lines, graphite pontil, green, 7½"	**50.00**	**70.00**
☐	17	**DANIEL BAHR**		
		In three line, graphite pontil, green, 7½"	**6.00**	**9.00**
☐	18	**BAKER, JOHN S., SODA WORK**		
		On 2 panels, panel bottle, aqua, 7¼"	**35.00**	**50.00**
☐	19	**JOHN C. BAKER & CO.**		
		Aqua, 7½"	**6.00**	**9.00**

☐ 20	**J. ED BAKER 417 WASHINGTON ST. NEWBURGH, N.Y.**		
	On front slug plate, aqua, 7⅛"	6.00	9.00
☐ 21	**THE PROPERTY OF MRS. J. ED. BAKER, NEWBURGH, N.Y.**		
	On front in oval slug plate, blob top, clear, 9"	7.00	10.00
☐ 22	**JOHN S. BAKER SODA WATER T.B.I.N.S.**		
	Eight-sided, green, 7½"	7.00	10.00
☐ 23	**BARCLAY STREET**		
	In center 41, N.Y., applied lip, green, 7"	10.00	15.00
☐ 24	**BARTH, ELIAS**		
	In ¼ moon letters, under it in 2 lines Burlington, N.J., blob top, squat type bottle, aqua, 7"	17.00	23.00
☐ 25	**BARTLETT BOTTLING WORK**		
	Clear or amethyst, 6½"	7.00	10.00
☐ 26	**BARTOW BOTTLING WORKS**		
	Aqua, root under bottom, 7½"	5.00	8.00
☐ 27	**F. BAUMAN, SANTA MARIA, CAL.**		
	In a circle, SODA WORKS in center, aqua, 7¼"	7.00	10.00
☐ 28	**BAY CITY POP WORKS M.T. REGISTERED BAY CITY, MICH.**		
	On front in slug plate, This Bottle Not To Be Sold, on opposite side, blob top, quart, apple green, 8¾"	9.00	12.00
☐ 29	**BAY CITY SODA WATER CO., S.F.**		
	Star symbol, blue, 7"	9.00	13.00
☐ 30	**B. & C., S.F.**		
	Applied lip, cobalt, 7¼"	22.00	32.00
☐ 31	**R.M. BECKER'S HYGEIA BOTTLE WORKS TRADE MARK**		
	In a shield, B on bottom, crown top, aqua, 7½"	7.00	10.00
☐ 32	**THE BENNINGTON BOTTLE CO., NO. BENNINGTON, VT.**		
	In a sunken panel, under bottom E.S. & H., ten-sided base, clear or amber, 7¾"	9.00	12.00
☐ 33	**BELFAST COCHRAN & CO.**		
	On front and back of tear drop bottle, 7—16" size letters, aqua, 9¼"	11.00	16.00
☐ 34	**BELFAST DUBLIN**		
	Cantrell, Cochrane, See that cork is branded around bottles on bottom, pop top, aqua, round bottom, 9½"	6.00	9.00
☐ 35	**BELFAST**		
	Round bottom, aqua, 9¼"	5.00	8.00
☐ 36	**BELFAST**		
	Plain flat bottom, aqua, 9"	4.00	7.00
☐ 37	**BELFAST ROSS**		
	Round bottom, aqua, 9¼"	5.00	8.00
☐ 38	**BELFAST ROSS**		
	Plain, aqua and clear, 9½"	5.00	8.00
☐ 39	**C. BERRY & CO., 84 LEVETT ST., BOSTON, REGISTERED**		
	On shoulder in oval slug plate, crown top, emerald green, 9⅜"	6.00	9.00
☐ 40	**C. BERRY & CO., 84 LEVERETT ST., BOSTON**		
	In oval slug plate, crown top, clear, 9½"	3.00	5.00
☐ 41	*Same as above except amber, 9¼"*	3.00	5.00
☐ 42	*Same as above except blob top, clear, 9"*	6.00	9.00
☐ 43	**SAMUEL BESKIN, FISHKILL LANDING, N.Y.**		
	On front in oval slug plate, blob top, aqua, 9⅜"	7.00	10.00
☐ 44	*BEVERAGE, plain, aqua, opalescent, pop type, 6¼"*	5.00	8.00

☐	45	*BEVERAGE, plain, Belfast type, aqua, 9"*	**4.00**	**6.00**
☐	46	*BEVERAGE, plain, clear, aqua*	**4.00**	**6.00**
☐	47	**WEISS BEER**		
		Under bottom Carl Hutten, N.Y., blob top, aqua, 7¼"	**10.00**	**15.00**
☐	48	**BIG 4 MF'G. CO.**		
		1120 and three dots under bottom, aqua, 7¾"	**7.00**	**10.00**
☐	49	**BIG HOLLOW LETTER "B"**		
		Applied crown top, light green, 8½"	**7.00**	**10.00**
☐	50	**E.L. BILLINGS, SAC. CITY, CAL.**		
		Reverse Geyser Soda, blob top, blue, 7"	**10.00**	**15.00**
☐	51	**BLACKHAWK GINGER ALE**		
		Dark green, 6½"	**6.00**	**9.00**
☐	52	**J.A. BLAFFER & CO., NEW ORLEANS**		
		Squat type, blob top, amber, 6½"	**17.00**	**24.00**
☐	53	**T. BLAUTH, 407 K. ST., SACRAMENTO, CALIF., BOTTLING WORKS**		
		Aqua, 6¾"	**7.00**	**10.0 0**
☐	54	**BLUDWINE BOTTLING CO.**		
		Aqua, machine made, 7½"	**7.00**	**10.00**
☐	55	**BLUDWINE**		
		Clear or amethyst, 8"	**5.00**	**8.00**
☐	56	**BLUFF CITY BOTTLING**		
		In horseshoe shape, in center of horseshoe Co. Memphis, Tenn., on bottom, on one panel, B.G. Co. in very small letters and next to it 199, aqua	**7.00**	**10.00**
☐	57	**BOARDMAN**		
		Blue, ground pontil, 7½"	**30.00**	**40.00**
☐	58	**GEO. BOHLEN**		
		Brooklyn, in a round slug plate in center 358 Hart St., blob top, aqua, 7¼"	**7.00**	**10.00**
☐	59	**BOLEN & BYRNE**		
		In a dome shape under it EAST 54th ST. N.Y., reverse T.B.N.T.B.S., aqua, 7¾"	**10.00**	**15.00**
☐	60	**BOLEN & BYRNE**		
		Opposite side N.Y., aqua, 8¼"	**10.00**	**15.00**
☐	61	**BOLEN & BYRNE, NEW YORK**		
		Round bottom, aqua, 9"	**7.00**	**10.00**
☐	62	**BOLEY & CO., SAC. CITY, CAL., UNION GLASS WORKS, PHILA.**		
		Cobalt, 7½"	**50.00**	**65.00**
☐	63	**BOLEY & CO., SAC. CITY, CAL.**		
		In slug plate, reverse Union Glass Works, Phila., graphite pontil, blob top, cobalt, 7¼"	**50.00**	**65.00**
☐	64	**BOLEY & CO.**		
		Sac City, Calif. in 2 lines, blob top, graphite pontil, cobalt, 7¼"	**50.00**	**65.00**
☐	65	**THE BONHEUR CO. INC., SYRACUSE, N.Y.**		
		In script, clear, 14 fl. ounce on bottom, under bottom diamond shape figure, machine made, 7½"	**7.00**	**10.00**
☐	66	**BONODE 5**		
		Clear or amber, 6¾"	**6.00**	**9.00**
☐	67	**BORELLO BROS. CO., FRESNO (B.B. CO.)**		
		On bottom, crown top, light aqua blue, 7¾"	**5.00**	**8.00**

☐ 68	**R. BOVEE, TROY, N.Y.**		
	Clear, 7½"	7.00	10.00
☐ 69	*Bowling type bottle, applied crown top, light green and*		
	dark green, 9"	24.00	33.00
☐ 70	*Same except blob top, aqua*	17.00	24.00
☐ 71	**W.H. BRACE, AVON, N.Y.**		
	On front in slug plate, blob top, aqua, 9¼"	6.00	9.00
☐ 72	**C.W. BRACKETT & CO. 61 & 63 ANDREW ST., LYNN, MASS.**		
	On front in oval slug plate, clear, 9⅛"	7.00	10.00
☐ 73	**H. BRADER & CO.**		
	Penalty For Selling This Bottle, SLLR Soda Work, 738 Broadway, S.F. on eight-panel, blob top, aqua, 7¼"	12.00	17.00
☐ 74	**BREIG & SCHAFFER, S.F.**		
	Picture of a fish under it, aqua, 6½"	10.00	15.00
☐ 75	**BREMEKAMPF & REGAL, EUREKA, NEV.**		
	Clear or aqua, 7¼"	10.00	15.00
☐ 76	**BREMENKAMPF & REGLI**		
	In ½ moon letter under it Eureka, Nev., 7"	55.00	75.00
☐ 77	**BRENHAM BOTTLING WORK**		
	Aqua, 8¼"	7.00	10.00
☐ 78	**W.E. BROCKWAY**		
	In hollow letters, NEW YORK, graphite pontil, squat type, blob top, blue green, 6¾"	55.00	75.00
☐ 79	**BROWN BROS CHEMISTS, GLASGOW**		
	Round bottom, blob top, aqua, 9½"	7.00	10.00
☐ 80	**H.L. & J.W. BROWN**		
	In hollow letters, HARTFORD, CT., squat type, tapered top, olive, 7"	16.00	23.00
☐ 81	**I. BROWNLEE**		
	In dome shaped lines, under it NEW BEDFORD, in back T.B.N.S., blob top, blue	10.00	15.00
☐ 82	**J. BRUNETT**		
	Big hollow letter A, big B, aqua, 7"	11.00	16.00
☐ 83	**THE BRUNNER BOTTLING CO. 669 to 673 GRAND ST., BROOKLYN, N.Y., 1889, AUG.**		
	Blob top, 7½"	10.00	15.00
☐ 84	**FILLIPPO BRUNO & CO., 298-300 NORTH ST. & 50 FLEET ST., BOSTON, MASS.**		
	On front in oval slug plate on shoulder, clear, 8⅞"	6.00	9.00
☐ 85	**R. W. BUDD**		
	Aqua, 7¼"	6.00	9.00
☐ 86	**BURKE**		
	E & J under bottom, amber, 7½"	6.00	9.00
☐ 87	**HENRY BURKHARDT**		
	H.B. under bottom, aqua, 6¾"	6.00	9.00
☐ 88	**W.H. BURT, SAN FRANCISCO**		
	Blob top, graphite pontil, aqua, 6½"	40.00	50.00
☐ 89	**BURT, W.H.**		
	San Francisco, in 2 lines, blob top, graphite pontil, dark green, 7¼"	70.00	90.00
☐ 90	**W.H. BURT, SAN FRANCISCO**		
	aqua, 7½"	7.00	10.00

☐ 91 **J.G. BYARS**
In center, 1882 No. Hoosick, N.Y., reverse T.B.N.T.S.,
aqua, 7" 11.00 16.00

C

☐ 92 **C.A.**
Aqua, 10" 7.00 10.00
☐ 93 **CALHOUN FALLS**
In center, BOTTLING WORKS, CALHOUN FALLS, S.C.,
clear or amber, 7½" 8.00 12.00
☐ 94 **CALIFORNIA BOTTLING WORK, T. BLAUTH, 407 K ST.,
SACRAMENTO**
Clear, 7" 6.00 9.00
☐ 95 **CALIFORNIA SODA WORKS**
With an arrow under it, H. FICKEN, S.F., in back an
embossed eagle, blob top, green, 7" 17.00 24.00
☐ 96 **CALVERT BOTTLE WORKS**
Calvert, Texas, aqua, soda water, 7¼" 5.00 8.00
☐ 97 **D. CAMELIO CO., 10 LEWIS ST., BOSTON, MASS.**
On shoulder in oval slug plate, clear, 2⅞" 7.00 10.00
☐ 98 **CAMPBELL & LYON**
Aqua, 9" 6.00 9.00
☐ 99 **CANADA DRY**
14 I Ginger Ale Incorporated under bottom, carnival glass,
crown top, machine made, 10½" 13.00 18.00
☐ 100 **P. CANTERBURY, GALVESTON, TEXAS**
Blob top, aqua, 6¼" 8.00 12.00
☐ 101 **M. J. CANTRELL, YONKERS N.Y., M. J. C.**
Monogram, amethyst or clear, 6½" or 11½" 7.00 10.00
☐ 102 **CANTRELL & COCHRANE'S**
Aerated Water, Dublin & Belfast, aqua, round bottom,
8¾" 6.00 9.00
☐ 103 **CANTRELL & COCHRANE'S**
Aerated Waters, Dublin & Belfast runs up and down,
round bottom, aqua, 8¾" 7.00 10.00
☐ 104 **CANTRELL & COCHRANE**
Belfast & Dublin Medicated Aerated Water around bottle,
round bottom, aqua, 9¼" 8.00 11.00
☐ 105 **CANTRELL & COCHRANE**
Belfast & Dublin around bottle, round bottom, aqua, 9" .. 8.00 11.00
☐ 106 **N. CAPPELLI, 327 ATWELLS AVE., PROVIDENCE, R.I.,
REGISTERED**
On font, blob top, clear, 8¼" 7.00 10.00
☐ 107 **CAPRONI BROS. CO., PROV., R.I., REGISTERED**
Written inside of shield, blob, top, clear, 9¼" 7.00 10.00
☐ 108 **CARBONATING APPARATUS COMPANY, BUFFALO, N.Y.
REG.**
Marble inside bottle, clear 11.00 16.00
☐ 109 **M. CARNEY & CO., LAWRENCE, MASS.**
With MC & Co. monogram all inside of slug plate circle,
blob top, clear, 9¼" 7.00 10.00

☐110 **HUGH CASEY EAGLE SODA WORKS, 51 K ST., SAC. CAL.**
Aqua, 7¼" **7.00 10.00**

☐111 **OWEN CASEY EAGLE SODA WORKS**
On front, Sac. City on back, blob top, aqua blue, 7¼" **10.00 15.00**

☐112 **OWEN CASEY EAGLE SODA WORKS**
Dark blue, 7¼" **10.00 15.00**

☐113 **CASWELL & HAZARD & CO., NEW YORK, GINGER ALE**
In vertical line, round bottom, blob top, aqua, 9" **10.00 15.00**

☐114 **C. B. SODA**
*Quality Coca Cola Bottling Co. on back, aqua, machine
made, St. Louis on bottom, 8"* **5.00 8.00**

☐115 **C.C., PORTLAND, ORG., T.M., REG.**
T.B.N.T.B.S., amber, 7½" **9.00 13.00**

☐116 **C. C. S. & M. CO., 1118 TOLL 26 ROYAL ST., NEW
ORLEANS**
Crown top, aqua, 8" **6.00 9.00**

☐117 **CELERY COLA**
C under bottom, amber, 7½" **7.00 10.00**

☐118 **CELERY COLA**
Clear or amethyst, 7½" **4.00 6.00**

☐119 **CENTRAL CITY BOTTLING CO.**
Clear or amethyst, 7¾" **5.00 8.00**

☐120 **CENTRAL CITY BOTTLING CO.**
*On back Bottle Not To Be Sold, clear or amethyst, (note
misspelling), 7¾"* **7.00 10.00**

☐121 **CENTRAL CITY BOTTLING CO.**
*(Note misspelled Selma), Bottle Not To Be Sold on back,
clear, 7¾"* **17.00 23.00**

☐122 **CHADSEY & BRO.**
*2" hollow letters, N.Y., blob top, graphite pontil, cobalt,
7½"* **55.00 75.00**

☐123 **CHAMPAGNE MEAD**
On 2 panels, 8 panels, blob top, aqua, 7" **22.00 24.00**

☐124 **CHCRO-COLA**
Savannah, Ga. on back, aqua, 7½" **5.00 8.00**

☐125 **CHECOTAH BOTTLING WORKS, CHECOTAH I.T.**
Light blue, 7¼" **23.00 29.00**

☐126 **CHERO COLA BOTT. CO.**
Raised X pattern, Tyler, Texas, aqua, 7⅝" **3.00 5.00**

☐127 **CHICAGO BOTTLING CO.**
Root on bottom, aqua, 7" **7.00 10.00**

☐128 **CHRISTIAN SCHLEPEGRELL & CO.**
Eight panels, ground pontil, blue, 8¼" **45.00 60.00**

☐129 **THE CINCINNATI**
*On shoulder, under it in horseshoe letters SODA WATER
& GINGER ALE CO. in center, aqua* **7.00 10.00**

☐130 **THE CITY BOTTLING CO.**
On label, marble in center of neck, aqua, 7¼" **8.00 11.00**

☐131 **CITY BOTTLING WORKS, CLEVELAND, OHIO**
Aqua, 7" **10.00 15.00**

☐132 **CITY BOTTLING WORK, DETROIT, MICH**
*In back G. Norris & Co., A.&D.H.G. on base, blob top, blue,
7¾"* **18.00 24.00**

☐133 **CITY ICE & BOTTLING WORKS**
Aqua, 7½" **6.00 9.00**

☐134	**C & K** *In hollow letters, EAGLE SODA WORK, SAC. CITY, blob top, cobalt, 7"*	33.00	45.00
☐135	**C. CLARK** *Ground pontil, green, 7½"*	33.00	45.00
☐136	**CHARLES CLARK** *Ground pontil, green, 7¾"*	33.00	45.00
☐137	**CLEBURNE BOTTLING WORK** *Cleburne, Tex., paneled trunk, wire "pop" stopper, 7¼"*	7.00	10.00
☐138	**CLINTON BOTTLING WORKS** *Aqua, 8"*	8.00	11.00
☐139	**CLYSNIC** *Under bottom, green, 7½"*	3.00	5.00
☐140	**G. B. COATES** *G.B.C. monogram, LYNN, MASS. in a slug plate, clear, 8½"*	5.00	8.00
☐141	**M.H. COBE & CO. BOTTLERS, BOSTON** *In large letters on front, clear, 8⅛"*	7.00	10.00
☐142	**COCA COLA** *(Christmas Coke), Patd. Dec. 25, 1923, Zanesville, Ohio on bottom, ABM, crown top, aqua, 7⅝"*	14.00	19.00
☐143	**COCA COLA CO., SEATTLE, WASH.** *Clear or aqua, 8½"*	6.00	9.00
☐144	**COCA COLA IDEAL BRAIN TONIC SUMMER & WINTERS BEVERAGE FOR HEADACHE AND EXHAUSTION** *All on label, clear, 9½"*	55.00	75.00
☐145	**COCA COLA, TOLEDO, OHIO** *Amber, 7"*	13.00	19.00
☐146	**COCA COLA BOTTLING WORKS, TOPEKA, KAN.** *Aqua, 6"*	7.00	10.00
☐147	**COCA COLA, BUFFALO, N.Y.** *Clear or amethyst, 7¾"*	7.00	10.00
☐148	**DAYTONA COCA COLA BOTTLING CO.** *Clear or amethyst, 8½"*	9.00	12.00
☐149	**COCA COLA** *Wilmington N.C. around bottom of bottle, under it small letters D.O.C. 173, aqua, clear, 7¼"*	6.00	9.00
☐150	**COCA COLA MACON GA.** *Property of the Coca Cola Bottling Co on back, aqua, 7¾"*	6.00	9.00
☐151	**COCA COLA BOTTLING CO., ROME, GA.** *Trade Mark Reg. on back, This Bottle Not To Be Sold on base, clear, 7½"*	6.00	9.00
☐152	**COCA COLA MACON (reverse N), GA.** *Aqua, 7"*	13.00	18.00
☐153	*Same as above with different town in U.S.A.*	6.00	9.00
☐154	**COCA COLA** *In center of bottle, under it Trade Mark Registered, around bottom of bottle Waycross, Ga., on back, in small letter, O.B.Co., aqua, clear, 7¼"*	6.00	9.00
☐155	*Same as above with different towns in U.S.A.*	6.00	9.00
☐156	**COCA COLA BOTTLING WORK** *6¼ Flu ozs on lower trunk, also in center of shoulder, clear or aqua, 7¼" or various sizes*	6.00	9.00

☐ 157	Also in amber, vertical arrow, under it the name of different towns, some have only Coca Cola	10.00	15.00
☐ 158	Also machine made	7.00	10.00
☐ 159	**COCA COLA** On crown top, amber, under the bottom S B & G CO. #2, diamond shape label, 7¼"	16.00	23.00
☐ 160	**COCA COLA** Name on shoulder in center, also on trunk, aqua, clear, 7¾"	6.00	9.00
☐ 161	**COCA COLA BOTTLING CO.** Charleston, S.C. on front of shoulder, other side Trade Mark Registered, under the bottle Root, aqua or clear, 7¼"	6.00	9.00
☐ 162	**COCA COLA** (Not in script) in center, clear or aqua, 8½"	6.00	9.00
☐ 163	**COCA COLA** Around bottom base Trade Mark Registered, around shoulder Portland, Oregon, this bottle never sold, amber, 7½"	5.00	8.00
☐ 164	**COCA COLA** In ½ circle, under it Berlin, N.H., slim bottle, around bottom Contents 7 fl. oz., machine made, green, 8¾"	6.00	9.00
☐ 165	**PROPERTY OF COCA COLA BOTTLING CO.** On small embossed bottle, four square panels, six panels above shoulder, aqua, 7¾"	6.00	9.00
☐ 166	**PROPERTY OF COCA COLA** Six stars on shoulder, Tyler, Texas on bottom, square, aqua, 7¾"	5.00	8.00
☐ 167	**COCA COLA** On two sides of sample bottle, Clear Soda Water, 2½" ...	1.50	2.35
☐ 168	**COCA COLA BOTTLING CO.** Property of Waco, Drink Delicious Bludwine For Your Health Sake, sunken middle, aqua, 7 flu. ozs., 7½"	6.00	9.00
☐ 169	**COCA COLA** Some bottled in pottery and pop bottles or Hutchinson with diamond shape labels in 1900's	13.00	18.00
☐ 170	**COCA COLA BOTTLING CO.** Lakeland, Fla. in a circle, above it in script, Indian Rock Ginger Ale, on bottom panel, 7 fluid oz., ten pin type, about 1908, aqua, 8½"	6.00	9.00
☐ 171	**COCA COLA** Amber, 6"	13.00	18.00
☐ 172	**COCA COLA** On back shoulder Trade Mark Registered, aqua, root on bottom, semi-round bottom, 3¾" round	9.00	12.00
☐ 173	**COCA COLA** Clear or amethyst, semi-round bottom, 7¾"	8.00	11.00
☐ 174	**COCA COLA** Amber, S.B.&G. CO. on bottom, 6"	13.00	18.00
☐ 175	**COCA COLA** Aqua, 7"	6.00	9.00
☐ 176	**COCA MARIANI, PARIS FRANCE** Green, 8½"	6.00	9.00
☐ 177	**COCHRAN & CO.** Tear drop shape, Belfast on back, 9"	9.00	12.00

☐ 178 **COD SODA**
*Embossing, STAR BRAND SUPER STRONG with star at
base on front, marble closure, aqua, 9¼"* 7.00 10.00

☐ 179 **L. COHEN NEW YORK**
This Bottle is Reg. Not To Be Sold on back, 2 under bottom, aqua, 7½" 6.00 9.00

☐ 180 **COLE'S SODA by N. J. COLE, SO. ACTON, MASS.**
Clear or amber, 7" 9.00 12.00

☐ 181 **COMSTOCK COVE & CO., 139 FRIEND ST., BOSTON**
*On front, C.C. & CO. in large letters on back, blob top,
aqua, 7"* 9.00 12.00

☐ 182 **F.A. CONANT, 252 GIROD ST., N.O.**
Graphite pontil, blob top, olive, 7¼" 50.00 70.00

☐ 183 **CONCORD BOTTLING CO., CONCORD, N.H.**
Aqua, 6½" 7.00 10.00

☐ 184 **JAS. CONDON, WALDEN, N.Y.**
C. J. monogram, Cont. 7 oz., amethyst or clear, 6¾" 7.00 10.00

☐ 185 **CONKLIN BOTTLING WORK, PEEKSKILL, N.Y.**
On front in arched shape slug plate, blob top, aqua, 7⅛" . 8.00 11.00

☐ 186 **CONNOR & McQUAIDE**
Aqua, on back C & S, 8" 7.00 10.00

☐ 187 **CONNOR & MCQUAIDE**
Aqua, 6½" 6.00 9.00

☐ 188 **CONSUMERS**
C under bottom, aqua, 7¾" 5.00 8.00

☐ 189 **CONSUMERS B.B. CO.**
Amber, 9" 12.00 16.00

☐ 190 **H. CORTES, GALVESTON, TEXAS**
Clear, 7" 7.00 10.00

☐ 191 **H. CORTES & BRO., TEXAS BOTTLING WORK,
GALVESTON, TEXAS**
In back Belfast Ginger Ale & Soda Water, blob top, aqua . 12.00 16.00

☐ 192 **COSCROUL JAMES**
*Charleston, S.C. in a circle in center of circle & Son in
back this bottle not to be sold aqua, 8¼"* 12.00 16.00

☐ 193 **J. COSGROVE**
Aqua, 7" 6.00 9.00

☐ 194 **COTTAN & MAGG** *(C & M monogram)*, **BOSTON, MASS.**
On front aqua, 7½" 6.00 9.00

☐ 195 **JOHN COTTER**
Aqua, 7¾" 6.00 9.00

☐ 196 **COTTLE POST & CO., PORTLAND**
Blob top, blue, 7½" 14.00 19.00

☐ 197 **COTTLE POST & CO.**
*In center an eagle under it, PORTLAND, ORG. blob top,
green, 7¼"* 18.00 24.00

☐ 198 **JOHN COYLE, NEWBURGH, N.Y.**
*Inside of circular slug plate on front THIS BOTTLE NOT
TO BE SOLD also on front blob top, clear, 9¼"* 7.00 11.00

☐ 199 **C.R. CRAMER & JACKY**
In a dome line under it, PHILLIPSBURG, MON. aqua, 6¾" 7.00 11.00

☐ 200 **C.W. CRELL & CO.**
Ground pontil, blue green 50.00 70.00

148

150

171

172

173

174

175

177

187

188

189

206

207

224

238

239

240

255

☐201	**M. CRONAN, 230 K ST., SACRAMENTO**		
	On front Sac. Soda Works on bottom aqua, 6¾"	9.00	13.00
☐202	**M. CRONAN, 230 K ST., SACRAMENTO, SODA WORKS**		
	Blob top, aqua, 6½"	9.00	13.00
☐203	**CROWN BOTTLING WORKS, DELAWARE O.**		
	In a circle light green, 6¾"	7.00	10.00
☐204	**THE CROWN CORK & SEAL CO. BALTIMORE**		
	Crown top, sample, clear, 3¾"	9.00	13.00
☐205	**CRYSTAL BOTTLING CO., CHARLESTON, W. VA.**		
	Panel base, aqua, 7¼"	7.00	10.00
☐206	**CRYSTAL BOTTLING WORKS**		
	C.B.W. under bottom aqua, 7½"	6.00	9.00
☐207	**CRYSTAL BOTTLING WORKS**		
	C.B.W. under bottom aqua, 7¾"	6.00	9.00
☐208	**CRYSTAL SODA WORKS CO., S. F.**		
	Aqua or light green, 7¼"	7.00	10.00
☐209	**CRYSTAL SPRING BOTTLING CO., BARNET, VT.**		
	Clear or amber, 7¼"	7.00	10.00
☐210	**CRYSTAL** (Soda in center) **WATER CO.**		
	In back, Pat. No. 12-1872, Taylors U.S.P.T. blob top, blue, 7½"	7.00	10.00
☐211	**A.W. CUDWORTH & CO., S.F.**		
	Aqua, 7¼"	6.00	9.00
☐212	**CULVER HOUSE PURE NATURAL LEMONADE SPECIAL-TY**		
	In back Registered Trade Mark with house in center golden amber, 9"	22.00	29.00
☐213	**CUNNINGHAM & CO., PHILA.**		
	Blob top, aqua, 7"	7.00	10.00
☐214	**T. & J. CUNNINGHAM, PHILA.**		
	Blob top, green, 7"	9.00	12.00
☐215	**JOHN CUNEO**		
	269 under bottom, aqua, 9"	6.00	9.00

D

☐216	**DR. DADIRRIAN'S ZOOLAK**		
	Vertical around neck in two lines aqua, 7¼"	6.00	9.00
☐217	**M.D'AGASTINO**		
	Aqua, 1223 under bottom 7¼"	6.00	9.00
☐218	**DANNENBURG BROS., C.C. T.M.R.**		
	In center GOLDSBORO, N.C. clear or aqua, 7¾"	10.00	15.00
☐219	**E. DANNENBURG, AUTHORIZED BOTTLER** of **C.C. WILSON-GOLDSBORO, N.C., U.S.A.**		
	In a circle on the T.B.N.T.B.S. clear or amber, 8"	13.00	18.00
☐220	**C. DAVIS, PHOENIXVILLE**		
	In slug plate squat type, graphite pontil, green, 7"	40.00	55.00
☐221	**J. DAY & CO.**		
	In two lines blob top, aqua, 7¾"	7.00	10.00
☐222	**DEACON BROWN MFG. CO., MONTGOMERY, ALA.**		
	On base T.B.N.T.B.S. aqua, 8¾"	5.00	8.00

☐223	**DEAMER**		
	In hollow letters Glass Valley in back W.E.D. in hollow letters blob top, aqua, 7¼"	**7.00**	**10.00**
☐224	**W. DEAN**		
	Small kick-up pontil, blue green, 6½"	**22.00**	**31.00**
☐225	**WM. DEAN**		
	Pale blue, 7¾"	**7.00**	**10.00**
☐226	**DEARBORN, 83 3rd AVE., N.Y.**		
	Blob top, green, 7"	**10.00**	**15.00**
☐227	**E. T. DELANEY & CO.**		
	In center BOTTLERS PLATTSBURG, N.Y. aqua, 7"	**7.00**	**10.00**
☐228	**H. DELMEYER**		
	In center, 1861 BROOKLYN in back XX in hollow letters, Porter squat bottle, blob top, aqua, 6½"	**13.00**	**18.00**
☐229	**DeMOTT'S CELEBRATED SODA or MINERAL WATER**		
	In back, Hudson County, N.J. cobalt, 7¼"	**21.00**	**28.00**
☐230	**G.V. DeMOTT'S**		
	Graphite pontil, green, 7½"	**40.00**	**55.00**
☐231	**DeMOTT'S PORTER & ALE**		
	Squat body, blob top, green, 6½"	**30.00**	**42.00**
☐232	**H. DENHALTER & SONS**		
	In a dome-shaped line in center SALT under it SALT LAKE CITY, UT. aqua, 7"	**8.00**	**12.00**
☐233	**D.G.W.**		
	Script type letters blob top, aqua, 7¼"	**7.00**	**10.00**
☐234	**JOHN DIETZE, WINONA, MINN.**		
	On front inside of slug plate crown top, aqua, 8⅛"	**5.00**	**8.00**
☐235	**J. DINETS, SUPERIOR SODA WATER, CHICAGO**		
	In panel six panels, graphite pontil, blue, 8"	**55.00**	**75.00**
☐236	**DISTILLED & AERATED WATER CO., MITCHELL, S.D.**		
	Aqua, 3½"	**10.00**	**15.00**
☐237	**DISTILLED SODA WATER CO. OF ALASKA**		
	Aqua, 7½"	**10.00**	**15.00**
☐238	**DIXIE CARBONATING CO.**		
	Thick bottom, clear or amethyst, 9"	**6.00**	**9.00**
☐239	**DIXIE CARBONATING CO.**		
	Back shoulder Trade Mark, Augusta, Ga., clear or amethyst, 8"	**6.00**	**9.00**
☐240	**DIXIE CARBONATING CO.**		
	Aqua, 8"	**6.00**	**9.00**
☐241	**HENRY DOWNES**		
	On back The City Bottling Works of New York, aqua, 7½"	**6.00**	**9.00**
☐242	**DOOLY, CORDELE, GA.**		
	Panel base, clear, 7"	**8.00**	**12.00**
☐243	**DR. PEPPER**		
	Label, aqua, 7"	**3.00**	**5.00**
☐244	**DR. PEPPER KING OF BEVERAGE**		
	Reg. Dallas Bottling Co., Dallas, Tx., amethyst, 8¼"	**7.00**	**10.00**
☐245	**DR. PEPPER**		
	In script, under it King of Beverages, on shoulder Registered, on base Artesian Mfg. & Bot. Co., Waco, Tex., clear, amethyst	**7.00**	**10.00**

□246	**D.S. & CO., SAN FRANCISCO**		
	Blob top, cobalt blue, 7"	14.00	19.00
□247	**E. DUFFY & SON**		
	Green, 7"	16.00	23.00
□248	**FRANCIS DUSCH, T.B.N.T.B.S., 1866**		
	Blob top, blue, 7¼"	14.00	19.00
□249	**DUTCHESS BRAND BEVERAGES MADE IN VERBANK VILLAGE, 7 OZ.**		
	On front, amethyst, 8½"	4.00	6.00
□250	**JAMES N. DYER, CATSKILL, N.Y.**		
	This Bottle Not To Be Sold, aqua, 6½"	8.00	12.00
□251	**DYOTTVILLE GLASS WORKS, PHILA.**		
	Squat type, graphite pontil, green, 6¼"	55.00	75.00

E

□252	EAGLE SYMBOL in a circle, marble closure, aqua, 8"	10.00	15.00
□253	**WM. EAGLE, N.Y. PREMIUM SODA WATER**		
	Paneled, blob top, graphite pontil, cobalt, 7¼"	60.00	80.00
□254	**W. EAGLE, CANAL ST., N.Y.**		
	Reverse side, Phila. Porter, blob top, squat type, dark green, 6¾"	50.00	65.00
□255	**EAGLE BOTTLING WORKS**		
	D under bottom, clear, 7¾"	6.00	9.00
□256	**EAGLE BOTTLING WORKS, BIRMINGHAM, ALA.**		
	Eagle symbol, crown top, aqua, 8"	8.00	12.00
□257	**ALEX EASTON, FAIRFIELD, IOWA**		
	In a circle, Hutchinson, aqua, 6½"	14.00	19.00
□258	**E.B. CO., EVANSVILLE, IND.**		
	B under bottom, panels around bottle, aqua, 7"	6.00	9.00
□259	**G. EBBERWEIN**		
	Savannah, Geo. on front, Ginger Ale vertical on back, short neck, amber, 7¾"	27.00	36.00
□260	**EEL RIVER VALLEY SODA WORKS**		
	In center, SPRINGVILLE, CAL., aqua, 7"	8.00	11.00
□261	**EL DORADO**		
	Tapered top, aqua, 7¼"	9.00	12.00
□262	**ELECTRO BRAND**		
	Jackson, Tenn. on back, R.O. Co. under bottom	7.00	10.00
□263	**ELEPHANT BOTTLING CO.**		
	D under bottom, aqua, 7¾"	6.00	9.00
□264	**ELLIOTT, TRENTON, N.J.**		
	Blob top, aqua, 7¼"	10.00	15.00
□265	**EL RENO, B. W.**		
	Aqua, 7¼"	10.00	15.00
□266	**ELSBERRY BOTTLING WORKS, ELSBERRY, MO.**		
	On front in oval slug plate, ABM, crown top, 8"	3.00	5.00
□267	**G. L. ELWICK, LINCOLN, NEB.**		
	Light blue, 6¾"	5.00	8.00
□268	**EMMERLING**		
	Amber, 9½"	7.00	10.00

☐ 269 **EMPIRE SODA WORKS, VALLEJO, CAL.**
Crown top, aqua, 6½" **6.00** **9.00**
☐ 270 **EMPSORRS**
In fancy script, tall blob top, panel base, amber, 9¼" **8.00** **12.00**
☐ 271 **F. ENGLE**
Big E in back, aqua, 7½" **10.00** **15.00**
☐ 272 **ENSLEY BOTTLING WORKS, ENSLEY, ALA.**
Crown top, clear or aqua, 7½" **4.00** **6.00**
☐ 273 **ENTERPRISE BOTTLING WORKS, DAVIS & CO. PROP., LINCOLN, ILL.**
On panels, ten panels, aqua, 6¾" **9.00** **12.00**
☐ 274 **EPPS-COLA**
John C Epping, Louisville, Ky, Reg. 7 Fluid Oz. around bottle, E under bottom, snap-on top, aqua, 8" **7.00** **10.00**
☐ 275 **C. ERNE'S CITY BOTTLING WORKS, 348 & 350 PIENVILLE ST. N.O., T.B.N.T.B.S.**
Blob top, 8¼" **10.00** **15.00**
☐ 276 **CHARLES EUKER**
Reverse T.B.N.T.B.S. 1866, Richmond, Va., blob top, light blue, 7" **14.00** **19.00**
☐ 277 **STOLEN FROM EUREKA BOTTLING WORKS**
Aqua, 6¾" **9.00** **12.00**
☐ 278 **JAMES EVERADO, NEW YORK**
Clear or amethyst **6.00** **9.00**

F

☐ 279 **M. FAIRBANKS & CO., HOWARD ST., BOSTON, MASS.**
On front, large F & Co. on back, aqua **6.00** **9.00**
☐ 280 **F.B.W., FAIRFIELD, IOWA**
Tenpin type, blob top, aqua, 6½" **11.00** **15.00**
☐ 281 **J. A. FALSONE**
Clear or amethyst, 6¾" **5.00** **8.00**
☐ 282 **S. H. FARNHAM**
In center, AMERICAN FLA., WESTERLY, R.I., vertical, aqua, 7½" **10.00** **15.00**
☐ 283 **J. E. FARRELL, MAIN ST., COLD SPRING**
On front in oval slug plate, clear, 9⅛" **6.00** **9.00**
☐ 284 **FEIGENSON BROS., REG. DETROIT, MICH.**
On front in oval slug plate, aqua, 6⅛" **7.00** **10.00**
☐ 285 **FEIHENSPAN P.O.N. TRADE MARK AGENCY, NEWBURGH, N.Y.** *in oval slug plate,*
Crown top, aqua, 9¼" **6.00** **9.00**
☐ 286 **FERBER BROS., PHOEBUS, VA.**
Aqua, 7¼" **7.00** **10.00**
☐ 287 **E.M. FERRY, ESSEX, CONN.**
Blob top, clear, 9¼" **6.00** **9.00**
☐ 288 **C. P. FEY & CO.**
Light blue, 7½" **8.00** **12.00**
☐ 289 **S.C. FIELDS SUPERIOR SODA WATER**
Eight panels, ground pontil, cobalt, 7¼" **70.00** **90.00**

☐ 290 **B.H. FINK**
J instead of F, in back To Be Returned, ground pontil, blue
green, 7¼″ **50.00** **65.00**
☐ 291 **HENRY FINKS SONS**
Harrisburg, Pa., clear or amethyst, 9½″ **7.00** **10.00**
☐ 292 **FLEMING BROS., MEADVILLE, PA.**
In four lines, aqua, 6½″ **7.00** **10.00**
☐ 293 **J.C. FOX & CO., FOX T.M., SEATTLE, WASH.**
Aqua, 7½″ **8.00** **12.00**
☐ 294 **WM. FREIDMAN, CHAMPION SODA FACTORY,**
KEY WEST, FLA., T.B.N.T.B.S.
Clear or amber, 6½″ **6.00** **9.00**

G

☐ 295 **GADSDEN**
In center BOTTLING WORKS, GADSEN, ALA., clear, 6¾″ **7.00** **10.00**
☐ 296 **GAFFNEY & MORGAN, AMSTERDAM, N.Y.**
In a circle, panel base, aqua, 7½″ **7.00** **10.00**
☐ 297 **C.H. GAHRE BOTTLER, BRIDGETOWN, N.J.**
Aqua, 7″ **7.00** **10.00**
☐ 298 **GALLITZIN BOTTLING CO.**
326 under bottom, aqua **6.00** **9.00**
☐ 299 **GALLITZIN BOTTLING CO.**
Amber, 9½″ **6.00** **9.00**
☐ 300 **GALVESTON BREWING CO.**
Guaranteed Pure, Galveston, Tex., aqua, round, 7¾″ **6.00** **9.00**
☐ 301 **HENRY GARDENER TRADE MARK, WEST BROMWISH**
Emerald green, 7½″ **7.00** **10.00**
☐ 302 **GEO. GEMENDEN**
Savannah Ga on front, Eagle, Shield and Flag on back, improved pontil, green, blob top, 7¼″ **40.00** **55.00**
☐ 303 **WILLIAM GENAUST, WILMINGTON, N.C.**
In a circle, blob top, reverse side T.B.N.T.B.S., aqua, 9¼″ **8.00** **12.00**
☐ 304 **GEYSER SODA**
In back Natural Mineral Water, From Litton Springs,
Sonoma Co. Calif., blob top, aqua, 7″ **16.00** **23.00**
☐ 305 **GHIRARD ELLIS BRANCH, OAKLAND**
Three lines on front, blob top, blue, 7¾″ **9.00** **12.00**
☐ 306 **CHAS. GIBBONS, PHILAD.**
In a horseshoe shape, reverse a star, long neck, blob top,
amber, 8″ **16.00** **23.00**
☐ 307 **T.W. GILLETT, NEW HAVEN**
Eight panels, graphite pontil, blue, 7½″ **55.00** **75.00**
☐ 308 **GLOBE BOTTLING WORKS**
Savannah, Ga., in a circle in center on bottom, in back
This Bottle Is Never Sold, clear, 8½″ **5.00** **8.00**
☐ 309 **G.M.S. CO.**
Crown in center, REGISTERED, ALLIANCE, OHIO, panel
base, aqua, 7⅜″ **8.00** **11.00**
☐ 310 **GOLDEN GATE BOTTLING WORK**
In a horseshoe, under it SAN FRANCISCO, 7¾″ **9.00** **12.00**

□311	GOLDEN WEST S. & E. SODA WORKS, SAN JOSE, CAL.		
	Four-piece mold, aqua green, 8⅜"	7.00	10.00
□312	JOHN GRAF, MILWAUKEE		
	Panel base, reverse T.B.N.T.B.S., blue, 8½"	12.00	18.00
□313	JOHN GRAF		
	On other panels This bottle never sold, Please Return, When Empty, To The Owner, Cor. 17th & Greenfield Ave., Trade Mark The Best What Gives	17.00	24.00
□314	JOHN GRAF, MILWAUKEE, WIS.		
	On front, reverse T.B.N.T.B.S., The Best What Give trade mark, eight panels on base, aqua green, 6⅜"	8.00	12.00
□315	GRANT & UPTON		
	In a horseshoe shape, under it, COLUMBUS, OHIO, aqua, 6½"	11.00	15.00
□316	J & J GRANTHAM		
	Star under bottom, Kiner Bros Ltd on back, green, 8"	13.00	19.00
□317	JOHN GRANZ, CROTON FALLS, N.Y.		
	On front, T.B.N.T.B.S. on reverse side, blob top, aqua, 7½"	7.00	10.00
□318	GRAPE PRODUCTS CO. WALKERS		
	On bottom, clear or amethyst, 11"	4.00	6.00
□319	GRATTAN & CO. LTD.		
	Aqua, 9"	6.00	9.00
□320	GREAT BEAR SPRINGS, FULTON, N.Y.		
	Round bottom, aqua, 12"	9.00	12.00
□321	GREENWOOD BOTTLING & SUPPLY CO., GREENWOOD, S.C.		
	In a circle, crown top, aqua, 7½"	8.00	11.00
□322	G.T.B.		
	Under bottom, marble in center, aqua, 7¾"	5.00	8.00
□323	GUYETTE & COMPANY, DETROIT, MICH.		
	REGISTERED in center, G under bottom, cobalt, 6¾"	17.00	24.00

H

□324	H *In hollow letter, also* SAC. *with hollow P*		
	Clear or aqua, 7"	7.00	10.00
□325	HABENICHT BOTTLING WORKS		
	Columbia, S.C. in sunken panel, aqua, 9"	6.00	9.00
□326	HABENICHT		
	Next line Bottling Work, Columbia, S.C. in round sunken circle, blob top, amber, 9½"	13.00	18.00
□327	HAIGHT & O BRIEN		
	Graphite pontil, aqua, 7½"	27.00	36.00
□328	H. HALL, HILLTOWN		
	Ireland & New York at base in three lines, in center a hand in shield, under it Trade Mark, tapered top, semi-round, aqua, 9"	10.00	15.00
□329	HANNE BROTHERS		
	This Bottle Not To Be Sold in back, clear, 7½"	8.00	12.00
□330	HANSSEN BROS., GRASS VALLEY, CAL.		
	In center G.W.B., aqua, 7¼"	8.00	12.00
□331	C. J. HARGAN & CO., MEMPHIS, TENN		
	Blob top, aqua, 6¾"	9.00	12.00

□332	**P. HARRINGTON, MANCHESTER, N.H.,**		
	P.H. monogram all inside slug plate, blob top, clear, 9¼"	**10.00**	**15.00**
□333	**J. HARRISON**		
	In center 197 FULTON, N.Y., reverse, Phila. XXX Porter & Ale, squat type, green, 6½"	**35.00**	**48.00**
□334	**C. HARTMAN, CLEVELAND, O.**		
	Light blue and blue green	**10.00**	**15.00**
□335	**F. HARVEY & CO.**		
	This Bottle Not To Be Sold on back, amber, 8½"	**6.00**	**9.00**
□336	**J. HARVEY & CO.**		
	In hollow letters, 65½ Canal St., Providence, R. I., graphite pontil, tapered top, green, 7¾"	**55.00**	**75.00**
□337	**J. HARVEY & CO.**		
	In hollow letters, 65½ Central St., Providence, R.I., blob top, graphite pontil, green, 7½"	**50.00**	**65.00**
□338	**J. & J.W. HARVEY, NORWICH, CONN.**		
	Reverse hollow letter H, graphite pontil, blob top, green, 7¾"	**50.00**	**65.00**
□339	**HARVEY & BRO.**		
	In a dome shape, under it HACKETTSTOWN, N.J., in back, hollow letter H, green, 7"	**17.00**	**24.00**
□340	**HAWAIIAN SODA WORKS, HONOLULU, T.H.**		
	Aqua, 7½"	**9.00**	**12.00**
□341	**J.S. HAZARD, WESTERLY, R.I.**		
	Reverse side XX in hollow letters, blob top, aqua, 7¼" ...	**17.00**	**24.00**
□342	**H & D**		
	In raised letters 1½" tall, under this in two lines Savannah, Geo, squat bottle, aqua, 7", blob top, 7"	**15.00**	**22.00**
□343	**HEADMAN, PHILA.**		
	Reverse F.W.H. in hollow letters, graphite pontil, green, 7¼"	**50.00**	**70.00**
□344	**M.C. HEALD & CO. (M.C.H. CO) LYNN, MASS.**		
	Inside of slug plate on front, crown top, amethyst, 7½" ..	**7.00**	**10.00**
□345	**HEATLY BROS., MANGUM**		
	This Bottle Not To Be Sold reverse side, aqua, 6¾"	**17.00**	**24.00**
□346	**JOHN HECHT, BROOKLYN, N.Y. 1862**		
	Aqua, 7½"	**14.00**	**19.00**
□347	**JOHN HEINZERLING, BALTIMORE, MD.**		
	Aqua, 7½"	**8.00**	**12.00**
□348	**GEO. N. HEMBT, MONTICELLO, N.Y., REG.**		
	On front in slug plate, aqua, 6¾"	**6.00**	**9.00**
□349	**HEMPSTEAD BOTTLING WORK**		
	Hempstead, Tx. in a circle, amethyst, fluted bottom, 8" ..	**6.00**	**9.00**
□350	**HENNESSY & NOLAN GINGER ALE, ALBANY, N.Y.**		
	In panels, reverse H. & N. monogram, 1876, blob top, aqua, 7¼"	**11.00**	**15.00**
□351	**ED HENRY, NAPA, CAL.**		
	Monogram in center, aqua, 6¾"	**6.00**	**9.00**
□352	**GEO HENRY**		
	Aqua, 7½"	**7.00**	**11.00**
□353	**F. T. HELLER**		
	Aqua, 7½"	**7.00**	**11.00**
□354	**HERANCOURT BRG. CO.**		
	Amber, 8¼"	**6.00**	**9.00**

262   263   271   291   298   299

313   319   327   335   353   380

395   408   418   421   444   449

☐355	**J.C. HERRMANN, SHARON, PA.**		
	Hutchinson, aqua, 9"	13.00	18.00
☐356	**HEWLETT BROS., SALT LAKE CITY, UTAH**		
	Reverse T.B.N.T.B.S., aqua, 6½"	7.00	10.00
☐357	**T.E. HICKEY, PROVIDENCE, R.I.**		
	Aqua, 6¼"	7.00	10.00
☐358	**E. HIGGINS, OROVILLE**		
	In two lines, blob top, aqua, 7"	9.00	12.00
☐359	**E. HINECKE**		
	Louisville, K.Y., H under bottom, aqua, 7"	7.00	10.00
☐360	**HIPPO SIZE SODA WATER**		
	Prop. Of Alamo Bottling Wks., San Antonio, Tx., Nov. 2-1926, picture of hippopotamus, clear, 9½"	3.00	5.00
☐361	**HIRE'S**		
	On bottom, old crown top, aqua, 9¾"	3.00	5.00
☐362	**H.L. & J.W. HARTFORD, CONN.**		
	Amber, 6½"	6.00	9.00
☐363	**HOFFMAN BROS., CHEYENNE, W.**		
	Aqua	166.00	23.00
☐364	**LAWRENCE L. HOLDEN, FALL RIVER, MASS.**		
	Written at an angle, fancy, blob top, clear, 9¼"	7.00	10.00
☐365	*Same as above except amber, 8½"*	8.00	12.00
☐366	**HOLDENVILLE BOTTLING WORKS**		
	Aqua, 7½"	7.00	10.00
☐367	**HOLIHAN BROS**		
	Clear or amethyst, 9¼"	6.00	9.00
☐368	**HOLLAND RINK, BUTTE, MONT.**		
	In center BOTTLING WORKS, aqua, 6¾"	13.00	18.00
☐369	**HOME BREWING CO., RICHMOND, VA. (1895)**		
	Aqua, 6¾"	7.00	10.00
☐370	**R. A. HORLOCK CO., NAVASOTA, TEXAS**		
	Clear or amber, 8¼"	7.00	10.00
☐371	**HOUCK & DIETER**		
	In one of the six cathedral panels, Company in one, El Paso in another, Texas in another, two blank panels, under bottle H&D Co., applied crown top, aqua, 8"	17.00	24.00
☐372	**HOUCK & DIETER**		
	H & D Co. on bottom, aqua, 8"	8.00	12.00
☐373	**L. HOUSE & SONS, SYRACUSE, N.Y.**		
	Aqua, 7"	7.00	10.00
☐374	**J.F. HOWARD**		
	Haverhill, Mass. around the lower part of the trunk, round, fluted around, clear, 7¼"	6.00	9.00
☐375	**JOHN HOWELL**		
	Hollow letters under it, BUFFALO, N.J., blob top, aqua, 7"	13.00	18.00
☐376	**HOXSIE, ALBANY**		
	XOSI in back, blob top, aqua, 6½"	6.00	9.00
☐377	**HULSHIZER & CO., PREMIUM**		
	All on panels, graphite pontil, green, 8½"	70.00	90.00

□378 **HUNT & CO.**
Trade Mark, in two lines, Hunt & Co in script inside a square below, word Hickley below, in back near base, Dan Hylands Ld Sole Marke, Barnsley, 2½″ at base to pinch shoulder, neck tapers to applied top, also in neck a pinch, inside of neck a marble, aqua, 8¾″ 8.00 11.00
□379 *Same as above except no pinch in neck, 1¾″ at base,*
□380 **HUNTINGTON** *green, 6½″* 8.00 11.00
Machine made, amber, 7½″ 7.00 10.00
□381 **HUTCHINSON SODA BOTTLING WORKS, HUTCHINSON, MINN.**
Aqua, 7″ 7.00 10.00
□382 **E.L. HUSTING, MILWAUKEE, WIS.**
Vertical on side, aqua, 6½″ 6.00 9.00
□383 **HYDE PARK, ST. LOUIS**
Crown top, amber, 9¾″ 4.00 6.00
□384 **HYGEIA SODA WORKS, KAHULUI, H.**
In three lines, star under bottom, 7¼″ 13.00 18.00
□385 **HYGENIC DISTILLED WATER CO.**
In horseshoe shape lines under it, BROOKLYN, AND FAR ROCKAWAY L.I., in back H.D.W. Co. interlocking hollow letters, aqua, 7″ 11.00 16.00

I

□386 **IMBESCHEID & CO**
In center, Registered Jamaica plain mass all in a circle, on base Registered, in back T.B.N.T.B.S., under bottom Kare Hutter, 33 N, N.Y., blob top, aqua, 9″ 18.00 25.00
□387 **IMPERIAL BOTTLING WORKS, PORTLAND, OREGON**
Aqua, 7¾″ 11.00 15.00
□388 **INGALL'S BROS., PORTLAND, ME.**
Squat type, green, 7″ 12.00 17.00
□389 **INGALL'S BROS., PORTLAND, ME., BELFAST ALE,**
Vertical lines, round bottom, aqua, 8¼″ 11.00 15.00
□390 **ITALIAN SODA WATER MANUFACTOR, SAN FRANCISCO,**
In a horizontal line, reverse Union Glass Works, Phila, graphite pontil, emerald green, 7½″ 70.00 90.00

J

□391 **JACKSON BOTTLING WORKS, JACKSON, TENN.**
Aqua, 8″ 6.00 9.00
□392 **J. L. JACOBS, CAIRO, N.Y.**
In a round sunken panel, green, 7″ 10.00 15.00
□393 **J.L. JACOBS, CAIRO, N.Y.**
Reverse side, This Bottle Not To Be Sold, blob top, 7¾″ .. 7.00 10.00
□394 **THE JAMES BOTTLING CO.**
Aqua, 6¾″ 8.00 11.00

☐ 395	**F.W. JESSEN BOTTLING WORKS**		
	Amber, 9½"	7.00	10.00
☐ 396	**J.L. & C. LDC 1449**		
	Under bottom, aqua, 9½"	4.00	6.00
☐ 397	Same as above, only aqua	6.00	9.00
☐ 398	**JOHNSON & CORBETT, SOCORRO, N.M.**		
	In a circle, Hutchinson, aqua, 7"	13.00	18.00
☐ 399	**S. N. JOHNSON BOTTLING WORK, LAREDO, TEX.**		
	Blob top, aqua, 7½"	9.00	12.00
☐ 400	**JOHNSTON BROS.**		
	J on bottom, clear, 7½"	8.00	12.00
☐ 401	**JOHNSTON & CO., PHILADA**		
	Squat type, blob top, green, 7"	40.00	55.00
☐ 402	**D. JOHNSTON, ATLANTIC CITY, N.J.**		
	In back, J in hollow letter, blob top, aqua, 7"	13.00	18.00
☐ 403	**A. JONES**		
	Aqua, 6¾"	7.00	10.00
☐ 404	**GEO. JONES**		
	Aqua, 7"	6.00	9.00
☐ 405	**GEO. JONES, FONDA, N.Y.**		
	On front, G-J Co. monogram on back, clear, 7¼"	7.00	10.00

K

☐ 406	**DANIEL KAISER, KEOKUK, IOWA, P.A. & CO.**		
	In four lines, aqua, 7½"	9.00	12.00
☐ 407	**NICK KARL, GLOVERSVILLE, N.Y.**		
	On front in oval slug plate, This Bottle Not To Be Sold on back, aqua, 9¼"	7.00	10.00
☐ 408	**K.B. LD 7-122-1**		
	Under bottom, aqua, 7½"	3.00	3.00
☐ 409	**P. KELLETT, NEWARK, N.J.**		
	Squat type, graphite pontil, green, 6¾"	33.00	45.00
☐ 410	**P. KELLETT, NEWARK, N.J.**		
	Reverse K, 1857, green, 7½"	28.00	37.00
☐ 411	**KERYER & CO., EST. 1851, BELFAST**		
	In center, in center of Trade Mark a five-leaved flower, round bottom, aqua, tapered top, 9½"	7.00	10.00
☐ 412	**KIA-ORA. T.M. REG. BEVERAGES LEMON ORANGE & LIME MADE FROM REAL FRUIT JUICE, O-T LTD. INC. S.F., CAL.**		
	Clear or amber, 11"	10.00	15.00
☐ 413	**H.B. KILMER N.Y.**		
	Philada Porter & Ale in back, graphite pontil, green, 6½" .	50.00	65.00
☐ 414	**GEORGE KIMMERER, CANAJOHARIE, N.Y.**		
	On front in oval slug plate, aqua, 9½"	5.00	8.00
☐ 415	**KINSELLA & HENNESSY, ALBANY, N.Y.**		
	Blob top, aqua, 6¾"	8.00	12.00
☐ 416	**KINSELLA & HENNESSY**		
	In a dome shape under it, ALBANY, blob top, aqua, 7½" .	7.00	10.00
☐ 417	**CHAS. KOLSHORN & BRO. SAVANNAH, GA**		
	Blob top, aqua, 8"	7.00	10.00

☐418 **C. L. KORNAHRENS**
Aqua, C.L.K. in back, 7½" 8.00 11.00
☐419 **C.L., KORNAHRENS**
Charleston, S.C. in circle, Trade Mark in center, in back
This Bottle Not To Be Sold, aqua, 7¾" 7.00 10.00
☐420 **C.L. KORNAHRENS**
In a horseshoe shape, under it Charleston, S.C., blob top,
aqua, 7" 6.00 9.00
☐421 **C.L. KORNAHRENS**
Blue, 7⅜" 17.00 23.00
☐422 **KROGER BROS., BUTTE, MT.**
In a slug plate, aqua, 6¾" 10.00 15.00
☐423 **H.O. KRUEGER, GRAND FORKS, N.D.**
Aqua, 7½" 9.00 13.00
☐424 **A. KRUMENAKER**
New York in a slug plate circle, in center, two lines, 512 &
514 West 166th St., under it Registered, in back This Bot-
tle Not To Be Sold, blob top, aqua, 7¼" 7.00 10.00
☐425 **HENRY KUCK, 1878**
Savannah Ga. in four lines on front, green, blob top, 7½" . 18.00 25.00
☐426 *Same as above, no date* 12.00 17.00
☐427 **HENRY KUCK**
Savannah Ga in a slug plate on front, blob top, short neck,
aqua, 7½" 13.00 19.00
☐428 **HENRY KUCK**
Savannah, Ga. in three lines, Green, blob top, 7" 12.00 17.00
☐429 *Same except no Ga* 13.00 19.00
☐430 **THE JOHN KUHLMANN BREWING CO., ELLENVILLE, N.Y.**
On front in oval slug plate, aqua, 6¾" 6.00 9.00
☐431 **J. H. KUMP**
In hollow letters, MEMPHIS, TENN., blob top, aqua, 7½" . 8.00 12.00

L

☐432 **L & V**
In large hollow letters, blob top, pontil, aqua and green, 7"
.... 60.00 80.00
☐433 **Le LAGHTLEBEN-HACKENSACK, N.J. REGISTERED**
Slanted on front, blob top, aqua, 9¼" 7.00 10.00
☐434 **J. LAKE in hollow letters, SCHENECTADY, N.Y.**
Semi-round bottom, graphite pontil, cobalt, 8" 45.00 60.00
☐435 **LANCASTER GLASS WORKS, N.Y.**
Graphite pontil, blue, 7¼" 45.0 60.00
☐436 **LANCASTER GLASS WORKS, N.Y.**
Reverse in center XX, blob top, graphite pontil, aqua, 6¼" 70.00 90.00
☐437 **LANCASTER GLASS WORKS, N.Y.**
(Reverse N in LANCASTER), graphite pontil, cobalt blue,
7½" 70.00 90.00
☐438 **F. LANCKAHR, HIGGINSVILLE, MO.**
Aqua, 6¼" 8.00 12.00
☐439 **A. LANDT, LIVINGSTON, MT.**
Aqua, 7" 10.00 15.00

□440 **LARAMIE BOTTLE WORKS, LARAMIE, WYO.**
Crown top, aqua, 6½" 7.00   10.00

□441 **LARGE, KANSAS**
Reverse side on base, A. & D. H.C., blue, 7" 18.00   25.00

□442 **LAUREL CLUB, BOSTON**
Clear, 10" 6.00   9.00

□443 **LAWERENCE & SHAVER, GEORGETOWN, WASH.**
Aqua, 8¼" 6.00   9.00

□444 **LAWES & CO.**
Belfast Ginger Ale around bottom, aqua 8.00   11.00

□445 **L. & B.**
In hollow letters, blob top, graphite pontil, green, 7¼" ... 50.00   70.00

□446 **L & B**
In 2" hollow letters, blob top, aqua, 7" 5.00   8.00

□447 **LEBANON BOTTLING WORKS**
Aqua, 7½" 6.00   9.00

□448 **JULIUS LIEBERT**
C 4 under bottom, aqua, This Bottle Not To Be Sold in back, 9½" 7.00   10.00

□449 **LIME COLA**
On both sides, aqua, under bottom Duro-glas 9-47-G999, machine made 4.00   6.00

□450 **J.A. LINDSEY**
Clear or amethyst, 6¾" 6.00   9.00

□451 **L. LINDY, SAVANNAH**
In sunken panel, under it, Union Glass Works Phila in two lines, cobalt blue, slug plate, improved pontil, 6½" 32.00   45.00

□452 **LIFE PRESERVER**
Clear, 7" 9.00   12.00

□453 **C.C. LITTLE, GREENFIELD, MASS.**
Aqua, 7¼" 6.00   9.00

□454 **LOCKE & BELTZ BOTTLERS, BROWNSVILLE, PA.**
In a slug plate, aqua, 7" 6.00   9.00

□455 **LODI SODA WORKS**
Aqua, 6¼" 6.00   9.00

□456 **J A LOMAX**
J.L. under bottom, cobalt, 7¼" 23.00   32.00

□457 **LONGMONT BOTTLING WORKS, LONGMONT, COLO.**
Clear, 6¾" 12.00   18.00

□458 **LOS ANGELES**
In center, a star and SODA WORKS, crown top, clear, 6½"
.... 6.00   9.00

□459 **LOS ANGELES SODA CO.**
In a dome shape line under it, MINERAL WATER FAC-TORY, reverse side H.W. Stoll, blob top, aqua, 6¾" 13.00   18.00

□460 **LOS BANOS**
In center, L & B SODA WORKS, crown top, clear, 6½" ... 6.00   9.00

□461 **HENRY LUBS & CO.**
1885, Savannah Ga, green, blob top, 7½" 15.00   22.00

□462 **HENRY LUBS & CO.**
1885, Savannah Ga., short neck, aqua, blob top, 7¼" 15.00   22.00

□463 **LYMAN ASTLEY, CHEYENNE, WYO.**
Aqua, 7" 8.00   12.00

M

☐464 **MACON MEDICINE CO.**
Guinns Pioneer Blood Renerver on other side, amber, 11"   10.00   15.00

☐465 **MACKS BEVERAGE, SAN ANGELO, TEXAS**
Light green, 7½" 6.00   9.00

☐466 **M. MADISON, LARAMIE, W.T.**
Blob top, aqua, 7" 45.00   60.00

☐467 **MAGNOLIA BOTTLING CO., PASO, TEXAS**
Contents 7 fl. oz. around bottom and shoulder, crown top,
aqua, 7⅛" 4.00   6.00

☐468 **THOS MAHER**
In small letters on slug plate, ground pontil, dark green,
7½" 23.00   32.00

☐469 *Same, except larger ½" size letters*   12300   32.00

☐470 **THOS MAHER**
Slug plate, green, 6¾" 23.00   32.00

☐471 **THOS MAHER**
Slug plate, dark green, 7" 18.00   25.00

☐472 **MANUEL BROS., NEW BEDFORD, MASS**
On front in slug plate, blob top, amethyst, 9¼" 7.00   10.00

☐473 *MARBLE BOTTLE, Japan, two round holes on shoulder,*
green, 7½" 8.00   11.00

☐474 *MARBLE TEARDROP TYPE BOTTLE, aqua, 9¾"* 13.00   18.00

☐475 **THE MAR-COLA CO.**
Aqua, 7¾" 6.00   9.00

☐476 **MARION-BOTTLE WORKS**
In center M. & B. monogram, MARION, N.C., aqua, 6½" ..   13.00   18.00

☐477 **A. MAROTTA, 249-251 NORTH ST., BOSTON, MASS.**
Clear, 9¼" 6.00   9.00

☐478 **MARQUEZ & MOLL**
Ground pontil, aqua, 7¼" 40.00   55.00

☐479 **MARTHIS & CO.**
Aqua, 8" 4.00   6.00

☐480 **C.H. MARTIN & CO., SODA WORKS, AVON, WASH.**
Aqua, 7¼" 7.00   10.00

☐481 **B. MARSH & SON, DETROIT, MICH.**
Ten panels, blob top, aqua, 7½" 12.00   17.00

☐482 **MASON & BURNS, RICHMOND, VA. 1859**
Blob top, dark green, 7" 22.00   32.00

☐483 **S.M. MATTEAWAN, N.Y.**
S.M.M. monogram on back, ten panels at base, clear, 6¼"
....   7.00   10.00

☐484 **MAU & CO. H., EUREKA, NEVADA**
In 3 lines, blob top, plain bottom, aqua, 6½" 32.00   41.00

☐485 **M. B. & CO., 145 W. 35th ST., N.Y., 1862**
Blob top, aqua, 7¼" 11.00   15.00

☐486 **J.W. McADAMS TRADE MARK**
In center of a bunch of grapes, RICHMOND, VA., panel
base, aqua, 7" 10.00   14.00

☐487 **M. McCORMACK**
W.McC & CO. on back, amber, 7" 13.00   18.00

☐488	**McGEE, BENICEA**		
	In 2 lines, blob top, plain bottom, 6³⁄₄"	45.00	60.00
☐489	**THOS. McGOVERN, ALBANY, N.Y.**		
	Blob top, aqua, 7¹⁄₂"	8.00	12.00
☐490	**J. McLAUGLIN**		
	Green, 7¹⁄₂"	17.00	24.00
☐491	**McMAHONS WELL'S, FT. EDWARD, N.Y.**		
	T.B.N.T.B.S., blob top, clear or amber, 7¹⁄₂"	8.00	12.00
☐492	**McMINNVILLE BOTTLING WORKS**		
	This Bottle Not To Be Sold in back, amber, 7¹⁄₂"	6.00	9.00
☐493	**MEEHAN BROS., BARBERTON, OHIO**		
	In script, aqua, 6¹⁄₂"	11.00	16.00
☐494	**MEINCKE & EBBERWEIN**		
	In horseshoe shape in center 1882, under it in two lines Savannah, Geo, Ginger Ale vertical on back, amber, short neck, blob top, 8¹⁄₄"	25.00	37.00
☐495	**MEMPHIS BOTTLING WORKS, R.M. BECKER**		
	Aqua, 7¹⁄₂"	8.00	11.00
☐496	**JOSEPH MENTZE, MILTON, PA.**		
	Blob top, aqua, 7¹⁄₄"	12.00	17.00
☐497	**MERCER BOTTLING CO.**		
	This Bottle Is Registered Not To Be Sold on back, aqua, 9¹⁄₂"	8.00	11.00
☐498	**MERRITT & CO., HELENA, MONT.**		
	Blob top, aqua, 7¹⁄₄"	10.00	15.00
☐499	**MEXOTA**		
	Root under bottom, 11¹⁄₂"	7.00	10.00
☐500	**A.W. MEYER 1885, SAVANNAH, GA.**		
	In four lines on front, green, blob top, 8"	13.00	17.00
☐501	*Same except aqua*	13.00	17.00
☐502	**JOHN P. MEYER, FREEHOLD, N.Y.**		
	On front in oval slug plate, clear, 9"	7.00	10.00
☐503	**MIAMI BOTTLING WORKS**		
	Clear or amethyst, 7¹⁄₂"	6.00	9.00
☐504	**MIGUEL PONS & CO., MOBILE**		
	Blob top, graphite pontil, teal blue, 7¹⁄₂"	35.00	47.00
☐505	**C. MILLER**		
	Aqua, 9¹⁄₄"	6.00	9.00
☐506	**MILLERS BOTTLING WORKS**		
	Aqua, M under bottom, 8"	5.00	8.00
☐507	**MILLER, BECKER & CO., M.B. & CO., CLEVELAND, OHIO**		
	Apple green, blob top, 6³⁄₄"	7.00	10.00
☐508	**M. MINTZ, M.M.**		
	In center GLOVERSVILLE, N.Y., REGISTERED, blob top, clear, 8"	6.00	9.00
☐509	**MIRRIANS**		
	On shoulder, graphite pontil, cobalt, 7¹⁄₄"	35.00	47.00
☐510	**MISSION ORANGE DRY REG.**		
	Under bottom, black glass, 9¹⁄₂"	5.00	8.00
☐511	**C.A. MOELLER**		
	Karl Hutter 33 n New York under bottom, aqua, 9¹⁄₄"	9.00	12.00
☐512	**CHAS MOHR & SON**		
	5¢ for return of bottle, Mobile, Ala., clear, 7"	7.00	10.00

450

456

465

475

478

487

503

511

544

548

563

564

565

573

574

575

576

577

□513	**MONTANA BOTTLING CO., BUTTE CITY, MON.**		
	Blob top, clear or aqua, 6¾"	10.00	15.00
□514	**MONROE CIDER & VINEGAR CO., EUREKA, CAL.**		
	Clear or aqua, 7¼"	7.00	10.00
□515	**MORGAN & BRO., 232 W. 47th ST., N.Y.**		
	Reverse, M.B. Trade Mark, blob top, aqua, 7"	10.00	15.00
□516	**MORLEY C. VICTORIA, B.C.**		
	In 4 lines vertical, blob top, 6½"	55.00	75.00
□517	**MORRILL G.P.**		
	In 2 lines, blob top, plain bottom, aqua, 7"	25.00	34.00
□518	**T. & R. MORTON, NEWARK, N.J.**		
	In three lines, squat type, graphite pontil, green, 6¾"	50.00	70.00
□519	**L.C. MOSES BOTTLER, PARSONS, KANSAS AND BARTLESVILLE**		
	Crown top, aqua	13.00	18.00
□520	**MOUNT BOTTLING CO.**		
	This Bottle Not To Be Sold on back, 3 under bottom, aqua, 9½"	8.00	11.00
□521	**C. MOTEL**		
	Aqua, big M on bottom, 7"	8.00	11.00
□522	**MOXIE**		
	Aqua or clear, 6¾"	7.00	10.00
□523	**E. MOYLE**		
	Aqua, 7¼"	7.00	10.00
□524	**EDWARD MOYLE, SAVANNAH, GA.**		
	On front, Ginger Ale vertical on back, amber, 7½"	20.00	27.00
□525	**E. MOYLE, SAVANNAH, GA.**		
	In sunken circle, blob top, 1880, aqua, 7¼"	7.00	10.00
□526	**JOHN E. MUELHLECK, NELLISTON, N.Y.**		
	On front in arch slug plate, T.B.N.T.B.S. on reverse side, aqua, 6¾"	6.00	9.00
□527	**MUFF CO.**		
	Label, marble in center of neck, aqua, 7¼"	5.00	8.00
□528	**JAS. MULHOLLAND, SOUTH AMBOY, N.J.**		
	On front in oval slug plate, reverse side, T.B.N.T.B.S., blue aqua, 9½"	7.00	10.00
□529	**B.J.E. MULLENS**		
	Eagle in center, STANDARD GRADE BOTTLING WORK, ALBANY, N.Y. in script, crown top, aqua, 9¼"	7.00	10.00
□530	**T.F. MURPHY, BROOKFIELD, MASS.**		
	On front in slug plate, blob top, aqua, 9¼"	5.00	8.00
□531	**P.C. MURRAY, MONTICELLO, N.Y.**		
	On front in slug plate, aqua, 7"	7.00	10.00
□532	**MUSKOGEE BOTTLING WORKS, MUSKOGEE, I.T.**		
	Aqua, 6¾"	85.00	110.00

N

□533	**N.A. PA.** (star under it), **WOODS** (star under it), **SODA**		
	In back, Natural Mineral Water, blob top, blue, 7¼"	17.00	25.00

☐534 **OTIS S. NEALE CO., HOWARD ST., BOSTON, REGISTERED**
1893
With OSN monogram, all on front, blob top, amethyst,
9¼" **7.00** **10.00**

☐535 **NERVE PEPSIN CO.**
Trade Mark Registered on shoulder, clear, 8" **6.00** **9.00**

☐536 **NEUMANN & FUNKE, DETROIT, MICH.**
Hutchinson, aqua, 7" **13.00** **18.00**

☐537 **NEVADA CITY SODA WORKS**
L. Seibert in 4 lines, blob top, plain bottom, aqua, 7" **32.00** **43.00**

☐538 **NEW ALAMADEN/MINERAL WATER, W & W, 1870**
Same on reverse in large letters, blob top, aqua, 7½" **7.00** **10.00**

☐539 **NEW CASTLE BOTTLING CO., MT. KISCO, N.Y.**
On front in oval slug plate, amethyst, 9" **5.00** **8.00**

☐540 **NEWTON BOTTLING WORKS**
Aqua, 8" **4.00** **6.00**

☐541 **NONPAREIL, SODA WATER CO., S.F.**
In 3 lines, blob top, aqua, 6¾" **18.00** **25.00**

☐542 **NO. MAIN ST. WINE CO., 208-212 NO. MAIN ST., PROVIDENCE, R.I.**
With H in center inside of slug plate, blob top, clear, 9¼" **6.00** **9.00**

☐543 **NORTHERN COCA-COLA BOTTLING WORKS, INC., MASSENA, N.Y.**
Seltzer bottle type with pewter nozzle, cobalt, 9¼" **45.00** **60.00**

☐544 **NOVA KOLA**
This Bottle Not To Be Sold on base, clear or amethyst,
7¾" **5.00** **8.00**

O

☐545 **OAKLAND PIONEER SODA WORK CO., TRADE MARK**
(Embossed bottle inside of O), aqua, 8¼" **6.00** **9.00**

☐546 **OAKLAND STEAM SODA WORKS INC.**
In center in a wheel, on base, Bottle Not To Be Sold **10.00** **15.00**

☐547 **OCCIDENTAL BOTTLE WORKS, OCCIDENTAL, CAL.**
O.B.W. monogram, aqua or clear, 6¾" **7.00** **10.00**

☐548 **ODIORNE'S**
Clear, 8½" **4.00** **6.00**

☐549 **O'KEEFE BROS. BOTTLERS, MATTEAWAN, N.Y. REGISTERED**
On front, O.K.B. monogram on back, ten panels at base,
aqua or clear, 6½" **7.00** **10.00**

☐550 *Same as above except 9¼"* **8.00** **11.00**

☐551 **O.K. SODA WORKS**
In three lines, aqua, 7" **7.00** **10.00**

☐552 **OLSEN & CO., MEMPHIS, TENN.**
Blob top, cobalt, 7½" **70.00** **90.00**

☐553 **D.L. ORMSBY**
In 2" hollow letters, graphite pontil, blob top, cobalt, 7½" **50.00** **65.00**

☐554 **OZARK FRUIT CO., MEMPHIS, TENN**
In a circle, panels around base, aqua, 7½" . **10.00** **15.00**

☐555 *Same except crown top* **7.00** **10.00**

P

☐557	**J. PABST & SON, HUMILTON, OHIO**		
	In a circle, aqua, 6½"	8.00	11.00
☐558	**PACIFIC & PUGET SOUND SODA WORKS, SEATTLE, WASH.**		
	Aqua, 7"	9.00	12.00
☐559	**PACIFIC BOTTLING WORKS, PACIFIC, MO.**		
	ABM, aqua, 8"	4.00	6.00
☐560	**PACIFIC GLASS WORK**		
	All under bottom, blob top, label bottle, aqua, 6¾"	30.00	42.00
☐561	**PACIFIC SODA WORKS, SANTA CRUZ**		
	R in a hollow letter in center	7.00	10.00
☐562	**D. PALLISER, MOBILE, ALA.**		
	Aqua, 6¾"	7.00	10.00
☐563	**D. PALLISER**		
	Arthur Christian, 1875 Pat. April 13 under bottom, glass plunger for stopper, aqua ....:......	10.00	15.00
☐564	**D. PALLISIER**		
	(Palliser, misspelled), aqua, 7½"	13.00	18.00
☐565	**D. PALLISER**		
	Aqua, 7½"	8.00	11.00
☐566	**PALMETTO BOTTLING WORKS**		
	Clear or amethyst, 9¼"	9.00	12.00
☐567	**PARKER**		
	Graphite pontil, blue, 5"	40.00	55.00
☐568	**E. PARMENTER, GLENHAM, N.Y.**		
	On front in crude slug plate, aqua, 9¼"	7.00	10.00
☐569	**E. PARMENTER, MATTEAWAN, N.Y.**		
	On front in slug plate, T.B.N.T.B.S. reverse side, blob top, aqua	6.00	8.00
☐570	**PEARSON'S SODAWORKS**		
	Aqua, 7"	6.00	8.00
☐571	**PEPSI-COLA**		
	In center in script, also on bottom, 7 on top of shoulder, clear or aqua, crown top, not machine made	6.00	8.00
☐572	**PEPSI-COLA**		
	In script, Trade Mark on top, Memphis, Tenn. under it on slug plate, on back, Registered, 2322 under bottom, crown top, not machine made, amber	18.00	25.00
☐573	**PEPSI-COLA**		
	Newberry, S.C., This Bottle Not To Be Sold on back, 2¼" diameter, aqua, 8"	6.00	8.00
☐574	**PEPSI-COLA**		
	Aqua, 8¾"	5.00	9.00
☐575	**PEPSI-COLA**		
	Aqua, 7¾"	4.00	7.00
☐576	*PEPSI-COLA*		
	Aqua, 8"	4.00	7.00
☐577	**PEPSI-COLA, ALBANY BOTTLING CO., INC.**		
	Amber, 8"	31.00	39.00

☐578 **PEPSI-COLA, NORFOLK, VA**
This Bottle Not To Be Sold Under Penalty Of Law on back,
cross under bottom, amber, 8¾" 28.00   37.00
☐579 **P.W. PERKINS, TANNERSVILLE, N.Y.**
Aqua, 6½" 9.00   12.00
☐580 **PERRY MFG. CO., INC., SONORA, KY.**
Reverse side on base, REG. T.B.N.T.B.S., aqua, 8¼" 5.00   8.00
☐581 **M. PETERSON SODA WORKS, SAN RAFAEL**
(VA. CITY, NEV.)
Blob top, aqua, 7¾" 7.00   10.00
☐582 **JOHN V. PETRITZ**
In a dome, ANACONDA, MONT., aqua, 6¾" 10.00   15.00
☐583 **HENRY PFAFF, EL PASO**
Clear or amethyst, 8¼" 11.00   15.00
☐584 **HENRY PFAFF**
Clear or amethyst, 9¼" 10.00   14.00
☐585 **GEO. PFEIFFER JR.**
In a dome, CAMDEN N.J., blob top, aqua, 7½" 10.00   14.00
☐586 **PHILLIPSBURG (BOTTLE WORK in center)**
PHILLIPSBURG,
MONT.
Reverse side T.B.N.T.B.S., aqua, 6¾" 10.00   14.00
☐587 **PHOENIX BOTTLING WORKS**
On three panels, other seven panels are blank, light blue,
6½" 7.00   10.00
☐588 **PHOENIX GLASS WORK**
In a circle, under it BROOKLYN, blob top, graphite pontil,
aqua, 7¼" 45.00   60.00
☐589 **B. PIETZ, PIQUA, O.**
This Bottle Never Sold on back, aqua, 7¾" 9.00   12.00
☐590 **PIONEER**
In center a bear, soda water co. S.F., blob top, plain bot-
tom, aqua, 6¾" 50.00   65.00
☐591 **PIONEER BOTTLING WORKS**
P.B.W. under bottom, aqua, 7¾" 6.00   9.00
☐592 **PIONEER SODA WORKS**
A shield with word TRADE on one side, MARK on the
other, blob top, aqua, 7½" 13.00   18.00
☐593 **PIONEER SODA WORKS**
A shield on one side, Trade Mark on other, blob top, plain
bottom, aqua, 6½" 17.00   23.00
☐594 **PIONEER SODA WORKS, GILROY**
In large letters, 7⅞" 6.00   9.00
☐595 **PIONEER SODA WATER CO., S.F.**
In center of a bear, aqua, 6½" 10.00   15.00
☐596 **PIONEER SODA WORKS, SMITH & BRIAN, RENO, NEV.**
Aqua, 6" 9.00   13.00
☐597 **W. PIPE**
Sky blue, 7" 13.00   18.00
☐598 **JOSEPH C. PLANTE & CO., 631-635 ELM ST.,**
MANCHESTER N.H.
On front inside of slug plate, blob top, amethyst, 9¼" ... 6.00   9.00
☐599 **P. PONS & CO.**
Large P on back, ground pontil, aqua 45.00   60.00

☐600 **C.M. POPE BOTTLING, HOLLIDAYSBURG, PA.**
Blob top, aqua, 6¾" 8.00 11.00

☐601 **PORTLAND**
Picture of an eagle, above that TRADE MARK, THE EAGLE
SODA WORKS, P.O., blob top, aqua, 7¼" 13.00 18.00

☐602 **POST E.A.**
In center a eagle, under it Portland Org., all in
watermellow circle, blob top, plain bottom, aqua 45.00 60.00

☐603 **POST EXCHANGE BOTTLING WORKS, FORT RILEY, KAN.**
In a circle, crown top, aqua, 7" 7.00 10.00

☐604 **PRATT BOTTLING WORKS**
Amber, 8" 7.00 10.00

☐605 **PRESCOTT BOTTLING WORKS, PRESCOTT, A.T.**
In four lines, aqua, 6½" 65.00 85.00

☐606 **S. PRIESTER & BRO., HOUSTON, TEXAS**
Aqua, 7¼" 10.00 15.00

☐607 **PURITY BOTTLING & MFG. CO.**
Clear or amethyst, purity on bottom, 8" 6.00 9.00

Q

☐608 **M.T. QUINAN**
In horseshoe shape, in center, 1884, under it in two lines,
Savannah, Geo, in back, 2" monogram MTQ, on top,
Mineral and under, Water, under bottom, monogram MTQ,
cobalt, 7¾", blob top, 7¾" 35.00 47.00

☐609 **QUINAN & STUDER 1888, SAVANNAH, GA.**
Aqua, blob top, 7½" 13.00 18.00

R

☐610 **RADIUM SPRINGS BOTTLING CO.**
Machine made, R on bottom, clear, 7¾" 4.00 6.00

☐611 **RANDALL**
Clear or amethyst, 5¼" 4.00 6.00

☐612 **JAMES RAY'S SONS, SAVANNAH, GA.**
In center, Hayo-Kola in sunken circle, blob top, clear, 8" . 9.00 12.00

☐613 **JAMES RAY, SAVANNAH, GEO.**
In sunken circle, on back in one vertical line, GingerAle,
cobalt, blob top, 8" 26.00 34.00

☐614 **JAMES RAY, SAVANNAH, GA.**
In watermelon circle on back, monogram JR, dark amber,
7½" 26.00 34.00

☐615 **JAMES RAY, SAVANNAH, GA.**
In watermelon circle on back, monogram JR, aqua, 7½" . 26.00 34.00

☐616 **JAMES RAY & SONS 1876, SAVANNAH, GA.**
In a sunken circle on back, This bottle Registered, Not To
Be Sold, under bottom, B, clear or amethyst, 7½" 13.00 18.00

☐617 **JAMES RAY, SAVANNAH, GA.**
In a sunken circle, aqua, blob top, under bottom C24, 7½" 9.00 13.00

☐618 **JAMES RAY, SAVANNAH, GA.**
In a sunken circle on front, blob top, aqua, 7½" 8.00 12.00

☐619 **JAMES RAY & SONS 1876**
Same except on back RJ, hollow letters 26.00 37.00
☐620 **JAMES RAY**
Aqua, 8" 10.00 15.00
☐621 **JAMES RAY**
Aqua, 7¼" 9.00 12.00
☐622 **RAYNERS SPECIALTIES**
Aqua, 7½" 9.00 12.00
☐623 **R.C. & T., NEW YORK**
Graphite pontil, aqua, 7½" 60.00 80.00
☐624 **R CROWN SODA WORKS**
In large slug plate, ABM, aqua, 7⅞" 4.00 6.00
☐625 **READ'S DOG'S HEAD, LONDON**
On front around base, crown top, ABM, 9¼", emerald green, 9¼" 4.00 6.00
☐626 **REGISTERED**
In oval slug plate, T.B.N.T.B.S., crown top, amethyst, 9¼" 4.00 6.00
☐627 **C.H. RICHARDSON**
In a dome shape under it, TRENTON, N.J., green, 7" 16.00 23.00
☐628 **N. RICHARDSON, TRENTON, N.J.**
Graphited pontil, dark green, 7" 50.00 70.00
☐629 **THE RICHARDSON BOTTLING CO., MANSFIELD, OHIO**
In a circle, aqua, 6¾" 6.00 9.00
☐630 **RICHMOND PEPSI COLA BOTTLING CO., RICHMOND, VA.**
In a circle, slim shape, aqua, 9" 10.00 15.00
☐631 **W.R. RIDDLE, PHILAD.**
Reverse, large monogram, graphite pontil, blob top, blue, 7½" 50.00 65.00
☐632 **C.W. RIDER, WATERTOWN, N.Y.**
Frost green, 6¾ 17.00 23.00
☐633 **T. & H. ROBER, SAVANNAH, GEO.**
Graphite pontil, green, 7" 60.00 80.00
☐634 **JAMES M. ROBERTSON, PHILADA**
Reverse side T.B.N.T.B.S., blob top, aqua, 7¼" 7.00 10.00
☐635 **A.B. ROBINSON**
In a dome shape under it BANGOR, ME., blob top, aqua, 7¾" 11.00 15.00
☐636 **J.P. ROBINSON, SALEM, N.J.**
Reverse side, hollow letter R, blob top, green, 6½" 13.00 18.00
☐637 **R ROBINSON'S**
402 Atlantic Av. Brooklyn, N.Y. on back, aqua, 7¼" 10.00 15.00
☐638 **ROBINSON, WILSON & LEGALLSE, 102 SUDSBURYS, BOSTON**
Blob top, ice blue, 6⅜" 11.00 16.00
☐639 **ROCKY MOUNTAIN BOTTLING CO., BUTTE, MONT.**
In large letters, aqua, 6⅜" 13.00 18.00
☐640 **A.I. ROE**
Arcadia Fla. on panel, Coca Cola Bottling Co. on bottom, clear, machine made, 7¾" 5.00 8.00
☐641 **C. ROOS**
Aqua, 7⅝" 6.00 9.00
☐642 **ROSS'S BELFAST**
Aqua, 9" 7.00 10.00

☐643 **HENRY ROWOHLT**
HR Trade Mark Registered on back, aqua, 7½" 7.00 10.00

☐644 **JOHN RYAN**
In 2" letters around bottle, hollow letters under it Savannah, Geo, ground pontil, cobalt, 7" 55.00 75.00

☐645 **JOHN RYAN**
In 2" letters around bottle, under it Savannah, Geo, under it 1859, cobalt, 7" 60.00 85.00

☐646 **JOHN RYAN SAVANNAH, GA.**
In vertical line, in back, also vertical line Gingerale, on shoulder, 1852 Excelsior, amber or golden, 7½" 30.00 42.00

☐647 **JOHN RYAN 1866**
In front, in back Excelsior Soda-works, Savannah, Geo., cobalt, olive, blue, green and red, 7¼" 40.00 60.00

☐648 **JOHN RYAN**
In small no. 1866, blue, 7¼" 33.00 45.00

☐649 **JOHN RYAN**
On front J.R.S. 1852. T, Columbus, Ga., on back This bottle Is Never Sold 1883, on bottom R, cobalt, 7¾", round 55.00 75.00

☐650 **JOHN RYAN 1866 SAVANNAH, GA.**
On front, in back, 1" letters Cider, amber, 7½" 22.00 31.00

☐651 **JOHN RYAN SAVANNAH, GA.**
In center of it, 1852, blue, 7½" 39.00 50.00

☐652 **JOHN RYAN SAVANNAH, GA.**
In three vertical lines, round bottom, 8" 70.00 100.00

☐653 **JOHN RYAN JAMAICA GINGER**
In vertical line, aqua, 6" 21.00 27.00

☐654 **RYAN BROS.**
Gravitating Stopper Made By John Mathews N.Y. Pat 11, 1864 in a circle under bottom, aqua, 7" 18.00 24.00

☐655 **JOHN RYAN, SAVANNAH, GEO.**
Reverse XX, Philadelphia Porter, squat shape, blob top, green, 6½" 60.00 80.00

☐656 *Same as above except long tapered, blob top, graphite pontil, cobalt, 6¾"* 65.00 90.00

☐657 **JOHN RYAN EXCELSIOR MINERAL WATER SAVANNAH, GA.**
Reverse side This Bottle Never Sold, Union Glass Works, Phila., graphite pontil, cobalt, 7½" 65.00 90.00

☐658 **JOHN RYAN EXCELSIOR MINERAL WATER, SAVANNAH, GA.**
Reverse side U.G.W.P., T.B.N.T.B.S., blob top, graphite pontil, blue, 7¼" 65.00 90.00

☐659 *Same as above except no pontil, blob top, peacock blue* . 45.00 60.00

☐660 *Same as above except on base 1859, and graphite pontil, cobalt* 65.00 90.00

☐661 *Same as above except no pontil* 45.00 60.00

☐662 **JOHN RYAN**
In 2" hollow letters, SAVANNAH, GA. 1859, cobalt, 7½" . 65.00 90.00

☐663 *Same as above except no date, graphite pontil* 65.00 90.00

☐664 **JOHN RYAN**
In 1" hollow letters, PHILA. XX PORTER & ALE, squat type, blue, 6¼" 60.00 80.00

☐665 **JOHN RYAN, SAVANNAH, GEO.**
*Reverse side XX Philadelphia Porter, squat type, cobalt,
5¾"* 80.00 110.00

☐666 **JOHN RYAN 1866 SAVANNAH, GA.**
*Reverse side in 1" hollow letters, Cider, blob top, blue or
amber, 7½"* 70.00 90.00

☐667 **JOHN RYAN**
*in 1" hollow letters, PHILADELPHIA, 1866, reverse side XX
Porter & Ale, squat type, green* 70.00 90.00

☐668 **JOHN RYAN 1852, AUGUSTA & SAVANNAH, GA.**
*Reverse Philadelphia XX Porter & Ale, blob top, cobalt,
6¾"* 70.00 90.00

☐669 **JOHN RYAN, SAVANNAH, GA.**
In a circle in center 1852, blob top, aqua 45.00 60.00

☐670 *Same except amber* 70.00 90.00

☐671 **JOHN RYDER, MT. HOLLOW, N.J.**
Blob top, aqua, 7" 10.00 15.00

☐672 **RYE-OLA BOTTLING WORKS**
DOC 116 on base, clear or aqua, 8" 6.00 9.00

S

☐673 **ST. JAMES GATE, DUBLIN**
Machine made, amber 4.00 6.00

☐674 **ST. PETERSBURG BOTTLING WORK**
Clear or amethyst, 8" 7.00 10.00

☐675 **SALINAS SODA WORKS, STEIGLEMAN, SALINAS, CAL.**
BOTTLE NEVER SOLD, aqua, 7⅞" 7.00 10.00

☐676 **SALSA DIABLO**
On panels around bottle, clear, 6¾" 5.00 8.00

☐677 **SAMMIS & HENTZ, HEMSTEAD, L.I.**
Aqua, 7¼" 10.00 15.00

☐678 **SAN ANSELMO BOTTLING CO., SAN RAFAEL, CAL.**
Aqua, 6¾" 7.00 10.00

☐679 **H. SANDERS, SAVANNAH, GA.**
Amber, 8½" 27.00 36.00

☐680 **SAN FRANCISCO GLASS WORKS**
Blob top, aqua, 7⅛" 11.00 16.00

☐681 **SAN JOSE SODA WORKS, A.J. HENRY,
SAN JOSE, CAL.**
All on front, light blue, 8¼" 7.00 10.00

☐682 **SAN JOSE SODA WORKS**
(K missing in WORKS), blob top, aqua, 7½" 16.00 23.00

☐683 **SANTA BARBARA BOTTLING CO.**
In center, SANTA BARBARA, CAL., aqua, 7" 7.00 10.00

☐684 **SAPULA BOTTLING WORKS**
Clear, 7¼" 11.00 16.00

☐685 **SASS & HAINER, CHICAGO, ILL**
C & I on back, aqua, 7¼" 9.00 12.00

☐686 **C.L. SCHAUMLOLEFFEL, TRENTON, N.J. REG.**
T.B.N.T.B.S., crown top, aqua, 7½" 8.00 11.00

☐687 **P. SCHILLE**
*In center, monogram S. P. under it, COLUMBUS, O., aqua,
6¾"* 7.00 10.00

☐688 **A. SCHMIDT BOTTLER**
Aqua, 6¾" 6.00 9.00

☐689 **SCHOONMAKER & WILKLOW**
In center, ELLENVILLE, N.Y. in a sunken circle, blob top,
aqua, 7½" 10.00 15.00

☐690 **ALEX SCHOONMAKER, ELLENVILLE, N.Y.**
In an oval slug plate, clear, 6¾" 7.00 10.00

☐691 **CARL H. SCHULT**
Top vertical line, in center C-P, monogram M-S, three lines
Pat. May 4 1868 New York, tenpin type, aqua, 8½" 10.00 15.00

☐692 **FRANK SCUTT BOTTLER, VERBAND VILLAGE, N.Y. 702**
Inside of slug plate, crown top, amethyst, 7½" 5.00 8.00

☐693 **JOHN SEEDORFF**
Ground pontil, blue, 7½" 40.00 55.00

☐694 **SEITZ BROS., EASTON, PA.**
Large S on reverse side, blob top, graphite pontil, cobalt, 7½" 50.00 65.00

☐695 **SEITZ BR. CO.**
Large S in back, amber, 7¼" 8.00 11.00

☐696 **SEITZ BROS., EASTON, PA.**
Large S on reverse side, blob top, green, 7¼" 10.00 15.00

☐697 **SEITZ BROS**
Large S on back, blue green, 7" 13.00 18.00

☐698 **F. SETZ, EASTON, PA.**
On back, ground pontil, green, 7¼" 35.00 47.00

☐699 **7-UP**
Crown top, brown, squat type bottle, 6" 7.00 10.00

☐700 **E.P. SHAW'S**
Label, marble in center of neck, aqua, 7¼" 8.00 11.00

☐701 **E. SHEEHAN 1880, AUGUSTA, GA.**
Blob top, Return This Bottle reverse side, aqua, 9" 13.00 18.00

☐702 **E. SHEEHAN 1880, AUGUSTA, GA.**
Blob top, amber, 7¼" 35.00 47.00

☐703 **E. SHEEHAN 1880, AUGUSTA, GA.**
In an oval slug plate, reverse side R.T.B., cobalt, 7½" 110.00 140.00

☐704 **E. SHEEHAN, AUGUSTA, GA.**
Blob top, amber, 7½" 20.00 29.00

☐705 **E. SHEEHAN, 1880, AUGUSTA, GA.**
Blob top, green, 7¼" 23.00 31.00

☐706 **E. SHEEHAN, 1880 AUGUSTA, GA.**
Reverse side R.T.B., amber, 8¼" 23.00 31.00

☐707 **SHEYENNE BOTTLING, VALLEY CITY, N.D.,**
STEVENS & CO. PROP.
Aqua, 6¼" 12.00 17.00

☐708 **SHINER BOTTLING WORKS, SHINER, TEX.**
In a circle slug plate, aqua, 6½" 7.00 10.00

☐709 **SINALCO**
C in a triangle and 8 under bottom, snap-on, machine
made, amber, 7½" 5.00 8.00

☐710 **SIOUX BOTTLING WORKS, WATERTOWN, S.D.**
Clear, 7" 9.00 12.00

☐711 **SIP DRINKS TASTE LIKE MORE**
Around base SIP BOTTLING CORP., reverse side, a hand
with crossed fingers and embossing reading Make This
Sign, crown top, clear, 7½" 10.00 15.00

☐712 **A.P. SMITH**
Ground pontil, 7¼" 35.00   44.00
☐713 **B. SMITH REG. POUGHKEEPSIE, N.Y.**
In a slug plate, blob top, clear, 9¼" 6.00   9.00
☐714 **D. SMITH, YONKERS, N.Y.**
On front in shield slug plate, T.B.N.T.B.S., aqua, 9" 7.00   10.00
☐715 **D.H. SMITH, YONKERS, N.Y.**
In shield slug plate, blob top, clear, 11½" 7.00   10.00
☐716 **JOHN J. SMITH, LOUISVILE, KY.**
Aqua, 6¼" 10.00   15.00
☐717 **SMITH & CO.**
Panels around base, blue 22.00   30.00
☐718 **SMITH & CO.**
Seven panels, ground pontil, green 50.00   65.00
☐719 **SMITH & SWEENEY, MIDDLETOWN, N.Y.**
On front in oval slug plate, blob top, aqua, 7" 7.00   10.00
☐720 *SODA, label, graphite pontil, green, 7½"* 25.00   34.00
☐721 *SODA, plain, blob top with sunken circle, under it, Reg-is-*
tered, aqua, 7½" 6.00   9.00
☐722 *SODA, label, 1589 C on bottom, aqua, 7½"* 4.00   6.00
☐723 *SODA, label, clear or amethyst, 7½"* 4.00   6.00
☐724 *SODA, label, aqua, marble in neck, 9"* 7.00   10.00
☐725 *SODA, label, tear drop, flat top, aqua, 8½"* 17.00   23.00
☐726 *SODA, label, dark amber, 7½"* 11.00   16.00
☐727 *SODA, label, small kick-up, dark green, 7½"* 4.00   6.00
☐728 *SODA, label, This Bottle Not To Be Sold on back, aqua,*
9¼" 4.00   6.00
☐729 *SODA, label, Reg. This Bottle Not To Be Sold on back,*
anchor under bottom, clear or amethyst, 7½" 6.00   9.00
☐730 **SODA WATER BOTTLING CO., PROPERTY OF**
COCA COLA, PAT'D JUNE 1, 1926, MEMPHIS
On four panels on center, six panels on neck with stars,
ABM, green, 9¼" 5.00   8.00
☐731 **SOLANO SODA WORKS, VACAVILLE, CALIF.**
In four lines, aqua, 6¾" 8.00   12.00
☐732 **A. SOLARY**
Aqua, 7" 7.00   10.00
☐733 **SOUTHERN BOTTLING CO., ATLANTA, GA.**
Aqua, 6¼" 5.00   8.00
☐734 **SOUTHERN PHOSPHATE CO., COLUMBUS, MISS.**
Clear, 8" 6.00   9.00
☐735 **SOUTHERN PHOSPHATE CO.**
Aqua, 8" 5.00   8.00
☐736 **THE SOUTHWESTERN BOTTLING CO., TULSA**
Crown top, aqua, 7¾" 12.00   17.00
☐737 **SOUTHWICK & TUPPES, NEW YORK**
On eight panels, grpahite pontil, green, 7½" 50.00   70.00
☐738 **SQUEEZE**
Clear or amethyst, Ybor City Fla on bottom, machine
made, 8" 7.00   10.00
☐739 **STANDARD BOTTLING & EXRACT CO.**
Aqua, 9¼" 4.00   6.00

☐740 **STANDARD BOTTLING CO.**
Machine made, a star on bottom, aqua 4.00 6.00
☐741 **STANDARD BOTTLING CO., PETER ORELLO PROP.,**
SILVERTON, COLO.
Aqua, 6¾" 9.00 12.00
☐742 **STANDARD BOTTLING WORKS, MINNEAPOLIS, MINN.**
Amber, 6¾" 11.00 15.00
☐743 *STAR under bottom, aqua, 9½"* 5.00 8.00
☐744 **STAR BOTTLING WORKS, HOUSTON TEXAS,**
Written in a circle around a large star, tear drop shape,
blob top, aqua, 8" 45.00 60.00
☐745 **STAR MAIL ORDER HOUSE**
243 under bottom, clear or amethyst, 12¼" 11.00 15.00
☐746 **M & M STAR BOTTLING CO., OSKALOOSA, LA.**
Clear or aqua, 6¾" 8.00 11.00
☐747 **STAR SODA WORKS, GRIBLE & CO.**
In a circle in center, Nevada City, 7", clear, 7" 8.00 11.00
☐748 **E.B. STARSNEY**
Clear or amethyst, 8¼" 4.00 6.00
☐749 **STEINKE & KORNAHRNES**
On one panel, Charleston S.C. other panel, eight panels,
dark olive, ground pontil, 8½" 60.00 75.00
☐750 **H. STEWART, 253 ROOM ST., N.O.**
Blob top, graphite pontil, aqua, 7½" 55.00 70.00
☐751 **STILLMAN BOTTLING CO., 42 STILLMAN ST., BOSTON**
In a slug plate, blob top, 9¼" 6.00 9.00
☐752 **PETER STONITSCH**
Aqua, 9" 6.00 9.00
☐753 **STRAWHORN & SLAGO, REGISTERED, GREENWOOD,**
S.C., T.B.N.T.B.S. & MUST BE RETURNED
Crown top, aqua, 7¾" 9.00 12.00
☐754 **P. STUMPF & CO**
This Bottle Not To Be Sold on back, amber, 8½ 17.00 23.00
☐755 **J.P. SLLIVAN, SANTA ROSA**
Blob top, aqua, 6½" 6.00 9.00
☐756 **SUMMERS & ALLEN, ALEXANDRIA, VIRGINIA**
In three vertical lines, aqua, 7½" 7.00 10.00
☐757 **SUPERIOR BOTTLING WORK, SUPERIOR, WASH.**
Aqua, 6½" 7.00 10.00
☐758 **SUPERIOR SODA WATER, J.F. MILLER, DAVENPORT,**
IOWA
Blob top, fancy shoulder, five panels, blue 17.00 23.00
☐759 **SUPERIOR SODA WATER**
Other side, ground pontil, blue, 7½" 50.00 65.00
☐760 **SUPREME BOTTLING CO., WAUKESHA, WIS.**
On front in a slug plate, aqua, 6¾" 7.00 10.00
☐761 **ALBERT H. SYDNEY, PROVIDENCE, R.I.**
AHS monogram all inside slug plate, blob top, clear, 9¼" 7.00 10.00
☐762 **SYPHON CORP. OF FLORIDA**
Bottle made in Czechoslovakia under bottom, emerald
green, 9" 17.00 23.00

T

☐763	**TAMPA BOTTLING WORKS**		
	Pale green, 8"	7.00	10.00
☐764	**THE TAMPA PEPSI COLA BOTTLING CO.**		
	Semi-round bottom, aqua, 6"	8.00	11.00
☐765	**TANGO-COLA, RICHMOND, VA. REG.**		
	Star around neck, clear, 7½"	7.00	10.00
☐766	**B.F. TATMAN, OWENSBORO, KY.**		
	In center on 3-4" panel, other panels are plain, semi-round bottom, aqua	7.00	10.00
☐767	**TAYLOR SODA WATER MFG. CO., BOISE, IDA.**		
	Panel base, clear, 6¾"	10.00	15.00
☐768	**TAYLOR & WILSON**		
	Aqua, round bottom, 8½"	11.00	16.00
☐769	**TEAR DROP (or sunbeam), aqua, there are three or four different sizes, 8½"**	11.00	15.00
☐770	*TEAR DROP shape, crude blob top, dark olive 8"*	45.00	65.00
☐771	**THORNTON & CO.**		
	In ¼ moon letters under it in 2 lines, Hudson, N.Y., blob top, aqua	17.00	23.00
☐772	**TOLLE BOTTLING WORKS**		
	In center big T, LITCHFIELD, ILL., clear or amethyst, 6½"	8.00	12.00
☐773	**C.A. TOLLE**		
	In a circle in the center, A big C in center, REGISTERED LITCHFIELD, ILL., aqua, 6½"	7.00	10.00
☐774	**TONOPAH SODA WORKS, TONOPAH, NEV.**		
	In three lines, Hutchinson, clear, 6"	13.00	18.00
☐775	**TRI STATE BOTTLING CO.**		
	D.O.C. 1209 around base in back, 7½"	11.00	15.00
☐776	**TRY-ME BEVERAGE CO.**		
	Machine made, clear, 9"	1.50	2.25
☐777	**T. & S. PORT TOWNSEND SODA WORKS, P.T. W.T.**		
	Aqua, 6¼"	40.00	55.00
☐778	**T S, SAVANNAH, GEO.**		
	In three lines, on back, This Bottle Is Never Sold, emerald green, improved pontil, blob top, 6½"	25.00	37.00
☐779	**TUCSON BOTTLING WORKS, TUCSON, ARIZ., I.P.G. CO.**		
	Crown top, 7¼"	5.00	8.00
☐780	**T. & W.**		
	In hollow letter under it 1875, reverse side 141 Franklin ST. N.Y., blob top, aqua, 6½"	10.00	15.00
☐781	**TWITCHELL**		
	Aqua, 7½"	10.00	15.00
☐782	**G.S. TWITCHELL**		
	In center, hollow letter T, under it PHILA., reverse hollow letter T, blob top, green, 7"	10.00	15.00
☐783	**TWITCHELL, PHILADA**		
	In center, hollow letter T, same on back, green, 7½"	10.00	15.00
☐784	**TYLER BOTTLING WORKS**		
	Aqua, 7¼"	4.00	6.00
☐785	**TYLER UNION BOTTLING WORKS, T.B.N.T.B.S., TYLER, TEX**		
	Panel base, clear or amethyst, 7"	8.00	11.00

U

☐786 **U.C.B. CO.**
Contents 8 Fl. Oz. under bottom, clear, machine made, 8" 4.00 6.00
☐787 **WM. UNDERWOOD & CO. BOSTON**
Around base, amber or aqua, 7½" 10.00 15.00
☐788 **UNION BEVERAGE CO., JITNEY-COLA, KNOXVILLE, TENN., 6½ FLO. OZ.**
On shoulder, amber, 7¾" 7.00 10.00
☐789 **UNION BOTTLING CO., WILMINGTON, DEL., REGISTERED**
Aqua, 7½" 10.00 15.00
☐790 **UNION BOTTLING WORK**
In dome shape, under it VICTOR, COLO., aqua, 6¾" 17.00 23.00
☐791 **UNION GLASS WORK, PHILA.**
Blob top, graphite pontil, green, 7" 45.00 60.00
☐792 **UNION SODA WATER CO.**
W & C under bottom, This Bottle never Sold Please Return on back, aqua, 7½" 5.00 8.00
☐793 **UNITED GLASS LTD. ENGLAND**
Map of world and 1759-1959, these bottles were dropped in the ocean in 1959 with maps, etc., sealed inside to commemorate the Guinness Brewing Co. bicentennial, machine made, amber, 9" 8.00 11.00

V

☐794 **PROPERTY OF VALLEY PARK BOTTLING WORKS, VALLEY PARK, MO.**
On front, AMB, aqua, 7½" 6.00 9.00
☐795 **JOHN VICKERY, ENNIS, TEXAS**
Registered on shoulder, 62 under bottom, aqua, 8¼" 7.00 10.00
☐796 **VICKSBURG STEAM BOTTLING WORKS**
P under bottom, aqua, 6¾" 7.00 10.00
☐797 **VIG-O**
T. E. McLaughlin, Lynchburg, Va., aqua, 9½" 5.00 8.00
☐798 **VINCENT & HATHAWAY, BOSTON**
Reverse side, hollow letters V. & H., aqua, 7" 13.00 18.00
☐799 **VINCENT HATHAWAY & CO., BOSTON**
Blob top, round bottom, aqua, 7¼" 9.00 12.00
☐800 **VIRGINIA FRUIT JUICE CO.**
Machine made, clear or amethyst, thick bottom, 7½" 5.00 8.00
☐801 **VIVA BOTTLING WORKS**
This Bottle Not To Be Sold on base, CS6G CO under bottom, clear, 9" 4.00 6.00
☐802 **VOGELS BEVERAGES, SYLACAUGA, ALA.**
Aqua, 6¾" 5.00 8.00
☐803 **VOGEL SODA WATER CO., ST. LOUIS, MO.**
Squat, crown top, aqua, 7¼" 7.00 10.00

☐804 **ALBERT VON HARTEN, SAVANNAH, GA.**
In two vertical lines, in back, same except one line Ginger ale, dark green, blob top, 7" **22.00   31.00**

☐805 **ALBERT VON HARTEN, SAVANNAH, GA.**
In two lines, on back Genger Ale, 2" neck, blob top, green, 7" **17.00   23.00**

☐806 **VON HARTEN & GROGAN, SAVANNAH, GA.**
On front, dark green, blob top, 7¼" **18.00   24.00**

W

☐807 **WABASH BOTTLING WORKS, B.F. HEILMAN, 702 WABASH, IND.**
ABM, crown top, light blue, 7⅝" **4.00   6.00**

☐808 **WAGONER BOTTLING WORKS**
Panel base, aqua, 7" **10.00   15.00**

☐809 **WAINSCOTT'S DISTILLED WATERS, WINCHESTER, KY.**
In a circle, aqua, 7¼" **11.00   16.00**

☐810 **H.S. WARTZ & CO., 78, 80 & 82 LEVERETT ST., BOSTON, MASS.**
In oval slug plate, blob top, clear **7.00   10.00**

☐811 **WEACLE VESTRY, VARICK & CANAL ST.**
Prem Soda Water on back, graphite pontil, cobalt, 7½" . . **50.00   65.00**

☐812 **WEBBS**
London on back, amber, 9½" **10.00   15.00**

☐813 **JOSEPH WEBER**
Aqua, J.W. inside clover leaf, 7¼" **11.00   16.00**

☐814 **R.B. WEBSTER**
New York Ginger Ale around bottle, aqua, 7½" **10.00   15.00**

☐815 **A. WEGENER & SONS, DETROIT, MICH.**
In oval slug plate, aqua, 6⅜" **6.00   9.00**

☐816 **J.W. WELCH**
This Bottle Not To Be Sold on back, 4-X under bottom, aqua, 9¾" **10.00   15.00**

☐817 **GEO. WELLER, SCHENECTADY**
Blob top, aqua, 7½" **7.00   10.00**

☐818 **R. WELLER**
In center 176 SPRING ST., SARATOGA N.Y.: reverse T.B.N.T.B.S.: blob top, aqua, 7½" **13.00   18.00**

☐819 **CHAS. WESTERHOLM & CO., CHICAGO, ILL., TRADEMARK, W. CO.**
In a monogram on front, blob top, aqua, 6½" **8.00   11.00**

☐820 **WESTERN**
In center a deer head and trade mark, under it SODA WORK, P.O., aqua, 6¾" **10.00   15.00**

☐821 **HIRAM WHEATON & SONS**
Registered on bottom rim, 19 under bottom, 7½" **6.00   9.00**

☐822 **WHEELER BORS., WAUKESHA SODA WATER CO., WAUKESHA, WIS.**
In a slug plate, blob top, light green, 6½" **7.00   10.00**

☐823 **WHEELER & CO. UD CROMAC SPRING**
In line around base of round bottom bottle, under it Belfast, under bottom big W, in center a wagon wheel, between top spoke E.R., on bottom of wheel between spokes & Co, under wheel Registered, aqua, blop top, 9½" 9.00 12.00

☐824 **WHITE SPRING CO.**
Light aqua, 8" 6.00 9.00

☐825 **WILLIAMS BROS. SAN JOSE**
In oval slug plate, crown top, light aqua, 7⅝" 5.00 8.00

☐826 **S.M. WILLIAMS, MATTEAWAN, N.Y.**
SMW monogram on reverse side, ten vertical panels, blob top, clear, 6½" 7.00 10.00

☐827 **WILLITS SODA WORKS, WILLITS, CAL.**
Crown top, aqua, 7¾" 6.00 9.00

☐828 **C.C. WILSON, MARKED TREE, ARK.**
Clear, 7" 7.00 10.00

☐829 **HENRY WINKLE**
In a dome shape, SAC. CITY, blob top, graphite pontil, aqua, 7¼" 40.00 55.00

☐830 **WINKLER, AUG.**
S.B. in center, large letters Soda Works, all in a circle, blob top, aqua, 6¾" 22.00 29.00

☐831 **HERMAN WINTER**
In ½ circle, Savannah, G. under it, in back This Bottle Not To Be Sold in three lines, aqua, round, blob top, 8¼" 17.00 23.00

☐832 **HERMAN WINTER**
In a horseshoe shape, under it Savannah, Ga., 8", blob top, aqua, 3" diameter 19.00 28.00

☐833 **A.J. WINTLE & SONS, BILL MILLS, NR ROSS,**
T. TURNER & CO. MAKERS, DEWSBURY
Golden, 6¼" 12.00 18.00

☐834 **JACOB WIRTH & CO. INC.**
JW monogram, PROV., R.I. in a diamond slug plate, clear, 9¼" 8.00 12.00

☐835 **WISEOLA**
Star under bottom, clear or amethyst, 8¼" 5.00 8.00

☐836 **WISEOLA BOTTLING CO.**
Star under bottom, clear, 7" 13.00 18.00

☐837 **THE P.H. WOLTERS BREWING CO.**
This Bottle Never Sold in back, aqua, 9½" 4.00 6.00

☐838 **BY WOOTAN WELLS CO.**
(Written vertically on bottle), WOOTAN WELLS, TEXAS, Hutchinson, aqua, 6½" 12.00 18.00

☐839 **W.S. WRIGHT**
Under bottom, PACIFIC GLASS WORKS, blob top, green, 7½" 17.00 24.00

☐840 **WRIGHT'S**
Coca Cola on back, amber, 7" 13.00 19.00

☐841 **W.T. & CO.**
Star under bottom, aqua, 7¼" 10.00 15.00

☐842 **W. & W.**
In large letters, BURLINGTON, IOWA, blob top, aqua, 6¾" 10.00 15.00

Y

☐843 **X.L.C.R.**
*In ¼ moon letters, under it in 2 lines Soda Works, San
Francisco, Ca., blob top, aqua, 7"* 40.00   55.00

☐844 **YALE BOTTLING CO.**
*In center 268½ WOOSTER ST., NEW HAVEN, CONN.,
aqua, 7¼"* 10.00   15.00

☐845 **YETTER & MOORE**
Clear or amethyst, 8" 6.00   9.00

☐846 **J.H. YETTER**
Aqua, 7½" 13.00   18.00

☐847 **PHILIP YOUNG & CO., SAVANNAH, GA.**
*On front, on back, eagle, shield and flag, improved pontil,
green, blob top, 7½"* 60.00   80.00

Z

☐848 **MRS. B.Z. ZIMMERMAN, NEW BRUNSWICK, N.J.**
In a circle, under it, T.B.N.T.B.S., clear or amethyst, 6⅛" .. 7.00   10.00

☐849 **OTTO J. ZIPPERER**
This Bottle Is Never Sold on back, amber, 8½" 7.00   10.00

SPIRITS

This is, unquestionably, the largest single category in the bottle hobby in terms of the number of different bottles available. Among the spirits bottles you will find an enormous variety of sizes, colors, designs, and shapes — including the ornately figurals. In terms of age, they date well back into the 19th century up to modern times. Because collecting activity has been strong on spirits bottles for many years, the prices in general have gotten high and most of the scarcer and handsomer ones are well up into the double-digit range. The beginner may be best advised to specialize if he chooses to collect spirits bottles either by manufacturer, age, or in some other way, since this field as a whole is enormous. Flasks and bitters bottles, which are also spirits, are collected as a specialty in themselves and are listed in their own section in this book.

Winemaking is, of course, of great antiquity. Wine was extensively made throughout the ancient world in all societies and cultures. The Greeks gained an international reputation for their wine by the 4th century B.C. For a number of the small Greek city-states, winemaking was the chief industry and wine symbols were placed on their coins — bunches of grapes, amphorae (wine jugs), or portraits of Bacchus, the God of Wine. Winemaking also became a flourishing trade in Rome, and in some of the Roman colonies, such as Gaul (France) and Spain. French mastery in winemaking dates back to the Romans.

In the ancient world, wine played a far more important role than at any subsequent time. It was used not only as a beverage with meals, but as an ingredient in many kinds of foods and even as a sauce. Sherbet-like desserts were concocted by the Romans, who did not have ice-cream, by pouring wine over crushed ice. Since ice itself was hard to get, this was an expensive dish that only the rich indulged in. But in Northern Italy, where the climate was colder, peasants got all the sherbet they wanted by pouring cheap wine on freshly fallen snow.

Winemaking continued after the fall of Rome, uninterrupted to the present day. During the middle ages, winemaking was largely carried out by the monasteries and by noble estates. Commercial sale on a large scale did not resume again until the 15th century A.D. It has increased steadily since then all over the world.

Wine bottles usually hold a pint of liquid. The one to ten gallon containers used to transport or store wines were called carboys or demijohns. Carboys were so durable that they were also used to store corrosives. Demijohns basically had long necks. Both types were reusable and weighed thirty to forty pounds.

Shapes of wine bottles came to be associated with certain wine types by the mid 19th century. Seal bottles were also popular, especially among the affluent, from as early as the 17th century. Family crests and coats of arms were stamped on these bottles in the finishing process. The practice dwindled in the late 1800's after invention of the plate mold, which replaced hand stamping. Though some wines today still use seals to identify the bottle's contents, paper labels have become much more familiar.

In 1860, E. G. Booz of Philadelphia manufactured a whiskey bottle in the shape of a cabin. His name, the year 1840, the phrase "Old Cabin Whiskey," and the company's address were embossed on the bottle. Many believe that the popularity of Booz's product was responsible for hard liquor gaining the colloquial name "booze." As logical as that sounds, there is an alternative theory: a Dutch word, bouse, meaning liquor, was adopted into the English language in the 17th century. Local dialectic pronounciation could easily have transformed "bouse" into "booze."

The Booz bottle is credited with starting the practice of embossing brand names on spirits bottles.

Jack Daniel is one of the more popular brands. As a child, young Jack ran away from home and succeeded in obtaining a partnership in a distillery. By 1866, only three years later, he owned his own whiskey company in Tennessee.

Other spirits bottles are found in the figural shapes of cannons, clocks, and barrels. These and other figurals are the most sought-after spirits bottles among collectors.

After the repeal of Prohibition in 1933, all liquor bottles bore the inscription "Federal Law Forbids Sale or Re-Use of this Bottle." That practice was discontinued in 1964. It was designed to prevent cheap liquors from being sold as famous brands.

NOTE: A license is necessary to sell any liquor bottle containing alcoholic spirits.

SPIRITS

A

NO.	DESCRIPTION	PRICE RANGE	
☐ 1	**ACKER MERRALL**		
	Label, A9 under bottom, amber, 11"	8.00	11.00
☐ 2	**F.P. ADAMS AND CO.**		
	Boston, Mass., USA under bottom, decanter with handle, ring top, clear	18.00	27.00
☐ 3	**ADAMS, TAYLOR & CO.**		
	Full Qt. Registered on back, clear, 12½"	15.00	20.00
☐ 4	**ADAMS, TAYLOR & CO.**		
	Boston, Mass., Royal Hand Made Sour Mash Whiskey, clear, quart	10.00	15.00
☐ 5	**ADAM-BOOTH CO.**		
	In center anchor lean-to toward left, Sacramento, Cal. all in a circle, tapered top and ring, clear, 12"	32.00	45.00
☐ 6	**AGCS CO.**		
	Birds or eagle all around bottle on base, clear, 12"	11.00	15.00
☐ 7	**AGW**		
	On base, Cefrin type, aqua, quart	7.00	10.00
☐ 8	**ALAMEDA COMPANY**		
	Tremont and Bromfield Streets, Boston on front written in slug plate, flask, ring collar, side bands, amethyst, 8" ...	7.00	10.00
☐ 9	Same as above except ½ pint, monogram on center, 6⅛" .	7.00	10.00
☐ 10	**ALCOHOL**		
	In label, also Brandy, square bottle, clear, 8¼"	4.00	6.00
☐ 11	**ALDERNEY OLD RYE WHISKEY**		
	Around a cow, Chris Gallagher, 806 Lombard Street, Philadelphia, 7½"	16.00	23.00

☐	12	**ALMADEN VINEYARDS**		
		Green, 10"	1.50	2.25
☐	13	**AMBROSIAL B.M. & EAW & CO.**		
		In a seal on shoulder, pontil, amber, 9"	80.00	110.00
☐	14	**AMERICUS CLUB**		
		Amber, 7½"	7.00	10.00
☐	15	**AMERICUS CLUB PURE WHISKEY**		
		Clear or amethyst, 9½"	9.00	12.00
☐	16	**AMETGAN THERAPEUTIC CO.**		
		Green, 8"	10.00	15.00
☐	17	**AMIDON'S UNION**		
		Ginge Brandy Registered, in center lady with long hair, clear or amethyst, 11¾"	10.00	15.00
☐	18	**E.L. ANDERSON DISTILLING CO.**		
		Newport, Ky. on front in circle, round, tapered, graduated top and ring, clear	8.00	11.00
☐	19	**ANDRESEN & SON**		
		Western Importers, Minneapolis, Minn. & Winnipeg on back, amber, 5" x 4¾" x 3"	325.00	425.00
☐	20	**ANGELO MYERS**		
		Clear or amethyst, 6½"	4.00	6.00
☐	21	**ARONSON J.**		
		In center full-measure, Seattle, Wash., all in a circle, applied ring top, amber, 10½"	25.00	34.00
☐	22	**ARONSON J., SEATTLE, WASH.**		
		All in a circle, double rings top and neck (union oval flask), amethyst, ½ pt.	14.00	19.00
☐	23	**ASPASIA**		
		Tan and white crock, 10" x 9"	225.00	275.00

B

☐	24	**BAILEY'S WHISKEY**		
		Clear or amethyst, 9¾"	8.00	11.00
☐	25	*BANJO, label, lavender camphor glass, 10"*	27.00	35.00
☐	26	**THE BANTAM COCK, NORTHAMPTON**		
		Under bottom 64 H.32, aqua	30.00	40.00
☐	27	*Same as above except clear*	22.00	29.00
☐	28	*BAR BOTTLE, label, clear, 10¾"*	17.00	26.00
☐	29	*BAR BOTTLE, fancy, plain rib on bottom, clear, 10¼"*	11.00	16.00
☐	30	*BAR BOTTLE, clear cut glass type, plain, quart, 10¾"*	18.00	27.00
☐	31	*BAR BOTTLE, label, red, 10¾"*	50.00	75.00
☐	32	*BAR BOTTLE, label, pontil, dark amber, 10¼"*	26.00	38.00
☐	33	**BARCLAY**		
		Amber, 12"	50.00	65.00
☐	34	**BARCLAY 76**		
		Machine made, amber, 12"	11.00	15.00
☐	35	**BARKHOUSE BROS & CO**		
		Golddust, Ky., Bourbon, John Van Bergen, Sole Agents, amber, quart	85.00	110.00

☐	36	**A. BAUER & CO.**		
		Pineapple Rock & Rye, Chicago, USA, under bottom Design Patented, clear, 9¾"	**14.00**	**18.00**
☐	37	*Same as above except amber, 8½"*	**10.00**	**15.00**
☐	38	**B & B**		
		Clear or amber	**4.00**	**6.00**
☐	39	**B.B. EXTRA SUPERIOR WHISKEY**		
		In center a hand holding playing cards, blob neck, amber, 4½"	**17.00**	**24.00**
☐	40	**SOL. BEAR & CO.**		
		Wilmington, North Carolina, ring top, clear or aqua, 6" x 2½" x 1½"	**10.00**	**15.00**
☐	41	**BEECH HILL DISTILLING CO.**		
		B under bottom, amber, 12"	**10.00**	**15.00**
☐	42	*Same as above except letters closer together and longer neck*	**17.00**	**23.00**
☐	43	**BELFAST MALT WHISKEY FOR MEDICINE USE**		
		In a circle, aqua, 11"	**34.00**	**45.00**
☐	44	**BELLE OF NELSON**		
		Label, Whiskey, top one full quart, M.M. under bottom, clear, 12"	**6.00**	**9.00**
☐	45	**BELSINGER & CO. DISTILLERS**		
		Grar. Full Qt. on back, clear, 10"	**9.00**	**12.00**
☐	46	**BENEDICTINE**		
		Liquor cresent above shoulder, olive green	**11.00**	**15.00**
☐	47	*Same as above except machine made*	**4.00**	**6.00**
☐	48	**BERNARD CONATY CO., INC. PROVIDENCE, R.I.**		
		TBNTBS on base, letters and number under bottom, smoke, 9"	**9.00**	**12.00**
☐	49	**BERNHEIM BROS AND URI, LOUISVILLE, KY**		
		On seal, amber, 9½	**22.00**	**29.00**
☐	50	**E.R. BETTERTON & CO.**		
		Amber, 11"	**18.00**	**25.00**
☐	51	**E.R. BETTERTON & CO.**		
		Distillers Chattanooga, Tenn. in three lines in sunken panel in back, raised panel plain, flask, three ribs on each side, twenty ribs around neck, under bottom a diamond with letter Y, brown, ½ pint	**7.00**	**10.00**
☐	52	**E.R. BETTERTON & CO.**		
		White Oak on back, C in diamond under bottom, amber, 12" .	**19.00**	**25.00**
☐	53	**GEORGE BIELER & SONS, CINCINNATI**		
		On base, Brookfield Rye, B in center, clear, 9¼"	**14.00**	**19.00**
☐	54	**GEORGE BIELER & SONS, CINCINNATI RYE**		
		Fancy fluted neck, ring top, clear, 9½"	**13.00**	**17.00**
☐	55	**A. M. BININGER & CO.**		
		Distilled in 1848 around base, pontil, 8"	**175.00**	**225.00**
☐	56	**A.M. BININGER & CO.**		
		Kentuckey [sic] on front, No. 19 Broad St. N.Y., Biningers Old Kentucky Bourbon 1849 Reserve Dist in 1848 on side, amber, 9¼"	**85.00**	**110.00**
☐	57	**BINSWANGER & BRO.**		
		Simon W.L. Co., St. Joseph, Mo. on front, whiskey, clear or amethyst, 6¾"	**4.00**	**6.00**

☐ 58 **BINSWANGER & BRO.**
Simon in horseshoe, W.L. Co. St. Joseph, Mo. under it,
flask, clear 7.00   10.00

☐ 59 **BLACK AND WHITE WHISK Y**
E left out of whiskey, three-part mold, olive, one 10½ ",
other 11½ " 16.00   23.00

☐ 60 **G. O. BLAKE**
Clear or amethyst, 12⅝ " 8.00   11.00

☐ 61 **G. O. BLAKE KY. WHISKEY**
Aqua, 12½ " 8.00   11.00

☐ 62 **BLUTHENTHAL & BECKART/ATLANTA "B & B"**
CINCINNATI/HIGH GRADE LIQUORS
Vertical in slug plate, flask, clear, ½ pint, 6½ " 6.00   9.00

☐ 63 **BLUETHENTHAL & BICKART**
Clear or amethyst, 6¼ " 4.00   6.00

☐ 64 **BOB TAYLOR WHISKEY**
Jos. A. Magnus & Co., Cincinnati O. U.S.A., lion and arrow
monogram on back, amber, 9½ " 90.00   115.00

☐ 65 **C.T. BOND, MERCHANT & TRADER, NEW ALBANY, MISS.**
On back eagle in circle, C.T. Bond, golden amber, 6¼ " . . .   275.00   335.00

☐ 66 **W.E. BONNEY**
In center of barrel-shaped bottle, two rings encircling bot-
tle, three rings on top and bottom, stands up on one side,
aqua, 3" long x 1½ " wide, 2½ " 10.00   15.00

☐ 67 **BONNIE BROS.**
On top of circle, Louisville, Ky. on bottom, in center circle
Bonnie & Twiges, whiskey, clear, quart, 6½ " 8.00   12.00

☐ 68 **BONNIE BROS.**
In circle, Foliage and BONNIE in center, LOUISVILLE, KY.
on front, rectangular, amethyst, ½ pint, 7" 8.00   12.00

☐ 69 **E.C. BOOZ'S**
Broad sloping collar, smooth with circular depression,
Old Cabin Whiskey on one roof, on back roof 1840, short
neck on front door, three windows on back, plain on one
side, 120 Walnut St., two dots under St., Philadelphia on
other side, E.C. Booz's Old Cabin Whiskey on another side
. . . .   225.00   315.00

☐ 70 *Same as above except no dot under St., very short neck*
with large round collar, smooth with circular depression,
pale green 175.00   220.00

☐ 71 *Same as above except reproduction or machine made* . . .   5.00   8.00

☐ 72 **BOURBON**
In center, over it inside a diamond 131 F, amber, 3" round
bottle, 7½ " body, 2¾ " neck with a handle from neck to
shoulder 40.00   55.00

☐ 73 **BOURBON WHISKEY**
Bitters, 1875, amber, 9¼ " 100.00   135.00

☐ 74 *Same as above except puce* 140.00   170.00

☐ 75 **JOHN BOWMAN AND CO.**
Old Jewell Bourbon, San Francisco, amber 65.00   85.00

☐ 76 *Same except flask* 310.00   375.00

☐ 77 **S.W. BRANCH**
Amber, ½ gallon, 9½ " 22.00   29.00

☐ 78	**THE HENRY BRAND WINE CO.**		
	Toledo, Ohio, crown top, hock wine shape, amber, 14" ...	7.00	10.00
☐ 79	**BRANDY, CHICAGO FANCY**		
	Clear or amethyst, 11¾"	6.00	9.00
☐ 80	**BRANDY, CHICAGO FANCY**		
	Ruby red, 11¾"	11.00	15.00
☐ 81	*BRANDY, crescent on shoulder, amber, 10"*	5.00	8.00
☐ 82	*BRANDY, no crescent, clear or amethyst, 9¼"*	4.00	6.00
☐ 83	*BRANDY, plain, amber, 9¼"*	3.00	5.00
☐ 84	*BRANDY, plain, amber, 8½"*	3.00	5.00
☐ 85	*BRANDY, plain, olive, 12"*	3.00	5.00
☐ 86	*BRANDY, plain, olive, 11½"*	5.00	8.00
☐ 87	*BRANDY, plain with crescent, green, 11½"*	3.00	5.00
☐ 88	*BRANDY, plain, blob neck, red amber, 10½"*	5.00	8.00
☐ 89	*BRANDY, square type with crescent on shoulder, amber, 10"*	5.00	8.00
☐ 90	*BRANDY, plain, square type, clear or amethyst, 9¼"*	6.00	9.00
☐ 91	*BRANDY, plain, square type, amber*	5.00	8.00
☐ 92	*BRANDY, plain, beer type, amber, 8½"*	5.00	8.00
☐ 93	*BRANDY, plain, round, lady's leg neck, olive green, 12"* ..	4.00	6.00
☐ 94	*BRANDY, plain, round, lady's leg neck, olive green, 11½"*	4.00	6.00
☐ 95	*BRANDY, plain, crescent, round, amethyst or clear, 11⅝"* .	3.00	5.00
☐ 96	*BRANDY, plain, crescent, round, clear or amethyst, 12"* ..	4.00	6.00
☐ 97	*BRANDY, plain, beer type, blob neck, olive green, 9¾"* ...	4.00	6.00
☐ 98	*BRANDY, plain, round, short neck, amber, 11½"*	5.00	8.00
☐ 99	**BROOK SUNNY**		
	The Pure Food Whiskey, left medallion Grand Prize St. Louis 1904, right medallion Gold Med. St. Louis 1904, clear or amethyst, 10¾"	17.00	25.00
☐100	**BROOK SUNNY**		
	The Pure Food Whiskey, with two shields on front, Grand Prize, St. Louis 1904 on one side, Gold Medal St. Louis 1904 other side, clear, 10¾"	22.00	29.00
☐101	**BROOKVILLE DISTILLING CO. CINCINNATI, O. USA**		
	In circle, DISTILLERIES in center, Guaranteed full quart on back, fluting on neck and shoulders, graduated top and ring, amethyst, 9⅞"	11.00	15.00
☐102	**BROWN'S CATALINA**		
	Tapered, barber type neck, amber, 11"	23.00	30.00
☐103	**BROWN-FORMAN CO. DISTILLERS LOUISVILLE, KY**		
	On front, flask, double band collar, clear, pint, 7½"	6.00	9.00
☐104	**BROWN-FORMAN CO. LOUISVILLE, KY**		
	Machine made, amber or amethyst, quart	14.00	19.00
☐105	**BROWN-FORMAN CO.**		
	On one line, Louisville, Ky. on shoulder, whiskey, clear or amethyst	4.00	6.00
☐106	**BROWN-FORMAN CO, DISTILLER, LOUISVILLE, KY**		
	Flask, clear, ½ pint, 6¼"	7.00	10.00
☐107	**BROWN THOMPSON & CO.**		
	On one line, Louisville, Ky. on shoulder, beer type, lady's leg neck, opalescent, amber, 11"	7.00	10.00
☐108	**BUREAU THE**		
	In center crown, Portland, Or. all in a circle, pumpkin seed flask, double ring top, amethyst or clear, pt.	70.00	90.00

☐ 109 **SURSH BROWN**
Label, R.B.J. & Co. under bottom, clear, 8" **17.00** **24.00**

☐ 110 **BROWNSVILLE FRUIT DISTILLING CO.**
Native Wine Maker, Brooklyn, N.Y., clear, 13¼" **12.00** **16.00**

☐ 111 **BUFFALO OLD BOURBON**
George Dierssen & Co. of Sacramento, Calif., clear, quart **125.00** **160.00**

☐ 112 **BUFFALO SPRING**
With buffalo in center, Stomping Ground, Ky. Co., 7" **10.00** **15.00**

☐ 113 **SIR R. BURNETT & CO., TRADE MARK**
Between Co. and Trade is a circle with a crown in it on top
of shoulder, under it This Bottle Not To Be Sold But Remains Property of Sir R. Burnett & Co. London, England,
under the bottom B & Co., in center of bottom K B 57,
whiskey, clear or aqua, 12" **9.00** **13.00**

☐ 114 **SIR R. BURNETT & CO.**
Aqua, 8½" **9.00** **13.00**

☐ 115 **SIR R. BURNETT/& CO./LONDON/ENGLAND**
TRADEMARK
(Crown), This Bottle Is Not To Be Sold But Remains Property of, bulbous neck, gloppy square and ring top, round,
aqua, 11¾" **10.00** **15.00**

☐ 116 **BURNS & O'DONOHUE**
Amber, 10¼" **13.00** **18.00**

☐ 117 **BURROW MARTIN & CO.**
Norfolk, Virginia, round ring top, clear or aqua, 6" **13.00** **18.00**

C

☐ 118 **CAHN, BELT & CO.**
Clear, 8½" **6.00** **9.00**

☐ 119 **CAHN, BELT & CO.**
Clear, ½ pint, 7" **7.00** **10.00**

☐ 120 **CALEDONIA WHISKEY, B.C. DISTILLER CO. L.T.D.**
NEW WESTMINISTER, B.C.
Oval shape, graduated top, emerald green, quart **6.00** **9.00**

☐ 121 **CALLAHAN WHISKEY**
Clear or amethyst, 12⅛" **7.00** **9.00**

☐ 122 **CALLAHAN/WHISKEY/J. CALLAHAN & COMPANY**
(written fancy) **BOSTON, MASS/REGISTERED**
Round, amethyst, 12⅛" **7.00** **10.00**

☐ 123 **J.F. CALLAHAN & COMPANY/BOSTON, MASS**
At slant, clear, ½ pint, 6⅝" **6.00** **9.00**

☐ 124 **JOHN F. CALLAHAN, BOTTLED ONLY BY BOSTON,**
MASS
Round, slug plate, graduated top and ring, amethyst, 11" **11.00** **15.00**

☐ 125 **D. CANALE & CO.**
Memphis, Tenn. Old Dominick Bourbon other side, clear
or amethyst, 11" **14.00** **19.00**

☐ 126 **T.F. CANNON & COMPANY/BOSTON,**
MASS/GUARANTEED
FULL PINT
All in slug plate, 12 Devonshire St. on side, 28-30 Ex-
change St. on opposite side, rectangular, clear, pint, 8" . . **8.00** **11.00**

☐ 127	**CARLSON-BROS.**		
	In center wholesale and Retail in three lines, Astoria, are all in a circle, applied ring top, clear, ½" pint	16.00	23.00
☐ 128	**CARTAN, McCARTHY & COMPANY, SAN FRANCISCO, CALIF. FULL QUART**		
	With monogram at top, all vertically, rectangular, graduated top and ring, amber, 10¾"	22.00	29.00
☐ 129	**CASCADE**		
	Clear, 9½"	13.00	18.00
☐ 130	**J.W. CASHIN FAMILY LIQUOR STORE**		
	Clear or amethyst, 9½"	7.00	10.00
☐ 131	**CASPERS WHISKEY**		
	Cobalt, 10½"	120.00	165.00
☐ 132	**CEDARHURST**		
	Cont. 8 Oz. on back shoulder, amber, ½ pint, 7"	8.00	11.00
☐ 133	**CENTURY LIQUOR & CIGAR CO.**		
	B-8 under bottom, amber, pint	9.00	12.00
☐ 134	*CHAMPAGNE, cylindrical, 2" indented bottom, pale green, 11⅞"*	7.00	10.00
☐ 135	*CHAMPAGNE, plain, kick-up, opalescent, green 12" x 10" x 9"*	5.00	8.00
☐ 136	*CHAMPAGNE, plain, green, 4¼"*	4.00	6.00
☐ 137	*CHAMPAGNE, plain, kick-up, dark green, 8"*	4.00	6.00
☐ 138	**J. LABORDE CHAMPAGNE**		
	1815 Cosmac Bordraux in seal on shoulder, ring top, blob neck, green, 1 qt.	14.00	19.00
☐ 139	**CHAPIN & GORE, CHICAGO**		
	Hawley Glass Co. under bottom, amber, 8¼"	75.00	95.00
☐ 140	**CHAPIN & GORE**		
	Diamond shape on back for label, amber, 8¾"	50.00	65.00
☐ 141	**HENRY CHAPMAN & COMPANY**		
	Sole agents, Montreal in circle, pumpkin seed type, inside screw, Patent 78 on screw cap, amber, 5¼"	50.00	65.00
☐ 142	**CHEATHAM & KINNEY**		
	W. Mc & Co. under bottom, aqua, 8¾"	16.00	23.00
☐ 143	**CHESLEYS JOCKEY CLUB**		
	In center a jockey and running horse, under it Whiskey all in a circle, tapered top and ring, amber, 12"	170.00	230.00
☐ 144	*Same except clear*	100.00	135.00
☐ 145	*CHESTNUT BOTTLE, kick-up, handle, ring around top neck, squat, amber, 2" neck, 4" body, 3" x 4"*	22.00	29.00
☐ 146	*Same as above except larger, amber*	16.00	23.00
☐ 147	*Same as above except machine made*	7.00	10.00
☐ 148	*Same as above except clear or blue*	16.00	23.00
☐ 149	*CHESTNUT BOTTLE, kick-up, ring around top, pontil, blue, 4" body, 2" neck*	55.00	75.00
☐ 150	*CHESTNUT BOTTLE, 25 ribs, Midwestern, l.h. swirl, sheared top, green, 7½"*	75.00	100.00
☐ 151	*CHESTNUT BOTTLE, 24 vertical ribs, sheared neck, attributed to Zanesville, golden amber, 5¼"*	135.00	165.00
☐ 152	*CHESTNUT BOTTLE, light vertical rib plus 18 r.h. swirl ribs, sheared neck, attributed to Kent, green*	70.00	90.00

☐ 153 CHESTNUT BOTTLE, 16 vertical ribs, sheared neck, 6½".	90.00	120.00
☐ 154 CHESTNUT BOTTLE, swirl tooled top, pontil, green, 5¾"	80.00	110.00
☐ 155 Same as above except deep amber, 5¼"	110.00	140.00
☐ 156 CHESTNUT BOTTLE, long outward flared neck, bluish aqua, ½ pint	55.00	70.00
☐ 157 CHESTNUT BOTTLE, diamond, ¼" ground off top, attributed to Zanesville, yellow green, 10"	60.00	75.00
☐ 158 CHESTNUT BOTTLE, aqua, 5½"	27.00	36.00
☐ 159 CHESTNUT BOTTLE, twelve diamonds quilted over 24 vertical ribs, tooled mouth, clear, 5¾"	175.00	225.00
☐ 160 CHESTNUT BOTTLE, diamond, yellow green or clear, 5¼"	26.00	35.00
☐ 161 CHESTNUT BOTTLE, sixteen ribs, sheared neck, mantua, 6¼"	75.00	95.00
☐ 162 CHESTNUT BOTTLE, sixteen ribs, l.h. swirl, mantua, aqua, 6½"	75.00	95.00
☐ 163 CHESTNUT BOTTLE, kick-up, ring around top, pontil, amber, 6"	19.00	26.00
☐ 164 Same as above except clear	26.00	35.00
☐ 165 CHESTNUT BOTTLE, kick-up, squat body, handle ring around neck, light amber, 6"	10.00	15.00
☐ 166 Same as above except machine made, clear	7.00	10.00
☐ 167 **CHEVALIERS OLD CASTLE WHISKEY** San Francisco, spiral neck, aqua, quart	500.00	650.00
☐ 168 **CHICAGO FANCY BRANDY** Label, amber, 12"	13.00	18.00
☐ 169 **CHICAGO FANCY BOTTLER BRANDY** Ribs on shoulder and bottom, clear or amethyst, 11¾" ..	7.00	10.00
☐ 170 **CHICAGO FANCY BOTTLER BRANDY** Ribs on shoulder and bottom, ruby red, 11¾"	16.00	23.00
☐ 171 CIGAR BOTTLE, cigar-shaped, amber, 7½"	13.00	18.00
☐ 172 CIGAR BOTTLE, cigar-shaped, amber, 5½"	13.00	18.00
☐ 173 **CLARKE BROS & CO.** Amber, 11½"	7.00	10.00
☐ 174 CLOWN BOTTLE (front and back of bottle pictured), frost clear or amethyst, 17"	100.00	130.00
☐ 175 **COCA MARIANI** On one line, Paris on line near shoulder, liquor, whittle mold, green, 8¾"	4.00	7.00
☐ 176 **COCA MARIANI PARIS** In two lines, whittle effect, short body, long neck, green, 8½"	4.00	7.00
☐ 177 COFFIN TYPE, all basket weave except neck, clear or amethyst, ½ pint	8.00	12.00
☐ 178 COFFIN TYPE, two rings on shoulder, checker type body except neck, in center on front a circle for label, clear, amethyst, 5", 1¾" at bottom	8.00	12.00
☐ 179 **COGNAC CASTILLON** Depose under bottom, curved back, clear, 6½"	7.00	11.00
☐ 180 **GEO. COHN & CO.** Amber, 4½"	5.00	8.00
☐ 181 **GEORGE COHN & COMPANY** Louisville, Ky., blob neck, amber, 4¾"	7.00	11.00

☐ 182 **CONGRESS HALL WHISKEY BLEND**
The Fleischmann Company, Cincinnati, USA, amber, 11" . 16.00 23.00
☐ 183 *Same as above except dark amber* 26.00 35.00
☐ 184 **COOK & BERNHEIMER CO.**
Mount Vernon Pure Rye on one side, amber, 6" 13.00 19.00
☐ 185 **COOPER & CO.**
Portobello (Scotland) all in a circle under bottom, 2 pts. mold, small kick up, double ring top, black, 9¼" 16.00 23.00
☐ 186 **VERY OLD CORN**
From Casper Winston, North Carolina, Lowest Price Whiskey House, write for private terms, fancy with handle and glass top 60.00 80.00
☐ 187 **COWIE & CO. LTD.**
Clear, 8¾" 16.00 23.00
☐ 188 **S. CRABFELDER & CO.**
Amber, 7", 4" x 2" 8.00 11.00
☐ 189 **CREAMDALE**
Hulling, Mobile, Alabama, Cincinnati, Ohio, Refilling of This Bottle Will Be Prosecuted By Law under bottom, amber, 11¼" 13.00 18.00
☐ 190 **CREAM OF KENTUCKY "THEE WHISKEY"**
Clear, 11¼" 25.00 34.00
☐ 191 **CREME DE MENTHE**
Gold claws, green, 11" 16.00 23.00
☐ 192 **THE CRIGLER & CRIGLER CO.**
Clear or amethyst, 4½" 6.00 9.00
☐ 193 **CRIGLER & CRIGLER DISTILLERS**
Full Qt. Union Made other side, clear or amethyst, quart . 9.00 13.00
☐ 194 **CRIGLER & CRIGLER DISTILLERS, COVINGTON, KY.**
Vertical on one panel, Full Quart Union Made on next side, square body, lady's leg neck, graduated top and ring, amethyst, 10⅛" 17.00 24.00
☐ 195 **GET THE BEST, ORDER YOUR WHISKEY FROM J. CROSSMAN SONS**
New Orleans, La., amber, quart 10.00 15.00
☐ 196 **CROWN**
Label, whiskey pinch bottle, machine made, amber, 8½" . 8.00 11.00
☐ 197 **CROWN DISTILLERIES CO.**
Around monogram Crown & Co. in center, inside screw thread, amber, 10" 6.00 9.00
☐ 198 **CROWN DISTILLERIES COMPANY**
Under bottom, Sample Whiskey, round, clear or amethyst 4.00 6.00
☐ 199 **CROWN DISTILLERIES COMPANY**
In circle, CROWN & SHIELD, DC CO. monogram, on center, S.F. Whiskey, inside threads, embossed cork, round, amber, 11¼" 14.00 20.00
☐ 200 *Same as above except reddish amber, quart* 7.00 10.00
☐ 201 **CUCKOO**
Clear or amethyst, 11¾" 22.00 29.00
☐ 202 **CUCKOO**/*(bird, branches, leaves on center)* **WHISKEY/ M. BURKE/BOSTON/ TRADE MARK**
Flask, clear, ½ pint, 6½" 16.00 23.00

119

121

131

132

136

137

139

142

173

180

184

187

190

191

192

☐ 203 **CUCKOO/WHISKEY/M. BURKE/BOSTON/TRADE MARK**
All with embossed cuckoo bird in branches and leaves,
Full M.B. Quart on back, graduated top, round, amethyst,
12" **26.00** **35.00**

☐ 204 **CURNER & COMPANY**
80 Cedar Street, New York, three-part mold, olive, amber,
11½" **32.00** **41.00**

☐ 205 **J.H. CUTTER OLD BOURBON**
A.P. Hotaling & Company, Portland, Oregon, pewter screw
cap, round top, amber **320.00** **410.00**

☐ 206 **J.H. CUTTER OLD BOURBON**
A.P. Hotaling & Co., Portland, Oregon, 5th **39.00** **52.00**

☐ 207 **J.H. CUTTER OLD BOURBON**
Moorman Mfg. Louisville, Ky., A.P. Hotaling & Company
amber, quart **75.00** **100.00**

☐ 208 **J.H. CUTTER OLD BOURBON**
E. Martin & Company, amber, quart **115.00** **140.00**

☐ 209 **CUTTER, J. H.**
Old Bourbon under it a crown, around it bottled by A. P.
Hotaling & Co. all in a watermelon circle, tapered top and
ring, amber, 12" **35.00** **47.00**

☐ 210 **CUTTER, J.H.**
Old Bourbon, A.P. Hotaling & Co. sale agents all in five
lines, on shoulder a crown, tapered top and ring, chip
mold, light amber, 11¾" **240.00** **290.00**

☐ 211 **J.H. CUTTER/TRADE MARK** *(star and shield)/***E. MARTIN**
& COMPANY/ SAN FRANCISCO, CAL.
In circle, slug plate, graduated top, round, amber, 11" ... **14.00** **19.00**

☐ 212 **J.H. CUTTER OLD BOURBON**
by Milton J. Hardy & Company, Louisville, Ky., barrel in
center, amber, 12" **40.00** **55.00**

☐ 213 **J.H. CUTTER OLD BOURBON**
Louisville, Ky., amber, 5th **38.00** **52.00**

☐ 214 **J.H. CUTTER OLD BOURBON**
Barrel and crown in center, C.P. Moorman Mfg., Louisville,
Ky., A.P. Hotaling & Co., amber, quart **75.00** **100.00**

☐ 215 **CUTTER HOTALING**
Coffin type, 1886, amber **95.00** **120.00**

D

☐ 216 **DALLEMAND & CO. INC.**
Chicago around bottom, brandy, fancy, blob neck, amber,
11¼" **5.00** **8.00**

☐ 217 **DALLEMAND & CO.**
Cream Rye around bottom, fancy shoulders, amber, 2¾" **4.00** **6.00**

☐ 218 **DALLEMAND & CO. CHICAGO**
Design Pat 21509 Apr. 26, 1892 under bottom, amber, 11" . **12.00** **16.00**

☐ 219 **B.B. DAVIS & COMPANY, NEW YORK, CONTENTS**
8 FL. OZS.
Flask, graduated collar and ring, amethyst, ½ pint, 6¾" . **7.00** **10.00**

☐ 220 **DAVIS' MARYLAND**
Label, Guaranteed Full Pint in back, Davis & Drake, clear,
8½" **6.00** **9.00**

☐ 221 **PETER DAWSON LTD, DISTILLERS**
On bottom, graduated and flared collar, concave and convex circles (thumb prints) around shoulder and base, green, 11¾" **6.00** **9.00**

☐ 222 **DEEP SPRING**
Tennessee Whiskey, amber, quart, 7" **10.00** **15.00**

☐ 223 **DeKUYPER'S SQUAREFACE, WHO DeKUYPER'S NIGHT-LY**
TAKES, SOUNDLY SLEEPS AND FIT AWAKES
On two panels, vertical at slant, vase gin shape, ABM, thread top, grass green, 7⅛" **7.00** **10.00**

☐ 224 **R. DENNER WINE & SPIRIT MERCHANT**
Bridgewater in three lines on one side shoulder, crock with handle, coffin flask type, ring top, short neck, tan and cream, 2¼" x 3", 8½" **18.00** **27.00**

☐ 225 **DEVIL'S ISLAND ENDURANCE GIN**
Clear or amethyst, pint **6.00** **9.00**

☐ 226 **DE IL'S ISLAND**
V missing from Devil's, clear, 9" **12.00** **16.00**

☐ 227 **DIAMOND PACKING CO., BRIDGETON, N.J.**
Pat. Feb 11th 1870 on shoulder, aqua, 8" **11.00** **15.00**

☐ 228 *DIAMOND QUILTED FLASK, double collar, very light aqua, almost clear, quart, 9"* **16.00** **23.00**

☐ 229 **DIEHL & FORD**
Nashville, Tennessee around bottle, each letter in a panel, light amber, 9" **18.00** **27.00**

☐ 230 *DIP MOLD WINE, kick-up, pontil, dark amber* **8.00** **12.00**

☐ 231 **J.E. DOHERTY COMPANY, BOSTON, MASS**
Written vertically, flask, clear, ½ pint, 6¾" **5.00** **8.00**

☐ 232 **J.E. DOHERTY CO./BOSTON, MASS**
On shoulder, Regist. Full Qt. on back, three-piece mold, graduated top, lady's leg neck, amethyst, 11" **8.00** **12.00**

☐ 233 **N.F. DOHERTY, 181-185 CAMBRIDGE ST., BOSTON, GUARANTEED FULL PINT**
Vertically in slug plate, rectangular, graduated, collar and ring, amethyst, pint, 8¾" **7.00** **10.00**

☐ 234 **NEIL DOHERTY**
176 North St. Boston in circle, in center of circle Wine & Liquors, strap flask, light amber, 9⅝" **7.00** **11.00**

☐ 235 **DONALDSON & COMPANY FINE OLD MADERA, MADCIRA**
HOUSE, FOUNDED 1783
Label, aqua, quart, 12¼" **7.00** **10.00**

☐ 236 **DREYFUSS-WEIL & COMPANY, DISTILLERS, PADUCAH, KY, USA**
Clear, ½ pint ...., **6.00** **9.00**

☐ 237 **DREYFUSS-WEIL & CO.**
Clear or amethyst, 6½" **5.00** **8.00**

☐ 238 **D.S.G. COMPANY**
Under bottom, light amber, 7¾" **27.00** **35.00**

☐ 239 **DUFF GORDON SHERRY**
Three-part mold, aqua, 12" **9.00** **13.00**

☐ 240	**THE DUFFY MALT WHISKEY CO.**		
	Rochester N.Y.U.S.A. on front in watermelon circle, in center monogram D.M.W.Co., under bottom pat'd Aug.24-1886, different number or letter on bottom, round, amber, 10¼"	5.00	8.00
☐ 241	*Same as above except ½ pint or pint*	26.00	35.00
☐ 242	*Same as above except miniature*	17.00	26.00
☐ 243	*Same as above except machine made*	3.00	4.00
☐ 244	**THE DUFFY MALT WHISKEY COMPANY**		
	Baltimore, Md. U.S.A. in a circle monogram, in center a circle D.C.O, under bottom Pat. Aug. 24-86, Baltimore Md., some have letters or numbers, amber, approximate quart	7.00	10.00
☐ 245	*Same as above except machine made*	4.00	6.00
☐ 246	*Same as above except approx. pint*	16.00	23.00
☐ 247	*Same as above except machine made, approx. pint*	10.00	15.00
☐ 248	*Same as above except approx. ½ pint*	17.00	23.00
☐ 249	*Same as above except machine made, approx. ½ pint* . . .	7.00	10.00
☐ 250	*Same as above except sample* . . . .,.	17.00	23.00
☐ 251	**THE DUFFY MALT WHISKEY CO.**		
	Baltimore Md., U.S.A. in watermelon circle, in center of circle monogram D.M.W. Co., under bottom Pat. Aug. 24 '86, Baltimore Md., ½" ring around neck, amber	8.00	12.00
☐ 252	**THE DUFFY MALT WHISKEY COMPANY**		
	Patd Aug. 1886 in back, plain bottom, amber, 10½"	40.00	55.00
☐ 253	**DUKEHART & CO.**		
	Amber, 4"	22.00	30.00
☐ 254	**DURHAM**		
	Amber, 11½"	200.00	265.00
☐ 255	**DURKIN WHOLESALE AND RETAIL WINE AND LIQUOR**		
	Hill and Sprague Street, Spokane, Washington in front, tapered, ring top, 13½"	17.00	23.00
☐ 256	**JAMES DURKIN WINE & LIQUORS**		
	Wholesale & retail, Durkin Block Mill & Sprague, Spokane, Washington, Telephone Main 731, 32 ounce on front, blob neck, tapered top and ring, amber, 11⅜"	14.00	19.00
☐ 257	**DYOTTVILLE GLASS WORKS, PHILA**		
	On bottom, gloppy graduated and flared lip, round, green, quart, 11½"	17.00	23.00
☐ 258	**DYOTTVILLE GLASS WORKS, PHILA.**		
	Green, 6½"	45.00	60.00
☐ 259	**DYOTTVILLE, GASS WORKS PHILA**		
	All in a circle, under bottom, tapered and ring top, black, 11½"	35.00	48.00

E

☐ 260	**EAGLE LIQUEUR DISTILLERIES**		
	Olive, 7¾"	47.00	60.00
☐ 261	**NATIONAL'S EAGLE BLENDED WHISKEY**		
	Label, light amber, 4½"	5.00	8.00
☐ 262	**F.H. EARL, SPRING ST., NEWTON N.J.**		
	Full Qt. on shoulder, light green, 7½"	6.00	9.00

201   218

252

359

266

254

278

269   378   288

294

☐ 263	**EDGEMONT WHISKEY BLEND**		
	Label, The I. Trager Co., Cincinnati, Ohio, clear, 8"	11.00	15.00
☐ 264	**EDGEWOOD**		
	In gold lettering, clear, quart, 11"	18.00	26.00
☐ 265	**EDGEWOOD**		
	Panels on shoulders and base, clear or amethyst, 11" ...	18.00	26.00
☐ 266	**WEISS EICHOLD LIQUOR CO.**		
	Sheared top, 3 dots on bottom, clear or amethyst, 7"	8.00	11.00
☐ 267	**ELK RUN BR'G CO. PUNX'Y, PA.**		
	Golden amber, 9½"	8.00	11.00
☐ 268	**ELIXIR DE GULLIE**		
	In center G all in seal, dip mold, sheer top, applied ring, deep kick-up, green, 6½"	60.00	80.00
☐ 269	**ERIE CLUB**		
	Clear or amethyst, quart or fifth, 11"	13.00	18.00
☐ 270	**ESSENCE OF JAMAICA**		
	Label, clear or amethyst, 5"	7.00	10.00
☐ 271	Same as above except 7½"	12.00	16.00
☐ 272	**N.J. ETHRIDGE**		
	Macon, Ga., pure old Winchester rye whiskey, label, clear, 6½"	13.00	18.00
☐ 273	**EUREKA**		
	Clear or amethyst, 7¾"	7.00	10.00
☐ 274	**EVERETT-LIQUOR CO., EVERETT, WASH.**		
	All in a circle, applied ring top, amber, 11"	30.00	40.00
☐ 275	**EVANS & O'BRIEN**		
	1870 Stockton, amber or green	120.00	165.00

F

☐ 276	**FARMVILLE DISPENSARY, FARMVILLE, VA.**		
	In a circle, REGISTERED FULL PINT, ring collar, and below it tapered ring top, clear or amethyst	13.00	18.00
☐ 277	**FARMVILLE DISPENSARY, FARMVILLE, VA.** **REGISTERED FULL PINT**		
	Clear, pint flask, 8"	11.00	15.00
☐ 278	**FARRELL**		
	A Merry Christmas and a Happy New Year, label, sheared top, clear or amethyst, 4½"	13.00	18.00
☐ 279	**FRED FERRIS, ELMIRA, N.Y.**		
	Amber, 6¾"	10.00	15.00
☐ 280	**JOHN F. FITZGERALD WHISKEY**		
	Clear or amethyst, quart	10.00	15.00
☐ 281	Same as above except ½ pint	10.00	15.00
☐ 282	**FLEMING'S**		
	Bottled Expressly For Family & Medicinal Purposes in back, 1 Qt. on side, clear or amethyst, 8½"	23.00	30.00
☐ 283	**FOCKINR, WYNARD, AMSTERDAM**		
	All under bottom, sheer top and applied ring, black, 9½".	32.00	42.00
☐ 284	**JAMES FOX**		
	Full under bottom, clear or amethyst, 9½"	21.00	28.00

☐285 **FRAIELLT BRANCA, MILANO**
In crude blob seal on shoulder, two ring collar, turn mold,
green, 14" 13.00   18.00
☐286 **THE PURDUE FREDERICK CO, NEW YORK**
Inside of oval circle, PF CO. monogram in center, oval
flask, amethyst, pint, 8" 6.00   9.00
☐287 **FRIEDMAN KEILER & CO**
Distillers and Wholesale Liquor Dealers, Paducah, Ky., 1
under bottom, amber, 12" 11.00   16.00
☐288 **FRIEDMAN KEILER & SON**
Amber, 12" 11.00   16.00
☐289 **JOS FUHRER & SONS**
3701 Butler Street, Pittsburgh, Pa., tapered top, clear or
amethyst, 9½" 12.00   18.00

G

☐290 **GAELIC OLD SMUGGLER**
On bottom, round, square and ring collar, fat neck, olive
green, quart, 10" 10.00   15.00
☐291 **GAGLE GLEN WHISKEY**
29 Market Street, San Francisco, Werle & Willow 60.00   80.00
☐292 **GAHN, BELT & CO.**
Clear or amethyst, 8" 6.00   9.00
☐293 **GANNYMEDE**
Amber, 7½" 7.00   10.00
☐294 **GARRETT & CO.**
Established In 1835 on top, in center eagle and shield with
American Wines, on each side of it St. Louis, Mo., Norfolk,
Va., at bottom Registered Trade Mark, Refilling Pro-
hibited, fancy, clear or amethyst, quart, 12" 7.00   10.00
☐295 *Same as above except amber* 15.00   22.00
☐296 *Same as above except sample with Norfolk, Va., 4¾"* ... 7.00   10.00
☐297 **GARRETT & CO.**
Two types: crown top—14", applied top—12", clear or
amethyst, 14" 6.00   9.00
☐298 *12"* 8.00   11.00
☐299 **GARRETT & CO.**
Clear, 6½" 6.00   9.00
☐300 **GELLERT, J.M.**
In center 230 Washington St., Portland, Oregon, bulb neck
and applied tapered top, amber, 10¾" 70.00   90.00
☐301 **C.R. GIBSON, SALAMANCA, NEW YORK**
In shield, amber, pint 11.00   15.00
☐302 **OLD JOE GIDEON WHISKEY**
Amber, 11½" 35.00   47.00
☐303 **OLD JOE GIDEON**
Amber, ½ pint 9.00   12.00
☐304 **GILBERT BROS. & CO. BALTIMORE, MD**
On front, oval, graduated collar and ring, thick glass,
aqua, pint, 8¼" 8.00   11.00

☐305 **H & A GILBEY LTD.**
Aqua, 12" 5.00   8.00
☐306 **J.A. GILKA**
Vertically, J.A. GILKA/BERLIN vertically on side, THIS
BOTTLE D vertically on corner panel, NOT TO BE SOLD on
corner panel, SCHUTZEN STR. NO. 9 on side, graduated
collar and ring, light amber, quart, 9¾" 25.00 32.00
☐307 **J.A. GILKA BERLIN**
On side, J.A. GILKA on back, SCHUTZEN STR. NO. 9 on
opposite side, same as above except embossing, gloppy
collar, red amber, quart, 9¾" 25.00 32.00
☐308 **W. GILMORE & SON, PAVILION, N.Y.**
Kick-up, teal blue, 10¼" 13.00 18.00
☐309 **GINOCCHIO & CO.**
In center Importers 287 - First St. in two lines, Portland, all
in a circle, pumpkin seed flask, clear, pt. 110.00 135.00
☐310 **GLENBROOK DISTILLING CO/BOSTON, MASS**
Vertically, oval flask, aqua, ½ pint, 6¾" 9.00 13.00
☐311 **GLENBROOK**
On bottom, flask, amber, ½ pint 7.00 10.00
☐312 *Same as above except aqua* 6.00   9.00
☐313 **THE GLENDALE CO.**
Three-part mold, clear or amethyst, 12" 11.00 15.00
☐314 **I. GOLDBERG DISTILLER**
Five panels, clear, 13¼" 12.00 17.00
☐315 **I. GOLDBERG**
On one panel, next panel 171E Broadway, next Houston or
Clinton St., 5th Ave. cor, 115th St, next New York City,
Brooklyn, next Graham Ave. cor. Debevoise St. Pitkin cor.
Rockaway Ave., three panels blank for label, under bot-
tom different number, on shoulder I. Goldberg and Est.
1873, 12¼" 27.00 36.00
☐316 **I. GOLDBERG**
On one panel, next Distiller, next 171-E Broadway, next
Houston cor Clinton St., next 5th Ave cor 115th St New
York City, three panels blank for label, plain shoulder,
amber, 12¼" 18.00 25.00
☐317 **I. GOLDBERG**
Vertically on one panel, 171 E. BROADWAY on next,
Houston Cor Clinton St. 5th Ave. cor 115th St. on next
panel Gram Cor Debevoise Pitkin cor Rockaway Ave, on
next panel, eight large vertical panels, graduated collar,
amber, quart, 12½" 37.00 46.00
☐318 **GOLDEN & CO. SAN FRANCISCO, CAL.**
Inside of circle, Net Contents One Quart Full Measure on
front, round, graduated collar and ring, amber, 11¾" 22.00 29.00
☐319 **GOLDEN CREAM 1878 WHISKEY**
Weiss Echold Liquor Co., Mobile, Ala., Proprietors, clear
or amethyst, 8½" 10.00 15.00
☐320 **GOLDEN CREAM**
Seven panels, clear, fifth 11.00 16.00
☐321 **GOLDEN GATE CO. BALTIMORE CELERY RYE**
Pat. Apl. For under bottom, clear, quart 7.00 10.00
☐322 *Same as above except amethyst* 7.00 10.00

297

299

HONEST MEASURE
Lovsett-Williams
BALTIMORE, U.S.A.

GARRETT & CO.
REGISTERED
TRADE MARK
REFILLING PUNISHED
BY LAW

303

OLD
JOE GIDEON
WHISKEY
AWARDED
GOLD MEDALS
ST LOUIS 1904
PORTLAND ORE 1905

302

JOE GIDEON WHISKEY
AWARDED GOLD MEDALS
ST LOUIS 1904
PORTLAND ORE.

305

H & G TILLEY
LTD

326

Gold Thimble
Scotch Whisky

313

THE CLENEAL
JACKSONVILLE

335

S. CRABFELDER & CO.
DISTILLERS
LOUISVILLE,
KY.

336

S. CRABFELDER & Co.
DISTILLERS
LOUISVILLE
KY

314

I. COLDBERG
DISTILLER

337

S. CRABFELDER & CO.
DISTILLERS
LOUISVILLE,
K.Y.

338

S. CRABFELDER & CO.
DISTILLERS
LOUISVILLE, KY.

350

GUARANTEED
FULL
½ PINT 8 OZ

☐ 323 **GOLDEN HILL**
On base, #2 under bottom, two ring top, amber, 4½" **10.00** **15.00**

☐ 324 **GOLDEN WEDDING**
Jos. S. Fench & Co. Schenley Pa, label, whiskey sample,
4" **10.00** **15.00**

☐ 325 **GOLDIE-KLENERT CO, STOCKTON, CAL**
In slug plate, graduated collar, round, clear, quart, 11¼" . **7.00** **10.00**

☐ 326 **GOLD THIMBLE SCOTCH WHISKEY**
Blck Bros Glasgow, pinch bottle, amber, 8½" **22.00** **30.00**

☐ 327 **GOLDTREE BROS**
In slug plate, 1880, San Luis, amber, quart **330.00** **410.00**

☐ 328 **MORRIS T. GOMBERT, HOUSTON**
Clear or amethyst, 6" **10.00** **15.00**

☐ 329 **GEO. H. GOODMAN**
B on bottom, clear or amethyst, fifth **9.00** **13.00**

☐ 330 **GORDONS DRY GIN, LONDON, ENGLAND**
Square with wide beveled corners, boar on bottom, graduated and flared collar, aqua, quart, 8⅝" ......,...... **7.00** **10.00**

☐ 331 Same as above except oval back, old **5.00** **8.00**

☐ 332 Same as above except ABM **5.00** **8.00**

☐ 333 **G.P.R.**
Whiskey label, clear or amethyst, 7½" **5.00** **8.00**

☐ 334 **G.P.R.**
Baltimore G. Gump & Sons on shoulder, clear, 10¾" **10.00** **15.00**

☐ 335 **S. GRABFELDER & CO.**
I on bottom, amber, 5¾" **6.00** **9.00**

☐ 336 **S. GRABFELDER & CO.**
99A on bottom, amber, 7" **8.00** **11.00**

☐ 337 **S. GRABFELDER & CO.**
J on bottom, amber, 7¼" **9.00** **12.00**

☐ 338 **S. GRABFELDER & CO.**
Clear or amethyst, 6" **5.00** **8.00**

☐ 339 **GRAFFING & CO. N.Y.**
Under bottom, boy and girl climbing trees, clear, 12¼" .. **27.00** **35.00**

☐ 340 **C.E. GRANGER, WINE & LIQUORS, SUNBURY, OHIO**
Double collar, bottom—AMF & CO., clear, ½ pint, 6½" .. **12.00** **17.00**

☐ 341 **C.E. GRANGER, WINES & LIQUORS**
Double collar, flask, under bottom—AMF & CO. warranted
full measure, clear, ½ pint, 6½" **11.00** **15.00**

☐ 342 **E.E. GRAY & CO/IMPORTERS/BOSTON, MASS**
Vertically, Full Quart Registered on back, round,
graduated collar, seven rings, amethyst, quart, 12½" **11.00** **15.00**

☐ 343 **GREAT SEAL STYRON BEGGS & CO. NEWARK O**
Clear or amethyst, 6" **6.00** **9.00**

☐ 344 **GREAT SEAL**
Clear or amethyst, 6" **5.00** **8.00**

☐ 345 **GREEN & CLARK MISSOURI CIDER**
Registered, Aug. 27, 1878 in vertical lines under bottom, A
B & M Co., blob top, amber, 9½" **14.00** **19.00**

☐ 346 **GREENBRIER WHISKEY**
Label, The Old Spring Distilling Company, Cincinnati, H2
under bottom, clear, 11" **6.00** **9.00**

☐ 347 **B.S. GREIL & CO, CINCINNATI, OHIO**
Clear or amethyst, pint **7.00** **10.00**

□348 **THE GRIM REAPER**
Sandemong Cherry Black on back, Royal Doulton China under bottom, black, 10½" 30.00 40.00

□349 **GUARANTEED** *on ribbon,* **FULL PINT** *under ribbon at top, Graduated collar with ring, rectangular, 8¾"* 6.00 9.00

□350 **GUARANTEED FULL**
Amber, 6½" 7.00 10.00

□351 **GUITAR WHISKEY**
Label, amber, 15" 11.00 15.00

H

□352 **H**
On bottom, whiskey label, clear or amethyst, 6½" 4.00 6.00

□353 **L. HAAS & CO. TOLEDO, O.**
Label, horseshoe seal, clear, 12½" 6.00 9.00

□354 **HAIG & HAIG**
Clear, 8" 7.00 10.00

□355 *Same as above except amber* 14.00 19.00

□356 **HALL, LUHRS & CO. SACRAMENTO**
Monogram on the front pumpkin seed, amethyst, 6¾" ... 16.00 23.00

□357 *Ham on shoulder, shape of a whole ham, screw top, sheared top, amber, 6¼" tall, 3½" wide* 34.00 45.00

□358 *Handled whiskey jug, Chestnut type, amber, 7⅞"* 21.00 29.00

□359 **HANDMADE SOUR MASH**
Clear, 4½" 7.00 10.00

□360 *Same as above except amber* 11.00 15.00

□361 **HANNIS DISTLG CO.**
Pat April 1890 under bottom, amber, 8¾" 14.00 19.00

□362 **I.W. HARPER**
With like-new wicker, name shows through window in wicker, graduated collar, light amber, quart, 9¾" 27.00 39.00

□363 **I.W. HARPER**
Medal Whiskey in center; gold on front, anchor in gold, rope around neck, 3" pottery, very light tan, 4" square tapering to 3½" on shoulder 35.00 47.00

□364 **I.W. HARPER**
Whiskey, amber, 9½" 13.00 18.00

□365 **I.W. HARPER**
Clear or amethyst, 4" 16.00 23.00

□366 **ADOLPH HARRIS AND CO.**
San Francisco, amber, quart 28.00 38.00

□367 **ANDOLPH HARRIS & CO.** *(deer head)* **SAN FRANCISCO**
Cylindrical, amber, fifth 85.00 110.00

□368 **ALBERT H. HARRIS N.Y.**
Label, turn mold, amber, quart 7.00 10.00

□369 **HARVARD RYE**
With interlocking **HR**, *inside of rectangle, slug plate, vertical panels on neck and shoulder, fancy, graduated collar, round, amethyst, quart, 12"* 7.00 10.00

□370 **HARVARD RYE**
With interlocking **HR** *monogram in center, rectangular, double band collar, heavy glass, clear, pint, 7½"* 7.00 10.00

☐371	**HARVARD RYE**		
	Clear or amethyst, 7½"	**10.00**	**15.00**
☐372	**THE HAYNER DISTILLING CO.**		
	Dayton, Ohio & St. Louis Mo. Distillers, W on bottom, also Nov. 30th 1897, Whiskey, amethyst, 11½"	**12.00**	**17.00**
☐373	**THE HAYNER DISTILLING CO., DAYTON, ST. LOUIS, ATLANTA, ST. PAUL, DISTILLERS**		
	Design Patented Nov. 30th, 1897 under bottom, amber, 11½"	**10.00**	**15.00**
☐374	**HAYNER RICH PRIVATE STOCK PURE WHISKEY**		
	In back H.W. Distillers, Troy, Ohio, under bottom, Distillers, Pat. Nov 30th, 1897-F, clear, 11½"	**8.00**	**11.00**
☐375	**THE HAYNER WHISKEY DISTILLERS, TROY, OHIO**		
	Designed Patented Nov. 30th, 1897 on bottom, fluting around base 1" high, also on shoulder and neck, graduated collar and ring, round, ABM, clear, quart, 11½"	**7.00**	**10.00**
☐376	**HAYNER WHISKEY DISTILLERY, TROY O.**		
	Lower trunk and paneled shoulder, Nov. 30th 1897, F on bottom, round, amethyst	**12.00**	**17.00**
☐377	**HAYNERS DISTILLING CO., DAYTON, OHIO, USA, DISTILLERS & IMPORTERS**		
	In circle, design patented Nov. 30th, 1897 on bottom, 14 fancy vertical panels on shoulder and neck, 14 vertical 1" panels around base, graduated collar and ring, amethyst, liter, 12"	**7.00**	**10.00**
☐378	**W.H. HECKENDORN & CO.**		
	Label, 2 under bottom, three-part mold, golden amber, 12"	**9.00**	**12.00**
☐379	**EDWARD HEFFERMAN** *in center,* **REG. FULL PINT** *at top,* **8 PORTLAND ST. BOSTON, MASS**		
	All on front in slug plate, rectangular, light green, pint, 8½"	**5.00**	**8.00**
☐380	**W.H. HENNESSEY, 38 TO 44 ANDREW ST., LYNN, MASS**		
	Vertically, slug plate, rectangular, graduated collar and ring, amethyst, ½ pint, 6¾"	**7.00**	**10.00**
☐381	**HERE'S A SMILE TO THOSE I LOVE**		
	Clear, 5½"	**13.00**	**18.00**
☐382	**HERE'S A SMILE TO THOSE I LOVE**		
	Clear or amethyst, 5½"	**17.00**	**23.00**
☐383	**HERE'S HOPING—**		
	Clear, 8"	**10.00**	**15.00**
☐384	**HEWONTS SQUEAL**		
	Hog bottle	**30.00**	**42.00**
☐385	**HIGHCLIFF WHISKEY CINI O**		
	Label amber, ½ pint	**6.00**	**9.00**
☐386	**HOCK WINE**		
	Label sheared top and ring, red ground pontil, mold, 14" .	**18.00**	**25.00**
☐387	*Same as above except old teal blue, 11½"*	**7.00**	**10.00**
☐388	*Same as above except old teal blue, 14"*	**9.00**	**12.00**
☐389	*Same as above except old red amber, 11½"*	**5.00**	**8.00**
☐390	*Same as above except old light amber, 7"*	**7.00**	**10.00**
☐391	*Same as above except old ABM light amber, 14"*	**5.00**	**8.00**
☐392	*Same as above except old ABM green, 13½"*	**4.00**	**6.00**

☐393 **HOFHEIMER'S EAGLE RYE BLEND**
M. HOFHEIMER & CO. NORFOLK, VA.
(Large eagle embossed on shield) rectangular, clear, ½
pint, 6" 7.00 10.00
☐394 **HOFHEMIER'S EAGLE RYE BLEND**
Clear or amethyst, 6" 6.00 9.00
☐395 **HOLBERG MERCANTILE CO.**
Amber, 11" 12.00 17.00
☐396 **HOLLANDS**
In gold letters around it gold circle glass top with H fan-
cy, 9½ " 45.00 60.00
☐397 **HOLLYWOOD WHISKEY**
Round, graduated collar and ring, amber, quart, 11" 10.00 15.00
☐398 *Same as above except golden amber* 25.00 34.00
☐399 **HOLLYWOOD WHISKEY**
Amber, 12" 11.00 15.00
☐400 **HOLLYWOOD WHISKEY**
Kick-up, amber, 11¼ " 11.00 15.00
☐401 **HOLTON, CHAS. F.**
In center in hollow letters Hover lap C., Olympia, W.T., all
in a circle Shoo Fly Flask, pt., clear, ring top 135.00 165.00
☐402 **HOME SUPPLY CO.**
Wine label three-part mold, amber, 11¼ " 7.00 10.00
☐403 **HOME SUPPLY CO.**
Whiskey label three-part mold, amber, 11¼ " 7.00 10.00
☐404 **HONEST MEASURE**
Clear, 4¾ " 8.00 11.00
☐405 **HONEST MEASURE**
half pint on shoulder saddle flask, amber, ½ pint 7.00 10.00
☐406 *Same as above except clear* 4.00 6.00
☐407 *Same as above except clear, pint* 6.00 9.00
☐408 **W. HONEY GLASS WORKS**
Under bottom amber, 7½ " 25.00 34.00
☐409 **HOTALING CO. THE A.P.**
In center a crown, under it Portland, Or., sole agents all in
a watermellow circle, applied top, amber, 11" 225.00 285.00
☐410 **HOTEL DONNELLY, TACOMA, (MINIATURE)**
3", Pu top, clear 18.00 24.00
☐411 **HOTEL WORTH BAR, FORT WORTH TEXAS**
Inside screw, amber, 6" 85.00 105.00
☐412 **HUBER KUEMMEL LIQUEUR, B.S. FLERSHEIM MERC.**
CO.
Label amber, 10" 13.00 18.00
☐413 **H.W. HUGULEY CO., 134 CANAL ST. BOSTON**
Full Quart on back round, graduated collar and ring,
amethyst, 12" 10.00 15.00
☐414 **H.W. HUGULEY CO.**
Clear or amethyst, 11¾ " 10.00 15.00
☐415 **HURDLE RYE**
Clear panels, neck, letters etched, 3" 9.00 12.00

I

☐416 **IMPERIAL DISTILLING CO.**
Kansas City, Mo. in center IDCO fancy shoulder, clear, 4"
.... 11.00   15.00
☐417 **IMPERIAL**
In ribbon pint on back in ribbon oval, aqua, 9" 6.00   9.00
☐418 **IMPERIAL**
In back aqua, ½ pint, 7¾" 17.00   24.00
☐419 **IMPERIAL WEDDING WHISKEY BLEND**
Label clear or amethyst, 8" and other sizes 9.00   12.00
☐420 **IMPORTERS**
Vertically flask, clear, ½ pint, 6½" 8.00   11.00
☐421 **G. INNSEN & SONS, PITTSBURGH**
Under bottom green, quart 16.00   23.00

J

☐422 **JACK CRANSTON'S DIODORA CORN WHISKEY**
Jack Cranston Co., Baltimore, Md. in back U blank seal
clear, 12" 13.00   18.00
☐423 **JACK DANIEL'S GOLD MEDAL OLD NO. 7**
Clear, 7¾' 22.00   29.00
☐424 **JAMES BUCHANAN & CO. LTD.**
½ ring on each side 106 under bottom dark green, 7¼" . 17.00   24.00
☐425 **JESSE MOORE-HUNT CO.**
Amber, 11¾" 10.00   15.00
☐426 **J.M. & CO. BOSTON, MASS**
In slug plate oval flask, aqua, 10" 8.00   11.00
☐427 **JOHANN MARIA FARINA NO. 4, JULICRSPLATZ NO. 4**
Clear or amethyst, 4" 8.00   11.00
☐428 **JOHN HART & CO.**
On each side amber, 7¼" 33.00   41.00
☐428 **W.L. JOHNSON KENTUCKY**
Pontil, amber, 8¼" 75.00   95.00
☐429 **W.H. JONES & CO. ESTABLISHED 1851 IMPORTERS/**
HANOVER AND/BLACKSTONE STS/BOSTON, MASS
(Shield with bear) all on front flask, light green slug plate,
pint, 8¾" 17.00   24.00
☐430 **W.H. JONES AND CO.**
Clear, 9½" 13.00   18.00
☐431 *JUG, round base, bulbous neck, light green, gallon, 5¾"*
across, 13½" 19.00   27.00
☐432 **L.E. JUNG & CO, PURE MALT WHISKEY,**
NEW ORLEANS, LA.
Amber, 10¾" 13.00   19.00
☐433 **J & W HARDIE EDINBURGH**
On bottom three-piece mold, large square collar, emerald
green, 10¼" 8.00   11.00
☐434 **J&W.N. & CO.**
Under bottom aqua, 11" 7.00   10.00
☐435 *Same as above except clear, 10"* 5.00   8.00

K

☐ 436 **KANE, O'LEARY & CO.**
In center 221 & 223, under it Bush St. S.F., inside of square box enclosing, tapered top and ring, amber, 12" 170.00 230.00

☐ 437 **KELLY & KERR**
222 College St., Springfield, Mo., C.W. Stuart's, machine made, clear, amber or aqua, quart 6.00 9.00

☐ 438 **KELLY & KERR**
222 College St., Springfield, Mo., machine made, clear or aqua 4.00 6.00

☐ 439 **KENTUCKY GEM, S.M. COPPER DISTILLERS, WHISKEY**
T.G. Cockrill, San Francisco, quart 8.00 12.00

☐ 440 **KEYSTONE BURGUNDY**
Tapered top, amber, 8¾" 40.00 60.00

☐ 441 **KEYSTONE**
Whiskey label, clear or amethyst, 7½" 13.00 18.00

☐ 442 **KING BEE**
Ten panels, clear, 11¾" 17.00 24.00

☐ 422 **KIRBY'S**
243 College St., Springfield, Mo., 1870, quart, clear or aqua 10.00 15.00

☐ 444 **H.B. KIRK & CO.**
Amber, 11⅛" 13.00 18.00

☐ 445 **REMAINS THE PROPERTY OF H.B. KIRK & CO., N.Y.**
On back, three Indian heads embossed in circle on shoulder, trademark in ribbon, Registered U.S. on front, graduated collar and ring, round, amber, quart, 11¼" 17.00 23.00

☐ 446 **HENRY KLINKER, JR.**
The Owl, 748-10th ave., SE corner 51st Street, N.Y. in circle under it; Full Measure; double collar; under bottom LCMG, 182 Fulton Street, N.Y.; amber, 1½ pint 20.00 30.00

☐ 447 **C.F. KNAPP, PHILADELPHIA**
Pig slope, clear or amethyst, 3¼" x 2" 33.00 42.00

L

☐ 448 **CHATEAU LAFIETE 1896**
In circle, blob seal on shoulder, crude band collar, kick-up, green, 12" 9.00 12.00

☐ 449 **LAKE DRUMMOND PURE RYE, J & E MAHONEY**
Rectangular, clear, ½ pint, 6½" 7.00 10.00

☐ 450 **LAKE KEUKA VINTAGE CO., BATH, NEW YORK WINERY NO. 25**
Same shape and design as a Hayner Whiskey, graduated collar and ring, amethyst, 12" 9.00 12.00

☐ 451 **LAMBE & DENMARKE FINE WHISKEY**
Arkansas City, Ark., under bottom, L.C. & R CO., tapered top and ring, fancy bottom, clear or aqua, 8" 25.00 34.00

☐ 452 **LANGERT WINE CO.**
422 - Sprague Ave. Spokane, Wash. all in a circle, applied ring top, amethyst and clear, qt. 12.00 17.00

☐453 **JOHN LATREYTE**
Under bottom C. Pat'd, April 1, '84, clear or aqua, 7¼" ... **12.00** **17.00**

☐454 **LEIPPS**
In script, Chicago, tapered top, amber, 4½" **11.00** **15.00**

☐455 **LILIENTHAL, CINCINNATI, SAN FRANCISCO &**
NEW YORK, 1885
Yellow amber **160.00** **210.00**

☐456 **LILIENTHAL DISTILLERS**
Coffin type with crown, amber **160.00** **210.00**

☐457 **LICKING VALLEY CO.**
Clear, quart size **10.00** **15.00**

☐458 **LONE CREEK**
Amber, 11½" **17.00** **23.00**

☐459 **LOS ANGELES CO., 51 & 53 SUMMER ST.,**
BOSTON, MASS., LA CO.
Monogram, flask, ring collar, amethyst, ½ pint **7.00** **10.00**

☐460 **LOUISVILLE, KY. GLASS WORKS**
Aqua, 8¾" **60.00** **85.00**

☐461 **LYNDEBORS**
L.G. CO. on base, cylindrical, honey amber **27.00** **36.00**

☐462 **LYONS, E.Y. AND RAAS**
San Francisco, California, cylindrical, clear or amethyst . **14.00** **19.00**

M

☐463 **MACKENZIE & CO. FINE TAWNY PORT, MEDAL OF**
HONOR S.F. 1915
Label on front and back, round and flared band collar,
slight bulbous neck, emerald green, 11½" **9.00** **12.00**

☐464 **JOS MAGNUS & CO.**
Embossed dragon and CINCINNATI, OHIO, rectangular,
square collar, clear, ½ pint, 6" **6.00** **9.00**

☐465 **JOS. A. MAGNUS & CO.**
Clear or amethyst, 6½" **7.00** **10.00**

☐466 **J & E MAHONEY DISTILLERS, PORTSMOUTH AND**
ALEXANDRIA, VA.
Rectangular, flask, clear, 6¼" **7.00** **10.00**

☐467 **MAILHOUSE RYE**
Clear or amethyst, 8¼" **90.00** **120.00**

☐468 **MALLARD DISTILLING CO., BALTIMORE AND NEW**
YORK,
PATENT APPLIED FOR
Sunken sides, ½ pint, 6¼" **12.00** **17.00**

☐469 **MALLARD DISTILLING CO.**
Clear or amethyst, pint **4.00** **6.00**

☐470 **MAN'S FACE FIGURAL WHISKEY BOTTLE; label, clear or**
amethyst, 7½" **30.00** **42.00**

☐471 **ISAAC MANSBACH & CO.**
In a dome shaped line, under it, Fine Whiskeys,
Philadelphia, square, flat collar, ring, amber, quart **17.00** **24.00**

☐472 **ISAAC MANSBACH & CO.**
Philadelphia other side, Millionaires Club Whiskey around
shoulder, amber, 4¾" **13.00** **18.00**

☐473	**ISAAC MANSBACH & CO.**		
	In back, Millionaire Club on shoulder, amber, 4½"	10.00	15.00
☐474	**THE J.G. MARK'S LIQUOR CO. WHOLESALE**		
	On back, clear or amethyst, 9"	22.00	29.00
☐475	**THE J.G. MARKS LIQUOR CO.**		
	Three barrels trademark in back, clear or amethyst, 9¼" .	22.00	29.00
☐476	*MARRIAGE BOTTLE, crock, black, white, blue, tan, 8¾"* .	40.00	55.00
☐477	**MARTINI COCKTAILS, FOR MARTINI COCKTAILS USE ONLY MARTINI VERMOUTHS**		
	Champagne shaped, sand blasted or etched lettering, ABM, green, 12½"	6.00	9.00
☐478	**MAY & FAIRALL GROCERS, BALTIMORE**		
	Three-piece mold, slug plate, amber, quart, 11¼"	13.00	18.00
☐479	**MAYSE BROS. DISTILLERS RYE**		
	With seal, clear or amethyst, 10"	40.00	55.00
☐480	**McAVDY BREW CO.**		
	Amber, 8½"	6.00	9.00
☐481	**McDONALD & COHN**		
	San Francisco, Cal., amber, quart	17.00	23.00
☐482	**McHENRY**		
	Amber, 10"	11.00	15.00
☐483	**McKNIGHTS**		
	Amber, 10½"	13.00	18.00
☐484	*Same as above except clear, 9¼"*	10.00	15.00
☐485	**JOHN A. McLAREN**		
	In center, PERTH MALT WHISKEY, PERTH, ONT, saddle flask, 193 under bottom, two-ring top, 8"	13.00	18.00
☐486	**Mc. LAUGHLIN H.**		
	In center The Magnolia, San Nateo all in a circle, double ring top, picnic flask, clear, 5¼"	33.00	42.00
☐487	**MERIDITH'S CLUB PURE RYE WHISKEY**		
	East Liverpool, Ohio, white, 7¼"	13.00	18.00
☐488	**MERRY CHRISTMAS HAPPY NEW YEAR**		
	Quilted back, sheared top, clear, 6"	28.00	37.00
☐489	**MERRY CHRISTMAS & HAPPY NEW YEAR**		
	In center, clear or amethyst, 5"	17.00	23.00
☐490	**MERRY CHRISTMAS & HAPPY NEW CENTURY**		
	In back a watch with Roman letters and B I Co in center, pocket watch type, milk glass	22.00	29.00
☐491	*MEXICAN DRINKING BOTTLE, clear, 10" tall, 7" round* ..	11.00	15.00
☐492	**MEYER PITTS & CO.**		
	Clear or amethyst, 6"	4.00	6.00
☐493	**H. MICHELSEN**		
	In center, on top Bay Rum, under it St. Thomas, clear or a.nethyst, fifth	6.00	9.00
☐494	**I. MICHELSON & BROS.**		
	Clear or amethyst, 11"	16.00	23.00
☐495	**MIDLAND HOTEL**		
	Kansas City, Mo., panels on neck, clear, 3"	7.00	10.00
☐496	*MILK GLASS, 7¼"*	32.00	43.00
☐497	**J.A. MILLER, HOUSTON, TEXAS**		
	Clear or amethyst, ½ pint	10.00	15.00

☐498	MONK LABEL, amber, 10"	50.00	65.00
☐499	MONOGRAM No. 6, clear, 8¼"	85.00	110.00
☐500	**M & M T CO.**		
	Clear or amethyst, 3¼"	6.00	9.00
☐501	**J. MOORE OLD BOURBON**		
	Amber, 12"	60.00	80.00
☐502	**J. MOORE**		
	Amber, 11"	60.00	80.00
☐503	**JESSE MOORE & CO. LOUISVILLE, KY.**		
	Ringdeer Trade Mark, Bourbon & Rye, Moore Hunt & Co., sole agents, flask, amber	160.00	210.00
☐504	**JESSE MOORE & CO. LOUISVILLE, KY.**		
	Outer circle, C.H. MOORE BOURBON & RYE center, JESSE MOORE HUNT CO./SAN FRANCISCO at base, graduated collar and ring, quart, 11½"	75.00	95.00
☐505	Same as above except golden amber, 11¾"	75.00	95.00
☐506	**G.T. MORRIS**		
	A bunch of flowers on back, amber, 12"	160.00	210.00
☐507	MOSES IN BULRUSH, clear or amethyst, 5"	35.00	47.00
☐508	**MOUNT VERNON**		
	Machine made, amber, 8¼"	10.00	15.00
☐509	**MOUNT VERNON PURE RYE WHISKEY**		
	In three lines, back Hannis Dist'l'G Co., Full Five in two lines, two more lines Re-Use of Bottle Prohibited, under bottom Patented March 25 1890, amber, 3¼" square, neck 4", 4¼"	16.00	23.00
☐510	Same as above except sample, 3¼"	16.00	23.00
☐511	Same as above except machine made	4.00	6.00
☐512	**MULFORD'S DISTILLED MALT EXTRACT**		
	Embossed, J.F. Mulford & Co., chemists, Philadelphia, amber, 8¾"	6.00	8.00
☐513	**MUNRO, DALUHINNIL, SCOTLAND**		
	Reuse of bottle prohibited in 5 lines on front in back, House of Lords, whiskey, 2½" x 2½" square, blob neck, double ring top, improved pontil, dr. aqua, 12½"	33.00	41.00
☐514	**MURPHY THE**		
	In center Wine & Liquor Co., 308-310-Pike St., Seattle, Wash. all in a circle, applied ring top, amber, qt.	55.00	75.00
☐515	**MURRAY HILL MARYLAND RYE**		
	Sherbrook Distilling Co., Cincinnati, label, clear or amethyst, 6"	8.00	11.00
☐516	**JOHN MURRAY (JM) RYE WHISKEY**		
	Label only, flask, amber, ½ pint, 7"	6.00	9.00
☐517	**ANGELO MYERS**		
	Clear or amethyst, 6¼"	7.00	10.00
☐518	**H.C. MYERS COMPANY/NEW YORK, N.Y./AND/COVINGTON, KY., GUARANTEED FULL ½ PINT**		
	All on front, flask, amethyst, 6⅜"	7.00	10.00

N

☐519	**NEALS AMB PHTH**		
	In seal on shoulder, cobalt blue, 9⅛"	70.00	100.00

☐ 520 **NEWMAN'S COLLEGE**
San Francisco and Oakland, round like football, amber,
4¼" **22.00** **29.00**
☐ 521 **NIXON & CO. J.C.**
In center Seattle, W.T. all in a circle, flask, amber, ½ pt. ... **130.00** **160.00**

O

☐ 522 **O'HARE MALT, H. ROSENTHAL & SONS**
#1 under bottom, amber, 10¾" **17.00** **23.00**
☐ 523 **O'HEARN'S WHISKEY**
#1919 under bottom, side mold, inside screw, amber,
10¼" **23.00** **32.00**
☐ 524 **OHIO**
Expanded swirl bottle, 24 rib pattern, vertical over swirl to
left, club shaped, deep blue aqua, 7¾" **70.00** **90.00**
☐ 525 **OLD ASHTON**
Clear, 8½" **8.00** **12.00**
☐ 526 **THE OLD BUSHMILLS DISTILLING CO.,**
LIMITED TRADEMARK
Pure malt, established 1734, to 1903, 10" **9.00** **12.00**
☐ 527 *1915 up* **6.00** **9.00**
☐ 528 **OLD CHARTER WHISKEY, LOUISVILLE, KY.**
Label, amber, 11¾" **6.00** **9.00**
☐ 529 **OLD DUFFY'S 1842 APPLE JUICE, VINEGAR**
STERILIZED 5 YEARS
Around shoulder, amber, 10" **8.00** **11.00**
☐ 530 **OLD EDGEMONT WHISKEY**
Label, clear, ½ pint, 6½" **7.00** **10.00**
☐ 531 **OLD EDGEMONT WHISKEY, THE I TRAGER CO.**
CINCINNATI, OHIO
Label, clear, ¼ pint, 5" **7.00** **10.00**
☐ 532 **OLD FAMILY WINE STORE** *(diamond design)*/**ESTABLISH-**
ED
1857/JOS. CLEVE & CO/19821 CAMBRIDGE ST. BOSTON
In slug plate, narrow flask, ring collar, clear, ½ pint, 6½" **8.00** **11.00**
☐ 533 **OLD HENRY RYE**
In script, ring top, clear or aqua, 9½" **10.00** **15.00**
☐ 534 **OLD HUDSON**
Pinch bottle, clear, 6½" **27.00** **35.00**
☐ 535 **OLD IRISH WHISKEY**
(trademark—shield and crown), This Is the property of
Mitchell & Co. of Belfast, Ltd, Imperial Pint, all on front,
flask shape, graduated collar and flared band, ABM, aqua,
9½" **4.00** **6.00**
☐ 536 **OLD IRISH WHISKEY**
Imperial Pint on back, aqua, 10" **17.00** **24.00**
☐ 537 **OLD J.H. CUTTER V.F.O. RYE, LOUISVILLE, KY.**
Label, clear or amethyst, 11" **6.00** **9.00**
☐ 538 **OLD JOE GIDEON WHISKEY BROS.**
F under bottom, 11½" **18.00** **25.00**
☐ 539 **OLD KAINTUCK BOURBON**
Clear, 3¾" **9.00** **12.00**
☐ 540 **THE OLD KENTUCKY CO.**
Clear or amethyst, 11" **11.00** **15.00**

□541	**OLD PORT HALEY WHISKEY**		
	Swope & Mangold, Dallas, Texas, clear or aqua, quart ...	22.00	31.00
□542	**OLD PRENTICE WHISKEY**		
	Label, in back embossed J.T.S. Brown & Sons, Distillers,		
	Louisville, Ky., clear, 11"	6.00	9.00
□543	**OLD QUAKER**		
	1234 under bottom, clear, 6½"	5.00	8.00
□544	**OLD SERVITOR DISTRIBUTING CO. N.Y.**		
	Amber, 11"	6.00	9.00
□545	**THE OLD SPRING DISTILLING CO.**		
	Clear or amethyst, 8½"	7.00	10.00
□546	**OLD SPRING WHISKEY**		
	Clear or amethyst, 9¼"	10.00	15.00
□547	**OLD TIME**		
	First Prize Worlds Fair 1893, clear, 9½"	17.00	23.00
□548	**OPPENHEIM**		
	Fine Whiskey, Atlanta, Ga., amber, 8"	17.00	23.00
□549	**THE ORENE PARKER CO.**		
	Clear or amethyst, 11¼"	10.00	15.00
□550	**E. OTLENVILLE, A.G. D.H. CO.**		
	In back E.O., Nashville, Tenn., tapered top, amber, 9"	22.00	31.00

P

□551	**J.W. PALMER, NELSON COUNTY KY WHISKEY**		
	In four lines, in back Compliments of J.W. Seay, Savan-		
	nah, Ga., pottery jug, with handle, brown and tan, 3"	13.00	19.00
□552	**PARKER RYE**		
	In front of squat bottle, ribs under bottom, six panels on		
	neck, flat top, clear, 1½" neck, 3¼"	6.00	9.00
□553	**PARKER RYE**		
	Six panels, fancy, clear, 1¾" neck, 1½" body	9.00	12.00
□554	**PAROLE**		
	Amber, 10½"	80.00	100.00
□555	**PATENT**		
	On shoulder, three-part mold, round, amber, 10½"	3.00	5.00
□556	**PATENTED APRIL 3d, 1900**		
	At base on concave panel, oval back, two rings on neck,		
	unusual shape, amber, ½ pint, 6½"	5.00	8.00
□557	**PATTERSON'S LIQUOR STORE**		
	Wapakoneta, Ohio, flask, clear, 6½"	11.00	15.00
□558	**PATTERSON'S LIQUOR STORE**		
	Wapakoneta, Ohio in a circle, lined at bottom, clear, 6¼"	13.00	18.00
□559	**PAUL JONES 1908**		
	N8 under bottom, amber, pint	6.00	9.00
□560	**PAUL JONES BOURBON, LOUISVILLE, KY.**		
	In seal, amber, quart	13.00	19.00
□561	**PAUL JONES PURE RYE, LOUISVILLE KY.**		
	On blob seal, round, amber, 9¼"	12.00	16.00
□562	Same as above except WHISKEY	12.00	16.00
□563	Same as above except OLD MONONGAHELA RYE	15.00	21.00

☐564 **PAUL JONES & CO.**
In script on curved 1½" x 3" panel on one side, front and
back of bottle curved, off center neck, light green, 6½" to
top, 4½" to curved shoulder 23.00   32.00

☐565 **PAUL JONES**
(Enameled) ground pontil, clear 27.00   36.00

☐566 **PAUL JONES WHISKEY**
Label, amber, quart 14.00   19.00

☐567 **PAUL JONES WHISKEY**
Amber, 4" 10.00   15.00

☐568 **PAUL JONES & CO.**
718 in diamond shape under bottom, machine made,
amber, 12" 8.00   11.00

☐569 **PAUL JONES 1905**
22 under bottom, amber, 9" 7.00   10.00

☐570 **PAUL JONES PURE GIN, LOUISVILLE KY.**
In seal, green, 9½" 19.00   26.00

☐571 **PAUL JONES PURE RYE, LOUISVILLE, KY.**
In circle, small kick-up, amber, 5¾" 9.00   12.00

☐572 **PEARSONS/PURE OLD/ MALT WHISKEY**
At top, REDDINGTON & CO./PACIFIC COAST AGENTS at
base, round, graduated collar, clear, quart 9.00   12.00

☐573 **PEDRO**
1880, glop top, amber, quart 130.00   160.00

☐574 **S.F. PETTS &
CO./IMPORTERS/BOSTON/U.S.A./REGISTERED**
Horizontally, round, graduated collar and ring, amethyst,
12½" 8.00   11.00

☐575 *PICNIC FLASK or PUMPKIN SEED, there are many different sizes and colors, some embossed, some not* 7.00   10.00

☐576 **S.N. PIKES MAGNOLIA, CINCINNATI, OHIO**
The Fleischman, clear or amethyst, 12¼" 14.00   19.00

☐577 **PIKES PEAK OLD RYE**
Aqua, pint 50.00   65.00

☐578 **PIKESVILLE RYE**
Clear, 4" 6.00   9.00

☐579 *Same as above except Patented under bottom* 7.00   10.00

☐580 **PLANTER RYE, REGISTERED ULLMAN & CO., OHIO**
Amethyst, ½ pint 14.00   19.00

☐581 **PLANTER MARY LOU RYE**
Ullman & Co., Cincinnati, ground top, clear, 5½" 10.00   15.00

☐582 **PLANTER MARY LOU RYE**
Ullman & Co., Cincinnati, clear, 5½" 10.00   15.00

☐583 **POND'S ROCK & RYE WITH HOREHOUND**
R missing in Rock, E missing in Rye, aqua, 10" 17.00   23.00

☐584 **PREACHER WHISKEY**
Curved bottle, 3" round sides, off-center neck, clear or
amethyst, ½ pint, 6½" 24.00   32.00

☐585 **P & SP**
Under bottom, three-part mold, dark olive, 9½" 11.00   15.00

☐586 *Same as above except 11½", pontil* 26.00   34.00

☐587 *PUMPKIN SEED, small, on back and front, sunburst pattern, clear or amethyst, 5"* 18.00   25.00

☐588	*PUMPKIN SEED, plain, clear or amethyst, all sizes*	**9.00**	**12.00**
☐589	*PUMPKIN SEED PICNIC FLASK, double band collar, amethyst, 5½"*	**5.00**	**8.00**
☐590	*PUMPKIN SEED, amethyst, 6"*	**6.00**	**9.00**
☐591	*PUMPKIN SEED, label, amber, 4"*	**17.00**	**23.00**
☐592	*Same as above except dark aqua, 4½"*	**25.00**	**47.00**
☐593	**PURE MALT WHISKEY, PRIDE OF CANADA** *Tapered top, amber, 10½"*	**17.00**	**23.00**

Q

☐594	**QUAKER MAID WHISKEY** *Girl in center of label, S. Hirsch & Co. Kansas City, Mo., fancy shoulder, clear, 3½"*	**16.00**	**22.00**
☐595	**QUAKER MAID WHISKEY** *In center, S.C.H. & Co. in circle, embossed, fancy shoulder, clear, 3½"*	**16.00**	**22.00**
☐596	**QUAKER MAID WHISKEY** *Patented under bottom, clear or aqua, quart*	**14.00**	**19.00**
☐597	**QUARTERBACK RYE WHISKEY** *S. Silberstein, Philadelphia, Pa., clear, quart*	**25.00**	**34.00**
☐598	**QUEEN MARY SCOTCH WHISKEY** *Amber, quart*	**25.00**	**34.00**
☐599	**QUEENSDALE WHISKEY** *Label, amber, quart*	**6.00**	**9.00**
☐600	**QUININE WHISKEY CO. LOUISVILLE, KY.** *On bottom, amber, 5¼"*	**10.00**	**15.00**
☐601	**F. R. QUINN** *This Bottle Not To Be Sold on back base, aqua, 11½"* ...	**9.00**	**13.00**

R

☐602	**RCV NP** *On shoulder, on top a crown, 3 pt. mold, applied top, kick up, dark green, 9½"*	**35.00**	**47.00**
☐603	**W.J. RAHILY CO.** *W.J.R. on back shoulder, three-part mold, clear or amethyst, 11"*	**11.00**	**15.00**
☐604	**FRED RASCHEN CO. SACRAMENTO, CAL.** *In form of circle, F.R. CO. monogram, round, graduated collar and ring, amber, fifth, 12"*	**17.00**	**23.00**
☐605	**FRED RASCHEN, SACRAMENTO, CAL.** *Amber, fifth*	**22.00**	**30.00**
☐606	**REBECCA AT THE WELL** *Pontil, clear or amethyst, 8"*	**55.00**	**75.00**
☐607	**RECORDS AND GOLDBOROUGH, BALTIMORE, MD.** *Vertically on slug plate, rectangular, ring collar, clear, pint, 6"*	**6.00**	**9.00**
☐608	**RED CHIEF** *Fort Hood, Indiania, Ballina Rye, clear, 12"*	**14.00**	**19.00**

☐609 **RED TOP**
With Top on shoulder, R.D. Westheimer & Sons on bottom, under bottom, different numbers, flask, extra ring on bottom of neck, amber, ½ pint 6.00 9.00

☐610 **REGISTERED HONEST ONE PINT**
At top half, rectangular, graduated collar and ring, amethyst, pint and ½ pint 4.00 6.00

☐611 **REGISTERED**
Clear or amethyst, 8" 8.00 11.00

☐612 **E. REMY**
Champagne, cognac, machine made, A.R. on bottom, green, 4" 1.50 2.25

☐613 **RHEINSTROM BROS. PROPRIETORS**
On other side, Mother Putnam's Blackberry Cordial, amber, 11" 19.00 26.00

☐614 **J. RIEGER & CO. KANSAS CITY, MO.**
Flute shoulder, clear or aqua, 11½" 14.00 19.00

☐615 **W.R. RILEY DISTILLING CO. KANSAS CITY, MO.**
Clear, quart 10.00 15.00

☐616 **H.H. ROBINSON, BOSTON**
Label, Guaranteed Full Pt on back, clear or amethyst, 8¾" 3.00 5.00

☐617 **ROMA CALIFORNIA WINE, PRIDE OF THE VINYARD, R.C.W. CO.**
Monogram all on front, ABM, thread top, amber, 12⅛" ... 3.00 4.00

☐618 **L. ROSE & CO.**
Rose and vine bottle, applied crown, tapered, aqua, 7½" . 7.00 10.00

☐619 **ROSEDALE OK WHISKEY**
Siebe Bros. & Plagermann, San Francisco, amber, quart . 170.00 215.00

☐620 **ROSSKAM GERSTLEY & CO.**
Old Saratoga Extra Fine Whiskey on back, Philadelphia in seal, small kick-up, clear or amethyst, 9¼" 11.00 15.00

☐621 **ROSSKAM GERSTLEY & CO.**
Monogram No. 6, clear, 8¼" 32.00 43.00

☐622 **ROSSKAM GERSTLEY & CO.**
Clear, 9½", amber 22.00 30.00

☐623 **ROSS'S BRAND**
Aqua, 14¼" 10.00 15.00

☐624 **ROTH & CO., SAN FRANCISCO, CALIFORNIA**
Pocket flask 12.00 17.00

☐625 **ROTH & CO., SAN FRANCISCO**
Amber, quart 45.00 60.00

☐626 **ROTHENBERG & CO**
In center a roster, San Francisco, call all in a watermellon circle, tapered top and ring, lt. amber, 11½" 110.00 140.00

☐627 **ROXBORO LIQ. CO.**
Clear or amethyst, 8" 8.00 11.00

☐628 **AQUA DE RUBINAT**
Aqua, 11" 3.00 5.00

☐629 **CHAS. RUGERS, WINE & LIQUORS, HOUSTON, TEXAS**
#181 under bottom, amber, 6" 10.00 15.00

☐630 RUM, five rings, clear, 3¾" 6.00 9.00

☐631	**RUSCONI, FISHER & CO., SAN FRANCISCO** *In 3 lines, back full quart on shoulder, inside threads top,* *flask type bottle, amber, 11"*	32.00	41.00
☐632	*RYE, three-part mold, clear, 11"*	10.00	15.00
☐633	*RYE, ground pontil, silk glass, hand painted, 11"*	27.00	36.00
☐634	*RYE, Decanter, gold trim, clear, 9¼"*	28.00	37.00

S

☐635	**SAFE WHISKEY** *Aqua, 9¼"*	34.00	46.00
☐636	*SAILOR'S FLASK, crock, tan and brown, 8¼"*	85.00	110.00
☐637	**ST. JACOB'S** *10½"*	10.00	15.00
☐638	**ST. JACOBS MALT WHISKEY, CINCINNATI O. U.S.A.** *Amber, 9¾"*	10.00	15.00
☐639	**ST. THOMAS DOUBLE DISTILLED BAY RUM,** **ST. THOMAS, V.I.** *Label, ABM, 10⅛"*	6.00	9.00
☐640	**ST. THOMAS BAY RUM** *On bottom, St. Thomas, V.I. USA, graduated ring collar,* *emerald green, quart, 11"*	8.00	11.00
☐641	**L.A. CHRTEN, ST. THOMAS, D.W.I. BAY RUM** *All on label, graduated collar and ring, slight bulbous* *neck, emerald green, 11½"*	6.00	9.00
☐642	**SALLADE & CO.** *Aqua, 8"*	7.00	10.00
☐643	**M. SALZMAN CO., NEW YORK** *Label, same in back with Purity above all, Old Doctrine* *Club Whiskey, quart, 11¼"*	7.00	10.00
☐644	**THE SAM'L LEHMAN CO., CINCINNATI, OHIO** *Amber, 11½"*	16.00	22.00
☐645	**THOS. D. SAMUEL, WHOLESALE LIQUOR DEALER** *11 East 5th Street, Kansas City, Mo., 8¾"*	9.00	12.00
☐646	**T.W. SAMUELS BOURBON WHISKEY** *Label, clear, 11"*	7.00	10.00
☐647	**SAW PALMETTO** *Genuine Vernal Buffalo N.Y. on other sides, clear or* *amethyst, 10"*	11.00	15.00
☐648	**S.B. CO. CHICAGO** *In back, clear, 3"*	10.00	15.00
☐649	**S.B. & CO.** *Under bottom, amber, 12"*	7.00	10.00
☐650	**S.B.&G. CO.** *Under bottom, aqua, 8"*	8.00	11.00
☐651	**S.C. DISPENSARY** *Under monogram SCD, under bottom C.L.F.G.C.O., with* *palm tree also, clear, ½ pint, pint, quart*	28.00	37.00
☐652	**DANIEL SCHAEFFER'S LOG CABIN WHISKEY**	55.00	70.00
☐653	**SCHLESINGER & BENDER, PURE WINE & BRANDIES,** **SAN FRANCISCO, CAL.** *Amber, quart*	90.00	120.00

☐654	**BARNEY SCHOW**		
	Wholesale & Retail Wine & Liquors, Willits, California, net contents, 8 oz., screw cap, amber, 6"	30.00	40.00
☐655	**SCHUTZ-MARKE**		
	Eigenthym von A. Schenk Altona in back, amber, 11½" ..	14.0	19.00
☐656	**SCHWARTZ A.**		
	In center Liquor Dealer, 120 & 122 Main St. in two lines, Walla Walla W.T. all in a circle, Shoo Fly Flask, ring top, amethyst, pt.	140.00	170.00
☐657	**SCHWARZ ROSENBAUM & CO.**		
	B under bottom, amber, 11½" ....·..........	14.00	19.00
☐658	**SCOTCH**		
	Label, clear, 10"	10.00	15.00
☐659	**G.B. SEELY'S SON**		
	Clear, 11"	11.00	15.00
☐660	**SHEA-BACQUERAZ CO., SAN FRANCISCO, CAL.**		
	Vertically, round, graduated collar and ring, dark amber, quart, 11½"	17.00	23.00
☐661	**A.A. SHEAFFERS**		
	Label, three-part mold, amber, quart	8.00	11.00
☐662	**SHEEHAN'S MALT WHISKEY**		
	With monogram in center, Utica, N.Y., same shape as The Duffy Malt, round, graduated collar, amethyst, 10½"	11.00	15.00
☐663	**SHEFFIELD CO, NEW YORK**		
	Amber, 9¾"	26.00	35.00
☐664	*SHELL FIGURAL, whiskey, sheared top, clear or amethyst, 5"*	55.00	70.00
☐665	**S.H.M. SUPERIOR**		
	Old Bourbon, quart	90.00	115.00
☐666	*SHOE FLY or COFFIN FLASK, graduated collar and ring, clear, pint and ½ pint*	5.00	8.00
☐667	*SHOE FIGURAL, label, dark purple, 6" x 3½" x 1¼"*	55.00	75.00
☐668	**SHOOMAKERS**		
	1331 Famous Resort, Pa. Avenue, Washington, D.C., Registered Full Pint, side strap, ring top, clear, quart	17.00	23.00
☐669	**S.I.G.W.**		
	1 under bottom, aqua, 12"	3.00	5.00
☐670	**SILVER LEAF PURE RYE WHISKEY**		
	Virginia, Carolina Co., owners, Richmond, Virginia, U.S.A., clear, ½ pint	10.00	15.00
☐671	**SILVER LEAF RYE**		
	Virginia, Carolina Grocery Co., Richmond, Virginia, under bottom, B.R. G. CO., clear or amethyst, 6¼"	10.00	15.00
☐672	**SIMON BROS.**		
	Horseshoe seal on back shoulder, clear, 10"	7.00	10.00
☐673	**SIMON BROS.**		
	Plain seal on back, clear or amethyst, 13"	11.00	15.00
☐674	**SM & CO.**		
	Ground pontil, amber, 11"	80.00	100.00
☐675	**THOS. L. SMITH & SONS/BOSTON, MASS**		
	On shoulder, three-piece mold, bulbous neck, round, graduated collar and ring, amethyst, quart, 12¼"	7.00	10.00

☐676 **SOL. BEAR & CO.**
Clear or amethyst, 13¾" 10.00   15.00

☐677 **SOREL E.A.**
Altona all under bottom, double ring top, 3 pt. mold, dark amber, 8½" 25.00   34.00

☐678 **SOUTH CAROLINA DISPENSARY**
Clear, 9¼" 22.00   30.00

☐679 **SOUTH CAROLINA DISPENSARY & TREE**
Aqua, 9½" 70.00   90.00

☐680 **SOUTHERN COMFORT**
Clear, 11½" 1.50   2.25

☐681 **SOUTHERN LIQUOR CO., DALLAS, TEXAS**
In a circle, tapered top, clear or amethyst, 10½" 12.00   17.00

☐682 **WILLIAM H. SPEARS OLD PIONEER WHISKEY**
Bear in center, A. Fenkhauser & Co., sole agents, San Francisco, amber, quart 165.00   210.00

☐683 **JARED SPENCER**
Flask, flared top, green, pint 800.00   1100.00

☐684 **R.A. SPLAINE & CO., HAVERHILL, MASS.**
On shoulder, It Pays To Buy the Best written on shoulder on opposite sides, three-piece mold, round, graduated collar and ring, amethyst, quart, 11½" 8.00   11.00

☐685 **S.S.T. PATENT**
Amber, quart 9.00   12.00

☐686 *STAR in center with stars circling, clear, 4¾"* 8.00   11.00

☐687 *STAR WHISKEY LABEL, saddle strap, amber, pint* 6.00   9.00

☐688 **STEIN BROS. CHICAGO**
On bottom, round, graduated rows of beads swirled around on shoulder, graduated band and ring collar, amethyst, quart, 11¾" 17.00   23.00

☐689 **C.B. STEWART, ATLANTA, GEORGIA**
Double top, clear, pint 11.00   15.00

☐690 **C.B. STEWART, ATLANTA, GEORGIA**
Clear or aqua, pint 7.00   10.00

☐691 **STODDARD**
Label, wine, iron pontil, olive or amber, 8½" 35.00   47.00

☐692 **STONEBROOK**
Turn mold, amber, 9½" x 4" 7.00   10.00

☐693 **OLD HENRY WHISKEY, STRAUS GUNST & CO., RICHMOND, VA.**
Panels on shoulder, clear or amethyst, 11" 16.00   23.00

☐694 **STRAUS GUNST & CO., PROPRIETORS, RICHMOND, VIRGINIA**
Amber, ½ pint 16.00   23.00

☐695 **STRAUSS BROS. CO., CHICAGO, U.S.A.**
Deep green, 12¼" 16.00   23.00

☐696 **STRAUSS PRITZ & CO.**
Sheared top, clear or amethyst, 5½" 7.00   10.00

☐697 **THE STRAUSS PRITZ CO.**
Clear or amethyst, 6¼" 3.00   5.00

☐698 **C.W. STUARTS**
Amber, quart 16.00   23.00

☐699 **SWANS G.**
The-owl, 5160 Ballard Ave. Ballard, Wash. all in a circle, double ring top and neck flask, clear and amethyst, ½ pt. 13.00   18.00

T

☐ 700 **TACOMA, WASH.**
In a double circle in center Monty's, flask Pu top, clear, ½
pt. 13.00   18.00

☐ 701 **LOUIS TAUSSIG & CO./SAN FRANCISCO/NEW YORK**
Vertically on one side, Union Made C.B.B.A. Branch No.
22 on opposite side, square, graduated collar, clear, scant
quart, 10¼ " 7.00   10.00

☐ 702 **TAUSSING & CO. LOUIS**
In script on top, San Francisco, under bottom, New York
all in 2 vertical lines, square, tapered top and ring, 10" . . .   17.00   23.00

☐ 703 **LOUIS TAUSSIG, MAIN STREET, SAN FRANCISCO**
Flask, amber 170.00   220.00

☐ 704 **LT & CO**
Inside of circle, Patented Feb. 4th, 1902 on bottom, oval
front paneling, ribbed, panels at base on back, rectangular, graduated collar and ring, amber, quart, 10½ " .   7.00   10.00

☐ 705 **TAYLOR & WILLIAMS**
Clear or amethyst, 3¼ " 6.00   9.00

☐ 706 **TAYLOR & WILLIAMS**
Side strap, clear, 6½ " 3.00   4.00

☐ 707 **TAYLOR & WILLIAMS**
In a horseshoe shape, under it Louisville, Ky, in center
Whiskey, ring top, clear or amethyst, 4¾ " round 6.00   9.00

☐ 708 Same as above except 11⅜" 7.00   10.00

☐ 709 TEA CUP, Old Bourbon, Shea Bacqueraz & Co., San Fran-
cisco, amber, quart 240.00   315.00

☐ 710 **TEAKETTLE OLD BOURBON**
San Francisco, amber, quart 175.00   220.00

☐ 711 **TEXAS**
Flask, tapered top, whiskey, clear, quart, 11" tall, 1¾ "
neck, 8" wide at center, 4" x 3" at bottom 10.00   15.00

☐ 712 **JAS. THARP'S SONS**
In center, Wine & Liquor, Washington, D.C., saddle flask,
ring top, amber, 7¾ " 19.00   26.00

☐ 713 **A. THELLER**
On shoulder, under bottom of bottle, in a circle, Theller
Arnold, applied top, kick-up, dark olive, 9½ " 6.00   9.00

☐ 714 **THEODORE NETTER**
1232 Market St. Phila., Pa., 6", clear 14.00   19.00

☐ 715 **TOKJ**
In seal, small kick-up, clear, 11" 7.00   10.00

☐ 716 **TONSMEIRE & CRAFT, MOBILE, ALABAMA**
Amber, 11" 32.00   45.00

☐ 717 **THE I. TRAGER CO.**
Amber, 12" 10.00   15.00

☐ 718 **THE I. TRAGER CO., CINCINNATI, OHIO**
Inverted V instead of A in Cincinnati, amber, 12" 27.00   36.00

☐719	**THE I. TRAGER CO.**		
	Ring top, amber, ½ pint	**6.00**	**9.00**
☐720	**THE I. TRAGER CO.**		
	Ring top, amber, ½ pint	**4.00**	**6.00**
☐721	**THE I. TRAGER CO.**		
	Amber, ½ pint	**5.00**	**8.00**
☐722	**TROST BROS.**		
	Clear, 6½"	**6.00**	**9.00**
☐723	**TUCKER ALA**		
	On one panel, four running legs in circle on back panel, amber, 9¼"	**50.00**	**70.00**
☐724	**F.G. TULLEDGE & CO, PURE POP CORN WHISKEY, CINCINNATI, OHIO**		
	Clear, quart	**7.00**	**10.00**
☐725	*TWO FISH WHISKEY, clear or amethyst, 7½"*	**45.00**	**60.00**

U

☐726	**ULLMAN & CO.**		
	Planter Rye Registered on back, clear or amethyst, 6¼" .	**10.00**	**15.00**
☐727	**UNION MADE C.B.B.A. of US & C TRADEMARK**		
	In circle, flask, clear, pint, 8¾"	**5.00**	**8.00**
☐728	*Same as above except ½ pint*	**7.00**	**10.00**
☐729	**UNION SQUARE COMPANY, 239 UNION ST., LYNN, MASS.**		
	GUARANTEED FULL ½ PINT		
	All in slug plate, rectangular, clear, 7"	**3.00**	**4.00**
☐730	**N.M. URI & CO.**		
	B on bottom, amber, 4¾" x 1½"	**10.00**	**15.00**
☐731	**N.M. URI & CO. LOUISVILLE, KY.**		
	Amber, 5¾"	**10.00**	**15.00**
☐732	**U.S. MAIL**		
	Clear, 5½"	**70.00**	**90.00**

V

☐733	**W.B. VAIL**		
	Golden amber, 11½"	**18.00**	**25.00**
☐734	**VARWIG & SON, PORTLAND, ORE.**		
	Monogram in center, Full Measure, round, graduated collar and ring, amber, 12¼"	**27.00**	**36.00**
☐735	**L. VERETERRA OVIEDO**		
	On bottom, ring top, 12"	**3.00**	**5.00**
☐736	**THE NORTH VERNON DISTILLING CO., DISTILLERY OFFICE CINCINNATI, O.**		
	Round, ten fancy vertical panels on neck and shoulder, graduated collar and ring, amethyst	**10.00**	**15.00**
☐737	**VI**		
	On base, whiskey label, pontil, clear, 5¼"	**14.00**	**19.00**
☐738	**VIEUX COGNAC**		
	Three-part mold, small kick-up, old top, aqua, 8¾"	**7.00**	**10.00**

☐739	**VINOL**		
	Private Mold Pat April 18, 1898 under bottom, amber, 6½"	8.00	11.00
☐740	*VIOLIN, plain back, different colors and sizes*	10.00	15.00
☐741	*VIOLIN, label, plain back, different colors and sizes*	18.00	25.00
☐742	*VIOLIN, label, amber, 8½"*	21.00	29.00
☐743	*VIOLIN, label, music score on back, pontil, different colors, 9¾"*	26.00	35.00
☐744	*VIOLIN, in back, musical score, plain bottom, many colors, various sizes*	9.00	12.00
☐745	*VIOLIN FLASK, ring top, clear, 6" x 3"*	14.00	19.00

W

☐746	**WALKERS KILMARNOOK WHISKEY 1807**		
	On bottom, square, square band and ring, ABM, emerald green, 10¼"	7.00	10.00
☐747	**WALTERS & CO. BALTIMORE**		
	On back base,amber, 11¾"	22.00	29.00
☐748	**WARRANTED**		
	Flask, dark amber and golden amber, pint or ½ pint	7.00	10.00
☐749	**WARRANTED**		
	Flask, light aqua, pint and ½ pint	5.00	8.00
☐750	**WARRANTED**		
	Flask, side bands, double band collar, amber, pint and ½ pint	7.00	10.00
☐751	**WARRANTED**		
	Flask, side bands, double band collar, amethyst, pint and ½ pint	7.00	10.00
☐752	**LOUIS WEBER, LOUISVILLE, KY.**		
	H.W.M. Colly & Co., Pittsburg under bottom, three-part mold, olive, 10"	32.00	42.00
☐753	**EDWARD WEISS**		
	Leading West End Liquor House, corner of West and Calvert, Annapolis, Md., ring top, clear or aqua, 6"	8.00	11.00
☐754	**WEST BEND OLD TIMERS LAGER BEER**		
	Label, aqua, 9¼"	3.00	5.00
☐755	**WEST END WINE & SPIRITS CO.**		
	Full Qt. Registered on back, amber, 12¼"	34.00	43.00
☐756	**FERDINAND WESTHEIMER & SONS, CINCINNATI, USA**		
	In circle, Rectangular, graduated collar and ring, amber, ½ pint	4.00	6.00
☐757	**FERDINAND WESTHEIMER & SONS**		
	Amber, 6"	8.00	11.00
☐758	**FERDINAND WESTHEIMER & SONS**		
	Amber, 9½"	14.00	19.00
☐759	**W.F. & S.**		
	Under bottom, aqua, 9½"	3.00	5.00
☐760	**WHARTON'S WHISKEY**		
	Witter Glass Work Glasboro N.J. under bottom, amber, 10"	270.00	335.00
☐761	*WHISKEY DECANTER, inlaid with silver, crystal glass, clear or aqua, 11¼"*	13.00	18.00

☐762	WHISKEY, ½ barrel shape, in front a rooster in center, in 1¾" x 2¾" panel A Merry Christmas and a Happy New Year, in center of panel M.C. & H.N.Y. and a woman in an old dress holding a glass while sitting on barrel, ½ pint, 1¾" neck, 4" body	25.00	34.00
☐763	WHISKEY; ribs on shoulder and bottom, clear or amethyst, fifth	8.00	11.00
☐764	WHISKEY; ribs on shoulder and bottom, clear or amethyst, fifth, 4½"	8.00	11.00
☐765	WHISKEY; plain, 3¼" round, 4½" body tapering to a blob neck 4¼", ring around top and bottom of body with plain seal on shoulder, amber, quart	16.00	23.00
☐766	WHISKEY; plain, side strap or shoe fly, Union oval, light green, clear or amber, ½ amber	11.00	15.00
☐767	Same as above except pint	11.00	15.00
☐768	Same as above except quart	11.00	15.00
☐769	WHISKEY; plain, turn mold, emerald green, quart, 11¼" .	8.00	11.00
☐770	WHISKEY; plain, with ribbed shoulder, various numbers under bottom, clear or amethyst, quart	3.00	5.00
☐771	Same as above except pint	3.00	5.00
☐772	WHISKEY; plain, with ribbed shoulder, with various numbers under bottom, amber, pint	7.00	10.00
☐773	Same as above except quart	7.00	10.00
☐774	WHISKEY; plain, turn mold, kick-up, pontil, light olive, 11½" tall, 2½" diameter	14.00	19.00
☐775	WHISKEY; plain, three-piece mold, round, amethyst, 11" .	6.00	9.00
☐776	WHISKEY; plain, round, tapered shoulder, amethyst, 9⅞"	3.00	5.00
☐777	WHISKEY; plain, green, fifth	8.00	11.00
☐778	WHISKEY; label, sheared top, also pewter top, clear, 6" ..	14.00	19.00
☐779	WHISKEY; label, aqua, 6½"	9.00	12.00
☐780	WHISKEY; label, milk glass, sheared top, 8"	14.00	19.00
☐781	WHISKEY; label, seal on shoulder, H999 on bottom, 11½" tall, 2½" diameter	8.00	11.00
☐782	WHISKEY; label, three-part mold, whittle mark, a dot on bottom, aqua, 11½" tall, 3" diameter	9.00	12.00
☐783	WHISKEY; label, clear or amethyst, 8"	5.00	8.00
☐784	WHISKEY; label, small kick-up, turn mold, red amber, 10½"	5.00	8.00
☐785	WHISKEY; label, clear or amethyst, ½ pint	3.00	5.00
☐786	WHISKEY; label, shallow kick-up, turn mold, amber 9¼" .	6.00	9.00
☐787	WHISKEY; label, amber, 6¼"	5.00	8.00
☐788	WHISKEY; label, clear, 10" tall, 4" diameter	5.00	8.00
☐789	WHISKEY; label, three-part mold, clear or amethyst, 11" .	6.00	9.00
☐790	WHISKEY; label, sample, B on bottom, amber, 4"	3.00	5.00
☐791	WHISKEY; label, sample, round, amber, 4½"	3.00	5.00
☐792	WHISKEY; label, sample, amber, 4½"	3.00	5.00
☐793	WHISKEY; label, sample, round, amber, 5"	3.00	5.00
☐794	WHISKEY; label, sample, round, amber, 4⅞", ...	3.00	5.00
☐795	WHISKEY; label, sample, round, #4 on bottom, amber, 5½"	3.00	5.00
☐796	WHISKEY; label, press glass, clear or amethyst, 6½"	6.00	9.00
☐797	WHISKEY; label, amber, 10"	21.00	31.00
☐798	WHISKEY; label, two stars under bottom, clear, 6½"	3.00	5.00
☐799	WHISKEY; label, sample, kick-up, amber, 4½"	6.00	9.00
☐800	WHISKEY; label, sample, amber, 3¾"	3.00	5.00

☐801	WHISKEY; label, sample, three-part mold, dark amber, 5¾"	3.00	5.00
☐802	WHISKEY; label, sample, dark amber, 5¼"	6.00	9.00
☐803	WHISKEY; label, sample, B under bottom, dark amber, 5¾"	3.00	5.00
☐804	WHISKEY; label, sample, kick-up, light amber, 5⅛"	6.00	9.00
☐805	WHISKEY; label, turn mold, small kick-up, dark amber, 10" tall, 3½" diameter	10.00	15.00
☐806	WHISKEY; label, machine made, amber, 6¾"	3.00	5.00
☐807	WHISKEY or BITTERS, label, amber, 9"	10.00	15.00
☐808	WHISKEY; label, brown crock, 6½"	10.00	15.00
☐809	WHISKEY; label, sample, amber, 5½"	3.00	5.00
☐810	WHISKEY; label, amber, 9"	3.00	5.00
☐811	WHISKEY; label, amber, quart	6.00	9.00
☐812	WHISKEY; label, diamond shape with # under bottom, amber, 5"	6.00	9.00
☐813	WHISKEY; sample or medicine, clear, 3"	3.00	5.00
☐814	WHISKEY; label, two dots under bottom, amber, 4"	3.00	4.00
☐815	WHISKEY; label, sample, sheared top, 4"	3.00	5.00
☐816	WHISKEY; label, light gold, 6½"	5.00	8.00
☐817	WHISKEY; label, amber, 12"	6.00	9.00
☐818	WHISKEY or BITTERS; label, nine rings top and bottom, graphite pontil, amber	60.00	80.00
☐819	WHISKEY; decanter, E.B. & CO. LP REG. No709209 1886 under bottom, 7"	10.00	15.00
☐820	WHISKEY; decanter, label, clear, 10"	17.00	23.00
☐821	WHISKEY; decanter, label, 1 Qt. on shoulder, clear or amethyst	17.00	23.00
☐822	WHISKEY; decanter, painted with gold and other colors, 10½"	55.00	75.00
☐823	WHISKEY; label, olive, 3½"	22.00	32.00
☐824	WHISKEY; label, dark green, 8¼"	17.00	23.00
☐825	WHISKEY; label, clear, 3½"	3.00	5.00
☐826	WHISKEY; label, pontil, amber, 7¾"	70.00	90.00
☐827	WHISKEY; label, pontil, amber, 5½"	45.00	60.00
☐828	WHISKEY; label, turn mold, small kick-up, clear, 11½" ...	3.00	5.00
☐829	WHISKEY; label, three-part mold, olive, 8¾"	16.00	23.00
☐830	WHISKEY; label, pontil, aqua, 9"	85.00	110.00
☐831	WHISKEY; label, sheared top, clear or amethyst, 9½" ...	10.00	15.00
☐832	WHISKEY; sample, plain, amber, 4½"	6.00	9.00
☐833	WHISKEY; sample, plain, clear or amethyst, 3½"	3.00	5.00
☐834	WHISKEY; sample, plain, clear, 4¼"	3.00	5.00
☐835	WHISKEY; sample, plain, clear, 4"	3.00	5.00
☐836	WHISKEY; sample, plain, 506 under bottom, olive, 3¾" ..	3.00	5.00
☐837	WHISKEY; sample, plain, 506 under bottom, amber, 3½" .	3.00	5.00
☐838	WHISKEY; sample, plain, clear, 3¾"	3.00	5.00
☐839	WHISKEY; sample, plain, seal, clear, 3¾"	6.00	9.00
☐840	WHISKEY; sample, plain, 2 under bottom, clear, 3¾"	6.00	9.00
☐841	WHISKEY; sample, plain, 5 under bottom, clear, 4½'	3.00	5.00
☐842	WHISKEY; sample, plain, clear, 3¾"	5.00	8.00
☐843	**WHITE RYE** Label; Clear or amethyst, 11¾"	5800	6.00
☐844	**WILLIAM WHITELEY LEITH** Reuse of Bottle Prohibited in back, Whiteleys Leith Scotch Whiskey, applied top, aqua, 8½"	28.00	37.00

☐ 845	*Same as above except double ring top*	**15.00**	**22.00**
☐ 846	**WILLIAM, WHITELEY LEITH, SCOTLAND**		
	In 4 lines, all on front back, House of Lord Wiskey, blob neck, double ring top, clear, 8 x 3½ "	**16.00**	**22.00**
☐ 847	*WINE, decanter, clear, 8¼ "*	**7.00**	**10.00**
☐ 848	*WINE, decanter, leather cover, Italy machine made, lion head with ring in mouth, two small lions heads*	**11.00**	**15.00**
☐ 849	*WINE, label, cobalt, 12"*	**40.00**	**55.00**
☐ 850	*WINE, label, amber, 4"*	**10.00**	**15.00**
☐ 851	*WINE, label, clear or amethyst, 11"*	**7.00**	**10.00**
☐ 852	*WINE, label, aqua, 12"*	**14.00**	**19.00**
☐ 853	*WINE, label (fish), French wine, aqua, 11"*	**26.00**	**34.00**
☐ 854	*WINE, label, also with wicker, green, 9"*	**1.50**	**2.25**
☐ 855	*WINE TESTER, turn mold, green, 8½ "*	**7.00**	**10.00**
☐ 856	*WINE, label, clear, 11"*	**3.00**	**5.00**
☐ 857	*WINE, label, kick-up, aqua, 7¼ "*	**3.00**	**5.00**
☐ 858	*WINE, label, kick-up, clear, 4"*	**6.00**	**9.00**
☐ 859	*WINE, label, WT under bottom, carnival glass, 10½ "*	**6.00**	**9.00**
☐ 860	*WINE, label, machine made, clear, 8"*	**3.00**	**5.00**
☐ 861	*WINE, label, 200 to 300 yrs. old, pontil, blue green, 5½ " tall, 3½ " diameter*	**30.00**	**42.00**
☐ 862	*WINE, label, three-part mold, kick-up, pontil, whittle mark, light green, 14½ " tall, 5" x 4"*	**16.00**	**22.00**
☐ 863	*WINE, label, kick-up, olive, 13"*	**5.00**	**8.00**
☐ 864	*WINE, label, very crude, free blown, kick-up, olive, 11½ " .*	**13.00**	**18.00**
☐ 865	*WINE, label, pontil, small kick-up, light aqua, 9¾ "*	**13.00**	**18.00**
☐ 866	*WINE, label, small kick-up, amber, 11¼ "*	**6.00**	**9.00**
☐ 867	*WINE, label, aqua, 7¼ "*	**5.00**	**8.00**
☐ 868	*WINE, label, small kick-up, turn mold, dark green, 12" ...*	**5.00**	**8.00**
☐ 869	*WINE, label, pontil, double collar, olive green, 9"*	**17.00**	**24.00**
☐ 870	*WINE, plain, lady's leg, kick-up, light green, body 7", neck 6½ "*	**30.00**	**42.00**
☐ 871	*WINE, plain, turn mold, olive green, 8", 9½ " or 11½ " ....*	**3.00**	**5.00**
☐ 872	*WINE, plain, turn mold, green, 9¾ " or 11¼ "*	**3.00**	**5.00**
☐ 873	*WINE, plain, turn mold, jade green, 9¾ " or 11¼ " ....*	**3.00**	**5.00**
☐ 874	*WINE, plain, P on bottom, three-part mold, aqua, 12" ....*	**5.00**	**8.00**
☐ 875	*WINE, plain, turn mold, aqua, 12½ "*	**3.00**	**5.00**
☐ 876	**A.J. WINTLE & SON**		
	Pint Imperial on shoulder, dark olive, 8"	**7.00**	**10.00**
☐ 877	**W.M.**		
	In circle on shoulder, Whyle & MacKay on back, three-part mold, aqua, 8¾ "	**6.00**	**9.00**
☐ 878	**WOLTERS BROTHERS & CO.**		
	115-6 Front Street, San Francisco, red, quart	**55.00**	**75.00**
☐ 879	**WOOD POLLARD & CO/BOSTON, MASS**		
	Slanted on lower left to upper right, FULL QUART on front, blob seal on back, round bulbous neck, graduated collar and ring, amethyst, 12½ "	**10.00**	**15.00**
☐ 880	**WORMER BROS., SAN FRANCISCO**		
	Embossed vertically, flask, clear	**19.00**	**26.00**
☐ 881	**WORMER BROS.**		
	In semicircle, SAN FRANCISCO in horizontal lines, flask, clear	**19.00**	**26.00**
☐ 882	*Same as above except S.F. instead of SAN FRANCISCO .*	**19.00**	**26.00**

□883 **WORMER BROS., SAN FRANCISCO**
Fine Old Cognac, double rolled collar, flask, amber 90.00   120.00
□884 **WORMER BROS., S.F.**
Fine Old Cognac 1872, double rolled collar, flask, amber .   90.00   120.00
□885 **WORMSER BROS., SAN FRANCISCO**
Rummy ver. double ring top, flask type bottle, amber, pt. .   140.00   170.00
□886 **WRIGHT & TAYLOR DISTILLERS LOUISVILLE, KY.**
In large letters on one side of shoulder, Full Quart Regis-
tered on opposite side, large base, round, graduated col-
lar and ring, amber, 9" 22.00   30.00
□887 **WRIGHT & TAYLOR**
Full Quart Registered on back, A B Co. under bottom,
amber, 10½" 11.00   15.00
□888 **WYETH & BRO.**
Saddle flask, amber, 7½" 7.00   10.00
□889 **JOHN WYETH & BRO.**
Amber, 9" 8.00   11.00
□890 **JNO. WYETH & BRO.**
Amber, 9" 8.00   11.00

X

□891 **XERES**
In seal on shoulder, dip mold, applied ring, kick up, olive
green, 10½" 55.00   75.00

Y

□892 **YE OLD MOSSROFF BOURBON**
Label on panel, R.S. Roehling, 1 Schultz, Inc., Chicago,
cabin shape, amber, 9½" 11.00   15.00

Z

□894 **ZELLER SCHWARZE KATZ**
On base in center, Golden Cat on round base, under bot-
tom AC and misc. numbers, machine made, green, 13¼" .   10.00   15.00
□895 *Same as above except a monkey wrapped around bottle* . .   10.00   15.00
□896 **ZWACK**
Label seal, ZWACK around shoulder, each letter in a
flower, amber, 4¼" 10.00   15.00

NEW BOTTLES

NEW BOTTLE PRICING

The **RETAIL PRICE** is the price charged by a knowledgeable dealer, aware of values in the bottle market. Retail prices are affected by numerous factors including source, type of bottle, desirability and condition. Combined with these is the fact that many bottles are deliberately made as collectors' items, in limited quantities with no reissues. Given the above variables in the market, these prices can fluctuate sharply at anytime.

The **AVERAGE BUYING PRICE (A.B.P.)** is the sum a knowledgeable bottle dealer will pay for an item. When an item is purchased *from* a dealer it is removed from the market for a short while or perhaps permanently, depending on the fate of the buyer's collection. Each purchase contributes to scarcity, thus dealers welcome the opportunity to replenish their stock by buying from the public. A good "rule of thumb" would be to calculate the average buying price as 35 — 50% of the retail price. This will not, of course, hold true in every instance.Each dealer sets his buying price on the basis of his selling price. Therefore, a dealer who *sells higher* is likely to *buy higher*. Also, you may (in fact you invariably will, if you sell bottles frequently) encounter dealers who decline to purchase even at a very low price. They may be overstocked on that particular bottle, or bottles of that manufacturer; or they may have no customers for that kind of bottle.

Some of the rarest and most valuable of the contemporary bottles have been illegally reproduced. This practice will undoubtedly continue as long as the bottle market thrives. *Antique & historical flasks* are also reproduced.

The best protection against unknowingly acquiring a "repro" is to buy only from reputable dealers who make a specialty dealing in bottles. They have usually considerable expertise and a reputation to guard. Another means of protection is to buy filled bottles from a spirits retailer!

Most bottles in this book are priced for Mint Condition. Sales, purchases or trades cannot be equitably made unless both parties are aware of the definition of MINT CONDITION. Many bottles are bought and sold in conditions less than Mint. We herewith define the various condition grades, and show the proportion of discount that should be made for non-Mint specimens.

For your convenience, we suggest that you use the following record-keeping system to note the condition of your bottles in the checklist boxes that precedes each listing.

☐**MINT M**—An empty bottle complete with new intact labels. Color bright and clean, no chips, or scrapes, or wear. Tax stamp like new, but cut. Box in like new condition. All stoppers, handles, spouts like new.

☐**EXTRA FINE EF**—A bottle complete with labels, stamps, etc. All color clean and clear, slight wear on labels and tax strip, gold or silver embellishments perfect. Stoppers, handles, spouts in fine condition. Box or Container missing. **WORTH 10% LESS THAN LISTED RETAIL PRICE.**

☐**FINE F**—The bottle Shows slight wear, but color is clear and bright overall. Tax stamp complete but worn. Labels can be missing. Gold or silver embellishments perfect. Stoppers, handles. spouts complete and undamaged. No box or container. **WORTH 15% LESS THAN RETAIL PRICE.**

☐**VERY GOOD VG**—The bottle shows some wear, gold or silver slightly worn. Labels missing, Tax stamp missing. Stoppers, handles, spouts complete. No box or container. **WORTH 25% LESS THAN LISTED RETAIL PRICE.**

☐**GOOD G**—The bottle shows wear, complete but color faded. Gold or silver shows wear. Labels and tax stamp missing. Stoppers, handles, spouts complete. No box or container. **WORTH 40% LESS THAN LISTED RETAIL PRICE.**

☐**FAIR FR**—The bottle color is worn and the gold or silver embellishments are faded. Labels and tax stamp missing. Stoppers, handles, spouts complete but worn. An undesirable category. No box or container. **WORTH 50% TO 75% LESS THAN LISTED RETAIL PRICE.**

AVON

Avon has been calling for more than 50 years, and the call from collectors for imaginative, decorative toiletries and cosmetic bottles has brought a stampede upon the antique shops. As the modern leader in the non-liquor bottle field, Avon's vast range of bottles offers almost unlimited opportunities for the collector. Since none of their figurals are extremely rare, a complete collection of them is possible though it would contain hundreds of specimens.

Today, the Avon figurals — shaped as animals, people, cars, and numerous other objects — are the most popular of the company's bottles, but not always the most valuable. Some of the early non-figurals of the pre-World War II era sell for high prices because of their scarcity. Since there were virtually no Avon collectors in those days, very few specimens were preserved.

Avon collecting has become such a science that all of its bottles, and even the boxes that they came in, have been carefully catalogued. In fact, everything relating to Avon is now regarded as collectible, including brochures, magazines ads, and anything bearing the Avon name. Of course, the older material is more sought after than items of recent vintage.

Avon bottles are readily obtainable through specialized dealers and numerous other sources. Since some people who sell the Avons are unaware of their value, the collector can often find bargain prices at garage sales or flea markets.

Although it seems that every possible subject has been exhausted, Avon continues to bring out original bottles with a variety in sizes, colors, and decorative designs. The new figurals in its line are issued in limited editions with editions being rather large in order to accommodate the collector as well as the general public. Collectors of new Avons should purchase the new issues as soon as they reach the market since they often sell out quickly. When an Avon product has sold out, its price begins rising and can double in less than a year depending on its popularity. Even though this does not always happen, the original retail price will be lower than can be expected later on in the collector's market.

Although Avon is the oldest toiletry company issuing decorative bottles, collecting interest in its products did not become wide-spread until stimulated by the release in 1965 of an after shave lotion in a Stein decanter and a men's cologne in an amber boot. The interest created by those toiletries led many people to investigate the earlier Avon products, partly for collecting and partly for use as decorations. At that time they could be purchased inexpensively from secondhand shops and thrift bazaars. Unfortunately, by then many of the older ones had perished and were just not to be found.

By the late sixties, Avons were plentiful in antique shops with prices on the rise. Some collecting clubs were established. The early seventies saw further increases in collecting activity. The company, well aware of what was happening, expanded its line of figurals to meet public demand.

Many collectors doubt that modern Avon figurals can ever become really valuable because of the large quanities made. But with natural loss, passage of time, and increasing collector demand, Avon figurals may well reach respectable prices in five or ten years, making the 1983 prices look like great bargains.

Just as with many other collectibles, the Avons that prove least popular when issued sometimes end up being the scarcest and costliest. This is why collectors automatically buy each one as they come out.

Avon began as the California Perfume Company, founded by D.H. McConnell, a door-to-door salesman who gave away perfume samples to prevent doors from being slammed in his face. Eventually he started selling perfume and abandoned bookselling. Although it was located in New York, the name "Avon" was initially used in 1929 in conjunction with the California Perfume Company or C.P.C. After 1939 it was known exclusively as Avon. The C.P.C. bottles are naturally very desirable, having been issued in relatively small quanities and not having been well preserved. These bottles are impossible to date accurately because many designs were used with various preparations. In most cases, sales do not occur frequently enough to establish firm price levels. Therefore, the prices listed in this book should be regarded only as being approximate. All C.P.C. bottles in this section are indicated with a cross (+).

There are numerous possible approaches to Avon collecting. The most popular is to amass as many figurals as one's budget, time and energy (not to mention luck) allows. They can also be collected by subject matter, or according to the type of product they originally contained — such as making specialized collection of perfume bottles, or after shave bottles. Another favorite specialty is Avons with figural stoppers.

CPC — FRAGANCES

NO.	DESCRIPTION	PRICE RANGE	
☐ 1	**ATOMIZER PERFUME** (1908)		
	Six-sided bottle, cork stopper, green label on front and neck, 1 oz., sold in CPC Atomizer Sets. Original price $.50	90.00	110.00
☐ 2	**CALIFORNIA ROSE TALCUM** (1921)		
	Clear glass, brass cap, 3½ oz. Original price $.33	70.00	90.00
☐ 3	**CHRISTMAS PERFUME** (1907)		
	Clear glass, glass stopper, paper label, ribbon at neck, 2 oz. Original price $.75	120.00	140.00
☐ 4	**CPC PERFUME** (1918)		
	Clear glass, glass and cork stopper, sold in gift box set, ½ oz.	75.00	95.00
☐ 5	**CRAB APPLE BLOSSOM** (1908)		
	Clear glass, round bottle, glass stopper, paper label with Eureka trademark, 1 oz. Original price $.50 to $.75	140.00	200.00
☐ 6	**CUT GLASS PERFUME** (1915-20)		
	Square-shaped bottle of clear glass, round neck, round cut glass stopper, two different lables with gold embossing, 2 oz. Original price $2.25	170.00	200.00
☐ 7	**EXTRA CONCENTRATED PERFUME** (1916)		
	Glass stopper, paper labels on front and neck, 1 oz. Original price $.75	165.00	185.00
☐ 8	**EXTRACT ROSE GERANIUM PERFUME** (1887)		
	Narrow clear bottle, glass stopper with floral design, paper label, 1 oz. Original price $.40	180.00	220.00
☐ 9	**EXTRACT PERFUME** (1908)		
	Clear glass, glass stopper, paper label, 1 oz. Original price $.50	170.00	200.00

☐	10	**EXTRACT PERFUMES** *(1896)* *Clear glass, round glass stopper, 2 oz. Original price $.90 to $1.40*	140.00	190.00
☐	11	**EIGHT OUNCES PERFUME** *Clear glass, glass stopper, paper labels on front and neck, 8 oz. Original price $3.25*	165.00	195.00
☐	12	**FRENCH PERFUME** *(1896-1908)* *Clear glass, glass stopper, paper label with Eureka trademarks, ½ oz. Original price $.55*	140.00	160.00
☐	13	**FRENCH PERFUME** *(1896)* *Clear glass with embossing, cork stopper, ¼ oz. Original price $.25*	120.00	135.00
☐	14	**FRENCH PERFUME** *(1890)* *Clear glass, glass stopper, paper label, ¼ oz. Original price $.25*	120.00	140.00
☐	15	**HALF OUNCE PERFUME** *(1919)* *Clear glass, glass stopper with crown on top, ½ oz. Original price $.75*	75.00	95.00
☐	16	**HALF OUNCE PERFUME** *(1915)* *Clear glass, glass stopper set in cork, paper lables on front and neck, ½ oz. Original price $.25*	90.00	110.00
☐	17	**CPC PERFUME** *(1906)* *Clear glass, glass stopper, gold label on front and neck, 1 oz.*	140.00	190.00
☐	18	**CPC PERFUME** *(1916)* *Glass stopper, paper label on front and neck, 1 oz. Original price $.50*	120.00	140.00
☐	19	**FLORIDA WATER** *(1887)* *Glass stopper, labels on front and neck, 2 or 4 oz.*	90.00	110.00
☐	20	**CPC TOLIET WATER** *(1890)* *Glass stopper, front and neck labels of various designs, 2 oz. or 4 oz.*	90.00	110.00
☐	21	**EAU DE COLOGNE** *(1890)* *Glass stopper, paper labels on front and neck in various designs, 4 oz. Original price $.65*	90.00	110.00
☐	22	**FLORIDA WATER** *(1900)* *Glass stopper, ribbed bottle, 2 oz. Original price $.35*	165.00	185.00
☐	23	**LAVENDER WATER** *(1910)* *Glass stopper, paper label on front with Eureka trademark, 2 oz. Original price $.35*	140.00	160.00
☐	24	**BABY TOLIET WATER** *(1923)* *Clear bottle, brass and cork stopper, soldier on front label, blue label on neck, 2 or 4 oz. Original price $.48 or $.89*	65.00	85.00
☐	25	**LILAC VEGETAL** *(1928-29)* *Clear glass ribbd, cork stopper with metal crown on top, paper front and neck labels are pink, 2 oz.*	65.00	85.00
☐	26	**LITTLE FOLKS PERFUME** *(1908)* *Clear glass, cork stopper, front label, sold in Little Folks Set only*	65.00	85.00
☐	27	**LITTLE FOLKS PERFUME** *(1912)* *Clear glass, cork stopper, sold in Little Folks Set, various labels on front*	65.00	85.00
☐	28	**LITTLE FOLKS PERFUME** *(1915)* *Small bottle, cork stopper, front label, ribbon on neck* ...	65.00	85.00

☐ 29 **LITTLE FOLKS PERFUME** *(1925-32)*
Clear glass with brass screw on cap, sold in Little Folks
Set, ½ oz. **60.00**   **80.00**

☐ 30 **MUSK PERFUME** *(1896)*
Clear glass, glass stopper, paper label, 1 oz. **90.00**   **120.00**

☐ 31 **MUS PERFUME** *(1915)*
Clear glass, glass stopper, paper labels on front and neck,
1 oz. Original price $.75 . . . .   **140.00**   **160.00**

☐ 32 **ONE OUNCE PERFUME** *(1908)*
Clear glass, glass stopper, paper label with Eureka trade-
mark, 1 oz. Original price $.50 . . . .   **140.00**   **190.00**

☐ 33 **PERFUME** *(1890)*
Clear glass, glass stopper, different lables, neck ribbons,
1 oz. Original price $.25 . . . .   **90.00**   **110.00**

☐ 34 **PERFUME** *(1896)*
Clear glass, octagonally shaped, labels on front and neck
with Eureka trademark, cork stopper, 1 oz. **140.00**   **160.00**

☐ 35 **PERFUME** *(1906)*
Clear glass, round bottle, sold with Atomizer Perfume Set,
cork stopper, 1 oz. **90.00**   **110.00**

☐ 36 **PERFUME** *(1908)*
Clear glass, various designs of glass stoppers, gold
labels, band around neck, 1 oz. **140.00**   **170.00**

☐ 37 **PERFUME** *(1908-18)*
Clear glass, glass stopper, gold embossed design on
front and neck, 4 oz. Original price $2.75 . . . .   **140.00**   **190.00**

☐ 38 **PERFUME** *(1923)*
Clear glass, glass stopper with crown on top, labels on
front and neck, ½ oz. Original price $.59 . . . .   **90.00**   **100.00**

☐ 39 **PERFUME** *(1925)*
Ribbed bottle, glass stopper, paper labels on front and
neck, 1 oz. Original price $1.17 . . . .   **90.00**   **110.00**

☐ 40 **PERFUME AND ATOMIZER** *(1918)*
Clear bottle with atomizer, cork stopper, green label on
front and neck, 1 oz. Original price $1.50 . . . .   **80.00**   **100.00**

☐ 41 **PERFUME "FLORAL EXTRACTS"** *(1908)*
Clear glass, glass stopper, paper label with Eureka trade-
mark, 1 oz. Original price $.50 . . . .   **140.00**   **190.00**

☐ 42 **PERFUME FALCONETTE** *(1923)*
Clear glass, octagonal shaped bottle, long glass stopper,
with or without brass cap, neck label. Original price $.49 .   **70.00**   **95.00**

☐ 43 **PERFUME FALCONETTE** *(1925)*
Clear glass embossed, glass stopper, brass cap that fits
over stopper. Original price $1.10 . . . .   **80.00**   **100.00**

☐ 44 **PERFUME FALCONETTE** *(1925)*
Frosted glass with ribbing, long glass stopper, brass cap
that fits over stopper, paper label. Original price $.59 . . . .   **70.00**   **90.00**

☐ 45 **PERFUME FALCONETTE** *(1930-35)*
Clear glass with embossing, glass stopper, brass cap that
fits over stopper, "Avon" on cap. Original price $1.10 . . . .   **80.00**   **100.00**

☐ 46 **PERFUME — HIGHLY CONCENTRATED** *(1918)*
Clear glass, glass stopper set in cork with crown on top,
paper labels on front and neck, ½ oz. Original price $.50 .   **80.00**   **100.00**

☐ 47 **POWDER SACHET** *(1886-1912)*
Clear glass, gold cap, front label. Original price $.25 . . . . .   **90.00**   **110.00**

☐ 48 **CPC POWDER SACHETS** *(1886-1912)*
Clear glass, round bottle, gold cap, front label. Original price $.25 .... **90.00** **110.00**

☐ 49 **CPC POWDER SACHET** *(1890)*
Round glass, aluminum cap, front label. Original price $.25 .... **90.00** **110.00**

☐ 50 **POWDER SACHET** *(1915)*
Clear glass, gold cap, paper label. Original price $.25 .... **60.00** **90.00**

☐ 51 **POWDER SACHET** *(1919)*
Clear glass, gold cap, yellow label on front **80.00** **100.00**

☐ 52 **POWDER SACHET** *(1922-25)*
Clear glass, brass cap, black label on front. Original price $.72 .... **75.00** **95.00**

☐ 53 **POWDER SACHET** *(1922-25)*
Clear glass, brass cap, black label on front, small bottle. Original price $.49 .... **65.00** **85.00**

☐ 54 **POWDER SACHET** *(1923)*
Clear glass, brass cap, front label ...., ... **75.00** **95.00**

☐ 55 **ROSE PERFUME SAMPLE** *(1900)*
Clear glass, cork stopper, ½ oz. **115.00** **135.00**

☐ 56 **SWEET COLOGNE** *(1905)*
Cork stopper, paper labels on front and neck, or 4 oz. Original price $.65 .... **120.00** **160.00**

☐ 57 **SMOKERS TOOTH POWDER** *(1918)*
Cork stopper with metal top, 2¾″ oz. Original price $.50 .. **90.00** **100.00**

☐ 58 **SMOKERS TOOTH POWDER** *(1920)*
Cork stopper with metal top, paper labels on front and neck, 2¾″ oz. Original price $.50 .... **90.00** **100.00**

☐ 59 **TOLIET WATER** *(1896)*
Clear glass ribbed, glass stopper set in cork, paper labels on front and neck with Eureka trademark, 2 oz. Original price $.35 .... **165.00** **185.00**

☐ 60 **TOILET WATER** *(1906)*
Clear glass ribbed, glass and cork stopper, 2 oz. Original price $.35 .... **165.00** **185.00**

☐ 61 **TOLIET WATER** *(1910)*
Clear glass, glass stopper, paper labels on front and neck, 8 oz. Original price $1.25 .... **140.00** **160.00**

☐ 62 **TOLIET WATER** *(1916)*
Clear glass, metal spout cap set in cork, paper labels on front and neck, 2 oz. Original price $.35 .... **90.00** **110.00**

☐ 63 **TOLIET WATER** *(1916)*
Clear glass, cork stopper with crown made of metal, front labels in two different designs, 2 oz. Original price $.35 .. **90.00** **110.00**

☐ 64 **TOLIET WATER** *(1916)*
Clear glass, cork stopper with plain metal top, paper labels on front and neck, 4 oz. Original price $.65 .... **80.00** **100.00**

☐ 65 **TOLIET WATER** *(1923-29)*
Clear glass ribbed, cork stopper with metal crown, labels on front and neck, 2 oz. Original price $.59 .... **60.00** **80.00**

☐ 66 **TRAVELER'S PERFUME** *(1896-1910)*
Clear glass, octagonally shaped, glass stopper with metal cap that fits over it, gold label, ½ oz. Original price $.50 .. **110.00** **140.00**

☐ 67 **TRIPLE EXTRACT TOLIET WATER** *(1896)*
*Glass stopper, front label with Eureka trademark, various
label designs, 4 oz. Original price $.65* **140.00   180.00**

☐ 68 **TWO OUNCES PERFUME** *(1916)*
*Clear glass, glass stopper faceted or round, paper label
on front and neck, 2 oz. Original price $1.10* **130.00   170.00**

MEN'S AFTER SHAVE AND COLOGNES

☐ 69 **AFTER SHAVE LOTION** *(1932-36)*
*Clear glass, black caps, yellow paper labels, 4 oz. Original
price $.37* **45.00   55.00**

☐ 70 **AFTER SHAVE** *(1975-76)*
Clear glass, brown cap, 5 oz. Original price $3.00 .... **.25   1.50**

☐ 71 **AFTER SHOWER FOR MEN** *(1959-60)*
*Clear glass, gold cap, gold foil around neck, gold neck
cord, 8 oz. Original price $2.50 Original price $2.50* **45.00   55.00**

☐ 72 **BAY RUM** *(1936-49)*
Clear glass, maroon cap, 4 oz. Original price $.52 .... **25.00   35.00**

☐ 73 **BRAVO AFTER SHAVE** *(1969)*
Clear glass, black cap, pink label, 4 oz. **3.00   5.00**

☐ 74 **COLOGNE FOR MEN** *(1946-49)*
*Clear glass with shield design on paper label, maroon
cap, 6 oz. Original price $1.50* **65.00   75.00**

☐ 75 **COLOGNE FOR MEN** *(1948)*
Clear glass, maroon cap, 2 oz. **20.00   30.00**

☐ 76 **DELUXE AFTER SHAVE "WOOD TOP"** *(1961-63)*
*Clear glass with some having gold letters while others
have gold paper labels, 6 oz. Original price $1.79* **20.00   30.00**

☐ 77 **GENTLEMAN'S CHOICE** *(1969-70)*
*Clear glass embossed with silver, gold or black caps, 2 oz.
Original price $1.75* **2.00   4.00**

☐ 78 **GIFT COLOGNE FOR MEN** *(1974-75)*
Clear glass, gold cap, 2 oz. Original price $2.00 .... **.50   2.00**

☐ 79 **VIGORATE AFTER SHAVE** *(1959-60)*
Clear glass, white cap, 8 oz. Original price $2.50 .... **35.00   45.00**

MEN'S FIGURALS

☐ 80 **AFTER SHAVE ON TAP** *(1974-75)*
*Dark amber glass, gold plastic spigot cap, 5 oz. Original
price $3.00* **2.00   4.00**

☐ 81 **ALASKAN MOOSE** *(1974-75)*
*Amber glass, cream colored plastic antlers, 8 oz. Original
price $7.00* **6.00   8.00**

☐ 82 **ALPINE FLASK** *(1966-67)*
*Brown glass, gold cap and neck chain, 8 oz. Original price
$4.00* **40.00   55.00**

☐ 83 **AMERICAN BUFFALO** *(1975-76)*
*Amber glass, amber plastic head, ivory colored horns,
5 oz. Original price $6.00* **5.00   7.00**

☐ 84 **AMERICAN EAGLE** *(1971-72)*
*Dark amber glass, gold eagle head, 5 oz. Original price
$5.00* **2.00   4.00**

☐ 85	**AMERICAN EAGLE PIPE** *(1974-75)* *Dark amber glass, gold plastic top, black handle, 5 oz.* *Original price $5.00*	4.00	6.00
☐ 86	**AMERICAN SCHOONER DECANTER** *(1972-73)* *Blue glass, blue plastic end over cap, 4.5 oz.*	4.00	6.00
☐ 87	**ANGLER** *(1970)* *Fishing reel of blue glass, silver reel cap, 5 oz. Original* *price $5.00*	4.00	6.00
☐ 88	**ARMY JEEP** *(1974-75)* *Oliver green with plastic cover, 4 oz. Original price $5.00* .	4.00	6.00
☐ 89	**THE ATLANTIC 4-4-2** *(1973-75)* *Clear glass painted silver, silver plastic parts, 5 oz.*	7.00	10.00
☐ 90	**AT POINT AFTER SHAVE** *(1973-74)* *Redish brown glass, redish brown plastic head, 5 oz.*	3.00	5.00
☐ 91	**AVON CALLING FOR MEN** *(1969-70)* *Old fashioned telephone (stand variety) of clear glass* *painted gold, gold cap, black mouth piece, black plastic* *ear piece, 6 oz. Original price $8.00*	8.00	10.00
☐ 92	**AVON CALLING 1905 DECANTER** *(1973)* *Old fashioned telephone of brown glass, brown plastic* *top, 7 oz.*	8.00	10.00
☐ 93	**AVON ON THE AIR DECANTER** *(1975-76)* *Microphone of black glass, silver plastic stand, 3 oz.* *Original price $4.59*	3.00	5.00
☐ 94	**AVON OPEN GOLD CART** *(1972-75)* *Green glass with green plastic front, red plastic gold* *bags, 5 oz. Original price $6.00*	2.50	4.50
☐ 95	**AVON TRIUMPH-TR 3 '56** *(1975-76)* *Blue-green glass with plastic cap. Original price $4.00* ...	3.00	6.00
☐ 96	**AUTO LANTERN** *(1973-74)* *Clear glass painted gold with amber windows, 5 oz.*	10.00	14.00
☐ 97	**BARBER POLE** *(1974-75)* *White milk glass with red and blue stripes, white plastic* *cap, 3 oz. Original price $3.00*	2.00	4.00
☐ 98	**BARBER SHOP BRUSH** *(1976)* *Brown glass, black and white plastic brush cap, 1.5 oz.* *Original price $4.00*	2.00	4.00
☐ 99	**BAY RUM KEG AFTER SHAVE** *(1965-76)* *Clear glass painted brown and silver, 8 oz. Original price* *$2.50*	16.00	20.00
☐ 100	**BENJAMIN FRANKLIN DECANTER** *(1974-76)* *Bust of Franklin, white plastic head and clear glass* *painted white, 6 oz. Original price $6.00*	5.00	7.00
☐ 101	**BIG GAME RINO** *(1972-73)* *Green glass, green plastic head on cap, 4 oz.*	3.00	5.00
☐ 102	**BIG MACK** *(1973-75)* *Green glass with beige bed, 6 oz.*	4.00	6.00
☐ 103	**BIG RIG** *(1975-76)* *Blue glass cab, white and blue plastic trailer, 6 oz.* *Original price $10.00*	8.00	10.00
☐ 104	**BIG WHISTLE** *(1972-73)* *Blue glass, silver cap, 4 oz.*	2.00	4.00
☐ 105	**BLACKSMITH'S ANVIL** *(1972-73)* *Black glass, silver cap, 4 oz.*	3.00	5.00

□106	**BLACK VOLKSWAGON** *(1970-72)*		
	Black glass, black plastic cap	1.00	3.00
□107	**BLOOD HOUND PIPE** *(1976)*		
	Clear glass painted beige, brown and silver cap, 5 oz.		
	Original price $7.00	4.00	6.00
□108	**BLUE VOLKSWAGON** *(1973-74)*		
	Blue painted glass, plastic cap, 4 oz.	2.00	4.00
□109	**BLUNDERBUSS PISTOL 1780** *(1976)*		
	Dark amber glass, gold cap with plastic trigger, 5.5 oz.		
	Original price $12.00	8.00	10.00
□110	**BOOT "GOLD TOP"** *(1966-71)*		
	Amber glass with hook on cap, 8 oz. Original price $5.00 .	1.00	3.00
□111	**BOOT "SILVER TOP"** *(1965-66)*		
	Amber glass, silver cap with hook on cap, 8 oz. Original		
	price $5.00	5.50	8.50
□112	**BOTTLED BY AVON** *(1973)*		
	Clear glass, silver lift off cap, 5 oz.	2.00	4.00
□113	**BUCKING BRONCO** *(1971-72)*		
	Dark amber glass horse, bronze plastic cowboy hat, 6 oz.		
	Original price $6.00	2.00	4.00
□114	**BUFFALO NICKEL** *(1971-72)*		
	Coin-shaped bottle of clear glass, foil covering embossed		
	with Indian on one side, 5 oz.	3.00	5.00
□115	**BUGATTI '27** *(1974-75)*		
	Black glass with chrome colored plastic trim. Original		
	price $6.00	5.00	7.00
□116	**BULL DOG PIPE** *(1972-73)*		
	Cream colored milk glass, black stem 6 oz.	4.00	6.00
□117	**EIGHT BALL DECANTER** *(1973)*		
	Billard ball of black glass, black and white cap, 3 oz.	1.00	3.00
□118	**ELECTRIC CHARGER** *(1970-72)*		
	Black glass with red trunk cap and side decals, 5 oz.		
	Original price $4.00	3.00	6.00
□119	**ELECTRIC GUITAR DECANTER** *(1974-75)*		
	Brown glass, silver plastic handle, 6 oz.	3.00	5.00
□120	**CABLE CAR AFTER SHAVE** *(1974-75)*		
	Clear glass painted green, plastic green and white top,		
	4 oz.	6.00	8.00
□121	**CALABASH PIPE** *(1974-75)*		
	Yellow gold painted glass, yellow gold plastic cap, black		
	plastic stand, 3 oz. Original price $8.00	7.00	10.00
□122	**CAMPER** *(1972-74)*		
	Green glass truck with after shave, 5 oz.; beige plastic		
	camper with talc, 4 oz.	7.00	10.00
□123	**CANADA GOOSE** *(1973-74)*		
	Brown glass, black plastic head, 5 oz. Original price $6.00	6.00	8.00
□124	**CAPITOL DECANTER** *(1976)*		
	Replica of the Capitol in white milk glass, white cap, and		
	gold tip, 4.5 oz. Original price $4.00	3.00	6.00
□125	**CAPITOL DECANTER** *(1970-72)*		
	Replica of the Capitol in amber glass, gold cap, 4.5 oz.		
	Original price $4.00	3.00	5.00
□126	**CAPTAIN'S CHOICE** *(1964-65)*		
	Green glass, green paper label, gold cap, 8 oz. Original		
	price $2.50	6.00	8.00

☐ 127	**CAPTAIN'S LANTERN, 1864** *(1975-76)*	
	Black glass, black plastic cap, gold ring, 7 oz. Original	
	price $5.00	**4.00** **6.00**
☐ 128	**CASEY'S LANTERN** *(1966-67)*	
	Clear glass painted gold, gold cap, colored windows in	
	amber, red, green, 10 oz. Original price $6.00	**40.00** **50.00**
☐ 129	**CAPTAIN'S PRIDE** *(1970)*	
	White colored glass bottle with ship decal on side, tan	
	cap, blue lable around neck, black plastic stand, 6 oz.	
	Original price $5.00	**4.00** **6.00**
☐ 130	**CHEVY '55** *(1974-75)*	
	Glass painted green with plastic cover, 2 oz. Original price	
	$5.00	**4.00** **6.00**
☐ 131	**CHIEF PONTIAC CAR ORNAMENT CLASSIC** *(1976)*	
	Black ribbed glass, silver Indian head top, 4 oz. Original	
	price $8.00	**5.00** **7.00**
☐ 132	**CLASSIC LION** *(1973-75)*	
	Green glass, green plastic head, 8 oz. Original price $6.00	**5.00** **7.00**
☐ 133	**CLOSE HARMONY** *(1963)*	
	Barber bottle, white glass, gold letters and neck band,	
	pointed white cap, 8 oz. Original price $2.25	**12.00** **20.00**
☐ 134	**COLLECTOR'S PIPE** *(1973-74)*	
	Brown glass, black stem, 3 oz.	**4.00** **6.00**
☐ 135	**COLT REVOLVER 1851** *(1975-76)*	
	Amber glass, silver plastic barrel, 3 oz. Original price $9.00	**8.00** **10.00**
☐ 136	**CORD '37** *(1974-76)*	
	Glass painted yellow with yellow plastic cap and black	
	plastic top	**6.00** **8.00**
☐ 137	**CORNCOB PIPE AFTER SHAVE** *(1974-75)*	
	Amber glass, black plastic stem, 3 oz. Original price $3.00	**2.00** **4.00**
☐ 138	**CORVETTE STRINGRAY '65** *(1975)*	
	Green glass with green plastic cap. Original price $3.00 . .	**2.00** **4.00**
☐ 139	**COUNTRY VENDOR** *(1973)*	
	Brown glass with brown plastic top, fruits and vegetables	
	on the side, 5 oz.	**7.00** **10.00**
☐ 140	**COVERED WAGON** *(1970-71)*	
	Dark amber glass bottom, white painted top, gold cap,	
	6 oz. Original price $5.00	**3.00** **5.00**
☐ 141	**DAYLIGHT SHAVING TIME** *(1968-70)*	
	Pocket watch in clear glass painted gold, 6 oz. Original	
	price $5.00	**4.00** **6.00**
☐ 142	**DEFENDER CANNON** *(1966)*	
	Amber glass, brown plastic stand, gold caps, gold center	
	band with label, 6 oz. Original price $5.00	**18.00** **22.00**
☐ 143	**DOLLAR'S 'N' SCENTS** *(1966-67)*	
	White glass with green dollar painted on, silver cap, 8 oz.	
	Original price $2.50	**18.00** **22.00**
☐ 144	**DUCK AFTER SHAVE** *(1971)*	
	Glass with ducks painted on sides, gold cap, 3 oz.	**2.00** **4.00**
☐ 145	**DUELING PITOL 1760** *(1973-74)*	
	Brown glass, silver clamp on parts, silver cap, 4 oz.	**7.00** **10.00**
☐ 146	**DUELING PISTOL II** *(1975)*	
	Black glass, gold plastic clamp and cap, 4 oz.	**7.00** **10.00**
☐ 147	**DUNE BUGGY** *(1971-73)*	
	Blue glass, silver motor cap, 5 oz. Original price $5.00	**2.00** **4.00**

☐ 148 **FIELDER'S CHOICE** (1971-72)
Baseball mitt and ball; dark amber glass, black cap, 5 oz.
Original price $4.00 .... 2.00 4.00

☐ 149 **FIRE ALARM BOX** (1975-76)
Clear glass painted red, black cap, 4 oz. Original price
$3.00 .... 2.00 4.00

☐ 150 **FIRE FIGHTER 1910** (1975)
Glass painted red, red plastic back. Original price $6.00 .. 5.00 7.00

☐ 151 **FIRST CLASS MALE** (1970-71)
Mail box of blue glass, red cap, 4 oz. Original price $3.00 . 2.00 4.00

☐ 152 **FIRST DOWN** (1970)
Football of brown glass, white plastic base, 5 oz. Original
price $4.00 .... 3.00 6.00

☐ 153 **FIRST DOWN** (1973-74)
Football of brown glass, white base, 5 oz. 1.00 3.00

☐ 154 **FIRST VOLUNTEER** (1971-72)
Gold coated over clear glass, 6 oz. Original price $8.50 ... 4.00 6.00

☐ 155 **FUTURA** (1969)
Abstract man, clear glass painted silver, silver cap, 5 oz.
Original price $7.00 .... 10.00 15.00

☐ 156 **GAVEL** (1967-68)
Dark amber glass, brown plastic handle, 5 oz. Original
price $4.00 .... 8.00 12.00

☐ 157 **GENERAL 4-4-0** (1971-72)
Dark blue glass and cap, 5½ oz. Original price $7.50 ..... 4.00 6.00

☐ 158 **GOLD CADILLAC** (1969-73)
Clear glass painted gold, gold cap, 6 oz. Original price
$5.00 .... 5.00 7.00

☐ 159 **GOLDEN ROCKET 0-2-2** (1974-75)
Clear glass painted gold, gold plastic cap, 6 oz. Original
price $7.00 .... 6.00 8.00

☐ 160 **GONE FISHING AFTER SHAVE DECANTER** (1973-74)
Man fishing in boat of blue glass with white plastic man,
yellow fishing rod, 5 oz. 5.00 7.00

☐ 161 **THE HARVESTER** (1973-75)
Amber glass with amber plastic front, 5.5 oz. Original
price $5.00 .... 4.00 6.00

☐ 162 **HAYNES APPERSON 1902** (1973-74)
Green glass with green plastic front over the cap. Silver
steering rod 4.00 6.00

☐ 163 **HOMESTEAD** (1973-74)
Brown glass, gray plastic chimney over cap, 4 oz. Original
price $3.00 2.00 4.00

☐ 164 **HUNTER'S STEIN** (1972)
Clear glass with nickel covering, gray and black plastic
bottle inside, 8 oz. 8.00 12.00

☐ 165 **INDIAN HEAD PENNY** (1970-71)
Coin-shaped bottle of clear glass painted bronze, foil
covering embossed with Indian head, 4 oz. Original price
$4.00 .... 2.00 4.00

☐ 166 **INKWELL** (1969-70)
Amber with purple tint, black cap, gold or silver pen, 6 oz.
Original price $6.00 .... 5.00 7.00

☐ 167	**IT'S A BLAST** *(1970-71)* *Horn of clear glass painted gold, black rubber horn on* *cap, 5 oz. Original price $7.00*	4.00	6.00
☐ 168	**JAGUAR CAR** *(1973-76)* *Jade green glass with green plastic trunk, 5 oz.*	4.00	6.00
☐ 169	**KING PIN** *(1969-70)* *Bowling pin of white glass with white cap, and red label,* *4 oz. Original price $3.00*	2.00	4.00
☐ 170	**LONG DRIVE DECANTER** *(1973-75)* *Brown glass, black cap, 4 oz.*	4.00	6.00
☐ 171	**LONGHORN STEER** *(1975-76)* *Dark amber glass, amber plastic head, ivory colored* *horns, 5 oz. Original price $6.00*	5.00	7.00
☐ 172	**LIBERTY BELL** *(1971-72)* *Amber glass, brown cap, 5 oz. Original price $5.00*	4.00	6.00
☐ 173	**LIBERTY BELL** *(1976)* *Clear glass painted bronze, bronze cap, 5 oz. Original* *price $5.00*	4.00	6.00
☐ 174	**LIBERTY DOLLAR** *(1970-72)* *Clear glass painted silver, silver cap with eagle, 6 oz.* *Original price $5.00*	3.00	5.00
☐ 175	**LINCOLN BOTTLE** *(1971-72)* *Rectangular bottle with decal of Lincoln on front, gold* *eagle cap, 4 oz. Original price $3.50*	1.00	3.00
☐ 176	**MALLARD DUCK** *(1967-68)* *Green glass, silver head, 6 oz. Original price $5.00*	6.00	8.50
☐ 177	**MALLARD-IN-FLIGHT** *(1974-75)* *Amber glass, green plastic head, 5 oz. Original price $5.00*	5.00	7.00
☐ 178	**MAN'S WORLD** *(1969-70)* *World globe of clear glass painted gold held by brown* *plastic stand, 6 oz. Original price $5.00*	4.00	6.00
☐ 179	**MARINE BINOCULARS DECANTER** *(1973-74)* *Black paint over clear glass, gold caps, 4 oz.*	7.00	10.00
☐ 180	**MAXWELL 1923** *(1972-74)* *Green glass with beige plastic top and trunk*	4.00	6.00
☐ 181	**MG 1936** *(1974-76)* *Glass painted red, red plastic cap and white plastic top* ..	3.00	5.00
☐ 182	**MINI-BIKE** *(1972-74)* *Amber glass, amber plastic wheel, silver handle bars with* *black grips, 5.5 oz.*	5.00	4.00
☐ 183	**MINUTEMAN DECANTER** *(1975-76)* *White opal glass, plastic top, 4 oz. Original price $7.00* ...	6.00	8.00
☐ 184	**MODEL A** *(1972-74)* *Clear glass painted yellow with yellow cap, 4 oz.*	3.00	5.00
☐ 185	**NOBLE PRINCE** *(1975-76)* *Brown glass, brown plastic head, 4 oz. Original price $3.25*	2.00	4.00
☐ 186	**NO PARKING** *(1975-76)* *Fire hydrant of clear glass painted red, red cap, 6 oz.* *Original price $4.00*	3.00	5.00
☐ 187	**OLF FAITHFUL** *(1972-73)* *Brown glass, brown plastic head, gold keg, 5 oz.*	4.00	6.00
☐ 188	**PACKARD ROADSTER** *(1970-72)* *Amber glass with matching plastic ramble seat cap. Origi-* *nal price $6.00*	2.00	5.00

☐ 189 **PAID STAMP** *(1970-71)*
Hand stamp of dark amber glass, black cap, red rubber
paid stamp on bottom, 4 oz. Original price $4.00 . . . .   **2.00**   **5.00**

☐ 190 **PASS PLAY DECANTER** *(1973-75)*
Football figurine, blue grass, white plastic top over cap,
5 oz. Original price $5.00 . . . .   **4.00**   **6.00**

☐ 191 **PERFECT DRIVE DECANTER** *(1975-76)*
Golfer figurine, green glass, white plastic top over cap,
4 oz. Original price $6.00 . . . .   **5.00**   **7.00**

☐ 192 **PHEASANT** *(1972-74)*
Brown glass, green plastic head, 5 oz. Original price $6.00   **5.00**   **7.00**

☐ 193 **PIANO DECANTER** *(1972)*
Dark amber glass, white cap is a stack of sheet music,
4 oz. Original price $4.00 . . . .   **2.00**   **4.00**

☐ 194 **PIERCE ARROW '33** *(1975-76)*
Dark blue glass painted, beige plastic cap, 5 oz. Original
price $6.00 . . . .   **5.00**   **7.00**

☐ 195 **PIPE DREAM** *(1967)*
Dark amber glass, black cap, beige plastic base, 6 oz.
Original price $5.00 . . . .   **12.00**   **16.00**

☐ 196 **PIPE FULL** *(1971-72)*
Brown glass, black stem, 2 oz. **2.00**   **4.00**

☐ 197 **PONY EXPRESS** *(1971-72)*
Brown glass, copper-colored man on cap, 5 oz. **5.00**   **7.00**

☐ 198 **PONY EXPRESS RIDER PIPE** *(1975-76)*
White milk glass with black plastic stem, 3 oz. Original
price $5.00 . . . .   **4.00**   **6.00**

☐ 199 **PONY POST** *(1972-73)*
Bronze painted glass, bronze cap and nose ring, 5 oz.
Original price $5.00 . . . .   **4.00**   **6.00**

☐ 200 **PONY POST MINIATURE** *(1973-74)*
Clear glass, gold cap and ring, 1.5 oz. Original price $3.00   **1.00**   **3.00**

☐ 201 **PONY POST "TALL"** *(1966-67)*
Green glass, gold cap and nose ring, 8 oz. Original price
$4.00 . . . .   **5.00**   **7.00**

☐ 202 **PORSCHE '68** *(1976)*
Amber glass with amber plastic cap, 2 oz. Original price
$3.00 . . . .   **2.00**   **4.00**

☐ 203 **POT BELLY STOVE** *(1970-71)*
Black glass, black cap, 5 oz. Original price $4.00 . . . .   **3.00**   **5.00**

☐ 204 **PRESIDENT LINCOLN DECANTER** *(1973)*
Bust of Lincoln, white plastic head with remainder of
clear glass painted white, 6 oz. Original price $5.00 . . . . . .   **4.00**   **6.00**

☐ 205 **PRESIDENT WASHINGTON DECANTER** *(1974-76)*
Bust of Washington in clear glass painted white, white
plastic head, 6 oz. Original price $6.00 . . . .   **5.00**   **7.00**

☐ 206 **QUAIL** *(1973-75)*
Brown glass, gold cap, 5.5 oz. Original price $6.00 . . . .   **5.00**   **7.00**

☐ 207 **RAINBOW TROUT** *(1973-74)*
Green glass, green plastic head over cap, 5 oz. **4.00**   **6.00**

☐ 208 **RAM'S HEAD DECANTER** *(1975-76)*
White opal glass on brown plastic base, 5 oz. Original
price $5.00 . . . .   **4.00**   **6.00**

☐ 209 **RED VOLKSWAGON** *(1972)*
Glass painted red, red plastic cap, 4 oz. **2.00**   **4.00**

☐210 **REVOLUTIONARY CANNON** *(1975-76)*
Glass painted bronze, plastic cap, 2 oz. Original price
$4.00 .... **3.00** **5.00**

☐211 **ROAD RUNNER** *(1973-74)*
Blue glass with blue plastic front wheel, silver handle bars
with black grips, 5.5 oz. **5.00** **7.00**

☐212 **ROLLS ROYCE** *(1972-75)*
Glass painted beige with dark brown and silver parts **6.00** **8.00**

☐213 **ROYAL ORB** *(1965-66)*
Clear round bottle, gold cap, red felt band around neck,
8 oz. Original price $3.25 .... **15.00** **20.00**

☐214 **SCIMITAR** *(1968-69)*
Clear glass painted gold, red windows, gold cap, 6 oz.
Original price $6.00 .... **14.00** **18.00**

☐215 **SEA TROPHY** *(1972-73)*
Blue, plastic blue head over cap, 5.5 oz. **6.00** **8.00**

☐216 **SIDE WHEELER** *(1971-72)*
Dark amber glass, black plastic stacks, silver or gold cap,
5 oz. Original price $6.00 .... **2.00** **4.00**

☐217 **SILVER DUESENBERG** *(1970-72)*
Silver paint over clear glass, 6 oz. Original price $6.00 .... **4.00** **6.00**

☐218 **SHORT PONY** *(1968-69)*
Green glass, gold cap, 4 oz. Original price $3.50 .... **3.00** **4.00**

☐219 **SNOOPY SURPRISE** *(1969-71)*
White glass, blue hat, black ears, 5 oz. Original price $4.00 **2.00** **4.00**

☐220 **SNOWMOBIL** *(1974-75)*
Blue glass with yellow plastic front, black runners **5.00** **7.00**

☐221 **SPARK PLUG DECANTER** *(1975-76)*
White milk glass, gray cap, 1.5 oz. Original price $2.00 ... **1.00** **3.00**

☐222 **SPIRIT OF ST. LOUIS** *(1970-72)*
Clear glass painted silver, 6 oz. Original price $8.50 ...... **5.00** **7.00**

☐223 **SPORT OF KINGS** *(1975)*
Amber glass, plastic head, 5 oz. Original price $5.00 ..... **4.00** **6.00**

☐224 **STAGE COACH** *(1970-71)*
Dark amber glass with gold cap, 5 oz. Original price $5.00 **4.00** **6.00**

☐225 **STANLEY STEAMER** *(1971-72)*
Blue glass bottle with black plastic seats and tire caps.
Original price $5.00 .... **2.00** **4.00**

☐226 **STAR SIGNS DECANTER** *(1975-76)*
Ovoid-shaped bottle of black glass, gold cap, 4 oz.
Original price $3.50 .... **2.00** **5.00**

☐227 **STATION WAGON** *(1971-73)*
Green glass car with beige plastic top. Original price $6.00 **3.00** **6.00**

☐228 **STEIN — SILVER** *(1965-66)*
Clear glass painted silver, silver cap, 8 oz. Original price
$3.50 .... **7.00** **10.00**

☐229 **STRAIGHT 8** *(1969-71)*
Dark green glass with black trunk cap, 5 oz. Number 8 on
the hood. Original price $3.50 .... **3.00** **5.00**

☐230 **STERLING SIX** *(1968-70)*
Produced in four various shades of amber glass with
black tire cap. Original price $4.00 .... **3.00** **6.00**

☐231 **STERLING SIX** *(1973-74)*
Green glass with white tire cap **3.00** **6.00**

☐232 **STOCK CAR RACER** *(1974-75)*
Blue glass with blue plastic cap, 5 oz. Original price $6.00 **5.00 7.00**

☐233 **STUDEBAKER '51** *(1975-76)*
Blue glass with blue plastic parts. Original price $2.50 ... **1.50 3.50**

☐234 **SUPER CYCLE AFTER SHAVE** *(1971-72)*
Gray glass, 4 oz. **4.00 6.00**

☐235 **SUPER SHAVER** *(1973)*
Razor of blue glass, gray plastic top, 4 oz. **2.00 4.00**

☐236 **SURE WINNER BASEBALL DECANTER** *(1973-74)*
White ball with dark blue lettering and blue base **1.00 3.00**

☐237 **SURE WINNER RACING CAR** *(1972-75)*
Blue glass with blue cap, 5.5 oz. Original price $5.00 ..... **4.00 6.00**

☐238 **STUTZ BEARCAT 1914** *(1974-76)*
Glass painted red with black plastic seats and cap, 6 oz. . **5.00 7.00**

☐239 **SWINGER GOLF BAG** *(1969-71)*
Black glass, red and silver clubs, 5 oz. Original price $5.00 **4.00 6.00**

☐240 **TEN-POINT BUCK** *(1973-74)*
Redish brown glass, redish brown plastic head and hold antlers, 6 oz. Original price $7.00 .... **6.00 8.00**

☐241 **THEODORE ROOSEVELT DECANTER** *(1975-76)*
Bust of Roosevelt, white plastic head, clear glass painted white, 5 oz. Original price $7.00 .... **6.00 8.00**

☐242 **THOMAS FLYER** *(1974-76)*
Glass painted white with red and blue plastic parts, white tire cap on back, 6 oz. Original price $6.00 .... **5.00 7.00**

☐243 **TOTEM POLE DECANTER** *(1975)*
Dark amber glass, plastic cap, 6 oz. Original price $5.00 .. **4.00 6.00**

☐244 **TOURING T** *(1969-70)*
Black glass with black plastic top and tire cap, 6 oz. Original price $6.00 .... **5.00 7.00**

☐245 **TOURING TEST T** *(1969)*
Dark amber glass factory test bottle; also in clear glass which is less valuable **70.00 80.00**

☐246 **TOWN PUMP** *(1968-69)*
Old fashioned water pump, black glass, gold cap, plastic handle, 6 oz. Original price $5.00 .... **4.00 6.00**

☐247 **TRIBUTE RIBBED WARRIOR** *(1971-73)*
Bust of Trojan warrior, clear ribbed glass, silver cap, 6 oz. Original price $4.00 .... **1.50 3.50**

☐248 **TRIBUTE SILVER WARRIOR** *(1967)*
Bust of Trojan warrior in clear glass painted silver and blue, silver cap, 6 oz. Original price $4.50 .... **12.00 16.00**

☐249 **TRIPLE CROWN DECANTER** *(1974-76)*
Horseshoe-shaped bottle of brown glass, red plastic cap, horse and horse shoe embossed on front, 4 oz. Original price $3.00 .... **2.00 4.00**

☐250 **TWENTY DOLLAR GOLD PIECE** *(1971-72)*
Clear glass painted gold, gold cap, 6 oz. Original price $5.00 .... **3.00 5.00**

☐251 **UNCLE SAM PIPE** *(1975-76)*
White opal glass with blue band and blue plastic stem, 3 oz. Original price $5.00 .... **4.00 6.00**

☐252 **VIKING HORN** *(1966)*
Dark amber glass, gold cap and trim, 7 oz. Original price $5.00 .... **10.00 14.00**

☐253	**VOLKSWAGON BUS** *(1975-76)*		
	Glass painted red with silver grey motorcycle. With four stick-on labels. Original price $5.00	4.00	6.00
☐254	**WASHINGTON BOTTLE** *(1970-72)*		
	Rectangular bottle with decal of Washington on front, gold eagle cap, 4 oz. Original price $3.50	1.00	3.00
☐255	**WEATHER–OR–NOT AFTER SHAVE** *(1969-71)*		
	Barometer in dark amber glass, gold cap, 5 oz. Original price $5.00	4.00	6.00
☐256	**WESTERN BOOT AFTER SHAVE** *(1973-75)*		
	Dark amber glass, silver cap and lamp, 5 oz.	3.00	5.00
☐257	**WESTERN CHOICE (STEER HORNS)** *(1967)*		
	Brown plastic base with red center with two clear bottles, silver caps. Original price $6.00	16.00	20.00
☐258	**WESTERN SADDLE** *(1971-72)*		
	Brown glass, brown cap; saddle astride a fence, 5 oz.	5.00	7.00
☐259	**WHALE OIL LANTERN AFTER SHAVE DECANTER** *(1974-75)*		
	Green glass, silver plastic top and base, 5 oz. Original price $4.00	3.00	5.00
☐260	**WHALE ORGANIZER BOTTLE** *(1973)*		
	Ivory milk glass with dark blue seafaring designs, shaped like walrus tusks, 3 oz.	4.00	6.00
☐261	**WILD TURKEY** *(1974-76)*		
	Amber glass, silver and red plastic head, 6 oz. Original price $5.00	4.00	6.00
☐262	**WISE CHOICE OWL** *(1969-70)*		
	Amber with silver top, 4 oz. Original price $4.00	4.00	6.00
☐263	**WORLDS GREATEST DAD DECANTER** *(1971)*		
	Trophy-shaped bottle, clear glass, red cap, 4 oz. Original price $3.50	2.00	4.00

MEN'S MISCELLANEOUS

☐264	**AFTER SHAVE LOTION** *(1949-58)*		
	Clear glass, red cap, silver label, 4 oz. Original price $.69 .	6.00	8.00
☐265	**AFTER SHAVE LOTION** *(1958)*		
	Clear glass, red cap, paper label, black and white, ½ oz. .	5.00	7.00
☐266	**BAY RUM AFTER SHAVE** *(1964-65)*		
	Clear glass, black cap, label, 4 oz. Original price $1.25 ...	8.00	10.00
☐267	**BATH OIL** *(1969-72)*		
	Black glass bottle with red cap, 4 oz. Original price $2.50 .	1.00	3.00
☐268	**BLEND 7 EMOLLIENT AFTER SHAVE** *(1973-74)*		
	Clear glass with 7 design, black cap	3.00	5.00
☐269	**COLOGNE FOR MEN** *(1949-58)*		
	Clear glass, red caps, silver labels, 2 oz. Original price $.69	5.00	7.00
☐270	**COLOGNE FOR MEN** *(1953-54)*		
	Clear glass, red cap, green label, 4 oz.	12.00	18.00
☐271	**COLOGNE FOR MEN** *(1952-57)*		
	Clear glass, red cap, paper label with stagecoach, 4 oz. ..	8.00	10.00
☐272	**COLOGNE FOR MEN** *(1958)*		
	Clear glass, red cap, black and white label, 2 oz.	10.00	14.00
☐273	**CREAM HAIR LOTION** *(1949-58)*		
	Clear glass, red cap, silver label. Original price $.59	8.00	12.00

☐ 274 **CREAM HAIR LOTION** *(1953-54)*
Clear glass, red cap, 1 oz. 20.00 24.00

☐ 275 **DEEP WOODS AFTER SHAVE** *(1976)*
Clear glass, brown cap. Original price $3.00 .... .50 2.00

☐ 276 **DEODORANT FOR MEN** *(1949-58)*
Clear glass, red cap, green label. Original price $.63 ..... 5.00 7.00

☐ 277 **DEODORANT FOR MEN** *(1954-57)*
Clear glass, red cap, green label, 4 oz. 8.00 10.00

☐ 278 **DEODORANT FOR MEN** *(1958-62)*
Clear glass, red cap, black and white label, 2 oz. Original
price $.69 .... 8.00 10.00

☐ 279 **ELECTRIC PRE-SHAVE LOTION** *(1957-58)*
Clear glass, red cap, silver label. Original price $.89 ..... 8.00 10.00

☐ 280 **ELECTRIC PRE-SHAVE LOTION** *(1959-62)*
Clear glass, red cap, black and white label, 4 oz. Original
price $.89 .... 10.00 14.00

☐ 281 **EVEREST AFTER SHAVE** *(1976)*
Clear glass, bronze cap, 5 oz. Original price $4.00 .... .50 2.00

☐ 282 **EXCALIBUR COLOGNE** *(1969-73)*
Clear glass with sword design on front, three-dimensional
rock design inside the bottom of the bottle, gold cap, 6 oz.
Original price $5.00 .... 4.00 6.00

☐ 283 **FIRST CLASS MALE** *(1953-56)*
Clear glass cologne bottle for men, paper label, 6 oz.
Original price $1.50 .... 12.00 16.00

☐ 284 **FOAMY BATH FOR CLEANER HIDES** *(1957)*
Clear glass, red cap, paper label with picture of cow hide,
2 oz. 16.00 20.00

☐ 285 **HAND GUARD** *(1951-52)*
Clear glass, blue cap, red, white and black label with
soldier, 2 oz. 18.00 26.00

☐ 286 **HAIR LOTION** *(1940-49)*
Clear glass, maroon cap, 6 oz. Original price $.69 .... 30.00 40.00

☐ 287 **HAIR LOTION** *(1949-58)*
Clear glass, red cap, silver label. Original price $.59 ..... 8.00 12.00

☐ 288 **HAIR LOTION** *(1953-54)*
Clear glass bottle, red cap, green label, 1 oz. 20.00 24.00

☐ 289 **HAIR TONIC** *(1938-39)*
Clear glass, maroon cap and label, 6 oz. Original price
$.52 .... 30.00 40.00

☐ 290 **HAIR TONIC EAU DE QUININE** *(1936-38)*
Clear glass, turquoise cap, 6 oz. Original price $.78 ...... 18.00 24.00

☐ 291 **HAIR TRAINER FOR TRAINING WILD HAIR** *(1957)*
Clear glass, red cap, paper label with picture of cow hide,
2 oz. 16.00 20.00

☐ 292 **HAIR TRAINER** *(1957-58)*
Clear glass, white or blue cap, 6 oz. Original price $.79 ... 14.00 18.00

☐ 293 **ISLAND LIME AFTER SHAVE** *(1969-73)*
Green frosted glass, green cap with yellow printing, 6 oz.
Original price $4.00 .... 1.00 2.00

☐ 294 **LEATHER AFTER SHAVE LOTION** *(1968)*
Clear glass, red cap, 3 oz. 6.00 8.00

☐ 295 **LEATHER ALL PURPOSE COLOGNE** *(1966)*
Clear glass, red label, black cap, 4 oz. 10.00 14.00

☐296	**OLAND COLOGNE** *(1970-76)*		
	Embossed glass, brown cap, 6 oz. Original price $6.50 ...	**1.00**	**3.00**
☐297	**ORIGINAL AFTER SHAVE** *(1965-69)*		
	Clear glass, red cap, green label with stagecoach, 4 oz.		
	Original price $1.25	**3.00**	**5.00**
☐298	**STAGE COACH EMBOSSED BOTTLES** *(1960-61)*		
	Clear glass, red or white caps, foil label with embossed		
	stagecoach, 2 oz.	**16.00**	**20.00**
☐299	**SPICY AFTER SHAVE** *(1965-67)*		
	Clear glass, beige cap, 4 oz. Original price $.98	**6.00**	**8.00**
☐300	**SPICY AFTER SHAVE LOTION** *(1966)*		
	Clear glass, paper label with wood grain, white cap, 4 oz. .	**8.00**	**10.00**
☐301	**SPICY AFTER SHAVE** *(1967-74)*		
	Clear or amber glass, black cap, 4 oz.	**.50**	**1.50**
☐302	**SPICY COLOGNE PLUS** *(1965-67)*		
	Narrow rectangular bottle, clear glass, gold ribbed cap,		
	2 oz. Original price $2.50	**15.00**	**20.00**
☐303	**TRIBUTE AFTER SHAVE LOTION** *(1963-68)*		
	Clear glass, silver and blue cap, 6 oz. Original price $2.50 .	**4.00**	**8.00**
☐304	**TRIBUTE AFTER SHAVE** *(1968-72)*		
	Clear glass with blue and silver cap, blue label, 4 oz.		
	Original price $2.25	**2.00**	**4.00**
☐305	**TRIBUTE ALL PURPOSE COLOGNE** *(1967-68)*		
	Clear glass with blue and silver top, cap and neck tag,		
	4 oz. Original price $3.00	**8.00**	**14.00**
☐306	**TRIBUTE COLOGNE FOR MEN** *(1964-66)*		
	Clear glass with blue and silver top, cap and tag, 4 oz.		
	Original price $2.50	**8.00**	**14.00**
☐307	**TRIBUTE ELECTRIC PRE–SHAVE LOTION** *(1963-66)*		
	Clear glass with blue and silver cap, 4 oz. Original price		
	$1.75	**6.00**	**10.00**
☐308	**WILD COUNTRY AFTER SHAVE** *(1971-76)*		
	Clear glass with silver label, black cap, 4 oz. Original price		
	$4.50	**.75**	**2.00**

WOMEN'S FRAGANCE

☐309	**APPLE BLOSSOM COLOGNE MIST** *(1974-76)*		
	Clear glass, clear cap with inner pink and white cap, 2 oz.		
	Original price $3.00	**.50**	**1.00**
☐310	**APPLE BLOSSOM PERFUME** *(1941-42)*		
	Clear glass, gold cap, ⅛ oz. Original price $.75	**50.00**	**55.00**
☐311	**APPLE BLOSSOM PERFUME** *(1941-43)*		
	Clear glass, gold cap and label, ⅛ oz. Original price $.75 ..	**25.00**	**35.00**
☐312	**APPLE BLOSSOM TOLIET WATER** *(1941-42)*		
	Pink, white and blue glass, 2 oz. Original price $1.04	**30.00**	**40.00**
☐313	**APPLE BLOSSOM TOLIET WATER** *(1941-42)*		
	Clear glass, blue label on front, pink cap, 2 oz. Original		
	price $1.04	**30.00**	**40.00**
☐314	**ATTENTION TOILET WATER** *(1942)*		
	Clear glass, purple cap, 2 oz. Original price $.25	**35.00**	**45.00**
☐315	**BALLAD PERFUME** *(1945)*		
	Small bottle, clear glass, gold neck cord and label,		
	3 drams. Original price $3.50	**120.00**	**145.00**

☐316	**BALLAD PERFUME** *(1945-53)* *Clear glass, small bottle, glass stopper, gold neck cord* *and label, 3 drams. Original price $3.50*	120.00	130.00
☐317	**BIRD OF PARADISE COLOGNE DECANTER** *(1970-72)* *Clear glass in shape of bird with gold head, 5 oz.*	7.00	9.00
☐318	**BIRD OF PARADISE PERFUME ROLLETTE** *(1970-76)* *Clear glass, gold cap ⅓ oz. Original price $3.00*	1.00	2.00
☐319	**BLUE LOTUS AFTER BATH FRESHENER** *(1967-72)* *Clear glass with blue cap, 6 oz. Original price $3.00*	4.00	6.00
☐320	**BLUE LOTUS CREAM SACHET** *(1968-72)* *Blue frosted glass, blue cap, .66 oz. Original price $2.50* ..	1.00	3.00
☐321	**BRIGHT NIGHT COLOGNE** *(1954-61)* *Clear glass, gold speckled cap, gold neck cord and white* *paper label, 4 oz. Original price $2.50*	16.00	20.00
☐322	**BRIGHT NIGHT COLOGNE MIST** *(1958-61)* *Clear glass coated with white plastic, gold speckled gold* *cap, gold neck cord with white label, 3 oz. Original price* *$2.75*	16.00	22.00
☐323	**BRIGHT NIGHT PERFUME** *(1954-59)* *Clear glass, glass stopper, white label on gold neck cord,* *½ oz. Original price $7.50*	70.00	115.00
☐324	**BRIGHT NIGHT TOILET WATER** *(1955-61)* *Clear glass, gold speckled cap, gold neck cord with white* *label, 2 oz. Original price $2.00*	16.00	22.00
☐325	**BRISTOL BLUE BATH OIL** *(1975-76)* *Blue opaline glass, plastic inner bottle, 5 oz. Original price* *$6.00*	2.00	4.00
☐326	**BRISTOL BLUE COLOGNE** *(1975)* *Blue glass with raised designs, 5 oz. Original price $6.00* .	3.00	5.00
☐327	**BROCADE PERFUME ROLLETTE** *(1967-72)* *Brown frosted glass, gold cap, ribbed. Original price $3.00*	2.00	4.00
☐328	**BUTTERFLY COLOGNE** *(1972-73)* *Clear glass, gold cap with two prongs for antenna, 1.5 oz.* *Original price $3.00*	2.00	4.00
☐329	**BUTTONS 'N BOWS COLOGNE** *(1960-63)* *Clear glass, white cap, pink lettering on front, pink ribbon* *around neck, 2 oz. Original price $1.35*	14.00	16.00
☐330	**CHARISMA COLOGNE** *(1969-72)* *Red glass, red plastic cap trimmed in gold, 4 oz. Original* *price $6.00*	2.00	4.00
☐331	**CHARISMA COLOGNE MIST** *(1968-76)* *Clear glass coated with red plastic, gold trimming, 3 oz.* *Original price $8.00*	.50	3.00
☐332	**CHARISMA COLOGNE SILK** *(1969)* *Frosted glass, red cap, 3 oz. Original price $4.50*	3.00	5.00
☐333	**CHARISMA COLOGNE SILK** *(1970-71)* *Clear glass, red cap, 3 oz. Original price $4.50*	1.00	3.00
☐334	**CHARISMA PERFUME ROLLETTE** *(1968-76)* *Red glass, gold trimming, .33 oz. Original price $4.50*	.50	3.00
☐335	**COLOGNE ELEGANTE** *(1971-72)* *Tall bottle with red rose on gold cap, clear glass painted* *gold, 4 oz. Original price $5.00*	2.00	4.00

☐ 336	**COME SUMMER COLOGNE MIST** *(1975-76)* *Clear glass, green band, white cap with green band, 2 oz.* *Original price $3.00*	.50	2.00
☐ 337	**CORNUCOPIA SKIN–SO–SOLFT** *(1971-76)* *White glass, gold cap, 6 oz.*	4.00	6.00
☐ 338	**COUNTRY GARDEN FOAMING BATH OIL** *(1971-73)* *White glass, white cap, green ribbon around neck.* *Original price $5.50*	4.00	6.00
☐ 339	**COUNTRY KITCHEN MOISTURIZED HAND LOTION** *(1974-76)* *Red glass, plastic top, 10 oz. Original price $6.00*	5.00	7.00
☐ 340	**COURTSHIP PERFUME** *(1937)* *Clear glass, gold cap, ribbed cap, paper label with flower,* *2 drams*	45.00	55.00
☐ 341	**COURTSHIP PERFUME** *(1938)* *Clear glass, gold cap, paper label, 2 drams. Original price* *$.20*	45.00	55.00
☐ 342	**COTILLON BATH OIL** *(1950-53)* *Clear glass, pink cap, pink and white paper label, 6 oz.* *Original price $.95*	18.00	24.00
☐ 343	**COTILLION BATH OIL** *(1954-59)* *Clear glass with pink lettering, pink cap, 4½ oz. Original* *price $1.35*	8.00	12.00
☐ 344	**COTILLION BODY POWDER** *(1958-59)* *Frosted glass, pink cap, pink paper label, 3 oz. Original* *price $1.00*	8.00	12.00
☐ 345	**COTILLION COLOGNE** *(1950-53)* *Clear glass, pink cap, pink paper label, 4 oz. Original price* *$1.75*	18.00	24.00
☐ 346	**COTILLION COLOGNE** *(1946-50)* *Clear glass, pink cap, scallops along sides of bottle, 6 oz.* *Original price $1.50*	50.00	60.00
☐ 347	**COTILLION COLOGNE** *(1957)* *Clear glass, white cap, lettering painted on front, 3 drams*	10.00	15.00
☐ 348	**COTILLION COLOGNE** *(1960)* *Clear glass, pink paper label around neck, pink lettering* *on front, pink cap, 4 oz. Original price $2.50*	18.00	22.00
☐ 349	**COTILLION COLOGNE** *(1961)* *Clear glass, gold cap, pink band around neck, lettering* *painted on front, 2 oz. Original price $1.50*	18.00	24.00
☐ 350	**COTILLION COLOGNE** *(1961-63)* *Frosted glass, white cap, 4 oz. Original price $3.00*	8.00	12.00
☐ 351	**COTILLION COLOGNE** *(1961-71)* *Frosted glass, white pointed cap, { oz. Original price $2.00*	1.00	2.00
☐ 352	**COTILLION COLOGNE** *(1969-72)* *Clear glass, white pointed cap, ½ oz. Original price $1.50* .	1.00	2.00
☐ 353	**COTILLION COLOGNE MIST** *(1961-74)* *Clear glass coated with white plastic, white cap, 3 oz.* *Original price $4.00*	8.00	12.00
☐ 354	**COTILLION CREAM LOTION** *(1950-53)* *Clear glass, pink cap, pink and white paper label, 4 oz.* *Original price $.89*	18.00	24.00
☐ 355	**COTILLION CREAM LOTION** *(1954-61)* *Clear glass, pink lettering, pink cap, 4½ oz. Original price* *$.95*	6.00	10.00

☐356 **COTILLION FOUR OUNCES COLOGNE** *(1953-61)*
Clear glass, gold cap, pink band at neck, pink label, 4 oz.
Original price $2.00 .... **8.00** **12.00**

☐357 **COTILLION PERFUME** *(1935)*
Clear glass, metal cap, paper label on front, ½ oz. Original
price $.20 .... **50.00** **60.00**

☐358 **COTILLION PERFUME** *(1935)*
Clear glass, gold cap, green and gold paper label, ¼ oz.
Original price $.20 .... **50.00** **60.00**

☐359 **COTILLION PERFUME** *(1968-76)*
Clear glass, gold cap, 2 drams. Original price $.20 .... **45.00** **55.00**

☐360 **COTILLION PERFUME** *(1939)*
Clear glass, ribbed cap, paper label on front, 2 drams **50.00** **60.00**

☐361 **COTILLION PERFUME** *(1940)*
Clear glass, ribbed gold cap, paper label on front, 2 drams **50.00** **60.00**

☐362 **COTILLION PERFUME** *(1951-52)*
Clear glass, swirl bottle, glass stopper, white, pink and
blue floral neck tag at neck, 3 drams. Original price $3.50 . **100.00** **140.00**

☐363 **COTILLION PERFUME OIL FOR THE BATH** *(1963-64)*
Frosted glass, white pointed cap, ½ oz. Original price
$4.00 .... **8.00** **12.00**

☐364 **COTILLION SWIRL PERFUME** *(1948-50)*
Clear glass, swirl bottle, gold neck band, dome lid, paper
label, 3 drams. Original price $3.00 .... **70.00** **80.00**

☐365 **COTILLION TALC** *(1956-58)*
Frosted glass, pink cap, pink paper label, 3 oz. Original
price $1.00 .... **8.00** **12.00**

☐366 **COTILLION TOLIET WATER** *(1939)*
Clear glass, ribbed cap, paper label on front, with
flowered design **30.00** **40.00**

☐367 **COTILLION TOILET WATER** *(1950-53)*
Clear glass, pink cap and white paper label, 2 oz. Original
price $1.25 .... **18.00** **24.00**

☐368 **COTILLION TOILET WATER** *(1953-61)*
Clear glass, gold cap, pink band around neck, pink label,
2 oz. Original price $1.50 .... **12.00** **16.00**

☐369 **CREAMY DECANTER** *(1973-75)*
Clear glass painted yellow, design of basket and flowers
on front, 8 oz. Original price $5.00 .... **4.00** **6.00**

☐370 **CRIMSON CARNATION PERFUME** *(1946-47)*
Clear glass, white cap, paper label on front. Original price
$3.75 .... **90.00** **110.00**

☐371 **CRIMSON CARNATION TOILET WATER** *(1946-48)*
Clear glass, gold or plastic cap, long narrow paper label
on front. Original price $1.19 .... **40.00** **50.00**

☐372 **CRYSTAL COLOGNE** *(1966-70)*
Clear glass, patterned glass, matching plastic cap, gold
trim at shoulder, 4 oz. Original price $3.50 to $5.00 .... **3.00** **5.00**

☐373 **DACHSHUND COLOGNE DECANTER** *(1973-74)*
Frosted glass, gold cap, 1.5 oz. **2.00** **4.00**

☐374 **DAISIES WON'T TELL BUBBLE BATH** *(1957-58)*
Clear glass with rib around middle, painted lettering,
white cap, 4 oz. Original price $1.10 .... **6.00** **10.00**

☐375 **DAISIES WON'T TELL COLOGNE** *(1958-62)*
Clear glass, white cap, painted lettering on front, lace
bow around neck, 2 oz. Original price $1.19 . . . .   **6.00   8.00**

☐376 **DAISIES WON'T TELL COLOGNE** *(1962-64)*
Clear glass, white cap, lettering painted on front, daisies
on front, 2 oz. Original price $1.19 . . . .   **5.00   7.00**

☐377 **DEW KISS DECANTER** *(1974-75)*
Clear glass painted, pink lid, 4 oz. Original price $3.00 . . .   **2.00   4.00**

☐378 **ELEGANTE COLOGNE** *(1956-59)*
Clear glass, silver cap and neck tag, red ribbon, 4 oz.
Original price $2.50 . . . .   **35.00   45.00**

☐379 **ELEGANTE PERFUME** *(1956-59)*
Clear glass, silver cap and neck tag, red neck ribbon ½ oz.
Original price $7.50 . . . .   **100.00   140.00**

☐380 **ELEGANTE TOILET WATER** *(1957-59)*
Clear glass, silver cap and neck tag, red neck ribbon, { oz.
Original price $2.00 . . . .   **30.00   40.00**

☐381 **EMERALD BUD VASE COLOGNE** *(1971)*
Green glass, glass lid, 3 oz. Original price $5.00 . . . .   **2.00   4.00**

☐382 **FLORAL BUD VASE** *(1973-75)*
White milk glass, 5 oz. **4.00   6.00**

☐383 **FLOWERTIME COLOGNE** *(1949-53)*
Clear glass, pink cap, paper label on front, 4 oz. Original
price $1.75 . . . .   **15.00   25.00**

☐384 **FOREVER SPRING CREAM** *(1956-59)*
Clear glass, yellow cap, lettering painted on front, 4 oz.
Original price $.95 . . . .   **10.00   14.00**

☐385 **FOREVER SPRING ONE DRAM PERFUME** *(1951-52)*
Clear glass, ribbed, gold cap, 1 dram. Original price $1.75   **15.00   18.00**

☐386 **FOREVER SPRING PERFUME** *(1951-56)*
Clear glass, glass stopper, blue ribbon and tag on neck,
3 drams. Original price $5.00 . . . .   **75.00   85.00**

☐387 **FOREVER SPRING PERFUME** *(1956-59)*
Yellow cap with blue bird on top, lettering painted on
front, ½ oz. Original price $5.00 . . . .   **80.00   90.00**

☐388 **FOREVER SPRING TOILET WATER** *(1939)*
Clear glass with leaflet design in the glass, yellow plastic
cap in design of tulip, 2 oz. Original price $1.50 . . . .   **15.00   18.00**

☐389 **FOREVER SPRING TOILET WATER** *(1956-59)*
Clear glass, yellow cap, blue bird on cap, lettering painted
on front, 2 oz. Original price $1.50 . . . .   **12.00   16.00**

☐390 **FLOWERTIME TALC** *(1949-53)*
Clear glass, brass shaker lid, 5 oz. Original price $.89 . . . .   **15.00   25.00**

☐391 **FLOWERTIME TOILET WATER** *(1949-53)*
Clear glass, pink cap, paper label on front, 2 oz. Original
price $1.25 . . . .   **18.00   25.00**

☐392 **GARDEN OF LOVE SWIRL PERFUME** *(1948)*
Clear glass, swirl design, glass stopper, gold neck tag,
3 drams. Original price $3.00 . . . .   **85.00   95.00**

☐393 **GOLDEN PROMISE COLOGNE** *(1947-56)*
Clear glass, large gold dome shaped cap, lettering
painted on front around shoulder, 4 oz. Original price
$2.25 . . . .   **16.00   22.00**

☐394	**GOLDEN PROMISE PERFUME** *(1947-50)*		
	Clear glass, gold cap, lettering painted on front, ½ oz.		
	Original price $3.95	160.00	185.00
☐395	**GOLDEN PROMISE PERFUME** *(1949)*		
	Clear glass, some ribbing, large gold cap in dome shape,		
	¼ oz.	20.00	30.00
☐396	**GOLDEN PROMISE PERFUME** *(1950-54)*		
	Clear glass, glass stopper domed shaped, faceted bottle,		
	gold base label and neck cord, 3 drams. Original price		
	$4.00	90.00	110.00
☐397	**GOLDEN PROMISE PERFUME** *(1954-56)*		
	Clear glass, glass stopper with flat top, gold and white		
	label, ½ oz. Original price $3.95	110.00	140.00
☐398	**GOLDEN PROMISE PERFUME GIFT** *(1947)*		
	Clear glass, large gold cap dome shaped, gold paper label		
	with red lettering	45.00	55.00
☐399	**GOLDEN PROMISE TOILET WATER** *(1953-56)*		
	Clear glass, large dome shaped cap, lettering painted on		
	around shoulder, { oz. Original price $1.50	18.00	22.00
☐400	**HAPPY HOURS COLOGNE** *(1948-49)*		
	Clear glass, pink cap, paper label on front	20.00	25.00
☐401	**HAPPY HOURS PERFUME** *(1948-49)*		
	Clear glass, pink cap, paper label on front	60.00	70.00
☐402	**HAPPY HOURS TALC** *(1948-49)*		
	Clear glass, metal shaker cap, small paper label on front,		
	2¾ oz.	20.00	30.00
☐403	**HAWAIIAN WHITE GINGER ALE AFTER BATH**		
	FRESHENER *(1965-67)*		
	Clear glass, pedestal foot, large white flat cap, painted		
	lettering in white, 5 oz. Original price $2.00	4.00	6.00
☐404	**HAWAIIAN WHITE GINGER COLOGNE MIST** *(1971-72)*		
	Green glass, large white cap, wide decorative band		
	around neck, 2 oz. Original price $4.25	1.00	2.00
☐405	**HAWAIIAN WHITE GINGER COLOGNE MIST** *(1972-76)*		
	Clear glass, textured, clear plastic cap, green, red and		
	white inner cap, 2 oz. Original price $5.00	.50	1.00
☐406	**HERE'S MY HEART COLOGNE** *(1970-71)*		
	Clear glass, white plastic cap with scalloped and beaded		
	rim, lettering painted on front, ½ 4 oz. Original price $1.50	1.00	3.00
☐407	**HERE'S MY HEART CREAM LOTION** *(1958-68)*		
	Clear glass, white plastic cap with scalloped and beaded		
	rim, lettering painted on front, 4 oz. Original price $1.00 ..	2.00	4.00
☐408	**HERE'S MY HEART LOTION SACHET** *(1958)*		
	Clear glass, fan shaped, blue cap, also came in Persian		
	Wood	6.00	10.00
☐409	**HERE'S MY HEART PERFUME** *(1946-48)*		
	Clear glass, glass stopper with dome shape, pink ribbon		
	around neck, lettering painted on front, ½ oz. Original		
	price $7.50	90.00	120.00
☐410	**HERE'S MY HEART PERFUMED CREAM ROLLETTE**		
	(1963-65)		
	Clear glass, embossed, gold cap, .33 oz. Original price		
	$1.75	2.00	4.00
☐411	**HERE'S MY HEART PERFUME ROLLETTE** *(1967-68)*		
	Clear glass, ribbed, gold cap, .33 oz. Original price $3.00 .	2.00	4.00

☐ 412 **HERE'S MY HEART PERFUME** *(1948-49)*
Clear glass, glass stopper, heart shaped bottle, pink satin ribbon around neck, lettering painted on front, ½ oz. Original price $7.50 . . . .   **110.00   140.00**

☐ 413 **HERE'S MY HEART PERFUME OIL** *(1964-68)*
Clear glass, white plastic cap with scalloped rim and beading, lettering painted on front, ½ oz. Original price $3.50 . . . .   **5.00   8.00**

☐ 414 **HERE'S MY HEART PERFUME OIL FOR THE BATH** *(1963)*
Clear glass, white plastic cap with scalloped rim and beading, lettering painted on the front, ½ oz. Original price $3.50 . . . .   **10.00   14.00**

☐ 415 **HERE'S MY HEART TOILET WATER** *(1959-62)*
Clear glass, heart shaped bottle, white cap with scalloped and beaded rim, lettering painted on front, 2 oz. Original price $2.50 . . . .   **8.00   12.00**

☐ 416 **HERE'S MY HEART TWO OUNCES COLOGNE** *(1961-68)*
Clear glass, white plastic cap with scalloped rim and beading, lettering painted on front, 2 oz. Original price $1.75 . . . .   **1.00   2.00**

☐ 417 **HONEYSUCKLE AFTER BATH FRESHENER** *(1967-72)*
Clear glass, orange cap, orange band around center of bottle, 8 oz. Original price $3.00 . . . .   **1.00   3.00**

☐ 418 **HONEYSUCKLE COLOGNE MIST** *(1971-72)*
Yellow glass, yellow cap, 2 oz. Original price $4.25 . . . . . .   **1.00   3.00**

☐ 419 **HONEYSUCKLE COLOGNE MIST** *(1972-76)*
Clear glass, clear plastic cap, inner cap of yellow and green, 2 oz. Original price $3.25 . . . .   **2.00   5.00**

☐ 420 **HONEYSUCKLE CREAM SACHET** *(1967-75)*
Yellow glass, frosted, orange cap, .66 oz. Original price $2.50 . . . .   **.50   2.00**

☐ 421 **JARDIN D'AMOUR PERFUME** *(1929-33)*
Clear stopper, black label at neck, 1 or 2 oz. Original price $3.50 or $6.50 . . . .   **90.00   120.00**

☐ 422 **JARDIN D'AMOUR PERFUME** *(1954)*
Clear glass bottle that sits in a blue and gold bucket with gold cord that ties around the top of the bottle, clear plastic cap, gold label, 1 dram. Original price $15.00 . . . . .   **160.00   195.00**

☐ 423 **JASMINE AFTER BATH FRESHENER** *(1964-68)*
Clear glass, tall shaped bottle, yellow cap, lettering painted on front, 8 oz. Original price $2.50 . . . .   **1.00   3.00**

☐ 424 **JASMINE BATH SALTS** *(1945-52)*
Clear glass, black cap and label, 9 oz. Original price $.75 .   **25.00   35.00**

☐ 425 **JASMINE POWDER SACHET** *(1949)*
Clear glass, black cap and label, 1½ oz. Original price $1.25 . . . .   **35.00   45.00**

☐ 426 **JASMINE TOILET WATER** *(1946-48)*
Clear glass, gold cap, long narrow black label on front of bottle, 2 oz. Original price $1.19 . . . .   **25.00   35.00**

☐ 427 **JASMINE TOILET WATER** *(1949)*
Clear glass, black cap and label, { oz. Original price $1.25   **35.00   45.00**

☐ 428 **LEMON VELVET COLOGNE MIST** *(1972-76)*
Clear glass, clear plastic cap, yellow and green inner cap, 2 oz. Original price $4.25 . . . .   **1.00   3.00**

☐ 429	**LEMON VELVET CREAM SACHET** *(1971-75)*		
	Yellow glass and cap, .66 oz. Original price $3.00	1.00	3.00
☐ 430	**LEMON VELVET ROLLETTE** *(1972-74)*		
	Clear glass, green and yellow cap, .33 oz. Original price $2.50	.50	1.50
☐ 431	**LEMON VELVET MOISTURIZED FRICTION LOTION** *(1973)*		
	Yellow glass, gold cap, 8 oz. Original price $4.00	1.00	3.00
☐ 432	**LAVENDER POWDER SACHET** *(1961-68)*		
	Clear glass, glass and plastic stopper, pink and white labels on front and around neck, 9 oz.	4.00	6.00
☐ 433	**LAVENDER TOILET WATER** *(1934-37)*		
	Clear glass, ribbed, blue or gold cap, lavender label, 4 oz. Original price $.75	55.00	65.00
☐ 434	**LAVENDER TOILET WATER** *(1938-43)*		
	Clear glass, lavender cap, small paper label on front, 4 oz. Original price $.78	35.00	45.00
☐ 435	**LAVENDER TOILET WATER** *(1945-46)*		
	Clear glass, lavender cap, small paper label, 4 oz. Original price $.89	40.00	50.00
☐ 436	**LAVENDER TOILET WATER** *(1946)*		
	Clear glass, pink cap, small paper label on front, 4 oz. Original price $1.19	45.00	55.00
☐ 437	**LILAC AFTER BATH FRESHENER** *(1964-68)*		
	Clear glass, pink cap and label, 8 oz. Original price $2.50 .	20.00	30.00
☐ 438	**LILAC CREAM SACHET** *(1967-75)*		
	Purple frosted glass, gold and white cap, .66 oz. Original price $2.50	1.00	3.00
☐ 439	**LILAC CREAM SACHET** *(1975-76)*		
	Clear glass, white cap with lilacs, .66 oz. Original price $1.00	.50	1.00
☐ 440	**LILY OF THE VALLEY AFTER BATH FRESHENER** *(1964-68)*		
	Clear glass, green domed shaped cap, lettering painted on front, 8 oz. Original price $2.50	2.00	4.00
☐ 441	**LILY OF THE VALLEY TOILET WATER** *(1946-49)*		
	Clear glass, gold cap and label, 2 oz. Original price $1.19 .	40.00	50.00
☐ 442	**LILY OF THE VALLEY TOILET WATER** *(1949-52)*		
	Clear glass, white flat cap, paper label on front, 2 oz. Original price $1.25	30.00	40.00
☐ 443	**LIQUID MILK BATH** *(1975-76)*		
	Frosted glass, gold cap, paper label on front, 6 oz. Original price $5.00	4.00	6.00
☐ 444	**LULLABYE BABY OIL** *(1946-50)*		
	Clear glass, flat on the back, pink cap, lettering painted pink on front, 6 oz. Original price $1.00	1.00	2.00
☐ 445	**LUSCIOUS PERFUME** *(1950)*		
	Clear glass, gold cap and label, 1 dram. Original price $1.75	10.00	14.00
☐ 446	**LUSCIOUS PERFUME** *(1950)*		
	Clear glass, glass stopper, either painted on lettering or gold neck tag label, 3 dams. Original price $2.25	110.00	140.00
☐ 447	**LUSCIOUS PERFUME** *(1950-55)*		
	Clear glass, embossed gold cap, lettering painted on front, 1 dram. Original price $1.75	8.00	14.00
☐ 448	**LUSCIOUS PERFUME AWARD** *(1950)*		
	Clear circular bottle, glass stopper, 3 drams.	90.00	120.00

☐449 **MARIONETTE PERFUME** *(1938)*
Clear glass, gold cap with ribbing, ½ oz. Original price
$.20 .... **35.00** **45.00**

☐450 **MARIONETTE TOILET** *(1939-40)*
Clear glass, plastic cap, long narrow label on front,
2 oz. Original price $.20 .... **30.00** **40.00**

☐451 **ORCHARD BLOSSOMS** *(1941-45)*
Clear glass, bubble side bottle, white flat cap, paper label
on front with tree and flowers, 6 oz. Original price $1.50 .. **50.00** **60.00**

☐452 **ORCHARD BLOSSOMS** *(1945-46)*
Clear glass, bubbled sided bottle, pink flat cap, paper
label on front, 6 oz. Original price $1.50 .... **65.00** **75.00**

☐453 **PEAR LUMIERE** *(1975-76)*
Pear shape, clear glass, plastic gold leaf, 2 oz. Original
price $5.00 .... **4.00** **6.00**

☐454 **PERFUME CONCENTRE** *(1975-76)*
Clear glass with gold cap, 1 oz. **3.00** **5.00**

☐455 **PERSIAN WOOD COLOGNE** *(1960-63)*
Clear glass, gold cap, gold lettering painted on front, 4 oz.
Original price $2.75 .... **8.00** **14.00**

☐456 **PERSIAN WOOD COLOGNE** *(1961-66)*
Clear glass, gold cap, gold lettering painted on front, 2 oz.
Original price $1.75 .... **4.00** **6.00**

☐457 **PERSIAN WOOD CREAM LOTION** *(1961-63)*
Clear glass, gold cap, gold lettering and floral design
painted on front, 4 oz. Original price $1.25 .... **6.00** **10.00**

☐458 **PERSIAN WOOD PERFUME** *(1964-66)*
Clear glass, gold cap lettering painted on front, ½ oz.
Original price $3.50 .... **10.00** **14.00**

☐459 **PERSIAN WOOD PERFUME OIL FOR THE BATH** *(1963)*
Clear glass, gold domed shaped cap with decorative
design, lettering painted on front, ½ oz. Original price
$3.50 .... **10.00** **14.00**

☐460 **PERSIAN WOOD TOILET WATER** *(1959-61)*
Clear glass, gold cap with decorative dome shape, floral
design and lettering painted on front, 2 oz. Original price
$2.50 .... **10.00** **14.00**

☐461 **PETTI FLEUR COLOGNE** *(1969-70)*
Flower shaped, clear glass, gold cap, 1 oz. Original price
$2.50 .... **3.00** **5.00**

☐462 **PINE BATH OIL** *(1942-51)*
Clear glass, flat sided bottle, turquoise cap, paper label
on front, 6 z. Original price $.95 .... **20.00** **26.00**

☐463 **PINE BATH OIL** *(1944-45)*
Clear glass, green cap, flat sided bottle, brown label, 6 oz.
Original price $1.00 .... **20.00** **28.00**

☐464 **PINE BATH OIL** *(1955-57)*
Clear glass, green cap, paper label on front with pine
needles and cones, 4 oz. **25.00** **34.00**

☐465 **PRETTY PEACH COLOGNE** *(1964-67)*
Clear glass, large cap in shape of peach with green leaf,
lettering painted on front, 2 oz. Original price $1.50 ...... **6.00** **10.00**

☐466 **PURSE PETITE COLOGNE** *(1971)*
Purse shaped, embossed, gold trim, gold cap and chain,
1½ oz. Original price $4.00 .... **5.00** **7.00**

☐467 **QUAINTANCE BATH OIL** *(1949-56)*
Clear glass, rose shaped and colored cap, lettering painted on front, 4 oz. Original price $1.25 .... **18.00** **24.00**

☐468 **QUAINTANCE COLOGNE** *(1955-56)*
Clear glass, blue cap with narrow ribbing, large paper label on front, 2 oz. **12.00** **18.00**

☐469 **QUAINTANCE CREAM LOTION** *(1949-56)*
Clear glass, rose shaped and colored cap, lettering and decorative border painted on front, 4 oz. Original price $.89 .... **10.00** **14.00**

☐470 **QUAINTANCE FOUR OUNCES COLOGNE** *(1948-56)*
Clear glass, ribbed corners, rose shaped and colored cap, with green neck band, lettering painted on front, 4 oz. Original price $1.75 .... **20.00** **18.00**

☐471 **QUAINTANCE PERFUME** *(1948-50)*
Clear glass, with ribbed corners, large rose shaped cap, lettering and decorative borders painted on front, 1 dram. Original price $1.50 .... **65.00** **75.00**

☐472 **QUAINTANCE PERFUME** *(1950)*
Clear glass, small dome shaped red cap with green leaf, 3 drams. **110.00** **140.00**

☐473 **QUAINTANCE TOILET WATER** *(1953-56)*
Clear glass, ribbed corners, rose shaped and colored cap, with green leaf neck band, green painted lettering on front, 2 oz. Original price $1.25 .... **16.00** **24.00**

☐474 **RAPTURE HALF OUNCE COLOGNE** *(1969-72)*
Clear glass, bulbous shaped, large tulip shaped green cap, ½ oz. Original price $1.50 .... **1.00** **3.00**

☐475 **RAPTURE PERFUMED ROLLETTE** *(1965-69)*
Blue glass, ribbed, large cylinder shaped/cap, ⅓ oz. Original price $2.50 .... **5.00** **7.00**

☐476 **REGENCE PERFUME ROLLETTE** *(1967-68)*
Clear glass, ribbed, large cylinder shaped gold cap, .33 oz. Original price $3.00 .... **2.00** **4.00**

☐477 **REGENCE PERFUME ROLLETTE** *(1969-70)*
Clear glass, ribbed, large cylinder green cap, .33 oz. Original price $3.00 .... **1.00** **3.00**

☐478 **REGENCE BATH OIL SKIN SO SOFT** *(1967-71)*
Clear glass, faceted bottle, large domed shaped gold cap, 6 oz. Original price $5.00 .... **2.00** **4.00**

☐479 **REGENCE COLOGNE** *(1967-69)*
Clear glass, faceted, gold cap in dome shape, 2 oz. Original price $3.00 .... **1.00** **3.00**

☐480 **REGENCE HALF OUNCE COLOGNE** *(1970-71)*
Clear glass, gold domed cap with decorative designs, ½ oz. Original price $1.75 .... **2.00** **4.00**

☐481 **REGENCE PERFUME** *(1966-69)*
Frosted glass, gold plastic cap, urn shaped bottle, gold band around shoulder, gold neck tag, ½ oz. Original price $15.00 .... **12.00** **18.00**

☐482 **REGENCE PERFUME** *(1966-69)*
Frosted glass, glass stopper, urn shaped bottle, gold and green trimmings around neck and shoulder, 1 oz. Original price $30.00 .... **25.00** **35.00**

☐ 483 **REGENCE PERFUME OIL** *(1968-69)*
Clear glass, domed shaped cap with decorative designs,
either clear bottom label or gold neck tag, ½ oz. Original
price $6.00 .... **6.00** **10.00**

☐ 484 **ROSE GERANIUM AFTER BATH FRESHENER** *(1964-68)*
Clear glass, rose colored dome cap, lettering painted on
front, 8 oz. Original price $2.50 .... **5.00** **8.00**

☐ 485 **ROSE GERANIUM BATH OIL** *(1943-50)*
Clear glass, falt sided bottle, pink cap, 6 oz. Original price
$.95 .... **20.00** **28.00**

☐ 486 **ROSE GERANIUM BATH OIL** *(1956-57)*
Clear glass, red cap, oval shaped paper label on front,
8 oz. Original price $1.95 .... **15.00** **20.00**

☐ 487 **ROYAL JASMINE BATH OIL** *(1958-59)*
Clear glass, yellow cap, flowered label on front, 8 oz.
Original price $1.95................................... **18.00** **22.00**

☐ 488 **ROYAL JASMINE BATH SALTS** *(1954-57)*
Clear glass, yellow cap, 8 oz. Original price $.89 .... **18.00** **22.00**

☐ 489 **ROYAL PINE BATH OIL** *(1957-59)*
Clear glass, green cap, paper label with pine cones, 8 oz.
Original price $1.95 .... **22.00** **28.00**

☐ 490 **ROYAL PINE BATH SALTS** *(1954-57)*
Clear glass, green cap, green and brown label with pine
cone and needles, 8 z. Original price $.75 .... **18.00** **24.00**

☐ 491 **391 PERFUME** *(1931-33)*
Clear glass, glass stopper, ribbon at neck, 1 oz. Original
price $2.60.. **10.00** **140.00**

☐ 492 **391 PERFUME** *(1933-36)*
Clear glass, ribbed, large flat plastic cap with octagon
shape, large label on front, ½ oz. **40.00** **50.00**

☐ 493 **391 PERFUME FALCONETTE** *(1931-33)*
Clear glass with embossing, glass stopper with long dab-
ber, brass cap. Original price $1.30 .... **80.00** **90.00**

☐ 494 **TO A WILD ROSE BATH OIL** *(1953-55)*
Clear glass, contoured bottle, blue cap, with or without
embossed roses, 4 oz. Original price $1.25 .... **16.00** **20.00**

☐ 495 **TO A WILD ROSE BATH OIL** *(1956)*
Clear glass, large flat white cap, large paper label, 2 oz. .. **18.00** **22.00**

☐ 496 **TO A WILD ROSE BATH OIL** *(1956-59)*
White glass, large domed pink cap, paper label on front,
4 oz. Original price $1.35 .... **10.00** **15.00**

☐ 497 **TO A WILD ROSE BODY POWDER** *(1955-59)*
White glass, white flat cap with rose design, paper label
border around base, lettering painted on front, 4 oz.
Original price $1.00 .... **12.00** **16.00**

☐ 498 **TO A WILD ROSE BODY POWDER** *(1955-59)*
White glass, white flat cap with rose design on top, paper
label on front, 4 oz. Original price $1.00 .... **10.00** **15.00**

☐ 499 **TO A WILD ROSE COLOGNE** *(1950-55)*
Clear glass, contoured bottle, blue cap, blue label, 4 oz.
Original price $2.00 .... **18.00** **22.00**

☐ 500 **TO A WILD ROSE COLOGNE** *(1954)*
Clear glass, white flat cap, blue paper label on front, 2 oz. **18.00** **22.00**

☐501 **TO A WILD ROSE COLOGNE** *(1955)*
Clear glass, white flat cap, large paper label on front, 2 oz. **18.00** **22.00**

☐502 **TO A WILD ROSE COLOGNE** *(1955-63)*
*White glass, large pink domed cap, paper border around
base with floral design, lettering painted on front, 4 oz.
Original price $2.50* **12.00** **18.00**

☐503 **TO A WILD ROSE COLOGNE** *(1956)*
*Clear glass, large white flat cap, large paper label on
front, 2 oz.* **18.00** **22.00**

☐504 **TO A WILD ROSE COLOGNE** *(1957)*
White glass, pink domed cap, paper label on front, 2 oz. . . **16.00** **20.00**

☐505 **TO A WILD ROSE COLOGNE** *(1970-71)*
*White glass, domed pink cap, lettering painted on front,
½ oz. Original price $1.75* **1.00** **3.00**

☐506 **TO A WILD ROSE CREAM LOTION** *(1954)*
Clear glass, blue cap, paper label, 2 oz. **18.00** **22.00**

☐507 **TO A WILD ROSE CREAM** *(1956-65)*
*White glass, large domed pink cap, paper label on front,
4 oz. Original price $1.25* **6.00** **10.00**

☐508 **TO A WILD ROSE CREAM LOTION** *(1965-68)*
*White glass, large domed pink cap, lettering painted on
front, floral border around the base, 4 oz. Original price
$1.25* **5.00** **8.00**

☐509 **TO A WILD ROSE FOUR OUNCES COLOGNE** *(1960-61)*
*White glass, pink cap and neck ribbon, lettering painted
on front, 4 oz. Original price $2.50* **22.00** **28.00**

☐510 **TO A WILD ROSE LOTION** *(1957)*
White glass, paper label on front, large domed pink cap . . **16.00** **20.00**

☐511 **TO A WILD ROSE PERFUME** *(1950-56)*
*Clear glass, large blue cap, flower around the neck,
2 drams. Original price $4.50* **70.00** **80.00**

☐512 **TO A WILD ROSE PERFUME** *(1955-59)*
*White glass, large domed pink cap, lettering painted on
front, floral border around base ½ oz. Original price $5.00* **90.00** **120.00**

☐513 **TO A WILD ROSE PERFUME OIL** *(1964-68)*
*White glass, large domed pink cap, lettering painted on
front, ½ oz. Original price $3.50* **6.00** **8.00**

☐514 **TO A WILD ROSE PERFUME OIL FOR THE BATH** *(1963)*
*White glass, large domed pink cap, lettering painted on
front, ½ oz. Original price $1.50* **8.00** **12.00**

☐515 **TO A WILD ROSE TOILET WATER** *(1950-55)*
*Clear glass, contoured bottle, blue cap with or without
embossed roses, 4 oz. Original price $1.50* **18.00** **22.00**

☐516 **TO A WILD ROSE TOILET WATER** *(1956)*
*White glass, large domed pink cap, lettering painted on
front, ½ oz.* **22.00** **28.00**

☐517 **TO A WILD ROSE TOILET WATER** *(1956-72)*
*White glass, large domed pink cap, paper border around
base with floral design, lettering painted on front, 2 oz.
Original price $1.50* **8.00** **15.00**

☐518 **TO A WILD ROSE TWO OUNCES COLOGNE** *(1961-68)*
*White glass, large domed pink cap, lettering painted on
front, 2 oz. Original price $1.50* **2.00** **4.00**

☐519 **SOMEWHERE COLOGNE** *(1966-71)*
Clear glass, gold domed shaped cap, 2 oz. Original price
$2.50 .... 1.00 3.00

☐520 **SOMEWHERE COLOGNE** *(1961-66)*
Clear glass, pink cap with jeweled trim, sculptured bottle,
lettering painted around shoulder, 2 oz. Original price
$2.00 .... 4.00 6.00

☐521 **SOMEWHERE CREAM LOTION** *(1963-66)*
Clear glass, pink cap, sculptured bottle, lettering painted
around shoulder, 4 oz. Original price $1.50 .... 4.00 6.00

☐522 **SOMEWHERE CREAM LOTION** *(1967-68)*
Clear glass, large dome shaped gold cap, front paper
label, 4 oz. Original price $1.50 .... 5.00 8.00

☐523 **SOMEWHERE PERFUME** *(1961-63)*
Clear glass, pink cap, sculptured bottle, lettering painted
around shoulder, jeweled trim around cap and base of
bottle, 1 oz. Original price $20.00 .... 50.00 60.00

☐524 **SOMEWHERE PERFUMED OIL** *(1964-66)*
Clear glass, pink glass, sculptured bottle, lettering
painted around shoulder, ½ oz. Original price $4.00 ..... 6.00 10.00

☐525 **SOMEWHERE PERFUME OIL** *(1966-69)*
Clear glass, gold domed cap, front paper label, ⅓ oz.
Original price $4.00 .... 5.00 8.00

☐526 **SOMEWHERE PERFUMED OIL FOR THE BATH** *(1963)*
Clear glass, pink cap, sculptured bottle, lettering painted
around shoulder, ½ oz. Original price $4.00 .... 8.00 12.00

☐527 **SONNET TOILET WATER** *(1941)*
Clear glass, purple cap and label, narrow paper label
down the center, 2 oz. Original price $.20 .... 30.00 40.00

☐528 **SWAN LAKE BATH OIL** *(1947-49)*
Clear glass, flat sided bottle, pink cap, lettering and swan
painted on front, 6 oz. Original price $1.25 .... 50.00 60.00

☐529 **SWAN LAKE COLOGNE** *(1947-50)*
Clear glass, pink cap, lettering and decorative border
painted on front, 4 oz. Original price $1.35 .... 40.00 50.00

☐530 **SWEET HONESTY COLOGNE MIST** *(1973-74)*
Clear glass, horizontal ribbing, inner and outer caps, 2 oz. 1.00 3.00

☐531 **TOPAZE FOUR OUNCES COLOGNE** *(1959-63)*
Gold cap, faceted bottle, lettering painted on front, 4 oz. . 8.00 12.00

☐532 **TOPAZE FOUR OUNCES GIFT COLOGNE** *(1959-61)*
Clear glass, gold cap, 4 oz. 10.00 15.00

☐533 **TOPAZ HALF OUNCE COLOGNE** *(1970-71)*
Clear glass, gold cap, lettering painted on front, ½ oz.
Original price $1.50 .... 2.00 4.00

☐534 **TOPAZ CREAM LOTION** *(1959-67)*
Clear glass, tall narrow shaped bottle, yellow cap, 4 oz.
Original price $1.50 .... 6.00 10.00

☐535 **TOPAZ PERFUME** *(1959-63)*
Amber glass, amber jeweled glass stopper, faceted bottle,
1 oz. Original price $20.00 .... 90.00 120.00

☐536 **TOPAZ PERFUME OIL** *(1964-69)*
Clear glass, gold cap, lettering painted on front, ½ oz.
Original price $4.00 .... 50.00 60.00

☐537	**TOPAZ PERFUME OIL FOR THE BATH** *(1963)* *Clear glass, gold cap, lettering painted on front, ½ oz.* *Original price $4.00*	**50.00**	**60.00**
☐538	**TOPAZ TWO OUNCES COLOGNE** *(1960-71)* *Gold cap, faceted bottle, lettering painted on front, 2 oz.* *Original price $2.00*	**1.00**	**3.00**
☐539	**ULTRA COLOGNE** *(1975-76)* *Clear glass, gold cap, 1 oz. Original price $2.50*	**2.00**	**4.00**
☐540	**UNFORGETTABLE COLOGNE** *(1966-71)* *Clear glass, domed shaped bottle, large flat decorative* *cap, lettering painted on front, 2 oz. Original price $2.50* ..	**1.00**	**3.00**
☐541	**UNFORGETTABLE PERFUME OIL** *(1965-69)* *Clear glass, large decorative gold cap, lettering painted* *on front. Original price $5.00*	**6.00**	**10.00**
☐542	**VIOLET BOUQUET COLOGNE** *(1946-49)* *Clear glass, bubble sides, caps in different colors, 6 oz.* *Original price $1.00*	**80.00**	**100.00**
☐543	**WINTER GARDEN** *(1975-76)* *Tall bottle, clear glass, gold cap, 6 oz. Original price $5.00*	**4.00**	**6.00**

WOMEN'S FIGURALS

☐544	**BABY OWL** *(1975-76)* *Clear glass, gold cap, 1 oz. Original price $2.00*	**1.00**	**3.00**
☐545	**BATH URN** *(1971-73)* *White glass and cap with gold top band under the cap,* *5 oz.*	**3.00**	**5.00**
☐546	**BATH TREASURE SNAIL DECANTER** *(1973-76)* *Clear glass, gold head, 6 oz. Original price $6.00*	**5.00**	**7.00**
☐547	**BEAUTIFUL AWAKENING** *(1973-74)* *Clear glass, painted gold in shape of an alarm clock, with* *clock face on front, 3 oz.*	**4.00**	**6.00**
☐548	**BETTY ROSS DECANTER** *(1976)* *Clear glass painted white, 4 oz. Original price $10.00*	**6.00**	**10.00**
☐549	**BIRD OF HAPPINESS COLOGNE** *(1975-76)* *Blue glass, gold cap, 1.5 oz. Original price $3.00*	**2.00**	**4.00**
☐550	**BLUE DEMI-CUP BATH OIL** *(1968-70)* *White glass, blue cap and floral design, 3 oz. Original* *price $3.50*	**5.00**	**7.00**
☐551	**BLUE EYES** *(1975-76)* *Kitten figurine, opal glass, blue eyes 1.5 oz. Original price* *$4.00*	**3.00**	**5.00**
☐552	**BON BON COLOGNE** *(1972-73)* *Poodle figurine, white glass, white cap, 1 oz. Original* *price $2.00*	**2.00**	**4.00**
☐553	**BON BON COLOGNE** *(1973)* *Poodle figurine, black milk glass, black plastic cap, 1 oz.* *Original price $2.00*	**1.00**	**3.00**
☐554	**BRIDAL MOMENTS** *(1976)* *Clear glass painted white, figurine of a bride, gold cap,* *4 oz. Original price $9.00*	**6.00**	**8.00**
☐555	**CANDLESTICK COLOGNE** *(1966)* *Clear glass coated silver, silver cap, 3 oz. Original price* *$3.75*	**8.00**	**12.00**

☐556 **CANDLESTICK COLOGNE** *(1970-71)*
Red glass, gold cap with wide plastic collar, 4 oz. Original
price $6.00 .... **5.00** **7.00**

☐557 **CANDLESTICK COLOGNE** *(1972-75)*
Clear glass painted silver, 5 oz. **5.00** **7.00**

☐558 **CHARMLIGHT DECANTER** *(1975-76)*
Clear glass in shape of lamp with white shade, .88 oz.
Original price $7.00 .... **6.00** **8.00**

☐559 **CHIMNEY LAMP COLOGNE MIST DECANTER** *(1973-74)*
Clear glass, white plastic shade with pink floral design,
2 oz. **5.00** **7.00**

☐560 **CHRISTMAS BELLS COLOGNE** *(1974-75)*
Clear glass painted red, gold cap, 1 oz. **1.00** **3.00**

☐561 **CHRISTMAS TREE** *(1968-70)*
Clear glass painted red, green, gold and silver, 4 oz. Original price $2.50 .... **6.00** **8.00**

☐562 **CLASSIC DECANTER** *(1969-70)*
Figurine of women with bowl on her head, white glass,
gold cap, 8 oz. **6.00** **8.00**

☐563 **COLOGNE AND CANDLELIGHT** *(1975)*
Clear glass, short, round bottle, gold cap and clear plastic
collar, 2 oz. Original price $3.00 .... **2.00** **4.00**

☐564 **COLOGNE ROYALE** *(1972-74)*
Clear glass in shape of a crown, god cap, 1 oz. **2.00** **4.00**

☐565 **COMPOTE COLOGNE DECANTER** *(1972-75)*
White milk glass, gold cap, 5 oz. **4.00** **6.00**

☐566 **COUNTRY CHARM BUTTER CHURN DECANTER** *(1973-74)*
Clear glass, gold band around the body, gold cap, 1.5 oz. . **4.00** **6.00**

☐567 **COUNTRY KITCHEN DECANTER** *(1973-75)*
Rooster figurine, white milk glass, red plastic head, 6 oz. . **4.00** **6.00**

☐568 **COUNTRY STORE COFFEE MILL** *(1972-76)*
White milk glass, white plastic cap and handles, gold rim,
5 oz. **5.00** **7.00**

☐569 **COURTING CARRIAGE** *(1973-74)*
Clear glass in the shape of a carriage, gold cap, 1 oz. **2.00** **4.00**

☐570 **COURTING LAMP COLOGNE** *(1970-71)*
Blue glass base, white milk glass shade, blue velvelt ribbon, 5 oz. Original price $6.00 .... **8.00** **10.00**

☐571 **CRYSTALIER COLOGNE DECANTER** *(1975)*
Clear glass, large glass stopper, 2 oz. Original price $4.00 **3.00** **5.00**

☐572 **CRYSTALLITE COLOGNE** *(1970-71)*
Clear glass, gold cap, tall, textured. Original price $5.50 .. **4.00** **6.00**

☐573 **CRYSTAL SONG** *(1975-76)*
Red glass, frosted bow and handle, in shape of bell, 4 oz.
Original price $6.00 .... **3.00** **5.00**

☐574 **CRYSTALTREE COLOGNE DECANTER** *(1975)*
Clear glass in shape of tree, gold plastic cap shaped like a
star, 3 oz. Original price $6.00 .... **3.00** **5.00**

☐575 **DEAR FRIEND COLOGNE DECANTER** *(1974)*
Seated girl holding cat, clear glass painted pink, light pink
plastic top, 4 oz. **5.00** **7.00**

☐576 **DEMI-CUP BATH OIL** *(1969-70)*
White milk glass, floral design in red, red cap, 3 oz. Original price $3.50 .... **5.00** **7.00**

☐577 **DOLPHIN MINIATURE** *(1973-74)*
Clear glass, gold tail, 1.5 oz. Original price $3.00 . . . .   **2.00**   **4.00**

☐578 **DREAM GARDEN** *(1972-73)*
Pink frosted glass in design of a watering can, gold cap,
½ oz. Original price $5.00 . . . .   **6.00**   **8.00**

☐579 **DR. HOOT DECANTER** *(1975)*
Opal white glass, black cap shaped like a graduate's cap
with a gold tassel, 4 oz. Original price $5.00 . . . .   **4.00**   **6.00**

☐580 **DUTCH GIRL FIGURINE COLOGNE** *(1973-74)*
Clear glass painted blue, white plastic top, 3 oz. **5.00**   **7.00**

☐581 **DUTCH TREAT DEMI-CUPS** *(1971)*
White glass, floral designs on front, yellow, blue, or pink
cap, 3 oz. Original price $3.50 . . . .   **5.00**   **7.00**

☐582 **EIFFEL TOWER COLOGNE** *(1970)*
Clear glass, gold cap, 3 oz. **6.00**   **8.00**

☐583 **EIGHTEENTH CENTURY CLASSIC FIGURINE YOUNG
BOY** *(1974-75)*
Clear glass painted white, white plastic head, 4 oz. Origi-
nal price $5.00 . . . .   **4.00**   **6.00**

☐584 **EIGHTEENTH CENTURY CLASSIC FIGURINE YOUNG
GIRL** *(1974-75)*
Clear glass painted white, white plastic head, 4 oz. Origi-
nal price $5.00 . . . .   **4.00**   **6.00**

☐585 **ELIZABETHAN FASHION FIGURINE** *(1972)*
Clear glass painted pin on lower portion, top portion pink
plastic, 4 oz. **8.00**   **10.00**

☐586 **ENCHANTED FROG CREAM SACHET** *(1973-76)*
Colored milk glass, plastic lid, 1.25 oz. Original price $3.00   **2.00**   **4.00**

☐587 **ENCHANTED HOURS** *(1972-73)*
Blue glass, gold cap, 5 oz. **6.00**   **8.00**

☐588 **EVENING GLOW PERFUME DECANTER** *(1974-75)*
White milk glass, in shape of old-fashioned lamp, green
floral design on front, white and gold cap, .33 oz. Original
price $6.00 . . . .   **4.00**   **6.00**

☐589 **FAIRYTALE FROG** *(1976)*
Clear glass, gold frog, 1 oz. Original price $3.00 . . . .   **1.00**   **3.00**

☐590 **FASHION FIGURINE COLOGNE** *(1971-72)*
Clear glass painted white on lower portion, top portion
white plastic, 4 oz. **7.00**   **10.00**

☐591 **FLAMINGO DECANTER** *(1971-72)*
Clear glass shaped like a bird, gold cap, tall and narrow
shaped, 5 oz. **6.00**   **8.00**

☐592 **FLOWER MAIDEN COLOGNE DECANTER** *(1973-74)*
Figurine of a girl, clear glass painted yellow for the skirt,
white plastic top, 4 oz. **5.00**   **7.00**

☐593 **FLY-A-BALLOON** *(1975-76)*
Clear glass painted blue, boy figurine holding balloon on
a string, white top, red balloon, 3 oz. Original price $7.00 .   **6.00**   **8.00**

☐594 **FRAGANCE BELL COLOGNE** *(1965-66)*
Clear glass, plastic handle, neck tag, 4 oz. Original price
$3.50 . . . .   **12.00**   **16.00**

☐595 **FRAGANCE BELL COLOGNE** *(1968-69)*
Clear glass ribbed in shape of bell that actually rings, gold
handle, 1 oz. Original price $2.00 . . . .   **3.00**   **5.00**

☐596 **FRAGANCE HOURS COLOGNE** *(1971-73)*
White glass in shape of grandfather's clock, gold cap,
6 oz. 4.00 6.00

☐597 **FRAGANCE SPLENDER** *(1971-74)*
Clear glass, gold cap, frosted plastic handle, 4½ oz. Original price $5.00 . . . . 4.00 6.00

☐598 **FRAGANCE TOUCH** *(1969-70)*
White milk glass, tall shaped bottle, 3 oz. Original price
$5.00 . . . . 5.00 7.00

☐599 **FRENCH TELEPHONE** *(1971)*
White milk glass base, gold cap and trim, 6 oz. Original
price $22.00 . . . . 18.00 24.00

☐600 **GARDEN GIRL COLOGNE** *(1975)*
Clear glass painted yellow, figurine of girl, yellow plastic
top, 4 oz. Original price $3.50 . . . . 3.00 5.00

☐601 **GAY NINETIES COLOGNE** *(1974)*
Clear bottle painted orange in figurine of woman, white
top, orange hat, 3 oz. Original price $4.00 . . . . . ,. 4.00 6.00

☐602 **GOLDEN THIMBLE** *(1972-74)*
Clear glass on lower portion, gold cap, 2 oz. 3.00 5.00

☐603 **GOOD LUCK ELEPHANT** *(1975-76))*
Frosted glass, gold cap, 1.5 oz. Original price $3.00 . . . . . . 2.00 4.00

☐604 **GRACEFUL GIRAFFE** *(1976)*
Clear glass, plastic top, 1.5 oz. Original price $4.00 . . . . . . 3.00 5.00

☐605 **GRECIAN PITCHER** *(1972-76)*
Bust of woman with jar on her head, white glass, white
stopper, 5 oz. 4.00 6.00

☐606 **HANDY FROG MOISTURIZED HAND LOTION** *(1975-76)*
Large frog with red hat, white milk glass, 8 oz. Original
price $6.00 . . . . 5.00 7.00

☐607 **HEARTH LAMP COLOGNE DECANTER** *(1973-74)*
Black glass, gold handle, yellow and white shade, daisies
around neck, 8 oz. 7.00 10.00

☐608 **HEAVENLY ANGEL COLOGNE** *(1974-75)*
Clear glass, white top, 2 oz. Original price $4.00 . . . . 2.00 4.00

☐609 **HIGH–BUTTONED SHOE** *(1975-76)*
Clear glass in shape of a shoe, gold cap, 2 oz. Original
price $3.00 . . . . 2.00 4.00

☐610 **HOBNAIL BELL COLOGNE DECANTER** *(1973-74)*
White milk glass, gold handle, gold bell clapper, 2 oz. 3.00 5.00

☐611 **HOBNAIL BUD VASE** *(1973-74)*
White milk glass, red and yellow roses on front, long neck,
4 oz. 5.00 7.00

☐612 **HOBNAIL DECANTER FOAMING BATH OIL** *(1972-74)*
White opal glass, 4 oz. 5.00 7.00

☐613 **HURRICANE LAMP COLOGNE DECANTER** *(1973-74)*
White glass lower portion, clear glass for top portion, gold
cap, 6 oz. 8.00 12.00

☐614 **KEY NOTE PERFUME** *(1967)*
Clear glass in shape of key with gold plastic cap, ¼ oz.
Original price $5.50 and $6.50 . . . . 8.00 12.00

☐615 **KOFFEE KLATCH** *(1971-74)*
Clear glass painted yellow in shape of coffee pot, gold
top, 5 oz. 4.00 6.00

□616 **LA BELLE TELEPHONE** *(1974-76)*
Telephone figurine, clear glass, gold top, 1 oz. Original
price $7.00 .... 6.00 8.00
□617 **LADY BUG PERFUME DECANTER** *(1975-76)*
Frosted glass, gold cap, ½ oz. Original price $4.00 .... 2.00 4.00
□618 **LADY SPANIEL** *(1974-76)*
Opal glass, plastic head, 1.5 oz. Original price $3.00 ..... 2.00 4.00
□619 **LEISURE HOURS** *(1970-72)*
White milk glass in shape of clock with face of clock
design on the front, gold cap, 5 oz. Original price $4.00 ... 3.00 5.00
□620 **LEISURE HOURS MINIATURE** *(1974)*
White milk glass in shape of clock with face of clock on
front, gold cap, 1.5 oz. Original price $3.00 .... 2.00 4.00
□621 **LIBRARY LAMP DECANTER** *(1976)*
Clear glass with base covered with gold foil, gold cap,
4 oz. Original price $9.00 .... 4.00 6.00
□622 **LITTLE DUTCH KETTLE** *(1972-73)*
Shaped like coffee pot, clear glass painted orange, gold
cap, 5 oz. 4.00 6.00
□623 **LITTLE GIRL BLUE** *(1972-73)*
Clear glass painted blue, blue plastic cap, 3 oz. 5.00 7.00
□624 **LITTLE KATE** *(1973-74)*
Clear glass painted orange, figurine of girl, orange plastic
hat over the cap, 3 oz. 5.00 7.00
□625 **LOVE BIRD PERFUME** *(1969-70)*
Frosted glass in design of a bird, head as gold cap, ¼ oz.
Original price $7.50 .... 7.00 9.00
□626 **LOVE SONG DECANTER** *(1973-75)*
Frosted glass, gold cap, 6 oz. Original price $6.00 .... 5.00 7.00
□627 **MAGIC PUMPKIN COACH** *(1976)*
Clear glass, gold cap, 1 oz. Original price $5.00 .... 2.00 4.00
□628 **MING BLUE LAMP** *(1974-76)*
Blue glass in shape of lamp, white plastic shade, 5 oz.
Original price $6.00 .... 5.00 7.00
□629 **MING CAT COLOGNE** *(1971)*
Tall seated cat, white glass, blue trim, neck ribbon, 6 oz. . 7.00 10.00
□630 **ONE DRAM PERFUME** *(1974-76)*
Clear glass with ribbing, gold cap. Original price $4.25 ... 2.00 4.00
□631 **PARISIAN GARDEN PERFUME** *(1974-75)*
White milk glass, in shape of pitcher with floral design on
front, gold cap, .33 oz. Original price $5.00 .... 4.00 6.00
□632 **PARLOR LAMP** *(1971-72)*
Lower portion in white milk glass, top portion in light
amber glass, gold cap 3 oz. Original price $7.00 .... 7.00 10.00
□633 **PARTRIDGE COLOGNE DECANTER** *(1973-75)*
White milk glass, white plastic lid, 5 oz. Original price
$5.00 .... 4.00 6.00
□634 **PERFUME PETITE MOUSE** *(1970)*
Frosted glass, gold head and tail, ¼ oz. Original price
$7.50 .... 14.00 16.00
□635 **PERT PENGUIN** *(1975-76))*
Clear glass, gold cap, 1 oz. Original price $2.00 .... 1.00 3.00
□636 **PETITE PIGLET** *(1972)*
Clear glass, embossed, gold cap, in design of pig. Original
price $5.00 .... 7.00 9.00

☐637 **PINEAPPLE PETITE COLOGNE** *(1972-74)*
Clear glass in the shape of a pineapple, large gold cap,
1 oz. 2.00   4.00

☐638 **PRECIOUS SLIPPER** *(1973-74)*
Frosted glass, gold cap as bow on shoe, .25 oz. Original
price $4.00 .... 4.00   6.00

☐639 **PRECIOUS SWAN PERFUME DECANTER** *(1974-76)*
Frosted glass, gold cap, ⅛ oz. Original price $4.00 .... 2.00   4.00

☐640 **PRETTY GIRL PINK** *(1974-75)*
Clear glass painted pink on lower portion, top portion
light pink, 6 oz. Original price $4.00 .... 3.00   5.00

☐641 **QUEEN OF SCOTS** *(1973-75)*
White milk glass, figurine of dog, white plastic head, 1 oz. 2.00   4.00

☐642 **REGENCY CANDLESTICK COLOGNE** *(1973-74)*
Clear glass, faceted, tall bottle, 4 oz. 6.00   8.00

☐643 **REMEMBER WHEN SCHOOL DESK DECANTER** *(1972-74)*
Black glass, light brown plastic seat and desk top, red
apple for cap, 4 oz. ....,...... 6.00   8.00

☐644 **ROARING TWENTIES FASHION FIGURINE** *(1972-74)*
Clear glass painted purple, plastic purple top, 3 oz. 5.00   7.00

☐645 **ROBIN RED-BREAST COLOGNE DECANTER** *(1974-75)*
Red frosted glass, silver plastic cap, 2 oz. Original price
$4.00 .... 3.00   5.00

☐646 **ROYAL COACH** *(1972-73)*
White milk glass, in shape of coach with gold cap on top,
5 oz. Original price $5.00 .... 4.00   6.00

☐647 **ROYAL PEKINGNESE** *(1974-75)*
White milk glass, white plastic head, 1.5 oz. Original price
$3.00 .... 2.00   4.00

☐648 **ROYAL SWAN COLOGNE** *(1971-72)*
White glass, gold crown cap on swan's head, 1 oz. 3.00   5.00

☐649 **ROYAL SWAN COLOGNE** *(1974)*
Blue glass, gold crown on swan's head, 1 oz. 2.00   4.00

☐650 **SALT SHAKERS** *(1968-70)*
White glass with floral designs either in pink or yellow,
pink or yellow ribbon, 3 oz. Original price $2.50 .... 4.00   6.00

☐651 **SCENT WITH LOVE** *(1971-72)*
Frosted glass, cap is gold pen, gold and white label
around bottle, ¼ oz. Original price $6.00 .... 8.00   12.00

☐652 **SCENT WITH LOVE** *(1975-76)*
Glass base painted gold with plastic amber top, .66 oz.
Original price $4.00 .... 3.00   5.00

☐653 **SEA HORSE** *(1976)*
Clear glass, large sea horse figurine, 6 oz. 7.00   10.00

☐654 **SEA LEGEND DECANTER** *(1975-76)*
Sea shell design, clear glass, white cap, 6 oz. Original
price $5.00 .... 4.00   6.00

☐655 **SEA MAIDEN SKIN-SO-SOFT** *(1971-72)*
Mermaid figurine, clear glass, gold cap, 6 oz. 6.00   8.00

☐656 **SEA SPIRIT FOAMING BATH OIL DECANTER** *(1973-76)*
Light green glass, green plastic cap as tail, 5 oz. Original
price $5.00 .... 4.00   6.00

☐657 **SEWING NOTIONS** *(1975)*
Pink and white glass in design of a spool with silver cap
designed as a thimble, 1 oz. Original price $3.00 .... 2.00   4.00

☐658 **SKIP-A-ROPE** *(1975-76)*
Clear glass painted yellow, figurine of girl jumping rope,
yellow top, white plastic rope, 4 oz. Original price $7.00 .. **6.00** **8.00**

☐659 **SITTING PRETTY COLOGNE** *(1971-73)*
White milk glass, in shape of easy chair, gold cap in
shape of cat sitting on top of chair, 4 oz. Original price
$5.00 .... **6.00** **8.00**

☐660 **SONG BIRD COLOGNE** *(1971-72)*
Clear glass, gold cap as the base, 1.5 oz. Original price
$3.00 .... **4.00** **6.00**

☐661 **SONG OF LOVE COLOGNE MIST** *(1975)*
Clear glass, plastic top with white bird, 2 oz. Original price
$4.00 .... **3.00** **5.00**

☐662 **SMALL WONDER PERFUME** *(1972-73)*
Frosted glass in design of caterpillar, gold cap as head,
⅛ oz. Original price $2.50 .... **4.00** **6.00**

☐663 **SNAIL PERFUME** *(1968-69)*
Clear glass, gold cap as head, ¼ oz. Original price $6.25 . **10.00** **14.00**

☐664 **SNOW BUNNY** *(1975-76)*
Rabbit figurine, clear glass, gold cap, 3 oz. Original price
$4.00 .... **3.00** **5.00**

☐665 **SNOW MAN PETITE PERFUME** *(1973)*
Textured glass, eyes, mouth and scarf are pink, gold cap
as hat, .25 oz. Original price $4.00 .... **4.00** **6.00**

☐666 **SONG OF THE SEA EMOLIENT BATH PEARLS** *(1974-75)*
Blue-green glass, plastic head. Original price $7.00 ...... **6.00** **8.00**

☐667 **STRAWBERRY FAIR PERFUME** *(1974-75))*
Red glass, silver cap, ⅛ oz. Original price $4.00 .... **3.00** **5.00**

☐668 **SWAN LAKE COLOGNE** *(1972-76)*
White glass, white cap 3 oz. **4.00** **6.00**

☐669 **SWEET DREAMS COLOGNE** *(1974)*
Clear glass painted white in shape of girl, blue top, 3 oz.
Original price $4.00 .... **4.00** **6.00**

☐670 **SWEET SHOPPE PIN CUSHION CREAM SACHET**
DECANTER *(1972-74)*
White milk glass for lower portion of ice cream parlor
chair, white plastic back, pink pin cushion for the cushion
seat, 1 oz. **4.00** **6.00**

☐671 **SWISS MOUSE** *(1974-75)*
Mouse on cheese figurine, frosted glass, gold cap, 3 oz.
Original price $4.00 .... **3.00** **5.00**

☐672 **SUZETTE DECANTER** *(1973-76)*
Poodle figurine, milk glass, plastic head, pink ribbon, 5 oz. **4.00** **6.00**

☐673 **TABATHA COLOGNE SPRAY** *(1975-76)*
Stylized cat figurine, black glass with plastic head, 1.5 oz.
Original price $6.00 .... **5.00** **7.00**

☐674 **TEATIME POWDER SACHET** *(1974-75)*
Frosted white, gold cap, 1.25 oz. Original price $4.00 ..... **3.00** **5.00**

☐675 **TIFFANY LAMP COLOGNE** *(1972-74)*
Brown glass base, pink shade, pink and green floral
design on shade, 5 oz. **8.00** **10.00**

☐676 **TO A WILD ROSE DEMI-CUP** *(1969)*
White glass, red rose on front, pink cap, 3 oz. Original
price $3.50 .... **6.00** **8.00**

☐677	**TOUCH OF CHRISTMAS** *(1975)* *Green glass, red cap, in shape of Christmas tree, 1 oz.* *Original price $2.50*	**1.00**	**3.00**
☐678	**UNICORN COLOGNE DECANTER** *(1974-75)* *Seated unicorn, clear glass, gold cap as horn, 2 oz.*	**3.00**	**5.00**
☐679	**VICTORIAN FASHION FIGURINE** *(1973-74)* *Clear glass painted light green, green plastic top, 4 oz.* . .	**5.00**	**7.00**
☐680	**VICTORIAN LADY** *(1972-73)* *White milk glass, figurine of lady, white plastic cap, 5 oz.* .	**5.00**	**7.00**
☐681	**VICTORIAN MANOR COLOGNE DECANTER** *(1972-73)* *Clear glass painted white, pink plaster roof, 5 oz.*	**6.00**	**8.00**
☐682	*White glass, floral designs in either yellow, lavender, or* *orange, ribbon at neck, 3 oz. Original price $2.50*	**5.00**	**7.00**
☐683	*White glass in shape of an owl with gold eyes, 1½ oz.* *Original price $3.00*	**2.00**	**4.00**
☐684	**YULE TREE** *(1974-75)* *Green glass in shape of Christmas tree, green plastic top* *and star, 3 oz. Original price $4.00*	**2.00**	**4.00**

BALLANTINE

Ballantine figural bottles are made to contain Ballantine imported Scotch whiskey. These ceramic bottles are brightly colored, generally reading "Blended Scotch Whiskey, 14 Years Old." When the bottle represents an animal or human figure, the head is the cap. Most of the Ballantine figurals are on sporting themes, such as Fisherman, Duck, and Golf Bag. Also collectible are the older Ballantine bottles which are non-figurals but are often very decorative, such as a 3-inch pottery jug in which the company's product was marketed around 1930.

BALLANTINE

NO.	DESCRIPTION	PRICE RANGE	
☐ 1	**Ballantine, Duck**	10.00	15.00
☐ 2	**Ballantine, Fisherman**	14.00	20.00
☐ 3	**Ballantine, Golf Bag**	10.00	15.00
☐ 4	**Ballantine, Mallard Duck**	5.00	8.00
☐ 5	**Ballantine, Old Crow Chessman**	10.00	15.00
☐ 6	**Ballantine, Scottish Knight**	10.00	15.00
☐ 7	**Ballantine, Seated Fisherman**	15.00	22.00
☐ 8	**Ballantine, Silver Knight**	17.00	24.00
☐ 9	**Ballantine, Zebra**	17.00	24.00

BARDI

Bardi bottles are ceramics, usually large sized with offbeat themes. Even though the company has issued only a limited number of figurals, they have attained a collector following. The edition that brought Bardi its greatest attention in the collector's market was its Elephant and Donkey political pair, a theme that had earlier been utilized by Jim Beam.

BARDI

☐ 1	**Alaskan Totem Pole,** *Ceramic, 11½"*	15.00	22.00
☐ 2	**Mandolin,** *Ceramic, 12½"*	13.00	17.00
☐ 3	**Santa Claus,** *Ceramic, Red-White-Blk.*	15.00	22.00

BRALATTA BOTTLES

Even though the Bralatta company produces less figurals than competitors, its impressive Old World-style bottles have gained a reputation on the market. Mostly ceramics, they are sharply colored with highly detailed modeling. The tall ceramic Beefeater, The Constable at the Tower of London, is typical of Bralatta's work. It stands 21 inches high with authentic costuming down to the smallest detail.

BRALATTA BOTTLES

☐ 1	**Beefeater,** *Ceramic, Red & Black, 21"*	11.00	15.00
☐ 2	**Masks,** *10"*	12.00	19.00
☐ 3	**Masks,** *Black with Yellow & White Trim*	7.00	11.00

BARSOTTINI

The Barsottini bottle manufacturers from Italy, unlike other foreign companies do not use American or non-geographic themes for the avid U.S. market. Barsottini bottles mostly represent European subjects, such as architectural bottles of the Arc de Triomphe and the Eiffel Tower and the Florentine Steeple. Subjects from European history included an antique

Florentine cannon from the early days of gunpowder. Most Barsottini bottles are large ceramics, often in grey and white to represent the brickwork of buildings. Prices vary depending on quantities imported to this country and the extent of their distribution.

BARSOTTINI

☐	1	**Alpine Pipe,** *Ceramic, 10"*	7.00	11.00
☐	2	**Antique Automobile,** *Ceramic, Coupe*	5.00	8.00
☐	3	**Antique Automobile,** *Open Car*	5.00	8.00
☐	4	**Clowns,** *Ceramic, 12" each*	8.00	11.00
☐	5	**Eiffel Tower,** *Grey & White, 15"*	7.00	11.00
☐	6	**Florentine Cannon,** *Length, 15"*	13.00	19.00
☐	7	**Florentine Steeple,** *Grey & White*	8.00	11.00
☐	8	**Monastery Cask,** *Ceramic, 12"*	13.00	19.00
☐	9	**Paris Arc de Triomphe,** *7½"*	9.00	12.00
☐	10	**Pisa's Leaning Tower,** *Grey & White*	9.00	12.00
☐	11	**Roman Coliseum,** *Ceramic*	7.00	11.00
☐	12	**Tivoli Clock,** *Ceramic, 15"*	13.00	19.00
		Clock with Cherub	31.00	39.00

JIM BEAM

In their variety of styles, shapes, subjects, colors, and approaches to modeling, Jim Beam bottles are unrivaled. They provide a feast for the collector. With such a wide selection, the hobbyist can choose to collect them topically, such as Beam theatricals, or animals.

Jim Beam figurals were first issued in the 1950's, prior to the initial collecting interest in Avons. The history of the James B. Beam Distilling company dates to the late 1700's following the Revolutionary War. Founded in Kentucky in 1778 by Jacob Beam, the company now bears the name of Colonel James B. Beam, Jacob's grandson. Beam whiskey was popular throughout most of the south during the 19th and 20th centuries, though it was not manufactured on a large scale. Since it was difficult to obtain in the north during the 19th century, Northerners often boasted of possessing "genuine Kentucky whiskey" when they were able to purchase it.

The early Beam bottles, though they bear little resemblance to the company's modern figurals, are collectible, of course. Some are worth more because of their scarcity.

In 1953, the Beam Distilling Co. produced and sold bourbon in a special ceramic decanter for the Christmas/New Year holiday season. At that time, special packaging by any spirits distiller was rare. When the decanters sold widely, Beam realized that creative bottling could indeed increase sales. His development of decorative packaging on a large scale led to a variety of series in the 1950's.

They appeared in the following order:

Ceramics	1953	Customer specialities	1956
Executive	1955	Trophy	1957
Regal china	1955	State	1958
Political figures	1956		

127

5

80

194

4

21

46

55

100

The Executive Series, which consists of 22K gold decorated bottles, was issued to mark the corporation's 160th anniversary which distinguished the Beam Distilling Co. as one of the oldest American business enterprises.

In the same year, Beam started its Regal china series, one of the most popular series of Beam bottles. The Regal china bottles, issued annually at intervals, honor significant people, places or events, concentrating on subjects based on "Americana" and the contemporary scene. The sporting events figurals, a frequent subject for Beam Regal chinas, are handsome, striking, and very decorative bottles. The first Regal china bottle, the *Ivory Ash Tray,* still sells in the modest price range.

The following year in 1956 the Beam Political Figures series started off with the traditional elephant and donkey, representing the Republican and Democratic parties.

Customer Specialties, bottles made on commission for customers who are usually liquor dealers or distributors, had its inception with a bottle created for Foremost Liquor Stores of Chicago.

The Trophy Series bottles serve as trophies or awards, usually to mark an achievement within the liquor industry, such as to honor a distributor with the largest sales volume.

In 1958, the State series commemorated the admittance of Alaska and Hawaii into the Union during the 1950's. The Beam Distilling Co. continues to issue bottles in honor of other states with the intention of making bottles for each of the 50 states.

Over 410 types of Beam bottles have been issued since 1953. Beam's ceramic bottles, produced by the Wheaton Glass Co. of Millville, New Jersey, are considerably more popular than the glass bottles, probably because of their pleasing coloration.

JIM BEAM

A

NO.	DESCRIPTION	PRICE RANGE	
☐ 1	**AC SPARK PLUG** (1977)		
	Replica of a spark plug in white, green, and gold	8.00	12.00
☐ 2	**AIDA** (1978)		
	Figurine of character from the opera of the same name. Woman is dressed in blue and yellow with black coned-shaped hat. The first in the Opera Series, this bottle comes with a music box which plays a selection from the "Egyptian March."	275.00	375.00
☐ 3	**AHEPA 50TH ANNIVERSARY** (c. 1972)		
	This striking Regal China bottle was designed in honor of AHEPA'S (AMERICAN HELLENIC EDUCATION PROGRESSIVE ASSOCIATION) 50th anniversary. The Order's anniversary logo is reproduced on the front. Current officers listed on the back. The "Greek Key" design appears on both the bottle itself and on the stopper which is a hollow vase. The bottle's neck is a traditional Greek column. 12"	4.00	8.00

☐ 4 **AKRON RUBBER CAPITAL** (c. 1973)
A unique Regal China creation honoring Akron, Ohio, The Rubber Producing Capital of the World. This creation is in the shape of an automobile tire, and features a Mag Wheel . . . in the center of the wheel the inscription — Rubber Capital Jim Beam Bottle Club 8.00 12.00

☐ 5 **ALASKA** (c. 1958)
Star-shaped bottle in turqoise blue and gold. Symbols of Alaskan industry in corners of star, gold "49" in center. Regal China. 9½" 40.00 50.00

☐ 6 **ALASKA** (c. 1964-65), re-issued
As above 65.00 70.00

☐ 7 **ALASKA PURCHASE** (c. 1958)
Blue and gold bottle with star-shaped stopper. Mt. McKinley pictured with State flag on top. Regal China. 10"
.... 55.00 65.00

☐ 8 **AMERICAN SAMOA** (c. 1973)
The enchantment of one of America's outside territorial possessions is captured in this genuine Regal China bottle. The Seal of Samoa signifies friendship, the whip and staff signify authority and power held by the great chiefs 6.00 15.00

☐ 9 **ANTIOCH** (c. 1967)
The Regal China Company is located in Antioch, Illinois, This decanter commemorates the Diamond Jubilee of Regal. Large Indian head ("Sequoit") on one side. Blue and Gold diamond on reverse. Regal China. 10" 4.00 8.00
With arrow package 4.00 8.00

☐ 10 **ANTIQUE COFFEE GRINDER** (1979)
Replica of a box coffee mill used in the mid 19th century. Brown with black top and crank which moves, gold littering 18.00 22.00

☐ 11 **ANTIQUE GLOBE** (1908)
Represents the Martin Behaim globe of 1492. The globe is blue and rotates on the wooden cradle stand 28.00 36.00

☐ 12 **ANTIQUE TELEPHONE 1897** (1978)
Gold base with black speaker and ear phone. Replica of an 1897 desk phone. The second in the series of antique telephones 16.00 22.00

☐ 13 **ANTIQUE TRADER** (c. 1968-69)
The widely read ANTIQUE TRADER weekly newspaper of the trade forms this bottle with the front page clearly shown in black and red, along side the "1968 NATIONAL DIRECTORY OF ANTIQUE DEALERS" both are on a black base. Regal China. 10½" 4.00 8.00

☐ 14 **ARIZONA** (c. 1968-69)
Embossed scene of Canyon, river, and cactus in blue, yellow and brown, "THE GRAND CANYON STATE" "ARIZONA" in gold. Map embossed on stopper. Reverse has scenes of Arizona life. Regal China, 12" 4.00 8.00

☐ 15 **ARMANETTI AWARD WINNER** (c. 1969-70)
A pale blue bottle in the shape of the number "1", to honor Armanetti Inc. of Chicago as "LIQUOR RETAILER OF THE YEAR" in 1969. In shield, gold & blue lettering proclaims "ARMANETTI LIQUORS 1969 AWARD WINNER". Heavily embossed gold scrolls decorate the bottle 8.00 15.00

☐ 16 **ARMANETTI VASE** *(c. 1968-69)*
Yellow toned decanter embossed with many flowers and a
large letter "A" for Armanetti 6.00 10.00

B

☐ 17 **BARNEY'S SLOT MACHINE** *(1978)*
Replica of the world's largest slot machine which is
located in Barney's Casino on the South Shore at Lake
Tahoe, Nevada. Red with small black stopper at the top .. 28.00 36.00

☐ 18 **BASEBALL** *(c. 1969-70)*
To commemorate the 100th Anniversary of the professional sport, this baseball shaped bottle was issued.
"PROFESSIONAL BASEBALL'S 100th ANNIVERSARY —
1869-1969" in gold & black on the front. Decal of player in
action on top. Reverse has history of growth of baseball . 4.00 8.00

☐ 19 **BEAM'S EXECUTIVE** *(c. 1972)*
This elegantly handcrafted Regal China bottle is heavily
embellished with fired 22 karat gold and features a bouquet of tiny flowers about its mid-section. Each bottle
comes in its own handsome dark red presentation case
lined with velvet 8.00 12.00

☐ 20 **BEAM'S EXECUTIVE** *(c. 1973)*
An elegantly handcrafted genuine Regal China, heavily
embellished with 22 karat gold and features a floral
design on the front. Each bottle comes in its own handsome presentation case lined with velvet 6.00 10.00

☐ 21 **BEAM'S I.B.A.** *(c. 1973)*
A commemorative Regal China bottle honoring the Inter-
national Bartenders' Association on the first International
Cocktail Competition in the United States 6.00 10.00

☐ 22 **BEAM'S KING KAMEHAMEHA** *(c. 1972)*
A replica of the famous King Kamehameha statue, this
genuine Regal China bottle has been designed to commemorate the 100th Anniversary of King Kamehameha
Day. A hero of the Hawaiian people, King Kamehameha is
credited for uniting the Hawaiian Islands 12.00 20.00

☐ 23 **BEAM'S NATIONAL ASSOCIATION CONVENTION
BOTTLE** *(c. 1971)*
Created to commemorate the occasion of the 1st National
Convention of the National Association of Jim Beam Bot-
tle and Specialty Clubs hosted by the Rocky Mountain
Club, Denver, Colorado, June 1971. 11" 12.00 20.00

☐ 24 **BEAM NATIONAL CONVENTION** *(c. 1972)*
This beautiful Regal China creation honors the second
annual convention of the National Association of Jim
Beam Bottle and Specialty Clubs, held June 19 through 25
in Anaheim, California. Features as a stopper the national
symbol of the Beam Bottle Clubs. 13" 55.00 65.00

☐ 25 **BEAM POT** *(1980)*
Shaped like a New England bean pot, a colonial scene is depicted on the front. On the back, there is a large map of the New England states. The stopper is a large gold dome. This is the club bottle for the New England Beam Bottle and Specialties Club **22.00 28.00**

☐ 26 **BEAVER VALLEY CLUB** *(1977)*
Figurine of a beaver sitting on a stump wearing blue pants, a white shirt, a red jacket, and black bow and hat. The beaver is saluting. A club bottle to honor the Beaver Valley Jim Beam Club of Rochester **18.00 24.00**

☐ 27 **BELL SCOTCH** *(c. 1970)*
Tan center, gold base, brown top with coat-of-arms of Arthur Bell & Sons on front. Bottle is in the shape of a large handbell. Regal China. 10½" **8.00 12.00**

☐ 28 **THE BIG APPLE** *(1979)*
Apple shaped bottle with embossed Statue of Liberty on the front with New York City in the background and the lettering "The Big Apple" over the top **10.00 15.00**

☐ 29 **BING CROSBY 36TH** *(1976)*
Same as the Floro de Oro except for the medallion below the neck. Urn-shaped bottle with pastel wide band and flowers around the middle. Remainder of bottle is shiny gold with fluting and designs **28.00 36.00**

☐ 30 **BLACK KATZ** *(c. 1968)*
Same Kitty different color: black cat, green eyes, red tongue, white base. Both Katz are Regal China. 14½" ... **8.00 14.00**

☐ 31 **BLUE CHERUB** *(c. 1960)*
Blue and white decanter with heavily embossed figures of Cherubs with bow & arrows gold details. Scrolls and chain holding Beam Label around neck. Regal China. 12½" ... **125.00 175.00**

☐ 32 **BLUE DAISY** *(c. 1967)*
Also known as "ZIMMERMAN BLUE DAISY". Light blue with embossed daisies and leaves around bottle. Background resembles flower basket **4.00 8.00**

☐ 33 **BLUE JAY** *(c. 1969)*
Tones of sky blue on the birds body with black & white markings. Black claws grip "oak tree stump" with acorns — leaves embossed **8.00 12.00**

☐ 34 **BLUE GOOSE** *(1979)*
Replica of a blue goose with its characteristic greyish-blue coloring. Authenticated by Dr. Lester Fisher, director of Lincoln Park Zoological Gardens in Chicago **16.00 22.00**

☐ 35 **BING'S 31ST CLAM BAKE BOTTLE** *(c. 1972)*
An inspired Regal China bottle heavily decorated in gold. The front features a full 3-dimensional reproductions of the famous Pebble Beach, California wind-swept tree overlooking the Pacific Ocean. The back commemorates the 31st Bing Crosby National Pro-Amateur Golf Tournament at the World Famous Pebble Beach course, January, 1972. The stopper is the official seal of the Tourney. 10¾"
.... **28.00 36.00**

☐ 36 **BING CROSBY NATIONAL PRO-AM** *(c. 1970-73)*
The fourth in its series honoring the Bing Crosby Gold
Tournament, genuine Regal China bottle in luxurious fired
22 karat gold with a white stopper, featuring replicas of
the famous Crosby hat, pipe and gold club 8.00   12.00

☐ 37 **BLUE SLOT MACHINE** 15.00   20.00

☐ 38 **BOBBY UNSER OLSONITE EAGLE** *(1975)*
Replica of the racer car used by Bobby Unser. White with
black accessories and colored decals 35.00   45.00

☐ 39 **BOB HOPE DESERT CLASSIC** *(c. 1974)*
This Regal China creation honors the famous Bob Hope
Desert Classic. Bob Hope silhouette and the sport of golf
that he is so well known is a color feature of the bottle . . .   8.00   12.00

☐ 40 **BONDED MYSTIC** *(1979)*
Urn shaped bottle with fluting on sides and lid. Small
scroll handles, open work handle on lid. Burgundy colored
. . . . 10.00   16.00

☐ 41 **BOYS TOWN OF ITALY** *(c. 1973)*
A handsome genuine Regal China bottle created in honor
of the Boys Town of Italy. This home for Italian orphans
began after World War II. The bottle features a map of
Italy, showing the various provinces of that country 5.00   8.00

☐ 42 **BROADMOOR HOTEL** *(c. 1968)*
To celebrate the 50th Anniversary of this famous hotel in
Colorado Springs, Colorado, Beam issued this bottle
replica complete with details of windows, doors, roof tiles
and tower capped with a "roof" stopper. The base bears
the legend "1918 — THE BROADMOOR — 1968" in white
ovals on a black background 4.00   8.00

☐ 43 **BULL DOG** *(1979)*
Bull dog with yellow infantry helmet with "Devil Dogs"
embossed on front. Real leather collar with metal stud-
ding around his neck. The mascot of the United Stats
Marine Corps, this bottle honors their 204th anniversary . 18.00   22.00

C

☐ 44 **CABLE CAR** *(c. 1968-69)*
A grey-green bottle in the form of a San Francisco Cable
Car, complete with doors, windows and wheels. A gold
label with "Van Ness Ave., CALIFORNIA & MARKET
STREETS" in black on one end, "POWELL & MASON
STREETS" on the side. The stopper is the front light.
Regal China. 4½" high, 7" long 4.00   8.00

☐ 45 **CABOOSE** *(1980)*
Red caboose with black trim. Sign on side reads "New
Jersey Central." Has movable wheels, and gold laterns on
each side 30.00   38.00

☐ 46 **CALIFORNIA RETAIL LIQUOR DEALERS
ASSOCIATION** *(c. 1973)*
Made of genuine Regal China, this bottle was designed to
commemorate the 20th Anniversary of the California

Retail Liquor Dealers Association. The bottle depicts the emblem of the association showing a liquor store superimposed on the State of California **8.00** **12.00**

☐ 47 **CAL-NEVA** *(c. 1969)*
This is a standard square-bottle, green toned with "RENO 100 YEARS" deeply embossed and "CAL-NEVA, CASINO • HOTEL, RENO • LAKE TAHOE" in the oval shaped emblem. Regal China, 9½" **4.00** **8.00**

☐ 48 **CAMELLIA CITY CLUB** *(1979)*
Replica of the cupola of the State Capitol building in Sacramento surrounded with camellias since the capitol is known as "The Camellia Capitol of the World." **28.00** **34.00**

☐ 49 **CAMEO BLUE** *(c. 1965)*
Also known as the "Shepherd Bottle". Scenes of shepherd and dog in white, on the sky blue, square-shaped bottle. White glass stopper. Glass. 12¾" **4.00** **8.00**

☐ 50 **CANTEEN** *(1979)*
Replica of the exact canteen used by the armed forces with simulated canvas covering which has snap flaps and chained cap **15.00** **20.00**

☐ 51 **CAPTAIN AND MATE** *(1908)*
A sea faring captain with blue jacket, white cap, and yellow duffel bag over his shoulder. The captain has his other arm around the shoulders of a small boy dressed in a red jacket and blue pants. He holds a toy boat **18.00** **24.00**

☐ 52 **CARDINAL — *(c. 1968)*
(KENTUCKY CARDINAL)**
A bright red bird with a black mask, tail, and markings, perched on a dark "tree stump" base **45.00** **55.00**

☐ 53 **CARMEN** *(1978)*
Figurine of Carmen from the character in the opera of the same name, the third issue in the Opera Series, it is a woman dressed in Spanish clothes of white, blue, gold and red. She wears a small black coned-shaped hat. Music box plays "Habanera" which is from the opera **375.00** **450.00**

☐ 54 **CATHEDRAL RADIO** *(1979)*
Replica of one of the earlier dome-shaped radios. Brown with gold trim and a large domed-shaped lid **12.00** **16.00**

☐ 55 **CATS** *(c. 1967)*
Trio of three cats, Siamese, Burmese, and Tabby. Colors: Grey-blue eyes, dark brown & white-yellow eyes, and white with tan-blue eyes. Regal China, 11½" high **32.00** **40.00**

☐ 56 **CHARLIE MCCARTHY** *(1976)*
Replica of Edgar Bergen's puppet from the 1930's. A black ribbon is attached to his monocle **28.00** **34.00**

☐ 57 **CHERRY HILLS COUNTRY CLUB**
A very handsome genuine Regal China bottle, commemorating the 50th Anniversary of the famous Cherry Hills Country Club. Located in Denver, Colorado, Cherry Hills has hosted some of the top professional golf tournaments. The front of the bottle illustrates the many activities available at Cherry Hills, while the name of the club circles the bottle in luxurious 22 karat gold **8.00** **12.00**

□ 58 **CHEYENNE, WYOMING** (c. 1967)
Circular decanter in shape of a wheel. Spokes separate
scenes of Cheyenne history. Regal China **4.00**   **8.00**

□ 59 **CHICAGO SHOW BOTTLE** (1977)
Stopper is a gold loving cup standing on a black pedestal.
Commemorates the 6th Annual Chicago Jim Beam Bottle
Show **38.00**   **48.00**

□ 60 **CHURCHILL DOWNS—PINK ROSES** (c. 1969-70)
Same as below, pink embossed roses **4.00**   **8.00**

□ 61 **CHURCHILL DOWNS—RED ROSES** (c. 1969-70)
"CHURCHILL DOWNS—HOME OF THE 95th KENTUCKY
DERBY" is embossed in gold on the front, around the
main paddock building. The shell-shaped bottle comes
with both red roses framing the scene. Reverse:
"ARISTEDES", 1st Derby winner in 1875, on a decal. Regal
China. 10¾" **8.00**   **12.00**

□ 62 **CIRCUS WAGON** (1979)
Replica of a circus wagon from the late 19th century. Blue
with gold embossing, white wheels with red trim which
are movable **26.00**   **36.00**

□ 63 **CIVIL WAR NORTH** (c. 1961)
Blue and grey bottle depicting Civil War battle scenes.
Stopper has Lee's face on one side, Grant's on the other.
Regal China. 10¾" (when sold as a pair) **35.00**   **45.00**

□ 64 **CIVIL WAR SOUTH** (c. 1961)
One side portrays the meeting of Lee and Jackson at
Chancellorville. On the other side a meeting of southern
Generals. Regal China. 10¾" (when sold as a pair) **60.00**   **70.00**

□ 65 **CLEAR CRYSTAL SCOTCH** (c. 1966)
The original patterned embossed bottle. Glass stopper
("DOORKNOB"). Bottom is unpatterned and has number
and date of issue. Clear Glass. 11½" **10.00**   **15.00**

□ 66 **CLEAR CRYSTAL BOURBON** (c. 1967)
Patterned embossed glass bottle with "swirl" stopper.
Starburst design on base of the bottle. Clear Glass. 11½"   **6.00**   **10.00**

□ 67 **CLEAR CRYSTAL VODKA** (c. 1967)
Same as above **6.00**   **10.00**

□ 68 **CLEOPATRA RUST** (c. 1962)
Same as Cleo Yellow. Scene with Mark Anthony and Cleo-
patra in white on rust-red background **4.00**   **6.00**

□ 69 **CLEOPATRA YELLOW** (c. 1962)
Black purple, 2 handled, amphora-decanter. yellow
figures of Mark Anthony in armor, & Cleopatra beside the
Nile, Pyramid and Sphinx background. Egyptian border
design circles bottles, white stopper. Rarer than
Cleopatra Rust. Glass. 13¼" **12.00**   **16.00**

□ 70 **CLINT EASTWOOD** (c. 1973)
A handsome genuine Regal China bottle, commemorating
the Clint Eastwood Invitational Celebrity Tennis Tournament held in Pebble Beach. The bottle features two tennis
rackets across the front while the stopper features an exact likeness of Clint Eastwood. Two ribbons adorn the
front of the bottle, one with stars on a field of blue, the
other in red with the name of the tournament emblazoned
in 22 karat gold **4.00**   **8.00**

☐ 71 **COCKTAIL SHAKER** *(c. 1953)*
Glass, Fancy Diz. Bottle, 9¼" 5.00 10.00

☐ 72 **COFFEE WARMERS** *(c. 1954)*
Four types are known in Red, Black, Gold and White necks, plastic cord over cork. The Corning Glass Company made the Pyrex bottles. Round stoppers are made of wood. Pyrex Glass. 9" 8.00 14.00

☐ 73 **COFFEE WARMERS** *(c. 1956)*
Two types with metal necks and handles, black and gold stripes on one, gold neck with black handle on the other. White Star design on sides of Pyrex glass on both. Round black plastic tops. Some have holder type candle warmers. Pyrex Glass. 10" 3.00 6.00

☐ 74 **COHO SALMON** *(1976)*
Grey with black speckles. Official Seal of the National Fresh Water Fishing Hall of Fame is on the back 8.00 12.00

☐ 75 **COLLECTOR'S EDITION** *(c. 1966)*
Set of 6, Glass, Famous painting, The Blue Boy, on the Terrace, Mardi Gras, Austide Bruant, The Artist Before His Easel, Laughing Cavalier, Set No. 1 .... *each* 20.00 30.00

☐ 76 **COLLECTORS EDITION VOLUMNE XII** *(1977)*
A set of four bottles of painted glass, each painted a different color and having a different reproduction of James Lockhart's on the front. Each picture is framed with a gold border. German Shorthaired Pointer is black with gold mottling and black stopper, Labrador Retriever is dark purple 10.00 15.00

☐ 77 **COLLECTORS EDITION VOLUMNE XIV** *(1978)*
A set of four flask type bottles. Glass made to appear like brown leather with framed whildlife scenes on the front which are reproductions of paintings by James lockhart. Each picture has embossed details. The names and themes of the botles are: Racoon, Mule Deer, Red Fox, and Cottontail Rabbit 15.00 20.00

☐ 78 **COLLECTORS EDITION VOLUME XV** *(1979)*
A set of three flasks each with a different reproduction of Frederic Remington's paintings titled: The Cowboy 1902, The Indian Trapper 1902, and Lieutenant S.C. Robertson 1890 .... 10.00 15.00

☐ 79 **COLLECTORS' EDITION VOLUME XVI** *(1980)*
Set of three flasks with each depicting scenes of ducks in flight on the front with an oval background and a bamboo styled frame. Large domed lids. The Mallard, The Redhead, The Canvasback. Artwork by James Lockhart, one of the best known wildlife artists in America 10.00 15.00

☐ 80 **COLORADO** *(c. 1959)*
Light turquoise showing pioneers crossing the rugged mountains with snow capped peaks in background. "COLORADO" and "1859-1959" in gold. Bottle has a leather thong. Regal China, 10¾" 40.00 50.00

☐ 81 **COLORADO CENTENNIAL** *(1976)*
Replica of Pike's Peak with a miner and his mule in front with the word "Colorado" above the base 15.00 20.00

☐ 82 **CONVENTION NUMBER-6 HARTFORD** *(1976)*
Chart Oak and gold lettering on the front. A map of the U.S. is on the back. Commemorates the annual convention of the Jim Beam Bottle Club held in Hartford, Connecticut 16.00   24.00

☐ 83 **CONVENTION NUMBER-7 LOUISVILLE** *(1978)*
Designed to resemble a map partially unrolled. Lettering and designs embossed on front. Stopper is a cardinal on a green nest 15.00   20.00

☐ 84 **CONVENTION NUMBER-8 CHICAGO** *(1978)*
Embossed scene with the Sears Tower, Hancock Building, Marina City, and Water Tower with Lake Michigan at the base. Commemorates the 8th Beam convention held in Chicago 16.00   22.00

☐ 85 **CONVENTION NUMBER-9 HOUSTON** *(1979)*
The mascot of the Beam Clubs — a grey poodle named Tiffany — sits on the side of a space capsule. Commemorates the 9th Beam convention which was held in Houston 70.00   80.00

☐ 86 **CONVENTION NUMBER-10 NORFOLK** *(1980)*
The sailing ship the USS Beam passing between the spokes of a ship's helm, with a gold flag atop the mast. The USS Beam is located at the Norfolk naval base where the 10th convention was held 20.00   26.00

☐ 87 **COWBOY** *(1979)*
Either antique tan or multicolored. Cowboy leaning on a fence with one hand on his belt buckle and the other holding a rifle. His cowboy hat is the stopper. Awarded to collectors who attended the 1979 convention for the International Association of Beam Clubs 375.00   430.00

☐ 88 **CRAPPIE** *(1979)*
Figure of a silver and black speckled crappie commemorates the National Fresh Water Fishing Hall of Fame 10.00   15.00

D

☐ 89 **DARK EYES BROWN JUG** *(1978)*
Also in beige; both flecked with color — the brown jug has red flecks; the beige jug has brown flecks. Regular jug shape with small handle at neck with black stopper 5.00   8.00

☐ 90 **DELAWARE BLUE HEN BOTTLE** *(c. 1972)*
This diamond shaped bottle, fashioned of genuine hand crafted Regal China commemorates the state of Delaware. "The first state of the Union." The front of the bottle depicts the act of ratification of the Federal Constitution on December 7, 1787. The back shows the Delaware State House, a state map and the famous Twin Bridges 6.00   10.00

☐ 91 **DELCO FREEDOM BATTERY** *(1978)*
Replica of a Delco battery. Entire plastic top is removable 10.00   18.00

☐ 92 **DELFT BLUE** *(c. 1963)*
"Windmill Bottles" — reverse has scene of embossed Dutch windmills, on grey-white bottle. Dutch fishing boats under sail on front in "Delft" (dark blue handle and stopper). Glass 13" 3.00   6.00

☐ 93 **DELFT ROSE** *(c. 1963)*
(rarer than Delft Blue)
Same as above, sailing scene in pale blue and pink. Wind-mill scene embossed on reverse. Glass. 13" **5.00**   **8.00**

☐ 94 **DEL WEBB MINT** *(c. 1970)*
A large gold "400" and "DEL WEBB'S LAS VEGAS", embossed under crossed checkered flags. Stopper is gold dune buggy. Checkered flags on edge of bottle. "MINT" on front for the Vegas Hotel that originally had the bottle. Regal China. 13" **12.00**   **18.00**

☐ 95 **DIAL TELEPHONE** *(1980)*
Black reproduction of a 1919 desk model telephone with a movable dial. The fourth in a series of Beam telephone designs **15.00**   **20.00**

☐ 96 **DOE** *(c. 1963)*
Pure white neck markings, natural brown body. "Rocky" base. Regal China. 13½" **30.00**   **36.00**

☐ 97 **DOE — RE-ISSUED** *(c. 1967)*
As Above **25.00**   **30.00**

☐ 98 **DOG** *(c. 1959)*
Long-eared Setter Dog, soft brown eyes, black and white coat. Regal China. 15¼" **60.00**   **70.00**

☐ 99 **DON GIOVANNI** *(1980)*
Figurine of Don Giovanni from the Mozart opera of the same name. The fifth in the Operatic series, this bottle has a music box which plays the aria "La ci darem la mano." **180.00**   **240.00**

☐ 100 **DONKEY & ELEPHANT ASH TRAYS** *(c. 1956)*
They were made to be used as either ash trays w/coaster, or book ends. The stylized Elephant and Donkey heads are in lustrous grey china. The "Beam" label fits the round coaster section of the bottle. Regal China, 10" . . . . . **PAIR**   **30.00**   **38.00**

☐ 101 **DONKEY & ELEPHANT CAMPAIGNERS** *(c. 1960)*
Elephant is dressed in a brown coat, blue vest with a gold chain, he carries a placard stating "REPUBLICANS — 1960" and the State where the bottle is sold. Donkey is dressed in black coat, tan vest and grey pants. His placard reads "DEMOCRATS — 1960" and State where sold. Regal China, 12" . . . . **PAIR**   **30.00**   **38.00**

☐ 102 **DONKEY & ELEPHANT BOXERS** *(c. 1964)*
The G.O.P. elephant has blue trunks with red stripes, white shirt and black top hat with stars on the band. His gloves are brown. The donkey has red trunks with a blue stripe, and black shoes and top hat. The hat band is white with red and blue stars . . . . **PAIR**   **12.00**   **16.00**

☐ 103 **DONKEY & ELEPHANT CLOWNS** *(c. 1968)*
Both are dressed in polka dot clown costumes. Elephant has red ruffs and cuffs, with blue dots. Donkey has blue with red dots. Yellow styrofoam straw hat, and clown shoes on both elephant and donkey. Their heads are the stoppers. Regal China, 12" . . . . **PAIR**   **12.00**   **16.00**

☐ 104 **DONKEY NEW YORK CITY** *(1976)*
Donkey wearing blue coat and black patriot hat stands inside broken drum decorated with stars, banner, and

plaque in red, white, and blue. Commemorates the
National Democratic Convention in New York City **10.00** **16.00**

☐ 105 **DUCK** (c. 1957)
Green-headed Mallard, bright yellow bill, brown breast,
black wings. Regal China, 14¼ " **30.00** **40.00**

☐ 106 **DUCKS & GEESE** (c. 1955)
A scene of wild ducks and geese flying up from marshes
in white is featured on this clear glass decanter. A round,
tall bottle with a large base and slender tapering neck.
Tall gold stopper sits in a flared top glass, 13½ " **6.00** **10.00**

☐ 107 **DUCKS UNLIMITED BLUE WINGED TEAL** (1980)
Two ducks made of bisque, dark brown coloring with blue
markings. The seventh in a series **20.00** **24.00**

☐ 108 **DUCKS UNLIMITED CANVASBACK DRAKE** (1979)
Replica of a canvasback drake preparing to take off in
flight with his wings spread. Light grey with black and
burgundy coloring on wings and neck **20.00** **26.00**

☐ 109 **DUCKS UNLIMITED 40TH MALLARD HEN** (1978)
White bottle with base designed to appear as if it is
floating in water which also has a brown duck sitting on it.
The number 40 in green is on the front, plaques on the
base and at the neck of the bottle **15.00** **20.00**

☐ 110 **DUCKS UNLIMITED MALLARD** (1978)
Head of a Mallard duck on a semi-circular shaped bottle
with a medallion type stopper. Ducks Unlimited is a conservation organization **22.00** **28.00**

☐ 111 **DUCKS UNLIMITED WOOD DUCK** (1975)
Wood duck nestled against a tree stump with Duck
Unlimited logo on front **20.00** **28.00**

E

☐ 112 **EAGLE** (c. 1966)
White head, golden beak, deep rich brown plumage,
yellow claws on "tree trunk" base. Regal China, 12½ " ... **12.00** **18.00**

☐ 113 **ELDORADO** (1978)
Grey-blue or grey, tear drop-shaped bottle on pedestal
stand, domed-sahped stopper, mottled **12.00** **18.00**

☐ 114 **ELEPHANT AND DONKEY SUPERMEN** (1980)
SEt of two. Representing the Democratic and Republican
political parties, the elephant and the donkey are both
dressed as Superman in yellow and grey outfits. Each carries the world on his shoulders **35.00** **45.00**

☐ 115 **ELEPHANT KANSAS CITY** (1976)
Elephant standing inside broken drum decorated in red,
white, and blue with stars, banner and plaque. Commemorated the National Republican Convention in Kan-
sas City, Missouri **10.00** **16.00**

☐ 116 **NATIONAL FOUNDATION** (1978)
Medallion-shaped bottle, blue and brown with white em-
bossing of picture and lettering on the front **15.00** **20.00**

☐ 117 **EMERALD CRYSTAL BOURBON** (c. 1968)
Emerald Green bottle, patterned embossed glass. Flat
stopper, "swirl" embosses. Green Glass. 11½ " **3.00** **6.00**

☐ 118 **EMMETT KELLY** *(c. 1973)*
A delightful genuine Regal China creation. An exact
likeness of the original Emmett Kelly, as sad-faced Willie
the Clown, who has capitivated and won the hearts of
millions of friends over the years from the Big Top to tele-
vision 20.00   40.00

☐ 119 **ERNIE'S FLOWER CART** *(1976)*
Replica of an old-fashioned flower cart used in San Francisco. Wooden cart with movable wheels. In honor of Er-
nie's Wines and Liquors of Northern California 22.00   30.00

F

☐ 120 **FALSTAFF** *(1979)*
Replica of Sir John Falstaff with blue and yellow outfit
holding a gold goblet. Second in the Australian Opera
Series. Music box which plays "Va, vecchio, John."
Limited edition of 1000 bottles 250.00   350.00

☐ 121 **FANTASIA BOTTLE** *(c. 1971)*
This tall, delicately hand crafted Regal China decanter is
embellished with 22 karat gold and comes packaged in a
handsome midnight blue and gold presentation case
lined with red velvet. 16¼ " 12.00   18.00

☐ 122 **FIESTA BOWL** *(c. 1973)*
The second bottle created for the Fiesta Bowl. This bottle
is made of genuine Regal China, featuring a football
player on the front side 10.00   16.00

☐ 123 **FIGARO** *(1978)*
Figurine of the character Figaro from the opera "Barber of
Seville. Spanish costume in beige, rose, and yellow. Holds
a brown guitar on the ground in front of him. Music box
plays an air from the opera 325.00   425.00

☐ 124 **FIRST NATIONAL BANK OF CHICAGO** *(c. 1964)*
Note: Beware of reproductions
Issued to commemorate the 100th anniversary of the First
National Bank of Chicago, about 130 were issued, 117
were given as mementoes to the bank directors, none for
public distribution. This is the most valuable Beam bottle
known. Sky blue color, circular shape, gold embossed
design aroung banner lettered "THE FIRST NATIONAL
BANK OF CHICAGO". Center oval was ornate bank logo
"1st", and "100th Anniversary" in gold. Gold embossed
"1st" on stopper.
Bottom marked "CREATION OF JAMES B. BEAM
DISTILLING CO.—GENUINE REGAL CHINA".
Reverse: Round paper label inscribed "BEAM CON-
GRATULATES THE FIRST NATIONAL BANK OF CHICA-
GO—100th ANNIVERSARY. 100 YEARS OF SUCCESSFUL
BANKING" 2800.00 3600.00

☐ 125 **FISH** *(c. 1957)*
Sky blue Sailfish, pink underside, black dorsal fin and side
markings on "ocean waves" base. Regal China. 14" 30.00   40.00

☐ 126 **FIVE SEASONS** *(1980)*
The club bottle for the Five Seasons Club of Cedar Rapids
honors their home state, Iowa. The bottle is shaped like
Iowa with a large ear of corn. The top of the corn is the lid **28.00 36.00**

☐ 127 **FLORIDA SHELL** *(c. 1968-69)*
Shell-shaped bottles made in 2 colors, mother of pearl,
and iridescent bronze, for a shimmering luminescent
effect. Reverse has map of Florida, and "SEA SHELL
HEADQUARTERS OF THE WORLD." Regal China, 9¾" .. **4.50 8.00**

☐ 128 **FLORO DE ORO** *(1976)*
Urn-shaped bottle with pastel band around middle and
yellow and blue flowers, remainder of the bottle is gold
with fluting and designs, gold handle **12.00 18.00**

☐ 129 **FLOWER BASKET** *(c. 1961-62)*
Blue Basket filled with embossed pastel flowers and
green leaves resting on gold base, gold details and stop-
per. Regal China. 12¼" **45.00 55.00**

☐ 130 **FOREMOST—BLACK & GOLD** *(c. 1956)*
Pylon shaped decanter with a deep black body embossed
with gold nuggets. The sqare white stopper doubles as a
jigger. This is the first Beam bottle issued for a liquor
retailer. Foremost Liquor Store of Chicago, many others
have followed. Regal China **200.00 275.00**

☐ 131 **FOREMOST—GREY AND GOLD** *(c. 1956)*
Same as above. Tapered decanter with gray body and
gold nuggets. Both decanters are 15½" high and are
Regal China **250.00 300.00**

☐ 132 **FOREMOST—SPECKLED BEAUTY** *(c. 1956)*
The most valuable of the "Foremost" bottles. Also known
as the "Pink Speckled Beauty", was created in the shape
of a Chinese vase and spattered in various colors of pink,
gold, black and gray. The spattered colors may vary from
bottle to bottle since it was hand applied. Regal China,
14½" **600.00 675.00**

☐ 133 **FOOTBALL HALL OF FAME** *(c. 1972)*
This bottle is a reproduction of the striking new Profes-
sional Football Hall of Fame Building, executed in gen-
uine Regal China. The stopper is in the shape of half a
football. 9¾" **4.00 8.00**

☐ 134 **14TH ANNUAL DESERT CLASSIC** *(c. 1973)*
The first genuine Regal China bottle created in honor of
the Bob Hope Desert Classic, an annual charity fund rais-
ing golf tournament. A profile of Bob Hope is shown on
the front side, with a golf ball and tee perched at the tip of
his nose **12.00 18.00**

☐ 135 **FOX** *(c. 1965)*
Bushy-tailed Fox with white pants, dark green coat, and
scarlet cravat. Regal China. 12¼" **40.00 50.00**

☐ 136 **FOX—RE-ISSUED** *(c. 1967)*
As above **35.00 45.00**

☐ 137 **FRENCH CRADLE TELEPHONE** *(1979)*
Replica of a French Cradle telephone. The third in the
Telephone Pioneers of America series **20.00 26.00**

☐138 **FRESH WATER FISHING HALL OF FAME** (c. 1973)
*Created in honor of the National Fresh Water Fishing Hall
of Fame, located in Hayward, Wisconsin, scheduled for
completion in 1974. A genuine Regal China creation
designed after the Largemouth Bass. Its stopper feature
the Official Seal of the Hall of Fame* 8.00   16.00

G

☐139 **GALAH BIRD** (1979)
*Rose colored Galah bird which is part of the cockatoo
family from South Australia. It has a white plume on its
head and touches of grey and white feathers.* 12.00   18.00

☐140 **GEORGE WASHINGTON COMMEMORATIVE PLATE**
(1976)
*Plate-shaped bottle with a painting of George
Washington in the center bordered by a band of gold. The
bottle is blue with gold lettering around the outside rim.
Commemorates the U.S. Bicentennial* 12.00   18.00

☐141 **GERMAN BOTTLE—WEISBADEN** (c. 1973)
*This bottle, of genuine Regal China, depicts a map of the
famous Rhine wine-growing regions of Germany. Special
attention is given to the heart of this wine country at
Weisbaden* 5.00   10.00

☐142 **GIANT PANDA** (1980)
*Adult panda on the ground with two cubs climbing the
stump of a tree. Authenticated by Dr. Lester Fisher, Director of the Lincoln Park Zoological Gardens in Chicago* ... 20.00   28.00

☐143 **GLEN CAMPBELL 51ST** (1976)
*Guitar-shaped bottle with a bust of Glen Campbell
sculptured at top of guitar. Lid is the ends of gold clubs.
Honors the 51st Los Angeles Open, a gold tournament
held at the Rivera Country Club between February 16 to 20*
.... 8.00   14.00

☐144 **GOLDEN CHALICE** (c. 1961)
*Chalice with grey-blue body, gold accents. Band of em-
bossed pastel flowers on the neck. Gold scrolled neck and
base. Regal China. 12¼"* 65.00   75.00

☐145 **GOLDEN GATE** (c. 1969)
*This almond-shaped bottle has "LAS VEGAS" embossed
in bright gold in a banner on the front. Mountains, a
helicopter, a golfer, and gambling montage, with
"GOLDEN GATE CASINO" in gold on a shield are
featured. Regal China, 12½"* 50.00   60.00

☐146 **GOLDEN NUGGET** (c. 1969)
*Same as above "GOLDEN NUGGET" in gold on shield in
front. Regal China, 12½"* 50.00   60.00

☐147 **GOLDEN ROSE** (1978)
*Three versions of this urn-shaped bottle, yellow emboss-
ed rose with a blue background framed in gold band, remainder of bottle gold mottled with two handles. Yellow
Rose of Texas version has the name of this bottle beneath
the rose, the Haroulds Club VIP version has its title lettered under the rose also* 22.00   42.00

☐ 148 **GRAND CANYON** *(c. 1969)*
"*GRAND CANYON NATIONAL PARK 50th ANNIVER-SARY*" *in a circle around a scene of the Canyon in black with "1919-1969" in earth-red. A round bottle (same as Arizona) with a "stick up" spout and round stopper embossed with map of "ARIZONA". Regal China, 12½"* 10.00 18.00

☐ 149 **GRANT LOCOMOTIVE** *(1979)*
Replica of Grant Locomotive, black engine with gold trim and bells, red wheels that move 35.00 45.00

☐ 150 **GREAT DANE** *(1976)*
White with black markings with gold collar 5.00 10.00

☐ 151 **GREAT CHICAGO FIRE BOTTLE** *(c. 1971)*
This historical decanter was created to commemorate the great Chicago fire of 1871, and to salute Mercy Hospital which rendered service to the fire victims. This first hospital of Chicago was started in 1852 by the Sisters of Mercy. The new Mercy Hospital and Medical Center, opened in 1968, is depicted on the reverse side. The front of the bottle shows towering flames engulfing Chicago's waterfront as it appeared on the evening of October 8, 1871. The look of actual flames has been realistically captured in this Regal China masterpiece. 7½" 12.00 18.00

☐ 152 **GREEN CHINA JUG** *(c. 1965)*
Deep mottled green china jug, with embossed "PUSSY WILLOW" branches and buds on side. Solid handle. Regal China. 12½" 4.00 8.00

☐ 153 **GRECIAN** *(c. 1961)*
A pale blue glass, CLUB SLOT MACHINE" in tones of grey and tan. Gold pinwheel and black "H" on front. Regal China, 10" 5.00 8.00

☐ 154 **GREY CHERUB** *(c. 1958))*
Checkered design, bordered with scroll work, accented with 22 karat gold. 3 embossed cherubs on neck. Regal China, 12" 375.00 475.00

☐ 155 **GREY SLOT MACHINE** *(c. 1968-69)*
The famous "HAROLDS CLUB SLOT MACHINE" in tones of grey and tan. Gold pinwheel and black "H" on front. Regal China, 10" 5.00 8.00

H

☐ 156 **HANNAH DUSTON** *(c. 1973)*
A beautiful Regal China creation designed after the granite monument erected in her memory on Contoocook Island, in the Merrimack River north of Concord. This was where in 1697 Hannah Duston, her nurse and a young boy made their famous frantic escape from Indians, who held them captive for two weeks 20.00 28.00

☐ 157 **HANSEL AND GRETEL BOTTLE** *(c. 1971)*
The forlorn, lost waifs from the Brothers Grimm's beloved fable "Hansel and Gretel" are depicted on the front of this charming and beautiful Regal China bottle. Above them, the words "GERMANY . . . LAND OF HANSEL AND GRETEL" stand out in gold. 10¼" 4.00 8.00

□ 158 **HAROLDS CLUB—BLUE SLOT MACHINE** *(c. 1967)*
A blue-toned "One Armed Bandit" with 2 gold bells show-
ing in the window, and a gold colored handle, the money
slot is the stopper. "HAROLDS CLUB RENO" and a large
"H" on a pinwheel emblem are on the front. Regal China,
10⅜" **10.00** **16.00**

□ 159 **HAROLDS CLUB—COVERED WAGON** *(c. 1969-70)*
A Conestoga wagon with "HAROLDS CLUB" embossed
on the side pulled by a galloping ox, driven by a cowboy.
The bottle is "arch" shaped, framing Nevada's mountains
and the wagon. Regal China. 10" **4.00** **8.00**

□ 160 **HAROLDS CLUB—GRAY SLOT MACHINE** *(c. 1968)*
Same as above but with an overall grey tone. Regal China,
10⅜" **4.00** **8.00**

□ 161 **HAROLDS CLUB (MAN-IN-A-BARREL)** *(c. 1957-58)*
This was the first in a series made for the famous Harolds
Club in Reno, Nevada. The man-in-a-barrel was an adver-
tising logo used by the club. In 1957, Jim Beam issued a
bottle using the figure of "Percy" in-a-barrel with
"HAROLDS CLUB" embossed on the front. "Percy" has a
top hat, a monocle, a mustache, a white collar and a
bright red tie, and spats. He stands on a base of "Bad
News" dice cubes. Regal China, 14" **425.00** **485.00**

□ 162 **HAROLDS CLUB (MAN-IN-A-BARREL-2)** *(c. 1958)*
Twin brother of "Percy" No. 1. No mustache, "HAROLDS
CLUB" inscribed on base of the bottle. Regal China, 14" . **250.00** **285.00**

□ 163 **HAROLDS CLUB—NEVADA (GREY)** *(c. 1963)*
"HAROLDS CLUB OF RENO" inscribed on base of bottle
created for the "Nevada Centennial — 1864-1964" as a
State bottle. Embossed picture of miner and mule on the
"HAROLDS" side, crossed shovel and pick are on stop-
per. Embossed lettering on base is grey-toned and not
bold. This is a rare and valuable bottle **150.00** **185.00**

□ 164 **HAROLDS CLUB—NEVADA (SILVER)** *(c. 1964)*
Same as above. Base lettering now reads "HAROLDS
CLUB RENO". the letters are bolder and are bright silver . **150.00** **185.00**

□ 165 **HAROLDS CLUB—PINWHEEL** *(c. 1965)*
A round bottle supporting a design of a spinning pinwheel
of gold and blue, with gold dots on the edge. "HAROLDS
CLUB RENO" embossed in gold in the center, "FOR FUN"
on the stopper. Regal China. 10½" **60.00** **70.00**

□ 166 **HAROLDS CLUB—SILVER OPAL** *(c. 1957)*
Issued to commemorate the 25th Anniversary of Harolds
Club, bright silver color with a "snowflake" design center
and a red label. Glass, 11⅛" **20.00** **28.00**

□ 167 **HAROLDS CLUB—VIP EXECUTIVE** *(c. 1967)*
An "Alladins Lamp" shaped decanter. "HAROLDS CLUB
RENO" embossed gold label on bottle. Over-all gold &
green color on bottle. Limited quantity issued. Regal
China, 12½" **55.00** **65.00**

□ 168 **HAROLDS CLUB—VIP EXECUTIVE** *(c. 1968)*
An overall "bubble" pattern in cobalt blue with silver trim
and handle distinguishes this bottle. "HAROLDS CLUB
RENO" in silver, on an embossed oval emblem, is in the
center of the bottle. Regal China, 12¾" **55.00** **65.00**

☐169 **HAROLDS CLUB—VIP EXECUTIVE** *(c. 1969)*
An oval shaped decanter with an overall motif of roses.
"HAROLDS CLUB RENO" is embossed in gold on the
yellow-toned bottle. The bottle was used as a Christmas
gift to the Casino's executives. *Regal China, 12½"* 65.00   75.00

☐170 **HAROLDS CLUB VIP** *(1976)*
Same as Floro de Oro except for the Haold's Club patch
on the base. Urn-shaped bottles with pastel band and blue
and yellow flowers around the middle. Remainder of the
bottle has very shiny gold with fluting and designs 22.00   30.00

☐171 **HAROLD'S CLUB VIP** *(1979)*
Double urn shaped bottle with wide alternating bands of
gold and mother-of-peral with double scroll handles on
large screw off lid 35.00   45.00

☐172 **HARRAH'S CLUB NEVADA—GRAY** *(c. 1963)*
This is the same round bottle used for the Nevada Centennial and Harolds Club with the miner, and mule and lettered "NEVADA CENTENNIAL". The base has
"HARRAH'S RENO AND LAKE TAHOE" embossed on the
gray-tone base. *Regal China, 11½"* 240.00   285.00

☐173 **HARRAH'S CLUB NEVADA—SILVER** *(c. 1963)*
Same as above. Nevada Centennial bottle, "HARRAH'S
RENO AND LAKE TAHOE" embossed on base in silver.
Regal China, 11½" 150.00   225.00

☐174 **HARVEY'S RESORT HOTEL AT LAKE TAHOE** *(c. 1970)*
Glass, 11½" 10.00   18.00

☐175 **HAWAII** *(c. 1959)*
Tribute to 50th State. Panorama of Hawaiian scenes,
palm trees, the blue Pacific, outriggers, and surf
boarders. Gold "50" in star. *Regal China, 8½"* 55.00   65.00

☐176 **HAWAII—RE-ISSUED** *(c. 1967)*
As above 50.00   60.00

☐177 **HAWAII** *(c. 1971)* 6.00   10.00

☐178 **HAWAIIAN OPEN BOTTLE** *(c. 1972)*
Cleverly decorated to simulate a pineapple with the
famous "Friendly Skies" logo in gold, this genuine Regal
China Bottle honors the 1972 Hawaiian Open Golf Tournament. The reverse side commemorates United Air Lines'
25th year (1972) of air service to Hawaii. The stopper is de-
signed to look like pineapple leaves. 10" 6.00   10.00

☐179 **HAWAIIAN OPEN** *(c. 1973)*
The second bottle created in honor of the United
Hawaiian Open Golf Classic. Of genuine Regal China
designed in the shape of a golf ball featuring a pineapple
and airplane on front 6.00   10.00

☐180 **HAWAIIAN OPEN** *(c. 1974)*
Genuine Regal China bottle commemorating the famous
1974 Hawaiian Open Golf Classic 6.00   10.00

☐181 **HAWAII PARADISE** *(1978)*
Embossed scene of a Hawaiian resort framed by a pink
garland of flowers. Black stopper 20.00   28.00

☐182 **HEMISFAIR** *(c. 1968)*
The Lone Star of Texas crowns the tall grey and blue
"TOWER OF THE AMERICAS". "THE LONE STAR STATE"

is lettered in gold over a rustic Texas scene. The ½ map of Texas has "HEMISFAIR 68 — SAN ANTONIO". Regal China, 13" **6.00** **10.00**

☐ 183 **HOFFMAN** *(c. 1969-70)*
The bottle is in the shape of "HARRY HOFFMAN LIQUOR STORE" with the Rocky Mountains in the background. Beam bottles, and "SKI COUNTRY — USA" are in the windows. Reverse: embossed mountain & ski slopes with skier. Regal China, 9" **4.00** **8.00**

☐ 184 **HOME BUILDERS** *(1978)*
Replica of a Rockford Builders Bungalow, brown with touches of black. Oval medallion on the roof reads "Your Best Bet - A Home Of Your Own." This bottles commemorates the 1979 convention of the Home Builders ... **22.00** **28.00**

☐ 185 **HONGA HIKA** *(1980)*
Honga Hika is the most famous warchief of the Ngapuki tribe. This is the first in a series of authentic Maori Warrior bottles **125.00** **165.00**

☐ 186 **HORSE (BLACK)** *(c. 1962)*
Black Horse with white nose blaze, white hooves, and black tail. Regal China, 13½" **20.00** **28.00**

☐ 187 **HORSE (BLACK)—RE-ISSUED** *(c. 1967)*
As above **16.00** **22.00**

☐ 188 **HORSE (BROWN)** *(c. 1962)*
Brown Horse with white blaze on nose, black hooves and tail. Regal China, 13½" high **20.00** **28.00**

☐ 189 **HORSE (BROWN)—RE-ISSUED** *(c. 1967)*
As above **16.00** **22.00**

☐ 190 **HORSE (GREY)** *(c. 1962)*
Grey Mustang with grey flowing mane and tail. Regal China, 13½" **20.00** **28.00**

☐ 191 **HORSE (GREY)—RE-ISSUED** *(c. 1967)*
As above **16.00** **22.00**

☐ 192 **HORSESHOE CLUB** *(c. 1969)*
Same as above with "RENO'S HORSESHOE CLUB" and a horseshoe in yellow & black on the emblem **4.00** **8.00**

☐ 193 **HULA BOWL** *(1975)*
Brown football resting on a stand with a red helmet on the top. Medallion type plaque on the front football player in the center **10.00** **15.00**

I

☐ 194 **IDAHO** *(c. 1963)*
Bottle in the shape of a State of Idaho. Skiier on slope on one side and farmer on other side. Pick and shovel on stopper. Regal China, 12¼" **65.00** **75.00**

☐ 195 **ILLINOIS** *(c. 1968)*
The log cabin birth place of "Abe Lincoln" embossed on front, oak tree, and banner with 21 stars (21st state) and "Land of Lincoln". Made to honor the Sesquicentennial 1818-1968 of Illinois, home of the James B. Beam Distilling Company. Regal China, 12¾" **4.00** **8.00**

☐ 196 **INDIAN CHIEF** (1979)
Seated Indian chief with a peace pipe across his arm. Tan
colored with touches of brown, green, and red **28.00**   **36.00**
☐ 197 **INTERNATIONAL CHILI SOCIETY** (1976)
Upper body of a chef with recipe of C.V. Wood's World
Championship Chili Recipe **8.00**   **12.00**
☐ 198 **IVORY ASH TRAY** (c. 1955)
Designed for a dual purpose, as a bottle, and as an ash
tray. Bottle lies flat with cigarette grooves and round
coaster seat. Ivory color. Regal China, 12¾" **20.00**   **28.00**

J

☐ 199 **JACKALOPE** (c. 1971)
The fabulous Wyoming Jackalope, a rare cross twixt
Jackrabbit and Antelope. With the body and ears of the
Western Jackrabbit and the head and antlers of an
Antelope. Golden brown body on "prairie grass" base.
Regal China, 14" **8.00**   **12.00**
☐ 200 **JIM BEAM ELECTION BOTTLES** (c. 1972)
"Pick the winning team." The Democratic donkey and the
G.O.P.'s elephant are depicted in football costumes atop
genuine Regal China footballs in this 1972 version of
Beam's famous election bottle series. Each is 9½" **5.00**   **8.00**
☐ 201 **JOLIET LEGION BAND** (1978)
Shield-shaped bottle with embossed details resembling a
coat of arms in blue, green, and gold. Commemorates the
26 national championships won by the band **10.00**   **15.00**
☐ 202 **KAISER INTERNATIONAL OPEN BOTTLE** (c. 1971)
This handsome Regal China creation commemorates the
Fifth Annual Kaiser International Open Golf Tournament
played that year at Silverado in California's beautiful
Napa Valley. The stopper is a "golf ball" decorated with
the Kaiser International Open logo suspended over a red
tee. The logo is repeated, in gold against a blue field, in
the center of the front panel and is surrounded by a ring of
decorated golf balls. Listed on the back are the par-
ticulars of the tournament. 11¼" **4.00**   **8.00**
☐ 203 **KANGAROO** (1977)
Kangaroo with its baby in its pouch on a green pedestal.
The head unscrews as the stopper **18.00**   **26.00**
☐ 204 **KANSAS** (c. 1960-61)
Round, yellow-toned bottle shows harvesting of wheat on
one side and "KANSAS 1861-1961 CENTENNIAL"
embossed in gold. On the other side, symbols of the
modern age with aircraft, factories, oil wells, and dairies.
Leather thong. Regal China, 11¾" **60.00**   **70.00**
☐ 205 **KENTUCKY BLACK HEAD — BROWN HEAD** (c. 1967)
The stopper is a horse's head, some are made in brown,
some black. State map on bottle shows products of Kentucky. Tobacco, distilling, farming, coal, oil, and industries. Regal China, 11½"

	BLACK HEAD	12.00	18.00
	BROWN HEAD	20.00	28.00
	WHITE HEAD	12.00	18.00

☐206 **KENTUCKY DERBY BOTTLE** (c. 1972)
Designed to commemorate the 98th "Run For The Roses"
at Churchill Downs showing Canonero II, 1971 winner,
garlanded with the traditional American Beauty Roses.
The reverse side depicts famous Churchill Downs Club-
house in relief and etched in gold. The stopper is a replica
of an American Beauty Rose. 11" 6.00   10.00

☐207 **KING KONG** (1976)
Three-quarters body of King Kong. Commemorates the
Paramount Picture move release in December 1976 ..... 10.00   16.00

☐208 **KOALA BEAR** (c. 1973)
The Koala Bear, the native animal of Australia. A genuine
Regal China creation. The bottle features two Koala
Bears on a tree stump, the top of the Stump is its pourer,
with the name Australia across the front of the bottle 10.00   16.00

L

☐209 **LARAMIE** (c. 1968)
"CENTENNIAL JUBILEE LARAMIE WYO. 1868-1968"
embossed around cowboy on bucking bronco.
Locomotive of 1860's on reverse. 10½" 4.00   8.00

☐210 **LAS VEGAS** (c. 1969)
This bottle was also used for CUSTOMER SPECIALS —
CASINO SERIES. "Almond" shaped with gold embossed
"LAS VEGAS" in a banner, and scenes of Nevada, and a
gambling montage. Reverse: Hoover Dam and Lake Mead.
Regal China, 12½" 4.00   8.00

☐211 **LIGHT BULB** (1979)
Regular bottle shape with replica of a light bulb for the
stopper, picture of Thomas Edison in a oval, letter of
tribute to Edison on the back 10.00   15.00

☐212 **LOMBARD** (c. 1969-70)
A pear-shaped decanter, embossed with lilacs and leaves
around a circular motto "VILLAGE OF LOMBARD, ILLI-
NOIS — 1869 CENTENNIAL 1969" lilac shaped stopper.
Reverse has an embossed outline map of Illinois. Colors
are lavender and green 3.00   6.00

☐213 **LOUISVILLE DOWNS RACING DERBY** (1978)
Short, oblong-shaped bottle, scene with horse, buggy an
rider on the front framed by wide white band with gold let-
tering. Medallion type stopper 10.00   15.00

M

☐214 **MADAME BUTTERFLY** (1978)
Figurine of Madame Butterfly character from the opera of
the same name. Female dressed in blue and black kimono
holding a realistic fan make of paper and wood. Music
box plays "One Fine Day" from the opera 475.00   575.00

☐215 **THE MAGPIES** *(1977)*
Black magpie sitting on top of a football with the name "The Magpies" on the front. Honors an Australian football team 16.00 24.00

☐216 **MAINE** *(c. 1970)* 4.00 8.00

☐217 **MAJESTIC** *(c. 1966)*
Royal blue decanter with handle, on a base of golden leaves. Gold scrolled stopper, and lip. Regal China, 14½ " 30.00 38.00

☐218 **MARBLED FANTASY** *(c. 1965)*
Decanter on a blue marbled base, set in a cup of gold with a heavy gold ring around the center. Gold lip and handle, blue & gold stopper. Regal China, 15" 70.00 80.00

☐219 **MARINA CITY** *(c. 1962)*
Commemorating Modern Apt. complex in Chicago. Light blue with Marina City in gold on the sides. Regal China, 10¾ " 30.00 40.00

☐220 **MARK ANTHONY** *(c. 1964)*
Same as Cleo bottles, amphora-decanter, 2 handles, white stopper. Mark Anthony alone before Nile scene, white on rust background. Bottle color is black-purple. Glass. 13¼ " 20.00 28.00

☐221 **MARTHA WASHINGTON** *(1975)*
Designed like a collector's plate, with a portrait of Martha Washington encircled by a band of white with the outside rim in light blue and gold embossed lettering 10.00 15.00

☐222 **MEPHISTOPHELES** *(1979)*
Part of the Opera series, this figurine depicts Mephistopheles from the opera "Faust." The music box plays "Soldier's Chorus." 275.00 350.00

☐223 **MICHIGAN BOTTLE** *(c. 1972)*
The map of the "Great Lakes State" adorns the front of this striking commemorative Regal China bottle. The state flower and the major cities are shown along with an inset plaque of an antique automobile, one of Michigan's traditional symbols. A capsule description of the state, a drawing of the magnificent Mackinac Bridge and the state motto of the "Wolverine State" appear on a scroll on the back. The stopper depicts and antique wooden wheel on one side and a modern automobile wheel on the other. 11⅞ " 6.00 10.00

☐224 **MINNESOTA VIKING** *(c. 1973)*
A strikingly handsome Regal China creation designed after the famous Viking statue in Alexandria, Minnesota, known as the "Largest Viking in the World". The bottle features a helmet as its stopper. The back depicts a replica of the Kensington Runestone 6.00 10.00

☐225 **MINT 400** *(c. 1971-72-73)*
The annual Del Webb Mint 400 was commemorated by a striking Regal China sculpture which captures the feeling of the desert, surrounded by mountains, beneath a blue Las Vegas sky — Home of one of the racing world's most grueling off-road events. The bottle's most prominent feature is the gold-painted motorcycle racer on the stopper. Black and white checkered flags are crossed on the

front above large gold letters. Black and white checks
edge the sides. A decal on the reverse details information
about the race. 8¼" 8.00   12.00
Same as above (c. 1970) 8.00   12.00

☐226 **MINT 400 8TH ANNUAL** *(1976)*
Medallion-shaped bottle. White bottle with gold lettering
and gold center with black lettering. Commemorates the
Mint 400 — a road race sponsored by Del Webb's Hotel
and Casino in Las Vegas 16.00   24.00

☐227 **MISSISSIPPI FIRE ENGINE** *(1978)*
Replica of the 1867 Fire Engine, red and black with brass
simulated fittings. Bells, lanterns, water pump, and
engine mountings are authentic 45.00   55.00

☐228 **MODEL A FORD 1903** *(1978)*
Replica of Henry Ford's Model A Ford in red with black
trim or black with red trim. Simulated brass and trim.
Stopper at the rear of the car 38.00   48.00

☐229 **MODEL A FORD 1928** *(1980)*
Beige Model A with black accessories, authentic details
for the headlights, trim, and interior. Stopper underneath
the rear trunk and spare tire 35.00   45.00

☐230 **MONTANA** *(c. 1964)*
Tribute to gold miners. Names of "ALDER GULCH",
"LAST CHANCE GULCH, BANNACK" and "MONTANA,
1864 GOLDEN YEARS CENTENNIAL 1964" are embossed
on bottle. Regal China, 11½" 80.00   90.00

☐231 **MONTEREY BAY CLUB** *(1978)*
Based on the band stand in Watsonville city park, honors
the Monterey Bay Beam Bottle and Speciality Club 16.00   22.00

☐232 **MOTHER OF PERAL** *(1979)*
Double urn-shaped bottle with wide alternating bands of
gold and mother-of-pearl with double scroll handles on
large screw off lid. Identical to the Harold's Club VIP bot-
tle except no lettering on the front 20.00   28.00

☐233 **MORTIMER SNERD** *(1976)*
Country boy with buck teeth, straw hat, and bow tie.
Replica of famous character created by Edger Bergen ... 28.00   34.00

☐234 **MOTORCYCLE STOPPER** 10.00   20.00

☐235 **MOUNTAIN ST. HELENS** *(1980)*
Depicts the eruption of St. Helens on May 18, 1980. A
small vial of ash from the explosion is attached on the
back 12.00   16.00

☐236 **MR. GOODWRENCH** *(1978)*
Half-figure of Mr. Goodwrench based on the General
Motors advertisement. The figure is the stopper which
sits on a rectangular base. Blue and white 8.00   12.00

☐237 **MUSICIANS ON A WINE CASK** *(c. 1964)*
"Old time" tavern scene: musicians, guitar and accordian,
embossed on cask-shaped embossed bottle. Wooden bar-
rel effect, and "wood" base. Grey china color. Regal
China, 9¾" 4.00   8.00

N

☐ 238 **NATIONAL TOBACCO FESTIVAL** *(c. 1973)*
Regal China bottle commemorating the 25th Anniversary of the National Tobacco Festival. The festival was held in Richmond, Virginia, on October 6 through the 13th. On the base of the special bottle, historic data of the growth and development of the tobacco industry is featured . . . the unique closure is the bust of an American Indian . . . .　**80.00**　**12.00**

☐ 239 **NEBRASKA** *(c. 1967)*
Round bottle bears the words, "WHERE THE WEST BEGINS" with a picture of a covered wagon drawn by oxen. Regal China, 12¼" . . . .　**6.00**　**10.00**

☐ 240 **NEBRASKA FOOTBALL** *(c. 1972)*
This strikingly handsome genuine Regal China creation commemorates the University of Nebraska's national championship football team of 1970-71 season. The stopper features an exact likeness of Bob Devaney, the "Cornhuskers" head coach. 8¾" . . . .　**6.00**　**10.00**

☐ 241 **NEVADA** *(c. 1964)*
Circular silver and grey bottle, with silver "NEVADA", bearing outline of State with embossed mountain peaks, forests, and a factory. Reverse is a miner and donkey. Regal China, 11½". Same bottle used by Harold's Club and Harrah's . . . .　**150.00**　**200.00**

☐ 242 **NEW HAMPSHIRE** *(c. 1967-68)*
Blue-tone bottle in the shape of the state. Decal of state motto, seal, flower and bird. Stopper in the shape of "The Old Man of the Mountain". Regal China, 13½" . . . .　**6.00**　**10.00**

☐ 243 **NEW HAMPSHIRE EAGLE BOTTLE** *(c. 1968)*
Under the New Hampshire banner on this beautiful Regal China bottle, a solid gold eagle against a blue field stands as a proud reminder of the original symbol, a great carved wooden bird, which was placed atop the New Hampshire State House when it was built in 1818. On the back of the bottle, beneath the slogan "Granite State", a decal recounts the history of the first New Hampshire Eagle, 12½" . . . .　**8.00**　**12.00**

☐ 244 **NEW JERSEY** *(c. 1963-64)*
Grey map of State filled with embossed colorful fruits, vegetables, and flowers, set on pyramid shaped bottle. "NEW JERSEY — THE GARDEN STATE, FARM & INDUSTRY" in gold. Regal China,, 13½" . . . .　**65.00**　**75.00**

☐ 245 **NEW JERSEY YELLOW** *(c. 1963-64)*
Same as above, yellow toned map of New Jersey . . . .　**55.00**　**65.00**

☐ 246 **NEW MEXICO BICENTENNIAL** *(1976)*
Square-shaped bottle with blue center. White lettering and gold eagle embossed on front. The Govenor's home is on the back . . . .　**8.00**　**12.00**

☐ 247 **NEW MEXICO STATEHOOD** *(c. 1972)*
Commemorating New Mexico's 60 years of statehood. This dramatic genuine Regal China bottle has been designed to represent the historical Indian Ceremonial Wedding Vase, used through the centuries by the New Mexico Indians in tribal wedding ceremonies . . . .　**8.00**　**12.00**

☐248 **NEW YORK WORLD'S FAIR** *(c. 1964)*
The emblem of the N.Y. World's Fair of 1964 — the
Unisphere forms the shape of this bottle. Blue tone
oceans, grey continents crossed by space flight routes.
Emblem embossed in gold "1964 WORLD'S FAIR —
1965". Stopper has Unisphere. Regal China, 11½" 18.00   24.00

☐249 **NORTH DAKOTA** *(c. 1964)*
Embossed memorial picture of a pioneer family in NORTH
DAKOTA—75" embossed in gold in banner. Yellows,
greens and browns. Regal China, 11¾" 90.00   110.00
"NORTH DAKOTA—(75)" embossed in gold in banner ... 30.00   38.00

☐250 **NORTHERN PIKE** *(1978)*
Replica of the Northern Pike. Green and yellow with
pointed head. The sixth in a series of bottles designed for
the National Fresh Water Fishing Hall of Fame 10.00   18.00

☐251 **NUTCRACKER TOY SOLDIER** *(1978)*
Figurine based on the character the toy soldier in the
ballet "The Nutcracker Suite," this is not part of the opera
series. Small man dressed in red, white uniform with blue
suspenders and gold trim. The music box plays a selec-
tion from "The Parade of the Toy Soldiers." 275.00   375.00

O

☐252 **OHIO** *(c. 1966)*
Bottle in shape of State. One side bears State seal, other
side has pictures of State industries. Regal China, 10" 10.00   16.00

☐253 **OHIO** *(c. 1973)*
A handsome bottle made of genuine Regal China, created
in honor of the 120th Ohio State Fair 8.00   12.00

☐254 **OLYMPIAN** *(c. 1960)*
Another Green urn decanter. Chariot horses, and warriors
design in white on light blue bottle. White glass stopper,
embossed base. Glass, 14" 3.00   6.00

☐255 **ONE HUNDRED FIRST AIRBORNE DIVISION** *(1978)*
Honors the division known during World War II as "The
Screaming Eagles." A gold flying eagles on top a white
pedestal 10.00   15.00

☐256 **OPALINE CRYSTAL** *(1969)*
Milk glass bottle same pattern and embossing, and stop-
per. Milk glass. 11½" 4.00   8.00

☐257 **OREGON** *(c. 1959)*
Green-tone bottle to honor Centennial of the state.
Depicting famous scenery on both sides. Two beavers on
bottle neck. Regal China, 8¾" 40.00   50.00

P

☐258 **PEARL HARBOR MEMORIAL** *(c. 1972)*
Honoring the Pearl Harbor Survivors Association, this
handsome genuine Regal China bottle is emblazoned with
the motto: "REMEMBER PEARL HARBOR — KEEP
AMERICA ALERT". The stopper features the official seal

of the armed services that were present December 7, 1941
— Army, Navy, Marine Corps, and Coast Guard. The stop-
per is set off by an American eagle. 11½" **20.00 28.00**

☐ 259 **PEARL HARBOR SURVIVORS ASSOCIATION** *(1976)*
Medallion-shaped bottle with flying eagle in the center
with a blue background and white lettering around the
border. On the back, a scene of the island, Oahu, with
three battleships **8.00 12.00**

☐ 260 **PENNSYLVANIA** *(c. 1967)*
Keystone-shaped bottle in blue tones. Decal of state seal
"HISTORIC PENNSYLVANIA — THE KEYSTONE STATE"
on front. Reverse: scenes of history and industry. Keystone stopper with gold "1776". Regal China, 11½" **6.00 10.00**

☐ 261 **PERMIAN BASIN OIL SHOW** *(c. 1972)*
This dramatic genuine Regal China bottle is fashioned
after an oil derrick and its attendant buildings. Commemorates the Permian Basin Oil Show in Odessa, Texas,
October 18 through 21, 1972. The building is inscribed:
The E. E. "Pop" Harrison No. 1 well. The back of the "flag"
says "The oil industry provides energy, enterprise,
employment for the nation". The stopper is fashioned in
the shape of the logo for the Oil Field Workers Show with
their motto "let's go". 13" **4.00 8.00**

☐ 262 **PHEASANT** *(c. 1960)*
Ring-necked Pheasant with red-circled eyes, green and
blue head, and soft brown plumage perched on a "fence"
base. Regal China, 13" **18.00 26.00**

☐ 263 **PHEASANT** *(c. 1961)*
Re-issued also: '63, '66, '67, '68. As above **16.00 22.00**

☐ 264 **PHI SIGMA KAPPA** *(c. 1973)*
(CENTENNIAL SERIES)
A Regal China creation commemorating the 100th Anniversary of this National Fraternity . . . A Fraternity
dedicated to the Promotion of Brotherhood, the Stimulation of Scholarship, and the Development of Character.
The Fraternity insignia is in silver on a magenta
back-ground outlined in white and lavender **4.00 8.00**

☐ 265 **PIED PIPER OF HAMLET** *(c. 1974)*
This charming bottle of genuine Regal China was
especially produced for the United States Armed Forces
in Europe as a commemorative of the famous German
Legend, the PIED PIPER OF HAMLET **4.00 8.00**

☐ 266 **PONDEROSA** *(c. 1969)*
The home of the Cartwrights of "Bonanza" TV fame. A
replica of the Ponderosa Ranch log cabin in brown tones.
Reverse: Lake Tahoe. Bottles in green lined box are worth
more. Regal China, 7½" high, 10" wide **4.00 8.00**

☐ 267 **PONDEROSA RANCH TOURIST** *(c. 1972)*
Commemorating the one millionth tourist to the Ponderosa Ranch. This horseshoe shaped bottle of genuine
Regal China features the Ponderosa Pine and "P" symbol
that have made the ranch famous. The stopper is traditional ten gallon hat, made famous by Dan Blocker. 11" .. **10.00 16.00**

☐ 268 **PONY EXPRESS** (c. 1968)
*Clearly embossed figure of horse and Pony Express Rider
with "SACRAMENTO, CALIF. — OCTOBER 1861" and
"ST. JOSEPH, MO. — APRIL 1860" and stars around
figure. Reverse: Map of the Pony Express route. Yellow &
brown tones* 4.00   8.00

☐ 269 **POODLE—GREY & WHITE** (c. 1970)
*Both poodles sit up with one paw on a ball. The grey has a
green banded ball embossed "PENNY", the white has a
blue banded ball. Blackeyes, and nose and a gold color on
each. Regal China, 12"* .... **PAIR**   14.00   20.00

☐ 270 **PORTLAND ROSE FESTIVAL** (c. 1972)
*To commemorate the 64th Portland, Oregon Rose Festival
which began in 1889. The Regal China bottle is encom-
passed in a garland of red roses which is commemorative
of the oldest and largest rose show in America. On the
reverse side there is a brief description of the festival with
the very poignant line, "For You A Rose In Portland
Grows," 10¼"* 80.00   12.00

☐ 271 **PORTOLA TREK** (c. 1969)
*This gold glass bottle has a painting of "THE PORTOLA
TREK" reproduction in full color on the front. This bottle
was issued to celebrate the 200th Anniversary of San
Diego, and is a companion to the Regal China bottle* 4.00   8.00

☐ 271 **POULAN CHAIN SAW** (1979)
*Replica of the Poulan Chain Saw with a plastic handle
and blade. Green body with silver blade and black trim* ... 18.00   22.00

☐ 273 **POWELL EXPEDITION** (c. 1969)
*Another gold glass bottle with a full color painting
depict-ing John Wesley Powell's survey of the Colorado
River and his traversing the Grand Canyon* 4.00   8.00

☐ 274 **PRETTY PERCH** (1980)
*Spiny-finned fish with dark bands, touches of orange on
the fins, the eighth in a series, this fish is used as the official seal of the National Fresh Water Fishing Hall of Fame*
.... 16.00   20.00

☐ 275 **PRIMA-DONNA** (c. 1969)
*Same as "CAL-NEVA" with PRIMA-DONNA CASINO" and
show girls on the emblem* 4.00   8.00

☐ 276 **PYREX COFFEE WARMERS** (c. 1954)
Corning Glass Co., date on top. 9" 10.00   16.00

Q

☐ 277 **QUEENSLAND** (1978)
*In the shape of the province, Queensland, the "Sunshine
State" of Australia. Embossed lettering and details, gold
star on the back. Medallion type stopper with "Australia"
in center* 12.00   18.00

R

☐278 **RAINBOW TROUT** *(1975)*
Rainbow trout mounted on an oval plaque made to look like wood. Produced for the National Fresh Water Fishing Hall of Fame. Their official seal is on the back 8.00 12.00

☐279 **RALPH CENTENNIAL** *(c. 1973)*
Made of genuine Regal China, this bottle was designed to commemorate the 100th Anniversary of the Ralph Grocery Company in California. The bottle depicts two sides of a coin struck especially for the occasion and an early version of a Ralphs delivery wagon 8.00 12.00

☐280 **RAM** *(c. 1958)*
Stylized Ram in soft tans and browns. Calender mounted on green base, and a round thermometer in the curve of the horn. Regal China 12½" high (without thermometer worthless) 100.00 200.00

☐281 **RAMADA INN** *(1976)*
The Ramada Inn Attendant is shown as a sentinel at the door to a small narrow building of red, white, and blue. Gold shingles with a black lid on the chimney 5.00 10.00

☐282 **REDWOOD** *(c. 1967)*
Pyramid shaped bottle, Coast Redwoods embossed on front in tones of brown and green. "REDWOOD EMPIRE OF CALIFORNIA" lettered below tree. Reverse: scenes of Redwood country. Regal China, 12¾" 4.00 8.00

☐283 **RENEE THE FOX** *(c. 1974)*
This interesting Regal China bottle represents the com-panion for the International Association of Jim Beam bottle and specialty group's mascot. Renee the Fox is the life long companion of Rennie the Fox 8.00 12.00

☐284 **RENNIE THE SURFER** *(1975)*
Rennie the fox dressed in an old-fashioned bathing suit and a black top hat rides a small surfboard. He holds a bottle of Beam behind him with one hand 20.00 28.00

☐285 **RENO** *(c. 1968-69)*
"100 YEARS — RENO" embossed over skyline of downtown Reno. "THE BIGGEST LITTLE CITY IN THE WORLD" lettered over skyline. Reverse: "RENO 100 YEARS" and scenes of Reno. Regal China. 9¼" 8.00 12.00

☐286 **REPUBLIC OF TEXAS** *(1980)*
Star-shaped bottle with gold spout, handle and top. White with a red border, symbols of the state are represented on the front. The stopper is a gold star 35.00 45.00

☐287 **RICHARDS—NEW MEXICO** *(c. 1967)*
Created for Richards Distributing Company of Albuquerque, New Mexico. Lettered "NEW MEXICO" and "RICHARD SAYS DISCOVER NEW MEXICO", in blue. Embossed scene of Taos Rueblo. Picture of "Richard" on stopper and front. Regal China, 11" 4.00 8.00

☐288 **ROBIN** *(c. 1969)*
An olive grey bird with a soft red breast, dark toned head and tail. The Robin has a yellow beak and stands on a "tree trunk" with an embossed branch and leaves. Regal China, 13½" 6.00 10.00

☐ 289 **ROCKY MARCIANO** *(c. 1973)*
A handsome genuine Regal China bottle in honor of Rocky Marciano, the world's only undefeated boxing champion. The bottle takes the shape of a rock, with a likeness of Rocky Marciano on the front. The back of the bottle features Marciano's complete professional record of 49 fights, all victories, 43 knockouts and 6 decisions .. **8.00** **12.00**

☐ 290 **ROYAL CRYSTAL** *(c. 1959-67)*
Starburst design embossed on both sides on this clear flint glass decanter. Gold label on neck and flat black stopper. Starburst theme appears on label and stopper. Glass, 11½" **4.00** **8.00**

☐ 291 **ROYAL DI MONTE** *(c. 1957)*
Mottled design, black and white bottle. Hand painted with 22 karat gold and bordered in gold. Gold & black stopper. Regal China, 15½" **70.00** **80.00**

☐ 292 **ROYAL EMPEROR** *(c. 1958)*
Made in the Shape of a Classic Greek urn. Warrior figure with spear and helmet and fret design in white on purple-black glass. White glass stopper. Glass, 14" **4.00** **8.00**

☐ 293 **ROYAL GOLD DIAMOND** *(c. 1964)*
Diamond-shaped decanter set on a flaring base, all in mottled gold. Gold chain holds label. Regal China, 12" **50.00** **60.00**

☐ 294 **ROYAL GOLD ROUND** *(c. 1956)*
Mottled with 22 karat gold, in classic round shape with graceful pouring spout, and curved handle. Gold neck chain holds label. Regal China, 12" **125.00** **175.00**

☐ 295 **ROYAL OPAL** *(c. 1957)*
A round, handled bottle, of Opal glass. Embossed geometric design on one side. White glass stopper. Bottle made by Wheaton Glass of Millville, New Jersey. Same bottle was used for Harolds Club, 25th Anniversary in silver. Glass, 10¾" **6.00** **10.00**

☐ 296 **ROYAL PORCELAIN** *(c. 1955)*
Gleaming black decanter, tapered with a large flared pouring lip, white stopper, gold cord & tassel. Regal China, 14½" **400.00** **500.00**

☐ 297 **ROYAL ROSE** *(c. 1963)*
Decanter, gold embossed with hand painted roses on a background of soft blue, gold spout, stopper, base & handle. Regal China, 17" **45.00** **55.00**

☐ 298 **RUBY CRYSTAL** *(c. 1967)*
Amethyst colored, patterned embossed bottle. "Swirl" glass stopper. When bottle is filled with bourbon it's ruby red. Sunburst pattern on bottom. Amethyst Glass. 11½" . **10.00** **16.00**

☐ 299 **RUIDOSO DOWNS** *(c. 1968-69)*
A round decanter with a unique "horsehead" stopper. Embossed silver horseshoe, branding iron and cowboy hat, "RUIDOSO DOWNS — NEW MEXICO, WORLD'S RICHEST HORSE RACE" on front. Reverse: Red, white and blue emblem. The bottle is known in "Pointed & Flat Ears". Regal China, 12¾" **4.00** **6.00**
    Flat Ears **4.00** **8.00**

S

☐300 **SAHARA INVITATIONAL BOTTLE** (c. 1971)
Introduced in honor of the Del Webb 1971 Sahara Invitational Pro-Am Golf Tournament. The prominent feature of this Regal China Bottle is a large "Del Webb Pro-Am 1971" golf ball atop a red tee on the face. Listed on the back are the winners of this annual contest from 1958 through 1970. 12" 4.00   8.00

☐301 **SAN DIEGO** (c. 1968)
Issued by the Beam Company for the 200th Anniversary of its founding in 1769. Honoring Junipero Serra, Francisca missionary. Serra and Conquistador embossed on gold front. Regal China, 10" 4.00   8.00

☐302 **SANTA FE** (c. 1960)
Governor's Palace blue-toned sky, date 1610-1960 (350th Anniversary). Navaho woman with Indian basket on reverse. Gold lettering. Regal China, 10" 200.00   275.00

☐303 **SCREECH OWL** (1979)
Either red or grey shading. Birds are bisque replicas of screech owls, authenticated by Dr. Lester Fisher, director of the Lincoln Zoological Gardens in Chicago 18.00   26.00

☐304 **SEAFAIR TROPHY RACE** (c. 1972)
This dramatic genuine Regal China creation commemorates the Seattle Seafair Trophy Race, August 6, 1972, and features an unlimited hydroplane at speed with picturesque Mt. Rainier in the background. 11½" 8.00   12.00

☐305 **SEATTLE WORLD'S FAIR** (c. 1962)
"The Space Needle" as this bottle is known embossed in gold on one side, "CENTURY 21" on the other. Pylon shaped with color scenes of fruit, airplanes over mountains, salmon, etc. Stopper is the Fair's revolving restaurant. Regal China, 13½" 18.00   26.00

☐306 **SHORT DANCING SCOT** (c. 1963)
A short barrel-shaped bottle with the dancing Scot, and music box in the base. Square shaped stopper, a rare bottle. Glass, 11" 65.00   75.00

☐307 **SHORT TIMER** (1975)
Brown army shoes with arm helmet sitting on top. Produced for all who have served in the armed forces 28.00   34.00

☐308 **SHRINERS** (1975)
Embossed camel on front of bottle in blue, green, and brown with bright red blanket flowing from the camel's saddle. A gold scimitar and a gold star centered with a fake ruby is on the back 15.00   20.00

☐309 **SHRINERS' PYRAMID** (1975)
White and brown pyramid with embossed emblems on the sides 12.00   16.00

☐310 **SHRINERS RAJAH** (1978)
Pretzel-shaped bottle with a Shriner's sword in the center. Stopper is red and shaped like a Shriners cap with a black tassel 18.00   26.00

☐311 **SHRINER'S TEMPLE** *(c. 1972)*
This beautiful Regal China bottle features the traditional symbols of Moila Temple — the scimitar, star and crescent, the fez and the pyramid, and the stopper is the head of a Sphinx. This bottle is unique in that it features three simulated precious stones, two of them in the handle of the sword and the third is the center point of the star. 11½ " 30.00   40.00

☐312 **SIGMA NU FRATERNITY** *(1978)*
Rectangular bottle with the badge and coat of arms of the Sigma Nu Fraternity embossed on the front. White and gold lettering and designs. Medallion type stopper 8.00   12.00

☐313 **SMITH'S NORTH SHORE CLUB** *(c. 1972)*
Commemorating Smith's North Shore Club, at Crystal Bay, Lake Tahoe. This striking genuine Regal China bottle features the anchor, symbol of the club and is topped by a giant golden golf ball. 12" 10.00   16.00

☐314 **SMOKED CRYSTAL** *(c. 1964)*
Dark greenish in tone, and resembling a "Genie's" magic bottle, this tall bottle has a bulbous embossed base, and a slender tapering shape, topped by an embossed glass stopper. Glass, 14" 6.00   10.00

☐315 **SNOW GOOSE** *(1979)*
Replica of a white goose with black wingtips. Authenticated by Dr. Lester Fisher, director of Lincoln Park Zoological Gardens in Chicago 16.00   22.00

☐316 **SOUTH CAROLINA** *(c. 1970)* 6.00   10.00

☐317 **SOUTH DAKOTA—MOUNT RUSHMORE** *(c. 1969-70)*
The faces of Washington, Jefferson, T. Roosevelt, and Lincoln are shown in relief in white with blue sky and green forest. This landmark is called the Mount Rushmore National Memorial. Reverse: Scroll with information about Memorial. Regal China. 10½ " 6.00   10.00

☐318 **SOUTH FLORIDA FOX ON DOLPHIN** *(1980)*
A fox dressed in hunting garb rides a dolphin. This bottle was sponsored by the South Florida Beam Bottle and Specialities Club which is located in Miami 30.00   40.00

☐319 **SPENGER'S FISH GROTTO** *(1978)*
Designed as a small boat with the captain at the helm. Brown, yellow and some blue, made in conjunction with Spenger's Fish Grotto Restaurant in Berkeley, California . 16.00   24.00

☐320 **SPORTS CAR CLUB OF AMERICA** *(1976)*
Six-sided front with a Ridge-Whetworth wire wheel in the center on pedestal foot. Brief history of the club on the back 5.00   10.00

☐321 **STATUE OF LIBERTY** *(1975)*
Figural bottle with gold embossed Statue of Liberty on the front with light blue background. Green base with plaque 8.00   12.00

☐322 **ST. BERNARD** *(1979)*
Replica of a St. Bernard with a small cask of Beam around his neck held by a real leather collar 62.00   72.00

☐323 **ST. LOUIS ARCH** *(c. 1964-67)*
The silhouette of St. Louis with the Mississippi flowing past. The famous stainless steel arch frames the bottle

"ST. LOUIS, GATEWAY TO THE WEST" and "200 YEARS"
embossed in gold. The ferry boat "ADMIRAL" is on the
back. Regal China, 11" 20.00   30.00

☐324   **ST. LOUIS ARCH—RE-ISSUE** (c. 1967)
Same as above 18.00   24.00

☐325   **ST. LOUIS STATUE** (c. 1972)
This handsome Regal China bottle features the famous
statue of St. Louis on horseback atop its pedestal base.
The entire statue is fired gold. The back bears the inscription, Greater St. Louis Area Beam and Specialties Club.
13¼" 18.00   24.00

☐326   **STURGEON** (1980)
Exclusive issue for a group that advocates the preservation of sturgeons. Long brown colored fish 12.00   16.00

☐327   **STUTZ BEARCAT 1914** (1977)
Either yellow and black or grey and black. Replica of the
1914 4-cylinder Stutz Bearcat. Authentic details with
movable windshield. Stopper is under plastic trunk and
spare wheel 38.00   48.00

☐328   **SUBMARINE REDFIN** (c. 1970)
Embossed submarine on ocean-blue background. MANI-
TOWOC SUBMARINE MEMORIAL ASSOCIATION" in
black. Round stopper, with map of Wisconsin. Regal
China, 11½" 4.00   8.00

☐329   **SUPERDOME** (1975)
Replica of the Louisiana Superdome which opened in
August 1975. White and gold with black lettering around
the top 6.00   10.00

☐330   **SWAGMAN** (1979)
Replica of an Australian hobo — a Swagman — who
roamed that country looking for work during the depression. He wears a greyish outfit with red kerchief around
his neck. A brown dog and a sheep are curled around his
feet 12.00   18.00

☐331   **SYDNEY OPERA HOUSE** (1978)
Replica of the building housing the Sydney Opera in
Sydney, Australia. Music box is in the base 25.00   32.00

T

☐332   **TALL DANCING SCOT** (c. 1964-70)
A small Scotsman encased in a glass bubble in the base
dances to the music of the base. A tall pylon shaped glass
bottle with a tall stopper. No dates on these bottles.
Glass, 17" 12.00   18.00

☐333   **TAVERN SCENE** (c. 1959)
Two "beer stein" tavern scenes are embossed on sides,
framed in wide gold band on this round decanter. Regal
China, 11½" 65.00   75.00

☐334   **TELEPHONE** (1975)
Replica of a 1907 phone of the Magneto Wallset type
which was used from 1890 until the 1930's 28.00   34.00

☐335　**TEN-PIN** *(1980)*
Designed as a bowling pin with two red bands around the
shoulder and the neck. Remainder of the pin is white,
screw type lid .... **4.00　8.00**

☐336　**THAILAND** *(c. 1969)*
Embossed elephant in the jungle and "THAILAND — A
NATION OF WONDERS" on the front. Reverse: A map of
Thailand and a dancer. Regal China, 12½" .... **4.00　8.00**

☐337　**THOMAS FLYER 1907** *(1976)*
Replica of the 1907 Thomas Flyer, 6-70 Model K
"Flyabout," which was a luxury car of its day. Comes in
blue or white. Plastic rear trunk covers the lid to the bottle **60.00　70.00**

☐338　**TIFFINY POODLE** *(c. 1973)*
Genuine Regal China bottle created in honor of Tiffiny,
the poodle mascot of the National Association of the Jim
Beam Bottle & Specialties Clubs. Mr. and Mrs. Milton
Campbell, officers of the National Association, are the
proud owners .... **14.00　20.00**

☐339　**THE TIGERS** *(1977)*
Tiger head on top of a football which reads "The Tigers."
Honors an Australian football team .... **22.00　28.00**

☐340　**TITIAN** *(1980)*
Urn-shaped bottle, reproduces the designs created by the
Venetian artist Titian in his oil paintings. Long fluted
neck, with double scrolled handle .... **4.00　8.00**

☐341　**TREASURE CHEST** *(1979)*
Partially opened treasure chest with gold coins, pearls,
and jewelry. The lid is a screw off top .... **22.00　28.00**

☐342　**TROUT UNLIMITED** *(1978)*
Large traditionally shaped bottle with a large yellow trout
placed across the front of the bottle at the shoulder. Stop-
per reads "Limit Your Kill, Don't Kill Your Limit." To honor
the Trout Unlimited Conservation Organization .... **10.00　20.00**

☐343　**TRUTH OR CONSEQUENCES FIESTA** *(c. 1974)*
A ruggedly handsome Regal China bottle in honor of
Ralph Edward's famous Radio and television show and
the city of Truth or Consequences, New Mexico .... **4.00　8.00**

☐344　**TURQUOISE CHINA JUG** *(c. 1966)*
Regal China, Spec., 13¼" .... **4.00　8.00**

☐345　**TWIN BRIDGES BOTTLE** *(c. 1971)*
Designed to commemorate the largest twin bridge com-
plex of its kind in the world. The twin bridges connect
Delaware and New Jersey and serve as major link
between key East Coast cities. Handsomely accented in
gold and bearing the shield of the Twin Bridges Beam Bot-
tle and Specialty Club, this Regal China bottle portrays
the twin spans of the front and provides a descriptive
story on the back. The stopper is a replica of the bridge
toll house. 10½" .... **50.00　60.00**

U

☐346 **U. S. OPEN** *(c. 1972)*
Whimsically depicts Uncle Sam's traditional hat holding a full set of golf clubs. This charming Regal China creation honors the U. S. Open Golf Tourney as the famous Pebble Beach course in California. 10½ " 12.00 18.00

V

☐347 **VENDOME DRUMMER'S WAGON** *(1975)*
Replica of a delivery wagon, green and cream wood with yellow wheels which are plastic. Honored the Vendomes of Beverly Hills, California — a food chain store which was first established in 1937 .... 60.00 70.00

☐348 **V.F.W. BOTTLE** *(c. 1971)*
A handsome Regal China creation designed to commemorate the 50th Anniversary of the Department of Indiana V.F.W. This proclamation is made on the neck of the bottle, in a plaque in the shape of the state of Indiana, over a striking reproduction of the medal insignia of the V.F.W. 9¾ " 4.00 8.00

☐349 **VOLKSWAGEN COMMEMORATIVE BOTTLE (2) COLORS**
Commemorating the Volkswagen Beetle ... the largest selling single production model vehicle in automotive history. Handcrafted of genuine Regal China, this unique and exciting bottle will long remain a memento for bottle collectors the world over 10.00 18.00

W

☐350 **WALLEYE PIKE** *(1978)*
Tall blue bottle with a large figurine of a yellow pike at the base. Designed for the National Fresh Water Fishing Hall of Fame in Hayward, Wisconsin 8.00 12.00

☐351 **WASHINGTON** *(1975)*
Shaped like the state of Washington, with border and lettering in gold and white embossing. An apple and a fir tree sit on the pedestal before the map 14.00 18.00

☐352 **WASHINGTON — THE EVERGREEN STATE** *(c. 1974)*
A unique Regal China creation, honoring the state of Washington — The Evergreen State. Contoured to the shape of the state of Washington, this bottle features a dimensional carving of an evergreen on the front 12.00 18.00

☐353 **WASHINGTON STATE BICENTENNIAL** *(1976)*
Patriot dressed in black and orange holding drum. Liberty bell and plaque in front of drummer 12.00 20.00

☐354 **WATERMAN** *(1980)*
In pewter or glazed. Boatman at helm of his boat wearing rain gear. Glazed version in yellow and brown 175.00 225.00

☐355 **WESTERN SHRINE ASSOCIATION** *(1980)*
Designed to commemorate the Shriners' convention in
1980 which was held in Phoenix, Arizona. Rounded sur-
face with a desert scene, red stopper designed as a fez
with a tassel 28.00 32.00

☐356 **WEST VIRGINIA** *(c. 1963)*
Waterfall scene in blue and green with gold embossed
"BLACKWATER FALLS — WEST VIRGINIA — 1863 CEN-
TENNIAL 1963" surrounded by scrolled "picture frame"
bottle. Reverse: State bird-red cardinal and gold "35" in a
star. Bear's head and maple leaf on each side of stopper . 220.00 275.00

☐357 **WISCONSIN MUSKIE BOTTLE** *(c. 1971)*
This striking Regal China sculpture pays tribute to the
state fish of Wisconsin, as the mighty Muskellunge
dances on his powerful tail in a burst of gold flecked blue
water. 14" 18.00 26.00

☐358 **WOODPECKER** *(c. 1969)*
Bright glazed red head, white breast and markings, black
beak and dark wings and tails. "Woody" grips a "tree
trunk" base. Regal China, 13½" 8.00 12.00

☐359 **WYOMING** *(c. 1965)*
An embossed bucking bronco with a cowboy "Hangin'
On" with mountains in the background and "WYOMING
— THE EQUALITY STATE" in gold on tones of blue and
tan. A rectangle shape of a pyramid, with a gold buffalo
on the stopper. Reverse: State bird, flower, and Old Faith-
ful. Regal China, 12" 60.00 70.00

Y

☐360 **YELLOW KATZ** *(c. 1967)*
The emblem of the Katz Department Stores (Missouri), a
green-eyed meowing cat, is the head (and stopper) of this
bottle. The pylon shaped, orange color body has a curved
tail. The "Katz' commemorates the 50th birthday of the
store 20.00 28.00

☐361 **YOSEMITE** *(c. 1967)*
Oval shaped bottle with scenes from the Park, and trees,
embossed on the front. "YOSEMITE CALIFORNIA" let-
tered on front. Gold pine tree on stopper 3.00 6.00

Z

☐362 **ZIMMERMAN BELL — COLBALT** *(1976)*
Bell-shaped bottle in colbalt blue with flowers and foliage
embossed in blue and gold. Designed for Zimmerman
Liquor Stors of Chicago 10.00 15.00

☐363 **ZIMMERMAN BELL — LIGHT BLUE** *(1976)*
Bell-shaped bottle in light blue with lavender lid. Floral
and foliage designs embossed on the front 10.00 15.00

☐364 **ZIMMERMAN BLUE BEAUTY** *(c. 1969-70)*
The name "ZIMMERMAN'S LIQUORS" is embossed in
bright gold on a sky blue bottle decorated with flowers

and scrolls. Reverse has Chicago skyline embossed on blue toned bottle. Arrow with "ZIMMERMAN'S points to store. Regal China, 10" **12.00** **18.00**

□ 365 **ZIMMERMAN CHERUBS PINK & LAVENDER** (c. 1968-69) Winged cherubs and leaves and vines are embossed over the surface of these slender round bottles. They were issued for the Zimmerman Liquor Stores of Chicago. Regal China, 11½" **8.00** **12.00**

□ 366 **ZIMMERMAN—GLASS** (c. 1969) A white outline of the Chicago skyline with "ZIMMERMAN'S" store on front of this glass bottle. White stopper has "MAX ZIMMERMAN'S portrait. Glass, 11¼" **6.00** **10.00**

□ 367 **ZIMMERMAN'S THE PEDDLER BOTTLE** (c. 1971) This unusual bottle in genuine Regal China was made in honor of Zimmerman's, the world's largest liquor store, in Chicago, Illinois. Max Zimmerman, "The Peddler" himself, who specializes in personal service and works the counters of the store himself, is famous for his Stetson hat and cowboy boots. He is affectionately known in the trade as "Max the Hat". Zimmerman's has always been active in merchandising Beam's collector's bottles. 12" **20.00** **28.00**

□ 368 **ZIMMERMAN—TWO HANDLED JUG** (c. 1965) Shaped and colored like an avocado, this dark green bottle has embossed grapes and grape leaves on the front, and two side handles. Regal China, 10¼" **85.00** **120.00**

BISCHOFF

Founded at Trieste, Italy in 1777, Bischoffs was issuing decorative figurals in the 18th century long before the establishment of most companies who presently issue figural bottles. The early specimens are extremely rare, because of limited production and the loss over the years. Since sales do not occur often enough for firm values to be established, they are not included in this listing further.

Imported into the U.S. in 1949, the modern Bischoffs attracted little notice at first due to lack of interest of Americans in bottle collecting at that time. Most sales were made for gift giving. The bottles are produced by the foremost glass, pottery, and porcelain companies in Bohemia, Czechoslovakia, Murano, Italy, Austria, and Germany.

KORD BOHEMIAN DECANTERS. Handblown, hand painted glass bottles were created in Czechoslovakia by the Kord Company, based on a long tradition of Bohemian cut, engraved, etched, and flashed glass. Typical Bohemia themes were used to decorate the decanters. Complete bottles with stoppers and labels are very difficult to find today.

Cut glass and ruby-etched decanters, traditional forms of Bohemian glass, were imported into the U.S. in the early 1950's. Cut glass specimens are of lead crystal with hand cutting. The ruby-etched decanters are executed in the usual two-layer manner with the exterior ruby glass etched through to show the clear glass beneath. Designs are quite elaborate including leaping deer, castles, scrolls, foliage, wild birds, grapes, and latticework. The overall color can be amber or topaz with ruby the most common.

34   39   42

When the under layer of glass is opaque, the cut designs show very distinctly. Several of the etched decanters, made in Austria and Germany, should have labels indicating the place of origin. Most Bischoff Kord Bohemian decanters had matching sets of glasses.

The Double Dolphin, Hunter & Lady, and Horse's Head decanters are thick, handblown glass made in Czechoslovakia. Not as rare as the ruby-etched decanter since importation continues, they have value only when complete with stoppers.

VENETIAN GLASS FIGURALS. Bischoff's Venetian Glass Figurals are made in limited editions by the Serguso Glass Company in Murano, Italy, a town historically famous for its artistic glass. The Bischoff figurals, originally containing the firm's liquors, are quite unique in design and color. Chief themes depict natural subject, such as, birds, mammals, and fish.

BISCHOFF

A

NO.	DESCRIPTION	PRICE RANGE	
☐ 1	**AMBER FLOWERS** (c. 1952)		
	A two-toned glass decanter. Amber flowers, stems and leaves on a Pale Amber background. The long tapering neck is etched in panels and circles. The stopper is dark amber and hand-ground to fit, 15½"	13.00	19.00
☐ 2	**AMBER LEAVES** (c. 1952)		
	Multi-tone bottle with dark amber leaves, and flowers, on pale amber etched background. Stopper neck and base are cut in circles and panels. Round bottle with long neck, 13½"	13.00	19.00
☐ 3	**ANISETTE** (c. 1948-51)		
	Clear glass bottle with 2 handles and a ground glass stopper. Clear glass ribbing on sides of bottle, 11"	13.00	19.00

B

☐ 4 **BOHEMIAN RUBY ETCHED** (c. 1949-51)
Etched design in typical Bohemian style, castle, birds, deer and scrolls and curlecues in clear glass, ruby-red color "flashed" on bottle, except for etching and cut neck. Ground glass, etched stoppers on this tall, round, decanter, 15½", tapered neck **13.00** **19.00**

C

☐ 5 **CORONET CRYSTAL** (c. 1952)
A broad band of flowers, leaves and scrolls circle this multi-toned bottle. The designs are cut in dark amber glass revealing the opaque pale amber background. Stopper neck and base are cut in circles and panels. A round tall bottle 14" **12.00** **18.00**

☐ 6 **CUT GLASS DECANTER (BLACKBERRY)** (c. 1951)
A geometric design hand-cut over-all on this lead glass decanter. The stopper is cut and ground to fit the bottle, 10½" **27.00** **35.00**

☐ 7 **CZECH HUNTER** (c. 1958)
Round thick clear glass body with green collar and green buttons and heavy round glass base. The stopper-head is of glass with a jaunty green "Bohemian" hat with feather crowning, pop-eyes, white mustache and red button nose, 8½" **13.00** **19.00**

☐ 8 **CZECH HUNTER'S LADY** (c. 1958)
"Mae West" shaped decanter of "cracked" clear glass. Green collar at neck of bottle with amber glass stopper-head. Brown hair, glasses and yellow earrings make up the lady's head. She's taller than the Hunter, 10" **13.00** **19.00**

D

☐ 9 **DANCING—COUNTRY SCENE** (c. 1950)
Clear glass hand-blown decanter with hand-painted and signed colorful scene of peasant boy & girl doing a country dance beside a tree, Bohemian village background. Spider bold white lines painted on bottle and stopper. 12¼" **21.00** **27.00**

☐ 10 **DANCING—PEASANT SCENE** (c. 1950)
Colorful peasants in costume, dancing to music of bag-pipes, hand painted and signed. The decanter is of pale amber glass, fine black lines painted on bottle. Stopper is ground to fit and fine line painted. 12" high **21.00** **27.00**

☐ 11 **DOUBLE-DOLPHIN** (c. 1949-69)
Fish-shaped twin bottles joined at the "bellies". They are made of handblown clear glass and have fins and "fish tail" ground glass stoppers, each has fish eyes and mouth **16.00** **22.00**

F

☐ 12 **FLYING GEESE PITCHER** *(c. 1952)*
Same as below, but with green glass handle and stopper.
This pitcher has a glass base **17.00** **24.00**

☐ 13 **FLYING GEESE PITCHER** *(c. 1957)*
Clear crystal, handled pitcher. Hand-painted and signed,
colorful scene of wild geese flying over Czech marshes.
Gold neck, pouring lip, and stopper, 9½" **18.00** **25.00**

H

☐ 14 **HORSE HEAD** *(c. 1947-69)*
Pale amber colored bottle in the shape of a horse's head.
Embossed details of horse's features are impressed on
this hand-blown bottle. Round pouring spout on top, 8" .. **10.00** **15.00**

J

☐ 15 **JUNGLE PARROT—AMBER GLASS** *(c. 1952)*
Same as below, except bottle is "flashed" a yellow-amber
color **13.00** **19.00**

☐ 16 **JUNGLE PARROT—RUBY GLASS** *(c. 1952)*
Profusely hand-etched jungle scene with parrot, monkeys,
insects, flowers leaves, cut through the ruby "flashed"
body. A tall round decanter with tapering etched neck,
15½" **18.00** **25.00**

O

☐ 17 **OLD COACH BOTTLE** *(c. 1948)*
Old time coach and white horses hand-painted on a hand-
blown Bohemian glass bottle pale amber color. Round
ground glass stopper. Bottle and stopper are both
numbered. 10" **21.00** **27.00**

☐ 18 **OLD SLEIGH BOTTLE** *(c. 1949)*
Hand painted, signed, Czech winter old-time sleigh scene.
Driver sits on lead horse and blows trumpet, passengers
on top of coach are pouring drinks. Glass decanter has
fine white trace lines. Glass stopper is clear and painted.
10" **18.00** **25.00**

W

☐ 19 **WILD GEESE—AMBER GLASS** *(c. 1952)*
Same as below, except bottle is a "flashed" yellow-amber
color **18.00** **25.00**
Matching glasses were made for both the Ruby & Amber.

☐ 20 **WILD GEESE—RUBY GLASS** (c. 1952)
Etched design of wild geese rising above the marshes. A tall round decanter with tapering, etched neck, and etched hand-ground stopper. Ruby-red color "flashed" on bottle, 15½" 18.00   25.00

VENETIAN GLASS FIGURAL

NO.	DESCRIPTION	PRICE RANGE	
☐ 21	**BLACK CAT** (c. 1969)		
	Glass black cat, with curled tail, 12" long	18.00	25.00
☐ 22	**DOG—ALABASTER** (c. 1969)		
	Seated alabaster glass dog, 13"	13.00	19.00
☐ 23	**DOG—DACHSHUND** (c. 1966)		
	Alabaster long dog with brown tones, 19" long	13.00	19.00
☐ 24	**DUCK** (c. 1964)		
	Alabaster glass tinted pink & green, long neck, up-raised wings, 11" long	18.00	25.00
☐ 25	**FISH—MULTICOLOR** (c. 1964)		
	Round fat fish, alabaster glass. Green, rose, yellow	18.00	25.00
☐ 26	**FISH—RUBY** (c. 1969)		
	Long, flat, ruby glass fish, 12" long	18.00	25.00

CERAMIC DECANTERS & FIGURALS

Many of the most interesting, attractive and valuable Bischoff bottles are made of ceramic, stoneware or pottery. They have a "rougher" surface appearance than the glass or porcelain bottles. Values quoted are for complete bottles with handles, spouts and stoppers in mint condition.

☐ 27	**AFRICAN HEAD** (c. 1962)	18.00	25.00
☐ 28	**BELL HOUSE** (c. 1960)	13.00	19.00
☐ 29	**BELL TOWER** (c. 1960)	18.00	25.00
☐ 30	**BOY (CHINESE) FIGURAL** (c. 1962)	21.00	27.00
☐ 31	**BOY (SPANISH) FIGURAL** (c. 1961)	21.00	27.00
☐ 32	**CLOWN WITH BLACK HAIR** (c. 1963)	21.00	27.00
☐ 33	**CLOWN WITH RED HAIR** (c. 1963)	18.00	25.00
☐ 34	**DEER FIGURAL** (c. 1969)	21.00	27.00
☐ 35	**EGYPTIAN DANCING FIGURAL** (c. 1961)	13.00	19.00
☐ 36	**EGYPTIAN PITCHER 2 MUSICIANS** (c. 1969)	18.00	25.00
☐ 37	**EGYPTIAN PITCHER 3 MUSICIANS** (c. 1959)	18.00	25.00
☐ 38	**FLORAL CANTEEN** (c. 1969)	13.00	19.00
☐ 39	**FRUIT CANTEEN** (c. 1969)	13.00	19.00
☐ 40	**GIRL IN CHINESE COSTUME** (c. 1962)	25.00	34.00
☐ 41	**GIRL IN SPANISH COSTUME** (c. 1961)	23.00	32.00
☐ 42	**GREEK VASE DECANTER** (c. 1969)	13.00	19.00
☐ 43	**MASK—GRAY FACE** (c. 1963)	13.00	19.00
☐ 44	**OIL & VINEGAR CRUETS BLACK & WHITE** (c. 1959)	18.00	25.00
☐ 45	**VASE—BLACK & GOLD** (c. 1959)	21.00	27.00
☐ 46	**WATCHTOWER** (c. 1960)	13.00	19.00

BOLS

The Bols bottles from Holland are designed in the fashion of early Dutch Delftware, a rare and expensive earthenware from the city Delft. As with Delftware, the Bols bottles have an opaque white glaze decorated with a delicate blue. The firm issues bottles reminiscent of ones made in Holland during the 17th and 18th centuries. To compliment its ceramics, Bols occasionally issues pewter bottles also. Their historic flavor derives from the common use of pewter for bottles since early times.

BOLS (DUTCH) BOTTLES

NO.	DESCRIPTION	PRICE RANGE	
☐ 1	**DELFT-TYPE**, *Blue & white, 8"*	8.00	11.00
☐ 2	**DELFT-TYPE**, *Blue & white, 11"*	8.00	12.00
☐ 3	**DELFT-TYPE**, *Blue & white, 5¼"*	6.00	9.00
☐ 4	**DELFT-TYPE**, *Blue & white, 5", (On tray)*	6.00	9.00
☐ 5	**DELFT-TYPE**, *Blue & white, 3½", (On tray)*	7.00	10.00
☐ 6	**PEWTER** *(c. 1969) 5"*	13.00	19.00
☐ 7	**PEWTER** *(c. 1969) 8"*	10.00	14.00

BORGHINI

Borghini bottles, exported from Pisa, Italy, are ceramics of modernistic style, dealing mostly with historical themes. Their sizes vary more than bottles from other manufacturers. Easily obtainable in the U.S., as is often the case with imported bottles, their prices vary greatly in different parts of the country. The lowest values tend to be in areas either closest to the points of distribution or heaviest in retail sale. Most of the recent Borghini bottles are stamped "BORGHINI COLLECTION MADE IN ITALY."

BOLS   BORGHINI   BRIZARD

BORGHINI

NO.	DESCRIPTION	PRICE RANGE	
☐ 1	CATS, *Black with red ties, 6"*	11.00	15.00
☐ 2	CATS, *Black with red ties, 12"*	10.00	13.00
☐ 3	FEMALE HEAD, *Ceramic, 9½"*	11.00	15.00
☐ 4	PENGUIN, *Black & white, 6"*	8.00	11.00
☐ 5	PENGUIN, *(c. 1969) Black & white, 12"*	12.00	16.00

MARIE BRIZARD

The Marie Brizard bottles are ceramics, usually deep brown in color with distinctive modeling. New editions are issued only occasionally. The Chessman series, which consists of bottles representing figures from the chessboard, are their most popular products. Among the more valuable of the Brizard bottles is a large model of a Parisian kiosk or newsstand, standing 11½" high.

MARIE BRIZARD

NO.	DESCRIPTION	PRICE RANGE	
☐ 1	BISHOP, *Ceramic chessmen, dark brown*	11.00	14.00
☐ 2	CASTLE, *Ceramic chessmen, dark brown*	6.00	9.00
☐ 3	KIOSK, *Colorful Parisian signpost, 11½"*	13.00	19.00
☐ 4	KNIGHT, *Ceramic chessmen, dark brown*	7.00	10.00
☐ 5	LADY IN ERMINE CAPE, *7"*	9.00	13.00
☐ 6	PAWN, *Ceramic chessman, dark brown*	7.00	10.00

EZRA BROOKS BOTTLES

Ezra Brooks rivals Jim Beam as one of the chief American spirits companies manufacturing figural bottles. First issuing figurals in 1964, Brooks started a decade behind Beam, but became competive because of effective promotion and a heavy production schedule. Due to the creative design, imaginative choice of subjects and an efficient distribution network, the Ezra Brooks bottles are collected throughout the country.

Some of the Brooks figurals deal with traditional themes for bottles such as sports and transportation. But Brooks has designed bottles based on subjects that are both surprising and striking. The very realistic "Maine Lobster" is among its masterpieces—a bottle that looks good enough to eat. Especially popular with collectors are the Brooks bottles representing various antiques, a subject neglected by most manufacturers. These include an Edison phonograph, a grandfather clock, and a Spanish cannon.

While the number of bottles fluctuates each year, Brooks usually adds new editions annually, often highlighting an American historical event or anniversary.

The Ezra Brooks Distilling Co. located in Frankfort, Kentucky, manufactures bottles containing Kentucky bourbon. Before 1968, their most brisk sales occured around the Christmas/New Year season as the majority were bought for gift giving. When interest grew in the U.S. for figural bottles, most sales were to collectors.

EZRA BROOKS BOTTLES

A

NO.	DESCRIPTION	PRICE RANGE	
☐ 1	**ALABAMA BICENTENNIAL** *(1976)*	10.00	15.00
☐ 2	**AMERICAN LEGION** *(1971)* *Distinguished embossed star emblem born out of WWI struggle. Combination blue and gold. On blue base*	25.00	34.00
☐ 3	**AMERICAN LEGION** *(1972)* *Ezra Brooks salutes the American Legion, its Illinois Department, and Land of Lincoln and the city of Chicago, host of the Legion's 54th National Convention*	17.00	23.00
☐ 4	**AMERICAN LEGION** *(1973)* *Hawaii, our fiftieth state, hosted the American Legion's 1973 annual Convention. It was the largest airlift of a mass group ever to hit the islands. Over 15,000 Legionnaires visited the beautiful city of Honolulu to celebrate the Legion's fifty-fourth anniversary*	8.00	12.00
☐ 5	**AMERICAN LEGION** *(1977)* Denver	18.00	26.00
☐ 6	**AMERICAN LEGION** *(1973)* Miami Beach	5.00	10.00
☐ 7	**AMVETS** *(1974)* Dolphin	16.00	20.00
☐ 8	**AMVET** *(1973)* Polish Legion	16.00	22.00
☐ 9	**ANTIQUE CANNON** *(1969)*	5.00	8.00
☐ 10	**ANTIQUE PHONOGRAPH** *(1970)* *Edison's early contribution to home entertainment. White, black, "Morning Glory" horn, red. Richly detailed in 24k gold*	8.00	12.00
☐ 11	**ARIZONA** *(1969)* *Man with burro in search of "Lost Dutchman Mine", golden brown mesa, green cactus, with 22k gold base, "ARIZONA" imprinted*	5.00	8.00
☐ 12	**AUBURN 1932** *(1978)* Classic Car	20.00	28.00

B

☐ 13	**BADGER NO. 1** *(1973)* Boxer	14.00	20.00
☐ 14	**BADGER NO. 2** *(1974)* Football	16.00	24.00
☐ 15	**BADGER NO. 3** *(1974)* Hockey	16.00	24.00
☐ 16	**BALTIMORE ORIOLE WILD LIFE** *(1979)*	35.00	45.00
☐ 17	**BARE KNUCKLE FIGHTER** *(1971)*	6.00	10.00
☐ 18	**BASEBALL HALL OF FAME** *(1973)* *Baseball fans everywhere will enjoy this genuine Heritage China ceramic of a familiar slugger of years gone by*	16.00	21.00
☐ 19	**BASKETBALL PLAYER** *(1974)*	8.00	12.00
☐ 20	**BEAR** *(1968)*	5.00	8.00
☐ 21	**BENGAL TIGER WILD LIFE** *(1979)*	40.00	48.00
☐ 22	**BETSY ROSS** *(1975)*	12.00	18.00
☐ 23	**BIG BERTHA** *Nugget Casino's very-own elephant with a raised trunk, gray, red, white and black, yellow & gold trim. "Blanket" and stand* .	8.00	12.00
☐ 24	**BIG DADDY LOUNGE** *(1969)* *Salute to South Florida's "STATE" liquor chain, and "Big Daddy's lounges. White, green, red*	5.00	10.00

☐ 25 **BIGHORN RAM** *(1973)*
Bighorns still scramble up and down the Rockies from
Alaska to Mexico, choosing the highest, most rugged
peaks. 8.00 11.00
☐ 26 **BIRD DOG** *(1971)* 10.00 18.00
☐ 27 **BORDERTOWN**
Borderline Club where California and Nevada meet for a
drink. Brown, red, white. Club Building with Vulture on
roof stopper, and outhouse 5.00 10.00
☐ 28 **BOWLER** *(1973)* 5.00 10.00
☐ 29 **BRAHMA BULL** *(1972)* 10.00 15.00
☐ 30 **BUCKET OF BLOOD** *(1970)*
Fabled Virginia City, Nevada saloon. Bucket shape bottle.
Brown, red with gold lettering on reverse side 5.00 10.00
☐ 31 **BUCKING BRONCO** *(1973)* Rough Rider 12.00 18.00
☐ 32 **BUCKY BADGER** Football 22.00 28.00
☐ 33 **BUCKY BADGER** *(1975)* Hockey 20.00 26.00
☐ 34 **BUCKY BADGER** *(1973)* No. 1, Boxer 12.00 18.00
☐ 35 **BUFFALO HUNT** *(1971)* 6.00 12.00
☐ 36 **BULLDOG** *(1972)*
Mighty canine mascot and football symbol. Red, white .. 16.00 22.00
☐ 37 **BULL MOOSE** *(1973)*
The Alaskan moose may weigh as much as 1,800 pounds
and stand over 7 feet high at the shoulder. The entire antler
may span over 75 inches and weigh up to 60 pounds 10.00 15.00
☐ 38 **BUSY BEAVER**
This genuine Heritage China ceramic is a salute to the
beaver, truly one of nature's wonders. 6.00 10.00

☐ 39 **CABIN STILL**
Hillbilly, Papers From Company, Gallon 35.00 45.00
☐ 40 **CABLE CAR** *(1968)*
San Francisco's great trolley-car ride in bottle form. Made
in three different colors, green, gray and blue, with red,
black & gold trim. Open Cable Car with passengers cling-
ing to sides 4.00 8.00
☐ 41 **CALIFORNIA QUAIL** *(1970)*
Widely admired game bird shape bottle. Crested head
stopper. Unglazed finish. Green, brown, white, black, gray 9.00 12.00
☐ 42 **CANADIAN HONKER** *(1975)* 28.00 34.00
☐ 43 **CANADIAN LOON WILD LIFE** *(1979)* 40.00 48.00
☐ 44 **CARDINAL** *(1972)* 15.00 25.00
☐ 45 **CASEY AT BAT** *(1973)* 6.00 10.00
☐ 46 **CEREMONIAL INDIAN** *(1970)* 18.00 28.00
☐ 47 **CHAROLAIS** *(1973)* 12.00 16.00
☐ 48 **C.B. CONVOY RADIO** *(1976)* 5.00 8.00
☐ 49 **CHAROLAIS BEEF** *(1973)*
The Charolais have played an important role in raising the
standards of quality in today's cattle 8.00 12.00
☐ 50 **CHEYENNE SHOOT OUT** *(1970)*
Honoring the Wild West and her "Cheyenne Frontier
Days." Sheriff and outlaw shoot-out over mirrored bar.
Brown tone with multi-color 5.00 10.00

2

10

11

24

27

30

40

142

50

55

56

62

68

77

81

☐	51	**CHICAGO FIRE** *(1974)*	**25.00**	**32.00**
☐	52	**CHICAGO WATER TOWER** *(1969)*	**8.00**	**12.00**
☐	53	**CHRISTMAS DECANTER** *(1966)*	**5.00**	**8.00**
☐	54	**CHRISTMAS TREE** *(1979)*	**25.00**	**35.00**
☐	55	**CHURCHILL** *(1970))*		

Commemorating "Iron Curtain" speech at Westminster College, Churchhill at lectern with hand raised in "V" sign. Fulton, Mo. Gold color **9.00** **12.00**

☐ 56 **CIGAR STORE INDIAN** *(1968)*
Tobacconist's sidewalk statue bottle form. The original Wooden Indian first appeared in 1770. Dark Camel **5.00** **8.00**

☐ 57 **CLASSIC FIREARMS** *(1969)*
4 Bottle embossed gun set consisting of: Derringer, Colt 45, Peacemaker, Over & Under Flintlock, Pepper box. Green, blue violet, red **17.00** **23.00**

☐ 58 **CLOWN BUST** *(1979)*
No. 1, Smiley **32.00** **40.00**

☐ 59 **CLOWN BUST** *(1979)*
No. 2, Cowboy **32.00** **40.00**

☐ 60 **CLOWN BUST** *(1979)*
No. 3, Pagliacci **30.00** **38.00**

☐	61	**CLOWN SHRINE** *(1978)*	**30.00**	**38.00**
☐	62	**CLOWN WITH ACCORDION** *(1971)*	**12.00**	**18.00**
☐	63	**CLOWN WITH BALLOON** *(1973)*	**18.00**	**22.00**
☐	64	**CLOWN** *(1978) Imperial Shrine*	**20.00**	**28.00**
☐	66	**CLUB BOTTLE** *(1973)*		

The third commemorative Ezra Brooks Collector Club bottle is created in the shape of America. Each gold star on the new club bottle represents the location of an Ezra Brooks Collectors Club **21.00** **28.00**

☐ 66 **CLYDESDALE HORSE** *(1973)*
In the early days of distilling, Clydesdales carted the bottles of whiskey from the distillery to towns all across America .. **10.00** **16.00**

☐ 67 **COLT PEACEMAKER** *(1969) Flask* **4.00** **8.00**

☐ 68 **CONQUISTADORS**
Tribute to a great drum & bugle corps. Silver colored Trumpet attached to drum **6.00** **12.00**

☐	69	**CONQUISTADOR'S DRUM & BUGLE** *(1972)*	**10.00**	**18.00**
☐	70	**CORVETTE INDY PACE CAR** *(1978)*	**40.00**	**50.00**
☐	71	**CORVETTE** *(1976) 1957 Classic*	**38.00**	**44.00**
☐	72	**COURT JESTER**		

A common sight in the throne rooms of Europe. Yellow and blue suit, pointed cap **6.00** **10.00**

D

☐	73	**DAKOTA COWBOY** *(1975)*	**40.00**	**48.00**
☐	74	**DAKOTA COWGIRL** *(1976)*	**30.00**	**38.00**
☐	75	**DAKOTA GRAIN ELEVATOR** *(1978)*	**28.00**	**35.00**
☐	76	**DAKOTA SHOTGUN EXPRESS** *(1977)*	**25.00**	**32.00**
☐	77	**DEAD WAGON** *(1970)*		

To carry gunfight losers to Boot Hill, old-time hearse with Tombstones on side. Vulture adornment on stopper. White, with black details **6.00** **10.00**

☐	78	**DELTA BELLE** *(1969)* *Proud paddlewheeler on the New Orleans to Louisville* *passage steamboat shape with embossed details. White,* *brown, red with 22k gold trim*	**8.00**	**14.00**
☐	79	**DEMOCRATIC CONVENTION** *(1976)*	**10.00**	**16.00**
☐	80	**DERRINGER** *(1969) Flask*	**4.00**	**8.00**
☐	81	**DISTILLERY—CLUB BOTTLE** *(1970)* *Reproduction of the Ezra Brooks Distillery in Kentucky,* *complete with smokestack. Beige, black, brown with 22k* *gold color*	**8.00**	**12.00**
☐	82	**DUESENBERG** *Jaunty vintage convertible. Famous SJ model reproduc-* *tion complete with superchargers & white sidewalls. Blue* *& gold, or solid gold color*	**22.00**	**30.00**

E

☐	83	**ELEPHANT** *(c. 1973)* *Based on an Asian elephant. There are three distinct* *species of elephants — one Asiatic, two African . . .* *African elephants are the ones more often seen in jungle* *movies because of their impressively larger ears and* *tusks. An African's tusks can weigh close to 300 pounds* *and extend over 11 feet in* *length*	**8.00**	**12.00**
☐	84	**ELK** *(c. 1973)* *While the elk herd is still relatively scarce in the United* *States, the elk name flourishes as a symbol for many* *worthwhile organizations, expecially those whose pri-* *mary object is the practice of benevolence and charity in* *its broadest sense. Ezra Brooks salutes these organiza-* *tions with this genuine Heritage China Ceramic bottle* ...	**20.00**	**28.00**
☐	85	**ENGLISH SETTER—BIRD DOG** *(c. 1971)* *Happy hunting dog retrieving red pheasant. White flecked* *with black, yellow base.*	**10.00**	**15.00**
☐	86	**EQUESTRIENNE** *(1974)*	**5.00**	**10.00**
☐	87	**ESQUIRE Ceremonial Dancer**	**10.00**	**16.00**

F

☐	88	**FARTHINGTON BIKE** *(1972)*	**8.00**	**12.00**
☐	89	**FIRE ENGINE** *(1971)*	**12.00**	**16.00**
☐	90	**FIREMAN** *(1975)*	**20.00**	**28.00**
☐	91	**FISHERMAN** *(1974)*	**16.00**	**22.00**
☐	92	**FLINTLOCK** *(1969)* *Dueling pistol rich in detail. Japanese version has wooden* *rack, "Made in Japan" on handle. Heritage China gun has* *plastic rack, less detail. Gunmetal gray & brown, silver &* *gold trim.* *Japanese*	**4.00**	**8.00**
		Heritage	**10.00**	**15.00**

☐ 93	**FLORIDA 'GATORS'** *(c. 1973)*		
	To adversaries, the Florida Gators football team some-times appear to be a lot like their namesakes, the Florida alligator — strong, tough skinned, able to tear apart anything within reach, up to 500 pounds and 12 feet long..	13.00	18.00
☐ 94	**F.O.E. FLYING EAGLE** *(1979)*	20.00	28.00
☐ 95	**FOREMOST ASTRONAUT** *(1970)*		
	Tribute to major liquor supermart, Foremost Liquor Store. Smiling "Mr. Bottle-Face" clinging to space rocket on white base	6.00	12.00
☐ 96	**FOOTBALL PLAYER** *(1974)*	12.00	18.00
☐ 97	**FORD THUNDERBIRD** *(1976), 1956*	38.00	48.00
☐ 98	**FRESNO DECANTER**		
	Map of famed California grape center. Stopper and in-scription — gold finish. Blue, white	4.00	10.00
☐ 99	**FRESNO GRAPE WITH GOLD**	48.00	58.00
☐100	**FRESNO GRAPE** *(1970)*	10.00	18.00

G

☐101	**GAMECOCK** *(1970)*		
	All feathers and fury against rival birds. Red with yellow base	10.00	15.00
☐102	**GO BIG RED #1 & #2**		
	Football shaped bottle with white bands and laces on base embossed, "GO BIG RED". Brown, white, gold detail.		
	No. 1 with football (1972)	25.00	32.00
	No. 2 with hat (1971)	25.00	32.00
	No. 3 with Rooster (1972)	12.00	18.00
☐103	**GOLD PROSPECTOR** *(1969)*		
	Rugged miner with white beard panning for gold. Black, pink and gold trim	6.00	10.00
☐104	**GOLDEN ANTIQUE CANNON** *(1969)*		
	Symbol of Spanish power. Embossed details on barrel, wheels and carriage. Dark brown, with lavish 22k gold trim	5.00	5.00
☐105	**GOLDEN EAGLE** *(1971)*		
	Rich plummage, sitting on a branch. Gold color	10.00	14.00
☐106	**GOLDEN GRIZZLY BEAR** *(1970)*		
	A Bear shape bottle, on haunches. Brown with gold high-lights	7.00	11.00
☐107	**GOLDEN HORSESHOE** *(1970)*		
	Salute to Reno's Horseshoe Club. Good-luck symbol on horseshoe. 24k gold covered, in a blue base	16.00	21.00
☐108	**GOLDEN ROOSTER #1**		
	A replica of the famous solid gold Rooster on display at "Nugget Casino" in Reno, Nevada. Glowing Rooster in 22k gold on black base	23.00	32.00
☐109	**GO TIGER GO** *(1973)*	12.00	18.00
☐110	**GOLD SEAL** *(1972)*	10.00	15.00
☐111	**GOLD TURKEY)**	40.00	48.00
☐112	**GRANDFATHER CLOCK** *(1970)*		
	Brown with gold highlights, much embossed detail	6.00	10.00
☐113	**GRANDFATHER'S CLOCK** *(1970)*	12.00	20.00

☐114	**GREAT WHITE SHARK** *(1977)*	**12.00**	**20.00**
☐115	**GREATER GREENSBORO OPEN** *(1972)*		
	To commemorate this event, Ezra Brooks has designed this genuine Heritage Ceramic bottle	**25.00**	**34.00**
☐116	**GREAT STONE FACE—OLD MAN OF THE MOUNTAIN** *(1970)*		
	Famous profile found in mountain of New Hampshire. Stopper has seal of New Hampshire	**14.00**	**19.00**
☐117	**GREAT WHITE SHARK** *(1977)*	**12.00**	**20.00**
☐118	**GREATER GREENSBORO OPEN** *(1973)*		
	Gofler	**18.00**	**26.00**
☐119	**GREATER GREENSBORO OPEN** *(1974)*		
	Map	**35.00**	**45.00**
☐120	**GREATER GREENSBORO OPEN** *(1975)*		
	Cup	**42.00**	**52.00**

H

☐121	***HAMBLETONIAN*** *(1971)*		
	Harness Racer honors the N.Y town and race track that sired harness racing, trotting, horse pulling driver and sulky. Green, brown, white, yellow, blue, gold base	**8.00**	**14.00**
☐122	**HAPPY GOOSE** *(1975)*	**16.00**	**26.00**
☐123	**HAROLD'S CLUB DICE** *(1968)*		
	Lucky 7 dice combination topped with H-cube stopper, on round white base. Red and white with gold trim	**5.00**	**10.00**
☐124	**HEREFORD** *(1971)*	**12.00**	**16.00**
☐125	**HEREFORD** *(1972)*		
	Best beef on the hoof in bottle form. Brown, white face . .	**10.00**	**15.00**
☐126	**HISTORICAL FLASK** *(1970)*		
	Eagle Blue	**3.00**	**7.00**
☐127	**HISTORICAL FLASK** *(1970)*		
	Flagship, Purple	**3.00**	**7.00**
☐128	**HISTORICAL FLASK** *(1970)*		
	Liberty, Amber	**3.00**	**7.00**
☐129	**HISTORICAL FLASK** *(1970)*		
	Old Ironside, Green	**3.00**	**7.00**
☐130	**HISTORICAL FLASK** *(1970)*		
	Set of 4	**3.00**	**7.00**
☐131	**HOLLYWOOD COPS** *(1972)*		
	. . . .	**8.00**	**12.00**
☐132	**HOPI INDIAN** *(1970)*		
	"KACHINA DOLL". Creative tribe doing ritual song-and-dance. White, red ornamental trim	**16.00**	**20.00**
☐133	**HOPI KACHINA** *(1973)*		
	Genuine Heritage China ceramic reproduction of a Hummingbird Kachina Doll	**60.00**	**70.00**

I

☐ 134 **IDAHO—SKI THE POTATO** *(1973)*
Ezra Brooks salutes the beautiful state of Idaho, its incomparable ski resorts and famous Idaho potatoes, with this genuine Heritage China Ceramic bottle 10.00 14.00
☐ 135 **IOWA FARMER** *(1977)* 65.00 75.00
☐ 136 **IOWA GRAIN ELEVATOR** *(1978)* 30.00 40.00
☐ 137 **INDIAN HUNTER** *(1970)*
Traditional buffalo hunt. Indian on horseback shooting buffalo with bow & arrow. Horse white, buffalo brown, yellow base 11.00 15.00
☐ 138 **INDIAN CEREMONIAL**
Colorful tribal dancer from New Mexico Reservation. Multi-colored, gold trim 13.00 18.00
☐ 139 **INDIANAPOLIS 500**
Sleek, dual-exhaust racer. White, blue, black, silver trim .. 21.00 28.00
☐ 140 **IRON HORSE LOCOMOTIVE**
Replica of old-time locomotive, complete with funnel, cow-catcher and oil burning headlamp. Black and red with 22k gold trim 8.00 14.00

J

☐ 141 **JACK O' DIAMONDS** *(1969)*
The symbol of good luck, a bottle in the shape of the "Jack" right off the card. A Royal Flush decorates the front. White, Red, Blue & Black 6.00 10.00
☐ 142 **JAY HAWK** *(1969)*
Funny bird with a large head perched on a "tree trunk" base. Symbol of Kansas during and after Civil War. Yellow, red, blue and brown 8.00 12.00
☐ 143 **JESTER** *(1971)* 8.00 12.00
☐ 144 **JUG, OLD TIME**
1.75 Liter 12.00 18.00

K

☐ 145 **KACHINA DOLL** *(1971)*
No. 1 .... 85.00 95.00
☐ 146 **KACHINA DOLL** *(1973)*
No. 2, Hummingbird 38.00 48.00
☐ 147 **KACHINA DOLL** *(1974)*
No. 3 .... 28.00 38.00
☐ 148 **KACHINA DOLL** *(1975)*
No. 4 .... 10.00 18.00
☐ 149 **KACHINA DOLL** *(1976)*
No. 5 .... 25.00 35.00
☐ 150 **KACHINA DOLL** *(1977)*
No. 6, White Buffalo 22.00 30.00
☐ 151 **KACHINA DOLL** *(1978)*
No. 7, Mud Head 22.00 30.00

☐ 152	**KANSAS Jayhawk** *(1969)*	8.00	16.00
☐ 153	**KATZ CATS** *(1969)*		
	Seal point and blue point. Siamese cats are symbolic of Katz Drug Company of Kansas City, Kansas. Grey and blue, tan and brown	10.00	15.00
☐ 154	**KATZ CATS PHILHARMONIC** *(1970)*		
	Commemorating its 27th Annual star night, devoted to classical and pop music. Black tuxedo, brown face . **PAIR**	6.00	10.00
☐ 155	**KEYSTONE COP** *(1980)*	30.00	38.00
☐ 156	**KEYSTONE COPS** *(1971)*	14.00	18.00
☐ 157	**KILLER WHALE** *(1972)*		
	Although they're often found just off the Washington coast, they cruise throughout all the seas of the world, all year long. Their travels take them as far as the polar ice caps. Killer Whales talk to each other by clicking under-water. This clicking also serves as the whale's "radar" since he can judge distance by the echo	11.00	16.00
☐ 158	**KING OF CLUBS** *(1969)*		
	Figure of card symbol. Sword and orb symbolize wisdom and justice. Royal flush in Clubs in front. Yellow, red, blue, black and white with gold trim	6.00	10.00
☐ 159	**KING SALMON** *(1971)*		
	Bottle in shape of leaping salmon. Natural red	18.00	24.00

L

☐ 160	**LIBERTY BELL** *(1970)*		
	Replica of the famous bell complete with "wooden" sup-port. Dark copper color, embossed details	5.00	8.00
☐ 161	**LINCOLN CONTINENTAL MARK I** *(1941)*	30.00	38.00
☐ 162	**LION ON THE ROCK** *(1971)*	6.00	10.00
☐ 163	**LIQUOR SQUARE** *(1972)*	6.00	10.00
☐ 164	**LITTLE GIANT** *(1971)*		
	Replica of the first horse-drawn steam engine to arrive at the Chicago fire in 1871. Red, black with gold trim	11.00	16.00

M

☐ 165	**MAINE LOBSTER** *(1970)*		
	Bottle in Lobster shape, complete with claws. Pinkish-red color. Bottle is sold only in Maine	20.00	28.00
☐ 166	**MAINE LIGHTHOUSE** *(1971)*	16.00	20.00
☐ 167	**MAN-O-WAR** *(1969)*		
	"Big Red" captured just about every major horse-racing prize in turfdom. Replica of famous horse in brown and green, 22k gold base. Embossed, "MAN-O-WAR"	10.00	16.00
☐ 168	**M & M BROWN JUG** *(1975)*	18.00	24.00
☐ 169	**MAP** *(1972)*		
	U.S.A. Club Bottle	8.00	14.00
☐ 170	**MASONIC FEZ** *(1976)*	10.00	18.00
☐ 171	**MAX** *(1976)*		
	The Hat, Zimmerman	25.00	30.00
☐ 172	**MILITARY TANK** *(1971)*	15.00	22.00
☐ 173	**MINNESOTA HOCKEY PLAYER** *(1975)*	18.00	22.00

☐ 174	**MINUTEMAN** *(1975)*	12.00 18.00
☐ 175	**MISSOURI MULE** *(1972)*	
	Obstinate critter that can outperform horses. Brown	12.00 15.00
☐ 176	**MOOSE** *(1973)*	22.00 30.00
☐ 177	**MR. MAINE POTATO** *(1973)*	
	From early beginnings the people of Maine have built the small potato into a giant industry. Today potatoes are the number one agricultural crop in the state. Over thirty-six billion pounds are grown every year	6.00 10.00
☐ 178	**MR. FOREMOST** *(1969)*	
	An authentic reproduction of the famous Bottle-shaped symbol of Foremost Liquor stores, "Mr. Foremost" known for good wines and spirits. Red, white and black	9.00 12.00
☐ 179	**MR. MERCHANT** *(1970)*	
	JUMPING MAN, Whimsical, checkered-vest caricature of amiable shopkeeper, leaping into the air, arms outstretched. Yellow, black	8.00 12.00
☐ 180	**MOTORCYCLE**	
	Motorcycle rider and machine. Rider dressed in Blue pants, red jacket, w/stars 'n stripes helmet. Motorcycle black with red tank on silver base	8.00 12.00
☐ 181	**MOUNTAINEER** *(1971)*	
	Figure dressed in buckskin, holding rifle. "MOUNTAIN-EERS ARE ALWAYS FREE" embossed on base. Bottle is hand-trimmed in platinum. One of the most valuable Ezra Brooks figural bottles	40.00 60.00
☐ 182	**MUSTANG INDY PACE CAR** *(1979)*	12.00 18.00

N

☐ 183	**NEW HAMPSHIRE STATE HOUSE** *(1970)*	
	150-year old State House. Embossed doors, windows, steps. Eagle topped stopper. Gray building with gold	10.00 14.00
☐ 184	**NEBRASKA—GO BIG RED!** *(1972)*	
	Genuine Heritage China reproduction of a game ball and fan, trimmed in genuine 24k gold	10.00 14.00
☐ 185	**NORTH CAROLINA BICENTENNIAL** *(1975)*	10.00 14.00
☐ 186	**NUGGET CLASSIC**	
	Replica of golf pin presented to golf tournament participants. Finished in 22k gold	8.00 10.00

O

☐ 187	**OIL GUSHER**	
	Bottle in shape of oil drilling rig. All silver, jet black stopper in shape of gushing oil	5.00 8.00
☐ 188	**OLD CAPITAL** *(1971)*	
	Bottle in shape of Iowa's seat of government when corn State was still frontier territory. Embossed windows, doors, pillars. "OLD CAPITAL/IOWA 1840-1857" on base. Reddish color with gold dome stopper	15.00 22.00
☐ 189	**OLD EZ** *(1977)*	
	No. 1, Barn Owl	45.00 55.00

☐ 190	**OLD EZ** *(1978)*		
	No. 2, Eagle Owl	40.00	50.00
☐ 191	**OLD EZ** *(1979)*		
	No. 3, Snow Owl	20.00	28.00
☐ 192	**OLD MAN OF THE MOUNTAIN** *(1970)*	10.00	18.00
☐ 193	**OLD WATER TOWER** *(1969)*		
	Famous land mark. Survived the Chicago fire of 1871. Embossed details, towers, doors, stones, windows. Grey and brown gold base	12.00	16.00
☐ 194	**ONTARIO 500** *(1970)*		
	California 500 is a speedway classic with an "Indy" style racing oval. Red, white, blue and black with silver trim ...	18.00	22.00
☐ 195	**ORDER OF EAGLES F.O.E.** *(1978)*	25.00	35.00
☐ 196	**OVERLAND EXPRESS** *(1969)*		
	Brown stagecoach bottle.	8.00	12.00
☐ 197	**OVER-UNDER FLINTLOCK** *(1969)*		
	Flask	4.00	8.00

P

☐ 198	**PANDA—GIANT** *(1972)*		
	Giant Panda ceramic bottle	14.00	18.00
☐ 199	**PENGUIN** *(1972)*		
	Ezra Brooks salutes the penguin with a genuine Heritage China ceramic figural bottle	8.00	12.00
☐ 200	**PENNY FARTHINGTON HIGH-WHEELER** *(1973)*		
	Ezra Brooks salutes the millions of cyclists everywhere, and the new cycling boom with this genuine Heritage China ceramic of the Penny Farthington bicycle	10.00	15.00
☐ 201	**PEPPERBOX** *(1969)*		
	Flask	4.00	8.00
☐ 202	**PHOENIX BIRD** *(1971)*		
	Famous mythical bird reborn from its own ashes honoring Arizona. Blue bird with outstretched wings arising from gold flames	22.00	30.00
☐ 203	**PHOENIX JAYCEES** *(1973)*		
	Ezra Brooks is proud to honor the Phoenix Jaycees and the Rodeo of Rodeos with this Heritage China reproduction of a silver saddle	12.00	17.00
☐ 204	**PIANO** *(1970)*		
	An "Old Time" piano player and his upright piano. Player wears blue pants, striped shirt, red bow tie, black derby, and yellow vest. Piano is brown is gold trim	10.00	15.00
☐ 205	**PIRATE** *(1971)*		
	A swashbuckling sailor with beard and eye-patch and "hook" hand, who flew the Jolly Roger (skull & crossbones) o'er the 7-seas. Black hat & jacket & boots, yellow striped shirt, pistol, sword & treasure chest on gold base .	5.00	8.00
☐ 206	**POLISH LEGION AMERICAN VETS** *(1978)*	18.00	26.00
☐ 207	**PORTLAND HEAD LIGHTHOUSE** *(1971)*		
	It's guided ships safely into Maine Harbor since 1791. White, red trim, gold "Light" stopper. "MAINE" embossed on rock base	15.00	22.00

☐ 208 **POT-BELLIED STOVE** *(1968)*
"Old-Time" round coal burning stove with ornate legs and
"Fire" in the grate. Black and red 8.00 10.00

Q

☐ 209 **QUEEN OF HEARTS** *(1969)*
Playing card symbol with Royal flush in Hearts on front of
bottle 6.00 10.00

R

☐ 210 **RACCOON WILD LIFE** *(1978)* 40.00 50.00
☐ 211 **RAM** *(1973)* 20.00 26.00
☐ 212 **RAZORBACK HOG** *(1969)*
Bright red hog with white tusks and hooves running on
green grass 18.00 24.00
☐ 213 **RAZORBAC HOG** *(1979)* 30.00 38.00
☐ 214 **RED FOX** *(1979)*
Wild Life 40.00 46.00
☐ 215 **RENO ARCH** *(1968)*
Honoring the "biggest little city in the world", Reno,
Nevada. Arch shape with "RENO" embossed on yellow.
Front of bottle multi-color decal of: dice, rabbits foot,
roulette wheel, slot machine, etc. White and yellow, purple stopper 5.00 10.00
☐ 216 **SAN FRANCISCO CABLE CAR** *(1968)* 10.00 16.00

S

☐ 217 **SAILFISH** *(1971)*
Leaping deep water Sailfish with a sword-like nose and
large spread fin. Blue-green luminous tones on green
"waves" base 8.00 12.00
☐ 218 **SALMON** *(1971)*
Washington King 12.00 18.00
☐ 219 **SAN FRANCISCO CABLE CAR** *(1968)* 10.00 16.00
☐ 220 **SEA CAPTAIN** *(1971)*
Salty old seadog, white hair and beard, in blue "captains"
jacket with gold buttons and sleeve stripes, white cap,
gold band. Holding pipe, on "wooden" stanchion base .. 10.00 14.00
☐ 221 **SENATOR** *(1971)*
Cigar-Chomping, whistle-stopping State Senator, stump-
ing on a platform of pure nostalgia. Black "western" hat
and swallow-tail coat, red vest, string tie, gold, bladk red,
white 12.00 16.00
☐ 222 **SENATORS OF THE U.S.** *(1972)*
Ezra Brooks honors the Senators of the United States of
America with this genuine Heritage Ceramic "Old Time"
courtly Senator 12.00 16.00
☐ 223 **SETTER** *(1974)* 12.00 18.00
☐ 224 **SHRINE KING TUT GUARD** *(1979)* 30.00 38.00
☐ 225 **SILVER SADDLE** *(1973)* 24.00 30.00

□ 226 **SILVER SPUR BOOT** *(1971)*
Cowboy-boot shaped bottle with silver spur buckled on.
"SILVER SPUR—CARSON CITY NEVADA" embossed on
side of boot. Brown boot with platinum trim 8.00   14.00

□ 227 **1804 SILVER DOLLAR** *(1970)*
Commemorates the famous and very valuable "1804
Silver Dollar". Embossed replica of the Liberty Head
dollar. Platinum covered round dollar shaped bottle on
black or white base 5.00   8.00

□ 228 **SIMBA** *(1971)*
Beautifully detailed Lion is reddish-brown color. Head of
Lion is stopper. "Rock" base is dark grey 9.00   12.00

□ 229 **SKI BOOT** *(1972)*
Ezra Brooks salutes the exciting sport of skiing with this
genuine Heritage Ceramic Ski Boot 8.00   12.00

□ 230 **SLOT-MACHINE** *(1971)*
A tribute to the "Slots" of Las Vegas, Nevada. A replica of
the original nickle "LIBERTY BELL" slot machine
invented by Charles Fey in 1895. The original is in Reno's
Liberty Belle Saloon. Top window shows 2 horseshoes
and a bell, bottom panel shows prizes. Grey body with
gold trim 20.00   26.00

□ 231 **SNOWMOBILES** *(1972)*
The snowmobile is used for many things other than
merely having a good time. It has already replaced the
dog sled as the chief means of transportation in Alaska
and Canada. 10.00   15.00

□ 232 **SOUTH DAKOTA AIR NATIONAL GUARD** *(1976)* 20.00   28.00

□ 233 **SPIRIT OF '76** *(1974)* 4.00   8.00

□ 234 **SPIRIT OF ST. LOUIS** *(1977)*
50th Anniversary 8.00   14.00

□ 235 **SPRINT CAR RACER**
A decanter replica of the race car sponsored by Ezra
Brooks. Supercharged racer with black Firestone racing
tires, and silver and blue trim. Goggled driver in white and
red jump suit at wheel. Cream colored car with silver &
blue trim 20.00   28.00

□ 236 **STAN LAUREL BUST** *(1976)* 10.00   16.00

□ 237 **STOCK MARKET TICKER** *(1970)*
A unique replica of a ticker tape machine. Gold colored
mechanism with white market tape under plastic dome.
Black base with embossed plaque "STOCK MARKET
QUOTATIONS" 8.00   11.00

□ 238 **STONEWALL JACKSON** *(1974)* 26.00   34.00

□ 239 **STRONGMAN** *(1974)* 6.00   10.00

□ 240 **STURGEON** *(1975)* 20.00   28.00

□ 241 **JOHN L. SULLIVAN** *(1970)*
"The Great John L." mustached, last of the bare nuckle
fighters, in fighting stance. Red tights, gold belt cord,
white gym shirt. John stands on a gold base 12.00   17.00

□ 242 **SEALION-GOLD** *(1972)*
Ezra Brooks commemorates the great State of California
and her world-famous marine showmen, with the Califor-
nia Sealion ceramic bottle, hand detailed in 24 carat gold   10.00   15.00

☐ 243 **SYRACUSE-NEW YORK** *(1973)*
*Ezra Brooks salutes the great city of Syracuse, its past
and its present* 11.00   16.00

T

☐ 244 **TANK PATTON** *(1972)*
*Reproduction of a U.S. Army tank. Turret top with cannon
is the stopper. Embossed details on tracks, tools, etc.
Camouflage green and brown* 18.00   24.00
☐ 245 **BOWLING TEN PINS** *(1973)*
*In Colonial Days Massachusetts and Connecticut banned
"bowling at nine pins" along with dice and cards. But
bowlers avoided the law by simply adding a 10th pin. Thus
10 pin bowling was born. Today the sport of bowling is
enjoyed by more than 30,000,000 Americans* 10.00   15.00
☐ 246 **TECUMSEH** *(1969)*
*The symbol known as "The God of 25" (passing grade at
Annapolis). The figure head of the U.S.S. Delaware, this
decanter is an embossed replica of the statue at Annapolis. Feathers in quiver form stopper. Gold figure on brown
"wood" base* 6.00   10.00
☐ 247 **TELEPHONE** *(1971)*
*A replica of the "old-time" upright handset telephone.
24k. gold body, mouth piece, and base trim, black
receiver, wires, base and head. Mouthpiece and head form
the stopper* 10.00   15.00
☐ 248 **TENNIS PLAYER** *(1972)*
*Ezra Brooks salutes tennis lovers everywhere, with this
genuine Heritage China ceramic "Tennis Player" bottle* .. 8.00   12.00
☐ 249 **TERRAPIN** *(1974)*
Maryland 16.00   20.00
☐ 250 **TEXAS LONGHORN** *(1971)*
*Realistic longhorn on tall green Texas "grass" base.
Long-horned head is stopper. Reddish-brown body, white
horns and mask, gold trimmed base* 10.00   15.00
☐ 251 **TICKER TAPE** *(1970)* 8.00   14.00
☐ 252 **TOM TURKEY**
*Replica of the American White Feathered Turkey. Tail
spread, red head and wattles, yellow feet and beak. On a
brown "tree trunk" base* 18.00   24.00
☐ 253 **TONOPAH** *(1972)* 14.00   20.00
☐ 254 **TOTEM POLE** *(1972)*
*Ezra Brooks commemorates the totem art of the Amer-
ican Indian with this genuine Heritage China reproduction
of an ornate, intricately designed Indian totem pole* 10.00   14.00
☐ 255 **TOTEM POLE** *(1973)*
*The Indians of North America have a proud history. And in
many instances, that history is beautifully portrayed in
totem pole art. It is a truly remarkable art form that will
enrich the world for generations to come. Ezra Brooks
commemorates the totem pole art of the North American
Indian with this genuine Heritage China reproduction of
an ornate, intricately designed Indian totem pole* 12.00   18.00

☐256 **TIGER ON STADIUM** *(1973)*
*Many college teams have chosen him for their mascot.
The roar of the crowds "Go Tiger" cheers on the college
playing fields act as an impressive testimonial to the
spirit and enthusiasm of those individuals who call
themselves "Tigers".* 12.00 17.00

☐257 **TRACTOR** *(1971)*
*A model of the 1917 Fordson made by Henry Ford.
Embossed details of engine and hood seat and steering
wheel. Red tractor wheels, grey body with silver trim* 12.00 18.00

☐258 **TRAIL BIKE RIDER** *(1972)*
*Ezra Brooks salutes the trail bike riders of America with
this genuine Heritage China ceramic bottle.* 8.00 14.00

☐259 **TROJAN HORSE** *(1974)* 14.00 20.00

☐260 **TROJANS—U.S.C. FOOTBALL** *(1973)*
*In the last dozen years alone, the Trojans have given
U.S.C. seven Pacific-Eight Conference titles, six Rose
Bowl teams, 23 All-Americans, two Heisman Trophy win-
ners (Mike Garrett and O.J. Simpson), three undefeated
seasons, and three national championships* 8.00 20.00

☐261 **TRUCKIN & VANNIN** *(1977)* 12.00 18.00

☐262 **TROUT & FLY** *(1970)*
*The Rainbow Trout leaping and fighting the McGinty Fly.
A luminescent replica of this angler's dream on a blue
"water" base, complete with scales, fins and flashing tail* 8.00 12.00

V

☐263 **V.F.W.—VETRANS OF FOREIGN WARS** *(1973)*
*The V.F.W. holds its National Convention each year in an
American city. Ezra Brooks salutes the Veterans of
Foreign Wars of the United States and the 1.8 million
fighting men of five wars who wear the Cross of Malta
emblem linked by bonds of comradeship that only shared
overseas military service can forge* 6.00 10.00

☐264 **VERMONT SKIER** *(1972)*
*The smooth hills of Vermont boasted America's first ski-
tow, in 1934. The ski-tow revolutionized the sport all
across the country. Each year when the green mountains
of Vermont turn frosty white, and New England's winter
athletes take to the slopes, the people of Vermont
remember that historic event* 12.00 18.00

☐265 **VIRGINIA—RED CARDINAL** *(1973)*
*A glorious bird, the Cardinal represents this illustrious
state.* 12.00 18.00

W

☐266 **WALGREEN DRUGS** *(1974)* 20.00 28.00

☐267 **WEIRTON STEEL** *(1973)* 18.00 24.00

☐268 **WESTERN RODEOS** *(1973)*
*Ezra Brooks salutes the rodeo, from its early pioneers to
its professional circuit riders, with this genuine Heritage
China bottle* 17.00 23.00

☐269	**WEST VIRGINIA—MOUNTAINEER** *(1971)*	75.00	85.00
☐270	**WEST VIRGINIA—MOUNTAIN LADY** *(1972)*		
	The mountain lady remains an inspiration to American		
	womanhood	17.00	23.00
☐271	**WHALE** *(1972)*	12.00	18.00
☐272	**WHEAT SHOCKER** *(1971)*		
	The mascot of the Kansas football team in a fighting		
	pose. Wheat-yellow figure, with black turtle-neck sweater,		
	"WHEAT SHOCKER" embossed in yellow on front. Wheat		
	stalk tops are the stopper, wheat plants are the base	6.00	10.00
☐273	**WHISKEY FLASKS** *(1970)*		
	Reproductions of collectible American patriotic whiskey		
	flasks of the 1800's, Old Ironsides, Miss Liberty, American		
	Eagle, Civil War Commemorative. Embossed designs in		
	gold, on blue, amber, green and red	10.00	15.00
☐274	**WHITE TAIL DEER** *(1947)*	20.00	26.00
☐275	**WHITE TURKEY** *(1971)*	15.00	20.00
☐276	**WICHITA**	4.00	8.00
☐277	**WICHITA CENTENNIAL** *(1970)*		
	Replica of the Wichita's center of culture and commerce,		
	Century II, the round building with the square base. Blue		
	roof with gold airliner on top symbol of "Air Capital of the		
	World". Blue, brown, black and gold	6.00	10.00
☐278	**WINSTON CHURCHILL** *(1969)*	4.00	8.00

Z

☐279	**ZIMMERMAN'S HAT** *(1968)*		
	A salute to "Zimmerman's — WORLD'S LARGEST		
	LIQUOR STORE". A replica of the store, embossed win-		
	dows, doors, and roof. The "Zimmerman Hat" caps the		
	store and is the bottle stopper. Red, white, brown and		
	gold	5.00	8.00

J. W. DANT BOTTLES

The bottles of J.W. Dant Distilling Company from Louisville, Kentucky, are not as numerous as those of Ezra Brooks and Jim Beam, the other major Kentucky distilleries, but their following is strong. Introduced in 1968, the Dant figurals carry American themes, including patriotic events, folklore, and animal species such as the mountain quail, woodcock, and prairie chicken. Dant's preoccupation with American history originates from the period of its establishment in 1863 during the Civil War.

Most Dant bottles are conventionally shaped with historical scenes in full color. The back of all rectangular bottles carries an embossed American eagle and shield with stars. Several of the "Boston Tea Party" bottles have an error: the eagle's head faces his left side instead of his right.

All Dant bottles are limited editions and the company assures customers that the molds will not be reused.

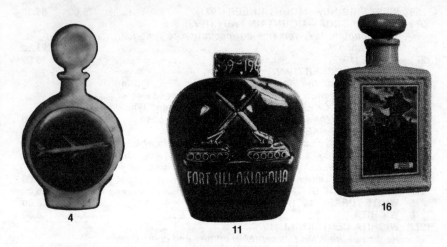

4

11

16

5   10   2

NO.	DESCRIPTION	PRICE RANGE	
☐ 1	ALAMO	7.00	10.00
☐ 2	AMERICAN LEGION	7.00	10.00
☐ 3	BOBWHITE	4.00	7.00
☐ 4	BOEING 747	7.00	11.00
☐ 5	BOSTON TEA PARTY	5.00	8.00
☐ 6	BOURBON	3.00	4.00
☐ 7	CALIFORNIA QUAIL	4.00	6.00
☐ 8	CHUKAR PARTRIDGE	5.00	8.00
☐ 9	DUEL BETWEEN BURR & HAMILTON	5.00	8.00
☐ 10	EAGLE	5.00	8.00
☐ 11	FORT SILL CENTENNIAL (c. 1969)	7.00	10.00
☐ 12	INDIANAPOLIS 500	8.00	10.00
☐ 13	MOUNTAIN QUAIL	5.00	8.00
☐ 14	MT. RUSHMORE	11.00	15.00
☐ 15	PATRICK HENRY	5.00	8.00
☐ 16	PAUL BUNYAN	4.00	7.00
☐ 17	PRAIRIE CHICKEN	3.00	4.00
☐ 18	REVERSE EAGLE	4.00	6.00
☐ 19	RING-NECKED PHEASANT	3.75	5.75
☐ 20	RUFFED GROUSE	3.75	5.75
☐ 21	SAN DIEGO	5.00	8.00
☐ 22	SPEEDWAY 500	5.00	8.00
☐ 23	TEA PARTY, WHITE	3.00	4.00
☐ 24	WASHINGTON CROSSING DELAWARE	5.00	8.00
☐ 25	WOODCOCK	4.50	7.00
☐ 26	WRONG WAY CHARLIE	14.00	19.00

GARNIER BOTTLES

The prestigeous figural bottles of the Garnier firm are among the oldest ones issued continuously since 1899 by a spirits company. But, during the American Prohibition and World War II, which eliminated the majority of the Garnier market, production ceased temporarily. Garnet et Cie, a French firm founded in 1858, is recognized as the pioneer of the modern "collector" bottle for liquor. Of course, figural and other decorative bottles for liquor existed before the Garnier products but these were not issued in the form of a series which encouraged the building up of a collection. Garnier actually had a line of figural bottles 50 years before Jim Beam. Some antique historians claim to have found a relationship between Garnier bottles and the later Hummel porcelain figurines, believing that the former inspired the latter. (Hummel fans may object to this since Garnier is a spirits company; but their approaches, in terms of types of figurals, are similar.)

The older Garniers, produced prior to World War II, are scarce and valuable. They are not listed because their price levels are difficult to establish. Some of the better known "old Garniers" are the Cat (1930), Clown (1910), Country Jug (1937), Greyhound (1930), Penguin (1930), and Marquise (1931). Garnier released its new figurals gradually with only 52 available within a 31 year span. But since 1930, new figurals have been produced more frequently.

80   68   31   77

PARIS   LONDON   NEW YORK

GARNIER BOTTLES

A

NO.	DESCRIPTION	PRICE RANGE	
☐ 1	**ALADDIN'S LAMP** (c. 1963)		
	Silver. 6½"	11.00	15.00
☐ 2	**ALFA ROMEO 1913** (c. 1970)		
	Red body, yellow seats, black trim, 4" x 10½"	5.00	8.00
☐ 3	**ALFA ROMEO 1929** (c. 1969)		
	Pale blue body, red seat, black trim, 4" x 10½"	4.00	7.00
☐ 4	**ALFA ROMEO RACER** (c. 1969)		
	Maroon body, black tires and trim, 4" x 10"	4.00	7.00
☐ 5	**ANTIQUE COACH** (c. 1970)		
	Multicolor pastel tones, 8" x 12"	4.00	7.00
☐ 6	**APOLLO** (c. 1969)		
	Yellow quarter-moon. Blue clouds, Silver Apollo Spaceship, 13½"	12.00	17.00
☐ 7	**AZTEC VASE** (c. 1965)		
	"Stone" Tan, Multicolor Aztec design, 11¾"	7.00	10.00

B

☐ 8	**BABY FOOT-SOCCER SHOE** (c. 1963)		
	Black with white trim, 3¾" x 8½"	4.00	7.00
	1962 Soccer Shoe—Large	8.00	11.00
☐ 9	**BABY TRIO** (c. 1963)		
	Clear glass, gold base, 6¼"	7.00	10.00
☐ 10	**BACCUS—FIGURAL** (c. 1967)		
	Purple, brown, flesh tones, 13"	11.00	15.00

☐ 11	**BAHAMAS**		
	Black Policeman, white jacket, hat, black pants, red stripe, gold details	11.00	15.00
☐ 12	**BALTIMORE ORIOLE** (c. 1970)		
	Multicolor, green, yellow, blue, approx. 11"	7.00	10.00
☐ 13	**BANDIT—FIGURAL** (c. 1958)		
	Pin ball shape, multicolor, 11½"	10.00	14.00
☐ 14	**BEDROOM CANDLESTICK** (c. 1967)		
	White with hand painted flowers, 11½"	11.00	15.00
☐ 15	**BELLOWS** (c. 1969)		
	Gold and red, 4" x .14½"	11.00	15.00
☐ 16	**BIRD ASHTRAY** (c. 1958)		
	Clear glass, gold stopper, 3"	3.00	4.00
☐ 17	**BURMESE MAN VASE** (c. 1965)		
	"Stone" Gray, multicolor eastern design, 12"	11.00	15.00
☐ 18	**BLUEBIRD** (c. 1970)		
	2 Blue birds, multicolor green, brown and yellow, approx. 11"	5.00	8.00
☐ 19	**BOUQUET** (c. 1966)		
	White basket, multicolor flowers, 10¾"	11.00	15.00
☐ 20	**BULL (& MATADOR)—ANIMAL FIGURAL** (c. 1963)		
	A "Rocking" bottle, bronze and gold, 12½" x 12½"	11.00	15.00

C

☐ 21	**CANADA**		
	"Mountie" in red jacket, black jodphur, brown boots	11.00	14.00
☐ 22	**CANDLESTICK** (c. 1955)		
	Yellow candle. Brown holder w/gold ring, 10¾"	11.00	15.00
☐ 23	**CANDLESTICK GLASS** (c. 1965)		
	Ornate leaves and fluting, 10"	16.00	23.00
☐ 24	**CANNON** (c. 1964)		
	With wheels and carriage. Mottled yellow-brown, 7½" x 13½"	16.00	23.00
☐ 25	**CARDINAL STATE BIRD—ILLINOIS** (c. 1969)		
	Bright red bird, green and brown "tree", 11½"	7.00	11.00
☐ 26	**CAT, BLACK** (c. 1962)		
	Black cat with green eyes, 11½"	10.00	15.00
☐ 27	**CAT, GREY** (c. 1962)		
	Greyish-white cat w/yellow eyes, 11½"	10.00	15.00
☐ 28	**CHALET** (c. 1955)		
	White, red, green and blue, 9"	11.00	15.00
☐ 29	**CHIMNEY** (c. 1956)		
	Red bricks and fire, white mantel with picture, 9¾"	11.00	15.00
☐ 30	**CHINESE DOG** (c. 1965)		
	Foo Dogs, carved, embossed. Ivory white on dark blue base, 11"	11.00	15.00
☐ 31	**CHINESE STATUETTE, MAN** (1970)		
	Yellow robe, dark skin, blue base, 12"	9.00	13.00
☐ 32	**CHINESE STATUETTE, WOMAN** (1970)		
	Ebony skin tones, Lavender robe, Blue base, 12"	9.00	13.00
☐ 33	**CHRISTMAS TREE** (1956)		
	Dark green tree, gold decorated, white candles, red flame, 11½"	14.00	19.00

- [ ] 34 **CITROEN, 1922** *(1970)*
  Yellow body, black trim wheels, 4" x 10½ " **4.00**   **7.00**
- [ ] 35 **CLASSIC ASHTRAY** *(1958)*
  Clear glass, round with pouring spout, 2½ " **5.00**   **8.00**
- [ ] 36 **CLOCK** *(1958)*
  Clear glass, round on black base. Working clock in center,
  9" **11.00**   **15.00**
- [ ] 37 **CLOWN HOLDING TUBA** *(1955)*
  Green clown with gold trim, 12¾ " **11.00**   **15.00**
- [ ] 38 **COFFEE MILL** *(1966)*
  White with blue flowers **11.00**   **15.00**
- [ ] 39 **COLUMBINE FIGURAL** *(1968)*
  Female partner to Harlequin. Green and blue, black hair
  and mask, 13" **10.00**   **14.00**
  HARLEQUIN **16.00**   **22.00**

D

- [ ] 40 **DRUNKARD—DRUNK ON LAMPOST**
  Figure in top hat and tails holding "wavy" lampost. Black,
  red, blue and white, 14¾ " **9.00**   **13.00**
- [ ] 41 **DUCKLING FIGURAL** *(1956)*
  Yellow duckling, white basket and red flowers, pink hat . .   **11.00**   **15.00**
- [ ] 42 **DUO** *(1954)*
  2 Clear glass bottles stacked, 2 pouring spouts, 7¼ " **11.00**   **15.00**

E

- [ ] 43 **EGG FIGURAL** *(1956)*
  White egg shape house, pink, red, green, 8¾ " **27.00**   **36.00**
- [ ] 44 **EIFFEL TOWER** *(1951)*
  Ivory with yellow tones, 13½ " **10.00**   **15.00**
  EIFFEL TOWER 12½ " **13.00**   **19.00**
- [ ] 45 **ELEPHANT FIGURAL** *(1961)*
  Black with ivory white tusks, 6¾ " **13.00**   **19.00**
- [ ] 46 **EMPIRE VASE** *(1962)*
  Green and white, gold design and trim, 11½ " **7.00**   **10.00**

F

- [ ] 47 **FIAT 500, 1913** *(1970)*
  Yellow body, red hub caps, black trim, 4" x 10¾" **10.00**   **14.00**
- [ ] 48 **FIAT NEUVO, 1913** *(1970)*
  Open top. Blue body and hub caps, yellow and black trim,
  4" x 10¾ " **4.00**   **7.00**
- [ ] 49 **FLASK GARNIER** *(1958)*
  Clear glass, embossed cherries, 3" **9.00**   **12.00**
- [ ] 50 **FLYING HORSE PEGASUS** *(1958)*
  Black Horse. Gold mane and tail, red "marble" candle
  holder, 12" **15.00**   **22.00**
- [ ] 51 **FORD, 1913** *(1970)*
  Green open body and wheels, black trim, 4" x 10¾ " **5.00**   **8.00**

☐ 52 **FOUNTAIN** *(1964)*
Brown with Gold Lion Head spout and embossing, 12½".   **11.00**   **14.00**

G

☐ 53 **GIRAFFE** *(1961)*
Yellow "marble", modern animal figure, 18" **11.00**   **14.00**
☐ 54 **GOLDFINCH** *(1970)*
*Yellow bird, black wings and tail, green and brown leaves
and limbs, 12"* **9.00**   **13.00**
☐ 55 **GOOSE** *(1955)*
*White with gold decoration. Modern swirl shaped goose,
9¼"* **11.00**   **14.00**
☐ 56 **GRENADIER** *(1949)*
*Light blue soldier with sword in uniform of 1880's.
(Faceless Figure), 13¾"* **13.00**   **19.00**

H

☐ 57 **HARLEQUIN WITH MANDOLIN** *(1958)*
*Seated comedy figure, mandolin and mask, white with
multicolored circles, black buttons and shoes, 14½"* **20.00**   **27.00**
☐ 58 **HARLEQUIN STANDING** *(1968)*
*Columbine's mate. Brown costume, blue cape, black cap
and shoes, 13¼"* **13.00**   **19.00**
☐ 59 **HORSE PISTOL** *(1964)*
Embossed brown antique pistol, gold details, 18" **11.00**   **14.00**
☐ 60 **HUNTING VASE** *(1964)*
Tan and gold with embossed hunting scene, 12¼" **12.00**   **17.00**
☐ 61 **HUSSAR** *(1949)*
*French Cavalry Soldier of 1800's holding sword. Maroon
color, 13¾"* **25.00**   **33.00**

I

☐ 62 **INDIA**
Turbaned figure. White jacket, blue kilts, red sash **10.00**   **14.00**
☐ 63 **INDIAN** *(1958)*
*"Big Chief" with headdress, bowling pin shape. Bright In-
dian design colors, 11¾"* **13.00**   **17.50**

J

☐ 64 **JOCKEY** *(1961)*
*Bronzed gold horse and jockey "rocking" bottle, 12½" x
12"* **13.00**   **17.00**

L

☐ 65 **LANCER** *(1949)*
Light green soldier holding drum, 13" **15.00**   **22.00**

☐ 66 **LOCOMOTIVE** (1969)
   Tan, old fashioned locomotive, 9" **11.00** **15.00**
☐ 67 **LOG—ROUND** (1958)
   *Brown and tan "log" shape, silver handle and
   spout, 10"* **10.00** **14.00**
☐ 68 **LONDON—"BOBBY"**
   Dark blue uniform, silver helmet shield **9.00** **13.00**
☐ 69 **LOON** (1970)
   Sitting bird, white, brown, tan, blue base, 11" **7.00** **10.00**

M

☐ 70 **MAHARAJAH** (1958)
   White and gold, Indian ruler with turban, 11¾" **10.00** **15.00**
☐ 71 **M.G. 1933** (1970)
   Green body, orange trim, white wheels, 4" x 11" **5.00** **8.00**
☐ 72 **MOCKINGBIRD** (1970)
   Black and white bird on "tree" stump, 11" **7.00** **10.00**
☐ 73 **MONTMARTRE JUG** (1960)
   Colorful Parisian Bohemian scene, green, 11" **10.00** **14.00**
☐ 74 **MONUMENTS** (1966)
   *A cluster of Parisian Monuments, Eiffel Tower spout,
   multicolor, 13"* **10.00** **14.00**

N

☐ 75 **NAPOLEON ON HORSEBACK** (1969)
   *Rearing white horse, Napoleon in red cloak, black hat and
   uniform, 12"* **10.00** **14.00**
☐ 76 **NATURE GIRL** (1959)
   Native girl under palm tree. Black with bronze, 13" **10.00** **14.00**
☐ 77 **NEW YORK**
   Dark blue uniform with gold shield and buttons **9.00** **13.00**

P

☐ 78 **PAINTING** (1961)
   Multicolor painting of girl, in tan "wood" frame, 12" **10.00** **14.00**
☐ 79 **PACKARD, 1930** (1970)
   Orange body, cream roof and wheels, black trim, 4" x 10" **6.00** **8.00**
☐ 80 **PARIS**
   French policemen in black, white gloves, hat and garness **10.00** **14.00**
☐ 81 **PARIS TAXI** (1960)
   *"Old-Time" cab, yellow body, red windows and
   headlights, black wire frame, 9" x 10½"* **14.00** **18.00**
☐ 82 **PARTRIDGE** (1961)
   Multicolor game bird, on "leaf" base, 10" **10.00** **14.00**
☐ 83 **PHEASANT** (1969)
   Multicolor game bird on "rocking" tree trunk base, 12" .. **10.00** **14.00**
☐ 84 **PIGEON—CLEAR GLASS** (1958)
   Bird-shape bottle, gold stopper, 8" **10.00** **14.00**
☐ 85 **PONY** (1961)
   "Modern" shaped horse, "wood" grain tan, 8¾" **12.00** **17.00**

☐ 86 **POODLE** *(1954) (Black & White)*
"Begging" Poodles in white or black with red trim, 8½" .. **12.00** **17.00**

R

☐ 87 **RENAULT, 1911** *(1969)*
Green body and hood, red hubs, black trim, 4" x 10¾" ... **10.00** **14.00**
☐ 88 **ROAD RUNNER** *(1969)*
Multicolor bird, green "cactus" pouring spout, 12" **9.00** **13.00**
☐ 89 **ROBIN** *(1970)*
Multicolor bird on "tree" stump with leaves, 12" **6.00** **9.00**
☐ 90 **ROCKET** *(1958)*
"Rocket" shape bottle, wire holder, yellow nose, 10¾ ... **11.00** **14.00**
☐ 91 **ROLLS ROYCE 1908** *(1970)*
Open touring car in yellow, red seats and hubs, black trim,
4" x 10½" **8.00** **11.00**
☐ 92 **ROOSTER** *(1952) (Black & Maroon)*
"Crowing" rooster with handle, black or maroon with gold
trim, 12" **10.00** **14.00**

S

☐ 93 **SAINT TROPEZ JUG** *(1961)*
Colorful French Riviera scene, tan jug, black handle **10.00** **14.00**
☐ 94 **SCARECROW** *(1960)*
Yellow "straw" body and hat, green jacket, red stripe face
and tie, bird on shoulder, 12" **11.00** **14.00**
☐ 95 **SHERIFF** *(1958)*
Two guns, badge and cowboy hat. "Pin-ball" shape. White
and gold, 12" **8.00** **10.00**
☐ 96 **SNAIL** *(1950)*
White and brown with spiral shell, 6½" x 10" **13.00** **18.00**
☐ 97 **SOCCER SHOE** *(1962)*
Black shoe, white laces, 10" long **14.00** **18.00**
☐ 98 **S.S. FRANCE—LARGE** *(1962)*
Commemorative model of ocean liner. Black hull, blue-
green decks, red and black stacks, with gold labels, 5" x
19" **37.00** **49.00**
☐ 99 **S.S. FRANCE—SMALL** *(1962)*
Same as above, 4½" x 14" **28.00** **37.00**
☐100 **S.S. QUEEN MARY** *(1970)*
Black hull, green-blue decks, blue "water", 3 red and
black stacks, 4" x 16" **13.00** **19.00**
☐101 **STANLEY STEAMER 1907** *(1970)*
Open blue car, yellow and black trim, 4" x 10½" **7.00** **10.00**

T

☐102 **TEAPOT** *(1961)*
Yellow and black striped body, black handle and spout,
8½" **11.00** **14.00**
TEAPOT, 1935 .... **16.00** **21.00**

☐ 103 **TROUT** *(1967)*
Gray-blue speckled leaping trout, "water" base, 11″ **10.00** **14.00**

V

☐ 104 **VALLEY QUAIL** *(1969)*
Black marked bird on "wood" base, 11″ **5.00** **8.00**
☐ 105 **VIOLIN** *(1966)*
White violin, hand painted flowers and details, 14″ **10.00** **15.00**

W

☐ 106 **WATCH-ANTIQUE** *(1966)*
Antique pocket watch, tan and gold, 10″ **11.00** **16.00**
☐ 107 **WATER PITCHER** *(1965)*
Glass body, silver base, handle and top, 14″ **10.00** **14.00**
☐ 108 **WATERING CAN** *(1958)*
Hand painted design, handle and pouring spout, 7″ **12.00** **17.00**

Y

☐ 109 **YOUNG DEER VASE** *(1964)*
Embossed figures. Tan color, 12″ **12.00** **17.00**

MINIATURES 1973/74

A new line of Garnier Fancy miniatures, featuring a colorful variety of safari animals, dogs, European houses, tropicms throughout the world. The collectors of miniatures have a choice of the regular replicas of the Garnier bottles, plus fancy ceramic, porcelain and glass figurals. The early surge in miniature collecting in the 1930's peaked again in the late 1960's and is still going strong today.

NO.	DESCRIPTION	PRICE RANGE	
☐ 110	**DOGS** *(1972)*		
	Collie, Dashchund, Toy Poodle, German Shepherd, Cocker Spaniel, Dalmatian . . . . **EACH**	**9.00**	**13.00**
☐ 111	**EUROPEAN HOUSES**		
	France, Holland, Italy, England, Switzerland, Spain **EACH**	**9.00**	**14.00**
☐ 112	**PLAYING CARDS**		
	Jack of Club, Jack of Hearts, Queen of Clubs, Queen of Hearts, King of Clubs, King of Hearts . . . . **EACH**	**9.00**	**13.00**
☐ 113	**SAFARI ANIMALS** *(1973)*		
	Lion, Elephant, Panda, Tiger, Giraffe, Zebra . . . . **EACH**	**9.00**	**14.00**
☐ 114	**SPORT FIGURES**		
	Hockey Player, Baseball Player, Football Player . . . **EACH**	**9.00**	**13.00**
☐ 115	**TROPICAL FISH** *(1974)*		
	Goldfish, Guppy, Gourami, Angelfish, Butterfly Fish, Zebra Sailfin . . . . **EACH**	**6.00**	**9.00**

HOFFMAN

The Hoffman bottles are limited editions ceramics. Each issue is restricted in the number of bottles made and when this designated number is reached the mold is destroyed to prevent reproductions in the future. Consequently, the "out of production" designs quickly become collectors' items achieving high prices on the market. Hoffmans have sometimes been called the Hummels of the bottle world because they often depict figures in European dress at various kinds of occupations. These include a shoemaker, a doctor, and a bartender. However, the firm also focused upon American themes, such as its 1976 centinnial bottles with "Pioneer of 1876" and "Hippie of 1976."

48

13

HOFFMAN

NO.	DESCRIPTION	PRICE RANGE	
☐ 1	**MR. BARTENDER with Music Box—** "He's a Jolly Good Fellow"	40.00	55.00
☐ 2	**MR. CHARMER with Music Box—** "Glow Little Glow Worm"	40.00	55.00
☐ 3	**MR. DANCER with Music Box—** "The Irish Washerwoman"	30.00	42.00
☐ 4	**MR. DOCTOR with Music Box—** "As Long As He Needs Me"	30.00	42.00
☐ 5	**MR. FIDDLER with Music Box—** "Hearts and Flowers"	30.00	42.00
☐ 6	**MR. GUITARIST with Music Box—** "Johnny Guitar"	30.00	42.00
☐ 7	**MR. HARPIST with Music Box—** "Do—Re—Mi"	20.00	32.00
☐ 8	**MR. LUCKY with Music Box—** "When Irish Eyes Are Smiling"	20.00	32.00

☐	9	**MRS. LUCKY with Music Box—**		
		"The Kerry Dancer"	30.00	42.00
☐	10	**MR. POLICEMAN with Music Box—**		
		"Don't Blame Me"	30.00	42.00
☐	11	**MR. SANDMAN with Music Box—**		
		"Mr. Sandman"	40.00	55.00
☐	12	**MR. SAXAPHONIST with Music Box—**		
		"Tiger Rag"	30.00	42.00
☐	13	**MR. SHOE COBBLER with Music Box—**		
		"Danny Boy"	26.00	37.00

BICENTENNIAL SERIES — *4/5 Quart*

☐	14	**BETSY ROSS with Music Box—**		
		"Star Spangled Banner"	28.00	40.00
☐	15	**GENERATION GAP**		
		Depicting "100 Years of Progress" — 2 ounce size	28.00	40.00
☐	16	**MAJESTIC EAGLE with Music Box—**		
		"America the Beautiful"	28.00	40.00

C. M. RUSSELL SERIES — *4/5 Quart Size.*

☐	17	**BUFFALO MAN**	23.00	34.00
☐	18	**FLATHEAD SQUAW**	23.00	34.00
☐	19	**LAST OF FIVE THOUSAND**	23.00	34.00
☐	20	**RED RIVER BREED**	23.00	34.00
☐	21	**THE SCOUT**	23.00	34.00
☐	22	**THE STAGE DRIVE**	23.00	34.00
☐	23	**TRAPPER**	23.00	34.00

DECOY DUCKS LIMITED *(Does not include Music Box)*

☐	24	**CANADA GOOSE**		
		8 ounce capacity	16.00	22.00
☐	25	**GREEN-WINGED TEAL**	16.00	22.00
☐	26	**MALLARDS**		
		2 ounce capacity	16.00	22.00
☐	27	**PINTAIL**	16.00	22.00
☐	28	**WOOD DUCKS**	16.00	22.00

MR. LUCKY SERIES — *2 ounce miniature Size. (Does not include music box)*

☐	29	**MR. DOCTOR**	14.00	19.00
☐	30	**MR. HARPIST**	11.00	15.00
☐	31	**MR. LUCKY**	14.00	19.00
☐	32	**MRS. LUCKY**	14.00	19.00
☐	33	**MR. SANDMAN**	14.00	19.00
☐	34	**SHOE COBBLER**	14.00	19.00

PISTOL SERIES *(without Music Box)*

☐	35	**45 AUTOMATIC**		
		2 ounce capacity	23.00	34.00
☐	36	**1776 TOWER FLINTLOCK**		
		8 ounce capacity	23.00	34.00
☐	37	**1851 CIVIL WAR COLT**		
		2 ounce capacity	23.00	34.00
☐	38	**DODGE CITY FRONTIER**		
		2 ounce capacity	23.00	34.00
☐	39	**KENTUCKY FLINTLOCK**		
		8 ounce capacity	23.00	34.00

RODEO SERIES — *4/5 Quart Size — Official Professional Rodeo Cowboys Assn. (without music box)*

☐	40	**BAREBACK RIDER—**		
		Complete with decal showing winners	28.00	40.00
☐	41	**BRAHMA BULL RIDER**	28.00	40.00
☐	42	**CALF ROPER**	28.00	40.00
☐	43	**CLOWN—**		
		Complete with decal showing All-Around Cowboy	28.00	40.00
☐	44	**SADDLE BRONC RIDER**	28.00	40.00
☐	45	**STEER WRESTLING—**		
		Complete with decal showing winners	28.00	40.00

SPECIALTY SERIES

☐	46	**FRACE CAR DECANTERS**	16.00	22.00

WILDLIFE SERIES — *4/4 Quart Size*

☐	47	**BEAR AND CUBS with Music Box—**		
		"Born Free"	28.00	40.00
☐	48	**DOE AND FAWN with Music Box—**		
		"Home on the Range"	28.00	40.00

HOLLY CITY BOTTLES

Holly City commemorative decanters are made by Clevenger Brothers of New Jersey. Each is individually mouth-blown, in the tradition of Casper Wistar who established the first glassworks in the colony of New Jersey in the 18th century. Clevenger Brothers retained the original formulas, enabling them to produce the same blue green, amethyst and amber colors of the much-admired Wistar glass. All Clevenger decanters made for Holly City Bottles are dated and embossed with their mark, "CB" and holly leaves.

HOLLY CITY BOTTLES

NO.	DESCRIPTION	PRICE RANGE	
☐ 1	**1973 CHRISTMAS "ST. NICK"** *(First run 200 bottles, amber)*	16.00	22.00
☐ 2	**DELAWARE BICENTENNIAL** *(First run 1,000 bottles, amber)*	14.00	19.00
☐ 3	**ISRAEL'S 25th ANNIVERSARY** *(First run 500 bottles, honey)*	16.00	22.00
☐ 4	**JOHN F. KENNEDY "ROCKING CHAIR" MEMORIAL** *(First run 1,000 bottles, blue)*	31.00	42.00
☐ 5	**PENNSYLVANIA BICENTENNIAL** *(First run 1,000 bottles, green)*	16.00	22.00
☐ 6	**SENATOR SAM ERVIN/SENATOR HOWARD BAKER** *(First run 500 bottles, topaz)*	16.00	22.00
☐ 7	**THE JERSEY DEVIL** *(First run 1,000 bottles, green - numbered)*	21.00	30.00
☐ 8	**WATERGATE** *(First run 500 bottles, amethyst)*	65.00	85.00
☐ 9	**WATERGATE** *(Second run 500 bottles, blue, 2 stars added)*	24.00	36.00
☐ 10	**WATERGATE** *(Third run 1,000 bottles, topaz, 3 stars and 3 birds added)* .	16.00	22.00

JAPANESE BOTTLES

Bottlemaking in Japan is an ancient art. Although the collectible bottles presently produced in Japan are mainly for exportation, they still reflect native designing in their characteristic shapes and handsome enameling. Japanese bottles are increasing in numbers on the American market but prices remain modest. Japan produces figural bottles also. The popular Kamotsuru bottles picture characters from Japanese mythology.

JAPANESE BOTTLES

NO.	DESCRIPTION	PRICE RANGE	
☐ 1	**DAUGHTER**	9.00	12.00
☐ 2	**FAITHFUL RETAINER**	14.00	20.00
☐ 3	**GOLDEN PAGODA**	6.00	8.00
☐ 4	**"KIKU" GEISHA**		
	Blue, 13¼"	14.00	20.00
☐ 5	**MAIDEN**	7.00	10.00
☐ 6	**NOH MASK**	9.00	13.00
☐ 7	**OKAME MASK**	9.00	13.00
☐ 8	**PLAYBOY**	8.00	12.00
☐ 9	**PRINCESS**	8.00	12.00
☐ 10	**RED LION MAN**	8.00	12.00
☐ 11	**SAKE GOD**		
	Colorful robe, Porcelain 10"	7.00	10.00
☐ 12	**SAKE GOD**		
	White, Bone China, 10"	7.00	11.00
☐ 13	**WHITE LION MAN**	8.00	12.00
☐ 14	**WHITE PAGODA**	6.00	8.00
☐ 15	**"YURI" GEISHA**		
	Pink, Red Sash, 13¼"	17.00	23.00

KIKUKAWA BOTTLES

NO.	DESCRIPTION		
☐ 16	**HARUNOBO**		
	Round flask, Geishas	10.00	14.00
☐ 17	**HOKUSAI**		
	Round flask, porcelain, multicolor	7.00	10.00
☐ 18	**TOYOKUNI**		
	Round flask, porcelain, Kabuki actor	13.00	19.00
☐ 19	**UTAMARO**		
	Oval flask, porcelain, multicolor	10.00	15.00

KAMOTSURU BOTTLES

NO.	DESCRIPTION		
☐ 20	**DAOKOKU**		
	God of wealth	9.00	13.00
☐ 21	**EBISU**		
	God of fisherman	9.00	13.00
☐ 22	**GODDESS OF ART**	7.00	11.00
☐ 23	**HOTEI**		
	God of Wealth	8.00	11.00

KENTUCKY GENTLEMAN BOTTLES

Kentucky Gentleman, another Kentucky whiskey distiller, issues figural bottles. Figurals are released less frequently than those of Beam or Brooks. To date, they have concentrated on ceramics, picturing costumes worn at various times in American history, especially from the Civil War period. Large sized, more than a foot high, they are impressively modeled and colored. Each stands on a rectangular base, the front of which reads "Kentucky Gentleman."

1   2   3   4   5   6

KENTUCKY GENTLEMAN

NO.	DESCRIPTION	PRICE RANGE	
☐ 1	**CONFEDERATE INFANTRY**		
	In gray uniform, with sword 13½"	19.00	25.00
☐ 2	**FRONTIERS MAN** (c. 1969)		
	Coonskin cap, fringed buckskin, powder horn and long		
	rifle, tan, 14"	23.00	32.00
☐ 3	**KENTUCKY BELLE** (c. 1969)		
	Long bustle skirt, feathered hat, parasol, pink, 13¾"	17.00	23.00
☐ 4	**KENTUCKY GENTLEMEN** (c. 1969)		
	Figural bottle, frock coat, top hat and cane, "Old		
	Colonel", gray ceramic, 14"	26.00	37.00
☐ 5	**REVOLUTIONARY WAR OFFICER**		
	In dress uniform, and boots, holding sword, 14"	15.00	22.00
☐ 6	**UNION ARMY SARGEANT**		
	In dress blue uniform, with sword 14"	13.00	17.00

LIONSTONE BOTTLES

Lionstone Distilleries, a relative newcomer into the ranks of figural bottle makers, has already garnered a substantial reputation. Their bottles stress realism in design with a great variety of subjects. Lionstone combines the better elements of classical porcelain-making with the traditional art of bottle manufacturing in their creations. Prices of the more popular issues have increased rapidly. Lionstone produced the most ambitious of all collector bottles in terms of components and detail. Their "Shootout At O.K. Corral," based upon an authentic incident in Old West history, consists of three bottles with nine human figures and two horses.

Lionstone issues all their bottles in series form, including the Oriental Worker series, Dog series, Sports series, Circus series, and Bicentennial series, with new ones added periodically. The most popular with collectors are the Western Figurals, a lengthy series depicting various characters from Western American history such as: Jesse James, SodBuster, Mountain Man, Highway Robber, and Gentleman Gambler. Lionstone's Annie Oakley bottle comes complete with guns and sharpshooter medals.

Since prices of Lionstones on the collector market continue to be firm, buyers should investigate the possibility of spirits dealers still having some old unsold stock on hand.

LIONSTONE BOTTLES

NO.	DESCRIPTION	PRICE RANGE	
☐ 1	AL UNSER #1	15.00	20.00
☐ 2	ANNIE CHRISTMAS	15.00	20.00
☐ 3	ANNIE CHRISTMAS	38.00	50.00
☐ 4	ANNIE OAKLEY	18.00	25.00
☐ 5	BARTENDER	18.00	25.00
☐ 6	BELLY ROBBER	18.00	22.00
☐ 7	BLACKSMITH	45.00	60.00
☐ 8	BUFFALO HUNTER	45.00	60.00
☐ 9	CALAMITY JANE	55.00	75.00
☐ 10	CASUAL INDIAN	16.00	22.00
☐ 11	CAVALRY SCOUT	15.00	21.00
☐ 12	COUNTRY DOCTOR	17.00	24.00
☐ 13	CAMP COOK	18.00	25.00
☐ 14	COWBOY	16.00	22.00
☐ 15	CAMP FOLLOWER	16.00	22.00
☐ 16	CHINESE LAUNDRYMAN	16.00	22.00
☐ 17	CIRCUIT JUDGE	16.00	22.00
☐ 18	CHERRY VALLEY CLUB	50.00	65.00
☐ 19	FRONTIERSMAN	45.00	60.00
☐ 20	GAMBELS QUAIL	40.00	55.00
☐ 21	GENTLEMEN GAMBLER	32.00	47.00
☐ 22	GOLD PANNER	45.00	60.00
☐ 23	HIGHWAY ROBBER	45.00	60.00
☐ 24	JESSE JAMES	45.00	60.00
☐ 25	JOHNNY LIGHTNING	40.00	55.00
☐ 26	JUDGE ROY BEAN	55.00	75.00
☐ 27	LONELY LUKE	55.00	75.00
☐ 28	LUCKY BUCK	45.00	60.00
☐ 29	MINIATURES WESTERN (6)	85.00	110.00

5

8

67

15

12

28

113

36

70

117

☐	30	MINT BAR WITH FRAME	700.00	900.00
☐	31	MINT BAR *w/nude & Fr.*	1000.00	1250.00
☐	32	MOLLY BROWN	45.00	60.00
☐	33	MOUNTAIN MAN	45.00	60.00
☐	34	PROUD INDIAN	30.00	42.00
☐	35	RAILROAD ENGINEER	35.00	47.00
☐	36	RENEGADE TRADER	45.00	60.00
☐	37	RIVERBOAT CAPTAIN	35.00	47.00
☐	38	ROADRUNNER	45.00	60.00
☐	39	SHEEPHERDER	60.00	80.00
☐	40	SHERIFF	32.00	43.00
☐	41	SOD BUSTER	45.00	60.00
☐	42	STP TURBOCAR	35.00	47.00
☐	43	STP TUBOCAR *w/gld & plt* ....PAIR	130.00	165.00
☐	44	SQUAWMAN	45.00	60.00
☐	45	STAGECOACH DRIVER	45.00	60.00
☐	46	TELEGRAPHER	45.00	60.00
☐	47	TINKER	45.00	60.00
☐	48	TRIBAL CHIEF	40.00	55.00
☐	49	WOODHAWK	45.00	60.00

BI-CENTENNIAL SERIES

☐	50	BETSY ROSS	50.00	65.00
☐	51	FIREFIGHTERS NO. 1 *(Old Item)*	60.00	80.00
☐	52	GEORGE WASHINGTON	50.00	65.00
☐	53	MAIL CARRIER	50.00	65.00
☐	54	MOLLY PITCHER	50.00	65.00
☐	55	PAUL REVERE	50.00	65.00
☐	56	SONS OF FREEDOM	50.00	65.00
☐	57	WINTER AT VALLEY FORGE	50.00	65.00

BI-CENTENNIAL WESTERNS

☐	58	BARBER	30.00	40.00
☐	59	FIREFIGHTER NO. 3	40.00	55.00
☐	60	INDIAN WEAVER	30.00	40.00
☐	61	PHOTOGRAPHER	30.00	40.00
☐	62	RAINMAKER	30.00	40.00
☐	63	SATURDAY NIGHT	27.00	38.00
☐	64	TRAPPER	30.00	40.00

BIRD SERIES
(1972-74)

☐	65	BLUEBIRD—WISCONSIN	45.00	60.00
☐	66	BLUEJAY	45.00	60.00
☐	67	PEREGRINE FALCON	45.00	60.00
☐	68	MEADOWLARK	40.00	55.00
☐	69	SWALLOW	50.00	65.00
☐	70	SCREECH OWL	50.00	70.00

CIRCUS SERIES
(Miniatures)

☐	71	BURMESE LADY	14.00	19.00
☐	72	THE BAKER....................................	12.00	17.00
☐	73	FAT LADY	13.00	17.00
☐	74	FIRE EATER	13.00	17.00
☐	75	GIANT WITH MIDGET	13.00	17.00

☐ 76	SNAKE CHARMER	13.00	17.00
☐ 77	STRONG MAN	13.00	17.00
☐ 78	SWORD SWALLOWER	13.00	17.00
☐ 79	TATTOOED LADY	13.00	17.00

DOG SERIES
(Miniatures)

☐ 80	BOXER	14.00	20.00
☐ 81	COCKER SPANIEL	12.00	17.00
☐ 82	COLLIE	14.00	20.00
☐ 83	POINTER	14.00	20.00
☐ 84	POODLE	14.00	20.00

EUROPEAN WORKER SERIES

☐ 85	THE COBBLER	50.00	65.00
☐ 86	THE HORSESHOER	50.00	65.00
☐ 87	THE POTTER	50.00	65.00
☐ 88	THE SILVERSMITH	50.00	65.00
☐ 89	THE WATCHMAKER	50.00	65.00
☐ 90	THE WOODWORKER	50.00	65.00

ORIENTAL WORKER SERIES

☐ 91	BASKET WEAVER	22.00	30.001
☐ 92	EGG MERCHANT	22.00	30.00
☐ 93	GARDNER	22.00	30.00
☐ 94	SCULPTOR	22.00	30.00
☐ 95	TEA VENDOR	22.00	30.00
☐ 96	TIMEKEEPER	22.00	30.00

SPORTS SERIES

☐ 97	BASEBALL	22.00	30.00
☐ 98	BASKETBALL	22.00	30.00
☐ 99	BOXING	22.00	30.00
☐ 100	FOOTBALL	22.00	30.00
☐ 101	HOCKEY	22.00	30.00

TROPICAL BIRD SERIES
(Miniatures)

☐ 102	BLUE CROWNED CHLOROPHONIA	12.00	16.00
☐ 103	EMERALD TOUCANET	12.00	16.00
☐ 104	NORTHERN ROYAL FLYCATCHER	12.00	16.00
☐ 105	PAINTED BUNTING	12.00	16.00
☐ 106	SCARLET MACAW	12.00	16.00
☐ 107	YELLOW HEADED AMAZON	12.00	16.00

OTHER LIONSTONE BOTTLES

☐ 108	BUCCANEER	50.00	70.00
☐ 109	COWGIRL	50.00	70.00
☐ 110	DANCE HALL GIRL	50.00	70.00
☐ 111	FALCON	55.00	75.00
☐ 112	FIREFIGHTER NO. 2	60.00	80.00
☐ 113	INDIAN MOTHER & PAPOOSE	55.00	75.00
☐ 114	ROSES ON PARADE	80.00	110.00
☐ 115	SCREECH OWLS	50.00	65.00
☐ 116	THE PERFESSER	50.00	65.00
☐ 117	UNSER-OLSONITE EAGLE	55.00	70.00

OTHER MINIATURES

☐118	CLIFF SWALLOW MINIATURE	13.00	18.00
☐119	DANCE HALL GIRL MINIATURE	15.00	22.00
☐120	FIREFIGHTER EMBLEM	24.00	31.00
☐121	FIREFIGHTER ENGINE NO. 8	24.00	31.00
☐122	FIREFIGHTER ENGINE NO. 10	24.00	31.00
☐123	HORSESHOE MINIATURE	14.00	20.00
☐124	KENTUCKY DERBY RACE HORSE *(Cannanade)*	33.00	43.00
☐125	SAHARA INVITATIONAL NO. 1	33.00	43.00
☐126	SAHARA INVITATIONAL NO. 2	33.00	43.00
☐127	SHOOT OUT AT THE OK CORRAL	320.00	375.00

LUXARDO BOTTLES

Made in Torreglia, Italy, the Girolamo Luxardo bottles boast a long and distinctive history. Importation into the U.S. began in 1930, gradually acquiring an impressive following among American collectors. Chiefly a manufacturer of wine, Luxardo also sells liquors.

The Luxardo line, extremely well modeled and meticulously colored, captures the spirit of Renaissance glass. Varying hues of color are blended on most specimens which radiate brilliantly when light shines through the bottles. The effective coloring techniques of the Luxardo bottles compare to those of ancient Egypt where color was the most important consideration. While Egyptian bottles were often colored garishly, the Luxardos carefully balance splashiness and restraint — the dominant colors never obscure the pastel shades.

Many of Luxardo's bottles, both glass and majolica, are figural. Natural history subjects as well as classical themes predominate. Most of the majolica decanters can be reused as vases, jars, lamp bases, or ash trays.

The firms maintains a regular schedule for its bottle production. Between three to six new designs are chosen each January for that year's production. The most popular, such as the *Cellini* bottle introduced in the early 1950's, continue to be used. Occasionally a design is discontinued after just one year. The Chess Set, produced in 1959, was discontinued because of manufacturing difficulty.

Unfortunately, the names and dates of production of the earlier Luxardo decanters are mostly unknown, due to many owners removing the paper identification labels.

The rare Zara decanters, made before World War II, are expected to increase further in value and scarcity. The *"First Born"* of the Murano Venetion glass, if ever located, will command a very strong price. Eventually, all the Naponelli "signed" decanters should rise markedly in value because of the small quantities issued.

Although the knowledgeable dealers are aware of the Luxardo prices, remarkable bargains are sometimes obtainable by shopping at garage sales, thrift stores and charity outlets.

Specimens in mint condition with the original manufacturer's label always command the highest sums. All prices listed are for empty bottles, in Fine to Mint condition.

If current or recent Luxardo bottles are not available at your local spirits dealer, the dealer can order them from the American distributor, Hans Schonewalk, American Beverage Brokers, 420 Market Street, San Francisco, California 94111.

A

NO.	DESCRIPTION	PRICE RANGE	
☐ 1	**ALABASTER FISH—FIGURAL** *(c. 1960-67-68)*	19.00	26.00
☐ 2	**ALABASTER GOOSE—FIGURAL** *(c. 1960-67-68)*		
	Green-white, wings, etc.	19.00	26.00
☐ 3	**AMPULLA—FLASK** *(c. 1958-59)*	14.00	19.00
☐ 4	**APOTHECARY JAR** *(c. 1960)*		
	Hand painted multicolor, green and black	11.00	16.00
☐ 5	**AUTUMN LEAVES DECANTER** *(c. 1952)*		
	Hand painted, 2 handles	10.00	15.00
☐ 6	**APPLE FIGURAL** *(c. 1960)*		
	Yellow apple, green leaves	10.00	15.00
☐ 7	**ASSYRIAN ASHTRAY DECANTER** *(c. 1961)*		
	Grey, tan and black	16.00	22.00

☐ 8 **AUTUMN WINE PITCHER** *(c. 1958)*
Hand painted country scene, handled pitcher **19.00** **26.00**

B

☐ 9 **BABYLON DECANTER** *(c. 1960)*
Dark green and gold **16.00** **23.00**
☐ 10 **BABY AMPHORAS** *(c. 1956)*
Six hand painted miniature bottles set vari-colored **16.00** **23.00**
☐ 11 **BAROQUE GOLD RUBY AMPHORA** *(c. 1955)*
Ruby red and gold. Gold handles **28.00** **37.00**
☐ 12 **BAROQUE GOLD TURQUOISE PITCHER** *(c. 1956)*
Turquoise bottle with gold handle and trim **22.00** **29.00**
☐ 13 ½ GOLD HANDLES and gold trim on ruby red bottle **20.00** **28.00**
☐ 14 **BIZANTINA** *(c. 1959)*
Gold embossed design white body **14.00** **19.00**
☐ 15 **BLUE FIAMMETTA or VERMILLIAN—**
Decanter *(c. 1957)* **20.00** **27.00**
☐ 16 **BLUE & GOLD AMPHORA** *(c. 1968)*
Blue and gold with pastoral scene in white oval **14.00** **19.00**
☐ 17 **BROCCA (PITCHER)** *(c. 1958)*
White background pitcher with handle, multicolor flowers,
green leaves **28.00** **37.00**
☐ 18 **BUDDHA GODDESS FIGURAL** *(c. 1961)*
Goddess head in green-gray stone **14.00** **19.00**
Miniature **11.00** **16.00**
☐ 19 **BURMA ASH TRAY—SPECIALTY** *(c. 1960)*
Embossed white dancing figure, dark green background . **13.00** **18.00**
☐ 20 **BURMA PITCHER—SPECIALTY** *(c. 1960)*
Green and gold, white embossed dancing figure **14.00** **19.00**

C

☐ 21 **CALYPSO GIRL—FIGURAL** *(c. 1962)*
Black West Indian girl, flower headress in bright color ... **14.00** **19.00**
☐ 22 **CANDLESTICK—ALABASTER** *(c. 1961)* **20.00** **28.00**
☐ 23 **CELLINI VASE** *(c. 1958-68)*
Glass and silver decanter, fancy **14.00** **19.00**
☐ 24 **CELLINI VASE** *(c. 1957)*
Glass and silver handled decanter, fancy, with serpent
handle **14.00** **19.00**
☐ 25 **CERAMIC BARREL** *(c. 1968)*
Barrel shape, barrel color, painted flowers, embossed
scroll with cameo head on decorative stand **14.00** **19.00**
☐ 26 **CHERRY BASKET—FIGURAL** *(c. 1960)*
White basket, red cherries **14.00** **19.00**
☐ 27 **CLASSICAL FRAGMENT—SPECIALTY** *(c. 1961)*
Embossed Classic Roman female figure and vase **25.00** **33.00**
☐ 28 **COCKTAIL SHAKER** *(c. 1957)*
Glass and silver decanter, silver plated top **14.00** **19.00**
☐ 29 **COFFEE CARAFE—SPECIALTY** *(c. 1962)*
"Old-time" coffee pot, with handle and spout, white with
blue flowers **14.00** **19.00**

☐ 30 **CURVA VASO VASE** *(c. 1961)*
Green, green and white, ruby red **22.00**   **29.00**

D

☐ 31 **DERUTA CAMEO AMPHORA** *(c. 1959)*
Colorful floral scrolls and cameo head on eggshell white 2
handled vase **20.00**   **27.00**
☐ 32 **DERUTA AMPHORA** *(c. 1956)*
Colorful floral design on white 2 handled decanter **11.00**   **16.00**
☐ 33 **DERUTA PITCHER** *(c. 1953)*
Multicolor flowers on base perugia, white single-handled
pitcher **11.00**   **16.00**
☐ 34 **DIANA—DECANTER** *(c. 1956)*
White figure of Diana with deer on black single handled
decanter **11.00**   **16.00**
☐ 35 **DOGAL SILVER & GREEN DECANTER** *(c. 1952-56)*
Hand painted gondola **14.00**   **19.00**
☐ 36 **DOGAL SILVER SMOKE DECANTER** *(c. 1952-55)*
Hand painted gondola **14.00**   **19.00**
☐ 37 **DOGAL SILVER SMOKE DECANTER** *(c. 1953-54)*
Hand painted gondola **11.00**   **16.00**
☐ 38 **DOGAL SILVER RUBY** *(c. 1952-56)*
Hand painted gondola, silver band neck **14.00**   **18.00**
☐ 39 **DOGAL SILVER SMOKE DECANTER** *(c. 1956)*
Hand painted silver clouds and gondola **11.00**   **16.00**
☐ 40 **DOGAL SILVER SMOKE DECANTER** *(c. 1956)*
Hand painted gondola, buildings, flowers, neck bands . . .   **14.00**   **18.00**
☐ 41 **DOGAL SILVER RUBY DECANTER** *(c. 1956)*
Hand painted Venetian scene and flowers **17.00**   **22.00**
☐ 42 **DOLPHIN FIGURAL** *(c. 1959)*
Yellow, green, blue **42.00**   **57.00**
☐ 43 **"DOUGHNUT" BOTTLE** *(c. 1960)* **CLOCK BOTTLE** *(c. 1959)*
Cherry este working clock in doughnut shape bottle **14.00**   **18.00**
☐ 44 **DRAGON AMPHORA** *(c. 1953)*
2 handled white decanter with colorful dragon and flowers . .   **14.00**   **18.00**
☐ 45 **DRAGON PITCHER** *(c. 1958)*
One handle, white pitcher, color dragon and scroll work . .   **14.00**   **18.00**
☐ 46 **DUCK-GREEN GLASS FIGURAL** *(c. 1960)*
Green and amber duck, clear glass base **20.00**   **27.00**

E

☐ 47 **EAGLE, ONYX** *(c. 1970)* **19.00**   **26.00**
☐ 48 **EGYPTIAN—SPECIALTY** *(c. 1960)*
2 handle amphora, Egyptian design on tan and gold back-
ground **14.00**   **19.00**
☐ 49 **EUGANEAN BRONZE** *(c. 1952-55)* **14.00**   **19.00**
☐ 50 **EUGANEAN COPPERED** *(c. 1962-55)*
Majolica **13.00**   **18.00**
☐ 51 **ETRUSCA DECANTER** *(c. 1959)*
Single handle black Greek design on tan background **14.00**   **19.00**
Except A, earthen brown **13.00**   **18.00**

F

☐ 52 **FAENZA DECANTER** *(c. 1952-56)*
Colorful country scene on white single handle decanter .. **21.00** **28.00**

☐ 53 **FIGHTING COCKS** *(c. 1962)*
Combination decanter and ashtray, black and red fighting birds **14.00** **19.00**

☐ 54 **FISH—GREEN & GOLD GLASS FIGURAL** *(c. 1960)*
Green and silver and gold, clear glass base **16.00** **21.00**

☐ 55 **FISH—RUBY MURANO GLASS FIGURAL** *(c. 1961)*
Ruby red tones of glass **26.00** **37.00**

☐ 56 **FLORENTINE MAJOLICA** *(c. 1956)*
Round handled decanter, painted pitcher, yellow, dragon, blue wings **21.00** **27.00**

G

☐ 57 **GAMBIA** *(c. 1961)*
Black princess, kneeling holding tray, gold trim, 10¾" ... **14.00** **19.00**

☐ 58 **GOLDEN FAKIR**
Seated snake charmer, with flute and snakes, gold **26.00** **37.00**
1961—Fakir 1960, black and gray **26.00** **37.00**

☐ 59 **GONDOLA** *(c. 1959)*
Highly glazed "abstract" gondola and gondolier in black, orange and yellow. Stopper on upper prow, 12¾" **21.00** **27.00**

☐ 60 **GONDOLA MINIATURE** *(c. 1959)*
Same as above, 4½" **11.00** **16.00**

☐ 61 **GONDOLA** *(c. 1960)*
Same as 1959, stopper moved from prow to stern **14.00** **19.00**
Miniature (c. 1960) **11.00** **15.00**

☐ 62 **GRAPES, PEAR FIGURAL** **14.00** **19.00**

M

☐ 63 **MAYAN** *(c. 1960)*
A Mayan temple God head mask, brown, yellow, black, white, 11" **14.00** **19.00**

☐ 64 **MOSIAC ASHTRAY** *(c. 1959)*
Combination decanter ashtray, mosaic pattern of rearing horse, black, yellow, green, 11½" **14.00** **19.00**
Miniature 6", black, green **8.00** **11.00**

N

☐ 65 **NUBIAN**
Kneeling black figure, gold dress and headress, 9½" **14.00** **19.00**
Miniature, as above, 4¾" **8.00** **11.00**

O

☐ 66 **OPAL MAJOLICA** (c. 1957)
Two gold handles, translucent opal top, pink base, also
used as lamp base, 10" **14.00**   **19.00**

P

☐ 67 **PENGUIN—MURANO GLASS FIGURAL** (c. 1968)
Black and white penguin, crystal base **26.00**   **37.00**
☐ 68 **PHEASANT—RED & GOLD FIGURAL** (c. 1960)
Red and gold glass bird on crystal base **23.00**   **35.00**
☐ 69 **PHEASANT—MURANO GLASS FIGURAL** (c. 1960)
Red and clear glass on a crystal base **26.00**   **37.00**
☐ 70 **PRIMAVERA AMPHORA** (c. 1958)
2 handled vase shape, with floral design in yellow, green
and blue, 9¾" **14.00**   **19.00**
☐ 71 **PUPPY—CUCCIOLO GLASS FIGURAL** (c. 1961)
Amber and green glass **26.00**   **37.00**
☐ 72 **PUPPY—MURANO GLASS FIGURAL** (c. 1960)
Amber glass, crystal base **26.00**   **37.00**

S

NO. **DESCRIPTION**
☐ 73 **SILVER BLUE DECANTER** (c. 1952-55)
Hand painted silver flowers and leaves **22.00**   **28.00**
☐ 74 **SILVER BROWN DECANTER** (c. 1952-55)
Hand painted silver flowers and leaves **26.00**   **37.00**
☐ 75 **SIR LANCELOT** (c. 1962)
Figure of English knight in full armor with embossed
shield, tan-gray w/gold, 12" **14.00**   **19.00**
☐ 76 **SPRINGBOX AMPHORA** (c. 1952)
Vase with handle, leaping African deer with floral and lat-
tice background, black, brown, 9¾" **14.00**   **19.00**
☐ 77 **SQUIRREL GLASS FIGURAL** (c. 1968)
Amethyst colored squirrel on crystal base **20.00**   **28.00**
☐ 78 **SUDAN** (c. 1960)
2 handle classic vase, incused figures, African motif in
browns, blue, yellow and gray, 13½" **14.00**   **19.00**

T

☐ 79 **TOWER OF FRUIT—MAJOLICAS**
TORRE BIANCA (c. 1962)
White and grey tower of fruit, 10¼" **14.00**   **19.00**
☐ 80 **TORRE ROSA** (c. 1962)
Rose tinted tower of fruit, 10¼" **15.00**   **22.00**
☐ 81 **TORRE TINTA** (c. 1962)
Multicolor tower of fruit, natural shades **14.00**   **19.00**
☐ 82 **TOWER OF FRUIT** (c. 1968)
Various fruits in natural colors, 22¼" **14.00**   **19.00**

McCORMICK

The McCormick bottles are made for retailing McCormick Irish Whiskey. There are four different series: Cars, Famous Americans, Frontiersman Decanters and Gunfighters. The category for cars includes various forms of transportation. The lengthiest series has been the Famous Americans, encompassing celebrities from colonial times to the 20th century. Released in limited numbers, the prices on all of the McCormick's are automatically higher than most figurals.

BARREL SERIES

NO.	DESCRIPTION	PRICE RANGE	
☐ 1	**BARREL WITH STAND AND SHOT GLASSES** *(1958)*	28.00	36.00
☐ 2	**BARREL** *(1968)*		
	With stand and plain hoops	14.00	18.00
☐ 3	**BARREL** *(1968)*		
	With stand and gold hoops	18.00	26.00

BIRD SERIES

NO.	DESCRIPTION	PRICE RANGE	
☐ 4	**BLUE JAY** *(1971)*	25.00	35.00
☐ 5	**WOOD DUCK** *(1980)*	25.00	35.00
☐ 6	**GAMBEL'S QUAIL** *(1982)*	25.00	35.00
☐ 7	**RING NECKED PHEASANT** *(1982)*	25.00	35.00

BULL SERIES

NO.	DESCRIPTION	PRICE RANGE	
☐ 8	**HEREFORD** *(1972)*	42.00	48.00
☐ 9	**BRAHMA** *(1973)*	40.00	46.00
☐ 10	**CHAROLAIS** *(1974)*	35.00	42.00
☐ 11	**MEXICAN FIGHTING** *(1974)*	30.00	38.00
☐ 12	**TEXAS LONGHORN** *(1974)*	34.00	40.00

CAR SERIES

NO.	DESCRIPTION	PRICE RANGE	
☐ 13	**THE PONY EXPRESS**	30.00	42.00
☐ 14	**THE SAND BUGGY COMMEMORATIVE DECANTER**	27.00	35.00

CONFEDERATE SERIES

NO.	DESCRIPTION	PRICE RANGE	
☐ 15	**JEFFERSON DAVIS**	16.00	23.00
☐ 16	**STONEWALL JACKSON**	16.00	23.00
☐ 17	**ROBERT E. LEE**	23.00	32.00
☐ 18	**JEB STUART**	16.00	23.00

COUNTRY & WESTERN SERIES

NO.	DESCRIPTION	PRICE RANGE	
☐ 19	**HANK WILLIAMS, SR.** *(1980)*	60.00	70.00
☐ 20	**HANK WILLIAMS, JR.** *(1980)*	60.00	70.00
☐ 21	**TOM T. HALL** *(1980)*	60.00	70.00

ELVIS PRESLEY SERIES

NO.	DESCRIPTION	PRICE RANGE	
☐ 22	**ELVIS '77** *(1978)*	70.00	90.00
☐ 23	**ELVIS BUST** *(1978)*	35.00	45.00
☐ 24	**ELVIS '55** *(1979)*	65.00	85.00
☐ 25	**ELVIS '68** *(1980)*	60.00	70.00
☐ 26	**ELVIS '77** *(1979) Mini*	32.00	40.00

☐ 27	ELVIS '55 *(1980) Mini*	32.00	40.00
☐ 28	ELVIS GOLD *(1979)*	200.00	250.00
☐ 29	ELVIS SILVER *(1980)*	180.00	225.00
☐ 30	ELVIS '68 *(1981) Mini*	32.00	40.00
☐ 31	ELVIS KARATE	55.00	65.00
☐ 32	ELVIS, DESIGNER I		
	Music box plays "Are You Lonesome Tonight?"	55.00	75.00
☐ 33	ELVIS, DESIGNER II		
	Music box plays "It's Now or Never."	55.00	75.00

FAMOUS AMERICAN PORTRAIT SERIES

☐ 34	ALEXANDER GRAHAM BELL		
	With Apron	28.00	40.00
☐ 35	GEORGE WASHINGTON CARVER	28.00	40.00
☐ 36	WILLIAM CLARK	23.00	31.00
☐ 37	THOMAS EDISON	33.00	44.00
☐ 38	HENRY FORD	30.00	42.00
☐ 39	ULYSSES S. GRANT		
	With coffee pot and cup of coffee	30.00	42.00
☐ 40	MERIWETHER LEWIS	26.00	35.00
☐ 41	ABE LINCOLN		
	With law book in hand	26.00	35.00
☐ 42	CHARLES LINDBERGH	35.00	47.00
☐ 43	ROBERT E. PERRY	26.00	35.00
☐ 44	POCAHONTAS	30.00	42.00
☐ 45	ELEANOR ROOSEVELT	26.00	35.00
☐ 46	CAPTAIN JOHN SMITH	29.00	39.00

FOOTBALL MASCOTS

☐ 47	ALABAMA BAMA	32.00	40.00
☐ 48	ARIZONA WILDCATS	22.00	28.00
☐ 49	ARIZONA SUN DEVILS	32.00	40.00
☐ 50	ARKANSAS HOGS *(1972)*	32.00	40.00
☐ 51	AUBURN WAR EAGLES	15.00	22.00
☐ 52	BAYLOR BEARS *(1972)*	22.00	28.00
☐ 53	DRAKE BULLDOGS *(1974))*		
	Blue helmet and jersey	20.00	28.00
☐ 54	GEORGIA BULLDOGS		
	Black helmet and red jersey	12.00	18.00
☐ 55	GEORGIA TECH YELLOWJACKETS	12.00	18.00
☐ 56	HOUSTON COUGARS *(1972)*	22.00	30.00
☐ 57	INDIANA HOOSIERS *(1974)*	12.00	18.00
☐ 58	IOWA HAWKEYES *(1974)*	45.00	55.00
☐ 59	IOWA CYCLONES *(1974)*	45.00	55.00
☐ 60	IOWA PURPLE PANTHERS	25.00	32.00
☐ 61	LOUISANA STATE TIGERS *(1974)*	12.00	18.00
☐ 62	MICHIGAN STATE SPARATANS	12.00	18.00
☐ 63	MICHIGAN WOLVERINES *(1974)*	22.00	30.00
☐ 64	MINNESOTA GOPHERS *(1974)*	12.00	18.00
☐ 65	MISSISSIPPI REBELS *(1974)*	12.00	18.00
☐ 66	MISSISSIPPI STATE BULLDOGS *(1974))*		
	Red helmet and jersey	12.00	18.00
☐ 67	MISSOURI UNIVERSITY TIGERS *(1974)*	28.00	36.00
☐ 68	NEBRASKA CORNHUSKERS *(1974)*	12.00	18.00

☐ 69	**NEW MEXICO LOBO**	30.00	38.00
☐ 70	**OKLAHOMA SOUTHER COWBOY** *(1974)*	28.00	36.00
☐ 71	**OKLAHOMA SOONERS WAGON** *(1974)*	20.00	28.00
☐ 72	**OREGON BEAVERS** *(1974)*	12.00	18.00
☐ 73	**OREGON DUCKS** *(1974)*	12.00	18.00
☐ 74	**PURDUE BOILERMAKER** *(1974)*	12.00	18.00
☐ 75	**RICE OWLS** *(1972)*	22.00	30.00
☐ 76	**S.M.U. MUSTANGS** *(1972)*	22.00	30.00
☐ 77	**TEXAS A&M AGGIES** *(1972)*	22.00	30.00
☐ 78	**TCU HORNED FROGS** *(1972)*	25.00	32.00
☐ 79	**TEXAS TACH RAIDERS** *(1972)*	22.00	30.00
☐ 80	**TEXAS HORNS** *(1972)*	22.00	32.00
☐ 81	**TENNESSEE VOLUNTEERS** *(1974)*	22.00	32.00
☐ 82	**WASHINGTON COUGARS** *(1974)*	12.00	18.00
☐ 83	**WASHINGTON HUSKIES** *(1974)*	12.00	18.00
☐ 84	**WISCONSIN BADGERS** *(1974)*	12.00	18.00

FRONTIERSMEN COMMEMORATIVE DECANTERS 1972

☐ 85	**DANIEL BOONE**	30.00	42.00
☐ 86	**JIM BOWIE**	30.00	42.00
☐ 87	**KIT CARSON**	23.00	32.00
☐ 88	**DAVIE CROCKETT**	26.00	35.00

GENERAL

☐ 89	**AIRPLANE — SPIRIT OF ST. LOUIS** *(1969)*	80.00	90.00
☐ 90	**AMERICAN BALD EAGLE** *(1982)*	30.00	40.00
☐ 91	**BUFFALO BILL** *(1979)*	45.00	55.00
☐ 92	**CAR — PACKARD 1937** *(1980)*		
	Black or cream. First in a series of classic cars. Rolling		
	wheels and vinyl seats	65.00	75.00
☐ 93	**CIAO BABY** *(1978)*	25.00	35.00
☐ 94	**CLOCK — CUCKOO** *(1971)*	25.00	35.00
☐ 95	**CLOCK — QUEEN ANNE** *(1970)*	25.00	35.00
☐ 96	**DE WITT CLINTON ENGINE** *(1970)*	40.00	50.00
☐ 97	**FRENCH TELEPHONE** *(1969)*	28.00	34.00
☐ 98	**GLOBE — ANGELICA** *(1971)*	25.00	32.00
☐ 99	**HUTCHINSON KANSAS CENTENNIAL** *(1972)*	12.00	18.00
☐ 100	**JESTER** *(1972)*	20.00	28.00
☐ 101	**JIMMY DURANTE** *(1981)*		
	With music box, plays "Inka Dinka Do."	35.00	45.00
☐ 102	**J.R. EWING** *(1980)*		
	With music box, plays theme song from "Dallas."	35.00	45.00
☐ 103	**JOPLIN MINER** *(1972)*	20.00	28.00
☐ 104	**JULIA BULETTE** *(1974)*	150.00	180.00
☐ 105	**LARGE MOUTH BASS** *(1982)*	20.00	28.00
☐ 106	**LOBSTERMAN** *(1979)*	45.00	55.00
☐ 107	**McCORMICK CENTENNIAL** *(1956)*	125.00	150.00
☐ 108	**MIKADO** *(1980)*	185.00	220.00
☐ 109	**MO. SESQUICENTENNIAL CHINA** *(1970)*	8.00	12.00
☐ 110	**MO. SESQUICENTENNIAL GLASS** *(1971)*	6.00	10.00
☐ 111	**MUHAMMAD ALI** *(1981)*	20.00	28.00
☐ 112	**U.S. MARSHAL** *(1979)*	35.00	45.00
☐ 113	**OZARK IKE** *(1979)*	45.00	55.00
☐ 114	**PAUL BUNYAN** *(1979)*	45.00	55.00

☐ 115	**PONY EXPRESS** *(1978)*	40.00	50.00
☐ 116	**PIONEER THEATRE** *(1972)*	8.00	12.00
☐ 117	**RENAULT RACER** *(1969)*	40.00	50.00
☐ 118	**THELMA LU** *(1982)*	15.00	20.00
☐ 119	**YACHT AMERICANA** *(1971)*	30.00	38.00
☐ 120	**MARK TWAIN** *(1977)*	25.00	35.00
☐ 121	**WILL ROGERS** *(1977)*	28.00	38.00
☐ 122	**HENRY FORD** *(1977)*	28.00	38.00
☐ 123	**STEPHEN F. AUSTIN** *(1977)*	25.00	35.00
☐ 124	**SAM HOUSTON** *(1977)*	25.00	35.00

GUNFIGHTER SERIES

☐ 125	**BLACK BART**	26.00	35.00
☐ 126	**WYATT EARP**	21.00	30.00
☐ 127	**DOC HOLIDAY**	28.00	37.00
☐ 128	**JESSE JAMES**	26.00	35.00
☐ 129	**CALAMITY JANE**	28.00	37.00
☐ 130	**BILLY THE KID**	26.00	35.00
☐ 131	**BAT MASTERSON**	28.00	37.00
☐ 132	**WILD BILL HICKOK**	21.00	30.00

JUG SERIES

☐ 133	**PLATTE VALLEY** *(1953)* *Traditional jug shape with two small handles from shoulders to neck*	10.00	16.00
☐ 134	**GIN JUG**	6.00	10.00
☐ 135	**VODKA JUG**	6.00	10.00
☐ 136	**OLD HOLIDAY BOURBON** *(1956)* *Embossed lettering in various sizes*	6.00	18.00

KING ARTHUR SERIES

☐ 137	**KING ARTHUR ON THRONE**	50.00	65.00
☐ 138	**MERLIN THE WIZARD WITH HIS WISE OLD MAGICAL ROBE** *(c. 1979)*	45.00	60.00
☐ 139	**QUEEN GUINEVERE, THE GEM OF ROYAL COURT**	45.00	60.00
☐ 140	**SIR LANCELOT OF THE THE LAKE IN ARMOR A KNIGHT OF ROUNDTABLE**	45.00	60.00

THE LITERARY SERIES

☐ 141	**TOM SAWYER** *(1980)* *Stands in front of a fence scratching his head*	40.00	50.00
☐ 142	**HUCK FINN** *(1980)* *Sets fishing, leaning on a tree trunk and smoking a pipe* .	40.00	50.00

MINIATURES

☐ 143	**PATRIOT MINIATURE SET (8)** *(1976)*	175.00	200.00
☐ 144	**MINIATURE SPIRIT OF '76** *(1977)*	20.00	30.00
☐ 145	**MINIATURE GUNFIGHTERS (8)** *(1977)*	110.00	140.00
☐ 146	**CONFEDERATES MINIATURE SET (4)** *(1978)*	50.00	75.00
☐ 147	**MINIATURE NOBLE** *(1978)*	14.00	20.00
☐ 148	**MARK TWAIN MINIATURE** *(1978)*	12.00	18.00
☐ 149	**WILL ROGERS MINIATURE** *(1978)*	18.00	18.00
☐ 150	**HENRY FORD MINIATURE** *(1978)*	18.00	18.00
☐ 151	**CHARLES LINDBERGH MINIATURE** *(1978)*	12.00	18.00

☐ 152	**ROSE COLLECTION** *(1980)*	80.00	90.00
☐ 153	**PONY EXPRESS MINIATURE** *(1980)*	20.00	30.00
☐ 154	**MINIATURE JUPITER 60 TRAIN** *(1980)*	65.00	75.00

THE PATRIOTS

☐ 155	**GEORGE WASHINGTON** *(1975)*	35.00	45.00
☐ 156	**BETSY ROSS** *(1975)*	30.00	40.00
☐ 157	**THOMAS JEFFERSON** *(1975)*	20.00	28.00
☐ 158	**BENJAMIN FRANKLIN** *(1975)*	20.00	28.00
☐ 159	**PAUL REVERE** *(1975)*	35.00	45.00
☐ 160	**JOHN PAUL JONES** *(1975)*	20.00	28.00
☐ 161	**JOHN HANCOCK** *(1975)*	20.00	28.00
☐ 162	**PATRICK HENRY** *(1975)*	20.00	28.00
☐ 163	**SPIRIT OF '76** *(1976)*	80.00	90.00

PIRATES SERIES

☐ 164	**PIRATE, NO. 1** *(1972)*	12.00	16.00
☐ 165	**PIRATE, NO. 2** *(1972)*	12.00	16.00
☐ 166	**PIRATE, NO. 3** *(1972)*	8.00	12.00
☐ 167	**PIRATE, NO. 4** *(1972)*	8.00	12.00
☐ 168	**PIRATE, NO. 5** *(1972)*	8.00	12.00
☐ 169	**PIRATE, NO. 6** *(1972)*	8.00	12.00
☐ 170	**PIRATE, NO. 7** *(1972)*	8.00	12.00
☐ 171	**PIRATE, NO. 8** *(1972)*	8.00	12.00
☐ 172	**PIRATE, NO. 9** *(1972)*	8.00	12.00
☐ 173	**PIRATE, NO. 10** *(1972)*	20.00	28.00
☐ 174	**PIRATE, NO. 11** *(1972)*	20.00	28.00
☐ 175	**PIRATE, NO. 12** *(1972)*	20.00	28.00

RURAL AMERICANA SERIES

☐ 176	**WOMAN WASHING CLOTHES** *(1980)* *Setting on a low table*	40.00	50.00
☐ 177	**WOMAN FEEDING CHECKENS** *(1980)* *Young woman with white bonnet and apron tossing feed* *two checkens at her feet*	40.00	50.00

SHRINE SERIES

☐ 178	**JESTER (MIRTH KING)** *(1972)*	35.00	45.00
☐ 179	**THE NOBLE** *(1976)*	25.00	32.00
☐ 180	**DUNE BUGGY** *(1976)*	30.00	40.00

SPORTS SERIES

☐ 181	**AIR RACE PYLON** *(1970)*	10.00	16.00
☐ 182	**AIR RACE PROPELLER** *(1971)*	15.00	20.00
☐ 183	**JOHNNY RODGERS NO. 1** *(1972)*	160.00	195.00
☐ 184	**JOHNNY RODGERS NO. 2** *(1973)*	70.00	85.00
☐ 185	**K.C. CHIEFS** *(1969)*	40.00	50.00
☐ 186	**K.C. ROYALS** *(1971)*	10.00	16.00
☐ 187	**MUHAMMID ALI** *(1980)*	45.00	55.00
☐ 188	**NEBRASKA FOOTBALL PLAYER** *(1972)*	22.00	30.00
☐ 189	**SKIBOB** *(1971)*	12.00	18.00

TRAIN SERIES

☐ 190	**JUPITER ENGINE** *(1969)*	30.00	40.00

☐ 191	**WOOD TENDER** *(1969)*	30.00	40.00
☐ 192	**MAIL CAR** *(1970)*	70.00	80.00
☐ 193	**PASSENGER CAR** *(1970)*	70.00	80.00

WARRIOR SERIES

☐ 194	**BERSAGLIERI** *(1969)*	16.00	24.00
☐ 195	**CENTURION** *(1969)*	16.00	24.00
☐ 196	**GARIBALDI** *(1969)*	16.00	24.00
☐ 197	**NAPOLEON** *(1969)*	16.00	24.00

THE BOTTLES LISTED BELOW WERE DESTROYED

GUNFIGHTER SERIES *(c. 1972)*
FRONTIERSMEN SERIES *(c. 1975)*
PATRIOT DECANTERS *(c. 1976)*
FAMOUS AMERICANS *(c. 1976)*

O.B.R. BOTTLES (OLD BLUE RIBBON)

Old Blue Ribbon (OBR) bottles are made to contain the company's liquors. With a relatively late start in issuing figural bottles, this firm has released a large number in recent years. The OBR bottles with historical themes are distinctive for their realism, such as the "Jupiter '60" series depicting various railroad cars from the 19th century. OBR is the only bottle maker with a Hockey Series; each bottle in this group relates to a different professional hockey team. The company also issues a Transportation Series, which includes such diverse representations as a hot-air ballon and a 5th Avenue New York Bus.

O.B.R. (OLD BLUE RIBBON)

NO.	DESCRIPTION	PRICE RANGE	
☐ 1	AIR RACE DECANTER (PYLON)	15.00	22.00
☐ 2	BLUE BIRD	14.00	19.00
☐ 3	CABOOSE MKT	13.00	17.00
☐ 4	JUPITER '60 MAIL CAR	13.00	17.00
☐ 5	JUPITER '60 PASSENGER CAR	16.00	23.00
☐ 6	JUPITER '60 WOOD TENDER	13.00	17.00
☐ 7	JUPITER '60 LOCOMOTIVE	15.00	22.00
☐ 8	K.C. ROYALS	18.00	24.00
☐ 9	PIERCE—ARROW	14.00	20.00
☐ 10	"SANTA MARIA" COLUMBUS SHIP	15.00	22.00
☐ 11	"TITANIC" OCEAN LINER	19.00	28.00

O.B.R. TRANSPORTATION SERIES

☐ 12	BALLOON	9.00	12.00
☐ 13	5TH AVE. BUS	12.00	16.00
☐ 14	PRAIRIE SCHOONER	15.00	22.00
☐ 15	RIVER QUEEN	15.00	22.00
	RIVER QUEEN—GOLD	18.00	24.00

O.B.R. HOCKEY SERIES

☐ 16	BOSTON BRUINS	13.00	17.00
☐ 17	CHICAGO BLACK HAWKS	10.00	15.00
☐ 18	DETROIT RED WINGS	14.00	19.00
☐ 19	MINNESOTA NORTH STARS	13.00	17.00
☐ 20	NEW YORK RANGERS	17.00	24.00
☐ 21	ST. LOUIS BLUES	17.00	24.00

1972-74

☐ 22	AGING BARREL WITH SPIGOT	11.00	15.00
☐ 23	ROBERT E. LEE	24.00	32.00
☐ 24	"PIRATES"		
	Different types of Costumes EACH	14.00	19.00
☐ 25	"PLATTE VALLEY" POTTERY JUG	13.00	17.00
☐ 26	YACHT "AMERICA"	13.00	17.00

OLD FITZGERALD—OLD CABIN STILL

Old Fitzgerald bottles are made by the Old Fitzgerald Distilling Co., to contain their whiskey and bourbon. Old Fitzgeralds are sometimes called Old Cabin Still bottles after one of the brand names under which they are sold. The company issues both decanter style and figural bottles. The decanters are ceramics in various styles and colors. Its figurals portray many different Irish and American subjects. New figurals are added to the line irregularly. The number of bottles issued by this firm is small.

OLD FITZGERALD—OLD CABIN STILL

NO.	DESCRIPTION	PRICE	RANGE
☐ 1	AMERICA'S CUP COMMEMORATIVE *(c. 1970)*	15.00	22.00
☐ 2	"BLARNEY" CASTLE *(c. 1970) Porcelain*	15.00	22.00
☐ 3	BROWSING DEER DECANTER *(c. 1967)*		
	Deer and woods scene, brown, tan and white, amber stopper	15.00	22.00
☐ 4	CALIFORNIA BICENTENNIAL *(c. 1970)*	15.00	22.00
☐ 5	CANDLELITE DECANTER *(c. 1955)*		
	Removable gold candle holder mounted on flint glass, pair	14.00	19.00
☐ 6	COLONIAL DECANTER *(c. 1969) Glass*	9.00	12.00
☐ 7	GOLD COASTER DECANTER *(c. 1954)*		
	Flint glass decanter, gold metal coaster	13.00	18.00
☐ 8	GOLD WEB DECANTER *(c. 1953)*		
	Flint glass, gold web and frame fused onto decanter	13.00	18.00
☐ 9	"GOLDEN BOUGH" DECANTER *(c. 1971) Glass*	7.00	10.00
☐ 10	HILLBILLY BOTTLE—PINT *(c. 1954)*		
	"Hillbilly" on Barrel with rifle, in brown, tan, black and green, 9⅛"	13.00	18.00
☐ 11	HILLBILLY BOTTLE—QUART *(c. 1954)*		
	Same as above, 11⅜"	13.00	18.00
☐ 12	HILLBILLY BOTTLE—GALLON *(c. 1954)*		
	Same as above, gallon size, very rare	60.00	85.00
☐ 13	HILLBILLY *(c. 1969)*		
	Same bottle as 1954 "HILLBILLY", more detail and color, 11½"	13.00	18.00
☐ 14	JEWEL DECANTER *(c. 1951-52)*		
	Flint glass, beveled neck	12.00	17.00
☐ 15	LEAPING TROUT DECANTER *(c. 1969)*	11.00	16.00

☐	16	**LEPRECHAUN BOTTLE** (c. 1968)		
		Porcelain bottle, gold band, green shamrocks, Irish verse, 10⅛"	13.00	18.00
☐	17	**LSU ALUMNI DECANTER** (c. 1970)	16.00	23.00
☐	18	**MAN O' WAR DECANTER** (c. 1969) Glass	7.00	11.00
☐	19	**MEMPHIS COMMEMORATIVE** (c. 1969) Porcelain	19.00	27.00
☐	20	**OLD CABIN STILL DECANTER** (c. 1958)		
		Gold letters "OLD CABIN STILL" infused on flint glass bottle, solid faceted stopper	16.00	23.00
☐	21	**OHIO STATE CENTENNIAL** (c. 1970)	16.00	23.00
☐	22	**PILGRIM LANDING COMMEMORATIVE** (c. 1970)	13.00	18.00
☐	23	**POINTING SETTER DECANTER** (c. 1965)		
		Dog on point, brown, tan and white, glass, 12"	16.00	23.00
☐	24	**QUAIL ON THE WING DECANTER** (c. 1968)		
		Round glass bottle, 3 color design, 12"	7.00	11.00
☐	25	**"REBEL YELL RIDER"—FIGURINE** (c. 1970)		
		Confederate cavalryman bottle in 6 colors, sold only in the South, 9¾"	23.00	32.00
☐	26	**RIP VAN WINKLE FIGURINE** (c. 1970)		
		Famous Catskill character with blunderbuss and elf, multicolor, 9¼"	7.00	11.00
☐	27	**SONS OF ERIN** (c. 1969) Porcelain	9.00	12.00
☐	28	**"SONGS OF IRELAND"** (c. 1972) Porcelain	13.00	18.00
☐	29	**SOUTH CAROLINA TRICENTENNIAL** (c. 1970)	16.00	23.00
☐	30	**WELLER MASTER PIECE** (c. 1963)		
		White; porcelain apothecary bottle, rebus design, gold bands, 10⅝"	26.00	35.00
☐	31	**"WINGS ACROSS THE CONTINENT"** (c. 1972)		
		Porcelain, Duck finial	16.00	23.00

WHEATON/NULINE DECANTERS

One of the oldest American manufacturers of decorative bottles, the Wheaton Company was founded in 1888. At first it produced a general line of hand-blown and pressed glassware. Wheaton Commemorative and Nuline bottles often illustrate portraits in the 19th century manner on flasks with raised designs. These honor famous Americans as well as American historical events. Unlike most of the bottles listed in this book, the Wheaton/Nuline have often been retailed empty in gift shops. Created in the style of 19th century flasks, the designs do not reproduce any actual antique bottles. Wheaton/Nuline bottles include the Campaign Series, Great American Series and Presidential Series. The Presidential Series includes recent Chief Executives as well as past ones. Issued in no particular order, the series began with a memorial issue for President Kennedy in 1967. The well-known Astronaut Series was instituted in 1969, concentrating on Moon Missions.

ASTRONAUT SERIES

NO.		DESCRIPTION	PRICE RANGE	
☐	1	**APOLLO 11** (c. 1969) Blue	16.00	23.00
☐	2	**APOLLO 12** (c. 1969) Ruby	22.00	31.00
☐	3	**APOLLO 13** (c. 1970) Burley	14.00	21.00

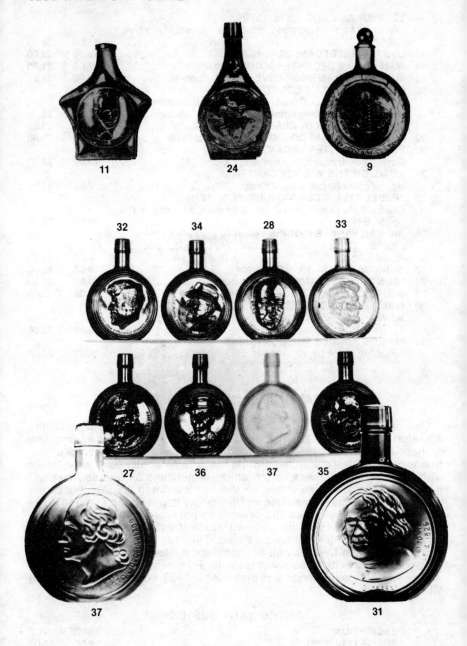

☐	4	**APOLLO 14** *(c. 1971) Aqua*	10.00	15.00
☐	5	**APOLLO 15** *(c. 1971) Green*	12.00	16.00
☐	6	**APOLLO 16** *(c. 1972) Iridescent Flint*	9.00	12.00

CAMPAIGN SERIES

☐	7	**HUMPHREY** *(c. 1969) Muskie Green*	16.00	23.00
☐	8	**NIXON-AGNEW** *(c. 1968) Topaz*	20.00	30.00

CHRISTMAS DECANTER SERIES

☐	9	**MERRY CHRISTMAS** *(c. 1971) Green*	13.00	18.00
☐	10	**SEASON'S GREETINGS** *(c. 1972) Topaz*	9.00	12.00

GREAT AMERICAN SERIES

☐	11	**HUMPHREY BOGART (Star Decanter)** *(c. 1971) Green*	7.00	10.00
☐	12	**THOMAS EDISON** *(c. 1969) Blue*	7.00	10.00
☐	13	**BEN FRANKLIN** *(c. 1970) Aqua*	12.00	17.00
☐	14	**REV. BILLY GRAHAM** *(c. 1970) Green*	10.00	15.00
☐	15	**JEAN HARLOW (Star Decanter)** *(c. 1972) Topaz*	10.00	15.00
☐	16	**CHARLES EVANS HUGHES** *(c. 1971) Blue*	7.00	10.00
☐	17	**JOHN PAUL JONES** *(c. 1970) Green*	9.00	12.00

☐	18	**HELEN KELLER** *(c. 1970) Frosty Flint*	**7.00**	**10.00**
☐	19	**ROBERT KENNEDY** *(c. 1967) Green*	**13.00**	**18.00**
☐	20	**MARTIN LUTHER KING** *(c. 1968) Amber*	**7.00**	**10.00**
☐	21	**ROBERT E. LEE** *(c. 1969) Green*	**13.00**	**18.00**
☐	22	**CHARLES LINDBERGH** *(c. 1968) Blue*	**7.00**	**10.00**
☐	23	**DOUGLAS MacARTHUR** *(c. 1968) Amethyst*	**13.00**	**18.00**
☐	24	**PAUL REVERE** *(c. 1971) Blue*	**9.00**	**18.00**
☐	25	**WILL ROGERS** *(c. 1969) Topaz*	**13.00**	**18.00**
☐	26	**BETSY ROSS** *(c. 1969) Ruby*	**10.00**	**15.00**

THE PRESIDENTIAL SERIES

☐	27	**GENERAL EISENHOWER** *(Special Memorial Issue)*	**16.00**	**23.00**
☐	28	**PRESIDENT EISENHOWER** *(c. 1969) Green*	**9.00**	**12.00**
☐	29	**PRESIDENT GRANT** *(c. 1972) Topaz*	**7.00**	**10.00**
☐	30	**ANDREW JACKSON** *(c. 1971) Green*	**13.00**	**18.00**
☐	31	**THOMAS JEFFERSON** *(c. 1970) Ruby*	**15.00**	**22.00**
☐	32	**JOHN F. KENNEDY*** *(c. 1967) Blue*	**20.00**	**30.00**
☐	33	**ABRAHAM LINCOLN** *(c. 1968) Topaz*	**9.00**	**12.00**
☐	34	**FRANKLIN D. ROOSEVELT** *(c. 1967) Green*	**9.00**	**12.00**
☐	35	**THEODORE ROOSEVELT** *(c. 1970) Blue*	**8.00**	**11.00**
☐	36	**WOODROW WILSON** *(c. 1969) Blue*	**9.00**	**12.00**
☐	37	**GEORGE WASHINGTON** *(c. 1970) Blue* *(c. 1969) Frosty Mint*	**16.00**	**23.00**

*VERY RARE — HAS BEEN "QUOTED" AS HIGH AS $100.00

MISCELLANEOUS

"Miscellaneous" covers all bottles not normally regarded as a major specialty of the hobby, including those for odd or short-lived products as well as products not generally sold in glass containers. This is not to say that some collectors are not making a specialty of these bottles. They certainly are, and interest in them is almost certain to increase in the future. All the "minor specialties" of today could well be major ones within a very few years.

Because prices on some bottles in the miscellaneous category are not firmly established, there are good opportunities for picking up bargains. Of course, you will need a bit of working knowledge, and we refer you for further information to the collector magazines and newspapers now on the market.

Commercially sold nursing bottles were first made of glass in 1841, when they were patented by Charles M. Winship of Roxbury, Massachusetts. They were not, however, the first nursing bottles. This vital accessory of the nursery had earlier been made of metal — yes, metal. Colonial American babies of middle-class parents nursed from pewter bottles, those of the well-to-do from silver, often elaborately ornamented. Metal, of course, had a big advantage over glass. It didn't shatter when a balky baby decided to fling it on the floor, but it was more expensive and mothers began to doubt the purity of milk kept in metallic bottles. After its introduction, the glass nursing bottle became so popular that the market for others collapsed.

Many nursing bottles of the late 1800's were designed to lie flat. A few were embossed with sayings or mottos, such as "Feed the Baby." By 1945 there were over 200 different kinds of nursing bottles in the U.S.

Sale of candy and related confections in glass bottles never became very widespread. Old-fashioned portion selling continued long after most other products were being packaged. Even when packaging became common, it was largely in paper boxes or cartons. Glass bottling was not considered suitable for candy on a large scale because it added to the cost without serving any real purpose. Usually, when candy was glass-bottled, it was for gift-giving and appeared in shops around holidays. Naturally, these bottles were very decorative. They were intended to be saved and used for further candy when the supplied quantity was consumed. Many were figurals of various colors. One was in the shape of the Liberty Bell and was made for sale at the Centennial Exposition at Philadelphia in 1876. This bottle has special appeal on the strength of being a figural, a bonafide antique (more than 100 years old), and a Centennial collectors' item. Others were in the form of lanterns, musical instruments, clocks, autos, airplanes, guns and battleships. Many converted into banks when empty which might account for their rather low survival rate.

A most unusual kind of collectible glass bottle is the "fire grenade." Fire grenades had their origins in Rome around the time of Nero (possibly developed as an aftermath of the Great Fire which devastated the city during his reign). Since all cooking and heating was then done with open flames, fires were common, and the means of fighting them very ineffective. Streets had no hydrants to which hoses could be attached. There were no pumpers, and really no means of getting water on a fire except by throwing it from buckets. So the fire grenade or bomb was relied upon. This was nothing more than a globular bottles, about the size of a baseball or slightly larger, filled with water. When fire broke out, it was thrown into the fire, where it would break, spill its contents and — hopefully — extinguish the flames. Laws were passed in Rome requiring all public buildings and places of assembly to keep certain quantities of fire grenades on hand. Of course, such a device was effective only if the fire was noticed immediately upon its outbreak. No amount of grenades could halt a fire that was already raging.

Alanson Crane of Fortress Monroe, Virginia, was granted the first American patent on a fire grenade in 1863. The best known maker, the Harden Hand Fire Extinguisher Co. of Chicago, was awarded a patent on August 8, 1871. Two months later the Great Chicago Fire destroyed much of the town.

Fire grenades were manufactured under various names, including Dash-Out, the Diamond, Harkness Fire Destroyer, Hazelton's High Pressure Chemical Firekeg, Magic Fire, and the Y-Burn. They were not superceded by the modern style of fire extinguisher until 1905.

Ornate little bottles with likenesses of theatrical stars, politicians or scenic pictures pasted on their surface and covered with glass were given away by barbers to favored clients in the 19th century. Most were personalized with the customer's name in gold lettering at the top. Brightly colored and found in a great variety of surface patterns, these bottles contained witch hazel, perfumed alcohol or other toiletries. Most American bottles of this kind were made at Glassboro, New Jersey. Their exquisite designing has made them popular with art collectors as well as bottle hobbyists.

Another variety of miscellaneous glass collectible — it might be stretching too far to call them "bottles" — is the insulator. Samuel Morse received a patent for the telegraph in 1840. A means of insulating the telegraph wires — which were exposed to rain and snow — was needed, and inventor Ezra Cornell suggesting using glass. Metallic insulators were not suitable, as they would not only conduct electricity but rust themselves. A non-conductive, non-rusting substance was needed. Cornell designed hollow glass bell-shaped caps to fit over the pegs on telegraph poles. Louis A. Cauvet, a New York carpenter, improved on the glass insulator by designing threaded caps that locked on to the pegs. Most electric insulators used today are porcelain instead of glass but they retain the bell shape.

Other types of interesting and collectible bottles include bar bottles, shoe polish bottles, glue bottles, snuff bottles (the Chinese always carried their snuff in bottles; Americans sometimes did, too), blueing bottles (laundry detergent), germicide bottles, cement bottles and oil bottles.

MISCELLANEOUS BOTTLES

A

NO.	DESCRIPTION	VALUE	
☐ 1	**A. MADE IN JAPAN**		
	Milk glass; 2½"	4.00	8.00
☐ 2	*ACID; plain; green, 6½"*	2.00	3.00
☐ 3	*ACID; plain; green, 6½"*	1.00	3.00
☐ 4	*ACID; plain; round; amber, 8"*	1.00	2.00
☐ 5	*ACID; plain; round; gold, 12"*	2.00	4.00
☐ 6	*ACID LINE; line around bottles; fire extinguisher; aqua or amethyst, 6"*	2.00	6.00
☐ 7	**AGUA CARABANA**		
	Small kick-up; aqua, 9½"	2.00	4.00
☐ 8	*AIRPLANE; figural candy container; clear; 4¼" long*	10.00	15.00
☐ 9	**ALMA POLISH**		
	On shoulder; M & Co. under bottom; aqua, 5"	2.00	6.00
☐ 10	**AMES**		
	Clear, 1¾"	2.00	4.00
☐ 11	**AMMONIA**		
	Flask type; aqua, all sizes	2.00	6.00
☐ 12	*APPLE BOTTLE, label; machine made; clear frosted, 7_0*	2.00	6.00
☐ 13	**APPLEBY & HELMES, RAIL ROAD MILLS**		
	Reverse side Snuff, 133 Waters, New York; flared top; amber, 4¾"	6.00	12.00
☐ 14	**ARMERS TOP NOTCH BRAND**		
	Chicago under bottom; clear or amethyst, 5½"	2.00	4.00
☐ 15	**ARNA'S 23**		
	Under bottom; amber, 8"	4.00	8.00
☐ 16	**E. ARNSTEIN, CHICAGO, ILL.**		
	Clear, 3¾"	2.00	6.00
☐ 17	*F. B. ASBURY, N.Y.*		
	Under bottom; large plain shield on front; amber, 12"	20.00	30.00
☐ 18	*AVERY LACTATE CO., BOSTON, MASS., U.S.A.*		
	In center; picture of a woman with a bucket of milk on her head and cow in back of her; two panels on each side; clear, 7"	8.00	20.00

B

☐ 19 **B**
Under bottom; label; clear or amethyst, 7½" 2.00 4.00

☐ 20 **B & B**
Under bottom; sheared top; amber, 3¾" 4.00 8.00

☐ 21 *BABY BOTTLE; OUNCES on front; cylindrical; ABM; clear,*
6⅞" 2.00 4.00

☐ 22 *BABY BOTTLE; flask; ABM; amethyst, 7"* 2.00 5.00

☐ 23 *Same as above except 4½"* 2.00 4.00

☐ 24 **H. A. BARTLETT & CO., PHILADE**
Shoe Dressing on bottom rim; aqua, 4½" 8.00 10.00

☐ 25 **BEECH NUT, CANAJOHARIE N.Y.**
On one line on shoulder; on bottom 23 N. 51; under bottom
B N P Co., A, 16 machine made; aqua, 9½" 2.00 3.00

☐ 26 **BENTON HOLLADAY & CO.**
Shoe polish; aqua, 4½" 4.00 8.00

☐ 27 **B.F.B. CO. 2845**
Under bottom; aqua, 8" 2.00 4.00

☐ 28 **BILUK**
Aqua, 4" tall, 2¼" x 2¼" base 10.00 25.00

☐ 29 **BIXBY**
Shoe polish; aqua, ¾" 3.00 4.00

☐ 30 **BIXBY**
Under bottle; round bottle tapering to round shoulder; short
neck; wide flared mouth; green, 4½" tall, 2¼" bottom 6.00 10.00

☐ 31 *Same as above except clear* 2.00 4.00

☐ 32 **BIXBY #15**
On bottom; shoe polish; dark green, 4" 4.00 6.00

☐ 33 **BIXBY 6-83**
On front; on bottom patented mch; shoe polish; conical;
aqua, 3⅞" 3.00 6.00

☐ 34 **BIXBY, PATENTED MCH. 6, 83**
Bulbous shoulders; flared narrow collar; aqua, 4" 2.00 4.00

☐ 35 **S. M. BIXBY & CO.**
Aqua, 4½" 4.00 6.00

☐ 36 **BIXBY'S FRENCH POLISH**
Fancy lettering; aqua, 3½" 4.00 8.00

☐ 37 *BLUING; label; different numbers on bottom; clear or*
amethyst, 4¾" 2.00 3.00

☐ 38 **THE BOYLE NEEDLE CO., CHICAGO**
On side 3 oz. full measure; machine made; clear, 6¼" 1.00 3.00

☐ 39 **BRAIN'S**
Cardiff on back; SAB under bottom; inside screw top;
machine made; amber, 10" 8.00 15.00

☐ 40 **BRAND BROS. CO. EIGENTHUMER ASETZLICH GESCHUTZT**
Three sides; fancy shape; amber, 5" 20.00 40.00

☐ 41 **BRYANT'S ROOT BEER**
THIS BOTTLE MAKES FIVE GALLONS, MFG. BY WIL-
LIAMS DAVIS BROOKS & CO. DETROIT, MICH.; amber,
4½" 4.00 8.00

☐ 42 **BULL DOG BRAND LIQUID GLUE**
Around shoulder; crude ring collar; aqua, 3½" **2.00** **4.00**

☐ 43 **BURN OLNEY CANNING CORP.**
Catsup; clear, 8" **4.00** **8.00**

C

☐ 44 **CALA NURSER BABY BOTTLE**
*Embossed in circular slug plate; ounces on back; ring on
neck; oval; ABM; clear, 7⅛"* **2.00** **6.00**

☐ 45 *CANDY BOTTLES shaped as telephone, train, gun, phonograph or lantern; screw top; clear* **10.00** **25.00**

☐ 46 *CAR FIGURAL; candy; clear, 4¾"* **10.00** **25.00**

☐ 47 **CAULK**
Square; clear, 1¾" **1.00** **2.00**

☐ 48 *CHILD'S FIRE EXTINGUISHER, UTICA, N.Y.; aqua, 6½"* .. **10.00** **20.00**

☐ 49 *CHILD'S FIRE EXTINGUISHER, UTICA, N.Y., SULPHURIC
ACID: 4 oz. line; aqua, 6¼"* **8.00** **20.00**

☐ 50 **CHRISTO MFG. CO.**
Amber, 9½" **4.00** **6.00**

☐ 51 *CIRCLE A. GINGERALE
On bottom; round; aqua, 7⅜" or 9¼"* **2.00** **4.00**

☐ 52 **CLEANFONT VENTED NURSING BOTTLE FOX FULLY &
WEBSTER, NEW YORK & BOSTON**
*Patented Oct. 25, 1892 on bottom; ring top; Aladdin's lamp
type; clear or amethyst, 5½"* **10.00** **25.00**

☐ 53 **C.L.G. CO.**
P under bottom; clear, 3½" **2.00** **4.00**

☐ 54 **CLOROX**
Machine made; nine-part mold; amber, 8" **1.00** **8.00**

☐ 55 **CM**
Under bottom; amber, 11½" **6.00** **8.00**

☐ 56 **COHEN COOK & CO., 229 WASHINGTON ST. NEW YORK**
Graphite pontil; aqua, 8¾" **35.00** **50.00**

☐ 57 **C185**
On bottom; label; amber, 3" **2.00** **3.00**

☐ 58 **C1637**
On bottom; label; aqua, 5" **2.00** **3.00**

☐ 59 **COOK & BERNHEIMER CO.**
*Full Quart, Refilling of This Bottled Prohibited; under bot-
tom C&B Bottling* **8.00** **12.00**

☐ 60 **R COTTER & CO., HOUSTON, TEX.**
*I.X.L. Sarsaparilla & Iodide Potassium on reverse side;
aqua, 9½"* **15.00** **30.00**

☐ 61 **COWDREY, E. T. CO.**
*In center; twirl top and bottom; screw top and sheared
top; 6¼"* **8.00** **15.00**

☐ 62 **CRIMAULT & CO.**
Clear, 6¼" **2.00** **6.00**

☐ 63 **CROWLEY'S MILK CO. BEACON, N.Y.**
*In circular slug plate; Liquid One Quart; large ring collar;
ABM; clear, 9¾"* **3.00** **4.00**

☐ 64 **C.W. & CO.**
Under bottom; kick-up; dot in center; three-part mold; dark olive, 5" body, 2" blob neck; 3" bottom 8.00 12.00

D

☐ 65 **DAIRYMEN'S LEAGUE CO-OPERATIVE ASSOCIATION INC. REGISTERED**
Dairylea Reg. U.S. Pat. Off., One Quart Liquid on back; large ring collar; ABM; clear, 9½" 2.00 6.00
☐ 66 *DECANTER; silver inlay; cobalt, 7"* 15.00 25.00
☐ 67 *DECANTER; whiskey label; fancy sides; wine color, 10½"* 8.00 15.00
☐ 68 **DEIMEL BROS. & CO.**
Under bottom; clear or amethyst, 4¾" 2.00 8.00
☐ 69 **DESIGN PAT'D, FEB 16TH 1886**
Under bottom in sunken circle; five different sizes of rings on top of shoulder; one ¼" ring on bottom (trunk); clear, 12¼" 10.00 20.00
☐ 70 **DETROIT CREAMERY CO. DETROIT, MICH. REGISTERED;**
DC CO. 12 OZ. LIQUID SEALED 48 on back; large ring collar; fourteen vertical ribs on shoulder; clear, pint, 5¼" . . . 6.00 15.00
☐ 71 **F. W. DEVOE & CO.**
Clear or amethyst, 3¼" 2.00 4.00
☐ 72 *DOG FIGURAL; candy; clear, 3¾"* 5.00 10.00
☐ 73 *DOG FIGURAL; beverage; clear, 10"* 8.00 10.00
☐ 74 **JOHN T DOYLE & CO., NEW HAVEN, CONN., BOKASKA LAUNDRY SOAP**
Clear or aqua 4.00 8.00
☐ 75 **DUNKLEY'S GENUINE**
Bulge at shoulder; screw top; round; amethyst, 6" 1.00 2.00
☐ 76 **D.W. & CO.**
Under bottom; aqua, 9½" 2.00 4.00
☐ 77 **DYSON NELSON, TRADE MARK**
Round; inside screw; aqua, 6¾" 2.00 6.00

E

☐ 78 **EASTMAN, ROCHESTER, N.Y.**
Clear, 5" 2.00 4.00
☐ 79 **ECLIPSE**
Number on bottom; dark amber, 4½" 3.00 4.00
☐ 80 **ECLIPSE**
Machine made; aqua, 4¼" 2.00 3.00
☐ 81 **THOMAS A. EDISON**
In script; BATTERY OIL; clear, 4¼" 2.00 4.00
☐ 82 **E.G.**
Label; D under bottom; aqua, 8" 2.00 4.00
☐ 83 **E.L.G. CO., BOSTON**
The Samson Battery No. 1 on one side; sheared top; aqua, 5¾" x 4" x 4" 8.00 12.00
☐ 84 **ELGIN MILKIN CO.**
Sheared top; aqua, 5½" 6.00 10.00

☐ 85 **CHARLES ELLIS & SON CO.**
Aqua, 7" 4.00   6.00

☐ 86 **EMPIRE NURSING BOTTLE**
Void on flat side; neck tapered; amethyst, 5¼" 6.00   10.00

☐ 87 **CARLO ERBA**
*On one panel; on back Milano; beveled corners; 1¾"
square, 6"* 8.00   10.00

☐ 88 *Same as above except 7¼"* 8.00   10.00

☐ 89 **EVERETT & BARRON CO., SHOE POLISH, PROVIDENCE, R.I.**
Oval; clear, 4¾" 3.00   6.00

☐ 90 **EVERLASTING BLACK DYE, BALTIMORE, MD.**
ABM; cobalt, 4¾" 4.00   8.00

☐ 91 **E Z STOVE POLISH**
#14 on bottom; aqua, 6" 2.00   8.00

F

☐ 92 **FAIR ACRES DAIRY, MOST MODERN DAIRY IN NEBRASKA,
PHONE 511**
In circular slug plate; large ring collar; ABM; clear, 5½" .. 4.00   8.00

☐ 93 **FALK**
*In sunken panel; IMPROVED FIRE EXT'R. in three panels;
on shoulder Pat. Appl'd For; green, 6½"* 35.00   85.00

☐ 94 **FIRE EXTINGUISHER MFG. CO., BABCOCK HAND GRENADE**
*On round panels; S. Des Plaines St. Chicago; non freezing;
ball shaped; fourteen rings around bottle; clear, 7½"* 10.00   25.00

☐ 95 *THIS BOTTLE LOANED BY F. W. FITCH CO. On lower
trunk; tapered neck; round; amethyst, 8"* 2.00   4.00

☐ 96 *FIVE DROPS On one panel; Chicago U.S.A. on the other;
rectangular; aqua, 5½"* 2.00   3.00

☐ 97 **W & J FLETT**
Aqua, 6¾" 15.00   20.00

☐ 98 **FLLI VIAHOV, PESCARA**
Clear, 11½" 30.00   50.00

☐ 99 **FLORIDA TROPICAL; 405 F.G. 2**
Under bottom; clear, 7½" 4.00   6.00

☐100 ROBT. H. FOERDERER, PHILADELPHIA, U.S.A.
Aqua, 4½" 2.00   4.00

☐101 **FOX TRADE MARK**
Clear or amethyst, 3¾" 2.00   4.00

☐102 *FRENCH GLASS; shoe polish; aqua or blue, 4½"* 4.00   6.00

☐103 *THIS BOTTLE CAN BE REFILLED AT THE FURST CO.;
clear or amethyst, 3¼"* 3.00   6.00

☐104 **FURST-MCNESE CO., FREEPORT, ILL.**
On front panel; rectangular; aqua, 8⅜" 2.00   3.00

G

☐105 **GAY OLA**
*In script; TRADE MARK REGISTERED; clear or amethyst,
7½"* 4.00   6.00

☐ 106 **GILLET'S**
A & DAC under bottom; aqua, 5½" 4.00   6.00
☐ 107 **GILT EDGE DRESSING**
Pat. May 13, 1889 under bottom; clear 4.00   8.00
☐ 108 GLUE, label; sheared top; clear or amethyst, 3" 3.00   4.00
☐ 109 GOOFUS GLASS; clear, 7" x 6½" 50.00   60.00
☐ 110 **GOLDEN STATE COMPANY LTD. ONE PINT**
Golden State Brand in shield on back; large G.S. on bottom; large ring collar; AMB; clear, 7¼" 6.00   8.00
☐ 111 **MARY T. GOLDMAN, ST. PAUL, MINN.**
On front panel; rectangular; 5½" 2.00   4.00
☐ 112 **B. F. GOODRICH CO.**
Amber, 4½" 4.00   6.00
☐ 113 **B. F. GOODRICH CO.**
Amber, 8" 10.00   15.00
☐ 114 GRADUATED NURSING BOTTLE; clear, 6½" 8.00   10.00
☐ 115 **GRAND UNION COMPANY**
Clear, 5¼" 2.00   4.00
☐ 116 **GREAT SEAL**
Aqua or amethyst, 5½" 2.00   6.00
☐ 117 **GRIMAULT & CO. INJECTION AUMATICO**
Clear, 6½" 4.00   6.00
☐ 118 **G.W.**
Under bottom; aqua, 5¾" 8.00   10.00

H

☐ 119 **HAGERTY'S GLASS WORKS, N.Y.**
Under bottom; aqua, 6½" 10.00   20.00
☐ 120 **HAMMER DRY PLATE CO., ST. LOUIS, MO.**
On panel; square; amethyst, 6¼" 4.00   8.00
☐ 121 HAND BLOWN; pontil on bottom; ⅝", applied sheared lip; round; long neck about 3½"; aqua, 8¾" 12.00   35.00
☐ 122 **HAND MFG. CO.**
On the shoulder; PHILA. on lower front; oval with front panel; clear, 5¼" 2.00   4.00
☐ 123 **HARDEN'S**—HNS on large diamond monogram in front and back; hand grenade fire extinguisher with four large and eight small diamond sides; round; light amber or golden, 3" neck 45.00   85.00
☐ 124 **HARDEN'S HNS**
On large diamond monogram in front; hand grenade fire extinguisher with two plain diamond and eight small diamond; cross on bottom; gold, quart 45.00   85.00
☐ 125 **HARDEN'S STAR HAND GRENADE**
Fire Extinguisher in back; blue, 6¾" 45.00   85.00
☐ 126 **HARKNESS FIRE DESTROYER**
Ball shaped; ten horizontal rings on body; five rings on neck; blue, 6¼" 10.00   25.00
☐ 127 **E. HARTSHORN & SONS**
Side mold; clear or amethyst, 5" 3.00   5.00

BOTTLE CLUBS

ALABAMA

Alabama Bottle Collectors Society — 2768 Hanover Circle, Birmingham, AL 35205. (205) 933-7902.

Mobile Bottle Collectors Club — 7927 Historic Mobile Parkway, Theodore, AL 36582. (205) 653-0713.

Montgomery, Alabama Bottle Club — 1940A Norman Bridge Court, Montgomery, AL 36104.

Montgomery Bottle & Insulator Club — 2021 Merrily Dr., Montgomery, AL 36111. (205) 288-7937.

Mobile Bottle Collectors Club — Rt. #4, Box 28, Theodore, AL 36582.

North Alabama Bottle & Glass Club — P. O. Box 109, Decatur, AL 35601.

Tuscaloosa Antique Bottle Club — 1617 11th Street, Tuscaloosa, AL 35401.

ALASKA

Alaska Bottle Club — (formerly The Anchorage Beam Club) — 8510 E. 10th, Anchorage, AK 99504.

ARIZONA

Arizona Territory Antique Bottle Club — P. O. Box 6364, Speedway Station, Tucson, AZ 85733.

Avon Collectors Club — P. O. Box 1406, Mesa, AZ 86201.

Fort Smith Area Bottle Collectors Association — 4618 So. "Q", Fort Smith, AZ 72901.

Kachina Ezra Brooks Bottle Club — 3818 W. Cactus Wren Drive, Phoenix, AZ 85021.

Pick & Shovel A.B.C. of Arizona, Inc. — P. O. Box 7020, Phoenix, AZ 85011. Meets 8:00 p.m. first Wednesday at 531 E. Bethany Home Rd., Phoenix. (Stuckey Ins. Agency) Newsletter: The Blister. Club formed 1969, has 40 family members.

Southern AZ Historical Collector's Association, Ltd. — 6211 Piedra Seca, Tucson, AZ 85718.

Vallley of the Sun Bottle & Specialty Club — 212 East Minton, Tempe, AZ 85281.

White Mountain Antique Bottle Collectors Association — P. O. Box 503, Eager, AZ 85925.

ARKANSAS

Fort Smith Area Bottle Collectors Assn. — 2201 South 73rd St., Fort Smith, AR 72903.

Hempsted County Bottle Club — 710 So. Hervey, Hope, AR 71801.

Little Rock Antique Bottle Collectors Club — #12 Martin Drive, North Little Rock, AR 72118. (501) 753-2623.

Madison County Bottle Collectors Club — Rt. 2, Box 304, Huntsville, AR 72740.

Southwest Arkansas Bottle Club — Star Route, Delight, AR 71940.

CALIFORNIA

A.B.C. of Orange County — P. O. Box 10424, Santa Ana, CA 92711. Meet first Monday at 7:30 p.m. Willard Jr. High School, Santa Ana. Newsletters: The Bottle Bulletin, Club formed 1968, has 60 members.

Amethyst Bottle Club — 3245 Military Avenue, Los Angeles, CA 90034.

Antique Bottle Collectors Association — P. O. Box 467, Sacramento, CA 95802.

Antique Bottle Collectors of Orange County — 223 E. Ponona, Santa Ana, CA 92707.

Antique Bottle Club Association of Fresno — P. O. Box 1932, Fresno, CA 93718.

Avon Bottle & Specialties Collectors — Southern California Division, 9233 Mills Avenue, Montclair, CA 91763.

Bidwell Bottle Club — Box 546, Chico, CA 95926.

Bishop Belles & Beaux Bottle Club — P. O. Box 1475, Bishop, CA 93514.

Beam Bottle Club of Southern California — 3221 N. Jackson, Rosemead, CA 91770.

California Ski Country Bottle Club — 212 South El Molino Street, Alhambra, CA 91801.

Camellia City Jim Beam Bottle Club — 3734 Lynhurst Way, North Highlands, CA 95660.

Central Calif. Avon Bottle & Collectible Club — P. O. Box 232, Amador City, CA 95601.

Cherry Valley Beam Bottle & Specialty Club — 6851 Hood Drive, Westminster, CA 92683.

Chief Solano Bottle Club — 4-D Boynton Avenue, Suisun, CA 94585.

Curiosity Bottle Association — Box 103, Napa, CA 94558.

First Double Springs Collectors Club — 13311 Illinois Street, Westminster, CA 92683.

Glass Belles of San Gabriel — 518 W. Neuby Avenue, San Gabriel, CA 91776.

Glasshopper Figural Bottle Association — P. O. Box 6642, Torrance, CA 90504.

Golden Bear Ezra Brooks Bottle Club — 8808 Capricorn Way, San Diego, CA 92162.

Golden Bear Jim Beam Bottle & Specialty Club — 8808 Capricorn Way, San Diego, CA 92126.

Golden Gate Historical Bottle Society — P. O. Box 2129, Alameda, CA 94501.

Greater Cal. Antique Bottle Collectors — P. O. Box 55, Sacramento, CA 95801.

High Desert Bottle Hunters — P. O. Box 581, Ridgecrest, CA 93558.

Hoffman's Mr. Lucky Bottle Club — 2104 Rhoda Street, Simi Valley, CA 93065.

Hollywood Stars-Ezra Brooks Bottle Club — 2200 North Beachwood Drive, Hollywood, CA 90028.

Humboldt Antique Bottle Club — P. O. Box 6012, Eureka, CA 95501.

Insulator Collectors Club, San Diego County, Inc.

Jim Beam Bottle Club — 139 Arlington, Berkeley, CA 94707.

Jim Beam Bottle Club of So. Calif. — 1114 Coronado Terrace, Los Angeles, CA 90066.

Juniper Hills Bottle Club — Rt. 1, Box 18, Valyerma, CA 93563.

Jewels of Avon — 2297 Maple Avenue, Oroville, CA 95965.

Kern County Antique Bottle Club — P. O. Box 6724, Bakersfield, CA 93306.

Lilliputian Bottle Club — 5119 Lee Street, Torrance, CA 90503.

Lionstone Bottle Collector's of America — P. O. Box 75924, Los Angeles, CA 90075.

Livermore Avon Club — 6385 Claremont Avenue, Richmond, CA 94805.

Lodi Jim Beam Bottle Club — 429 E. Lodi Avenue, Lodi, CA 95240.

Los Angeles Historical Bottle Club — P. O. Box 60762, Terminal Annex, Los Angeles, CA 90060. (213) 332-6751.

Mission Bells (Beams) — 1114 Coronada Terrace, Los Angeles, CA 90026.

Mission Trails Ezra Brooks Bottles & Specialties Club, Inc. — 4923 Bel Canto Drive, San Jose, CA 95124.

Mission Trail Historical Bottle Club — P. O. Box 721, Seaside, CA 93955. (408) 394-3257.

Modesto Old Bottle Club (MOBC) — P. O. Box 1791, Modesto, CA 95354.

Monterey Bay Beam Bottle & Specialty Club — P. O. Box 258, Freedom, CA 95019.

M. T. Bottle Club — P. O. Box 608, Solana Beach, CA 92075.

Mt. Bottle Club — 422 Orpheus, Encinitas, CA 92024.

Mt. Diablo Bottle Club — 4166 Sandra Circle, Pittsburg, CA 94565.

Mt. Diablo Bottle Society — 1699 Laguna #110, Concord, CA 94520.

Mt. Whitney Bottle Club — P. O. Box 688, Lone Pine, CA 93545.

Motherlode Bottle Club — P. O. Box 337, Angels Camp, CA 95222.

Napa-Solano Bottle Club — 1409 Delwood, Vallejo, CA 94590.

Northern California Jim Beam Bottle & Specialty Club — P. O. Box 186, Montgomery Creek, CA 96065.

Northwestern Bottle Club — P. O. Box 1121, Santa Rosa, CA 95402. Meet 4th Tuesday January, April, June, September, October, Coddingtown Community Meeting Room, Santa Rosa. Newsletter: The Glassblower. Club formed 1966, has 29 family members.

Northwestern Bottle Collectors Association — 1 Keeler Street, Petaluma, CA 94952.

Original Sippin Cousins Ezra Brooks Specialties Club — 12206 Malone Street, Los Angeles, CA 90066.

Peninsula Bottle Club — P. O. Box 886, Belmont, CA 94002.

Petaluma Bottle & Antique Club — P. O. Box 1035, Petaluma, CA 94952.

Queen Mary Beam & Specialty Club — P. O. Box 2054, Anaheim, CA 92804.

Relic Accumulators — P. O. Box 3513, Eureka, CA 95501.

Santa Barbara Beam Bottle Club — 5307 University Drive, Santa Barbara, CA 93111.

Santa Barbara Bottle Club — P. O. Box 30171, Santa Barbara, CA 93105.

San Bernardino County Historical Bottle and Collectible Club — P. O. Box 127, Bloomington, CA 92316. Meets 4th Tuesday, 7:30 p.m. San Bernardino Co. Museum, Redlands, CA, phone 714-244-5863. Newsletter: Bottle Nooz. Club formed 1967, has 60 members.

San Diego Antique Bottle Club — P. O. Box 536, San Diego, CA 92112.

San Diego Jim Beam Bottle Club — 2620 Mission Village Drive, San Diego, CA 92112.

San Joaquin Valley Jim Beam Bottle & Specialties Club — 4085 North Wilson Avenue, Fresno, CA 93704.

San Jose Antique Bottle Collector's Assn. — P. O. Box 5432, San Jose, CA

San Francisco Bay Area Miniature Bottle Club — 160 Lower Via Casitas #8, Kentfield, CA 94904.

San Luis Obispo Antique Bottle Club — 124-21 Street Paso Robles, CA 93446. Meets 3rd Saturday, private homes. Phone 238-1848. Club formed in 1965, has 30 family members.

Sequoia Antique Bottle Society — 1900 4th Avenue, Kingsburg, CA 93631.

Shasta Antique Bottle Collectors Association — Route 1, Box 3147-A, Anderson, CA 96007.

Sierra Gold Ski Country Bottle Club — 5081 Rio Vista Avenue, San Jose, CA 95129.

Ski-Country Bottle Club of Southern California — 3148 N. Walnut Grove, Rosemead, CA 91770.

South Bay Antique Bottle Club — 2589½ Valley Drive, Manhattan Beach, CA 90266.

Southern California Miniature Bottle Club — 5626 Corning Avenue, Los Angeles, CA 90056.

Southwestern Wyoming Avon Bottle Club — 301 Canyon Highlands Dr., Oroville, CA 95965.

Stockton Historical Bottle Society, Inc. — P. O. Box 8584, Stockton, CA 95204.

Sunnyvale Antique Bottle Collectors Association — 613 Torrington, Sunnyvale, CA 94087.

Superior California Bottle Club — P. O. Box 555, Anderson, CA 96007.

Taft Antique Bottle Club — P. O. Box 334, Taft, CA 93268.

Tehama County Antique Bottle Club — Rt. 1 Box 775, Red Bluff, CA 96080. Meets 7:30 p.m. first Wednesday at Lassen View School. Phone 916-527-1680. Club formed 1960, has 55 family members.

Teen Bottle Club — Route 1, Box 60-TE, Eureka, CA 95501.

Western World Collectors Assn. — P. O. Box 409, Ontario, CA 91761. Meets every third Wednesday, 7:30 p.m. at Upland Lumber Co., 85 Euclid Ave., Upland, CA. Phone 714-984-0614. Club formed in 1971, has 150 family members.

COLORADO

Alamosa Bottle Collectors — Route 2, Box 170, Alamosa, Colorado 81101.

Antique Bottle Collectors of Colorado — P. O. Box 63, Denver, CO 80201.

Avon Club of Colorado Springs, CO — 707 N. Farragut, Colorado Springs, CO 80909.

Colorado Mile-High Ezra Brooks Bottle Club — 7401 Decatur Street, Westminster, CO 80030.

Four Corners Bottle & Glass Club — P. O. Box 45, Cortez, CO 81321.

Horsetooth Antique Bottle Collectors, Inc. — P. O. Box 944, Fort Collins, CO 80521.

Lionstone Western Figural Club — P. O. Box 2275, Colorado Springs, CO 80901.

Northeastern Colorado Antique Bottle Club — P. O. Box 634, Fort Morgan, CO 80701.

Northern Colorado Antique Bottle Club — 227 W. Beaver Avenue, Ft. Morgan, CO 80701.

Ole Foxie Jim Beam Club — P. O. Box 560, Westminster, CO 80020.

Peaks & Plains Antique Bottle Club — P. O. Box 814, Colorado Springs, CO 80901.

Rocky Mountain Jim Beam Bottle & Specialty Club — Alcott Station, — P. O. Box 12162, Denver, CO 80212.

Telluride Antique Bottle Collectors — P. O. Box 344, Telluride, CO 8143.

Western Figural & Jim Beam Specialty Club — P. O. Box 4331, Colorado Springs, CO 80930.

Western Slope Bottle Club — 607 Belford Avenue, Grand Junction, CO 81501.

CONNECTICUT

Antique Bottle Club of Middletown — 15 Elam Street, Apt. 10, New Britain, CT 06053.

East Coast Mini Bo Club — 156 Hillfield Road, Hamden, CT.

Central Connecticut Antique Bottle Collector's Club — 210 Rolling Hill Lane, Southington, CT 06489. Phone 621-0502.

Connecticut Specialty Bottle Club, Inc. — P. O. Box 624, Stratford, CT.

Greenwich Antique Bottle Club — 18 Pond Place, Cos Cob, CT 06807.

Housatonic Antique Bottle Association — Falls Village, CT 06031.

The Nutmeg State Brooks Bottle Club — 191 W. Main Street, Meriden, CT 06450.

Southeastern New England Antique Bottle Club — 656 Noank Road, Mystic, CN 06355.

Somers Antique Bottle Club — P. O. Box 373, Somers, CT 06071. 203-487-1071.

So. Conn. Antique Bottle Collectors — 33 Spice Hill Dr., Wallingford, CT 06492.

Southern Connecticut Antique Bottle Collectors Association, Inc. — P. O. Box 346, Seymour, CT 06483.

DELAWARE

Mason-Dixon Bottle Collectors Association — P. O. Box 505, Lewes, DE 19958.

Tri-State Bottle Collectors and Diggers Club — 730 Paper Mill Road, Newark, DE 19711.

FLORIDA

Antique Bottle Collectors Assn. of Florida — 5901 S.W. 16th St., Miami, FL 33144. Meets 2nd Tuesday, 7:30 p.m. School. Phone 305-266-4854. Newsletter: Whittlemark. Club formed 1965, has 55 members.

Antique Bottle Collectors of North Florida — P. O. Box 14796, Jacksonville, FL 32210.

Antique Bottle Collectors of Florida, Inc. — 2512 Davie Boulevard, Ft. Lauderdale, FL 33312.

Bay Area Historical Bottle Collector — P. O. Box 3454, Apollo Beach, FL 33570.

Central Florida Insulator Club — 3557 Nicklaus Drive, Titusville, FL 32780. 305 267-9170.

Crossarms Collectors Club — 1756 N.W. 58th Avenue, Lauderhill, FL 33313. Meets every other month, 3rd Wednesday at above address. Phone 733-1053. Newsletter: Crossarms. Club formed 1975.

Everglades A.B.C. —6981 S.W. 19th St., Pompano, FL 33068. Club formed 1977, has 44 members.

Everglades Antique Bottle & Collectors Club — 400 So. 57 Terr., Hollywood, FL 33023. 305 962-3434.

Gold Coast Collectors Club — Joseph I. Frakes, P. O. Box 10183, Wilton Manors, FL 33305.

Halifax Historical Society — 224½ S. Beach Street, Daytona Beach, Fl 32018.

Harbor City — 1232 Causeway, Eau, FL 32935.

Longwood Bottle Club — P. O. Box 437, Longwood, FL 32750.

M. T. Bottle Collectors Assn., Inc. — P. O. Box 581, Deland, FL 32720.

Mid-State Antique Bottle Collectors — 88 Sweetbriar Branch, Longwood, FL 32750, 834-8914.

Northwest Florida Regional Bottle Club — P. O. Box 282, Port St. Joe, FL 32456.

Original Florida Keys Collectors Club — P. O. Box 212, Islamorada, FL 33036.

Oviedo Bottling Works — Maitland, FL 32751.

Pensacola Bottle & Relic Collectors Association — 1004 Freemont Avenue, Pensacola, FL 32505.

Ridge Area Antique Bottle Collectors — 1219 Carlton, Lake Wales, FL 33853.

Sanford Antique A.B.C. — 2656 Grandview Ave., Sanford, FL. Meets 2nd Tuesday, 8:00 p.m. 305-322-7181. Newsletter: Probe. Club formed 1966, has 50 members.

Sarasota-Manatee A.B.C. Assn. — Rt. 1, Box 74-136, Sarasota, FL 33583. Phone 813-924-5995. Meets 3rd Wednesday, 7:30 p.m. in member's homes. Newletter: The Glass Habit. Club formed 1969, has 20 members.

South Florida Jim Beam Bottle & Specialty Club — 7741 N.W. 35th Street, West Hollywood, FL 33024.

Suncoast Antique Bottle Club — P. O. Box 12712, St. Petersburg, FL 33733.

Suncoast Jim Beam Bottle & Spec. Club — P. O. Box 5067, Sarasota, FL 33579.

Tampa Antique Bottle Collectors — P. O. Box 4232, Tampa, FL 33607.

West Coast Florida Ezra Brooks Bottle Club — 1360 Harbor Drive, Sarasota, FL 33579.

GEORGIA

Bulldog Double Springs Bottle Collector Club of Augusta, Georgia — 1916 Melrose Drive, Augusta, GA 30906.

Coastal Empire Bottle Club — P. O. Box 3714, Station B, Savannah, GA 31404.

The Desoto Trail Bottle Collectors Club — 406 Randolph Street, Cuthbert, GA 31740.

Flint Antique Bottle & Coin Club — c/o Cordele-Crisp Co., Recreation Department, 204 2nd Street North, Cordele, GA 31015.

Georgia Bottle Club — 2996 Pangborn Road, Decatur, GA 30033.

Georgia-Carolina Empty Bottle Club — P. O. Box 1184, Augusta, GA 30903.

Macon Area Bottle Club — P. O. Box 5395, Macon, GA 31208. Meets 7:30 p.m. 2nd Monday, Robert Train Recreation Center. Newsletter: Glass Heart of Georgia. Club formed 1968, has 20 members.

Macon Antique Bottle Club — c/o 5532 Jane Ru Circle, Macon, GA 31206. Meets 7:30 p.m. 2nd Monday at Robert Train Rec. Newsletter: Heart of Georgia News, has 30 members.

The Middle Georgia Antique Bottle Club — 2746 Alden Street, Macon, GA 31206.

Peachstate Bottle & Specialty Club — 5040 Vallo Vista Court, Atlanta, GA 30342.

Southeastern Antique Bottle Club — P. O. Box 657, Decatur, GA 30033.

HAWAII

Hauoli Beam Bottle Collectors Club of Hawaii — 45-027 Ka-Hanahou Place, Kaneohe, HI 96744.

Hawaii Bottle Collectors Club — 6770 Hawaii Kal Dr., Apt. 708, Hawaii Kai, HI 96825.

IDAHO

Buhl Antique Bottle Club — 500 12th North, Buhl, ID 83316.

Em Tee Bottle Club — P. O. Box 62, Jerome, ID 83338.

Fabulous Valley Antique Bottle Club — P. O. Box 769, Osburn, ID 83849.

Gem Antique Bottle Collectors Assn., Inc. — P. O. Box 8051, Boise, ID 83707.

Idaho Bottle Collectors Association — 4530 South 5th Street, Pocatello, ID 83201.

Inland Empire Jim Beam Bottle & Collectors' Club — 1117 10th Street, Lewiston, ID 83501.

Rock & Bottle Club — Route 1, Fruitland, ID 83619.

ILLINOIS

A.B.C. of Northern Illinois — P. O. Box 23, Ingleside, IL 60041. Phone 815-338-2567. Meets 1st Wednesday 8:00 p.m. at Jones Island Meeting House, Grayslake, IL. Newsletter: Pick & Probe. Formed 1973, has 29 members.

Alton Area Bottle Club — 2448 Alby Street, Alton, IL. 618-462-4285.

Blackhawk Jim Beam Bottle & Specialties Club — 2003 Kishwaukee Street, Rockford, IL 61101.

Central & Midwestern States Beam & Specialties Club — 44 S. Westmore, Lombard, IL 60148.

Chicago Ezra Brooks Bottle & Specialty Club — 3635 West 82nd Street, Chicago, IL 60652.

Chicago Jim Beam Bottle & Specialty Club — 1305 W. Marion Street, Joliet, IL 60436.

1st Chicago A.B.C. — P. O. Box A-3382, Chicago, IL 60690. Meets 3rd Friday, 8:00 p.m. at St. Daniels Church, 5400 S. Nashville, Chicago. Newsletter: Mid-West Bottled News. Formed 1969, has 75 members.

Heart of Illinois Antique Bottle Club — 2010 Bloomington Road, East Peoria, IL 61611.

Illinois Bottle Club — P. O. Box 181, Rushville, IL 62681.

Illini Jim beam Bottle & Specialty Club — P. O. Box 13, Champaign, IL 61820.

International Association of Jim Beam — 4336 Saratoga Ave., Downers Grove, IL 60515.

Kelly Club — 147 North Brainard Avenue, La Grange, IL 60525.

Land of Lincoln Bottle Club — 2515 Illinois Circle, Decatur, IL 62526.

Lewis & Clark Jim Beam Bottle & Specialty Club — P. O. Box 451, Wood River, IL 62095.

Louis Joliet Bottle Club — 12 Kenmore, Joliet, IL 60433.

Metro East Bottle & Jar Association — 309 Bellevue Dr., Belleville, IL. Phone 618-233-8841. Meets 2nd Tuesday at O'Fallon Township Bldg., 801 E. State St., O'Fallon, IL. Newsletter: Metro-East Bottle & Jar & Insulator Relater. Club formed 1971, has 26 members.

Metro East Bottle & Jar Association — 1702 North Keesler, Collinsville, IL 62234.

Metro East Bottle & Jar Association — P. O. Box 185, Mascoutah, IL.

National Ezra Brooks Club — 645 N. Michigan Ave., Chicago, IL 69611.

Pekin Bottle Collectors Assn. — P. O. Box 372, Pekin, IL 61554. Phone 309-347-4441. Meets 3rd Tuesday, Pekin Memorial Arena. Club formed 1970, has 96 members.

Sweet Corn Capital Bottle Club — 1015 W. Orange, Hoopeston, IL 60942.

INDIANA

Fort Wayne Historical Bottle Club — 5124 Roberta Drive, Fort Wayne, IN 46306. Meets 2nd Wednesday at Library Branches. Club formed 1970, has 20 members.

Hoosier Jim Beam Bottle & Specialties Club — P. O. Box 24234, Indianapolis, IN 46224.

Indiana Ezra Brooks Bottle Club — P. O. Box 24344, Indianapolis, IN 46224.

Lafayette Antique Bottle Club — 3664 Redondo Drive, Lafayette, IN 47905. Phone 477-0038. Meets 4:00 p.m. 1st Sunday at Jenks Rest, Columbian Park, Lafayette, IN. Club formed in 1977, has 8 members.

Michiana Jim Beam Bottle & Specialty Club — 58955 Locust Road, South Bend, IN 46614.

Mid-West Antique Fruit Jar & Bottle Club — P. O. Box 38, Flat Rock, IN 47234.

The Ohio Valley Antique Bottle and Jar Club — 214 John Street, Aurora, IN 47001.

Steel City Ezra Brooks Bottle Club — R.R. #2, Box 32A, Valparaiso, IN 46383.

We Found 'Em Bottle & Insulator Club — P. O. Box 578, Bunker Hill, IN 46914.

IOWA

Iowa Antique Bottleers — 1506 Albia Rd., Ottumwa, IA 52501. 319-377-6041. Meets 4 times a year at various places. Newsletter: The Iowa Antique Bottleers. Club formed 1968, has 60 members.

Larkin Bottle Club — 107 W. Grimes, Red Oak, IA 51566.

KANSAS

Cherokee Strip Ezra Brooks Bottle & Specialty Club — P. O. Box 631, Arkansas City, KS 67005.

Flint Hills Beam & Specialty Club — 201 W. Pine, El Dorado, KS 67042.

Jayhawk Bottle Club — 7919 Grant, Overland Park, KS 66212.

Kansas City Antique Bottle Collectors — 5528 Aberdeen, Shawnee Mission, KS 66205. Phone 816-433-1398. Meets 6 p.m. 2nd Sunday at 1131 E. 77th, Kansas City, MO 64125. Newsletter: Privy Primer. Club formed 1974, has 15 family members.

Southeast Kansas Bottle & Relics Club — 115 N. Lafayette, Chanute, KS 66720. Phone 316-431-1643. Meets 7:30 p.m. 1st Wednesday at First National Bank Community Room. Newsletter: S.E. Kantique News. Club formed 1973, has 40 members.

Wichita Ezra Brooks Bottle & Specialties Club — 8045 Peachtree Street, Wichita, KS 67207.

KENTUCKY

Derby City Jim Beam Bottle Club — 4105 Spring Hill Road, Louisville, KY 40207.

Kentuckiana A.B. & Outhouse Society — 5801 River Knolls Drive, Louisville, KY 40222. 425-6995.

Kentucky Bluegrass Ezra Brooks Bottle Club — 6202 Tabor Drive, Louisville, KY 40218.

Kentucky Cardinal Beam Bottle Club — 428 Templin, Bardstown, KY 41104.

Louisville Bottle Collectors — 11819 Garrs Avenue, Anchorage, KY 40223.

LOUISIANA

Bayou Bottle Bugs — 216 Dahlia, New Iberia, LA 70560.

"Cajun Country Cousins" Ezra Brooks Bottle & Specialties Club — 1000 Chevis Street, Abbeville, LA 70510.

Cenia Bottle Club — c/o Pam Tullos, Rt. 1, Box 463, Dry Prong, LA 71423.

Dixie Diggers Bottle Club — P. O. Box 626, Empire, LA 70050.

Historical Bottle Association of Baton Rouge — 1843 Tudor Drive, Baton Rouge, LA 70815.

New Albany Glass Works Bottle Club — 732 N. Clark Boulevard, Parksville, LA 47130.

New Orleans Antique Bottle Club — c/o Ralph J. Luther, Jr., 4336 Palmyra St., New Orleans, LA 70119. Meets 7:30 p.m. last Friday of the month at Banks St. Social Club, 423 S. Lopez St. Newsletter: Crescent City Comments. Club formed 1969, has 42 family members.

North East Louisiana A.B.C. — P. O. Box 4192, Monroe, LA 71291. Phone 322-8359. Meets 7:00 p.m. 3rd Thursday at Ouachita Valley Library. Newsletter: Glass Treasures. Club formed 1972, has 25 family members.

Shreveport Antique Bottle Club — 1157 Arncliffe Dr., Shreveport, LA 71107. 221-0089.

MAINE

Dirigo Bottle Collectors Club — R.F.D. 3, Dexter, ME. Phone 207-924-3443. Meets 1st Tuesday at Eastern Maine Vocational Tec. Institute, Hogan Road, Bangor, ME. Newsletter: The Paper Label. Club formed 1969, has 21 members.

Dover Foxcroft Bottle Club — 50 Church Street, Dover Foxcroft, ME 04426.

The Glass Bubble Bottle Club — P. O. Box 91, Cape Neddick, ME 03902.

Jim Beam Collectors Club — 10 Lunt Road, Falmouth, ME 04105.

Kennebec Valley Bottle Club — 9 Glenwood Street, Augusta, ME 04330.

Mid Coast Bottle Club — c/o Miriam Winchenbach, Waldoboro, ME 04572.

New England Bottle Club — 45 Bolt Hill Road, Eliot, ME 03903.

Paul Bunyan Bottle Club — 237 14th Street, Bangor, ME 04401.

Pine Tree Antique Bottle Club — Buxton Road, Saco, ME 04072.

Tri-County Bottle Collectors Association — RFD 3, Dexter, ME 04930.

Waldo County Bottlenecks Club — Head-of-the-Tide, Belfast, ME 04915.

MARYLAND

Baltimore A.B.C. — 421 6 Ave. N.E., Glen Burnie, MD 21061. Meets 2nd Friday at Lutherville Elementary School, 1700 N. York Rd., Lutherville, MD 21093 at 7:30 p.m. Club formed 1970.

Blue & Gray Ezra Brooks Bottle Club — 2106 Sunnybrook Drive, Frederick, MD 21201.

Catoctin Beam Bottle Club — P. O. Box 2126, Silver Spring, MD 20902.

Mason Dixon Bottle Collectors Association — 601 Market Street, Denton, MD 21629.

South County Bottle Collector's Club — Bast Lane, Shady Side, MD 20867.

MASSACHUSETTS

Berkshire Antique Bottle Assn. — P. O. Box 753, Lenox, MA 01240.

The Cape Cod Antique Bottle Club — c/o Mrs. John Swanson, 262 Setucket Rd., Yarmouth, MA 02675.

Merrimack Valley Antique Bottle Club — c/o M. E. Tarleton, Hillside Road, Boxford, MA.

New England Beam & Specialty Club — 1104 Northampton Street, Holyoke, MA 01040.

Scituate Bottle Club — 54 Cedarwood Road, Scituate, MA 02066.

MONTANA

Hellgate Antique Bottle Club — P. O. Box 411, Missoula, MT 59801.

MICHIGAN

Central Michigan Krazy Korkers Bottle Club — Mid-Michigan Community College, Clare Ave., Harrison, MI 48625.

Chief Pontiac Antique Bottle Club — 13880 Neal Rd., Davisburg, MI 48019. c/o Larry Blascyk. 313 634-8469.

Dickinson County Bottle Club — 717 Henford Avenue, Iron Mountain, MI 49801.

Flint Antique Bottle Collectors Association — 450 Leta Avenue, Flint, MI 48507.

Flint Eagles Ezra Brooks Club — 1117 W. Remington Avenue, Flint, MI 48507.

Grand Valley Bottle Club — 31 Dickinson S.W., Grand Rapids, MI 49507.

Great Lakes Miniature Bottle Club — P. O. Box 245, Fairhaven MI 48023.

Huron Valley Bottle Club — 12475 Saline-Milan Road, Milan, MI 48160.

Kalamazoo A.B.C. — 628 Mill St., Kalamazoo, MI 49001. Phone 616-342-5077. Meets 2nd Monday at 628 Mill St. in Kalamazoo at 7 p.m. Club formed 1979, has 42 members.

Lionstone Collectors Bottle & Specialties Club of Michigan — 3089 Grand Blanc Road, Swartz Creek, MI 48473.

Manistee Coin & Bottle Club — 207 E. Piney Road, Manistee, MI 49660.

Metro & East Bottle and Jar Assn. — 309 Bellevue Park Drive, Fairview Heights, IL.

Metro Detroit Antique Bottle Club — 28860 Balmoral Way, Farmington Hills, MI 48018. Meets 3rd Thursday, 7:30 p.m. at Hazel Park Recreation Center. Has 50 family members.

Michigan Bottle Collectors Association — 144 W. Clark Street, Jackson, MI 49203.

Michigan's Vehicle City Beam Bottles & Specialties Club — 907 Root Street, Flint, MI 48503.

Northern Michigan Bottle Club — P. O. Box 421, Petoskey, MI 49770.

Old Corkers Bottle Club — RT 1, Iron River, MI 49935.

Traverse Area Bottle & Insulator Club — P. O. Box 205, Acme, MI 49610.

W.M.R.A.C.C. — 331 Bellevue S.W., Grand Rapids, MI 49508.

West Michigan Avon Collectors — 331 Bellevue S.W., Wyoming, MI 49508.

Wolverine Beam Bottle & Specialty Club of Michigan — 36009 Larchwood, Mt. Clemens, MI 48043.

World Wide Avon Bottle Collectors Club — 22708 Wick Road, Taylor, MI 48180.

Ye Old Corkers c/o Janet Gallup, Box 7, Gastr, MI 49927. Phone 906-265-485. Meets 7:15 p.m. at Bates Twp. School. Club formed 1968, has 20 members.

MINNESOTA

Arnfalt Collectors Beam Club — New Richard, MN 56072.

Dump Diggers — P. O. Box 24, Dover, MN 55929.

Lake Superior Antique Bottle Club — P. O. Box 67, Knife River, MN 55609.

Minnesota's First Antique B.C. — 5001 Queen Ave., North Minneapolis, MN 55430. Meets 8:00 p.m. 1st Thursday in member's homes. Newsletter: Bottle Diggers Dope. Club formed 1966, has 48 members.

North Star Historical Bottle Association, Inc. — P. O. Box 30343, St. Paul, MN 55175.

MISSISSIPPI

Middle Mississippi Antique Bottle Club — P. O. Box 233, Jackson, MS 39205.

Oxford Antique Bottlers — 128 Vivian Street, Oxford, MS 38633.

South Mississippi Antique Bottle Club — 203 S. 4th Avenue, Laurel, MS 39440.

South Mississippi Historical Bottle Club — 165 Belvedere Dr., Biloxi, MS, 388-6472.

MISSOURI

A.B.C. of Central Missouri — 726 W. Monroe, Mexico, MO 65265. Phone 314-581-1391. Meets 7:30 p.m. 1st Wednesday at Farm & Home Bldg., East Broadway, Columbia, MO. Newsletter: No Deposit No Return. Club formed in 1974, has 20 family members.

Antique Bottle & Relic Club of Central Missouri — c/o Ann Downing, Rt. 10, Columbia, MO 65210.

Bud Hastin's National Avon Club — P. O. Box 9868, Kansas City, MO 64134.

Greater Kansas City Jim Beam Bottle & Specialty Club — P. O. Box 6703, Kansas City, MO 64123.

Kansas City Antique Bottle Collectors Association — 1131 East 77 Street, Kansas City, MO 64131.

Mid-West Antique Bottle & Hobby Club — 122 Hightower Street, El Dorado Springs, MO 64744.

Mineral Area Bottle Club — Knob Lick, MO 63651.

Mound City Jim Beam Decanter Collectors — 42 Webster Acres, Webster Groves, MO 63119.

Northwest Missouri Bottle & Relic Club — 3006 S. 28th Street, St. Joseph, MO 64503.

St. Louis Antique Bottle Collectors Assn. — 306 N. Woodlawn Ave., Kirkwood, MO 63122.

St. Louis Ezra Brooks Ceramics Club — 42 Webster Acres, Webster Groves, MO 63119.

NEBRASKA

Mini-Seekers — "A" Acres, Rt. 8, Lincoln, NE 68506.

Nebraska Antique Bottle and Collectors Club — P. O. Box 37021, Omaha, NE 68137.

Nebraska Big Red Bottle & Specialty Club — N Street Drive-in, 200 So. 18th Street, Lincoln, NE 68508.

NEVADA

Jim Beam Bottle Club of Las Vegas — 212 N. Orland Street, Las Vegas, NV 89107.

Las Vegas Bottle Club — 3115 Las Vegas Blvd., No. Space 56, North Las Vegas, NV 89030. Phone 702-643-1101. Meets 7:30 p.m. 1st Wednesday at 2832 E. Flamingo Rd., Las Vegas. Newsletter: The Front Line. Club formed 1976, has 45 members.

Las Vegas Bottle Club — 884 Lulu Avenue, Las Vegas, NV 89119.

Lincoln County A.B.C. — P. O. Box 191, Callente, NV 89008. Phone 726-3655. Meets 7:30 p.m. 2nd Tuesday at Pioche Housing Admin. Bldg. Newsletter: Bottle Talk. Club formed 1971, has 30 members.

Nevada Beam Club — P. O. Box 426, Fallon, NV 89406.

Reno/Sparks A.B.C.— P. O. Box 1061, Verdi, NV 89439. Meets 3rd Wednesday at McKinley Park School. Newsletter: Diggers Dirt. Club formed 1965, has 30 members.

Southern Nevada Antique Bottle Club — 431 No. Spruce Street, Las Vegas, NV 89101.

Virginia & Truckee Jim Beam Bottle & Specialties Club — P. O. Box 1596, Carson City, NV 89701.

Wee Bottle Club International — P. O. Box 1195, Las Vegas, NV 89101.

NEW HAMPSHIRE

Bottleers of New Hampshire — 125A Central Street, Farmington, NH 03835.

Granite State Bottle Club — R.F.D. #1, Belmont, NH 03220.

Yankee Bottle Club — P. O. Box 702, Keene, NH 03431.

NEW JERSEY

Antique Bottle Collectors Club of Burlington County — 18 Willow Road, Bordentown, NJ 08505.

Artifact Hunters Association Inc. — c/o 29 Lake Road, Wayne, NJ 07470.

The Jersey Devil Bottle Diggers Club — 14 Church Street, Mt. Holly, NJ 08060.

The Jersey Shore Bottle Club — Box 995, Toms River, NJ 08753.

Lakeland A.B.C. — 18 Alan Lane, Mine Hill, Dover, NJ 07801. Phone 201-366-7482. Meets 3rd Friday except July and August on Roosevelt School on Hillside Ave., Suecasunna, NJ in the cafeteria. Has 50 members.

Lionstone Collectors Club of Delaware Valley — R.D. #3 Box 93, Sewell, NY 08080.

New Jersey Ezra Brooks Bottle Club — South Main Street, Cedarville, NJ 08311.

North New Jersey Antique Bottle Club Association — P. O. Box 617, Westwood, NJ 07675.

South Jersey's Heritage Bottle & Glass Club Inc. — Box 122, Glassboro, NJ 08028. Phone 609-423-5038. Meets 7:30 p.m. 4th Wednesday, September through June, at Owen's III. Club House, 70 Sewell St., Glassboro, NJ. Newsletter: The Heritage Newsletter. Club formed 1970, has 200 members.

Sussex County Antique Bottle Collectors — Division of Sussex County Historical Society, 82 Main Street, Newton, NJ 07860.

Trenton Jim Beam Bottle Club, Inc. — 17 Easy Street, Freehold, NJ 07728.

Twin Bridges Beam Bottle & Specialty Club — P. O. Box 347, Pennsville, NJ 08070.

West Essex Bottle Club — 76 Beaufort Avenue, Livingston, NJ 07039.

NEW MEXICO

Roadrunner Bottle Club of New Mexico — 2341 Gay Road S.W., Albuquerque, NM 87105.

Cave City Antique Bottle Club — Rt. 1 Box 155, Carlsbad, NM 88220.

NEW YORK

Auburn Bottle Club — 297 South St. Road, Auburn, NY 13021.

Catskill Mountains Jim Beam Bottle Club — Six Gardner Avenue, Middletown, NY 10940.

Chautauqua County Bottle Collectors Club — Morse Hotel, Main Street, Sherman, NY 14781.

Eastern Monroe County Bottle Club — c/o Bethlehem Lutheran Church, 1767 Plank Road, Webster, NY 14580.

Empire State Bottle Collectors Association — c/o Dr. L. Simpson, Rd. #3, Fulton, NY 13069.

Empire State Jim Beam Bottle Club — P. O. Box 561, Farmingdale Post Office, Main Street, Farmingdale, NY 11735.

Finger Lakes Bottle Club Association — P. O. Box 815, Ithaca, NY 14850.

Genessee Valley Bottle Collectors Assn.— P. O. Box 7528, West Ridge Station, Rochester, NY 14610. Phone 716-872-4015. Meets 7:30 p.m. 3rd Thursday at Klem Rd. School, Webster, NY. Newsletter: Applied Seals. Club formed 1969, has 155 family members.

Greater Catskill Antique Bottle Club — P. O. Box 411, Liberty, NY.

Hudson Valley Bottle Club — c/o Robert Jordy, 255 Fostertown Rd., Newburgh, NY 12550.

Hudson River Jim Beam Bottle and Specialties Club — 48 College Road, Monsey, NY 10952.

Northern New York Bottle Club Association — P. O. Box 257, Adams Center, NY 13606.

North Country Bottle Collectors Association — Route 1, Canton, NY 13617.

Rensselaer County Antique Bottle Club — Box 92, Troy, NY 12180.

Rochester New York Bottle Club — 7908 West Henrietta Road, Rush, NY 14543.

Southern Tier Bottle & Insulator Collectors Association — 47 Dickinson Avenue, Port Dickinson, NY 13901.

Suffolk County Antique Bottle Association of Coney Island, Inc. — P. O. Box 943, Melville, NY 11746.

Tryon Bottle Badgers — Box 146, Tribes Hill, NY 12177.

Twin Counties Old Bottle Club — Don McBride, Star Rt., Box 242, Palenville, NY 2463, 518-943-5399.

Upper Susquehanna Bottle Club — P. O. Box 83, Milford, NY 13807.

Warwick Valley Bottle Club — Box 393, Warwick, NY 10990.

Western New York B.C.A. — c/o 62 Adams St., Jamestown, NY 14701. Phone 716-487-9645. Meets 8 p.m., 1st Wednesday except January at Buffalo Savings Bank, Eastern Hills Mall, Clarence, NY. Newsletter: Traveler's Companion. Club formed 1967, has 51 club members.

Western New York Bottle Collectors — 87 S. Bristol Avenue, Lockport, NY 14094.

West Valley Bottleique Club — Box 204, Killbuck, NY 14748. Phone 716-945-5769. Meets 8:00 p.m. 3rd Thursday at West Valley American Legion, Rt. 240, West Valley, NY. Newsletter: The Bottleique Banner. Club formed 1967, has 36 family members.

NORTH CAROLINA

Blue Ridge Bottle and Jar Club — Dogwood Lane, Black Mountain, NC 28711.

Carolina Bottle Club — c/o Industrial Piping Co., Anonwood, Charlotte, NC 28210.

Carolina Jim Beam Bottle Club — 1014 N. Main Street, Burlington, NC 27215.

Goldsboro Bottle Club — 2406 E. Ash Street, Goldsboro, NC 27530.

Greater Greensboro Moose Ezra Brooks Bottle Club — 217 S. Elm Street, Greensboro, NC 27401.

Kinston Collectors Club, Inc. — 325 E. Lenoir, Kinston, NC 28501.

Wilmington Bottle & Artifact Club — 183 Arlington Drive, Wilmington, NC 28401. Phone 919-763-3701. Meets 1st Wednesday, Carolina Savings & Loan Board Room. Club formed 1977, has 25 members.

Wilson Antique Bottle & Artifact Club — Route 1 Box 414, Wilson, NC 27893.

Yadkin Valley Bottle Club — General Delivery, Gold Hill, NC 28071.

OHIO

The Buckeye Bottle Club — 229 Oakwood Street, Elyria, OH 44035.

Buckeye Bottle Diggers — Rt. 2 Box 77, Thornville, OH.

Buckeye Jim Beam Bottle Club — 1211 Ashland Avenue, Columbus, OH 43212.

Central Ohio Bottle Club — 931 Minerva Ave., Columbus, OH 43229.

Diamond Pin Winners Avon Club — 5281 Fredonia Avenue, Dayton, OH 45431.

Findlay Antique Bottle Club — P. O. Box 1329, Findlay, OH 45840, Phone 419-422-3183. Meets 2nd Sunday at 7:00 p.m. at Findlay College Croy Center, Findlay, OH. Newsletter: Whittlemarks. Club formed 1976, has 35 members.

First Capitol B.C. — c/o Maxie Harper, Rt. 1 Box 94, Laurelville, OH 43135.

Gem City Beam Bottle Club — 1463 E. Stroop Road, Dayton, OH 45429.

Heart of Ohio Bottle Club — Box 353, New Washington, OH 44854, 419-492-2829.

Jefferson County A.B.C. — 1223 Oakgrove Ave., Steubenville, OH 43952.

North Eastern Ohio Bottle Club — P. O. Box 57, Madison, OH 44057, 614-282-8918.

Northwest Ohio Bottle Club — 104 W. Main, Norwalk, OH 44857.

Ohio Bottle Club — P. O. Box 585, Barberton, OH 44203.

Ohio Ezra Brooks Bottle Club — 8741 Kirtland Chardon Road, Kirtland Hills, OH 44094.

Rubber Capitol Jim Beam Club — 151 Stephens Road, Akron, Ohio 44312.

Sara Lee Bottle Club — 27621 Chagrin Boulevard, Cleveland, OH 44122.

Southwestern Ohio Antique Bottle and Jar Club — Box 53, North Hampton, OH. Meets 1st Sunday at 1:30 p.m. at Meat Cutters Local 430 Hall, 1325 E. 3rd St., Dayton, OH. Newsletter: Shards. Formed 1976, has 29 family members.

Tri State Historical Bottle Club — P. O. Box 409, East Liverpool, OH 43920.

OKLAHOMA

Bar-Dew Antique Bottle Club — 817 E. 7th Street, Dewey, OK 74029.

Little Dixie Antique Bottle Club — P. O. Box 741, Krebs, OK 74501.

McDonnel Douglas Antique Club — 5752 E. 25th Place, Tulsa, OK 74114.

Ponca City Old Bottle Club — 2408 Juanito, Ponca City, Ok 74601.

Southwest Oklahoma Antique Bottle Club — 35 S. 49th Street, Lawton, OK 73501.

Tulsa Antique Bottle & Relic Club — P. O. Box 4278, Tulsa, OK 74104.

OREGON

Central Oregon Bottle & Relic Club — 671 N.E. Seward, Bend, OR 97701.

Central Oregon Bottle & Relic Club — 1545 Kalama Avenue, Redmond, OR 97756.

Central South Oregon Antique Bottle Club — 708 South F. Street, Lakeview, OR 97630.

Emerald Empire Bottle Club — P. O. Box 292, Eugene, OR 97401.

Frontier Collectors — 504 N.W. Bailey, Pendleton, OR 97801.

Gold Diggers Antique Bottle Club — 1958 S. Stage Road, Medford, OR 97501.

Lewis & Clark Historical Bottle & Collectors Soc. — 8018 S.E. Hawthorne Blvd., Portland, OR.

Lewis & Clark Historical Bottle Society — 4828 N.E. 33rd, Portland, OR.

Molalla Bottle Club — Route 1 Box 205, Mulino, OR 97042.

Oregon Antique Bottle Club — Route 3 Box 23, Molalla, OR 97038.

The Oregon Beaver Beam Bottle & Specialties — P. O. Box 7, Sheridan, OR 97378.

Oregon B.C.A. — 3661 S.E. Nehalem St., Portland, OR 97202. Meets 8:00 p.m. every 3rd Saturday, except July and August. Newsletter: The Bottle Examiner. Club formed 1966, has 60 family members.

Pioneer Fruit Jar Collectors Association — P. O. Box 175, Grand Ronde, OR 97347.

Siskiyou Antique Bottle Collectors Assn. — P. O. Box 1335, Medford, OR 97501.

PENNSYLVANIA

Antique Bottle Club of Burlington County — 8445 Walker St., Philadelphia, PA 19136.

Beaver Valley Jim Beam Club — 1335 Indiana Avenue, Monaca, PA 15061.

Bedford County Antique Bottle Club — 107 Seifert St., Bedford, PA 15522.

Camoset Bottle Club — Box 252, Johnstown, PA 15901.

Classic Glass Bottle Collectors — 1720 Memorial Ave., (soon to be in Aug. at R.D. #2, Cogan Station, PA 17728.

Delaware Valley Bottle Club — 12 Belmar Road, Hatboro, PA 19040.

Del-Val Bottle Club — Rt. 152 & Hilltown Pike, Hilltown, PA. Mailing address: Duffield's, 12 Belmar Rd., Hatboro, PA 19040.

East Coast Double Springs Specialty Bottle Club — P. O. Box 419, Carlisle, PA 17013.

East Coast Ezra Brooks Bottle Club — 2815 Fiddler Green, Lancaster, PA 17601.

Endless Mountain Antique Bottle Club — P. O. Box 75, Granville Summit, PA 16926.

Erie Bottle Club — P. O. Box 373, Erie, PA 16512.

Flood City Jim Beam Bottle Club — 231 Market Street, Johnstown, PA 15901.

Forks of the Delaware Bottle Collectors, Inc. — Box 693, Easton, PA 18042.

Friendly Jim's Beam Club — 508 Benjamin Franklin H.W. East, Douglassville, PA 19518.

Indiana Bottle Club — 240 Oak Street, Indiana, PA 15701.

Laurel Valley Bottle Club — 618 Monastery Dr Latrobe, PA 15650. Phone 412-537-4800. Meet at 8:00 p.m. last Saturday at Oak Grove Civi Center. Newsletter: Digger's Delight. Forme 1975, has 35 members.

Middletown Area B.C.A. — P. O. Box 1, Middle town, PA 17057. Phone 717-939-0288. Meets 2n Tuesday, 7:30 p.m. at Middletown Elks Lodge Emaus St., Middletown. Club formed 1973, ha 54 members.

The Pennsylvania Bottle Collectors Association — 825 Robin Road, Lancaster, PA 17601.

Pennsylvania Dutch Jim Beam Bottle Club — 812 Pointview Avenue, Ephrata, PA 17522.

Philadelphia Coll. Club — 8445 Walker St., Phil adelphia, PA. Meets 1st Monday at 8:00 p.m. a Trevose Savings Bank, L St. and Hunting Par Ave. Club has 25 members.

Philadelphia Bottle Club — 8203 Elbero Avenue, Philadelphia, PA 19111.

Pittsburgh Bottle Club — P. O. Box 401, In gomar, PA 15127.

Pittsburgh Bottle Club — 1528 Railroad Street Sewickley, PA 15143.

Tri-County Antique Bottle & Treasure Club — R.D. #2 Box 30, Reynoldsville, PA 15851.

Washington County Bottle & Insulator Club — R.D. #2 Box 342, Carmichaels, PA 15320. Phone 412-966-7996. Meets 7:30 p.m. 1st Tuesday a Washington Library. Newsletter: Bottle Nu News.

RHODE ISLAND

Little Rhody Bottle Club — 3161 West Shore Road, Warwick, RI 02886.

SOUTH CAROLINA

Greer Bottle Collectors Club — Box 142, Greer SC 29651.

Lexington County Antique Bottle Club — 20 Roberts Street, Lexington, SC 29072.

Piedmont Bottle Collectors — c/o R. W. Leizear Route 3, Woodruff, SC 29388.

South Carolina Bottle Club — 1119 Greenbridge Lane, Columbia, SC 29210. Meets 8:00 p.m. 1s Thursday at Dewey's Antiques. Newsletter South Carolina Bottle News. Club formed 1970 has 35 members.

Union Bottle Club — 107 Pineneedle Road Union, SC 29379.

Upper Piedmont Bottle and Advertising Collec tors Club — Rt. 3, Woodruff, SC, c/o R. W Leizear.

TENNESSEE

Cotton Carnival Beam Club — P. O. Box 17951 Memphis, TN 38117.

Memphis Bottle Collectors Club — 232 Tifton Rd., Memphis, TN 38111, 901-272-8998.

Middle Tenn. Bottle Collector's Club — P. O Box 120083, Nashville, TN 37212. Phone 615 269-4402. Meets 2nd Tuesday at 7:00 p.m. Don elson Branch Public Library. Newsletters: Note From a Bottle Bug. Club formed March 1969 has 45 members.

TEXAS

Alamo Chapter Antique Bottle Club Association — 701 Castano Avenue, San Antonio, TX 78209.

Austin Bottle & Insulator Collectors Club — 1614 Ashberry Drive, Austin, TX 78723, 453-7900.

El Paso Insulator Club — Martha Stevens, Chairman, 4556 Bobolink, El Paso, TX 79922.

The Exploration Society — 603 9th St. NAS, Corpus Christie, TX 78419, 992-2902.

Foard C. Hobby Club — P. O. Box 625, Crowell, TX 79227.

Fort Concho Bottle Club — 1703 West Avenue, N. San Angelo, TX 76901.

Foursome (Jim Beam) — 1208 Azalea Drive, Longview, TX 75601.

Gulf Coast Beam Club — 128 W. Bayshore Drive, Baytown, TX 77520.

Gulf Coast Bottle & Jar Club — Box 1754, Pasadena, TX 77501. Phone 713-592-3078. Meets 7:30 p.m. 1st Monday at 1st Pasadena State Bank, Corner of Southmore and Tarter. Newsletter: Gulf Coast Bottle & Jar Club News. Club formed 1969, has 55 family members.

Republic of Texas Jim Beam Bottle & Specialty Club — 616 Donley Drive, Euless, TX 76039.

San Antonio Antique Bottle Club — c/o 3801 Broadway, Witte Museum-Auditorium, San Antonio, TX 78209.

Texas Longhorn Bottle Club — P. O. Box 5346, Irving, TX 75060.

UTAH

Utah Antique Bottle and Relic Club — 1594 W. 500 No., Salt Lake City, UT 84116, 328-4142.

Utah Antique Bottle Club — P. O. Box 15, Ogden, UT 84402.

VIRGINIA

Apple Valley Bottle Collectors Club — P. O. Box 2201, Winchester, VA 22601. Meets 2 p.m. 3rd Sunday at Gore-Volunteer Fire Hall, U.S. 50. Newsletter: Bottle Worm. Club formed 1973, has 36 members.

Bottle Club of the Virginia Peninsula — Box 5456, Newport News, VA 23605.

Dixie Beam Bottle Club — Route 4 Box 94-A, Glen Allen, VA 23060.

Hampton Roads Area Bottle Collector's Assn. — Virginia Beach Federal Savings & Loan, 4848 Virginia Beach Blvd. in Virginia Beach.

Historical Bottle Diggers of Virginia — Route 3 Box 226, Harrisburg, VA 22801.

Metropolitan Antique Bottle Club — 109 Howard St., Dumfries, VA 22026, 221-8055.

Potomac Bottle Collectors — 6602 Orland St., Falls Church, VA 22043. Phone 703-534-7271 or 534-5619. Meets 8:00 p.m. 1st Monday at Coca-Cola Plant, Seminary Road. Club formed 1972, has 156 members.

Richmond Area B.C. Assn — 7 N. 8th St., Richmond, VA 23219. Meets 7:30 p.m. 3rd Monday at Bank of Va., 8th and Main. Newsletter: The Bottle Digger. Club formed 1970, has 20 members.

Tidewater Beam Bottle & Specialty Club — P. O. Box 14012, Norfolk, VA 23518.

Ye Old Bottle Club — General Delivery, Clarksville, VA 23927.

WASHINGTON

Antique Bottle and Glass Collectors — P. O. Box 163, Snohomish, WA 98290.

Capitol Collectors & Bottle Club — P. O. Box 202, Olympia, WA 98507.

Cascade Treasure Club — 254 N.E. 45th, Seattle, WA 98105.

The Chinook Ezra Brooks Bottle Club — 233 Kelso Drive, Kelso, WA 98626.

Evergreen State Beam Bottle & Specialty Club — P. O. Box 99244, Seattle, WA 98199.

Klickital Bottle Club Association — Goldendale, WA 98620.

Inland Empire Bottle & Collectors Club — 7703 E. Trent Avenue, Spokane, WA 99206.

Mt. Rainer Ezra Brooks Bottle Club — P. O. Box 1201, Lynwood, WA 98178.

Northwest Jim Beam Bottle Collectors Association — P. O. Box 7401, Spokane, WA 99207.

Northwest Treasure Hunter's Club — East 107 Astor Drive, Spokane, WA 99208.

Pacific Northwest Avon Bottle Club — 25425 68th South, Kent, WA 98031.

Seattle Jim Beam Bottle Collectors Club — 8015 15th Avenue N.W., Seattle, WA 98107.

Skagit Bottle & Glass Collectors — 1314 Virginia, Mt. Vernon, WA 98273.

South Whedley Bottle Club — c/o Juanita Clyde, Langley, WA 98260.

Washington Bottle Collectors Association — P. O. Box 80045, Seattle, WA 98108. Meets 5 p.m. 2nd Saturday at King Co. Recreations Center, 46th and 188th St. Newsletter: Ghost Town Echo. Club formed 1966, has 30 family members.

WEST VIRGINIA

Wild & Wonderful West Virginia Ezra Brooks Bottle & Specialty Club — 1924 Pennsylvania Avenue, Weirton, WV 26062.

WISCONSIN

Badger Bottle Diggers — 1420 McKinley Road, Eau Claire, WI 54701.

Badger Jim Beam Club of Madison — P. O. Box 5612, Madison, WI 53705.

Cameron Bottle Diggers — P. O. Box 276, 314 South 1st Street, Cameron, WI 54822.

Central Wisconsin Bottle Collectors — 1608 Main Street, Stevens Point, WI 54481.

Milwaukee Antique Bottle Club — N 88 W 15211 Cleveland Avenue, Menomonee Falls, WI 53051.

Milwaukee Jim Beam Bottle and Specialties Club, Ltd. — N. 95th St. W. 16548 Richmond Drive, Menomonee Falls, WI 53051.
Milwaukee Antique Bottle Club, Inc. — 2343 Met-To-Wee Lane, Wauwatosa, WI 53226. Phone 414-257-0158. Meets 7:30 p.m., 1st Wednesday, 8701 W. Chambers St., Cooper Park. Newsletter: Cream City Courier. Club formed 1973, has 57 members.
Shot Tower Jim Beam Club — 818 Pleasant Street, Mineral Point, WI 53565.
South Central Wisconsin Bottle Club — c/o Dr. T. M. Schwartz, Route 1, Arlington, WI 53911.

WYOMING
Cheyenne Antique Bottle Club — 4417 E. 8th St., Cheyenne, WY 82001.
Insubott Bottle Club — P. O. Box 34, Lander, WY 82520.

CANADA
St. John B.C. — 25 Orange St., St. John N.B. E2L 1L9. Phone 652-3537. Meets 8 p.m. 1st Monday at N.B. Museum. Newsletter: The Historical Flask. Club formed 1969, has 25 members.

BOTTLE DEALERS

ALABAMA
BIRMINGHAM — Steve Holland, 1740 Serene Dr., Birmingham, AL 35215. 853-7929. *Bottles dug around Alabama.*
BIRMINGHAM — Walker's Antique Bottles, 2768 Hanover Circle, Birmingham, AL 35205. (205) 933-7902. *Medicines, crown sodas.*
FORT PAYNE — Terry & Katie Gillis, 115 Mountain Dr., Fort Payne, AL 35967. (205) 845-4541.
FORT PAYNE — C. B. and Barbara Meares, Rt. 3, Box 161, Ft. Payne, AL (205) 638-6225.
MOBILE — Bottles and Stuff, Clinton P. King, 4075 Moffatt Road, Mobile, AL 36618. (205) 344-2959. *Pontiled medicines, local bottles, black glass, pottery.*
MOBILE — Loretta and Mack Wimmer, 3012 Cedar Cresent Dr., Mobile, AL 36605.
OZARK — Old Time Bottle House and Museum, 306 Parker Hills Dr., Ozark, AL 36360. *Old bottles, stone jugs, fruit jars.*
SPANISH FORT — Elroy and Latrelle Webb, 203 Spanish Main, Spanish Fort, AL 36527. (205) 626-1067.
THEODORE — Ed's Lapidary Shop, 7927 Historic Mobile Parkway, US HWY #90, 36582. Call (205) 653-0713. *Locally dug bottles.*

ARIZONA
PHOENIX — The Brewery, 1605 N. 7th Ave., Phoenix, AZ 85007. 252-1415. *Brewery items.*
PHOENIX — Tom and Kay Papa, 3821 E. Mercer Lane, Phoenix, AZ 85028. (602) 996-3240.
PINETOP — Ray and Dyla Lawton, Box 374, Pinetop, AZ 85935. (602) 366-4449.

ARKANSAS
JACKSONVILLE — Charles and Mary Garner, 620 Carpenter Dr., Jacksonville, AR 72076. (501) 982-8381.
RISON — Rufus Buie, P. O. Box 226, Rison, AR 71665. (501) 325-6816.
ASHDOWN — Buddy's Bottles, 610 Park Ave., Ashdown, AR 71822. (501) 898-5877. *Hutchinson sodas, medicines. Arkansas bottles always wanted.*

CALIFORNIA
AROMAS — Bobbie's Country Store, in the Big Red Barn, 1000 El Camino Real, HWY 101, P. O. Box 1761, Carmel, CA 93921. (408) 394-3257.
BEVERLY HILLS — Alex Kerr, 9584 Wilshire Blvd., Beverly Hills, CA 90212. (213) 762-6320.
BUENA PARK — Walter Yeargain, 6222 San Lorenzo Dr., Buena Park, CA 90620. (714) 826-5264.
BUTLER — Wayne Hortman, P. O. Box 183, Butler, CA 31006. (912) 862-3699.
CHICO — Randy Taylor, 566 E. 12th St., (916) 342-4928.
CITRUS HEIGHTS — Duke Jones, P. O. Box 642, Citrus Heights, CA 95610. (916) 725-1989. *California embossed beers.*
CONCORD — Stoney and Myrt Stone, 1925 Natoma Dr., Concord, CA 94519. (415) 685-6326.
CORONA — Russell Brown, P. O. Box 441, Corona, CA 91720. (714) 737-7164.
CYPRESS — Gary and Harriet Miller, 5034 Oxford Dr., Cypress, CA 90630. (714) 828-4778.
FILLMORE — Mike and Joyce Amey, 625 Clay St., Fillmore, CA 93015. (805) 524-3364.
HESPERIA — Gene and Phyllis Kemble, 14733 Poplar St., Hesperia, CA 92345. (714) 244-5863.
HUNTINGTON BEACH — Larry Caddell, 15881 Malm Circle, Huntington Beach, CA 92647. (714) 897-8133.
LONG BEACH — Omar and Helen Sherwood, 4700 Lakewood Bl. #4, Long Beach, CA 90808. (213) 421-9124.
LOS ALTOS — Louis and Cindy Pellegrini, 1231 Thurston, Los Altos, CA 94022. (415) 965-9060.
MARIETTA — John and Estelle Hewitt, 366 Church St., Marietta, CA 30060. (404) 422-5525.
REDDING — Byrl and Grace Rittenhouse, 3055 Birch Way, Redding, CA 96002. (916) 243-0320.
REDDING — Ralph Hollibaugh, 2087 Gelnyose Dr., Redding, CA 96001. (916) 243-4672.
SACRAMENTO — George and Rose Reidenbach, 2816 - "P" St., Sacramento, CA 95816. (916) 451-0063.
SACTO — Peck and Audie Markota, 4627 Oakhallow Dr. Sacto, CA 95842. (916) 334-3260.

SAN FRANCISCO — Bill Groves, 2620 Sutter St., San Francisco, CA 94115. (415) 922-6248.

SAN JOSE — Terry and Peggy Wright, 6249 Lean Ave., San Jose, CA 95123. (408) 578-5580.

SOLANA BEACH — T.R. Schweighart, 1123 Santa Luisa Dr., Solana Beach, CA 92075.

STOCKTON — Frank and Judy Brockman, 104 W. Park, Stockton, CA 95202. (209) 948-0746.

SUTTER CREEK — The Glass Bottle, now in "Creekside Shops," 22 Main St., Sutter Creek, HWY 49. Mailing address, Box 374, Sutter Creek, CA 95685. (209) 267-0122. *Old figural, perfumes, whiskey, milk.*

WESTWOOD — Whitman's Bookkeeping Service, 219 Fir St., P. O. Drawer KK 96147. (916) 256-3437. *Soda.*

WINDSOR — Betty and Ernest Zumwalt, 5519 Kay Dr., Windsor, CA 95492. (707) 545-8670.

YREKA — Sleep's Siskiyou Specialties, 217 West Miner, P. O. Box 689, Yreka, CA. 96097.

COLORADO

SNOWMASS VILLAGE — Jim Bishop, Box 5554, Snowmass Village, CO 81615. 923-2348. *Miniature liquor.*

CONNECTICUT

ASHFORD — Woodlawn Antiques, P. O. Box 277, Mansfield Center, Ashford, CT 06250. (203) 429-2983. *Flasks, bitters, inks.*

FAIRFIELD — Stephen Link, 953 Post Rd., Fairfield, CT 06430.

HARTFORD — B'Thea's Cellar, 31 Kensington St., Hartford, CT 06112. 249-4686.

LIME ROCK — Mary's Old Bottles. White Hollow Road, Lakeville, CT 06039. (203) 435-2961. *Bottles.*

MYSTIC — Bob's Old Bottles, 656 Noank Rd. RT. 215, Mystic, CT 06355. (203) 536-8542.

NEW HAVEN — Gerald "J." Jaffee and Lori Waldeck, P. O. Box 1741, New Haven, CT 06507. (203) 787-4232. *Poisons (bottles), insulators.*

NIANTIC — Albert Corey, 153 W. Main St., Niantic, CT 06357. (203) 739-7493. *No. Eastern bottles, jars, stoneware.*

SAYBROOK — Bill Stankard, 61 Old Post Rd., Saybrook, CT 06475. (203) 388-4235.

WATERTOWN — George E. Johnson, 2339 Litchfield Rd., Watertown, CT 06795. (203) 274-1785.

WOODSTOCK — Norman and Elizabeth Heckler, Woodstock Valley, CT 06282. (203) 974-1634.

FLORIDA

BROOKSVILLE — E.S. and Romie MacKenzie, Box 57, Brooksville, FL 33512. (904) 796-3400.

FORT MEADE — M and S Bottles and Antiques, Marlaine and Steve, 421 Wilson St., Mail address: Rt. 2, Box 84B3, Fort Meade, FL 33841. 285-9421.

FT. PIERCE — Gore's Shoe Repair, 410 Orange Avenue, Ft. Pierce, FL 33450. *Old bottles, Florida bottles, black glass.*

HOLLISTER — This-N That Shop (Albert B. Coleman), P. O. Box 185, Hollister, FL 32047. (904) 328-3658.

HOLLYWOOD — Hickory Stick Antiques, 400 So. 57 Terr., Hollywood, FL 33023. 962-3434. *Canning jars, black glass, household.*

JACKSONVILLE — The Browns, 6512 Mitford Rd., Jacksonville, FL 32210. 771-2091. *Sodas, min. waters, milk, glass, black glass.*

KEY LARGO — Dwight Pettit, 33 Sea Side Dr. Key Largo, FL 33037. (305) 852-8338.

NEW PORT RICHEY — Gerae and Lynn McLarty, 6705 Dogwood Ct, New Port Richey, FL 33552. (813) 849-7166.

ORMOND BEACH — Mike Kollar, 50 Sylvania Pl., Ormond Beach, FL 32074.

PALMETTO — Jon Vander Schouw, Box 1151, Palmetto, FL 33561. (813) 722-1375.

SANFORD — Hidden-Bottle-Shop, 2656 Grandview, Sanford, FL 32771. 322-7181.

TALLAHASSEE — Harry O. Thomas, 2721 Parson's Rest., Tallahassee, FL 32308. (904) 893-3834.

TITUSVILLE — Insulators - L. L. Linscott, 3557 Nicklaus Drive, Titusville, FL 32780. (305) 267-9170. *Fruit jars, porcelain insulators.*

GEORGIA

BUTLER — Wayne's Bottles, Box 183, Butler, GA 31006. (912) 862-3699. *Odd colors, odd shapes.*

DUNWOODY — Carlo and Dot Sellari, Box 888553. Dunwoody, GA 30338. (404) 451-2483.

EATONTON — James T. Hicks, Rt. 4, Box 265, Eatonton, GA 31024. (404) 485-9280.

LAURENCEVILLE — Dave and Tia Janousek, 2293 Mulligan Circle, Laurenceville, GA 30245.

MACON — Schmitt House Bottle Diggers, 5532 Jane Rue Circle, Macon, GA 31206. (912) 781-6130. *Indiana, Kentucky bottles.*

NEWNAN — Bob and Barbara Simmons, 152 Greenville St., Newnan, GA 30263. (404) 251-2471.

HAWAII

HONOLULU — The Hawaiian Antique Bottle Shop, Kahuku Sugar Mill, P. O. Box 495, Honolulu, HI 96731. 293-5581. *Hawaiian soda, whiskey, medicine, milk.*

HONOLULU — The Hawaii Bottle Museum, 1044 Kalapaki St., P. O. Box 25153, Honolulu, HI 96825. (808) 395-4671. *Hawaiian bottles, Oriental bottles and pottery.*

IDAHO

SILVER CITY — Idaho Hotel, Jordan Street, Box 75, Murphy, ID 83650. (208) 495-2520.

BUHL — John Cothern, Rt. #1, Buhl, ID 83316. (208) 543-6713.

ILLINOIS

ADDISON — Ronald Selcke, 4N236 8th Ave., Addison, IL 60101. (312) 543-4848.

ALTON — Sean Mullikin, 5014 Alicia Dr., Alton, IL 62002. (312) 466-7506.

ALTON — Mike Spiiroff, 1229 Alton St., Alton, IL 62002. (618) 462-2283.

BELLEVILLE — Wayne and Jacqueline Brammer, 309 Bellevue Dr., Belleville, IL 62223. (618) 233-8841.

CERRO GORDO — Marvin and Carol Ridgeway, 450 W. Cart, Cerro Gordo, IL 61818. (217) 763-3271.

CHAMPAIGN — Casad's Antiques, 610 South State St., Champaign, IL 61820. (217) 356-8455. *Fruit jars, milk bottles, Avons.*

CHICAGO — Tom and Gladys Bartels, 5315 W. Warwick, Chicago, IL 60641. (312) 725-2433.

CHICAGO — Ernest Brooks, 9023 S. East End, Chicago, IL 60617. (312) 375-9233.

CHICAGO — 1st Chicago Bottle Club, P. O. Box A3382, Chicago, IL 60690.

CHICAGO — Fruit Jars, 5003 West Berwyn, Chicago, IL 60630. (312) 777-0443. *Fruit jars.*

CHICAGO — Joe Healy, 3421 W. 76th St. Chicago, IL 60652.

CHICAGO — William Kiggans, 7747 South Kedzie, Chicago, IL 60652. (312) 925-6148.

CHICAGO — Carl Malik, 8655 S. Keeler, Chicago, IL 60652. (312) 767-8568.

CHICAGO — Jerry and Aryliss McCann, 5003 W. Berwyn, Chicago, IL 60630. (312) 777-0443.

CHICAGO — Louis Metzinger, 4140 N. Mozart, Chicago, IL 60618. (312) 478-9034.

CHICAGO — L. D. and Barbara Robinson, 1933 So. Homan, Chicago, IL 60623. (312) 762-6096.

CHICAGO — Paul R. Welko, 5727 S. Natoma Ave., Chicago, IL 60638. (312) 582-3564. *Blob top and Hutchinson sodas.*

CHICAGO HTS. — Al and Sue Verley, 486 Longwood Ct., Chicago Hts., IL 60411. (312) 754-4132.

DEERFIELD — Jim Hall, 445 Partridge Lane, Deerfield, IL 60014. (312) 541-5788.

DEERFIELD — John and Claudia Panek, 816 Holmes, Deerfield, IL 60015. (312) 945-5493.

DIETERICH — Ray's and Betty's Antiques, Dieterich, IL 62424. (217) 925-5449. *Bitters.*

ELMWOOD PARK — Keith and Ellen Leeders, 1728 N. 76th Ave., Elmwood Park, IL 60635. (312) 453-2085.

GODFREY — Jeff Cress, 3403 Morkel Dr., Godfrey, IL 62035. (618) 466-3513.

HICKORY HILLS — Doug and Eileen Wagner, 9225 S. 88th Ave., Hickory Hills, IL 60457. (312) 598-4570.

HILLSBORO — Jim and Penny Lang, 628 Mechanic, Hillsboro, IL 62049. (217) 532-2915.

INGELSIDE — Art and Pat Besinger, 611 Oakwood, Ingelside, IL 60041. (312) 546-2367.

LAGRANGE — John Murray, 301 Hillgrove, LaGrange, IL 60525. (312) 352-2199.

LAKE VILLA — Lloyd Bindscheattle, P. O. Box 11, Lake Villa, IL 60046.

LEMONT — Russ and Lynn Sineni, 1372 Hillcrest Rd., Lemont, IL 60439. (312) 257-2648.

MOKENA — Neal and Marianne Vander Zande, 18830 Sara Rd., Mokena, IL 60448. (312) 479-5566.

MORRISON — Emma's Bottle Shop, Emma Rosenow, RR3, Morrison, IL 61270. (815) 778-4596. *Beers, inks, bitters, sodas.*

O'FALLON — Tom and Ann Feltman, 425 North Oak St., O'Fallon, IL 62269. (618) 632-3327.

PARK FOREST — Vern and Gloria Nitchie, 300 Indiana St., Park Forest, IL 60466. (312) 748-7198.

PARK RIDGE — Ken's Old Bottles, 119 East Lahon, Park Ridge, IL 60068. (312) 823-1267. *Milks, inks, sodas and whiskies.*

PEKIN — Harry's Bottle Shop, 612 Hillyer St., Pekin, IL 61554. (309) 346-3476. *Pottery, beer, sodas and medicines.*

PEKIN — Oertel's Bottle House, Box 682, Pekin, IL 61554. (309) 347-4441. *Peoria pottery, embossed picnic beer bottles, fruit jars.*

RIVERDALE — Bob and Barbara Harms, 14521 Atlantic, Riverdale, IL 60627. (312) 841-4068.

SAUK VILLAGE — Ed McDonald, 3002 23rd St., Sauk Village, IL 60511. (312) 758-0373.

TRENTON — Jon and Char Granda, 631 S. Main, Trenton, IL 62293. (618) 224-7308.

WHEATON — Ben Crane, 1700 Thompson Dr., Wheaton, IL 60187. (312) 665-5662.

WHEATON — Scott Garrow, 2 S. 338 Orchard Rd., Wheaton, IL

WHEELING — Hall, 940 E. Old Willow Rd., Wheeling, IL 60090. (312) 541-5788. *Sodas, inks, medicines, etc.*

WHEELING — Steve Miller, 623 Ivy Ct., Wheeling, IL 60090. (312) 398-1445.

WOODSTOCK — Michael Davis, 1652 Tappan, Woodstock, IL 66098. (815) 338-5147.

WOODSTOCK — Mike Henrich, 402 McHenry Ave., Woodstock, IL 60098. (815) 338-5008.

QUINCY — Bob Rhinberger, R.R. 7, Quincy, IL 62301. (217) 223-0191.

INDIANA

BOGGSTOWN — Ed and Margaret Shaw, R. 1, Box 23, Boggstown, IN 46110. (317) 835-7121.

CLINTON — Tony and Dick Stringfellow, 714 Vine, Clinton, IN 47842. (317) 832-2355.

FLORA — Bob and Morris Wise, 409 E. Main, Flora, IN 46929. (219) 967-3713.

FORT WAYNE — Annett's Antiques, 6910 Lincoln HWY-East, Fort Wayne, IN 46803. (219) 749-2745.

GOSHEN — Gene Rice, 61935 CR37, R. 1, Goshen, IN 46526.

GOSHEN — Wayne Wagner, 23558 Creek Park Dr., Goshen, IN 46526.

GREENFIELD — George and Nancy Reilly, R10, Box 67, Greenfield, IN 46140. (317) 462-2441.

INDIANAPOLIS — John and Dianna Atkins, 3168 Beeler Ave., Indianapolis, IN 46224. (317) 299-2720.

NOBELSVILLE — Rick and Becky Norton, R.R. G, Box 166, Noblesville, IN 46060. (317) 844-1772.

PERU — Herrell's Collectibles, 265 E. Canal St., Peru, IN 46970. 473-7770.

SCOTTSBURG — Fort Harrod Glass Works, 160 N. Gardner St., Scottsburg, IN 47170. (812) 752-5170.

TERRE HAUTE — Harry and Dorothy Frey, 5210 Clinton Rd., Terre Haute, IN 47805. (812) 466-4642.

WESTFIELD — Doug Moore, #9 Northbrook Circle Westfield, IN 46074. (317) 896-3015.

IOWA

ELKADER — The Bottle Shop, 206 Chestnut, S.E., Mailing address, Box 188, Max Hunt, Elkader, IA 52043. (319) 245-2359. *Sarsaparilla and bitters.*

STORM LAKE — Ralph and Helen Welch, 804 Colonial Circle, Storm Lake, IA 50588. (712) 732-4124.

KANSAS

HALSTEAD — Doanald Haury, RT #2, Halstead, KS 67056. (316) 283-5876.

LAWRENCE — Mike Elwell, R.R. 2, Box 30, Lawrence, KS 66044. (913) 842-2102.

MERRIAM — Dale Young, 9909 West 55th St., Merriam, KS 66203. (913) 677-0175.

PAOLA — Stewart and Sons Old Bottle Shop, 610 E. Kaskaskia, Paola, KS 66071. (913) 294-3434. *Drugstore bottles, blob top beers.*

TOPEKA — Joe and Alyce Smith, 4706 West Hills Dr., Topeka, KS 66606. (913) 272-1892.

KENTUCKY

ALEXANDRIA — Michael and Kathy Kolb, 6 S. Jefferson, Alexandria, KY 41001. (606) 635-7121.

JEFFERSONTOWN — Paul Van Vactor, 10004 Cardigan Dr., Jeffersontown, KY 40299.

LOUISVILLE — Gene Blasi, 5801 River Knolls Dr., Louisville, KY 40222. Phone: (502) 425-6995.

LOUISVILLE — Jerry and Joyce Phelps, 6013 Innes Trace Rd., Louisville, KY 40222.

LOUISVILLE — Paul and Paulette Van Vactor, 300 Stilz Ave., Louisville, KY 40299. (502) 895-3655.

PADUCAH — Earl and Ruth Cron 808 N. 25th St., Paducah, KY 42001. (502) 443-5005.

LOUISIANA

BATON ROUGE — Sidney and Eulalie Genius, 1843 Tudor Dr., Baton Rouge, LA 70815. (504) 925-5774.

BATON ROUGE — Bobby and Ellen Kirkpatrick, 7313 Meadowbrook Ave., Baton Rouge, LA 70808.

BATON ROUGE — Sheldon L. Ray, Jr. (Summer address): 2316 Amalie, Monroe, LA 71201. Mail address: P. O. Box 17238 LSU, Baton Rouge, LA 70893. (504) 388-3814.

JENNINGS — Cajun Pop Factory, P. O. Box 1113, Jennings, LA 70546. (318) 824-7078. *Hutchinsons, Blob-tops and pontil sodas.*

MONROE — Everett L. Smith, 100 Everett Dr., Monroe, LA 71202. 325-3534. *Embossed whiskies.*

NATCHITOCHES — Ralph and Cheryl Green, 515 Elizabeth St., Natchitoches, LA 71457.

NEW ORLEANS — Bep's Antiques, 3923 Magazine St., New Orleans, LA 70115. 891-3468. *Antique bottles, import bottles.*

NEW ORLEANS — Dr. Charles and Jane Aprill, 484 Chestnut, New Orleans, LA 70118. (504) 899-7441.

RUSTON — The Dirty Digger, 1804 Church St., Ruston, LA 71270. 255-6112.

RUSTON — Bob and Vernell Willett, 1804 Church St., Ruston, LA 71270. (318) 255-6112.

MAINE

BETHEL — F. Barrie Freeman — antiques, Paradise Hill Rd., Bethel, ME 04217. (207) 824-3300.

BRYANT POND — John and Althea Hathaway, Bryant Pond, ME 04219.

EAST WILTON — Don McKeen Bottles, McKeen Way. P. O. Box 5A, E. Wilton, ME 04234.

HALLOWELL — The Mini Shop, 176 Main St., Hallowell, ME 04347.

MILFORD — Spruce's Antiques, Main Street, Box 295, Milford, ME 04461. 827-4756.

SEARSPORT — Morse and Applebee Antiques, U.S. Route 1. Box 164, Searsport, ME 04974. 548-6314. *Early American glass.*

WALDOBORO — Wink's Bottle Shop, Rt. #235, Waldoboro, ME 04572. (207) 832-4603.

WALDOBORO — Daniel R. Winchenbaugh, RFD #4, Box 21, Waldoboro, ME 04572. (207) 832-7702.

MARYLAND

NORTH EAST — Pete's Diggins, Route 40 West, RR #3, Box 301, North East, MD 21901. (301) 287-9245.

SUDLERSVILLE — Fran and Bill Lafferty, Box 142, Sudlersville, MD 21668.

MASSACHUSETTS

DUXBURY — Joe and Kathy Wood, 49 Surplus St., Duxbury, MA 02332. (617) 934-2221.

LEVERETT — Metamorphosis, 46 Teewaddle Rd., RFD #3, Leverett, MA 01002. *Hairs, medicines.*

LITTLETON — The Thrift & Gift Shop, Littleton Common, Box 21, Littleton, MA (617) 486-4464.

MANSFIELD — Shop in my home, 211 East St., Mansfield, MA 02048. (617) 339-6086. *Historic flasks.*

NORTH EASTON — The Applied Lip Place, 26 Linden St., North Easton, MA 02356. (617) 238-1432. *Medicines, whiskies.*

WELLESLEY — Carlyn Ring, 59 Livermore Road, Wellesley, MA 02181. (617) 235-5675.

WEST SPRINGFIELD — Leo A. Bedard, 62 Craig Dr., Apt. 7A, West Springfield, MA 01089. *Bitters, whiskeys, medicines.*

YARMOUTH — Gloria Swanson Antiques, 262 Setucket RD., Yarmouth, MA 02675. 398-8648. *Inks.*

MICHIGAN

ANN ARBOR — John Wolfe, 1622 E. Stadium Blvd., Ann Arbor, MI 48104. (313) 665-6108.

BLOOMFIELD HILLS — Jim and Robin Meehan, 25 Valley Way, Bloomfield Hills, MI 48013. (313) 642-0176.

BUCHANAN — Old Chicago, 316 Ross Dr., Buchanan, MI 49107. (616) 695-5896. *Hutchinson sodas, blob beers.*

CLARKLAKE — Fred and Shirley Weck, 8274 S. Jackson Rd., Clarklake, MI 49234. (517) 529-9631.

DAVISBURG — Chief Pontiac Antique Bottle Shop, 13880 Neal Rd., Davisburg, MI 48019. (313) 634-8469.

DETROIT — Michael and Christina Garrett, 19400 Stout, Detroit, MI 48219. (313) 534-6067.

DUNDEE — Ray and Hillaine Hoste, 366 Main St., Dundee, MI 48131. (313) 529-2193.

GAINES — E & E Antiques, 9441 Grand Blanc Road, Gaines, MI 48436. (517) 271-9063. *Fruit jars, beer bottles, milks.*

GRAND RAPIDS — Dewey and Marilyn Heetderks, 21 Michigan N.E., Grand Rapids, MI 49503. (616) 774-9333.

IRON RIVER — Sarge's, 111 E. Hemlock, Iron River, MI 49935. (906) 265-4223. *Old mining town bottles, Hutchinsons.*

KALAMAZOO — Mark and Marty McNee, 1009 Vassar Dr., Kalamazoo, MI 49001. (616) 343-9393.

KALAMAZOO — Lew and Leon Wisser, 2837 Parchmount, Kalamazoo, MI 49004. (616) 343-7479.

LATHRUP VILLAGE — The Jar Emporium, Ralph Finch, 19420 Saratoga, Lathrup Village, MI 48076. (313) 569-6749. *Fruit jars.*

MANISTEE — Chris and Becky Batdorff, 516 Maple St., Manistee, MI 49660. (616) 723-7917.

MONROE — Don and Glennie Burkett, 3942 West Dunbar Rd., Monroe, MI 48161. (313) 241-6740.

STAMBAUGH — Copper Corner Rock & Bottle Shop, 4th & Lincoln, Stambaugh, MI 49964. (906) 265-3510. *Beer, Hutch's, medicines.*

ST. JOSEPH — Anvil Antiques, 2 blocks So. of exit 27, I-94, 3439 Hollywood Rd., St. Joseph, MI 49085. (616) 429-5132. *Bottles, insulators.*

STUGIS — John and Kay Petruska, 21960 Marathon Rd., Sturgis, MI 49091. (616) 651-6400.

WUCHANAN — James Clengenpeel, 316 Ross Dr., Wuchanan, MI 49107. (616) 695-5896.

MINNESOTA

DOVER — Dave and Ruth Stagner, Box 24, Dover, MN 55929. (507) 932-4964.

EXCELSIOR — Jim Conley, P. O. Box 351, Excelsior, MN 55331. (612) 935-0964.

MINNEAPOLIS — Steve Ketcham, P. O. Box 24114, Minneapolis, MN 55424. (612) 920-4205.

MINNEAPOLIS — Neal and Pat Sorensen, 132 Peninsula Rd., Minneapolis, MN 55441. (612) 545-2698.

RICHFIELD — Ron and Vernie Feldhaus, 6904 Upton Ave., S. Richfield, MN 55423. (612) 866-6013.

ST. PAUL — J & E, 1000 Arcade St., St. Paul, MN 55106. 771-9654.

MISSISSIPPI

BILOXI — Vieux Beloxie Bottlery Factory Restaurant, US 90 E., Biloxi, MS 39530. 374-0688. *Mississippi bottles.*

COLUMBIA — Robert A. Knight, 516 Dale St., Columbia, MS 39429. (601) 736-4249. *Mississippi bottles & jugs.*

McCOMB — Robert Smith, 623 Pearl River Ave., McComb, MS 39648. (601) 684-1843.

STARKVILLE — Jerry Drott, 710 Persimmon Dr., P. O. Box 714, Starkville, MS 39759. 323-8796. *Liniments, drug stores.*

VICKSBURG — Ted and Linda Kost, 107 Columbia Ave., Vicksburg, MS 39180. (601) 638-8780.

MISSOURI

ELSBERRY — Dave Hausgen, Rt. 1, Box 164, Elsberry, MO 63343. (314) 898-2500.

GLENCOE — Sam and Eloise Taylor, 3002 Woodlands Terrace, Glencoe, MO 63038. (314) 273-6244.

HANNIBAL — Bob and Debbi Overfield, 2318 Chestnut St., Hannibal, MO 63401. (314) 248-9521.

INDEPENDENCE — Mike and Carol Robison, 1405 N. River, Independence, MO 64050. (816) 836-2337.

KANSAS CITY — Donald Kimrey, 1023 W. 17th St., Kansas City, MO 64108. (816) 741-2745.

KANSAS CITY — Robert Stevens, 1131 E. 77th, Kansas City, MO 64131. (816) 333-1398.

LINN CREEK — The Bottle House, 1 mile north of Linn Creek on HWY 54, Route 1, Box 111, Linn Creek, MO 65052. (314) 346-5890.

ST. LOUIS — Gene and Alberta Kelley, 1960 Cherokee, St. Louis, MO 63126. (314) 664-7203.

ST. LOUIS — Jerry Mueller, 4520 Langtree, St. Louis, MO 63128. (314) 843-8357.

ST. LOUIS — Terry and Luann Phillips, 1014 Camelot Gardens, St. Louis, MO 63125. (314) 892-6864.

ST. LOUIS — Hal and Vern Wagner, 10118 Schuessler, St. Louis, MO 63128. (314) 843-7573. *Historical flasks, colognes, early glass.*

TAYLOR — Barkely Museum, one mile South Taylor, MO on U.S. 61 (service road). (314) 393-2408.

TIPTON — Joseph and Jean Reed, 237 E. Morgan, Tipton, MO 65081. (816) 433-5937.

WESTPHALIA — Randy and Jan Haviland, American Systems Antiques, Westphalia, MO 65085. (314) 455-2525.

NEBRASKA
OMAHA — Born Again Antiques, 1402 Williams St., Omaha, NE 68108. 341-5177.

OMAHA — Karl Ferson, 10210 "W" St., Omaha, NE 68127. (402) 331-2666.

OMAHA — Fred Williams, 5712 N. 33rd St., Omaha, NE 68111. (402) 453-4317.

NEVADA
FALLON — Don and Opal Wellman, P. O. Box 521, Fallon, NV 89406. (702) 423-3490.

SPARKS — Don and Bonnie McLane, 1846 F. St., Sparks, NV 89431. (702) 359-2171.

NEW HAMPSHIRE
AMHERST — Dave and Carol Waris, Boston Post Rd., Amherst, NH 03031. (603) 882-4409.

DOVER — Bob and Betty Morin, RD 3, Box 280, Dover, NH 03820.

EXETER — Lucille Stanley, 9 Oak St., Exeter, NH 03833. (603) 772-2296.

HAMPSTEAD — Murray's Lakeside Bottle Shop, Benson Shores, Hampstead, NH 03841, P. O. Box 57. (603) 329-6969. *All types, pontils, bitters, sarsaparillas, balsams, hairs, labeled, medicines, general line. Open 7 days, mail order too.*

MANCHESTER — Jim and Joyce Rogers, Harvey Road, Box 776, Manchester, NH 03103. (603) 623-4101.

TROY — House of Glass, 25 High St., Troy, NH 03465. (603) 242-7947.

NEW JERSEY
BRANCHVILLE — Richard and Lesley Harris, Box 400, Branchville, NY 07826. (201) 948-3935.

CALIFON — Phil and Flo Alvarez, P. O. Box 107, Califon, NJ 07830. (201) 832-7438.

ENGLEWOOD — Ed and Carole Clemens, 81 Chester Pl. Apt. D-2, Englewood, NJ 07631. (201) 569-4429.

FLEMINGTON — John Orashen, RD 6, Box 345-A, Flemington, NJ 08822. (201) 782-3391.

HOPEWELL — Tom and Marion McCandless, 62 Lafayette St., Hopewell, NJ 08525. (609) 466-0619.

HOWELL — Howell Township, Bruce and Pat Egeland, 3 Rustic Drive, Howell, NJ. 07731. (201) 569-0556. *Second shop open 7 days a week at shop #106, building #3, Red Bank Antique Center, West Front St., and Bridge Ave., Red Bank, N.J.*

MICKLETON — Sam Fuss, Harmony Rd., Mickleton, NJ 08056. (609) 423-5038.

SALEM — Old Bottle Museum, 4 Friendship Dr., Salem, NJ. 08079. (609) 935-5631. *Sodas, medicines, milks.*

NEW MEXICO
ALBUQUERQUE — Irv and Ruth Swalwell, 8826 Fairbanks NE, Albuquerque, NM 87112. (505) 299-2977.

DEMING — Krol's Rock City & Mobile Park, 5 miles east of Deming on State HWY 26, Star RT. 2, Box 15A, Deming, NM. 88030. *Hutch sodas, inks, Avons.*

NEW YORK
AUBURN — Brewster Bottle Shop, 297 South St. Road, Auburn, NY. 13021. (315) 252-3246. *Milk bottles.*

BALLSTON LAKE — Tom and Alice Moulton, 88 Blue Spruce Lane, RD #5, Ballston Lake, NY 12019.

BINGHAMTON — Jim Chamberlain, RD 8, 607 Nowland Rd., Binghamton, NY 13904. (607) 772-1135.

BINGHAMTON — Jo Ann's Old Bottles, R.D. 2, Box 638, Port Crane, NY 13833. (607) 648-4605.

BLODGETT MILLS — Edward Pettet, Box 1, Blodgett Mills, NY 13738. (607) 756-7891. *Inks.*

BLOOMING GROVE — Old Bottle Shop, Horton Rd., Box 105, Blooming Grove, NY 10914. (914) 496-6841.

CENTRAL VALLEY — J. J.'s Pontil Place, 1001 Dunderberg RD., Central Valley, NY (914) 928-9144.

CLIFTON PARK — John Kovacik, 11 Juniper Dr., Clifton Park, NY 12065. (518) 371-4118.

CLIFTON PARK — Richard Strunk, Rd. 4, Grooms Rd., Clifton Park, NY 12065. *Bottles, flasks, bitters, Saratogas.*

CRANBERRY LAKE — The Bottle Shop Antiques, Box 503, Cranberry Lake, NY (315) 848-2648.

ELMA — Leonard and Joyce Blake, 1220 Stolle Rd., Elma, NY 14059. (716) 652-7752.

LEROY — Kenneth Cornell, 78 Main, Leroy, NY 14482. (716) 768-8919.

LOCH SHELDRAKE — The Bottle Shop, P. O. Box 24, Loch Sheldrake, NY 12759. (914) 434-4757.

MONTICELLO — Manor House Collectibles, Rt. 42, South Forestburgh, RD #1, Box 67, Monticello, NY 12701. (914) 794-3967. *Whiskeys, beers, sodas.*

NEW WINDSOR — David Byrd, 43 E. Kenwood Dr., New Windsor, NY 12550. (914) 561-7257.

NEW YORK CITY — Chuck Moore, 3 East 57th St., N.Y.C., NY 10022.

NEW YORK CITY — Bottles Unlimited, 245 East 78th St., N.Y.C., NY 10021. (212) 628-8769. *19th and 18th century.*

ROCHESTER — Burton Spiller, 169 Greystone Lane, Apt. 31, Rochester, NY 14618. (716) 244-2229.

ROCHESTER — Robert Zorn, 23 Knickerbocker Ave., Rochester, NY 14615. (716) 254-7470.

WEBSTER — Dick and Evelyn Bowman, 1253 LaBaron Circle, Webster, NY 14580. (716) 872-4015.

NORTH CAROLINA

BLOWING ROCK — Vieve and Luke Yarbrough, P. O. Box 1023, Blowing Rock, NC 28605. (704) 963-4961.

CHARLOTTE — Bob Morgan, P. O. Box 3163, Charlotte, NC 28203. (704) 527-4841.

DURHAM — Clement's Bottles, 5234 Willowhaven Dr., Durham, NC. 27712. 383-2493. *Commemorative soft drink bottles.*

GOLDSBORO — Vernon Capps, Rt. 5, Box 529, Goldsboro, NC 27530. (919) 734-8964.

GOLD HILL — Howard Crowe, Box 133, Gold Hill, NC 28071. (704) 279-3736.

RALEIGH — Rex D. McMillan, 4101 Glen Laurel Dr., Raleigh, NC. 27612. (919) 787-0007. *N.C. blobs, saloon bottles, colored drug store.*

NORTH DAKOTA

MANDAN — Robert Barr, 102 N. 9th Ave. N.W., Mandan, ND 58554.

OHIO

AKRON — Don and Barb Dzuro, 5113 W. Bath Rd., Akron, OH 44313. (216) 666-8170.

AKRON — Jim Salzwimmer, 3391 Tisen Rd., Akron, OH 44312. (216) 699-3990.

BEACHWOOD — Allan Hodges, 25125 Shaker Blvd., Beachwood, OH 44122. (216) 464-8381.

BLUFFTON — Schroll's Country Shop, 3 mi. east of county line on Co. Rd. 33. (419) 358-6121.

BYESVILLE — Albert and Sylvia Campbell, RD 1, Box 194, Byesville, OH 43723. (614) 439-1105.

CINCINNATI — Kenneth and Dudie Roat, 7755 Kennedy Lane, Cincinnati, OH 45242. (513) 791-1168.

CLEVELAND — Joe and Mary Miller, 2590 N. Moreland Blvd., Cleveland, OH 44120. (216) 721-9919.

DAYTON — Don and Paula Spangler, 2554 Loris Dr., Dayton, OH 45449. (513) 435-7155.

DUBLIN — Roy and Barbara Brown, 8649 Dunsinane Dr., Dublin, OH 43017. (614) 889-0818.

FRANKFORT — Roger Durflinger, Box 2006, Frankfort, OH 45628 (614) 998-4849.

HANNIBAL — Gilbert Nething, Box 96, Hannibal, OH. 43931. *Hutchinson sodas.*

LANCASTER — R. J. and Freda Brown, 125 S. High St., Lancaster, OH 43130. (614) 687-2899.

LEWISTOWN — Sonny Mallory, Box 134, Lewistown, OH 43333. (513) 686-2185.

NORTH HAMPTON — John and Margie Bartley, 160 South Main, North Hampton, OH 45319. (513) 964-1080.

POWHATAN POINT — Bob and Dawn Jackson, 107 Pine St., Powhatan Point, OH 43942. (614) 795-5567.

REYNOLDSBURG — Bob and Phyllis Christ, 1218 Creekside Place, Reynoldsburg, OH 43068. (614) 866-2156.

SPRINGFIELD — Ballentine's Bottles, 710 W. First St., Springfield, OH 45504. 399-8359. *Antique bottles.*

SPRINGFIELD — Larry R. Henschen, 3222 Delrey Rd. (513) 399-1891.

STEUBENVILLE — Tom and Deena Caniff, 1223 Oak Grove Ave., Steubenville, OH 43952. (614) 282-8918.

STEUBENVILLE — Bob and Mary Ann Villamagna, 711 Kendall Ave., Steubenville, OH 43952. (614) 282-9029.

STOW — Doug and Joann Bedore, 1483 Ritchie Rd., Stow, OH 44224. (216) 688-4934.

TORONTO — Bob Villamagna, 1518 Madison Ave., Box 56, Toronto, OH. 43964. (614) 537-4503. *Tri-state area bottles, stoneware.*

WASHINGTONVILLE — Al and Beth Bignon, 480 High St., Washingtonville, OH 44490. (216) 427-6848.

WAYNESVILLE — The Bottleworks, 70 N. Main St., Box 446, Waynesville, OH 45068. (513) 897-3861.

WELLINGTON — Elvin and Cherie Moody, Trails End, Wellington, OH 44090. (216) 647-4917.

XENIA — Bill and Wanda Dudley, 393 Franklin Ave., Xenia, OH 45385. (513) 372-8567.

OKLAHOMA

ENID — Ronald and Carol Ashby, 831 E. Pine, Enid, OK 73701.

OKLAHOMA CITY — Joe and Hazel Nagy, 3540 NW 23, Oklahoma City, OK 73107. (405) 942-0882.

SANDSPRINGS — Larry and Linda Shope, 310 W. 44th, Sandsprings, OK 74063. (918) 363-8481.

OREGON

HILLSBORO — Robert and Marguerite Ornduff, Route 4, Box 236-A, Hillsboro, OR 97123. (503) 538-2359.

PORTLAND — Alan Amerman, 2311 S.E. 147th, Portland, OR 97233. (503) 761-1661. *Fruit jars.*

PORTLAND — The Glass House, 4620 S.E. 104th, Portland, OR 97266. (503) 760-3346. *Fruit jars.*

PENNSYLVANIA

ALBURTIS — R. S. Riovo, 686 Franklin St., Alburtis, PA 18011. (215) 965-2706. *Milk bottles, dairy go-withs.*

BRADFORD — Ernest Hurd, 5 High St., Bradford, PA 16701. (814) 362-9915.

BRADFORD — Dick and Patti Mansour, 458 Lambert Dr., Bradford, PA 16701. (814) 368-8820.

CANONSBURG — John and Mary Schultz, RD #1, Box 118, Canonsburg, PA 15317. (412) 745-6632.

EAST GREENVILLE — James A. Hagenbach, 102 Jefferson St., East Greenville, PA 18041. (215) 679-5849.

COUDERSPORT — The Old Bottle Corner, 508 South Main St. Mailing address: 102 West Maple St., Coudersport, PA 16915. (814) 274-7017. *Fruit jars, blob tops.*

EAST PETERSBURG — Jere and Betty Hambleton, 5940 Main St., East Petersburg, PA 17520. (717) 569-0130.

HATBORO — Al and Maggie Duffield, 12 Belmar Rd., Hatboro, PA 19040. (215) 675-5175. *Hutchinson's and inks.*

LANCASTER — Barry and Mary Hogan, 3 Lark Lane, Lancaster, PA 17603.

LEVITTOWN — Ed Lasky, 43 Nightingale LN., Levittown, PA 19054. (215) 945-1555.

MARIENVILLE — Harold Bauer Antique Bottles, 136 Cherry St., Marienville, PA 16239.

McKEES ROCKS — Chuck Henigin, 3024 Pitch Fork Lane, McKees Rocks, PA 15136. (412) 331-6159.

MUNCY — Harold Hill, 161 E. Water St., Muncy, PA 17756. (717) 546-3388.

PIPERSVILLE — Allen Holtz, RD 1, Pipersville, PA 18947. (215) 847-5728.

PITTSBURGH — Carl & Gail Onufer, 210 Newport Rd., Pittsburgh, PA 15221. (412) 371-7725. *Milk bottles.*

ROULETTE — R. A. and Esther Heimer, Box 153, Roulette, PA 16746. (814) 544-7713.

STRONGSTOWN — Butch and Gloria Kim, RD 2, Box 35, Strongstown, PA 15957.

RHODE ISLAND

KENYON — Wes and Diane Seemann, Box 49, Kenyon, RI 02836. (203) 599-1626.

SOUTH CAROLINA

EASHEY — Bob Durham, 704 W. Main St., Eashey, SC 29640.

MARION — Tony and Marie Shank, P. O. Box 778, Marion, SC 29571. (803) 423-5803.

TENNESSEE

KNOXVILLE — Ronnie Adams, 7005 Charlotte Dr., Knoxville, TN 37914. (615) 524-8958.

McMINNVILLE — Terry Pennington, 415 N. Spring St., McMinnville, TN 37110. *Jack Daniels, amber Coca Cola.*

MEMPHIS — Bluff City Bottlers, 4630 Crystal Springs Dr., Memphis, TN 38123. (901) 353-0541. *Common American bottles.*

MEMPHIS — Larry and Nancy McCage, 3772 Hanna Dr., Memphis, TN 38128. (901) 388-9329.

MEMPHIS — Tom Phillips, 2088 Fox Run Cove, Memphis, TN 38138. (901) 754-0097.

TEXAS

AMARILLO — Robert Synder, 4235 W. 13th St., Amarillo, TX 79106.

EULESS — Mack and Alliene Landers, P. O. Box 5, Euless, TX 76039. (817) 267-2710.

HOUSTON — Bennie and Harper Leiper, 2800 W. Dallas, Houston, TX 77019. (713) 526-2101.

PASADENA — Gerald Welch, 4809 Gardenia Trail, Pasadena, TX 77505. (713) 487-3057.

PORT ISABEL — Jimmy and Peggy Galloway, P. O. Drawer A, Port Isabel, TX 78578. (512) 943-2437.

RICHARDSON — Chuck and Reta Bukin, 1325 Cypress Dr., Richardson, TX 75080. (214) 235-4889.

SAN ANTONIO — Sam Greer, 707 Nix Professional Bldg., San Antonio, TX 78205. (512) 227-0253.

VERMONT

BRATTLEBORO — Kit Barry, 88 High St., Brattleboro, VT 05301. (802) 254-2195.

VIRGINIA

ALEXANDRIA — A. E. Steidel, 6167 Cobbs Rd., Alexandria, VA 22310.

ARLINGTON — Dick and Margie Stockton, 2331 N. Tuckahoe St., Arlington, VA 22205. (703) 534-5619.

CHESTERFIELD — Tom Morgan, 3501 Slate Ct., Chesterfield, VA 23832.

FREDERICKSBURG — White's Trading Post, Boutchyards Olde Stable, Falmouth, VA. 1903 Charles St., Fredericksburg, VA 22401. (703) 371-6252. *Fruit jars, new and old bottles.*

HINTON — Vic and Betty Landis, Rt. 1, Box 8A, Hinton, VA 22801. (703) 867-5959.

HUNTLY — Early American Workshop, Star Route, Huntly, VA 22640. (703) 635-8252. *Milk bottles.*

MARSHALL — John Tutton, Rt. 1, Box 261, Marshall, VA 22115. (703) 347-0148.

RICHMOND — Lloyd and Carrie Harnish, 2936 Woodworth Rd., Richmond, VA 23234. (804) 275-7106.

RICHMOND — Jim and Connie Mitchell, 5106 Glen Alden Dr., Richmond, VA.

WASHINGTON

BELLEVUE — Don and Dorothy Finch, 13339 Newport Way, Bellevue, WA 98006. (206) 746-5640.

BREMERTON — Ron Flannery, 423 NE Conifer Dr., Bremerton, WA 98310. (206) 692-2619.

SEATTLE — John W. Cooper, 605 N.E. 170th St., Seattle, WA 98155. (206) 364-0858.

WISCONSIN

ARLINGTON — Mike and Carole Schwartz, Route 1, Arlington, WI 53911. (608) 846-5229.

MEQUON — Jeff Burkhardt, 12637 N. River Forest Cir., Mequon, WI 53092. (414) 243-5643.

MEQUON — Bor Markiewicz, 11715 W. Bonniwell Rd., Mequon, WI 53092. (414) 242-3968.

OSKOSH — Richard Schwab, 65-5 Larsen Rd., Oskosh, WI 54901. (414) 235-9962.

STEVENS POINT — Bill and Kathy Mitchell, 703 Linwood Ave., Stevens Point, WI 55431. (715) 341-1471.

WAUTOMA — George and Ruth Hansen, Rt. 2, Box 26, Wautoma, WI 54982. (414) 787-4893.

FOREIGN

CANADA

BADEN, ONTARIO — John and Sara Moore, R.R. 2, Baden, ONT.

DOLLARD-DES-ORMEAUX, P.Q. — Richard Davis, 39 Brunswick #115, Dollard-Des-Ormeaux, P.Q. (314) 683-8522.

OTTAWA, ONT. — Paul Hanrahan, 292 Byron Ave. #2, Ottawa, ONT, Canada. (613) 929-56-75.

ENGLAND

TRENT — David Geduhon, Box 85, Cayuga Ind. & Burton-on-Trent, England. (317) 494-3027.

YORKSHIRE — John Morrison, 33 Ash Grove, Leeds G., Yorkshire, England.

DESCRIPTION	DATE PURCHASED	COST	DATE SOLD	PRICE	CONDITION

DESCRIPTION	DATE PURCHASED	COST	DATE SOLD	PRICE	CONDITION

How did your plates do?

Reco's "Little Boy Blue" by John McClelland

UP 214% in 1 Year

Some limited edition plates gained more in the same year, some less, and some not at all . . . But Plate Collector readers were able to follow the price changes, step by step, in Plate Price Trends, a copyrighted feature appearing in each issue of the magazine.

Because The Plate Collector is your best source guide . . . has more on limited editions than all other publications combined . . . and gives you insight into every facet of your collecting . . . you too will rate it

Your No. 1. Investment
In Limited Editions.

In 1972, Plate Collector was the first to feature limited editions only. It's expanded, adding figurines, bells and prints, earning reader raves like you see below.

To bring you the latest, most valuable information, our editors crisscross the continent. Sometimes stories lead them to the smaller Hawaiian Islands, or to the porcelain manufactories of Europe.

Their personal contact with artisans, hobby leaders, collectors, artists and dealers lets you share an intimate view of limited editions.

Each fat, colorful issue brings you new insight, helps you enjoy collecting more.

You'll find Plate Collector a complete source guide. Consider new issue information and new issue announcements, often in full color. Use the ratings of new releases and wide array of dealer ads to help you pick and choose the best.

Read regular columns, including one on Hummels, and check current market values in Plate Price Trends to add to your storehouse of knowledge.

You'll profit from tips on insurance, decorating, taxes . . . just a sample of recurring feature subjects.

Read Plate Collector magazine to become a true limited edition art insider. Order now. See new and old plates in sparkling color. Enjoy 2 issues every month, delivered to your home at savings up to 37% from newsstand price.

12 issues (6 months) $17.50
24 issues (year) $30
The PLATE COLLECTOR
P.O. Box 1041-HC   Kermit, TX 79745

To use VISA and MasterCard, include all raised information on your card.

Here is Plate Collector, as viewed by our readers in unsolicited quotes . . .

"Objective and impartial," has *"great research,"* yet is warm and personal . . . *"I am delighted in 'our' magazine."* A New York couple says flatly, *"It is the best collector magazine on the market."*

"Quality printing is valuable to me because there are no stores near me where I can view and decide," says an Arizona reader. It is *"a major guide to the plates I buy,"* says a Massachusetts reader, while *"It is the best investment in a magazine I ever made,"* comes from Illinois.

"I enjoy your articles on artists," *"The full-color pictures are great,"* *"Your staff was most helpful,"* *"I depend on Plate Collector,"* and *"I look forward to receiving it twice a month,"* are other reader reactions.

A California reader said simply, *"I am glad there is a Plate Collector."*

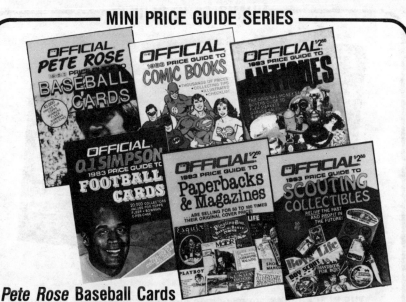

THE BLACKBOOKS are more than just informative books, they are the most highly regarded authority on the nation's most popular hobbies.

1983 Blackbook Price Guide of United States Coins

A coin collector's guide to current market values for all U.S. coins from 1616 to date—over *16,000 prices.* **THE OFFICIAL BLACKBOOK OF COINS** has gained the reputation as the most reliable, up-to-date guide to U.S. Coin values. This new special 1983 edition features, an exclusive gold and silver identification guide. Learn how to test, weigh and calculate the value of any item made of gold or silver. Proven professional techniques revealed for the first time. Take advantage of the current ''BUYERS' MARKET'' in gold and silver. *ILLUSTRATED.*
$2.95-21st Edition, 288 pgs., 4″ x 5½″, paperback, Order #: 342-2

1983 Blackbook Price Guide of United States Paper Money

Over *8,200 buying and selling prices* covering U.S. currency from 1861 to date. Every note issued by the U.S. government is listed and priced, including many Confederate States notes. Error Notes are described and priced, and there are detailed articles on many phases of the hobby for beginners and advanced collectors alike. *ILLUSTRATED.*
$2.95-15th Edition, 240 pgs., 4″ x 5½″, paperback, Order #: 343-0

1983 Blackbook Price Guide of United States Postage Stamps

Featuring all U.S. stamps from 1847 to date pictured in full color. Over *18,750 current selling prices.* You will find new listings for the most current commemorative and regular issue stamps, a feature not offered in any other price guide, at any price! There were numerous important developments in the fast moving stamp market during the past year and they are all included in this *NEW REVISED EDITION. ILLUSTRATED.*
$2.95-5th Edition, 240 pgs., 4″ x 5½″, paperback, Order #: 344-9

══*For your convenience use the handy order form.*══

SEND ORDERS TO: **THE HOUSE OF COLLECTIBLES,** *ORLANDO CENTRAL PARK*
1900 PREMIER ROW, ORLANDO, FL 32809 PHONE (305) 857-9095

☐ *Please send the following price guides — (don't forget to add postage & handling):*

____ 188-8 @ $9.95 + (1.50)	____ 183-7 @ $9.95 + (1.50)	____ 315-5 @ $2.50 + (.75)
____ 184-5 @ $9.95 + (1.50)	____ 325-X @ $9.95 + (1.50)	____ 314-7 @ $2.50 + (.75)
____ 190-X @ $9.95 + (1.50)	____ 191-8 @ $9.95 + (1.50)	____ 342-2 @ $2.50 + (.75)
____ 172-1 @ $9.95 + (1.50)	____ 185-3 @ $9.95 + (1.50)	____ 343-0 @ $2.50 + (.75)
____ 354-6 @ $9.95 + (1.50)	____ 186-1 @ $9.95 + (1.50)	____ 344-9 @ $2.50 + (.75)
____ 350-3 @ $9.95 + (1.50)	____ 159-4 @ $9.95 + (1.50)	____ 173-X @ $2.50 + (.75)
____ 180-2 @ $9.95 + (1.50)	____ 348-1 @ $9.95 + (1.50)	____ 171-3 @ $6.95 + (1.00)
____ 181-0 @ $9.95 + (1.50)	____ 322-8 @ $2.50 + (.75)	____ 300-7 @ $6.95 + (1.00)
____ 324-4 @ $9.95 + (1.50)	____ 345-7 @ $2.50 + (.75)	____ 301-5 @ $6.95 + (1.00)
____ 349-X @ $9.95 + (1.50)	____ 323-6 @ $2.50 + (.75)	____ 302-3 @ $6.95 + (1.00)
____ 189-6 @ $9.95 + (1.50)	____ 308-2 @ $2.50 + (.75)	

☐ Check or money order enclosed $_____

(include postage and handling)

☐ Please charge $_____ to my: ☐ MASTER CHARGE ☐ VISA

My account number is:_____ (all digits)

Expiration date _____

NAME (please print)_____

ADDRESS_____ APT. #_____

CITY _____ STATE_____

ZIP_____ PHONE _____

SIGNATURE_____

SEND ORDERS TO: **THE HOUSE OF COLLECTIBLES,** *ORLANDO CENTRAL PARK*
1900 PREMIER ROW, ORLANDO, FL 32809 PHONE (305) 857-9095

☐ *Please send the following price guides — (don't forget to add postage & handling):*

____ 188-8 @ $9.95 + (1.50)	____ 183-7 @ $9.95 + (1.50)	____ 315-5 @ $2.50 + (.75)
____ 184-5 @ $9.95 + (1.50)	____ 325-X @ $9.95 + (1.50)	____ 314-7 @ $2.50 + (.75)
____ 190-X @ $9.95 + (1.50)	____ 191-8 @ $9.95 + (1.50)	____ 342-2 @ $2.50 + (.75)
____ 172-1 @ $9.95 + (1.50)	____ 185-3 @ $9.95 + (1.50)	____ 343-0 @ $2.50 + (.75)
____ 354-6 @ $9.95 + (1.50)	____ 186-1 @ $9.95 + (1.50)	____ 344-9 @ $2.50 + (.75)
____ 350-3 @ $9.95 + (1.50)	____ 159-4 @ $9.95 + (1.50)	____ 173-X @ $2.50 + (.75)
____ 180-2 @ $9.95 + (1.50)	____ 348-1 @ $9.95 + (1.50)	____ 171-3 @ $6.95 + (1.00)
____ 181-0 @ $9.95 + (1.50)	____ 322-8 @ $2.50 + (.75)	____ 300-7 @ $6.95 + (1.00)
____ 324-4 @ $9.95 + (1.50)	____ 345-7 @ $2.50 + (.75)	____ 301-5 @ $6.95 + (1.00)
____ 349-X @ $9.95 + (1.50)	____ 323-6 @ $2.50 + (.75)	____ 302-3 @ $6.95 + (1.00)
____ 189-6 @ $9.95 + (1.50)	____ 308-2 @ $2.50 + (.75)	

☐ Check or money order enclosed $_____

(include postage and handling)

☐ Please charge $_____ to my: ☐ MASTER CHARGE ☐ VISA

My account number is:_____ (all digits)

Expiration date _____

NAME (please print)_____

ADDRESS_____ APT. #_____

CITY _____ STATE_____

ZIP_____ PHONE _____

SIGNATURE_____